Discover Australia

ROAD GUIDE

The wai

After a 10 year wait, the all new 1998

is over.

Patrol is here. Just wait 'til you drive it.   NISSAN

Discover Australia

ROAD GUIDE

Edited by Ron and Viv Moon

 RANDOM HOUSE

Published in Australia by
Random House Australia Pty Ltd
20 Alfred St, Milsons Point, NSW 2061, Australia
tel 61 2 9954 9966 fax 61 2 9954 9008
http://www.randomhouse.com.au

ISBN 0 09 183774X

Sydney New York Toronto London Auckland Johannesburg and agencies
throughout the world

First published in 1998

Random House Australia has made every effort to include the latest
changes to all roads and highways at the time this publication went to
press.

Use of maps: Should you be interested in using any of the maps
or other material in this publication, please contact Sarah Sherlock
on tel 61 2 9954 9966 or fax 61 2 9954 9008.

Cartographic coordinator: Gordon Cheers

The Publisher would be pleased to receive additional or updated material,
or suggestion for future editions. Please address these to Gordon Cheers,
Random House Australia Pty Ltd, 20 Alfred St, Milsons Point, NSW 2061,
Australia. Tel 61 2 9954 9966 or fax 61 2 9954 9008.

National Library of Australia
Cataloguing-in-Publication Data

Moon, Ron
Discover Australia : road guide

Includes index.
ISBN 0 09 183774X.

1. Automobile travel – Australia – Guidebooks. 2. Australia
– Guidebooks. I. Moon, Viv. II. Title.

919.940465

Printed by Dah Hua, Hong Kong
Film separation Pica Colour Separation, Singapore

For information about purchasing books for use in mail order catalogues,
as corporate gifts or as premiums, please contact Sarah Sherlock, Random
House Australia on tel 61 2 9954 9966 or fax 61 2 9954 9008.

Publisher's Note:
Distances of towns from capital cities given in the text have been taken
from the maps. In general, they have been calculated following the most
direct route. However, in some areas a longer route has been taken,
usually to avoid unsealed roads. The accommodation listings given at the
end of each town or city are a sample only of the range available.

Publisher	Gordon Cheers
Chief consultants	Ron and Viv Moon
Managing editors	Heather Jackson
	Margaret Olds
Contributors	Ron and Viv Moon
	Ian Glover
	David Moon
	Sharyn Vanderhorst
Designer	Robert Taylor
Production designers	Max Peatman
	Deborah Clarke
Cover design	Bob Mitchell
Cartographer	John Frith
Cartographic consultants	Brian Stokes
	Bruce Whitehouse
Map coordinator	Valerie Marlborough
Map editors	Marlene Meynert
	Janet Parker
	Jane Cozens
	Joan Sutter
	Denise Imwold
	Heather Martin
	Jenny Lake
Editors	Doreen Grézoux
	Jenni Bruce
	Denise Imwold
Keyboarding	Dee Rogers
Index	Heather Martin
Line drawings	Tony Pyrzakowski
Photo research	Gordon Cheers
	Marie-Louise Taylor
Publishing manager	Linda Watchorn
Publishing coordinator	Sarah Sherlock

PHOTOGRAPHS
Half title: Countryside near Lithgow, New South Wales
Page iv: Countryside near Nimbin, New South Wales
Pages viii–ix: Mt Ossa, Cradle Mountain–Lake St Clair National Park,
Tasmania
Pages xii–xiii: Warrumbungle National Park, New South Wales

Legend for town maps

Freeway	▬▬▬▬	Destination arrow	→	Carpark	🅿
Highway	▬▬▬▬	Direction of traffic flow	→	Caravan park	▭
Major road	▬▬▬▬	Tourist information	ℹ	Special-use area	▭
Minor road	▬▬▬▬	Public toilets	🚻	Park or reserve	▭
Railway	─┼─┼─┼─	Camping	⛺	Mall	_ _ _ Mall _ _ _

KEY TO ROAD MAPS

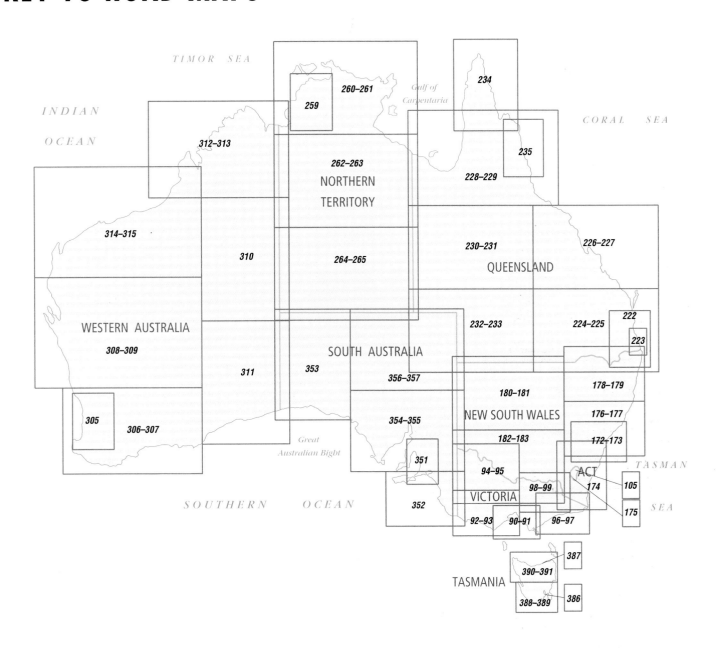

Legend for road maps

Freeway with national route number		Built-up area		Major river	
Highway with State route numbers		State or Territory capital	★	Watercourse	
Major sealed road with Metroad number		Major regional centre	⊙	Mountain peak	▲
Minor sealed road		Other towns	○ ○	Perennial lake	
Major unsealed road		Homestead	■	Dry or intermittent lake	
Minor unsealed road or track		Ruin	□	Dry or intermittent lake in national park or reserve	
Total and intermediate road distances (km)	11 7 18	Mine	⚒	Prohibited Area boundary	
Railway with station	Watson	Landmark or tourist feature	▪	State or Territory border	
Railway (underground)		Bridge		Marine park or reserve boundary	
Ferry route		Gate		Aboriginal land	
Walking track		Grid		National or conservation park or reserve	
Major linear feature (as noted)	Dog Fence	Bore, well or waterhole	∘	Coral reef	
International airport	✈	Tank	▪		

CONTENTS

THE STATES AND TERRITORIES

For many Australians a long-held dream is to travel around this great continent of ours. Most see it as a thing to do after they retire, but for a growing number of people it is something to be enjoyed earlier in life, before starting a family, before the kids start school, or, for some young people, just out of school and with a driver's licence fresh in their pocket, even before university, or before starting a career. No matter when it occurs, though, it is one of the great adventures of life, and life and living will never be the same again. Some who have tried it cannot stop travelling, the endless stretch of bitumen or dirt in front of them egging them on; the magic of the wide and wild open spaces, the hidden jewels that dot Australia, drawing them back time and time again. Travelling, for them, is a lifestyle in itself.

Most of us, though, have a far less enviable life. The vast majority of people live in the major cities that spread along the Australian shoreline and for us the road is a ribbon that ties us to work, school and home. Normally we share that road with hundreds, if not thousands, of often

A long straight road out of Hay, New South Wales

disgruntled drivers clogged together on a three- or four-lane freeway on our way to work. On weekends and holidays we escape and take to the open road, heading for a favourite destination, a beach, mountainside retreat, or some Outback hideaway.

This is the real Australia, away from the concrete jungle, traffic lights and parking meters of the suburbs. As we travel away from the cities, the small manicured hobby farms give way to rolling plains of yellow waving wheatfields, or stubble grazed by a thousand or more head of woolly sheep or soft-eyed cattle. Gnarled red gums dot the fields and along the streams a tangle of verdant green climbs into the hills where the forests take over. Further afield the orderly fenced farmland gives way to a wilder more untamed country and you enter the Outback.

The coastline of the Tasman Peninsula in south-east Tasmania

INTRODUCTION

Buildings in the historic township of Campbell Town, south-east of Launceston

For Sydneysiders the Outback begins somewhere around Cobar and south of Bourke; Victoria misses out altogether, as do Tasmania and the ACT; for South Australians, Port Augusta, at the top of Spencer Gulf and the stepping-off point for the run north on the Stuart Highway to the Northern Territory, or west across the Eyre Highway and the Nullarbor to Western Australia, sits on the boundary of the Outback. In Western Australia, anywhere away from the south-west corner of the state is Outback, while in the Northern Territory, most Territorians would say it is *all* Outback.

Here cattle and sheep still roam, but the stations—Americans and Canadians would call them 'ranches'—now stretch for kilometres and they get bigger the further you travel. In the Kimberley region of Western Australia, or in the Territory, the stations are often a million hectares or more, while the larger, such as Wave Hill or Victoria River Downs, both in the north-west of the Northern Territory are over 5000 sq km. That is bigger than many European countries, and such an area could easily encompass Sydney and Melbourne combined.

Then there is the desert country where spinifex, desert oak and the red, raw vestiges of mountains hold sway. Here, wild camels roam and the vastness is touched only by the occasional sandy track, remote Aboriginal community or mining camp.

A country as vast as Australia demands an equally large and impressive road network, and in the 200 or so years of European history on this great island continent the wheelmarks of modern man have crisscrossed the land, giving access to much of our coastline and the sweep of rolling plains that make up so much of the interior.

In all, there are over 807 000 km of dirt, formed gravel and bituminised roads in Australia and a near incalculable amount of forestry 4WD tracks and rough sandy bush tracks in the more unsettled parts of the country. As is to be expected, the vast majority of the 'official' road network lies within the more populated areas of the nation, with New South Wales having around 183 000 km, Queensland 176 000 km, and much smaller Victoria with about 160 000 or so kilometres of road. South Australia has around 95 000 km, Western Australia 145 000 km, with over 100 000 of that dirt or gravel, and the Northern Territory with just 21 000 km of road, less than 8000 of which is blacktop—some of it awfully narrow blacktop as well! The island state of Tasmania has around 25 000 km of road, while the Australian Capital Territory has close to 2500 km of roadway, much of that, it would seem, in gigantic roundabouts!

Well over half of the total amount, in all around 505 000 km, is gravel or dirt, so for anyone thinking of travelling around this magnificent country, sooner or later they will be leaving the bitumen for a gravel or dirt road.

But if that seems a little daunting, it is incredible to think that it was only just over 10 years ago that the final section of bitumen was laid down on Highway 1, giving Australia, finally, a ribbon of blacktop completely circumnavigating the continent.

But there would appear to be some confusion here. Look at most maps and Highway 1 has a major gap in it. The section between Three Ways in the Northern Territory and Normanton on the Gulf in Queensland, where Highway 1 is supposed to run, is not blacktop, and is not marked as Highway 1, except in some publications. This route is paralleled by a ribbon of tar a little further south across the Barkly Tablelands—an alternative Highway 1, but really Route 66. The Barkly and Flinders Highways, both parts of Route 66, depending on what side of the Northern Territory/Queensland border you are on, heads east, meeting with the Burke Developmental Road, now known more widely as part of the Matilda Highway. This road then heads north to join the marked and official Highway 1, just south of Normanton.

Highway 1, though, for all its peculiarities, is Australia's premium highway and cuts through all the capital cities except Canberra, the nation's capital. It even makes it to Tasmania where it runs from Burnie to Launceston, down through the Midlands to Hobart. For much of its length it hugs the coast, in places hardly above the high-tide mark, while across the Nullarbor it is just a stone's throw from the cliffs that mark the Great Australian Bight. Only in the far north, around the Kimberley, through the Northern Territory, and across the bottom of Cape York Peninsula in northern Queensland does it stray far from the ocean. In all, it is just under 15 000 km—give or take 100 or 200 km, depending on which map you use—all the way round. It is a mighty trip and one of the world's great journeys.

Only a couple of years before Highway 1 was sealed, the Stuart Highway, through the very heart of Australia, was bituminised for its complete length, while the long ribbon of tar that is the crossing of the Nullarbor had only been completed in the early 1980s. Before the blacktop arrived, the horror strips of dirt west of Ceduna to the Western Australian border on the Nullarbor run, or north from Kingoonya on the then dirt Stuart Highway, or on Highway 1 between Fitzroy Crossing and Halls Creek, were where vehicles literally shook themselves to pieces and potholes were marked by a tyre standing upright in them! The 'improved dirt' surface was in places churned to the consistency of fine talcum powder, the 'bulldust' creating its own hazard of choking clouds of dust

behind any vehicle, while it settled on the road hiding some devastatingly big potholes or washaways.

Today, you can still find bulldust, potholes, washaways and corrugations, but only if you head off the blacktop onto the more remote Outback roads and tracks.

However, that does not mean that you will need a 4WD vehicle to travel around Australia. Far from it. Highway 1, the Stuart Highway, the Matilda Highway through central Queensland and a host of other highways, are very good bitumen roads where the major problems are wandering stock, wildlife and the long stretches of apparent emptiness where boredom can set in and losing concentration is the real problem.

Many of the lesser roads, those deemed gravel, or improved surfaces, and formed dirt roads, are generally passable to normal vehicles, with the dirt roads the first to break up or to close after heavy rain. However, most of them are usually in pretty good condition and while you may not be able to cruise along them at a freeway speed of 110 kph, you can still travel at 80 kph or more. A word of warning here, though, is appropriate. The ever changing and often loose surface of a dirt road needs to be traversed with care, especially if you are hauling a van or a trailer. It is easy to lose control and the consequences can be dire.

No, you do not need a 4WD to travel around Australia, but there is no doubt you will see more with one, and when it does rain or a flood comes down a creek you will have a better chance of sneaking through. There are times though, when even the bitumen roads get cut—during one of the not-so-infrequent storms in the north. Then no matter whether you are in a normal car, a 4WD or a huge road train, everyone waits for the rain to stop and the rivers to subside. It's just one of the hazards of travelling this great country of ours, part of the excitement and part of the adventure. Be a part of the adventure, soon!

The majestic coastline of Lord Howe Island

TOURING AUSTRALIA

Touring this great country of ours can be exciting, enjoyable, an adventure and also a challenge.

A day visit to a nearby place of scenic interest, for example, can be a most enjoyable way to spend a few hours. At the opposite end of the scale is a visit to a national park on the other side of the state or to a distant part of the country. Clearly this would involve much more detailed planning, particularly if travelling off road through the Outback is part of your trip.

It will pay you to check the equipment you have and what you will need to take before setting out on any trip, whatever its length or duration.

The main ideas are to have an itinerary—a flexible one—and to enjoy yourself. Enjoying yourself will be a lot easier if you have not got a cast-iron set of times and places to stick to.

A peaceful setting for a picnic in Tarra-Bulga National Park in Gippsland, Victoria

PLANNING THE ITINERARY

Once you have decided on where you are going and for how long, you need to do a little planning. Distances to be travelled, how long you will be away, and where to stay will all be important when working out costs. At that point you will need a budget, and while food costs may be a little higher on the road than they are at home, the big cost for most travellers is fuel.

Plan ahead and thoroughly check the condition of all the equipment you take away with you—from your vehicle, to the tent, and the zips on the sleeping-bags.

Before you go, let somebody know your travel plans, and if you are going away for any length of time and you say you are going to contact them every week, make sure you do! If you are heading into very remote country, of course, this becomes even more important.

Should you need more information than is given here, there are a host of places to go, including state government tourist offices, state national park bodies, the state motoring organisations, dedicated map shops that sell a wide range of maps and guides, as well as the local tourist information centres.

TRAVELLING LONG DISTANCES

Setting off on any trip is not to be undertaken too lightly and you should set yourself modest goals in terms of distance covered each day and the time you estimate it will take you to travel from one place to another.

Long-distance truckies might be able to sit behind the wheel for six to eight hours on end, but most people cannot. A lot of accidents happen on holidays because people try to drive too far too quickly. So take it easy, plan plenty of breaks and try not to drive for more than ten hours a day.

If the road is rougher than you expected, the weather rainy and windy, or if you are towing a trailer or caravan, you should travel far more slowly, allow yourself more time, and stop earlier than you had planned as you will find that driving in these conditions will be more tiring.

It goes without saying that your lights should always be in first-class condition, and this is especially important if you plan to any night driving.

TRAVELLING WITH KIDS

Ah, the joys of travelling with kids! Be they tiny tots or teenagers, they bring a new dimension to touring and camping.

Taking the kids camping and touring can be an enjoyable and rewarding experience—it just takes a little effort, planning and compromise.

These days, when work and family commitments make it difficult to spend much time as a family unit, camping and touring provide a great opportunity to enjoy each other's company amid the delights of the bush.

Keep in mind that, for both parents and children, being confined to the vehicle for long periods with nowhere to go to get away from each other can lead to tempers flaring and disagreements and arguments. Kids need regular breaks every couple of hours, as do most adults.

If you start taking the children camping when they are young you sort of 'advance' with their needs as they grow.

Life on the road can also be a lot easier if you travel in the company of friends who also have children.

Around Camp

We have found that kids usually disappear once you get to your camp site. While this may be a relief after a full day's travel, you should set clear guidelines on how far they can go when exploring around the camping area. It is very easy for them to get lost in the bush.

It is also very important to have strict rules around the campfire and near water. A fire for cooking your meals and to sit around at night is one of the great experiences of camping in the bush, but keep a watchful eye on young children especially.

It is worth mentioning that most snakes are nocturnal and are active at night, so do not let the kids go wandering off in the bush unsupervised. If they need to go to the toilet, make sure they carry a torch with them. In fact, children should each have their own torch, which they can also take to bed with them.

TRAVELLING WITH PETS

For many, the family pet is part of the family, and the thought of parting with your much loved companion is hard to envisage. Not only are pets great company, but a dog also offers some security, helping to guard your camp and deter would-be intruders.

However, while a day-trip would pose no problems, depending on where you plan to go, for a longer trip it may not be possible or practical. For example, with a cat or dog you are prohibited from entering any national park, and very few parks and camping grounds allow pets.

One other point should be stressed that is relevant to touring with your pet—*never* leave an animal locked in a fully closed vehicle. The sun shining through a window increases the temperature inside the vehicle and a pet left inside will quickly overheat, dehydrate, and can die.

LEGAL ISSUES

We are relatively lucky in this country that the road rules are similar right across the board.

Driving licenses, car registration and the like are all valid wherever you are in Australia. Likewise, you will be liable for a speeding fine or an unroadworthy vehicle sticker no matter what state you are in or where you come from.

SPEED LIMITS

All speed limits are well signposted: on the open highway it is between 100 and 100 kph, except in the Northern Territory where at present there is an open speed limit.

TRAVELLING IN PASTORAL AREAS

- Don't impose on property owners along the way for help unless you are in *real* trouble. Property owners are not geared up to receive or resupply tourists. Before planning to enter private property write to the owner for permission. At the very least, if you enter a property, proceed directly to the homestead and speak to the manager or owners.
- Leave all gates as you find them unless otherwise requested by the occupier. A gate may have been left open to allow stock to get to water.
- Refrain from lighting fires unless approved by the occupier. If you do have a fire, cover it completely with earth and ensure it is out before going to sleep or leaving camp. One small spark can start a devastating bushfire.
- Littering is an offence by law, the same as anywhere else, and plastics and tin cans can be fatal if chewed or swallowed by livestock. Remove all litter and rubbish.
- Chasing or upsetting livestock can cause broken fences, injuries and even death, especially around calving time.
- Livestock need water too, so please do not bathe, swim or wash clothes in water tanks or troughs, and do not camp near a watering place as stock will not come in to drink.
- Fences must not be cut, removed or driven over.
- Travelling on wet, unsealed roads can cause expensive damage and take months to repair. You could be made to pay, so always check with the local Shire office, Department of Transport or the occupier before driving on unsealed roads after rain.

Careless acts by insensitive, non-thinking people have spoilt it for others, as well as themselves if they ever want to come back. Please take care and consider the rights of others.

WILDLIFE

One of the attractions of travelling our great continent is the wildlife that inhabits it. Ever since the first seafarers landed on our shores our unique animals have amazed and delighted people. Modern travellers are no different. For those who want a good idea of what there is to see, and also help in identifying what they see, a good field guide to wildlife is essential.

Birds

There are over 700 species of birds which call Australia home either all the time or for at least part of the year. Found in every region, from arid desert country to the most dense rainforest, they range in size from tiny bush birds the size of a matchbox to the emu which is taller than a man. Any time in the bush can be enhanced by watching birds and a long trip will be appreciated more if you take the time to watch and learn about birds and their habits.

There are some excellent guide books available, including *The Birds of Australia* by Simpson and Day and *A Field Guide to the Birds of Australia* by G. Pizzey.

Mammals

The mammals of this country vary from the seals that inhabit many of our southern offshore islands to the majestic kangaroo, to the introduced species that have caused so much damage to the land and the native and unique marsupials.

For most people the larger kangaroos are the most common native mammal seen, while luckier or more observant people will spy koalas, possums, wallabies and small marsupials. Most of our native fauna will go unnoticed by the majority of travellers, which is rather sad.

Reptiles and Frogs

Snakes and lizards may send a shiver up most people's spines, but Australia has a vast array of reptiles and outdoor people are sure to meet up with some. One species of crocodile and several snakes are dangerous, so unless you know what you are looking at, leave well alone!

The lizards are a variable lot, ranging from tiny geckoes to large monitor lizards over a metre in length. While not dangerous, the larger animals can bite and scratch if cornered, so once again leave them alone.

The frog fauna of Australia takes in the whole of the continent, with some specially adapted frogs making their home in ephemeral pools in the central deserts of Australia. They are incredible.

Looking Out for Wildlife

When travelling you need to take a little care as far as our wildlife if concerned. Wombats wander quiet country roads in the mountains of the south-east, and kangaroos or other marsupials can be found on most country roads at one time or another, as can many of our birds.

A lace monitor, or goanna, often encountered on camping trips

Without getting too melodramatic about it, the toll of wildlife on our roads is shocking. It is near impossible to travel the Outback and not add to the carnage, but you can lessen the toll by driving more slowly, watching out for animals on the side of the road and keeping travelling at night, in the early morning, or the evening, to a minimum.

If you do hit an animal on an Outback road, do the right thing: stop and make sure it is dead. It is not nice, but it is better than leaving the animal to die a painful and lingering death.

Approaching Wildlife

Remember that the animals you see in a national park or in the bush, are wild! Most animals will tolerate a human approaching to within a certain distance and then they will want to flee. If you are in their way they could very well attack you. Feeding wild animals is a definite no-no!

Dangerous Wildlife

Barring the animal that will attack you because it feels threatened or trapped, we have very few animals that could really be called dangerous.

Snakes

There are a few species of snake that will attack with little provocation and others that may not be so willing to attack but are still poisonous. Generally the best rule by far is to leave them well and truly alone and they will do the same. I have yet to hear of the snake that has gone out of its way to spring an unprovoked, surprise attack on a human! Wear above-ankle boots or similar, and take particular care when walking through thick undergrowth or gathering wood for a campfire.

Prevention is much better than any cure, but we have included information about snakebite in the First Aid section of this book, just in case.

Sharks

There are a few shark attacks on humans each year in Australia, most of them around the well-populated areas of our coastline.

There is only one sure way of not getting attacked and that is not to go swimming in the ocean or in a river that has unrestricted access to the sea. However, the chances of being attacked are pretty slim and most of us take the risk each summer.

When travelling in more remote areas the same risks apply, but you may be a little further from help than if an attack happened on a major suburban beach.

Our section on First Aid has details on how to stop bleeding (under Bleeding), in the unlikely event that an attack occurs.

A kookaburra, a symbol of the Australian outdoors

Crocodiles

When travelling north for the first (or even the twentieth) time, this is the animal that strikes fear into most people's hearts.

Australia has two species, the freshwater crocodile and the estuarine (or saltwater) crocodile.

The freshie only inhabits freshwater streams, waterholes and billabongs; it grows to around 3 metres and is a shy, retiring creature. Basically, it will not hurt you, but again, it will bite if you corner it. In a word, do the right thing and they are not a problem.

Salties are an entirely different matter. They can grow to well over 6 metres, live in fresh and salt water, and have been recorded 300 km offshore as well as hundreds of kilometres upstream. They are aggressive, cunning and eat large mammals. If you are in their territory you are potential prey!

ENJOYING THE GREAT OUTDOORS

There are a variety of things to do while you are touring, from simply soaking up the scenery and atmosphere or having a picnic, to more adventurous pursuits such as bushwalking, climbing and diving.

Nature Watching

Many national parks, beaches, and the like, close to major populated areas are great spots to watch the delights of nature. You need nothing more than a good pair of eyes and some patience, but in some places the latter is not even required.

Animals

In a number of parks and reserves animals have become so used to seeing humans in close proximity that they either ignore them, pester them for food, or sneak food at the earliest opportunity. In rare instances the animals have become such a problem that the authorities have had to erect enclosures for the humans, so that they are not molested by over-friendly animals looking for a free feed.

Even so, there have been some magical moments in parks and other places when animals have visited us, or allowed us to approach them closely. Children will love this interaction with animals, to the point where you may have to subdue their enthusiasm, and noise, a little. By being quiet and moving slowly, the animals will allow you to get closer, for longer. Do not use food to tempt wildlife as animals soon realise that humans mean food and they will become a pest. They may also be harmed by eating foodstuffs that are not part of their natural diet.

Out in the more remote areas, especially in national parks, where kangaroos and eagles roam, you will find that animals will tolerate people in a vehicle more easily than they will a person on foot, so getting close is easy—just stay in the car! Remember, though, that in a national park you must stay on the road or track—heading into the scrub off the track in a vehicle is definitely frowned on, and liable to a fine!

Remember, too, that no matter how friendly an animal appears, it is a wild creature and deserves respect, not only for what it is, but also for what it can do. A kangaroo, even if it is not large, can easily hurt a young person, while a large red kangaroo can disembowel an adult human with one swift kick. An emu can do likewise. Watch and enjoy!

Birdwatching

This can be an all-consuming pastime and, in fact, can be the main reason for travelling to different areas of Australia.

A good pair of binoculars, such as an 8 x 40 or even a 10 x 40 roof prism, is ideal, but can be expensive. The generally cheaper porro prism binoculars are the most common but they are heavier and bulkier. Whichever type you choose, get the best you can afford, with Nikon, Tasco and Pentax, to name a few, being a good starting range.

There are a number of good bird books available for birdwatchers and no matter how keen or experienced you are, you definitely need a guidebook. Choose a general, all-Australian guide at a good bookshop.

Plants and Flowers

Viewing the flora is another enjoyable pastime, and some places are a kaleidoscope of colour at certain times of the year. In the Alps, daisies and other plants burst into life in early summer while in the desert, colour adorns each and every dune four to six weeks after rain. In Western Australia the south-west puts on one of the great displays of wildflowers in Australia with the flush of colour appearing to the north of Perth in early spring and then rolling down to the south coast later in the summer. Early spring is also good for wildflowers in the Flinders Ranges.

Remember that no matter how tempting it is, you are not allowed to pick plants in a park, and in most places in south-western Western Australia you are not even allowed to pick wildflowers from the roadside. At times the flowers can be so profuse it is hard not to walk on them, but please take care.

Once again, there are some excellent field guides on wildflowers, but the best ones are those that describe plants from a particular region or group of plants. Check out the bookshops in the area or information centres in towns and national parks for the appropriate books, or browse through a good bookshop in any of the major cities.

PHOTOGRAPHY

Bringing back treasured memories from the bush is what photography is all about and it can be as simple, or as demanding (read expensive), as you want to make it.

Most people own a camera, and they have become so easy to use and so good in recent years that even the most basic camera can take reasonable shots of scenery and the like. Once your interest extends to taking photos of delicate flowers or wildlife, or if you want more than just a sunlit scene, then you need to purchase something a little better.

Autumn leaves near Bright in Victoria

An SLR camera with interchangeable lenses is what you need, preferably a good camera with a couple of zoom lenses. If you have a 30–70 mm zoom and a 70–200 mm lens, you will have enough equipment to give you quite professional results.

However, even though you do not need to be an expert photographer, and even if you own the best photographic equipment, taking a good photo is more than just pointing and shooting. Composition, perspective, depth of field and exposure all contribute to making a photo and by reading a little (there are heaps of books available on photography from good bookshops around Australia) and practising in the field, you will soon be turning out stunning photos of your latest trip.

Once again, it is a hobby that can become the main reason for visiting a particular area or travelling around Australia and many hours of enjoyment can be had by just chasing that special shot.

WALKING

The simplest and possibly the most enjoyable pastime is walking. It demands the least equipment, no training, and gives each of us the opportunity to get back to basics.

There is, however, a certain amount of skill required in travelling on foot in the bush and those that have it seem to simply glide across the ground, using a minimum of effort and making the least amount of noise. On the other hand, some of us crash our way along a track, stumbling over a rock here, tripping over a tree root there and tiring ourselves out in the process. Yes, you do get better with practice, but it seems silly to practise walking. Just get out and do it—and enjoy!

Day Walks

If you are heading off on a walk that is longer than a stroll to a favoured lookout or a top swimming hole, you really ought to do some planning and carry some extra gear.

Wear good walking shoes. A good pair of runners will do for most jaunts, but if you have them, your favourite walking boots would be more suitable. Carry a daypack with a few snacks, and maybe even lunch, if you are going further afield. When you are up in the mountains, or when the weather is changeable, make sure you carry a waterproof jacket because the weather can go from delightful to diabolical in just a few hours, or even less. Do not forget to include a box of matches or a lighter, along with a compass, a pocket knife and a torch in the pack. A water bottle, containing nothing more than water, is essential, and if there is the slightest chance of heading off the track, or if you are in an unfamiliar area, then make sure you have a map. Sunglasses, sunscreen and a hat should be either worn or carried. If you have children with you make sure they are suitably attired and protected from the elements; they burn easily and get colder more quickly. They also run out of energy, so take enjoyable snacks as well as a few drinks.

Longer Bushwalks

From gentle day walks it is a natural progression to overnight hikes and longer forays into the bush. But that step needs more equipment and more skills and experience. Backpacks, sleeping-bags, tents, lightweight cooking stoves and other essentials will be required for most of us to enjoy an overnight bushwalk. There is a wide choice of equipment available and many books that can help you, not only in the choice of equipment but also where and when to go.

Stores such as Paddy Pallin, Mountain Design, Kathmandu and other specialty backpacking stores in every major city around Australia are a good starting point as most of the staff in these places are keen bushwalkers. Each capital city has a number of bushwalking clubs, as do the major regional centres, and the Federation of Bushwalking Clubs will also be pleased to help. You should find them in the *White Pages* of the telephone directory in each state's capital city.

SKIING

Downhill and cross-country skiing are such vastly different activities that the only thing they have in common is snow—even the skis are quite different, as is all the equipment.

Downhill skiing is the glamour winter activity of the High Country. In Kosciuszko National Park the hills around Thredbo, Perisher Valley, Smiggin Holes and others are cut by the long line of poles and cables of the chairlifts that carry thousands each day to the top of the ski runs.

Cross-country skiers generally shun such places, heading as quickly as possible to the quieter back country for a day's skiing or for longer overnight excursions.

While most resorts hire out cross-country skis, anything more than an easy day run should be left to those who are well equipped and experienced. Even on an easy day trip it is imperative that a small daypack is carried with warm and protective clothing, including gloves, a warm cap, waterproof jacket and overpants, a down vest and a pile jacket. And do not forget such things as sunscreen and sunglasses. Something to sit on, such as a foam mat, will come in handy, as will lots of high-energy snacks along with lunch and a water bottle or a thermos.

There are a number of adventure tour operators who organise trips into the High Country during winter and joining an operator is one of the best ways to experience the back country with the right equipment and the right support. Once again, stores such as Paddy Pallin are great places to start learning about cross-country skiing. It is a fabulous experience and one easy to get hooked on.

CANOEING

Canoeing is such a diverse activity it encompasses everything from lazily paddling a canoe across a tranquil inlet, to paddling down a remote wilderness river, to shooting huge rapids. It brings to any region a completely different aspect and experience.

It does not matter where you go, a canoe will add to your appreciation of the region. Down along the delightfully peaceful rivers of the Victorian Croajingolong coast, or up on the Cooper Creek near Innamincka in

Downhill skiing in the Snowy Mountains near Thredbo, New South Wales

north-eastern South Australia, or paddling under the cliffs in Yardi Creek Gorge in north-western Western Australia, a canoe will add pleasure and excitement to any trip.

There are a number of basic styles of canoe but most people will opt for an open Canadian canoe for their first experience as these are best for gentle paddles or trips down wide, open rivers that have few or no rapids.

A good quality buoyancy vest should be worn by all while helmets and protective spray decks should be used if you are travelling through whitewater or rapids.

There is a great deal more to handling a canoe properly than first meets the eye and if you want to do more than a very lazy paddle it would be best to do some reading or attend a basic course on the main points of canoeing. Sweep strokes, J-strokes and bow strokes will help you become a more efficient paddler and you will enjoy the experience much more.

CLIMBING

Climbers have some of the best rocks and mountains to climb within national parks and other areas dotted around Australia, while in winter the Alps offer snow and ice climbing.

Mt Buffalo in the north-east, the Grampians and Mt Arapiles in the west of Victoria are well-known spots, with Arapiles considered to have the finest rock climbing in Australia.

In New South Wales the vertical walls of the Blue Mountains make find climbing venues, while in South Australia the southern walls of Wilpena Pound are considered the best in the state.

For ice-climbing buffs the area around Blue Lake in Kosciuszko National Park and Mt Feathertop in the Alpine National Park, across the border in Victoria, offer the only real chance for mountaineering experience on this continent.

There are a host of other spots and the best place to start is at a specialty outdoor shop or within the pages of magazines such as *Wild* and *Rock*. There are also a number of climbing schools located around Australia, generally close to the best climbing areas, or in the capital cities where you can learn the skills required. While you need to be fit to climb the top grades, most of us would be capable of tackling the minor climbs and getting a fantastic buzz out of it. Give it a try!

DIVING

All around the coast of Australia there are stretches of spectacular coastline that are perfect for divers and snorkellers. In some areas marine parks have been established while in others underwater trails have been marked where divers can follow a series of signs to wrecks or other points of interest.

While SCUBA diving is a skill that demands training and a range of expensive equipment, snorkelling can be enjoyed by most people—with a minimal outlay on equipment. Both open up a whole new world, with fish colour and movement surrounding you wherever you choose to go. Of course, snorkelling on a coral reef is everyone's dream, but southern Australia also offers plenty of fabulous opportunities to delight in the underwater world.

For snorkelling, you will need fins that fit firmly but comfortably, a mask that seals around the face and is comfortable, and a snorkel. While you could spend well over $200 on these three items alone, for $70 or so you should be able to buy some reasonable gear. And, because it is expensive and you want to keep it in good condition, wash your equipment in fresh water after you have used it.

Of course, there are a few skills to learn, but the most common mistake for first-timers is that, as they lie on the surface looking down, they splash too much with their fins, using up energy and scaring away any fish. Keep your fins down and under water and use slow, steady strokes to propel yourself along.

Most of the dive shops around the country can arrange to teach you SCUBA diving, but if snorkelling is all you want to do you can learn most of the basics from a book and with practice you will soon be snorkelling with the best of them.

Once again, diving can become an all-encompassing passion and the prime reason for travelling and visiting our wild, magnificent places.

FISHING

Fishing is the biggest recreational pastime in Australia and it is no wonder that thousands of people each year pack their vehicles and head off fishing.

Some save up for that one big trip north to the barramundi capitals of the Territory or the Cape: others with less time head up to a local stream for a weekend's trout fishing or along the coast after a snapper or mulloway. It is an activity that is worth millions to the economy, and one that in recent years has become more and more controlled. It is not that governing bodies want people to stop fishing, but they want to manage the resource so that the fishing will be just as good in years to come.

Fishing Regulations

Fishing regulations vary from state to state. However, recreational fishing in a marine environment is normally free of any licensing requirements unless you want to use nets, pots or take selected species like crayfish; in these cases state requirements vary.

Fishing in freshwater habitats generally requires a licence of some sort. Once again the regulations vary by state.

Most states have minimum sizes for all fish and other marine life. Some species also have maximum sizes, while other species are protected altogether. Bag limits also apply and once again the requirements vary from state to state.

Most states have areas of coastline that are marine habitat reserves, or marine national parks. These can include areas where no fishing, collecting or the removal of any item from the water is allowed, as well as others where there are bag and size limits. Check with each state body or the individual parks and reserves concerned as to their regulations.

MOUNTAIN BIKING

Designed for riding on rough and rocky trails, the mountain bike is an ideal way to see and experience many of our wild places. Day trips and longer overnight forays are possible on a mountain bike. In national parks these bikes often suffer the same restrictions as motor vehicles. In other words, you are often confined to public roads and tracks, with walking trails and even Management Vehicles Only (MVO) tracks being out of bounds. There does not seem to be a standard ruling on mountain biking, even within parks in the same state, so it pays to check before setting out on two wheels.

In some places, such as Thredbo, you can hire mountain bikes (though riding to the crest of Mt Kosciuszko is not allowed). Otherwise you could spend a lot of dollars buying a mountain bike, with prices topping out at an incredible $8000!

Clothing for bike touring needs to be light and snug fitting, and you need good windproof and waterproof gear as well. Much the same gear as for bushwalking needs to be carried for either day jaunts or extended overnight trips.

Mountain biking is a much faster way to travel through the back country than on two feet and there is ample opportunity for excitement on exhilarating descents and narrow trails.

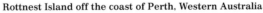
Rottnest Island off the coast of Perth, Western Australia

VEHICLE TOURING

In many parts of the country, vehicle-based touring is a pleasant and easy way to enjoy what the area has to offer. It does not matter whether you have a 4WD or the family car, most places close to the more settled areas of Australia have access routes and through routes which are suitable to explore, and the chances of finding a delightful place to camp are good.

In the more remote country a 4WD is a better choice, but even so there are many places around the country, even fairly remote areas such as some national parks—Sturt National Park in far north-western New South Wales or the Big Desert National Park in Victoria, to name just two—that can be visited and enjoyed in the family car, driven with care.

If you intend to visit a national park and you are not sure of the road conditions, contact the ranger headquarters of the particular parks you wish to visit and they will let you know which roads and tracks are suitable for you and your vehicle, and if there are any seasonal closures or roads temporarily closed due to recent rains or floods.

Travel in remote areas demands some special precautions such as carrying some water, maybe an extra spare tyre, as well as tools, camping gear, food and drink.

OTHER ACTIVITIES

Canyoning, caving, paragliding and a host of other activities can all be enjoyed in wilderness areas and in parks. Whatever your particular interest, it can be found somewhere in this great country.

ABORIGINAL COMMUNITIES AND LAND

Much of inland Australia is Aboriginal land. These areas can be cattle stations that are now owned and run by Aboriginal communities, or vast areas of old reserve land that have been deeded to an Aboriginal community as freehold land, or areas of Crown land that have been handed back to a particular group of Aboriginal people. In the Northern Territory over 50 per cent of the land is now owned by Aboriginal groups, while other states have lesser amounts.

Permits and Access

You need an access permit to enter or to cross most Aboriginal land. While some permits can be easy to obtain, like those needed to use the Gunbarrel Highway west of Uluru (Ayers Rock), other areas are almost impossible to enter.

For further information and requirements concerning access permits, write to or contact the Aboriginal authorities concerned—allow plenty of time before your planned trip as it can take months to get a permit.

FUEL

Getting fuel in the Outback is not as easy as it may seem. In big towns and on the major highways it is not a problem, but once you start heading into remote country fuel is just a little harder to organise.

Autogas may be common on the east coast, but away from the main highways elsewhere it can be hard to get. For example, north of Cooktown on Cape York you cannot get autogas. For the autogas vehicle owner there are a couple of annually updated guides that list outlets. These are essential for planning. The RAA of SA has an LPG Outlets Directory, or alternatively, contact the Energy Information Centre in Adelaide.

A Queenslander, an historic style of home, in Maryborough, south-east Queensland

MONEY MATTERS

Do not expect to find your bank while travelling around the country. Once you are away from major town centres, most small communities have only one or two banks represented. You cannot count on the banks having full banking facilities, and if the computers go down, it can create problems.

When touring in more remote areas, it pays to have a Commonwealth Bank passbook account—not just a keycard account—as every post office in Australia is a Commonwealth Bank agency, and even though they may not be able to offer EFTPOB (Electronic Funds Transfer Point of Banking) facilities for you to use your keycard, they can certainly let you withdraw money from a passbook account.

These days electronic banking is becoming more readily available even in isolated communities, but it should not be relied upon. It is also possible to do a lot of transactions, such as shopping and buying fuel, through EFTPOS (Electronic Funds Transfer at Point of Sale) terminals.

While credit cards, especially Mastercard, Bankcard and Visa are widely accepted as payment, they cannot be depended upon, and trying to get a cheque accepted as payment for goods and services and be difficult. Australian dollar travellers cheques can also be used and cashed in many places, but once again they are not universally accepted and we would not suggest that they be your main source of cash, especially in Outback areas.

In many cases you will find that cash is the only form of money accepted, so try to gauge how much you will need for fuel and food, along with incidentals, between banking points, especially if you do not have a Commonwealth Bank passbook account.

INSURANCE

Travelling off the beaten track in this vast country does open one up to a new range of experiences, including exposure to having equipment lost, stolen or damaged in ways not covered by your normal insurance policies.

AUTOMOBILE ASSOCIATION MEMBERSHIP

We are great believers in joining your state motoring organisation, particularly if you are about to set off on a long trip around Australia. It might also pay to upgrade your membership to include any extra benefits the association might offer in your home state.

Not only does membership give you access to a vast range of cheap, often free, touring and accommodation information, there are also the roadside assist schemes that are a great help when touring. The Plus schemes give even more coverage, including such things as return fares home, hire cars, accommodation, and more. It can pay to belong.

The amount of planning and preparation you will need to do for a trip away from home will depend on where you are going and how long you will be away. For a day's jaunt you may only need to take a portable cooler with a few cool drinks and lunch. For an overnight trip you may need to plan where you will stay and what you would like to see. Obviously, if you intend to camp you will also need a swag or a tent plus sleeping gear and food.

On long trips you will need to do a lot more planning and take much more gear. Questions about fuel requirements, and a dozen other things, need to be answered before you set off. This section aims to give you some idea of what you require, but you will need to think about the trip you have planned, the style of accommodation or camping you enjoy, and your gear. There are places where you should not go if you have not got the right equipment. While Cape York is fine without a High Frequency (FH) radio, a more remote and difficult trip to the Simpson Desert or any Outback, isolated area really demands at least one HF radio in your group.

PLANNING THE TRIP

- Make a plan of your proposed trip—where, what season, time allowed, distance, fuel.
- Check on fuel availability, where you can resupply, places to see, history, attractions and things to do
- Make a rough, and flexible, itinerary
- Apply for any permits that may be necessary, such as for certain national parks and Aboriginal land. Advance bookings are necessary for camp sites in some national parks, and during holiday periods they often operate on a ballot system. It is also very important to apply well ahead for any permits for access to Aboriginal land as these can take some time to obtain.
- It is always advisable to book accommodation at some of the more popular destinations.
- If you are going bush, let someone know your itinerary and if you change it significantly, contact them so they do not panic. Keep in regular touch.
- For some areas it will be necessary to check the conditions of the roads, whether they are open to vehicular traffic, whether conventional or 4WD only.

PREPARING THE VEHICLE

Your vehicle is your lifeline. If you were to break down on a remote track in a mountainous area, for instance, you could be in for a long, hard walk. If you have the same sort of breakdown in the Kimberley or the Gulf Country your bones, bleached by the sun, may be all they find.

It pays to have a well-set up vehicle, and remember that a vehicle that can handle a 300 km day trip to the mountains may not be at all suitable for a long trip that covers rough stretches of terrain and vastly differing road and weather conditions.

Checking the Mechanicals

Many people can service and maintain their own vehicle and that will certainly be of help if you are heading for the bush. It does not take a lot of skill and knowledge to do a basic service on your vehicle—it always helps to be able to diagnose a problem. It would also be a good idea to learn to do a basic service before you head off into the wild.

However, if you are not at all mechanically minded, make sure before setting off that your vehicle is checked by a reputable mechanic.

PACKING A VEHICLE

Everyone knows how to pack a vehicle for a short trip, but packing for a long trip is a skill: it gets easier—and better—with practice. Once you have done it a few times you will know the things you require to be kept handy and those you can afford to bury.

Keep in mind the equipment and stores you will be using all the time. Cameras, a lolly jar and a pillow, plus a few cassette tapes you may want always at hand, while everyday food items, water and the basic cooking gear need to be pretty close. On the other hand, the stores required to cook bread over the campfire can be buried a little deeper because you will not be doing that every day.

The clothes bag will need to be fairly handy, as will a basic first aid kit.

Depending on where you are going the shovel and toilet paper need to be very handy as you will need it whenever anyone wants a nature walk.

A basic tool-roll should always be part of your equipment along with a can of WD40 and the vehicle manual.

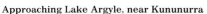

Approaching Lake Argyle, near Kununurra

CAMPING

One of the real delights of a trip away from home is setting up a tent and being close to nature. Today there is absolutely no reason why you cannot be comfortable when you are in the bush: good tents to keep the bugs and elements at bay, refrigerators to keep the food and beer cold, showers to keep you clean and sleeping gear that is comfortable and warm all provide the ingredients for a happy and successful camping trip.

What camping equipment you buy will really depend on how much money you have to spend, how much time you are going to be in the scrub and where you plan to go. Whatever you do, buy the very best you can afford. Not only will it keep you drier and warmer, it will last longer and if you want to sell it later you will get more for it.

CAMPING GEAR

What you take with you will depend on where you go and for how long. A swag may be good for the Outback, but a tent is better for the Alps in spring or autumn when it can rain at any time. If you are on the road for a long time a camper may be the best answer as it does give a lot more luxury. Decide on your style of camping and buy the appropriate gear.

Wild Dog Hill in Whyalla Conservation Park, South Australia

Swags

A swag is an excellent option for sleeping when touring the Outback. It is quick: while everyone else is struggling with a tent, a swag is a throw-down winner. Although they are basically just a protected sleeping cocoon, the models of swags now available keep you comfortable and secure from all the elements. They are especially suitable for trips in central Australia, or up north in the warmer areas, and there is no greater feeling than sleeping under a clear, star-studded sky.

A basic swag consists of a large piece of good quality canvas in which you put all your sleeping gear—mattress, blankets or sleeping-bag, pillow and mossie net. Today, however, you can get swags that are more like a

small tent and these are definitely better in the rain. This type also prevents the bugs and creepy crawlies from getting into your sleeping gear, while still having all the advantages of the normal traditional swag.

As with buying a tent, make sure you are getting a high standard of workmanship, that good quality material is used in the canvas, flywire and zips, and that the mattress is made of high density foam.

Tents

Tents are the long term favourite of Australians going bush and how you camp will depend on which is the best for you. Think about your requirements, then buy the very best tent you can afford.

Are you a tourer or a stay-in-one-place camper, an overnight bush-walker or a vehicle-based camper? Clearly, weight and packed size are of prime importance to bushwalkers and mountain climbers. A 'minute camper' that is easy to erect is great for overnight stops, while a more palatial tent may suit longer stays but is a pain to erect each and every night. The smaller tents, with a floor size of around 3 metres square, are acceptable for overnighting.

It is hard to beat an Australian or New Zealand made tent. Look for quality when you are choosing a tent: quality of canvas, floor material, zips (go for the YKK brand and check to make sure that they are protected from the weather), even and close sewing, reinforced seams, corner peg points, and even the poles, pegs and ropes, are all important. Flyscreens on the windows should be double-stitched; fibreglass screens will generally outlast nylon. Do not select by floor size alone, as lower wall heights and sloping walls will greatly reduce the amount of usable space.

When you get your new tent home, hose it down and saturate the tent thoroughly so that the new canvas stretches and fills up any sewing holes—you do not want it leaking on your first outing simply because you could not be bothered to give it a thorough soaking at home.

Never put your tent away wet. If you have to pack it wet, erect it again as soon as possible to dry out the canvas, or the canvas will deteriorate.

CAMPING AND PERSONAL REQUIREMENTS CHECKLIST

Portable light	Boots/shoes
Torch	Hat
Tent or swag	Wet weather gear
Sleeping gear	Sunglasses
Clothes—to suit where you are going	
Portable refrigerator/ice chest	First aid kit (see First Aid)
Jerrycan(s) of water	Paper and pencils
Folding chairs	String
Fire extinguisher	Plastic sheet
Toilet paper	Tarpaulin
Toiletries bag	Poles, ropes and pegs
Camera, film and spare batteries	Bucket
Compass and maps	Shovel, Axe
Insect repellent	Food
Sunblock cream	Cooking equipment

If purchasing a tent made from a synthetic like nylon, stick to the better brands such as Fairydown, Tatonka or Eureka. Tents made from these materials can vary in size from a one-person bivvy, through small bush-walking dome and tunnel tents to larger family-style dome and A-frame tents.

Be aware that nylon is usually not UV stabilised and can lose its colour and become weak in areas constantly exposed to heat and sunlight. Make sure you get a double skin tent, or one with a fly. Also ensure that stress areas like peg loops and seams are reinforced and as with canvas tents, that zippers are a good quality (such as YKK). It is worth noting that alloy poles are more durable than fibreglass poles.

Good outdoor shops such as Paddy Pallin, found around Australia, are the best places for tents, but the top of the line ones are expensive.

Caravans

The choice of vans available for the tourer is immense and your choice will be determined by where you want to go. There are only a few that come anywhere near real off-road capability. The final choice will depend on your wallet and the layout of the van.

No matter what style and size, a van will limit your travels. In places such as Cape York and the Simpson Desert, to name just two, you will be forced to leave the van behind and take a tent or a swag.

Sleeping Gear

You spend nearly a third of your life in bed asleep and it is not much different when you are in the bush, so it pays to be comfortable and warm.

Mattresses

You can use a layer of foam, a camp stretcher, a normal air mattress or one of the newer, self-inflating air mattresses.

While the latter may be the most expensive, they have the advantage of taking up a minimum amount of room when packed, they are well padded for sleeping on and being insulated they keep the cold from the ground away from you. There are a number of different sorts of self-inflators around.

A layer of foam is the simplest form of mattress and is very comfortable. Its main drawback is its size when packed.

Camp stretchers are comfortable, yet they tend to break at the most inappropriate times. The original canvas stretcher is still available, but today there is a wider selection of makes and models.

Normal air mattresses are fine once you have learnt to inflate them to suit your own requirements, and they pack down to a small size for travelling.

Sleeping-bags

Sleeping-bags come in all shapes and sizes, but it is what is on the inside that makes the difference—and that makes the choice confusing. Be guided by the price—the more expensive the bag is, the better it will be. It certainly pays to select a bag from a specialised camping store where the staff are well qualified to guide you.

Sleeping-bags are priced according to their filling and lining. At the lower end of the market, acrylic and polyester filled bags are only suitable for home use or strictly in warmer climates. Hollofill is a good all-round filling and Quallofill, which is lighter in weight than Hollofill, has good heat retention, even if wet.

The warmest, and the fill that packs down to the smallest size, is down and the best you will find consists of 90 per cent down/10 per cent feathers. Some of the cheaper down bags will be less than 50 per cent down—so they are bulkier and colder!

You need to keep your bag clean as the things that destroy a bag's insulating qualities are dust, dirt and body oils. While most bags are washable, it pays to keep washing to a minimum. To do that and to preserve your bag the best idea is to make up an inner bag out of an old sheet that will fit nicely into your new sleeping-bag. That will not only keep the bag clean, it is great for warm nights when you can use it on its own, and on cold nights it adds a little more insulation.

Another point well worth remembering when sleeping out is that it is no use just throwing blankets on top of you if you are cold—the cold will come in from underneath you as well. So either wrap yourself and bag in a blanket or put one blanket on the bottom and one on the top!

Upon returning home, do not leave the bag in its stuffsack. Store it loosely and that way the filling will not break down so quickly.

Whatever you do, think about your needs and shop around at specialty camping stores. Remember the old adage. You get what you pay for.

THE TRAVELLING COOK

Cooking in the bush, whether it be from a van or tent, using a camp oven or a gas stove, need not be a daunting task. Make a rough plan of the meals you hope to cook—this will give you an idea of the staples you will need to carry. If you go through your favourite recipes you can list the necessary ingredients and include them in your shopping list. A great help

Waves breaking over Dudley Beach near Newcastle, New South Wales

in this regard is to start your own camping cookbook, a ready reckoner for camping meals.

As well, make a list of the items you think you might need for each meal. For example: Breakfast—cereal, toast, bacon and eggs for the first few mornings, tea/coffee, sugar, milk, etc. Do the same thing for lunch and dinner, then estimate how many days you might be away from civilisation and a corner shop. From this you can gauge your food requirements.

Space and Time Savers

With weight and space at a premium in most vehicles or backpacks on any trip, dehydrated and long-life products make catering for wilderness camping much easier. However, no matter how hard you try you cannot get away from taking some canned food.

CAMP HYGIENE

Let us say something about camp hygiene. Please do not use any form of soap in a river, stream, waterhole or lake. It is not necessary, does nothing for the water quality (even if you feel the amount is inconsequential), does nothing for the people downriver except give them belly aches and does nothing for the aquatic life (plant and animal) except kill them!

If you want to swim and wash in a river or lake, it is not a problem: wet yourself and then with a bucket of water, walk a whole 15 metres or so from the water's edge, soap yourself up and then rinse it off, making sure the waste water does not run down the bank back into the river or dam. Then you can go back and enjoy the swim.

Toilets should be erected well away from a water source, a short distance from camp. We all like our privacy but if you need a cut lunch and a water bottle to get to the loo it is a bit far!

For a toilet pit, dig a deep hole about a metre long and 40 cm wide. A folding toilet seat makes it more comfortable. Always cover any waste with soil and leave a shovel or trenching tool at the toilet for this purpose. When you are moving on, make sure the trench is covered with a deep layer of soil before you pack the shovel.

For the quick loo stop you will need a shovel—a small garden one or a trenching tool is ideal. Scrape a hole at least 20 cm deep and once you have finished, bury all the waste with soil. Better still, before burying the waste, burn the paper and then bury what remains. Obviously, you need to be careful not to start a fire or let young kids out into the scrub with matches lighting paper at the drop of a hat!

When setting up a toilet, remember not to erect it where wastes can run back into the water system.

INSECT PROBLEMS

Bush flies can be a real hassle and at times can spoil a great holiday. And insect repellent is not too effective either. In warm weather in central Australia or places further north, a fly veil or a hat with a set or corks is a must. At mealtimes an insect-free enclosure, either inside the vehicle or in a specially erected insect-screened gazebo may be the answer.

Young kids can be driven to despair by flies, so make sure they have a fly veil during the day when the flies are bad and a net that keeps the insects away when they are having a nap.

Mosquitoes too can be a problem in the Outback. Claypans and waterholes topped up with occasional seasonal rains provide ideal breeding places. In the evening and at night they can be a real pest Insect repellents work well on these insects, with Rid or tropical strength Aeroguard being the best. Even so, a long-sleeved shirt or an insect-free enclosure, either a tent or a fly-screen gazebo, is more effective.

In northern Australia, anywhere near the coast or an estuary, sandflies can drive you insane. Once bitten, the damage is done—the bites will itch and itch. If you are in sandfly country cover up, especially just before sunset, and use plenty of insect repellent on exposed flesh.

We make up our own north Queensland-proven anti-sandfly mix of baby oil and Dettol in an 8:1 ratio. You can add 1 part methylated spirits, along with some citronella for that little extra something that may help.

SETTING UP CAMP

This is one aspect of camping that you learn as you go along. We will give some pointers here, but there is nothing like experience to teach you what you have done wrong. It is easy to say, 'Do not set up your camp on low ground'. But sometimes it is only when it rains that you know where the low ground is!

Camp Sites

Many people are happy in camping grounds and caravan parks. We tend to look for uncrowded camp sites where we and a few travelling companions can enjoy some peace and the delights of the bush.

Getting away from it all does not mean the back of beyond. It just takes a little forethought. Nearly every summer, over the school break, we take a beachside holiday. We stay away from the east coast though, saving our favourite camping spots in the Myall Lakes National Park or Fraser Island for when school is back. No, over the Christmas break we head for the west coast of South Australia where believe it or not, you can still camp and have a beach to yourself.

If you want an east coast holiday it is surprising how quickly the crowds drop away just a few kilometres inland from the coast. We have often camped beside a delightful steam within easy distance of the Gippsland 'Riviera' coast and not seen another soul from one day to the next.

Overnight Bushcamps

Travelling down the main highway it is not easy to find a good camp site, though you can be lucky. The more remote the area, the better your chances of finding a good site near the road. Even so, you will have a better

A 4WD vehicle makes towing a caravan across a beach look easy

camp, quieter and more private, if you head off the road a short distance. Use your maps and head along a side road: ones that follow a creek or cross a river or stream often give access to small areas ideal for a camp. Unless you are in a hurry it is best to set up camp while there is some daylight left, especially if are unfamiliar with your equipment. Setting up camp at night after a long day's drive is bound to bring tempers to the boil.

If you want to get away in the morning and have dry canvas when you do, make sure your tent or camper is sited to catch the early morning sun.

If you are not in a hurry and you are working to a flexible timetable, do not drive past a great looking camp site, even if it is only mid-afternoon. Chances are it will be the last decent one you see.

Choosing a Camp Site

Pick a site protected from the wind. A line of trees or scrub can break the wind while a small hollow tucked into the side of a hill can be a very sheltered spot. If you are in a vehicle, it can, at a pinch, act as a windbreak. The prevailing winds can often be picked, especially near the coast, by the trees and scrubs all leaning in one direction. In the mountains, stay away from ridges and saddles between two hilltops; when on the coast, avoid those bare unprotected heathlands.

Do not select the lowest ground. Water can gather there, while in a valley or larger depression cold air can be trapped, keeping your camp cool, while just a little higher both you and the camp could be warmer.

Check out where the shade is going to be. You will need to know where north is to do this, so use a compass, or a watch, and work out the sun's path. If it is blistering hot during the day you will want to try and be in the shade during those hot hours. If it is a winter camp you will be happier if your tent or camper trailer catches some sun. Select the site accordingly.

Do not camp underneath old gum trees. This rule is probably broken by everyone sooner or later. Those shady red gums along the river can be a delight on a hot summer's day. However, red gums, yellow box gums and the like are notorious for dropping branches. Visible dead branches are a sign that should be heeded. We have seen cars crushed by a fallen branch, so you can imagine what a large bough would do to a tent with people!

Do not camp in a dry river or creek bed. West of the Great Divide and away from the well-watered regions of this country, you will come across many dry river beds. Flat, soft and sandy, with few of the weeds and burrs that mar the surrounding areas, they seem to offer an ideal camp site. They can be a trap! A distant rainstorm can send down a torrent of water to catch you unprepared, and even steady rain can produce enough water to bog your vehicle.

A river flat or a sandy tropical beach front may look a nice spot to camp, but the insects, mosquitoes especially, can drive you nuts. It might be better to camp away from the stream and the floodplain, or the beach, by just 100 metres or so—the difference in annoying insect life is amazing.

Two other things make for an ideal camp. Being close to a good, reliable water supply makes life a lot easier. Remember, though, in the Outback not to crowd a water point. It may be the only waterhole for kilometres, which all the wildlife and stock in the area depend on. Your actions could cause them to go thirsty and die a horrible death.

Wood for a fire makes for an easy camp. You will be surprised how quickly the easily collected wood is used up and you will then have hunt around for more. Use wood conservatively and do not cut or chop down live trees and scrub to feed a fire. It will not burn well and you will destroy the area. Bring out the gas stove if there is no firewood.

There is one other point to consider before setting up your canvas home. Is there anybody else there? Most people who are camping in the bush prefer not to have somebody camp right on their doorstep. If there is another site not far away, or even a kilometre or so, think before you crowd up close to someone else. Ask if they mind, they might be pulling out next morning and then you will have the site to yourself.

CAMPING AND TOURING ETIQUETTE

It's one of the greatest disappointments of a trip to travel through pristine wilderness and come across a delightful camping site marred—no, vandalised—by rubbish! For everybody's sake
• Leave the camp site clean and take ALL your rubbish out with you. Don't even bury it, as wild animals, other people and flooding rivers can uncover the junk and spread it over the countryside.
• Use a shovel to dig a deep hole for your toilet requirements; keep it away from running water and other campers.
• Set up camp well away from any stock or water point.
• Don't use soap, shampoo or detergent in streams, waterholes, dams or water troughs. Use a bucket or a bush shower well away from the water to wash and rinse yourself. Also use a bucket to wash clothes and dishes, away from where animals and other humans may drink. Nobody likes to drink water tainted by soap!
• Take care with fire—clear an area around the fireplace before lighting it. Before you leave, make sure the fire is completely out.
• Use old fireplaces—don't erect new ones.
• Observe all fire restrictions.
• Observe all rules and regulations pertaining to the use of public land.
• Keep to constructed vehicle tracks, never 'bush bash'.
• Avoid areas which are easily damaged, such as swamps, alpine snow plains and vegetated sand dunes.
• Respect our wildlife.
• Respect private land. Always ask permission before crossing pastoral land.
• Leave gates as you find them.
• Observe all park regulations; when in doubt consult the ranger.

Setting Up The Camp

Once you have found an area that looks good, pick a flat-looking site, making sure there is enough room for your tent, swag or camper. Once the tent is up, the camper erected or the swag laid out (the latter is the easiest and quickest of the three), the pegs hammered in and everything ship-shape, it is time to think about what the weather will do.

If it is about to rain or you think a storm is likely, it will pay to dig a gutter or two to keep any flooding water away from your canvas home. You do not need to dig a gutter all the way around your tent. One across the slops on the high side of your tent will be fine.

A colourful beach scene at Barwon Heads. Victoria

FIRST AID AND SURVIVAL

You may think you will never need to be proficient at first aid but everybody should have some training in this essential skill. Prompt action, correctly carried out, can go a long way to save lives.

There are quite a few good handbooks on first aid, such as those produced by the St John Ambulance association and the Red Cross, and one is essential in any glovebox.

PRACTICAL FIRST AID

In the bush the main aspect of first aid is clear, logical thinking, prompt action and the ability to improvise. We have included the treatment for some of the more dangerous situations and the more common situations travellers will come across. Much of the information has been taken from the free book *Aids to Survival* produced by the WA Police Force.

IN AN EMERGENCY

The acknowledged order of urgency when assessing a situation is
D R A B C
Danger—move the cause from the patient or the patient from the cause
Response—shake and shout
Airway—maintain an open and clear airway
Breathing—look, listen and feel
Circulation—check the carotid pulse

Further Action
• Stop bleeding
• Minimise pain
• Reassure the patient
• Seek further aid if necessary
Always attend to the most urgent needs first

Making a Diagnosis
Before you can commence rational treatment a diagnosis must be made. You need to find out quickly:
HISTORY—how the injury occurred
SYMPTOMS— what the patient feels
SIGNS—what you can observe by examining the patient

UNCONSCIOUSNESS

A patient may be unconscious for many reasons including heart attack, drowning, electrocution, a head injury, fainting, and smoke inhalation.

Diagnosing an unconscious patient is a little more difficult than a conscious one. Apply principles of DRABC, then check the level of consciousness by seeing if the patient responds to speech or reacts to a more painful stimulus.

Check head, neck, spine and upper and lower limbs for any sign of injury. Treat as required and place the patient in the coma position.

See our chart for the resuscitation of an unconscious patient.

SHOCK

Shock is brought on by a fall in blood pressure: if unchecked it can result in death or irreversible damage. The onset of clinical shock is often delayed, that is, when a person first starts bleeding, they may not be shocked, but if they go on bleeding (externally or internally) they will eventually go into shock.

Early detection, or better still, anticipation or prevention of shock and commencement of treatment are extremely important, because the patient's condition can deteriorate very quickly.

Signs and Symptoms of Shock
• Patient is cold, clammy and pale, has a rapid, feeble pulse and may have fast, shallow breathing
• Thirst
• Weakness, anxiety, restlessness, incoherence
• Nausea

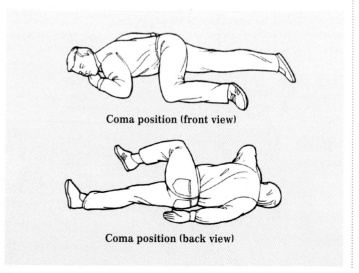

Coma position (front view)

Coma position (back view)

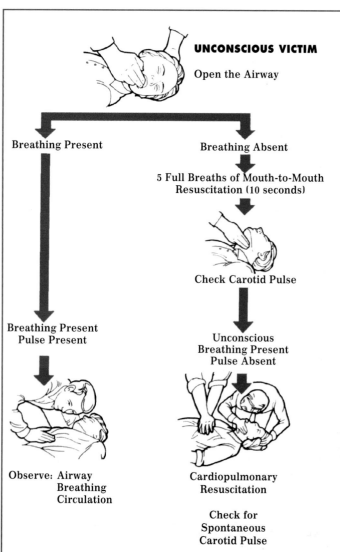

UNCONSCIOUS VICTIM
Open the Airway

Breathing Present

Breathing Absent

5 Full Breaths of Mouth-to-Mouth Resuscitation (10 seconds)

Check Carotid Pulse

Breathing Present
Pulse Present

Unconscious
Breathing Present
Pulse Absent

Observe: Airway
Breathing
Circulation

Cardiopulmonary
Resuscitation

Check for
Spontaneous
Carotid Pulse

Treatment of Shock

Cover patient and keep warm, raise the legs, protect from the elements, minimise fluid loss (e.g., from bleeding), reassure, moisten lips and DO NOT give alcohol.

FRACTURES

The key to the treatment of fractures is immobilisation. A mobile fracture is painful, may cause internal bleeding, may become compound (break through the skin) and is a major cause of shock.

Treatment of Fractures

Check and assess—can you immobilise the limb?

Reduction (repositioning) can be dangerous. Only reduce a fracture if you must, say, to move the person to safety. In this case, if the patient faints with pain, do not stop! Reduce and splint the fracture while the patient is unconscious.

Methods of Immobilisation

Finger—strap the broken one to the adjacent finger
Leg—strap legs together or splint
Pelvis—strap legs together
Upper arm—collar and cuff sling, then bandage upper arm to chest
Ribs—leave alone

Fractures of the Spine

Fractures of the spine may be complicated by damage to the spinal cord. Therefore, to avoid permanent damage, careful protective handling aimed at minimising spinal cord damage is essential. The signs and symptoms may range from severe pain to loss of sensation and lack of control over limbs.

Treatment
- The aim is to prevent further damage by immobilising the spine
- If patient is unconscious, normal resuscitation procedures MUST take precedence
- The patient should then be immobilised by strapping the legs together, maintaining body position with improvised padding and keeping the head straight and in extension to ensure an open airway.

SPRAIN

Sprains result form abnormal stretching or partial tearing of the supporting ligaments of any joint. Ankles are the most common. There is pain, swelling, tenderness and bruising, but the patient can still use the joint or limb.

Treatment
- In a bushwalking situation it may be better NOT to remove the boot if the boot comes above the ankle.
- Otherwise, remove shoe, elevate and support the foot and apply a cold compress for 15 minutes, then support joint with a firm elastic bandage.

HEAD INJURY

If a patient is unconscious and has not obviously been electrocuted or drowned, etc., think of head injury. There may be no obvious signs. Bleeding from the nose, mouth or ears may indicate a fracture of the skull.

If a patient who has been unconscious recovers and then loses consciousness again, you may assume head injury.

Treatment
- Put patient into recovery position.
- Transport to hospital.

BURNS AND SCALDS

These can happen anywhere around a camp and can be very painful.

Treatment
- Apply cold water to any burn.
- Do not attempt to remove clothing from burned area.
- Do not use butter
- Leave blisters intact.
- For minor burns and all peripheral burns apply antibiotic cream or Betadine and cover. (Antibiotic cream or Betadine can help to prevent infection.)

BLEEDING

Blood flows through a system of arteries and veins. If there is a break or a hole in them, bleeding occurs.

Primary Treatment

Plug the hole. Do not worry about whether it is arterial or venous bleeding. If there is a lot of bleeding the patient will develop shock quickly.
- First wipe away any blood (or remove clothing) so you can see where the bleeding is coming from.
- Apply direct pressure with a pad or bandage (or your hand) to the source of the bleeding.
- Elevate the bleeding site, if practicable, to reduce blood flow.

Tourniquets

A big NO-NO—only to be used if you cannot stop the bleeding in any other way. Tourniquets can cause damage and the patient may lose the limb altogether. However, use common sense. If the limb is severed, use a tourniquet first up—you cannot do any more damage to a limb that is missing.

SNAKE BITE

Ninety per cent of snake bites in Australia are at the ankle or below, 8 per cent occur on the hand and 2 per cent elsewhere. Hence the best guard against snake bite is protection. If you wear above-ankle boots, and/or thick socks and/or long trousers, you are less likely to be bitten.

Treatment
- Apply a pressure bandage straight over the bite, then wind the bandage up the limb towards the body.
- Do not cut or bleed the site of the bite. A cut will only allow poison into the body.
- Do not wipe or wash the site of the bite because the residual venom on the skin may be identifiable in the laboratory when the patient arrives at the hospital. Venom is harmless on skin contact.
- The patient should avoid excessive activity; carry or walk them slowly.
- Reassure the patient.
- Endeavour to get medical aid within eight hours.

A sea snake on Stradbroke Island, Queensland

FIRST AID AND SURVIVAL

Poeppels Corner on the border of Queensland and South Australia

BITES AND STINGS

The only fatal bites from an insect come from ticks. Funnel web spider bites can cause death; redback spiders and scorpions cause pain but almost never death.

Bees, Wasps, Ants

The major problem with stings of bees, wasps and ants is an allergy to the bite. If you know you are allergic to insect bites, be careful, and carry the appropriate medicine/first aid treatment. A liquid antihistamine is often of some help while an antihistamine tablet has a slower effect.

Ammonia and methylated spirits may be useful as counter irritants.

In the case of bee stings, the poison sac is attached to the sting which, as it is barbed, will often remain in the skin. It should be removed with the edge of a knife, or the edge of a piece of paper, not with fingers. Fingers can squash the venom sac and inject more venom.

Ticks and Leeches

In areas where ticks and leeches are prevalent you can reduce your chances of attracting them by covering up (long trousers, socks and boots, long-sleeved shirt, a hat) and applying Rid or similar to your boots, socks, neck and wrists.

Leeches are mainly a nuisance; they feed, injecting an anticoagulant into your bloodstream, which makes the tiny wound bleed profusely, then they drop off. Wash the wound to remove the anticoagulant, then apply a dressing until the bleeding stops.

Ticks, on the other hand, can cause paralysis, breathing failure, even death, if not removed. At the end of the day, check your body carefully for ticks, particularly soft skin areas (armpits, groin, navel, behind ears, etc.). Check children similarly.

If a tick is attached to/embedded in the skin, DO NOT pull it off: this could leave the toxin-containing mouthparts there. Do not prick or burn the tick as it will release more toxin; do not apply petrol or kerosene.

To remove the tick, use fine-point tweezers to grasp the tick's mouthparts, and then pull gently, with steady pressure; do not jerk or twist the tick. When it is removed, wash the area carefully with soap and water, pat dry and apply Betadine. If you are unable to remove the tick, seek medical attention urgently.

Spiders and Scorpions

Treat as for snake bite, with a pressure bandage (see Snake Bite). Seek medical aid and if possible, take the spider or scorpion for identification.

CUTS AND ABRASIONS

These are common on any bush trip and treatment is simple:
- Clean with water.
- Apply antiseptic cream or solution as this may prevent infection later.
- Cover with a Bandaid, dressing, or bandage.

BLISTERS

Everybody will get them if they are doing a fair amount of walking.
- Leave them intact.
- Pad away from the area causing pressure (use 4 Bandaids, 2 felt strips, or a felt pad with a hole cut in it). Do not put the dressing on the blister, as this increases pressure.

HYPOTHERMIA

Hypothermia is the abnormal lowering of body temperature and can cause death.

Mild Hypothermia
- Skin feels cold
- Skin looks blue or livid (mottled)
- Patient shivers
- Patient complains of feeling cold

Severe Hypothermia
- Skin cold and mottled
- No shivering—shivering response has failed
- Irrational behaviour and speech; may be uncooperative
- May be unconscious; if so the patient is near death!

    Note: A victim of cold can be resuscitated after a much longer period of 'technical death' (when no pulse or breathing can be detected) than a patient at normal temperature.

Treatment
- Shelter in warm, dry environment.
- Replace wet clothing with dry clothing.
- Leave arms and legs cold, but insulate body with blankets to minimise further heat loss.
- Rewarm critical areas—chest, neck and head—by body-to-body contact with two or more persons, or by placing heated objects (such as hot rocks wrapped in towels to prevent burning the skin) about these areas, particularly the sides of the chest.
- Breathe warm air in the vicinity of the patient's mouth (several people if possible) to warm the air breathed into the lungs.
- If conscious, rehydrate with warm drinks (non-alcoholic).
- If unconscious, transport to hospital; leave the patient cold while transporting, just insulate with blankets to prevent further heat loss.

HYPERTHERMIA

Hyperthermia is heat stroke. This can occur quite easily in the Outback.

Factors Influencing Development
- High air temperatures—reduces radiation.
- High humidity—reduces sweat evaporation.
- Clothing—reduces sweat evaporation.
- Level of exercise—sustained exercise causes internal heat generation.
- Level of fitness—an unfit person will have poor blood flow to muscles and skin.

- Body build—big, well-muscled or fat people are more susceptible.
- Dehydration—reduces blood volume.
- Age—babies and the elderly are at higher risk
- Acclimatisation to hot conditions reduces risk

Recognition (in Hot Conditions)
- Skin feels hot
- Face flushed
- Rapid pulse at rest
- Dizziness
- Excessive fatigue
- Lethargy; no will to go on
- Irrational behaviour
- Cessation of sweating

Treatment
- Transfer to a cool, shaded location.
- Immerse in cold water or apply ice packs, water or alcohol to the skin.
- Concentrate on cooling head, neck and chest.
- Rehydrate by giving cool fluids orally.
- Keep at rest.

FIRST AID KIT CHECKLIST

A basic first aid kit including a manual from the Australian Red Cross should always be carried in the vehicle and updated as items are used so the kit is always intact. Bushwalkers should carry as many of the following items as possible. Include items such as
- Antiseptic fluid (Betadine, Dettol, or similar)
- Antiseptic cream
- Eye bath and eyestream drops
- Assorted Bandaids, strips, spots
- Steristrip wound closures
- Elastic and crepe bandages for sprains and snake bite
- Sterile gauze bandages (50 and 75 mm)
- Triangular bandages to support limbs and hold dressings in place
- Adhesive tape, cotton wool, tissues
- Scissors, safety pins
- Thermometer
- Calamine lotion, Stingose or similar for insect bite
- Fine-point tweezers

PLANNING FOR THE UNEXPECTED

If you become stranded or lost, the first rule of survival is: Do Not Panic!

Once you realise that you are stranded or lost there are certain questions you must sit down and ask yourself. How much water do I have? How much food do I have? How much food or water is in the surrounding? What protection from the elements do I have?

If you have a radio, use it.

If you have notified someone of your intended route and dates, then it might just be a matter of sitting tight, opening a good book and waiting patiently for a search party to arrive. Meanwhile, concentrate on the four main requirements of water, food, shelter and warmth, until help arrives.

If you have a vehicle, stay with it as it is a source of shelter and contains all your supplies. Only leave your vehicle if you know, absolutely, that there is help within walking distance in the direction you have come.

Water
The average person can expect to survive without water for three to four days, depending on the climate and what you try to do. It is possible to perish after only hours if you do anything too strenuous. Water is needed to replace fluid loss, so by conserving body fluid you need less water.

Your body loses fluid in six ways: perspiring, breathing, urinating, vomiting, crying and talking.
- Perspiring and urinating are normal bodily processes that cannot be ceased, but if you stay still in the shade your body will perspire less.
- Move around in the evening only; your body will retain more fluid. A person standing still in the heat requires about three times more fluid than someone standing still in the shade.
- Crying and talking should be avoided, and vomiting can be prevented by not eating contaminated or potentially harmful food.
- Cover as much of the body as possible to avoid sunburn as blistering causes water loss. By keeping your clothes on, you slow down the rate at which perspiration evaporates: this maximises the cooling effect.
- Light coloured clothing is recommended as it reflects the sun: loosen clothing at the neck, waist, wrists and ankles for better ventilation.
- Take advantage of cool breezes and try not to rest on the ground: the temperature may be up to 16°C cooler 30 cm above the ground than it is on the ground.
- If near the sea, keep your clothes wet during the day to cool your body.

What Water Can I Drink?
- Do not drink salt water.
- Infection and sickness must be avoided: dirty water can only be drunk after it has been boiled and strained through a piece of cloth.
- Urine should not be drunk, but it can be used on the surface to cool the skin.
- Do not suck on stones as it encourages salivation.
- A good idea is to carry a filter-style drinking straw, available from bushwalking stores and the like. These can be used to filter water but are no use for filtering salt water.

Shelter
When you erect your tent to wait for rescue, the following points should be considered:
- Select your camp site carefully.
- Look for shelter that is near fuel (wood).
- Do not place a tent on a windswept ridge, in a draughty gully, or on a river bed at the base of a steep slope or cliff.
- Do not face the tent into the wind.

If you have not got a tent, construct a shelter of some sort to protect you from wind, cold and sun. Shelter, as survival experts will tell you, is the most important thing to have and must be organised before anything else.

Conserving Food and Energy
It is important that you plan for an extended stay, and ration the water and food accordingly.
- Estimate the number of days you expect to be stranded, divide food into thirds: allow two-thirds for the first half, one-third for the second half.
- If members of your party go back for help, divide food and give them twice as much as is allocated for those at camp.
- Eating increases thirst. If you have minimal water, avoid dry, starchy food, highly flavoured foods and meats.
- The best foods to eat are those that are high in carbohydrates: sugar, cereals and fruit.
- Do as little work as possible.
- If you have plenty of water, drink more than normal.
- Eat regularly and cook all food, if possible, to avoid sickness.

VICTORIA

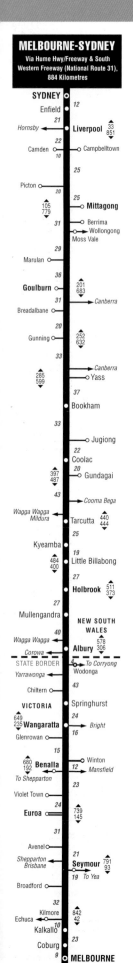

MELBOURNE-SYDNEY
Via Hume Hwy/Freeway & South
Western Freeway (National Route 31),
884 Kilometres

SYDNEY
Enfield   12
          21
Hornsby ←   Liverpool   33
          22   851
Camden   Campbelltown
          10
          25
Picton
          20
          105   25
          779   Mittagong
          31   Berrima
                Wollongong
                Moss Vale
          29
Marulan
          36
Goulburn   201
          31   683
Breadalbane   Canberra
          20
Gunning   252
          33   632
          285   Canberra
          599   Yass
          43   37
          Bookham
          33
                Jugiong
          22   Coolac
          397   20
          487   Gundagai
          43   Cooma Bega
Wagga Wagga
Mildura   Tarcutta   440
          25   444
Kyeamba
          19
          484   Little Billabong
          400
          27
Holbrook   511
          27   373
Mullengandra   NEW SOUTH
          40   WALES
Wagga Wagga   578
Corowa   Albury   306
STATE BORDER   To Corryong
Yarrawonga   Wodonga
Chiltern   43
VICTORIA   Springhurst
          649   24
          235 Wangaratta   Bright
Glenrowan   16
          15
          680 Benalla   Winton
          192   12   Mansfield
To Shepparton   23
Violet Town
          24
Euroa   739
          145
          31
Avenel
          21   Seymour   791
Shepparton   93
Brisbane   19   To Yea
Broadford
          32
Kilmore   842
Echuca   42
Kalkallo   10
Coburg   23
          9   MELBOURNE

The state of Victoria in the southeast of Australia offers a diverse range of attractions. In this state you can dine out at one of the many magnificent restaurants of Melbourne, take a drive along the Great Ocean Road and view the rugged western coastline, play a round of golf in the north of the state beside the mighty Murray River or look over the magnificent snow-capped Dividing Range from a chalet at a ski resort. As Victoria is a small state, the ideal way to tour is by road—within one day you can visit magnificent beaches, take in the desert country in the north-west of the state or visit one of the many national parks or reserves that are found right across the state.

Victoria can be easily divided up into 12 different regions that will help you plan your holiday, all of which are in easy reach utilising the state's excellent road system.

The city of Melbourne, sitting on Port Phillip Bay, is an exciting town and plays host to many international events such as the Formula One Grand Prix, and Australia's biggest horse race, the Melbourne Cup. Here you will find an interesting beach environment in St Kilda, and the Yarra River with its surrounding parkland is ideal for picnics or a leisurely lunchtime stroll. This city also features a wide range of excellent restaurants, museums, the Crown Casino, an exciting night life and world-class sporting venues. There are also numerous parks and gardens which can be explored by foot or bicycle and a great tramway system for getting around town.

To the north-east of Melbourne is the Yarra Valley and Dandenong Ranges, home to a large number of Victoria's wineries. This region is favoured by Melbournians as a quiet retreat. The Dandenong Ranges feature lush, ferny forests and a drive along the scenic road to the top of Mt Dandenong offers magnificent mountain scenery. Once at the top, the view reveals the city of Melbourne and the surrounding area out to Port Phillip Bay which put on a spectacular light show at night.

Melbourne and much of Central Victoria were built from the profits of the extensive gold rush that swept the state in the mid to late 1800s, just as the state was beginning to take shape. A trip to the goldfields region, which is bordered by the towns of Bendigo, Ballarat and Maryborough, is only an hour from Melbourne.

The large towns of Bendigo and Ballarat have many attractions including the superb theme park, Sovereign Hill, while the historic towns of Castlemaine and Maldon with their wide streets and restored antique and cottage craft shops will take you back in time.

The Goulburn River starts its journey from the Murray River on the New South Wales border and winds its way down through the centre of the state to Lake Eildon, less than three hours' drive from Melbourne. This river provides an important

The mighty Murray River and its red sandy banks at Happy Valley near Robinvale

irrigation system throughout the region supporting a rich dairy and fruit growing industry. The waters of the Goulburn also feed into many reservoirs such as Lake Nagambie and Lake Eildon which are popular with water sport enthusiasts and anglers.

Perched on the extreme western edge of the Great Dividing Range to the west of Melbourne is a series of blue peaks known as Gariwerd which forms a striking outline on the horizon. This rugged mass of sandstone pinnacles, part of the Grampians National Park, provide a playground for walkers, abseilers and climbers. During spring the whole region is covered in a mosaic of colourful wildflowers, while in winter, water tumbles down over the rugged escarpments to waterways below. This region is a haven for wildlife with many birdwatchers frequenting the region, especially in spring.

Winding its way along the west Victorian coastline, the Great Ocean Road offers some of the world's most spectacular coastal scenery including the famous natural sculptures known as the Twelve Apostles and London Bridge. Sandy beaches nestle in between towering cliffs while dolphins and whales can be seen playing in the roaring seas to the south. Originally built as a monument to those who served in World War I, the Great Ocean Road leads to some of Victoria's best surfing locations and exciting coastal holiday towns.

The rugged, western coastline and open seas have seen many ships meeting their end and the region is often referred to as the 'Shipwreck Coast'. Here divers can explore many of the wrecks which foundered, from Port Phillip Bay to the border of Victoria and South Australia and beyond.

The peninsula region of South Gippsland, south-east of Melbourne, has plenty to offer visitors including the magnifi-

cent Wilsons Promontory National Park with its granite land-scapes and pristine beaches. This park is one of Victoria's earliest parks and its diverse landscape of lush rainforests and coastal heath land contains a large range of walking tracks.

Closer to Melbourne is the nature wonderland of Phillip Island. It is here that you will find one of Victoria's greatest international attractions, the Penguins on Parade. Every evening thousands of penguins swim to the shores of this island and return to their burrows. This island, which is also home to seals and koalas, is the perfect seaside destination offering excellent surfing and swimming too. The island is connected to the mainland by a bridge for easy access.

Gippsland is a rich dairy farming district and is also rich in coal deposits which have been mined since the 1800s. Coal Creek in Korrumburra is a theme park which outlines the history of coalmining in Victoria while tours of the large power stations in the heart of Gippsland offer an insight into the state's energy system.

Further east lies the magnificent lakes district on the coast bordered by Ninety Mile Beach. Here you can sail in the protected waters of the lakes, or head out to open sea waters at Lakes Entrance. A major fishing region, Lakes Entrance is also an ideal holiday destination. Croajingolong National Park, to the far south-east of the state, is an important coastal parkland. Cool freshwater streams trickle down the mountains in this park through temperate rainforests, before filtering through the sand dunes and merging with the sea. This region is popular with campers, walkers and anglers.

The Dividing Range cuts through the centre of Victoria and is commonly referred to as the High Country. Here towns nestle in small valleys between towering mountains. This is also where the legends of the High Country were made, and there are still cattle wandering over the mountains, and cattle-men riding their horses across this vast mountain wilderness.

During winter snow covers the peaks and numerous ski resorts offer superb international class skiing, with plentiful numbers of ski lifts and excellent accommodation and restaurants. Mt Buller and Mt Baw Baw are only three hours' drive from Melbourne, while the larger peaks of Hotham, Falls Creek and Mt Buffalo can be found further to the north-east.

Melbournians have a special weekend spa retreat less than two hours' drive from town over the Macedon Ranges. The delightful towns of Daylesford and Hepburn Springs are rich in history which is reflected in their rustic appearance. It is, however, the soothing mineral waters that beckon visitors to the region, along with fine dining, excellent wineries and the peaceful surroundings.

Mt Macedon is also a popular weekend retreat, offering stunning views and magnificent old gardens and parks with many walking tracks.

With its beginnings in the High Country to the north-east of the state, the Murray River winds its way along the northern border of Victoria This river offers plenty of holiday opportunities and is home to some of Victoria's

best golf courses. Paddle-steamers once transported goods along the river but now houseboats and ski-boats have replaced these old vessels, although there are still some fine, restored paddle-steamers operating along the mighty Murray.

Once an inland port, the major town of Echuca lies north of Melbourne on the shores of the Murray and is one of Victoria's more popular historic tourist towns. Here you can either stay in one of the many hotels or camp along the banks of the river, surrounded by red gum trees and waking to the calls of the Major Mitchell cockatoos.

Proving just how diverse Victoria is, the north-west of the state features a desert oasis that is so rich in wildlife and flora that numerous parks and reserves have been created to protect thisregion's fragile and important environment.

Here the waters of the Murray River flow out to small streams and creeks to form lakes in the Hattah–Kulkyne National Park, creating a haven for bird life, while the Murray–Sunset Park plays host to undulating sand hills covered in mallee scrub, and heathlands opening up to a series of pink salt lakes.

A superb irrigation system in the region allows the far north-west to produce copious quantities of citrus fruit as well as grapes for sultanas around the townships of Swan Hill and Mildura.

Scattered right across the state, from the north-west desert country through to the coastal peninsula areas, are the wine regions of Victoria. This state has been producing fine wines since the late 1800s and today there are more than 230 wineries operating throughout the state. Popular regions include the Yarra Valley, and the Mornington and Bellarine Peninsulas, Macedon Ranges and Rutherglen.

Many of the smaller wineries allow you to talk to the wine-makers themselves and sit out under a shady gum tree and picnic on the premises. The larger vineyards offer restaurants which serve food to complement the wines, while all of the major wine regions feature a festival during the year to celebrate their produce.

Victoria really is a great holiday destination, and with so many great attractions within easy reach, the most difficult decision for any traveller will be choosing which way to go.

MacKenzie Falls in full flow in the Grampians National Park

MELBOURNE-ADELAIDE
South Eastern Fwy & Princes Hwy
(National Route 1), Dukes & Western
Hwys (National Route 9), 732 Kilometres

MELBOURNE
   19
Deer Park
   18
Melton
   16
   53 / 679 → Bacchus Marsh
   25
→ Ballan
   36
Daylesford   Ballarat 114 / 618
Avoca   Geelong
   23
Burrumbeet
   25
Beaufort
   20
Buangor   182 / 550
   22
Avoca → Ararat   Halls Gap
   17
221 / 511   Great Western
Stawell   13   Halls Gap
   28
Dadswells Bridge
   39
301 / 431   Horsham   Hamilton
Warracknabeal ←   Naracoorte
   17
Pimpinio
   18
Warracknabeal ←   Dimboola
   26
Kiata
   14   376 / 356
Nhill
   40
Kaniva
   24   **VICTORIA**
- - - - - - - STATE BORDER
   17
457 / 275   → Naracoorte
Bordertown
SOUTH AUSTRALIA   46
Keith → Naracoorte
   38
Tintinara   541 / 191
   28
Coonalpyn
   23
592 / 140   Yumali
   41
Sturt Hwy Pinnaroo   Meningie
Tailem Bend   Mt Gambier
   26
Murray Bridge   659 / 73
   39
Littlehampton   Mt Barker
Hahndorf   8
   26
ADELAIDE

MELBOURNE

POPULATION: 3.1 MILLION

MAP REFERENCE: PAGE 90 G3

The financial focal point of Australia and the capital city of Victoria, Melbourne is commonly referred to as the Garden City because of its tree-lined streets and delightful parklands and gardens which hug the Yarra River.

Trams still play a vital part in Melbourne's transport system

With beaches and bayside suburbs lining Port Phillip Bay and the Dandenong Ranges providing a backdrop to the north-east, this picturesque city has much to offer residents and visitors.

The township of Melbourne was originally settled by graziers, the first being John Batman, who took up land north of Port Phillip Bay. Many other graziers also ventured to these rich river flats of the Yarra River without permission to colonise the area. Captain William Lonsdale was sent from Sydney to negotiate the land sales in this region. The township was established in 1835, named after the then British Prime Minister Lord Melbourne, and was integrated into New South Wales. It was not until 1851 that Victoria was established as a separate colony.

Melbourne plays host to a variety of different architectural styles as illustyrated by the Gothic ANZ Bank building, the art deco Town Hall and the modern skyscrapers. There are several fine buildings in the city, many of which were financed by the gold rush of the mid to late 1800s. Examples of such buildings include the Magistrates Court, Town Hall, State Library and the impressive Exhibition Buildings which have been restored and are surrounded by magnificent gardens. There are also some impressive churches. They too have undergone extensive renovations, and include St Paul's and St Patrick's Cathedrals. Como House in Toorak is an elegant mansion surrounded by superb gardens, while the Block Arcade, built in the 1890s and fully restored, is a delightful centre for shoppers. One of the more unusual buildings of Melbourne is the Adelphi Hotel with a swimming pool that juts out over Flinders Lane offering swimmers a view of the streetscape below.

The city is set out following a typical nineteenth-century pattern with a grid system of streets taking the names of early settlers and dignitaries that are easy to remember. The main streets leading away from the main railway station, Spencer Street Station, are King, William, Queen, Elizabeth, before reaching the main shopping area of Swanston Street—clever indeed!

Melbourne features many parks where you can go to relax, have a picnic or jog in beautiful surroundings. The Royal Botanic Gardens are world renowned and were originally established in 1846. With large exotic trees and plants that are up to 150 years old, this garden is one of Melbourne's finest. Set on the banks of the Yarra River it is also home to a number of majestic black swans and flying foxes, or fruit bats.

The Fitzroy and Treasury Gardens take up 32 hectares of prime Melbourne real estate and is where Captain Cook's Cottage is sited. This stone building once stood in Great Ayrton in England, and, built in 1755, was home to Captain Cook's parents. The building was bought in 1933 by Sir Russell Grimwade who gave it to the Victorian Government. It was transported to Melbourne and erected in the gardens in 1934. A delightful ivy-covered cottage, it is a fine monument to this great explorer.

Other beautiful parklands include the Queen Victoria Gardens which feature a magnificent floral clock. This is 9 metres in diameter and more than 7000 plants are used to create this intricate floral display. The clock actually tells the time and is synchronised to chime with the clock on the Town Hall.

The Royal Melbourne Zoological Gardens can be found on the edge of the city, and with over 3500 animals it is considered one of the world's finest. During the summer months Melbourne Zoo features a Twilight Jazz Festival where patrons bring picnic hampers and enjoy the music in very unusual surroundings. Within an hour's drive of the city there are two other notable wildlife parks, the Werribee Zoo and the Healesville Sanctuary.

Life is never boring in this city and if there isn't a major sporting event scheduled, then there is probably a festival in town, or maybe both. A diverse mix of races and cultures sees Melbourne come alive with a variety of exciting and unusual carnivals year round.

The most popular festival, held in March, is Moomba, which means 'getting together and having fun'. A well-known identity is crowned the 'Moomba Monarch', and leads the festivities which include a huge street parade with enormous floats, always a hit with families. The event has a real carnival atmosphere: a fair is set up on the banks of the Yarra River where fireworks are set off each night and waterskiing events take place during the day. Other events coincide with this festival including the Formula One Grand Prix and the Melbourne Motor Show.

Other festivals occur in March, including the Annual Yarra Valley Grape Grazing Festival which is celebrated by a number of wineries in the Yarra Valley Region. This region produces much of Australia's superb wines and during the festival delicious food from a selection of restaurants is matched up with the wineries to present gastronomic delights. Jazz adds to the festival feel of this event.

Festivities head indoors during the winter months with the Melbourne International Film Festival and Victoria State Opera season. Spring brings Melbournians outside again for the Royal Melbourne Show and a range of horticultural shows which take place during September. The outdoor tradition flows through to Christmas when thousands of Melbournians head to the Myer Music Bowl on Christmas Eve for the famous 'Carols By Candlelight' concert.

It is well documented that Melbourne people love sport whether it be football, tennis, car racing or a totally foreign sport to the Victorian state such as rugby. Many large sporting events are held in Melbourne.

Melbourne is the home of Australian Rules Football and a visit to Melbourne should include a trip to the Melbourne Cricket Ground (MCG)

where, apart from cricket being played in summer, the Aussie Rules Grand Final is held on the third Saturday of September. Tours can be had of the venue and include a walk on the hallowed turf of the MCG. During the week of the Grand Final the town has football fever; it is a great time to visit and there are a number of festivities in town.

Melbourne Park is home to the Australian Open, the first round of the World Grand Slam Tennis Circuit. The main feature of this impressive tennis venue is the centre court which has a roof that can be opened or closed. With Melbourne's reputation of having four seasons in one day, this has proved very useful.

Melbourne Park is also the venue for concerts and productions all through the year and the outside courts are available for hire.

Melbourne also hosts the first round of the Formula One Grand Prix circuit, and this is truly an exciting time to be in Melbourne, when the Albert Park Lake area is transformed into an award-winning track with thousands of people joining in on the festivities which run over four days. Grand Prix ticket holders have free use of the Melbourne trams and after the racing each day the city comes alive as racegoers venture into town and head for the restaurants, clubs or even the Melbourne International Motor Show.

Horseracing is popular in Melbourne with excellent racing at the Autumn and Spring Racing Carnivals. The Spring Carnival features the Melbourne Cup, Australia's most famous horserace which is run on the first Tuesday in November and is honoured by a public holiday for Victorians. The festivities involved around this horserace are fabulous, and it is a real Australian tradition to 'have a bet on the race'. Melbournians go along and have some fun, with many dressing up in either their Sunday best, including a hat, or fancy dress.

Victoria also plays host to a round of the 500cc Motorcycle Grand Prix Circuit and this is held at Phillip Island to the south of Melbourne. The Air

The spectacle of the 1996 AFL Grand Final at the Melbourne Cricket Ground

MELBOURNE

The Melbourne skyline at dusk

Down Under International Air Show is another annual event and features aircraft from all around the world which demonstrate the latest innovations in aviation and aerospace technology. The show is held at the Avalon Airport near Geelong during February.

Melbourne is the ideal destination for shoppers. It has its own fashion festival in summer. In the centre of Melbourne there are a couple of splendid arcades that allow you to shop in superb historical surroundings: the Block Arcade has mosaic tiled floors and grand architecture, and the Royal Arcade has its unique speciality shops.

Large shopping complexes also beckon including Melbourne Central which features a number of retail outlets including the Japanese-owned department store Daimaru. This magnificent building has a large glass pyramid roof and shot tower. Nearby are the huge department stores of Myer and David Jones. The Crown Entertainment Complex and Southgate also have an enormous range of exclusive shops, many from overseas. In the suburbs, you will find streets which are considered 'the' places to shop such as Chapel Street in South Yarra for fashion, Bridge Road, Richmond, for seconds outlets, High Street, Armadale, for exclusive boutiques and Maling Road, Canterbury, for antiques.

The city of Melbourne has a large migrant population and the food and restaurants are influenced by this diversity of cultures: almost any international cuisine is available in this city.

The central business district features many fine restaurants but the town is traditionally split into cultural sectors such as Lygon Street in Carlton for Italian and Richmond for Vietnamese or Greek food. Little Bourke Street features a sector called Little China with superb Chinese cuisine. Melbourne loves to celebrate the Chinese New Year in February when thousands of people head to the Chinatown precinct to bring in the new year. Large dragons wind their way through the crowd and firecrackers pop and drums beat in the background.

The suburb of Southgate, an area situated on the banks of the Yarra, features restaurants and the Crown Entertainment Complex. This enormous complex is home to the Crown Casino and contains theatres, a hotel and many shops, clubs and restaurants. On a sunny day in Melbourne you will see people sitting at restaurants on the edge of the Yarra from St Kilda Road all the way to Spencer Street. Of an evening this sector of town also comes alive with clubs and restaurants open until the early hours.

A great way to get to most of Melbourne's attractions is by taking a free Circle Tram ride. The Circle Trams are painted a distinctive burgundy colour as opposed to the traditional green Melbourne Tram, and they circle the city utilising Flinders, Spencer, LaTrobe and Spring Streets.

The numerous attractions in the city of Melbourne are perhaps best appreciated by a visitor on a guided tour which can be organised through the tourist office in the city.

Government House originally occupied La Trobe Cottage and this, together with the present-day Government House, can be toured. The Melbourne Stock Exchange also offers tours of the bustling complex while the Bureau of Meteorology presents an impressive display which includes

interactive television screens on the self-guided tour.

The Yarra River is an integral part of the city and a cruise along the waterway is an ideal way to view the city.

The Old Melbourne Gaol is another fascinating attraction, depicting life in a nineteenth-century Australian prison. It is here that Victorian hangings took place, 135 in total, including the infamous bushranger Ned Kelly. Death masks made of those hanged can be viewed here.

The Old Treasury building underwent a significant restoration in 1994 and it is one of the more significant nineteenth-century buildings in Melbourne. This building features changing exhibitions representing Australian history.

Built in 1872, the Royal Mint hosts two major displays, one pertaining to the Royal Mint, the other set up by the Royal Historical Society of Melbourne and outlines a comprehensive history of Melbourne.

Melbourne boasts many fine galleries with a diverse range of styles and exhibitions. The National Gallery of Victoria on St Kilda Road is located within the Victorian Arts Precinct and contains an enormous stained glass ceiling. This gallery has a magnificent art collection made up of paintings, sculptures, drawings and photographs. Also on St Kilda Road is the Victorian Arts Centre which

which are very popular with both children and adults. This centre is built around an old pumping station in Spotswood and is open every day.

The Melbourne Maritime Museum has, as its central exhibit, the tall ship *Polly Woodside*, which was built in Belfast in 1885. The Rialto Towers

Flinders Street Station, the main railway station in Melbourne

provides a number of different venues for the performing arts. A feature of this centre is the tall spire on the rooftop which changes colours at night.

The Aboriginal Gallery of Dreamings offers international visitors the chance to view works of art that are unique to Australia, including Aboriginal dot paintings, boomerangs and didgeridoos. The centre in Bourke Street features more than 2500 paintings.

The Museum of Victoria houses some magnificent exhibits, including Aboriginal displays, the famous racehorse Phar Lap, and dinosaur displays. It is here you will also find the Melbourne Planetarium.

The Ancient Times House was established in 1954 and is the largest archaeological museum in Melbourne with exceptional displays from Mesopotamia and Egypt, including replicas of artefacts from the tomb of Tutankhamen.

The Shrine of Remembrance is a memorial to the people who served Australia in the wars and features 42 books of remembrance which contain the names of 116 000 Victorians who served overseas during World War I. A fascinating feature of the building which stands proud between Domain and St Kilda Roads is the inner sanctuary and the stone of remembrance which is lit by sunlight precisely at 11 am on 11 November—Remembrance Day—every year.

There are many other great attractions in the city including Scienceworks, a science and technology centre with interactive displays

Observation Deck offers a superb 360 degree view of the city and the surrounding area from Melbourne's tallest building.

Queen Victoria Market is the place to go for fresh produce and a bargain with over 1000 traders offering everything from fresh fruit and seafood, through to clothing and leathergoods. This historic complex was established in 1878 and is the largest outdoor market in the world.

ACCOMMODATION

CBD: Grand Hyatt Melbourne Hotel, ph (03) 9657 1234; Le Meridien Hotel at Rialto Melbourne, ph (03) 9620 9111; The Regent Hotel Melbourne, ph (03) 9419 3311; Sheraton Towers Hotel, ph (03) 9696 3100; Savoy Plaza Hotel, ph (03) 9622 8888; Crown Towers Hotel, ph 132138

East side: Melbourne Hilton on the Park Hotel, ph (03) 9419 3311; Park Royal Hotel on St Kilda Road, ph (03) 9529 8888; Birches Boutique Apartments, ph (03) 9417 2344

West side: Ramada Inn, ph (03) 9380 8131; Station Pier Condominiums, ph (03) 9647 9665; Footscray Motor Inn, ph (03) 9687 6877

North side: Parkville Place Motel, ph (03) 9387 8477; The Townhouse Hotel, ph (03) 9347 7811; City Gardens Holiday Apartments, ph (03) 9320 6600

TOURIST INFORMATION: Ph (03) 96588 9955

THE VICTORIAN ALPS

The Australian Alps are ever-changing; snow covers the upper reaches for most of winter, while summer brings heat to the lower reaches and the mountains. The weather can change from extreme heat to freezing temperatures very quickly, and snow is not uncommon during the warmer months.

MAP REFERENCE: PAGE 96 D2

LOCATION: ACCESS BETWEEN 230 AND 500 KM FROM MELBOURNE

BEST TIME: YEAR ROUND, 4WD LATE SPRING TO EARLY AUTUMN

MAIN ATTRACTIONS: NATURAL BEAUTY OF THE MOUNTAINS, SKIING IN WINTER, OUTDOOR ACTIVITIES IN SUMMER, HISTORIC INTEREST

INFORMATION: PARKS VICTORIA AT BRIGHT, PH (03) 5755 1577; WHITFIELD, PH (03) 5729 8266; MANSFIELD, PH (03) 5775 2788; HEYFIELD, PH (03) 5148 2355

ACCOMMODATION: SEE TOWN LISTINGS FOR MANSFIELD, MOUNT HOTHAM DINNER PLAIN AND OMEO

Camping in the Victorian Alps

Be prepared for any weather and always carry warm clothing and adequate food and water.

Seasonal road closures apply in winter due to snow and heavy rainfalls. Check the local Parks Victoria office for details of track closures before planning your trip.

With most of the continent being relatively flat, the Great Dividing Range protects a myriad wildlife species, many of which are endangered. It also provides a playground for Melbournians.

Perhaps the most enduring image of the High Country is that of tall timbers: the area is dominated on the lower reaches by eucalypts such as the mountain gum and stringybark, on the higher peaks by the alpine ash, and above the snow line, by the colourful, gnarled, stunted snow gum. During spring, as the winter snow melts, a carpet of alpine daisies, alpine marsh marigold and the alpine hovea greet walkers who utilise the ski tracks for their treks.

The changing weather and the different types of vegetation lead to a diversity in the wildlife, particularly the bird life. Species include the noisy gang-gang cockatoo and the distinctive long-beaked wattlebird.

Patient visitors will be rewarded by chance meetings with kangaroos, bats, echidnas or the hearty wombat, which can be found foraging at night. There are also some reclusive emus but they are rarely spotted. Many species of animals are endemic to the region, including the brush-tailed rock wallaby and the mountain pygmy possum, the latter once thought to be extinct.

History

Aborigines resided in this mountain region for thousands of years, but it was in 1824 that Hume and Hovell explored and named the Australian Alps. However, it was not until George McKillop pushed south from the Monaro in southern New South Wales to the present site of Omeo that the mountains of Victoria started to give up their secrets.

The first to push a route right across the mountains to the southern coast was Angus McMillan in 1839. Once again it was the quest for new pasture land by Monaro pastoralists that initiated the search, with McMillan taking up land for his sponsors on the Tambo River near present-day Ensay. In further expeditions he opened up a route from the Monaro Plains in New South Wales to the coast at Corner Inlet.

In 1840 Paul Edmund de Strzelecki, a Polish geologist, was sponsored by the wool baron James Macarthur to find new pastoral country; in so doing he named, but did not climb, Australia's highest peak, Mt Kosciuszko. Crossing the Indi or Murray River above present-day Corryong, he pushed south to the Omeo Plains and from there to Bruthen and the coast.

With the discovery of gold in Victoria at places close to the mountains, it was not long before hardy bushmen in search of wealth were combing every gully of the Great Divide looking for the precious metal. The diggers came up the Mitta Mitta River and then up Livingstone Creek to where Omeo now stands. By 1856 there were more than 600 miners on the field.

During the 1850s, Baron Ferdinand von Mueller extensively explored the botany of the alpine region and thus expanded our knowledge of the diverse alpine flora.

In 1860 A. W. Howitt was appointed to lead an expedition in search of new fields; he explored the Mitchell and the headwaters of the Dargo River, as well as the Wentworth, and found gold on the Crooked River.

In 1864 the government commissioned Angus McMillan to lead an expedition to blaze a series of tracks through the mountains. In 12 months over 350 km of track were cut from the Wonnangatta over the Snowy Plains to the top of the range at the Moroka River. Other tracks from Dargo to Harrietville and from the Wellington to the Moroka and from Jordon to Mt Tamboritha were also cut.

When the alluvial gold ran out the search for reef gold continued, and slowly but surely the mountains were opened up. The loggers and the mountain cattlemen were never far behind and when the mountains had given up most of their gold the loggers and the cattlemen stayed, giving us much of today's heritage.

During the 1950s controls were imposed on graziers to limit stock numbers and prohibit grazing of sheep and horses in the High Country. These controls were later extended even further when concern arose over the impact the cattle were having on the fragile environment and many grazing licences were withdrawn. Today, very few permits allowing cattle to graze in the spectacular High Country are still valid.

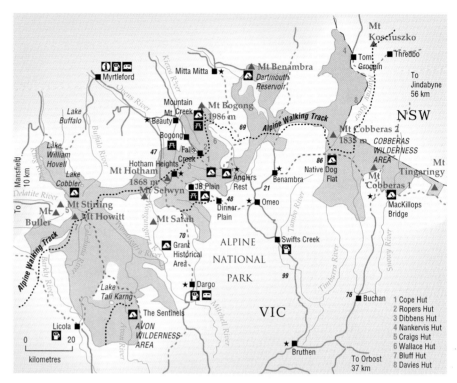

LEGEND

Sealed/Unsealed Rd	★ 26 ★
Four Wheel Drive	
Walks	
Rest Area (Picnic Area)	
Caravan Park	
Camping Area	
Accommodation	
Information	
Fuel Supplies	

1 Cope Hut
2 Ropers Hut
3 Dibbens Hut
4 Nankervis Hut
5 Craigs Hut
6 Wallace Hut
7 Bluff Hut
8 Davies Hut

N

ALPINE NATIONAL PARK

The Alpine National Park, Victoria's largest park, covers a vast area of 635 580 hectares. One of Australia's finest parks, it offers rugged mountains, powerful rivers, remote snowfields, open plains where cattle once grazed and deep gorges which open out to reveal green valleys. Reaching far across the Dividing Range this park forms an important natural corridor for its unique flora and fauna.

The push for a national park first came from the newly formed Victorian National Parks Association during the 1960s, but it was not until several public enquiries had been held and there was a change in attitude in many of the users that the Alpine National Park was proclaimed in December 1989.

The park is best treated as 6 sectors: Mt Hotham–Feathertop; Wombargo–The Cobberas; Tingaringy; Bogong High Plains; Wonnangatta–Moroka; and Mt Buller–Stirling.

Access

Many bitumen and good quality roads lead to the main regions of the Alpine National Park.

The Mt Buller–Stirling area can be reached via Mansfield, north of Melbourne, along good quality gravel roads.

The Wonnangatta–Moroka area is accessed via Licola, following a well-maintained gravel road, or from Dargo on 4WD tracks.

Mt Hotham is serviced by a good bitumen road from Harrietville to the north and Dargo from the south.

The Snowy River Road provides access for the Tingaringy section while Benambra and the Black Mountain Road lead to the Cobberas region.

Mt Hotham–Feathertop

Mt Feathertop, standing at 1922 metres, and Mt Hotham, a mere 1862 metres, are two of Victoria's highest peaks and provide a perfect play-ground for skiers and snowboarders in winter and walkers and cyclists during summer.

Situated in the heart of the Alpine National Park, this sector is best known for its winter activities with regular snowfalls on the higher reaches during winter. The Hotham Heights village caters for the downhill skier, while the surrounding area boasts a remote mountain range for the ski tourer. Many cross-country skiers base themselves at nearby Dinner Plain while the adventurous head cross-country along the Razorback trail to Mt Feathertop. This is an 18 km trek that can be completed in a day, with snow camping possible near Federation Hut below the summit of Feathertop.

Walking tracks abound after the snow melts, and the Alpine Walking Track cuts through this region towards Falls Creek.

Wombargo–The Cobberas

With only one access road suitable for conventional vehicles, this northern section abuts Kosciuszko National Park to the north of the park, and the Buchan Headwaters Wilderness Area to its south. Although there are still some 4WD tracks in the area, visitors with conventional vehicles should use Black Mountain Road to access the popular camping areas of Native Dog Flat, Willis on the Snowy River and the Cobberas Wilderness Area.

The peaks of Mt Cobberas One and Two are popular bases for walkers, as is Cowombat Flat where there is a wreck of a DC-3 aircraft which crashed in 1954, killing one crew member.

Tingaringy

As the highest peak east of the Snowy River, Mt Tingaringy offers commanding views of the Kosciuszko Range and the peaks down south towards the Snowy River. Most of this region is classified as a wilderness area. At the border with New South Wales it adjoins the Kosciuszko National Park and Byadbo Wilderness Area. Because vehicles, and all other mechanical means of transport, are not permitted, it is mainly bushwalkers who use this remote region. Water can be scarce here in summer, so bushwalkers need to be well prepared and self-sufficient.

Bogong High Plains

The Bogong High Plains saw, in the early 1900s, the birth of skiing in Victoria, but long before that pioneers had grazed their cattle on the lush, grassy plains during summer. Today the area is popular with visitors in both summer and winter as it offers snow skiing, bushwalking, bike and horse riding. There is also trout fishing available in the Rocky Valley Dam and Pretty Valley Pondage.

Popular walks include the 5 km moderate trek from the Rocky Valley Dam up to Ropers Lookout which takes 1½ hours return, or the difficult day journey along the Mt Bogong Staircase which is 16 km return and for the seriously fit only.

South of the Rocky Valley Dam you will find Wallaces Hut, built by the Wallace Brothers in 1889,. This is the oldest of the huts still standing in the park. The woollybutt roof shingles were replaced by galvanised iron in the 1930s and it is now classified by the National Trust. The hut is not far from the Bogong High Plains Road, near Falls Creek.

Wonnangatta–Moroka

This section of the park, only 335 km from Melbourne, is one of the more popular, offering a wide range of walking and 4WD tracks, ski trails in winter for cross-country skiers, and excellent camping areas, many of which have access for conventional vehicles. For many, the main attraction is the Wonnangatta Valley with its majestic green valley floor where many pioneers settled last century.

Hidden deep in the mountains at the head of the Wellington River is the jewel of the High Country, Lake Tali Karng, which is accessible on foot, and can only be viewed from the Sentinel and Echo Point on Rigalls Spur. Many walkers enjoy the 28 km return descent to the lake which should be undertaken only by the fit and healthy. The trek takes 2 days and is best enjoyed by spending more than one night camped by the sapphire blue lake.

Another excellent walk is along the Moroka Gorge where sections of the Moroka River have carved their way through the rock. There are three waterfalls and excellent swimming holes in summer when the water level is low. A walking track leading to the gorge can be found at the popular camping area of Horseyard Flats.

Further east, the Moroka Road heads to the Pinnacles Lookout where a fire tower watches over the surrounding country. You can drive to within 1 km of the peak, then take the moderate walking track to the lookout from where you will enjoy breathtaking views.

Mt Buller–Stirling and Lake Cobbler

Only 2½ hours' drive from Melbourne, Mt Buller and Mt Stirling stand atop the Delatite Valley where the cool streams of the Delatite and King Rivers flow. These two mountains are Melbourne's playgrounds, with Stirling offering excellent cross-country skiing and popular walking trails while Buller caters for downhill skiers. With many trails surrounding the two mountains and leading up to Lake Cobbler, 4WD touring and cycling are popular pastimes.

Huts of the High Country

Scattered throughout the Alpine National Park are a number of huts which represent part of the rich cultural heritage of the region. Many of these

The famous Snowy River near McKillops Bridge

Kelly's Hut, one of many such huts built by the early settlers

huts once belonged to the pioneers who grazed their cattle on the high plains during summer. Today, the huts are visited for their historical significance and can be used as temporary or emergency shelters.

The popular huts to visit include Wallaces Hut on the Bogong High Plains, and Bluff Hut and Bindaree Hut, which, along with Craigs Hut, are in the region near Mansfield. Off the Howitt Road, north of Licola, you will find Guys Hut and the ruins of the Old Wonnangatta Station, while in the north of the state is Davies Plain Hut.

4WD Touring

In recent years, the 4WD vehicle has become a very popular way to enjoy the park where access is impossible by conventional vehicles.

One of the most popular areas to visit, Wonnangatta Valley, is in the centre of the park, north of Licola. Zeka Spur Track, the road into Wonnangatta from the Howitt High Plains Road, was once a very challenging track, but with the increase in visitors the track has been upgraded and should not pose a problem for novice drivers of 4WD vehicles.

An ideal weekend jaunt would be to camp on the Wellington River outside Licola on Friday night, then travel the 72 km north to the Zeka Spur Track which winds down for 30 km to the valley floor. This is now of a moderate standard and should take you 3 or 4 hours from Licola. There is camping aplenty in the valley and attractions include the site of a burnt-out homestead on the banks of Conglomerate Creek and a cemetery which is perched on the hillside under towering pine trees.

Other interesting tours in the alpine park include Dargo and the Crooked River–Talbotville area, Jacksons Crossing on the Snowy River, and the Deddick Trail. The more adventurous and experienced might like to tackle Butcher Country Track or the mountain country around Davies Plain in the north.

Walking for Fun

This park is extremely popular with walkers. Popular short walks include the return trek from the Bogong High Plains to Wallaces Hut, one of the most picturesque. This easy walk of 2 km will take less than an hour.

Another easy walk is to Bryces Gorge which starts at Howitt Road, 70 km north of Licola. It is 8 km return and takes in Bryces Plain and Gorge, Guys Hut and the Pieman Falls. Allow 3 hours for the journey.

While there are many short walks, by far the most impressive is the Alpine Walking Track which extends a lengthy 650 km from the old goldmining town of Walhalla in Gippsland, across the rugged mountain range, into New South Wales, finally finishing in the Australian Capital Territory at the Namadgi Visitor Centre. The Alpine Walking Track was devised in 1968, before the area was declared a national park, and passes through areas rich in history and natural wonders.

The entire trail takes more than 10 weeks to complete, but most walkers tackle it in sections.

Other Activities

The Alps of Victoria represent premium mountain-bike riding country, with tracks running alongside deep river gorges, imposing clifftops, large plateaus and verdant valleys.

Cyclists must remember that temperatures in the Alps are generally lower than the rest of the state, with the peaks rarely recording temperatures above 20°C, even in summer.

There are restrictions imposed on cyclists in parks and wilderness areas so it is best to check before assuming you may use vehicular or Management Vehicle tracks.

Other recreations that can be enjoyed in the park include canoeing, which is popular on the Wellington, Macalister and Snowy Rivers, and horse riding along the mountaintops.

Camping

Remote camping is the best way to experience the magnificent alpine park in areas where there are no facilities provided. There are, however, a number of popular camping sites where toilets and fireplaces can be found. For conventional vehicle access, MacKillops Bridge on the Snowy River in the north-east is a great camping area, as are Sheepyard Flat and Lake Cobbler near Mt Buller, Wellington River north of Licola, Anglers Rest north of Omeo and the numerous camping sites at the top end of the Snowy River Road.

Drivers of 4WDs might like to try areas such as Wonnangatta Valley, Grant Historical Area, Rams Head at the Cobberas, or Davies Plain.

Walkers have the best camping opportunities and can take in the delights of the wilderness areas within the national park at the Avon and Buchan Headwaters Wilderness Zones.

THE ALPINE TREK

This trek takes in some of the finest country in Australia and easily rates as one of the great national trips to be undertaken by 4WD. It is also some of the hardest country any four wheeler is likely to tackle and therefore it is not one for the beginner.

The trek can easily take a week or longer, but as the route crosses major roads and passes through the odd town it can also be done in easy two or three day stages.

Mansfield to Bindaree Hut

There is no better place to start a trip into the mountains than at the town of Mansfield—a cattleman's town if there ever was one. It is also the gateway to the snow resort of Mt Buller, and because of this dual role, the town caters well for all of a four wheeler's requirements.

Head towards Mt Buller, pass through Merrijig 19 km later, and at Mirimbah, 32 km from Mansfield, turn left onto the Mt Stirling road. You will pass through a toll gate which operates in winter only, and 6.5 km later you will be at Telephone Box Junction (TBJ) where you need to veer right up the hill.

The road you are now on is Circuit Road and 7 km from TBJ you will pass through Howqua Gap. The road is generally pretty good as it winds along the edge of the mountain where the occasional landslip has narrowed the road.

Turn right off the Circuit Road at a major track junction where a large dugout is located, 11 km from the Gap, or 18 km from TBJ. This is Bindaree Creek Track and while it is an easy route for a high clearance 4WD, it is not suitable for normal cars. The 8 km to a T-junction at the bottom of the hill is slow. Once at the junction, turn right, and keep straight ahead at the next junction, just a few hundred metres further on.

The track is very rough from this point on as it parallels the Howqua River, which it crosses 1.5 km from the T-junction. The crossing is rough but rocky, and once across you are at Bindaree Hut (**GPS** 37°10'27" S, 146°33'13"E) and the flat of the same name, which is an ideal camp site. The river, although small, often produces pan-size trout. You are just 65 km from Mansfield, but you will need a couple of hours to get to this point, and from now on the going is much slower!

Bindaree Hut to Zeka Spur

Head up the hill from Bindaree Hut, sticking to the main route. A track on the right 4.5 km later leads down to a good camp site on the Howqua, while another, just 200 metres past the first, leads down to Pikes Flat. This is a popular camp for horse riders, as the nearby horseyards testify. It is a lovely camp site and the river is magnificent here.

Head past the hut and up the hill to the main track, and 0.5 km later you will cross a narrow rocky creek; then, a similar distance further, you will cross a wider stream—16-Mile Creek—and almost straight away the track turns and begins to head steeply uphill.

This track, known as 16-Mile Track, is fairly easy in the dry but it can be a terror when it is wet. The climb is for about 3.5 km, and you cross the creek once in that time. At the top you meet a large clearing with a dam on your right and a track junction a little further after that. Turn right onto 16-Mile Road.

Less than a kilometre further along this good dirt road, turn left onto a track signposted 'Bluff Hut'. This track climbs steeply for just over a kilometre to Bluff Hut, which is worth a long stop to check around.

The Stoney family, mountain cattlemen, own this hut and used to run cattle on this High Country lease. They now run horse treks, and in the winter cross-country ski trips, from the hut. The hut is generally open and when not used by the family, like all the huts of the High Country, it is open to any traveller. There is an emergency shelter at one end and a toilet just up the hill from the hut. The view from the cliff edge, 30 metres from the track on the left, is great, marred only by the man-made scars on nearby Mt Buller. Such views are what made the film *The Man from Snowy River* world famous.

Keep to the main track; it has been re-aligned in recent times and much work has been done to keep it open, and to keep the occasional snow plain which it crosses free from bogs. You will pass through a gate just before getting to Lovick's Hut, 5 km from Bluff Hut. The Lovick family, too, are mountain cattlemen who now run horse rides from this hut.

Less than 2 km later a track junction is reached where the main track veers around to the right. For one of the greatest views anywhere, turn left, drive 50 metres and stop. Walk over to the edge of the cliff, and in front of you is a sea of ridges and peaks stretching away to the horizon. This is a great spot to stop on a clear day for lunch—you will never tire of the view!

Back on the main route, the track deteriorates from this point on, and the next 2.5 km to the crossroads at King Billy No. 2 is slow and often boggy. Take your time. You are just 21 km from Bindaree Hut. King Billy No. 2 (**GPS** 37°12'56"S, 146°36'21"E) is on a high saddle dotted with tall

gnarled snow gums; if the weather is good it makes a fine camp. There is no water, so if you are planning to camp you will need to bring some.

At the crossroads you need to turn left. Straight ahead leads out to Mt Clear, and right leads down the Jamieson River Valley on the relatively good Brocks Road.

About 4.5 km down the hill from King Billy you will cross King Billy Creek, the first of a couple of crossings, and then 1.5 km later you come to a track junction where you need to turn left across the creek again. From this crossing the track follows and crosses the headwaters of the Macalister River. After 2 km the track begins to climb, through a number

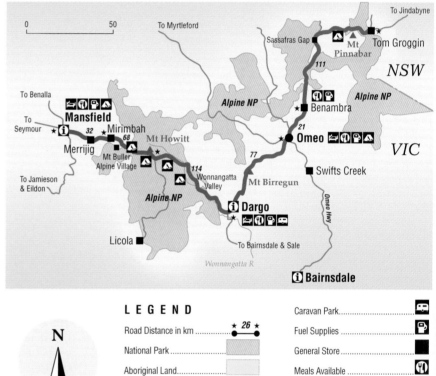

LEGEND

Road Distance in km	★ 26 ★	Caravan Park	
National Park		Fuel Supplies	
Aboriginal Land		General Store	
Accommodation		Meals Available	
Camping Area		Rest Area (Picnic Area)	
		Tourist Information	

of switchbacks, to the top of the range. Another 3.5 km will see you on top of the range, and in the interim you have gone from a densely wooded valley to open snow plains. Within a kilometre you will be at the car park for the walking trail out to Macalister Springs.

Macalister Springs has a hut and makes a pleasant camp for those who are keen enough to walk the 5 km to the site. It is an easy walk, though, for the most part across snow plains. From the hut it is a 2 km walk out to the crest of Mt Howitt, at 1742 metres one of the highest mountains in Victoria.

Less than 2 km east of the car park you will come to the Zeka Spur Track (**GPS** 37°12'48"S, 146°41'31"E) on your left. This is the only access route from this side of the valley into the fabled Wonnangatta Valley—the Hidden Valley of the Alps. At this point you are 14 km from King Billy, 35 km from Bindaree and 100 km from Mansfield.

The Route South to Licola

The main road heads south to Licola, 72 km south from the Zeka Spur track. For many coming to the Wonnangatta this is their favoured route.

Licola is 54 km north of Heyfield and is on the Macalister River. The town has a general store which can supply basic food items and fuel.

Heading north from Licola the road follows the Wellington River and there are a number of good camps along this pleasant stream. The dirt road begins 23 km north of Licola where the final bridge crosses the Wellington River.

You cross over the Tamboritha Saddle 14.5 km later and then, at Arbuckle Junction 8.5 km further on, you need to veer left. The Zeka Spur Track leaves the main road 26 km north of Arbuckle Junction, or 72 km north of Licola.

The Wonnangatta Valley

Completely surrounded by mountains, the Wonnangatta was the 'Lost Valley' of the Alps. First discovered by A. W. Howitt during his wanderings through the high plains looking for gold in 1860, Wonnangatta Station was taken up soon after, probably by the American prospector Oliver Smith. John Bryce entered the scene a bit later, taking over the lease around 1866.

In 1917–18 the infamous Wonnangatta Murders took place. The murderers of James Barclay, then manager of Wonnangatta Station, and his cook, John Bamford, are still not known today. Some say Bamford, in one of his angry argumentative moods, killed Barclay, and then a friend of Barclay's (he had many) killed Bamford. Others thought both were killed by rustlers. We will probably never know, but it all adds to the mystery and character of this beautiful hidden valley.

The first vehicle to enter the valley was in 1945 when a horse track was widened to take the legendary Harry Smith to Sale for burial. Harry, who was 98 and son of the American Oliver Smith, had lived all his life in and around the valley and was one of the great horsemen of the region.

The original homestead built by Smith and enlarged by the Bryce family was accidentally burnt down, probably by bushwalkers, in May 1957. Sold a number of times after the death of the last Bryce family member, the station freehold land was finally purchased by CNR in 1988. Today, as part of the Alpine National Park, it is popular for activities including 4WD, camping, bushwalking and deer shooting.

While it does get busy on summer long weekends, its many secluded camping sites along the river ensure an enjoyable stay.

Zeka Spur to Eaglevale

The descent down the Zeka Spur is interesting to say the least. While it is steep and slippery in the wet, it is the couple of rock steps that really test a driver's skill and the vehicle. Luckily you are heading down them, so it is not as hard as coming up.

Keep to the main marked track. There has been a lot of roadwork around here and a number of tracks have been closed off, but the main track is easy to follow. There are some good views along the way and it pays to take your time.

Once you get to the bottom of the ridge the track turns south and about 23 km from where you left the High Plains road you arrive at a track junction. The valley stretches away in front of you, and on all sides the mountains rear up from the flat plains to their lofty peaks. Left leads out of the valley to Myrtleford and is probably the easiest way out.

Continue straight ahead at the junction and 3.5 km later you will cross Zeka Creek. Once again there are numerous tracks along here. Keep to the main one and avoid the mud holes that dot the tracks where they cross the flat floodplain. A number of tracks off to the left lead to camp sites on the river, about 500 metres from the tree line. The tiny historic cemetery is

Mallee fowl mound

found 3.5 km further along and another 1 km on, near a dense clump of trees, is the remains of the Wonnangatta Homestead (**GPS** 37°12'35"S, 146°49'55"E). The hut is the only thing really standing and it can still be used. The camping amongst the trees is also popular; it is shady in summer, but can be a little too shady when the weather is cool.

There are numerous camps along the river and these are idyllic, with pleasant swimming holes and spots to catch a feed of fish.

Keep heading south on the main track and nearly 9 km from the Wonnangatta Homestead you will cross the river and come to a track junction. Signposted 'Wombat Spur' and 'Herne Spur', you have a choice of routes to take out of the valley.

Herne Spur is the steepest climb; if taking this route, continue to follow the river downstream for another 4 km, crossing the river a few times in the process. The track then swings steeply uphill and it is steep, so it is only advisable in the driest of times.

Taking the Wombat Spur route, the track first follows the Humffray River and crosses it a couple of times until, 3 km from the Wonnangatta River crossing, a track heads steeply uphill on your right. Nearly 3 km later, and on top of the ridge, the Herne Spur route comes in on the right.

The track continues along the ridge, giving some excellent views of the surrounding mountains, and 6.5 km from the Spur junction a track on the right leads to a helipad and the top of Mt Von Guerard. Continue along the main track south and 6 km later, on the crest of Mt Cynthia, you will come to another track junction. Turn right and almost immediately you will begin to descend steeply.

The 4 km to the bottom of the hill can be hairy if the track is wet, but is relatively easy when it is dry. You will end up almost in the front yard of Eaglevale Homestead at the bottom of the hill, so stick to the track which cuts in close to the front of the house and then turn right, dropping into the Wonnangatta River.

Once across the steam and on the flat land you can sit back and relax, as it is fairly easy travelling from here on—well, for the next few kilometres anyway. You are just 32 km from the heart of the Wonnangatta Valley, 63 km from the top of Zeka Spur and 163 km from Mansfield. The 63 km from the top of Zeka Spur is a few hours' travelling, should you want to do it that quickly!

Eaglevale to Dargo

From the river crossing, head across the flat land, taking any of the tracks to the left, or in a downstream direction. Once you get onto the main track, continue heading down the valley and as you progress the road will get start to get better.

You will cross Kingwells Bridge 22 km from Eaglevale and then just afterwards the turn-off, on your left, to Crooked River. Watch out for the junction, 21 km after the bridge, where you need to turn left onto Shortcut Track, and follow this to the main road 2 km further on.

Veer left and follow this main bitumen road 6 km to the small township of Dargo and its pub. You are 51 km from Eaglevale and 83 km from the very heart of the 'Hidden Valley'. Mansfield is 214 km behind you.

The Bridge Hotel has accommodation and meals, and the general store across the road has fuel and basic supplies. The Dargo Caravan Park caters for vanners and campers.

There is so much four wheeling available around this mountain town it is hard to know where to start. The town is 325 km from Melbourne via good roads.

Dargo to Omeo

You can always follow the main road north to Mt Hotham, 62 km away, then east, 55 km to Omeo. It is a very pleasant mountain trip, full of great views and lots of snow plains.

Our 4WD trek goes to Omeo a shorter way, but it will take you longer and be a little more adventurous as well.

Head north out of town and just over 5 km from the pub, at Farm Junction, veer right off the Dargo High Plains Road and keep following the Dargo River northwards. You will cross a small creek about 2 km north and then 5 km further on you come to a junction where you need to veer right and cross the main river. This crossing can get very deep and the river powerfully fast, so make sure it is not too deep before you plunge in!

Jones Road, as the track is called, climbs steeply uphill for 5 km to a track junction close to the top of Mt Steve. Turn left onto the Birregun Road. This road leads all the way east to Livingstone Creek and meets the main Cassilis–Omeo road.

At Rudolf Gap, 2 km north, veer left, staying on the main road. Keep left at the next intersection, 6 km further on, and veer right where Birregun Creek Track comes in from the left, nearly 5 km further on again.

Near the top of Mt Birregun, 5 km later, turn right, past the helipad. Keep straight ahead at the next two intersections, and 6.5 km from the top of the mount veer right.

About 3 km north you will come to a track junction. Veer right here for Dog's Grave, just a kilometre off the main road. It is a touching tribute to man's best friend, and nearby there is a pleasant camp. Down the hill a little way is a stream where you can get water.

Veer right and head more easterly 2.5 km later, where Dinner Plain Track joins the main track. Stick on the main track and 6 km later you will come to a creek crossing with a hut beside it, on the right.

Keep on the main route and 8 km after the hut you will come to the Livingstone Creek Track, which quickly becomes Livingstone Creek Road. Turn left onto this easier road and follow it for another 6 km,

Turn left here (**GPS** 37°10'24"S, 147°33'22"E), onto the Cassilis–Omeo Road, cross the bridge and 7 km later you will veer right onto the main Omeo–Mt Hotham Road. Another 3 km will see you in the heart of Omeo— capital of the Alps. You are just 75 km from Dargo via this slower route, and Mansfield is 289 mountainous kilometres west of you.

Omeo

Omeo is the biggest town you will pass through on this trip, apart from Mansfield at the very start. Founded during the gold rushes, the Omeo area was first opened up by pioneer cattlemen from the Monaro district in New South Wales, who pushed their way south in the 1830s. Gold was discovered here supposedly as early as 1850.

Much of the area that was worked by sluicing and by Chinese prospectors is now protected in a small reserve just out of town, which is worth a visit.

Omeo caters for travellers heading for the snow in winter or those going fishing, hunting or camping in summer. The town has all the facilities a traveller would need.

Omeo to Tom Groggin

Head north out of town on the main Omeo Highway to Mitta Mitta. About 4 km from the centre of town turn right onto the Benambra Road. Once you get to Benambra, 18 km further on, where a store can supply fuel and basic food and the pub can supply a cold beer, continue to head north on the main road to Corryong.

This road at first passes through flat rich grazing land; then the bitumen runs out about 12 km north of town and the road begins to climb through forested country. It continues as a good dirt road, and about 24 km north of Benambra when it meets with the Gibbo River it turns and heads up this river valley. Keep a lookout for the giant logging trucks that use this road.

It follows the river closely for 14 km, crossing it a few times, and then heads north away from the river, climbing all the time. Sassafras Gap, the top of the Great Dividing Range, is reached after travelling another 12 km. A track on the left is the main access track to the back end of Lake Dartmouth, 12 km due west but well and truly out of sight. From here the road starts to descend.

Nearly 10 km north of the Gap, and about 82 km north of Omeo, you will come to the Wheelers Creek Logging Road which leaves the main road on your right. Turn right here and follow this road into the forest. Once again the tall gums of the mountains tower over you and it is great to be back in the forest again. This track gets chopped up by the traffic that uses it, and as there is a fair amount of logging activity going on throughout this area keep a sharp eye on the trip meter and a good lookout for any new tracks and signs.

About 11.5 km into the forest you will come to Wheelers Creek Hut on your right. This cattlemen's hut and flat are pleasant enough, but the track you need is about 1 km back along the track you have come in on. Backtrack to this junction and veer right onto Cattlemens Track. Again, watch for re-aligned tracks all through this forest.

Keep on this track, and left at the Y-junction less than a kilometre north of where you left the logging road. Just over 3 km north from leaving the Wheelers Creek road veer right, and then 500 metres later hard right, onto Shady Creek Lower Track. You will cross a couple of creeks, and less than 5 km from the last junction you come to Gibson's Hut. This is a fine spot to stop or camp on the edge of a mountain stream. The hut is a private hut and could well be in use, but like all cattlemen's huts it is open for all to use, though not to abuse! From here, you are just 10 km from Wheelers Creek Hut.

Once you leave Gibson's, head east, keeping left at the junction just east of the hut. From this point the track heads further north, crosses a stream and then swings back almost west, before heading north again to meet with Dunstans Logging Track and Dead Finish Track, 4 km north of the hut. Turn right onto Dead Finish Track and then right again, just over 2 km later. Less than a kilometre later veer right onto the Pinnibar Jeep Track.

Keep right at the next junction just over 3 km further on, and 2 km later you will be on the crest of Mt Pinnibar (**GPS** 36°32'16"S, 148°00'06"E), with its trig point nearby and one of the finest views in the High Country. You are just 34 km from Sassafras Gap and 116 km from Omeo. Those with a phone in their 4WD can dial home and tell them how unlucky they are not to be at this magnificent spot. The main Kosciuszko Range is off to the east, while magnificent mountains fill the view to the south.

Ignore the track that heads south from this point and continue on the Pinnibar Track eastward, which begins to drop pretty steeply once you are off the top. Descending about 11 km from the top—and if it is wet, the track will be slippery—you will come onto open land which is part of Tom Groggin Station.

Stick to the track, which is faint in parts, especially in the flush of rich grass in late spring. There are a few small creeks to cross, and these can be a little boggy, but at least the route is obvious. The official route is not down the valley but swings up the valley before striking eastward—signs will help you stay on track. Just over 2 km after entering the property you will be on the treeline and come to a defined track junction where you will turn left (right leads back south on the Tom Groggin Track). You go for 3 km through the forest to another junction, where you need to turn left once again.

As you approach the River Murray, less than a kilometre further on, the track swings left through a gate, cuts a corner in the paddock and goes through another gate, just a few hundred metres from the first. Do not deviate from this route.

Once through the second gate you are on top of the bank of the River Murray. Check this crossing before plunging in—it can be tricky! There is normally a deep hole immediately on your right as you enter the water. Needless to say, stick left, but not so far as to get washed off the shallow water of the ford—the current is generally pretty strong. It is not a wide crossing, but you will be glad to get to the other bank.

If the river crossing is too daunting, backtrack through the gates and back along the track past the junction where you turned left. The track skirts the river and 2 km further on another track comes in on the left. Turn left here, but before sliding down the bank check the slope of the track. Quite a few people come to grief here before they get into the water. The water is shallower than at the other crossing—the banks are the major problem at this spot!

Once through the river at this point, you are in New South Wales and the Kosciuszko National Park. Veer left and follow the main track, basically north for nearly 3 km to the picnic/camping ground (**GPS** 36°32'29"S, 148°08'07"E). There are a few tracks around the area, but they all end up in the same general place. The road in front of you is the Alpine Way.

Back at the first crossing, once you are across the river you are again in the park, but less than 1 km from the main Alpine Way. Again, there are a few tracks around here, but basically head east and you will get to the road, just west of the picnic and camping ground, and about 18 km from the top of Mt Pinnibar.

At this point you are about 20 km south of Thredbo Village if you turn right onto the main road. If you turn left onto the Alpine Way you are 57 km south of Khancoban . You are now 134 km from Omeo and 423 km from Mansfield.

If you have done the whole distance in a week you have been rushing it—take two as a minimum. The adventure is over, but what a trip!

The stunning view from the the Bluff in the Alpine National Park

AIREYS INLET

118 KM SOUTH-WEST OF MELBOURNE
POPULATION: 675   MAP REF: PAGE 93 L8

Aireys Inlet on the magnificent and scenic Great Ocean Road, south-west of Melbourne, is one of the oldest coastal settlements in this region. Once a base for pirates, it is now a renowned seaside resort.

Named after John Airey, a settler who came to this area in 1846, this town played an important role along the coast with its Split Point Lighthouse. Built in 1891 and still in operation, it dominates the Great Ocean Road view and is visible to all coming in from the sea. A walking track leads to a clifftop lookout over to the lighthouse which is said to be haunted.

Aireys Inlet is on the eastern boundary of the Angahook–Lorne State Park, a huge parkland encompassing 21 340 hectares of coastal hinterland and fern-filled ravines. It is an ideal area for bushwalking, scenic drives or cool, restful picnics during the warmer months. The Allen Noble Sanctuary on the Great Ocean Road is also an excellent reserve with plenty of bird life.

This area is extremely popular during school holidays and it is best to book accommodation in advance. Many hotels or cottages will only take week-long bookings during the peak holiday season in summer and over Easter.

ACCOMMODATION: Lightkeepers Inn Motel, ph (03) 5289 6666; Lorneview (B&B), ph (03) 5289 6430; Aireys Inlet Getaway, ph (03) 5289 7021
ACTIVITIES: Bushwalking, fishing, scenic drives, water sports
TOURIST INFORMATION: Ph (03) 5237 6529

ANGLESEA

168 KM SOUTH-WEST OF MELBOURNE
POPULATION: 1975   MAP REF: PAGE 93 L8

Anglesea features safe, sandy beaches, along with abundant coastal bushland which comes alive with

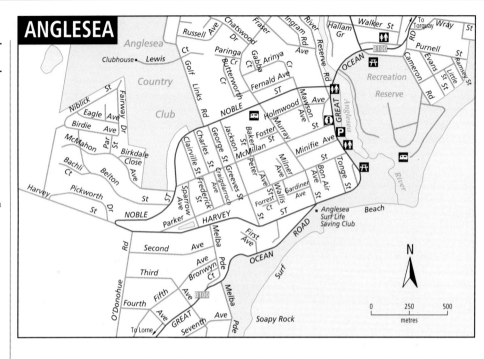

The white sands of Anglesea Beach

colourful wildflowers in spring. The small seaside town is situated at the start of the Great Ocean Road, a scenic trek which winds its way around Victoria's western coastline offering superb views of the ocean. The town offers all the delights of a seaside resort with plenty of sandy beaches or grassy knolls on which to sit and take in the scenery.

At the end of the River Reserve Road in town is the Coogaoorah Park. This incorporates unique waterways with natural coastal bushland and is ideal for fishing, canoeing and picnics. A series of raised boardwalks and platforms allows walkers to view this magnificent wetland without disturbing it.

Anglesea is also within easy reach of the magnificent Otway National Park and the Angahook–Lorne State Park, both of which offer scenic drives amongst cool temperate forests and delightful walks to small fern-lined creeks.

Walkers can also delight in the Heathland Cliff Walk, a 3.5 km circuit which takes around one hour to complete. Beginning from the car park at the end of Purnell Street, this walk takes you past massive cliff formations and coastal heathlands, with a viewing platform offering excellent views out to Bass Strait.

ACCOMMODATION: Anglesea Homestead Motor Lodge, ph (03) 5263 2600; Surfcoast Resort Anglesea, ph (03) 5263 3363; Debonair Motel Guesthouse, ph (03) 5263 1440
ACTIVITIES: Bowls, fishing, golf, hang gliding, horse riding, scenic drives, tennis, water sports
TOURIST INFORMATION: Ph (03) 5237 6529

ALEXANDRA

128 KM NORTH-EAST OF MELBOURNE
POPULATION: 2200   MAP REF: PAGE 98 D8

This small country town is typical of many found in Central Victoria with much of the surrounding countryside cleared and utilised for farming. Alexandra is situated near the popular holiday destination of Lake Eildon with the Lake Eildon National Park offering campers a lakeside camp on the foreshores. This lake is well liked by swimmers, waterskiers, watercraft enthusiasts, including those with houseboats, while anglers try their luck for brown and rainbow trout and redfin.

The town was originally known as Redgate Diggings during the gold rush days in the late 1800s but its name was later changed to Alexandra in honour of the then Princess of Wales.

In Station Street lies the Timber and Tramway Museum which is housed in the old railway station. This museum displays a range of photographs and artefacts from the pioneer days when timber was felled in the region. There are also steam engines on display and rides available on both steam and diesel locomotives at certain times.

ACCOMMODATION: Mt Pleasant Hotel, ph (03) 5772 1083; Alexandra Motor Inn, ph (03) 5772 02077
ACTIVITIES: Bushwalking, fishing, national park access, scenic drives, tennis, water sports
TOURIST INFORMATION: Ph (03) 5772 2169

APOLLO BAY

189 KM SOUTH-WEST OF MELBOURNE
POPULATION: 2000   MAP REF: PAGE 93 K9

While Apollo Bay itself is a fantastic seaside resort, the journey there from Melbourne travels along the Great Ocean Road and passes through the quaint villages of Skenes Creek and Wye River. You will find many lookouts and viewing platforms along this route which offer panoramic views of the coastline and out to Bass Strait, while the picturesque rainforests of the Otway Ranges stand tall in the background.

Once an important harbour, the sheltered waters have silted up and the size of vessel now able to enter the port is restricted. The small bay and foreshore are the focus of the town and this magnificent stretch of beach is a haven for beach lovers, swimmers and surfers. It is here that the local fishing boats come in with their haul of fresh fish and seafood.

There are two museums in town. The Bass Strait Shell Museum features a huge display of shells from all around the world, and information on shipwrecks that have occurred off this treacherous western coastline; the Historical Museum has thousands of photographs showcasing the area's shipping history.

The region lends itself to scenic drives around the coast or inland through the parks. Apollo Bay is within easy reach of the Otway National Park and Cape Otway, the most southerly point on this coastline. A steep and narrow road will take you to Mariners Lookout east of town, where a short walk leads to spectacular views of the township and the coastline. A drive down Barham River Road will lead to the 3 km walk through lush forest beside a creek to Mariners Falls. Other falls in the area include Beauchamp and Hopetoun Falls.

ACCOMMODATION: Apollo International, ph (03) 5237 6100; Great Ocean View Motel, ph (03) 5237 6527; Seafarers Holiday Retreat, ph (03) 5237 6507
ACTIVITIES: Bowls, fishing, golf, hang gliding, horse riding, national park access, scenic drives, tennis, water sports
TOURIST INFORMATION: Ph (03) 5237 6529

ARARAT

205 KM WEST OF MELBOURNE
POPULATION: 8300   MAP REF: PAGE 92 G4

Founded in 1839, Ararat is an important town in a district which is famous for wool and wheat production. Situated on the outer edge of the gold-fields region of Victoria, near the south-eastern ridges of the Grampians National Park, Ararat forms part of the Goldfields Touring Triangle Route which extends to the old goldmining centres of Ballarat and Bendigo.

Horatio Wills was the first settler in this region in 1841, and the first gold nugget was uncovered in 1854. It was to take three years before the big gold rush hit this district when a large alluvial deposit was found at Canton Lead.

By the late 1800s vines had been planted in the area and today there are a number of wineries situated in this region. The small wine-growing township of Great Western, with the Grampians as a backdrop, can be found 17 km from Ararat. Best Wines and Seppelts Great Western are the largest wineries in town.

Ararat boasts many attractions including the magnificent Alexandra Gardens, Green Hill Lake which is popular with water-sport enthusiasts, and One Tree Hill Lookout which offers spectacular views of the surrounding ranges. Langi Morgala Museum—the name is Aboriginal for 'home of yesterday'—displays Aboriginal relics, along with other artefacts from this town's history.

A monument commemorating Ararat's gold rush days

ACCOMMODATION: Ararat Colonial Lodge, ph (03) 5352 4644; Ararat Central Motel, ph (03) 5352 4444; Golden Gate Motel, ph (03) 5352 2474
ACTIVITIES: Bowls, bushwalking, croquet, fishing, golf, horse riding, horseracing, national park access, scenic drives, swimming, tennis, trotting, wineries
TOURIST INFORMATION: Ph (03) 5352 2836

AVOCA

182 KM NORTH-WEST OF MELBOURNE
POPULATION: 1032   MAP REF: PAGE 93 J3

This agricultural and mining town sits on the banks of the Avoca River with the nearby Pyrenees Ranges and the rich, fertile soil of the valley within easy reach. Avoca was named by explorer Major Thomas Mitchell in 1836 and by the 1850s was part of a huge gold rush which extended for miles around to include such towns as Maryborough, Ballarat and Stawell.

Located near the centre of the Goldfields Touring Route, Avoca makes an ideal base from which to explore these old goldmining towns.

There are a couple of magnificent bluestone buildings in town, including the chemist shop which dates back to 1854 and the old bluestone gaol. The Avoca Rock Museum can be found in High Street and it contains specimens of rocks, gemstones and minerals from all over Australia along with historic photographs and information on Avoca.

Nestled in the Pyrenees Valley are a number of excellent wineries including the Blue Pyrenees Estate, Dalwhinnie, Mount Avoca and Taltarni. The Avoca Wool and Wine Festival is held in October.

ACCOMMODATION: Motel Avoca, ph (03) 5465 3464; Avoca Heritage School (B&B), ph (03) 5465 3691; The Old Rectory Guesthouse, ph (03) 5465 3560
ACTIVITIES: Bowls, bushwalking, gold prospecting, golf, horse riding, horseracing, river fishing, river swimming, scenic drives, squash, tennis, wineries
TOURIST INFORMATION: Ph (03) 5465 3767

BACCHUS MARSH

53 KM WEST OF MELBOURNE
POPULATION: 11 000   MAP REF: PAGE 93 M5

A dairy and pastoral township, Bacchus Marsh is a short drive from Melbourne in a charming valley which lies between the Lerderderg and Werribee Gorges. The town is named after Captain W. H. Bacchus who bought a portion of swamp land from the area's first settler Mr K. Clarke. Bacchus built a two-storey brick mansion in 1840 which still stands.

The most impressive feature of the town is the Avenue of Honour which comprises 232 giant elm trees. There were planted in 1918 to commemorate servicemen who fought for Australia in World War I.

Adjacent to the railway station in Grant Street is Maddingley Park where nearly 10 hectares are available for picnics and other recreational activities.

Outside town on the road to Melton is the Djerriwarrah Bridge, a spectacular sandstone structure built in 1858–59. To the south of Bacchus Marsh is the Werribee Gorge while to the north lies the Lerderderg State Park, home to the Lerderderg Gorge. This conservation area boasts the largest single area of eucalypt forest in north-central Victoria, and it is also home to koalas, which lives in the large ribbony manna gums.

Gold was mined in this region many years ago and there are still relics to be found in the park including old machinery. This is a popular region with gem fossickers, walkers and four wheel drivers.

ACCOMMODATION: Bacchus Marsh Avenue Motel, ph (03) 5367 3766; Sunnystones Farm, ph (03) 5367 1984
ACTIVITIES: Golf, horse riding, rock climbing, tennis, walking, wineries
TOURIST INFORMATION: Ph (03) 9658 9972

BAIRNSDALE

288 KM EAST OF MELBOURNE
POPULATION: 10 690   MAP REF: PAGE 96 E6

Sitting at the southern boundary of the Victorian High Country and surrounded by the tall timbers of the forestry industry and cleared farmlands, Bairnsdale is a major regional centre. The town's name originated from the Isle of Skye, the birthplace of Archibald McLeod who established his station Bernisdale here in 1844.

With fertile land, this region has always supported vegetable farming and cattle and sheep grazing. Much produce was initially supplied to the goldfields scattered through the hills to the north.

Before road transport was viable, this town, sitting as it does on the Mitchell River, was a major port and used by river steamers. It is still a major supply point for the region, along with being a gateway to the High

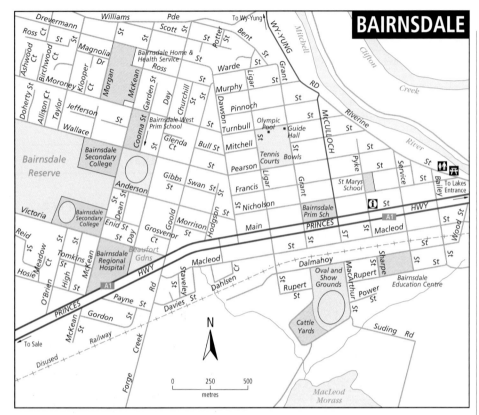

BAIRNSDALE

Country to the north and the splendid lakes system that lies just south of the town on the coast.

The town features galleries, craft shops and museums. The Hillmay House Antique Museum is an 1890s furnished historic home which contains a nursery with an excellent display of baby furniture and dolls. The Historical Museum and Resource Centre is a two-storey building housing memorabilia while the grounds are scattered with machinery from a bygone era. In Main Street you will find St Mary's Roman Catholic Church which was built in 1913 and is noted for its exquisite murals.

Paynesville and Lakes Entrance to the south offer sailing and cruising on the Gippsland Lakes while the picturesque town of Dargo, nestled in the Victorian Alps, is less than two hours' drive from Bairnsdale.

ACCOMMODATION: Bairnsdale Motor Inn, ph (03) 5152 3004; Bairnsdale Kansas City Motel, ph (03) 5152 6266; Mitchell Motor Inn, ph (03) 5152 5012

ACTIVITIES: Bowls, bushwalking, croquet, fishing, golf, horse riding, horseracing, scenic drives, tennis, water sports

TOURIST INFORMATION: Ph (03) 5152 3444

BALLARAT

111 KM WEST OF MELBOURNE
POPULATION: 63 802   MAP REF: PAGE 93 K5

The large town of Ballarat is a major regional centre. It prospered during the gold rush and is now known as a most picturesque tourist town. The city literally glows in autumn when the leaves of its deciduous trees change colour. The botanic gardens near Lake Wendouree are a tranquil spot in this beautiful city.

Ballarat's origins extend back to 1837 when William Yuille and his men camped on the edge of the Black Swamp, an area that has been reclaimed and is now known as Lake Wendouree. Yuille settled here—the name Ballarat comes from an Aboriginal word 'ballarat' which means 'camping or resting place'.

It was not long before the first gold nugget was found by Thomas Hiscock—from the ground near the cemetery in 1851. It was not until two years later, however, that two main lodes were found and thousands of miners rushed to the region to try their hand at gold prospecting. Their 'settlement' was a huge tent city.

The Eureka Stockade incident followed in 1854 when there was a major clash over miners' rights and taxes: the miners eventually lined up and simultaneously burnt their licences in a huge campfire. This revolt was led by Peter Lalor under the blue and white Eureka flag, and within days a fight ensued between the miners and government soldiers. Over 30 people were killed. Sent to trial, the agitators were found not guilty and Lalor went on to become a member of the Victorian Parliament. You will still see the famous flag flying throughout this town today. A Eureka Stockade Memorial sits on the corner of Stawell and Eureka Streets while an exhibition of this event can be found on Eureka Street.

Gold provided a great deal of wealth to this area and it is here that the world's second biggest gold nugget was found. The Welcome Nugget weighed 68 956 grams and was found at Bakery Hill in 1858.

The Arch of Victory forms an entrance to the town and to the Avenue of Honour, along which nearly 4000 trees are planted in honour of ex-servicemen.

Without doubt the biggest attraction is Sovereign Hill, a theme park re-creating the old gold rush days. Its staff members dress in period costume, and it contains realistic stores and banks. It is situated on the old Sovereign Hill Quartz Mining Site.

The Great Southern Woolshed can be found on the Western Highway. Based around the wool industry, it features displays of sheep shearing, working sheep dogs and an animal nursery. Ballarat Wildlife Park is set amongst 116 hectares of scenic peppermint forest with native wildlife such as koalas, kangaroos, emus and wombats.

South of town is the theme park Kryal Castle, the world's third largest castle which features Gothic architecture. The staff dress as medieval characters and put on shows. The armour, torture chamber, glass-blowing display and stone maze are popular.

There were many Chinese present in the gold rush days: it is said that up to one-third of the population during the 1800s was of Chinese descent.

The beautiful and peaceful botanic gardens of Ballarat

The numerous Chinese graves on McArthur Street reinforce this belief.

Other features in town include the Ballarat Aviation Museum which houses a huge collection of vintage and classic planes, models and memorabilia. You will also find a gold museum which contains a great collection of the alluvial gold nuggets.

ACCOMMODATION: The Ansonia Hotel, ph (03) 5332 4678; Sovereign Park Motor Inn, ph (03) 5331 3955; Ballarat Colony Motor Inn, ph (03) 5334 7788; Gardens House (B&B), ph (03) 5331 4957

ACTIVITIES: Bowls, fishing, golf, greyhound racing, horse riding, horseracing, scenic drives, squash, tennis, water sports

TOURIST INFORMATION: Ph (03) 5332 2694

BALNARRING

80 KM SOUTH-EAST OF MELBOURNE
POPULATION: 1425   MAP REF: PAGE 93 P8

This small township overlooks Westernport Bay and features many holiday houses which are utilised during the weekends and holiday periods by Melbournians escaping the city and looking for the beach and the sea.

Situated on the Mornington Peninsula, this town is close to the surf beaches of Point Leo and Somers on the east and to the bustling seaside resorts of Rosebud and Dromana on the west of the peninsula.

This peninsula has many fruit farms and wineries such as Balnarring Vineyard and the Hofferts Balnarring Estate, both of which can be found on the Bittern–Dromana road.

Popular in the area are the markets, such as Red Hill and Emu Plains, which are held during summer and autumn on varying Saturdays.

ACCOMMODATION: Balnarring Village Hotel, ph (03) 5983 5222; Warrawee Homestead, ph (03) 5983 1729

ACTIVITIES: Bowls, markets, tennis, wineries

TOURIST INFORMATION: Ph (03) 5987 3078

BEACONSFIELD

47 KM SOUTH-EAST OF MELBOURNE
POPULATION: 2065   MAP REF: PAGE 91 J4

Once a small farming community on the outskirts of Melbourne, the less hectic lifestyle and spacious real estate have led to the growth of Beaconsfield over the past ten years. It is now an extension of Melbourne's suburbs and many people commute from this town to their jobs in Melbourne 50 km away.

The town was once known as Little Berwick, an extension of its neighbouring town, but in 1881 it received its own identity and name. The town was named after the British Prime Minister, Benjamin Disraeli, the first Earl of Beaconsfield, who died that same year.

Situated on the Princes Highway, it is the start of many a journey to Gippsland in the east of the state.

ACCOMMODATION: Farthings of Fernhill (B&B), ph (03) 5944 3116

ACTIVITIES: Bushwalking, golf, horse riding, scenic drives, tennis

TOURIST INFORMATION: Ph (03) 9658 9972

BEAUFORT

158 KM WEST OF MELBOURNE
POPULATION: 1200   MAP REF: PAGE 93 J4

Now the centre of a rich pastoral and agricultural district, Beaufort was once a bustling goldmining town originally known as Fiery Creek Diggings. A hectic gold rush began in 1854 at Yam Holes Creek and thousands of prospectors quickly moved from surrounding mining locations to chance their luck at this new find. However, by 1914 most had left as the gold supply was depleted.

The Country Garden on Caramballac Road is a traditional English garden established in 1909 and is open to the public on weekdays.

Other features in the town include the historic court house which was built in 1863 from handmade bricks manufactured from quartz from the goldfields.

Beaufort is also close to Lake Burrumbeet where swimming, waterskiing and boating can be enjoyed.

ACCOMMODATION: Beaufort Motel, ph (03) 5349 2297; Wirranee Park (B&B), ph (03) 5349 7267

ACTIVITIES: Bowls, bushwalking, croquet, fishing, gold prospecting, golf, rock climbing, scenic drives, squash, tennis, water sports

TOURIST INFORMATION: Ph (03) 5332 2694

BEECHWORTH

275 KM NORTH-EAST OF MELBOURNE
POPULATION: 3700   MAP REF: PAGE 98 G4

Nestled amongst the natural beauty of the Northern Victorian Alps is the historic goldmining town of Beechworth. It is history that draws visitors to this town with more than 30 of its buildings classified by the National Trust; it is currently the best preserved gold town in Victoria.

The town was settled in 1853 and with the discovery of gold there were soon over 8000 gold diggers lining Spring and Reedy Creeks. Beechworth Historic Park encompasses 1130 hectares of the town and features treasures from the old goldmining days. The self-guided Woolshed Historic Walk in the park takes around one hour to complete and goes past diversion tunnels and old mining relics.

Other attractions include the restored powder magazine which was built of local stone in the 1850s for the safe storage of the gunpowder used to extract the gold from the ground.

A memorial to the large number of Chinese prospectors who mined this region—the Chinese Burning Towers and Cemetery—stands on Cemetery Road. There you will find the remains of towers, altars and headstones of some of the 1600 Chinese who are buried there.

Loch Street Museum has a display on Robert Burke, of Burke and Wills fame, who once served as police chief in the district. The gaol cell which held a young Ned Kelly and where he was imprisoned before his execution is also in Beechworth.

ACCOMMODATION: Beechworth Motor Inn, ph (03) 5728 1301; Carriage Motor Inn, ph (03) 5728 1830; The Old Priory (guesthouse), ph (03) 5728 1024; Alba Country Rose Private B&B, ph (03) 5728 1107

ACTIVITIES: Bowls, croquet, fishing, gem fossicking,

Beechworth's Carriage Museum

golf, historic interest, horse riding, scenic drives, tennis, water sports

TOURIST INFORMATION: Ph (03) 5728 3233

BENALLA

198 KM NORTH-EAST OF MELBOURNE
POPULATION: 9200   MAP REF: PAGE 98 E5

It was the famous explorer Major Thomas Mitchell who first trekked alongside the Broken River and camped in 1836 at the site of Benalla; a fountain was later placed in the town gardens in honour of this event. The name was originally Benella, an Aboriginal name meaning 'musk duck', but was later changed.

The centre of a large agricultural and pastoral area, Benalla services the surrounding smaller towns and farms. It is known as the 'Glider Capital of Australia' and these silent flyers can often be seen in the skies above town. The Gliding Club of Benalla offers passenger flights daily.

Bushrangers frequented this region and the old court house had two visits from the famous Ned Kelly. The Costume and Pioneer Museum in Mair Street houses a magnificent collection of fascinating costumes including Ned Kelly's cummerbund.

In the warmer months the huge trees of the Benalla Gardens offer welcome shade, while hundreds of magnificent colourful roses bloom not only in the gardens which were established in 1949, but throughout town. This is where Benalla gets its name as 'The City of Roses' and the Rose Festival is held every November.

The Benalla Art Gallery, situated in the gardens, has a fine collection of Australian artwork and exhibitions, while there is an excellent display of dolls and toys at the Enchantable Collectibles.

Broken River was dammed in 1974. This created a picturesque lake in the centre of town which is popular with swimmers and boating enthusiasts. On the foreshore of the lake is the Ceramic Mural Garden where potters, helped by local school children, have decorated more than 1000 ceramic tiles.

ACCOMMODATION: Avondel Motor Inn, ph (03) 5762 3677; Glider City Motel, ph (03) 5762 3339

ACTIVITIES: Art galleries, bowls, fishing, golf, horse riding, horseracing, scenic drives, tennis, water sports

TOURIST INFORMATION: Ph (03) 5762 1749

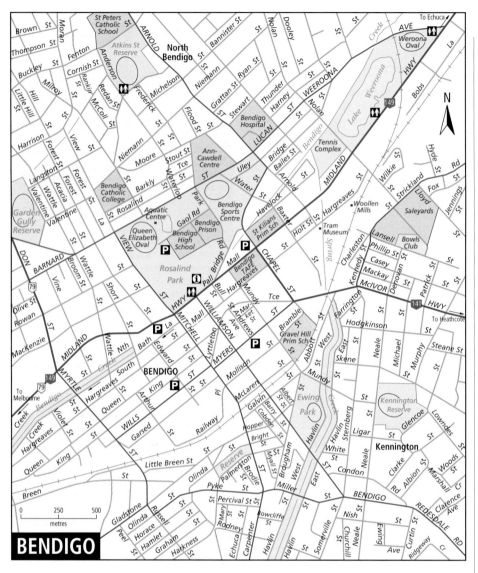

BENDIGO

BENDIGO

152 KM NORTH-WEST OF MELBOURNE
POPULATION: 70 000   MAP REF: PAGE 93 M2

Lying on the fertile flats of the Campaspe and Loddon Rivers, this sprawling town in the heart of Victoria acts as a service centre for much of the outlying area. Gold was discovered in Bendigo in 1851 and the mines around Bendigo went on to produce more than 595 million grams of gold, making it one of the richest goldfields in the world. Mining ceased in 1954 when the Central Deborah Gold Mine closed down. The 422-metre-deep mine reopened in 1972 and now tours are conducted to the second of the 17 levels underground, while surface tours are also available. The Gold Mining Museum in Eaglehawk has a good collection of artefacts and mining relics.

Pall Mall, the main street in town, features numerous historic buildings dating back to the nineteenth century including the Post Office, Law Courts and the impressive Shamrock Hotel which is still in operation. A quartz fountain, using more than 20 tonnes of the superb stone, was given to the city of Bendigo by the 'Quartz King' George Lansell in 1881.

Other superb buildings include the Sacred Heart Cathedral on Wattle Street, believed to be the last Gothic cathedral built in the world.

Nearly as old as the mining industry is the famous Bendigo Pottery, founded in 1857 by a Scottish potter, George Guthrie. Another of Bendigo's greatest attractions is the Vintage Talking Tram on which visitors can take an hour long journey through this historic city. At the depot are a number of vintage trams, many of which are restored. Also of interest are the fully restored Joss House and the Golden Dragon Museum, both of which highlight the contributions made by the Chinese in this town.

Off the Loddon Valley Highway in Eaglehawk is Sandhurst Town, which is actually two towns, one representing Bendigo during the gold rush and the other a small country town typical of this region. These two impressive representations are connected via a full sized railway.

On the outskirts of Bendigo are the Whipstick and Kamarooka Parks which are home to the blue eucalyptus. This stunted eucalypt has adapted to the harsh growing conditions of the region and produces excellent eucalyptus oil. Harland's Eucalyptus Factory can be toured. The distillery has been operating since 1890 and still produces the popular oil and soaps.

ACCOMMODATION: Shamrock Hotel, ph (03) 5443 0333; All Seasons International Motor Inn, ph (03) 5443 8166; Bendigo Colonial Motor Inn, ph (03) 5447 0122

ACTIVITIES: Bowls, croquet, greyhound racing, golf, historic interest, horseracing, swimming, tennis

TOURIST INFORMATION: Ph (03) 5444 4433

Bendigo's famous Shamrock Hotel, built in the nineteenth century and still a hotel today

BIRCHIP

312 KM NORTH-WEST OF MELBOURNE
POPULATION: 850   MAP REF: PAGE 94 G8

Situated in the heart of the Wimmera Country, Birchip services a large agricultural and wheat growing area. The town was first settled in 1880 and has been farmed ever since. The Dingo Fence, built to keep dingoes out of the region, ran through this district, from South Australia up to the Murray River and the township of Swan Hill. Much of it has been destroyed, but sections of the fence can still be found.

The Pioneer Fountain is a symbol of the importance of water in this region; it was also erected in memory of the area's pioneers. The Soldiers Memorial Park features huge Moreton Bay fig trees and is a popular picnic area. Lake Tchum, which is ideal for water sports, is only 10 km from town.

ACCOMMODATION: Birchip Motel, ph (03) 5492 2566; Commercial Hotel, ph (03) 5492 2413

ACTIVITIES: Bowls, fishing, golf, tennis, water sports

TOURIST INFORMATION: Ph (03) 5398 1632

BRIGHT

319 KM NORTH-EAST OF MELBOURNE
POPULATION: 2000   MAP REF: PAGE 99 H6
A very picturesque country town in the Ovens Valley,
Bright offers colourful blooms in spring, huge shady
trees in the warm summer months, a kaleidoscope of
colour in autumn when the leaves turn amber and
fiery red, while in winter they fall to the ground
allowing the eye to scan the landscape, taking in
snow-capped mountain tops.

Alluvial gold was uncovered here in 1853 and the
town's original name was Morses Creek. This was
changed in 1862 to Bright, after the English political
reformer, John Bright. Today it is the timber industry
built on the surrounding pine and eucalypt forests
from which this town prospers, along with a
successful tourist industry.

Positioned at the gateway to much of the High
Country, Bright is often frequented by snow skiers in
winter, and walkers, mountain bikers, hang gliders
and four wheel drivers from spring thorough to
autumn.The Bright Autumn and Spring Festivals
celebrate the change of seasons.

There are a number of walks in the region. The
town has many interesting shops and different
galleries to browse through.
ACCOMMODATION: High Country Inn (motel),
ph (03) 5755 1244; Bright Avenue Motor Inn, ph
(03) 5755 1911; Riverbank Park Motel and Apartments, ph (03) 5755 1255; Mystic Valley Cottages,
ph (03) 5750 1502; Forest Lodge Holiday Chalets, ph
(03) 5755 1583
ACTIVITIES: Bowls, bushwalking, fishing, 4WD
touring, gold prospecting, golf, hang gliding, horse
riding, scenic drives, snow skiing, swimming, tennis
TOURIST INFORMATION: Ph (03) 5755 2275

BROADFORD

74 KM NORTH OF MELBOURNE
POPULATION: 3000   MAP REF: PAGE 93 P4
The township of Broadford services the surrounding
pastoral and agricultural industry and features a
large paper mill which dates back to 1890.

It is the surrounding areas, though, which attract
visitors, including the Tallarook State Forest to the
east which offers 4WD tracks, camping, and peaceful
picnic areas. The State Forest of Mt Disappointment
south-east of Broadford is named after the towering
peak which explorers Hume and Hovell climbed in an
attempt to view Port Phillip Bay. Much to their
disappointment a sight of the bay was not possible,
but there is an excellent panorama of Melbourne and
the outer suburbs.

Less than 5 km south-west of town is the Mt Piper
Education Reserve which, with much cleared grazing
land around, has been set aside to protect the local
flora and fauna.
ACCOMMODATION: Sugar Loaf Motel, ph
(03) 5784 1069
ACTIVITIES: Bowls, 4WD touring, golf, swimming,
tennis
TOURIST INFORMATION: Ph (03) 9568 9972

BUCHAN

361 KM EAST OF MELBOURNE
POPULATION: 400   MAP REF: PAGE 96 G4
Buchan, nestled amongst cleared rolling farmland
and native bushland, is very charming, but its main
feature for more than a century has been the large
cave system, reserved in 1897.

Formed by underground rivers cutting their way
through limestone, it is the formations of stalactites
and stalagmites, produced by droplets of the
dissolved limestone, that give these caves their
character. Two caves in the system are open to the
public for guided tours: the Fairy and Royal Caves.
North of the township, off the Gelantipy Road, is the
Shades of Death Cave, also open to visitors.

A drive north of the town leads into the Alpine
and Snowy River regions where you will find
delightful camping areas, magnificent scenery,
remote unsealed roads and rugged 4WD tracks.
ACCOMMODATION: Buchan Motel, ph (03) 5155 9201;
Sherrington Holiday Apartments, ph (03) 5159 9221;
Buchan Caves Caravan Park (park and cabins),
ph (03) 6453 7242
ACTIVITIES: Bushwalking, caving, fishing, 4WD
touring, golf, horse riding, scenic drives, swimming
TOURIST INFORMATION: Ph (03) 5152 3444

CASTERTON

371 KM WEST OF MELBOURNE
POPULATION: 2000   MAP REF: PAGE 92 C5
This grazing and agricultural community can be
found on the Glenelg River west of the large country
municipality of Hamilton. First settled in 1840, the
town's name means 'walled city', a reference to the
surrounding hills which give the illusion that the town
is enclosed. The town was named after Casterton in
Westmoreland, in the north of England.

Explorer Thomas Mitchell passed through this
region and was so impressed by its beauty that he
named it 'Australia Felix', meaning 'this wonderful
land', because it contrasted with the dry, arid country

Sheep in the yards ready for shearing at Casterton

he had recently travelled through. Francis Henty was
one of the first settlers, taking up land in 1837.

The Historical Museum is housed in the old
railway building on Jackson Street and has a wide
collection of historic items and photographs from
this district.

The region boasts natural features such as Baileys
Rocks, 30 km north-west of town, which is an outcrop
of large green-coloured granite boulders; the Bluff
which offers superb views of the surrounding
countryside; and Bilston's Tree, said to be Australia's
largest red gum.

On Warrock Road, 29 km north of town, is
Warrock Homestead, where visitors can explore a
number of century-old buildings including a
blacksmith's building, stables, woolshed and the
homestead itself.
ACCOMMODATION: Albion Hotel, ph (03) 5581 1092;
Casterton Hotel, ph (03) 5581 1317; Glen-Aron House
(B&B), ph (03) 5581 2350
ACTIVITIES: Bushwalking, gem fossicking, golf,
horseracing, scenic drives, swimming, tennis
TOURIST INFORMATION: Ph (03) 5581 2070

CASTLEMAINE

122 KM NORTH-WEST OF MELBOURNE
POPULATION: 7140   MAP REF: PAGE 93 L3
Castlemaine is an historic goldmining town in the
heart of the former goldmining belt of Central
Victoria and is a great weekend destination.

The town was first named both Forest Creek and
Mount Alexander in the 1850s. Later its name was
changed to Castlemaine in honour of Viscount
Castlemaine. It was gold, however, that kept the town
prosperous for its first two decades.

Herons Creek, south-west of town, is an historic
gold digging area which was mined from 1851 to the
late 1930s and is now classified by the National Trust.

Castlemaine features a number of historic
buildings, many of which are classified by the
National Trust and built from sandstone mined from
local quarries. Buda is one such home open for
inspection; it was built in 1861 and is set amongst two
hectares of magnificent gardens. The Castlemaine
Market building has unusual architectural styling and
is now used as an art and craft market—which also
houses antiques. The botanic gardens in town were
established in 1860 using land that was once a
goldmining site. The beauty of the town and
surrounding area is best appreciated from the Burke
and Wills Monument which stands on Wills Street
overlookng the town. This monument was placed in
honour of Robert Burke who served as a policeman in
Castlemaine from 1858 to 1860 , after which he set off
on his exploration of Central Australia.
ACCOMMODATION: Castlemaine Colonial Motel,
ph (03) 5472 4000; Castle Motel, ph (03) 5472 2433;
Coach and Rose (B&B), ph (03) 5472 4850; Old
Castlemaine Goal (guesthouse), ph (03) 5470 5311;
Wisteria House (B&B), ph (03) 5470 6604; Campbell
Street Motor Lodge, ph (03) 5472 3477
ACTIVITIES: Bowls, bushwalking, croquet, fishing,
gold prospecting, golf, historic interest, horse riding,
scenic drives, tennis, water sports
TOURIST INFORMATION: Ph (03) 5470 6200

CHARLTON

247 KM NORTH-WEST OF MELBOURNE
POPULATION: 1400   MAP REF: PAGE 95 J9

This small country town on the Avoca River is in the centre of a large wheat-growing district which also farms sheep for wool production and lambs.

One of the town's greatest distinctions is that the former Australian Prime Minister John Curtin attended the Charlton State School as a child.

Other history of the region can be found at the town's musum which is situated in the old Mechanics Institute Hall. Here that you can learn of the production of wheat and wool in this West Victorian town.
ACCOMMODATION: Foundary Palms Motel, ph (03) 5491 1911; Charlton Motel, ph (03) 5491 1600
ACTIVITIES: Boating, bowls, croquet, fishing, golf, swimming, tennis, trotting, waterskiing
TOURIST INFORMATION: Ph (03) 5382 1832

CHILTERN

276 KM NORTH-EAST OF MELBOURNE
POPULATION: 1200   MAP REF: PAGE 98 G3

This small town near the border of Victoria and New South Wales has been previously known as Black Dog Creek and New Ballarat.

Historically a gold town, it is unique in that the prospectors who first discovered gold here in the 1850s decided not to spread the news of their finds, in order to keep the site to themselves. But word escaped and soon the small site had thousands of people searching for gold. With much of the goldmining ceasing by 1910, the now peaceful and smaller town concentrates on an agriculture and pastoral industry.

Features of this town include the Athenaeum Library Museum which was built in 1866 during the boom years and now houses a collection of books, photographs and artefacts from the goldmining and agricultural days. The old printing works in Main Street which were built in 1859 are still standing.
ACCOMMODATION: Chiltern Colonial Motor Inn, ph (03) 5726 1788; The Mulberry Tree Restaurant (B&B), ph (03) 5726 1277
ACTIVITIES: Bowls, bushwalking, scenic drives, tennis
TOURIST INFORMATION: Ph (03) 5744 1989

CLUNES

145 KM NORTH-WEST OF MELBOURNE
POPULATION: 817   MAP REF: PAGE 93 K4

The first gold discovery in Victoria was made on a property called Clunes—by William Campbell in 1850. The find was not made public until the following year when James Esmonds found rich quartz nearby.

Unlike many of the surrounding sites, the gold at Clunes was buried deep in quartz and extraction was not easy and to many prospectors seemed too expensive. In the early 1870s miners were worried about the lack of safety measures and this, along with a dispute over shift hours, led to a strike in 1873. The owners were not concerned and engaged Chinese labour to work the shafts. Outraged, the miners took to the streets and destroyed houses meant for the imported workers. It all came to a head when the Chinese were prevented from entering the town—the mine managers agreed to back down.

Along the road from Clunes to Creswick there is another significant site, the Australasia Mine, where 22 workers were killed in a mining disaster in 1882.

The Clunes Museum on Fraser Street is a legacy of these goldmining days and this historic bluestone building houses interesting artefacts and photographs of that era.
ACCOMMODATION: Clunes Motel, ph (03) 5345 3092; Keebles of Clunes (B&B), ph (03) 5345 3220
ACTIVITIES: Bowls, fishing, historic interest, scenic drives, tennis
TOURIST INFORMATION: Ph (03) 5332 2694

COBRAM

252 KM NORTH OF MELBOURNE
POPULATION: 4600   MAP REF: PAGE 98 C2

The delightful town of Cobram sits on the Murray River which snakes its way to South Australia, forming the border between Victoria and New South Wales. It is surrounded by rich fruit growing and pastoral properties.

This area was part of a huge soldier settlement scheme after World War II and many soldiers established themselves here on dairy and fruit farms.

Today the region is best known for its holiday activities which are based on the river. Its New South Wales sister town is Barooga.

Many people gather on Thompsons Beach near the bridge for waterskiing, swimming and picnics. Horseshoe Lagoon is another favourite location with swimmers and bushwalkers.

Other attractions around the town include the Cobram Matata Deer Farm on the Benalla–Tocumwal road where visitors can view red deer. The wineries in the region include Strathkellar Winery.
ACCOMMODATION: The Charles Sturt Motor Inn, ph (03) 5872 2777; Regency Court Motel, ph (03) 5872 2488; Cobram Classic Motel, ph (03) 5872 1633
ACTIVITIES: Bowls, bushwalking, fishing, golf, scenic drives, tennis, trotting, water sports
TOURIST INFORMATION: Ph (03) 5872 2132

Cattle on the move near Cobram

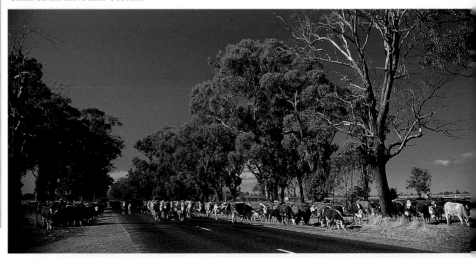

COHUNA

301 KM NORTH OF MELBOURNE
POPULATION: 2070   MAP REF: PAGE 95 L8

This town, sitting on a branch of the Murray River, is a popular tourist destination for waterskiiers, anglers and boating enthusiasts—nearby Gunbower Island provides the perfect base for these water activities.

The Gunbower Island State Forest has magnificent red gum trees. The region also plays host to a variety of wildlife including kangaroos, possums and bird life which are protected by the Gunbower Island Wildlife Sanctuary, a part of the state forest. Summer brings warm to hot weather while the winter sees the roads in this forest reserve become very slippery and passable by 4WD only.

The barefoot waterskiing championships which are held during April each year are extremely popular with visitors.

The region is famous for animal skeletal finds, some of which date back more than 14 000 years.
ACCOMMODATION
West End Motel, ph (03) 5456 6297; Cohuna Hotel/Motel, ph (03) 5456 2604; Cohuna Caravan Park, ph (03) 5456 2562
ACTIVITIES: Bowls, bushwalking, fishing, horse riding, scenic drives, tennis, water sports
TOURIST INFORMATION: Ph (03) 5453 3100

COLAC

151 KM SOUTH-WEST OF MELBOURNE
POPULATION: 12 000   MAP REF: PAGE 93 J8

Colac is a provincial centre south-west of Melbourne and gateway to the rainforest region of the Otway Ranges. Rich in farmland, the fertile lands are the result of volcanic activity in the region thousands of years ago. Old volcanic headlands surround the town offering spectacular views of the region.

A major source of recreation is Lake Colac which is a base for boating, waterskiing and fishing, while magnificent botanic gardens surround the foreshore providing the perfect picnic location. Lake Corangamite, 25 km north of town, is Victoria's largest lake and home to a wide variety of bird life.

Waterfowl can also be found at the Floating Island Reserve west of Colac where six islands of separated peat float in a lagoon and offer refuge to wildlife.

The Otway Ranges lie to the south and the tall timber logged from these forests has provided residents of Colac with a thriving timber industry. Other industries include wool, lambs and beef.
ACCOMMODATION: Baronga Motor Inn, ph (03) 5231 2100; Colac Mid City Motel, ph (03) 5231 3311; Prince of Wales Guest House, ph (03) 5231 3385
ACTIVITIES: Bushwalking, fishing, golf, horse riding, horseracing, scenic drives, tennis, water sports
TOURIST INFORMATION: Ph (03) 5231 3730

COLERAINE

342 KM WEST OF MELBOURNE
POPULATION: 1089   MAP REF: PAGE 92 D5
Nestled in the Wannon Valley, north of Hamilton in the heart of Victoria's west, Coleraine is a quaint town. There is much for visitors to see, including the Points Reserve Arboretum which can be found off the Portland Road. This 40 hectare property features one of the world's largest assortments of eucalypt species.

The Koonongwootong Reservoir off the Glenelg Highway is the water supply for Coleraine and neighbouring towns and is popular with trout anglers.

One of the town's most famous former residents was the world renowned cosmetics manufacturer Helena Rubinstein who spent her childhood here and opened her first shop in Wyte Street. The shop is now a museum dedicated to her achievements.
ACCOMMODATION: National Hotel, ph (03) 5575 2064; Coleraine Caravan Park, no phone
ACTIVITIES: Bowls, gem fossicking, horseracing, scenic drives, swimming, tennis
TOURIST INFORMATION: Ph (03) 5572 3746

CORRYONG

435 KM NORTH-EAST OF MELBOURNE
POPULATION: 1274   MAP REF: PAGE 99 M4
Corryong is the gateway to the Snowy Mountains and was home to Jack Riley, on whom A. B. 'Banjo' Paterson based 'The Man From Snowy River'. Riley is buried in the Corryong Cemetery in 1914 where you can find his grave along with information on this High Country horseman's life. The Man From Snowy River Folk Museum contains a replica of a pioneer's hut.

It is the majestic mountain country that brings visitors to Corryong, coupled with the excellent trout fishing in the slow-flowing headwaters of the mighty Murray River.

The first settlers in this region came here in 1837 and realised the potential this fertile land offered for cattle grazing. Three years later the explorer Paul Strzelecki passed through on his way south to Gippsland. It was not long after that pastoralists took up cattle runs in this valley—the High Country cattle tradition continues today in this town.

Corryong is not far from Australia's highest mountain, Mt Kosiuszcko, and the Kosiuszcko National Park lies to the north of town. Victoria's rugged Alps lie to the south.

Corryong, gateway to the Snowy Mountains

ACCOMMODATION: Corryong Country Inn Motel, ph (03) 6096 1333; Pinnibar Motel, ph (03) 6076 1766; Alpine Gateway Lodge (B&B), ph (03) 6076 1269
ACTIVITIES: Bowls, bushwalking, fishing, 4WD touring, gold prospecting, golf, hang gliding, national park access, scenic drives, snow skiing, swimming, tennis
TOURIST INFORMATION: Ph (03) 6076 1381

COWES

150 KM SOUTH OF MELBOURNE
POPULATION: 2400   MAP REF: PAGE 91 J6
Cowes is the main town of Phillip Island, a small island which lies at the mouth of Westernport Bay. The island is accessible via a long bridge from the mainland town of San Remo.

Cowes was initially a sealing and whaling base but settlement stepped up in the 1840s when grazing and chicory farming commenced.

This seaside town offers everything needed for a summer holiday with a magnificent foreshore and plenty of restaurants, cafés, guesthouses and shops.

The Phillip Island Heritage Centre features displays of the island's history dating back to the original inhabitants.

There are many attractions here including the fairy penguin parade: each night these small birds emerge from the ocean onto Summerland Beach returning to their nests. Koalas were introduced onto the island many years ago and now they are abundant. There is also a fur seal colony near the Nobbies on the far west edge of the island.

Visitors are able to mingle with the animals at the Phillip Island Wildlife Park. There you will be able to glimpse, and even touch, native Australian wildlife. The Koala Conservation Centre is another great place to view koalas, from platforms amongst the treetops.
ACCOMMODATION: Banfields Motel, ph (03) 5952 2486; Kaloha Motel, ph (03) 5952 2179; Seahorse Motel, ph (03) 5952 2269; First Class Bed and Breakfast, ph (03) 5956 8329; Cliff Top Country House (B&B), ph (03) 5952 1033; Park View Holiday Units, ph (03) 5952 1496
ACTIVITIES: Fishing, golf, horse riding, scenic drives, tennis, water sports
TOURIST INFORMATION: Ph (03) 5952 2650

CRANBOURNE

53 KM SOUTH-EAST OF MELBOURNE
POPULATION: 14 005   MAP REF: PAGE 91 J5
While it is some distance from Melbourne, the urban sprawl that has occurred over the past twenty years sees Cranbourne as an outer suburb of Melbourne.

The area had settlers as early as 1836 when an inn was built but it was not until 1861 that the town was officially gazetted and named.

During 1860 the Cranbourne district was subjected to a falling meteorite and a large portion of this is in the museum in Melbourne. A full scale model can be found in Cranbourne.

On Ballarto Road you will find the botanic gardens with 334 hectares of native plants while farms in the region offer fruit such as berries for sale.
ACCOMMODATION: The Terrace Motel at Cranbourne, ph (03) 5996 3366; Mahogany Park Motel, ph (03) 5996 8555; Fourth Furlong Motel, ph (03) 5996 7500
ACTIVITIES: Bowls, golf, greyhound racing, horse riding, sightseeing, swimming
TOURIST INFORMATION: Ph (03) 9658 9972

CRESWICK

129 KM NORTH-WEST OF MELBOURNE
POPULATION: 2800   MAP REF: PAGE 93 K4
Creswick is just a short drive north of Ballarat, and as with many of the towns in this region, its beginnings go back to the gold rush days of the 1800s.

The town's name comes from John, Charles and Henry Creswick, brothers who squatted in this area in 1842 and named it Creswick Creek. Ten years later gold was found here and it is believed that at the height of the rush there were more than 60 000 prospectors searching for gold in the Creswick area.

Flanked on one side by the Creswick State Forest, the town is home to the Victorian School of Forestry. The first of its kind, it was set up in 1911. Nearby is St Georges Lake, surrounded by bush and pine forests.

Creswick was the birthplace of former Prime Minister John Curtin and also of the famous artist and author, Norman Lindsay. You will find some of Lindsay's and his family's works of art displayed in the Creswick Museum at the Town Hall.
ACCOMMODATION: Creswick Motel, ph (03) 5345 2400; Belfield (B&B), ph (03) 9763 6097; Hillview Host Farm, ph (03) 5345 2690
ACTIVITIES: Bowls, bushwalking, fishing, gold prospecting, scenic drives, swimming, tennis
TOURIST INFORMATION: Ph (03) 5345 2676

DAYLESFORD

110 KM NORTH-WEST OF MELBOURNE
POPULATION: 3500   MAP REF: PAGE 93 L4
Daylesford and the nearby township of Hepburn Springs are popular weekend and holiday destinations. They are set in tranquil scenic countryside on Australia's largest collection of

mineral springs. The mineral springs were discovered at the same time as gold was found in the region—in 1854—but after the gold rush was over, the town became known for its mineral spas and the therapeutic qualities these waters possessed.

The Hepburn Springs Spa Complex has Australia's only mineral bath facility. You can also head out to the many natural freshwater springs around the town for a tasting of this delightful water, or trek to the blowhole and frolic in the soothing waters in a natural surrounding.

With many wineries in the region including Sunbury, Macedon, Lancefield and Hanging Rock wineries, together with a wide variety of restaurants, this is definitely a gourmet getaway.

Other attractions of the town include the Lake Daylesford Central Springs Reserve on Wombat Creek, Jubilee Lake, Wombat Hill Gardens, Lavendula Lavender Farm and the Central Highlands Tourist Railway. It is beside the tourist railway that you will find the Sunday markets which are always very popular for antiques, bric-a-brac and local produce. The Historical Society Museum has an excellent display of photographs, mining equipment and paraphernalia from the town's past.

ACCOMMODATION: Royal Hotel Daylesford, ph (03) 5348 2205; Lake House Hotel, ph (03) 5348 3329; Paganetties Country House (B&B), ph (03) 53483892; Jarawong Country Cottages, ph (03) 5476 4362
ACTIVITIES: Bowls, bushwalking, fishing, golf, historic interest, mineral springs, scenic drives, swimming, tennis
TOURIST INFORMATION: Ph (03) 5348 1339

DIMBOOLA

342 KM NORTH-WEST OF MELBOURNE
POPULATION: 1500   MAP REF: PAGE 92 E1
The small township of Dimboola lies in the west of Victoria, in between Wyperfeld and Little Desert National Parks. Based on the agricultural industry, this town is typical of those found in the Wimmera.

Ebenezer Mission on the Dimboola–Japarit road was established in 1858 by missionaries. This mission was only in operation for 45 years, but remains of some of its buildings and a cemetery can be found near the banks of the Wimmera River.

Using Dimboola as a base, a visit to the national parks near this town is a great way to experience the desert country. There is family car access into the Wyperfeld National Park to the north and Little Desert National Park to the south but a 4WD is the best way to explore these parks. Camping in this remote environment is very tranquil. Wildflowers bring the desert to life in spring, which is the best time for a visit. Kangaroos and mallee fowl which build large mound nests for their young are also a feature of these parks.

ACCOMMODATION: Dimboola Motel, ph (03) 5389 1177; Riverside Host Farm (cabins), ph (03) 5389 1550; Little Desert Log Cabins and Cottage, ph (03) 5389 1122
ACTIVITIES: Bowls, bushwalking, fishing, 4WD touring, golf, national park access, scenic drives, tennis, water sports
TOURIST INFORMATION: Ph (03) 5382 1832

DUNOLLY

195 KM NORTH-WEST OF MELBOURNE
POPULATION: 720   MAP REF: PAGE 93 K2
Sheep were grazed in this country region north of Melbourne by a Scots farmer who took up residence here in 1845. He named the site after his clan's castle in Scotland. It was, however, the discovery of gold and the finding in 1869 of the largest gold nugget in this country that has put Dunolly on the map.

The 'Welcome Stranger', as it is known, weighed a hefty 64 kg and was dug out from the ground 13 km north-west of the town. The Welcome Stranger Monument on Goldsborough–Moliagul road marks the site where it was uncovered, while the Historical Museum in town features models of famous nuggets, mining equipment and Aboriginal relics. The old Courthouse on Market Street was built in 1862 and originally used as a town hall; now it is a Gold Discovery Information Centre and houses a replica of the 'Welcome Stranger'.

Water sports take place on the Laanecoorie Reservoir, 13 km east of Dunolly.
ACCOMMODATION: Golden Triangle Motel, ph (03) 5468 1166
ACTIVITIES: Bowls, fishing, historic interest, tennis, water sports
TOURIST INFORMATION: Ph (03) 5460 4511

ECHUCA

220 KM NORTH OF MELBOURNE
POPULATION: 10 000   MAP REF: PAGE 95 N9
Echuca is the Aboriginal word for 'meeting of the waters'; this major regional centre was built where the Campaspe and Goulburn Rivers meet the Murray.

Begun in 1853, this is one of the oldest river towns in Victoria. An inn was built on the banks of the Murray River by Henry Hopwood who was an ex-convict. Then a punt was used to ferry passengers across the river and it was from this that the port of Echuca was born.

Being on a major route between Victoria and New South Wales, Echuca grew rapidly, with passengers and produce crossing the Murray here. A railway line opened from Bendigo in 1864 and both produce and passengers travelled on the river.

By the 1880s Echuca was Victoria's second largest port. The Echuca Wharf was an impressive sight in those days: by 1884 the length of the wharf had grown to 1.2 km long and was built on three different levels to accommodate the different water heights experienced during various seasons. A wood shortage at the turn of the century meant that the paddle-steamers could no longer run as often and the port slowed down. By 1944 the wharf was in disrepair, but has since been partially restored by the National Trust. They have also other many historic buildings in the area.

The old port is now a museum and there are a handful of paddle-steamers which have been done up and returned to their former glory, including the *Emmylou*, *Canberra* and *Pride of the Murray*.

The Murray River is popular for water-based activities including fishing for the massive Murray cod. Houseboats are a great way to explore the river and these can be hired at Echuca from a number of different operators.

There are many other attractions in town including the Echuca Historical Society Museum, World in Wax Museum, and the Coach House Carriage Collection which features more than 25 restored coaches from around the world. Car lovers will delight in the Holden Motor Museum.

Echuca has several festivals and events including the Southern 80, a waterski race along the Murray which is held on the second weekend in February. The Rich River Festival is run over one week in October with many different events.
ACCOMMODATION: Port of Echuca Motor Inn, ph (03) 5482 5666; All Rivers Motor Inn, ph (03) 5482 5677; Caledonian Hotel Motel Echuca, ph (03) 5482 2100; Rich River Houseboats, ph 1800 032 643; Dinky-Di Houseboats, ph (03) 5482 5223
ACTIVITIES: Bowls, bushwalking, croquet, fishing, golf, historic interest, horse riding, horseracing, scenic drives, tennis, trotting, water sports
TOURIST INFORMATION: Ph (03) 5480 7555

Paddle-steamer *Emmylou* travelling on the Murray River near Echuca

EDENHOPE

401 KM WEST OF MELBOURNE
POPULATION: 1000   MAP REF: PAGE 92 B3

Edenhope, situated on the shores of Lake Wallace near the Victorian/South Australian border, is one of the oldest grazing towns in Victoria. George and James Hope, pioneers from Scotland, first set up pastoral runs here in 1845 and the area is still mainly sheep and cattle country.

William Wallace was the first European to come across Lake Wallace—in 1843. When full, it is 7 metres deep. It is a popular venue with local residents for boating, waterskiing, swimming, and fishing for trout and redfin. The wetlands around this lake form an extremely important habitat for waterfowl. Much of the region can be explored through a series of walking tracks.

The first Aboriginal cricket team, which toured England in the late nineteenth century, trained here and there is a monument in the town which commemorates this event.

Events include the Henley-on-Lake Wallace Carnival in February, Edenhope Cup Race Meeting on Labour Day and an annual show in November.
ACCOMMODATION: Edenhope Motor Inn, ph (03) 5585 1369
ACTIVITIES: Birdwatching, bowls, fishing, golf, tennis, water sports
TOURIST INFORMATION: Ph (03) 5382 1832

EILDON

136 KM NORTH-EAST OF MELBOURNE
POPULATION: 650   MAP REF: PAGE 98 D8

Eildon sits on one of Melbourne's favourite holiday destinations, Lake Eildon. The town itself is quite small, but it is the waters of the lake and the 600 km of shoreline that attract visitors who enjoy camping on the water's edge or cruising on houseboats.

This region originally supported a timber and mining industry but between 1915 and 1927 a dam was built which was 47 metres deep and had a storage capacity of 33 700 megalitres. In the 1950s it was decided that this storage system of the Goulburn River was to be extended and Eildon was established to house the workers for this massive project. A new dam wall was erected that stood 79 metres in height and the end result was a massive lake which now holds 3.38 million megalitres of water for irrigation—six times the amount in Sydney Harbour.

Houseboats and other water craft can be hired at the lakeside towns. Fishing is a big sport as the lake offers brown and rainbow trout along with redfin. Nearby are Lake Eildon National Park and Fraser Inlet which are popular with campers, bushwalkers and waterskiers. It is here that you will often catch a glimpse of the local kangaroos.

Events include the Lake Eildon Triathlon in late March, Navigation Rally for motorbikes in April and the Horseman's Carnival in January.
ACCOMMODATION: Eildon Parkview Motor Inn, ph (03) 5774 2165; Golden Trout Motel, ph (03) 5774 2508; Eucalypt Ridge Private Country Retreat (guesthouse, weekends only), ph (03) 5774 2033; High Country Houseboats, ph (03) 5777 3899
ACTIVITIES: Bowls, bushwalking, 4WD touring, fishing, golf, horse riding, national park access, scenic drives, tennis, water sports
TOURIST INFORMATION: Ph (03) 5774 2909

EMERALD

54 KM EAST OF MELBOURNE
POPULATION: 4054   MAP REF: PAGE 91 J4

Tulip time in Emerald

Tall eucalypt trees and long-reaching tree ferns surround the aptly named township of Emerald. This town sits on a scenic hilltop in the Dandenong Ranges, only a short drive from Melbourne and is a favoured destination for scenic day drives.

Emerald was one of the first towns established in the hills of the Dandenongs in 1858 and it now draws a continuous weekend crowd, offering, in summer, a cool respite from the heat. This is also the end of the railway line which carries Puffing Billy, a famous Melbourne steam train, through the Dandenongs from Belgrave. The train is a favourite with children and families who take the scenic journey through the temperate forest and over trestle bridges to Emerald and back to Belgrave.

Another of the town's attractions is the Emerald Lake Park which contains a huge lake covering more than 50 hectares. It is here that you can enjoy swimming, paddleboats and a giant water slide. An excellent picnic location, the park also features many walking tracks. The park houses the Emerald Lake Model Railway, one of the largest working small-scale railways in Australia.

Another water source close to town is the Cardinia Reservoir which is a water storage area for Melbourne and a popular spot for picnics.
ACCOMMODATION: Inglewood Country Accommodation (B&B), ph (03) 5968 3796; The Nook (B&B), ph (03) 5968 4080; Timbertop Lodge (B&B), ph (03) 5968 5476
ACTIVITIES: Bowls, bushwalking, fishing, golf, scenic drives, swimming, tennis
TOURIST INFORMATION: Ph (03) 9752 6554

EUROA

156 KM NORTH-EAST OF MELBOURNE
POPULATION: 2800   MAP REF: PAGE 98 C6

Euroa, in the north-east of the state, is a primary producer of fine wool. Nestled on the edge of the Strathbogie Ranges, this region is popular with walkers and owners of 4WD vehicles.

Explorers Hovell and Hume travelled through the region in 1824 but it was the local bushrangers that have made Euroa famous. In 1878 the notorious Kelly gang raided the town and incarcerated 50 people in the local police station while they robbed the bank. It was here that Ned Kelly forced a local station owner to sign over a cheque worth thousands of pounds which he then cashed at gun point at the bank.

Attractions in this town include the Farmers Arms Museum which is housed in an historic inn over 100 years old. The Forlonge Memorial pays tribute to the two pioneering women who introduced the Merino sheep to this district in 1851, while a 2.7 km heritage trail takes in the town and all its features.

Seven Creeks Run demonstrate sheep shearing and has displays relating to the wool industry.

A parachute school offers half or full day courses in skydiving while balloon flights present a more sedate way of viewing the magnificent scenery of the Strathbogie Ranges.

Annual events include the Garden Expo in March, Euroa Wool Week Festival in September and the Agricultural Show in October.
ACCOMMODATION: Jolly Swagman Motor Inn, ph (03) 5795 3388; Castle Creek Motel, ph (03) 5795 2506; Euroa Motel, ph (03) 5795 2211
ACTIVITIES: Balloon flights, bowls, bushwalking, fishing, golf, historic interest, horse riding, scenic drives, skydiving, squash, swimming, tennis
TOURIST INFORMATION: Ph (03) 5794 2647

FOSTER

180 KM SOUTH-EAST OF MELBOURNE
POPULATION: 1107   MAP REF: PAGE 91 N7

The township of Foster is the gateway to one of Victoria's most popular seaside national parks, Wilsons Promontory National Park.

The area of Foster was originally named Stockyard Creek and was a goldmining region, but by the early 1900s this had given way to dairy farming on the lush fertile soils of south-west Gippsland.

There are numerous vantage points where this majestic land can be viewed, including Foster North Lookout on the South Gippsland Highway. Mt Nicoll Lookout off the Foster–Fish Creek road is also a superb site, offering uninterrupted views as far as Corner Inlet and Waratah Bay.

There is a museum in town which displays photographs and other memorabilia from the goldmining days of Foster in the 1870s.

Wilsons Promontory, or the Prom as it is referred to, is a delightful park featuring sandy beaches and large rocky outcrops which extend into the ocean waters. It also has a myriad bushwalks of varying lengths and degrees. The town, together with thousands of loyal park users, fought off attempts to commercialise the park during 1997.

ACCOMMODATION: Foster Motel, ph (03) 5682 2022; Wilsons Promontory Hotel, ph (03) 5682 2055; Hillcrest Farmhouse (B&B), ph (03) 5682 2769

ACTIVITIES: Bowls, bushwalking, fishing, golf, horse riding, national park access, scenic drives, tennis, water sports

TOURIST INFORMATION: Ph (03) 5655 2233

GEELONG

76 KM SOUTH-WEST OF MELBOURNE
POPULATION: 145 335   MAP REF: PAGE 93 M7

The bayside suburb of Geelong is Victoria's second largest town and is a city in its own right, featuring many outer suburbs around Corio Bay at the western side of Port Phillip Bay.

The first settlers to this region were J. H. Cowie and David Stead who established a property called Cowies Creek. Soon after, in 1840, two pioneering women took up residence at South Corio and the Bellarine Peninsula. Within a year the town boasted many buildings including a post office and store and was producing the *Geelong Advertiser*, said to be Australia's oldest morning paper.

The countryside was used for sheep grazing over the next decade until gold was discovered in 1851. Geelong was then an entry point for immigrants hoping to strike it rich on the goldfields and also a port from which to export the gold. Today it is a large regional centre and the gateway to the Bellarine Peninsula and the western districts of Victoria.

The Barwon River runs through the township and nestled on its banks is Barwon Grange, an historic homestead which dates back to 1856 and features a magnificent veranda.

A well-laid out mall in Geelong

The National Wool Museum gives a fine interpretation of the wool industry in Australia.

Situated on the coast, the sea has also played a major role in this town's heritage and the Naval and Military Museum displays a range of records, photographs and wartime relics along with plenty of information on shipwrecks off the Victorian coastline. The museum is housed in the old Royal Australian Naval College buildings which were the site of the first Australian submarine base.

Eastern Beach on the edge of Corio Bay is within easy walking distance from central Geelong and features piers, the Bay City Marina, along with saltwater swimming pools and lawned parkland. The beach area extends into Eastern Park, a popular recreation area in Geelong East with walking tracks.

There are interesting walks in Geelong, including Bayside Bollard Walk, which goes from Rippleside Park to Limeburners Point along a sealed path. Along its route are a number of large colourful bollards representing characters from Geelong's past. The Heritage Trail explores the city streetscapes taking in the early history and buildings.

Festivals in the town include the Pako Festa (a food and music festival) and National Aquatic Festival which are both held in February. The Bells Beach Surf Carnival is held at Easter while the Geelong Spring Festival and Geelong Show are in October. The Strawberry Fair and Geelong Speed Trials take place during November.

ACCOMMODATION: Ambassador Geelong Hotel, ph (03) 5221 6844; Admiralty Motor Inn, ph (03) 5221 4288; Shannon Motor Inn, ph (03) 5222 4355; Golden Palms Motel, ph (03) 5243 1077; Duneed Guest House (B&B), ph (03) 5264 1436

ACTIVITIES: Bowls, bushwalking, birdwatching, fishing, golf, greyhound racing, horseracing, scenic drives, squash, tennis, trotting, water sports

TOURIST INFORMATION: Ph (03) 5222 2900

GISBORNE

54 KM NORTH-WEST OF MELBOURNE
POPULATION: 4200   MAP REF: PAGE 90 F1, PAGE 93 N5

Named after Henry Gisborne, Commissioner of Crown Lands, the town was laid out in 1851. The Cobb & Co horse-drawn coaches used Gisborne as a stopover during their journey from Melbourne north-west to the goldfields in Castlemaine and Bendigo.

A stroll through the town will uncover many delightful galleries and shops including the Wooden Horse craft shop, Jackson Creek Trading which features Australian gift ware, and the Black Forest Gallery which offers paintings and pottery for sale.

Wineries near Gisborne include the Mount Macedon Winery, Hanging Rock Winery and Mount Aitken Estate. Spectacular wines are also made in the Macedon Ranges region and these are available for tasting at the Macedon Budhurst Wine Celebration which is held in late October. In February a Harvest Picnic is held at nearby Hanging Rock.

Markets are held in town on the first Sunday of every month and the Gisborne Festival is held in early December.

ACCOMMODATION: Gisborne Motel, ph (03) 5482 2139

ACTIVITIES: Bowls, bushwalking, craft shops, fishing, golf, horse riding, scenic drives, swimming, tennis, wineries

TOURIST INFORMATION: Ph (03) 5427 2033

GLENMAGGIE

228 KM EAST OF MELBOURNE
POPULATION: 200   MAP REF: PAGE 96 B6

Sitting on the edge of the Glenmaggie Weir is the hamlet of Glenmaggie, named by the McFarlanes, Scottish settlers who ran cattle at the headwaters of the Macalister and Thomson Rivers in the 1840s.

The original village of Glenmaggie was established when gold was mined in the vicinity, and while not much of the precious metal was extracted from the Glenmaggie region, the township stocked supplies for the mines to the north-east.

A weir was built in 1927 to supply water to the township of Maffra and for irrigation purposes. Glenmaggie was flooded when the weir was built and only three buildings—the Anglican church, Town Hall and Glenmaggie Store—were relocated to their present position. The weir is much used by waterskiers, swimmers and sailors, and while Glenmaggie has remained small, Coongulla, a town on the other side of the weir, houses most of the locals and holiday residences.

This region is a stepping-off point for the Alpine National Park to the north. The Avon Wilderness where the magnificent Avon River meets the Turton, is only a short drive from Glenmaggie by 4WD.

ACCOMMODATION: Paradise Valley Caravan Park, ph (03) 5148 0291

ACTIVITIES: Fishing, 4WD touring, golf, national park access, scenic drives, water sports

TOURIST INFORMATION: Ph (03) 5174 3199

GLENROWAN

221 KM NORTH-EAST OF MELBOURNE
POPULATION: 216   MAP REF: PAGE 98 F5

Located just off the main highway from Melbourne to Sydney, Glenrowan came into prominence when the notorious bushranger Ned Kelly made his last stand in this town. Ned and his brothers brought havoc to the towns of central Victoria during the 1870s. It was at the Glenrowan Inn that Ned and his gang were besieged and all of the gang except for Ned were shot down. Kelly was later tried for the murder two years previously of Constable Thomas Lonigan at Stringybark Creek. He was found guilty and hanged on 11 November 1880.

Ned Kelly lives on in Glenrowan, however, where he stands tall as a statue wearing his famous metal armour. Throughout the town you will also find many other artefacts and literature relating to the famous bushranger.

There are a number of wineries in this region, extending along the Ovens and King Valleys. These include Auldstone Cellars, Baileys of Glenrowan and HJT Vineyards.

Water sports take place at Lake Mukoan, on the east side of Glenrowan.

ACCOMMODATION: Glenrowan Kelly Country Motel, ph (03) 5766 2202

ACTIVITIES: Fishing, historic interest, scenic drives, water sports, wineries

TOURIST INFORMATION: Ph (03) 5766 2367

HALLS GAP

265 KM NORTH-WEST OF MELBOURNE
POPULATION: 300   MAP REF: PAGE 92 F3

Halls Gap is the tourist centre of the Grampians region. Extending for over 80 km and up to 50 km wide, the Grampians are the beginning of the Great Dividing Range which eventually ends near Cooktown in Queensland.

Thomas Mitchell in 1836 was the first European to explore this region and it was not long after that graziers occupied the foothills of the mountains. The gap is named after C. Hall who set up cattle runs through here, discovering the mountain pass in 1841 when trying to walk cattle over the range. The Grampians themselves are named after the mountain range in Scotland.

Other settlers to the area included goldminers and loggers, whose activities were stopped when the Grampians National Park was formed in 1984.

The main attractions around Halls Gap concentrate on the national park and the outdoor activities associated with it. Popular with many tourists is bushwalking along designated tracks, or rock climbing on the rugged peaks. Hang gliding is practised here, as is wildflower study in spring when the mountain range glows with a mass of brilliant colours. The area is also a haven for birdwatchers.

This region is of great significance to the local Aborignes. The Brambuk Living Cultural Centre houses Aboriginal arts and crafts along with cultural displays and exhibitions. The Brambuk Café allows you to experience true Aboriginal bush tucker.

Nearby Lake Bellfield is ideal for sailboats and fishing while Rocklands Reservoir offers a playground for power boat owners, waterskiers and swimmers.

Wildflowers come alive in spring and that is when the Halls Gap Wildflower Exhibition is held, featuring hundreds of species of flora from the Grampians.

The Grampians is a diverse region and features a number of excellent wineries including Bests Great Western. The Grampians Gourmet Weekend is an exciting event held in May offering fine wines, food and entertainment with a backdrop of the rugged Grampians Ranges.

ACCOMMODATION: Halls Gap Colonial Motor Inn, ph (03) 5356 4344; Pinnacle Holiday Lodge, ph (03) 5356 4249; Mountain View Motor Inn and Lodges, ph (03) 5356 4364; Grampians Wonderland Cabins, ph (03) 5356 4264
ACTIVITIES: Bushwalking, camping, fishing, golf, national park access, rock climbing, scenic drives, tennis, water sports, wildflower study, wineries
TOURIST INFORMATION: Ph (03) 5358 2314

HAMILTON

312 KM WEST OF MELBOURNE
POPULATION: 10 131   MAP REF: PAGE 92 E6

In the heart of the state's west, Hamilton is the centre of Victoria's fine wool industry and a major regional centre for the small farming communities.

Explorer Major Thomas Mitchell came across this grazing land in 1836 and pastoralists soon followed, setting up what is often referred to as 'the wool capital of the world'. During the 1850s, large towns to the east of Hamilton, such as Ararat and Stawell, were involved in Victoria's gold rush and the grazing land of Hamilton meant that the new settlers of the town could prosper by providing the hungry prospectors with food supplies.

At the Big Woolbales in Hamilton, visitors can learn about the wool industry and see sheep being sheared; the Pastoral Museum houses many pieces of old farm equipment. Another notable feature in the town is the Sir Reginald Ansett Transport Museum, who started his career here in the 1930s.

Nigretta Falls to the north-west of Hamilton

Visitors to this country centre will enjoy walks around Lake Hamilton on the eastern edge of town where there is an excellent aquatic centre, playground, swimming area and small boats for hire.

Local wildlife can be viewed at the Institute of Rural Learning which comprises 5 hectares of parkland and a series of walking tracks. The elusive eastern barred bandicoot can be found here.

Nigretta Falls to the north-west of the town are a magnificent sight when in full flow.

Events include the Wool Heritage Week and the Sheepvention field days during July, Garden Expo in October and Picnic Races held in November.
ACCOMMODATION: Grange Burn Motor Inn, ph (03) 5572 5755; Goldsmith Motel, ph (03) 5572 4347; Caledonian Hotel/Motel, ph (03) 5572 1055
ACTIVITIES: Art galleries, bowls, croquet, fishing, go-karting, golf, horse racing, scenic drives, tennis, trotting, water sports
TOURIST INFORMATION: Ph 1800 807 056

HARRIETVILLE

344 KM NORTH-EAST OF MELBOURNE
POPULATION: 275   MAP REF: PAGE 99 J7

A picturesque town at the foot of the Victorian Alps, Harrietville sits on the banks of the Ovens River which runs through the magnificent Ovens Valley in the north-east of the state.

Goldminers were the first settlers in 1852, but the rush did not last and residents took up farming and ultimately tourism. Quiet streets offer country-style fare and hospitality, with small delightful shops for browsing and a range of different accommodation.

The region surrounding Harrietville is ideal for bushwalking, scenic drives, 4WD touring, with the Alpine National Park presenting plenty of camping opportunities too. A drive to Mount Hotham Village in summer offers commanding views of the blue-toned alpine mountain ranges, while in winter they are capped with brilliant white snow.

The town is central to the popular mountain ski resorts of Mount Hotham, Dinner Plain, Mount Buffalo, Mount Beauty and Falls Creek.

Harrietville and the ranges beckon anglers who come here to try their hand at trout fishing. If this clever fish eludes you, a visit to the Mountain Fresh Trout and Salmon Farm may help to ensure a catch.

The Market and Fair Day is held in January while the winter brings with it plenty of activities.
ACCOMMODATION: Snowline Hotel/Motel, ph (03) 5759 2524; Cas-Bak Flats, ph (03) 5759 2531; Alpine Lodge Inn (guesthouse), ph (03) 5759 2525; Feathertop Chalet (guesthouse), ph (03) 5759 2688
ACTIVITIES: Bushwalking, 4WD touring, national park access, scenic drives, snow skiing, trout fishing
TOURIST INFORMATION: Ph (03) 5755 2275

HEALESVILLE

58 KM EAST OF MELBOURNE
POPULATION: 9169   MAP REF: PAGE 98 C10

Nestled in the lush Yarra Valley less than two hours from Melbourne via the Maroondah Highway is Healesville, well known for its surrounding forests and beautiful scenery.

The town was first settled in 1860 and was named in honour of Sir Richard Heales, the then Premier of Victoria. Timber milling was the main industry but now much of the region's fine forests have become national parks or catchment areas. The Healesville Sanctuary is a popular tourist attraction. Opened in 1934, it has the largest collection of Australian native species in the world including snakes, birds,

The Maroondah Highway en route to Healesville

kangaroos, koalas, emus and wombats. The best feature of this park is that the animals roam the grounds amongst the onlookers.

The Yarra Valley is now one of Australia's premier wine-growing districts offering world-class vintages. Domaine Chandon, the Australian winery of French champagne manufacturers Möet et Chandon, has a vineyard here. St Huberts Winery in Coldstream, one of the oldest in the region, offers fine wines and food along with a jazz festival on the last Sunday of the month during summer. Other wineries include Coldstream Hills, De Bortoli, Eyton on Yarra and Yarra Ridge, all of which produce excellent wines.

One of outer Melbourne's most scenic drives is along the Black Spur, north of Healesville, which winds across the Dividing Range through catchment areas of tall mountain ash and broad towering tree-ferns. At the end of the range the canopy opens up to reveal the small village of Narbethong and the Black Spur Inn, a delightful pub. Accommodation is offered here at the inn as well as at the Hermitage, a National Trust building, deep in the mountain range.

Another lovely drive north-west of town takes a less well-used road—with large, lush, green tree-ferns draping its edges—to the timber township of Toolangi.

Annual events include the Healesville Show in February, Grape-Grazing Festival (a wine and food festival) on the first weekend in March, Gateway Festival with market stalls in November.

ACCOMMODATION: Healesville Motor Inn, ph (03) 5962 5188; Healesville Therapy Centre and The Retreat (B&B), ph (03) 5962 4502; Black Spur Inn (motel), ph (03) 5963 7153; The Hermitage (B&B), ph (03) 59637120

ACTIVITIES: Bowls, bushwalking, canoeing, fishing, 4WD touring, golf, greyhound racing, horse riding, scenic drives, swimming, tennis, wineries

TOURIST INFORMATION: Ph (03) 5962 2600

HEATHCOTE

113 KM NORTH OF MELBOURNE
POPULATION: 1725   MAP REF: PAGE 93 N3

A small grazing and agricultural town, Heathcote sits on the McIvor Creek not far from the regional centre of Bendigo. Major Mitchell explored this area and named the creek McIvor after a member of his party; the town was later to be known as McIvor Diggings when gold was discovered in 1853. With forests nearby, the town soon created a timber industry and with the abundance of heath in the district, the town's name was changed to Heathcote.

The main street is wide and sprawling, featuring small cafés, restaurants, a delicious bakery and basic shops to supply the surrounding farms.

Lake Eppalock to the north is a popular venue for water sports such as boating and waterskiing. This reservoir was built to irrigate farmland in the region and to the west, while it is also a great place for fishing and camping.

A rodeo is held at Easter and the Gold 'n' Grapes Festival is held the weekend prior to the Melbourne Cup in November.

ACCOMMODATION: Heathcote Motor Inn, ph (03) 5433 2655; The Commercial Hotel/Motel, ph (03) 5433 2944; Argyle Lodge (B&B), ph (03) 5433 3413

ACTIVITIES: Bowls, bushwalking, fishing, golf, horseracing, horse riding, scenic drives, tennis, water sports

TOURIST INFORMATION: Ph (03) 5433 3677

HEPBURN SPRINGS

113 KM NORTH-WEST OF MELBOURNE
POPULATION: 750   MAP REF: PAGE 93 L4

Hepburn Springs is a small town only 9 km from the larger town of Daylesford and together they comprise one of Victoria's favourite weekend destinations. The ground around these towns contains mineral springs, which have been proven to have therapeutic qualities. The Hepburn Spa Complex features a huge heated spa and pool along with many private therapies such as hyrdobaths, massages, flotation tanks and beauty treatments.

The Hepburn Mineral Springs Reserve on the Main Road features a number of springs which run freely and can be used for drinking. Walking tracks and BBQ facilities make this reserve ideal for a picnic.

A larger park, the Hepburn Regional Park, features wonderful wildflower displays during spring and scenic attractions such as the Blowhole and Sailors Falls. An excellent walking trail, the Tipperary Walk, covers 16 km of the park and while most of it is an easy stroll taking around four hours to complete, there are some steep sections.

Fishing can be enjoyed at Hepburn Reservoir and the nearby creeks.

In Shepherds Flat, 5 km north of town, lies the Lavendula Lavender Farm which comes alive in summer with brilliant mauve and purple hues of the lavender heads. The property features an historic stone and clay farmhouse that was built in the 1850s and the barn houses an array of crafts and lavender products for sale.

The township has many interesting shops and eateries, such as the Old Billiard Hall Gallery which is filled with local pottery and crafts.

An art and craft market is held in town every Sunday. Wineries in the vicinity include those in Trentham and Woodend area to the east of Hepburn Springs.

ACCOMMODATION: Hepburn Springs Motor Inn, ph (03) 5384 3234; Springs Hotel/Motel, ph (03) 5348 2202; Genoa Accommodation Hepburn Springs (B&B), ph (03) 5348 1151

ACTIVITIES: Bowls, bushwalking, fishing, golf, horse riding, mineral springs, scenic drives, tennis, wineries

TOURIST INFORMATION: Ph (03) 5348 1339

HEYFIELD

209 KM EAST OF MELBOURNE
POPULATION: 1614   MAP REF: PAGE 96 B6

Just to the south of the Glenmaggie Weir and sitting on the banks of the Thomson River is the township of Heyfield, once a stopping point for prospectors trekking to the goldfields to the north.

Situated at the base of the Victorian Alps, Heyfield supported a strong grazing and dairy industry and

was also a busy timber town. Still a major dairy and timber town, Heyfield is a stopping-off point before heading either to the shores of Lake Glenmaggie for waterskiing and camping, or to the hills for bushwalking or 4WD touring.

Licola in the north is perfect for a single-day drive and offers spectacular scenery down into the valleys and up into the High Country. The high plains of the Alps are often under snow and Mt Skene has good cross-country skiing, with skis available for hire from the Licola Store. The region is also popular with anglers and deer hunters, while Lake Tali Karng, a turquoise jewel in the nearby mountain valley and accessible only by bushwalking, is an interesting full day's trek both in and out.

A large timber festival is held in the town during January and the Gippsland Historical Automobile Club Rally is held in August.

ACCOMMODATION: Broadbents Motor Inn, ph (03) 5148 2434; Abington Bed and Breakfast, ph (03) 5148 2430

ACTIVITIES: Bowls, bushwalking, fishing, 4WD touring, golf, horse riding, scenic drives, tennis, water sports

TOURIST INFORMATION: Ph (03) 5144 1108

HORSHAM

305 KM NORTH-WEST OF MELBOURNE
POPULATION: 13 300   MAP REF: PAGE 92 E2

Horsham, known as the capital of the Wimmera region of Victoria, lies at the junction of three major highways, the Western, Henty and Wimmera.

The first settler to the region was James Darlot who ventured west in the 1840s after Thomas Mitchell's exploration of the region. He set up a

Aerial view of Horsham

property and homestead, although the surrounding town was not well developed until the 1870s. The town's name comes from Darlot's home town in Sussex, England.

Horsham and the Wimmera produce a substantial amount of Victoria's wheat. Apart from wheat, sheep and wool are the major income earners. On Golfcourse Road is the Wool Factory, a community based enterprise where disabled workers specialise in fine wool production.

The magnificent botanic gardens on the banks of the Wimmera River were originally designed in the 1870s but not finished until the 1930s. There are picnic facilities here, along with playgrounds and toilets.

With so many roads leading from this major centre, there are plenty of regions to discover outside of town, including the Grampians Ranges and the Grampians National Park. There are plenty of walking tracks, Aboriginal art and natural bushland to explore. Nearby Mt Arapiles is well known to climbers and at the weekend many climbers can be seen making their way to the peak. A road also leads to the top where the magnificent views can be enjoyed without expending so much energy. Numerous lakes can be found in the west near Horsham, including Pine Lake, a recreational reserve which is a good spot for anglers and for yabbying.

To the north of Horsham lies Victoria's desert country and the national parks of Little Desert, Big Desert and Wyperfeld. These offer spectacular desert scenery, colourful wildflowers in spring and delightful camping areas.

The Apex Fishing Competition is held over the Labour Day weekend, the Horsham Annual Show is held in late September, a Spring Garden Festival takes place in October and Kannamaroo Festival in late November.

ACCOMMODATION: Country City Motor Inn, ph (03) 5382 5644; Golden Grain Motor Inn, ph (03) 5382 4741; Town House Motel, ph (03) 5382 4691

ACTIVITIES: Bushwalking, cycling, fishing, 4WD touring, golf, greyhound racing, horseracing, horse riding, national park access, orienteering, rock climbing, tennis, trotting, water sports

TOURIST INFORMATION: Ph (03) 5382 1832

INVERLOCH

150 KM SOUTH-EAST OF MELBOURNE
POPULATION: 2100   MAP REF: PAGE 91 L7

A popular holiday seaside town and fishing port, Inverloch sits at the mouth of Anderson's Inlet on the Victorian coast, only two hours from Melbourne.

A diverse coastal area, the shoreline has mud flats of mangrove swamps during low tide, or exposed rock pools. A sandy surf beach lies to the south of Point Norman, outside the inlet on Venus Bay, along with another beach which is more protected for swimming.

Windsurfers and sailors use the inlet for safe boating: the yacht club is at Point Hughes, while further along the Esplanade is the angling club. A road stretches all the way along the coast—the foreshore is a reserve which also offers camping in designated areas.

The Shell Museum houses one of the world's largest private shell collections as well as a large reference library. Shells and handcrafts can also be purchased here.

There are now many wineries being established in South Gippsland including the Lyre Bird Hill Winery and the Bass Phillip Winery.

The Inverloch Fun Festival is held on the last weekend in January while the Jazz Festival is on the Labour Day long weekend in March.

ACCOMMODATION: Inverloch Central Motor Inn, ph (03) 5674 3500; Hill Top House (B&B), ph (03) 5674 3514; Eagles Nest Cottage By The Sea (cottages), ph (03) 5674 2255

ACTIVITIES: Bowls, fishing, golf, horse riding, scenic drives, tennis, water sports, wineries

TOURIST INFORMATION: Ph (03) 5674 2706

JAMIESON

186 KM NORTH-EAST OF MELBOURNE
POPULATION: 250   MAP REF: PAGE 98 E8

The quaint country township of Jamieson sits at the junction of the Jamieson and Goulburn Rivers near the shores of Lake Eildon.

Originally a goldmining district, there are many relics and abandoned mines around Jamieson. A scenic drive takes in the neighbouring goldmining townships of Kevington, Woods Point and Gaffneys Creek. There are many 4WD tracks and walking trails which head up into this rugged country, some which lead to old mine sites and many have great views of the surrounding mountain range. There are still people who head for these hills to try their hand at gold fossicking although anglers will probably have more luck with fishing in the Goulburn River or Lake Eildon which contains rainbow and brown trout. Lake Eildon is also much used for water sports and offers camping on its shores.

North of Jamieson is the Howqua Hills Historic Area which covers 1300 hectares where there is still an old water race and brick chimney, relics of the goldmining past. Other remains include Tunnel Bend where miners dug a 100-metre tunnel through rock in the 1880s to link the Howqua River with their water race. A short walk off the main road provides access to this tunnel. The Tunnel Bend Reserve is off the Jamieson–Woods Point road, along with cemeteries at Aberfeldy and mining relics and cemetery at the historic Woods Point township.

ACCOMMODATION: Jamieson Lakeside Hotel/Motel, ph 903) 5777 0515; Duck Inn Jamieson (B&B), ph (03) 5777 0554; The Jamieson Cottages, ph (03) 5777 0670

ACTIVITIES: Bushwalking, fishing, 4WD touring, gold fossicking, scenic drives, tennis, water sports

TOURIST INFORMATION: Ph (03) 5775 1464

KANIVA

417 KM NORTH-WEST OF MELBOURNE
POPULATION: 900   MAP REF: PAGE 94 B10

This small Wimmera farming township sits on the Western Highway near the border of South Australia and Victoria. It is best known for its spring wildflowers.

Kaniva was originally settled in 1845 and was at first known as Budjik. The desert areas to the north and south are protected parks and wilderness areas with sectors set aside for camping, walking and 4WD touring.

An interesting 4WD trek, the Border Track, runs through a corridor of farming land and over small red sand dunes from the border, north to the Mallee Highway. Another track continues across the highway and zigzags its way north, staying with the border for the most part. This scenic drive will take you to Aboriginal rockholes, tall sandhills and offers superb views of the mallee scrub from small bluffs. Spring is the best time to visit when the weather is mild and the wildflowers are out.

In Kaniva, the Historical Museum has a display of local history—it is open by appointment only. Three kilometres from town is Serviceton which features an historic brick station built in 1887; it now houses memorabilia from the area, and local arts and crafts.

ACCOMMODATION: Kaniva Midway Motel, ph (03) 5932 2515; Parlawidgee (guesthouse and farm), ph (03) 5392 2613

ACTIVITIES: Bowls, bushwalking, 4WD touring, golf, horse riding, scenic drives, squash, swimming, tennis

TOURIST INFORMATION: Ph (03) 5392 2418

KERANG

286 KM NORTH OF MELBOURNE
POPULATION: 4030   MAP REF: PAGE 95 K7

A number of lakes and swamps can be found in the region around Kerang, where the waters from the Loddon River gather. The Middle Lake features an

Lester Smith Lookout Tower in Kerang

ibis rookery, one of the largest in the world, while Lake Charm is preferred for waterskiing and boating activities and the shallower First Lake for swimming.

Nesting season is particularly popular with birdwatchers, when literally thousands of birds arrive to nest during August to April. During the duck season, many hunters descend on the region.

The town's beginnings were an inn situated by a bridge which crossed the Loddon River. It was built in 1863 by the earliest settler to the region, Woodful

Patchell. It was not long after settlement that this Irish farmer started to use the water from the lakes and rivers to irrigate his property. This system of irrigation has since been widely adopted through the northern regions of Victoria.

Farming remains the main industry in the region, although tourism, especially in the summer months, has added to the town's economy.

The town's museum contains many artefacts and photographs of the area's history. The Lester Smith Lookout Tower which once used to store the town's water is now the tourist centre. A climb to the top gives excellent views of the surrounding waterways.

There is an annual show held in town in the first week of October.

ACCOMMODATION: Downtown Motor Inn, ph (03) 5452 1911; Motel Kerang, ph (03) 5452 1311; Motel Loddon River, ph (03) 5452 2511
ACTIVITIES: Birdwatching, bowls, bushwalking, croquet, fishing, golf, horse riding, horseracing, scenic drives, tennis, water sports
TOURIST INFORMATION: Ph (03) 5452 1860

KILMORE

63 KM NORTH OF MELBOURNE
POPULATION: 3500   MAP REF: PAGE 93 P4

Originally a supply town for those heading north to the goldfields of Beechworth or Bendigo, little has changed in Kilmore.

First settled in 1841, it is one of Victoria's oldest inland settlements. The town still services travellers although visitor numbers did drop when the town was by-passed by the Hume Freeway which heads north-east towards Seymour. As an alternative route to Bendigo, the Northern Highway offers a chance to look at this historic town.

Some of the town's history is outlined at the Bylands Museum. This museum also houses a number of interesting cable cars and trams, and tram rides can be taken through the picturesque countryside when the museum is open.

Farming uses much of the land around Kilmore but the area is also an important region for horseracing. A racecourse in town is the venue for the popular Kilmore Racing Cup and the Kilmore

Whitburgh Cottage in Kilmore

Pacing Cup, two important race meetings on the provincial harness-racing calendar.

The town comes alive every year in early December, when the Agricultural Show is held.
ACCOMMODATION: Kestrel Motor Inn, ph (03) 5782 1457; Kilmore Country Motel, ph (03) 5782 1346; Laurel Hill Cottage, ph (03) 5782 1630
ACTIVITIES: Bowls, golf, horseracing, swimming, tennis, trotting
TOURIST INFORMATION: Ph (03) 5781 1319

KOO-WEE-RUP

75 KM SOUTH-EAST OF MELBOURNE
POPULATION: 1096   MAP REF: PAGE 91 K5

Lush green pastures and a good supply of rainfall are what makes Koo-wee-rup an important dairy farming and agricultural region to the south-east of Melbourne. Situated inland from Westernport Bay, this township is also a supply stop for tourists along the Gippsland–Bass Highways.

The unusual name of this town comes from the Aboriginal term for blackfish swimming. The area was originally settled by Europeans in the 1840s. There was much swamp land in the region which was drained to make way for grazing land in the 1860s. Thirty years later the railway arrived and Koo-wee-rup became a major milk supplier for Melbourne.

Bayles Fauna Park is situated at nearby Bayles on the South Gippsland Highway and features a large number of birds and animals native to this region. Tooradin Inlet on the edge of Westernport Bay is an excellent picnic location with a jetty which is ideal for fishing and where many pelicans congregate. Swamp Observation Tower, east of Tooradin, offers fine views of Westernport Bay and French Island, which sits in the centre of the bay.

The Koo-Wee-Rup Festival is held here during March.
ACCOMMODATION: Koo Wee Motel, ph (03) 5997 1880
ACTIVITIES: Bowls, swimming, tennis
TOURIST INFORMATION: Ph (03) 9658 9972

KOROIT

285 KM WEST OF MELBOURNE
POPULATION: 1490   MAP REF: PAGE 92 F8

Koroit sits on rich agricultural land near the large regional centre of Warrnambool and, with its large Irish population, is most famous for its production of onions and potatoes. The town was established in the 1800s and a walk through the streets will reveal a number of historic buildings. Koroit Galleries displays interesting prints and artwork while the Old Courthouse Inn contains cottage crafts and gifts.

The most significant feature of the area is an extinct volcano in nearby Tower Hill State Game Reserve, which covers 636 hectares of land. Tower Hill is one of Victoria's most recently active volcanoes and has a large island in the middle. A 16 km-long track takes visitors round the edge of the crater and offers great views into the volcano and the Southern Ocean in the distance. Information on the volcano can be obtained at the Natural History Centre which also has

Aboriginal and geological exhibits along with history on the settlement of this region.

Port Fairy is a charming seaside fishing village close to Koroit.
ACCOMMODATION: Bourkes Koroit Hotel, ph (03) 5565 8201; Limuru House (B&B), ph (03) 5565 8203
ACTIVITIES: Bowls, croquet, historic interest, scenic walks
TOURIST INFORMATION: Ph (03) 5564 7837

KORUMBURRA

126 KM SOUTH-EAST OF MELBOURNE
POPULATION: 2773   MAP REF: PAGE 91 L6

Korumburra's origins are coalmining. Coal was a very important energy source in the nineteenth century. Mining began at Korumburra on a large scale in 1889. There were more than 2000 men in the area working on the mines and the township blossomed, servicing the mines and workers. The mines were worked well into the first half of the twentieth century, but then began to decline, with the last mine closing in 1958.

Coal Creek Historical Village, set in the original Coal Creek Tunnel, depicts the coalmining era.

Another tourist attraction is the giant Gippsland earthworm which is found in the ground around Korumburra. Known as 'karmai' to the local Aborigines, it is a rare and now protected species and can grow to an incredible 3 metres in length while remaining at around 2.5 cm in diameter. At nearby Bass you will find the Giant Worm and Wombat Attraction where displays enable you to see the giant earthworm, watch movies in a theatre and crawl through the stomach of a giant-sized replica of one of these earthworms.

Events in the township include the Coal Creek Coin Day in October, Karmai Festival in March and the Twilight Music Show in February. Bush markets are held at nearby Junbunna, usually on the last Sunday of each month.
ACCOMMODATION: Korumburra Motor Inn, ph (03) 5655 1822; Pindari (B&B), ph (03) 5662 2005; Fairview Homestead (cottages), ph (03) 5657 3270
ACTIVITIES: Bowls, croquet, fishing, golf, horse riding, scenic drives, swimming, tennis
TOURIST INFORMATION: Ph (03) 5655 2233

KYABRAM

198 KM NORTH OF MELBOURNE
POPULATION: 5600   MAP REF: PAGE 98 A4

The irrigation systems channelled through the Goulburn Valley in the north of the state feed the fruit-growing district of Kyabram. The land here was settled in the 1840s by Mitchell Scobie and was originally used for grazing and wheat growing. The main industry changed, however, with irrigation which was established in the 1890s. Plentiful water, combined with good soils and excellent climate, meant the area was good for fruit growing, especially stone fruits. A fruit-processing plant and cannery were established, providing more employment.

The Fauna and Waterfowl Park is situated on Lake Road and comprises 555 hectares. There are over

RSL Memorial Walk at Kyabram

400 different species of bird life and mammals living within their own natural environment in the park.

Other features include the Stables, also on Lake Road, where renovated horse stables now house a large range of arts and crafts. The Western Gums Egg Experience at the Western Gums Caravan Park has a display of eggs in the Fabergé style featuring intricate carving and paintings.

The Kyabram Show is held in November, a rodeo in March, while Market Day is in November.

ACCOMMODATION: Country Roads Motor Inn, ph (03) 5852 3577; Kyabram Motor Inn, ph (03) 5852 2111

ACTIVITIES: Bowls, croquet, fishing, golf, squash, tennis, water sports

TOURIST INFORMATION: Ph (03) 5852 2883

KYNETON

85 KM NORTH-WEST OF MELBOURNE
POPULATION: 3940   MAP REF: PAGE 93 M4

The historic township of Kyneton, with more than 30 buildings classified by the National Trust, resembles an English town, with its large ornate buildings, hedges and extensive grazing land. The town is named after Kyneton in England and while it was once a supply and stopping point on the way to the goldfields, Kyneton is now a farming community.

Old mill wheels in the historic town of Kyneton

There are numerous old buildings including many bluestone structures which date back to the mid-1800s. The museum is housed in a bluestone building which used to be the old bank. Built in 1855, it is a good representation of the era and contains fine examples of furniture of the period.

The Steam Mill is a unique historic flour mill dating from 1862. It was only in 1964 that this mill closed but it has since been restored and, along with photographs and memorabilia, offers a fine display.

Other attractions include two wineries, Knight Granite Hills and Cobaw Ridge, together with parklands such as Blackhill Reserve, and the Lauriston and Upper Coliban Reservoirs. These are popular for trout fishing.

On the banks of the Campaspe River are the botanic gardens which date back to 1866 and have a number of magnificent old trees. Amongst these are exotic shrubs which were donated by Ferdinand von Mueller who was Director of the Melbourne Botanic Gardens when the Kyneton gardens were established.

A daffodil exhibition and the Arts Festival are held in September while the Kyneton Show takes place in November.

ACCOMMODATION: Central Highlands Motor Inn, ph (03) 5422 2011; Kyneton Motel, ph (03) 5422 1098; Kyneton Country House (guesthouse), ph (03) 5422 3556

ACTIVITIES: Bowls, bushwalking, croquet, fishing, golf, horseracing, scenic driving, swimming, tennis

TOURIST INFORMATION: Ph (03) 5422 6110

LAKES ENTRANCE

324 KM EAST OF MELBOURNE
POPULATION: 4625   MAP REF: PAGE 96 G6

The town of Lakes Entrance and the lake system it sits beside have long been popular for holidays.

Apart from being a tourist resort the town operates one of the largest fishing fleets in Australia, with the Entrance, as it is known, providing access and shelter to the Gippsland Lakes from the Tasman Sea. The town's name comes from an artificial entrance that was established in 1889—there had always been a natural entrance, but it was unpredictable and did not provide a safe passage. There are many fishing boats at the jetty in town,

and fresh fish can be purchased from here.

Five major waterways, including the Tambo and Dargo Rivers, find their way to the Gippsland Lakes which are separated from the ocean by only a narrow stretch of dunes, known as the Ninety Mile Beach. This region forms part of the Gippsland Lakes Coastal Park and the Lakes National Park.

A great way to explore the waters of the lakes system is by boat, either on one of the passenger ferries or cruisers, or by hiring a sailing boat and exploring the area yourself. You will find plenty of boating craft for rent, including the paddle-boats at Cunninghame Arm near the footbridge.

There are many areas to explore by foot and the footbridge over Cunninghame Arm connects the beach with the Esplanade, while a walking track leads from the centre of town to the entrance itself.

The Ninety Mile Beach offers great views of the coast and is popular with surfers and anglers, while the nearby Nyerimilang Park offers fantastic views of the lakes. This 178 hectare property, which features a homestead built in 1892, is surrounded by semi-formal gardens. They provide a home to birds and wildlife. The park is ideal for picnics.

Other attractions include an antique car and folk museum (which can be found at Charma, an 1860s cottage), and a recreation park with waterslides, mini golf and other family activities. The Sea Shell Museum features over 80 000 shells and corals along with a large aquarium and model railway. Train buffs should also visit the Stoney Creek Railway Bridge on Colquhourn Road where the 276-metre-long trestle bridge lies. This bridge was built of local timber in 1916 and is more than 18 metres high.

A Sunday market is held at the Mayfair Entertainment Complex, while the Lions Club Fish Tasting is held each year on Good Friday. Other events include a fishing expo in November and a fantastic New Year's Eve fireworks display.

ACCOMMODATION: Banjo Paterson Motor Inn, ph (03) 5155 2933; Bellvue Motor Inn, ph (03) 5155 3055; George Bass Motor Inn, ph (03) 5155 1611; Ocean Breeze Flats, ph (03) 5155 1369

ACTIVITIES: Bowls, bushwalking, fishing, golf, scenic drives, tennis, water sports

TOURIST INFORMATION: Ph (03) 5155 1966

LEONGATHA

141 KM SOUTH-EAST OF MELBOURNE
POPULATION: 4500   MAP REF: PAGE 91 M7

Leongatha lies at the bottom of the Strzelecki Ranges in South Gippsland. The land at the base of the ranges is today dominated by rolling pastures, but this region was once heavily forested with magnificent mountain ash trees. The area was cleared for dairy use during the 1870s, and this industry continues today.

Leongatha is close to Wilsons Promontory and Lakes Entrance. Moss Vale Park off the Leongatha–Mirboo road lies on the Tarwin River and has 5 hectares of fine English trees; it is the perfect location for a summer picnic.

Gippsland is home to a number of wineries such as Bass Phillip on Tosch's Road in Leongatha South and Lyre Bird Hill on the Inverloch Road.

Other things to do around Leongatha include visiting the Fireling Museum which has an excellent collection of antique lanterns and firearms, some of which are more than 400 years old. The Woorayl Shire Historical Society, housed in the old Mechanics Institute and classified by the National Trust, houses memorabilia from the region's past.

Events in Leongatha include the Daffodil and Rotary Art Festival which is held in September.

ACCOMMODATION: Leongatha Motel, ph (03) 5662 2375; Opal Motel, ph (03) 5662 2321; Peaceful Gardens (B&B) ph (03) 5664 0020

ACTIVITIES: Bowls, croquet, golf, horse riding, scenic drives, squash, swimming, tennis

TOURIST INFORMATION: Ph (03) 5655 2233

LILYDALE

39 KM EAST OF MELBOURNE
POPULATION: 9505   MAP REF: PAGE 91 J3

The gateway to the Yarra Valley region, the township of Lilydale is now considered an outer suburb of eastern Melbourne.

This region with its rich, fertile soil was once farming and grazing land and the surrounding area that is not used for housing is still mainly farmland.

The Lilydale Lake was formed in recent years and with a walking track, picnic area and playgrounds, is extremely popular with locals.

The Lilydale Museum on Castella Street was built in 1889 and originally housed the shire offices. Now it is home to a large collection of photographs and documents relating to the region. There is also plenty of information on the famous opera singer, Dame Nellie Melba, who once resided at Combe Cottage in neighbouring Coldstream. Her father, David Mitchell, lived in Lilydale and owned the large limestone quarry clearly visible as you drive down into the town. Dame Nellie Melba's grave is in Lilydale Cemetery.

Lilydale is one of the oldest wine-growing regions in Victoria with the first vines being planted in 1838 at nearby Yering. Today there are many wineries in the Yarra Valley, and they include well-known names such as De Bortoli, Yarra Yering, Domaine Chandon and Coldstream Hills.

The herb farm on Mangans Road in Lilydale is well worth a visit.

A raft race is held on the Lilydale Lake during summer while a large agricultural show is put on in November. The Yarra Valley Grape-Grazing takes place during March.

ACCOMMODATION: Billanook Country Inn Motel, ph (03) 9735 3000; Lilydale Motor Inn, ph (03) 9735 5222; Lilydale Herb Farm (B&B), ph (03) 9735 0486

ACTIVITIES: Bowls, bushwalking, fishing, golf, horse riding, scenic drives, swimming, tennis, wineries

TOURIST INFORMATION: Ph (03) 5962 2600

LORNE

142 KM SOUTH-WEST OF MELBOURNE
POPULATION: 1170   MAP REF: PAGE 93 L8

Sitting at the foothills of the magnificent Otway Ranges on Loutit Bay, Lorne has, for more than

The beach at Lorne, popular with residents and visitors for over 100 years

100 years, been a popular seaside resort. The bay is named after Captain Loutit who sought shelter in its protected waters in 1841. The town, which was established in 1871, is named in honour of the Marquis of Lorne, a Scottish peer.

The opening of the Great Ocean Road in 1932 gave a real boost to the town. This road is itself a tourist attraction, winding along the coastline from Torquay to near Warrnambool, offering fantastic coastal views. During the peak times of summer, the township is very busy—indeed, for much of the year, accommodation needs to be booked well in advance.

Seafood here is as fresh as you can get it: a small fishing fleet comes in every day with their catch which includes fish and crayfish.

Apart from the sun and surf there are plenty of things to do in town including a visit to its many craft shops, or a stroll around the Historical Society Building on Mountjoy Parade (which features plenty of photographic memorabilia), or the shell museum.

Outside of town Teddy's Lookout offers magnificent views of the coastline. The Erskine Falls is at the end of a walk through a picturesque fern-lined valley. The waterfall tumbles down over moss-covered rocks. Lorne is also close to the Otway Ranges and its associated parks which are ideal for bushwalking, scenic drives and picnics.

ACCOMMODATION: Lorne Main Beach Motor Inn, ph (03) 5389 1199; Kalimna Motel, ph (03) 5289 1407; Lorne Hotel, ph (03) 5289 1409; Cumberland Lorne Resort (apartments), ph (03) 5289 2400

ACTIVITIES: Boating, fishing, national park access, scenic drives, bushwalking, tennis, water sports

TOURIST INFORMATION: Ph (03) 5289 1152

MACEDON

60 KM NORTH-WEST OF MELBOURNE
POPULATION: 1800   MAP REF: PAGE 93 M4

Macedon sits on the edge of the Great Dividing Range and Mt Macedon, which towers behind it, is actually a 1000 metre volcano, not a mountain. This region is heavily forested and is often affected by bushfires. During the summer of 1983 much of Macedon was burnt in the Ash Wednesday fires, but the township still remains and many of the buildings, some which were grand historic structures, are being restored.

The area has always been forest land and timber was taken from this region and used in the mines during the gold rush. It was when the timber became scarce that orchardists moved to the region and built large mansions surrounded by spectacular gardens. One such property is Ard Choille, set on 98 hectares.

The Macedon Regional Park encompasses more than 3200 hectares of land which can be used for bushwalking, horse riding and scenic drives. Within the park you will find the Major Mitchell Lookout and Camel's Hump. The large Memorial Cross, originally built in honour of World War I soldiers, was restored during 1996 and is visible from afar.

There are more than 20 km of walking trails in the bush around Macedon, and during autumn the large European trees which dot the landscape come alive with warm copper tones.

A large collection of enormous boulders originally formed by lava pushed up from the earth's surface, forms Hanging Rock, a site which is steeped in Aboriginal history. It was also the setting for Joan Lindsay's famous book and the subsequent film, *Picnic at Hanging Rock*. This is the site for harvest picnics and festivals during the year or for a quiet BBQ.

ACCOMMODATION: Black Forest Motel, ph (03) 5426 1600; Ard Choille (B&B), ph (03) 5247 2482; Braeside Mt Macedon (cottages), ph (03) 5426 2025; Linden Cottage, ph (03) 5426 1592

ACTIVITIES: Bowls, bushwalking, golf, horse riding, scenic drives, rock climbing, tennis

TOURIST INFORMATION: Ph (03) 5427 2033

MAFFRA

220 KM EAST OF MELBOURNE
POPULATION: 3880   MAP REF: PAGE 96 C6

Maffra took its name from a property of an early settler. He had spent time in Mafra in Portugal during the Peninsular Wars and named his run accordingly. Maffra is surrounded by rich pastoral land within the irrigation system which feeds off the Macalister River. The town was established in 1875 and is now a service centre to the smaller outlying towns and farms at the base of the Alps. In 1929 the Glenmaggie Weir was established to form the basis for the irrigation system to feed the Maffra region; it was increased in size during the 1950s. The small town of Coongulla grew around the shores of the weir and is a popular holiday destination for waterskiers and sailors.

The township of Maffra is very picturesque. Before irrigation and the dairy industry, Maffra was involved in the sugar beet industry between 1890 and 1940. The venture proved to be unsuccessful and the history of this undertaking can be found at the Maffra Sugar Beet Museum on River Street.

Other attractions include the herb garden on Foster Street and the Wa-De-Lock Vineyard.

There are some small and interesting towns outside Maffra, including Tinamba which is home to the Schoenmaekers Tavern and Tinamba Hotel. The tavern offers a genuine Dutch feast, while the atmosphere in the hotel is also a blend of country Australia and Holland.

Heading north from Maffra leads you to the alpine country and towns such as Licola which are a great base for bushwalking, 4WD touring or scenic drives. In winter the snow-covered mountains above Maffra are great for cross-country skiing.

The Gippsland Harvest Festival is held in March, the Farming Festival in April and the Agricultural Show in October.

ACCOMMODATION: Motel Maffra, ph (03) 5147 2111; Metropolitan Hotel, ph (03) 5147 1809; Powerscourt Country House (guesthouse, circa 1859), ph (03) 5147 1897

ACTIVITIES: Bowls, bushwalking, croquet, fishing, 4WD touring, golf, horse riding, scenic drives, swimming, tennis

TOURIST INFORMATION: Ph (03) 5144 1108

MALDON

141 KM NORTH-WEST OF MELBOURNE
POPULATION: 1300   MAP REF: PAGE 93 L3

Gold was discovered in the Maldon region in 1853 and mined until as recently as the 1930s. A stroll down the street beneath the line of verandahs will take you back to the gold era as you pass antique shops, small quaint retail stores and art galleries. This historic town was declared Australia's first 'Notable Town' by the National Trust.

Dabb & Co, an old general store in Maldon

Evidence of the town's heritage is visible through the large mullock heaps outside of town, now covered in grass, and the Beehive Mine Chimney on Main Street. The Beehive Mine was established in the 1860s and named by a group of Cornish miners who saw a swarm of bees near the mine. The chimney was built in 1862 and although it fell into disrepair after mining ceased, it has since been fully restored.

The Porcupine Township, 3 km out of Maldon, recreates an old goldmining town. Carmen's Tunnel Gold Mine is a journey back in time where visitors can walk through the tunnel by candlelight.

Excellent views can be had from Anzac Hill Lookout. The Pioneer Cemetery is most interesting. Another attraction of Maldon is the Vintage Railway which journeys through picturesque forest from Maldon to Muckleford on the way to Castlemaine, towed by an authentic steam engine. The railway was originally opened in 1884 during the rush and was in operation for nearly 100 years.

ACCOMMODATION: Maldon's Eaglehawk Motel, ph (03) 5475 2750; Clare House (B&B), ph (03) 5475 2152; Heritage Cottages of Maldon, ph (03) 5475 2927

ACTIVITIES: Bowls, bushwalking, croquet, fishing, golf, historic interest, scenic drives, swimming, tennis

TOURIST INFORMATION: Ph (03) 5475 2569

MALLACOOTA

531 KM EAST OF MELBOURNE
POPULATION: 960   MAP REF: PAGE 97 N5

The tranquil fishing and holiday resort town of Mallacoota is perched in the remote eastern corner of the state near the border of New South Wales.

A whaling port was established here by Ben Boyd and the Imlay Brothers in the 1840s. By the end of the century the township was established as a fishing base. Abalone is dived for in these waters. In summer tourists come for the boating, fishing and surfing.

There are many beautiful places to visit, including Shady Gully Walk within town which leads down through a reserve to Shady Gully. Bastion Point can be found at the end of Bastion Road where a viewing platform gives outstanding views of the entrance to Mallacoota Inlet, Croajingolong Park, Howe Range and out to Gabo Island.

Parks in the surrounding area offer excellent bushwalking, scenic drives and 4WD touring including Croajingolong National Park which is an important forest region on the coast with superb beaches. Visitors following the Genoa River northward from Mallacoota Inlet will discover the delights of the green timberland regions at the edge of the Great Dividing Range above Genoa.

Events include the Easter Carnival in Coota and the Mallacoota Cup soccer weekend in October.

ACCOMMODATION: Mallacoota Hotel/Motel, ph (03) 5158 0455; Silver Bream Motel Suites and Flats, ph (03) 5158 0305; Adobe Mudbrick Flats, ph (03) 5158 0329

ACTIVITIES: Bowls, bushwalking, fishing, golf, national park access, scenic drives, tennis, water sports

TOURIST INFORMATION: Ph (03) 5158 0788

MANSFIELD

174 KM NORTH-EAST OF MELBOURNE
POPULATION: 2500   MAP REF: PAGE 98 E7

Mansfield, at the foot of the Victorian Alps, is well known as the gateway to the High Country. It first achieved notoriety in 1878, when three policemen were killed by the notorious Kelly Gang at Stringybark Creek. The three men are buried in the Mansfield Cemetery and a monument can be found in the centre of a roundabout in the town's main street.

Set amongst some of Victoria's most magnificent mountain scenery, Mansfield is busy in both summer and winter. There is the popular holiday destination of Lake Eildon to the south and the snowfields of Mt Buller and Mt Stirling are not far away. For most of the year the surrounding countryside and mountains are a playground for bushwalkers, 4WD tourers, and campers. It is even possible to take a camel trek or a balloon ride in this region.

A popular destination near Mansfield is Craigs Hut, which was built on Clear Hills overlooking the valley below for the movie *Man From Snowy River*. The hut can be accessed by the family car and then on foot for the last 2 km, or by 4WD right to the hut. The area is not accessible during winter as the main Circuit Road is closed.

Mansfield is an ideal starting point for a High Country jaunt in a 4WD vehicle, visiting such places as Matlock, Licola, Wonnangatta Station and Dargo. It is also possible to enjoy the scenery through a series of gravel roads in the region which head through Jamieson and the old goldmining towns of Woods Point and Walhalla.

There are plenty of activities in the area, including bush markets on the Saturday of most long weekends, Mansfield Harvest and Merrijig Rodeo on Labour Day Weekend, the High Country Hot Air Balloon Festival in late March, Mansfield High Country Festival in November and the High Cs in the High Country—an open-air concert held at Mt Buller on New Year's Eve.

ACCOMMODATION: Mansfield Valley Motor Inn, ph (03) 5775 1300; Arlzburg Inn (motel), ph (03) 5775 2367; Mansfield Country Resort (cottage), ph (03) 5775 2679

ACTIVITIES: Bowls, bushwalking, fishing, 4WD touring, golf, horse riding, scenic drives, snow skiing, tennis, water sports

TOURIST INFORMATION: Ph (03) 5775 1464

MARLO

399 KM EAST OF MELBOURNE
POPULATION: 380   MAP REF: PAGE 97 J6

This small fishing village lies at the mouth of the Snowy River, along the east coast of the state. Here, south of Orbost, the Snowy River flows into a small channel before running out into the Tasman Sea. This is an ideal fishing area much used by anglers wanting to avoid the larger coastal towns.

Apart from the quaint town which survives on fishing and tourism, Marlo's greatest asset is that it is close to the Cape Conran Foreshore Reserve, a picturesque park to the east of town which is ideal for fishing, SCUBA diving, surfing and bushwalking. Swimming is also popular but tides and currents can be strong especially around the mouth of the Snowy River. The best places to swim are Yeerung Beach and Banksia Bluff. Both the Snowy and Yeerung Rivers are suitable for canoeing. Campers can use Banksia Bluff which has fireplaces and toilets.

From Marlo you can access the temperate rainforests north of Orbost by way of gravel roads. The magnificent scenery is worth the drive.

ACCOMMODATION: Padies Units, ph (03) 5154 8364; Tabbara Lodge Marlo (holiday units), ph (03) 5154 8231; AA Relocation and Holiday Homes (cottages), ph (03) 9873 3060

ACTIVITIES: Bushwalking, fishing, horse riding, scenic drives, tennis, water sports

TOURIST INFORMATION: Ph (03) 5154 2424

MARYBOROUGH

171 KM NORTH-WEST OF MELBOURNE
POPULATION: 7850   MAP REF: PAGE 93 K3

Historic Maryborough is in the 'golden triangle' of Victoria west of Castlemaine, and is a thriving industrial town surrounded by grazing land.

The first settlers to the region were three Scottish brothers who set up a run in 1840 to graze their

Maryborough's historic railway station, considered to be one of the finest in Victoria

sheep. When gold was discovered at White Hills in 1854, the town became a major supply point for the gold rush which spread through the centre of Victoria. The town was named by the Gold Commissioner after his home town in Ireland.

Mining continued in the region until 1918, after which the town's economic base is that of a service and industrial centre.

There are many magnificent old buildings in town, but the most impressive is the Maryborough Railway Station which is not just an historic site, it is also a tourist complex. The railway station has been meticulously restored and is considered one of the finest in Victoria. In the complex are the Maryborough Station Antique Emporium which has antiques, collectables and old wares. There is also an art gallery, café and markets with country crafts, on what is believed to be one of the longest railway platforms in the southern hemisphere.

Other interesting buildings include an historic bluestone cottage built in 1894 which now houses the Museum of Creative Arts and Sciences. Worsley Cottage built in 1894 by Arthur Worsley is the base for the Midlands Historical Society and features a collection of memorabilia which dates back to 1854.

Further afield, the Bristol Hill Lookout Tower in the Bristol Hill Reserve offers spectacular views of the city. There are Aboriginal drinking wells which can be found off Shoreham Drive. The five small wells are formed from granite outcrops and were used by the local Aborigines for obtaining water.

Wineries in this area include Kangderaar, Newstead and Tipperary Estate, which offer wine tasting and cellar sales.

Events include the Maryborough Golden Wattle Festival which is held in September, and the Maryborough Highland Gathering Championships and Gift which are held on New Year's Day.

ACCOMMODATION: Golden Country Caratel (motel), ph (03) 5461 2344; Bristol Hill Motor Inn, ph (03) 5461 3833; Junction Motel Maryborough, ph (03) 5461 1744

ACTIVITIES: Bushwalking, bowls, croquet, fishing, gold fossicking, golf, historic interest, horse riding, scenic drives, trotting, water sports

TOURIST INFORMATION: Ph (03) 5460 4511

MARYSVILLE

93 KM EAST OF MELBOURNE
POPULATION: 650   MAP REF: PAGE 98 D9

Deep in the heart of the Yarra Ranges is the quaint country town of Marysville, a popular day and weekend destination with Melbournians.

The township was named after Mary Steavenson, the wife of the town's founder, John Steavenson, who first settled here in 1863. Gold was discovered nearby, in the hills around Mattock and Woods Point, and Marysville was a stopping point on the way to and from Melbourne. It also held supplies for the prospectors and travellers heading up into the mountain range.

Surrounded by tall mountain timber, Marysville has long been a timber town and a sawmill still exists here today. Other industries in the region include tourism and grazing.

Snow skiing and tobogganing can be enjoyed at Lake Mountain above the town while Cumberland Scenic Reserve covers 300 hectares of mountain bushland including old growth forest. Here also are Cumberland Falls and Sovereign View lookout which provides excellent views over Warburton. Keppels Lookout on Plains Road is also popular and a three hour walk will reward the energetic with magnificent mountain ash forest scenery and views of the Steavenson River and Marysville.

The Wirreanda Festival is held in October and features a number of activities including a horse gymkhana, motorcycle rally cross, and market day.

ACCOMMODATION: The Cumberland Hotel, ph (03) 5963 3203; Tower Motel, ph (03) 5963 3225; The Birches Resort (motel), ph (03) 5963 3392; Mountain Lodge Marysville (guesthouse), ph (03) 5963 3270; Marylands Country House (guesthouse), ph (03) 5963 3204

ACTIVITIES: Bowls, bushwalking, fishing, 4WD touring, golf, horse riding, mountain bike riding, scenic drives, snow skiing, swimming, tennis

TOURIST INFORMATION: Ph (03) 5963 4567

MILAWA-OXLEY

240 KM NORTH-EAST OF MELBOURNE
POPULATION: 270   MAP REF: PAGE 98 F5

The small town of Milawa in the north-east of the state is in the centre of a pastoral and wine producing district and is home to the famous Brown Brothers Winery. This company is a major producer of Victorian wines and the winery now features an Epicurean Centre which offers international cuisine made from local produce. To complement the wine there is the Milawa Cheese Company which is housed in the old Milawa Butter Factory on Factory Road.

Home-made mustards can also be purchased in the region from Milawa Mustards who stock varieties varying from mild to hot.

ACCOMMODATION: Milawa Lodge Motel, ph (03) 5727 3326

ACTIVITIES: Bowls, scenic drives, squash, tennis, wineries

TOURIST INFORMATION: Ph (03) 5721 5711

MILDURA

550 KM NORTH-WEST OF MELBOURNE
POPULATION: 17 990   MAP REF: PAGE 94 E2

Located on the banks of the Murray River in the far north-west of the state is Mildura, a town surrounded by hundreds of hectares of farmland producing grape vines and citrus fruit in the heart of the Sunraysia region. With the constant warm to hot weather, little rain and the plentiful waters of the Murray River, it is a great holiday destination. The name Mildura comes from the Aboriginal word meaning 'red rock' or 'red earth' which is a description of the deep red soil found in the region.

Pastoralists Hugh and Bushby Jamieson settled in the area in 1847, and because of the arid land, an irrigation system was set up in the 1880s which now sees water pumped from the Murray River to provide year-round water for the crops. A variety of crops continue to be produced including grapes for sultanas and wine, olives and citrus fruits. Visitors can learn of the citrus production in the area at the Citrus Shop and Information Centre while Sultana Sam offers a guided tour of a vineyard.

The heart of the town is the Murray River and it is home to many boats and old paddle-steamers. These huge vessels used to cruise the waters of the Murray picking up loads of wool from stations and shipping them to inland ports. There are still some paddle-steamers using the Murray around Mildura, including the *Melbourne*. This still retains its original engine and boiler and operates cruises down to Lock 11 taking around two hours for the round trip. The vessel was built in 1912 for the Victorian Government and was restored in 1965. The *Rothbury* also operates on the Murray and takes visitors to the Golden River Zoo and Trentham Winery.

The Mildura Arts Centre is based around the home of William Chaffey, irrigation pioneer. Built from Murray pine, red gum and red brick, it was completed in 1899. The Centre is an art gallery and theatre. It houses an excellent collection of Australian and European paintings and sculptures.

Wineries in the region include Capagreco and Trentham Estate.

Further south of town are the Murray–Kulkyne Park and Hattah–Kulkyne National Park, both of which lie west of the Murray River. They encompass a typical mallee environment of natural cypress pine woodland and vast areas of mallee scrubland. The Hattah Lakes provide a life source for waterfowl, and there are camping areas and sandy 4WD tracks.

Events in town include the Mildura Vintage and Arts Festival which is held in March, the Mildura Golf Week in July, Country Music Week in September and the Festival of the Oasis Rose during November. For wine buffs there is a Sunraysia Wine and Jazz Festival which takes place during November.

ACCOMMODATION: Boulevard Motor Inn, ph (03) 5023 5023; Central Motel, ph (03) 5021 1177; Chaffey International Motor Inn, ph (03) 50235833; Mildura Holiday Houseboats, ph (03) 5021 4414
ACTIVITIES: Bowls, fishing, golf, horse riding, national park access, scenic drives, squash, swimming, tennis, trotting, water sports, wineries
TOURIST INFORMATION: Ph (03) 5021 4424

Old Gippstown, a restored pioneer village at Moe

MOE

155 KM SOUTH-EAST OF MELBOURNE
POPULATION: 16 720   MAP REF: PAGE 91 N5

The industrial town of Moe is in the heart of the coalmining region of the Latrobe Valley in Gippsland. It is situated in the foothills of the High Country, and nearby is the old town of Walhalla which has been extensively renovated over the past years. The name of the town comes from the Aboriginal word 'mouay' meaning swamp. Originally the region supported a dairy and pastoral industry, but with brown coal deposits being found under the swamp, the town's interest soon turned to the coal and the energy it produces. The nearby township of Yallourn was actually relocated to enable mining of the coal. Moe now houses coal workers although there are still many farms in the region.

Old Gippstown sits at the freeway exit to Moe and has been established to represent an old pioneer town with 30 buildings which have been transported from throughout Gippsland for the display. These authentic homes were then restored on-site and apparently include the home of Angus McMillan, who explored the region and settled here in 1840.

On the way to Walhalla you will find Moondarra Reservoir which offers spectacular views from near the spillway and a range of walking tracks.

Nearby Blue Rock Lake holds 200 000 megalitres of water and is popular with residents for swimming, waterskiing and fishing.

Walhalla has many old buildings and a large old goldmine and tunnel which is now open for tours. Further north lies the Alpine National Park which is a playground for bushwalkers, owners of 4WD vehicles, horse riders, and cross-country skiers in winter.

ACCOMMODATION: Moe Motor Inn, ph (03) 5127 1166; The Park Motor Inn, ph (03) 5127 3344
ACTIVITIES: Bowls, bushwalking, croquet, fishing, 4WD touring, golf, horse riding, horseracing, national park access, scenic drives, tennis, water sports
TOURIST INFORMATION: Ph (03) 5127 308

MONBULK

47 KM EAST OF MELBOURNE
POPULATION: 3839   MAP REF: PAGE 91 J3

Monbulk is a small town in the middle of a large fruit-growing district that has everything from cherries to peaches and strawberries. The rich red soils in the valleys of the Dandenong Ranges and the good rainfall which the area experiences combine to provide excellent growing conditions. In spring the countryside comes alive with blooms destined for the cut flower industry along with the pink and white blossoms of the cherries and plums.

Nearby Silvan is home to Tesselaar's Tulip Farm which hosts a huge Tulip Festival when the flowers are in bloom during September. During spring there are also a number of flower shows throughout the Dandenongs and neighbouring Yarra Valley region.

Located close to Melbourne, this region also boasts a large residential population with many people commuting to the city and inner suburbs for work, whilst retaining the picturesque uncrowded lifestyle of the Dandenong Ranges.

The town hosts a local market on the third Sunday of every month.

ACCOMMODATION: Bluegum Heights (B&B), ph (03) 9756 7434; Spring Waters Retreat (cottages), ph (03) 67566332; Camp Waterman (lodge), ph (03) 9756 6120
ACTIVITIES: Bowls, bushwalking, fishing, 4WD touring, horse riding, scenic drives, swimming, tennis
TOURIST INFORMATION: Ph (03) 9752 6554

MORNINGTON

54 KM SOUTH OF MELBOURNE
POPULATION: 14 150   MAP REF: PAGE 91 H5

Overlooking Port Phillip Bay, Mornington is a seaside resort on the west of the Mornington Peninsula, long popular with Melbournians during the summer.

The splendid fountain in Kernot Lake, Morwell

Matthew Flinders was the first European to land in this area and soon this region, being not far from Melbourne, was settled. Originally the town was known as Schnapper Point, but the name was changed in 1864 to Mornington in honour of the Earl of Mornington. A unique feature of the town is the number of century-old private changing huts on the beach. These and other historic buildings in the town date back to the 1880s when the resort first began attracting large crowds from the city.

With white sandy beaches, safe waters for swimming and its proximity to the suburbs of Melbourne, it is hardly surprising that this beach and town are so popular. A large number of restaurants and cafés also attract visitors. Surfers are catered for further down the peninsula at Portsea or over on the eastern side at Point Leo.

Along the seaward edge of the peninsula facing the Bass Strait is the Mornington Peninsula National Park. Port Nepean and the old military fort were closed to the public for many years. Now open, they and the quarantine staion and cemetery are among the main attractions of the park. Other drawcards include the wide, sandy beaches and the coastal heathland. The Cape Schanck Lighthouse is situated on the most southern point of the peninsula.

In the centre of the peninsula there are a number of good vineyards to explore. These include Dromana Estate and Main Ridge Estate. The best way to sample the wines of the district is to visit one of the festivals, such as the Mornington Peninsula Queen's Birthday Wine Weekend in June or the Mornington Peninsula Carnival of Wine during October/November.

ACCOMMODATION: Brooklands of Mornington (motel), ph (03) 5975 1166; Ranch Motel, ph (03) 5975 4022; Rosemont on the Beach (holiday units), ph (03) 5981 0136

ACTIVITIES: Bowls, fishing, golf, horseracing, national park access, squash, tennis, water sports, wineries

TOURIST INFORMATION: Ph (03) 5975 1644

MORWELL

155 KM SOUTH-EAST OF MELBOURNE
POPULATION: 17 000   MAP REF: PAGE 96 A8

Coal is the mainstay of Morwell, in the heart of the Latrobe Valley. Open-cut mining began in Morwell in 1916 by the then State Electricity Commission (SEC), although privatisation of government resources now sees independent companies operating the state's power supply.

The Hazelwood Power Station was due to open in 1971 and this led to the construction of the Hazelwood pondage. This body of water is heated by the power station and provides delightful warm water for swimming and is very popular with waterskiers.

Tours of the open-cut mine, power station and the briquette factory can be organised through the Powerworks Visitors Centre who also run spectacular night tours from November through to May.

Before the establishment of the coal industry, dairying was the mainstay of the region.

In town the Morwell Centenary Rose Garden on Commercial Road is one of Victoria's finest rose gardens. It covers about 1.5 hectares of landscaped beds containing over 2000 different varieties of roses.

The more adventurous might like to head to the Thomson River for whitewater rafting.

To the south of the town lies Morwell State Park which is popular with bushwalkers who enjoy the fern-lined gullies and tall stringybark forests.

ACCOMMODATION: Del Spana Motor Inn, ph (03) 5134 4155; Coal Valley Motor Inn, ph (03) 5134 6211; Morwell Southside Motel, ph (03) 5134 8266

ACTIVITIES: Bowls, bushwalking, croquet, fishing, 4WD touring, golf, horse riding, scenic drives, tennis, water sports

TOURIST INFORMATION: Ph (03) 5135 3415

MOUNT BEAUTY

350 KM NORTH-EAST OF MELBOURNE
POPULATION: 2100   MAP REF: PAGE 99 J6

As the name suggests, Mount Beauty is a magnificent country town, situated in the foothills of Mt Bogong in the Upper Kiewa Valley. Originally built as an accommodation town for workers on the Kiewa hydro-electricity scheme in the 1940s, the town soon became popular with tourists because of its proximity to the Bogong High Plains and the ski resort of Falls Creek.

During winter skiers converge on this quaint town where they can stock up on supplies, find a bed for the night or hire their ski gear. Many people also take advantage of the coachline which ferries skiers to the slopes of Falls Creek.

During the rest of the year the area offers magnificent scenery and many bushwalking trails. The tree-lined roads are great for cycling, especially in autumn when the roads are edged with golden hues. The large pondage, used for the hydro-electricity scheme, is great for water-based activities such as waterskiing, windsurfing and fishing.

An excellent visitors centre in the town provides information on the hydro-electricity scheme, the town's history through an informative museum, and details of attractions in the area.

An annual race is held in March to the top of Mt Bogong and a community market is held on the first Saturday of each month.

ACCOMMODATION: Snowgum Motel, ph (03) 5754 4508; Bogong Moth Motel, ph (03) 5754 4644; Jane's Bed and Breakfast, ph (03) 5754 4036

ACTIVITIES: Bowls, bushwalking, fishing, 4WD touring, golf, horse riding, scenic drives, snow skiing, tennis, water sports

TOURIST INFORMATION: Ph (03) 5754 3172

MOUNT HOTHAM AND DINNER PLAIN

365 AND 370 KM NORTH-EAST OF MELBOURNE
POPULATION: 370   MAP REF: PAGE 99 J7

The small alpine villages of Mount Hotham and Dinner Plain sit in the snowfields of the Victorian Alps. In winter they are covered in a thick blanket of snow. When the snow melts in spring, the mountain top is covered in alpine grass and wildflowers.

Dinner Plain is a small community nestled amongst the snow gums. Its architecture is uniquely Australian and blends in beautifully with the surrounding scenery. Cross-country skiing can be undertaken from this village, while a shuttle bus operates between the two resorts taking downhill skiers to the chairlifts and slopes of Mount Hotham only 8 km further along the Alpine Road.

Mount Hotham offers a large snowfield with many lifts and excellent skiing for beginners right through to those who play on the black runs. There is also plenty of night life on this mountain. The attractions are not restricted to the winter months as during summer and spring the mountain attracts bushwalkers, sightseers and rock climbers.

The region is surrounded by the Alpine National Park and is home to a variety of wildlife including the mountain pygmy possum, once thought to be extinct.

Events include New Year's Day Celebrations with the annual Cattlemen's Horse Race. The Winter Classic Triathlon starts here on the last weekend in July.

ACCOMMODATION: Alpine Haven (holiday flats), ph (03) 5759 9522; Lawlers Apartments, ph (03) 5759 3606; Dinner Plain Accommodation Booking Service, ph (03) 9790 2121

ACTIVITIES: Bushwalking, horse riding, rock climbing, scenic drives, snow skiing

TOURIST INFORMATION: Ph (03) 5759 3550

MURCHISON

150 KM NORTH OF MELBOURNE
POPULATION: 860   MAP REF: PAGE 98 B5

This small township, known as the River Bank Garden Town, lies on the western banks of the Goulburn River and is surrounded by vast amounts of flat grazing land. The town was initially settled by pioneers heading to the Waranga goldfield in 1840. The original settlement on the banks of the Goulburn has now been preserved as tranquil gardens.

The Waranga Basin north of town is a huge reservoir which supplies water through more than 350 km of irrigation channels to the Wimmera and the Mallee in the state's west. The basin was originally built to supply water to Portland in the south-west of the state. It is now also popular for boating, waterskiing and angling.

Nearby Whroo Historic Area is a natural reserve which was once the site of the old goldmining township of Whroo (pronounced 'roo'). The town's name is Aboriginal for 'waterhole' and there is an Aboriginal rock-well here along with ruins of the town and a historic cemetery.

A community fete is held in April while a cross-country run is held during mid-July each year.

ACCOMMODATION: Murchison Motel, ph (03) 5826 2488; Komali-on-the-Goulburn (B&B), ph (03) 5826 2388

ACTIVITIES: Bowls, bushwalking, fishing, golf, horse riding, scenic drives, tennis, water sports

TOURIST INFORMATION: Ph (03) 5794 2647

MYRTLEFORD

286 KM NORTH-EAST OF MELBOURNE
POPULATION: 3600   MAP REF: PAGE 98 G5

The delightful old gold town of Myrtleford lies at the junction of the Buffalo and Ovens Rivers and is named after Myrtle Creek, a tributary of the Ovens. Surrounded by a large mountain range with Mt Buffalo looming overhead, the fertile flats of this town are used for cattle-raising and growing crops such as hops, walnuts, tobacco, hemp and fruit.

Gold was discovered nearby in 1853 which led to the town being surveyed in 1856 by Henry Davidson and then established during 1859. It was not, however, until the railway line opened up in 1883 that the town really started to grow.

The Old School Museum provides an insight into the town's heritage. Built in 1870 this historic building contains a restored classroom, kitchen, living room, old printing machinery and memorabilia from World War I. The museum is open on Sunday afternoons or by appointment.

The surrounding mountain ranges offer plenty of attractions for outdoor enthusiasts with Mt Buffalo providing snow skiing in winter and delightful trails

The peaceful countryside around Myrtleford

for bushwalking in summer. Lake Buffalo is also excellent for angling and swimming while a scenic lookout on Reform Hill gives panoramic views of the town and countryside.

A bush market is held in January, and the Tobacco, Hops and Timber Festival is held on Labour Day in March. An annual show features in October and the rodeo on Boxing Day.

ACCOMMODATION: Golden Leaf Motor Inn, ph (03) 5721 1566; Standish Street Motel, ph (03) 5752 1583; Myrtleford Country Motel, ph (03) 5752 1438

ACTIVITIES: Bowls, bushwalking, croquet, fishing, golf, scenic drives, squash, swimming, tennis

TOURIST INFORMATION: Ph (03) 5752 1727

NAGAMBIE

125 KM NORTH OF MELBOURNE
POPULATION: 1500   MAP REF: PAGE 93 P2

A large lake in the centre of town is the main feature of Nagambie. The artificial lake was constructed in 1887, using the plentiful waters of the Goulburn River. It is a favourite with waterskiers while the quieter waters upstream are sought after by canoeists, or anglers trying their luck at landing trout or redfin.

To the north of town is the Goulburn Weir which supplies irrigation channels and is linked to the Waranga Basin near Murchison. This weir was built at around the same time as Lake Nagambie. The surrounding countryside is mainly used for grazing.

The Historical Society and Folk Museum, housed in the old court house, contains exhibits illustrating the town's history.

There are several wineries in the region including Mitchelton Winery and Goulburn Valley. Chateau Tahbilk Winery and Vineyard is housed on a magnificent historic property. The cellars are classified by the National Trust and a visit to this historic property is a must.

ACCOMMODATION: Centre Town Motel Nagambie, ph (03) 5794 2511; Nagambie Motor Inn and Conference Centre, ph (03) 5794 2833; Nagambie Lake Motel, ph (03) 5794 2300

ACTIVITIES: Bowls, croquet, fishing, golf, scenic drives, tennis, water sports, wineries

TOURIST INFORMATION: Ph (03) 5794 2647

NELSON

439 KM WEST OF MELBOURNE
POPULATION: 200   MAP REF: PAGE 92 A7

Nelson is a fishing hamlet located at the mouth of the Glenelg River in the far south-west of the state, 5 km from the border of South Australia and Victoria. Surrounded by the Discovery Bay Coastal Park and the Lower Glenelg National Park, it is the natural features around the town that attract visitors.

The Glenelg River flows out into Discovery Bay and anglers are drawn here in the hope of landing bass, southern black bream or Australian salmon. Boating is popular along the estuary and up into the park, especially canoeing, which is the best way to view the outstanding cliffs of the gorge area of the Glenelg River. Powerboats can use the lower section of the river outside the park area.

The Nelson Endeavour River Cruise is another way to view the scenery. This cruise also visits the Princess Margaret Rose Caves with their spectacular examples of stalactites, stalagmites and columns.

The Great Southwest Walk, a 250 km trek along the south-west of Victoria, runs through the Lower Glenelg Park. This is an arduous journey that takes about ten days and should be undertaken only by the fit, during the cooler months.

ACCOMMODATION: Motel Black Wattle, ph (03) 8738 4008; Pinehaven Chalet Motel, ph (03) 8738 4041

ACTIVITIES: Bushwalking, fishing, national park access, scenic drives, tennis, water sports

TOURIST INFORMATION: Ph (03) 5523 2671

NHILL

378 KM NORTH-WEST OF MELBOURNE
POPULATION: 1900   MAP REF: PAGE 94 C10

Located at the halfway point between Melbourne and Adelaide, Nhill is an important centre for the wheat industry in the Wimmera region. The town was first established in 1877 and wheat soon became the major industry in these vast western plains. Today Nhill boasts a huge turnover with a large wheat silo in town that can hold 2.25 million bushels of the golden grain.

South of Nhill lies the Little Desert National Park while to the north are the Big Desert Wilderness Park and Wyperfeld National Park. These parks offer a chance to drive or walk through the mallee scrub where you may catch a glimpse of the elusive mallee

fowl, a bird which builds a large mound to incubate its eggs. Wildflowers bloom throughout the parklands in spring, while the mallee bush is covered in yellow blooms. Carry water with you in these parks. Summer is extremely hot in this region and it is advisable not to travel into these parks during the warmer months.
ACCOMMODATION: Zero Inn, ph (03) 5391 1622; Nhill Oasis Motel, ph (03) 5391 1666; Motel Wimmera, ph (03) 5391 1444
ACTIVITIES: Bowls, bushwalking, fishing, golf, horseracing, horse riding, national park access, scenic drives, swimming, tennis
TOURIST INFORMATION: Ph (03) 5391 3086

NUMURKAH

215 KM NORTH OF MELBOURNE
POPULATION: 3600   MAP REF: PAGE 98 C3
A town surrounded by good soil, plentiful water and a constantly warm climate, Numurkah is an excellent base for the orchard industry. Only 35 km north of Shepparton, it is close to the fruit canning factories of Ardmona and the Shepparton Preserving Co. (SPC). Visitors can tour the SPC factory.

The area was first inhabited by squatters in the 1830s with more settlers arriving during the 1880s.

Brookfield Historic Farm has a restored hut, built in 1876 and used by early settlers, and a homestead which is set amid a large garden. The woolshed and farm machinery used by the pioneers can be seen.

The expansive waters of the Goulburn Valley region provide a natural haven for birds and wildlife, and the Murray River, only a short drive from Numurkah, offers excellent swimming, boating, fishing and birdwatching.
ACCOMMODATION: El Toro Motel, ph (03) 5862 1966; Numurkah Motel, ph (03) 5862 1922; Brookfield Historic Farm (cottages), ph (03) 5862 2353
ACTIVITIES: Bowls, fishing, golf, tennis, water sports
TOURIST INFORMATION: Ph (03) 5862 1866

OCEAN GROVE–BARWON HEADS

103 AND 99 KM SOUTH-WEST OF MELBOURNE
POPULATION: 8155   MAP REF: PAGE 93 M8
The twin townships of Ocean Grove and Barwon Heads are at the mouth of the Barwon River where it flows out into Bass Strait. Set amongst a picturesque seaside scene with more than 6 km of sandy beaches, these towns service the large number of tourists that flock to the Bellarine Peninsula every summer.

The township of Ocean Grove was originally settled in 1854 and apart from fishing, leather tanning was a major industry, utilising the bark from the many wattle trees in the area.

Smiths Beach is the major swimming area frequented by the local residents and tourists, while the waters off the beach are also popular with surfers, SCUBA divers, sailors and waterskiers.

Local attractions include A Maze N Things, which is popular with children. The complex has a large wooden maze along with mini-golf and a puzzle centre. The Moorfield Wildlife Park allows visitors to feed kangaroos and native birds in a natural setting.

The popular beach at Ocean Grove

Bushwalkers will delight in the parklands in the Foreshore Reserve and the Nature Reserve. Both of these parks have several walking trails. The foreshore offers magnificent views of the coast and Bass Strait.

Events in town include the Collendia Cup Ocean Grove Festival in March.
ACCOMMODATION: Ocean Grove Motor Inn, ph (03) 5256 2555; Boat Ramp Motel, ph (03) 5255 2018; The Terrace Lofts Bed and Breakfast (holiday units), ph (03) 5255 4167
ACTIVITIES: Bowls, bushwalking, fishing, golf, horse riding, scenic drives, tennis, water sports
TOURIST INFORMATION: Ph (03) 5222 2900

OMEO

408 KM EAST OF MELBOURNE
POPULATION: 274   MAP REF: PAGE 96 E3
High up in the hills above Bairnsdale is the historic township of Omeo, visited by snow skiers on their way to Mount Hotham and Dinner Plain. Owners of 4WD vehicles and horse riders also pass through during much of the year. This is true mountain cattle country and the flats down by the Livingstone and Tambo Rivers are home to the region's main industry of cattle farming.

The town was named by James McFarlane on his journey south, originally calling it 'Omeo B' and it served as a stopping point and cattle station for many years. There are a number of buildings in town including the court house which can be found in the Historical Park along with a large waterwheel.

Gold was discovered in Omeo during the early 1850s and thousands of prospectors besieged the township. The Omeo diggings, high up in the Alps, were among the roughest in Victoria. Two kilometres west of the town is the Oriental Claims Historical Area where the Chinese miners worked during the gold rush.

Fishing is popular in the local rivers along with gold panning in the Livingstone, while snow skiing

can be enjoyed at the higher towns of Dinner Plain and Mount Hotham.

Exploring by 4WD is popular in the region; this way you can visit some of the old goldmining sites and huge stampers that remain as a reminder of the era.

The Omeo Show is held in November, the Bush Picnic and Races in March and a Rodeo during Easter.
ACCOMMODATION: Omeo Motel, ph (03) 5159 1297; The Omeo Golden Age Private Hotel, ph (03) 5159 1344; Conbungra View Holiday Units, ph (03) 5159 1467
ACTIVITIES: Bowls, bushwalking, fishing, 4WD touring, gold fossicking, golf, historic interest, horse riding, scenic drives, tennis, water sports
TOURIST INFORMATION: Ph (03) 5159 1411

ORBOST

384 KM EAST OF MELBOURNE
POPULATION: 2515   MAP REF: PAGE 97 H5
The timber town of Orbost sits high in the forested mountains that support its main industry. First occupied during 1838, by 1842 settlers were using the flat swampland by the Snowy River to grow their crops. Today there are still crops flourishing in these fertile river flats.

The highly prized timber has always been a major industry and most of the hardwood is sent to the Brodribb Mill for processing. Much of the area is protected as parkland and the Rainforest Centre run by the Conservation Department details the intrinsic value of the temperate rainforests found in the area.

North of Orbost the Snowy River National Park offers excellent walking tracks and the Snowy River is popular with rafters and canoeists. Errinundra National Park further east is a plateau that is home to a magnificent cool temperate rainforest which features raised walking platforms and information boards. The slippery unsealed tracks also provide a challenge for drivers of 4WD vehicles.

The Slab Hut Information Centre on the edge of town was built by John Moore in 1872 and provides a wealth of information on the township of Orbost and the surrounding area. The hut is in parkland which is ideal for picnics.

The Snowy River Country Music Festival is held near here in January while the Orbost Show takes place in March.
ACCOMMODATION: Orbost Country Roads Motor Inn, ph (03) 5154 2500; Countryman Motor Inn, ph (03) 5154 1311; Killarney Bed and Breakfast, ph (03) 5154 1804
ACTIVITIES: Bowls, bushwalking, canoeing, fishing, 4WD touring, golf, national park access, scenic drives, squash, swimming, tennis
TOURIST INFORMATION: Ph (03) 5154 2424

OUYEN

442 KM NORTH-WEST OF MELBOURNE
POPULATION: 1335   MAP REF: PAGE 94 E5
Ouyen began as a railway station on the track from Melbourne to Mildura in the early 1900s. It was not

until 1910—quite late for settlement by Victoria's standards—that the town was opened up for settlement. Almost immediately sheep farming and wheat production began.

The pioneers of this region worked extremely hard removing the mallee scrub, including the large root ball at its base, in an effort to clear the land for wheat production. In town you can see the largest Australian mallee stump which remains in honour of the first settlers in Ouyen. The Local History Resource Centre also pays tribute to the town's heritage.

The Hattah–Kulkyne and Murray–Kulkyne parks are situated north of town. Stretching as far as the Murray River, the parks feature lagoons and waterways off this large watercourse. Another park worth visiting in the area is the Murray Sunset National Park with its undulating desert country, mallee scrub and large salt lakes, often referred to as the Pink Lakes as they take on a pink hue in overcast weather. All these parks offer a chance to glimpse the mallee fowl or any other of a number of birds which inhabit this region, especially along the lagoons of the Murray. Wildflowers are a beautiful sight in spring. The parks are best visited in a 4WD vehicle. Camping sites are available but visitors should take their own drinking water.

Festivals include the Mallee Festival and Vintage Train Trip in March, and the Ouyen Farmers' Festival in November.

ACCOMMODATION: Mallee View Motel, ph (03) 5092 2195; Hilltop Motel, ph (03) 5092 1410; Ouyen Motel, ph (03) 5092 1397
ACTIVITIES: Bowls, bushwalking, croquet, golf, horse riding, national park access, scenic drives, tennis, trotting, water sports
TOURIST INFORMATION: Ph (03) 5092 1763

PAYNESVILLE

306 KM EAST OF MELBOURNE
POPULATION: 2447   MAP REF: PAGE 96 E6

The boating resort town of Paynesville sits amongst the sheltered waters of the McMillan Straits in Gippsland near the large coastal community of Lakes Entrance. The inland waters of the lakes are protected by dunes and coastal headlands. Large powerboats and yachts are used on the lakes and yacht races are held in summer.

The influence of the boating community is also evident on a most unusual church, St Peter by the Lake, built in 1961. It has a limestone spire that is shaped like a lighthouse and a pulpit designed to resemble the bow of a fishing boat. Like a beacon, the cross of the church can be seen by anglers on the lakes and church-goers can look out onto Lake Victoria through tall windows behind the altar.

Raymond Island is popular with bushwalkers and can be accessed by a car ferry from the township of Paynesville. Rotamah Island lies between the Ninety Mile Beach and Lake Victoria, providing a protected bird and wildlife habitat in the coastal woodland and sand dunes. This island is perfect for bushwalking and birdwatching.

Other parkland includes the Lakes National Park and Gippsland Lakes Coastal Park, both of which offer protection of the fragile seaside environment.

A Sunday market is held every second week on the Esplanade with handicrafts and home-made produce for sale while yachting championships are held during Easter and Christmas.

ACCOMMODATION: Mariners Cove Resort (motel), ph (03) 5156 7444; The Crowes Nest Bed and Breakfast, ph (03) 5156 6699; Crystal Cruises (cruisers), ph (03) 5156 6971
ACTIVITIES: Bowls, fishing, golf, horse riding, national park access, scenic drives, tennis, water sports
TOURIST INFORMATION: Ph (03) 5152 3444

PENSHURST

282 KM WEST OF MELBOURNE
POPULATION: 483   MAP REF: PAGE 92 E?

On the Hamilton Highway between Hamilton and Mortlake in the west of the state is Penshurst, a small farming town that also services the smaller communities in the region.

Perched above Penshurst is Mt Rouse which is 339 metres high and offers commanding views of the countryside and the Grampians district which lies to the north of the town.

The Grampians represent the starting point of the Great Dividing Range. The Grampians National Park is popular with bushwalkers, climbers and bird-watchers. During spring the area is covered with wildflowers and the birds are active making nests.

There are also lakes in the area which are popular for water sports and swimming. They include Lake Linlithgow and Lake Swallow which are both on Chatsworth Road and where yachting, waterskiing and fishing can be enjoyed year round.

The Penshurst Agricultural Show is held in December.

ACCOMMODATION: Burnbrae Bed and Breakfast, ph (03) 5576 5499
ACTIVITIES: Bowls, croquet, golf, horse racing, national park access, scenic drives, tennis, water sports
TOURIST INFORMATION: Ph (03) 5572 3746

PETERBOROUGH

246 KM WEST OF MELBOURNE
POPULATION: 210   MAP REF: PAGE 92 G9

Peterborough is in the west of the state on the Great Ocean Road. The famous road winds its way along the coastline from Torquay and provides spectacular coastal views of huge cliffs towering above the road and of the beaches below. The township is at the entrance of Curdies Inlet where the surfing is good while swimming and windsurfing are favoured sports in the relevant safety of the protected waters of Curdies Inlet.

The coastline is the major attraction of the area. Off the coast along the Great Ocean Road near Peter-borough is the Bay of Islands, a unique cluster of rocks that have formed small islands. Another similar group is the Bay of Martyrs which also has these rock pillars. More rock formations and rugged cliffs can be found at Crofts Bay and Childers Cove. Massacre Bay offers a secluded beach area popular with anglers.

The rugged coastline at Peterborough

The road between Peterborough and Port Campbell offers magnificent views of the natural rock pillars and cliffs of Loch Ard Gorge, London Bridge and the Arch, all of which are protected in the Port Campbell National Park.

ACCOMMODATION: Peterborough Motel, ph (03) 5598 5251; Schomberg Inn (hotel/motel), ph (03) 55985285
ACTIVITIES: Bushwalking, fishing, golf, national park access, scenic drives, tennis, water sports
TOURIST INFORMATION: Ph (03) 5237 6529

PHILLIP ISLAND

130 KM SOUTH OF MELBOURNE
POPULATION: 4995   MAP REF: PAGE 91 H7

This island, which is connected to the mainland via a long bridge between Newhaven and San Remo, has long been a popular holiday resort for Melbournians. Its attractions have grown recently, with the Phillip Island Race Track hosting rounds of the Motorcycle Grand Prix and the World Superbike Championships.

The first European to see the island was George Bass in 1798. First known as Snapper Island, its name was later changed to honour Governor Phillip. It was used as a military settlement in the early 1800s before farmers moved in during the 1840s.

Cowes is the main town on the island and has safe beaches for swimming. It makes an excellent base for touring the island. The other main towns are Newhaven, Ventnor and Rhyll.

Wildlife has always been an attraction of Phillip Island. The fairy penguin parade is one of Victoria's main attractions and each evening busloads of tourists venture to Summerland Beach to watch these tiny creatures walk onto the beaches to their burrows.

Koalas can be seen at various locations on the island. For a closer look you can go to the Koala Conservation Centre at Summerland Beach.

Phillip Island also boasts a large colony of fur seals, at times as many as 6000, and these can be seen at Seal Rock on the Cowes–Nobbies road. A ferry also runs each day from Cowes to the north of the island allowing exceptional views of the seals at play. The

Reefworld Marine Aquarium has a tropical aquarium that is home to more than 4000 fish.

Natural features include the Blow Hole, the Nobbies (a large stack of rocks), and magnificent sandy beaches combined with a rugged coastline.

The Phillip Island Heritage Centre in Cowes outlines the history of the island from Aborigines through to the whalers, sealers and farmers.

Wineries are relatively new to the island but are worth visiting: the Phillip Island Vineyard and Winery is the only permanently netted vineyard in Australia. The nets protect the grapes from birds and from the powerful wind gusts that blow in from Bass Strait.

ACCOMMODATION: Also see Cowes listing. The Continental Phillip Island Motel, ph (03) 5052 2316; Watini Waters (B&B), ph (03) 5956 6300; Coleshill Lodge Motel, ph (03) 5956 9304; The Gatehouse Cottage, ph (03) 5956 9406

ACTIVITIES: Bowling, bushwalking, fishing, golf, horse riding, scenic drives, tennis, water sports, wildlife

TOURIST INFORMATION: Ph (03) 5956 7447

POINT LONSDALE

105 KM SOUTH-WEST OF MELBOURNE
POPULATION: 1740   MAP REF: PAGE 93 N8

The town of Point Lonsdale at the small entrance into Port Phillip Bay originally served as a signal station in 1854 for ships entering the bay. The signal station was replaced by a large lighthouse in 1902 which is still in service. Point Lonsdale has always played a major part in Port Phillip's shipping industry.

The 'rip', as the treacherous waters of the entrance are known, has taken its toll on many ships over the years. Vessels can be seen sailing in and out of the rip at Rip View Lookout.

Swimming is best enjoyed on the Front Beach inside Port Phillip Bay while the surf beach is on the Bass Strait side of the head. Walking tracks and a cycling track follow the foreshore right around the head. The area is also protected in reserves.

On the Point Lonsdale Road the Marconi Memorial marks the site where the first broadcast was made to Tasmania in 1906. It is named after the radio equipment which was supplied by Marconi Wireless Company.

The lighthouse at Point Lonsdale, built in 1902

Point Lonsdale is close to the seaside town of Queenscliff; a ferry crosses the bay from here to Sorrento each day.

ACCOMMODATION: Lighthouse Resort Motel, ph (03) 5281 1142; Queenscliff Motel, ph (03) 5258 2970; Lonsdale Villas (holiday units), ph (03) 5258 4533

ACTIVITIES: Bowls, fishing, horse riding, scenic drives, tennis, water sports

TOURIST INFORMATION: Ph (03) 5222 2900

POREPUNKAH

310 KM NORTH-EAST OF MELBOURNE
POPULATION: 385   MAP REF: PAGE 96 B1

Set in the picturesque Buckland Valley where the Ovens and Buckland Rivers meet is the township of Porepunkah. The eastern border of the Mount Buffalo National Park lies on the edge of the town while the Alpine National Park is off to the east.

The township owes its start to a gold rush in the 1850s when many miners came to the Ovens Valley. Eventually the gold petered out and farming became the main industry.

With the attractions of the nearby parkland and the beautiful towns of Bright and Mount Beauty, this area is perfect for scenic drives. It is particularly lovely in autumn when the leaves on the trees turn to shades of copper and gold.

Snow skiing is popular at Mt Buffalo in winter while bushwalking, horse riding, 4WD touring, rock climbing and hang gliding are enjoyed through the rest of the year.

Wineries based in the Ovens Valley include Boynton's of Bright, famous for its hospitality and magnificent views of Mt Buffalo.

ACCOMMODATION: Buffalo Motel, ph (03) 5756 2242; Porepunkah (hotel/motel), ph (03) 5756 2391; Buckland Valley Bed and Breakfast, ph (03) 5756 2656

ACTIVITIES: Bushwalking, fishing, gold fossicking, golf, hang gliding, horse riding, national park access, rock climbing, scenic drives, snow skiing, swimming

TOURIST INFORMATION: Ph (03) 5755 2275

PORT ALBERT

231 KM SOUTH-EAST OF MELBOURNE
POPULATION: 310   MAP REF: PAGE 96 B9

The coastal town of Port Albert lies on the coast south of Yarram behind Sunday Island, part of Nooramunga Marine and Coastal Park.

The harbour was first sighted by Angus McMillan in 1841. The township was originally known as New Leith, but this was changed to honour Prince Albert, husband of Queen Victoria. The port was most important in the early days and it was the only port for Gippsland until the 1870s. The railway was finally linked all the way to Sale in 1878 when rail became the preferred method of travel.

The port today is mainly used by a fishing fleet, along with recreational anglers who frequent the sheltered waters of this quiet little town. Robertson's Beach is ideal for swimming and there are other good beaches further along the coastline towards Seaspray in the east.

The Maritime Museum in Tarraville Road displays a large range of artefacts and photographs of maritime activities along with navigational equipment. There is also a reference library at this museum.

ACCOMMODATION: Port Albert Holiday Homes (cottages), ph (03) 5183 2677

ACTIVITIES: Bushwalking, fishing, historic interest, scenic drives, water sports

TOURIST INFORMATION: Ph (03) 5655 2233

PORT CAMPBELL

234 KM WEST OF MELBOURNE
POPULATION: 200   MAP REF: PAGE 93 H9

Situated near the major attractions of the Great Ocean Road in the south-west of the state, Port Campbell is a small crayfishing village. It also plays host to the large number of tourists who visit this coast renowned for its shipwrecks.

On the lengthy voyage to and from England during the 1800s and early 1900s, the ruthless southern coastline of Australia was considered one of the worst stretches of the journey. Many ships met their end along the coastline of what is now the Port Campbell National Park. The most famous is the *Loch Ard* which was wrecked in 1878 claiming the lives of

The Twelve Apostles in Port Campbell National Park

52 people. The Loch Ard Gorge is on the stretch of road from Port Campbell, east to Princetown, along with a number of other notable clusters of islands off the coastline such as the Blow Hole, Mutton Bird Island and Elephant Rock. London Bridge is another formation which was once a double arch resembling

London Bridge, but it collapsed in 1990, stranding sightseers, and is now a detached landmass.

Without doubt the most spectacular landmark on the whole of the Victorian coastline and the most photographed is the Twelve Apostles, offshore stacks which have eroded over the years, with only eight now left standing above the water line.

A number of walks can be found near Port Campbell including the Port Campbell Discovery Walk which covers 2.5 km. It starts near the Port Campbell beach and takes in some of the delights of the national park. To the north is the township of Timboon where a 5 km walk leads to a magnificent railway trestle bridge.

ACCOMMODATION: Port Campbell Motor Inn, ph (03) 5598 6222; Southern Ocean Motor Inn, ph (03) 5598 6231; Loch Ard Motor Inn, ph (03) 5598 6328

ACTIVITIES: Bushwalking, fishing, national park access, scenic drives, tennis, water sports

TOURIST INFORMATION: Ph (03) 5237 6529

PORT FAIRY

293 KM WEST OF MELBOURNE
POPULATION: 2505   MAP REF: PAGE 92 E8

The fishing town of Port Fairy is one of the main ports supplying a major share of Victoria's abalone and crayfish catch. Port Fairy is one of the state's oldest ports and many of the buildings date back to the nineteenth century with more than 50 classified by the National Trust. Situated at the mouth of the Moyne River, this was originally a whaling centre, but fishing and tourism are now the main industries.

A walk through the town highlights many of the historic buildings such as Motts Cottage in Sackville Street. The restored stone home of pioneer Charles Mills can be found on Woddbine Road. The Port Fairy Historical Society located in the old court house contains displays of photographs and memorabilia.

Another interesting walk is along the jetty on the Moyne River where the fishing fleet dock.

Griffith Island, off the eastern coast of Port Fairy, was once the site of a large whaling station. It is now home to a colony of muttonbirds that make their nests on the island in September. The Port Fairy Lighthouse is at the far eastern point of the island.

Further afield is Mount Eccles National Park, home to an extinct volcano.

The Moyneyana Festival is held over January while the Port Fairy Folk Festival features in the Labour Day festivities.

ACCOMMODATION: Seacombe House Motor Inn, ph (03) 5568 1082; Lady Julia Percy Motel, ph (03) 5568 1800

ACTIVITIES: Bowls, fishing, golf, national park access, scenic drives, squash, tennis, water sports

TOURIST INFORMATION: Ph (03) 5568 2682

PORTARLINGTON

105 KM SOUTH-WEST OF MELBOURNE
POPULATION: 2565   MAP REF: PAGE 93 N7

Safe ocean swimming and excellent beaches see the population of Portarlington swell during the summer months. Situated on the Bellarine Peninsula, only 32 km from Geelong, there is reputedly good fishing in these waters of Port Phillip Bay.

The town was originally named after Lord Arlington in 1851; it grew quickly and a steam-powered flour mill was in operation by 1856. This enormous four-storeyed sandstone building is now classified by the National Trust. It houses historic displays from the area along with those pertaining to local Aboriginal history.

The waters of Portarlington are used for a range of activities including sailing, fishing and snorkelling.

Portarlington's historic steam-powered flour mill

The Bellarine Peninsula has a proud history of wine-making. Near Portarlington is Kilgour Estate on McAdams Lane in Bellarine and Mt Duneed winery is on Feehans Road.

The Geelong Gourmet Wine and Food Fair is held on Australia Day in January.

ACCOMMODATION: Portarlington Beach Motel, ph (03) 5259 3801; Claremont House Portarlington (B&B), ph (03) 5259 3551; Portarlington Holiday Resort (holiday flats), ph (03) 5259 2910

ACTIVITIES: Bowls, croquet, fishing, golf, tennis, water sports, wineries

TOURIST INFORMATION: Ph (03) 5258 3403

PORTLAND

367 KM WEST OF MELBOURNE
POPULATION: 11 000   MAP REF: PAGE 92 C8

The historic town of Portland is surrounded by rich grazing land and has a large number of buildings which are classified by the National Trust. Portland was originally established as a whaling and sealing port in the early 1800s because of the deep waters of Portland Bay, but that industry gave way to fishing and grazing when the number of whales decreased in the mid-1800s. Farmers used the port to ship their goods to Melbourne, as this was quicker than travelling by road. The area still relies on grazing and fishing along with tourism.

An aluminium smelter has been established in the town and this has helped boost the town's economy.

Amongst the classified buildings are the Old Steam Packet Inn which was built in 1842 using timber from Tasmania and local bluestone, and Burswood which was built in 1856 and is now a bed and breakfast accommodation house with impressive gardens. In the botanic gardens near Henty Park is a delightful old cottage which has been fully restored and furnished in its original 1857 style.

A walking track from the park circles Fawthrop Lagoon and leads to the vintage car club museum. This wetland is fed by the incoming tide and contains unusual plant life and numerous birds which take refuge in the wildlife reserve. Penguins also frequent Portland and can be found at Henty Beach on the harbour foreshore. An artificial habitat has been created for these birds which have declined in numbers over the years.

Attractions in the region include the Great South West Walk, a 250 km trek along the coastline of western Victoria which begins just west of Portland. The walk is divided into 17 separate sections which vary in length from 8 to 22 km. A more leisurely walk can be enjoyed amidst the unique sandstone formations near Cape Bridgewater which is known as the Petrified Forest. Cape Bridgewater is also home to the last manned lighthouse in Victoria and can be found to the west of town.

The Portland Show is held in February while the Dahlia Festival is on show during the long weekend in March. The Three Bays Running Marathon takes place in mid-November while the Surfboat Marathon is held in December.

ACCOMMODATION: Hotel Bentinck (hotel/motel), ph (03) 5523 2188; The Richmond Henty Hotel (hotel/motel), ph (03) 5523 1032; Victorian House Portland (private hotel) classified by National Trust, ph (03) 5521 7577

ACTIVITIES: Bowls, bushwalking, croquet, fishing, golf, horse riding, scenic drives, tennis, water sports

TOURIST INFORMATION: Ph (03) 5523 2671

PORTSEA

95 KM SOUTH OF MELBOURNE
POPULATION: 750   MAP REF: PAGE 93 N8

Portsea has long been a favourite holiday destination for Melbournians, especially the wealthy, as is clear from the number of large and expensive homes that grace the area. It is also well known as the place where the then Australian Prime Minister Harold Holt disappeared in 1967 when swimming in the waters off Cheviot Beach.

Despite this unfortunate accident, Portsea has some excellent beaches for swimming, although it is surfing that is the real attraction to many. The back beach of Portsea has become legendary amongst surfers. Here you will also find plenty of rockpools to investigate at low tide.

Portsea has always been regarded as the 'fashionable' place to be seen down at the beach, along with the neighbouring suburb of Sorrento and the strip of coast between these two towns. Here are a number of trendy cafés and restaurants as well as fish and chip shops that serve up the local catch.

The historic mansion Delgany Country House Hotel, built as a castle in 1920, is now a privately owned guesthouse.

The Mornington Peninsula has a large number of wineries which are open to the public, mostly on the weekends. The more interesting include Peninsula

Estate at Red Hill where you can listen to a jazz band while tasting the wines on long weekends, or Hann's Creek Estate at Merricks North where you can try your hand at a game of boule.

Portsea was named by a settler in the area, James Ford, after an area in Portsmouth, his home town in England. Originally a lime burner settlement, a quarantine station was built in town during 1856 after disease killed more than 80 men who were aboard the ship *Ticonderoga* anchored in the waters of the bay. The area was also used as a School of Army Health as part of Portsea's Military Area. Tours are available of the old Quarantine Station Museum and the Army Health Services Museum which are part of the Mornington Peninsula National Park.

Portsea Surf Beach and the surf beaches of Sorrento, Rye and Gunnamatta also form part of the Mornington Peninsula National Park. There are a number of interesting walking tracks, the most popular being the Farnsworth Track which covers the area from Portsea to the London Bridge rock formation taking in heathlands and beach areas and offering excellent coastal views from the clifftops.

ACCOMMODATION: Delgany Country House Hotel, ph (03) 5984 4000
ACTIVITIES: Bushwalking, fishing, golf, national park access, tennis, water sports
TOURIST INFORMATION: Ph (03) 5984 5678

POWELLTOWN

85 KM EAST OF MELBOURNE
POPULATION: 120   MAP REF: PAGE 91 L3

The small settlement of Powelltown is based on the timber which can be found deep in the mountain ash forests on the edge of the Great Dividing Range and across the east of the state. It was named in honour of the Powell timber company that worked the timber processing plant. Mills have been operating in Powelltown for over a century and a mill still operates in the town.

In the early 1900s tramlines were established with gentle grades so that the logs could be hauled by teams of horses, providing the only access into the thick forest. By 1915, steam engines were brought in to haul the logs, and later these were superseded by motorised locomotives. A huge fire ravaged the area in 1939 and unfortunately much of the timber and the infrastructure of the timber industry were destroyed. Logging roads were then built and large trucks were used to haul the timber. An excellent forestry office in Powelltown has brochures and information on scenic drives along with forest walks.

This region lends itself to scenic drives, whether on the bitumen or well-formed gravel roads with either a conventional vehicle or a 4WD. With the latter you can take some of the logging and forestry roads and get a close look at the tall timbers.

Attractions of the area include the Seven Acre Rock which is a rocky outcrop offering superb views of the nearby Bunyip State Park and even as far as Western Port Bay on a clear day.

There are many interesting walks in the forest and a 3.6 km loop will take you to the Ada Tree, an enormous mountain ash tree which is believed to be more than 300 years old. The tree is 76 metres tall and with a circumference of 15 metres dwarfs everything around it. The Ada Tree is accessed via the Ada River Road off the Powelltown–Noojee road.

ACCOMMODATION: Bush camping sites outside town
ACTIVITIES: Bushwalking, 4WD touring, scenic drives
TOURIST INFORMATION: Ph (03) 5966 7203

QUEENSCLIFF

108 KM SOUTH-WEST OF MELBOURNE
POPULATION: 1935   MAP REF: PAGE 93 N7

Victoria has many seaside resorts on its shores, but nothing that is as elegant as Queenscliff on the Bellarine Peninsula. A short trip on a car ferry from Sorrento takes you to Queenscliff where grand historic hotels offer superb dining and accommodation.

In 1842 Queenscliff was a settlement for the customs house, lighthouse and pilot station at the entrance to Port Phillip Bay. By 1880 this seaside town had become a very fashionable resort for Melbournians who would travel by steamboat across the waters of the bay.

While it is the grand hotels and magnificent views that attract tourists, there are plenty of historic attractions to investigate on a visit to Queenscliff. The Maritime Museum has recorded the maritime history of the bay and houses artefacts such as the town's old lifeboat. Photographs, maps and records of early life in Queenscliff and the Port Phillip Bay Heads region can be found at the Historical Museum in the centre of town. Fort Queenscliff is one of the largest historic military fortresses in Australia and has been preserved as a museum.

Every Sunday steam train enthusiasts operate the Bellarine Peninsula Railway offering visitors a journey from Queenscliff to Lakers Siding 5 km away, or to Drysdale on the other side of the peninsula. The train is hauled by authentic steam engines which the group has acquired from around Australia and is a must for train buffs.

ACCOMMODATION: Ozone Hotel (classified by National Trust), ph (03) 5258 1011; Vue Grand Hotel (private hotel), ph (03) 5258 1544; Maytone by the Sea (guesthouse), ph (03) 5258 4059
ACTIVITIES: Bowls, bushwalking, croquet, fishing, golf, horse riding, scenic drives, tennis, water sports
TOURIST INFORMATION: Ph (03) 5258 3403

RED CLIFFS

532 KM NORTH-WEST OF MELBOURNE
POPULATION: 5440   MAP REF: PAGE 94 E2

Situated only 8 km south of Mildura in the heart of Victoria's Sunraysia country, Red Cliffs has expanded over the years to become a suburb of Mildura. This region boasts a true Mediterranean climate which is why a visit will reveal endless rows of vineyards and large crops of citrus fruit and olives growing in the red sandy soil.

Named after the vivid red cliffs which form the banks of the nearby Murray River, the town was first established in the 1890s when the Chaffey brothers from Canada selected land in the area with the

Red Cliffs is well known for its vineyards

intention of installing irrigation systems, as had been successfully carried out in nearby Renmark, utilising the copious quantities of water found in the Murray River. The towering red cliffs, however, were to prove an obstacle for their scheme and the area remained undeveloped for many years.

After World War I the region was part of the soldier settlement scheme and was cleared to make way for farming land. The mallee scrub with its huge root system is tough to remove from the soil and horses and tractors were used to flatten the land.

Modern technology has meant that water can now easily be pumped up over the imposing cliffs and this has seen the growth of the town in the latter half of the twentieth century. The Red Cliffs Pumping Station irrigates more than 5000 hectares of land and Cliff View near the station overlooks the Murray, more than 70 metres below.

Wineries include Lindeman's Karadoc south of Red Cliffs which is an enormous vineyard.

The Country Music Festival is held in late September, while the Lunarfest is held in late March.

ACCOMMODATION: Red Cliffs Colonial Motor Lodge, ph (03) 5024 1060; Big Lizzie Motor Inn, ph (03) 5024 2691; Mirrabinda (B&B), ph (03) 5024 1520
ACTIVITIES: Bowls, bushwalking, croquet, fishing, golf, horse riding, scenic drives, tennis, water sports, wineries
TOURIST INFORMATION: Ph (03) 5024 2866

ROCHESTER

181 KM NORTH OF MELBOURNE
POPULATION: 2540   MAP REF: PAGE 93 N1

Originally known as Rowe's Camp, this town, situated on the banks of the Campaspe River 47 km south of Echuca, went through two name changes, first becoming Rowechester, before finally settling on the

current name Rochester in 1865. Dr John Rowe was the first European settler in the region—he set up a hotel catering for travellers. The town remained small until the railway from Bendigo to Echuca was built in 1864 and with this new form of transport available for produce and people, the town flourished.

The establishment of nearby reservoirs for irrigation such as the Waranga Basin and Lake Eppalock meant that the area could support dairy farming, fruit orchards and lucerne crops.

The dairy industry is the mainstay of the community today and Rochester is home to a large dairy processing plant, one of many to be found throughout the Goulburn Valley region.

Rochester was the birthplace of the champion cyclist, Hubert 'Oppy' Opperman; the Autumn Family Festival in April holds cycling races and a triathlon. The Great Northern Show is held in February.

ACCOMMODATION: Rochester Motel, ph (03) 5484 1077

ACTIVITIES: Bowls, fishing, golf, horse riding, scenic drives, squash, tennis, water sports

TOURIST INFORMATION: Ph (03) 5480 7555

ROSEBUD

78 KM SOUTH OF MELBOURNE
POPULATION: 13 275   MAP REF: PAGE 93 N8

Many Melbournians remember holidays on the Rosebud Foreshore, where hundreds of caravans and tents merged during the summer months to form a seashore community. Other families built or rented beach houses and would come from Melbourne every weekend to enjoy the sun and beach. The district is still popular today, although the seaside town has grown considerably.

Rosebud and the neighbouring town of Dromana are on the edge of Port Phillip Bay and have safe swimming beaches and shady foreshores. The township is named after a vessel which ran aground in this part of the bay in 1851.

The Mornington Peninsula has many attractions to offer visitors including the large Mornington Peninsula National Park on the south-western side of the peninsula where you will find the surf beaches of Gunnamatta and Sorrento Back Beach. There are also opportunities for bushwalking and the Coastal Walk stretching from Cape Schanck near the lighthouse to Bushrangers Bay at the southern end of the park is a scenic trek of 6 km.

On the third Saturday of every month markets are held on Boneo Road, in nearby Boneo, offering handcrafts and fresh produce.

ACCOMMODATION: Bayview Motor Inn, ph (03) 5981 1333; The Admiral Motel, ph (03) 5986 8933; Copper Lantern Motel, ph (03) 5986 2220

ACTIVITIES: Bowls, bushwalking, fishing, golf, horse riding, tennis, water sports

TOURIST INFORMATION: Ph (03) 5987 3078

ROSEDALE

193 KM EAST OF MELBOURNE
POPULATION: 1155   MAP REF: PAGE 96 B7

Rosedale is situated on the banks of the Latrobe River between the regional centres of Traralgon and Sale. Originally used as a stopping point for the stage coach which ran between these towns, Rosedale is now the centre of a pastoral region.

Rosedale occupies the land that was originally the Holey Plain Cattle Run which was taken up by Edward Crooke. He used the property to hold cattle that he drove down from Omeo before they were transported to market by sea. The Holey Plains State Park, to the east of town on the Princes Highway, is named after the property. This park is home to a diversity of trees and plants, many endemic to this region, such as the Gippsland grey box, golden grevillea and the rare Holey Plains mintbush.

Merriman Creek flows to the south of the park and waterfowl make use of the Big Winch Swamp and the clear waters of the lake. A network of walking trails allow visitors to explore this whole area. In spring wildflowers carpet much of the ground and this is the best time for a visit.

ACCOMMODATION: Coach Lamp Motel, ph (03) 5199 2301; Rosedale Motel, ph (03) 5199 2555

ACTIVITIES: Bowls, bushwalking, fishing, golf, scenic drives, squash, swimming, tennis

TOURIST INFORMATION: Ph (03) 5144 1108

RUSHWORTH

168 KM NORTH OF MELBOURNE
POPULATION: 1000   MAP REF: PAGE 93 P1

Gold was discovered in this region in 1853 and this eventually led to the establishment of the town of Rushworth, 100 km north of Bendigo in the Goulburn Valley. At the peak of the gold rush there were 26 mines operating in the area with more than 40 000 miners. The early name for the area was Nuggety and the prosperous Nuggety–Whroo goldfields were active until the 1870s.

Many of the buildings in the old mining town of Rushworth are classified by the National Trust, including St Paul's Church of England, the Imperial Hotel and the band rotunda.

The Waranga Basin on the outskirts of town is a huge reservoir which supplies water via more than 350 km of irrigation channels to the Wimmera and the Mallee in the state's west. Built between 1903 and 1905 on a large swamp, it is contained by a large earthen embankment more than 7 km long and with a capacity of 410 000 megalitres. This basin is also popular for boating, waterskiing and fishing.

ACCOMMODATION: Rushworth Resorts (hotel/motel), ph (03) 5856 1090; Waranga Holiday Camp (lodge), ph (03) 5856 1243

ACTIVITIES: Bowls, bushwalking, fishing, gold fossicking, golf, horse riding, scenic drives, tennis, water sports

TOURIST INFORMATION: Ph (03) 5831 4400

RUTHERGLEN

277 KM NORTH-EAST OF MELBOURNE
POPULATION: 1880   MAP REF: PAGE 98 F3

Rutherglen is a major wine producing region and lies in the north-east of the state, although its origins began in the gold rush. Gold was first discovered in the 1850s, but Rutherglen's original wine-maker, Lindsay Brown, was not smitten with the lust for gold and planted vines in the area instead.

The gold fever was not to last and unfortunately the vineyards also suffered, first through the demise of the gold rush, then because of disease which struck the plants, and finally as a result of the depression years of the 1930s.

At this time the fields were ploughed and sheep and cattle grazing took over the land and it was not

Cheviot Beach in the Mornington Peninsula National Park, south of Rosebud

until the 1970s that the wine industry started to revive once again in this area.

Wineries to visit include the R. L. Buller and Sons Rutherglen Winery, the Morris Winery, and Campbells Winery. Many of the region's wineries are within a short drive from town and you can hire bicycles and pedal your way around the vineyards.

Other attractions include the old water tower which is shaped like a wine bottle, and the local museum which is housed in the old school building. The main street has several historic buildings including the old hotel, post office and court house, all of which are classified by the National Trust.

A Spring Wine and Arts Show is held in the region during September.

ACCOMMODATION: Rutherglen Motor Inn, ph (03) 6032 9776; Star Hotel Motel, ph (03) 6032 9625; Wine Village Motor Inn, ph (03) 6032 9900
ACTIVITIES: Boating, bowls, cycling, fishing, golf, scenic drives, wineries
TOURIST INFORMATION: Ph (03) 6032 9166

RYE

83 KM SOUTH OF MELBOURNE
POPULATION: 7285   MAP REF: PAGE 90 G6
Rye is a popular bayside resort on the edge of Port Phillip Bay. It was originally known as White Cliffs because of the limestone deposits from which lime was produced for use in mortar in the 1800s. There is a reconstructed lime kiln on the foreshore.

Road access was a problem in the early years and it was not until a port and jetty were built in 1860 that this isolated township began to grow.

Rye has both a back beach and front beach; the front, or Foreshore Reserve, is frequented by families. This sandy stretch offers safe swimming, foreshore camping, a boat ramp and the Rye Jetty. Fishing is popular here with flathead, snapper, whiting and mullet among the most commonly caught. The back beach is situated in the Mornington Peninsula National Park and is popular with surfers as it offers more of a challenging swim. Australian salmon and mullet can be caught here.

Other popular seaside towns near Rye include Sorrento, Rosebud, Dromana and Portsea, while on the other side of the Mornington Peninsula, looking out to Phillip and French Islands, are the quiet beach villages of Somers, Merricks and Hastings.
ACCOMMODATION: Hilltonia Homestead (B&B), ph (03) 5985 2654; Moonlight Bay Resort, ph (03) 5985 7499; Annies Cottage, ph (03) 5988 7097
ACTIVITIES: Bowls, fishing, golf, horse riding, tennis, water sports
TOURIST INFORMATION: Ph (03) 5987 3078

ST ARNAUD

247 KM NORTH-WEST OF MELBOURNE
POPULATION: 3480   MAP REF: PAGE 93 H1
St Arnaud on the Sunraysia Highway was, like many towns in this region, originally part of a farming community which then grew when gold was discovered in 1855. Many of the prospectors who

descended on the town came from other mining regions and the town was named 'New Bendigo' in the hope that it would yield the same rewards as the fields in Bendigo. Unfortunately not all the miners struck it rich in St Arnaud and the last of the mines closed in 1926, giving way to the pastoral industry.

Like many of the towns built during the gold-mining era, there are substantial buildings in the main streets, many of which have ornate lace work on their verandas. The town was named after a French commander in the Crimean War and the streets are named in honour of the British commanders.

Pioneer Park in the centre of town is home to the angling club and local swimming pool. Other notable parks include King George's, Bicentennial Park and Queen Mary Gardens. The latter has a pond that was once the watering hole for bullock teams that hauled goods in the region. The Historical Museum is housed in an old building which was once the fire station while the old post office is now home to an art gallery.

Annual events in the town include the St Arnaud Show which is held on the first Saturday in October.
ACCOMMODATION: St Arnaud Country Road Inn (motel), ph (03) 5495 2255; Motel St Arnaud, ph (03) 5495 1755; Old Post Office Bed and Breakfast, ph (03) 5495 2313
ACTIVITIES: Bowls, bushwalking, croquet, fishing, golf, horse riding, horseracing, scenic drives, tennis, trotting, water sports
TOURIST INFORMATION: Ph (03) 5495 2313

ST LEONARDS

114 KM SOUTH-WEST OF MELBOURNE
POPULATION: 1023   MAP REF: PAGE 93 N7
A delightful seaside town on the eastern edge of the Bellarine Peninsula, St Leonards and its small sister town of Indented Head are popular summer retreats.

Matthew Flinders landed here in 1802. A stone cairn in Batman Park at Indented Head indicates the site where John Batman landed during his expedition along the coast in 1835.

The area was first settled during the 1850s when pioneers ran a leather tanning industry using the bark from the wattle trees for tanning the leather. A timber industry was also established, along with fishing which was lucrative in the waters of Port Phillip Bay.

St Leonards boasts a golf course and a delightful foreshore where camping is allowed to the north of the jetty. South of town, on the foreshore past the yacht club, is Edwards Point State Fauna Reserve which provides a habitat for birds including the rare orange-bellied parrot.

St Leonards is close to the popular resort of Queenscliff where the car ferry sails every day to and from Portsea and Sorrento.

Vineyards have been established on the Bellarine Peninsula for years and close to St Leonards is Kilgour Estate and Scotchman's Hill, the largest of the wineries on the peninsula.
ACCOMMODATION: St Leonards Hotel, ph (03) 5257 1408
ACTIVITIES: Bowls, fishing, golf, tennis, water sports, wineries
TOURIST INFORMATION: Ph (03) 5222 2900

SALE

220 KM SOUTH-EAST OF MELBOURNE
POPULATION: 13 858   MAP REF: PAGE 96 C7
Surrounded by pastoral land in the heart of Gippsland is the regional centre of Sale which services the outlying farm areas and smaller communities. It also acts as an administrative centre for the offshore oil and gas fields of eastern Victoria.

The town is some 25 km overland to the coast, but Sale was connected to the Gippsland Lakes by way of the Thomson and Latrobe Rivers. A canal was built allowing paddle-steamers to carry produce to Lakes Entrance from where it was shipped to Melbourne.

The Sale Canal and port can be found just off the main highway at Cullen Park. Further along the canal is the swing bridge, built across the Latrobe River in 1883. The bridge provided a route across the river to Port Albert, the main port of entry to Gippsland in the mid-1800s. Trade in the town increased with the arrival of the Eastern Railway Line.

Our Lady of Sion Convent in Sale, built of pressed brick

The name Sale comes from a general in the British Army, Sir Robert Sale, who died in battle on the Northwest Frontier Province in India.

There are many features of interest in this old town, including the ornate St Paul's Cathedral which was originally built in 1885; Bishops Court, residence of the Bishop of Gippsland, constructed in 1885; and the Our Lady of Sion Convent, built in 1892–1901.

Bon Accord Tea Rooms are housed in an attractive Victorian homestead surrounded by farmland and lush gardens.

Lake Guthridge in the centre of town houses a bird sanctuary. Situated near Lake Guthridge is the Historical Museum which offers a well-documented history of the town and the region.

Sale is also a gateway to the outer Gippsland region and the alpine High Country to the north.
ACCOMMODATION: The King Avenue Motor Inn, ph (03) 5143 2222; Aspen Motor Inn, ph (03) 5144 3888; Midtown Motor Inn, ph (03) 5144 1444
ACTIVITIES: Bowls, bushwalking, croquet, fishing, golf, greyhound racing, horse riding, horseracing, scenic drives, tennis, water sports
TOURIST INFORMATION: Ph (03) 5144 1108

SEA LAKE

333 KM NORTH-WEST OF MELBOURNE
POPULATION: 980   MAP REF: PAGE 94 G7

Sea Lake is a wheat growing and pastoral centre in the Mallee region of north-western Victoria. Five kilometres north of Sea Lake is the large inland saltwater lake, Lake Tyrell, which is surrounded by masses of saltbush and sand hills. It is because of this large lake and two other smaller lakes, Washpool and Timboran, that the town receives its name.

Over the years salt has been mined from the lake and the main feature of the town is the Cheetham Saltworks which visitors may visit. There is also a viewing platform at Lake Tyrell which overlooks the lake and surrounding countryside.

To the west of Sea Lake is the desert country of western Victoria and the Wyperfeld National Park. This park contains a large number of lakes which are connected by Outlet Creek which runs north–south through the park. The lakes used to fill on a 20-year cycle, but irrigation systems built further north have prevented the lakes and creek system of the Wyperfeld National Park from flourishing. It is, however, an interesting region which is home to a myriad birds, such as the sulphur-crested cockatoo, and native animals like the kangaroo.

ACCOMMODATION: Motel Thistledome, ph (03) 5070 1252

ACTIVITIES: Croquet, golf, horse riding, national park access, scenic drives, swimming, tennis

TOURIST INFORMATION: Ph (03) 5032 3033

SEYMOUR

101 KM NORTH OF MELBOURNE
POPULATION: 7800   MAP REF: PAGE 98 A7

A large farming community and nearby army base support the rural township of Seymour, on the banks of the Goulburn River north of Melbourne.

During 1909 Lord Kitchener declared that Seymour be a military base, but it was not until World War I that the establishment of the base took place. Later, in World War II, the base was extended and situated near Puckapunyal, west of Seymour.

The Royal Australian Armoured Corps Tank Museum at Puckapunyal is home to one of the largest displays of veteran tanks and armament in the southern hemisphere. The Royal Australian Corps of Transport Museum complements it and has a large number of military vehicles from World War I through to the present day, with most in operating condition.

While the town services the military base, it also caters to the outlying farms and tourists.

Of interest in town is the old log gaol which was built in 1858 and the Royal Hotel which dates back to 1849. New Crossing Place in Emily Street features a park with bushwalking tracks and was once the site of the old punt used to cross the Goulburn River.

Farming is a big industry and there are some unconventional farms in the region including the Capalba Park Alpaca Farm where there is a range of different animals such as alpacas, kangaroos, monkeys, emus, deer, camels and wombats. On sale here are by-products of the emu, such as emu oil. The Spotted Jumbuck in Highlands Road features animals such as lambs, sheep and rabbits with uniquely spotted coats. There are also sheepskin products and local crafts for sale.

There is a great deal of fertile land out on the river flats. Grapes enjoy this soil and climate, and some wineries worth visiting are Michelton, Hankin Estate and Somerset Crossing Vineyard.

The Seymour Alternative Farming Expo is a popular event and is held each year in February. The Agricultural show takes place in October and the Rafting Festival on the Goulburn River is held over Labour Day weekend in March.

ACCOMMODATION: New Crossing Place Motel, ph (03) 5792 2800; Wattle Motel, ph (03) 5792 2411; Bellbourie Estate Bed and Breakfast, ph (03) 5792 3505

ACTIVITIES: Bowls, fishing, golf, horse riding, horseracing, scenic drives, swimming, tennis

TOURIST INFORMATION: Ph (03) 5794 2647

SHEPPARTON

182 KM NORTH OF MELBOURNE
POPULATION: 25 450   MAP REF: PAGE 98 B4

Shepparton in the state's north is set amongst rich fertile land, watered by the Goulburn River Irrigation System. Surrounding the town are large orchards, dairy farms and cattle, all benefiting from the warm climate, good soil and excellent water supply.

Shepparton was originally a crossing point of the Goulburn River in the 1850s and McGuires Punt was used to ferry passengers and their wares across the river. In 1912 the town expanded when the irrigation system was implemented and fruit growing and farming became widespread. Because of the freight problems associated with fresh fruit, processing plants and a cannery were established and Shepparton became a strong regional centre.

The Shepparton Preserving Co. (SPC), is one of the oldest canneries in Australia and the factory is open for viewing of the processing and canning during the fruit season, which is generally during the warmer months. Visitors can also purchase SPC products direct from the factory. Other major factories in the town include Campbells Soups and Australian Country Spinners (Cleckheaton).

Shepparton is also home to Furphy's Foundry Museum, where you will find displays of old implements and memorabilia pertaining to the Furphy Foundry which has been manufacturing cast-iron products, such as the old-fashioned Australian camp ovens, for over a century. John Furphy established the foundry in 1874 and during World War I supplied the military with metal water carts.

Shepparton's history can easily be traced through the Historic Precinct at the corner of Highland and Welsford Streets where four buildings contain items pertaining to the town's heritage which date from 1850 through to 1950.

Victoria Park with its 20 hectare lake provides a haven for native wildlife. It is also popular for water sports such as sailboarding, waterskiing and boating. A large aquatic centre is located at the northern end of the lake which includes a giant waterslide. Other attractions of the park include picnic areas and a solar powered telephone.

An excellent and unusual feature of the town is the International Village Park where a number of pavilions representing a wide variety of countries are situated beside the waterways that run through the 23 hectare park.

ACCOMMODATION: Parklake Motor Inn, ph (03) 5821 5822; Pines Country Club Motor Inn, ph (03) 5831 1204; Sherbourne Terrace (hotel/motel), ph (03) 5821 4977

ACTIVITIES: Bowls, croquet, fishing, golf, greyhound racing, scenic drives, squash, tennis, trotting, water sports

TOURIST INFORMATION: Ph (03) 5831 4400

The International Village Park at Shepparton, with pavilions representing different countries

SORRENTO

91 KM SOUTH OF MELBOURNE
POPULATION: 1160 MAP REF: PAGE 93 N8

Sorrento and the nearby town of Portsea are popular seaside resorts on the Mornington Peninsula near the entrance to Port Phillip Bay. Within easy reach of Melbourne, this region has long been a favourite summer holiday destination for Melbournians.

Land in the region has always been sought after, particularly by the wealthy. A drive through Sorrento's tea-tree lined streets will reveal an abundance of stylish holiday homes while the main street features large ornate Victorian hotels which were built in the late 1800s.

Just off the Nepean Highway on Leggett Way is Collins Settlement Historic Site which is where Lieutenant-Colonel David Collins landed and settled in 1803. Because of the lack of drinking water the settlement was abandoned within a year and the group moved on to Hobart.

The Nepean Historical Society Museum can be found in the Mechanics Institute Hall which was built in 1876 and is now classified by the National Trust.

Sorrento Beach, along the Nepean Highway, is ideal for swimming in the safe waters while the back beach with its tall imposing cliffs, large waves and strong currents is favoured by surfers.

Along the foreshore of Sorrento Beach is parkland with bike paths, picnic facilities, kiosk, toilets and a boat ramp. An interesting walk which allows you to fully enjoy the rugged coastal scenery and superb sandy beaches is Coppins Track, from St Pauls to Sorrento, which was established in 1890 in honour of Queen Victoria's Diamond Jubilee. Meandering along the coastline, it takes in a section of the walking track through the Mornington Peninsula National Park from London Bridge, down to Cape Schanck at Bushrangers Bay in the south.

Attractions in Sorrento include the Marine Aquarium on St Albans Way where visitors can see the seals being fed, or take a cruise in Port Phillip Bay and swim with dolphins and seals.

The Sorrento car ferry heads across Port Phillip Bay five times a day to the resort town of Queenscliff. Here you can explore the historic buildings or try one of the acclaimed restaurants.

ACCOMMODATION: Hotel Sorrento, ph (03) 5984 2206; Tower House Resort Sorrento (B&B), ph (03) 5984 1343; Motel Saltair, ph (03) 5984 1356
ACTIVITIES: Bowls, diving, fishing, golf, tennis, water sports
TOURIST INFORMATION: Ph (03) 5984 5678

STAWELL

239 KM NORTH-WEST OF MELBOURNE
POPULATION: 6700 MAP REF: PAGE 92 G3

Stawell was first settled after gold was discovered here in 1853; a huge gold rush that lasted until the 1860s followed. When much of the easily extracted alluvial gold had been recovered and prospectors moved on to easier diggings, Stawell started to establish itself as a farming town.

Central Park in Stawell where the Stawell Gift Hall of Fame Museum is situated

The Pleasant Creek Quartz Mine was established at this time and their large operation worked the gold reefs deep down in the ground around Stawell until 1920. Gold has continually been found in the area and even today there are people mining around Stawell.

The famous Stawell Gift foot race is held over Easter every year. This event, run by the Stawell Athletic Club, has been conducted since the club was first formed in 1878 and is the oldest professional running race in Australia. The Stawell Gift Hall of Fame in Central Park features videos of events dating back as far as 1927 along with other memorabilia.

Stawell is close to the rugged Grampians which are ideal for bushwalking and rock climbing. The Wimmera wheat region and the old goldfield towns of central Victoria can also be reached from Stawell.

The Yabby Farm on the Halls Gap road has yabbies and trout for sale. With rod and bait supplied, you can even have a go at catching them yourself.

Sisters Rocks are a collection of huge granite boulders which can be found on the side of the Western Highway. They are named after the three Levi Sisters who camped in the area during the gold rush days. Today the boulders are covered in graffiti.

The Pioneer Lookout and Memorial is situated on the 'Big Hill' and is the best place to view the town and surrounding area. A memorial was laid here in 1935 to commemorate the pioneers who opened up this region last century.

Markets are held on the first Sunday of each month at the State Emergency Services Headquarters in Sloane Street.

ACCOMMODATION: Goldfields Motor Inn, ph (03) 5358 2911; Magdala Motor Lodge, ph (03) 5358 3877; Central Park Motel, ph (03) 5382 2417
ACTIVITIES: Bowls, bushwalking, croquet, fishing, gold fossicking, horse riding, horseracing, scenic drives, swimming, tennis, trotting
TOURIST INFORMATION: Ph (03) 5358 2314

STRATFORD

236 KM EAST OF MELBOURNE
POPULATION: 1300 MAP REF: PAGE 96 C6

The delightful country township of Stratford in Gippsland was settled in the 1840s by William Raymond who grazed his sheep on the fertile plains beside the Avon River. Raymond also set up the Shakespeare Hotel in 1847.

The town is believed to have been named after William Shakespeare's birthplace, Stratford-on-Avon, in England. Locals and Shakespearean buffs honour the naming of this town with occasional Stratford-on-Avon Shakespeare Festivals.

Stratford is situated near the townships of Sale and Maffra and the gateway to the Victorian High Country. It was originally a supply town for people heading to the goldfields to the north and today it is a supply point and stopover for people heading to the Alps, and for the outlying farms.

Knob Reserve can be found close to the Avon River and the lookout in this 57 hectare park offers excellent views of the Avon River and of the surrounding farmland.

The Stratford Highway park on the Princes Highway is easily accessed and features large red gums surrounding a lakeland reserve for native birds and a walking track.

Stratford is only a short drive from the Ninety Mile Beach on the Gippsland coastline and lakes Wellington and Victoria. This region is favoured by anglers, campers, and water sport enthusiasts.

ACCOMMODATION: Stratford Motel, ph (03) 5145 6500

ACTIVITIES: Bowls, fishing, horse riding, scenic drives, tennis, water sports

TOURIST INFORMATION: Ph (03) 5144 1108

SWAN HILL

343 KM NORTH-WEST OF MELBOURNE
POPULATION: 9600   MAP REF: PAGE 95 J6

Sitting on the banks of the Murray River is Swan Hill, often referred to as the 'Heart of the Murray'. This large regional centre is surrounded by rich land which produces a variety of crops such as citrus fruits and grapes. A major part of the town's economy is tourism: it has even been said that Swan Hill enjoys more sunny days than Queensland's Gold Coast.

Named for the large black swans that kept explorer Thomas Mitchell awake when he camped here in 1836, the town was first settled in 1840. Farms were soon established in the region and by 1850 a large port was constructed in town. Paddle-steamers were used to ship produce along the river.

The Pioneer Settlement Park pays tribute to these pioneering days of Swan Hill and comprises 4 hectares of buildings, machinery, artefacts and streets which date back to 1830. Also at the park is the PS *Pyap* which offers cruises on the Murray River.

Another important feature of town is the Military Expo. With over 5000 rare and interesting items it is the largest collection of military paraphernalia in the country. Other attractions in town include the Giant Murray Cod, a tribute to an elusive fish that was once prevalent in these waters: the replica stands more than 11 metres tall. On Curlewis Street is a huge Moreton Bay fig tree, believed to be the largest of its type in Australia.

There are a number of parks and sporting facilities in town including six golf courses, the most favoured being the award winning Murray Downs Golf Course. Other activities include boating, fishing, swimming and canoeing on the Murray River.

South of Swan Hill is Lake Boga which is excellent for waterskiing, boating and parasailing. There is also camping available on the foreshore.

Wineries in the region include Buller's and Bests, both large-volume producers of Australian wines.

ACCOMMODATION: Burke and Wills Motor Inn Swan Hill, ph (03) 5032 9788; Lady Augusta Motor Inn, ph (03) 5032 9677

ACTIVITIES: Bowls, croquet, fishing, golf, horse riding, horseracing, scenic drives, squash, tennis, water sports, wineries

TOURIST INFORMATION: Ph (03) 5032 3033

TATURA

169 KM NORTH OF MELBOURNE
POPULATION: 2778   MAP REF: PAGE 98 B5

A rich agricultural town in the north of Victoria, Tatura, like the nearby townships of Shepparton and Rushworth, benefits from the huge irrigation system which was established in the region in the early 1900s.

The town was officially gazetted in 1874 and the area was used for grazing sheep, wheat growing and a strong dairy industry. The region has always been a major producer of quality butter and the dairy industry is still an important contributor. Wheat was produced in large quantities in the late 1800s and the Tatura Wheat Export Movement was set up to export the grain to the United Kingdom.

The area has links with the two world wars as it played host to three prisoner-of-war camps during World War II and four internee camps. The Tatura German Military Cemetery here contains the graves of 250 German internees from both world wars. In a program organised by the German Government, bodies were exhumed from cemeteries all around Australia in 1958 and buried here. An insight into the history of Tatura and the irrigation system is given in the Irrigation and Wartime Camps Museum.

Attractions of the town include Cussen Park which has a swamp area set aside as a bird sanctuary. Nearby Lake Bartlett is popular for water sports and features parkland that is perfect for picnics.

ACCOMMODATION: Whim-Inn Motel, ph (03) 5824 1155

ACTIVITIES: Bowls, fishing, golf, horse riding, horseracing, squash, swimming, tennis

TOURIST INFORMATION: Ph (03) 5831 4400

TORQUAY

98 KM SOUTH-WEST OF MELBOURNE
POPULATION: 4887   MAP REF: PAGE 93 M8

The village of Torquay beside the ocean is a surf city and with long stretches of golden sandy beaches and great waves, this is where the surfers 'hang out' during summer. This is also the start of the Great Ocean Road, a magnificent long, winding stretch of road that offers superb coastal views whilst also taking in some of the region's more spectacular rainforest areas.

Bells Beach, the world-famous surf beach where national and international challenges are held, is near here. The Bells Easter Classic, a top competition for professional surfers, was established in 1961.

The town was originally known as Spring Creek, named by the Scammell brothers whose clipper *Joseph Scammell* ran aground on rocks outside Torquay in 1891. They later developed a shipping company here. The town's name was changed to Torquay after the English seaside resort in Devon.

Being a surfing town, it is only fitting that this is the location for Australia's only surfing museum, Surfworld. It is situated in Surfworld Plaza which is open every day and features videos, interactive displays and a wave-making tank. You can also purchase surfing gear here.

Other attractions in the town include Scammell House, a home which was built using the deckhouse of the clipper *Joseph Scammell*.

For a spectacular view of the Great Ocean Road and its famous landmarks, you can head for the skies in an authentic Tiger Moth plane.

Surfing competitions are held from November through to April with the major competitions held during Easter. Torquay High Tide Festival is held in early December.

ACCOMMODATION: Surf City Motel, ph (03) 5261 3492; Torquay Tropicana Motel, ph (03) 5261 2951; Torquay B&B, ph (03) 5261 4127

ACTIVITIES: Bowls, bushwalking, fishing, golf, hang gliding, horse riding, squash, tennis, water sports

TOURIST INFORMATION: Ph (03) 5261 4219

The Great Ocean Road and its splendid coastal views, south-west of Torquay

TRARALGON

169 KM EAST OF MELBOURNE
POPULATION: 19 235   MAP REF: PAGE 96 A7

Traralgon has always been a stopping-off place on the way to somewhere else. In the early days it was frequently used by either graziers on their way to the mountain country, or prospectors heading to the goldfields. When the railway arrived in 1877, it became a stopping point for the railway which continued on to the east. While today the town itself has a large commercial base, with paper and power industries in the area, it is still used as a stopover on the way to the Alps or the lakelands of Gippsland.

The town has grown significantly over the past few decades, but its history is evident in buildings such as the post office and court house which were both built in 1887. The Traralgon Hotel, with its ornate iron lace work veranda, is classified by the National Trust.

The Tambo Cheese Factory is based in Traralgon and offers a wide variety of Gippsland cheeses along with local crafts.

Traralgon is close to the Moondara State Park and reservoir and Baw Baw National Park. Mt Baw Baw is a fascinating mountain and in winter the great combination of slopes are enjoyed by both downhill and cross-country skiers. Snowboarders also enjoy it.

The nearby Thomson River is excellent for white-water rafting while the Blue Rock Lake near Moe is used for all kinds of water sports. Traralgon is also not far from the historic township of Walhalla which used to be a major goldmining town in the 1800s.

ACCOMMODATION: Latrobe Motel and Convention Centre, ph (03) 5174 2338; Connells Motel, ph (03) 5174 5221; Fernhill Motor Inn, ph (03) 5174 7277
ACTIVITIES: Bowls, croquet, fishing, golf, greyhound racing, horse riding, horseracing, scenic drives, skiing, swimming, tennis, trotting, whitewater rafting
TOURIST INFORMATION: Ph (03) 5174 3319

WALHALLA

202 KM EAST OF MELBOURNE
POPULATION: 30   MAP REF: PAGE 91 P4

Nestled into a deep valley on Stringers Creek in Gippsland, Walhalla only just managed to survive the decline of the goldmining era and is now an historic town, popular with tourists. The small township has a few residents although most use the town as a week-end retreat—it is still not supplied with electricity.

Many buildings have been restored and there are numerous ruins to be explored, along with the cemetery and mines. Fossicking is still allowed and the rivers are an excellent playground in summer.

This town also signifies the start of the well-used Australian Alps Walking Trail which ends at the ACT more than 760 km away.

The Long Tunnel Extended Mine which was operational from 1865 until 1911 was the fifth richest in Victoria, bringing in 14 tonnes of gold. Guided tours are conducted through the 300 metre opening into the hillside.

The rotunda has been standing in the main street since 1896 and is still used during festivals. A small path on the main road leads to an interesting old cemetery terraced on a steep hillside, while a visit to the museum, also in the main street, is a great insight into the town's history.

One of Victoria's most spectacular railway journeys was reborn here in 1994 when the old Walhalla Gold Fields Railway was restored as a tourist attraction. Now that the Thomson River Trestle Bridge has been fully restored, passengers can cross the bridge and wind their way up through the lush forest area of Stringers Creek Gorge. The railway is still being built and will eventually finish at Happy Creek where there will be a picnic ground and railway station.

ACCOMMODATION: The Old Hospital (guesthouse), ph (03) 9803 9365
ACTIVITIES: Bushwalking, gold fossicking, historic interest, scenic drives
TOURIST INFORMATION: Ph (03) 5165 6250

WANGARATTA

238 KM NORTH-EAST OF MELBOURNE
POPULATION: 15 985   MAP REF: PAGE 98 F4

Wangaratta in the state's north is a very large regional centre at the junction of the King and Ovens Rivers. The area was first explored by Hume and Hovell in 1824 and settlement began in 1837. The town itself was eventually established in 1849 and started its life as a supply base and stopover for miners in the surrounding goldfields.

Woollen mills were set up here in the 1920s and that was when the town started to develop into what is today a large commercial and agricultural centre.

There are several historic buildings in town, reminders of the pioneers that first settled here. The impressive Holy Trinity Cathedral took 56 years to build, with the works initiated in 1909 and not completed until 1965. The main features of this magnificent cathedral are the stained glass windows and the timber belfry which houses eight bells cast in England in 1806 and originally used in a church there.

Other historic places of interest in Wangaratta include the North-East Historical Society Museum and the Pioneer Cemetery.

The House In Miniatures is 2.5 metres long, 1.8 metres high and 1.6 metres wide and took ten years to construct. This twentieth-century villa is built to scale and includes furnishings such as fireplaces with logs, crockery and minute cotton reels in the sewing basket.

Located on an old Aboriginal camp is the King George Gardens on Ovens Street, where an English-style garden was built in 1936. It was named after King George V who died while the garden was being built. Two large cannons used in the Crimean War are in the grounds.

Air World Aviation Museum houses a number of antique aircraft along with aviation memorabilia.

The Wangaratta Agricultural Show is held in October while the Wangaratta Festival of Jazz is presented in November.

ACCOMMODATION: Gateway Wangaratta (motel), ph (03) 5721 8399; Advance Motel, ph (03) 5721 9100; Hermitage Motor Inn, ph (03) 5721 7444
ACTIVITIES: Bowls, croquet, fishing, gem fossicking,

Air World Aviation Museum in Wangaratta

golf, greyhound racing, horseracing, horse riding, scenic drives, swimming, tennis, trotting
TOURIST INFORMATION: Ph (03) 5721 5711

WARBURTON

78 KM EAST OF MELBOURNE
POPULATION: 2005   MAP REF: PAGE 91 L3

Nestled in a lush valley where the Yarra River snakes its way downwards to Port Phillip Bay, this country town is a delight for day or weekend visits.

Gold was discovered here in 1864 and when the gold rush ended the settlers turned to clearing the land. Timber mills were soon scattered through the mountains. Today forestry is still a major industry in Warburton, although tourism is also significant.

Warburton has always had a large Seventh Day Adventist community with Melbourne Adventists moving to the area in 1904 and building a printing works. In 1923 the Sanitarium Health Food Factory was established. Warburton is also home to the Warburton Health Care Centre which offers therapeutic services for busy city people.

Tommy Finns Trout Farm can be found just outside the town entrance. Here a series of lakes set amongst the magnificent ranges offer a chance to catch a trout.

Warburton is the perfect base from which to explore the surrounding ranges, visiting such interesting places as the historic goldmining towns of Matlock or Woods Point high up in the hills. Mt Donna Buang is only 6 km from the town and is popular with families from Melbourne seeking a day in the snow. Tobogganing is popular here, as is cross-country skiing at nearby Lake Mountain.

The mountain area is also popular with bushwalkers, 4WD owners, mountain and trail bike riders and canoeists.

ACCOMMODATION: Mt Victoria Motel, ph (03) 5966 2037; Magnolia Country Retreat (B&B), ph (03) 5966 9469; Warburton Health Care Centre (guesthouse), ph (03) 5966 4444
ACTIVITIES: Bowls, bushwalking, fishing, 4WD touring, golf, horse riding, scenic drives, snow sports, tennis, water sports
TOURIST INFORMATION: Ph (03) 5962 2600

WARRACKNABEAL

346 KM NORTH-WEST OF MELBOURNE
POPULATION: 2687   MAP REF: PAGE 94 F9

Warracknabeal, now an important service centre for the outlying wheat communities in the Wimmera, was first settled in 1844 when the Scott brothers set up the Warracknabeal sheep run.

A severe drought affected the region at the end of the nineteenth century and it was from this disaster that the Wimmera–Mallee water supply was initiated, bringing relief to the drought-stricken farmers. Apart from sheep, wheat has also contributed to the town's economy and enormous wheat silos can be seen throughout the region.

The Historical Centre which houses a collection of artefacts from former residents includes furniture, a pharmaceutical collection and documents that date back more than 100 years.

Visitors can take a self-guided tour of the town, called the Black Arrow Tour. It passes the National Trust buildings and the old Commercial Hotel which was built in 1872.

The Yarriambiack Creek which flows through the town features a recreational area and a flora and fauna park on its shores. This is an ideal area for walking and picnics.

ACCOMMODATION: Warrack Motel, ph (03) 5398 1633; Warracknabeal Country Roads Motor Inn, ph (03) 5398 1811; Werrigar Motel, ph (03) 5398 2144
ACTIVITIES: Bowls, bushwalking, croquet, fishing, golf, horse riding, horseracing, tennis, water sports
TOURIST INFORMATION: Ph (03) 5398 1632

WARRAGUL

109 KM SOUTH-EAST OF MELBOURNE
POPULATION: 8910   MAP REF: PAGE 91 M5

About 100 years ago the area on which the township of Warragul is situated consisted mostly of swamp land, but through the hard work and determination of the pioneers, the marshland was filled in and a successful dairy industry established on the green fertile flats. The historic centre in the old shire hall outlines the history of the dairy industry in the region.

Warragul is in a rich agricultural area and a Gourmet Deli Trail leads visitors on a gastronomic tour of the region, taking in farms, wineries, restaurants and food shops.

The old drive-in site is home to the Lillco Garden Railway, where a miniature railway system is housed, featuring landscaped surroundings and rides on miniature engines.

Only 8 km to the east of town is Darnum, home to the Darnum Musical Village which houses a superb collection of musical instruments.

To the north of town lies the Dividing Range and the old timber towns of Noojee and Powelltown with its trestle bridges and old milling tram tracks, while south is the Mount Worth State Park. Here you will find the Standing Giant, a huge mountain ash tree which is more than 300 years old.

Events include the Warragul Springfest in October and the Gippsland Field Days in March.

The peaceful Civic Gardens in Warragul

ACCOMMODATION: Edinburgh Motor Inn, ph (03) 5622 3339; Freeway Motor Inn, ph (03) 5623 5222; Warragul Motel, ph (03) 5623 2189
ACTIVITIES: Bowls, bushwalking, croquet, golf, greyhound racing, horse riding, scenic drives, swimming, tennis, trotting, wineries
TOURIST INFORMATION: Ph (03) 5624 2411

WARRNAMBOOL

265 KM WEST OF MELBOURNE
POPULATION: 25 500   MAP REF: PAGE 92 F8

The delightful town of Warrnambool is set on the western coastline of Victoria on the Great Ocean Road. This site was chosen because of the harbour access and it was originally settled by whalers and sealers. The town has now emerged as a fishing, farming and tourist town.

Ships sailing from England stopped here on their way to the ports of Melbourne and Sydney. Many ships met their demise on this rugged coastline and the region is often referred to as the 'shipwreck coastline'. Information on the coastline and shipwrecks can be found at the Flagstaff Hill Maritime Museum, arguably the best attraction in Warrnambool. The Flagstaff Hill Maritime Museum uses restored and re-created buildings to depict an early coastal settlement. Features include an operating lighthouse and a number of historic vessels. The *Loch Ard* is one of Australia's better known shipwrecks which lies off the coast along the Great Ocean Road. The Loch Ard Peacock, an ornate statue which was plucked from the shipwreck is housed in this museum.

Warrnambool has many magnificent parks and gardens. A fine example of this is the Fletcher Jones clothing factory which is surrounded by gardens featuring delightful floral displays which are floodlit at night. So popular are these gardens that they are regularly hired out for wedding ceremonies.

Cannon Hill offers panoramic views of the bay and Lake Petrobe. Lake Petrobe Adventure Park offers plenty of fun for the whole family with a maze, boats, islands and walking tracks.

Other attractions include the fairy penguins at Middle Island where a colony of these tiny creatures

Hopkins Falls, also known as 'Little Niagara', north-east of Warrnambool

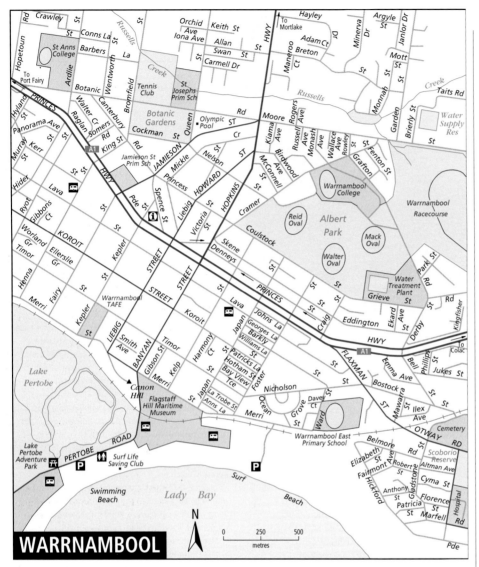

WARRNAMBOOL

0 | 250 | 500
metres

N

1950s when gold nuggets worth $20 000 were found in one resident's backyard. Then, in 1979 the Beggary Lump, an enormous gold nugget valued at $50 000, was discovered.

Memorabilia can be seen at the General Store Museum, built in 1910. There is also a coach building and blacksmith's shop here.

Seventeen kilometres outside of town is the Wychitella Flora and Fauna Reserve, a 3930 hectare park which is believed to support the most concentrated population of mallee fowl, a large bird which inhabits the mallee region of western Victoria. Flora and fauna in the reserve are protected and gold prospecting is not allowed here.

An annual Gold Dig is held in March.

ACCOMMODATION: Wedderburn Motel, ph (03) 4594 3002

ACTIVITIES: Bowls, bushwalking, fishing, gold fossicking, golf, scenic drives, swimming, tennis, trotting

TOURIST INFORMATION: Ph (03) 5444 4433

WINCHELSEA

115 KM SOUTH-WEST OF MELBOURNE
POPULATION: 1180   MAP REF: PAGE 93 L7

The small township of Winchelsea sits on the banks of the Barwon River, a large body of water which flows down towards Geelong before running into the sea at Barwon Heads.

Originally a stopping point between the towns of Geelong and Colac, the township is now surrounded by farmland and serves the rural community.

The town features historic bluestone buildings, bridges and shops from the nineteenth century along with magnificent gardens. One notable property is Barwon Park on Inverleigh Road 3 km out of town. It is a superb two-storey bluestone mansion which was completed in 1871 by Thomas Austin, a wealthy English grazier who brought animals such as pheasants, quail and foxes to Australia for game sport. He was also responsible for introducing the rabbit which was later to become a pest throughout Australia while the fox has also caused much disturbance to native flora and fauna.

The river is good for swimming; also the town is not far from the seaside towns of Barwon Heads and Geelong where there are beaches and ocean swimming and surfing.

ACCOMMODATION: Wincheslea Motel/Roadhouse, ph (03) 5267 22930; Sea Mist Palomino Stud (lodge), ph (03) 5288 7255

ACTIVITIES: Bowls, fishing, golf, scenic drives, tennis, water sports

TOURIST INFORMATION: Ph (03) 5222 2900

WODONGA

308 KM NORTH OF MELBOURNE
POPULATION: 23 640   MAP REF: PAGE 99 H3

Wodonga and its twin city Albury across the waters of the Murray River in New South Wales have combined to become a major service centre. Situated on the Hume Highway between Melbourne and Sydney, the

have made their burrows. Access is only at low tide when it is possible to wade across to the island.

Breakwater Rock is at the south-west end of town where there is the yacht club and the Breakwater Aquarium. This contains many different species of fish found locally, along with a large seashell collection. Adjacent to the aquarium is Thunder Point Coastal Reserve with walking tracks leading to fantastic views of the Southern Ocean.

Hopkins Falls, on Hopkins Falls Road, 15 km north-east of town, are often referred to as 'Little Niagara'. These falls are at their best after rainfall and during summer eels migrate down the river and can be seen falling over the edge.

The Tower Hill State Game Reserve on the Princes Highway west of the town is based on an extinct volcano. You can climb to the top of the rim where you will be rewarded with excellent views of the volcano itself and the surrounding countryside.

Sunday markets are held every week at the showgrounds while the racing carnival is held in May. The Melbourne to Warrnambool Cycle Classic and the annual show are held in October.

ACCOMMODATION: Central Court Motor Inn, ph (03) 5562 8555; Olde Maritime Motor Inn, ph (03) 5561 1545; Western Coast Motel, ph (03) 5562 2755

ACTIVITIES: Bowls, croquet, fishing, golf, greyhound racing, horse riding, horseracing, scenic drives, squash, tennis, water sports

TOURIST INFORMATION: Ph (03) 5564 7837

WEDDERBURN

216 KM NORTH-WEST OF MELBOURNE
POPULATION: 795   MAP REF: PAGE 93 J1

This town, once one of the state's richest gold producers, is located on the Calder Highway only 74 km north of the regional centre of Bendigo. The township was originally settled by squatters in the 1840s but from the time gold was first struck here in 1852, the region was inundated with prospectors hoping to find a nugget.

While gold was still being mined, swampland surrounding the diggings was reclaimed by a man called Duncan McGregor and an engineer, Carlo Catani. It is suggested that at the peak of this project in 1889, there were more than 500 men involved.

The dense mallee scrub around the town was difficult to clear and for many years much of the thick scrub outside of town was not cleared. As the town grew and these areas were eventually cleared, gold discoveries continued to be made, some as late as the

area is used as a major stopover point on the journey between the two capital cities.

The explorers Hume and Hovell travelled through this region in 1824 but it was not until the 1830s that sheep runs were taken up in the area. Charles and Paul Huon, who have a lake in town named after them, were the first to take up land. From here the twin towns, known collectively as Albury–Wodonga, grew to eventually become Australia's first major decentralised city in 1973.

Stoneleigh Cottage, built in the High Street in 1857 by Paul Huon, is Wodonga's oldest building. The Sumsion Gardens overlook Lake Huon and were renovated extensively during the 1950s. Here you will find picnic facilities and a playground.

During the early years a customs house was established in Wodonga as this was the only major crossing of the Murray River for many miles. It was also an important part of the mail run between the two major capital cities. Because of its location, Wodonga also served as a cattle market and was at one stage the largest between Melbourne and Sydney.

A military camp was established outside of town in 1940 and it also served as a migrant camp. The large Bandiana Military Camp south-east of Wodonga was established in 1942 and a large number of army personnel have been stationed here over the last half of the twentieth century. The Royal Australian Army Ordnance Corps Museum is housed at the Bandiana Camp and displays a large range of tanks, weapons and armoured vehicles.

Across the waters of the Murray and just out of Albury in New South Wales is the Ettamogah Pub, a tourist attraction and pub which was designed and built from a cartoon drawn by artist Ken Maynard. This unusual hotel has out-of-square walls and a Chevrolet truck sitting on the uneven roof. The name Ettamogah comes from the Aboriginal word for 'good drinking place'.

East of Wodonga is Lake Hume, a large reservoir that is also extensively used for water sports such as waterskiing, boating, angling and swimming.

The Wodonga Show is held four weeks before Easter each year. A community market is held every second Sunday morning while a Food and Wine Festival is held in September.

ACCOMMODATION: The Blazing Stump Motel, ph (060) 563 433; Belvoir Village Motel, ph (060) 245 344; Best Western Stagecoach Motel, ph (060) 243 044

ACTIVITIES: Bowls, fishing, golf, scenic drives, squash, tennis, water sports

TOURIST INFORMATION: Ph (060) 413 875

Local government buildings in Wodonga

WONTHAGGI

150 KM SOUTH-EAST OF MELBOURNE
POPULATION: 6710   MAP REF: PAGE 91 K7

A large commercial and industrial centre in the south Gippsland region of Victoria, Wonthaggi lies only 2 km from the Cape Paterson coastline of Bass Strait.

This region is best known for the black coal which was discovered here in 1824 by the explorer William Hovell. It was mined at Cape Paterson from 1859 to 1864. Miners eventually gave up on the operation as transporting the coal was made difficult because the ships could not find safe anchorage in Venus Bay.

The coal was left underground until a major strike in the Newcastle coalfields of New South Wales in 1910 led to the Victorian Government encouraging mining in the Wonthaggi coalfield. Much of the coal was used by the government to keep the state railway system running. Camps, and eventually houses, were set up to support the coal miners and the area grew until the State Coal Mine was closed in 1968.

A portion of the coalmine can be viewed today with information available at the Orientation Centre at the East Area Mine.

Wonthaggi is close to the township of Inverloch which offers plenty of seaside activities such as swimming, surfing, sailboarding and fishing. Wilsons Promontory National Park is also a pleasant drive from Wonthaggi offering an enormous network of walking tracks and spectacular coastline.

The Picnic Races are held here in January while the Coal Skip Competition is on during Easter.

ACCOMMODATION: Wonthaggi Motel, ph (03) 5672 2922; Miners Rest Motor Inn, ph (03) 5672 1033; Caledonian Hotel, ph (03) 5672 1002

ACTIVITIES: Bowls, bushwalking, fishing, golf, horse riding, scenic drives, tennis, water sports

TOURIST INFORMATION: Ph (03) 5672 2484

WOODS POINT

181 KM NORTH-EAST OF MELBOURNE
POPULATION: 50   MAP REF: PAGE 91 N2

The old goldmining town of Woods Point is a tourist attraction, especially for owners of 4WD vehicles who head to this mountainous country and stay in town on the banks of the Goulburn River. The last mine closed down in this remote town in 1963 and the residents then hoped that tourism would keep the town alive. Its isolation, however, has meant that it is only just surviving, supported by a small number of passing tourists who are on their way to the mountains north-east of Melbourne.

In 1861 gold was discovered on Gooley's Creek and the township of Woods Point grew rapidly and by 1864 the town supported two newspapers, four banks, two schools, three churches and 23 hotels. The Morning Star Mine established in 1861 was the most prosperous in the area and continued to operate after the rush. By a cruel twist of fate, the entire town was destroyed in the 1939 bushfires which ravaged the mountains around Melbourne. Without the plentiful gold for income, very few houses were rebuilt and the ones that remain are mainly used as weekend accommodation. The Morning Star Mine, however, was rebuilt and continued to operate until 1963.

The drive to Woods Point is a very scenic one indeed. However, unless you have a 4WD vehicle it should be undertaken in the warmer months only as snow can fall in these mountains at any time of year if it is cold enough. A steep road heads out of the township of Warburton up to the Cumberland Junction where a gravel road leads to Mt Matlock. Along the way you will come to a large flat area that was once a township, built to house the workers for the Thomson Dam project in the late 1960s and removed once the project was complete.

After descending Mt Matlock and arriving at the township of Woods Point you can venture along

The countryside around Woods Point

another gravel road which leads to Lake Eildon National Park and the small towns of Jamieson and Gaffneys Creek.

Anglers will enjoy fishing in the waters of the Goulburn River while bushwalkers can explore the old mining sites around Woods Point.

ACCOMMODATION: Commercial Hotel, ph (03) 27778224; J. H. Scott Camping Reserve, Woods Point Road (no power)
ACTIVITIES: Bushwalking, fishing, 4WD touring, gold fossicking, historical interest, scenic drives, swimming
TOURIST INFORMATION: Ph (03) 5963 4567

YACKANDANDAH

298 KM NORTH-EAST OF MELBOURNE
POPULATION: 700   MAP REF: PAGE 99 H4

Yackandandah is a perfect example of an old goldmining town from the nineteenth century. Gold was discovered here in 1852. Because of the significant number of old buildings, the whole town has been classified by the National Trust. Interesting buildings include the Bank of Victoria which is now a museum, along with many others which are now used to house art and craft shops and tearooms.

The township of Yackandandah has several handicraft shops. On High Street is Ray Riddingtons Gallery, which is housed in a store that is nearly 100 years old. Inside is a collection of leather goods, pottery, woodwork and glass-blown items. Wild Thyme features an excellent range of dried flower arrangements, baskets and handicrafts. The Yackandandah Workshop and Craft Gallery is in the town's old winery and has a range of woollen products as well as spinning wheels.

On the Beechworth Road, the Lavender Patch Plant Farm, settled in a most picturesque valley, has more than 15 varieties of lavender plants for sale. The farm also sells herbs along with toiletries and crafts

manufactured from the lavender plant. The farm is open from September through to May.

Yackandandah is not far from another significant historic township, Beechworth, which features extraordinary buildings which date back to the gold rush era.

ACCOMMODATION: Cottage Yackandandah (B&B), ph (03) 6027 1713; Downham House (B&B), ph (03) 6027 1690; Serendipity Bed and Breakfast (B&B), ph (03) 6027 1881
ACTIVITIES: Bowls, bushwalking, fishing, golf, horse riding, scenic drives, tennis, water sports
TOURIST INFORMATION: Ph (060) 413 875

YARRA GLEN

52 KM NORTH-EAST OF MELBOURNE
POPULATION: 2095   MAP REF: PAGE 91 J2

First known as Yarra Flats, the township of Yarra Glen is flanked on one side by the Yarra River as it winds its way through the river flats of the Yarra Valley on its way to Melbourne and Port Phillip Bay. The area around Yarra Glen is so low that after a heavy downpour the Yarra River rises and cuts off the town from the neighbouring towns of Lilydale and Coldstream. Fortunately this occurs infrequently.

Though the township is small it houses one of the more magnificent hotels in the region, the Grand Hotel, which is on the main road and has recently been restored.

Gulf Station on the Melba Highway just out of Yarra Glen was established in the 1850s and is one of the oldest farms in the Yarra Valley region. The whole farm is one of the most complete groups of solid timber buildings still standing in Victoria. A visit will reveal many of the machines and utensils used in the early pioneering days.

Yarra Glen is at the heart of the winery region of the Yarra Valley, one of Victoria's oldest and most successful wine growing regions. Wineries worth visiting are Tarrawarra, Yarra Ridge, Yering Station and the nearby vineyard of Domaine Chandon, a branch of the French Möet et Chandon house.

The Grape Grazing Festival and the Yarra Glen Show are both held in March.

ACCOMMODATION: The Grand Hotel, ph (03) 9730 1230; The Valley Gallery (guesthouse), ph (03) 9730 1822; Art at Linden Gate (B&B), ph (03) 9730 1861
ACTIVITIES: Bushwalking, fishing, 4WD touring, horseracing, horse riding, water sports, wineries
TOURIST INFORMATION: Ph (03) 5962 2600

YARRA JUNCTION

68 KM EAST OF MELBOURNE
POPULATION: 1120   MAP REF: PAGE 91 K3

Yarra Junction lies on the edge of the Yarra River at the foot of the Yarra Ranges. There are a couple of theories as to how the town got its name: one is that it is where the Little Yarra and Yarra Rivers meet, while the other is that it was named after the junction of the Victorian Railway Line and the smaller three-foot gauge of the Powelltown Tramway.

The area supports a large timber and farming industry and along with the neighbouring towns of Warburton, Marysville and Powelltown, Yarra Junction once supported a huge forestry industry with many sawmills operating in the area.

Much of the region's history is recounted in the Upper Yarra Historical Museum which is housed in the old railway station. This was formerly the Lilydale Station and was moved to its present location in 1901.

Yarra Junction is home to Yarra Burn Winery which was the first winery in the Yarra Valley to manufacture sparkling wines.

The drive from Lilydale along the Warburton Highway to Yarra Junction offers spectacular views of the rich grazing and fruit growing regions outside Melbourne, along with the magnificent Yarra Valley.

ACCOMMODATION: Tarrango Farm (B&B), ph (03) 5967 2123; Langbrook Farm Cottage, ph (03) 5967 1320
ACTIVITIES: Bowls, bushwalking, fishing, 4WD touring, mountain bike riding, scenic drives, tennis, water sports, wineries
TOURIST INFORMATION: Ph (03) 5962 2600

YARRAWONGA

263 KM NORTH-EAST OF MELBOURNE
POPULATION: 3390   MAP REF: PAGE 98 E3

Yarrawonga sits beside the Murray River where its waters flow into the man-made Mulwala Lake in the north of Victoria. This lake was originally created in the 1930s as a storage for the waters of the Murray River and covers an area of 6000 hectares. The Murray River and the lake are perfect for water sports such as waterskiing, swimming, boating and sailboarding. The quieter backwaters are great for fishing, canoeing and birdwatching.

The first settler to the region was Elizabeth Hume, sister-in-law of the explorer Hamilton Hume. Elizabeth came here in 1842 and it is believed that because her husband had been killed by bushrangers she designed her homestead so that she had a commanding view of all who approached.

Apart from activities on and around the lake, other attractions of the town include the Pioneer Museum, the Tudor House Clock Museum and Linley Park Animal Farm. The information centre features the Old Yarra Mine Shaft, a simulated mine with many tunnels, one of which includes glow worms along with displays of various minerals and gems.

The MV *Paradise Queen* is a fine old vessel which offers cruises along the Murray River and Lake Mulwala, leaving from the Yarrawonga foreshore. The *Lady Murray* also offers river cruises, but in a more modern vessel, this time heading along the Murray from Yarrawonga to Corowa.

Speedboat races are held in January while the Yarrawonga Show is held during October. The Red Cross Murray River Marathon starts here on 26 December each year.

ACCOMMODATION: Central Yarrawonga Motor Inn, ph (03) 5744 3817; Belmore Motor Inn, ph (03) 5744 3685; Lakeview (motel), ph (03) 5744 1555
ACTIVITIES: Bowls, bushwalking, croquet, fishing, golf, scenic drives, squash, tennis, water sports
TOURIST INFORMATION: Ph (03) 5744 1989

The Otway National Park

BAW BAW NATIONAL PARK

This park lies 95 km north of Moe and, apart from the Alpine National Park, is the only other Victorian park with subalpine vegetation such as the twisted snow gum and the wildflowers that carpet the area in summer. The park has become a base for walkers and cross-country skiers. The busiest time for this alpine park is during winter, when many skiers head downhill in the village area or cross-country on the many and varied tracks. Fantastic views of the Thomson Dam can be had from the Silvertop Picnic Ground. Wildlife includes the amphibian Baw Baw frog and the rare Leadbeater's possum, as well as numbats, cockatoos and lyrebirds.

BEECHWORTH HISTORIC PARK

Situated in north-eastern Victoria, 40 km from Wangaratta, this park lies amid the natural beauty of the Victorian Alps. The old goldmining town of Beechworth has been so well preserved that it allows visitors to assimilate the lifestyles of the earlier diggers. The forests of brittle gum and peppermint are a natural drawcard but it is history that brings visitors to the park. In the Lock Street Museum there is a display on Robert Burke, of Burke and Wills fame, who was a police chief in the district's early years. Of interest, too, are the Chinese Burning Towers, and

headstones in the cemetery, a reminder of the many Chinese who worked on the goldfields. Browsing, walking, fishing, horse riding and swimming are all on offer in this interesting area of northern Victoria.

BRISBANE RANGES NATIONAL PARK

The Brisbane Ranges National Park is 105 km west of Melbourne and just over one hour's drive away. The park is renowned for its wildflowers and native plants, which are especially prolific in the west of the park on the plateau area. Eucalypt woodlands, with a dense understorey of heaths, are also found on the plateau. During the gold rush years, much of this forest was cut down for mining timbers, building material and firewood. The park is cut by deep gorges and gullies created over the millennia by water eroding the ancient slate and sandstone of the ranges. Visitors will enjoy the abundant flora and bird life, and the pleasant walks and scenic drives.

CROAJINGOLONG NATIONAL PARK

Situated in the far eastern corner of Victoria, 450 km east of Melbourne, this park stretches for 100 km along the coast south from the New South Wales border. One of Victoria's largest parks, it has a wide diversity of landforms. The vegetation is also

varied with soft-leaved subtropical species, cool-temperate communities, and hardier plants that are resistant to fire and drought. While road travel throughout the park is restricted, there are numerous dirt tracks giving good access to some interesting places, especially the inlets. At Shipwreck Creek you can enjoy some pleasant walks in the surrounding areas as well as paddle a canoe on the creek. The Thurra River inlet is set in an unspoilt forest close to the ocean beach. The shallow waters of the river provide safe swimming as well as canoeing, and you can fish along the coast. There are also bush and beach walks.

DANDENONG RANGES NATIONAL PARK

The verdant sanctuary of the Dandenong Ranges, 40 km east of Melbourne, has been a popular picnic ground for Victorians for more than 70 years. This suburban park stretches across three sections of Mt Dandenong. The Ferntree Gully block boasts natural bushland and offers a variety of interesting walks, while the Sherbrooke section has the tumbling Sherbrooke Falls. The Doongalla section offers spectacular views and rugged bush trails leading down the western side of the mountain. The large tree-ferns, the variety of eucalypts, the sounds of many bellbirds and the spectacular song of the lyrebird will reward visitors to this park so close to the bustling city of Melbourne

GIPPSLAND LAKES COASTAL PARK

The Lakes National Park and the Gippsland Lakes Coastal Park encompass the region from Seaspray to Lakes Entrance and boast such natural features as The Ninety Mile Beach and the inland coastal lakes system. The lakes were formed aeons ago when the sea forced sand onto the shore, creating a series of barriers along the coast. The park is rich in wildlife and is a retreat from the bustling seaside villages that dot the coast. Kangaroos can be seen feeding on the plains along Bartons Hill Track, while seabirds of all kinds are always nearby. Dolphins and seals are regularly spotted searching for food near Barrier Landing, accessible only by boat. The region offers fishing, boating, canoeing, swimming, bushwalks, wildlife spotting, and of course long walks on the beach and family fun of all kinds.

GRAMPIANS NATIONAL PARK

This park is 260 km west of Melbourne and 25 km south-west of Stawell. Rugged sandstone ranges of the westernmost heights of the Great Divide make up the Grampians National Park, protecting a region rich in native flora, fauna and Aboriginal art sites. A wide variety of soils, topography and localised weather patterns brings a great wealth of botanical species. Eucalypts dominate the forests, while higher up heaths carpet the terrain. In spring, the wildflower display is superb. Animal life is just as varied and the Grampians are host to mammals both large and small. Kangaroos abound in some areas. Hundreds of kilometres of vehicle and walking tracks give easy access to some of the state's most spectacular scenery. Just about every outdoor activity can be undertaken, from waterskiing, fishing, hunting, bushwalking and rock climbing to just enjoying the magnificent panoramas.

HATTAH-KULKYNE NATIONAL PARK

This national park runs east of the Calder Highway between Ouyen and Mildura, and combined with the Murray–Kulkyne Park the area offers many opportunities for outdoor recreation. The Hattah Lakes system forms the heart of the national park, filling when the Murray River floods. Imposing river red gums line the banks of the Murray River, and around the lakes red gums, black box, native grasses and water plants are well established. The lakes are a haven for bird life and many species of birds breed here. Depending on water levels, canoeing is an excellent way to survey the lakes, while there are unlimited walking opportunities. There is also a good network of vehicle tracks through the park; however they are often very sandy and better suited to 4WDs, and can become impassable after rain.

KINGLAKE NATIONAL PARK

This park is 65 km north-east of Melbourne and is the largest national park near Melbourne. It is situated on the north-western slopes of the Great Dividing Range, with vehicle tracks meandering through eucalypt forests and fern gullies. One of the major attractions is Masons Falls, found in the western part of the park. It is reached via one of the park's 24 walking trails. Other tracks lead to panoramic viewpoints.

While bushwalking is a popular pastime, visitors can also enjoy some great birdwatching.

LAKE EILDON NATIONAL PARK

Located on the southern and western shores of Lake Eildon, this park is the result of Fraser National Park combining with the larger Eildon State Park. Visitors to the park will be rewarded by many different species of native wildlife including possums and koalas. Bird life is plentiful with cockatoos, rosellas and miners filling the air with their cries, while on the lake can be found herons, coromants, pelicans and ibis, among other water birds. The vegetation consists of red box, red stringybark and narrow and broad-leafed peppermints Canoeing, fishing, boating, windsurfing and swimming are the main attractions of the area, and pleasant bushwalks crisscross the park. The profusion of forestry tracks in the area to the south of the of the lake, in the old state park, is popular with owners of 4WD vehicles. The park is 145 km north-east of Melbourne.

LITTLE DESERT NATIONAL PARK

The park runs south of the Western Highway from Dimboola to the South Australian border and is divided into three blocks—western, central and eastern. It is 375 km north-west of Melbourne. The sandy plains which make up much of this park are dominated by mallee and stringy-bark eucalypts, along with a diverse range of other eucalypts, pines, melaleuca, heaths, banksias and broombush. With dazzling displays of spring wildflowers and the excellent variety of bird life and fauna, this park is a must for nature lovers. In such a dry landscape, the Wimmera River in the eastern block, with its woodlands of river red gum and black box on the floodplains, gives a different aspect to the surrounding countryside. While much of the park can be explored on foot, sandy tracks, really only suited to 4WDs, criss-cross the park, and in fact the central and western blocks are only accessible to 4WD vehicles.

LOWER GLENELG NATIONAL PARK

The Glenelg River begins its journey to the sea in the Grampians in western Victoria, 400 km away. The lower reaches of the river are protected within the national park, taking in the Glenelg River Gorge. It is possible to launch small boats and canoes at several spots along the river. Other activities which can be enjoyed are fishing and swimming, while waterskiing is permitted only in designated zones. Numerous vehicle and walking tracks offer plenty of opportunities to view the fauna and flora. There is a magnificent display of wildflowers in spring in the eastern section of the park.

MITCHELL RIVER NATIONAL PARK

A remote mountain wilderness park, it is popular with 4WD owners, canoeists and bushwalkers. One of its attractions is the Den of Nargun, a limestone cave filled with stalactites. There is an excellent walking track of about 3 km which takes in the cave, the Bluff Outlook and the Mitchell River. Drivers of 4WD vehicles have a choice of varied tracks to follow in the park. The Mitchell River is a favourite stretch of water in spring with canoeists and rafters. There are numerous bush camping sites, especially along the banks of the river. The park is 200 km east of Melbourne.

MORNINGTON PENINSULA NATIONAL PARK

Port Nepean and the old military fort are now incorporated in this park. This area was formerly known as the Point Nepean National Park but ten years ago it was amalgamated with the Cape Schanck Coastal Park and now covers a region of craggy headlands, sandy beaches and an abundance of marine life. The old Port Nepean Quarantine Station is also included in the area, as well as a historic fort, built in 1882 in response to fears of attack from countries such as Russia. Point Nepean can be explored on a tractor-pulled train and once a month the fort area is opened for cyclists to ride around the park. There is plenty of surfing, swimming, walking and fishing available on Gunnamatta Beach and Sorrento Back Beach. The park is for day-use only. It is 95 km south of Melbourne on the eastern side of the entrance to Port Phillip Bay.

MOUNT BUFFALO NATIONAL PARK

Encircled by the Ovens, Buffalo and Buckland Rivers, this park offers snow-covered mountaintops in winter and clear, warm days in summer. It is 320 km north-east of Melbourne via the Hume Highway. This rugged park beckons a wide variety of outdoor enthusiasts. Bushwalking is a popular activity after the snow melts and there are more than 90 km of marked tracks in the park. During winter, cross-country skiers are well catered for while downhill skiers have many trails to choose from. Anglers will find brown trout in Lake Catani.

MURRAY–SUNSET NATIONAL PARK

Located only six hours from Melbourne, in the very north-west of the state, this park is the second largest in Victoria. The region contains disparate environments, from the wetlands, lakes and billabongs of the Murray River system, to the seemingly infertile semi-arid interior of Victoria's desert country. But first appearances can be deceptive as this dry region supports a well-adapted community rich in flora and fauna. Sandhills, saltpans, occasional grasslands and mallee scrub cover the vast areas of desert, and spring is the time to visit, when much of the heath country and even the mallee is in flower. The park is renowned for the magnificent Pink Lakes in the southern section, where there are some enjoyable walks. Bird life and fauna are plentiful.

OTWAY NATIONAL PARK

This park stretches from Apollo Bay south to Princetown, with spurs of the Otway Range reaching down to the striking and ruggedly beautiful coastline of Bass Strait. The southern section of the range is one of the wettest areas in Victoria, sustaining a diverse range of vegetation from mountain ash, blue and mountain grey gum, to gullies of myrtle beech rainforest interspersed with tree-ferns, while mosses form a thick carpet over the ground and any fallen logs. Logging flourished in the Otways as early as 1848, and the old tramway tracks through the forests are now used as walking tracks. While bushwalking is a favourite pastime along the forest tracks and beaches, swimming, snorkelling, canoeing, surfing and fishing are also popular activities.

SNOWY RIVER NATIONAL PARK

This spectacular park, with its splendid river scenery, impressive deep gorges, picturesque forests and diverse vegetation and fauna, protects Victoria's largest forest wilderness, adjoining the Alpine National Park. Numerous vehicle tracks offer opportunities for visitors to explore the region; the Deddick Trail is suitable for 4WDs only. The Snowy River is also a mecca for canoeists. The southern part of the park is 390 km east of Melbourne.

WILSONS PROMONTORY NATIONAL PARK

With its pristine beaches, spectacular granite rock formations, magical fern gullies and remarkable variety of vegetation and wildlife, Wilsons Promontory National Park, or 'The Prom' as it is usually called, is one of Victoria's most popular parks. Surrounded on three sides by sea, a number of marine parks and reserves also stretch along the coastline and the area has long been a favourite for fishing and boating. Activities include surfing, diving, snorkelling, bushwalking and photography. The shallow waters of Tidal River make it a great place for kids to splash around in, while the nearby beaches are ideal for walking, swimming or simply lazing about. There are many walking trails in the park leading to secluded sandy beaches, or you could hike to the southernmost tip of mainland Australia and visit the lighthouse there. The park is 200 km south-east of Melbourne.

WYPERFELD NATIONAL PARK

Reached via Hopetoun, or the small township of Rainbow, the Wyperfeld National Park features a series of lakes and rivers which are normally dry lake beds connected by Outlet Creek. Only after exceptionally heavy rain do the river courses run. The vegetation varies considerably. In the west of the park the sand-plains are covered in heath, with mallee dominating the eastern section. Cypress pine woodlands prefer the sand dunes encircling the lakes, and river red gum and black box woodlands cover the floodplains of Outlet Creek and the lakes. This semi-arid environment comes alive in the spring when wildflowers put on a magnificent display, especially after rain. The bird life is one of the major attractions, and birdwatchers will find plenty to occupy their time. Emus and western grey kangaroos are also plentiful, along with stumpy-tail lizards and sand goannas. Many of the vehicle tracks in the park are suitable only for 4WDs. The park is 450 km north-west of Melbourne.

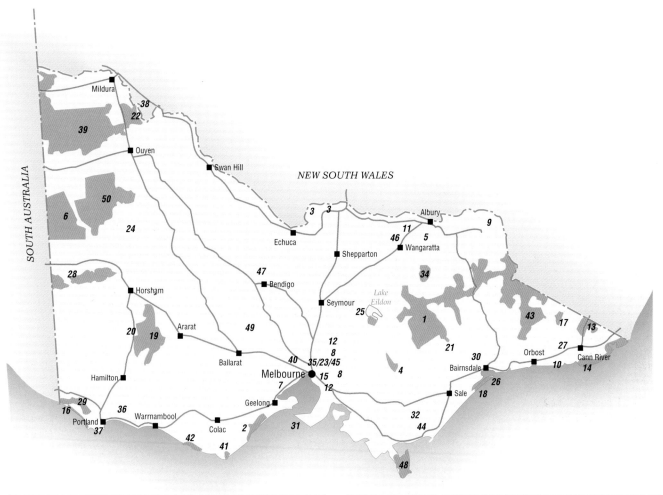

Popular Parks

	Camping	Caravans	Wheel Chairs	4WD Access	Picnic Area	Toilets	Walking Trks	Kiosk	Information
1 Alpine NP	■			■	■	■	■		■
2 Angahook-Lorne SP	■	■	■	■	■	■	■		■
3 Barmah SP & SF	■			■	■	■	■		■
4 Baw Baw NP	■		■		■	■	■	■	■
5 Beechworth Historic Park				■	■	■	■		■
6 Big Desert Wilderness	Access by foot only								
7 Brisbane Ranges NP	■				■	■	■		
8 Bunyip SP	■			■	■	■	■		■
9 Burrowa-Pine NP	■			■	■	■	■		
10 Cape Conran Foreshore Reserve	■		■		■	■	■		
11 Chiltern RP	■			■	■	■	■		
12 Churchill NP					■	■	■		
13 Cooracambra NP	■			■					
14 Croajingalong NP	■	■		■	■	■	■		■
15 Dandenong Ranges NP					■				
16 Discovery Bay CP	■	Dune Buggy Area		■	■	■	■		■
17 Errinundra NP	■			■	■	■	■		
18 Gippsland Lakes Coastal Park	■			■	■	■	■		
19 Grampians NP	■	■		■	■	■	■		■
20 Grampians SF	■	■		■	■	■	■		
21 Grant Historic Area	■			■	■	■	■		
22 Hattah-Kalkyne NP	■	■		■	■	■	■		■
23 Kinglake NP	■			■	■	■	■		■
24 Lake Albacutya RP	■	■		■	■		■		
25 Lake Eildon NP	■	■	■	■	■	■	■		■

Popular Parks

	Camping	Caravans	Wheel Chairs	4WD Access	Picnic Area	Toilets	Walking Trks	Kiosk	Information
26 Lakes NP	■	■			■	■	■		
27 Lind NP			■		■	■	■		
28 Little Desert NP	■	■		■	■	■	■		■
29 Lower Glenelg NP	■	■		■	■	■	■		■
30 Mitchell River NP	■			■	■	■	■		
31 Mornington Peninsula NP			■		■	■	■		■
32 Morwell NP					■	■	■		
33 Mt Buangor SP/Mt Cole SF	■			■	■	■	■		
34 Mt Buffalo NP	■	■	■	■	■	■	■	■	■
35 Mt Disappointment SF	■			■	■		■		
36 Mt Eccles NP	■	■	■		■	■	■		■
37 Mt Richmond NP					■	■	■		
38 Murray-Kulkyne Park	■			■	■	■	■		
39 Murray-Sunset NP	■			■	■	■	■		■
40 Organ Pipes NP					■	■	■		■
41 Otway NP	■	■		■	■	■	■		■
42 Port Campbell NP	■	■			■	■	■		■
43 Snowy River NP	■			■	■	■	■		
44 Tarra-Bulga NP					■	■	■		■
45 Toolangie SF/Murrindindi SR	■			■	■	■	■		■
46 Warby Range SP	■	■		■	■	■	■		
47 Whipstick SP					■	■	■		■
48 Wilsons Promontory NP	■	■	■		■	■	■	■	■
49 Wombat SF (Hepburn Springs)	■	■		■	■	■	■		■
50 Wyperfeld NP	■	■		■	■	■	■		■

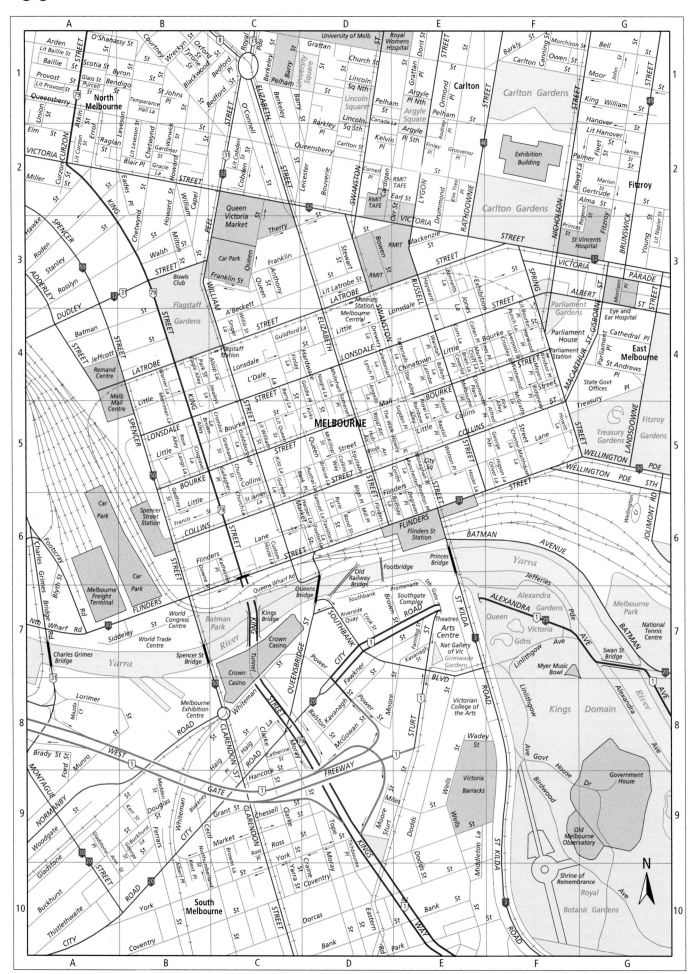

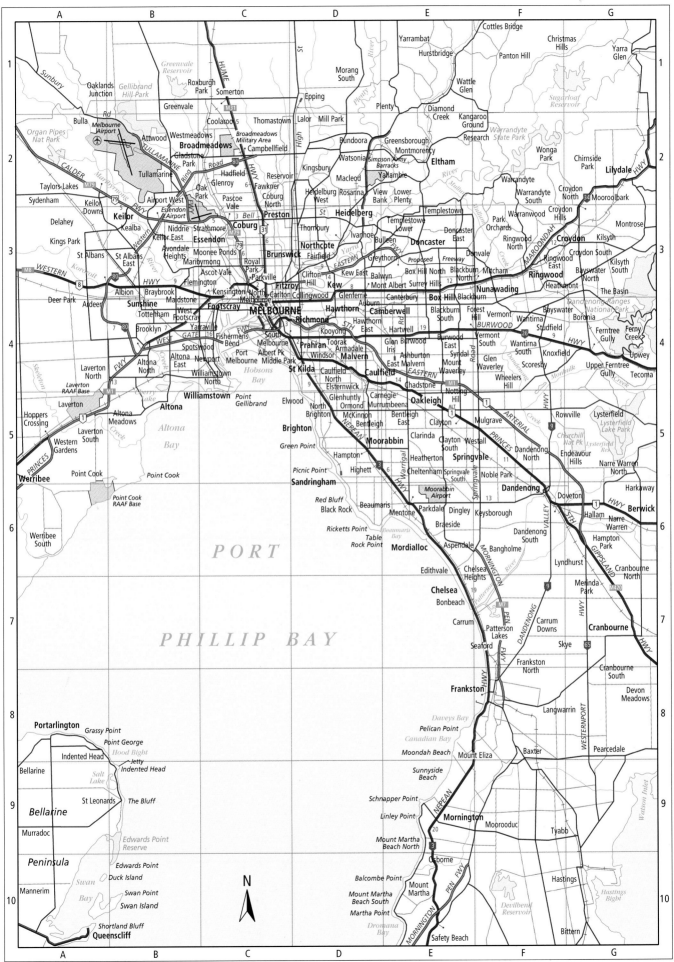

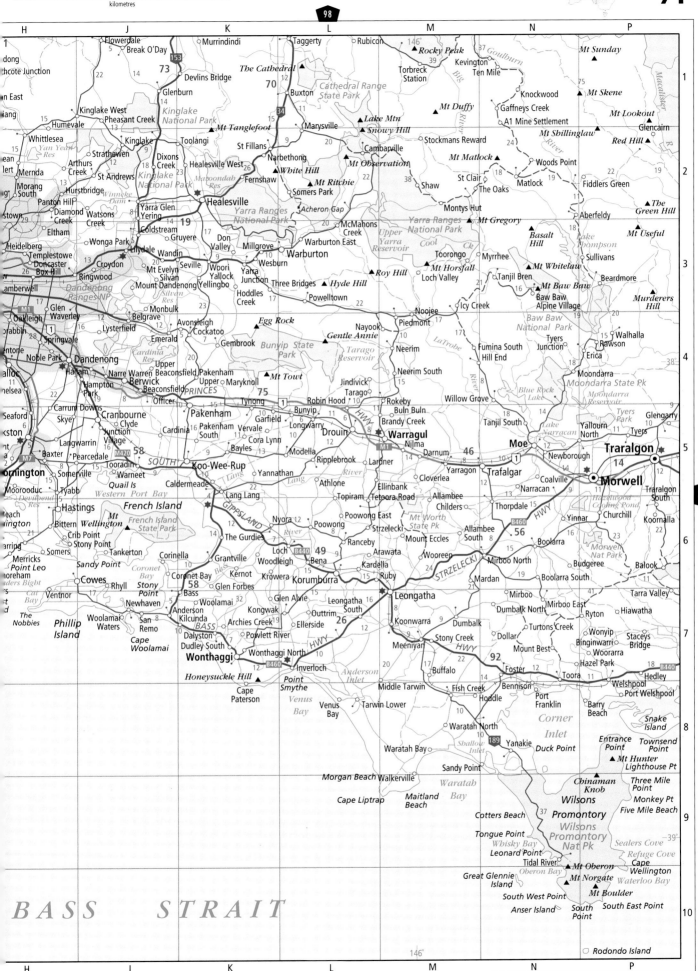

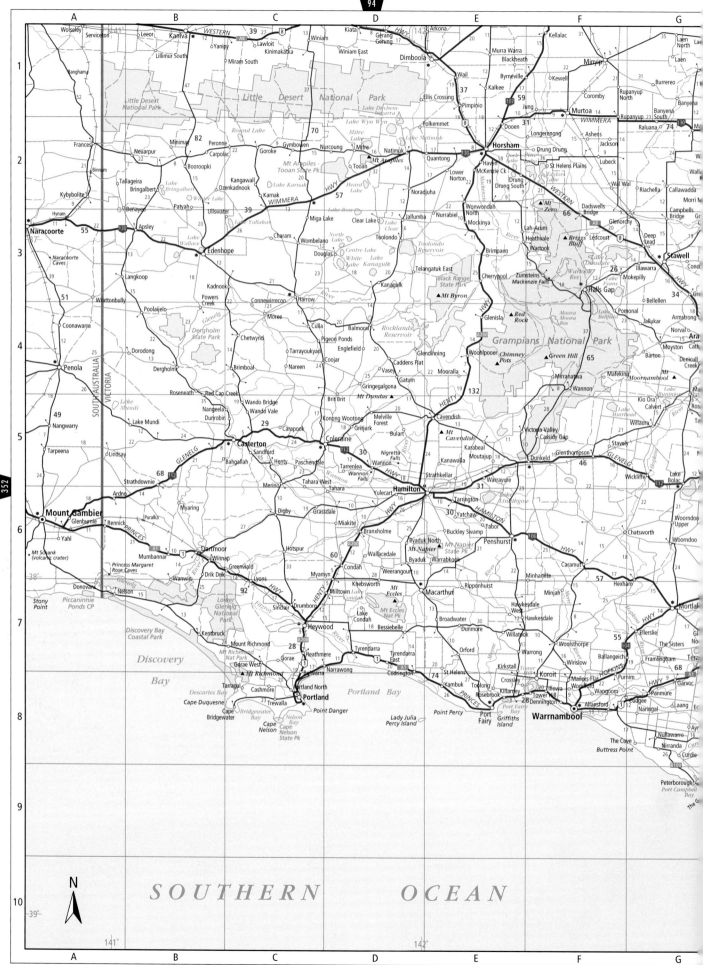

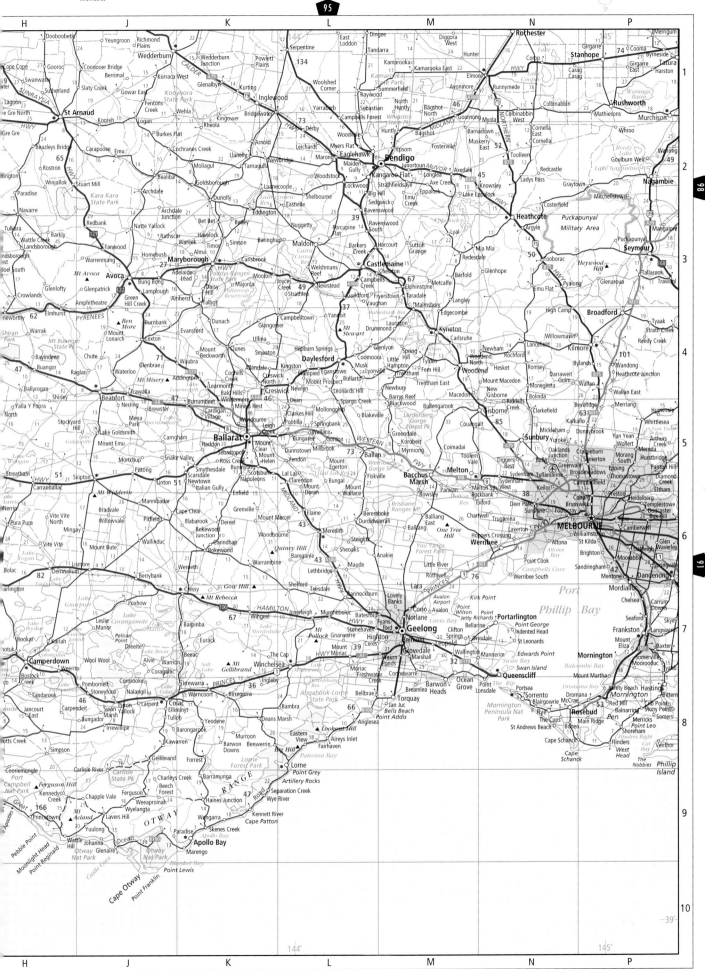

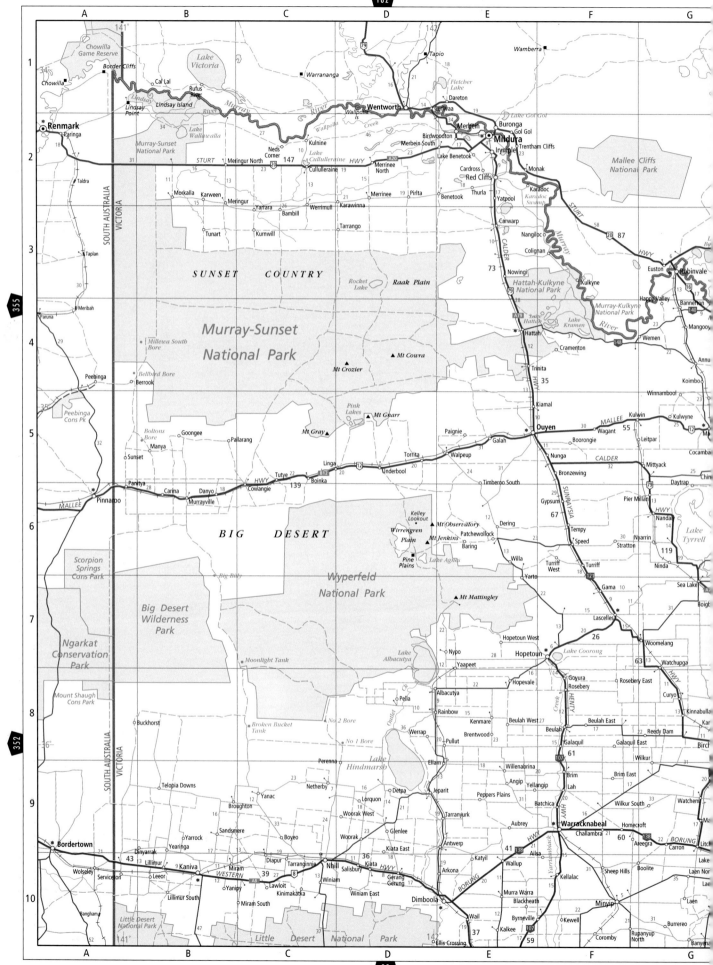

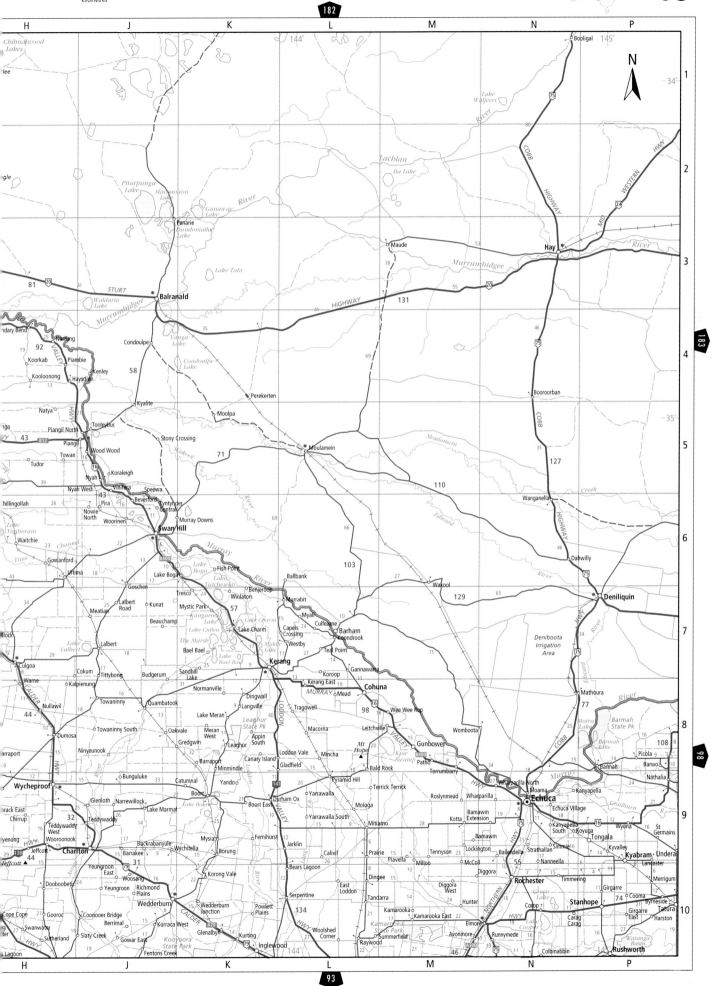

0 10 20 30 40 50
kilometres

183

98

H   J   K   L   M   N   P

Booligal
Lake Waljeers
Lachlan River
Ita Lake
Pitarpunga Lake
Macammon Lake
Ganaway Lake
Penarie
Dundomallee Lake
Lake Tala
Maude
Murrumbidgee
Hay
COBB HIGHWAY
MID WESTERN HWY

STURT
Balranald
Waldaria Lake
Murrumbidgee
HIGHWAY 131
Condoulpe
Yanga Lake
Condoulpe Lake
Booroorban

Nerring
Piambie
Koorkab
Kooloonong
Haysdale
Kenley
Kyalite
Perekerten
Moolpa

Natya
Toolevbuc
Piangil North
Stony Crossing
Moulamein
Wanganella
Piangil
Wood Wood
Towan
Murray Downs
Tudor
Nyah
Koraleigh
Speewa
Deniliquin
Nyah West
Vinifera
Beverford
Tyntynder Central
Pira
Woorinen
Swan Hill
Murray River
Deniboota Irrigation Area
Nowie North
Waitchie
Gowanford
Lake Boga
Fish Point
Ballbank
Wakool
Dahwilly
Ultima
Lake Boga
Benjeroop
Murrabit
129
Tresco
Winlaton
Myall
Goschen
Mystic Park
Kunat
Capels Crossing
Culfearne
Barham
Meatian
Lake Charm
Westby
Koondrook
Beauchamp
Bael Bael
Teal Point
Lalbert
Lake Bael Bael
Kerang
Mathoura
Tulgoa
Cokum
Tittybong
Sandhill Lake
Koroop
Gannawarra
Moira Lake
Barmah State Pk
Warne
Kalpienung
Budgerum
Normanville
Kerang East
Cohuna
Mead
108
Nullawil
Towaninny
Dingwall
Langville
98
Wee Wee Rup
Picola
Dumosa
Towaninny South
Oakvale
Meran West
Leaghur State Pk
Tragowell
Leitchville
Womboota
Barmah
Barwo
Ninyeunook
Gredgwin
Leaghur
Appin South
Macorna
Gunbower
Nathalia
Barraport
Bunguluke
Catumnal
Yando
Minmindie
Canary Island
Gladfield
Mt Hope
Bald Rock
Patho
Torrumbarry
Wharparilla North
Kanyapella
Wycheproof
Boort
Durham Ox
Yarrawalla
Pyramid Hill
Terrick Terrick
Roslynmead
Wharparilla
Echuca
Echuca Village
Glenloth
Narrewillock
Lake Marmal
Boort East
Yarrawalla South
Mologa
Mitiamo
Bamawm Extension
Kotta
Kanyapella South
Koyuga
Wyuna
St Germains
Chirrup
Teddywaddy West
Wooroonook
Mysia
Fernihurst
Calivil
Prairie
Tennyson
Bamawm
Lockington
Ballendella
Strathallan
Simmie
Kyvalley
Tongala
Charlton
Barrakee
Wychitella
Borung
Jarklin
Milloo
McColl
Nanneella
Kyabram
Underal
Jeffcott
Yeungroon East
Woosang
Korong Vale
Bears Lagoon
Dingee
Piavella
Diggora
Rochester
Timmering
Girgarre
Merrigum
Dooboobetic
Yeungroon
Richmond Plains
Serpentine
East Loddon
Tandarra
Diggora West
Hunter
Corop
Stanhope
Girgarre East
Cooma
Tatura
Wedderburn
Wedderburn Junction
Powlett Plains
134
Kamarooka
Kamarooka East
Elmore
Avonmore
Runnymede
Carag Carag
Harston
Swanwater
Gooroc
Coonooer Bridge
Berrimal
Kurraca West
Glenalbyn
Kurting
Inglewood
Woolshed Corner
Summerfield
Raywood
Colbinabbin
Rushworth
Cope Cope
Sutherland
Slaty Creek
Gowar East
Fentons Creek

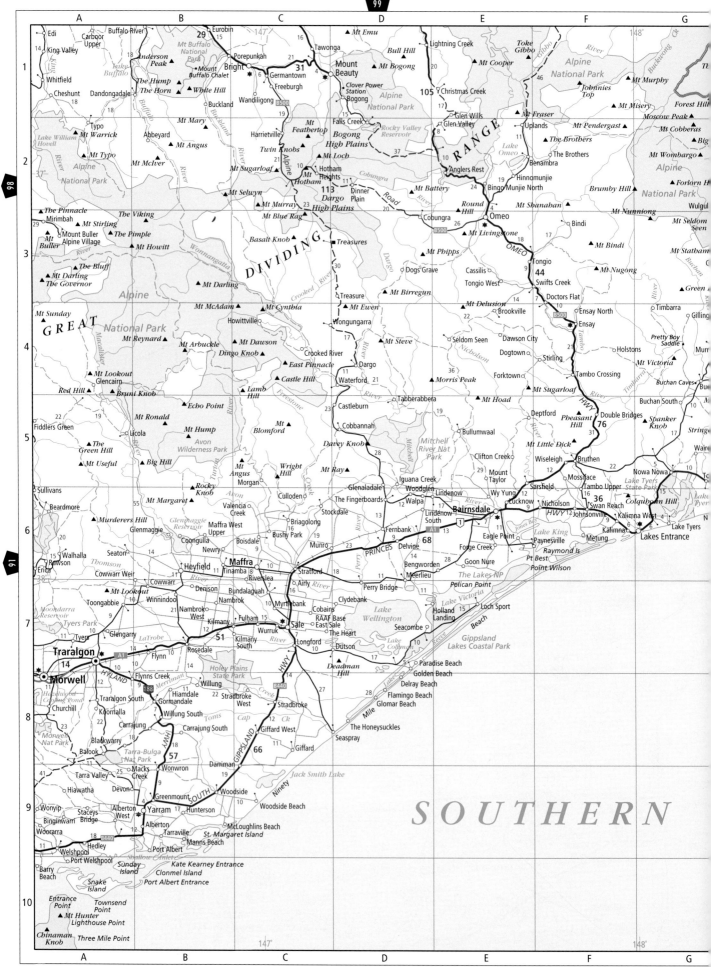

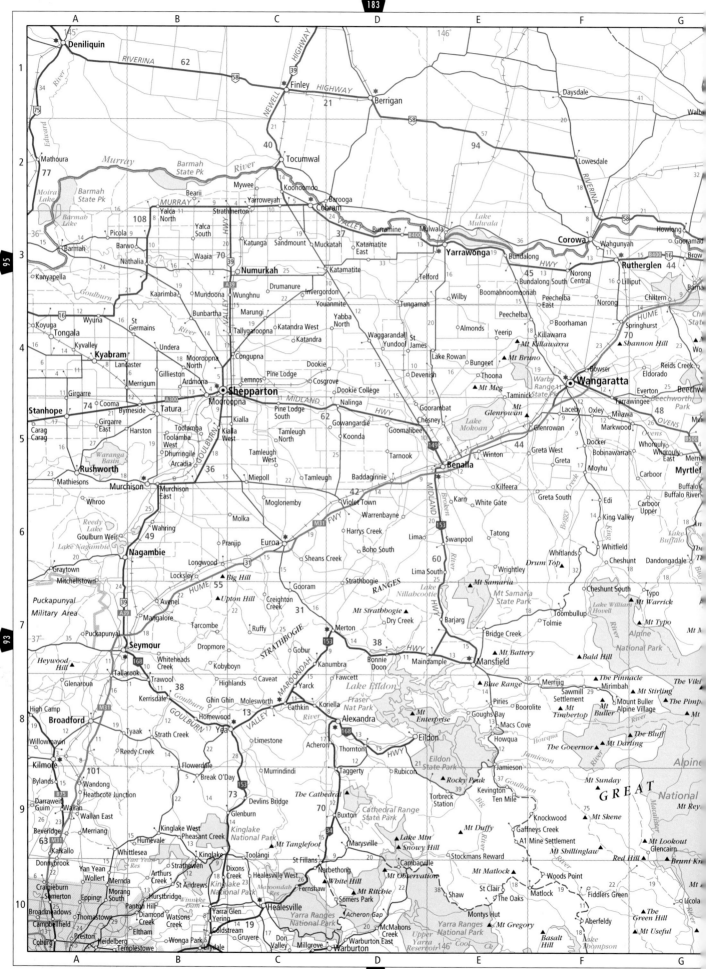

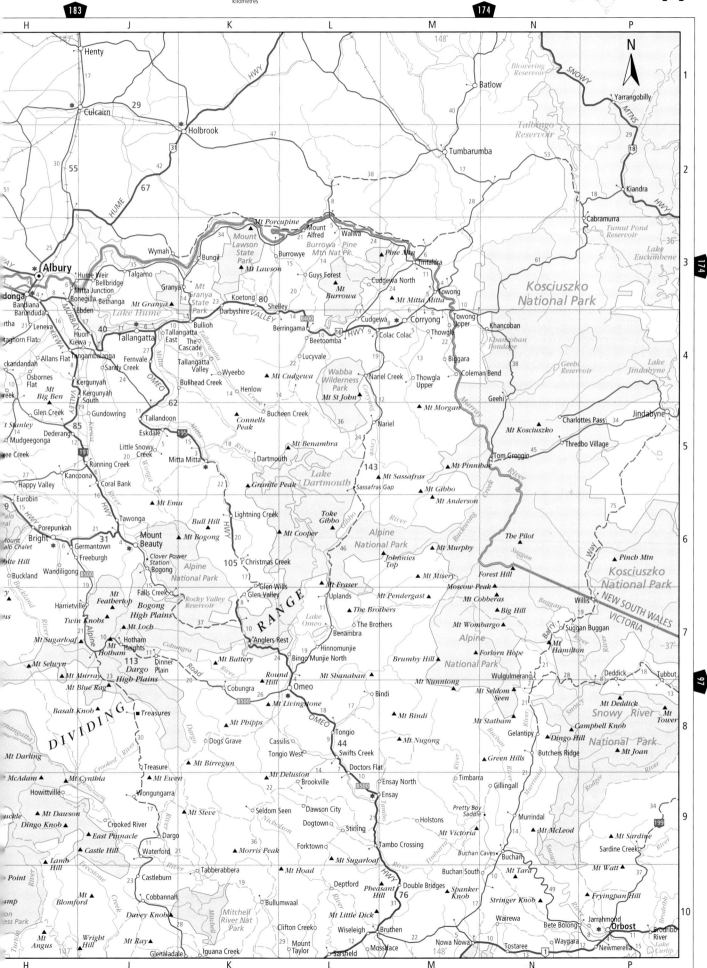

THE AUSTRALIAN CAPITAL TERRITORY

Section 125 of the Commonwealth Constitution Act of 1900 provided that the seat of Australian Government should lie in Commonwealth Territory. Nine years of prolonged political debate preceded the choice of Canberra as the nation's capital, with 2330 square kilometres ceded by New South Wales making the surrounding Australian Capital Territory.

The ACT is approximately halfway between Sydney and Melbourne. The primary road routes in are the Monaro Highway (which heads almost straight north from Cooma), the Barton Highway (which comes in from the northwest just out of Yass), and the Federal Highway (which travels alongside most of the western shore of Lake George and originates just southwest of Goulburn). Lake George, by the way, is an enigma. Its waters regularly recede for no apparent reason, then fill again, often without the benefit of heavy rains.

Over 40 per cent of the ACT is taken up by Namadgi National Park, the most northerly alpine environment in Australia. Though devoted mainly to wilderness areas, the park allows horse riding in designated areas and its streams attract trout fishermen. There are also picnic and camping areas along the main access roads and the visitors' centre on Naas Road provides not only information on the park but has audiovisuals and hands-on displays.

Another park worth visiting in the adjoining area is Brindabella, with some terrific 4WD tracks which eventually lead the visitor out of the park and through to Yarrangobilly Caves. Drivers should be aware, however, that local farmers are trying to block access to the more rugged areas. Magnificent mountain scenery and old cattlemen's huts, however, more than make up for any inconvenience.

Europeans first explored the region in 1821, when explorer/surgeon Charles Throsby Smith came in as far as Black Mountain, where Telstra's 195 metre high tower now stands. Famous botanist Allan Cunningham followed, and the area was named Limestone Plains, regarded as suitable for pastoral pursuits. In 1824, the first European settler, Joshua Moore, arrived to set up his property 'Canberry' and the following year, wealthy Sydney merchant Robert Campbell, blazed out another property that he called 'Duntroon'. It is now, of course, Australia's most famous military college, and has been since 1910.

What is less well known is that the Australian Capital Territory has an adjunct at Jervis Bay. The same Act which proclaimed the need for an independent capital also demanded that the Federal Government have access to the sea, so an area of 5 square kilometres—later increased to 72.5 square kilometres—was also ceded by the New South Wales Government to the Federal Government. Throughout most of its history, Jervis Bay has been the preserve of the Royal Australian Navy, and in the late 1990s, was the subject of bitter debate about its future.

History buffs should make time to visit Lanyon, some 30 km south of Canberra. Lanyon preserves life as it was as a nineteenth century homestead and has the National Trust's highest classification. There are many original Sidney Nolan paintings in the house, including some of the well-known 'Ned Kelly' series. Further south on the banks of the Murrumbidgee is Cuppacumbalong homestead, which has a private cemetery, a craft centre, a restaurant and areas for picnicking and swimming.

Other places worth visiting include Cockington Green, a miniature English village 9 km north of Canberra on the Barton Highway;

Hot-air balloons getting ready to rise into the sky over the ACT

Glorious parkland in the ACT

Ginanderra, which features craft and art galleries, shops and a restaurant; the National Dinosaur Museum (directly opposite); and Bywong Mining Town, a recreation of late 1880s mining settlements, which is off the Gundaroo Road. Though somewhat overshadowed by other radio telescopes such as the one at Parkes, Mt Stromlo Observatory was one of the first in Australia.

At Tidbinbilla, about 40 km south of Canberra, is the Canberra Deep Space Communications Complex, which has models of spacecraft and some exciting audiovisual displays.

Visitors coming this far should also take in the Tidbinbilla Nature Reserve, where kangaroos and koalas can be easily viewed and there are good picnic and BBQ facilities. Corin Forest Recreation Area, with its 1 km alpine slide and interesting bushwalks, and Cotter Dam Reserve, with river swimming, a children's playground and again, picnic and camping areas, are two popular spots for locals as well as tourists.

One out-of-the-way monument that is rarely alluded to in any tourist information can be found on a dirt track that spurs off the Canberra–Queanbeyan road. It commemorates a disastrous 1940 plane crash in which top-ranking Air Force officers, cabinet ministers and civil servants lost their lives. Coming in the darkest days of World War II, it could not have occurred at a worse time.

The ACT is one of the country's major tourist areas, having varied countryside, historic dwellings, musuems and wildlife parks to explore, as well as being home to the nation's capital and seat of government.

Kangaroos in the beauting setting of Tidbinbilla Nature Reserve

CANBERRA

POPULATION: 307 000

MAP REFERENCE: PAGE 305 B5

The name 'Canberra' (supposedly Aboriginal for 'meeting place') evokes mixed feelings in most Australians.

On the one hand, it is the seat of the Federal Government, and as such, is deserving of respect. On the other hand, as the seat of the Federal Government it is the target of collective rancour against elected officials whom many people see as self-serving—anything *but* servants of the public.

In contrast to most Australian cities and towns, Canberra is a fully planned city, and lacks the chaotic charm of places that grew up from a random collection of tents clustered on the banks of a river or by a goldfield. So while the nation's capital is undeniably well ordered, with a fast network of well-signposted roads and highways, there is a certain sterility about the place which means the tourist has to dig a little deeper than normal to find the living core. Many do not bother, seeing Canberra as a roadblock on the way south to the snowfields (or skirt it entirely, going via Queanbeyan), but that is doing the city a disservice. Canberra is clean, its suburbs following the sweeping lines of avenues and cul-de-sacs called for in the original plan. What relatively little industry exists is confined to suburbs like Fishwyck, Hume and Mitchell. Finally, that super-efficient road network takes some getting used to, and if you miss a turn you may find yourself inexorably borne kilometres out of your way. Study the road map carefully before setting off, or make sure you have a good navigator.

Canberra's genesis lies in bitter and hostile dispute. Prior to Federation in 1901, intercolonial controversy raged over the site of the new nation's capital. So, at the Premiers' Conference of 1899, it was proposed that the Federal capital would be in New South Wales, but not within 100 miles (161 km) of Sydney. Many Sydneysiders opposed the resolution, as did Melbournians. Both felt their cities would make fine capitals, though few proponents were willing to cede the land that would become the Australian Capital Territory. Competition from New South Wales towns outside the forbidden zone was fierce as well. Ultimately the Yass–Canberra site was agreed upon.

Since 1823, the site of Canberra had been used for grazing sheep and was originally known as Limestone Plains. Canberry was a property run by Joshua Moore.

Crimson rosellas can seen in the parks around Canberra

While Melbourne became the temporary capital (a situation which persisted until 1927), an international competition was announced for the design of Canberra, and once again, controversy raged. Objections to the terms and conditions by the Royal Institute of British Architects meant that Empire architects boycotted the competition, and first prize went to American Walter Burley Griffin. His plan used free-flowing lines, in contrast to the other entries. However, nothing ran smoothly. Committees changed Burley Griffin's design, incorporating elements of the other entries, and it was not until 1915 that this unharmonious scheme was rejected. Burley Griffin continued to fight over design changes with the government, and his employment was terminated in 1920, long before construction was completed. There is little doubt that many Australians opposed spending lavish amounts on a 'bush capital' long after Burley Griffin had departed.

Canberra grew slowly. Though construction had begun in 1911, World War I interrupted proceedings. The politicians moved to Canberra in 1927, but the huge, lumbering public service remained behind in Melbourne until well after World War II. Development was much quicker after 1955, with Canberra rapidly becoming Australia's largest inland city. The Molonglo River was not dammed until 1964, creating Lake Burley Griffin, the centrepiece of the city.

Though now a thoroughly modern city, Canberra lacks nightlife compared with Sydney or Melbourne. It is not as bad as it used to be, but the nation's capital is still more for visitors interested in architecture and monuments than strip clubs and cabaret. However, Canberra does lay claim to a casino.

The best way to gain an appreciation of Canberra is to visit any of the lookouts on the surrounding hills. Telstra Tower, on Black Mountain, is 195 metres high and has viewing galleries and a revolving restaurant. On the summit of Mt Pleasant are memorials to the Australian Artillery and Armoured Corps, while Red Hill overlooks Parliament House, southern Canberra and the Woden Valley. From Mt Ainslie the visitor can see central Canberra and Lake Burley Griffin, which has a shoreline of over 35 km, complete with cycling and walking tracks.

On the southern foreshore of the lake is the National Gallery of Australia, which houses not only an excellent collection of Aboriginal art, but works by modern and post-modernist artists, including a number of Australians like Arthur Boyd, Tom Roberts, Arthur Streeton, Sidney Nolan and Brett Whitely. In the grounds, sculptures blend with the natural environment and the gallery's restaurant is situated in an artificial fog sculpture by Japanese artist Fujiko Nakaya.

The National Gallery is connected to the High Court by a footbridge. With its lofty public gallery and murals by Jan Senbergs, Australia's final court of appeal should be put on the visiting list.

Also on the foreshore is the National Library of Australia, opened in 1968. An eclectic building designed in neo-Classical style, the library contains more than 5 million books, as well as photographs, documents, newspapers and periodicals. Its exterior features 44square columns of Carrara marble, and inside Aubusson tapestries (made from Australian wool). It also contains stained glass windows by Australian artist Leonard French.

Between the National Library and the High Court is Questacon, the National Science and Technology Centre, which features interactive displays and DIY experiments. Further south is the Canberra Railway Museum, which boasts Australia's oldest working steam locomotive (1878) and other railway memorabilia.

On the lake itself are three landmarks: the Captain Cook Memorial, a 150 metre water jet known irreverently to Canberrans as 'the Royal Flush'; the Carillon, a three-column belltower that was a gift from the British Government to mark Canberra's Jubilee, and the National Capital Exhibition on Regatta Point.

Aerial view of Canberra with the War Memorial in the foreground, with Anzac Parade leading to Lake Burley Griffin and Old Parliament House

Lake Burley Griffin is set in parklands, including Commonwealth Park and Weston Park. Bicycles can be hired so that you can cycle round the lake, or alternatively, take a sightseeing cruise. Paddleboats, windsurfers and sailing boats can also be hired.

Burley Griffin designed Canberra as a centre of politics rather than an urban living area. The crown of his plan consists of a triangle formed by Kings, Constitution and Commonwealth Avenues, with the apex dominated by Capital Hill and Parliament House. The new Parliament House, finished in 1988, is built into the top of the hill, so that the building would merge into its surroundings, with the result that a grass walkway exists on the roof. It contains fine paintings and artefacts, and is well worth a visit.

One of the most popular attractions in Canberra is the Australian War Memorial, at the end of Anzac Parade. It houses a huge collection of relics, models and paintings commemorating the sacrifices of Australians in all theatres of war. A very moving place, the War Memorial is a grand structure. It also houses the Pool of Remembrance and the Tomb of the Unknown Soldier.

One of the early homesteads—Yarralumla—is now the official residence of the Governor-General, and the Prime Minister's Lodge is on the corner of Adelaide Avenue and National Circuit. The Royal Australian Mint, which presses all Australian coin and also prints notes, is in Deakin.

Canberra is also home to Australia's best-known military school, Duntroon Royal Military College. The Officers' Mess at Duntroon is actually the old stone homestead of the Campbell family, early pioneers in the district. Robert Campbell is commemorated in a stained glass window in the Church of St John the Baptist, near Anzac Park. The graveyard there offers the visitor an insight into the area's early history, as does the adjacent schoolhouse which has been converted into a museum. Other folkloric relics are kept in Blundell's Farmhouse, which can be found on the northern shore of the lake.

For those who like their sightseeing potted rather than discovered, there is the Canberra Explorer bus service, which runs every hour seven days a week on a 25 km route around the city. There are 19 stops, and passengers can get off and rejoin the tour at any time. .

As expected in a city that hosts many diplomatic embassies, Canberra's restaurants are of good standard and very diverse, offering cuisines ranging from contemporary Australian to Asian, Mediterranean and the even more exotic Turkish and Russian. The city has over 300 restaurants to choose from, and diners should also sample some local wine. Though the district's viticulture does not yet have the reputation of New South Wales'

famous Hunter Valley or Mudgee, it has a distinct style, naturally based on cool climate grapes. There are 16 or so wineries in the area, around the nearby townships of Hall, Murrumbateman and Bungendore.

Hall also has a market fostering home produce and folk art on the first Sunday of every month, and Bungendore is a town that has been totally classified by the National Trust. Its village square has an historic recreation of the tale of a local bushranger of the 1850s.

Visitors should be aware that Canberra has four very distinct seasons. Summers are hot and winters often see light snowfalls and more regularly, heavy fogs that can and do close the airport.

Canberra hosts a number of festivals and events, the most famous of which is probably Floriade, in September, when the gardens and parks provide visitors with stunning views of flowers and plants. However, the event that brings the most 'heads' and tourist dollars to Canberra is vastly different—almost counterculture to the city's normally staid, white collar existence. Every December, just after Christmas, Canberra throbs to the roar of V8 engines as the Street Machine Summernats are held. This is an event featuring what used to be called 'hot rods'—modified and heavily accessorised saloon cars, usually Holdens and Fords. There are wet T-shirt competitions, no T-shirt competitions, 'burn-outs' and what could be called concourse d'inelegances. It is rowdy Australian fun. Young fun. The Summernats is an experience no one should miss.

January sees the Canberra World Cup Showjumping; February the Royal Show, Multicultural Festival and St Valentine's Jazz Festival; March horseracing, the Canberra Festival and the PGA Seniors Golf; April the Anzac Day Parade and Service at the War Memorial, and the ACT and Australian Science Festivals. Other notable events are the Festival of Contemporary Arts in October and the Canberra Rally in November.

ACCOMMODATION

Hyatt Hotel Canberra (grand hotel at Yarralumla), ph (02) 6270 1234; Capital Parkroyal (grand hotel in the city), ph (02) 6247 5504; Embassy Motel (Deakin), ph (02) 6281 1322; Tall Trees Lodge Motel (Ainslie), ph (02) 6247 9200; Capital Executive Apartments (serviced, in the city), ph (02) 6243 8333; Argyle Executive Apartments (serviced, in the city), ph (02) 6275 0800; City Walk Hotel, ph (02) 6257 0124; Gazebo Hotel (city), ph (02) 6247 6344; Holiday Haven Tourist Parks (camping/caravans), ph 1800 626 054

TOURIST INFORMATION: Ph (02) 6205 0666

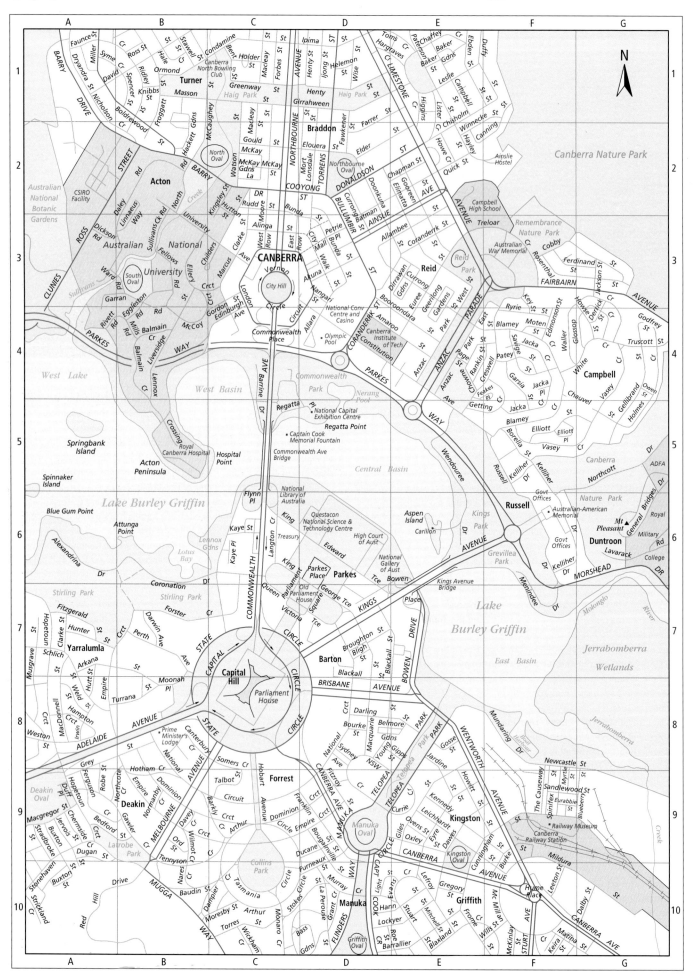

kilometres
0 5 10 15 20

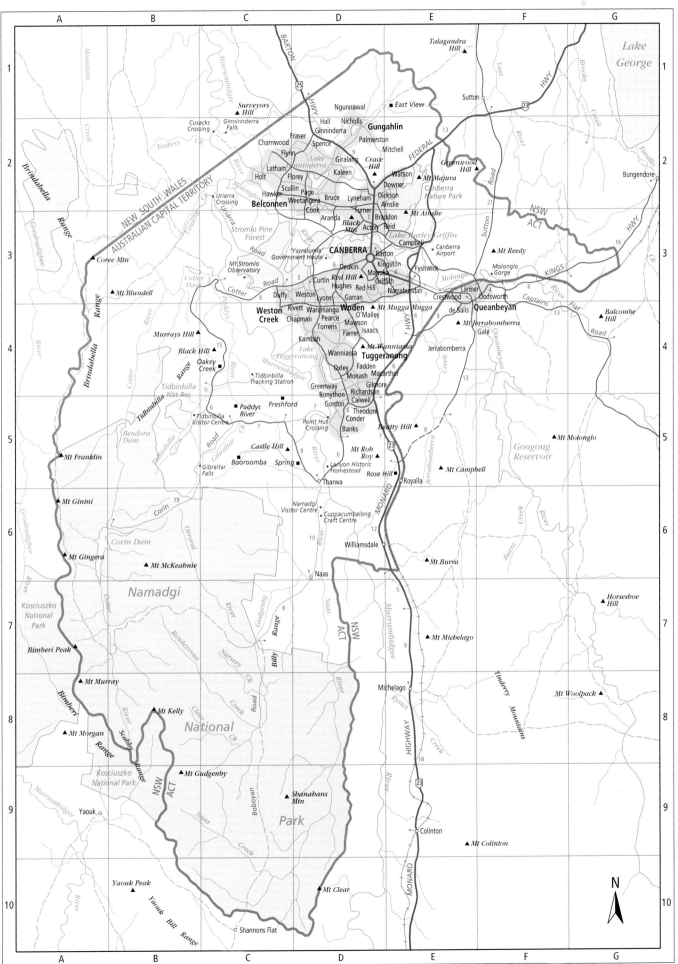

NEW SOUTH WALES

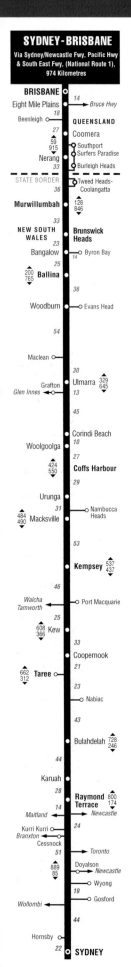

SYDNEY - BRISBANE
Via Sydney/Newcastle Fwy, Pacific Hwy
& South East Fwy, (National Route 1),
974 Kilometres

BRISBANE
Eight Mile Plains
— 14 — *Bruce Hwy*
Beenleigh — 18 —
QUEENSLAND
— 27 —
Coomera
— 59 / 915 — Southport
Surfers Paradise
Nerang
— 33 — Burleigh Heads
STATE BORDER
— 36 — Tweed Heads–
Coolangatta
Murwillumbah
— 128 / 846 —
— 33 —
NEW SOUTH WALES
Brunswick Heads
— 23 —
Bangalow
— 14 — Byron Bay
— 25 —
— 200 / 765 — **Ballina**
— 36 —
Woodburn — Evans Head
— 54 —
Maclean
— 30 —
Grafton — Ulmarra — 329 / 645
Glen Innes — 13 —
— 45 —
Corindi Beach
Woolgoolga — 10 —
— 27 —
— 424 / 550 — **Coffs Harbour**
— 29 —
Urunga
— 31 — Nambucca Heads
— 484 / 490 — Macksville
— 53 —
Kempsey — 537 / 437
— 46 —
Walcha — Port Macquarie
Tamworth — 25 —
— 608 / 366 — Kew
— 33 —
Coopernook
— 21 —
— 662 / 312 — **Taree**
— 23 — Nabiac
— 43 —
Bulahdelah — 728 / 246
— 44 —
Karuah
— 28 —
Raymond Terrace — 800 / 174
— 14 —
Maitland — Newcastle
Kurri Kurri — 24 —
Branxton
Cessnock — Toronto
— 51 —
Doyalson
— 889 / 85 — Newcastle
— 19 — Wyong
Wollombi — Gosford
— 44 —
Hornsby
— 22 —
SYDNEY

For the tourist, the prime attraction of New South Wales is that it encompasses everything from sophistication to remote serenity. You can enjoy a *café latte* in Double Bay one morning and the next be brewing some billy tea on the banks of the Darling River, civilisation light years behind you. Home to Australia's largest city, the state offers great regional diversity, from the snow-covered peaks of the Snowy Mountains to tropical rainforests, beaches beyond compare, the stirring magnificence of the Great Dividing Range running like a spine just west of the coast, and beyond that, wheat plains to rival Canada's. Further out is semi-desert that would please the most ardent desert-lover, with beacons like the Walls of China, in Mungo National Park, or the placid tranquillity of Lake Cawndilla in Kinchega National Park where Burke and Wills had their last taste of 'civilised' living. It is all out there.

Once New South Wales encompassed the whole of Australia, at least theoretically. When Arthur Phillip arrived with the First Fleet in 1788, Sydney Cove represented a landmark of continental sovereignty. As the other states and territories came into being, New South Wales shrank to its current size of over 800 000 sq km. This represents more than 10 per cent of the total landmass of Australia; it is still a lot bigger than Texas.

New South Wales has an excellent network of roads based on the tracks carved out of the virgin bush by the early explorers. They were followed by settlers and goldminers, generating in the process what are now the major routes. These highways, apart from servicing the state, offer visitors access to New South Wales's myriad tourist attractions.

The coastal Pacific Highway (Highway 1) runs from Timbilica in the south to Tweed Heads in the north, though it is called the Princes Highway from Melbourne to Sydney. Along that route are places like Eden, famous as a whaling station and now a wonderful holiday destination; as are Merimbula, Bega, Narooma and Moruya, which share the generic name of the 'Sapphire Coast'.

Further north are Batemans Bay—gateway to some terrific hinterland national parks— and Ulladulla, New South Wales's abalone fishing capital, while further on is Nowra which, for the traveller, represents a significant point in the road. From here you can either cut through the picturesque Kangaroo Valley to join the Hume Highway/Freeway at Mittagong, or take the longer but more diverting route to Sydney up through historic Berry, Wollongong and the coastal resort towns of Austinmer, Thirroul and Stanwell Park, cutting through Australia's oldest national park, the Royal, before hitting the traffic of Sydney's outskirts. (Another alternative, equally leisurely, is to take the Old Hume Highway through places like Picton and Tahmoor.)

From the time you cross the Sydney Harbour Bridge from Sydney's Central Business District and head into North Sydney, you are on the Pacific Highway, which runs through the city's North Shore until it reaches Wahroonga, when those in a hurry can divert onto the inappropriately named Newcastle Freeway, as it now runs clean past Newcastle to the New England Highway to the north, with a left hand turn to Maitland and beyond and a right hander to Raymond Terrace, back on the Pacific Highway proper. This road north will take you past legendary holiday destinations like the Myall Lakes, through the 'driver's road' sections of the Bulahdelah Mountain, and on to the North Coast with its recreational meccas like Port Macquarie, Coffs Harbour, Ballina, Byron Bay and, finally, the twin towns of Tweed Heads and Coolangatta. The other major route north for Sydneysiders is the New England Highway, which effectively begins just out of Newcastle and runs through more rural land, initially through wineries and pastoral areas of the Hunter Valley, then the mighty coal-producing districts around Muswellbrook and into the horse stud areas of Scone and Murrurundi. North is the Country Music Capital of Australia, Tamworth; then Uralla, where bushranger Captain Thunderbolt is buried; Armidale,

Port Maquarie on the Mid-North Coast with its beautiful beaches

the centre of rural education in New South Wales; and finally Tenterfield the town immortalised by songwriter Peter Allen in his ode to his grandfather, George Woolnough just before the Queensland border.

For the north-bound traveller who wishes to 'circumnavigate' the state, highway options soon dwindle. The Bruxner

Highway runs west from Lismore to Tenterfield (encompassing some magnificent Great Divide scenery). It runs out at Boggabilla, with the adventurous explorer forced onto secondary tar and then dirt to reach Mungindi and Collarenabri, Walgett and Brewarrina (where you can still see the rocks in the river which the Aborigines fashioned into fish traps), Bourke, then the real adventure of the Outback journey to Wanaaring and through to Milparinka on the Silver City Highway—a distance of some 1330 km from coast to corner. The real Corner Country, however, is to the north of Milparinka in Sturt National Park and Cameron Corner, where a general store sells fuel, drink and food.

The Silver City Highway runs from Warri Gate through Tibooburra and Milparinka almost due south through the mining giant of Broken Hill to Wentworth. There, the circumnavigator's journey becomes complicated. Initially, the Sturt Highway more or less follows the course of the Murray River, which forms the border between Victoria and New South Wales, but soon peels away to the east to Hay and on through Narrandera to Wagga. The Cobb Highway, which begins at Wilcannia, once known as the 'Queen of the West' and now more infamous for racial tension, would take the traveller south to Deniliquin to join the Riverina Highway through the Murrumbidgee Irrigation Area and the towns of Finley, Berrigan and finally Albury. To reach the coast again requires using the Snowy Mountains and Monaro Highways—no great hardship, as both traverse some of the most spectacular alpine country in Australia.

Other highways crisscross the state, beckoning the traveller. The Hume Highway, known to the truck drivers who regularly travel between Sydney and Melbourne as 'Sesame Street', has diversions to Gundagai, where the dog 'sat' on the tuckerbox, and runs through Holbrook, originally called Germanton, but rechristened in World War I after the commander of a British submarine. Where the georgraphy of New South Wales used to be remembered by schoolchildren by the names of its rivers (Clarence, Macleay, Manning and so on), perhaps now the highways are better indicators of geographic positioning.

The Gwydir runs from Grafton (famous for its jacaranda trees) through the gem-fossickers' paradise of Glen Innes through Warialda, Moree and finally Collarenebri.

The Oxley Highway begins on the coast at Wauchope, traverses the Great Divide to reach Walcha, then runs through to Gunnedah on the Black Soil Plains, Coonabarabran (gateway to the Warrumbungles), Gilgandra and finally Warren, on the fringes of the Macquarie Marshes, a spectacular haven for waterfowl and other wetlands inhabitants.

The old goldmining city of Bathurst spawns two major road arteries. The first is the Mitchell Highway, which runs northwest through Orange, Wellington (with its limestone caves), Dubbo (with its famous gaol), the citrus-growing centre of Narromine, Trangie, flood-beleaguered Nyngan, Bourke, Enngonia and finally Barringun, on the Queensland border—just a pub (but what a pub!). The second is the Mid-Western Highway, which spurs south-west through Blayney, historic Carcoar, Cowra, the goldmining town of Grenfell, the trucking hub of New South Wales, West Wyalong, and across the plain to Hay. Bathurst is also the terminus for the Great Western Highway, which approximately follows the route across the Blue Mountains built by convict labour in 1815.

Fly fishing on the Goodradigbee River near Brindabella

One of the longest highways in New South Wales is the Newell, which runs from Tocumwal in the south of the state through historic Jerilderie, Narrandera, West Wyalong, the bushranging district of Forbes, Parkes (with its huge astronomical telescope), Peak Hill, the hub of the West—Dubbo, Gilgandra, where the famed Coo-ee March began, Coonabarabran, Narrabri, Moree, and finally Boggabilla, right on the Queensland border.

Then there are the lesser-known highways like the Castlereagh, which links the opal fields of New Angledool with Walgett and towns further south like Coonamble, Gulargambone, Gilgandra and Dubbo. Or the remote Barrier Highway, stretching from Nyngan through the copper city of Cobar through Wilcannia to Broken Hill and beyond. And the highway in name only: the Lachlan, which links the isolated outposts of Booligal, Hillston and Lake Cargellico with a road that is mainly dirt.

For the visitor to New South Wales, there is a never-ending diversity of natural and man-made wonders to enjoy: the World Heritage listed areas and national parks are there to be explored, either on foot, on horseback or in a 4WD vehicle; the beaches and waterways beckon anglers, swimmers, and water sports enthusiasts alike, while the towns and cities offer contact with the past and a vitality and enthusiasm for the present. New South Wales has it all.

The statue of the champion pacer Paleface Adios in Temora

SYDNEY-MELBOURNE
Via Hume Hwy/Freeway & South Western Freeway (National Route 31), 884 Kilometres

SYDNEY
Enfield — 12
21
Hornsby — Liverpool — 33 851
22
Camden — Campbelltown
10
25
Picton
20
25 — Mittagong
105 779
31 — Berrima
Wollongong
Moss Vale
29
Marulan
36
Goulburn — 201 683
31 — Canberra
Breadalbane
20
Gunning — 252 632
33
285 599 — Canberra
Yass
37
Bookham
33
Jugiong
22
Coolac
20 — Gundagai
397 487
43
Cooma Bega
Wagga Wagga Mildura — Tarcutta — 440 444
25
Kyeamba
19
484 400 — Little Billabong
27
Holbrook — 511 373
27
Mullengandra — NEW SOUTH WALES
40
Wagga Wagga — Albury — 578 306
Corowa
STATE BORDER — To Corryong Wodonga
Yarrawonga
Chiltern
43
VICTORIA — Springhurst
649 235 — Wangaratta
24 — Bright
Glenrowan
16
15
680 192 — Benalla — Winton
12 — Mansfield
To Shepparton
23
Violet Town
24
Euroa — 739 145
31
Avenel
Shepparton Brisbane — Seymour — 791 93
21
19 — To Yea
Broadford
32
Kilmore — 842 42
Echuca
10
Kalkallo
23
Coburg
9 — MELBOURNE

SYDNEY

POPULATION: 3.9 MILLION

MAP REFERENCE: PAGE 305 B5

Sydney is the birthplace of modern Australia. When the First Fleet arrived on 26 January 1788, Governor Phillip, his troops and convicts all faced the same task: to take what they saw as a wilderness and transform it into a humble imitation of what they regarded as normal and expected in eighteenth-century Georgian Britain.

The fact that there were people already living in the Sydney Basin seemed irrelevant to them because the times in which they lived represented an epoch of expanding colonialism—an age of white is right. It was an age where human life—even white life—was cheap (unless you were an aristocrat); an age where people could be hanged for stealing a loaf of bread, or worse, sentenced to transportation to Botany Bay.

The little settlement—the tiny 'outpost of civilisation'—grew around the Tank Stream, which bubbled from the ground in what is now Hyde Park and flowed beneath today's buildings between Pitt and George Streets. Other buildings clung to the foreshores of Sydney Cove, but went no further than the present site of Bridge Street. But by 1794 there were 700 wooden dwellings in Sydney, plus the Government buildings, which, by contrast, were made of brick. And today the Sydney metropolitan area covers some 5000 square kilometres.

If Melbourne is establishment, Sydney is nouveau (though it has its share of old money and dynastic families). If Adelaide is old school tie, Sydney is entrepreneurial (though it is home to some of the best private schools in Australia).

Sydney is like Los Angeles without the pejoratives—it is big, sprawling, brash at times and sensitive at others. Perhaps more than any other city in Australia, Sydney is complex, almost schizophrenic, where the literally breathtaking beauty of the Opera House and the harbour on a warm summer day lives side by side with the industrial bleakness of Silverwater. Yet it is Sydney's very diversity that makes it appealing, makes it one of the great cities of the world.

Going into the twenty-first century, Sydney is admirably racially tolerant. That is probably because, of all Australian cities, it is the most polyglot. Though many new immigrants band together in suburban enclaves—Vietnamese in Cabramatta, Chinese in Strathfield, Japanese on the North Shore—that behaviour is understood and tolerated by Sydneysiders, who appreciate that a commonality of interests, language and custom initially needs the reinforcement of proximity. They know, too, that this will change. When Greek and Italian migrants came to Sydney in the Fifties and Sixties, they too gathered together in suburbs like Marrickville and Leichhardt. Now, many have dispersed to other parts of Sydney, their children sounding more Australian than Paul Hogan.

As it is, Asians have added a new dimension to Australia's biggest city. Someone driving through Campsie, for example, could think they had been teleported to somewhere—anywhere—in South-East Asia, with shopfronts bearing unfamiliar characters to advertise their trade. The Asian migration has broadened Sydney culturally and, of course, from a culinary perspective, just as the Italians and Greeks did 30 years ago. Where they introduced now-everyday items like garlic and chili, the Asians have brought with them ingredients such as daikon (Japanese radish) and lemongrass, so now chefs and suburban cooks alike can buy them fresh instead of processed. As a natural corollary, Sydneysiders have a profusion of choices when eating out: every cuisine in the world is represented from Argentinian to Zulu.

Tall ships on Sydney Harbour on Australia Day 1998

Because Sydney has such a wonderful climate (tending more to be hot than cold) its citizens spend their leisure time in the outdoors. The barbecue—long socially accepted as *the* way to entertain friends on the weekend—has become almost a religious rite. Sydneysiders spend their summers at the beaches that stretch from Palm Beach in the north to Maroubra in the south, or sail anything from boards to maxis in the Harbour, Pittwater or Port Hacking. Fishing and golf are other very popular pastimes.

The Central Business District (CBD) is geographically and figuratively Sydney's core. Part of Sydney's appeal is its energy, and like New York, much of that has to do with business drive. Sydney is one of the most

important commercial and financial centres of the Pacific Rim. Yet while its more modern skyscrapers are jaggedly angular, preservation orders have meant that the architectural charm and comparative softness of last century have remained a part of the cityscape. So, dwarfed by glass, steel and concrete, the Victorian extravagance of the Town Hall and Queen Victoria Building, the neo-Gothic of St Andrew's and St Mary's Cathedrals and the colonial genius of Francis Greenway's Macquarie Street buildings survive as a restful contrast to the new, encapsulating the ethos of the city itself. Only in the Rocks—that time capsule of Sydney's past, fronting Circular Quay and winding around to Campbell's Cove—is there any sense of architectural homogeneity. Warehouses may now be restaurants, and

brothels art galleries, but visitors wishing to know what Sydney looked like when it was younger and even more cocksure, should begin here. But instead of larrikins and touts and shady characters in the Argyle Cut, the Rocks is now full of tourists, souvenir shops, good pubs and live music. (Other suburbs have retained the grace of the bygone: Glebe, Balmain and Paddington are probably the best examples.)

Exploring Sydney from the CBD is like peeling the layers of an onion—from the inside. To the east are the traditional lairs of Sydney's 'elite': Rose Bay, Darling Point, Double Bay; also Bondi—to Kiwis what Earls Court was to expatriate Aussies in London in the 1960s—and Randwick, with its famous racecourse. Closer in is Oxford Street, the mecca of the gay

SYDNEY

The Archibald Fountain in Hyde Park

community and scene of the biggest homosexual ritual in the world—the Gay and Lesbian Mardi Gras, which takes place in February each year and is televised globally. Oxford Street is also famous for its cafés, cheap (but imaginative) eateries and coffee shops.

To the south is Kingsford Smith Airport and the suburbs of Mascot and Rockdale. The busiest aerodrome in Australia sits on Botany Bay, the site selected by James Cook as the most likely place of settlement and rejected by Arthur Phillip in favour of Port Jackson—now Sydney Harbour. Further on is the first national park proclaimed in Australia and among the first in the world—the Royal, which despite its proximity to the city, still retains rugged areas where the visitor can find inspiration from natural bushland.

Across 'the Coathanger' (the Harbour Bridge) is North Sydney, which became a secondary business district in the 1960s. Now it is filled with advertising agencies, smart eateries and smart young things. (Further up the line, Chatswood, and in the west, Parramatta and Blacktown, are currently experiencing the same metamorphosis from residential to commercial that North Sydney went through 40 years ago.) The outer north and the peninsula hold Sydney's alternative 'prestige' suburbs: Palm Beach, Whale Beach, Wahroonga, Turramurra and Pymble are all sought-after residential areas. Many people are now moving even further out to 'acreages', as they are known—large blocks of land on the periphery of the north-western metropolitan area—in suburbs like Dural, Annangrove and Glenorie.

But the west is the most dynamic player in Sydney's twenty-first century development. As Sydney galloped across the Cumberland Plain, engulfing previously separate entities such as Parramatta, Campbelltown and Liverpool, the outskirts have now become an integral part of the societal whole. Unlike Melbourne, where people are perhaps more cosmopolitan and think it perfectly normal to live in a flat or an apartment, Sydney best epitomises the realisation of the Australian dream of 'owning your own quarter-acre': it is regarded almost as a birthright.

Already the location for Sydney's fourth university—the University of Western Sydney, near Penrith, which joins Sydney, New South Wales and Macquarie Universities as centres of higher learning—the outer west is growing faster than anywhere else. A comparatively young residential group has seen the expression 'population explosion' made real. And with a high average disposable income, the west is becoming wealthier and worldlier. The west also contains some of Sydney's most popular drawcards, such as Australia's Wonderland which is great for children, and Eastern Creek Raceway, which hosts international motorsport events.

Sydney is similar to many other large cities in that not all of its workforce lives locally. Thanks to improved road networks like the northern

expressway, people commute from the Central Coast and the Blue Mountains every weekday.

Sydney has landmarks, both geographical and cultural: White City, aspiration of every young tennis player; a revitalised Taronga Park Zoo; the Mitchell Library, surely the best reference source in the country; Bradley's Head, with gun emplacements that never fired a shot in anger; Bondi Beach, which every overseas visitor *has* to see; Kings Cross, seedy by day, steamy by night; Homebush Bay, home of the Sydney 2000 Olympics. Though it perhaps lacks the international sporting sanctity of Lords in the United Kingdom, the Sydney Cricket Ground is hallowed ground for followers of both the willow and the pigskin, for not only have some of the greatest cricket test matches been played there, but all Rugby League Grand Finals. It is also impossible to omit from a list of Sydney's landmarks the Entertainment Centre, where performers ranging from the world's best rock bands to Julio Iglesias and Australia's own Dame Joan have thrilled audiences for some years now.

All in the one day, Sydney has karaoke in a Camden club and Rimsky-Korsakov in the Opera House, ice-skating in Ryde and eisteddfods in the Town Hall, rages in Rydalmere and romantic dinners in Darlinghurst, street parties in Padstow and Heidelberg School paintings in Paddington galleries. It is a great city where you can get anything you want.

Ferries are used by Sydneysiders as an alternative means of public transport. A ride across one of the finest natural harbours in the world will take you to Manly, which is full of footpath cafés and restaurants. Though not as famous as Bondi Beach, Manly usually has better surfing, and nearby Fairy Bower is very popular with boardriders.

On the way across on the ferry, you would have seen Fort Denison, a martello (small, round) tower built after an unannounced visit by a fleet of American warships in 1839 prompted concerns that the harbour should have some defences. Despite this, it was not completed until 1857, after the Crimean War gave rise to a 'Russian scare'. Before the fort was built, the small island known to the Aborigines as 'Mat-te-wa-ye', a 'favourite rest place', was termed Pinchgut because really troublesome convicts in the First Fleet were put there with practically no food. Australia's brutal colonial past is told in the story of convict Francis Morgan, who was condemned to hang there in chains. Three years later, the skeleton still remained on view and Aborigines completely avoided the place.

Something else you would have seen on the ferry ride would have been the Royal Botanic Gardens, 24 hectares of parkland right in the middle of the city, on the foreshores of what used to be called Farm Cove. They contain a stone wall that marks the site of Australia's first vegetable garden, planted at the instigation of Governor Phillip. The Gardens boast huge, old Moreton Bay figs and its national herbarium displays plant specimens collected by botanist Joseph Banks on his voyage of discovery with Captain James Cook in 1770.

Alternatively, you could take a leisurely walk through Hyde Park (named, of course, after the famous park in London). Hyde Park is in the centre of Sydney and its most outstanding feature is the Archibald Fountain, a legacy to Sydney from the first publisher of *The Bulletin* to commemorate the association of Australia and France in World War I. In those days of cultural cringe, a French artist, François Sicard, was chosen to execute the work. (Nowadays, the likes of Russell Drysdale, William Dobell, Sidney Nolan and Brett Whitely have forever changed the conception that Australians are second-raters in the artistic world.) The fountain features three tableaux, one of which depicts Theseus slaying the Minotaur. The original design had Hercules slaying the lion, but as the lion is the symbol of Britain, the politically correct authorities of the late 1920s suggested a substitute.

Just across Collins Street is the Australian Museum, a vast, rambling structure with some fantastic exhibits, and north of Hyde Park is the Art Gallery of New South Wales, an imposing neo-Classical building.

Sydney has some excellent restaurants, representing all types of cuisine, and many of which have set new standards in food presentation. From the intimate eatery to world-class hotel restaurants, from the café to the innovative, trendsetting restaurant, from the informal to the formal, Sydney has it all in the line of eating establishments.

Even on weekdays, Darling Harbour, to the west of the CBD, throngs with crowds eager to shop, eat or simply walk around. The Darling Harbour complex houses a number of exhibition halls, some of which are used to stage Sydney's International Motor Show in the last quarter of every year. The aquarium there is one of the greatest in the world and on the other side of the National Trust-classified Pyrmont Bridge is the Powerhouse Museum, exhibiting planes, boats, cars and steam engines and is well worth a look. Abutting Darling Harbour is Sydney's Chinatown, where visitors can choose from a bewildering array of restaurants or buy specialist ingredients for cooking, or herbal medicines. They should also stroll through the Chinese Gardens, incorporating the Garden of Friendship, a gift to Sydney from the people of Quandong Province in China.

If sushi is more enticing, just a little further west at Pyrmont are the Sydney Fish Markets, where you can not only buy superb fresh seafood, but dine at one of the many fish restaurants. Many people, particularly locals, go there at weekends, order a bottle of wine and sit outside savouring lunch and the views of the harbour.

If you keep heading west, eventually you will reach the Blue Mountains, which, like Bowral and Moss Vale in the Southern Highlands, used to be the summer escape of Sydney's rich. Now they are accessible to everyone, offering a wealth of scenic bushwalking trails, B&Bs, gracious old guesthouses and some real landmarks. The Paragon Café in Katoomba for example, has been famous for its chocolates since the 1930s, and also in Katoomba, the Carrington Hotel is an institution. Further up from Katoomba is the Hydro Majestic Hotel at Medlow Bath, which used to be notorious for illicit weekends away. The Blue Mountains' most famous landmark is natural, appearing on postcards almost as often as the Opera House. The Three Sisters is an eroded, sandstone rock formation. It can be climbed, but, like many of the deep gorges and cliff faces in this part of the Great Dividing Range, only by the well-equipped and experienced.

Sydney hosts a number of events and festivals. In January, the Sydney Festival has highlights including Opera in the Park, held in the Domain, and shares time with the Sydney Fringe Festival, based at Bondi. The Gay and Lesbian Mardi Gras is a highlight in February, while March sees Clean Up Australia, and the Walk Against Want. In April it is time for the Royal Easter Show, held now at Sydney Showground, Homebush Bay, and National Trust Heritage Week.

June sees in the Sydney Film Festival and the Darling Harbour Jazz Festival, and July, the International Music Festival. August is the time for the annual City to Surf, a run from the centre of the city to Bondi, raising money for charity. November is for the Australian Craft Show and December for Carols in the Domain, the Sydney to Hobart Yacht Race and New Year's Eve celebrations, which include a spectacular fireworks display, televised practically throughout the world.

ACCOMMODATION

CBD: Inter-Continental Hotel, ph (02) 9230 0200; Park Hyatt Hotel, ph (02) 9241 1234; Observatory Hotel, ph (02) 9256 2222; Regent Hotel, ph (02) 9238 0000; Renaissance Hotel, ph (02) 9372 2233; Hilton Hotel, ph (02) 9261 8651; Ritz-Carlton Hotel, ph (02) 9252 4600; Sheraton on the Park Hotel, ph (02) 9286 6000; Nikko Hotel, ph (02) 9299 1231; Novotel Hotel, ph (02) 9934 0000; Parkroyal Hotel, ph (02) 9261 1188; Downtown Apartments, ph (02) 9261 4333; Miramar Apartments, ph (02) 9211 2601; Metro Inn 1800 122 523; The York Apartments, ph (02) 9210 5000; Carrington Apartments, ph (02) 9290 1577

East side: Frisco Hotel (Woolloomooloo), ph (02) 9357 1800; Hotel Capital (Kings Cross), ph (02) 9358 2755; Macleay Serviced Apartments (Potts Point), ph (02) 9357 7755; Lords Hotel (Rushcutters Bay), ph (02) 9331 2520; Montpellier Private Hotel B&B (Elizabeth Bay), ph (02) 9358 6960; Hughenden Boutique Hotel (Woollahra), ph (02) 9363 4863; Racecourse Hotel (Randwick), ph (02) 9399 3588; Paddington Inn Hotel, ph (02) 9380 5913; City Beach Motor Inn (Bondi), ph (02) 9365 3100; Clairvaux Guest House (Vaucluse), ph (02) 9371 8625

North side: Harbourside Apartments (serviced, McMahons Point), ph (02) 9963 4300; Northside Gardens Hotel (North Sydney), ph (02) 9922 1311; Steyne Hotel (Manly), ph (02) 9977 4977; Mercure Hotel & Conference Centre (St Leonards), ph (02) 9439 6000; Shore Inn (Lane Cove), ph (02) 9460 7777; Greengate Hotel (Killara), ph (02) 9498 3577; Ascot Motor Inn (Wahroonga), ph (02) 9487 3355

South Head and lighthouse, at the entrance to Port Jackson and Sydney Harbour

West side: Mercure Hotel Lawson (Ultimo), ph (02) 9211 1499; Glebe Lodge B&B, ph (02) 9552 3830; Pension Albergo B&B (Leichhardt), ph (02) 9560 0179; Archie's at the Victoria Hotel B&B (Annandale), ph (02) 9564 5605; El Toro Motor Inn (Warwick Farm), ph (02) 9602 7077; Ryde Motor Inn (West Ryde), ph (02) 9874 0231; Country Comfort Inn (Pennant Hills), ph (02) 9980 6999; The Hills Lodge Boutique Hotel B&B (Castle Hill), ph (02) 9680 3800; O.K. Caravan Corral (Rouse Hill), ph (02) 9629 2652; Casa Paloma Caravan Park (Leppington), ph (02) 9606 5470

South side: The Petra (hotel, Surry Hills), ph (02) 9319 7594; The Chelsea Guest House B&B (Darlinghurst), ph (02) 9380 5994; Hilton Sydney Airport (Arncliffe), ph (02) 9597 0122; Hurstville Ritz Hotel, ph (02) 9580 1324; Novotel Brighton Beach (Brighton le Sands), ph (02) 9597 7111; Silver Beach Caravan Park (Kurnell), ph (02) 9668 8215; Cronulla Carapark (caravan/camping), ph (02) 9523 4099; Engadine Motor Inn, ph (02) 9520 8166

TOURIST INFORMATION: Ph (02) 9235 2424

THE BLUE MOUNTAINS

The visitor to the Blue Mountains will be astounded at the raw beauty of the sandstone cliffs and the deep gorges. There are many activities to pursue in the Blue Mountains.

MAP REFERENCE: PAGE 176 F8

LOCATION: 100 KM WEST OF SYDNEY

BEST TIME: SPRING, SUMMER AND AUTUMN

MAIN ATTRACTIONS: SUPERB LOOKOUTS, WALKING TRAILS, WILDFLOWERS IN SPRING, WALKS, ABSEILING, ROCK CLIMBING AND CANYONING

INFORMATION: GOVETTS LEAP, PH (02) 4787 8877; GLENBROOK, PH (02) 4739 2950

ACCOMMODATION: SEE TOWN LISTINGS FOR KATOOMBA, LEURA AND LITHGOW

These range from sitting in an opulent bed and breakfast sipping champagne and watching a fiery sunset reflect off the giant cliff faces, to dangling precariously on the end of a rope as you abseil down a waterfall into a valley from the Jurassic era.

History

The sandstone which forms the dramatic scenery was originally deposited by river systems that drained into a coastal plain more than 275 million years ago. Then 50 million years ago the area was uplifted, forming the Great Dividing Range. Volcanoes added to the dramatic scene before the weathering process began to etch the landscape. The deep gorges and towering cliffs of today are the result of this continual weathering action.

The mountains formed a natural barrier to the early settlers in Sydney. However in 1813 Blaxland, Wentworth and Lawson found a route. The rich plains to the west ensured that a rough road was quickly cut into the thick, scrubby bush that clung to the sandstone plateaus. The present-day Great Western Highway follows closely the route of the first coach trail. At Mt York the coach track followed a switchback route down the ridge line to the Hartley Valley. It is possible to follow this track on foot from Mt York, and you will marvel at the ability of the horse-drawn carriages to negotiate the steep grade.

An alternative route, via Richmond on the Hawkesbury River, was discovered in 1823 by Archibald Bell, a local landholder, and Robert Hoddle surveyed the original route of Bells Line; it served as a stock route and then a coach track for the remainder of the nineteenth century.

The development of the area was hastened when oil shale seams were discovered in the Wolgan Valley in the 1860s, but the mountains remained sparsely populated until 1868 when the Great Western Railway was built. This brought the scenic beauty of the mountains within reach of the growing Sydney population and the area was quickly recognised for its tourism value.

Small mining operations were performed in Wolgan Valley until 1903 when the New South Wales Shale and Oil Company commenced large scale mining. The town of Newnes was established at the head of the valley.

One of the greatest engineering feats of its time was the building of the railway from Newnes to Lithgow. It would require the construction of viaducts and tunnels over the almost impossible terrain of cliff faces and deep gullies. Amazingly, the line was completed within one year, in 1907. However, high operational costs and the discovery of more oilfields throughout the world soon had a dramatic effect on the Newnes mine, and it had closed by 1933.

As early as the 1890s reserves were established to protect the natural areas within the mountains. The Blue Mountains National Park was proclaimed in 1959.

There is a great deal of evidence of Aboriginal occupation in the form of art sites and grinding-stone marks in the sandstone cliffs which have been dated back 14 000 years.

BLUE MOUNTAINS NATIONAL PARK

The Blue Mountains National Park has the highest number of visitors of any park in New South Wales. It is little wonder considering it is virtually

The dramatic landscape of the Blue Mountains National Park

in sight of Sydney, being only 100 km west of the Harbour Bridge. It has some of the most spectacular scenery of any of Australia's parks, and is a favourite with many overseas visitors who are as familiar with photographs of the Three Sisters as they are with Uluru.

Access

The park lies to the west of Sydney and is best accessed along the Great Western Highway. It stretches in the east from Glenbrook, virtually at the foot of the mountains, to west of Katoomba near Mt Victoria where the road descends onto the western plains. Its northern boundary is the Bells Line of Road where the Wollemi National Park continues northwards and its southern section stretches all the way to Wombeyan Caves, west of Mittagong.

The park has three distinct regions: the Glenbrook section covering the lower Blue Mountains down to Lake Burragorang and west to Wentworth Falls; the south-western section, which includes the Jamison Valley and the Three Sisters, and is the most remote area, extending south towards Kanangra Boyd National Park and on to Wombeyan Caves; and the

northern section between the Great Western Highway and the Bells Line of Road which includes the Grose Valley and contains some of the best lookouts and walking trails.

Major Attractions

There are a number of activities to occupy you in the Blue Mountains, ranging from simply sightseeing at the many excellent lookouts, to bushwalking deep in the Grose Valley, abseiling off the sheer sandstone cliffs or canyoning and whitewater rafting. Tourism is big in the mountains and there are plenty of options in relation to accommodation and unusual ways to enjoy the natural wonders. Two good examples are the Scenic Railway with its near vertical drop and the Skyway cable car that stretches across deep, fern-filled gullies.

The most famous attraction in the mountains is the Three Sisters rock formation. Situated within the confines of the town of Katoomba, there is very easy access, parking being the only problem due to the huge number of tourists that flock to the area.

Bushwalking is another great activity and the park has many wonderful trails. Some are quite easy and include the scenic lookouts, while others require a degree of fitness and an overnight camp as they extend into deep river valleys. The National Parks and Wildlife Service (NPWS) have excellent publications detailing the many walks and giving their degree of difficulty and duration.

Things to Do

Around the major towns of Katoomba, Leura and Blackheath there are lookouts accessible by everyone. There is the already mentioned Three Sisters where there are viewing platforms, walks to the base of the rock formations and a well-stocked information and souvenir shop. From Katoomba it is possible to follow the cliff drive which passes several other lookouts over the Jamison Valley as well as some great picnic locations both east and west of Katoomba. Along this route you will find the Skyway and the Scenic Railway. At Leura there are several excellent lookouts over Sublime Point, within an easy five minute walk from the car park.

In the Glenbrook area there are good walks with views over the Nepean River as well as hand stencils to view at Red Hands Cave. Abseiling off the cliffs in this part of the park is also popular and every weekend you will find groups enjoying this exhilarating pastime.

There are a number of adventure tour companies who can safely take you on abseiling trips off huge cliffs, rock climbing expeditions or canyoning through narrow gorges where waterfalls plunge into deep pools of icy cold water.

West of Katoomba, around Blackheath, there are several roads out to lookouts above the Grose Valley. This is one of the most spectacular regions as the rock faces of the cliffs are several hundred metres high. The better known lookouts include Evans, Govetts Leap, Perrys Lookdown and Victoria Falls. There are several easy walking trails along the top of the escarpment which will occupy at the most two hours.

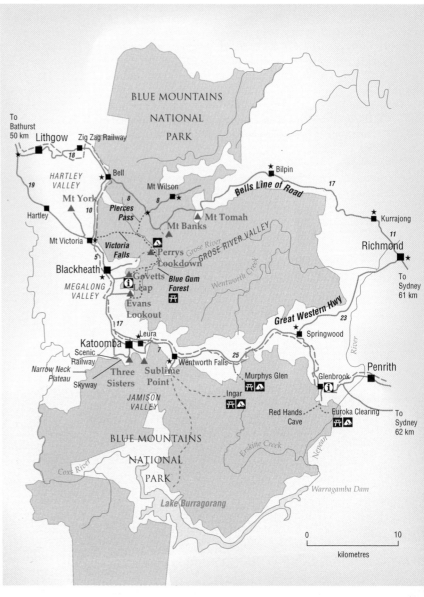

LEGEND

Sealed/Unsealed Rd	★ 26 ★ ─●─ ─ ─ ─
Four Wheel Drive	─ ─ ─ ─ ─ ─
Walks	⋯⋯⋯⋯
Rest Area (Picnic Area)	🏕
Caravan Park	🚐
Camping Area	⛺
Accommodation	🛏
Information	ⓘ
Fuel Supplies	⛽

The most renowned walks in the Blue Mountains are those that descend into the Grose Valley from Govetts Leap and Perrys Lookdown. You will need to be fit to tackle the steep trails and you must always be prepared for dramatic changes in the weather. Because the mountains are at quite a high altitude, sudden temperature drops and even snowfalls are common. Heavy rain can cut tracks in the valleys and the area should be avoided in this type of weather. There are several walks in the Grose Valley with the Blue Gum Forest being one of the better known attractions. If you are planning a walking trip into the Grose Valley, it is suggested that you contact the Heritage Centre at Govetts Leap to obtain maps and advice on your intended walk. It is very wise to let someone reliable know of your intended route and time of return in order to avoid any unnecessary searching.

There are some good lookouts off the Bells Line of Road also. These are found a few minutes off the main road at Pierces Pass, Mt Banks, and Mt Tomah, where there is the excellent High Country botanical garden.

Camping

It is best to look at each area individually. The Glenbrook section is primarily a day-use area but there is a camping ground at Euroka Clearing. Accessed from the park entrance at Glenbrook, it is necessary to book your site and pay a small fee at the Glenbrook Visitor Centre. There are also camping locations at Ingar and Murphys Glen which are accessed off the highway at Wentworth Falls, but it is a 5 km walk to Murphys Glen as it is closed to vehicle access. Camping elsewhere in the Glenbrook section is not encouraged.

In the northern section, or the Grose Valley, there is one official camp site at Perrys Lookdown. This is accessed off the Great Western Highway at Blackheath. There are toilets and BBQs but you should bring your own water. This section of the park is very popular with bushwalkers: however, bush camping is permitted in only two places in the Grose Valley—Acacia Flat and Burra Korain Flat. In other areas outside the Grose Valley it is possible to bush camp—away from roads and walking trails.

As an alternative there is access off the Bells Line of Road to Burralow Creek where there is a large grassy camping area. The road to this location is gravel and a little rough in places but it does provide car-based camping. It is possible to follow the fire trail all the way up to Kurrajong which makes it a round trip. Look for the track 1 km east of the Fruit Bowl at Bilpin on the Bells Line of Road.

The southern section of the park is much more remote, and if you are walking in this area you will need to be very experienced. You will almost certainly have to bush camp overnight. Camping within 3 km of Lake Burragorang is not permitted as this is the catchment for Sydney's water supply. It is important to note that, despite their clean and fresh appearance, all streams in the Blue Mountains are polluted with run-off from residential areas on the plateaus. Travellers are strongly advised to boil all water.

THE BLUE MOUNTAINS TREK

The Blue Mountains contain some of the most spectacular scenery in Australia. Much of the area is wilderness, but Newnes and the Newnes State Forest, on the southern fringe of Wollemi National Park, offer interesting places to explore by 4WD.

Wollemi, the second largest national park in New South Wales, abuts the Blue Mountains National Park along the Bells Line of Road. Our trek goes from the Zig Zag Railway at Clarence, through to the Glow Worm Tunnel created by the shale oil railway, and finishes in the Wolgan Valley at the town of Newnes.

Generally there are very limited facilities in this area—some camping spots in the pine forests around Lithgow and a camping area in the Wolgan Valley near Newnes. None has reliable water supplies and pit toilets are only found at the Newnes camp. No fees apply.

This area can get very cold in winter, it may even snow, so go prepared for below-zero temperatures and biting winds at that time of year.

Sydney to Bungleboori

From Sydney, take the Bells Line of Road over the Blue Mountains via the towns of Richmond and Kurrajong. This route passes the apple orchards of Bilpin, the botanic garden at Mt Tomah and the quiet settlements of Mt Wilson and Bell.

At Bell, continue west towards Lithgow. After passing through Clarence you will see the historic Zig Zag Railway on the right. This railway could occupy your attention for a day on its own. It now operates as a tourist venue and three times a day the old steam locomotive chugs up and down the mountain behind Lithgow.

At the railway (**GPS** 33°28'37"S, 150°13'19"E), turn right onto the gravel road and follow it past the Clarence Sawmill and on past the Boral Sand Quarry. This is the old Bells Line of Road. After approximately 7 km, at a T-junction (**GPS** 33°25'33"S, 150°12'01"E), the road joins the main road from Lithgow to the Glow Worm Tunnel; turn right here. At this point you can do a little four wheel driving by following the tracks under the power lines which are on the left side of the Glow Worm Tunnel road.

Many challenging walks descend into the Grose Valley at Govetts Leap

If you decide to follow the power line road, do so until there is a steep, low-range hill climb. At the top of this climb, turn left at the crossroad.

If you prefer to follow the main gravel road, do so for 2 km, until you come to the Bungleboori picnic ground.

Bungleboori to the Lost City

From here it is worth making a small detour to your left to view the rock formations known as the Lost City. With Bungleboori camp site on your left, turn left onto Blackfellows Hand Road and then turn immediately left again. Look for the Lithgow Water Supply sign in the trees (**GPS** 33°24'22"S, 150°11'33"E). Within 100 metres you will cross under the power lines. (This is where you will join the track if you decide to follow the 4WD track under the power lines.)

Heading to the Lost City, keep left at the next two Y-junctions and then go straight ahead at the track on your right which comes up 1.5 km from the power lines. The track continues for another kilometre, and finishes at the Lost City. The last 200 metres are low range 4WD, but the unusual rock formations sculpted by wind and rain are well worth it. Please take care exploring this area on foot, as the sandstone formations are very fragile. Deep in the gullies you will find two old dams; this was the original Lithgow water supply.

To Deep Pass

Our route backtracks now to the Bungleboori camp site, but if you wish you could explore the tracks that lie off to your left as you return. There are the ruins of an old mine to see, plus a challenging hill climb.

From Bungleboori, continue north down the Glow Worm Tunnel road. Another interesting detour can be taken approximately 8 km further down the road. It would be best to arm yourself first with the appropriate topographic maps, which are Lithgow, Rock Hill and Cullen Bullen in the 1:25 000 series.

Approximately 5 km along the forestry trails is a place known as Deep Pass. It is necessary to walk into the pass these days, but the rock formations and crystal-clear creeks are well worth the exercise. The first rock scramble from the locked gate is the most difficult; after that the walk enters a large, wide valley.

A brush-tail possum with its young, often seen in the Blue Mountains

LEGEND

Road Distance in km	★ 26 ★
National Park	
Aboriginal Land	
Accommodation	
Camping Area	
Caravan Park	
Fuel Supplies	
General Store	
Meals Available	
Rest Area (Picnic Area)	
Tourist Information	

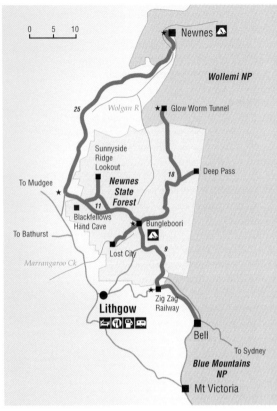

Follow the gully to your left, towards a huge sandstone rock. The walking track leads to a giant split in the rock mountain where you can walk right through the centre of the mountain.

Alternatively, as you enter the wide open clearing, keep to your right and follow the creek bed. Here the track crisscrosses a pleasant creek until it ends in a pool fed by a cascading waterfall, an absolutely beautiful sight. You will need at least two hours to enjoy the walk into Deep Pass.

To the Glow Worm Tunnel

Backtrack to the Glow Worm Tunnel road. It is easy going on this potholed and corrugated road which only requires 4WD after rain; continue for another 10 km. Along the way you will pass Deans Siding to your right. By now the road is beginning to follow the route of the old railway line, and eventually it passes through the first of the two tunnels. You can drive right through this tunnel. It is then only another kilometre to the end of the road.

From here you need to walk the last kilometre to the Glow Worm Tunnel. Take a torch, as the old rail tunnel is very long and pitch black. There are plenty of glow worms to see, just take your time—walk in quietly, then switch your torch off to see the thousands of tiny lights.

At the opposite end of the tunnel the wet gullies are being reclaimed by tree-ferns and a walk along the route of the old railway line will leave you in awe of the engineering marvel. It is possible to walk all the way to Newnes, but allow at least six hours for this walk.

To Newnes

Following your visit to the Glow Worm Tunnel, retrace your wheel tracks back to the Bungleboori camp site. This time, turn right onto Blackfellows Hand Road.

After 2.5 km the road forks, with Sunnyside Road to your right (**GPS** 33°23'28"S, 150°10'52"E). This can be followed all the way to its end,

approximately 11 km. It finishes at a magnificent lookout (**GPS** 33°17'49"S, 150°08'10"E) over the Wolgan Valley. Along the way you could also deviate to Bird Rock which offers another fine view.

From Sunnyside retrace your route 4.5 km, then turn right. This track is a shortcut between Sunnyside Road and Blackfellows Hand Road and includes some difficult rock steps and climbs. The track is only 4 km long but it passes through some magnificent gorge country and will require low range.

At a T-junction, this track rejoins Blackfellows Hand Road. Turn right here and follow the stony track through another very pretty gully for 2.8 km, then look for a large clearing on your left 500 metres further on (**GPS** 33°19'22"S, 150°05'55"E), which marks the walking track to Blackfellows Hand Cave. It is only a short walk up the hillside from the car park and the hand stencils are easily seen under the rock overhang. There are many similar rock art sites in the area and again, if you have time, it would be worth exploring the escarpment on foot.

From the car park, continue west for another kilometre and turn right onto the bitumen road. This is the Wolgan Valley Road and it is only 25 km to the site of Newnes.

Not much is left of the old town, even the pub has closed its doors. The camp site is large and there is a pit toilet. The road crosses the Wolgan River just past the old rail carriages and continues for another 500 metres. There are various bush camps along the way. The ruins of the old mining town are upstream, reached on foot.

From Newnes back to Lithgow is approximately 35 km; just retrace your route along the Wolgan Valley and keep going until you reach the Mudgee road, where you turn left and follow the signs to Lithgow.

The Three Sisters, a famous landmark in the Blue Mountains

ADAMINABY

459 KM SOUTH-WEST OF SYDNEY
POPULATION: 300   MAP REF: PAGE 174 B6

Winter gateway to the Snowy Mountains, Adaminaby lies at the end (or beginning) of the exciting section on one of the greatest drivers' roads in Australia—the looping, circuitous Snowy Mountains Highway. The town is a pleasant hamlet whose main tourist attraction is trout fishing in nearby Lake Eucumbene—in fact, the site of the original township, 9 km south-west of the present one, lies under its waters. It was flooded in 1957 as part of the Snowy Mountains Hydro-Electric Scheme, but the original village was moved in its entirety to its present location.

Adaminaby sprang up because of its proximity to the Kiandra goldfields last century, but now farming, grazing and tourism are the main industries.

Cross-country skiers who take to the slopes of Mt Selwyn and Blue Cow will often choose to stay at Adaminaby. It is also a favourite with tourists as Aboriginal cultural tours are available, as well as trips to Providence Portal which offers a unique view of water cascading into the lake.

ACCOMMODATION: San Michele Country Resort, ph (02) 6454 2229; Snow Goose Motel, ph (02) 6454 2202; Lake Eucumbene Units, ph (02) 6454 2444; Gooandra Alpine Cottages, ph (02) 6454 2327; Happy Valley B&B, ph (02) 6454 2434; Rainbow Pines Caravan Park, ph (02) 6454 2317; Providence Holiday Park, ph (02) 6454 2357;
ACTIVITIES: Boating, fishing, horse riding
TOURIST INFORMATION: Ph (02) 6450 1742

ADELONG

432 KM SOUTH-WEST OF SYDNEY
POPULATION: 855   MAP REF: PAGE 174 A5

Only a short distance (21 km) west of Tumut on the Snowy Mountains Highway, Adelong still bears visible scars of its origins as a goldmining town. In its time, it was the richest alluvial field in New South Wales, and diggings and craters can be seen almost everywhere.

Buildings from that era are National Trust listed and present an insight into the goldmining period.

A visit to the Adelong Falls, 2 km to the north on the Tomblong–Gundagai road, is well worth the effort.
ACCOMMODATION: Adelong Hotel, ph (02) 6946 2009; Adelong Caravan Park, ph (02) 6946 2282
ACTIVITIES: Golf, horse riding, trout fishing
TOURIST INFORMATION: Ph (02) 6947 1849

ALBURY

583 KM SOUTH-WEST OF SYDNEY
POPULATION: 41 790   MAP REF: PAGE 183 M8

On the banks of the Murray River, Albury and its twin town Wodonga represent an immense regional growth centre. They are situated on the main road (the Hume Highway) between Sydney and Melbourne.

Founded near the spot where Hume and Hovell, on the journey to Port Phillip in 1824, first came

The main street of Albury

across the Murray, the town site was named after a village in Surrey, England.

Though initially slow to grow (three years after gazetting, the population had grown to seven), Albury became significant as a port for the paddle-steamers plying up and down the river. The thriving local wine industry can trace its roots back to the German settlers who first arrived in 1840.

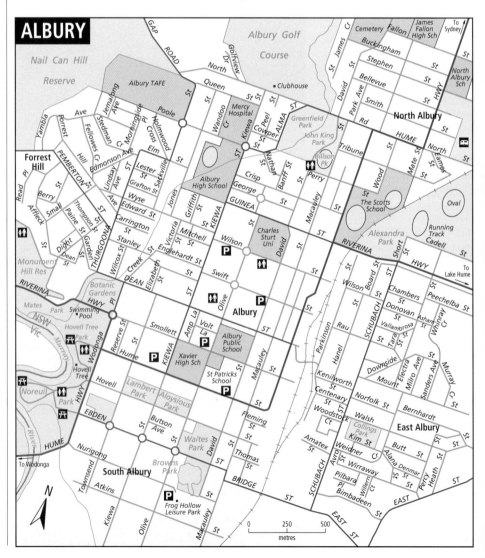

As befits an energetic rural city, Albury boasts everything a traveller could want, from restaurants offering international cuisine to plenty of things to see and do. A walk around town will reveal fascinating insights into the past, as the architecture dates from the late nineteenth century in many places.

Albury is home to both Charles Sturt University and a vast array of manufacturing enterprises including woollen and newsprint mills. The famous Ettamogah Pub, immortalised in the cartoons and comics of the same name, is only 15 km to the north and is now a complex where the needs of both adults and children can be catered for.

Lake Hume is 12 km from town and offers opportunities for water sports. The *Cumberoona*, a paddle-steamer replica from the 1880s, plies up and down the river, and you can even take an Iron Horse Motorcycle Tour.

ACCOMMODATION: Albury Georgian Motor Inn, ph (02) 6021 8744; Carlton Albury Motel, ph (02) 6021 5366; Albion Hotel/Motel, ph (02) 6021 3377; Albury Tourist Haven, ph (02) 6025 1619; Albury Central Caravan Park, ph (02) 6041 1844

ACTIVITIES: Fishing, water sports, wineries

TOURIST INFORMATION: Ph (02) 6021 2694

ALSTONVILLE

791 KM NORTH OF SYDNEY
POPULATION: 3678   MAP REF: PAGE 179 P3

Alstonville is located on the Bruxner Highway which runs between Ballina and Tenterfield and eventually out to Boggabilla in the central north-west. Originally a timber-getting area, its industries now consist of macadamia, avocado and other tropical fruit propagation. There are a number of unique nurseries in the area that supply all of Australia.

Alstonville is essentially a central point for excursions elsewhere. Bundjalung National Park lies to the south and to the north are the twin parks of Nightcap and Mount Jerusalem.

An agricultural show is held in late October.

ACCOMMODATION: Alstonville Settlers Motel, ph (02) 6628 5285; Federal Hotel, ph (02) 6628 0719; Alstonville Leisure Village (camping/caravans), ph (02) 6628 0146

ACTIVITIES: Bowls, national park access, squash, swimming, tennis

TOURIST INFORMATION: Ph (02) 6686 3484

ARALUEN

317 KM SOUTH-WEST OF SYDNEY
POPULATION: 100   MAP REF: PAGE 174 E6

Reachable on 22 km of tar from Braidwood to the north, or on dirt from Captains Flat to the west and Moruya to the south-east, Araluen is now a mere shell of what it was in its glory days when the valley was home to one of the state's most lucrative goldfields. Sixty years of exploitation sprang from when Alexander Waddell discovered gold in 1851, and poets Charles Harpur and Henry Kendall, and novelist Rolf Boldrewood all spent time there (no doubt at the pub—a great historic hostelry).

The Araluen Valley was also a hole-in-the-wall for the Clarke brothers' bushranging gang, who terrorised the area for two years in the 1860s.

Araluen owes its name to the Aboriginal word 'arralyin', meaning 'place of waterlilies'. Nowadays, local industry consists of grazing and fruit growing.

The valley is sandwiched between Deua National Park to the south and Budawang National Park in the north. Araluen is also a base from which to explore the old mining centres of Majors Creek and Captains Flat, which bear far more evidence of metallurgical activity than this quiet, naturalist painters' paradise.

ACCOMMODATION: The Old Court House B&B, ph (02) 4846 4053

ACTIVITIES: Gold panning, historic goldfields, national park access, walking

TOURIST INFORMATION: Ph (02) 4842 2310

ARMIDALE

566 KM NORTH OF SYDNEY
POPULATION: 23 500   MAP REF: PAGE 179 J8

Almost halfway between Sydney and Brisbane, Armidale is one of the prettiest, stateliest rural cities in New South Wales. The area where the city now stands was home to the Anaiwan Aborigines for 10 000 years and an Aboriginal painting site can be found at Mt Yarrowyck, 30 km west of Armidale.

The first white settler was William Dumaresq, who took up land in 1835, and four years later the Commissioner of Crown Land, G. J. Macdonald, established a head station. He named it Armidale, after his father's estate in Scotland.

Gazetted in 1849, Armidale is now the principal city of New England. The area is known for high-grade fine wool and as the source for bloodlines for noted sheep studs, but timber processing, dairying and the production of stone fruits and potatoes also feature.

The city is renowned as an educational and ecclesiastical centre. It has two cathedrals—St Peter's (Anglican) and St Mary's (Roman Catholic)—and the town is host to not only New England University and the Armidale Technical College and TAFE, but a number of exclusive private schools.

Thirty-five of Armidale's buildings have been classified by the National Trust, and there are two historic homesteads: Saumarez, to the south, and Booloominbah, in the grounds of the University of New England. One of many museums worth visiting is the New England Regional Arts Museum

There is a heritage walk which runs for 3 km around Armidale, and you should also visit the Aboriginal Cultural Centre and Keeping Place.

Less than two hours' drive from Armidale is New England National Park, which is on the World Heritage List. Near by are four other national parks: Oxley Wild Rivers; Guy Fawkes; Cathedral Rock and Dorrigo. Natural attractions include Wollomombi Falls, Hillgrove Gorge and Ebor Falls.

ACCOMMODATION: Cattleman's Motor Inn, ph (02) 6772 7788; Regency Hallmark Inn, ph (02) 6772 9800; Beambolong Guest House, ph (02) 6771 2019; Poppy's B&B, ph (02) 6775 1277; Highlander Van Village, ph (02) 6772 4768

ACTIVITIES: Abseiling, bushwalking, canoeing, fishing, gliding, golf, horse riding, national park access, squash, tennis, water sports

TOURIST INFORMATION: Ph (02) 6773 8527

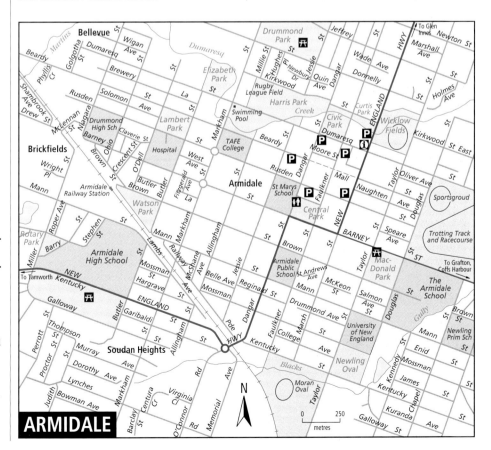

ARMIDALE

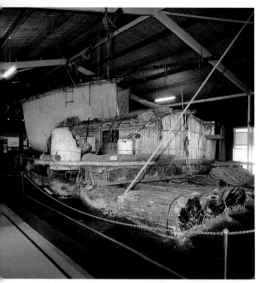

A balsa wood raft in the Maritime Museum at Ballina

BALLINA

789 KM NORTH OF SYDNEY
POPULATION: 12 500   MAP REF: PAGE 179 P3

Ballina sits at the estuary of the Richmond River, now the heart of a thriving fishing industry. Originally, the first white residents were cedar-getters, but farmers and graziers took up when they left. Tourism is now also an important local industry, and with ready access to surf beaches, Ballina is a magnet to visitors.

There are heaps of things to do around Ballina. There are the usual water sports of surfing, sailing and SCUBA diving, plus whitewater rafting on the upper reaches of the Richmond River. There is even a 'Skirmish' adventure park!

Slightly less taxing are camel trekking, fossicking for gold, 4WD in the hinterland and whale watching during spring and autumn.

For lovers of Australian kitsch, a visit to the Big Prawn is a must, but you can also visit a 'castle' (a family fun attraction), inspect the naval museum, the opal and gem museum, or go to a tea-tree or macadamia nut plantation.

Ballina holds its annual Kingsford Smith Festival in September.

ACCOMMODATION: Ballina Beach Resort, ph (02) 6686 8888; Ballina Club Resort, ph (02) 6686 7001; Avlon Motel, ph (02) 6686 4044; Lobster Pot Hotel/ Motel, ph (02) 6686 2135; Allan's Leisure-Lee Holiday Units, ph (02) 6686 2426; Boomerang Caravan Park, ph (02) 6686 2220; Tinkerbell Caravan Park, ph (02) 6686 3133
ACTIVITIES: Abseiling, bowls, bushwalking, climbing, cycling and mountain biking, golf, hang gliding, horse riding, parachuting, skydiving, water sports
TOURIST INFORMATION: Ph (02) 6686 3484

BALRANALD

889 KM SOUTH-WEST OF SYDNEY
POPULATION: 1450   MAP REF: PAGE 182 F5

Balranald lies on the Murrumbidgee River, some 130 km west of Hay. Further west is Mallee Cliffs National Park, and to the north-west is the unique Mungo National Park. The town's links with history include Charles Sturt (who visited the region in 1830), Thomas Mitchell, and Burke and Wills. The town was a busy river port in the mid-nineteenth century. The Homebush Hotel was established in 1878.

One hundred kilometres north of Balranald is Boree Plains, a 51 000 hectare sheep and cattle station adjoining Mungo National Park, which offers accommodation in the shearers' quarters and camping. You can hire a 4WD there, see the School of the Air classroom in a 100-year-old train carriage and see mallee fowl, kangaroos and emus close up.

ACCOMMODATION: Balranald Motor Inn, ph (03) 5020 1104; Capri Motel, ph (03) 5020 1201; Colony Inn, ph (03) 5020 1302; Balranald Shire Council Caravan Park, ph (03) 5020 1321
ACTIVITIES: Fishing, golf, national park access, swimming
TOURIST INFORMATION: Ph (03) 5020 1599

BANGALOW

820 KM NORTH OF SYDNEY
POPULATION: 700   MAP REF: PAGE 179 P3

Bangalow is a rustically quaint village set in the Byron Bay hinterland. The town has many art, craft and antique shops and is a regional centre for the dairy industry and fruit and vegetable production. There is an fine secondhand bookshop (Uncle Pete's Books) in Byron Street.

There is also an excellent walking track that leaves from town and winds its way along the banks of Byron Creek. Bangalow is best used as a base from which to explore other areas by car.

On the last Saturday of every month rural markets are held in Bangalow.

ACCOMMODATION: Bangalow Palms Resort, ph (02) 6687 1216; Talofa Lodge (B&B), ph (02) 6687 1494; Camarra Holiday Cottage, ph (02) 6687 1956
ACTIVITIES: Shopping, sightseeing, walking
TOURIST INFORMATION: Ph (02) 6685 8050

BAROOGA

711 KM SOUTH-WEST OF SYDNEY
POPULATION: 700   MAP REF: PAGE 183 K8

If you take the picturesque Murray Valley Highway west from Albury and turn north-west at Cobram, you will come to the holiday town of Barooga, on the banks of the River Murray. It boasts excellent (inland) beaches and very pretty countryside where the local industry is citrus and grape-growing.

Seppelts has a winery in the district, and there is also a good golf course with very reasonable rates.

Visitors can loll on sandy beaches by the Murray River, visit the Dalveile Gallery with its antique oil lamp collection, or take a stroll through Barooga's Botanical Gardens.

Across the Murray River, in Victoria, is Cobram, Barroga's sister town.

ACCOMMODATION: El Sierra Motel, ph (at the golf course) 1800 63 1082
ACTIVITIES: Golf, swimming, winery
TOURIST INFORMATION: Ph (02) 6021 2694

BARRABA

532 KM NORTH-WEST OF SYDNEY
POPULATION: 1550   MAP REF: PAGE 179 G7

Barraba is the centre for a pastoral area producing high-grade fine wool. Earlier, asbestos mining at nearby Woods Reef augmented the area's economy, but the mining has now ceased.

A monument in the town commemorates Allan Cunningham's crossing of the Manilla River in 1827; Thomas Mitchell is also associated with the area.

Barraba is also close to two magnificent national parks: Mount Kaputar to the west, and the tiny Warrabah Park to the south-east. Mount Kaputar in particular is worth a visit, reserving almost 37 000 hectares of forest-clad mountains and volcanic peaks. Its diverse conditions provide habitats for an immense variety of wildlife including koalas, walleroos and kangaroos, gliders, possums, wedge-tailed eagles, honeyeaters, parrots and treecreepers.

ACCOMMODATION: Barraba Motel, ph (02) 6782 1555; Blue Gum Caravan Park, ph (02) 6782 1067
ACTIVITIES: Fishing, national park access
TOURIST INFORMATION: Ph (02) 6768 4462

BATEMANS BAY

297 KM SOUTH OF SYDNEY
POPULATION: 7950   MAP REF: PAGE 174 E6

James Cook named Batemans Bay in 1770 after the captain of the *Northumberland*, and the town that sits beside the bay was first settled in 1840.

Batemans Bay is situated on the mouth of the Clyde River (known as 'Bhundoo' to the local Aborigines), which boasts very pure water—the local oysters are excellent, as is the fishing.

As befits a town with a strong tourist industry, the weather is near perfect—whether winter or summer. Surfing beaches and quiet backwaters abound, and the local lakes—Durras, Coila and Tuross—are popular for aquatic activities. Lake Coila is also famous for its prawns.

Besides any and all things aquatic (including boat hire), Batemans Bay caters for most tastes. Nearby Pigeon House Mountain in Morton National Park is renowned among bushwalkers, and there are walking trails like the Corn Trail, which follows the route down the Clyde Mountain used by the early settlers to bring produce to the coast.

Craft lovers are catered for by many local stores and by those at nearby Mogo, just south of Batemans Bay, which also feature Koori crafts.

Birdland, with its display of exotic birds, is certainly worth a look, as is the Mogo Zoo which has a variety of native species.

Nearby national parks offer different attractions: Murramarang boasts Pebbly Beach, where kangaroos and wallabies mingle freely with visitors; Budawang, Eurobodalla and Deua have spectacular scenery.

ACCOMMODATION: Lincoln Downs Country Resort, ph (02) 4472 6388; Coachhaven Marina Resort, ph (02) 4472 4392; Mariners Lodge (motel), ph (02) 4472 6222; Batemans Bay Tourist Park, ph (02) 4472 4972

An inlet at Batemans Bay, sparkling in the sun

ACTIVITIES: Bushwalking, national park access, water sports
TOURIST INFORMATION: Ph (02) 4472 6900

BATHURST

203 KM WEST OF SYDNEY
POPULATION: 27 840   MAP REF: PAGE 176 D7
Marking the end of the Great Western Highway out of Sydney, Bathurst is a city for history buffs. Being Australia's oldest inland city, Bathurst has some truly magnificent buildings, reflecting its heritage: the Court House in particular is one such example.

Governor Macquarie named Bathurst after the then Secretary of State for the Colonies, Earl Bathurst. Gold was discovered in 1851 at Summer Hill Creek, about 50 km to the north-west, and the rush saw towns like Ophir, Sofala, Rockley and O'Connell spring up overnight. The news of easy wealth also brought bushrangers such as Frank Gardiner, Johnny Gilbert, Ben Hall, O'Meally and Vane into the area.

In 1862, Cobb & Co established its first service in New South Wales, with Bathurst as the headquarters.

Charles Darwin visited Bathurst in 1836, and a plaque in Machattie Park commemorates the event. More recently, J. B. Chifley, who took over from John Curtin as Labor Prime Minister after Curtin's death in 1945, was born in Bathurst in 1885, and was buried in Bathurst Cemetery in 1951. The house where he grew up is in Busby Street.

Even more recently, Bathurst has been home to the Mt Panorama racing circuit, site of 'the Great Race' watched by millions of Australians every year.

The Macquarie River, on which Bathurst is situated, is a mecca for canoeists, who often use the nearby Bridle Track to access camping bases such as Bruinbun. The convict-built Bridle Track is a spectacular drive in itself, ending up at the historic goldmining town of Hill End.

Nearby Mountain View is a picturesque sheep, cattle and cherry property and wildlife refuge. This is an old goldmining area and there is also a museum and relics. You can also fossick for gold and sapphires, fish for trout and ride horses. There is accommodation available here and also at Yarrabin, a 400 hectare sheep grazing and wildlife refuge.
ACCOMMODATION: Bathurst Motor Inn, ph (02) 6331 2723; Capri Bathurst Motel, ph (02) 6331 2723; Railway Hotel, ph (02) 6331 2864; Bathurst Caravan Park, ph (02) 6331 8286
ACTIVITIES: Fishing, fossicking, historic interest, horse riding, tennis, water sports
TOURIST INFORMATION: Ph (02) 6333 6288

BATLOW

467 KM SOUTH-WEST OF SYDNEY
POPULATION: 1275   MAP REF: PAGE 174 A5
Originally known as Reedy Flat, Batlow was named after the surveyor who planned the town. Once in the middle of a vast goldmining area, now it is the centre of a fruit industry, specialising in apples and pears. Indeed, some people argue that Batlow apples are the best in Australia, and the Big Red Apple Tourist Complex capitalises on this fact. The complex also provides great views of the Bogan Ranges.

The Blowering Reservoir is used by residents for water sports, while the Hume and Hovell's Lookout commemorates the expedition through the region by the two explorers in 1824. Mt Selwyn is only an hour's drive from Batlow and many locals are keen skiers.

The Apple Harvest Festival and the Batlow Show both take place in March.
ACCOMMODATION: Batlow Digger's Rest Motel, ph (02) 6949 1342; Batlow Hotel, ph (02) 6949 1001; Batlow Caravan Park, ph (02) 6949 1444
ACTIVITIES: Bowls, bushwalking, golf, scenic drives, skiing, tennis, water sports
TOURIST INFORMATION: Ph (02) 6947 1849

BEGA

443 KM SOUTH OF SYDNEY
POPULATION: 4310   MAP REF: PAGE 174 E8
Bega is a major rural business district hub. The main industries are dairy farming, timber and tourism, but its most famous product is undoubtedly Bega cheese. Bega cheddar is the number one seller in Australia, grossing some 86 million dollars a year. The factory employs over 100 people and is worth visiting to see how cheese is made.

Reached by either the Princes Highway or the Snowy Mountains Highway, Bega is thought to derive its name from the Aboriginal word 'biggah', meaning either 'beautiful' or 'big meeting place'. Bega is proud of its history, and the new Heritage Centre chronicles the region's past, its ancestors and cultural society.

Rich in natural beauty, Bega is surrounded by national parks: east on the coast are Mimosa Rocks and Bournda; to the north, Mumbulla; the north-west, Wadbilliga (containing the Brogo Wilderness area), and to the south, the newly created South-East Forests National Park.

Owners of 4WDs praise the scenery and driving challenge in the Bega hinterland, while the Earth Craft Gallery caters for art and craft lovers.

Kameruka Estate with its beautiful gardens is National Trust listed and should not be missed.
ACCOMMODATION: Bega Downs Motor Inn, ph (02) 6492 2944; Bega Hotel, ph (02) 6492 1120; Crown Tree Farm Cottage B&B, ph (02) 6494 2133; South Bega Caravan Park, ph (02) 6492 2303.
ACTIVITIES: Bushwalking, fishing, 4WD touring, golf, horse riding, national park access, scenic drives
TOURIST INFORMATION: Ph (02) 6492 3313 or (02) 6492 2045

Mist rolling in near Bega

BELLINGEN

568 KM NORTH OF SYDNEY
POPULATION: 11 420   MAP REF: PAGE 179 M8
Bellingen is a truly beautiful town, located on the Bellinger River only 40 km from the major coastal centre of Coffs Harbour. It marks the beginning of a spectacular drive over the Great Divide to Dorrigo.

Originally called 'Boat Harbour', Bellingen was once the backwater from where red cedar was floated down to the mouth of the Bellinger River (first encountered by timber-getters in 1841).

Farmers followed the sawyers and the area is now a prosperous district with a strong agricultural heritage. Dairy farming and the production of pigs, maize and fruit are the predominant industries. A more contemporary venture—Advanced Wind Technologies, which specialises in energy-producing windmills—can be found on the Waterfall Way.

Bellingen is more for the contemplative visitor than the active, abounding in art and craft shops and upmarket coffee and teahouses, and it is a great place to unwind.

Of interest is Mac's House of Rocks which features lapidary work, opals and other gemstones.

Dorrigo National Park is to the north-west of the town, while Bongil Bongil National Park is on the coast, just south of Sawtell.

Bellingen holds a jazz festival in August each year.
ACCOMMODATION: Bellingen Valley Inn, ph (02) 6655 1599; Bliss Lodge Farmstay, ph 1800 803 007; Blue Gum (B&B), ph (02) 6655 1592; Jelga (B&B), ph (02) 6655 2202 ; Bellingen Caravan Park, ph (02) 6655 1338
ACTIVITIES: Canoeing, golf, historic interest, shopping, swimming
TOURIST INFORMATION: Ph (02) 6652 1522

BELMONT

155 KM NORTH OF SYDNEY
POPULATION: 6250   MAP REF: PAGE 177 J6
Belmont is the opposite of Bellingen. Were it not for
the fact that the Australian artist, Sir William Dobell's
home (open to the public) is situated at nearby Wangi,
Belmont could almost be a culture-free zone. Sport's
the name of the game here, with fishing and yachting
being the most visible activities. Belmont is, in fact, a
huge yachting centre, situated on the eastern shore of
Lake Macquarie.
ACCOMMODATION: Lake Macquarie Flag Motor Inn, ph
(02) 4947 7149; Belmont Hotel, ph (02) 4945 0444;
Belmont Pines Tourist Park, ph (02) 4945 4750;
Belmont North Caravan Park, ph (02) 4945 3653
ACTIVITIES: Fishing, swimming, yachting
TOURIST INFORMATION: Ph (02) 4958 0221

BERMAGUI

400 KM SOUTH OF SYDNEY
POPULATION: 1000   MAP REF: PAGE 174 E8
Bermagui is an angler's paradise. Indeed, it achieved
international fame way back in the 1930s when the
American novelist Zane Grey regularly chartered big
game boats from here. The reason why those looking
for black marlin and yellowfin tuna are almost
invariably successful is because the continental shelf
is closest to the mainland here, so there is great
fishing just off the shoreline.

Nowadays, the charter boats include other deep-
sea fishing and also SCUBA diving. The surf beaches
are excellent and very popular.

Bushwalking is a favourite pastime at nearby
Wallaga Lake—the biggest in New South Wales and a
significant breeding area for black swans. Wallaga has
special significance for the Yuin Aborigines, and
cultural tours are regularly organised by the local
Kooris to explain why. (The name 'Bermagui' is the
Aboriginal term for 'canoe with paddles'.)

Bermagui market is held on the last Sunday of
each month and features the homemade and
handmade.
ACCOMMODATION: Bermagui Motor Inn, ph
(02) 6493 4311; Bermagui Horseshoe Bay Hotel/Motel,
ph (02) 6493 4206; The Captain's Quarters Luxury
Townhouses, ph (02) 6493 4946; Bermagui Blue Pacific
Flats/Hostel, ph (02) 6493 4921; Ocean Lake Caravan
Park , ph (02) 6493 4055
ACTIVITIES: Billiards, bowls, bushwalking, fishing,
golf, indoor bowls, water sports
TOURIST INFORMATION: Ph (02) 6493 4174

BERRIDALE

447 KM SOUTH OF SYDNEY
POPULATION: 700   MAP REF: PAGE 174 C7
Situated halfway between Cooma and Jindabyne,
Berridale lies on the Murray River. Its name is
thought to derive from the Aboriginal 'berri', meaning
'wide bend in the river'. It is close to Lake Eucumbene

and its trout farm, but drivers should be aware that
the town is notorious for booking speeding motorists.

Berridale comes into its own in the ski season,
when it is a popular stop-off spot for people to grab a
cup of coffee or something to eat—even hire skis or
snow chains! (There are a few eateries, and one
delightful country pub.)
ACCOMMODATION: Cooba Holiday Motel, ph
(02) 6456 3150; Snowy Mountains Coach & Motor Inn,
ph (02) 6456 3283; Southern Cross Motor Inn and
Tourist Park, ph (02) 6456 3289; Snowy Station Lodge
(B&B), ph (02) 6456 5086
ACTIVITIES: Horse riding, trout fishing
TOURIST INFORMATION: Ph (02) 6450 1742

BERRIGAN

726 KM SOUTH-WEST OF SYDNEY
POPULATION: 1000   MAP REF: PAGE 183 K7
Situated on the Riverina Highway between Albury
and Deniliquin, Berrigan boasts many old buildings
dating back to the 1880s. It lies in the middle of rich
agricultural lands, but has long been synonymous
with horseracing: the historic Kilfenora Stables are
quite close to the racecourse. The course and the
racing club have been going since the 1890s, and now
Berrigan holds five meets a year, the major one being
the Berrigan Gold Cup.
ACCOMMODATION: Berrigan Country Club Motor
Inn, ph (03) 5885 2409; Finley Palm Motor Inn,
ph (03) 5885 2077; Berrigan Hotel, ph (03) 5885 2029
ACTIVITIES: Golf, historic interest, horseracing,
tennis
TOURIST INFORMATION: Ph (02) 6021 2694

in the Southern Highlands, the town boasts
Australia's oldest gaol (construction began in 1834),
now a minor offenders' institution. It housed in its
time a number of infamous bushrangers.

Berrima also has Australia's oldest continually
licensed inn, the Surveyor-General, named after Sir
Thomas Mitchell, who camped on the site in 1829 and
proclaimed it an excellent place for a town. There are
many other sandstone Georgian buildings in town,
the most notable being Berrima House (1835), the two
churches and the Post Office (1836).

Although situated on the old Hume Highway in
the midst of farming and grazing lands, coalmining
and cement manufacture are also important local
industries. However, there are many artists and
artisans who live in Berrima, and it is the arts and
crafts that they produce which attract visitors just as
much as the history of the town. (On weekends,
Berrima can be as crowded as George Street in
Sydney in rush hour!)

Although Berrima is extremely popular with
cyclists, it tends more to the sedentary pursuits, and
contains a number of coffee houses and restaurants of
very high standard.

The Berrima District Museum (in Market Street)
is well worth a visit, plus there are antique stores to
tempt collectors. Berkelouw's Books—known to
bibliophiles throughout Australia—is just out of town
on the old Hume Highway.
ACCOMMODATION: Bakehouse Motel, ph
1800 670 370; Surveyor-General Inn, ph (02) 4877 1266;
Coach and Horses Inn (B&B), ph (02) 4877 1242;
Berrima Lodge (B&B), ph (02) 4877 1755
ACTIVITIES: Arts and crafts, bicycling, historic
interest
TOURIST INFORMATION: Ph (02) 4871 2888

The Surveyor-General Inn at Berrima, Australia's oldest, continually licensed inn

BERRIDALE

BERRIMA

135 KM SOUTH-WEST OF SYDNEY
POPULATION: 600   MAP REF: PAGE 176 F10
Like Bathurst, Berrima is steeped in history and is
even more popular as a tourist destination because of
its proximity to both Sydney and Canberra. Situated

BERRY

164 KM SOUTH OF SYDNEY
POPULATION: 1400   MAP REF: PAGE 174 G3
Berry is another town of high historic importance as it
occupies part of what was a 28 300 hectare property
owned by Alexander Berry in the early nineteenth

century. The National Trust has classified many of Berry's buildings, including the Bunyip Inn, an historic guesthouse that dates from 1889, when it was a bank building. The Coolangatta Historic Village Resort is housed in cottages once used by convicts.

Originally occupied by Wadi Wadi Aborigines, the district was invaded initially by timber-getters, then dairy farmers. Dairying is still an important industry.

Towards the end of last century, settlers planted extended stands of English oaks, elms and beeches, creating a distinctly British feel which Berry perpetuates today. Within reasonable reach of Sydney, antique shops, the museum, art galleries and good restaurants draw people to the town, particularly in autumn, when natural beauty complements the other attractions. (The town's most famous doughnut shop—a caravan on the main street—has been unchanged for many years, and is now a tourist drawcard in itself.)

You can visit Brango Park Blueberries and there are two local wineries. An agricultural show is held each February. Local markets are set up each month in the showground.

ACCOMMODATION: Coolangatta Historic Village Resort, ph (02) 4448 7131; The Bunyip Inn, ph (02) 4464 2064; Bangalee Motel, ph (02) 4464 1305; Victoria's Guesthouse, ph (02) 4464 2211; Amelia's Country House B&B, ph (02) 4464 2534
ACTIVITIES: Scenic drives, sightseeing, wineries
TOURIST INFORMATION: Ph (02) 4464 2177

BLAYNEY

235 KM WEST OF SYDNEY
POPULATION: 2610   MAP REF: PAGE 176 C8
Blayney is in the centre of a rich agricultural district producing wool, fat lambs, wheat, vegetables and fruit. There are also a number of sheep, cattle, horse and pig studs in the area, but for many years Blayney has been most famous for its abattoir.

Visitors, however, will be more interested in its arts and crafts shops, and its proximity to the historic village of Carcoar. The local residents use Carcoar Dam in summer for water sports. Be aware that Blayney can be extremely cold in winter.
ACCOMMODATION: Blayney Goldfields Motor Inn, ph (02) 6368 2000; Blayney Central Motel, ph (02) 6368 3355; Blayney Caravan Park, ph (02) 6368 2799
ACTIVITIES: Historic interest, horse riding, water sports
TOURIST INFORMATION: Ph (02) 6333 6288

BODALLA

349 KM SOUTH OF SYDNEY
POPULATION: 260   MAP REF: PAGE 174 E7
Like Bega, Bodalla is perhaps best known for its cheese, but the town has important links with early Australia. Thomas Sutcliffe Mort, most famous for his pioneer work in exporting frozen meat to Great Britain in refrigerated ships, established Bodalla as a model farm in 1856, and incidentally founded a rural tradition of dairying for the district. (Mort was buried on his property at Bodalla.)

As part of the Sapphire Coast group of towns (which includes places like Bega and Narooma), Bodalla places a great deal of emphasis on tourism.

Bodalla caters for all manner of guests. It has art galleries, restaurants and gardens. On the other hand, its proximity to surf beaches and rivers gives it a different appeal. There is also great scenery close at hand. The village of Nerrigundah, famous for its bushrangers, is only a short drive away.
ACCOMMODATION: Motel Bodalla, ph (02) 4473 5201; Bodalla Arms Hotel, ph (02) 4473 5206; McConkey's Hotel, ph (02) 4473 5233; Blackfellow Point Camp Ground, ph (02) 4473 5312
ACTIVITIES: Historic interest, water sports
TOURIST INFORMATION: Ph (02) 6492 3313

BOGGABRI

555 KM NORTH-WEST OF SYDNEY
POPULATION: 571   MAP REF: PAGE 178 E8
Boggabri derives its name from an Aboriginal dialect, meaning 'place of creeks'. The town is the centre of a rural district that produces wool, wheat, fat lambs and cattle. The district also has an important connection with horses. Many of the members of the 1st Australian Light Horse came from Boggabri, mainly due to the efforts of Lt-Col Ken Mackay who, in 1897, travelled throughout New South Wales searching out the best horsemen.

Two local geographical features—Barbers Pinnacle and Barbers Lagoon—owe their names to an escaped convict known as 'the Barber', who lived with the local Aboriginal tribe for many years.

Some 20 km to the north is Leard State Forest, which is a prime gemstone fossicking location. (A licence is available from the local post office.)

Boggabri holds its annual picnic races in July.
ACCOMMODATION: Boggabri Nestle Inn (motel), ph (02) 6743 4308
ACTIVITIES: Fishing, fossicking, historic interest
TOURIST INFORMATION: Ph (02) 6792 3583

BOMADERRY

177 KM SOUTH OF SYDNEY
POPULATION: 10 100   MAP REF: PAGE 174 F4
Bomaderry is part of North Nowra, but is interesting in its own right, being an important industrial centre and the terminus of the South Coast Railway Line. It boasts a good shopping centre for those who wish to stock up on supplies without the congestion of Nowra.

There is a nice signposted walk along Bomaderry Creek; there are also 4WD tours over some of the Shoalhaven's more spectacular scenery. Skydiving is also an attraction in the region.
ACCOMMODATION: Avaleen Lodge Motor Inn, ph (02) 4421 8244; Balan Village Motel, ph (02) 4423 1111; Bomaderry Motor Inn, ph (02) 4421 0111; Shoalhaven Ski Park, ph (02) 4423 2488; Treehaven Village (camping/caravans), ph (02) 4421 3494; Nowra Animal Park Camping Reserve, ph (02) 4421 3949
ACTIVITIES: Bushwalking, 4WD touring, skydiving
TOURIST INFORMATION: Ph (02) 4421 0778

BOMBALA

533 KM SOUTH-WEST OF SYDNEY
POPULATION: 1500   MAP REF: PAGE 174 C9
The tourist blurb describes Bombala as 'Tranquillity in the middle of everything', and it *is* a hidden rural treasure between the Snowy Mountains and the Sapphire Coast. Three hours south of Canberra, it is a stunning blend of the treeless plains of the Monaro district, the rainforests of the Errinundra Plateau and dense native forests. Wildlife is abundant. There are even platypuses in the town itself. The quiet visitor on a relaxed evening stroll along the riverbank will perhaps be rewarded with a glimpse of this shy creature. (Bombala has the highest density of platypuses in New South Wales.)

Bombala is perhaps the most famous trout fishing centre in the state, and there are many places to stay very close to great spots on the river.

The town is also famous for the vivid jumpers created by the Toorallie Woollen Mill.

In January Bombala has a wool and wood festival.
ACCOMMODATION: Motel Maneroo, ph (02) 6458 3500; Kangaroo Camp Retreat, ph (02) 6458 3737; Mail Coach Restaurant (motel), ph (02) 6458 3721; Bibbenluke Lodge & Lavender Nursery (B&B), ph (02) 6458 5235; Bombala Caravan Park, ph (02) 6458 3270
ACTIVITIES: Bushwalking, fishing, gold fossicking
TOURIST INFORMATION: Ph 1800 633 012

BOURKE

778 KM NORTH-WEST OF SYDNEY
POPULATION: 3090   MAP REF: PAGE 181 K4
Of all New South Wales towns, Bourke has the most legendary folkloric reputation. Self-proclaimed as 'The Gateway to the Outback', the town has long been synonymous as the last outpost of civilisation, and expressions like 'back o' Bourke' merely scratch the surface of a rich cultural history. 'No work in Bourke',

The Darling River at Bourke

'Bourke shower' (a dust storm) and many other catchphrases also make it part of our linguistic heritage. And literary heritage: Henry Lawson made the Carriers Arms (a Cobb & Co staging station) home for quite some time in 1892.

Thomas Mitchell built Fort Bourke here in 1835—a wooden palisade against the warlike local Aboriginal tribes. It was the highest town on the Darling River from which wool could be shipped downstream in the halcyon days of the riverboat trade.

From Sydney, Bourke is reached via the Mitchell Highway, which, after Nyngan, becomes hedged by relentlessly grey-green scrub and red earth. Despite the dry surroundings, Bourke is incredibly verdant, as it is irrigated for citrus and cotton crops. But it is still an Outback town, an outpost, a frontier marker. Every Aussie should see Bourke at least once in their lives.

Fishing on the Darling River is a major attraction, but local festivals are worth marking in the calendar. The Bourke Mateship Festival, held since 1992 in September, features water sports, paddleboats, art and historical exhibitions, an old time ball and damper cooking, while the Back O'Bourke Stampede—essentially a professional bull riding contest and rodeo—is held in October.

ACCOMMODATION: Major Mitchell Motel, ph (02) 6872 2311; Bourke Riverside Motel and Gallery, ph (02) 6872 2539; Bourke Cottage (B&B), ph (02) 6872 2837; Paddlewheel Caravan Park, ph (02) 6872 2277; Central Australian Hotel, ph (02) 6872 2151; Carriers Arms Hotel, ph (02) 6872 2040
ACTIVITIES: Fishing, historic interest
TOURIST INFORMATION: Ph (02) 6872 2280

BOWRAL

127 KM SOUTH OF SYDNEY
POPULATION: 7410   MAP REF: PAGE 174 F3
Just as the expatriate English in the days of the British raj in India left behind the searing summer heat of the plains by escaping to the hill stations, so Sydney's wealthy at the turn of the century would set up in Bowral. Situated in the Southern Highlands, Bowral has a generally mild summer climate (but can be bitterly cold in winter). Bowral derives its name from the Aboriginal 'bowrel', which the local tribe bestowed on the giant rock which towers over the town; it is now known as 'The Gib' (after Gibraltar).

John Oxley was the first settler in the district, naming his homestead Wingecarribee—perpetuated in the shire name today. Bowral still has a very English ambience about it, with stately homes and magnificent gardens to delight the visitor.

While the town attracts Sydneysiders in droves, it is also a magnet for cricket lovers. Though born in Cootamundra, Sir Donald Bradman grew up in Bowral, and the self-guided Bradman Walk visits some of the town sites associated with the man whom many would argue was the greatest batsman of all. The Bradman Oval and Museum further commemorate Sir Donald's name. Amongst other memorabilia, the museum houses the bat the great man used at Headingly in 1934 to notch up his second highest ever Test score of 304.

Bowral has its famed Tulip Festival in September every year.

ACCOMMODATION: Oxley View Motel, ph (02) 4861 4211; Port-O-Call Motor Inn, ph (02) 4861 1779; Briars Country Lodge, ph (02) 4868 3566; Boronia Lodge (motel), ph (02) 4861 1860; Bowral Heritage Park Resort, ph (02) 4861 4833; Bowral Hotel, ph (02) 4862 2646; Craigieburn Family Resort, ph (02) 4861 1277
ACTIVITIES: Historic interest, sightseeing, walking
TOURIST INFORMATION: Ph (02) 4872 2280

BRAIDWOOD

292 KM SOUTH OF SYDNEY
POPULATION: 1000   MAP REF: PAGE 174 E5
Situated on Gillamatong Creek—a tributary of the Shoalhaven River—Braidwood bears the name of pioneer settler Thomas Braidwood Wilson, who also served as surgeon to the convicts. It is an historic gold town classified by the National Trust, lying halfway between Canberra and Batemans Bay on a superb stretch of 'driver's road'. The road from Braidwood to Batemans Bay over the Clyde Mountain offers spectacular views, but is subject to very heavy fog.

Certain buildings 'must' be seen, in particular the Post Office and the Tallagandra Shire Council Chambers, both restored by the Heritage Council. The gaol, the infirmary and the Catholic and Presbyterian churches are also worth seeing.

Braidwood nestles in the Budawang Ranges, and is very popular as a base for four-wheel drivers. The terrain is challenging and the scenery very diverse. There are three state forests and three national parks nearby to explore.

Braidwood is also famous as the location for Mick Jagger's 1969 re-creation of the character of Ned Kelly—a fitting site, as the Clarke Brothers gang of bushrangers used to hole up in the nearby Araluen Valley in the goldrush days.

Braidwood is a local arts and crafts centre with something to suit the taste of every tourist including a trout farm, a museum and a racecourse.

The local rural show is held in February/March, Heritage Week in April and stockhorse events take place in December.

ACCOMMODATION: Braidwood Cedar Lodge Motel, ph (02) 4842 2244; Braidwood Colonial Motel, ph (02) 4842 2027; Royal Mail Hotel, ph (02) 4842 2488; Shoalhaven River Retreat (B&B), ph (02) 4844 5344
ACTIVITIES: Bushwalking, fishing, 4WD touring, golf, horseracing, national park access, squash, swimming, tennis
TOURIST INFORMATION: Ph (02) 4842 2310

BREWARRINA

783 KM NORTH-WEST OF SYDNEY
POPULATION: 1250   MAP REF: PAGE 181 M3
Known as 'Bree' to the locals, Brewarrina lies 100 km east of Bourke on the Barwon River. Still the centre of a vast pastoral district extending to the Queensland border, in the old days Brewarrina was famous for the size of the wool clip loaded at the paddle-steamer wharf. Because the river was shallow at this point, it was also originally the site of a stock crossing.

The name derives from an Aboriginal word meaning 'the fisheries', and even today, visitors can see the old Aboriginal fish traps in the river. Made from partially submerged boulders, the traps consist of funnels through which fish were driven into shallow holding ponds.

Like most Outback New South Wales country towns, Brewarrina has had its share of racial tensions over the years. Last century, it was the scene of the infamous Breakfast Creek massacre. However, local residents are actively working to promote mutual understanding, and the Aboriginal Cultural Museum gives a great insight into the local Aboriginal history.

In terms of European culture, there is the Settlers' Museum and on the eastern edge of town there is a milk bar that is obviously a relic from the 1950s. Worth an ice-cream soda or two!

Fishing is the name of the game, both in the Barwon and at Narran Lake, 40 km east, and perch, cod and freshwater catfish are the prizes.

The town holds the Festival of the Fisheries in early September.

ACCOMMODATION: Swancrest Motel, ph (02) 6839 2397; Brewarrina Hotel, ph (02) 6839 2019; Brewarrina Caravan Park, ph (02) 6839 2106
ACTIVITIES: Fishing, historic interest
TOURIST INFORMATION: Ph (02) 6872 2280

BROKEN HILL

1163 KM NORTH-WEST OF SYDNEY
POPULATION: 21 560   MAP REF: PAGE 180 B8
Almost all the streets of Broken Hill have names relating back to mining operations or ores—a legacy of what made the Silver City the only sizeable town in the far west of New South Wales.

In 1883 German-born boundary rider and part-time prospector Charles Rasp found what he thought were tin samples on a rise explorer Charles Sturt had diarised as 'a broken hill'. Rasp formed a syndicate to mine the ore, which turned out to be extremely rich silver-lead-zinc, and Broken Hill Proprietary Ltd

An old mine at Broken Hill

(BHP) was born. More than a third of the world's silver has come from Broken Hill, but now the ore is finally running out, and the townsfolk, all of whom in one way or another have been dependent on the mine for their livelihood, are turning to tourism.

Signs of the times consist of large boards in the streets noting sites of interest like historic buildings, including the Town Hall and the Post Office.

An air of cosmopolitanism has started to pervade Broken Hill. Not that the Hill has been culture-less in the past: it has long been the home of the Brushmen of the Bush, a select group including Pro Hart and Jack Absalom.

Apart from Pro Hart's Gallery, visitors should go and see the Living Desert Sculpture Park, where sculptors from all over the world have created massive works from Wilcannia sandstone. These are sited to be visible for over 100 km and represent an arcing flow from the Pinnacle Hills to Fred Hollows' grave at Bourke.

Broken Hill affords all the customary diversions any large city does. But the most fascinating activity that Broken Hill can offer is mine tours.

A drive out to Silverton—an historic town in its own right—is well worth the effort, and if you go beyond the town, you will see the plains where the action shots for *Mad Max* were staged.

Broken Hill also makes a very civilised base for visiting other Outback locations like Menindee, Kinchega and Sturt National Parks, or the isolated Mootwingee National Park. The Barrier Ranges offer good 4WD touring, and if you're unsure about your cross-country skills, there are a number of 4WD tour operators in the Hill.

ACCOMMODATION: Theatre Royal Hotel, ph (08) 8087 3318; Old Willyama Motor Inn, ph (08) 8088 3355; Broken Hill Overlander Motor Inn Motel, ph (08) 8088 2566; Charles Rasp Cottage (B&B), ph (08) 8087 1988; Broken Hill Historic Cottages (B&B), ph 1800 639696; Broken Hill City Caravan Park, ph (08) 8087 3841

ACTIVITIES: Art galleries, 4WD touring, historic interest, mine tours, national park access

TOURIST INFORMATION: Ph (08) 8087 6077

Fishing boats at Brunswick Heads

BRUNSWICK HEADS

842 KM NORTH OF SYDNEY
POPULATION: 1600   MAP REF: PAGE 179 P2
Captain Rous was the first European to come across the Brunswick River in 1828 and he named it after Queen Caroline of Brunswick, wife of King George IV.

Today, the town of Brunswick Heads maintains a maritime connection with the tidy commercial fishing fleet moored in the harbour. Brunswick is famous for its fishing, and its fish—many pundits claim that the North Coast's best seafood is available at Fins, situated on the riverfront.

The town has a good art gallery. Brunswick Heads Nature Reserve with local flora and fauna is well worth a look.

The Brunswick Heads Festival of Fish and Chips is held in January.

ACCOMMODATION: Brunswick Heads Motel, ph (02) 6685 1851; Casa Blanca Motor Inn, ph (02) 6685 1353; Brunswick Heads Hotel, ph (02) 6685 1236; Terrace Reserve Caravan Park, ph (02) 6685 1233

ACTIVITIES: Bowls, fishing, golf, scenic drives, tennis, water sports

TOURIST INFORMATION: Ph (02) 6686 3484

BULAHDELAH

261 KM NORTH OF SYDNEY
POPULATION: 1100   MAP REF: PAGE 177 L4
On the Pacific Highway, Bulahdelah is the main aquatic gateway to the splendours of Myall Lakes and is surrounded by water, bush and mountain scenery. The word 'Bulahdelah' has seen 13 different spellings since the original 'boola-deela', which comes from Kattang, language of the Worimi, ancestral inhabitants of the Great Lakes. It means 'place beneath the mountain where the two rivers meet'; the rivers are the Myall and the Crawford.

Since the early nineteenth century, the area has been a supplier of high quality hardwood, and numerous local state forests still supply the industry. They also house a diverse range of flora and fauna including 275 species of birds, 45 species of mammals

and 41 species of reptiles and frogs. There are some rare animals in this list, including the yellow-bellied glider, golden-tipped bat, sooty owl and the nocturnal tiger quoll. On Bulahdelah Mountain, there are 16 species of orchid.

Things to see in and around Bulahdelah include the historic Court House, the old inn which was a staging post for Cobb & Co, the Bulahdelah Steam Logging Railway, the Mungo Brush and the old trestle bridge. And of course, there's the Grandis (*Eucalyptus grandis*), the tallest tree in the state.

The hiring of houseboats to explore the Lakes system is a popular activity, as is bushwalking.

ACCOMMODATION: Bulahdelah Motor Lodge, ph (02) 4997 4520; Bulahdelah Mount View Motel, ph (02) 4997 4292; Forest Lodge Country Resort (B&B), ph (02) 4997 4511; Bulahdelah Myall Shores Camping Area, ph (02) 4997 4495; Alum Mountain Tourist Caravan Park, ph (02) 4997 4565

ACTIVITIES: Birdwatching, bushwalking, fishing, houseboats, horse riding, rainforest exploration, trail bike riding, water sports

TOURIST INFORMATION: Ph (02) 4929 9299

BUNDANOON

152 KM SOUTH OF SYDNEY
POPULATION: 1500   MAP REF: PAGE 174 F3
Together with Bowral, Bundanoon used to be a favourite spot in the Southern Highlands for Sydney's elite, and with streets lined with oaks, elms and poplars, it has retained its genteel charm. Now, the visitor demographic is far more democratic, with sightseers, bushwalkers, backpackers and golfers making up the weekend clientele at coffee shops, restaurants and art nooks. It is also popular with cyclists, who can use Bundanoon as a base for easy runs up to Sutton Forest, Moss Vale and back (33 km), or for more arduous exercise through neighbouring Kangaroo Valley.

Bundanoon is very close to Morton National Park, which boasts a labyrinth of walking tracks, spectacular lookouts, deep canyons and cliffs. There is also the Glow Worm Glen (best seen at night) and a Thai Buddhist monastery which welcomes visitors.

In April Bundanoon celebrates its Gaelic roots by holding the Highland Gathering, with traditional Scottish games, bands and country dances.

ACCOMMODATION: Killarney Guest House and Motel, ph (02) 4883 6224; Bundanoon Hotel, ph (02) 4883 6005; Tree Tops Guest House (B&B), ph (02) 4883 6372, Mildenhall Guest House (B&B), ph (02) 4883 6643

ACTIVITIES: Bowls, bushwalking, golf, horse riding, national park access, sightseeing

TOURIST INFORMATION: Ph (02) 4872 2280

BYRON BAY

832 KM NORTH OF SYDNEY
POPULATION: 4150   MAP REF: PAGE 179 P2
Once an unspoilt backwater on the state's north coast, Byron Bay is now a mix of cultures (including the alternative) and lifestyles. Byron—'where the sun

The beautiful countryside around idyllic Byron Bay

first hits the sand'—has a year-round subtropical climate, with summer temperatures dominated by a cooling onshore breeze. It is idyllic, which explains its burgeoning population, and its attraction as a holiday destination.

Named by Captain Cook after a pillar of the English establishment, sailor Sir John Byron (who was also the grandfather of the famed poet), Byron Bay now is very international. Restaurants embrace almost every national cuisine, and services with origins all around the globe, like shiatsu massage, tarot readings and tai chi, are available.

Cape Byron, the easternmost point of Australia, is a great spot from which to watch migrating whales and frolicking dolphins.

Byron Bay has a number of surf beaches, and the breaks are famous all around the world. Watego's Beach, with its white sands and crystal waters, also has a break that is popular with bodysurfers and boogie boarders. It is just under the Cape Byron light. The crystal clear waters are also popular with snorkel and SCUBA divers.

There are also some great drives in the Byron hinterland, with spectacular views to the coast.

Regular events at Byron are the Whale and Dolphin Festival in August, the Byron Kiteflyers' Picnic in July, the famed East Coast Blues Festival which takes place in June.

ACCOMMODATION: Beach Hotel, ph (02) 6685 6402; Byron Motor Lodge, ph (02) 6685 6522; Mariner Bay Apartments, ph (02) 6685 5272; Beachfront Apartments, ph (02) 6685 6354; On the Bay Beachhouse (B&B), ph (02) 6685 5125; Byron Bay Beach Resort (B&B), ph (02) 6685 8000; Glen Villa Resort (camping and caravans), ph (02) 6685 7382
ACTIVITIES: Fishing, scenic drives, water sports, whale and dolphin watching
TOURIST INFORMATION: Ph (02) 6686 3484

CAMDEN

61 KM SOUTH-WEST OF SYDNEY
POPULATION: 7600   MAP REF: PAGE 174 G2
With Sydney sprawling like Los Angeles, Camden could now almost be called a suburb, but to do so would be to do this fine historic village a disservice.

The Camden (and indeed Campbelltown) saga dates back to 1795, when two convicts discovered wild cattle—descendants of a herd that had originally strayed from Sydney—in the vicinity. Hence its early name 'Cowpastures', now perpetuated in the Cowpastures Road heading south from Sydney.

In 1805 John Macarthur was granted two properties (2000 hectares in all), one of which he named Camden Park after the Secretary of State for the Colonies, Lord Camden, who had authorised the grants, and here he carried on his wool-growing experiments. Today, industries include dairying, agriculture, fruit-growing, viticulture, raising fat lambs, beef cattle, pigs and poultry.

Founded in 1839, the town boasts an excellent example of Gothic Revival architecture in the Anglican Church, its spire visible for kilometres.

Camden also has ties with aviation: the Macquarie Grove aerodrome, owned by the Federal Government, was developed from a private field and a military installation located here during World War II.

Nowadays, the town houses the University of Sydney Rural Veterinary Centre.

In October Camden hosts a rural agricultural show which is held on 20 hectares of parkland on what was once part of Camden Park. It features rural food and fibre industries, cottage crafts, commercial exhibitions, sheep and dog trials, bush bands, fishing and horse events.

ACCOMMODATION: Crown Hotel/Motel, ph (02) 4655 2200; Plough & Harrow Hotel, ph (02) 4655 8189; Camden Country Club (motel), ph (02) 4655 8402; Poplar Caravan Park, ph (02) 4658 0485
ACTIVITIES: Bowls, golf, historic interest, sightseeing, tennis
TOURIST INFORMATION: Ph (02) 4658 1370

CAMPBELLTOWN

52 KM SOUTH-WEST OF SYDNEY
POPULATION: 40 150   MAP REF: PAGE 174 G2
This really is now a suburb of sprawling Sydney, but originally was a quiet country village named by Governor Macquarie after his wife's maiden name.

Now its dairies supply much of Sydney's milk and the district also produces poultry and fruit. Architectural landmarks include St Peter's Church (completed in 1824), and Glenalvon and Richmond Villa, two of the original houses.

Campbelltown sponsors an annual festival in November: the Fisher's Ghost Festival. Activities include a massive street parade of floats and marching bands, fireworks, a Mardi Gras, and arts and crafts. The Ghost, according to Australian colonial folklore, is that of Frederick Fisher, a Campbelltown farmer, who was murdered by a fellow ex-convict. Four months later Fisher's 'ghost' was 'seen' by a local man and subsequent investigation led to Fisher's grave and the murderer admitted his guilt. Fisher's Ghost Creek is a local watercourse perpetuating the legend.

ACCOMMODATION: Rose & Crown Hotel, ph (02) 4625 4314; Court Tavern, ph (02) 4265 1016; Colonial Motor Inn, ph (02) 4625 2345; Motel Formula One, ph (02) 4628 7340; Maclin Autolodge Motel, ph (02) 4625 2338
ACTIVITIES: Bowls, golf, historic interest, scenic drives, sightseeing, tennis
TOURIST INFORMATION: Ph (02) 4620 1510

CANOWINDRA

302 KM WEST OF SYDNEY
POPULATION: 1720   MAP REF: PAGE 176 B8
Even today, newsreaders pronounce Canowindra phonetically, not as it should be: 'Ca-nown-dra'. The name comes from an Aboriginal term for 'home'.

Canowindra is the service centre for a district which produces lucerne, wheat, wool and fat lambs.

Up until fairly recently, Canowindra was most famous as the ballooning capital of New South Wales, a title the town can still rightly claim. The best time for going aloft is between April and October.

Canowindra's historic claim to fame is that the town was taken over for three days by bushrangers Ben Hall and Frank Gardiner, holding the population in Robinson's Hotel (now the Royal) and forcing them to party. The group included the town's policeman!

Latterly, a scientist named Dr Alex Ritchie has been responsible for spreading Canowindra's name all over the world. He has been researching an enormous fossil find. Local stone beds contain

detailed impressions of more than 100 Late Devonian fish—one of the world's greatest fossil discoveries. The local people, with the help of some government aid, are building an 'Age of Fishes' Museum which will draw even more tourism into the district. An entire industry—including an Internet website—has sprung up because of the ichthyological discovery!

ACCOMMODATION: Junction Hotel, ph (02) 6344 1365; Canowindra Hotel, ph (02) 6344 1407; Blue Jacket Motel, ph (02) 6344 1002; Poppy's & the Galah Guesthouse and Restaurant, ph (02) 6344 1009; Mount Cole Guest Property, ph (02) 6344 7142; Falls Guesthouse, ph (02) 6344 1293

ACTIVITIES: Ballooning, fossil viewing, historic interest, scenic drives

TOURIST INFORMATION: Ph (02) 6344 1399

CARCOAR

250 KM WEST OF SYDNEY
POPULATION: 450   MAP REF: PAGE 176 C8

One of the prettiest towns in the state, Carcoar sits perched on a hill with the River Belubula at its base. It is the third oldest town west of the Blue Mountains.

Carcoar is another town for history buffs: it was the site of Australia's first bank robbery in 1863, and it also has many fine examples of Georgian architecture, including the stables at Stoke House. The Church of the Immaculate Conception—built in the 1870s—is most innovative in that it allows air to be drawn into the building through cavities in its walls. The air cools the edifice as it escapes out of the specially designed window sills.

There is also an interesting Firearms Museum, housed in the 1877 Commercial Bank building designed by architect Allan Mansfield (who was also responsible for the Royal Prince Alfred Hospital in Sydney). The structure is solid brick with stucco rendering. Most internal joinery is made from Australian red cedar, including the bank counter. Originally, lighting was supplied by gas created at the building's own generating plant.

Firearms have been collected over the past 15 years and many represent the work of the English gunsmith William Tranter (1816–90), who was one of the first gunmakers to utilise the rimfire cartridge.

Carcoar is also a popular cycling destination. An established track starts in Canberra, goes via Wyangala Dam and ends in Carcoar—475 km over sealed and gravel roads.

In January, the annual Australia Day Handicraft Fair is held, featuring craft stalls and music.

ACCOMMODATION: Dalebrook Guesthouse (B&B), ph (02) 6367 3149

ACTIVITIES: Cycling, historic interest

TOURIST INFORMATION: Ph (02) 6333 6288

CASINO

741 KM NORTH OF SYDNEY
POPULATION: 11 800   MAP REF: PAGE 179 N3

Casino derives its name from the fact that in the 1840s Henry Clay and George Stapleton, two early settlers, called their station Cassino (sic), after the town in southern Italy. Timber-getting (especially cedar) and cattle raising were the principal early industries, but to some extent these have given way to dairying and pig raising.

Casino is now also an important air, rail and road junction for north coast tourist traffic. It is a bustling, busy place and has a large variety of sports venues, clubs and restaurants.

Straddling the Richmond River, the town has a large milk-products factory and a meatworks that is one of the biggest of its kind in the southern hemisphere. It also houses the north coast headquarters of the Forestry Commission.

The local anglers have success in Cook's Weir and in the river. For those who are interested in history and culture, there are totemic Aboriginal rock carvings on the Tenterfield road. There is also a museum in the town.

Casino is also known as the Beef Capital, and every May/June the town holds Beef Week, where the town's local butchers set up BBQs in the main street between 7 and 9 am and cook for all and sundry. The entertainment is extremely varied and includes comedy, a milking competition, several live bands, street performers, a street parade, fashion parades, art exhibitions, a cattle auction and a talent quest.

ACCOMMODATION: Commonwealth Hotel, ph (02) 6662 1145; Cecil Hotel, ph (02) 6662 1047; Casino Motor Inn, ph (02) 6662 1777; Milgate Motel, ph (02) 6662 1022; Canberra Guest House, ph (02) 6662 1094; Norway Guest House, ph (02) 6662 2648; Brown's Caravan Park, ph (02) 6662 1840

ACTIVITIES: Fishing, golf, sightseeing, tennis

TOURIST INFORMATION: Ph (02) 6662 3566

CENTRAL TILBA

390 KM SOUTH OF SYDNEY
POPULATION: 100   MAP REF: PAGE 174 E7

Central Tilba is one of the prettiest and most historic towns in the state. A National Trust village, the architecture spans the last years of the nineteenth century and the early ones of the twentieth. Its Victorian timber buildings represent an important example of a bygone age and lifestyle. The only constructions still standing are the original weatherboard residences and shops, and the local hotel and general store are particularly evocative of the pioneering days. Many TV commercials have been filmed there, as the only concessions to modernity are the power lines.

The town nestles under the sacred 'Gulaga', named Mt Dromedary by James Cook because its peak resembled the camel's back.

The area was originally inhabited by the Yuin tribe (in their language, 'tilba' means 'wind'), but the first white settler was Henry Bate, who subdivided the area. The Bate family is synonymous with the history of Tilba. On a sweeping headland overlooking the sea is the grave of politician Jeff Bate, with a head-stone bearing a dedication to 'a brave man'. The stone was donated by his widow Dame Zara, also the widow of drowned Prime Minister Harold Holt.

Gold changed sleepy Tilba into a booming and roisterous place, but the find was shortlived, and peace returned quickly. Dairying replaced digging, and the manufacture of cheese (which still goes on today), became one of the village's means of survival.

Central Tilba is now totally dedicated to the tourist trade. As such, it has three craft galleries—the Tilba Wood-turning Gallery, Mangrove Craft Gallery and the Gulaga Gallery. Many artisans work in the town. There are leatherworkers, wood-turners, jewellers and cheesemakers.

Nearby is Tilba's winery, and a deer farm, both of which are open to the public.

A festival which features live music, theatre and exhibitions, is held annually on Easter Saturday.

ACCOMMODATION: Dromedary Hotel, ph (02) 4473 7223; Central Tilba Farm Cabins, ph (02) 4473 7353

ACTIVITIES: Arts and crafts, historic interest, winery

TOURIST INFORMATION: Ph (02) 4476 2099

CESSNOCK

266 KM NORTH OF SYDNEY
POPULATION: 17 500   MAP REF: PAGE 177 H6

Like Lithgow, Cessnock suffers the stigma of being a coalmining town, but it has much to offer the tourist.

The township of Central Tilba with Mt Dromedary in the background

Cessnock was named after Cessnock Castle in Scotland by pioneer Scots settler John Campbell, who received a land grant of 2560 acres in 1826 from Governor Darling. His estate was subdivided in 1853 and a village developed. In 1856 coal was discovered and by the turn of the century this had brought prosperity to the district and a security of employment.

Running parallel with mining ventures was wine production. Today, Hunter Valley wines are regarded as being amongst the best in Australia—particularly its best reds.

The Cessnock area, once a favourite haunt of bushrangers as it was close to Sydney but backed onto wild bush, now encompasses over 20 towns and villages, with many descendants of the pioneer settlers of 150 years ago among the residents. Free settlers and ticket-of-leave convicts became graziers, timber-getters, miners and grape-growers. Now, while the coal is still important, local industries include dairying, cattle breeding, mixed farming, timber milling, pottery and clothing manufacture.

There is a lot to do in Cessnock. It is a very strong racing town, with both harness and greyhound events occurring on a regular basis. Then, of course, there are tours of the wineries, all of which have cellar door sales. Some of these wineries have been in the same families since the first vines were planted, and the upper Hunter has some superb views as you journey from one vineyard to the other.

Worth visiting is the historic twin-gabled timber building of Marthaville on the Wollombi Road at Cessnock. It was the home of George Brown, a man of many talents. In his day he was builder, sawmiller, prospector, magistrate, coroner, councillor and vigneron! Built in the 1880s, Marthaville is now home to many local art and craft exhibitions.

Four-wheel drivers will find plenty to do in the nearby Watagan Mountains, and people with conventional cars will have plenty to see on scenic drives throughout the district.

ACCOMMODATION: Cessnock Hotel, ph (02) 4990 1002; Caledonia Hotel, ph (02) 4990 1212; Heritage Inn, ph (02) 4991 2744; Cessnock Motel, ph (02) 4990 2699; Cessnock Cabins and Caravan Park, ph (02) 4990 5819
ACTIVITIES: Bowls, 4WD touring, golf, horseracing, horse riding, hot-air ballooning, swimming, tennis, wineries
TOURIST INFORMATION: Ph (02) 4990 4477

COBAR

704 KM NORTH-WEST OF SYDNEY
POPULATION: 5500   MAP REF: PAGE 181 K7

Cobar sits in isolation in western New South Wales. Most people come into Cobar on the Barrier Highway from either Nyngan or Wilcannia, but the more adventurous may prefer to travel the dirt from either Bourke or Louth to the north or Lake Cargellico, Condobolin or Hillston to the south.

Cobar derives its name from the Aboriginal 'coburra', meaning 'burnt earth used as body decoration'. The coloured earth is Cobar's raison d'être. In 1870, three men drilling for water found some red-coloured stones which they showed to a Cornishwoman living on Priory Station. She recognised them as copper ore and the boom began. What started as a tent city soon had a population of 10 000, and at one stage the Great Cobar copper mine was reputed to be the largest in the world.

Several buildings of those halcyon days survive, including the Great Western Hotel, which claims to have the longest verandah in Australia.

Cobar experienced a revival in the 1960s, when mining giant CSA ran a water pipeline 135 km from Nyngan into the town. Cobar now has tree-lined streets and is literally an oasis in predominantly semi-arid, dusty country.

The Great Cobar Outback Heritage Centre is worth a visit. Housed in the Great Cobar Copper Mine's Edwardian administration building (1910), it has wheelchair access, souvenirs, refreshments and guided tours of the museum and surrounds. It covers all aspects of Cobar's industrial, pastoral and Aboriginal history. Interpretive signs guide visitors through the grounds and there is an amazing collection of mining and transport artefacts.

For those with a more cultural bent, the work of local artists is on display at the Gloria Gallery, while others may like to participate in an underground mine tour. By arrangement, visitors can inspect the Aboriginal cave paintings 40 km out on the Wilcannia road (Barrier Highway).

ACCOMMODATION: Great Western Cobar Hotel/Motel, ph (02) 6836 2503; New Occidental Hotel, ph (02) 6836 2111; Town & Country Motor Inn, ph (02) 6836 1244; Cobar Caravan Park, ph (02) 6836 2425
ACTIVITIES: Aboriginal cave paintings, bowls, copper mines, golf, historic interest, swimming
TOURIST INFORMATION: Ph (02) 6836 2448

COFFS HARBOUR

582 KM NORTH OF SYDNEY
POPULATION: 60 000   MAP REF: PAGE 179 N7

Thought to be a corruption of Korff's Harbour (some people still pronounce it that way), Coffs owes its name to John Korff, a cedar-getter in the 1850s.

Originally two towns (the other was Coffs Harbour Jetty) which gradually merged, Coffs is one of Australia's major timber ports. It is also now the commercial centre of the mid-north coast, and has been assessed by the CSIRO as having one of the best climates in the country—more hours of sunshine than areas further south and less humidity than those further north. Needless to say, this feature has been one of the many contributory factors for making Coffs Harbour a popular holiday resort.

Now regarded by many sailors as one of New South Wales' safest all-weather ports, originally Coffs Harbour was shunned by captains as too dangerous until the lighthouse was built in 1878. Not surprisingly, the town now has a yacht club, a refurbished marina and a large commercial fishing fleet.

Other industries in the region include banana growing, dairying, engineering and sawmilling.

Coffs Promenade is a popular attraction, with many specialty shops and restaurants. Coffs Harbour

St Laurence Catholic Church, a magnificent building in Cobar

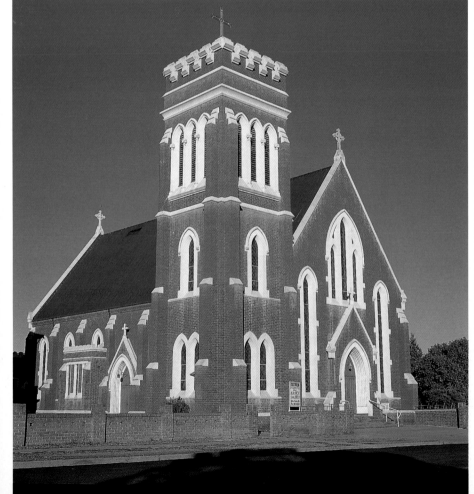

The marina at Coffs Harbour with the fishing fleet moored in the background

has a beautiful botanic gardens with a mangrove boardwalk; other enticements include art, crafts and antique shops.

For families, there is the zoo, the Big Banana Theme Park, the Butterfly House and the Plaster Fun House. Coffs Harbour Jetty Foreshores makes an ideal picnic spot, with great views over the beaches, which are great for surfing or swimming.

Active people can enjoy whitewater rafting on the nearby Nymboida River. There are also a number of 4WD adventure safaris available, and those who own their own 4WD vehicle can explore the rugged hinterland. Owners of conventional cars will greatly enjoy delightful scenic tours of the district.

Every Sunday, markets are held on the jetty and every October, the Festival of Golf runs for nine days. It is open to both men and women, with events like the Coffs Harbour Cup, the Ladies' Open and the North Coast Amateur Open.

ACCOMMODATION: Novotel Opal Cove Resort, ph (02) 6651 0510; Pelican Beach Resort, ph (02) 6653 7000; Aanuka Beach Resort, ph (02) 6652 7555; Nautilus on the Beach Resort, ph (02) 6653 6699; Zebra Motel, ph (02) 6652 1588; Split Solitary Caravan Park, ph (02) 6653 6212

ACTIVITIES: Fishing, 4WD touring, golf, horse riding, scenic drives, sightseeing, water sports

TOURIST INFORMATION: Ph (02) 6652 1522

COLEAMBALLY

675 KM SOUTH-WEST OF SYDNEY
POPULATION: 600   MAP REF: PAGE 183 K5
For those who follow Henry Ford's dictum 'history is bunk', Coleambally should be a mecca, for it could lay claim to being the least historic town in the state. Founded in the 1950s, Coleambally is the commercial hub for a 95 000 hectare irrigation area specialising in producing wheat, wool, cotton and most importantly, rice. The initial impetus for the town and district was World War II soldier settlement blocks.

ACCOMMODATION: Brolga Hotel, ph (02) 6954 4009; Coleambally Motel and Restaurant, ph (02) 6954 4233; Kingfisher Caravan Lodge, ph (02) 6954 4100

ACTIVITIES: Bowls, golf, horse riding, swimming, tennis

TOURIST INFORMATION: Ph (02) 6954 4100

CONDOBOLIN

467 KM WEST OF SYDNEY
POPULATION: 3500   MAP REF: PAGE 183 M1
Regarded as the geographic centre of New South Wales, 'Condo' is situated on the Lachlan River on red soil plains. The name derives from the Aboriginal word for 'hop bush'.

The district survives on wool, wheat, cattle and pigs. However, in 1896 when gold was discovered at Overflow Station (made famous by A. B. 'Banjo' Paterson's 'Clancy of the Overflow'), an influx of prospectors, particularly Chinese, swelled the community. The gold ran out, but fossicking still attracts the tourists.

One of the last Aboriginal chiefs of the area is buried about 40 km out of town.

Lake Condobolin Recreation Area is popular with residents for water sports.

ACCOMMODATION: Condobolin Hotel/Motel, ph (02) 6895 2040; Condobolin Motor Inn, ph (02) 6895 2233

ACTIVITIES: Bowls, fishing, golf, tennis, water sports

TOURIST INFORMATION: Ph (02) 6895 2377

COOLAH

384 KM WEST OF SYDNEY
POPULATION: 900   MAP REF: PAGE 176 D3
If the phrase 'beyond the black stump' means anything, Coolah has the best credentials to claim to be the site. Not only did the Kamileroi Aborigines call the area 'Weetalibah-Wallangan' ('place where the fire went out and left a burnt stump'), but in the early days Coolah had a wine bar named the Black Stump Wine Saloon. The bar and staging post were erected in the 1860s by John Higgins. He saw the need for a place where fellow teamsters and coach drivers could stop and prepare for the long journey west. The original Black Stump Wine Saloon burnt down in 1908.

The first white man to see the Coolah area was Allan Cunningham, who reached Pandora's Pass in June 1823. Tommy Governor, father of the Aborigine Jimmy Governor—the anti-hero of Thomas Keneally's *The Chant of Jimmie Blacksmith*—discovered silver at Leadville in 1887 and this led to the formation of a mining enterprise which employed over 500 men.

Visiting Pandora's Pass with its magnificent vista over the Liverpool Plains and Coolah Valley is a must, as is a detour to Aboriginal rock sites at nearby Ulan and Uarbry. There are also local fossil sites to inspect and bushwalkers should explore both Norfolk and Bald Hill Creek Falls.

ACCOMMODATION: Hotel Coolah, ph (02) 6377 1231; Coolah Valley Hotel, ph (02) 6377 1210; Black Stump Motel, ph (02) 6377 1208

ACTIVITIES: Bushwalking, fossil sites, historic interest, silver mines

TOURIST INFORMATION: Ph (02) 6884 1422

COOLAMON

521 KM SOUTH-WEST OF SYDNEY
POPULATION: 1300   MAP REF: PAGE 183 M5
Thirty kilometres north-west of Wagga Wagga, between Junee and Mandera, lies Coolamon in the centre of a rich wheat and fat lamb district.

When the railway arrived in 1881, the town was laid out on the original Coolemon Holes run, but the spelling soon changed to more closely reflect the Aboriginal word 'coolamon', meaning a hollowed-out piece of wood suitable for carrying water or food.

Known as 'the turkey capital' because of the large numbers of these birds produced in the district, it is also famous for its antique shops, museums and historic buildings which abound throughout the area. The Ardlethan Walking Track is close by.

A strong racing town, special events through the year are the Anzac Day Races, the Pacers' Cup and the South-west and Riverina Pacers' Derby.

Coolamon has a number of festivals. In March, there's the Vintage Tractor Pull; in August, the Agricultural Show; in September, a Hootenanny (folk festival) and in October, the Canola Festival.

ACCOMMODATION: Coolamon Hotel, ph (02) 6927 3028; Royal Tavern Hotel, ph (02) 6927 3015; Coolamon Caravan Park, ph (02) 6927 3206

ACTIVITIES: Historic interest, horseracing

TOURIST INFORMATION: Ph (02) 6923 5402

COOMA

415 KM SOUTH OF SYDNEY
POPULATION: 7750   MAP REF: PAGE 174 C7

In the heart of the Snowy Mountains, the Cooma district boasts gentle country hospitality, crisp, clean air, tranquil riverbanks and waterfalls, forest glades and treeless plains. In winter it throngs with holiday-makers using it as a base for their skiing activities.

The townsite was first surveyed in 1849, boomed when gold was discovered at Kiandra in 1860, but declined in the late 1880s. But as headquarters for the famed Snowy Mountains Hydro-Electric Scheme in the 1950s, the town again exploded, with some 10 000 workers billeted around the area.

'Cooma' is derived from the Aboriginal word 'coombah', meaning either 'big lake' or 'open country'.

Lambie Street, predominantly Georgian in design, is an historic precinct. There is also a statue in town perpetuating the legend of A. B. 'Banjo' Paterson's *Man From Snowy River*. The airliner *Southern Cloud* crashed close to Cooma in 1931, and a memorial was erected to these early aviators.

Cooma also has a number of special events throughout the year. In January, the races and a trade fair are held; in March, another race day and in April, Heritage Day. In October/November, Coomafest is held, featuring a rock & roll picnic, a talent quest and fun run. In November, there are two events: the Snowy Mountains Chainsaw Classic (which also features axemen) and the Snowy Mountains Trout Festival, which has prize money totalling $35 000.

Every third Sunday, markets are held at Centennial Park.

ACCOMMODATION: Coffey's Hotel, ph (02) 6452 2064; Alpine Hotel, ph (02) 6452 1466; Cooma Gateway Holiday Motel, ph (02) 6452 1592; Bunkhouse Motel, ph (02) 6452 2983; Rose Valley Farm Holidays, ph (02) 6452 2885; Mountain View Caravan Park, ph (02) 6452 4513

ACTIVITIES: Horse racing, snowskiing, tennis, trout fishing, water sports

TOURIST INFORMATION: Ph (02) 6450 1742

COONABARABRAN

454 KM NORTH-WEST OF SYDNEY
POPULATION: 3800   MAP REF: PAGE 176 C1

Coonabarabran started life in 1860, the first buildings being a courthouse and prison (restored in 1967 and still in use). It was at Coonabarabran that Australia's only Chinese bushranger, Sam Poo, shot and wounded a police constable. He was tracked down, captured and hanged.

Coonabarabran (the name means 'an inquisitive person') is the closest centre to the famed Warrum-bungles, a volcanic plateau that literally erupts from the surrounding plains. It consists of over 21 000 hectares under the supervision of the National Parks and Wildlife Service, and is full of kangaroos, koalas, emus and an abundance of bird life. A walk over the Grand Hightops is unforgettable, and though it takes from 4 to 6 hours, it is accessible even with children.

White Gum Lookout and Gurianama walks are suitable for prams and wheelchairs. There is a powered camp site at the park with an amenities block, cleared sites and electric BBQs.

Visitors have a number of opportunities in the Coonabarabran area. They can take a scenic flight over the Bungles, or go on an ecotour with Coonabarabran Country Tours, or gain some appreciation of Aboriginal life with Milton Judd's Aboriginal Site Tours.

Siding Springs Observatory, 24 km to the west, has the southern hemisphere's largest optical telescope.

Crystal Kingdom is within easy walking distance of the main shopping centre and Shea's Miniland, with its life-size animated dinosaurs and fantasy stone age train which carries visitors through natural bush settings and the exhibits, is 9 km from Coona-barabran on the Warrumbungle road. It has BBQs and picnic settings, plus 'Paddle-O-Saurus' boats, a bush puppet theatre, a museum and a waterslide.

ACCOMMODATION: Imperial Hotel, ph (02) 6842 1023; Royal Hotel, ph (02) 6842 1816; Acacia Motor Lodge, ph (02) 6842 1922; Everton Guesthouse, ph (02) 6842 2619; Castlereagh Village Caravan Park, ph (02) 6842 1706; 'Brooklyn' (farmstay), ph (02) 6842 8281

ACTIVITIES: Aboriginal site tours, bushwalking, national park access, sightseeing

TOURIST INFORMATION: Ph (02) 6842 1441

COONAMBLE

562 KM NORTH-WEST OF SYDNEY
POPULATION: 3125   MAP REF: PAGE 178 A9

A town of the inland plains, Coonamble is the natural centre of a rich pastoral district. Wool, wheat, fat lambs and beef cattle are the principal products of the district. Coonamble lies in the artesian belt and has a reticulated supply of bore water. The site of the town was established in 1817 and it became a watering place for stockmen. The town takes its name from the initial run in the area, Koonamble.

Coonamble is in close proximity to the Warrumbungles and the Pilliga Scrub. The famed Macquarie Marshes are also close to Coonamble. For bird lovers, the Marshes offer an experience which can rarely be duplicated anywhere in Australia.

You can also go boating or swimming at nearby Warrana Weir.

Coonamble is also big on horseracing, with six meetings held annually. The Wool Festival Gold Cup, held in association with the Coonamble Festival each October, is one of the richest inland one-day race meetings in Australia. The Coonamble Show is held in May.

ACCOMMODATION: Clubhouse Hotel, ph (02) 6822 1663; Sons of the Soil Hotel, ph (02) 6822 1009; Coonamble Motel, ph (02) 6822 1400; Castlereagh Lodge Motel, ph (02) 6822 1999

ACTIVITIES: Birdwatching, fishing, sightseeing, water sports

TOURIST INFORMATION: Ph (02) 6822 3040

COOTAMUNDRA

427 KM SOUTH-WEST OF SYDNEY
POPULATION: 6400   MAP REF: PAGE 183 P5

Like Bowral, Cootamundra (the name means 'turtles', 'low flying' or 'a marsh') is tied up with Sir Don Bradman. He was born here in 1908 and 'Bradman Cottage' has been restored and converted into a museum full of cricketing memorabilia. It is open to the public seven days a week between 8.30 am and 4.30 pm. (At the time of Bradman's birth, it was a local midwife's hospital.) Sir Donald's grandparents are buried in Cootamundra cemetery.

The fertile land around Coonabarabran, with the Warrumbungles in the background

First settled in the 1830s, today the town is a major rail junction for the western and Riverina lines. It is also an important stock-selling centre and the surrounding district supports grazing, agriculture and mixed farming. There is also a great deal of secondary industry within the town.

This is the home of the Cootamundra wattle (*Acacia baileyana*), one of the best known of all cultivated acacias.

Cootamundra is a big racing town—both harness racing and gallopers.

August is a good time to visit Cootamundra, when the Wattle Time Festival takes place.

ACCOMMODATION: Globe Hotel, ph (02) 6942 1446; Cootamundra Hotel, ph (02) 6942 1290; Motel Wattle Tree, ph (02) 6942 2688; Bradman Motor Inn, ph (02) 6942 2288; Caravan Park Cootamundra, ph (02) 6942 1080
ACTIVITIES: Historic interest, sightseeing
TOURIST INFORMATION: Ph (02) 6942 4212

COROWA

636 KM SOUTH-WEST OF SYDNEY
POPULATION: 4650   MAP REF: PAGE 183 L8
Corowa sits on the Murray River and is the centre of a prosperous district growing wool, cereal crops, fat stock and wine grapes. Secondary industries include wine-making, timber milling, and the processing of malt and stock feed. The name is of Aboriginal origin, and means a pine which exudes gum for affixing spear heads.

Corowa was surveyed in 1857 and marked an important crossing place for stock. Later, it was used by miners rushing to the Victorian goldfields.

Federation was extremely important to Corowa, as when New South Wales and Victoria were separate colonies, customs posts were stationed at every crossing point on the Murray River. Federation gave much easier access to the markets of Victoria. The Federation Museum has on display memorabilia and documents relating to that historic event.

There are delightful bushwalks in the hinterland, and the river provides good opportunities for birdwatching.

Corowa also boasts the world's largest bowling club!
ACCOMMODATION: Arcadia Motor Inn, ph (02) 6033 2088; Corowa Golf Club Motel, ph (02) 6033 4188; Murray Banks Holiday Units, ph (02) 6033 2922; Bindaree Holiday Park, ph (02) 6033 2500
ACTIVITIES: Birdwatching, bowls, bushwalking, fishing, golf, river cruising, swimming, tennis
TOURIST INFORMATION: Ph (02) 6033 3221

COWRA

307 KM WEST OF SYDNEY
POPULATION: 8500   MAP REF: PAGE 176 B9
Cowra takes its name from the Aboriginal meaning 'rocks'—no doubt because of the granite outcrops that overlook the town. In the early days, the Wiradjuri people moved along the Lachlan River from Forbes to Goolagong and onto Cowra where they split into

three clans, one moving to Carcoar, another to Reids Flat, the third remaining in Cowra—the Erambie Aboriginal Reserve was declared there in 1891.

The district chiefly produces fat lambs, cattle, wool, wheat, lucerne, asparagus and other vegetables. There are a number of secondary industries as well.

Though the Cowra district is rich in colonial history, that is somewhat dwarfed by the Japanese prisoner of war breakout of 1944, in which four Australian guards were killed and 247 prisoners lost their lives. The Japanese dead are buried in a separate cemetery, suitably marked, on the outskirts of town. Rather than creating lasting racial enmity, this event has actually made Cowra one of the most tolerant towns in New South Wales. Its calendar of events and festivals now mirrors those of Japan's (see below) and its Japanese gardens, designed by Ken Nakajima, are based on the Imperial Gardens in Kyoto. They are well worth seeing.

Visitors can also see Australia's World Peace Bell, a replica of the one in the UN Building in New York.

Less well known is that Cowra also housed European migrants after World War II. In 1948, the first arrived and were housed in the World War II army base. Three thousand people from East European countries, including Poland, Czechoslovakia, Estonia, Latvia and Germany, arrived. The men were sent to work on projects like the Snowy Mountains Scheme while the women and children stayed in camp, where they were taught English. The migrants had a tremendous impact on Cowra. The women worked as domestics, cooks and fruit pickers. Many set up businesses. Edgell's was a major employer. Hundreds of children were educated and many moved on to illustrious careers. There was a huge reunion held in Cowra in 1998.

Bellevue Nature Reserve and Observatory is a scenic lookout and nearby Conimbla National Park offers rustic camping and birdwatching. There are water sports available at Wyangala Dam. The bridge over the Lachlan has its pylons adorned with Aboriginal art and Darby's Falls Observatory reveals the secrets of the stars.

Cowra's Museum is an interactive war, rural and rail experience, with over 8000 exhibits, including one of Australia's largest operating model railways.

There's a craft shop in the town, and you can go horse riding at one of the local properties.

In April Cowra holds a Moon Viewing at the Japanese Gardens. In May Japanese Children's Day is observed with activities and games. Also in May, Cowra hosts the largest dog show in New South Wales: the Kennel Club Championship Dog Show. June sees the National Bush Tucker and Home Brewing Championships, July the Cowra Picnic Races and Wine Show, August Japanese Bon (food) Day, with folk dancing and a special dinner, September the Agricultural Show. October is a big month, with both the Japan Cowra Cup Races and the Sakura (cherry blossom) Matsuri (festival), which features Japanese tea ceremonies, pottery, kite flying, martial arts and calligraphy demonstrations.
ACCOMMODATION: Cowra Hotel, ph (02) 6342 1925; Lachlan Valley Hotel/Motel, ph (02) 6342 2900; Town House Motor Inn, ph (02) 6342 1055; Countryman's Motor Inn, ph (02) 6342 3177; Caravan City Holiday Resort, ph (019) 659 333; Pine Trees Caravan Park, ph (02) 6542 1850

ACTIVITIES: Birdwatching, hiking, historic interest, national park access, star gazing, water sports
TOURIST INFORMATION: Ph (02) 6342 4333

CROWDY HEAD

373 KM NORTH OF SYDNEY
POPULATION: 50   MAP REF: PAGE 177 M3
Crowdy Head is popular for just-caught prawns from the local fish co-op and for the Crowdy Head

The wide sweep of one of Crowdy Head's beaches

lighthouse, taking in sweeping views from Cape Hawke to Middle Brother Mountain. It boasts an excellent surf club and long stretches of Crowdy Head National Park to explore on foot or by 4WD.

To the north is Diamond Head, a craggy headland of unsurpassed beauty that provides a haven for campers, wildflower enthusiasts, SCUBA divers and boardriders.
ACCOMMODATION: Crowdy Head Motel & Restaurant, ph (02) 6556 1206
ACTIVITIES: Bushwalking, 4WD touring, national park access, water sports
TOURIST INFORMATION: Ph (02) 6552 1900

CULCAIRN

545 KM SOUTH-WEST OF SYDNEY
POPULATION: 1150   MAP REF: PAGE 183 M7
Culcairn lies on the Olympic Highway between Albury and Wagga Wagga. This is the area over which bushranger Mad Dan Morgan held sway in the 1860s. There is a statue of the bushranger in the town.

National Trust classification has been given to many buildings in the main shopping centre. The Station Trust Museum is housed in the restored former residence of the station master and is furnished to suit the 1880s time frame.

Culcairn's water comes from one of the country's biggest artesian supplies and this accounts for the lushness of its gardens.
ACCOMMODATION: Culcairn Hotel, ph (02) 6029 8501; Culcairn Morgan Country Motel, ph (02) 6029 8233; Farmhost and Farm Holidays, ph (02) 6029 8621
ACTIVITIES: Arts and crafts shops, historic interest, scenic drives
TOURIST INFORMATION: Ph (02) 6029 8521

DENILIQUIN

789 KM SOUTH-WEST OF SYDNEY
POPULATION: 8500   MAP REF: PAGE 183 H7

Situated on the Edward River in south-west New South Wales, Deniliquin is the centre for a renowned Riverina sheep-breeding and wool-growing industry. It is the third largest centre in the Riverina.

Deniliquin was established in 1845 by Benjamin Boyd as a personal holding. In 1849, a town was established with the name 'Sandhills', but two years later was gazetted as 'Deniliquin', a corruption of the name 'Denilakoon', a leader of the local Aboriginal tribe who was 2 metres tall and immensely powerful.

In the early days, the town was a busy crossing point for livestock, and agriculture was already the base for Deniliquin's economy. Today the town is surrounded by highly developed farms and grazing land. Irrigation made the land more reliable and enabled extensions of crops. Rice is now an integral part of all this, along with wheat, barley, oats, oil seeds and lucerne.

Deniliquin lies at the junction of the Cobb and Riverina Highways and has more sunshine per year than Queensland's famed Gold Coast.

Deniliquin has beautiful parks, gardens, forests and waterways, and offers abundant recreation and sporting facilities. Major tourist attractions revolve around history, like the Peppin Heritage Centre and the Court House, but also include the Edward River Island Sanctuary, Barmah Forest and the Lawson Syphon (an irrigation marvel).

The town holds a jazz festival at Easter.

ACCOMMODATION: Edward River Hotel, ph (02) 5881 2065; Deniliquin Golf Leisure Resort, ph (02) 5881 3835; White Lion Hotel/Motel, ph (02) 5881 2699; Deniliquin Car-O-Tel & Caravan Park, ph (02) 5881 1732

ACTIVITIES: Bowls, clay target shooting, golf, horseracing, squash, swimming, tennis

TOURIST INFORMATION: Ph (02) 5881 2878

DENMAN

299 KM NORTH OF SYDNEY
POPULATION: 800   MAP REF: PAGE 176 G4

Six vineyards and some spectacular scenery surround the traditional rural town of Denman. The Upper Hunter is a beautiful part of the state, with rich farmland, rolling pastures and rugged scrub-covered mountains. The area is, of course, known for its wines: Rosemount has been in operation here since the 1850s, and other notable wineries include Arrowfield, Horseshoe Vineyard and Inglewood. Like Scone, Denman is also a centre for horse breeding and has magnificent horse studs.

The Upper Hunter is well served by guesthouses, hotels, motels and excellent restaurants.

ACCOMMODATION: Royal Hotel, ph (02) 6547 2226; Denman Hotel, ph (02) 6547 2207; Denman Motor Inn, ph (02) 6547 2462; Denman Van Village, ph (02) 6547 2590

ACTIVITIES: Scenic drives, wineries

TOURIST INFORMATION: Ph (02) 6545 1526

DORRIGO

599 KM NORTH OF SYDNEY
POPULATION: 1200   MAP REF: PAGE 179 M7

As graziers moved east from Armidale in search of more pastures in the 1840s, they discovered rich volcanic soils around what became Ebor and Dorrigo, but the credit for the original European discovery of the Dorrigo Plateau goes to an escapee from Moreton Bay Penal Settlement, Richard Craig. He recognised the potential of vast stands of red cedar, and others soon followed into what became known as the 'Don Dorrigo Scrub'. (The name commemorates the Spanish general Don Dorrigo, but coincidentally, is Aboriginal for 'stringybark'.)

Dangar Falls at Dorrigo in full flow

Nowadays, the local district is famed for its potatoes, but dairying, beef cattle and timber are other important resources.

Dorrigo stands at the entrance to Dorrigo National Park, one of Australia's most accessible rainforest areas. The Skywalk, Walk With Birds and other areas have been designed to provide easy access and impressive viewing points. The Rainforest Visitors' Centre houses a 50-seat video theatrette featuring the history, ecology and beauty of rainforests in the state.

Dorrigo is an historic town with many older buildings refurbished and restored to their original appearance. (The Dorrigo Hotel is listed by the National Trust.) The town has one of the few bakeries in Australia that still uses a wood-fired oven, and the local paper is still printed in town on original presses.

Nearby Dangar Falls and Griffiths Lookout are certainly worth a visit. There are viewing platforms and facilities. Dorrigo also has a thriving arts and crafts movement, ranging from wood-turning to woolcraft. Another attraction is the Steam Railway and Museum, which has 57 locomotives, 300 carriages and wagons, and thousands of small exhibits. It is the largest collection of railway memorabilia in the southern hemisphere.

The drive east from (or to) Dorrigo—the Waterfall Way—is also spectacular, with great vistas and some stunning plant life, ranging from gigantic trees, clinging vines and elkhorns to staghorns and bird's-nest ferns.

ACCOMMODATION: Dorrigo Hotel/Motel, ph (02) 6657 2016; Commercial Hotel/Motel, ph (02) 6657 2003; The Lookout Motor Inn, ph (02) 6657 2511; Meriden Heights Farm Retreat, ph (02) 6657 2823; Dorrigo Mountain Resort (caravan park), ph (02) 6657 2564

ACTIVITIES: Arts and crafts shops, bushwalking, historic interest, national park access, scenic drives, steam railway

TOURIST INFORMATION: Ph (02) 6657 2486

DUBBO

404 KM WEST OF SYDNEY
POPULATION: 36 430   MAP REF: PAGE 176 B4

Dubbo, the 'Hub of the West', is the only city in the area. It was proclaimed in 1966.

The area was first visited by John Oxley in 1818, on his way to the Macquarie Marshes. In 1824 the first pastoralists arrived, followed, in 1833, by Robert Dulhunty who took up a property which he called Dubbo (the name has various interpretations, from 'red earth' to 'foggy' to 'head covering' and 'possum fur head covering'). In 1841, recognising that Dubbo was an important stopping place on the stock route to Victoria, Frenchman Jean Serisier opened a store on the banks of the Macquarie River. Eight years later, in 1849, a village was proclaimed.

Nowadays, the area produces wheat, wool, fat lambs, dairy cattle, poultry, fruit and vegetables. Secondary industries include an abattoir, a flour mill, timber mills, a brick and pipe works, joinery, clothing and an air engine works.

Dubbo is probably most famous for the Western Plains Zoo, the first open-range zoo in Australia. Just outside of town, on the Peak Hill Road, the zoo covers 300 hectares and houses a great variety of animals—it is well known for its breeding program of the endangered black rhino. You can drive the 6 km track, hire a bike or even walk.

Dubbo Military Museum has wheelchair access and guided tours. This private collection of World War II memorabilia includes planes, tanks, guns, vehicles, uniforms and documents. There are over 50 major exhibits.

Old Dubbo Gaol is also worth a look. It has been faithfully restored after being closed down in 1966. The gallows, which were dismantled early in the twentieth century, have been re-erected. Seven men were hanged on the gallows in the period 1877–1904, the last of whom was Chinese, Ah Chick, who killed a Peak Hill grazier. The most notorious to die was Jacky Underwood, a participant in the Breelong massacres of 1900, with Jimmy Governor (later immortalised in Thomas Keneally's *The Chant of Jimmie Blacksmith*).

Dubbo hosts a three day jazz festival in August, and in September, the Festival of the Red Earth, which celebrates all art forms, runs over ten days.

ACCOMMODATION: Amaroo Hotel, ph (02) 6882 3533; Civic Hotel, ph (02) 6882 3688; Aberdeen Motor Inn,

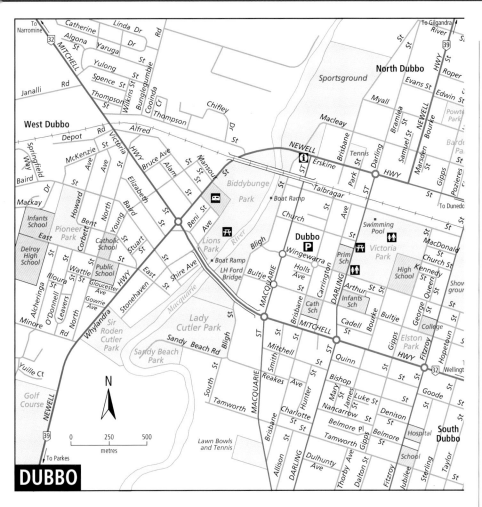

DUBBO

EDEN

497 KM SOUTH OF SYDNEY
POPULATION: 4000   MAP REF: PAGE 174 E9

Eden is aptly named. Located on Twofold Bay, it features golden sandy beaches and rugged cliffs.

Eden started as a whaling town, but is now the main port of the south coast and a major commercial fishing centre. Chartering boats is popular with visitors. So is visiting the Killer Whale Museum, which details the history of shore-based whaling in the country. It houses the skeleton of 'Old Tom', a killer whale, and showcases equipment used in the now-defunct whaling industry. Local history also features.

Whale watching is another popular pastime. Humpbacks, southern rights, minke and the endangered blue whales are often sighted.

In town, there is the McCulloch Campbell Gallery, Eden Shells Gallery and the Harris Daishowa Chipmill, which is open to visitors by appointment.

The beaches are excellent. Surfers should try Aslings, while families will enjoy Corcora. There are sea caves to explore at Snug Cove.

Ben Boyd National Park is spectacular, featuring stunning coastal scenery with rugged cliffs, rock formations and sea caves. The park perpetuates the name of Ben Boyd who established whaling operations in the area in 1842, and built his folly—Boyd Town—across the bay, wanting it to rival Eden. You can also visit the old Davidson Whaling Station.

South of Eden and in the hinterland, there is fabulous 4WD touring. You can go escorted or pick your own way through to places like Bendethera and Deua National Park.

ACCOMMODATION: Great Southern Hotel, ph (02) 6496 1515; Boydtown Sea Horse Inn Hotel, ph (02) 6496 1361; Twofold Bay Motor Inn, ph (02) 6496 3111; Eden's B&B, ph (02) 6496 1575; Boydtown Caravan Park, ph (02) 6496 1361

ACTIVITIES: Bushwalking, fishing, 4WD touring, historic interest, national park access, water sports, whale watching

TOURIST INFORMATION: Ph (02) 6492 3313

---

ph (02) 6884 1700; Country Apartments, ph (015) 459 030; Leura Farm Holidays, ph (02) 6887 6254; Dubbo Cabins and Caravan Parkland, ph (02) 6884 8633; Dubbo Sports World Cabins, ph (02) 6882 5740

ACTIVITIES: Bowls, fishing, historic interest, tennis, water sports, zoo

TOURIST INFORMATION: Ph (02) 6884 1422

DUNGOG

241 KM NORTH OF SYDNEY
POPULATION: 3425   MAP REF: PAGE 177 J4

Birthplace of famed cricketer Doug Walters, Dungog means 'a clear hill' or 'a thickly wooded hill'. It nestles in the Williams River Valley. The town was firmly established by the 1840s. In the mid-1800s a military guard of horse-troopers was stationed here to protect the area against bushrangers.

The Gringai were the local tribe and the first white settlers were timber-getters. When timber was king, it had to be freighted to Clarence Town, which was then head of navigation for the Williams River.

Now the local economy relies on dairying, grazing, forestry and to a lesser extent, poultry and deer farming, hydroponics and tourism. It is an excellent base from which to explore the Barrington Tops National Park.

Dungog's annual festival (held in September), is heavily focused on cycling, but features other events like street entertainment and the Great Dungog Gumboot Race!

ACCOMMODATION: Royal Hotel, ph (02) 4992 3070; Courthouse Hotel, ph (02) 4992 1615; The Bank Hotel, ph (02) 4992 1701; Tall Timbers Motel, ph (02) 4992 1547

ACTIVITIES: Birdwatching, bushwalking, cycling, 4WD tours, fishing, horse riding, national park access, water sports

TOURIST INFORMATION: Ph (02) 4992 2212

The coastline at Eden, with golden, sandy beaches

EVANS HEAD

767 KM NORTH OF SYDNEY
POPULATION: 2800　MAP REF: PAGE 179 P4

With idyllic holiday torpor about it, Evans Head is a very popular destination for tourists. Evans Head was known as 'Gummingar' by local Aborigines, and there are a number of important indigenous sites in the area, including Goanna Headland.

These days, the primary industry is fishing. Delicious prawns are also netted locally, and with its sweeping, clean beaches and surrounding national parks, there is plenty to see and do.

Close by are the Broadwater and Bundjalung National Parks. The Broadwater has unspoilt beaches and heathland that becomes a colour fest in spring.

The name 'Bundjalung' perpetuates the language of the local Aboriginal tribe—a dialect which ranged from the Clarence River to Beenleigh, from Beaudesert to Tenterfield and Warwick. The park is full of wildlife and some Aboriginal relics.

In June, Evans Head hosts the Evinrude Seafarer Fishing Classic and over the New Year, the Great Eastern Fly-in. Local markets are held regularly.

ACCOMMODATION: Illawong Hotel, ph (02) 6682 4222; Evans Head Pacific Motel, ph (02) 6682 4318; Doyle's Holiday Flats, ph (02) 6682 5445; Silver Sands Caravan Park, ph (02) 6682 4212

ACTIVITIES: Bowls, fishing, national park access, tennis, water sports

TOURIST INFORMATION: Ph(02) 6682 4611

FORBES

371 KM WEST OF SYDNEY
POPULATION: 8500　MAP REF: PAGE 183 P2

On the banks of the Lachlan River, Forbes commemorates the name of the first Chief Justice of New South Wales, Francis Forbes, who did much to ensure that trial by jury was introduced to the colony. John Oxley was the first explorer to track the area in

The Town Hall at Forbes

1817, but gold drew large numbers (over 30 000) to the district in 1861. For the next four years it was a magnet to honest people, as well as bushrangers like Ben Hall and Frank Gardiner. Hall is buried in Forbes cemetery after being shot by troopers (at age 27) at Bogan Gate to the north. Another celebrity in the graveyard is Ned Kelly's sister Kate.

When gold ran out at the end of the 1860s, Forbes reverted to an agricultural and pastoral centre. Now, local industries include wool, fat lambs, beef cattle, poultry and pigs, as well as wheat, lucerne, wine grapes, fruit and dairy products.

Forbes is rich in history. The Albion Hotel was originally a Cobb & Co depot—tunnels used to transport gold to and from the banks still exist beneath the building, and the lookout tower can be seen on the roof.

Lachlan Vintage Village re-creates the community as it was in the nineteenth century, with early buildings reconstructed on site and displays of goldmining and machinery. Included are Ben Hall's cottage and the home of poet Henry Lawson.

In the Historical Museum in Cross Street are relics of the bushranging days; the museum itself began life as Osborne Hall, a dance hall attached to the Osborne Hotel. All facets of Forbes' history, from Aboriginal lifestyle and artefacts to furniture, photographs, clothing, household items and machinery are on display. Naturally, quite a lot of space is devoted to Ben Hall.

South of the town on the Newell Highway is Gum Swamp, which has a specially constructed hide for viewing waterbirds. There are two wineries on the outskirts of town: Sandhills Wineyard and Lachlan Valley Wines.

Forbes also has a great racecourse. The town hosts a five-day jazz festival in January.

ACCOMMODATION: Forbes Inn Hotel/Motel, ph (02) 6852 1555; Albion Hotel, ph (02) 6851 1881; Country Mile Motor Inn, ph (02) 6852 4099; Lachlan View Caravan Park, ph (02) 6852 1055; Apex Caravan Park, ph (02) 6852 1929

ACTIVITIES: Bowls, fishing, gold panning, golf, historic interest, horseracing, squash, tennis, water sports, wineries

TOURIST INFORMATION: Ph (02) 6852 4155

FORSTER

326 KM NORTH OF SYDNEY
POPULATION: 15 000　MAP REF: PAGE 177 L4

Forster and its twin town Tuncurry are linked by one of the longest pre-stressed concrete bridges in the southern hemisphere. Forster sits on a narrow strip of land between Wallis Lake (which is one of the Myall Lakes) and the Pacific Ocean.

Forster is renowned for its great beaches and its fishing—especially flathead, whiting, bream and tailor. Ten kilometres from the town is Booti Booti National Park, which offers a dramatic range of scenery from tropical rainforest to beaches. Forster also has a number of art and craft galleries.

In April the town hosts the Australian International Ironman Triathlon, while in June a country music festival and a national sports fishing convention are held. In August there is a dramafest

Evening light on Wallis Lake at Forster

and in September, the Great Lakes Lifestyle and Leisure Expo. Australia Day celebrations are also big in the town.

ACCOMMODATION: Forster View Motel, ph (02) 6554 6365; Golden Sands Motor Inn, ph (02) 6554 6222; Forster Holiday Villas Retreat, ph (02) 6554 6837; Merryland RSL Holiday Units, ph (02) 6554 6264; Coastal Resort Caravan Park, ph (02) 6559 2719; Palms Oasis Caravan Park, ph (02) 6554 0488

ACTIVITIES: Bowls, fishing, golf, national park access, water sports

TOURIST INFORMATION: Ph (02) 6546 8799

GERRINGONG

147 KM SOUTH OF SYDNEY
POPULATION: 2400　MAP REF: PAGE 174 G3

The Gerringong area was first settled in the 1820s, initially by cedar-getters, but as the land was cleared, dairying became the main industry and remains so today, along with tourism.

Gerringong is a coastal village where green fields seem to drop into the sea. Those impressive views are coupled with terrific beaches and friendly locals.

Seven Mile Beach, where Charles Kingsford Smith took off in the *Southern Cross* for his flight to New Zealand in 1933, has become part of a national park that contains a monument to the famous aviator.

Apart from excellent surfing and fishing, visitors can detour via Wild Country Park, a local wildlife refuge, which is home to kangaroos, emus, wombats and many colourful species of parrot. You can also visit the Gerringong & District Historical Society. With its primary focus on the dairy industry, the museum also houses models of early Gerringong and a photographic record of motor racing on Seven Mile Beach in the 1920s.

ACCOMMODATION: Gerringong Hotel, ph (02) 4234 1451; Anchor Motel, ph (02) 4234 2222; Beachview Resort Motel & Conference Centre, ph (02) 4234 1359; Werri Beach Holiday Park, ph (02) 4234 1285

ACTIVITIES: Bushwalking, national park access, nature study, scenic drives, surfing

TOURIST INFORMATION: Ph (02) 4232 3322

GILGANDRA

448 KM NORTH-WEST OF SYDNEY
POPULATION: 5160   MAP REF: PAGE 176 B2

Situated on the Castlereagh River, 'Gilgandra' derives from the Aboriginal word for 'long waterhole'.) Its European origins began in the 1830s with settlers grazing their flocks by the river. It was also once called 'the windmill town' because of the plethora of windmills which brought up water from the Great Artesian Basin. However, these have mostly gone as the town now uses mains water.

Gilgandra was also the scene of the first 'Coo-ee' (the traditional bushman's cry for help) army recruitment march of 1915, after the Gallipoli disaster. This set an example to the rest of Australia and many other similar marches followed nationwide.

Gilgandra Observatory has been operating for 22 years, giving the public a chance to view the night skies through a 2-metre-long telescope with a 31 cm diameter mirror. Open every night, the Observatory also houses a good collection of meteorites, rocks and fossils. It is surrounded by a renowned garden with over 80 varieties of roses. Gilgandra Flora Reserve has an excellent display of wildflowers in spring.

The Gilgandra Coo-ee Festival is held in October and features a variety of activities highlighted by a street parade, stalls, the Australian Coo-ee Calling Championships, a country music quest, goat races, the Gilgandra Gift footraces and a bushman's relay.
ACCOMMODATION: Castlereagh Motor Inn, ph (02) 6847 2697; Alfa Motel, ph (02) 6847 1188; Gilgandra Lodge (B&B), ph (02) 6847 2431; Wyanna Farmstay B&B, ph (02) 6848 8246; Barney's Van Park, ph (02) 6847 2636; Gilgandra Rotary Caravan Park, ph (02) 6847 2423
ACTIVITIES: Bowls, golf, sightseeing, swimming (pool), tennis
TOURIST INFORMATION: Ph (02) 6847 2045

GLEN INNES

667 KM NORTH OF SYDNEY
POPULATION: 6250   MAP REF: PAGE 179 J5

Long before Europeans reached the Northern Tablelands, the Nugumbul tribe migrated there seasonally. They called the place 'Eehrindi' which means 'wild strawberry'.

John Oxley was the first white explorer to visit the Glen Innes district in 1818 and 36 years later, the town was proclaimed and named after Major Innes, principal landowner in the district.

In 1872, the discovery of tin at Vegetable Creek (known today as Emmaville) caused a population explosion, and other minerals and gems which followed in the wake were antimony, gold, bismuth, molybdenite, emeralds and sapphires.

Besides mining, current local industries include dairying, raising beef and sheep, mixed farming and the growing of vegetables.

Glen Innes still produces top quality sapphires and is popular with fossickers. Fishing is another local pastime. The town has beautiful parks, some of which line Rocky Ponds Creek. It also boasts some well-cared-for nineteenth-century buildings, one of

which contains the Land of the Beardies Folk Museum. (The area is known as 'Land of the Beardies' after two early stockmen who sported long beards.)

Nearby Gibraltar Range National Park has a range of bushwalks. In Centennial Parklands' Martins Lookout are the Australian Standing Stones, a sculptural group dedicated to the contribution made to Australia by people of Celtic origin.

Glen Innes commemorates its Celtic background with two festivals: the Australian Celtic Festival in May and the Land of the Beardies Festival in November. Other festivals are the Minerama in September, an annual gem and mineral fest, and the Australian Music Festival in October.
ACCOMMODATION: Alpha Motel, ph (02) 6732 2688; Amber Motel, ph (02) 6732 2300; New Tattersall's Hotel/Motel, ph (02) 6732 3011; Boolabinda Holiday Homestead, ph (02) 6732 2215; Fossicker Caravan Park & Service Station, ph (02) 6732 4246
ACTIVITIES: Bushwalking, fossicking, golf, national park access, sightseeing
TOURIST INFORMATION: Ph (02) 6768 4462

GLOUCESTER

279 KM NORTH OF SYDNEY
POPULATION: 2600   MAP REF: PAGE 177 K3

Flanked on the east by the Mograni Range, Gloucester is bounded to the west by a range of unusual-looking monolithic hills called the Bucketts. The name derives from the Aboriginal word 'buccans', meaning 'big rocks', also commemorated by Bucketts Way, the road which leads into the town from the south and Raymond Terrace. Other major access routes are from Nabiac, on the Pacific Highway to the east, from Walcha to the north—involving some dirt sections—and from the west across the Barrington Tops from Scone, which is also largely unsealed.

The first white man in the district was Surveyor Henry Dangar, early in 1826, but by the early 1830s, a number of farms were established along the Barrington River. The town is now the centre of a rich dairying, cattle-raising and mixed farming district.
ACCOMMODATION: Gloucester Country Lodge, ph (02) 6558 1812; Gloucester Hotel/Motel, ph (02) 6558 1816; Avon Valley Inn Hotel, ph (02) 6558 1016; Hookes Creek Forest Resort, ph (02) 6558 5544; Altamira Holiday Ranch, ph (02) 6550 6558; Arrowee House (B&B), ph (02) 6558 2050; Gloucester Tops Riverside Caravan Park, ph (02) 6558 3155
ACTIVITIES: Bowls, bushwalking, fishing, golf, squash, tennis, water sports
TOURIST INFORMATION: Ph (02) 6558 1408

GOSFORD

88 KM NORTH OF SYDNEY
POPULATION: 42 190   MAP REF: PAGE 177 H7

Gosford is located between Sydney and Newcastle in a region called the Central Coast. It is a favourite tourist and holiday destination.

Planned in 1839, the town was named by Governor Gipps after the 2nd Earl of Gosford, with whom he had served on a commission of inquiry in Canada.

A festival of the arts, held in Gosford

Initially, the town grew in tandem with neighbouring East Gosford, a private township of Sydney tea merchant Samuel Peek, but the two were amalgamated into a municipality in 1886, and Gosford Shire was declared in 1947.

Thanks to an efficient rail service and the Sydney–Newcastle Expressway, it is possible for hundreds of Gosford residents to commute to Sydney each day, making it almost a satellite town. Local industries include growing citrus fruit—a dominant crop since the 1880s—passionfruit and vegetables, dairying, poultry farming, mixed farming and timber cutting. A particularly fine sandstone is quarried close to town and numerous secondary industries support a buoyant economy.

The whole area is a tourist playground; it is for its water sports that Gosford is famous. The fishing is excellent, and the area is a surfer's paradise. For boardriders, MacMasters, Avoca and Forresters Beaches are legendary, while bodysurfers and families may prefer Terrigal, Killcare, Copacabana or Wamberal. There really is a beach environment in the area to suit the tastes and needs of everybody. SCUBA divers also love the crystal-clear waters of the Central Coast, with plenty of wrecks to explore off Terrigal.

Henry Kendall's cottage, where the poet lived in the 1870s, is now a colonial museum.

The Australian Reptile Park—one of the first major tourist attractions on the Central Coast—is popular with visitors and regularly supplies anti-venom vaccine from snakes and spiders to countries around the world.

For families, Old Sydney Town—a realistic re-creation to scale of Sydney as it was in 1810, including the Tank Stream, Sydney Cove, Government House and soldiers' huts—is close to Gosford.

Nine kilometres south-west of Gosford is Brisbane Water National Park, which offers panoramic views from 100-metre-high cliffs overlooking the Hawkesbury River. It comes alive with Christmas bells and waratahs during November and December. There is also Aboriginal art carved into sandstone boulders and rockfaces.

In town itself, the court house and prison are the oldest buildings on the Central Coast.
ACCOMMODATION: Union Hotel, ph (02) 4324 1267; Hotel Gosford, ph (02) 4324 1634; Metro Inn Gosford, ph (02) 4328 4666; Gosford Motor Inn, ph (02) 4323 1333; Ourimbah-Gosford Caravan Park, ph (02) 4362 1071
ACTIVITIES: Bowls, bushwalking, national park access, scenic drives, sightseeing, squash, tennis, water sports
TOURIST INFORMATION: Ph (02) 4385 4430

GOULBURN

206 KM SOUTH OF SYDNEY
POPULATION: 21 530   MAP REF: PAGE 174 D3

Goulburn was named after Henry Goulburn, Under-Secretary for the Colonies at the time explorers James Meehan and Hamilton Hume came through the district in 1818, though John Oxley was the first white man to actually cross the site of the city.

For a number of years after Goulburn was gazetted in 1833, it was a garrison town and became a centre for police parties hunting bushrangers.

Early experiments with wheat were supplanted by sheep after the western regions gained supremacy in cereals, and wool is still the primary industry. Goulburn has the distinction of being the last town in the British Empire to be declared a city, in 1864, by being created a bishopric by Royal Letters Patent.

Today, Goulburn is an important rail centre and has a number of thriving secondary industries (including textiles, carpets and knitting yarns) both in town and around the district. Marulan, 39 km away, has one of the largest limestone quarries in the southern hemisphere.

As an historic town, Goulburn has much of interest. In the Gothic Revival style, St Saviour's Cathedral was designed by famed colonial architect Edmund Blacket and was completed in 1884, with the tower and spire finally added over a century later. National Trust-classified buildings abound throughout the area, many of which are open to the public. There is also a regional art gallery with a wide range of art and craft forms, often in exhibitions combining the works of local and other artists.

At the other end of the scale is Goulburn's answer to Coffs Harbour's Big Banana and Taree's Big Prawn. It is the Big Merino, a three-storey concrete ram in which you can see a wool history display and gaze out on Goulburn and environs through a sheep's eyes.

Motor racing buffs will be interested in visiting Wakefield Park, south-east of the town. It is a privately owned circuit used for many race events. It is favoured by vintage car racing buffs and has been used for many new vehicle releases, including the MG-F, which heralded the return of the MG marque to Australia after an absence of more than 20 years.

To the south also is Bungonia State Recreation Reserve, which offers bushwalking, climbing, abseiling, caving, canoeing and some great views from spectacular lookouts. Another natural feature in the vicinity is Wombeyan Caves, with its spectacular limestone formations, but visitors should be careful on the road into the valley, which has nasty switchbacks and blind curves flanking very steep drops.

Tarlo National Park, 30 km north of Goulburn, is a refuge for platypuses, long-necked tortoises, waterbirds, wallabies and wombats.

In October, Goulburn holds the Lilac City Festival.
ACCOMMODATION: Astor Hotel, ph (02) 4821 1155; Coolavin Hotel, ph (02) 4821 2498; Heritage Motor Lodge, ph (02) 4821 9377; Countrywide Stay (B&B), ph (02) 4822 1091; Goulburn South Caravan Park, ph (02) 4821 3233
ACTIVITIES: Bowls, fishing, 4WD touring, national park access, scenic drives, sightseeing, squash, tennis
TOURIST INFORMATION: Ph (02) 4821 5343

Magnificent jacarandah trees, for which Grafton is famous

GRAFTON

667 KM NORTH OF SYDNEY
POPULATION: 18 500   MAP REF: PAGE 179 M5

'The Jacaranda City', Grafton is famous for its 7000 trees, graceful old buildings, beautiful parks and its mighty river, the Clarence. As with Dorrigo, escaped convict Richard Craig was the first white man in the district. For a pardon and 100 pounds he brought a party of cedar-getters back to the area and they were followed by pastoralists.

The town was proclaimed in 1851 and named after the Duke of Grafton by his grandson, Governor Fitzroy. City status was conferred in 1885.

The list of buildings classified by the National Trust ranges from the serene (Christ Church Cathedral) to the infamous (Grafton Gaol). The council has purchased and restored many fine old homesteads, like Schaeffer House—which now houses exhibits belonging to the Clarence River Historical Society—and Prentice House, now the regional art gallery. There are a number of craft galleries, art studios and antique shops in town, or visitors can take a drive up to Ulmarra, 12 km north of Grafton, which has been classified by the National Trust and also has craft, bric-a-brac and antique stores.

Alumy Creek School has displays of how schooldays were at the turn of the century. Visitors can also take a boat to Susan Island. It is home to the largest fruit bat colony in the southern hemisphere.

Houseboats and cruisers are available for hire to explore the Clarence River's islands and river towns.

The annual Jazz Festival is held at Easter, while in July visitors can lay a few bets at the Racing Carnival, especially on the Grafton Cup, reputedly the richest horserace in rural Australia. (The Grafton Jockey Club is one of the oldest in the country.)

October sees the Bridge to Bridge Ski Race on the Clarence, and Grafton's most famous occasion, the Jacaranda Festival, which was first held in 1935. If you are still around in November, the Sailing Classic is on. The community markets are held on the last Saturday of each month.

ACCOMMODATION: Roches Family Hotel, ph (02) 6642 2866; Fitzroy Motel, ph (02) 6642 4477; Jacaranda Motel, ph (02) 6642 2833; The Gateway Village Caravan Park, ph (02) 6642 4225; Big River Ski Lodge & Caravan Park, ph (02) 6644 9324
ACTIVITIES: Canoeing, fishing, gliding, golf, greyhound racing, horse riding, bowls, water sports, tennis
TOURIST INFORMATION: Ph (02) 6642 4677

GRENFELL

363 KM WEST OF SYDNEY
POPULATION: 2040   MAP REF: PAGE 183 P3

Grenfell is an agricultural and pastoral centre first settled by graziers in the 1830s. The area boomed with the discovery of gold at Emu Creek on John Woods' 'Brundah' run in 1866. The town was marked out a year later, and named after J. G. Grenfell, district Gold Commissioner, who had been shot by bushrangers at Narromine not long before. In its heyday, Grenfell boasted 30 pubs.

Though the McCabe family lived in the town for some time, and the museum in Camp Street has some unusual cricket photos (born in Grenfell, Stan McCabe was a superb batsman, first-class fieldsman and useful medium pace bowler), the town's main claim to historical fame is that Henry Lawson was born on the diggings there, at One Mile, and a monument marks the spot.

Weddin Mountains National Park is 19 km to the south. It has walking trails winding through indigenous plant growth where native animals are also readily seen. Its best known attraction is Ben Hall's Cave, used by the bushranging gang as a refuge. The cave was also used as a base for forays to pillage the Gundagai–Yass Cobb & Co run.

O'Brien's Lookout, on the Cowra road, provides good views over the town and old gold diggings.

First held in 1958, the Henry Lawson Festival of the Arts is celebrated over the Queen's Birthday weekend in June each year.

The Rudd Family bronze in Gundagai

ACCOMMODATION: Exchange Hotel, ph
(02) 6343 1034; Railway Hotel, ph (02) 6343 1807;
Grenfell Motel, ph (02) 6343 1333; Grenfell Caravan
Park, ph (02) 6343 1194
ACTIVITIES: Bushwalking, gold fossicking, historic
interest, national park access, scenic drives,
sightseeing
TOURIST INFORMATION: Ph (02) 6343 1612

GRIFFITH

615 KM SOUTH-WEST OF SYDNEY
POPULATION: 13 500   MAP REF: PAGE 183 K4

Griffith is a comparatively modern town designed in
1914 by Walter Burley Griffin, the architect of
Canberra. It is named after Sir Arthur Griffith, who
was the first Minister for Public Works in the New
South Wales government.

Thanks to irrigation (pioneered by the McCaughey
brothers), what was once largely barren land now
supports a thriving agricultural economy. All varieties
of fruit, grapes, vegetables, rice, wheat and cotton are
produced, as well as sheep and wool.

The wine industry of Griffith has undergone a
transformation in recent years. While years ago
Griffith's wines were regarded as inferior, it now
produces some first-rate wines, including those of De
Bortoli, McWilliams Hanwood (known for its port) and
Miranda. There are 15 local vineyards in all.

The Murrumbidgee River provides plenty of
opportunities for fishing and water sports, while visits
to the vineyards are obviously popular. The view from
Scenic Hill shows what lushness irrigation has
brought the surrounding countryside. Pioneer Park
Museum is to the north of the town, as is Cocoparra
National Park. Griffith holds an annual Wine and
Food Festival. Music, song and street theatre are
integral components.
ACCOMMODATION: Acacia Motel, ph (02) 6962 4422;
Yambil Inn, ph (02) 6964 1233; Shearers' Quarters
Guest House, ph (02) 6962 4196; Tourist Caravan
Park, ph (02) 6964 2144; Griffith Caravan Village, ph
(02) 6962 3785
ACTIVITIES: Bowls, fishing, golf, national park access,
scenic drives, water sports
TOURIST INFORMATION: Ph (02) 6962 4145

GULGONG

303 KM NORTH-WEST OF SYDNEY
POPULATION: 2250   MAP REF: PAGE 176 D4

The Town on the Ten Dollar Note has become The
Town on the Old Ten Dollar Note. Gulgong made
much use of its appearance on the currency—a
couple of shop fronts from the gold rush days, frozen
by the photography of Henry Beaufoy Merlin, from the
collection of Bernard Holtermann.

Like Hill End, Gulgong (the name means 'deep
waterhole') owes its existence solely to the discovery
of gold in 1866. By 1872, Gulgong and its satellite
villages boasted a population of 20 000: a mix of
Greeks, Italians, Bulgarians, Scots, Irish, Chinese,
English, Americans, Canadians, and of course, native-
born Australians. It was a rowdy, boisterous town in

those days, inciting a visiting English clergyman to
proclaim 'Why man, there's nothing like it... Gulgong
is the hub of the world!'

Nowadays Gulgong is a quiet country town, one of
the best preserved gold rush towns in New South
Wales, with winding, narrow streets, National Trust
classified buildings and hitching posts on the paths.

The Pioneers' Museum, converted from a bakery
and produce store, has probably the best collection of
Australiana in the country. It covers half a hectare
and is a must for lovers of history.

The Prince of Wales Opera House, unchanged
from the rush days, has supposedly seen Lily Langtry,
Lola Montez and Dame Nellie Melba perform, but
some definites are boxer Les Darcy, William Morris
Hughes (delivering a fiery oration on the necessity of
conscription in World War I) and, more recently,
pianist Roger Woodward.

The Henry Lawson Centre has a magnificent
collection of Lawson memorabilia including paintings,
books and poems. Though born in Grenfell, Lawson
moved to the area with his family while still a boy, and
many of his writings allude to Gulgong. The Henry
Lawson Birthday Celebrations are held in June.

To the north-east, the immense Ulan Coal Mine,
which has the longest conveyor belt in the southern
hemisphere, can be inspected by the public.

Gulgong also has a craft shop with fetching pieces
made from local woods and clays. Pratt's Winery is
2 km outside of town on the Mudgee road. Gulgong is
also within easy reach of the many wineries around
Mudgee.
ACCOMMODATION: Post Office Hotel, ph
(02) 6374 1031; Prince of Wales Hotel, ph (02) 6374 1166;
Goldfields Motor Inn, ph (02) 6374 1111; Gulgong
Motel, ph (02) 6374 1122; Willow Vale Cottage, ph (02)
6374 1446; Stables Guesthouse, ph (02) 6374 1668;
Henry Lawson Caravan Park, ph (02) 6374 1294
ACTIVITIES: Bowls, coal mines, golf, historic interest,
wineries
TOURIST INFORMATION: Ph (02) 6372 5874

GUNDAGAI

399 KM SOUTH-WEST OF SYDNEY
POPULATION: 4200   MAP REF: PAGE 174 A4

The name Gundagai has intriguing origins. It derives
from the Aboriginal 'gundabandoobingee', which
means either 'going upstream' or more intriguingly,
'to cut sinews behind the knee with a tomahawk'.
Moved uphill after a disastrous 1852 flood which
claimed 98 lives, the town is now the centre for a
rural economy based on sheep and cattle, though
asparagus, wheat, maize and lucerne are also grown.

Gundagai is most famous for the Jack Moses'
poem commemorating the bullocky's story of a dog
doing its business on a tuckerbox—there is a monument sculpted by Frank Rusconi 8 km north of town.
Rusconi also sculpted his 'Marble Masterpiece', a
miniature replica of the altar of St Maria's Cathedral
in Paris. Also immortalised in bronze are the Rudd
Family (Dad, Dave, Mum and Mabel), characters from
On Our Selection by Steele Rudd.

Gundagai Historical Museum has some
interesting folkloric exhibits, such as the saddlecloth
that Phar Lap wore in the last race before he died.

Many of the buildings in town date back 130 years,
and the courthouse saw the trial of bushranger
Captain Moonlight. Prince Alfred Bridge is the
longest wooden bridge in the southern hemisphere.

The town hosts the Dog on the Tuckerbox Festival
in November, with a two-day race meeting climaxed
by the running of the Snake Gully Cup, but also
featuring country music, dog sporting events, market
stalls and a breakfast at the Dog on the Tuckerbox.
ACCOMMODATION: Hotel Gresham, ph (02) 6944 1028;
Lott Family Hotel, ph (02) 6944 1019; Gundagai Motel,
ph (02) 6944 1066; Garden Motor Inn, ph (02) 6944 1744;
Carowa Village, ph (02) 6944 1057; Gundagai River
Camping & Caravan Park, ph (02) 6944 1702
ACTIVITIES: Bowls, fishing, golf, squash, tennis, water
sports
TOURIST INFORMATION: Ph (02) 6944 1341

GUNNEDAH

515 KM NORTH OF SYDNEY
POPULATION: 10 000   MAP REF: PAGE 178 F9

In the heart of the wheat belt, Gunnedah is built on a
hillside overlooking the Namoi and Mooki Rivers. The
name means 'many white stones', and the site of the
town was originally the principal crossing place on
the Namoi, hence a major centre for teamsters.

First settled by Europeans in 1834, it is the
birthplace of poet Dorothea Mackellar. There is a life-
size bronze memorial to her in Anzac Park, while
another memorial honours a great Aboriginal warrior
and leader of the Gunnedarr people, Combo
Gunnerah. He was immortalised by Ion L. Idriess in
his book *Red Chief*.

Housing the archives of the local historical society,
the Water Tower Museum was originally the town's
water reservoir, built in 1908. Other historic buildings
include the Town Hall, Court House, Brunton's Flour
Mill, the Catholic convent and Cohen's Bridge. The
Rural Museum has many items on display ranging
from shovels to steam engines and purportedly has
the largest gun display in northern New South Wales.

Lake Keepit is only half an hour's drive from
Gunnedah, and is the town's playground, offering all
sorts of water sports. The Lake Keepit Soaring Club
organises joyflights over the dam.

If you are driving off the beaten track near Gunnedah, bear in mind that the surrounding country is largely black-soil plains, and that when it becomes wet, even 4WDs and tractors can become stuck!

In January, Gunnedah hosts the Tomato Festival and Australia Day celebrations. In April, there's the Gunnedah Show and Rodeo and Campdraft; in May, the Spinners and Weavers Expo, and an eisteddfod; in June, the Gold Cup Horse Races and the Lake Keepit Sailing Regatta; and in August, Gunnedah's most famous event—Agquip, agricultural field days.

ACCOMMODATION: Regal Hotel, ph (02) 6742 2355; Parkview Hotel, ph (02) 6742 2212; Alyn Motel, ph (02) 6742 5028; Gunnedah Motor Inn, ph (02) 6742 2377

ACTIVITIES: Bowls, bushwalking, fishing, gliding, scenic drives, tennis, water sports

TOURIST INFORMATION: Ph (02) 6742 4300

GUNNING

253 KM SOUTH OF SYDNEY
POPULATION: 500   MAP REF: PAGE 174 C3
Explorer Hamilton Hume first established a station here in 1821, and plans for the town were approved in 1838. One year later, it was home to 20 horses and 95 people, and included a store and a pub.

Now Gunning boasts antique stores and art and craft shops. It also has a number of historic buildings, including London House, the post office, Royal Hotel and the old court house (now a church).

ACCOMMODATION: Telegraph Hotel, ph (02) 4845 1217; Gunning Motel, ph (02) 4845 1191; Do Duck Inn Guesthouse, ph (02) 4845 1207

ACTIVITIES: Bowls, scenic walks, tennis, trout fishing

TOURIST INFORMATION: Ph (02) 4845 1191

HARRINGTON

366 KM NORTH OF SYDNEY
POPULATION: 1185   MAP REF: PAGE 177 M3
Harrington is on the Manning River, where it meets the sea. A popular holiday destination, the town offers safe swimming in a lagoon, and good fishing off the breakwater.

Pilot Hill Lookout offers great views along the coast, and nearby is a small cemetery containing the graves of pilots who used to guide ships over the Harrington bar on their way to load timber and grain at Taree and Wingham.

ACCOMMODATION: Harrington Hotel, ph (02) 6556 1205; Cabana Motel, ph (02) 6556 1141; Sea Breeze Holiday Units, ph (02) 6556 1234; Colonial Leisure Village, ph (02) 6556 3312;

ACTIVITIES: Water sports

TOURIST INFORMATION: Ph (02) 6552 1900

HARTLEY

123 KM WEST OF SYDNEY
POPULATION: UNDER 200   MAP REF: PAGE 176 E8
On the Great Western Highway just below Victoria Pass, the protected historic site of Hartley reflects the simplicity of life in the mid-1800s. Once a thriving settlement that went into decline when the railway bypassed it, the township includes three old inns, two churches, and private homes. Of the churches, only St John's Anglican is still in regular use, but the other— St Bernard's—is still sanctified.

The Court House was the scene of trials of hundreds of convicts and is now a museum, brought vividly to life by tape recordings based on actual trial transcripts. Guided tours are available from National Parks and Wildlife Service.

ACCOMMODATION: Little Hartley Farm, ph (02) 6355 2244; Venice Caravan Park, ph (02) 6355 2106

ACTIVITIES: Bushwalking, 4WD touring, sightseeing

TOURIST INFORMATION: Ph (02) 6351 2307

HAY

758 KM SOUTH-WEST OF SYDNEY
POPULATION: 2985   MAP REF: PAGE 183 H5
Originally known as Lang's Crossing, Hay was once a Murrumbidgee sheep fording point. Charles Sturt passed by on his way down the river in 1829, and in 1858, that legendary riverboat identity responsible for opening up much of both the Murrumbidgee and the Darling Rivers—Francis Cadell—opened a store here. The town was named in 1859 after local politician and pastoralist, Sir John Hay.

Today, Hay is an essential service centre for a vast pastoral area. The major crop is wool, but there are several world famous sheep studs in the area.

At the junction of three highways—Sturt, Midwestern and Cobb—and midway between Sydney and Adelaide, Hay represents an ideal stop-off point for travellers.

Hay is indeed a welcome sight for travellers journeying from Sydney after the long drive across the Hay Plain from West Wyalong—surely the most boring drive in New South Wales.

An old saying pertinent to the district is 'The three hottest places in New South Wales are Hay, Hell and Booligal—in that order'. Booligal is the next stop north on the Cobb Highway, 78 km away.

Hay Gaol Museum was built in 1878 and houses an impressive collection of local memorabilia. Hay was regularly served by Cobb & Co and the original coach, *Sunbeam*, which plied the Deniliquin–Hay–Wilcannia run until 1901, is housed in the town.

Ruberto's Winery is open to visitors.

ACCOMMODATION: Highway Inn Hotel, ph (02) 6993 1069; Caledonian Hotel, ph (02) 6993 1024; Bishop's Lodge Motel, ph (02) 6993 3003; Cobb Highway Inlander Motel, ph (02) 6993 1901; Hay Plains Holiday Park, ph (02) 6993 1875; Hay Caravan Park, ph (02) 6993 1415

ACTIVITIES: Sightseeing, water sports, wineries

TOURIST INFORMATION: Ph (02) 6993 2102

HENTY

542 KM SOUTH-WEST OF SYDNEY
POPULATION: 100   MAP REF: PAGE 183 M7
Named after the Henty family of pioneer pastoralists, this town was originally called Doodle Cooma.

For 32 years the town has hosted one of the most important agribusiness events in Australia: the Henty Machinery Field Days. This event commemorates the unveiling of a harvester-header at the 1914 Henty Agricultural Show by local farmer Headlie Taylor. The Taylor Header subsequently revolutionised grain farming and is regarded by many to be the single greatest contribution to the grain industry. (An original header is on display in a special building in Henty Park.)

Henty Machinery Field Days showcase over 200 million dollars' worth of farming equipment and technology. Held in September over three days, the event regularly attracts over 50 000 visitors, who also come to see the fashion, crafts and cooking displays.

Just to the west of the town is a memorial plaque for a Sergeant Smyth, who was shot dead there by 'Mad' Dan Morgan.

ACCOMMODATION: Doodle Cooma Arms Hotel, ph (02) 6929 3013

ACTIVITIES: Scenic drives, sightseeing

TOURIST INFORMATION: Ph (02) 6929 3013

An abandoned hotel outside Hay

HILL END

276 KM WEST OF SYDNEY
POPULATION: 200   MAP REF: PAGE 176 D6

There are three ways into Hill End, a former gold rush town that has been an official Historic Site since 1967. The most picturesque route is via the Bridle Track, from Kelso, just out of Bathurst. This convict-built road winds beside the Macquarie River and features some spectacular views. An alternative is an equally winding road from the other goldmining town of Sofala, and the third option is to come in from Mudgee via yet another gold town—Hargraves. All roads are dirt and warrant extreme care.

Like Gulgong, Hill End owes its existence solely to the discovery of gold. In 1851, the first strike was made and in its heyday the population was in excess of 20 000. By 1873, Hill End had 53 hotels and shops catering to every need and appetite.

Hill End's biggest find was the Holtermann Nugget, a massive conglomerate of reef gold 1.5 metres high by 0.5 metre across. It weighed 236 kg and had a gold content of over 8.5 kg. As with all boom towns, by the time gold finally ran out in 1895, Hill End was a ghost town.

Now the town is administered by the National Parks and Wildlife Service. Throughout the town are plaques marking sites where significant buildings once stood. There is a general store operating and the Royal Hotel (built in 1872) still serves cold beers.
ACCOMMODATION: Royal Hotel, ph (02) 6337 8261
ACTIVITIES: 4WD touring, gold fossicking, sightseeing
TOURIST INFORMATION: Ph (02) 6337 8206

HILLSTON

734 KM WEST OF SYDNEY
POPULATION: 1000   MAP REF: PAGE 183 J2

Hillston, on the Lachlan River, is the centre for a wool and wheat economy in the western districts. It also has a thriving citrus industry. The town can be reached from Ivanhoe in the north-west, Hay in the south-west, Griffith to the south, and West Wyalong and Lake Cargellico to the east.

One of the first settlers in the area was the explorer William Hovell. In 1863 a pub was built named The Red Bank—presumably because the Aboriginal name for the district was 'melnunnu', meaning 'red earth'. Hillston was named after the first publican, William Hill.
ACCOMMODATION: Motel Hillston, ph (02) 6967 2573; Kidman Way Motor Inn, ph (02) 6967 2151; Hillston Caravan Park, ph (02) 6967 2575
ACTIVITIES: Scenic drives, sightseeing
TOURIST INFORMATION: Ph (02) 6962 4145

HOLBROOK

516 KM SOUTH OF SYDNEY
POPULATION: 1400   MAP REF: PAGE 183 N7

Changing the names of towns was a popular pastime during World War I (particularly in South Australia,

A replica of Cdr Holbrook's submarine, in Holbrook

which had a high proportion of early German immigrants). In New South Wales, Germanton, halfway between Sydney and Melbourne on the Hume Highway, was rechristened 'Holbrook' after a Victoria Cross-winning British submarine commander. A replica of Commander Holbrook's submarine is visible from the highway as you drive through town.

In the nineteenth century, Germanton was an important staging post on the Cobb & Co Melbourne–Sydney run, and the main street has many buildings from that era, including the Woolpack Inn. Built in 1895, almost 80 years later it was turned into a museum, with 22 rooms housing turn-of-the-century fashions, furniture and artefacts.

The racecourse has been in use since the end of the nineteenth century and the major event held is the Commander Holbrook Cup, on Anzac Day.
ACCOMMODATION: Riverina Hotel, ph (02) 6036 2523; Holbrook Hotel, ph (02) 6036 2099; Holbrook Skye Motel, ph (02) 6036 2333; Town Centre Motor Inn, ph 1800 676 227
ACTIVITIES: Scenic drives, sightseeing
TOURIST INFORMATION: Ph (02) 6036 2131

HUSKISSON

196 KM SOUTH OF SYDNEY
POPULATION: 1600   MAP REF: PAGE 174 G4

On the shores of Jervis Bay, this town was probably named after William Huskisson, who was the Colonial Secretary from 1827 to 1828. Huskisson is a 20 minutes' drive from Nowra.

At the turn of the century, a major boat-building industry was based here, and it produced, among others, the *Lady Denman*, a ferry that plied Sydney Harbour for many years. Today, the ferry occupies pride of place in the Lady Denman Heritage Complex, which is also a more general maritime museum.

Fishing and tourism are now the town's main industries, but Huskisson also offers some interesting shopping, with an Aboriginal arts and crafts centre and a trading post stocked with antiques and bric-a-brac. For travellers, the town also has a comprehensive shopping centre.
ACCOMMODATION: Jervis Bay Hotel, ph (02) 4441 5781; Huskisson Beach Motel, ph (02) 4441 6387; Anglesea Motel & Holiday Lodges, ph (02) 4441 5057; Husky Pub, ph (02) 4441 5001; Husky Holiday Units, ph (02) 4441 6580; Leisurehaven Caravan Park, ph (02) 441 5046
ACTIVITIES: Bowls, bushwalking, fishing, golf, tennis, water sports
TOURIST INFORMATION: Ph (02) 4421 0788

INVERELL

733 KM NORTH OF SYDNEY
POPULATION: 10 000   MAP REF: PAGE 179 H6

Known as 'the Meeting Place of the Swans' or 'the Sapphire City', and surrounded by a prosperous mixed farming district, Inverell is situated on the Gwydir Highway. The first commercial venture was in 1863, when Colin and Rosanna Ross started a general store for the settlers who had moved into the district. (Nearby Ross Hills carries on their family name.)

The man who gave the town its Gaelic name was Alexander Campbell, a Scot who in 1835 established a property—Inverell—in the district.

Inverell Pioneer Village perpetuates the old way of life. A collection of authentic buildings relocated from their original sites in the area, the village includes Goonoowigall school; The Grove homestead; Paddy's Pub; a blacksmith's hut and miner's hut; Oakwood Hall, a printer's shop; and Gooda Cottage, which houses an excellent collection of gemstones.

Good gemstones—including diamonds, sapphires and zircons—have long been found in the area, along with tin, silver and bauxite. Fossicking areas abound, and equipment can be hired in town.

Buildings in town worth a visit include the Court House, completed in 1887. Nearby is the Town Hall and just around the corner is the Arts and Crafts Gallery, which holds many local and visiting exhibitions and has many fine examples of ceramics, woodwork, painting and needlework on sale.

The most recent building is the Bicentennial Memorial, which has three courtyards: one devoted to the Tertiary Period and Aboriginal tribal culture, another to the period from 1788 to 1888, and the third from 1888 to 1988 and beyond.

Lake Inverell Reserve is an aquatic sanctuary covering 100 hectares and is home to a large variety of waterbirds, platypus, wallabies and black swans. The area is great for bushwalking and fishing.

Commanding views of the town and the surrounding district can be had from McIlveen Park Lookout, west of town. Also worth a visit are Morris' Honey Farm and the Bottle Museum.

Copeton Dam has a 939 hectare recreation area. There is whitewater rafting below the dam and on the eastern foreshores near Tingha, bushwalking can include exploring the old mining settlement, but care should be taken in the diggings.

Gwydir Ranch Park, a recreation area close to the river and the dam is accessible only by 4WD. It is private property, but visits can easily be arranged.

The Draught Horse Centre shows visitors the five different breeds of draught horse that played a role in the pioneering of Australia. Gilgai winery—at an elevation of 760 metres, one of the highest vineyards in Australia—produces limited quantities of wines.

Wildlife abounds at Goonoowigall Wilderness Reserve and marked tracks provide peaceful walks by cool rapids and huge granite outcrops. Remains of Chinese earth ovens and mines can be found here.

Green Valley Farm provides unusual fun rides and has a native and exotic zoo and beautiful gardens. The famous Smith's Museum from Tingha is housed here and features a rare collection of gems and minerals from all over the world.

Also worth seeing are the Ashford Limestone Caves and Macintyre Falls.

Inverell Hobby Market is held on the first Sunday of each month and the Sapphire City market on the third Sunday.

In January, Australia Day celebrations are held in the Pioneer Village. February sees the Inverell Show and March the Inverell Motorshow and the Bowling Club Easter Bowling Carnival. The Grafton–Inverell Cycling Classic is held in September, and the Sapphire City Floral Festival in October. The year concludes with both the Venetia Carnival and the Inverell Cup Racing Carnival.

ACCOMMODATION: Royal Hotel/Motel, ph (02) 6722 2811; Australian Hotel, ph (02) 6722 1611; Cousins Motor Inn, ph (02) 6722 3566; Sapphire City Motel, ph (02) 6722 2500; Dejon Sapphire Centre (B&B), ph (02) 6723 2222; Four Winds (B&B), ph (02) 6723 1323; Fossicker's Rest Caravan Park, ph (02) 6722 2261

ACTIVITIES: Bowls, fishing, fossicking, golf, scenic drives, tennis, water sports, wineries

TOURIST INFORMATION: Ph (02) 6722 1693

JERILDERIE

692 KM SOUTH-WEST OF SYDNEY
POPULATION: 1000   MAP REF: PAGE 183 K6
A town in the Riverina district, Jerilderie lies on plains noted for Merino studs, the production of wool, fat lambs, cattle and wheat. Jerilderie (the name means 'a reedy place') houses a small community that is proud of its place in Australian history and today provides many sporting facilities and amenities not found in towns of similar size.

Ned Kelly Post Office, in Powell Street (named after the 1850s founder of the town, John Caractacus Powell), was the original telegraph station sabotaged by the Kelly gang in 1879 who robbed the Bank of New South Wales of more than 2000 pounds. The Willows houses local archives and items of farming and historic significance.

The home of John Monash, one of Australia's greatest generals, can be found in Jerilderie.

ACCOMMODATION: Colony Inn Hotel/Motel, ph (03) 5886 1220; New Riverina Hotel, ph (03) 5886 1325; Jerilderie Motor Inn, ph (03) 5886 1360; Jerilderie Motel, ph (03) 5886 1301

ACTIVITIES: Bowls, golf, horseracing, tennis, water sports

TOURIST INFORMATION: Ph (03) 5886 1666

JERVIS BAY

208 KM SOUTH OF SYDNEY
POPULATION: 5000   MAP REF: PAGE 174 G4
Pronounced 'jarvis', Jervis Bay is an extensive inlet and holiday resort on the south coast of New South Wales. The bay was named in 1791 by Lieutenant Bowen of the transport *Atlantic* in honour of Sir John Jervis, with whom he had served. Later, as the areas inland were settled, the bay was used as a port for small coastal ships that took produce to Sydney and returned with provisions for the settlers.

Jervis Bay has been the site for some ambitious schemes, none of which came to fruition, but part of the area is still owned by the Commonwealth Government. The Seat of Government Act of 1908 decreed that the capital of the nation should have access to the sea. In the late 1990s, that ownership and what should be done with the land was the subject of heated debate between environmentalists and those who wished to develop the area.

ACCOMMODATION: Jervis Bay Hotel, ph (02) 4441 5781

ACTIVITIES: Bushwalking, SCUBA diving, swimming

TOURIST INFORMATION: Ph (02) 4421 0778

JINDABYNE

457 KM SOUTH OF SYDNEY
POPULATION: 2000   MAP REF: PAGE 174 B8
For New South Wales skiers, Jindabyne is truly the gateway to the Snowy Mountains, just 40 minutes away from the winter playgrounds of Thredbo and Perisher Blue. For many, it is a last chance to fuel up, hire snow chains (mandatory in Kosciuszko National Park in the snow season), or skis and snowboards. For others, cheaper accommodation than in the resorts means that Jindabyne is a good base for a skiing holiday, despite long drives and missing out on the schnapps with bratwurst at lunchtime.

The original town is now under Lake Jindabyne, flooded as part of the Snowy Mountains Hydro-Electric Scheme in 1966. The surrounding district supports sheep and cattle, but Jindabyne's raison d'être is tourism, whether it be for the trout seekers who come to cast a line in the lake, the alpine tourists or the snow enthusiasts.

In summer, too, Jindabyne has much to offer. At 910 metres above sea level and with a capacity of almost 690 000 gigalitres, the lake gives visitors the chance to sail, windsurf or waterski. There is an annual regatta for sailors in the first weekend of December, but be warned, most of the local craft are multi-hulled and therefore very fast!

ACCOMMODATION: Alpine Resort Motel, ph (02) 6456 2522; Thredbo Valley Lodge (motel), ph (02) 6456 1428; Lake Jindabyne Hotel/Motel, ph (02) 6456 2203; Pioneers Tavern Bay (hotel),

Alpine buttercups growing on hills near Jindabyne

ph (02) 6456 2696; Bungarra Alpine Centre (serviced apartments), ph (02) 6456 2688; Amber Apartments, ph (02) 6456 2266; Karoonda Flats, ph (02) 6456 7188; Steiner Ski Lodge (B&B), ph (02) 6456 2308; Sonnblick Lodge, ph (02) 6456 2472; Pat's Patch Caravan Park, ph (02) 6456 2354; Snowline Caravan Park, ph (02) 6456 2099

ACTIVITIES: Abseiling, fishing, gliding, mountain biking, national park access, skiing, water sports

TOURIST INFORMATION: Ph (02) 6456 2444

JUNEE

446 KM SOUTH-WEST OF SYDNEY
POPULATION: 5000   MAP REF: PAGE 183 N5
Aboriginal for 'speak to me', Junee calls itself the Rail & Jail Town. The 'Rail' is easy to explain, as Junee is an important train centre on the Riverina lines. On 29 September 1947, the largest circular railway loco-motive roundhouse in the southern hemisphere was opened here, with a 32 metre turntable and 42 repair bays. The 'Jail' refers to a high-tech, privately owned and operated correctional centre.

Situated on the Murrumbidgee River about halfway between Sydney and Melbourne on the Olympic Way, the town is the centre of a grazing and agricultural district though gold was mined in the area last century at Old Junee, Junee Reefs and Illabo. Nowadays, BHP also operates an ethanol plant at Junee, and the district is the largest producer of canola in the state. Junee has the largest wheat terminal in the southern hemisphere, with a storage capacity of 153 000 tonnes.

'Jewnee Run', established in 1845, was the original property in the district. In 1876, Christopher Crawley built what is currently the Hotel Junee, and 22 years later he erected Monte Cristo Homestead, now an award-winning tourist attraction, faithfully restored and boasting an impressive collection of antiques and horse-drawn carriages. In February, the town hosts a Pro Rodeo; in March, a Billycart Derby; in April, a Vintage and Veteran Car Rally; in June, Kennel Club Championships; in September, the Monte Cristo Charity Ball and in October, an Agricultural Show.

ACCOMMODATION: Red Cow Motel, ph (02) 6924 1985; Crossing Motel, ph (02) 6924 3255; Loftus Hotel/Motel, ph (02) 6924 1511; Junee Hotel, ph (02) 6924 1124; Junee Willow Caravan Park, ph (02) 6924 1316

ACTIVITIES: Bowls, golf, horseracing, swimming, tennis

TOURIST INFORMATION: Ph (02) 6923 5402

KATOOMBA

104 KM WEST OF SYDNEY
POPULATION: 16 930   MAP REF: PAGE 176 F8
Originally called 'Crushers' after a local quarry, in 1877 this coalmining area was given an Aboriginal name—'Katoomba'—meaning 'falling water' or 'falling together of many streams'. It is now the admin-istrative centre of the Blue Mountains, and is also the gateway to some spectacular scenery.

The environs of Katoomba attract some three million visitors a year. Most will visit Echo Point and

The view from Cahill's Lookout, one of many such vistas in the Blue Mountains near Katoomba

the Three Sisters, known in Aboriginal mythology as Mennhi, Wimlah and Gunnedoo. These have recently been incorporated into the Blue Mountains National Park, a move that will doubtless stop rock climbers from further eroding the geologically fragile sandstone formations.

Fitter visitors can climb the Giant Stairway—a descent of almost 1000 steps leading to the floor of the Jamieson Valley—but there are many easier bushwalks which lead along the edge of the escarpments above the Jamieson and Grose Valleys, overlooking natural attractions such as the Ruined Castle and Mount Solitary.

For the less active, there is the Scenic Railway, originally designed to take coalminers 250 metres down the cliff face and reputedly the steepest in the world, or the Skyway cable car, offering superb views over the Katoomba Falls and the valley floor.

Other spots worth seeing include the oldest pub in the Blue Mountains, the Carrington Hotel, built in 1880, temporary home to the rich, famous and royal, and the Paragon Café, with mouthwatering chocolates to tempt the taste buds of even the most fastidious health fanatic.

Explorers' Tree—a blaze tree marked by Blaxland, Wentworth and Lawson, the first men to find a way through the mountains to the fertile western plains— lies on the road just west of Katoomba township. The Edge Maxvision Cinema has a six-storey high screen showing Blue Mountains views as well as feature films.

Katoomba holds local markets on the first and third Saturdays each month, and in February hosts the Blue Mountains Folk Festival. In June, the Winter Magic Festival is held, a part of Yulefest, which runs from June through to August throughout the district.

ACCOMMODATION: Lillianfels (resort), ph (02) 4780 1200; Katoomba Town Centre Motel, ph (02) 4782 1266; Alpine Motor Inn, ph (02) 4782 2011; Gearins Hotel, ph (02) 4782 4395; Narrow Neck Lodge (apartments), ph (02) 4782 5626; Lurline Lavender B&B, ph (02) 4782 6230; Avonleigh Country House (B&B), ph (02) 4782 1534; Crystal Lodge (chalet), ph (02) 4782 5122; Katoomba Falls Caravan Park, ph (02) 4782 1835
ACTIVITIES: Bowls, bushwalking, 4WD touring, golf, horse riding, national park access, swimming, tennis
TOURIST INFORMATION: Ph (02) 4782 0756

KEMPSEY

463 KM NORTH OF SYDNEY
POPULATION: 9050   MAP REF: PAGE 179 M9

Named after the Valley of Kempsey in Worcestershire, England, the Kempsey that we know today began life in the early 1830s. In 1836 Enoch Rudder, who later subdivided his land to create a village, operated a punt service across the Macleay River.

The economic base is dairying and timber-getting, though some light industry exists in the area, including the famed Akubra hat factory. Tourism is important, and the area has many and varied activities on offer, from skydiving and fishing to scenic flights. History buffs will be interested in the Macleay River Historical Society Museum and Settler's Cottage as well as a number of nineteenth-century buildings in the town.

In March, Kempsey holds Country Music Heritage Week and the Festival of the River, which embraces water sports, street theatre, linedancing and an art

exhibition. In July, a round of the Australian Off Road Racing Championship is held; in September, another Country Music Festival; in October, the Truck Show, and in November, a Classic Bike Rally.
ACCOMMODATION: All Nations Hallmark Inn (motel), ph (02) 6562 1284; Skyline Motel, ph (02) 6562 4888; Hotel Kempsey, ph (02) 6562 8588; Netherby Guest Houses, ph (02) 6563 1777; Tall Timbers Caravan Park, ph (02) 6562 4544
ACTIVITIES: Cycling, 4WD touring, fishing, horse riding, horseracing, scenic flights, skydiving, water sports
TOURIST INFORMATION: Ph (02) 6563 1555

KIAMA

120 KM SOUTH OF SYDNEY
POPULATION: 10 000   MAP REF: PAGE 174 G3

Its name is thought to derive from the Aboriginal 'kiaram-a' (meaning 'where the sea makes a noise'). Tourists flock to see the blowhole, which shoots water into the air up to a height of 60 metres and was first chronicled by George Bass, who anchored his small boat there in 1797.

Also popular are the National Trust-classified row of restored timber terrace cottages in Collins Street,

The rolling hills around Kiama

which now house craft and antique shops. Other visitors come to trace their lineage in the records of the Family History Centre.

Bordered on one side by the sea, with an excellent surfing beach, and on the other by the rugged Minamurra Rainforest, Kiama now relies on tourism to augment a local economy built on dairying, blue metal mining and fishing. The town has been in existence since 1839.

In June, Kiama hosts an Australian Folk Festival, and in November, a Seaside Festival and Colonial Ball. In December the town lays claim to Australia's largest regional Carols by Candlelight and in February, there's a Jazz Festival.
ACCOMMODATION: The Grand Hotel, ph (02) 4232 1037; Terrace Motor Lodge, ph (02) 4233 1100; Beachfront Motel, ph (02) 4232 1533; Kiama Inn, ph (02) 4232 1166; Cranford Lodge (guesthouse), ph (02) 4232 1060; East's Beach Van Park, ph (02) 4232 2124
ACTIVITIES: Bowls, bushwalking, fishing, golf, scenic drives, surfing
TOURIST INFORMATION: Ph (02) 4232 3322

KYOGLE

796 KM NORTH OF SYDNEY
POPULATION: 2750   MAP REF: PAGE 179 N2

This 'Gateway to the Rainforest' takes its name from an early cattle run, which in turn borrowed from the Aboriginal 'kauiou-gal', meaning brush turkey, or bustard. Situated on the headwaters of the Richmond River, nestled between the McPherson, Tweed and Richmond Ranges, Kyogle is adjacent to World Heritage-listed Border Ranges National Park. The park offers a variety of marvellous walks, ranging from 50 metres to 10 km. The most spectacular is the three hour return walk to The Pinnacle, which offers panoramic views over the Tweed Valley.

Once reliant on timber (first cedar, then hoop pine) for its existence, Kyogle is now the centre of a rich agricultural and dairying district, with Norply (a ply timber mill) employing a large proportion of the town's workforce. The town has a large number of Heritage buildings to see, and homesteads in the area dating back to the early 1800s. Amateur anthropologists will be fascinated by a large number of Aboriginal sites. You can swim, camp or fish at nearby Toonumbar Dam.

Kyogle has an average annual rainfall of 1100 mm so, as the locals say—bring your brolly!

There is a rodeo in July, an agricultural show in October, and in November a festival and golf tournament.

ACCOMMODATION: Kyogle Motel, ph (02) 6632 1070
ACTIVITIES: Bowls, bushwalking, camping, fishing, golf, national park access, scenic drives, swimming, tennis
TOURIST INFORMATION: Ph (02) 6632 1044

LEETON

560 KM SOUTH-WEST OF SYDNEY
POPULATION: 7000   MAP REF: PAGE 183 L5

Named after C. A. Lee, Minister for Public Works when the Murrumbidgee Irrigation Area (MIA) was being developed, Leeton was the first of many Riverina towns designed by American architect Walter Burley Griffin, in 1912.

Leeton is the administrative centre for the MIA, with many Government departments based there. The local economy relies predominantly on agriculture, the town housing major food processing organisations, such as the Ricegrowers Cooperative, Leeton Citrus Juices and a stock-killing centre. (In 1940, the Letona cannery—another important local employer since 1914—established a record of canning 419 609 tins of fruit in one day.)

Visitors can inspect the Quelch juice factory, visit a sheep milking farm, see the historic Hydro Hotel, built in 1919, or call in at the Whitton Court House Museum. Two local wineries—Toorak and Lillypilly Estate—are open for tastings and just 2 km out of town is Fivebough Swamp, a waterfowl sanctuary. Harness racing, gliding and hot-air ballooning are popular tourist attractions.

Leeton holds a ten-day Country Festival during Easter in even-numbered years.

ACCOMMODATION: Bygalorie Motor Inn, ph (02) 6953 4100; Gilgal Family Holiday Centre (camping/caravans), ph (02) 6953 3882; Leeton Caravan Park, ph (02) 6953 3323
ACTIVITIES: Bowls, gliding, golf, horseracing, hot-air ballooning, sightseeing, water sports, wineries
TOURIST INFORMATION: Ph (02) 6953 2832

LEURA

107 KM WEST OF SYDNEY
POPULATION: 3622   MAP REF: PAGE 176 F8

'Leura' is Aboriginal for 'lava', and while the Blue Mountains are predominantly sandstone, many volcanic rocks have been found in the area. Of all the mountain resort villages, Leura is probably the most prestigious, as some of the grand houses in the district proclaim. Leura Mall is charming and olde worlde, with coffee shops, restaurants and art galleries all in Heritage colours. There are strict council controls on any development.

Along Cliff Drive are the Leura Cascades, which provide a great spot for family picnics or BBQs, and the drive also offers access to many beautiful waterfalls, like Leura, Linda, Lila and Bridal Veil Falls.

But it is the gardens and mansions most visitors come to see. Everglades Gardens, owned by the National Trust, was designed by the famous Danish landscaper, Paul Sorenson. Nearby Leuralla, which is another magnificent home, also houses the largest collection of toys, dolls, teddy bears and model railways in Australia.

The view from Sublime Point is also worth seeing, while the more active can play golf at either Fairmont Resort, or the equally famous Leura Golf Club, which boasts fine greens and traps.

Leura Fair and Garden Festival are held in October each year, while the local markets are on the first Sunday of each month.

ACCOMMODATION: Fairmont Resort, ph (02) 4782 5111; Menabilly Guest House (motel), ph (02) 4784 2418; Leura Gardens Ibis Resort (hotel), ph (02) 4784 1331; Megalong Manor (B&B), ph (02) 4784 1461; Bygone Beauty's Cottages (self-contained), ph (02) 4784 3117; Little Brown Cottage (self-contained), ph (02) 4573 2228; Leura Village Caravan Park, ph (02) 4784 1552
ACTIVITIES: Bowls, bushwalking, golf, national park access, scenic drives, sightseeing, swimming
TOURIST INFORMATION: Ph (02) 4739 6266

LIGHTNING RIDGE

760 KM NORTH-WEST OF SYDNEY
POPULATION: 7000   MAP REF: PAGE 181 P2

Thirty years ago, Lightning Ridge consisted of a general store and the tiny, spartan Diggers' Rest Hotel. The access roads were all unsealed, and if it rained—a rare occurrence—you got out quickly unless you wanted to be trapped by mud for weeks.

These days, sealed roads enable adventurous visitors, keen to see the only place in the world where black opal is found, to come in droves. The Diggers' Rest has a long bar, carpets on the floors, even pool

An opal mine at Lightning Ridge

tables! The massive Lightning Ridge Bowling Club now dominates the town. The 3600 members enjoy fine dining, including fresh seafood flown in daily. With both a synthetic green and a more recently added natural one, the club hosts the Black Opal Classic tournament in October. Players from all over Australia come to test their skills, attracted by $25 000 in prize money.

Mining methods have changed too. Whereas in the old days, prospectors used picks and buckets to bring the ore to the surface, now they use jackhammers and massive industrial vacuum cleaners. There are also open-cut operations on the fields.

You can, of course, buy opal in Lightning Ridge, but there are plenty of other things to do. You can fossick the mullock heaps (a practice known as 'noodling'), visit the cactus nursery, take a joy flight or soak away tired muscles in the hot mineral baths. There are underground mine tours, or you can watch a master lapidarist fashion opal into jewellery. The Bottle House Museum, which features collections of bottles, mining relics and minerals, is worth a visit, as is the Bush Moozeum just out of town at Simm's Hill. The Goondee Aboriginal Keeping Place features artefacts and educational tours.

Lightning Ridge is purportedly the fastest growing town in north-west New South Wales. More than 50 different nationalities are represented around the fields, which is where most of the population lives. Some may be rich, but their accommodation remains fairly primitive by city standards. Visitors, however, are well catered for.

In July, the town hosts the Gem and Opal Festival; over Easter, the Great Goat Races; while in June a Pistol Shoot is held.

ACCOMMODATION: Wallangulla Motel, ph (02) 6829 0542; Lightning Ridge Motor Village, ph (02) 6829 0304; Tram-O-Tel, ph (02) 6829 0448; Diggers' Rest Hotel, ph (02) 6829 0404; Crocodile Caravan & Camping Park, ph (02) 6829 0437
ACTIVITIES: Bowls, fossicking, golf, horse riding, swimming, tennis
TOURIST INFORMATION: Ph (02) 6829 1466

LISMORE

821 KM NORTH OF SYDNEY
POPULATION: 27 250   MAP REF: PAGE 179 N3

Though the Aboriginal name for the area was 'Tuckurimba', this rich agricultural centre took its name from the property Lismore owned by an early station owner, William Wilson.

One of the most densely populated rural areas in Australia, dairying, pig farming, bacon curing, banana growing, sugar cane, sawmilling and engineering are the dominant local industries. Early pastoral efforts centred on sheep, but the area made them prone to liver fluke, footrot and catarrh.

For humans, however, the subtropical climate is excellent, with mild to warm temperatures all year and good rainfall. The original inhabitants had a fairly wide-ranging territory, travelling as far as the Bunya Mountains in Queensland for the annual bunya nut food crop. Aboriginal relics can be seen at the Richmond River Historical Society Museum.

Lismore is in the centre of an area known as 'The Big Scrub'. Visitors can take an indoor rainforest walk, and Wilsons Park still has residual rainforest, giving some idea of what the country must have been like before the cedar-getters moved in. Visitors can also take a river cruise or visit Macadamia Magic, a processing plant and tourist complex.

In March, there is a Square Dance Festival; in May, the Trinity Arts Festival; in August, Lismore Street Festival; in September, Lismore Cup Race Day and Garden Week; in October, the Northern Rivers Folk Festival and the North Coast National Show.
ACCOMMODATION: Northern Rivers Hotel, ph (02) 6621 5797; Currendina Lodge (motel), ph (02) 6621 6118; Lismore City Motor Inn, ph (02) 6621 4455; McDermotts B&B, ph (02) 6624 1158; Melville House B&B, ph (02) 6621 5778; Lismore Lake Caravan Park, ph (02) 6621 2585
ACTIVITIES: Bowls, golf, scenic drives, squash, swimming, tennis, waterskiing
TOURIST INFORMATION: Ph (02) 6622 0122

LITHGOW

143 KM WEST OF SYDNEY
POPULATION: 13 500   MAP REF: PAGE 176 E7

Lithgow has been a coal town since 1841 but has a lot to offer the visitor in things to see and do. Named after William Lithgow, a New South Wales Auditor-General, the town was the birthplace of Olympic runner Marjorie Jackson—the 'Lithgow Flash'.

Blast Furnace Park is a monument to the town's industrial history. The first iron and steel cast in Australia were produced here in 1886, when William Sandford established a blast furnace. Production continued until 1928, when the entire industry moved to Port Kembla.

Eskbank House is an historic house with period furniture, a blacksmith's forge, a coach house and a display of Lithgow pottery. Australia's oldest commercial pottery, it was established in 1833.

The Small Arms Museum in Methven Street commemorates a long era in Lithgow's history. It houses one of Australia's most comprehensive collections of machine-guns, rifles and related items. Lithgow State Mine Railway Heritage Park is on the site of the former Lithgow Power Station and colliery.

There are also a number of national parks in the area, such as Blue Mountains and Wollemi, and the old mining town of Newnes, with its famous glow-worm tunnel. But Lithgow's greatest tourist attraction continues to be the Zig Zag Railway. This was the first rail link to the western region of New South Wales, traversing spectacular mountain scenery, where one engine pulled and another pushed up terrifying grades. Now, the return journey covers 12 km, and is a very popular family entertainment.

The local markets are held every second month on the first Saturday in the month.
ACCOMMODATION: Donnybroook Hotel, ph (02) 6351 3063; Grand Central Hotel, ph (02) 6351 3050; Colonial Motor Inn, ph (02) 6352 2471; Holly Lodge Guest House (B&B), ph (02) 6355 2742; Clarence House (B&B), ph (02) 6355 2643; Goollooinbion Station (farmstay), ph (02) 6379 7247; Binalong Bird Sanctuary (farmstay), ph (02) 6379 7326
ACTIVITIES: Bushwalking, 4WD touring, golf, national park access, scenic drives
TOURIST INFORMATION: Ph (02) 6353 1859

LORD HOWE ISLAND

700 KM NORTH-EAST OF SYDNEY
POPULATION: 320

Lord Howe Island lies off Australia's east coast and is roughly crescent-shaped, about 11 km long and 1.5 km wide. The island—a volcanic eruption from a submarine ridge running from the South Island of New Zealand to the Chesterfield Reefs—was first sighted by Henry Lidgbird Ball, commander of HM tender *Supply* in 1788, on a voyage from Sydney to Norfolk Island. He named it after Admiral Lord Howe.

Thick tropical vegetation and isolation made early settlement attempts fairly unsuccessful, but by 1851 the population consisted of 16 people who had become entirely self-sufficient. They traded fresh produce with ships, primarily whalers, but ultimately more profitable was trade in kentia palms, which subsequently became one of the most popular palms in the world. Lord Howe is the only place in the world where the kentia palm grows naturally.

In 1981 70 per cent of the island was made a Permanent Park Reserve and a year later, the island was placed on the World Heritage List.

There are only a few cars on the island and visitors either hire bicycles or walk.
ACCOMMODATION: Pinetrees Lodge (resort), ph (02) 6563 2177; Lorhiti Apartments, ph (02) 6563 2081; Palm Haven (holiday units), ph (02) 6563 2177; Broken Banyan Flats, ph (02) 6563 2024; Beachcomber Lodge (B&B), ph (02) 6563 2032
ACTIVITIES: Birdwatching, coral viewing, cycling, duty free shopping, fishing, mountain climbing, walking, water sports
TOURIST INFORMATION: Ph (02) 6563 8261

MACKSVILLE

519 KM NORTH OF SYDNEY
POPULATION: 2800   MAP REF: PAGE 179 M8

Originally called 'Macks Village' after two early Scots settlers, Macksville lies at the junction of Taylors Arm Creek and the Bowra River, where they become the Nambucca River. The fertile district supports maize, bananas, vegetables, timber-getting and dairying.

Picnicking and fishing are popular pastimes on the banks of the Nambucca River. BBQs and tables are available north of the bridge.

At Taylors Arm, 20 km upriver, is the Cosmopolitan, reputedly the original 'pub with no beer' immortalised by Slim Dusty on the only 78 rpm record to go gold in Australia.

Macksville hosts a number of festivals through the year. In April, there are both the Nambucca Country Music Festival and the Agricultural Show. In May,

Lord Howe Island, looking towards the southern end of this most beautiful island

another two events: the Autumn Orchid Show and the Annual Trek to the Pub with No Beer. In July, the Eungai Art & Craft Show and in September, the Annual Flower Show.

ACCOMMODATION: Nambucca Hotel, ph (02) 6568 1033; Mid Coast Motor Inn, ph 1800 25532; Golden Emblem Motel, ph (02) 6568 1977; Nambucca River Tourist Park, ph (02) 6568 1850

ACTIVITIES: Fishing, 4WD touring, golf, horseracing, water sports

TOURIST INFORMATION: Ph (02) 6568 6954

MACLEAN

703 KM NORTH OF SYDNEY
POPULATION: 3000   MAP REF: PAGE 179 N5
Originally known as Rocky Mouth, Maclean was established in the early 1860s by Scots pioneers. Situated on the confluence of the north and south arms of the Clarence River, the town is the commercial centre of an area where sugar cane, fishing and timber-getting are the important industries.

The town has several historic buildings, including Stone Cottage. The Bicentennial Museum tells of the history of the area. To celebrate its Scottish heritage, a Highland gathering is held in town over Easter.

ACCOMMODATION: Maclean Motel, ph (02) 6645 2473; Water View Motel, ph (02) 6645 2494; Gables (B&B), ph (02) 6645 2452; Maclean Riverside Caravan Park, ph (02) 6645 2987

ACTIVITIES: Fishing, water sports

TOURIST INFORMATION: Ph (02) 6645 4121

MAITLAND

191 KM NORTH OF SYDNEY
POPULATION: 50 000   MAP REF: PAGE 177 J5
Older than Melbourne and 16 years younger than Sydney, Maitland lies on the banks of the Hunter River. Originally called Wallis's Plains, it was renamed in the 1820s after Sir Frederick Lewis Maitland, Admiral of the Fleet, to whom Napoleon surrendered in 1815.

Maitland's imposing architecture is a reminder that in the nineteenth century the city was a rival to Sydney. Many of Maitland's heritage-protected buildings date back to the 1820s. Significant places of interest abound. Walka Water Works was constructed between 1882 and 1887 to provide Newcastle with a more hygienic and reliable source of fresh water. Classified by the National Trust, historic features are the pumphouse and the sand-stone reservoir wall. This is a popular recreation area.

Grossman House (1862) and Brough House (1870), of classic Georgian design, form a unit with St Mary's Anglican Church and Rectory (1867 and 1881). Maitland Heritage Mall is noted for its rotunda, fountain and 1860 drawing of the town inlaid in the pavement. The Black Boy statue, erected more than 135 years ago, was originally a hitching post for horse-drawn vehicles.

Windermere House, believed to be the oldest homestead in the Hunter Valley, was built by convicts in 1821 and has historic photographs and equipment.

To the south are the Watagan Mountains, which offer rock climbing, hang gliding and terrific 4WD

touring, while to the north are the famed Barringtons, where you can self-drive or take 4WD tours.

The Hunter Valley's biggest family market day is held at Maitland Showground on the first Sunday of each month excluding January, and on the first and third Sunday in November and December. In April, the city celebrates the Hunter Valley Steamfest, together with Heritage Week and the Maitland City Festival of Visual Arts. The Maitland Garden Ramble is held in September.

ACCOMMODATION: Belmore Hotel, ph (02) 4933 6351; Country Comfort Inn, ph (02) 4932 5288; Siesta Motel, ph (02) 4932 8322; Cintra (B&B), ph (02) 4932 8483; Coachstop Caravan Park, ph (02) 4933 2950

ACTIVITIES: Antique buying, arts and crafts, 4WD touring, national park access, scenic drives

TOURIST INFORMATION: Ph (02) 4933 2611

MENINDEE

1133 KM NORTH-WEST OF SYDNEY
POPULATION: 800   MAP REF: PAGE 180 C9
Situated on the banks of the Darling, Menindee lies amongst the overflow lakes that form the Menindee Lakes Storage. Menindee was the first town built on the Darling. In 1849, river navigation pioneer Francis Cadell established a store at a spot named in 1835 by explorer Thomas Mitchell as 'Laidley's Chain of Ponds'. Burke and Wills stayed in Maiden's Hotel before venturing off for their date with destiny. One of their Afghan camel drivers is buried just outside town and historic markers abound throughout the town.

The local lakes provide important breeding grounds for many bird species. The wreck of the paddle-steamer *Providence* is worth seeing, and fishing for perch or cod is possible along the river.

Kinchega National Park is very close to town, with its multiple Aboriginal sites in a landscape of grey soil plains and red sandridges. It houses the original Kinchega Station woolshed, which in its time saw six million sheep shorn. Numerous species of waterfowl live in the overflow lakes and the Darling.

Mungo National Park is a little further to the south-west. It is World Heritage listed, representing a remarkable record of Aboriginal life dating back 40 000 years. There is an abundance of wildlife and bird life, plus the visually stunning Walls of China, a 30 km crescent dune of orange, grey and white earth.

ACCOMMODATION: Maiden's Menindee Hotel, ph (02) 8091 4208; Burke & Wills Motel, ph (08) 8091 4313; Menindee Lakes Caravan Park, ph (08) 8091 4315

ACTIVITIES: Birdwatching, fishing, 4WD touring, national park access, scenic drives, water sports

TOURIST INFORMATION: Ph (08) 8091 4274

MERIMBULA

476 KM SOUTH OF SYDNEY
POPULATION: 4000   MAP REF: PAGE 174 E9
A holiday destination on the Sapphire Coast, Merimbula features clean tidal lakes and all manner of beaches. Boats can be hired and one of the most popular fishing spots is Merimbula Wharf.

Bournda National Park is a short drive away, and there is also bushwalking in the ancient forests in the

foothills of the South Coast Range, with small adjoining towns like Candelo (famous for its arts and crafts) and the pioneering towns of Kameruka and Wyndham providing interesting diversions.

For children, the Magic Mountain Complex is a must. Merimbula also has an aquarium and winery.

ACCOMMODATION: Hillcrest Motor Inn, ph (02) 6495 1587; Black Dolphin Resort Motel, ph (02) 6495 1500; Albacore Luxury Holiday Apartments, ph (02) 6495 3187; Holiday Hub Caravan Park, ph (02) 6495 6363

ACTIVITIES: Bowls, cycling, fishing, horse riding, national park access, tennis, water sports, wineries

TOURIST INFORMATION: Ph (02) 6492 3313

MERRIWA

348 KM NORTH-WEST OF SYDNEY
POPULATION: 1100   MAP REF: PAGE 176 F4
Merriwa is in the Upper Hunter and is the centre of an agricultural and cattle-raising district. The Old Stone Cottage dates from 1847, and is now the local history museum. The post office dates from 1880, while the Anglican church was built in 1899. To the south-west is a designated gem fossicking area and a little further on is Goulburn River National Park, which features walks on wide sandy riverbanks under orange cliffs. The visitor is likely to see wombats, eastern grey kangaroos and emus.

ACCOMMODATION: El Dorado Motel, ph (02) 6548 2273; Hidden Valley Lodge (B&B), ph (02) 6548 8515

ACTIVITIES: Bushwalking, fossicking, national park access, nature walks, scenic drives

TOURIST INFORMATION: Ph (02) 6548 2607

MITTAGONG

123 KM SOUTH OF SYDNEY
POPULATION: 6500   MAP REF: PAGE 176 F10
A town in the Southern Highlands, Mittagong was originally intended to become an industrial centre. Instead, the district is given over to dairying, poultry farming and growing fruit and vegetables, though some industrial activity also contributes to the local economy. 'Mittagong' means either 'little mountain' or 'plenty of native dogs'.

The first white men to traverse the area were led by John Wilson in 1798, but the first land grant was

The Old Pot Factory, a feature of Mittagong

made in 1821, to William Chalker. The nucleus of a village grew in the 1830s. Buildings from the 1860s now provide visitors with sightseeing opportunities, and there are also a butterfly house and a maze. Within the town are several walking trails. The area is also popular with drivers of 4WD vehicles.

ACCOMMODATION: Lion Rampant Hotel, ph (02) 4871 1090; Mittagong Motel, ph (02) 4871 1277; Welby Park Manor (B&B), ph (02) 4871 1732; Mittagong Caravan Park, ph (02) 4871 1574

ACTIVITIES: Bushwalking, 4WD touring, scenic drives

TOURIST INFORMATION: Ph (02) 4871 2888

MOAMA

864 KM SOUTH OF SYDNEY
POPULATION: 8500   MAP REF: PAGE 183 H8

Moama is the twin of the Victorian town of Echuca and lies directly across the Murray River, connected to Echuca by a bridge. Originally called Maidens Punt, the town was renamed in 1851 after the Aboriginal name for the area.

These two towns represent a monument to the paddle-steamer days, as taking a river cruise will demonstrate. Horseshoe Lagoon is a reserve near the bridge consisting of 16 hectares of natural bushland, and visitors can take in the history of Old Moama Wharf, and the recently restored Moama slipway, or simply enjoy the tranquillity and the bird life.

ACCOMMODATION: Moama Riverside (resort), ph (03) 5482 3241; Sportslander Motor Inn, ph 1800 037 074; Old Charm Holiday Villas, ph (03) 5480 9532; Shady River Caravan Resort, ph (03) 5482 5500

ACTIVITIES: Birdwatching, canoeing, fishing, river cruising, sightseeing, swimming

TOURIST INFORMATION: Ph 1800 804 446

MOLLYMOOK

248 KM SOUTH OF SYDNEY
POPULATION: 12 295   MAP REF: PAGE 174 F5

Mollymook is a pleasant getaway spot on the south coast. Here, life centres around the beach, a white expanse stretching for kilometres. Two other attractions are the Bogey Hole—a natural rockpool—and nearby Collers Beach. Ulladulla, 2 km to the south, provides all the shopping and entertainment facilities the holidaymaker could want.

ACCOMMODATION: Mollymook Shores Resort, ph (02) 4455 5888; Seascapes Motel, ph (02) 4455 5777; Bannisters Point Lodge (B&B), ph (02) 4454 3044; Mollymook Caravan Park, ph (02) 4455 1939

ACTIVITIES: Golf, water sports

TOURIST INFORMATION: Ph (02) 4455 1269

MOLONG

291 KM WEST OF SYDNEY
POPULATION: 1565   MAP REF: PAGE 176 B6

Centre for a rural economy based on fine wool and wheat, cattle, fat lambs, orchards and vineyards,

Molong gets its name from the Aboriginal word meaning 'place of rocks'. A government stockyard was established at Molong in 1828, and in 1845, a copper mine was opened.

Today poplar trees line the road into town from Orange. The grave of Sir Thomas Mitchell's Aboriginal guide Yuranigh is just outside Molong.

There are several historic buildings in the town, including a museum.

The state sheepdog trials are held here in March.

ACCOMMODATION: Freemason Hotel, ph (02) 6366 8012; Molong Motor Inn, ph 1800 028 295; Millamolong (B&B), ph (02) 6367 5241; Rooney Gardens Guest House, ph (02) 6369 6244; Molong Caravan Park, ph (02) 6366 8328

ACTIVITIES: Bowls, fishing, golf, swimming, tennis

TOURIST INFORMATION: Ph (02) 6361 5226

MOREE

705 KM NORTH-WEST OF SYDNEY
POPULATION: 10 460   MAP REF: PAGE 178 E5

Situated on the Mehi River, Moree derives its name from an Aboriginal word meaning either 'waterhole' or 'rising sun'. A sheep station took up the name in 1848. Explorer Allan Cunningham was the first European through the area in 1827, and Sir Thomas Mitchell followed in 1832. The village of Moree was established in 1852, when the Brands family opened a general store and later a pub. The famed artesian mineral spas, which are sought after by sufferers of arthritis and rheumatism, were sunk in 1895, and in 1900 the town had its own brewery!

Moree was home to the first pecan nut farm in Australia (1966) and has been the centre for an important cotton growing industry since the 1960s.

Moree Art Gallery houses an extensive collection of Aboriginal art, and the Mary Brand Park is named after one of the town's founders.

ACCOMMODATION: Spa Village Travel Inn, ph (02) 6752 4033; Dragon & Phoenix Motor Inn, ph (02) 6752 5555; Gwydir Caravan Park, ph (02) 6752 2723; Mehi River Van Park, ph (02) 6752 7188

ACTIVITIES: Fishing, swimming, 'taking the waters'

TOURIST INFORMATION: Ph (02) 6872 2280

MORPETH

199 KM NORTH OF SYDNEY
POPULATION: 1120   MAP REF: PAGE 177 J5

Morpeth's earliest name was Green Hills, and there has been a settlement here since 1834. On the Hunter River, the town became the Hunter Valley's busiest port until 1850, when the railway arrived.

Several buildings in the town have been classified by the National Trust, most notably Closebourne House, which was built by Edward Charles Close. Other buildings worth inspecting include the old Commercial Bank, the courthouse, police station and Roman Catholic church.

Morpeth has many antique and bric-a-brac shops. It has been a suburb of the city of Maitland since 1944.

Morpeth hosts a jazz festival in May.

ACCOMMODATION: Royal River Inn, ph (02) 4933 6202;

Bentley's Guest House, ph (02) 4934 1068

ACTIVITIES: Antiques, scenic drives, sightseeing

TOURIST INFORMATION: Ph (02) 4933 2611

MORUYA

325 KM SOUTH OF SYDNEY
POPULATION: 2400   MAP REF: PAGE 174 E6

Although the smallest of the three major towns on the Eurobodalla coast, Moruya is the administrative head of the district, as it is in the centre of the shire and one of the oldest towns in the region. Moruya developed in the 1850s as a gateway to the Araluen and Braidwood goldfields, and later became important as settlers like Thomas Mort developed the pastoral industries that still operate today.

The town has a number of historic buildings, but it is as a holiday resort that Moruya is best known. Great surfing beaches like Congi, Bingi and Moruya Heads are only 10 km to the east, and the fishing is good too, particularly on the Deua River and the coastal headlands. Nearby Deua National Park also offers some great 4WD challenges and bushwalks.

Commercially operated entertainments include camel trekking, mountain biking, and an historic bus tour of 1½ hours' duration, which takes in Kiora House, the first homestead built by convicts.

Moruya has country markets every Saturday morning and an annual rodeo, held at Easter.

ACCOMMODATION: Moruya Motel, ph (02) 4474 2511; Motel Luhana, ph (02) 4474 2722; Hotel Monarch, ph (02) 4474 2433; Adelaide Hotel, ph (02) 4474 2084; Moruya Caravan Park, ph (02) 4474 2242

ACTIVITIES: Bowls, fishing, 4WD touring, golf, national park access, swimming (heated pool), tennis

TOURIST INFORMATION: Ph (02) 4933 2611

MOSS VALE

135 KM SOUTH-WEST OF SYDNEY
POPULATION: 6100   MAP REF: PAGE 174 F3

Moss Vale was named in the 1860s after an old resident, Jemmy Moss. High in the Southern Highlands, it is surrounded by lush farming areas and spectacular scenery. Nearby attractions are Fitzroy Falls, in the 154 000 hectare Morton National Park, and the Wombeyan Caves. In town, Leighton Gardens provide colourful blooms for most of the year.

One of Moss Vale's beautiful gardens

Many old buildings have been restored in the town. Tudor House (a prep school for boys) welcomes visitors, who should also inspect the memorial fountain and clock tower. Throsby Park is a magnificent colonial mansion once owned by the pioneering Throsby family, who lived in it for five generations, from the 1830s.

The famed Bong Bong picnic races are held close by each October.

ACCOMMODATION: Golf Ball Motel, ph (02) 4868 1511; Bong Bong Motel, ph (02) 4868 1033; Moss Vale Hotel, ph (02) 4868 1007; Southdowns Caravan Lodge, ph (02) 4868 1215; Moss Vale Village Park, ph (02) 4868 1099

ACTIVITIES: Bushwalking, golf, national park access, shopping, sightseeing

TOURIST INFORMATION: Ph (02) 4871 2883

MOUNT WILSON

140 KM NORTH-WEST OF SYDNEY
POPULATION: 100   MAP REF: PAGE 176 F8

In the 1860s, Mount Wilson was subdivided into 62 portions and was put up for auction in 1870. There was little interest as the area was regarded as almost inaccessible. With the opening of Bell railway station in 1875, however, the land sold quickly.

Mount Wilson is still a rustic mountain village where Sydney's wealthy have their country retreats. It is famous for its cool-climate gardens which are popular with daytrippers from Sydney. Some are open all year round; others in spring and autumn.

Unlike most of the Blue Mountains, which are predominantly sandstone, Mount Wilson is capped with volcanic rock, so plant growth is luxuriant, with one area—for obvious reasons—being known as the Cathedral of Ferns.

Visitors can enjoy English-style Devonshire teas, or buy antiques or crafts from tiny stores. The Mount Tomah Botanic Gardens, on the Bells Line of Road before the Mount Wilson turn-off, is also spectacularly beautiful and worth visiting.

ACCOMMODATION: Withycombe (B&B), ph (02) 4756 2106

ACTIVITIES: Garden viewing, sightseeing, walking

TOURIST INFORMATION: Ph (02) 4739 6266

MUDGEE

271 KM NORTH-WEST OF SYDNEY
POPULATION: 7500   MAP REF: PAGE 176 D5

Mudgee's name comes from the Aboriginal word 'moothi'—'a nest in the hills'. It was established in 1838, making it the second oldest town west of the Great Divide (after Bathurst). The area was initially explored by James Blackman and William Lawson, and the first settlers were the Cox brothers. Mudgee was settled 14 years before Melbourne, and the town was considered to be so well laid out that surveyor Robert Hoddle followed the same principles when asked to survey the City of Melbourne.

Mudgee is cradled in an upland valley of the Cudgegong River (a tributary of the Macquarie), which runs through rich lucerne flats and fertile grazing country and alongside vine-clad red soil slopes, all of which contribute to making Mudgee the centre of a wool and wheat growing district.

For many years the only mode of travel from Wallerawang, near Lithgow, was by Cobb & Co coach. Relics of the coaching days can still be seen on the Lithgow–Mudgee road.

Nowadays, Mudgee is renowned for its wines. Though the industry has been extant in the area for almost 150 years, in the 1950s Mudgee was famous for its fortified wines. Now, over 20 vineyards in the region produce rich, full-flavoured reds, and some good chardonnays as well.

Nearby attractions include Munghorn Gap—34 km north of the town, it is the second oldest declared nature reserve in New South Wales. It features great bird life, including satin bowerbirds, superb lyrebirds, wonga pigeons and gang gang cockatoos. There are walking trails, picnic area, and caves to explore.

Wollemi National Park is also close by. Covering 450 000 hectares, it is the state's largest wilderness area. Within it are wonderful Aboriginal carvings, cave drawings, hand stencils and grinding grooves.

Frog Rock is a natural rock formation by the side of the Cassilis road, in the shape of a crouching frog. Hands on the Rock, closer to Gulgong, has stencilled Aboriginal hands from hundreds of years ago. To the south-east, Windamere Dam provides great opportunities to fish, sail, swim and canoe.

From July to September, Mudgee opens its gardens for viewing, and from August into September, the Mudgee Spoonful (souvenir arts and crafts) is held. September sees the Rotary Art Show, and the Land Rover Mudgee Wine and Food Festival.

ACCOMMODATION: Central Motel, ph (02) 6372 2268; Cudgegong Valley Motel, ph (02) 6372 4322; Allambie Guest House (B&B), ph (02) 6372 2185; Weeroona Farm Holidays, ph (02) 6373 6533; Mudgee Tourist and Van Resort, ph (02) 6372 1090

ACTIVITIES: Garden viewing, national park access, scenic drives, wineries, water sports

TOURIST INFORMATION: Ph (02) 6372 5875

MULLUMBIMBY

842 KM NORTH OF SYDNEY
POPULATION: 2500   MAP REF: PAGE 179 P2

Proclaimed a village in 1888, Mullumbimby's dairying and agricultural industries developed rapidly after the opening of the railway in 1894. Now, the area around the town produces dairy products, cattle, pigs, bananas, pineapples, avocados and timber. Tourism has also become an important part of the local economy.

The town has an art gallery and heritage park, and is set in a beautiful, lush environment, making it perfect for scenic drives and walks. Wanganie Gorge and Rainforest are popular destinations, along with Nightcap National Park and Tuntable Falls.

Mullumbimby has its annual show in October.

ACCOMMODATION: Chincogan Hotel, ph (02) 6684 1550; Lyrebird Motel, ph (02) 6684 1725; Adriz Motel, ph (02) 6684 1651; The Sakura Farm (B&B), ph (02) 6684 1724

ACTIVITIES: Bushwalking, national park access

TOURIST INFORMATION: Ph (02) 6672 1340

MURRURUNDI

347 KM NORTH-WEST OF SYDNEY
POPULATION: 2345   MAP REF: PAGE 176 G2

Now the centre for a cattle, sheep and horse breeding district, Murrurundi is an historic town with many buildings classified by the National Trust. The Royal Hotel was built in 1863 on land purchased by surveyor Henry Dangar. Except that it originally had wooden pillars to support the verandah, the pub is exactly the same as it was when the coaches drew up.

Just 30 minutes' drive away are the Timor Caves, on the Isis River. Most are accessible to the public, though some—with a very high carbon dioxide content—have been sealed up. The most famous cave is Main Cave, which bears the signature of Fred Ward (Captain Thunderbolt), the bushranger.

Also close to town is Wallabadah Rock; according to some, only Uluru (Ayers Rock) and Mt Augustus in Western Australia are bigger monoliths. It measures 61 hectares around the base and is 950 metres high. It is on private property, so permission must be sought from the Council to inspect the site.

ACCOMMODATION: Motel Murrurundi, ph (02) 6546 6082; Valley View Motel, ph (02) 6546 6044; White Hart Hotel, ph (02) 6456 6242

ACTIVITIES: Bushwalking, historic interest

TOURIST INFORMATION: Ph (02) 6546 6205

MURWILLUMBAH

874 KM NORTH OF SYDNEY
POPULATION: 8200   MAP REF: PAGE 179 N1

Situated on the Tweed River, about 30 km from its mouth, Murwillumbah (or 'Murbah', as it is known to

The Tweed River flows through Murwillumbah

the locals) is the centre for a rich agricultural district growing sugar cane and bananas and raising dairy cattle. The name means 'good camping ground' or 'place of many possums'.

Always at the mercy of floods, the town has been damaged many times. The local historical society has a collection of photographs documenting the floods, and also of the disastrous fire of 1907.

Murwillumbah is close to four World Heritage listed national parks. Mount Warning National Park is situated around an eroded volcanic plug, named by James Cook in 1770. A walk to the top of Mt Warning (first achieved in 1868) takes an average fit adult from 4 to 5 hours return, and affords stupendous views.

Nightcap National Park takes in Terania Creek, site of massive anti-logging demonstrations in the late 1970s. Its subtropical rainforests are home to several endangered species of birds and animals.

Border Ranges National Park is 38 km west of Murwillumbah. Finally, there is Lamington National Park, which straddles the New South Wales/Queensland border.

ACCOMMODATION: Bushranger Country Resort, ph (02) 6679 7121; Murwillumbah Motor Inn, ph (02) 6672 2022; Poinciana Motel, ph 1800 063 850; Imperial Hotel, ph (02) 6672 1036; Greenhills Caravan Park, ph (02) 6672 2035
ACTIVITIES: Bowls, bushwalking, golf, national park access, swimming, tennis
TOURIST INFORMATION: Ph (02) 6672 1340

MUSWELLBROOK

281 KM NORTH OF SYDNEY
POPULATION: 11 080   MAP REF: PAGE 176 G4
Originally called 'Muscle Brook' (and still pronounced that way), Muswellbrook is both a coalmining town and the centre of an important pastoral and dairying area. In addition, some of the best wines of the Hunter region come from Muswellbrook's vineyards.

Muswellbrook Mine is estimated to have 170 million tonnes of coal reserve. Operating both as an open-cut and underground mine, it produces 2.2 million tonnes of coal a year.

Muswellbrook is part of the Upper Hunter horse stud scene and its race meetings are important events. Nearby Wollemi National Park is a favourite with bushwalkers.

The Spring Wine Festival is held in October.
ACCOMMODATION: Baybrook Motor Inn, ph (02) 6543 4888; John Hunter Motel, ph (02) 6543 4477; Eaton's Hotel, ph (02) 6543 2403; Thetford B&B, ph (02) 6547 9155; Denman Van Village, ph (02) 6547 2590; Pinaroo Leisure Park, ph (02) 6543 3905
ACTIVITIES: Bushwalking, national park access, scenic drives, wineries
TOURIST INFORMATION: Ph (02) 6543 3599

NAMBUCCA HEADS

532 KM NORTH OF SYDNEY
POPULATION: 5000   MAP REF: PAGE 179 N8
Popular both as a stopover and a holiday destination, Nambucca Heads is a tidy town with a history based

around boatbuilding, agriculture and timber-getting. It was here that shipwright John Campbell Stewart built many boats including the *Royal Tar*, which in 1876 was the largest ship built in New South Wales. In 1893 and 1894, it took members of the socialist, teetotal New Australia Association to Paraguay to build new lives there.

The Copenhagen Mill and Shipyard foreshore walk allows visitors to see how huge logs supported the keels of ships being built a hundred years ago.

The Vee Wall Breakwater provides an outdoor gallery for graffiti artists. The breakwater ensures safe water for small boats, sailboards and swimmers. Water sports and fishing are very popular in Nambucca.

Markets are held every second Sunday. In April both the Nambucca Country Music Festival and the local agricultural show are held. In May, the annual 'Trek to the Pub with No Beer' (at Taylors Arm) takes place. The town also has a Septemberfest.
ACCOMMODATION: Destiny Motor Inn, ph (02) 6568 8044; Nambucca Motor Inn, ph (02) 6568 6300; Scotts Guest House, ph (02) 6568 6386; White Albatross Holiday Centre (van park), ph (02) 6568 6468
ACTIVITIES: Bowls, fishing, 4WD touring, golf, horseracing, water sports, tennis
TOURIST INFORMATION: Ph (02) 6568 6954

NAROOMA

370 KM SOUTH OF SYDNEY
POPULATION: 3000   MAP REF: PAGE 174 E7
Popularly called 'Narooma' for many years, it was not until 1972 that the name was officially altered from 'Noorooma' (meaning 'blue water'), the name of an early cattle station. Narooma is a tourist resort, renowned for its big-game fishing. Sawmilling and oyster farming are important industries.

Tuross Lake and Lake Corunna are major attractions, particularly for fishing, and there are many great surfing beaches including Blackfellows Point, Mystery Bay and Bar Beach. Eight kilometres offshore is Montague Island, a flora and fauna reserve.
ACCOMMODATION: Lynch's Hotel, ph (02) 4476 2001; Motel Narooma, ph (02) 4476 4270; Narooma Golfers Lodge (units), ph (02) 4476 2428; Amooran Court (B&B), ph (02) 4476 2198; Island View Beach Resort (camping/caravanning), ph (02) 4476 4600
ACTIVITIES: Fishing, scenic drives, water sports
TOURIST INFORMATION: Ph (02) 4476 2099

NARRABRI

608 KM NORTH-WEST OF SYDNEY
POPULATION: 7300   MAP REF: PAGE 178 E7
'Nurruby' Station was taken up in 1834, and the township of Narrabri was surveyed some 25 years

South Beach at Nambucca Heads

later. Today it is the cotton capital of Australia, and visitors in April through to June will see everything covered by the 'snow' of white cotton.

Several buildings in town date from the late nineteenth century, including the post office. Just west of town, at Culgoora, is the Australia Telescope, which links to others in western New South Wales.

Mount Kaputar National Park lies 53 km to the east. Mount Kaputar is the remnant of an 18-million-year-old volcano, and has slopes covered by open forest and savannah woodland. This national park is very popular with rockclimbers, but also has some short wilderness walks.

Horseracing is a popular pastime, and the town boasts a good racecourse.

Narrabri has an agricultural show in April and a spring festival in October.
ACCOMMODATION: Nandewar Motor Inn, ph (02) 6792 4000; Tommo's Motor Lodge, ph (02) 6792 1922; Council Caravan Park, ph (02) 6792 1294
ACTIVITIES: Bowls, bushwalking, golf, national park access, rock climbing, swimming, tennis
TOURIST INFORMATION: Ph (02) 6872 2280

NARRANDERA

584 KM SOUTH-WEST OF SYDNEY
POPULATION: 5000   MAP REF: PAGE 183 L5
One of the Riverina's earliest settlements, Narrandera was proclaimed in 1863, taking its name from an early pastoral holding. (The name means 'place of lizards'.)

The town is the centre for an economy based on wheat, oats, barley, wool, lucerne, fruit, fat lambs, beef cattle and poultry. Narrandera is on the Murrumbidgee River, which, together with nearby Lake Talbot, means an abundance of water and wildlife.

Narrandera's Race Club has a long history, dating back to 1879, and hosts five major meets each year.

The town also has art galleries and antique shops, and the Parkside Cottage Museum is of interest. Many of the town's buildings have been classified but are being used as restaurants or galleries.

ACCOMMODATION: Narrandera Hotel, ph (02) 6959 2057; Charles Sturt Hotel, ph (02) 6959 2042; Country Roads Motor Inn 1800 028 591; Figtree Hotel/Motel, ph (02) 6959 1888; Historic Star Lodge (B&B), ph (02) 6959 1768; Lake Talbot Caravan Park, ph (02) 6959 1302

ACTIVITIES: Bowls, bushwalking, fishing, golf, horse riding, scenic drives, water sports

TOURIST INFORMATION: Ph (02) 6959 1766

NARROMINE

444 KM WEST OF SYDNEY
POPULATION: 3390   MAP REF: PAGE 176 A4

The town was established by William O'Neill in 1878, almost in the geographic centre of New South Wales, and became famous for its citrus fruits, wheat, prime lambs, wool, vegetables and, latterly, cotton.

Narromine's main non-pastoral claim to fame is its association with flying. Besides having the oldest country aero club in Australia, Narromine was also the landing place for Ross and Keith Smith on their 1920 record-breaking flight from England to Australia. A memorial stone and plaque where their Vickers Vimy came to rest is on the golf course, not far from the clubhouse, and a look at the Aero Club's visitors' book reveals a pageant of Australian aeronautical history: Charles Kingsford Smith, Charles Ulm, Nancy Bird and others.

Today, Narromine continues its love affair with flying: it is the gliding capital of New South Wales and the Australian Gliding Championships are held here.

This town on the Macquarie River—its fertile flats fed by irrigation from Burrendong Dam—has also produced a number of sporting champions, including Olympic sprinter Melissa Gainsford-Taylor and world champion clay target shooter, Kevin Heywood.

ACCOMMODATION: Narromine Hotel/Motel, ph (02) 6889 1017; Stockman Motor Inn, ph (02) 6889 2033; Aerodrome Caravan Park, ph (02) 6889 2129; The Old Farm Caravan Park, ph (02) 6889 1558

ACTIVITIES: Bushwalking, gliding, golf, horseracing, polo and polocrosse, tennis, water sports

TOURIST INFORMATION: Ph (02) 6889 4596

NELSON BAY

224 KM NORTH OF SYDNEY
POPULATION: 5500   MAP REF: PAGE 177 K5

A popular tourist resort on the south-eastern shores of Port Stephens, Nelson Bay was home in the 1800s to a group of Chinese fishermen who caught and salted fish for shipment to China. Commercial fishing is still an important industry, although the tourist dollar is equally important.

This 'blue water wonderland' has an abundance of beaches and wildlife, offering good fishing—both beach and offshore—SCUBA diving in the marine reserves off Fly and Halifax Points, plus bike riding on the tracks around the shoreline.

Little Beach at Nelson Bay

ACCOMMODATION: Leilani Court Motel, ph (02) 4981 3304; Port Stephens Motor Lodge, ph (02) 4981 3366; Dowling Real Estate (apartments), ph (02) 4981 1577; Halifax Holiday Park, ph (02) 4981 1522

ACTIVITIES: Bike riding, bowls, fishing, game fishing, golf, tennis, walking, water sports, whale watching

TOURIST INFORMATION: Ph (02) 4981 1579

NEWCASTLE

173 KM NORTH OF SYDNEY
POPULATION: 500 000   MAP REF: PAGE 177 J6

The largest non-capital city in Australia, Newcastle has also the sixth largest urban area, with more people than Canberra, Darwin, Wollongong or the Gold Coast! Its area extends from Catherine Hill Bay in the south to Nelson Bay in the north and out to Cessnock in the west.

Newcastle has a reputation as being a dirty, brawling industrial city, but its residents and visitors are actually well served with modern air-conditioned shopping centres, activities aplenty and an abundance of things to see. Some of the city's finest Victorian and Edwardian buildings can be found in the Hunter Mall, established in the 1980s. Tourism will become even more important for Australia's answer to Sheffield or Manchester as industry grinds inexorably to a halt, relocated elsewhere. The city started out badly, being a penal settlement for convicts who had transgressed while serving their original sentences. Its reputation even then was 'unsavoury'. The convicts were employed as cedar-getters, miners and lime-burners.

In 1797, the site of the city of Newcastle was discovered by Lieutenant John Shortland, looking for escaped convicts who had stolen a government boat, the *Cumberland*. He sailed up the coast as far as Nelson Bay, and on the return journey, hugging the shore to make sure the convicts had not landed, noticed a small island a short distance from the mainland. He christened it 'The Nob' (now known as Nobbys). The island had obscured an opening to a fine harbour, and as he climbed a hill (now Fort Scratchley) to get a better view of the river and surrounding district, he noticed a seam of coal protruding from the ground, so named the river the 'Coal River'. Fortunately for winemakers who came later, the name was changed to the Hunter River in 1804, in honour of the then Governor of New South Wales. (Coal Valley chardonnay does not exactly have a good marketing ring to it.)

After the penal settlement was moved to Port Macquarie on the instigation of potential settlers, surveyor Henry Dangar was commissioned to supervise and design the layout of Newcastle, but was resisted by free settlers who had taken over the convict cottages, explaining the somewhat chaotic layout of modern-day Newcastle.

One of Newcastle's many beaches

Early industries included coal and timber, later followed by shipbuilding, salt manufacture and copper smelting. This was then supplanted by iron smelting and a steelworks.

Newcastle has had its share of natural disasters, most significant of which was a 1989 earthquake that destroyed buildings and claimed human lives. These days, the city is completely recovered, and seems to have more civic pride than ever before.

Of historical interest is Fort Scratchley, the site of a Japanese submarine attack in 1942 and now home to the Newcastle Region Maritime Museum. In the centre of the city, the Newcastle Regional Museum is a must for everyone. It contains Supernova, Newcastle's Science and Technology exhibits.

On a hill just south of the city is an obelisk which was erected in 1847 when sailors complained that the demolition of a landmark windmill interrupted the correct plotting of their bearings.

Newcastle is close to one of the great 4WD beaches in Australia. To the north is Stockton, a long, treacherous sand trap even for the experienced. Stockton Beach can have the worst sand conditions in Australia, especially when it has been hot, dry and windy. It is a favourite location of fishermen, who run customised 4WDs with wide sand tyres and, usually, V8 engines. Permits are required and are available from the pie shop, 1 km north of the Ladis Lane entrance to the beach.

ACCOMMODATION: Noah's on the Beach (hotel), ph (02) 4929 5181; Lucky Country Hotel, ph (02) 4929 1997; Novocastrian Motor Inn, ph (02) 4926 3688; Tyrell Towers Serviced Apartments, ph (02) 4929 6515; Broadmeadow Motel (Adamstown), ph (02) 4961 4666; Motel Newcastle Heights (Charlestown), ph (02) 4943 3077; Commonwealth Hotel (Cooks Hill), ph (02) 4929 3463; Redhead Beach Caravan Park, ph (02) 4944 8306
ACTIVITIES: Newcastle has everything for the visitor
TOURIST INFORMATION: Ph (02) 4929 9299

NIMBIN

847 KM NORTH OF SYDNEY
POPULATION: 1270   MAP REF: PAGE 179 N2

Nimbin lies north-west of Lismore, just outside the foothills of Nightcap National Park. Before European settlement, it was a place of 'men's business' and male initiation for the Bundjalung tribe. In 1973 the Australian Union of Students selected it as the location for the Aquarius Festival, and Nimbin's fate was sealed. It became a focus for alternative lifestyles and, more significantly, the environmental movement. In real terms, it halted a rural decline in the local dairying industry.

Shop facades still display the original psychedelic murals that were all a part of the 'flower power' of the 1970s, and the Nimbin Museum—devoted to social history—follows a Rainbow Snake through eight rooms, tracing in chronological order: Aboriginal culture, the pioneer days and the hippy era. (The latter includes displays like Kombi vans rescued from lantana bushes, decorated with original 1970s murals.) There is no entry fee, just a voluntary donation. Nimbin is an interesting living social document for those who didn't experience the culture of free love and Jefferson Airplane.

To the northern end of the Nimbin Valley lies Nimbin Rocks, an escarpment covered with forest and containing caves inhabited by bentwing bats.
ACCOMMODATION: The Motel Abode of Peace, ph (02) 6689 1420; Grey Gum Lodge (motel), ph (02) 6689 1713; Rainbow Retreat (B&B), ph (02) 6689 1269; Hotel Freemasons, ph (02) 6689 1246; Nimbin Caravan Park, ph (02) 6689 1402
ACTIVITIES: National park access, scenic drives, walks
TOURIST INFORMATION: Ph (02) 6622 0122

NOWRA

179 KM SOUTH OF SYDNEY
POPULATION: 20 080   MAP REF: PAGE 174 F4

Nowra (an Aboriginal word meaning 'black cockatoo') is a bustling centre for the Shoalhaven district, an area given to dairying, vegetable growing and timber milling. The best way to appreciate the coastal plains on which the city stands is to come in through Kangaroo Valley and look out from the Cambewarra Range, which rises some 600 metres above the surrounding countryside.

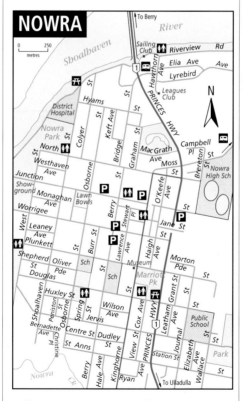

Tourism is very important to Nowra, and it has a lot to offer, including surfing and tranquil lakeside beaches, offshore and riverside fishing.

Meroogal, an historic home built in 1886, is open for public inspection, and Nowra also has an excellent historic museum.

Nowra has long been associated with the Navy's Fleet Air arm, and the base, HMAS *Albatross*, is 9 km south-west of the town. It contains an aviation museum with a magnificent collection of military aircraft, uniforms, engines and memorabilia.
ACCOMMODATION: Empire Hotel, ph (02) 4421 2433;

Kelly's Hotel, ph (02) 4423 3377; Nowra Motor Inn, ph (02) 4421 0555; City Centre Motel, ph (02) 4421 3455; Armstrong's White House (B&B), ph (02) 4421 2084; Coral Tree Lodge (camping/caravans), ph (02) 4447 1358; Crookhaven Heads Tourist Park, ph (02) 4447 2849
ACTIVITIES: Bowls, fishing, golf, scenic drives, squash, tennis, walking, water sports
TOURIST INFORMATION: Ph (02) 4421 0778

NUNDLE

423 KM NORTH-WEST OF SYDNEY
POPULATION: 350   MAP REF: PAGE 177 H2

Located at the foot of the Great Divide, Nundle is an excellent destination for those seeking the peace of quiet walks—alongside the banks of the Peel River— or the majestic beauty of the mountains.

The town sprang up in the goldrush of the 1850s, and visitors can still pick up a little colour here and there with the pan. Prospectors last century took out more than 1.5 million dollars in alluvial gold, but it is thought there is still a great deal of the yellow metal left to be discovered locally. In fact, Nundle is a fossicker's dream, with quartz crystals and other semi-precious stones filling out the wish list. Equipment can be hired in town.

While the historical museum will take hours to see properly, the active are also catered for with trout in well-stocked streams and sailing, swimming and fishing at nearby Chifley Dam.

The Hanging Rock picnic and camping area (not the famous one; that is in Victoria, near Mt Macedon), and Sheba Dams, have some great bushwalks.
ACCOMMODATION: The Peel Inn (hotel), ph (02) 6769 3377; Hills of Gold Motel, ph (02) 6769 3222; Nundle Caravan Park, ph (02) 6769 3355
ACTIVITIES: Bowls, bushwalking, fishing, forest drives, fossicking, tennis, water sports
TOURIST INFORMATION: Ph (02) 6766 9422

NYMBOIDA

683 KM NORTH OF SYDNEY
POPULATION: 350   MAP REF: PAGE 179 M6

Nymboida houses an important power station which supplies electricity right up to the Queensland border. However, it is for whitewater rafting that the town and the river of the same name are famous. This is some of the best, most adrenalin-pumping rafting available in Australia, with rapids like the Devil's Cauldron living up to its name. Not for nothing is the Nymboida Cup canoeing contest held here every September.

Those of more gentle inclination can, however, relax beside the river enjoying live music at the Nymboida Coaching Station—a reference to the old days when Nymboida was a stopover on the Cobb & Co route from Grafton to Armidale.

Nymboida is close to the Nymboi–Binderay National Park, which contains part of the Nymboida and Little Nymboida Rivers and the recreational spots of Cod Hole and the Junction. These embrace areas of rainforest and old-growth forests. There are no defined tracks, but experienced and well-equipped bushwalkers will revel in the conditions.

ACCOMMODATION: Nymboida Canoe Centre, ph (02) 6649 4155

ACTIVITIES: Bushwalking, camping, canoeing, national park access, whitewater rafting

TOURIST INFORMATION: Ph (02) 6642 4677

NYNGAN

571 KM NORTH-WEST OF SYDNEY
POPULATION: 2500   MAP REF: PAGE 181 M7

When Sir Thomas Mitchell came through this outer western district in 1835, he recorded the name 'nyingan', which he took to be 'long pond of water'.

Nyngan during the April 1990 floods

Over the years, Nyngan has had its fair share of water, the most recent disastrous floods being in 1990 and 1997. A social history museum—'The Story of Nyngan'—in Pangee Street, concentrates on the flooding, but covers other aspects of the town's history. It is chiefly an audiovisual museum, housed in the old railway refreshment room.

The district is mostly pastoral, with a number of famous sheep studs in the area. Early stations often had to be abandoned due to conflict with the local Aborigines, but now Nyngan is relatively free of racial tension. Reminders of those early days, and the days before European settlement, can be found on several carved trees in the district, fashioned by the Bogan-gal tribe to commemorate important events.

North of Nyngan is a series of creeks flowing from the Macquarie River into the Bogan River. They are a magnet to inland anglers, attracted to the prospect of catching golden perch, catfish and cod. Bird life is common all along the rivers. The wetlands of the Macquarie Marshes, with their abundance of bird life, are 80 km away to the north-east.

Nyngan's copious reserves of water supply the copper town of Cobar. The area also hosts a number of waterskiing carnivals each year.

In the district, also, is the grave and memorial marker of Mitchell's botanist, Richard Cunningham, who became lost during one of his forays in search of specimens and was killed by Aborigines.

Situated on the Mitchell Highway, Nyngan is the gateway to the legendary Outback towns, with Cobar, Wilcannia and Broken Hill off to the west along the Barrier Highway, and Bourke to the north-west. Bourke is at the end of a 212 km drive along a basically straight road, the journey broken only by the whistle-stops of Girilambone, Coolabah and Byrock.

The Nyngan district has much to offer the adventurous visitor, but tourists should be warned that the summer months can be extremely hot.

ACCOMMODATION: Barrett's Hotel, ph (02) 6832 1028; Canonba Hotel/Motel, ph (02) 6832 1559; Alamo Motor Inn, ph (02) 6832 1660; Illabunda Country Holdings (units), ph (02) 6833 7598; Nyngan Caravan Park & Squash Centre, ph (02) 6832 1705; Riverside Caravan Park, ph (02) 6832 1729

ACTIVITIES: Birdwatching, bowls, fishing, golf, Outback touring, squash, tennis, water sports

TOURIST INFORMATION: Ph (02) 6832 1155

ORANGE

257 KM WEST OF SYDNEY
POPULATION: 33 000   MAP REF: PAGE 176 C7

The location in which the mid-western city of Orange stands was originally known as Blackman's Swamp, after the chief constable of Bathurst, who had accompanied explorer John Oxley into the region in 1818. Fourteen kilometres north-east of Mt Canobolas—an extinct volcano and the highest peak (1395 metres) between the Blue Mountains and the Indian Ocean—Orange was named by Thomas Mitchell, who had fought in the Peninsular War with the Prince of Orange, later King of Holland.

Orange is now the centre for a fertile, productive district. Sheep, cattle and pigs are raised, and wheat, potatoes, peas and other crops are grown. Apple and cherry growing, dairying, and forestry also play a part in the region's economy.

The city has grown from a rich mining past as well. In the 1850s, gold was discovered at nearby Ophir and Lucknow, and regional museums display mining relics, as well as demonstrating what life was like back in the 1880s. Country mansions and historic homes will delight history buffs who take the sign-posted Heritage Trail which winds through the city.

Now, the boom could be on again. Cadia Goldmine—an open-cut gold and copper mine some 25 km from Orange—is operational and should bring new prosperity to an already affluent district.

Orange is justifiably proud of being a sophisticated, cosmopolitan and cultural town. Two of Australia's foremost poets were born there. The first was A. B. 'Banjo' Paterson, and a monument marking the site of his home is located just out of town. An annual festival celebrates the poet's life in Orange. The second was Kenneth Slessor, who spent his early years there before moving to Sydney.

There is a growing cottage industry in unusual culinary produce, such as venison and pickled walnuts, and the town has some good restaurants.

Orange's parks and gardens will also delight the visitor. Cook Park is the most acclaimed. It has a begonia house, a sunken rose garden and huge, ancient trees. Orange Botanic Gardens feature an historic church, a billabong and native trees.

Mt Canobolas is worth visiting as well. Often snowcapped in winter, it has walking trails, lookouts and picnic spots. Visitors can glimpse black-tail wallabies, wombats and many varieties of birds. At the base of the mountain is Lake Canobolas with a picnic spot and swimming hole.

ACCOMMODATION: Canobolas Hotel, ph (02) 6362 2444; Marshall's Carrington Club Hotel, ph (02) 6362 2919; Central Caleula Motor Lodge, ph (02) 6362 6969; Apple City International Motel, ph (02) 6362 6033; Sale Terrace Apartments, ph (02) 6362 6966; Duntry League Guest House, ph (02) 6362 3602; Robinhill B&B, ph (02) 6365 3336; Canobolas Caravan Park, ph (02) 6362 7279

ACTIVITIES: Bowls, bushwalking, golf, historic interest, motocross, swimming,

TOURIST INFORMATION: Ph (02) 6362 4215

PARKES

359 KM WEST OF SYDNEY
POPULATION: 9150   MAP REF: PAGE 176 A6

Goldmining was the original industry in the Parkes district. In 1862, reef gold was found there and was worked for about five years, and then a little later, important finds of alluvial gold were made. The settlement that formed was known as Bushman's, after a mine called Bushman's Lead, but the name was changed in 1873 to honour statesman Sir Henry Parkes (then plain Mr Parkes).

Now the district produces wheat, wool, fat lambs, cattle and pigs, and the town is an important wheat storage centre.

Many people come to Parkes to inspect the CSIRO radio telescope, with its 64 metre diameter saucer-shaped antenna. It is located in the Parkes region because it is a very low radio-interference

The CSIRO telescope at Parkes

zone and normally has low wind speed. The Visitors Centre—open daily—has an excellent audiovisual presentation on how the telescope works.

Other attractions in Parkes include the Henry Parkes Historical Museum (in Clarinda Street, named after the Father of Federation's first wife, Clarinda Varney), which features relics and items from the pioneering and goldmining days. Pioneer Park boasts a collection of historic agricultural implements and machinery and the Motor Museum–Craft Corner has 18 cars on display.

The Parkes Show is held in August while each October long weekend, several hundred people converge on Parkes for an antique motorbike rally.

ACCOMMODATION: Broadway Hotel, ph (02) 6862 2400; International Motor Inn, ph (02) 6862 5222; Parkview Motor Inn, ph (02) 6862 2888; Spicer Park Caravan Park, ph (02) 6862 6162;

ACTIVITIES: Scenic drives, sightseeing, swimming (pool), walking

TOURIST INFORMATION: Ph (02) 6862 4365

PATERSON

207 KM NORTH OF SYDNEY
POPULATION: 50   MAP REF: PAGE 177 J5

Paterson is named after William Paterson, Lieutenant Governor of New South Wales from 1801 to 1809. It was in 1801 that he explored the Hunter River and discovered its two main tributaries, which Governor King named the Paterson and the William Rivers. First European settlement along the banks of the Paterson was in 1820.

Now, with the river trade gone, Paterson is a delightful, placid town with most of its buildings classified by the National Trust. Some of the more notable are: Annadale, an historic residence built in 1839 for Major Edward Johnstone, the local magistrate; the Paterson Tavern (1845), formerly the Commercial Hotel; St Paul's Church and cemetery (1845); the Paterson Court House Museum (1860), which fulfilled its legal function for over 100 years and became a museum in 1974; and St Ann's (1846), the oldest Presbyterian church in Australia still in use.

Not all the classified buildings are nineteenth century: the Paterson School of Arts was built in 1935 and was used as a community hall and movie hall in the 1950s. A quiet stroll through Paterson's streets, largely unchanged since the late 1800s, is very

rewarding, and while some of the private residences are obviously not open to the public, commercial buildings such as the hotels are.

Paterson is close to Tocal Agricultural College.

ACCOMMODATION: Most visitors to the area stay in Dungog, but to the north of Paterson, past Vacy, is Eaglereach Wilderness Resort, ph (02) 4938 8233

ACTIVITIES: Historic interest, scenic drives, walking

TOURIST INFORMATION: Ph (02) 4933 2611

PENRITH

54 KM WEST OF SYDNEY
POPULATION: 84 125   MAP REF: PAGE 176 G8

Say 'Penrith' to any Sydneysider and two images immediately spring to mind. First is Penrith Panthers—reputedly the world's largest club—headquarters of the football club of the same name. Set on over 80 hectares, Panthers has cable water-skiing, mini-car racing, waterslides, swimming pools, a tennis complex and a lake where visitors can windsurf, canoe or have fun with paddle-boats. Inside the building are six restaurants and an array of poker machines to make Las Vegas look deficient.

The second is the Head of the River, the annual rowing competition between the major Sydney boys' private schools. The stretch of the Nepean River used for this contest is so well suited to the sport that Penrith is host city to the canoe and rowing events for the Sydney 2000 Olympics.

Penrith was named by Governor Macquarie after a town in Cumberland, England. (The Aboriginal name for the area was 'mulgoa'—now a suburb in Sydney's outer west, very close to Penrith.) The first European to see this section of the Nepean valley was Captain Watkin Tench in 1879; later Blaxland, Wentworth and Lawson crossed the Nepean at Emu Ford on their way to the Blue Mountains. The town began growing after William Cox built the road over the Blue Mountains, and it experienced a boom when the gold rushes began, as it was the last staging post before the western plains.

Penrith is one of Sydney's fastest-growing areas. Though agriculture and animal raising are still carried on in the district, Penrith is losing its semi-rural appearance. The town has its own personality—a bustling, thriving one.

ACCOMMODATION: Panthers Resort, ph (02) 4721 7700; Penrith Hotel/Motel, ph (02) 4721 2060; Grey Gums Hotel/Motel, ph (02) 4733 1801; Penrith Valley Inn (motel) 1800 021 262; Peachtree Inn (hotel), ph (02) 4731 3444

ACTIVITIES: Bowls, historic interest, squash, tennis, water sports

TOURIST INFORMATION: Ph (02) 4732 7671

PICTON

80 KM SOUTH-WEST OF SYDNEY
POPULATION: 2000   MAP REF: PAGE 176 G10

When the old Hume Highway went through Picton, it was always a traffic bottleneck of epic proportions. Since the expressway bypassed the town, Picton has reverted to a quiet, pleasant village in a rural setting.

Picton has a wonderful historic atmosphere, with its old pub, railway viaduct and narrow streets. It is a useful base from which to visit other attractions like the Thirlmere Railway Museum, or quietly tour the old Hume Highway, now almost deserted.

Picton is also home to the Sydney Skydiving Centre—the largest training facility of its type in the southern hemisphere—catering to experienced jumpers and first timers alike. If you have ever had the urge to jump out of a plane from 4000 metres, this is for you. The Skydiving Centre also has a BBQ and picnic area and offers free camping to its clients.

ACCOMMODATION: Picton Village Motel & Restaurant, ph (02) 4677 2121; Hotel Picton, ph (02) 4677 1416; Wollondilly Caravan Park Community Worker, ph (02) 4677 2689.

ACTIVITIES: Scenic drives, skydiving, walking

TOURIST INFORMATION: Ph (02) 4677 1167

PORT MACQUARIE

425 KM NORTH OF SYDNEY
POPULATION: 39 000   MAP REF: PAGE 177 M2

Named after Governor Macquarie by explorer John Oxley in 1818, 'Port' has had an interesting and varied history. On Oxley's return to Sydney, Macquarie thought the place suitable as a penal settlement for those convicted of crimes in New South Wales. The convicts could be used there to cut down timber and ship it back to Sydney, as timber supplies from the then penal settlement of Newcastle were becoming scarce. So, in October 1821, there were 102 people living in Port Macquarie, plus their military guard.

In 1823, the first sugar cane to be cultivated in Australia was planted here, but by 1830 an influx of free settlers saw the penal settlement come to an end.

Today Port Macquarie services a district where dairying, timber-getting, fishing and oyster farming are the principal industries, but it is also a town where the tourist is king. With two major shopping centres and more than 60 local restaurants ranging from five star to fish and chips, Port is perfect for holidays, or for the transient visitor to restock and revitalise. Located at the mouth of the Hastings River, the town has 85 km of coastline stretching north and south. With good surf, secluded rock pools and sand dunes on hand, the visitor can indulge in any water-based activity, from hiring a jetski to chartering a deep-sea fishing boat.

The area also caters for eco-tourism, with a range of tours through the river systems, rainforest and wilderness locations. Alternatively, camel safaris along the beach or overnight camping by a lagoon, are possible, or taking a river cruise which visits the oyster farm, the canal system and Settlement Point.

For families, there is Peppermint Park, full of outdoor activities, with BBQ facilities. Fantasy World has ghosts, castles and dragons, and train rides. It too has a BBQ and picnic area.

Nearby Wauchope also has Timbertown, a re-creation of life in the pioneering days.

Because it is one of the oldest towns in New South Wales, Port Macquarie has plenty to interest amateur historians. On the corner of Clarence and Hay Streets is the old courthouse, with its high-pitched roof and sweeping verandah. Built in 1868, it originally had a

Crescent Head and its beautiful beaches, to the north of Port Macquarie

lockup and even a post office. There are guided tours daily in the school holidays. Tacking Point Lighthouse, erected in 1879, is also worth a visit.

November is a busy month in Port Macquarie, with both a Novemberfest and the Hastings Valley Expo taking place.

ACCOMMODATION: Sails Resort, ph (02) 6583 3999; Port Pacific Resort, ph (02) 6583 8099; Golden Beaches Motor Inn, ph (02) 6583 8899; Port Macquarie Hotel/Motel, ph (02) 6583 1011; Settlers Inn Hotel, ph (02) 6583 3100; Limeburners Lodge B&B, ph (02) 6583 3381; Shelly Beach Resort (units), ph (02) 6582 3978; Breakers Holiday Units, ph (02) 6583 1625; Leisure Caravan Park & Units, ph (02) 6583 1261; Edgewater Holiday Park, ph (02) 6583 2799

ACTIVITIES: Bowls, fishing, golf, historic interest, surfing, swimming, tennis, theme parks, water sports

TOURIST INFORMATION: Ph (02) 6583 1293

QUEANBEYAN

313 KM SOUTH-WEST OF SYDNEY
POPULATION: 27 000   MAP REF: PAGE 174 C5

There were two tribes, the Ngunawal and the Ngarruga, in the Queanbeyan district when Europeans first arrived in the early 1820s. One settler borrowed a word from them to call his property 'Quinbean' ('clear waters'); this became Queanbeyan.

One of the fastest growing towns in New South Wales due to its proximity to Canberra—it is a favourite with commuters—Queanbeyan represents a delightful blend of modern conveniences and a wonderful sense of history. Many of the old buildings are being used for vastly different purposes than originally intended. The museum is housed in an 1876 building which was originally the police sergeant's residence; Hibernia Lodge, a two-storey cottage in spacious grounds built in 1865 for the Queanbeyan Clerk of Petty Sessions, is now a private residence and gallery.

Of added interest in the town is a memorial to a local resident, William James Farrer, who developed rust-resistant strains of wheat on his property.

Queanbeyan makes a good base for touring the countryside. Nearby is historic Bungendore, and further on, Braidwood. The nation's capital is literally, 'just up the road'.

ACCOMMODATION: Hotel Queanbeyan, ph (02) 6297 3299; Walsh's Hotel, ph (02) 6297 1001; Burley Griffin Motel, ph (02) 6297 1211; Rainbow Motel, ph (02) 6297 2784; Village Cabins, ph (02) 6297 1255; Crestview Tourist Park (camping/caravans), ph (02) 6297 2443

ACTIVITIES: Bowls, fishing, golf, historic interest, scenic drives, squash, swimming, tennis, walking

TOURIST INFORMATION: Ph (02) 6298 0241

QUIRINDI

383 KM NORTH-WEST OF SYDNEY
POPULATION: 3100   MAP REF: PAGE 176 G2

The district surrounding Quirindi, part of the fertile Liverpool Plains, produces wool, grain and seed crops, lucerne, lambs, cattle, pigs, poultry, dairy products and vegetables. Thomas Mitchell, in 1831, referred to the area as 'Cuerindi', thought to be an Aboriginal word for 'nest in the hills'. Squatters had already moved in by the 1820s and the town was proclaimed in 1856.

One of the first towns in New South Wales where polo was played, Quirindi continues its equine love affair with a polo meeting in August, as well as the Quirindi Rodeo and regular race meetings. The Turf Club has been in existence for over 50 years and considers its racecourse to be the 'showcourse of country racing'.

There is also a small folklore museum housed in an historic cottage.

ACCOMMODATION: Motel Quirindi, ph (02) 6746 1777; Quirindi Heritage Motel, ph (02) 6746 1742; Quirindi Caravan Park, ph (02) 6746 2407

ACTIVITIES: Bowls, golf, horse riding, horseracing, polo, scenic drives, tennis

TOURIST INFORMATION: Ph (02) 6768 4462

RAYMOND TERRACE

201 KM NORTH OF SYDNEY
POPULATION: 9250   MAP REF: PAGE 177 J5

Governor Macquarie visited Raymond Terrace in 1812 and 1818. It was known even then by that name. The village was gazetted in 1837 and the court house, built in 1838, is still in use. By the 1840s the town was really booming, a busy centre where wool, transported by road from the New England district, was shipped to Sydney via the river. These days, agriculture and dairying are the principal primary industries, but the area supports a number of productive secondary industries.

Situated on the Pacific Highway, Raymond Terrace is always busy, but the visitor should escape from the traffic and noise to take the Heritage Walk and wander around the historic buildings of the town—not only the court house but also the first homestead, Irrawang (built in 1830), the Anglican church and its rectory. Some 8 km out of town is Sketchley Pioneer Cottage and at nearby Williamtown, the RAAF has an aircraft museum.

Raymond Terrace is a good base for 4WD tours and for anglers who want to spend extended time on nearby Stockton Beach, just past Williamtown.

ACCOMMODATION: Spinning Wheel Hotel, ph (02) 4987 2381; Clare Castle Hotel, ph (02) 4987 2078; Colonial Motel, ph (02) 4987 2244; Sleepy Hill Motel, ph (02) 4987 2321;Pacific Gardens Caravan Park, ph (02) 4987 6636

ACTIVITIES: Bowls, 4WD touring, golf, swimming

TOURIST INFORMATION: Ph (02) 4987 3122

RICHMOND

60 KM NORTH-WEST OF SYDNEY
POPULATION: 15 500   MAP REF: PAGE 176 G8

In 1789 Governor Phillip climbed a hill near the junction of the Hawkesbury and Grose Rivers and named it Richmond Hill. In the next ten years, farmers grew wheat on the lowlands by the river, often suffering disastrously due to flooding. In 1810, Governor Macquarie founded Richmond, one of five Hawkesbury River towns that would be above the high-water mark (or so the theory went). The schoolhouse (1813) was the first building, and it also served as a church.

These days vegetables and corn are grown on the river flats and dairy cows are raised. The RAAF has a base here from where it conducts pilot training, usually in Hercules transports, and the University of Western Sydney's campus is just south of the town.

Visits to the local cemeteries are useful for those interested in Australian history. Roadbuilder William Cox, for example, is buried in the grounds of St Peter's Church, built in 1841.

Richmond Estate, where connoisseurs can taste and purchase fine wines, is close by.

ACCOMMODATION: Richmond Inn Motel, ph (02) 4758 1044

ACTIVITIES: Scenic drives, sightseeing, wineries

TOURIST INFORMATION: Ph (02) 4587 7388

ROBERTSON

143 KM SOUTH OF SYDNEY
POPULATION: 300   MAP REF: PAGE 174 F3

Famous for its potatoes, Robertson sits high at the crest of Macquarie Pass, and is about halfway between the coast and the Southern Highlands. A

pretty little village, it offers many nearby vantage points for spectacular views right down the coast. It can also get very cold in winter, so visitors should choose their timing.

Robertson is very close to natural attractions like Fitzroy Falls. Nearby Morton National Park provides bushwalkers with some wonderful walking trails.

ACCOMMODATION: Country Inn Hotel, ph (02) 4885 1202; Motel Robertson Country, ph (02) 4885 1444; Ranelagh House (B&B), ph (02) 4885 1111

ACTIVITIES: Bushwalking, national park access

TOURIST INFORMATION: Ph (02) 4871 2888

RYLSTONE

241 KM NORTH-WEST OF SYDNEY
POPULATION: 800   MAP REF: PAGE 176 E4

A picturesque town with many historic buildings, Rylstone is some 50 km south-east of Mudgee. The town was surveyed in 1842, and a counter lunch at one of the pubs can almost have you believing that you are back in those days.

Many visitors come to see the Aboriginal painting on sandstone overhangs not far from the town centre. Rylstone's proximity to Lake Windamere also has great tourist appeal. Lake Windamere offers all sorts of water sports, with a large picnic area and many boat ramps. It is extremely popular with fishermen.

Using Rylstone as a base, the visitor is in striking distance of all of Mudgee's wineries, or by heading north-east through Wollemi and Goulburn River National Parks, the vineyards of the Hunter. (The latter is a very pretty drive, but the roads are narrow and wind up and down the mountain ranges, so exercise care.)

ACCOMMODATION: Apex Caravan Park, ph (02) 6379 1165

ACTIVITIES: Aboriginal art sites, fishing, national park access, scenic drives, swimming, wineries

TOURIST INFORMATION: Ph (02) 6372 5874

SAWTELL

580 KM NORTH OF SYDNEY
POPULATION: 6500   MAP REF: PAGE 179 N7

For centuries Aborigines hunted and fished on the waterway known now as Bonville Creek, at Sawtell. Then came the cedar-getters in 1863, and slowly, more Europeans followed. A village was proclaimed in 1923 and named after Oswald Sawtell, a landowner. Now it is a thriving holiday centre, with fishing, boating and swimming the major attractions.

Just 6 km south of Coffs Harbour, Sawtell has tree-lined streets and a rustic village atmosphere. It boasts a fully restored cinema, shops, restaurants and cafés, a million dollar RSL club and on the first Saturday of the month, street markets.

There are plenty of sporting facilities too. Besides beach swimming, there are alternatives in a safe rockpool and sandy creeks. Sawtell also has an 18-hole golf course. Anglers can choose between beach, rock and estuary fishing, and there are boat ramps at Bonville Creek and Boambee Creek.

In January, Sawtell celebrates with a Country Music Festival; in June, the mood changes with an annual Jazz and Blues Festival; and there is a big Street Party in December.

ACCOMMODATION: Boambee Bay Resort, ph (02) 6653 2700; Sawtell Hotel, ph (02) 6653 1213; The Coasters Motel, ph (02) 6653 1541; Sawtell Motel Beach Haven, ph (02) 6653 1659; Town Terrace (units), ph (02) 6653 1989; Sawtell Beach Caravan Park, ph (02) 6653 1379

ACTIVITIES: Bowls, croquet, fishing, golf, tennis, water sports

TOURIST INFORMATION: Ph (02) 6652 1522

SCONE

306 KM NORTH-WEST OF SYDNEY
POPULATION: 4235   MAP REF: PAGE 176 G3

'The Horse Capital of Australia', Scone is surrounded by rich pastoral country in the Upper Hunter Valley. There are 65 horse studs—a veritable honour roll, with 'Alabama', 'Arrowfield', 'Segenhoe' and 'Wakefield' being merely the tip of the top. Some studs are open to the public on certain days during the Scone Horse Festival in May. For horse lovers, the Australian Stock Horse Museum in Kelly Street is also worth visiting.

Besides horse studs and some noted sheep stations, the district also produces some fine wines—the vineyard of Birnam Wood is the latest addition to the viticultural register.

Scone is a wealthy town with all modern conveniences, but for the average tourist, it is probably what is around the town that will excite the most interest. Twenty kilometres to the north of town, up the New England Highway, is the Burning Mountain, a burning coal seam that is believed to have been alight for 1000 years. The Aborigines called it 'the Stone Woman of Fire'.

Middlebrook Station is closer to town. It is a working property with displays of shearing and mustering and is owned by the Henderson family. Groups of ten or more can have morning tea, lunch or afternoon tea in a converted shearing shed.

On the other side of town, on the Gundy road, is Belltrees historic homestead, which welcomes visitors. This property, with its shearing shed, museum, chapel and stables, has been in the White family for seven generations. Further out are the old goldmining areas at Moonan Flat (where there is a very good pub!) and Moonan Brook. On the same road you will eventually come to the famed Barrington Tops.

It is a magnificent drive into the Tops from Moonan Flat, climbing constantly, with superb views over the entire Upper Hunter Valley. The road, however, is dirt and very corrugated, so care must be taken at all times. At the top of the climb there is a large dingo gate which must be opened—and closed! The variation in altitude from valley floor to top of the range is so great that you can see subtropical rainforest, Antarctic beeches and snow gums all in the same day. (The Tops is the highest range in Australia after the Snowy Mountains.)

Once on the plateau, visitors can make use of many walking tracks, or, by arrangement with the

National Parks and Wildlife Service, 4WD trails. Polblue Swamp is most unusual: it is a large sphagnum moss swamp bisected by channels of icy cold water. There are duckboard walking paths so visitors can appreciate the beauty without damaging this unique environment. From there, it is down the other side to Gloucester, but be warned that there is no fuel between Moonan Flat and Gloucester—a distance of 65 km.

Further south is Glenbawn Dam—Scone's aquatic playground. Twice the size of Sydney Harbour, the Lake Glenbawn State Recreation Area provides sweeping views, boating, water sports, bushwalking, fishing, golf, horse riding and picnic and BBQ facilities. Cottages, cabins and camping spots are available for those who want to stay longer than a day.

The rural landscape around Scone

ACCOMMODATION: Golden Fleece Hotel, ph (02) 6545 1357; Aberdeen Hotel, ph (02) 6543 7381; Airlie House (motel), ph (02) 6545 1488; Folly Foot Motel, ph (02) 6545 3079; March House B&B, ph (02) 6545 2076; Belltrees (farmstay), ph (02) 6545 1688; Highway Caravan Park, ph (02) 6545 1078; Scone Caravan Park, ph (02) 6543 7193

ACTIVITIES: Bushwalking, fishing, 4WD touring, golf, hockey, horse riding, horse trials, national park access, polo, polocrosse, water sports, wineries

TOURIST INFORMATION: Ph (02) 6545 1526

SHELLHARBOUR

130 KM SOUTH OF SYDNEY
POPULATION: 2000   MAP REF: PAGE 174 G3

Shellharbour gets its name from the large number of Aboriginal middens in the area, all listed by the Heritage Commission and regarded as archaeologically significant. In the 1830s Shellharbour was used as a port and by 1855, an embryonic village had formed, but with the coming of the railway, its importance declined—until tourism.

Just 22 km south of Wollongong, Shellharbour is extremely popular with surfers, but there are other things to do. To the north, surrounded by a 25 km cycleway, Lake Illawarra affords the opportunity of waterskiing, sailboarding, canoeing, paddleboating, fishing and prawning. To the south is the Marine Aquatic Reserve at Bushrangers Bay, a favourite spot for snorkellers and SCUBA divers. The rainforest at Macquarie National Park is also a big attraction.

ACCOMMODATION: Blackbutt Motel, ph (02) 4295 1317; Ocean Beach Hotel/Motel, ph (02) 4296 1399; Shellharbour Beachside Tourist Park, ph (02) 4295 1133

ACTIVITIES: Bowls, bushwalking, fishing, golf, national park access, prawning, scenic drives, water sports

TOURIST INFORMATION: Ph (02) 4228 0300

SILVERTON

1186 KM NORTH-WEST OF SYDNEY
POPULATION: 50   MAP REF: PAGE 180 A8

Originally known as Umberumberka, Silverton achieved its current name in 1880 following the discovery of rich silver-lead ore. In 1883 extensive rushes again occurred and the town was surveyed, but rich finds at Broken Hill, 25 km to the south-east, attracted the miners and from housing a population of 3000, Silverton quickly declined. The final straw was the closure of the Silverton Tramway—a private railway linking Broken Hill with Cockburn, South Australia, via Silverton—in 1970.

With its red earth and blue sky, its harsh, unyielding landscape, Silverton is popular with filmmakers. Indeed, *Mad Max II*, *A Town Like Alice* and *Razorback* were all shot there. (Visitors should see the vast Mundi Mundi Plains, where the chase scenes in *Mad Max* were filmed.)

The Silverton Hotel

Silverton has many historic buildings, including the old gaol and the museum. The town is full of artists and galleries. Visitors can ride camels, go underground at nearby Day Dream Mine, which opened in 1885, picnic at Umberumberka Reservoir or camp at Penrose Park. There is also a two-hour walking trail which winds through creeks, valleys and the town itself. The Visitors' Centre is a tiny schoolhouse where Dame Mary Gilmour, the poet, was once a teacher.

ACCOMMODATION: Silverton Hotel, ph (08) 8088 5313

ACTIVITIES: Historic interest, sightseeing

TOURIST INFORMATION: Ph (08) 8087 6077

SINGLETON

234 KM NORTH OF SYDNEY
POPULATION: 19 000   MAP REF: PAGE 177 H5

On the New England Highway in the Hunter Valley, Singleton is an elegant town with historic buildings and old-style rose gardens. European settlement dates back to the early 1800s, but before that the district was home to the Wanuaruah people. The first white man to arrive was John Howe, chief constable of Windsor. Benjamin Singleton, a member of his party, settled there on a grant of land and in 1836 subdivided part of his land as the town of Singleton. He put his residence near a ford across the Hunter and the town grew up around him. Coal has been mined in the district since 1870.

Now Singleton services both the miners and a district producing milk and cheese, fat lambs, beef cattle, wool, stock feed, fruit and vegetables. There are also a number of wineries in the area.

Singleton boasts the southern hemisphere's largest sundial and visitors should also inspect the gardens at the historic house, Townhead. Nearby Lake St Clair, formed by the Glennies Creek Dam in 1983, is 26 km from Singleton via the Bridgeman Road. The recreation area has free electric BBQs, hot water, showers and toilet facilities. Overnight camping is allowed, and there is a boat ramp. Canoeing, sailing, sailboarding, swimming and fishing are popular local pastimes. There are plenty of opportunities for bushwalking as well, as Wollemi, Yengo and Barrington Tops National Parks are within easy striking distance.

ACCOMMODATION: Charbonnier in the Hunter (motel), ph (02) 6572 2333; Benjamin Singleton (motel), ph (02) 6572 2922; Agricultural Hotel/Motel, ph (02) 6572 1511; Caledonian Hotel, ph (02) 6572 1356; Club House Hotel, ph (02) 6572 1274; The Terraces (serviced units), ph (02) 6572 1088; Downahill B&B, ph (02) 6577 5608; Fairoak Guesthouse & B&B, ph (02) 6571 1586; Country Acres Park (camping/caravanning), ph (02) 6572 2328; Wyland Caravan Park, ph (02) 6571 1744

ACTIVITIES: Bushwalking, coalmine inspections, fishing, golf, national park access, scenic drives, sightseeing, tennis, water sports, wineries

TOURIST INFORMATION: Ph (02) 6572 4197

SOFALA

243 KM NORTH-WEST OF SYDNEY
POPULATION: 100   MAP REF: PAGE 176 D6

In the Turon River Valley, Sofala is the oldest gold town in Australia. Settled only three weeks after the strike at Ophir, the population quickly swelled to around 40 000. It is a little different today, but Sofala, with its weathered buildings and picturesque setting, is very much worth a visit. You can still get a beer at the Royal Hotel, and do a little fossicking as well.

The surrounding district grows superfine wool, and most of the properties have relics and remnants of the old days. One, Chesleigh Homestead, contains 7 km of the original Cobb & Co coach road to Hill End. It also has extensive underground mines, alluvial diggings, water-races (used to sluice river gravel to

The beautiful township of Sofala

search for gold), old shanties and hectares of land and history to explore. The 1400 hectare property has 3 km of river frontage, horses, tennis courts, games room, gold-fossicking equipment, fishing tackle, a swimming pool and spa. It takes house guests.

ACCOMMODATION: Chesleigh Homestead, ph (02) 6337 7077

ACTIVITIES: Fossicking, 4WD touring, scenic drives, sightseeing

TOURIST INFORMATION: Ph (02) 6132 1444

SOUTH WEST ROCKS

498 KM NORTH OF SYDNEY
POPULATION: 3100   MAP REF: PAGE 179 N9

The largest seaside town in the Macleay Valley, South West Rocks boasts a variety of beautiful beaches and a rich history. Trial Bay Gaol, for example, was first occupied in 1886, and was used to intern 500 German prisoners in World War I. Smoky Cape Lighthouse, the highest in New South Wales, has terrific views and is well worth seeing. Before the lighthouse was built, several ships were wrecked locally, including the *Koodooloo*, whose rusting remains can be seen off Main Beach. A fully restored boatman's cottage provides tourist information, maritime history—even local art and crafts.

South West Rocks also has an aquarium, and visitors can charter boats for marine adventures. The area is extremely popular with divers.

Nearby Arakoon State Recreation Area and Hat Head National Park are good for bushwalking.

The town has good restaurants, and its varied accommodation and both family and surfing beaches make it an ideal getaway spot.

ACCOMMODATION: Sea Breeze Hotel, ph (02) 6566 6205; Bay Motel, ph (02) 6566 6909; South West Rocks Motel, ph (02) 6566 6330; South West Rocks Holiday Villas, ph (02) 6566 6126; Macleay Valley Caravan Park, ph (02) 6566 6264; Arakoon State Recreation Area (camping), ph (02) 6566 6168

ACTIVITIES: Bowls, bushwalking, fishing, golf, national park access, squash, tennis, water sports
TOURIST INFORMATION: Ph (02) 6563 1555

SPRINGWOOD

72 KM WEST OF SYDNEY
POPULATION: 5885   MAP REF: PAGE 176 F8
On his way to Bathurst in 1815, Governor Macquarie was impressed by 'a pretty wooded Plain near a Spring of very good fresh Water'. He called the place 'Spring-Wood'. Today Springwood is a residential centre and tourist resort in the lower Blue Mountains, 310 metres above sea level.

Most people who come to Springwood are bushwalkers, and there are a number of tracks, ranging from easy to sweaty, in close proximity to the village. More sedentary folk may like to browse through the antique stores or visit the Local History Centre and community art gallery. These are both housed in Braemar, a National Trust Federation home. Springwood railway station is also a listed property. The grave of Sir Henry Parkes, Father of Federation and after whom the central western town of Parkes was named, lies in Springwood cemetery.
ACCOMMODATION: Pioneer Way Motel, ph (02) 4751 2194
ACTIVITIES: Bushwalking, national park access, scenic drives, sightseeing
TOURIST INFORMATION: Ph (02) 4739 6299

STROUD

163 KM NORTH OF SYDNEY
POPULATION: 500   MAP REF: PAGE 177 K4
In 1826, the Australian Agricultural Company purchased 400 000 hectares of land in the Port Stephens area and proceeded to develop Stroud as a company headquarters. Built by convicts, Stroud's construction was overseen by Sir Edward Parry, a former Arctic explorer. His wife supervised the construction of St John's Anglican Church, a Gothic Revival structure made from the clay bricks of the area. Another building using the same materials, also convict-built, was the Australian Inn, the first pub in Stroud and, like the church, erected in 1833.

In 1918, Alfred Bowen bought the inn—by now a dilapidated remnant of its past—and painstakingly demolished it brick by brick. Using those same materials—bricks, fireplaces, cedar doors and skirting boards—he then built Chalford House, which remained in the Bowen family until 1996, when it was bought by the current owners. It is now once again opened to travellers.

Stroud is full of history and classified buildings, and one unusual event. Every year, it holds an international brick-throwing contest between four centres named Stroud: one here, one in England, one in Canada and one in the United States.
ACCOMMODATION: Central Hotel, ph (02) 4994 5197; Chalford House (B&B or extended stays), ph (02) 4994 5429
ACTIVITIES: Scenic drives, sightseeing
TOURIST INFORMATION: Ph (02) 6554 8799

SWANSEA

58 KM NORTH OF SYDNEY
POPULATION: 7900   MAP REF: PAGE 177 J6
Now practically a suburb of Newcastle, Swansea began life as Pelican Flats and, like many Australian towns, had a somewhat dubious history. In the 1830s, a salt works was established here, but when it went bankrupt, escaped convicts used the deserted buildings as hideouts—a practice that continued into the late 1840s, with bushrangers joining the convicts.

In the 1850s, a family of boatbuilders called Boyd moved into the area and began salt-curing fish, and by the 1860s, many small farms had sprung up to supply a burgeoning marine cargo trade in timber and coal. However, any hopes locally entertained that Pelican Flats would become a mighty shipping port were ill-founded. The opening of the railway from Sydney to Newcastle in 1889 diminished the importance of shipping.

Now Swansea is a popular fishing and boating spot. Tourism is a valuable money-spinner.
ACCOMMODATION: Blue Pacific Motor Inn, ph (02) 4971 1055; Swansea Motel, ph (02) 4971 1811; Swansea Hotel, ph (02) 4971 1227; Swansea Gardens Tourist Park, ph (02) 4971 2869; Sunstrip Caravan Park, ph (02) 4971 1165
ACTIVITIES: Fishing, water sports
TOURIST INFORMATION: Ph (02) 4929 9299

TAMWORTH

440 KM NORTH OF SYDNEY
POPULATION: 55 000   MAP REF: PAGE 176 G1
Tamworth was named after the Staffordshire town represented by British Prime Minister Robert Peel, after whom the Peel River was named. John Oxley was the first white explorer in the district in 1818. By 1830 squatters had moved in but they were dispossessed in 1834 when the Australian Agricultural Company was granted two massive holdings, the larger of which took in the site of Tamworth.

The town was gazetted in 1850. The discovery of gold at nearby Nundle further stimulated growth in Tamworth which, even at that stage, was an important coaching station.

Sometimes called 'The City of Light' Tamworth was the first town in Australia to have electric street lighting. At the centennial celebrations for this event in 1988, the Power Station was made into a museum.

Proclaimed a city in 1946, Tamworth is famous Australia-wide for its annual Country Music Festival, an 11-day event featuring all branches of 'country', from ballads to bluegrass and bush poetry. There is a harmonica championship, guitar workshops, even a street parade. The event regularly attracts around 30 000 visitors. As a result of the festival, the Gallery of Stars (a waxworks of the Country & Western famous) and the Hands Of Stone Corner (handprints) have been set up in the city.

Calala Cottage is a townhouse built in 1875 for Philip Gidley King, first Mayor of Tamworth. ('Calala', incidentally, means 'place of battle' and was the Aborigines' name for the Peel River.)

The Art Gallery has works by Hans Heysen and Julian Ashton, and an excellent collection of Australian silver and ivory figurines. The Pyramid Planetarium, north of the town, has a display of the solar system reproduced in miniature.

There are many natural attractions in the area, including Warabah National Park and Sheba Dams Reserve. Keepit State Recreation Area, with its availability of water sports, is 57 km to the south.
ACCOMMODATION: Good Companions Hotel, ph (02) 6766 2850; Powerhouse Boutique Motor Inn, ph (02) 6766 7000; Riley's Motel Australia, ph (02) 6765 9258; Roseville Apartments (serviced), ph (02) 6765 3644; Quince's B&B, ph (02) 6766 2589; Rex Guest House, ph (02) 6766 1030; Paradise Caravan Park, ph (02) 6766 3120
ACTIVITIES: Bowls, clay target shooting, horse riding, national park access, scenic drives, squash, tennis, water sports
TOURIST INFORMATION: Ph (02) 6768 4462

Line dancers at Tamworth's Country Music Festival

TAREE

333 KM NORTH OF SYDNEY
POPULATION: 17 125   MAP REF: PAGE 177 L3

'Taree' is a diminutive of the Aboriginal word 'tareebit', which described a particular fig tree growing in the Manning Valley. It stands on a grant of land made to William Wynter, first permanent settler on the Manning, who moved to the area in about 1831. A private town was laid out by Henry Flett, Wynter's son-in-law, in the early 1850s.

Now the town is the commercial and industrial centre of a district given chiefly to dairying, timber cutting, mixed farming and fishing. It offers much to the tourist: river cruises, horse riding, 4WD tours, but its chief appeal lies in nearby attractions.

Crowdy Bay National Park is 35 km to the north and is noted for fishing and surfing. Diamond Head is the main camping area in the park, with BBQ and toilets, but visitors must bring in their own water—something that holds true for the entire 6000 hectare reserve of coastal plains. There are good walking trails in the park as well. Australian author Kylie Tennant wrote the novel *The Man on the Headland* in a self-built hut on Diamond Head.

Boorganna Nature Reserve—the second one declared in the state—covers 396 hectares and is just over 6 km west of town. It features a walking track through rainforest.

Five kilometres south of town is Kiwarrack State Forest, perfect for car tourers, as it offers a magnificent scenic drive. The best spots are the Pines Picnic Area and Breakneck Lookout. All up, it is a 16 km drive through the forest. Another area worth visiting is Coopernook State Forest, which offers spectacular views of the Manning Valley. Middle Brother Forest has several walking trails, one of which passes the two largest blackbutt trees in the state—'Bird Tree' and 'Benaroon'.

In June Taree hosts its annual Envirofair; in August, the Gold Cup Racing Carnival and in October, the Taree Show and Spring Expo.
ACCOMMODATION: Exchange Hotel, ph (02) 6552 1160; Fotheringham's Hotel, ph (02) 6552 1153; City Centre Motor Inn, ph (02) 6552 5244; Caravilla Motor Inn, ph (02) 6552 1822; Cabbage Tree Island (caravans & camping), ph (02) 6553 3222; Twilight Caravan Park, ph (02) 6552 2857
ACTIVITIES: Bowls, fishing, 4WD touring, golf, greyhound and horse racing, national park access, scenic drives, sightseeing, squash, tennis, water sports
TOURIST INFORMATION: Ph (02) 6552 1900

TATHRA

461 KM SOUTH OF SYDNEY
POPULATION: 1300   MAP REF: PAGE 174 E8

Smallest of the towns on the Sapphire Coast, Tathra lies between Bermagui and Merimbula, and is rich in history and marine tradition. The historic timber wharf has been restored by the National Trust and now houses a museum in its old cargo shed. It is a mecca for anglers, history lovers and photographers.

Tathra Beach is 3 km long and is patrolled in summer. Offering good surfing, it also gives anglers the chance at salmon and tailor. Mogareka Inlet is safer for small children. There is also good SCUBA diving at Tathra, with local corals, underwater caves and shipwrecks providing plenty of interest.

Visitors can also camp and bushwalk at nearby Mimosa Rocks National Park and Bournda State Recreation Area.
ACCOMMODATION: Surfside Motel, ph (02) 6494 1378; Tathra Hotel/Motel, ph (02) 6494 1101; Tathra Beach House Holiday Apartments (serviced), ph (02) 6494 1944; The Waves Holiday Units, ph (02) 6494 1465; Tathra Lodge Guest House B&B, ph (02) 6494 4084; Tathra Beach Motor Village (camping/caravans), ph (02) 6494 1577
ACTIVITIES: Bowls, bushwalking, fishing, national park access, scenic drives, tennis, water sports
TOURIST INFORMATION: Ph (02) 6494 4062

TEMORA

458 KM SOUTH-WEST OF SYDNEY
POPULATION: 4600   MAP REF: PAGE 183 N4

With a name thought to be of Celtic rather than Aboriginal origin, Temora services the Riverina's wheat district.

The first white settlers came in the 1850s and 1860s, carving themselves huge runs, but the population remained small until Temora Goldfield was proclaimed in 1880, bringing 20 000 people into the district. There were some great finds, including the Mother Shipton nugget, a facsimile of which is in the town's Rock and Mineral Museum. This is housed inside the award-winning Temora Rural Museum, and also features Temora Greenstone, much sought after by lapidarists. A special exhibit is the Paragon Gold Project, near town.

During World War II, over 10 000 RAAF personnel passed through training at Temora, and with one of the most fog-free strips in the state, it continues its aviation traditions today with civilian training, gliding and skydiving.

Temora holds its annual show in September and has markets every last Saturday of the month except for December and January.
ACCOMMODATION: Goldtera Motor Inn, ph (02) 6977 2433; Aromet Motel, ph (02) 6977 1877; Temora Budget Motel, ph (02) 6977 1866; Temora Council's Caravan Park, ph (02) 6977 1712
ACTIVITIES: Fossicking, flying, gliding, sightseeing, skydiving
TOURIST INFORMATION: Ph (02) 6978 0500

TENTERFIELD

758 KM NORTH OF SYDNEY
POPULATION: 3400   MAP REF: PAGE 179 K3

Tenterfield began in the 1840s, when a resident gave the name to his property. It is now the centre of a cattle-raising district which also produces wool, maize and cold-climate fruits.

Tenterfield is justifiably proud of its history, and there are two historic walks for visitors. One takes an hour or so and takes in the Post Office (1881), with its Italianate façade, clock tower and metal mansard roof. The walk also passes the School of Arts where, on 24 October 1889, Henry Parkes made an impassioned speech which started the impetus for independence and culminated in Federation on 1 January 1901. The walk also includes St Stephen's Presbyterian Church (1884), where the social event of 1903 was the marriage of Alice Walker to A. B. 'Banjo' Paterson. The Technical College (1870) was used by Cobb & Co as a change station for horses. The Centenary Museum and Petrie Cottage, also en route,

Bald Rock in Bald Rock National Park, north of Tenterfield

house interesting collections of Tenterfield memorabilia. Also on the walk is the Tenterfield Saddlery, immortalised by Peter Allen in the song about his grandfather, George Woolnough, and family. Built in 1860 of hand-cut blue granite, it is the town's most popular tourist destination.

The building that housed the Tenterfield *Star* is another feature. *The Star* was first published in 1870 and one of its editors was Major J. F. Thomas, who defended 'Breaker' Morant at his court martial in South Africa during the Boer War.

A second walk takes in Salisbury House, built for Isaac Whereat, who had been first mate on Nelson's flagship *Victory* before coming to Australia.

There are natural attractions in the vicinity of Tenterfield as well. Bluff Rock—a huge piece of granite 10 km south of town on the New England Highway—commemorates a dark page in the district's history. Following attacks by Aborigines on shepherds and sheep, the hands at Bolivia Station attacked them at Pye's Creek, drove them towards Bluff Rock, then, legend has it, threw them over.

Woollool Woolloolni, also close to town, has been declared an Aboriginal Place. This 370 hectare reserve features a massive mushroom-shaped rock standing out from the other boulders, and is sacred to the Aborigines, who now run cultural tours to tell the Dreamtime story. A 4WD vehicle is needed to get right up to the site.

Ghost Gully, an unusual example of erosion, is beloved by photographers, and the famous Bald Rock National Park is only 29 km to the north.

ACCOMMODATION: Commercial Hotel, ph (02) 6736 1027; Jumbuck Motor Inn, ph (02) 6736 2055; Tally-Ho Motor Inn, ph (02) 6736 1577; Royal Hotel/Motel, ph (02) 6736 1833; Spring Valley Cottage (B&B), ph (02) 6736 1798; Barney Downs (B&B), ph (02) 6732 2610; Seven Knights Caravan Park, ph (02) 6736 2005; Craig's Caravan Park, ph (02) 6736 1585

ACTIVITIES: Bowls, golf, national park access, scenic drives, sightseeing, swimming, tennis

TOURIST INFORMATION: Ph (02) 6736 1082

TERRIGAL

98 KM NORTH OF SYDNEY
POPULATION: 7500   MAP REF: PAGE 177 J7
Terrigal translates as 'place of little birds'. This town and tourist resort on the Central Coast of New South Wales stands on the same stretch of surfing beach as the adjoining town of Wamberal. Nearby lagoons are shark-free and attract many visitors for swimming, boating, fishing and prawning.

Jutting into the ocean just south of Terrigal is an impressive headland called the Skillion. Bouddi National Park, which is great for bushwalkers, campers and anglers, is also close by.

ACCOMMODATION: Hotel Terrigal, ph (02) 4384 1033; Country Comfort Inn (motel), ph (02) 4384 1166; Terrigal Beach Motel, ph (02) 4384 1423; Miami Guest House, ph (02) 4384 1919; Bellbird Caravan Park, ph (02) 4384 1883

ACTIVITIES: Bushwalking, fishing, national park access, prawning, water sports

TOURIST INFORMATION: Ph (02) 4384 6577

THE CHANNON

782 KM NORTH OF SYDNEY
POPULATION: 100   MAP REF:
Situated between Nimbin and Byron Bay, The Channon combines the laid-back with the chic. It is most famous for its craft market, with a great variety of homemade or hand-crafted goods. Vendors are not allowed to sell anything manufactured.

Visitors can have an open-air haircut, a camel ride, tarot reading or a session of crystal healing, or listen to buskers, musicians or storytellers. There are also dancers and puppets shows. Occasionally, there are even live bands.

ACCOMMODATION: Most people who visit the markets stay in Byron Bay.

ACTIVITIES: Scenic drives, sightseeing

TOURIST INFORMATION: Ph (02) 6685 8050

THE ENTRANCE

103 KM NORTH OF SYDNEY
POPULATION: 38 250   MAP REF: PAGE 177 J7
The Entrance gets its name from its position on the waterway that leads from Tuggerah Lake to the Tasman Sea. One of the first settlers was farmer Thomas Cade Batley, who built a house on Homestead Hill in 1836. Dairying became the major industry but inevitably caved in to tourism.

About halfway between Sydney and Newcastle, the principal weekend attractions are fishing—both lake and ocean—prawning, swimming, boating and waterskiing. It has clean beaches and pleasant picnic spots along the lakeside. Visitors can also enjoy cruises on Tuggerah Lake.

ACCOMMODATION: Sapphire Palms Motel, ph (02) 4332 5799; The Entrance Hotel, ph (02) 4332 2001; Surfside Palms Beach Resort (units), ph (02) 4333 1902; Myola Flats, ph (02) 4332 2018; Two Shores Caravan Park, ph (02) 4332 2999

ACTIVITIES: Bowls, fishing, prawning, water sports

TOURIST INFORMATION: Ph (02) 4432 9282

THE ROCK

511 KM SOUTH-WEST OF SYDNEY
POPULATION: 750   MAP REF: PAGE 183 M6
The Rock pretty much says what it is all about: a giant outcrop some 363 metres high.

The town is 32 km south-west of Wagga and is surrounded by quite distinct scenery which appeals to photographers. The bird life is also varied and will attract birdwatchers.

Walking trails run through the Rock Nature Reserve culminating at the summit.

ACCOMMODATION: King's Own Hotel/Motel, ph (02) 6920 2011

ACTIVITIES: Birdwatching, sightseeing, walking

TOURIST INFORMATION: Ph (02) 6923 5402

TIBOOBURRA

1311 KM NORTH-WEST OF SYDNEY
POPULATION: 130   MAP REF: PAGE 180 C2
Thought to mean 'heap of granite rock', Tibooburra is in the extreme north-west of the state, in a very dry area where some wool is produced. This remote township can be the hottest in Australia on most summer days—it is what the Outback is all about.

Tibooburra is a 'ghost town' of the late 1800s: another boomer and crasher. (Just as with Arltunga in the Northern Territory, water became more valuable than gold in extremely harsh conditions.) Now, two pubs and a smattering of shops service the surrounding countryside. It has the only hospital in the district and, of course, provides a link with the Royal Flying Doctor Service.

Many of the historic buildings are constructed from the local granite, including Braybrooks' House, the Family Hotel (which possesses a 24-hour liquor licence), and the Tibooburra Hotel. The Mount Stuart Aboriginal Artefact Collection is also worth seeing.

Sturt National Park starts at Tibooburra and consists of 310 634 hectares of eroded cliff-rimmed mesas and gibber plains. Temperatures can reach

A dirt road leading to Tibooburra, typical of roads in the Outback

50°C in summer, so prospective visitors should perhaps consider a beach holiday instead. In winter, it can be quite cold at night, but beautiful during the day. At the very extreme of the state, in the park, is Cameron Corner, the junction of the borders of New South Wales, Queensland and South Australia. Here, you can see the longest fence in the world. Five thousand kilometres in length, it theoretically keeps Queensland dingoes out of sheep country and is known colloquially as the 'dog fence'.

On the New South Wales Labour Day Weekend, Tibooburra hosts a famous gymkhana and rodeo.

ACCOMMODATION: Tibooburra Hotel, ph (08) 8091 3310; Family Hotel, ph (08) 8091 3314; Granites Motel & Caravan Park, ph (08) 8091 3305
ACTIVITIES: 4WD touring, national park access, sightseeing
TOURIST INFORMATION: Ph (08) 8087 6077

TINGHA

721 KM NORTH-WEST OF SYDNEY
POPULATION: 850   MAP REF: PAGE 179 H6
Almost 30 km east of Inverell, Tingha is well known to gem fossickers, with sapphires, zircons and quartz crystal there for the taking. Smith's Mining and Natural History Museum is situated on the banks of Copes Creek and boasts a good New England mineral and gemstone collection, together with period clothing, Aboriginal artefacts and antiques.
ACCOMMODATION: Tingha Gems Caravan Park, ph (02) 6732 3234
ACTIVITIES: Fossicking, scenic drives, sightseeing
TOURIST INFORMATION: Ph (02) 7623 3434

TOCUMWAL

727 KM SOUTH-WEST OF SYDNEY
POPULATION: 1500   MAP REF: PAGE 183 J7
While the Aboriginal name translates as 'a bottomless pit in the river', the town, situated on the Murray River, has a long association with aviation. In World War II, it had the biggest airstrip in the southern hemisphere and there are still two gliding and flying schools here. The Sportavia Soaring Centre encompasses all flying activities.

Founded in 1862, Tocumwal is an historic town, with many fine examples of colonial architecture listed by the National Trust. There are four historic pubs, open gardens, display gardens, working woodturners, art studios, an emu farm, antiques and wineries. Attractions for children include a miniature world of railways, mini-golf and an extensive foreshore playground and family picnic area with free BBQs. The magnificent sandy beaches, surrounded by red gum forests, have been popular with tourists for over 100 years!
ACCOMMODATION: Tattersalls Hotel, ph (03) 5874 2016; Tocumwal Motel, ph (03) 5874 3022; Greenways Holiday Units, ph (03) 5874 2882; Tocumwal Caravan Park & Swimming, ph (03) 5874 2114
ACTIVITIES: Bowls, fishing, flying, golf, horseracing, horse riding, sightseeing, water sports, wineries
TOURIST INFORMATION: Ph (03) 5874 5271

TOORAWEENAH

488 KM NORTH-WEST OF SYDNEY
POPULATION: 100   MAP REF: PAGE 176 B2
Rustic little Tooraweenah, like Coonamble and Coonabarabran, is yet another gateway to the magical Warrumbungles. Visitors can take gliding flights over the surrounding countryside with the Warrumbungle Gliding Club on weekends and there are many scenic drives in the area, including one which has sections of unsealed road into the Warrumbungle National Park.
ACCOMMODATION: Hotel-Motel Mountain View, ph (02) 6848 1017; Warrumbungle Caravan Court, ph (02) 6848 1066
ACTIVITIES: Bushwalking, gliding, national park access, scenic drives, sightseeing
TOURIST INFORMATION: Ph (02) 6847 2045

TORONTO

153 KM NORTH OF SYDNEY
POPULATION: 8600   MAP REF: PAGE 177 J6
Driving up the Pacific Highway, once you reach Toronto, you know Newcastle is not too far away. Situated on Lake Macquarie, Toronto dates back to 1829 when Governor Darling granted just over 500 hectares to Reverend Lancelot Threlkeld to found an Aboriginal mission. The reverend later became a very wealthy man after investing in a coal mine.

Toronto is attractive to fishermen, sailors and water-sport fanatics, but it also provides easy access to Awaba and Heaton State Forests.
ACCOMMODATION: Toronto Hotel/Motel, ph (02) 4959 1033; Palm Shores Motel, ph (02) 4950 4133; Palm Shores (motel), ph (02) 4959 1311
ACTIVITIES: Fishing, scenic drives, water sports
TOURIST INFORMATION: Ph (02) 4929 9299

TOUKLEY

110 KM NORTH OF SYDNEY
POPULATION: 7125   MAP REF: PAGE 177 J7
Toukley is popular with sailors. It is also a hit with families who like the safe swimming the lake provides, though surf beaches are easily accessible.

Situated between Budgewoi and Tuggerah on the Central Coast, Toukley is a favourite prawning spot. Nearby Munmorah State Recreation Park and Red Gum Forest appeal to bushwalkers.
ACCOMMODATION: Toukley Motor Inn, ph (02) 4396 5666; Toukley Motel, ph (02) 4397 1999; Carr's Caravan Court, ph (02) 4396 4203; Canton Beach Tourist Park, ph (02) 4396 3252
ACTIVITIES: Bowls, bushwalking, water sports
TOURIST INFORMATION: Ph (02) 4396 4666

TRANGIE

478 KM NORTH-WEST FROM SYDNEY
POPULATION: 1000   MAP REF: PAGE 181 P8
Trangie (Aboriginal for 'quick') derives its name from Trangie Station, which was first owned by J. C. Ryrie. The first settler, however, was John Campbell, who arrived from Dubbo in 1883, setting up a farm and a pub, the Swinging Gate. Trangie's subsequent growth resulted from it becoming a staging centre for Cobb & Co on the route from Dubbo to Bourke. The town was also well used by the teamsters who carried goods into (and wool out of) stations like Emereran, Panjee and The Overflow.

The construction of Burrendong Dam was a boon to the landholders at Trangie. With an average district rainfall of only 457 mm, the irrigation schemes saw Trangie facing a new prosperity, forever banishing images of aridity with a maze of irrigation channels and different crops. Cotton is now the economic base.
ACCOMMODATION: Trangie Hotel/Motel, ph (02) 6888 7554; Trangie Caravan Park, ph (02) 6888 7511
ACTIVITIES: Fishing, sightseeing
TOURIST INFORMATION: Ph (02) 6884 1422

TUMBARUMBA

507 KM SOUTH-WEST OF SYDNEY
POPULATION: 1600   MAP REF: PAGE 174 A6
Halfway between Sydney and Melbourne in the western foothills of the Snowy Mountains, Tumbarumba is like Jindabyne on the other side of the range: a good base for skiers in winter. In Tumbarumba's case the snow venue is Mount Selwyn.

Tourism is only one industry for the district, with fat stock, wool, timber and dairying also contributing

Spring wildflowers in Kosciuszko National Park, to the east of Tumbarumba

to the local economy. In the 1850s, however, the magnet for people—particularly the Chinese—was gold. The rush did not last very long.

Tumbarumba is named after the Tumbarumba Creek run, which in turn borrowed the name from a local Aboriginal dialect. It means 'sounding ground', and was used to describe the sound of kangaroos bounding over certain areas of the hills.

There is plenty for the visitor to do. There are nearby walking tracks, including one named after Hume and Hovell that has picnicking and camping facilities. In designated areas fossicking for gold, sapphires and zircons is permitted. Other alternatives are trail rides or High Country horseback safaris. There is also canoeing and whitewater rafting, mountain biking and 4WD touring, or perhaps a visit to the Snowy Mountains hydro-electric power stations. Tumbarumba lies to the east of Kosciuszko National Park and so is a good base from which to explore the national park.

Horseraces have been held here since 1882 and there is a local vineyard! The town has an histoirc museum and a wool and craft centre.

In January, Tumbarumba holds its annual rodeo, February sees the running of the Tumbarumba Cup, March is Showtime and there is a Polocrosse Carnival in May. In November the Tumbarumba Heritage Week and Street Parade is held.

ACCOMMODATION: Tumbarumba Motel, ph (02) 6948 2494; Hackey's Union Hotel, ph (02) 6948 2013; Tumbarumba Hotel, ph (02) 6948 2562; Runaway Resort (camping/caravans), ph (02) 6948 2562; Captain Cook Caravan Park, ph (02) 6948 2097

ACTIVITIES: Bushwalking, fossicking, 4WD touring, horse riding, national park access, scenic drives, skiing, sightseeing, water sports

TOURIST INFORMATION: Ph (02) 6948 2805

TUMUT

434 KM SOUTH-WEST OF SYDNEY
POPULATION: 6500 MAP REF: PAGE 174 A5

A tranquil, pretty town with poplar-lined avenues, Tumut owes its name to the Aboriginal 'doomut', or 'quiet resting place by the river'. On their way to Port Phillip Bay, Hume and Hovell passed through this lush valley with its meandering watercourse in 1824. The first settler in the district was Thomas McAlister, who founded Darbalara Station in the early 1830s. (This station subsequently produced the Darbalara shorthorn strain of cattle.) By 1887 Tumut was a municipality.

Today, Tumut's economy relies on agricultural and pastoral pursuits, but softwood timber milling is an important contributor. The state forests in the district contribute to a certain European ambience in Tumut particularly around nearby Blowering Dam, where the mountains come down to meet the water. The local residents waterski and sail on Blowering Dam and, of course, fish for trout and perch. Camping is permitted on the foreshores.

Canoeing is exciting on the Tumut and Goobraganda Rivers, or visitors can opt to go horse riding. In winter, skiers will find Mount Selwyn quite easily accessible. Yarrangobilly Caves are nearby and visitors can go on guided or self-guided tours through

Morning mist over the township of Tumut

the limestone caverns. You can relax in a thermal pool there that stays at a constant 27°C.

The town claims it has the oldest racing club in New South Wales. The course is set on the banks of the Tumut River and features two magnificent grandstands, built in 1909. Seven races are held each year, the major event being the Tumut Cup.

ACCOMMODATION: Tumut Star Hotel, ph (02) 6947 1102; Commercial Hotel, ph (02) 6947 1040; The Elms Motor Inn, ph 1800 819 497; Farrington Motel, ph (02) 6947 1088; Ribbonwood Holiday Cottages, ph (02) 6947 2527; Caravan Park Riverglade, ph (02) 6947 2528; Blowering Holiday Park, ph (02) 6947 1383

ACTIVITIES: Bushwalking, exploring, fishing, 4WD touring, horse riding, horseracing, scenic drives, skiing, water sports

TOURIST INFORMATION: Ph (02) 6947 1849

TWEED HEADS

907 KM NORTH OF SYDNEY
POPULATION: 5150 MAP REF: PAGE 179 P1

Tweed Heads is bustling, busy, sometimes frantic, and is the northernmost town on the New South Wales coast. The Tweed River was named by John Oxley after one of the members of his 1823 expedition in the *Mermaid*. However, the original name of the settlement was 'Cooloon'.

Tweed Heads shares its main street with the Queensland town of Coolangatta—they are in fact

twin towns at the mouth of the Tweed River. In the old days when poker machines were illegal in Queensland but not in New South Wales, large clubs sprang up in Tweed Heads to cater for large groups of gambling Queenslanders who would have a flutter and then head back across the border. This created much better restaurants and night clubs than one would expect in a town of its size.

Tweed Heads has excellent surfing beaches (not as crowded as on the nearby Gold Coast) and boats are for hire to fish in the Tweed estuary or on Cobaki Lakes. River cruises are a popular tourist choice.

ACCOMMODATION: Tweed Heads Hotel, ph (07) 5536 1010; Cook's Endeavour Motor Inn, ph (07) 5536 5399; Tweed Harbour Motor Inn, ph (07) 5536 6066; Sea Drift Holiday Units, ph (07) 5536 8855; Haven Flats, ph (07) 5536 5112; Whitehall Sunset Lodge B&B, ph (07) 5536 3233; Border Caravan Park, ph (07) 5536 3134

ACTIVITIES: Bowls, fishing, golf, scenic drives, tennis, water sports

TOURIST INFORMATION: Ph (07) 5536 4244

ULLADULLA

246 KM SOUTH OF SYDNEY
POPULATION: 7500 MAP REF: PAGE 174 F5

Ulladulla owes its name to the Aboriginal word for 'safe harbour'. One of its earliest settlers was the Reverend Thomas Kendall, grandfather of the poet Henry Kendall, who was born there. Though timber was its raison d'etre in the 1820s, nowadays it is fishing and tourism that pays the bills.

Ulladulla has a large fishing fleet, and every Easter there is a Blessing of the Fleet, culminating in a fireworks display on the night of Easter Sunday. It is a tradition that originated in Italy. Ulladulla is also the centre for New South Wales abalone divers, complete with a processing plant on the harbour. Most of the product is exported to Japan.

Ulladulla's neighbours are Milton, Mollymook and Burril Lake, all on the east side of the Budawang Range. (This is where the Clyde River, with its famous oysters, rises.) Often the towns of Milton and Ulladulla are referred to as a complete entity, but in reality they are very different. Milton sits high in the hills, while Ulladulla is right on the coast, where visitors can enjoy all kinds of water sports.

Beaches like Mollymook can be both great for kids and at the same time host surf titles, but if it is too rough there are other spots to swim, including Wairo, Racecourse and Narrawallee. And, of course, the lakes such as Burril, Cajola and Tabourie are always calm. Ulladulla also offers great fishing for the amateur, and waterskiing for those who want it.

Within easy range are other natural attractions, such as Pigeon House Mountain, named by James Cook as he sailed up the coast in 1770. To the south is Murramarang National Park, where the kangaroos eat out of your hand on Pebbly Beach.

Ulladulla holds a fishing carnival in May, apart from the Blessing of the Fleet at Easter.

ACCOMMODATION: Pigeon House Motor Inn, ph (02) 4455 1811; Albacore Motel, ph (02) 4455 1322; Marlin Hotel, ph (02) 4455 1999; Malabar Holiday Flats, ph (02) 4455 4344; Ulladulla Guest House, ph (02) 4455 1796; Beach Haven Holiday Resort (camping/caravans), ph (02) 4455 2110; Seabreeze Tourist Village (camping/caravans), ph (02) 4455 2348
ACTIVITIES: Bushwalking, croquet, fishing, golf, national park access, tennis, water sports
TOURIST INFORMATION: Ph (02) 4455 1269

URALLA

544 KM NORTH-WEST OF SYDNEY
POPULATION: 2300   MAP REF: PAGE 179 J8
Situated on the New England Highway between Tamworth and Armidale, Uralla is surrounded by a district producing fine Merino wool, cold-climate fruits and oats. A gold rush in 1852 created a tent city which in turn became a village. This was gazetted in 1855. (Fossickers may still find some 'colour' at the old Rocky River diggings.)

Uralla is perhaps best known for having a celebrity in its cemetery. In 1870, the gentleman bushranger Fred Ward, otherwise known as Captain Thunderbolt, was killed in a shoot-out with police at Kentucky Creek. Flowers are still put on his grave.

Prospective visitors should be warned that at a height of 1017 metres above sea level, Uralla can be bitterly cold in winter.

ACCOMMODATION: Coachwood and Cedar Hotel/Motel, ph (02) 6778 4110; Thunderbolt Inn (hotel), ph (02) 6778 4048; Uralla Motel, ph (02) 6778 4326; Altona Motel, ph (02) 6778 4007; Country Road Caravan Park, ph (02) 6778 4563;

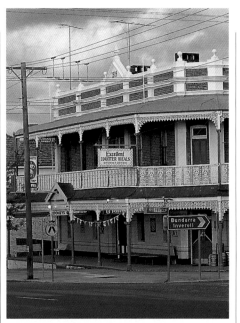
Decorative lacework on a Uralla hotel

Uralla Caravan Park, ph (02) 6778 4763
ACTIVITIES: Fossicking, scenic drives, sightseeing
TOURIST INFORMATION: Ph (02) 6778 4144

URUNGA

554 KM NORTH OF SYDNEY
POPULATION: 2340   MAP REF: PAGE 179 N8
Situated where the estuaries of the Kalang and Bellinger Rivers combine, Urunga is only 32 km south of Coffs Harbour. Its name translates as 'long white beach'. The first Europeans to see the region were the crew of the *Northumberland,* captained by William Wright, when the ship entered the estuary in 1841.

The basis for the town's existence was cedar-getting, sawmilling and shipbuilding, but now it is popular for its fishing and its beautiful river, ocean and mountain setting. A broad lagoon provides safe swimming for children and is great for sailboarding and gentle boating.

ACCOMMODATION: Sudden Comfort Motel, ph (02) 6655 6900; Kalang River Motel, ph (02) 6655 6229; Hungry Head Retreat (serviced apartments), ph (02) 6655 6736; Paringa Holiday Flats, ph (02) 6655 6305; Hungry Head Holiday Cabins, ph (02) 6655 6208; Gundamain Caravan Park, ph (02) 6655 6373; Urunga Heads Caravan Park, ph (02) 6655 6355
ACTIVITIES: Fishing, water sports
TOURIST INFORMATION: Ph (02) 6655 6160

VINCENTIA

193 KM SOUTH OF SYDNEY
POPULATION: 380   MAP REF: PAGE 174 G4
Vincentia is another of the South Coast's tiny holiday resorts, nestled across the Moona Moona Creek from better known Huskisson.

It offers the usual diversions: fishing, swimming and generally lazing about, but there are shops and a nine-hole golf course. The views over Jervis Bay are

superb, and Plantation Point has a picnic area with toilet facilities.
ACCOMMODATION: Dolphin Shores Motor Inn, ph (02) 4441 6895
ACTIVITIES: Fishing, golf, water sports
TOURIST INFORMATION: Ph (02) 4421 0778

WAGGA WAGGA

486 KM SOUTH-WEST OF SYDNEY
POPULATION: 53 630   MAP REF: PAGE 183 N6
Wagga Wagga is more commonly known simply as 'Wagga' (which means 'crow' in the language of the Wiradjuri, the largest tribe in New South Wales, who first settled in the area). The city is situated on the Murrumbidgee River, with Cootamundra and Temora to the north, Narrandera to the west, Albury to the south and Tumut in the east. It forms the hub of a vast district that supports the production of wheat, fat lambs, the dairy industry and mixed farming.

For once, settlers beat the explorers to the district: Charles Sturt was almost ten years behind the land-seekers when he came through in 1829. Robert Holt Best founded the Wagga Wagga run in 1832. Now the city is an important business, agricultural, educational and industrial centre, one of the bigger settlements in the southern region.

Students of history can participate in the three walks arranged by the National Trust, passing by buildings which date from 1865. Other attractions are the zoo, art gallery, botanic gardens and Historical Museum. With prolific gardens and parks, including a formal Shakespearian garden, the city can be a visual treat in spring. Music lovers can enjoy an orchestral concert at the outdoor music bowl and entertainment centre. Charles Sturt University even has its own winery which is open for tastings and sales.

ACCOMMODATION: Romano's Hotel, ph (02) 6921 2013; Astor Hotel, ph (02) 6921 4328; Heritage Motor Inn, ph 1800 028 508; Country House Motor Lodge, ph (02) 6922 7256; Red Hill Lodge (B&B), ph (018) 693 471; Crepe Myrtle Guest House, ph (02) 6921 4757; Carinya Caravan Park, ph (02) 6933 1256; Wagga Tourist Caravan Park, ph (02) 6921 2540
ACTIVITIES: Bowls, bushwalking, croquet, fishing, golf, greyhound racing, horseracing, tennis, trotting, water sports, wineries
TOURIST INFORMATION: Ph (02) 6923 5402

WALCHA

456 KM NORTH-WEST OF SYDNEY
POPULATION: 1750   MAP REF: PAGE 179 J9
Walcha's name is an Aboriginal term for the sun. When Hamilton Sempell carved a station in the upper Apsley Valley in 1832, he called it Wolka. This apparently is how the town's name should be pronounced. John Oxley, first European in the district, preceded Sempell by 16 years.

Now the district produces mainly fine Merino wool, cattle and hardwood. This is rugged country, as visits to nearby Oxley Wild Rivers and Werrikimbe National Parks will attest, but there are things to do

for those who want to stay in town. The home of Abraham Nivison is the oldest surviving in New England, and there are several historic sites of interest in Walcha, including a pioneer cottage and museum complex where visitors can experience what life was like in the early days.

Walcha is on the Oxley Highway between Port Macquarie and Bendemeer—one of the best 'driver's roads' in the state.

ACCOMMODATION: New England Hotel/Motel, ph (02) 6777 2532; Walcha Road Hotel, ph (02) 6777 5829; New Royal Hotel, ph (02) 6777 2550; Walcha Caravan Park, ph (02) 6777 2501
ACTIVITIES: Bushwalking, 4WD touring, national park access, scenic drives, sightseeing
TOURIST INFORMATION: Ph (02) 6777 2272

WALGETT

679 KM NORTH-WEST OF SYDNEY
POPULATION: 2300   MAP REF: PAGE 181 P4
Torn by strained racial relations for many years, Walgett has still much to offer the visitor. Its name means 'meeting of the waters', presumably because the town stands near the junction of the Barwon and Namoi Rivers. The name was first used in 1838 by station owner John Campbell for his property.

Sturt originally came through in 1829, and found 'an unbroken sheet of water, evidently very deep and literally crowded with pelicans and other wildfowl'. Today Walgett rides on the sheep's back, with cotton as an additional crop.

Walgett is the gateway to the opal fields at Lightning Ridge, Angledool, Glengarry and, most recently, Grawin Tanks. The Grawin was first a boom field in the 1920s, particularly when 'The Light of the World'—an opal as big as a fist weighing 450 grams—was dug out on Richard's Hill. (It is now in the United States.) The Grawin has recently experienced a renaissance, but whereas the old-time miners used a pick, shovel and a bucket, nowadays it is done with jackhammers and giant vacuum cleaners.

Burren Junction is about 100 km east of Walgett over bad dirt. It boasts a superb hot artesian bath, open 24 hours a day.

On the other side of town, about 100 km to the west, is Narran Lake, one of the largest and least known lakes in Australia, abounding in native animal and bird life. The best way to see it is by plane, arranged through the Walgett Aero Club.
ACCOMMODATION: Coolabah Motel, ph (02) 6828 1366; Leisure World Motel & Spa Resort, ph (02) 6828 1154; Two Rivers Caravan Park, ph (02) 6828 1381
ACTIVITIES: Fossicking, 4WD touring, sightseeing, 'taking the waters'
TOURIST INFORMATION: Ph (02) 6828 1399

WARIALDA

681 KM NORTH-WEST OF SYDNEY
POPULATION: 1440   MAP REF: PAGE 178 F5
'A place of wild honey' in the Aboriginal lexicon, Warialda is on the Gwydir Highway between Inverell

and Moree. The centre of a rich pastoral, agricultural and stud cattle area, the University of New England has a research station nearby.

Most people come to try their luck at gem fossicking, to bushwalk or to watch the horse races. Cuddell Animal Kingdom is popular with children.
ACCOMMODATION: Sunflower Motel, ph (02) 6729 1344; Motel Sunflower, ph (02) 6729 1320
ACTIVITIES: Bushwalking, fossicking, horseracing, sightseeing
TOURIST INFORMATION: Ph (02) 6729 1016

WARREN

533 KM WEST OF SYDNEY
POPULATION: 2500   MAP REF: PAGE 181 P7
There is some confusion over where Warren derived its name. It is believed that it comes from one of the following Aboriginal words: 'warrien' (a large root); 'wurren' (strong), or 'wurrena' (level and flat).

The first Europeans in the region were explorers John Oxley (in 1818) and Charles Sturt ten years later. Oxley made his journey during a very wet period and was unable to penetrate the Macquarie Marshes, to the north-west of the present town. When Sturt came through, it was much drier, and he managed to ascertain that the Macquarie River, far from feeding a vast inland sea, actually fed into the Darling River.

The country around Warren was taken up initially by William Lawson (a son of the explorer who forged the way across the Blue Mountains with Wentworth and Blaxland), and Thomas Readford in 1845. The first 'town' building was not erected until 1850.

Today Warren is the centre of a pastoral district which services legendary sheep studs like Haddon Rig and Mumblebone. The construction of the Burrendong Dam brought guaranteed supplies of water and pastoralists branched out into crops like cotton, forage crops and grain sorghum.

Sometimes described as 'the Randwick of the West', Warren's showground/racecourse complex is one of the best in the state, with facilities for racing, trotting, rodeos and other equestrian activities.

The Macquarie River offers excellent fishing along its banks, with good catches of yellowbelly, cod, freshwater bream and catfish almost surefire.

Warren's main attraction is the Macquarie Marshes. Whereas the marshes defeated Oxley and

other explorers who followed, they are a delight to today's visitors. This is the largest wildfowl breeding area in eastern Australia. As many as 120 different species of birds have been observed in the area.

The Warren Show is held in May.
ACCOMMODATION: Warren Motor Inn, ph (02) 6847 4404; Macquarie Valley Motor Inn 1800 656 188; Sandy Creek Cabins, ph (02) 6847 4666; Macquarie Caravan Park, ph (02) 6847 4706; Warren Caravan Park, ph (02) 6847 4968
ACTIVITIES: Birdwatching, bowls, fishing, golf, tennis, water sports
TOURIST INFORMATION: Ph (02) 6847 4604

WAUCHOPE

422 KM NORTH OF SYDNEY
POPULATION: 4250   MAP REF: PAGE 177 M2
Wauchope (pronounced 'war-hope', not 'watch-a-pee', as in the Northern Territory), is the timber town of New South Wales. It is also the centre of a cattle, dairying and mixed farming district. It was named after an early settler, Captain Robert Wauch.

The town's major attraction is Timbertown, where both children and adults can return to the bygone days of horsedrawn wagons, steam trains, bullock teams and woodcutters.

Mount Seaview, 55 west of Wauchope, offers excellent 4WD driving for those with their own vehicles. There are also organised safaris for those who have not.
ACCOMMODATION: Wauchope Motel, ph (02) 6585 1933; Hastings Hotel, ph (02) 6585 2003; Mount Seaview Resort, ph (02) 6587 7199; Cowarra Homestead, ph (02) 6585 3531; Mount Seaview Resort/Campsite Bunkhouse, ph (02) 6587 7177
ACTIVITIES: 4WD touring, scenic drives, sightseeing
TOURIST INFORMATION: Ph (02) 6583 1077

WEE WAA

650 KM WEST OF SYDNEY
POPULATION: 2110   MAP REF: PAGE 178 D7
In the 1840s two squatters called Campbell and Ryan ran a station in the area called Weeawaa, thought to be Aboriginal for 'fire thrown away'.

A wooden bridge over the Namoi River at Wee Waa

Today Wee Waa is famous for cotton, wool, meat, wheat and other cereals.

Drivers who prefer tarred roads will find Wee Waa is the end of the line. Having come in off the Newell Highway from Narrabri, they will have to be content with what Wee Waa has to offer, unless they want to continue further west to Burren Junction's artesian spa. More adventurous travellers can experience the Pilliga Scrub by cutting west-southwest, or go west through Burren to the opal fields north of Walgett.

ACCOMMODATION: Cottonfields Motel & Restaurant, ph (02) 6795 4577; Wee Waa Motel, ph (02) 6795 4522; Mainway Caravan Park, ph (02) 6795 4268
ACTIVITIES: Boating, fishing, sightseeing
TOURIST INFORMATION: Ph (02) 6792 3583

WELLINGTON

354 KM NORTH-WEST OF SYDNEY
POPULATION: 5550   MAP REF: PAGE 176 B5

Explorer John Oxley named the Wellington Valley after his hero, Arthur Wellesley, the Duke of Wellington who defeated Bonaparte at the Battle of Waterloo. Oxley came down the Macquarie River in 1818 in search of the fabled inland sea, and on the basis of his report, a penal settlement was established in the Wellington district in 1823, under the command of Lieutenant Percy Simpson. The penal settlement did not last long, as pioneers soon came into the area to set up properties.

Today Wellington is the service centre for a rich agricultural and pastoral district of some 4000 sq km. The district produces wool, wheat, sheep and cattle, with some market gardening and dairying on the fertile flats of the Bell and Macquarie Rivers.

The Wellington Caves are the area's main attraction. Though not as extensive as the caves of Jenolan, they boast the largest stalagmite in the world—15 metres high and 32 metres around the base. Because it is thought to resemble the Virgin Mary, the cave in which it can be seen is called Cathedral Cave. The only other cave open to the public, the Gaden Cave, is smaller but possesses more exquisite formations, while the third cave, Bone Cave, contains the fossilised skeletons of animals which roamed the Wellington Valley millions of years ago. It is reserved for scientific study. The caves are thought to have been discovered by George Ranken in 1830, when he accidentally fell into one!

Nearby Burrendong Dam provides access to many water sports. Built originally to mitigate flood damage, the dam supplies irrigation water as far west as Warren. It backs up the Cudgegong River for 26 km and the Macquarie for 35 km. It is also home to an arboretum which preserves native plant life.

Gold was discovered at Wellington in 1849 at a place known as Mitchell's Creek. Gold was also found at Ironbarks, known today as Stuart Town.

ACCOMMODATION: Wellington Hotel, ph (02) 6845 2083; Bridge Motel, ph (02) 6845 2555; Wellington Motor Inn, ph (02) 6845 1177; Wellington Caves Holiday Complex (camping/caravans), ph (02) 6845 2970
ACTIVITIES: Bowls, cave exploration, fishing, fossicking, golf, scenic drives, tennis, water sports
TOURIST INFORMATION: Ph (02) 6845 2001

Houseboats at Wentworth are a most pleasurable way to enjoy the Darling River

WENTWORTH

1076 KM SOUTH-WEST OF SYDNEY
POPULATION: 1400   MAP REF: PAGE 182 C4

Situated near the junction of the Murray and Darling Rivers, Wentworth is just over 30 km west of Mildura. It was named after William Charles Wentworth and in the 1850s was an important river transport centre for wool and provisions. Now, it is the centre for a fruit and wool district.

The first residence went up in 1851. St John's Anglican Church (built in 1871) is only one of many buildings in town of interest to historians.

The Buronga Winery and the Cod River Aquarium are both worth a visit. A relic of the old days of Wentworth, the paddle-steamer *Ruby*, is moored at one of the wharves. Visitors can hire houseboats to explore the river systems and catch their supper in the process.

ACCOMMODATION: Royal Hotel/Motel, ph (03) 5027 3005; Captain Sturt Hotel/Motel, ph (03) 5027 3051; Cod River Lodge, ph (03) 5027 3071; Two Rivers Motel, ph (03) 5027 3268; River Junction Holiday Units, ph (03) 5027 2022; Willow Bend Caravan Park, ph (03) 5027 3213
ACTIVITIES: Fishing, scenic drives, swimming, wineries
TOURIST INFORMATION: Ph (03) 5027 3624

WERRIS CREEK

408 KM NORTH-WEST OF SYDNEY
POPULATION: 2050   MAP REF: PAGE 176 G1

Where gold has more often than not been the reason behind settlements in New South Wales generating almost spontaneously, the town of Werris Creek (originally 'Werres Creek' or 'Weery's Creek') owes its

existence to the railways. In the 1870s only a few families had settled in the area, but when the railway came through, Werris Creek became a major junction. Later, in 1896, it became a railway maintenance centre. Even more workshops were added in 1917 and the volume of work grew to the extent that in 1925, a coal mine to supply fuel for the steam locomotives was opened in the district.

But just as paddle-steamers and the railway put an end to Cobb & Co, and more efficient road networks put paid to the river trade, the introduction of diesel locomotives in the 1960s caused the closure of the coal mine and the decline of Werris Creek.

Visitors should take a look at the size (and grandeur) of Werris Creek railway station to get some impression of what a bustling town it must have been in the old days. Apart from the station, however, it is just a sleepy little country town.

The road through Werris Creek makes an interesting diversion when travelling on the New England Highway. Take the turn off at Tamworth towards Werris Creek. You will rejoin the New England at Willow Tree. Another more interesting (albeit longer) detour involves leaving the Oxley Highway at Tamworth and journeying to Coonabarabran via Werris Creek.

ACCOMMODATION: Signal Hotel, ph (02) 6768 7045
ACTIVITIES: Scenic drives, sightseeing
TOURIST INFORMATION: Ph (02) 6766 9422

WEST WYALONG

524 KM WEST OF SYDNEY
POPULATION: 3700   MAP REF: PAGE 183 M3

On the Mid-Western Highway, West Wyalong is the last real outpost of civilisation before Hay, 260 km away. Now the commercial hub of a lucrative wool, wheat and mixed farming area, West Wyalong owes its existence to a gold strike in 1893. The original

strike had been made at Wyalong, a few kilometres to the north-east, but when it ran out and the 'main camp' proved to have more water, West Wyalong came into being. Though one of the richest fields in New South Wales in its day, mining ceased in 1914.

Like Gulgong, the town retains images of its former glory days in its narrow, winding streets and some architectural remnants. The District Museum has a scale model of a working goldmine, and the Aboriginal Art Centre holds some fascinating artefacts from Central Australia.

East of West Wyalong is Weddin Mountains National Park. For squatters taking up land in the western district, the Weddin Mountains marked the beginning of the plains, known as the Bland, or the Levels. In the 1850s and 1860s, bushrangers used them as a base from which they emerged to steal horses from squatters or gold from the coaches.

The father of one bushranger, John O'Meally, ran a pub somewhere up in the ranges, but after Frank Gardiner robbed the Eugowra gold escort of 14 000 pounds in 1862, troopers looking for him set fire to O'Meally's pub and burnt it to the ground. The money was never found.

Camping is possible in the national park, but you have to bring in your own water. Bushwalkers should be warned that there are few tracks in the park.
ACCOMMODATION: Top Town Tavern (hotel), ph (02) 6972 2166; Country Roads Motor Inn, ph 1800 025 215; Charles Sturt Motor Inn, ph (02) 6972 2422; West Wyalong Caravan Park, ph (02) 6972 3133
ACTIVITIES: Birdwatching, horse trotting, national park access, scenic drives, sightseeing, water sports
TOURIST INFORMATION: Ph (02) 6972 3645

WHITE CLIFFS

1063 KM WEST OF SYDNEY
POPULATION: 205   MAP REF: PAGE 180 E5
Like Coober Pedy in South Australia, White Cliffs is a town that has seen humans turn into moles because

Underground living at White Cliffs

of the extreme heat: they live underground. (The average temperature in summer is 35°C and in winter, 17°C.) White Cliffs opal field, established in 1884, is the oldest in Australia. The town reached its peak in the early 1900s, with between 4500 and 5000 searching for the elusive 'colour'. The population is dramatically less today but opal mining still goes on, with jewelled opal 'pineapples' being a unique local find. The opalised skeleton of a plesiosaur was discovered in 1976 and can be seen in the town.

White Cliffs is the site of Australia's first solar power station which was opened in 1983. There are several historic buildings worth inspecting in town, including the old police station and post office. Tourists should be warned that summer is not the best time to visit White Cliffs.
ACCOMMODATION: Dugout Motel & Restaurant, ph (08) 8091 6647; White Cliffs Hotel, ph (08) 8091 6645; White Cliffs Hotel, ph (08) 8091 6606
ACTIVITIES: Fossicking, 4WD touring, opal buying
TOURIST INFORMATION: Ph (08) 8091 6614

WILCANNIA

962 KM WEST OF SYDNEY
POPULATION: 750   MAP REF: PAGE 180 E7
On the junction of the Darling and Paroo Rivers, Wilcannia was once known as 'the Queen City of the West', the third largest inland port in Australia when the paddle-steamers plied back and forth to Adelaide carrying wool one way and supplies the other. The first riverboat was taken by inland waterway legend Francis Cadell to Mount Murchison Station in 1859. The following year a post office was established and in 1866, the first store. By the 1870s, Wilcannia was an important coaching station for travellers to the western goldfields.

There is a self-guided tour that takes in some of Wilcannia's historic sandstone buildings. Still the centre for a vast wool district, Wilcannia is situated in the hottest part of the state and suffers from very unpredictable rainfall.

ACCOMMODATION: Wilcannia Motel, ph (08) 8091 5802; Graham's Motel, ph (02) 8091 5040; Club Hotel, ph (08) 8091 5009
ACTIVITIES: Fishing, historic interest, Outback exploration
TOURIST INFORMATION: Ph (08) 8091 5909

WINDSOR

54 KM WEST OF SYDNEY
POPULATION: 1870   MAP REF: PAGE 176 G8
Windsor was one of five town sites selected by Governor Macquarie. Originally it was developed to provide a safe haven when the Hawkesbury flooded—which was fairly often. At first called Green Hills, Macquarie changed the name because of a supposed similarity with the English Windsor.

The town is one for history buffs and lovers of colonial architecture—St Matthew's Anglican Church, for example, is the oldest Anglican church in Australia. However, there are other things to do, particularly if you are travelling with children. Fairly close is Australian Pioneer Village, where the oldest timber dwelling in Australia, Rose Cottage, is located. A blacksmith displays his trade on certain days, and there are BBQ and picnic spots and a lake with paddle-boats. Cattai National Park, 14 km to the north-east, also has activities to interest young folk, including canoe hire.

Windsor has a craft market each Sunday in the Mall. It is also the scene of three famous 'Bridge to Bridge' races. One, for power boats, is held in May, another, for canoes, is held in October, and the third (for waterskiers) is in November.
ACCOMMODATION: Radisson Rum Corps Resort, ph (02) 4577 4222; Windsor Terrace Motel, ph (02) 4577 5999; Windsor Motel, ph (02) 4577 3626; Macquarie Arms Hotel, ph (02) 4577 2206; Hawkesbury Hotel, ph (02) 4577 3050; Riverside Van Park, ph (02) 4575 1571
ACTIVITIES: Art, craft and antique shopping, national park access, scenic drives, sightseeing
TOURIST INFORMATION: Ph (02) 4588 5895

WINGHAM

345 KM NORTH OF SYDNEY
POPULATION: 4407   MAP REF: PAGE 177 L3
Known as 'the Friendly Town', Wingham is also the oldest town on the Manning River and was built around an English-style village green. This is surrounded by 13 buildings including two pubs, the post office and court house, all of which have been classified by the National Trust as being of historic significance. The Historical Museum displays Aboriginal activist Jimmy Governor's cell.

Dairying and timber-getting are the biggest local industries.

Nearby Wingham Brush is one of the few subtropical floodplain rainforests left in New South Wales. It is now a major maternity site for the grey-headed flying fox. There are walks through the forest and you can have lunch there at one of the picnic sites or on the riverbank. Facilities are provided.

Wingham makes a good starting point for the Bulga Forest Drive, which features Ellenborough Falls, at 160 metres, the longest single drop falls in Australia. Bulga has walk trails and camping areas.

Wingham holds a rodeo in January and its Agricultural Show in March. There is also an annual Bush Music Festival.

ACCOMMODATION: Motel Wingham, ph (02) 6553 4295; Wingham Hotel, ph (02) 6553 4007; Kimbriki Homestead (B&B), ph (02) 6550 6140
ACTIVITIES: Camping, scenic drives, walking
TOURIST INFORMATION: Ph (02) 6552 1900

WISEMANS FERRY

66 KM NORTH-WEST OF SYDNEY
POPULATION: 400   MAP REF: PAGE 177 H7
Wisemans Ferry is named after Solomon Wiseman, an ex-convict who ran a ferry service over the Hawkesbury River and later established an inn here. Described by the local clergyman as a man 'deeply read in the corruption of human nature', Wiseman is believed to have killed his wife by pushing her down the steps of the inn whilst arguing over beer. Her ghost is said to haunt the hotel, which still stands.

Nearby Dharug National Park, named after one of the local Aboriginal tribes, contains a wealth of indigenous rock engravings, some of which are up to 8000 years old. The convict-built Old Northern Road forms the park's western boundary. A feat of engineering, the road is open to cyclists and walkers.
ACCOMMODATION: Wisemans Ferry Inn Hotel, ph (02) 4566 4301; Wisemans Ferry Country Retreat (B&B), ph (02) 4566 4422; Del Rio Resort (camping/caravans), ph (02) 4566 4330; Torrens Waterski Gardens (camping/caravans), ph (02) 4566 4208
ACTIVITIES: Bushwalking, national park access, scenic drives, water sports
TOURIST INFORMATION: Ph (02) 4588 5895

WOLLOMBI

606 KM NORTH-WEST OF SYDNEY
POPULATION: 500   MAP REF: PAGE 179 K8
Just south-west of Cessnock, Wollombi is reached via dirt roads. It is a pretty little village with a small museum and some noteworthy colonial buildings, including St John's Anglican Church, the post office and the court house. The Endeavour Museum contains interesting relics of the area's social history, and a local brew—Dr Jurd's Jungle Juice—is worth trying. Once.

Wollombi holds a village fair in June and a folk festival in September.
ACCOMMODATION: Wollombi House B&B Farmstay, ph (02) 4998 3316; Capers Cottage (B&B), ph (02) 4998 3211; Yango Park House (B&B), ph (02) 4998 8322
ACTIVITIES: Bushwalking, scenic drives
TOURIST INFORMATION: Ph (02) 4990 4477

WOLLONGONG

104 KM SOUTH OF SYDNEY
POPULATION: 211 417   MAP REF: PAGE 176 G10
Colloquially known as 'the Gong', this city was incorporated in 1859 as Australia's first country municipality and is now the third largest city in New South Wales.

Navigators Bass and Flinders landed at Lake Illawarra in 1796 and the area was first traversed by Europeans in 1797, when survivors from the wreck of the *Sydney Cove* discovered coal at Coalcliff. For many years, due to the ruggedness of the surrounding ranges, all visits to the district were by sea, but in 1815, on the advice of Aborigines, explorer and pastoralist Charles Throsby pushed a mob of cattle

through to good pasture. Others followed, cedar-getting became an important industry and a town was planned in 1834. The name Wollongong is thought to be an onomatopoeic attempt by the Aborigines to duplicate the sound of waves breaking on the beach.

These days, Wollongong has a reputation of being 'smog city', largely due to the proximity of Port Kembla—a steel-producing centre since 1928—and as such, considered not worth visiting. Nothing could be further from the truth.

The local lighthouse was built in 1872. The Illawarra Historical Society Museum has a Victorian parlour. Mount Kembla Village has a pioneer kitchen, blacksmith's shop, original miners' huts and a reconstruction of a tragic mining disaster in 1902.

At Bald Hill Lookout, overlooking Stanwell Park Beach, is a monument to the aviation pioneer Lawrence Hargreaves. It is also a spot very popular with hang gliders.

The more active can also enjoy good surfing beaches, playing with the kids in foreshore parks, or prawning, fishing or sailing—hire boats are available—on Lake Illawarra.

As Wollongong is completely ringed by national parks—indeed, there is a chronic shortage of building land into which Wollongong can expand—there are also plenty of walking trails in the district. Panoramas from the Illawarra Range, particularly Mt Kiera and Sublime Point, above Austinmere, are stunning.
ACCOMMODATION: Novotel Northbeach Hotel, ph (02) 4226 3555; Boat Harbour Motel, ph (02) 4228 9166; Motel Surfside 22, ph (02) 4229 7288; Illawarra Hotel, ph (02) 4229 5411; City Pacific Hotel & Function Centre, ph (02) 4229 7444; Belmore Deluxe Apartments Hotel, ph (02) 4224 6500; Caprice Serviced Apartments, ph (02) 4226 2210; Coo-ee Guest House, ph (02) 4229 1615
ACTIVITIES: Bushwalking, fishing, national park access, prawning, scenic drives, sightseeing, water sports
TOURIST INFORMATION: Ph (02) 4228 0300

WOOLGOOLGA

608 KM NORTH OF SYDNEY
POPULATION: 3660   MAP REF: PAGE 179 N7
The town, which describes itself as 'the Missing Piece of Paradise', is known to the locals as 'Woopi'.

Woolgoolga derives its more formal name from landowner Thomas Small, who in 1874 called his place Weelgoolga, the name thought to be used by the Yaggir people to describe the area in general and lilly pilly trees in particular. Banana and vegetable growing—and tourism—are now the main industries.

Coming in from Coffs Harbour up the Pacific Highway, the first landmark that is visible, high on the crest of a hill, is the Guru Nanak Sikh Temple. This is a massive, imposing building erected by the Punjabi Sikhs whose ancestors had originally been brought to Australia as labourers on the canefields of Queensland, but moved south to become banana planters. This was the first Sikh temple built in Australia, and the town also has the Raj Mahal Indian Cultural Centre, an Indian theme park.

Woolgoolga looks out to sea and the Solitary Island Marine Reserve, one of the most significant

Crossing the Hawkesbury River at Wisemans Ferry

group of islands on the New South Wales coast. It is popular with SCUBA divers and snorkellers because of the tremendous array of marine life, with schools of pelagic fish, rays, turtles, clown fish and numerous varieties of coral.

There are good, local surfing beaches and fishing spots, together with great views from the headland over tiny neighbouring villages like Emerald Beach, Red Rock and Corindi and the coastline itself.

Nearby forests like Wedding Bells and Woolgoolga Creek Flora Reserve have striking examples of hoop pine and silver quandong.

ACCOMMODATION: Woolgoolga Motor Inn, ph (02) 6654 1534; Balcony View Motor Inn, ph (02) 6654 1289; Emerald Beach Holiday Units, ph (02) 6656 1370; Seaside Holiday Units, ph (02) 6654 1349; Woolgoolga Beach Caravan & Camping, ph (02) 6654 1373
ACTIVITIES: Bushwalking, fishing, sightseeing, water sports
TOURIST INFORMATION: Ph (02) 6652 1522

WOOLI

695 KM NORTH OF SYDNEY
POPULATION: 460   MAP REF: PAGE 179 N6
The coastal village of Wooli is located on a peninsula with the Wooli River on one side and Solitary Island Marine Reserve on the other. Behind it is Yuraygir National Park. The town is almost hidden by nature.

Wooli has a burgeoning oyster industry. It is proud of the fact that the waters of the river are completely surrounded by the national park, creating exceptionally clean water untainted by industry.

The marine park is a favourite for anglers and also for divers, and boats can be chartered for fishing, diving, whale and dolphin watching or scenic cruises.
ACCOMMODATION: Wooli River Lodge, ph (02) 6649 7750; Bushland Holiday Park (camping/caravans), ph (02) 6649 7519; Wooli Caravan Park, ph (02) 6649 7671
ACTIVITIES: Fishing, national park access, sightseeing, water sports, whale and dolphin watching
TOURIST INFORMATION: Ph (02) 6642 4677

WOY WOY

100 KM NORTH OF SYDNEY
POPULATION: 12 205   MAP REF: PAGE 177 H8
Woy Woy (the name means 'deep water') relies almost entirely on tourism for its community income, although being within commuting distance of Sydney, a number of city workers live in Woy Woy.

Originally known as Webbs Flat after the first European in the area, James Webb, who arrived in 1834, the name Woy Woy was conferred in 1888.

These days, fishing, boating and swimming—along with the beautiful scenery—attract large numbers of visitors. There are also important national parks in the area, including Brisbane Water, which contains the Bulgandry Aboriginal rock carvings and has an abundance of wildflowers, bushwalks and bird life. The wreck of the *Maitland* is within Bouddi National

Fishing on the Hawkesbury River near Woy Woy

Park, which features good bushwalking, swimming and fishing areas. Near the entrance to the park, Marie Byles Lookout has great views of Sydney.

In November Woy Woy celebrates the Oyster and Wine Festival.
ACCOMMODATION: Glades Country Club Motor Inn, ph (02) 4341 7374; Woy Woy Hotel, ph (02) 4341 1013; Bay View Hotel, ph (02) 4341 2088
ACTIVITIES: Bushwalking, fishing, national park access, scenic drives, sightseeing, water sports
TOURIST INFORMATION: Ph (02) 4343 2200

WYONG

109 KM NORTH OF SYDNEY
POPULATION: 3902   MAP REF: PAGE 177 J7
Now a popular tourist resort, Wyong was founded on timber-getting in the 1840s and 1850s. The name means 'place of running water'. The chief industries of the district are timber milling, dairying, poultry farming and citrus fruit.

The District Museum has some interesting relics of the early logging days, as well as material relating to early ferry services across the surrounding lakes. The system of lakes stretches from Lake Munmorah in the north to Killarney Vale in the south, and also embraces Budgewoi and the more famous Tuggerah Lake, which is the largest and the only one offering access to the sea (at The Entrance).

The Wyong hinterland is popular with bush-walkers and campers, and to the north, the state forests also offer some fun for drivers of 4WDs. There are some superb lookouts in the forests, much appreciated by photographers.
ACCOMMODATION: Central Coast Motel, ph (02) 4353 2911; Dam Hotel/Motel, ph (02) 4392 3333; Warners Lodge, ph (02) 4352 1161
ACTIVITIES: Bushwalking, camping, fishing, 4WD touring, greyhound racing, trotting, water sports
TOURIST INFORMATION: Ph (02) 4392 4666

YAMBA

715 KM NORTH OF SYDNEY
POPULATION: 3710   MAP REF: PAGE 179 N5
The largest resort town in the Clarence Valley, Yamba translates as 'edible shellfish'. The earliest known European contact with the area occurred in 1799, when Matthew Flinders moored near the estuary, but it was 1861 before the town was surveyed.

Yamba is noted for its fishing and mild climate, and its surfing beach is regarded as one of the safest on the coast.

For those of an historical bent, the Story House Museum contains a photographic display of early life in the town.

For the active person, Yamba offers sea, lake and river fishing, and boats are available for hire. At Brushgrove, 35 km to the south-west, you can also hire houseboats. Daily passenger ferries run to Iluka, and there are also river cruises. Good fishing and prawning is available at Lake Wooloweyah, and the superb Yuraygir National Park, with its sand ridges and banksia heath, is close by.

At Angourie, 5 km to the south is a freshwater pool, known as the Blue Pool. Only 50 metres from the ocean, it is a favourite spot with families for picnics and swimming.

Yamba holds a community market on the last Sunday of each month and in September/October, the Family Fishing Festival takes place.
ACCOMMODATION: Pacific Hotel, ph (02) 6646 2466; Yamba Shores Tavern (hotel), ph (02) 6646 1888; Moby Dick Waterfront Motel, ph (02) 6646 2196; Oyster Shores Motel, ph (02) 6646 1122; Seascape Beachfront Units, ph (02) 6646 2694; Jane's of Yamba (units), ph (02) 6646 2982; Yamba Waters Caravan Park, ph (02) 6646 2930; Blue Dolphin Holiday Resort (camping/caravans), ph (02) 6646 2194
ACTIVITIES: Bushwalking, fishing, national park access, prawning, water sports
TOURIST INFORMATION: Ph (02) 6645 4121

YANCO

607 KM SOUTH-WEST OF SYDNEY
POPULATION: 650   MAP REF: PAGE 183 L5

You can learn a lot about Yanco by visiting the Powerhouse Museum in town. The Yanco Power-house was built in 1913 to supply power to the Murrumbidgee Irrigation Area (MIA) and closed down in 1957, when electricity from the Snowy Mountains Scheme became available. The building is five storeys high and is made entirely of concrete. It now displays farm machinery and items of local history and also has a theatrette seating 60.

On Yanko Station, Samuel McCaughey first experimented with the irrigation procedures that led to the creation of the MIA. Though his mansion is now an agricultural high school, it is open to the public.

There are extensive red gum forests along the Murrumbidgee, and scenic drives that lead to pleasant swimming and fishing spots.
ACCOMMODATION: Hotel Yanco, ph (02) 6955 7253
ACTIVITIES: Fishing, scenic drives, swimming
TOURIST INFORMATION: Ph (02) 6953 2832

YARRANGOBILLY

497 KM SOUTH-WEST OF SYDNEY
POPULATION: 10   MAP REF: PAGE 174 B6

This historic village is a shadow of what it once was, with only Cotterill's Cottage (named after the family who lived there until the 1950s) and some public facilities still standing. Yarrangobilly means 'flowing stream' in Aboriginal. In winter, the village is frequently covered in snow.

Yarrangobilly is a great camping and fishing spot, with fascinating spongy tundra-type vegetation. The Yarrangobilly River is chillingly clean. The nearest 'hot running water' accommodation is at Talbingo. Alternatively, stay at Tumut or Adaminaby.

Most people come to the region to look at Yarrangobilly Caves, which were carved by the river out of limestone some 440 million years ago. There are some good bushwalks around the area.
ACCOMMODATION: Camping sites
ACTIVITIES: Bushwalking, caving, fishing, sightseeing
TOURIST INFORMATION: Ph (02) 6949 5334

YASS

292 KM SOUTH-WEST OF SYDNEY
POPULATION: 4828   MAP REF: PAGE 174 C4

Originally called McDougall's Plains by the first Europeans to see the area, explorers Hume and Hovell, the town of Yass was gazetted in 1837. The name means 'running water'. Nowadays Yass is the centre of a fertile agricultural and pastoral area, with fine Merino wool, and sheep and cattle studs.

Close to the junction of two major highways, the Hume and the Barton, Yass was once thought to be a good site for the proposed Federal capital. Hamilton Hume, who is buried in Yass cemetery in a tomb of his own design, settled in Yass and his house, Cooma

Cooma Cottage, once Hamilton Hume's home, in Yass

Cottage, is listed by the National Trust and is open for inspection by visitors.

Yass has always been a prosperous town, and fine buildings attest to this. (There are still hitching rails along the street.) The museum in Comur Street is worth visiting to see just how Yass made its money in the old days compared with today.

The nearby Gooradigbee River offers excellent trout fishing. Further south is Carey's Cave, with some marvellous limestone formations. Burrinjuck Dam is also to the south and offers the visitor a chance to bushwalk, fish, or indulge in water sports.

Yass holds its agricultural show in March and a rodeo in November.
ACCOMMODATION: Colonial Lodge Motor Inn, ph 1800 807 686; Hamilton Hume Motor Inn, ph (02) 6226 1722; Club House Hotel, ph (02) 6226 1042; Royal Hotel, ph (02) 6226 1005; Swaggers Conference & Function Centre (B&B), ph (02) 6226 3188; Yass Caravan Park, ph (02) 6226 1173
ACTIVITIES: Bushwalking, fishing, scenic drives, sightseeing, water sports
TOURIST INFORMATION: Ph (02) 6226 2557

Cherry trees in flower at Young

YENDA

599 KM SOUTH-WEST OF SYDNEY
POPULATION: 695   MAP REF: PAGE 183 L4

Yenda is a small farming town in the Murrumbidgee Irrigation Area and had most of its development after World War I, when returned servicemen were given the opportunity for a rural existence on what were called 'soldier settlement blocks'. The land now supports wheat, rice and citrus fruits.
ACCOMMODATION: Yenda Hotel, ph (02) 6968 1014
ACTIVITIES: Scenic drives
TOURIST INFORMATION: Ph (02) 6962 4145

YOUNG

378 KM SOUTH-WEST OF SYDNEY
POPULATION: 6666   MAP REF: PAGE 176 A10

The undisputed cherry capital of New South Wales, Young came into being because of a gold rush in the 1860s. Lambing Flat, as the township was known, was the site of the infamous anti-Chinese riots. The town was eventually renamed after Sir John Young, Governor of New South Wales between 1861 and 1867.

Today the Young district produces wheat, wool, lucerne and fat lambs. In town, the Lambing Flat Folk Museum and the Burrangong Art Gallery should not be missed.

Four kilometres south-east of town, the Chinaman's Dam recreation area has picnic and BBQ facilities, a children's playground and scenic walks. Two local wineries—Wodonga Hill and Demondrille Vineyard—are open for tastings.
ACCOMMODATION: Federation Motor Inn, ph 639 988; Townhouse Motor Inn, ph (02) 6382 1366; Young Tourist Park (camping/caravans), ph (02) 6382 2190
ACTIVITIES: Bushwalking, scenic drives, wineries
TOURIST INFORMATION: Ph (02) 6382 5433

The sandy landscape of the World Heritage-listed Mungo National Park

BALD ROCK NATIONAL PARK

This park is located 29 km north of Tenterfield on the Wodenbong road. The centrepiece of this park is the huge dome-shaped granite monolith of Bald Rock itself, weathered in stripes of grey, brown and pink, which rises above the surrounding eucalypt forest and rainforest. Smaller outcrops of rock are scattered through the park. A walk to the summit of Bald Rock, with magnificent views west and north across the border to Girraween National Park and east to the Pacific, will take about two hours return.

BARRINGTON TOPS NATIONAL PARK

Barrington Tops and Gloucester Tops form a high plateau on the Great Divide between Scone and Gloucester on the Mid North Coast. It is an area of high rainfall and sudden, dramatic weather changes—storms and even snowstorms. The park gained a World Heritage listing for its magnificent and diverse vegetation, which ranges from snow gums and heathlands at the higher altitudes to cool-temperate rainforest with Antarctic beeches in more sheltered gullies and subtropical rainforest in the lower valleys.

BEN BOYD NATIONAL PARK

Extending north and south of Eden on the Far South Coast, this park protects the superb stretches of rocky coastline on either side of Twofold Bay. There are great surfing beaches, sheltered coves and inlets, sea caves and headlands. At Long Beach the colourful red and white rocks have been eroded to form the spectacular columns of the Pinnacles. The coastal heathlands produce spectacular wildflowers in late spring, and further inland banksia forests give way to dense, tall eucalypts. Some of the access roads can be slippery after rain and are better suited to a 4WD than a conventional vehicle. The ruins of Benjamin Boyd's old whaling station near Twofold Bay, established in the 1840s, are worth a visit.

BOOTI BOOTI NATIONAL PARK

This small park, on a narrow strip of land between the Pacific Ocean and Wallis Lake in the beautiful Myall Lakes district of the Mid North Coast, is 10 km south of Forster. The area is renowned for its great surfing beaches, sailing and windsurfing opportunities on the saltwater lake, and fishing.

BORDER RANGES NATIONAL PARK

With its dramatic setting on the rim of an extinct volcano, of which Mt Warning is the remnant core, this is one of the most scenic parks in New South Wales. It is part of a World Heritage listed area to preserve its cool-temperate and subtropical rainforests, and a number of rare plant and animal species. The Tweed Ranges scenic drive makes a large loop through the park, and there are excellent walks along the way; do not miss the Antarctic beech trees in the rainforest walk at Bar Mountain and the Pinnacle walk with its breathtaking views across the Tweed Valley to Mt Warning. Roads in the park are gravel and steeply graded, and a 4WD vehicle would be useful in wet conditions.

BOUDDI NATIONAL PARK

Protecting the northern foreshore at the entrance to Broken Bay, this small park has a magnificent coastline of rocky cliffs and headlands, sheltered bays and fine surf beaches, backed by coastal heathlands, with open forest and pockets of rainforest further inland. A special feature of the park is the 280 hectare marine extension which offers great opportunities for skindiving and snorkelling—but not fishing!

BRISBANE WATER NATIONAL PARK

Set in the rugged sandstone country in the lower reaches of the Hawkesbury River, just an hour's drive north of Sydney, this park is a boating paradise, with peaceful bays and mangrove-fringed inlets for fishing, broad reaches for waterskiing, plus deep gorges with rainforest, heavily timbered slopes and walking tracks through superbly scenic terrain. There is bush camping without facilities, and no 4WD tracks.

BUNDJALUNG NATIONAL PARK

Bundjalung National Park protects a stretch of coast and heathland between Iluka and Evans Head on the North Coast. With long sandy beaches, lagoons and mangrove swamps, it is a great place for fishing, surfing and canoeing.

CATHEDRAL ROCK NATIONAL PARK

Set high on the Great Divide in the New England area, this park is 77 km east of Armidale. Its main feature is the huge free-standing granite boulders, Cathedral Rock and others, which are balanced one on top of another like piles of pebbles, here and there across the Snowy Range. There are excellent views from the top of Cathedral Rock and Woolpack Rocks if you have the energy for the climb. The vegetation is mainly open eucalypt forest, with snow gums at higher altitudes.

KANANGRA–BOYD NATIONAL PARK

This park is located west of Sydney, near the Jenolan caves. Famous for its rugged terrain and wilderness areas, the park occupies the southwest corner of the group of parks that protect the Blue Mountains and the Hawkesbury. With sandstone cliffs and gorges, caves, waterfalls and panoramic views, this is a park for experienced, well-equipped bushwalkers, and there is a labyrinth of tracks. Frequent snowfalls in winter and sudden thunderstorms in summer mean that you need to carry appropriate clothing at all times. Vegetation is mainly eucalypt forest, with heathlands on exposed ridges and rainforest in sheltered gullies.

KOSCIUSZKO NATIONAL PARK

This magnificent park in the Snowy Mountains, by far the biggest national park in New South Wales, contains many of the country's top ski fields and offers a range of year-round activities. Walking, horse riding, trout fishing and even canoeing are enjoyed in the warmer months. The landscape ranges from high plains, with their spectacular display of wildflowers in summer, through mountain slopes with gnarled and twisted snow gums, to sheltered valleys at lower altitudes with fine stands of mountain ash and stringybark. The rare mountain pygmy possum inhabits the high plains, while kangaroos, wallabies, wombats and possums live on the lower slopes. During winter all vehicles to the park must carry snow chains and fit them when advised.

KU-RING-GAI CHASE NATIONAL PARK

Located in the northern suburbs of Sydney, this park has magnificent views across Broken Bay to Palm Beach and Brisbane Water National Park. Some of the sandstone caves and shelters contain Aboriginal engravings and drawings, and the Garigal Aboriginal Heritage Walk takes you to a selection of them. Naturally enough, the park is popular at weekends, but there is a marvellous range of bushwalking tracks along creeks and ridgelines; also picnic facilities, and boat ramps at Cottage Point and Akuna Bay.

MORTON NATIONAL PARK

This vast park stretches south along the Great Divide, from near Moss Vale to where it adjoins the Budawang National Park. The northern portion of the park offers the stunning mountain scenery of Kangaroo Valley and Bundanoon, high sandstone ridges and deep gorges cut by the Shoalhaven River and its tributaries, and the magnificent Fitzroy Falls. The southern section is a rugged wilderness area of deep sandstone cliffs and weathered gorges: a bushwalkers' paradise. During spring, the wildflowers put on a wonderful display. There is a visitor information centre.

MUNGO NATIONAL PARK

An area of saltbush plains, dry lakebeds and parched claypans, this park is listed as a World Heritage area to preserve records of Aboriginal existence dating back more than 40 000 years. At that time, Lake Mungo was a freshwater lake stocked with fish and shellfish; shell middens and fireplaces on its shores reveal that the Aboriginal people lived and ate well here. Other archaeological finds give information about many aspects of Aboriginal culture over thousands of years, as the climate changed and the lake dried out. Another reminder of the ancient past is the Walls of China; this natural formation on the shore of Lake Mungo is a 30 km long crescent of orange and white sand dunes sculptured by wind and rain

into fantastic shapes, then coloured and hardened with deposits of salt, clay and mud. Camping is available but bookings may be necessary. The park is north-east of Mildura, off the Sturt Highway, in the south-west of the state.

MYALL LAKES NATIONAL PARK

Two-thirds of the area of this magnificent park consists of a series of shallow, connected coastal lakes, separated from the Pacific Ocean by high sand dunes. It is the largest coastal lake system in New South Wales and is very popular, especially in school holidays. The tranquil lakes provide wonderful opportunities for fishing, sailing, windsurfing and canoeing, while the ocean beaches offer excellent surf as well as beach fishing. The park is 230 km north of Sydney via Tea Gardens.

ROYAL NATIONAL PARK

Gazetted in 1879, the Royal National Park is the oldest national park in Australia and the second oldest in the world. Just 32 km south of Sydney, bordered by the Pacific Ocean and the shores of Port Hacking, it is an area of quiet beaches and bays, with headlands and sea caves carved out of the sandstone; inland, there are creeks, waterfalls and clear rockpools. Banksia heathlands cover the stony ground, making glorious displays of wildflowers in spring, while open forest and rainforest are found further from the coast. A range of walking tracks lead to isolated beaches, or follow tree-lined streams. It is possible to bush camp (with a permit) along some of the walking tracks.

STURT NATIONAL PARK

This huge park occupies the far north-west corner of the state, the borders of Queensland and South Australia forming its northern and western boundaries. The post that marks Cameron Corner, the point where the borders of the three states meet, is within the park; it is named for John Cameron, who first surveyed this area in the 1880s. This is semi-arid desert country, the Outback, with gibber plains and flat-topped jump-ups (mesas) on the horizon; spectacular red sand ridges run parallel to each other, and between them are lake beds that fill with water after heavy rains. River red gums line the waterholes, and the stony plains are sparsely covered

with spinifex. There are camping areas at Mt Wood, Dead Horse Gully (near Tibooburra), Fort Grey and Olive Downs.

WADBILLIGA NATIONAL PARK

Inland from Narooma on the Far South Coast, the rugged eastern escarpment and plateau of the Great Divide are protected in this park, which almost meets Deua National Park on its northern boundary. The Tuross, Wadbilliga and Brogo Rivers rise in these mountains and have carved their wide, deep valleys through the granite of the park; walking tracks to the spectacular Tuross Falls and the Tuross Gorge are recommended for experienced and well-equipped bushwalkers. Although this park is primarily wilderness, it does allow 4WD access via roads from Cobargo and Eurobodalla. You can bush camp at the Cascades.

WARRUMBUNGLE NATIONAL PARK

This park is 27 km west of Coonabarabran in central New South Wales. Volcanic activity over millions of years, followed by erosion of the less durable rocks, has produced the dramatic landforms and scenery of the Warrumbungle Range. The remnants of ancient volcanic plugs now tower above the forested slopes, the most distinctive and widely photographed of these being the tall, thin, jagged spire of the Breadknife. Bushwalking and mountain climbing are the main activities in the park; there is a good range of walking tracks, from an easy nature walk of 1 km to more challenging walks and climbs to lookouts with spectacular views. The Blackman camping ground has good facilities; Pincham and Wambelong have basic facilities. You need a camping permit, obtainable in advance or from the visitor centre. Note that this is a low rainfall area, so carry sufficient water for your needs within the park.

WERRIKIMBE NATIONAL PARK

On the eastern slopes of the New England Tablelands, 90 km north-west of Port Macquarie, lies this World Heritage listed park. Three rivers, the Hastings, Forbes and Kunderang Brook, rise in these mountains and tumble down in cascades and waterfalls, through gorges and steep-sided valleys to the coast. With its range of altitudes,

Werrikimbe National Park protects a great diversity of flora, from the subtropical rainforest gullies of Cobcrofts Brush, through temperate rainforest with fine Antarctic beech trees, to snow gums, and alpine heaths and swamps. The area teems with wildlife, especially kangaroos and wallabies. Gravel roads should be avoided in wet weather as they become very slippery; winter snowfalls can occur, so go prepared for very cold weather. There is great camping (with basic facilities) at Cobcrofts and Mooraback on the western side of the park and Brushy Mountain on the eastern edge.

WILLANDRA NATIONAL PARK

In the late 1880s Big Willandra Station was a famous Merino stud occupying 290 000 hectares of the flat red sandplains of central western New South Wales. Over the years close settlement led to subdivision, and the final leasehold was resumed in 1972 to form Willandra National Park; the old homestead, woolshed, stables and other station buildings were later added to the park. Willandra Creek forms the northern boundary of the park, and Willandra Billabong attracts many species of waterbirds. Coolibahs and black box trees line the banks of the creek and waterhole; away from water, the semi-arid sandplains are sparsely covered with saltbush and native grasses. Emus and kangaroos are abundant. It is possible to stay in the old homestead, however bookings are essential. There is also a camp site near the homestead. Fees apply for both.

WOLLEMI NATIONAL PARK

This huge park, west of Sydney in the Blue Mountains, stretches from the Bells Line of Road, where it abuts the Blue Mountains National Park, north to the Hunter Valley. Much of the park is designated wilderness, protecting some of the most rugged mountain country in Australia— sheer cliffs and ridges, deep canyons, cool rivers and ancient vegetation. This is excellent country for the experienced bushwalker but, because it is so remote, you need to be well prepared. From Bells Line of Road it is possible to reach the old train tunnels of the Newnes mining area, visiting the canyons of Deep Pass and the rock gardens of the Lost City on the way. Camping with basic facilities is available at Newnes and Wheeney Creek.

Popular Parks	Camping	Caravans	Wheel Chairs	4WD Access	Picnic Area	Toilets	Walking Trks	Kiosk	Information
1 Bald Rock NP	■				■	■	■		
2 Barrington Tops NP	■			■	■	■	■		
3 Ben Boyd NP	■		■		■	■	■		
4 Blue Mountains NP	■	■	■	■	■	■	■	■	■
5 Boonoo Boonoo NP	■				■	■	■		
6 Booti Booti NP	■				■	■	■		
7 Border Ranges NP	■				■	■	■		
8 Bouddi NP	■				■	■	■		
9 Bournda NP	■	■	■		■	■	■		
10 Brisbane Water NP					■	■	■		
11 Broadwater NP					■	■	■		
12 Budawang NP	■			■			■		
13 Budderoo NP			■		■	■	■	■	■
14 Bundjalung NP	■		■	■	■	■	■		
15 Cathedral Rock NP	■				■	■	■		
16 Cocoparra NP	■			■	■	■	■		
17 Conimbla NP					■	■			
18 Crowdy Bay NP	■				■	■	■		
19 Deua NP	■			■		■	■		
20 Dharug NP	■			■	■	■	■		
21 Dorrigo NP			■		■	■	■	■	■
22 Gibraltar Range NP	■	■			■	■	■		■
23 Goulburn River NP	■				■		■		
24 Guy Fawkes NP	■		■	■	■	■	■		
25 Heathcote NP	■				■	■	■		

Popular Parks	Camping	Caravans	Wheel Chairs	4WD Access	Picnic Area	Toilets	Walking Trks	Kiosk	Information
26 Kanangra-Boyd NP	■	■	■	■	■	■	■		
27 Kinchega NP	■	■		■	■	■			
28 Kosciuszko NP	■	■	■		■	■	■	■	■
29 Ku-ring-gai Chase NP	■		■		■	■	■	■	■
30 Macquarie Pass NP					■		■		
31 Mootwingee NP	■	■	■	■	■	■	■		
32 Morton NP	■				■	■	■	■	■
33 Mount Kaputar NP	■				■	■	■		
34 Mount Warning NP					■		■		
35 Mungo NP	■	■		■	■	■	■		
36 Murramarang NP	■	■			■	■	■		
37 Myall Lakes NP	■	■			■	■	■		
38 Namadgi NP	■		■		■	■	■		
39 Nattai NP							■		
40 New England NP	■				■	■	■		■
41 Royal NP	■				■	■	■	■	■
42 Sturt NP	■			■	■	■			
43 Wadbilliga NP	■			■			■		
44 Wallaga Lake NP					■				
45 Warrumbungle NP	■	■	■		■	■	■		■
46 Washpool NP	■				■	■	■		
47 Werrikimbe NP	■				■	■	■		
48 Willandra NP	■				■	■	■		
49 Wollemi NP	■				■	■	■		
50 Yengo NP	■			■	■	■	■		

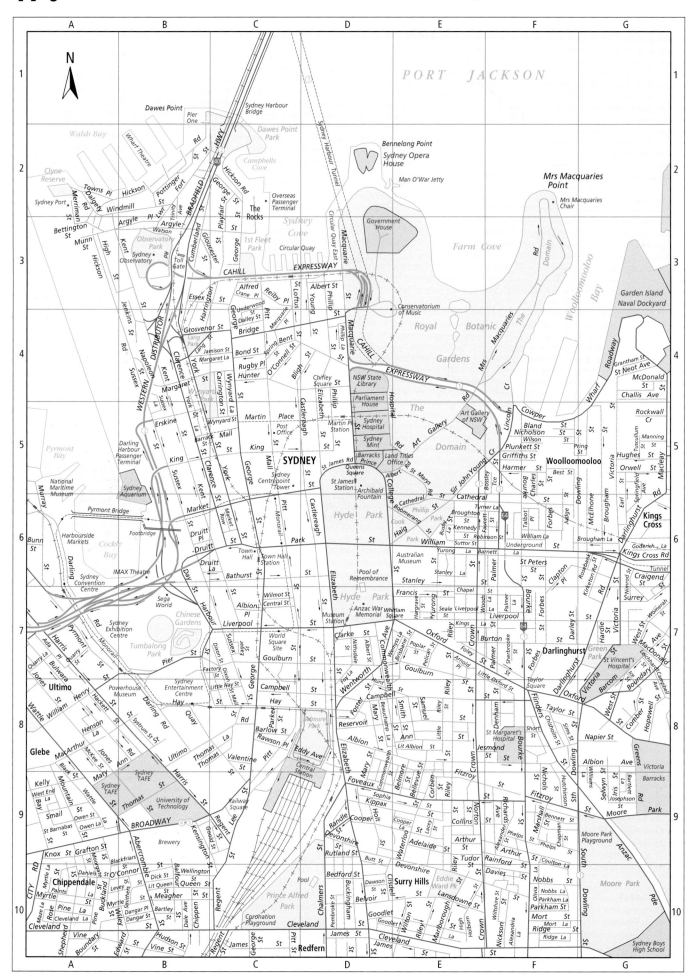

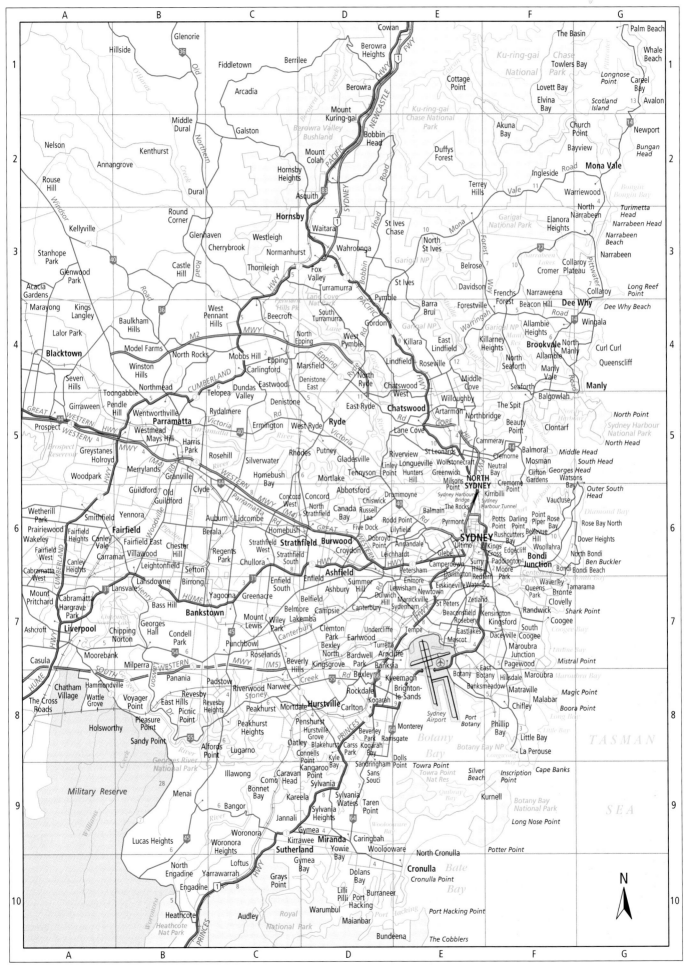

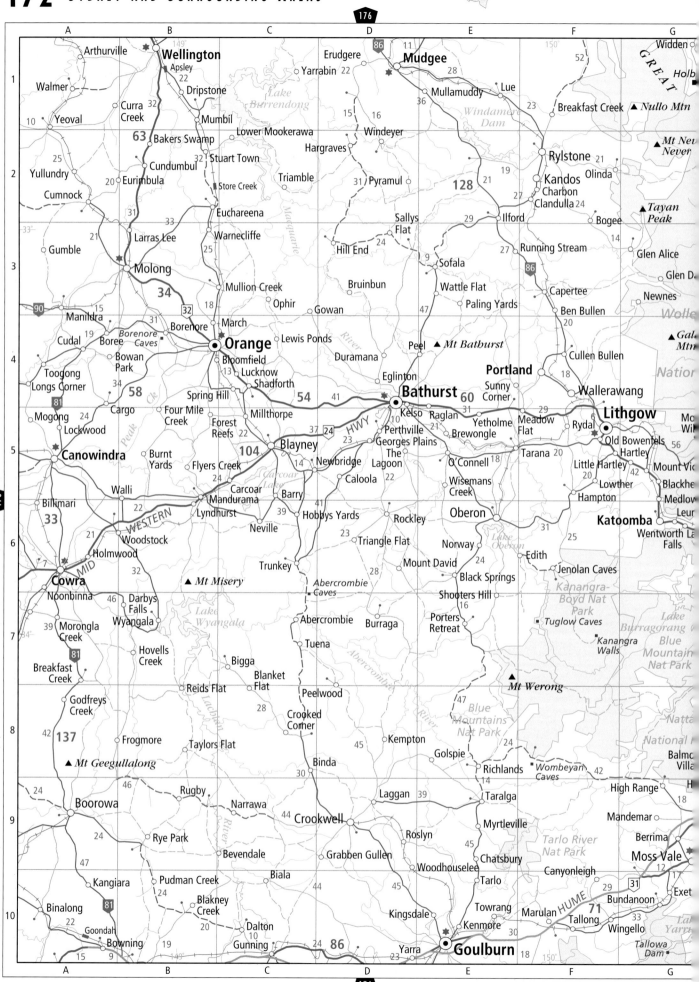

0   10   20   30   40   50
kilometres

H | J | K | L | M | N | P

1
rami Creek | Glen Gallic | Doyles Creek | Maison Dieu | Redbournberry | Vacy | Martins Creek | Clarence Town | Allworth | 26 | 152 | 22 | Mungo Brush
Warkworth | Singleton | Paterson | Limeburners Creek | 88
Mt Wambo ▲ | 10 | Branxton | Woodville | Seaham | Karuah | 21 | 1 | Tea Gardens
ollemi National Park | 11 | Belford | Greta | 22 | Wallalong | Swan Bay | 17 | Hawks Nest
Bulga | 16 | 21 | Rutherford | Morpeth | Medowie | Soldiers Point
Coriaday | 37 | 43 | **Maitland** | Metford | 9 | **Raymond Terrace** | 51 | **Nelson Bay**
Broke | Rothbury | 36 | Abermain | 28 | Kurri Kurri | 18 | Beresfield | Williamtown | Anna Bay | Boat Harbour
▲ *Kindarun Mtn* | *Yellow Rock* | **Cessnock** | 37 | Sandgate | Fern Bay | *Newcastle Bight*
27 | 69 | 31 | Bellbird | 27 | Pelaw Main | 19 | Wallsend | Stockton | *Port Hunter*
Howes Valley | 30 | Paxton | Kearsley | Kitchener | 37 | Broadmeadow | **Newcastle**
▲ *Mt Yengo* | Ellalong | Brunkerville | Boolaroo | Charlestown
Putty | Wollombi | Warners Bay | 18
Laguna | 23 | Dora Creek | Belmont
3
Yengo | Bucketty | Cooranbong | Morisset | Swansea
Nat Park | Cedar Brush Creek | 23 | Gwandalan | *Lake Macquarie*
19 | 1 | Wyee | 46 | Catherine Hill Bay
Kulnura | Dooralong | Lake Munmorah
St Albans | Yarramalong | Doyalson | Budgewoi
27 | Jilliby | 85 | Toukley
4
Colo Heights | Central Mangrove | **Wyong** | *Norah Head*
69 | Wisemans Ferry | Peats Ridge | Tuggerah | *Tuggerah Lake*
unt Irvine Bilpin | *Dharug Nat Pk* | Calga | 19 | Ourimbah | The Entrance
Stanley Park | Maroota | 21 | **Gosford**
40 | 28 | *Marramarra Nat Pk* | Kariong | Terrigal
5
Kurrajong | Cattai | 44 | Woy Woy | *Bouddi NP*
Richmond | Berowra Waters | Killcare | *SOUTH*
6 | Windsor | Brooklyn | Umina | *Broken Bay*
Londonderry | Box Hill | 88 | Palm Beach | *Ku-ring-gai Chase NP*
Springwood | Cranebrook | **Hornsby** | Mona Vale
6
Blaxland | 21 | Parklea | Narrabeen | *TASMAN*
odford | 18 | Blacktown | Terrey Hills | 28 | *Long Reef Point*
Penrith | St Marys | 25 | Pymble | 25 | Manly
31 | Chatswood | *PACIFIC*
34 | Erskine Park | **Parramatta** | North Sydney
7
Warragamba | Kemps Creek | 14 | 23 | *Port Jackson*
Bringelly | **Liverpool** | **SYDNEY** | *SEA*
ombi | 69 | Bankstown | Bondi Junction
dale | 27 | Narellan | 20 | Eagle Vale | Hurstville | Botany | 34
Camden | Heathcote | 55 | Caringbah | *Botany Bay*
8
Picton | 89 | **Campbelltown** | Como | Cronulla
moor | 28 | 18 | Sutherland | *Port Hacking*
Buxton | Appin | Waterfall | Bundeena
Bargo | Wilton | 104 | Helensburgh | *Royal National Park* | *OCEAN*
41 | 69 | 31 | Stanwell Park | Coalcliff
Yanderra | *Lake Cataract*
9
Yerrinbool | Corrimal | Thirroul
ylmerton | Balgownie
tagong | **Wollongong**
ral | Unanderra | *Red Point*
Kangaloon | 61 | Dapto | **Port Kembla**
48 | Albion Park | *Lake Illawarra*
Robertson | 21 | **Shellharbour** | *Bass Point*
10
75 | Minnamurra
Jamberoo | **Kiama**
Kangaroo Valley | 42 | Werri Beach
Berry | Gerringong
17 | HWY
pers Brush | Gerroa | N
151 | 152

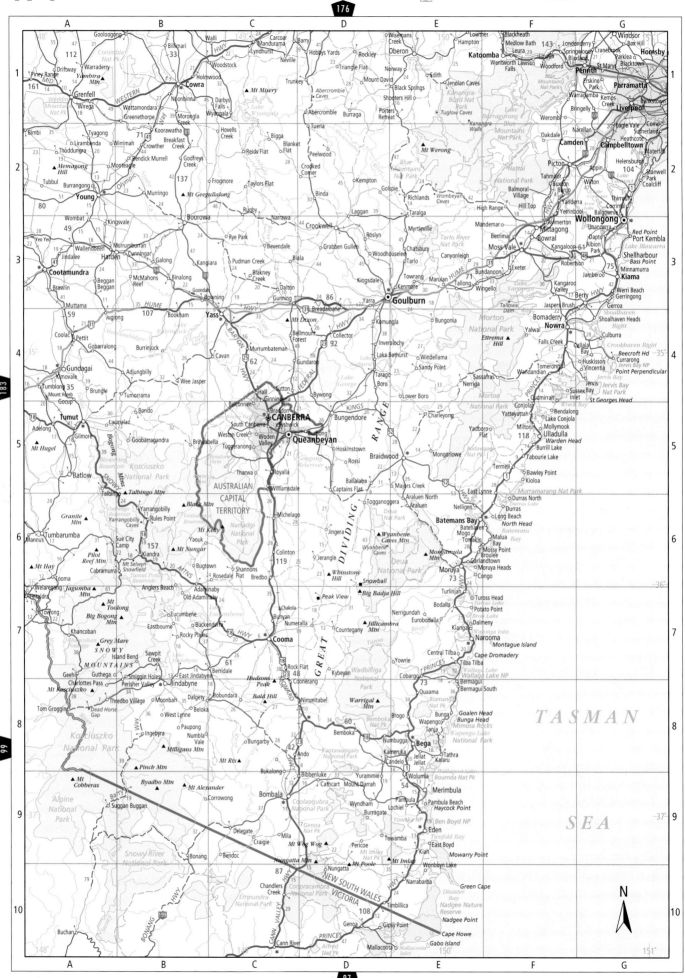

© Random House Australia Pty Ltd

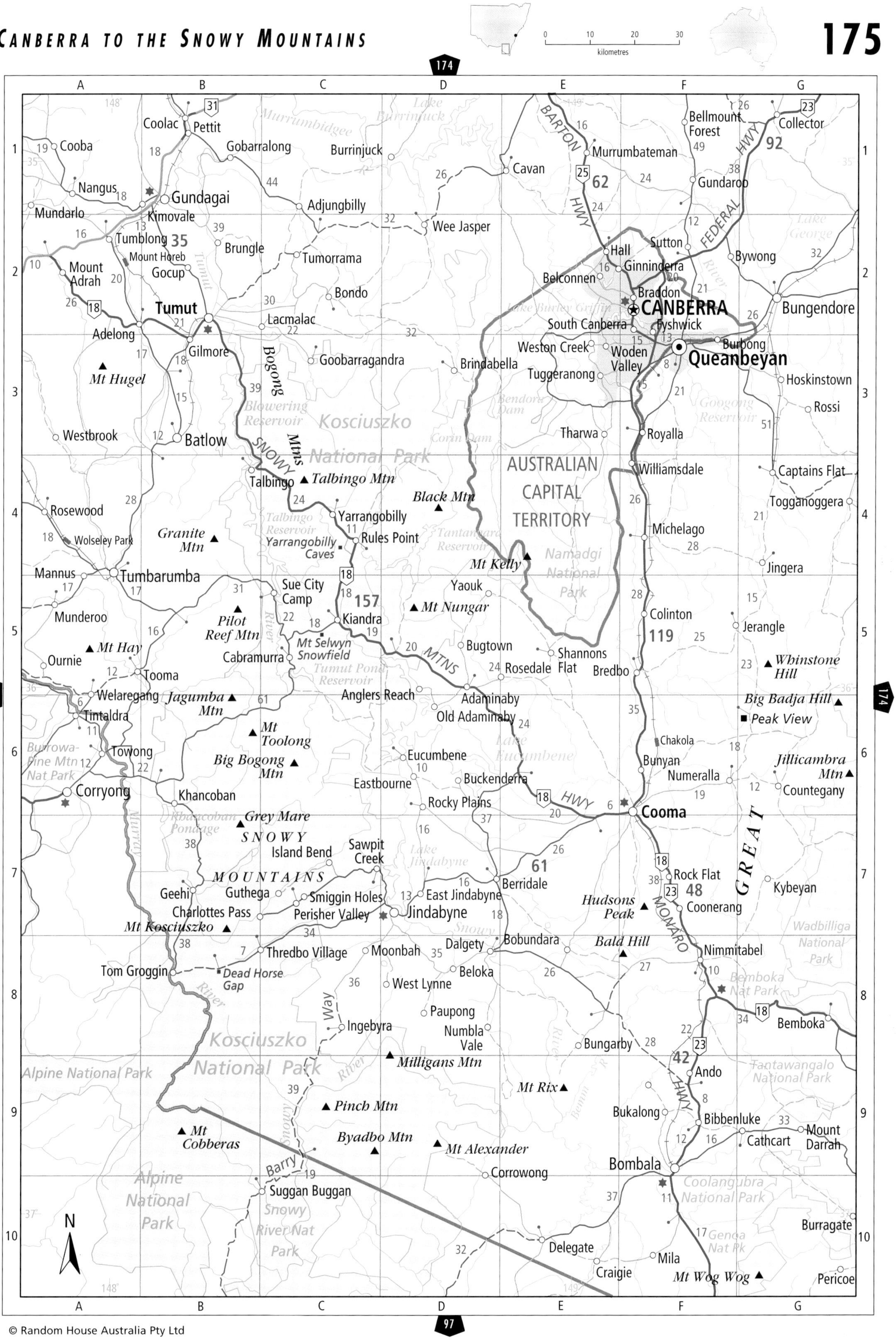

kilometres

Coolac
Pettit
31
Gobarralong
Burrinjuck
Cooba
19
35
Nangus
18
Gundagai
Kimovale
13
Mundarlo
16
Tumblong 35
39
Mount Horeb
Brungle
Mount Adrah
Gocup
10
20
Tumorrama
Bondo
26
18
Tumut
30
Lacmalac
Adelong
21
22
32
17
Gilmore
18
Goobarragandra
Mt Hugel
15
39
Westbrook
12
Batlow
Talbingo
Talbingo Mtn
Black Mtn
24
Yarrangobilly
Rosewood
28
11
Rules Point
Granite Mtn
Yarrangobilly Caves
18
Wolseley Park
18
Mannus
Sue City Camp
18 157
Tumbarumba
31
18
Mt Nungar
17
17
22
Kiandra
18
19
Munderoo
16
Pilot Reef Mtn
Mt Selwyn Snowfield
20
Bugtown
Mt Hay
Cabramurra
Ournie
Tumut Pond Reservoir
Tooma
12
Anglers Reach
24
Rosedale Flat
Welaregang
Jagumba Mtn
61
Adaminaby
Tintaldra
6
Old Adaminaby
11
Towong
22
Mt Toolong
24
Corryong
Big Bogong Mtn
Eucumbene
10
Khancoban
Buckenderra
Eastbourne
Grey Mare
Rocky Plains
18
Island Bend
Sawpit Creek
16
37
SNOWY
Geehi
Guthega
MOUNTAINS
Smiggin Holes
13
East Jindabyne
Charlottes Pass
Perisher Valley
Jindabyne
61
Berridale
Mt Kosciuszko
34
38
Tom Groggin
7
Thredbo Village
Moonbah
Dalgety
Bobundara
Dead Horse Gap
36
West Lynne
35
Beloka
Ingebyra
Paupong
26
Milligans Mtn
Numbla Vale
Pinch Mtn
39
Mt Rix
Mt Cobberas
Byadbo Mtn
Mt Alexander
Corrowong
Barry
19
Suggan Buggan
Snowy River Nat Park
Delegate
32
Craigie
Mila

148°
Murrumbidgee
Lake Burrinjuck
Adjungbilly
Wee Jasper
44
32
Cavan
16
Murrumbateman
Bellmount Forest
26
Collector
25 62
49
92
24
Gundaroo
38
12
Bywong
32
Lake George
Hall
Sutton
16
Ginninderra
Belconnen
Braddon
21
26
CANBERRA
South Canberra
Fyshwick
Bungendore
Weston Creek
Woden Valley
15 13
Queanbeyan
Burbong
Tuggeranong
8
Hoskinstown
Brindabella
15
21
Rossi
Tharwa
Royalla
51
AUSTRALIAN CAPITAL TERRITORY
Williamsdale
Captains Flat
Togganoggera
21
Mt Kelly
Michelago
26
28
Jingera
Yaouk
15
Colinton
Jerangle
119
25
23
Whinstone Hill
Shannons Flat
Bredbo
35
Big Badja Hill
Peak View
Chakola
18
Bunyan
Jillicambra Mtn
Numeralla
12
Countegany
18 HWY
20
6
Cooma
19
GREAT
18
Rock Flat
23 48
Kybeyan
Hudsons Peak
38
Coonerang
Bald Hill
Nimmitabel
Wadbilliga National Park
27
MOMARO
10
Bemboka Nat Park
34 18
Bemboka
22
Bungarby
28
23 42
Ando
Mt Wog Wog
8
Bukalong
Bibbenluke
33
Mount Darrah
12
16
Cathcart
Bombala
37
11
Coolangubra National Park
Tantawangalo National Park
17
Genoa Nat Pk
Burragate
Pericoe

183
174
97

© Random House Australia Pty Ltd

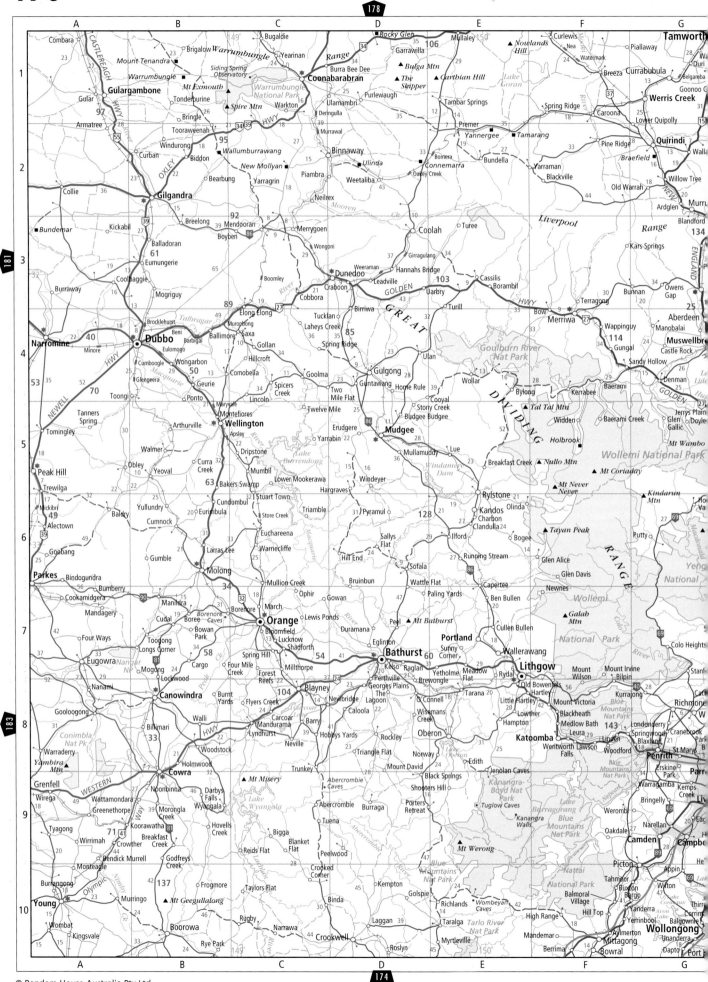

0 10 20 30 40 50
kilometres

H   J   K   L   M   N   P

N

Map labels (NSW mid-north coast):

Piallamore, Aberbaldie, Dungowan, Weabonga, Glen Morrison, Brackendale, Kangaroo Flat, Kemps Pinnacle, Mt Banda Banda, South Kempsey, Hat Head NP

Woolomin, Niangala, Mt Sugarloaf, Yarrowitch, Mt Werrikimbe, Upper Rollands Plains, Crescent Head, Kundabung

Ogunbil, Bowling Alley Point, Riamukka, Myrtle Scrub, Mount Seaview, Forbes River, Kindee, Rollands Plains, Limeburners Creek NR, Point Plomer

Nundle, Hanging Rock, Nowendoc, Raffles Peak, Ellenborough, Bagnoo, Byabarra, Pappinbarra, Pembrooke, Beechwood, Wauchope, Port Macquarie, Tacking Point, Saltwater Lake

Wombramurra, Barry, Bralga Tops, Bulga, Elands, Comboyne, Herons Creek, Kendall, Lake Cathie, Bonny Hills, Lake Innes Nature Res

Timor, Ellerston, Woko Nat Pk, Bretti, Number One, Bobin, Mooral Creek, Apple Tree Flat, Central Lansdowne, Lansdowne, Kew, North Haven, Laurieton, Watson Taylor Lake

Moonan Flat, Upper Bowman, Tibbuc, Mount George, Kimbriki, Cedar Party, Johns River, Coopernook, Moorland, Coralville, Crowdy Bay National Park

Woolooma, Belltrees, Mt Barrington, Rawdon Vale, Copeland, Rookhurst, Barrington, Wingham, Taree, Killawarra, Tinonee, Burrell Creek, Crowdy Head

Davis Creek, Mt Royal, Salisbury, Maudville, Forbesdale, Gloucester, Faulkland, Stratford, Rainbow Flat, Krambach, Nabiac, Old Bar, Wallabi Point, Diamond Beach, Hallidays Point, Harrington, Manning Point, Farquhar Inlet

Barrington Tops National Park, Chichester, Gloucester Tops, Craven, Dyers Crossing, Falford, Tuncurry, Forster

Bowmans Creek, Halton, Munni, Bendolba, Main Creek, Fosterton, Markwell, Wootton, Forster Keys, Coomba, Elizabeth Bay, Blueys Beach, Booti Booti National Park

St Clair, Allynbrook, Gresford, Dungog, Stroud Road, Stroud, Elizabeth Beach, Pacific Palms, Smiths Lake, Sugarloaf Bay

Ravensworth, Camberwell, Tyraman, Wallarobah, Booral, Girvan, Bulahdelah, Bungwahl, Seal Rocks, Myall Lakes National Park

Matson Dieu, Glendon Brook, Vacy, Martins Creek, Brookfield, Clarence Town, Allworth, Nerong, Bombah Point, Mungo Brush, The Broadwater, Broughton Island

Singleton, Branxton, Greta, Paterson, Seaham, Karuah, Limeburners Creek, Tea Gardens, Hawks Nest

Belford, Rothbury, Rutherford, Woodville, Wallalong, Swan Bay, Soldiers Point, Shoal Bay, Anna Bay, Boat Harbour, Nelson Bay

Broke, Maitland, Metford, Raymond Terrace, Williamtown, Medowie

Cessnock, Ahermain, Kurri Kurri, Pelaw Main, Sandgate, Fern Bay, Newcastle Bight

Yellow Rock, Bellbird, Kearsley, Kitchener, Beresfield, Stockton, Port Hunter

Paxton, Ellalong, Boolaroo, Broadmeadow, Wallsend, Newcastle

Wollombi, Brunkerville, Warners Bay, Toronto, Charlestown, Redhead, Lake Macquarie

Laguna, Bucketty, Cooranbong, Morisset, Dora Creek, Belmont, Swansea

Cedar Brush Creek, Gwandalan, Wyee, Catherine Hill Bay

Kulnura, Dooralong, Yarramalong, Jilliby, Doyalson, Budgewoi, Lake Munmorah

Central Mangrove, Wyong, Toukley, Norah Head, Tuggerah Lake

Peats Ridge, Ourimbah, Tuggerah, The Entrance

Calga, Kariong, Gosford, Terrigal

Kion, Woy Woy, Bouddi NP, Killcare

Brooklyn, Umina, Broken Bay, Palm Beach, Ku-ring-gai Chase NP

Terrey Hills, Mona Vale, Narrabeen, Long Reef Point, Manly

North Sydney, Port Jackson

SYDNEY, Bondi Junction, Botany, Hurstville, Caringbah, Cronulla, Botany Bay, Bundeena, Port Hacking, Royal National Park

Ocean labels:

SOUTH PACIFIC OCEAN

TASMAN SEA

-32°, -33°, -34°

152°, 153°

1 2 3 4 5 6 7 8 9 10

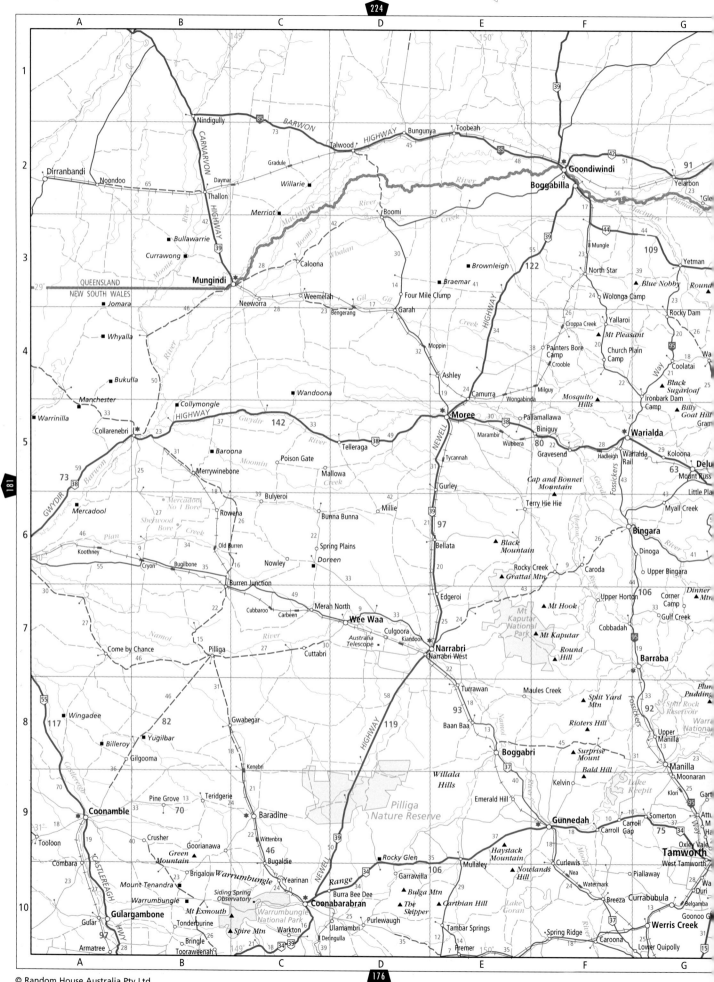

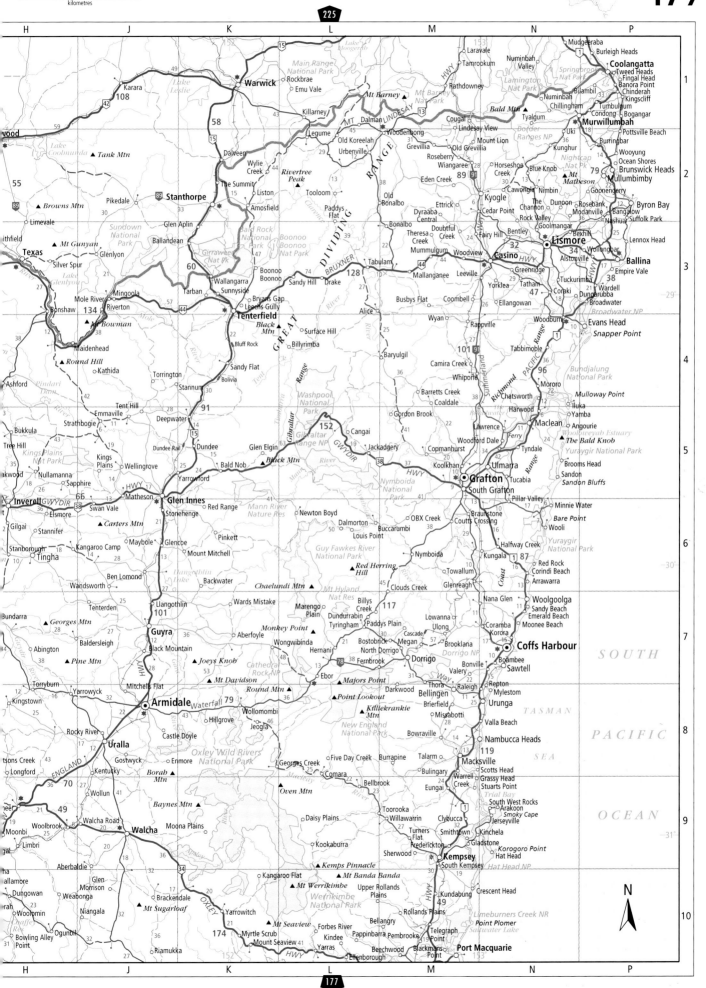

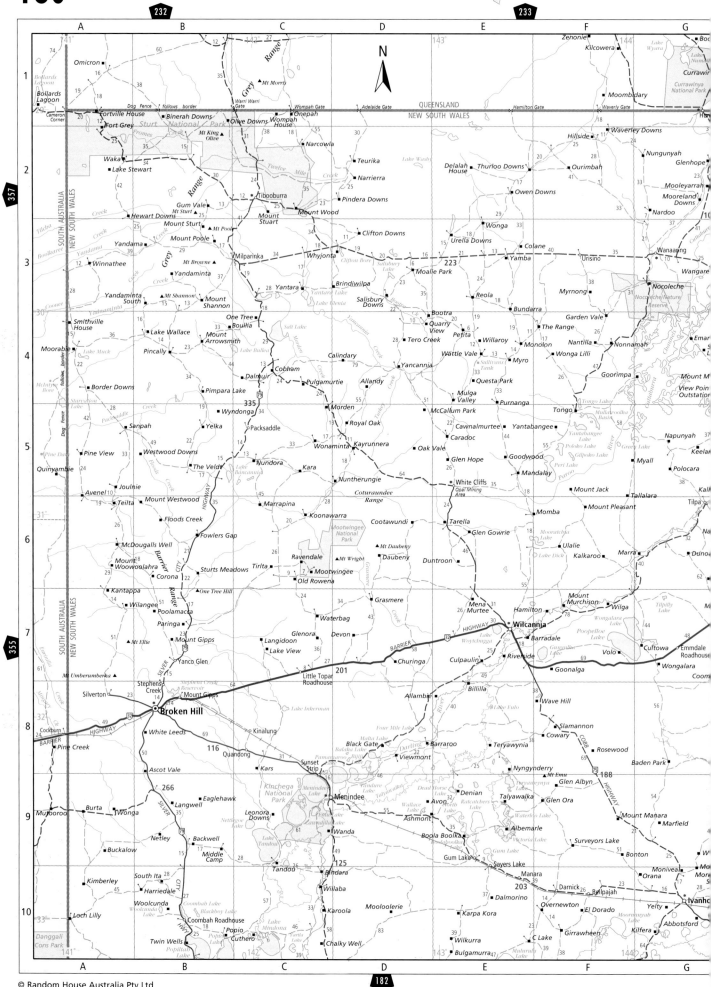

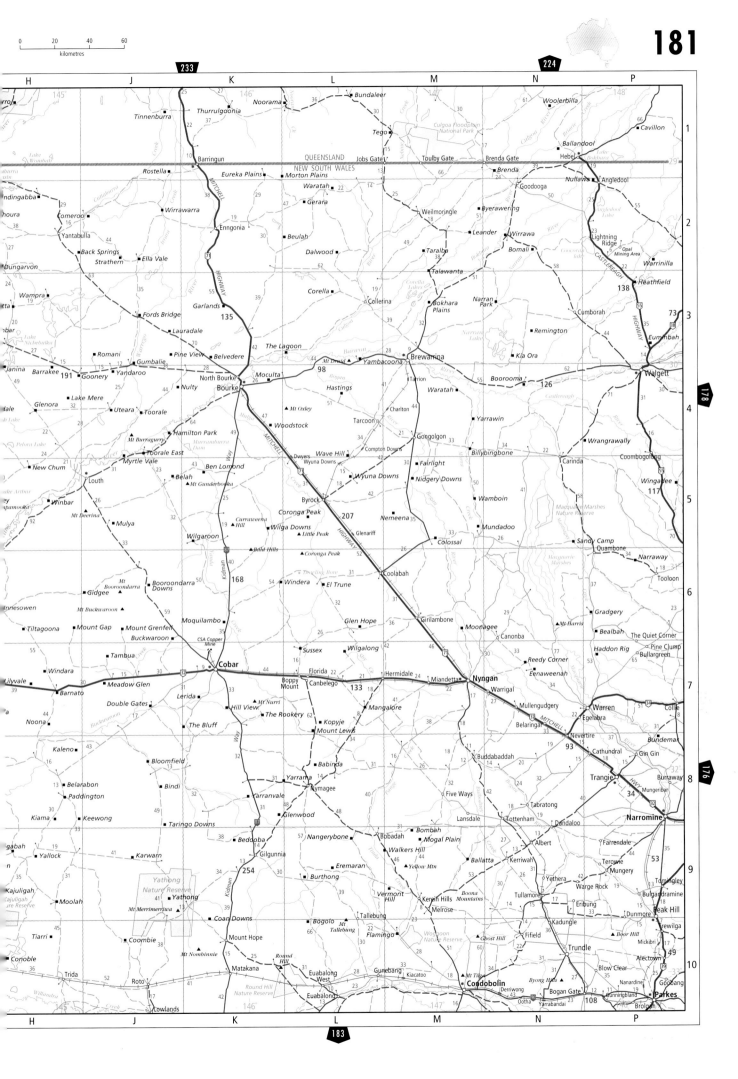

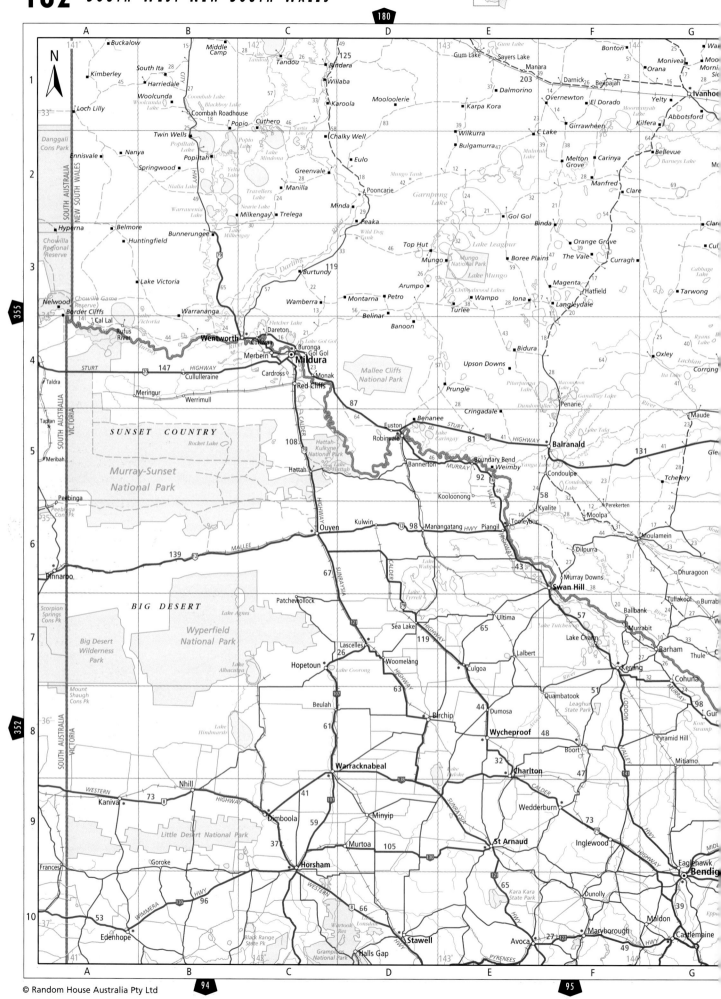

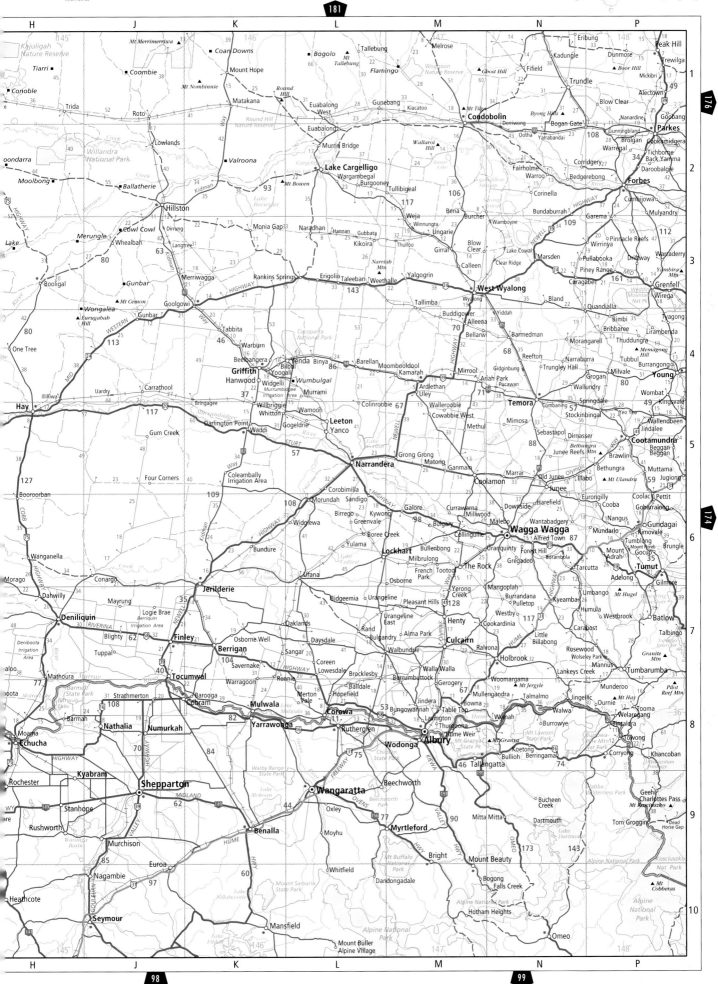

QUEENSLAND

BRISBANE-DARWIN
Via Cunningham Hwy 15, & Warrego Hwy 54
Landsborough Hwy 71 & 61, Barkly Hwy 66
& Stuart Hwy 87, 3484 Kilometres

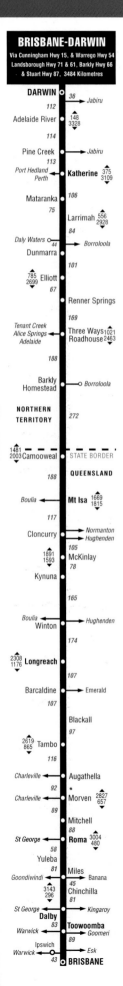

DARWIN	36 → Jabiru
112	
Adelaide River	148 / 3328
114	
Pine Creek	→ Jabiru
113	
Port Hedland / Perth	**Katherine** 375 / 3109
Mataranka	106
75	
	Larrimah 556 / 2928
84	
Daly Waters	→ Borroloola
Dunmarra	44
	101
785 / 2699 Elliott	
67	
	Renner Springs
	169
Tenant Creek / Alice Springs / Adelaide	Three Ways 1021 / Roadhouse 2463
	188
Barkly / Homestead	→ Borroloola
NORTHERN / TERRITORY	272
1481 / 2003 Camooweal	STATE BORDER
	QUEENSLAND
	188
Boulia	**Mt Isa** 1669 / 1815
	117
Cloncurry	→ Normanton / → Hughenden
	105
1891 / 1593	McKinlay
	78
Kynuna	
	165
Boulia / Winton	→ Hughenden
	174
2308 / 1176 **Longreach**	
	107
Barcaldine	→ Emerald
107	
	Blackall
	97
2619 / 865 Tambo	
	116
Charleville	Augathella
92	•
Charleville	Morven 2827 / 657
89	
	Mitchell
	88
St George	**Roma** 3004 / 480
	Yuleba
81	
Goondiwindi	Miles → Banana
3143 / 296	45 Chinchilla
	81
St George	→ Kingaroy
	Dalby
Warwick	83 **Toowoomba** → Goomeri
	89
Ipswich	
Warwick	→ Esk
	43 **BRISBANE**

Queensland, the second largest state in Australia and with a population approaching 3.2 million, is the fastest growing state in Australia. Its percentage growth rate each year continues to exceed the national growth rate. Even with over 60 per cent of the population residing in the south-east corner of the state, Queensland's population is the least centralised of all the mainland states of Australia. It is interesting to note that in 1938 the population was one million and that it took until 1974, a period of 36 years, to reach two million and then only another 18 years to exceed three million, in March 1992. The people of Queensland are not spread evenly across the state. Instead, they live on the narrow strip of rich, fertile land between the coast and the Great Dividing Range. Queensland, in common with most other developed regions, is experiencing a 'greying' of the population, with increasing median ages and a higher proportion of people in the 65 years and over age group. This trend is expected to accelerate, as the state moves into the twenty-first century, when those people born in the 'baby boom era'—post World War II—reach retirement age. It is anticipated that Queensland's population will increase from approximately 3.2 million in 1994 to between 4.1 and 4.3 million by the year 2011.

Queensland is a big state. From Coolangatta, on the New South Wales border, to the tip of Cape York is 3000 km. From the Northern Territory border in the west to Sandy Cape in the east the distance is more than 1350 km. Queensland's infrastructure is necessarily huge, given that it has to service the state's burgeoning and widely spread population. A network of over 176 635 kilometres of roads, 9357 kilometres of rail, ten major airports including two international airports—one in Brisbane and one in Cairns—and 15 major ports connect and work together to service Queensland.

Geographically, Queensland can be divided into four main regions, all running from north to south. First there is the rich, fertile coastal strip with reliable rainfall and good weather and where the bulk of the population lives. This section in the far north is typically tropical with high rainfall, and access is difficult, with lush rainforests coming in places right down to the sea and the reef. Further south the rainfall is not as reliable as in the north but there are also sections of subtropical rainforest as far south as the New South Wales border and Lamington National Park.

Next there is the Great Dividing Range, a complex mountain system running right through the state from north to south. To the west of the range is the third main region, the rolling and timbered tablelands, typified by the Atherton Tablelands and Darling Downs. These consist generally of volcanic, black soil which is particularly fertile and highly productive. Finally, in the west are the grasslands that make up more than half the area of the state. This is grazing country with a very unreliable rainfall and where droughts are not unusual. It is also the country of waving plains of Mitchell grass, the only natural grass of Australia. A major part of it is also mulga country, where forests of near impenetrable mulga trees stretch away to the horizon. A lifesaver to the land owner when the feed is burnt off and it has not rained for months, the mulga survives to sustain the stock through the drought.

Overlooking Noosa Heads

This part of Australia is also rich in history. This is the country where Banjo Paterson wrote the words of the unofficial national anthem of Australia, *Waltzing Matilda*. It is also the birthplace of the Australian Labor Party which had its beginnings as a result of the shearers' strike. QANTAS (Queensland and Northern Territory Aerial Services), one of the world's leading international airlines, was conceived, born and took to the air in this area of Australia. John Flynn, the visionary who started the Royal Flying Doctor Service, a unique and the world's first medical service of its kind, was a Queenslander. Even the rivers in this part of the country,

The Matilda Highway stretching north from the New South Wales border

Barcoo, Diamantina, Georgina, Cooper, Thomson, Paroo to name a few, bring to mind the days of long ago and the hardships that our early settlers had to endure to open up this unpredictable and beautiful country. In memory of these people, both men and women, is the outstanding Australian Stockman's Hall of Fame at Longreach.

The state of Queensland had a fairly inauspicious beginning as the site of Brisbane was selected for a convict penal colony. For a period, the settlement in Queensland was for convicts only, but as free settlers started to populate the Darling Downs the penal settlement was abandoned. The population increased dramatically as the rich farming land drew more and more settlers. Eventually it was agreed a new colony should be formed and in 1859 the colony of Queensland was declared. The new colony relied almost entirely on farming, including sugarcane in the northern areas. In a replay of the United States' experience, the sugar farmers, who were using forced labour ('kanakas') brought in from the Pacific Islands to work their properties, considered seceding to form another state when this practice fell into disfavour. Fortunately, the move to secede was unsuccessful and in 1904 indentured labour was banned altogether.

Around 1867, Queensland was in a slump when the discovery of gold at Gympie revived the colony's fortunes. This was followed by further goldfields opening around Charters Towers and Palmer River. The economy of Queensland has always relied on agriculture and mining although in the twentieth century the growth industry of tourism has been added. Now the state has a prosperous future, and even though the ratios between the three industries of mining, agriculture and tourism may vary from time to time, the balance for a sound economic future is assured.

Queensland is blessed with having a great climate and is worthy of the name the Sunshine State. Probably for this reason alone, Queensland has attracted, and continues to attract, many Australians to move there.

Stretching along the coastline is a myriad islands with North and South Stradbroke, Moreton and Fraser Islands in the south, all easily reached from Brisbane and with high visitation rates. Further north there are Great Keppel, Heron, the Whitsunday group, Magnetic Island off Townsville, Dunk,

Hinchinbrook, Lizard and Green Islands, to name just a few. Add to that the eighth wonder of the world, the Great Barrier Reef, which parallels the Queensland coast for almost its entire length, and it can be easily realised why people in their millions, from overseas and within Australia, make this state their holiday destination.

The Great Barrier Reef, a wonderland of coral atolls, reefs and islands, is the world's largest and the most famous coral formation. All the reef is now protected as part of a World Heritage Park and administered by the Great Barrier Reef Marine Authority. Visitors and scientists come from all over the world to study and admire this magnificent and beautiful marine paradise. The reef has its problems with natural phenomena such as cyclones, or predators like the crown of thorns starfish which at odd times multiplies and causes severe damage to localised sections of the reef. However, given all that, the Great Barrier Reef is still the greatest single tourist attraction in Queensland.

Even though the international visitor appears to have the highest profile it is worth remembering that most of the visitors to the state of Queensland are from within Australia. The number of overseas visitors is steadily increasing but Australians account for the majority of tourists.

Inland Queensland also has much to offer the traveller. From Carnarvon Gorge National Park to the Gulf Country and the wilderness of Cape York, and all the historic cities and towns in between, there is an endless variety of sights and sounds to delight the visitor.

Queensland is a growing state and an essential contributor to the Australian economy and even though the coastal strip with the bulk of the population and its endless attractions will continue to claim most of the attention, it is the sparsely populated hinterland that, for the foreseeable future anyway, provides the basis of a substantial and growing economy built on mining and agriculture.

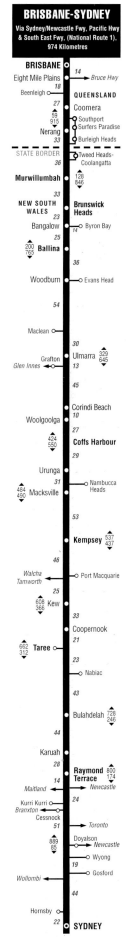

BRISBANE-SYDNEY
Via Sydney/Newcastle Fwy, Pacific Hwy
& South East Fwy, (National Route 1),
974 Kilometres

BRISBANE
Eight Mile Plains — 14 → Bruce Hwy
Beenleigh — 18
QUEENSLAND
27
Coomera
59
915 — Southport
Surfers Paradise
Nerang — Burleigh Heads
33
STATE BORDER — Tweed Heads-Coolangatta
36
Murwillumbah — 128
846
33
NEW SOUTH WALES — **Brunswick Heads**
23
Bangalow — 14 → Byron Bay
25
Ballina 200
765
36
Woodburn — Evans Head
54
Maclean
30
Grafton — Ulmarra 329
645
Glen Innes — 13
45
Corindi Beach
Woolgoolga — 10
27
Coffs Harbour 424
550
29
Urunga
31 — Nambucca Heads
Macksville 484
490
53
Kempsey 537
437
46
Walcha — Port Macquarie
Tamworth
25
Kew 608
366
33
Coopernook
21
Taree 662
312
23 — Nabiac
43
Bulahdelah 728
246
44
Karuah
28
Raymond Terrace 800
174
14 — Newcastle
Maitland
24
Kurri Kurri
Branxton
Cessnock
51 — Toronto
889
85 — Doyalson → Newcastle
— Wyong
19 — Gosford
Wollombi
44
Hornsby
22
SYDNEY

BRISBANE

POPULATION: 306 700

MAP REFERENCE: PAGE 222 G5

Brisbane, with its hot, humid summers and mild winters, has a much more relaxed attitude and a far more casual atmosphere than its southern cousins. Maybe it is due in no small part to the city retaining a 'little bit of country'.

With all its dramatic growth, both skywards and outwards, the Brisbane city folk appear to get things done without having to resort to a hectic, tearing pace. Maybe it is a by-product of a superb climate.

Brisbane River was named by John Oxley after Thomas Brisbane, the governor of New South Wales in 1823. As Oxley rowed up the river he spotted a glorious patch of subtropical jungle and he stopped for breakfast. This is now a commercial and industrial area known as Breakfast Creek. A landmark since it was first erected in 1889 is the Breakfast Creek Hotel. This hotel has established a name for serving one of the best steaks in town. And for those who have never tried it, have a beer 'off the wood'.

In about 1824, the city started life as a penal colony and at one time was the largest penal colony on the Australian mainland with over 1000 convicts. At that time free settlers were not allowed to come within 80 kilometres of the settlement. But change was inevitable and slowly the free settlers moved in, until by 1839 the penal colony had ended. Queensland became a separate colony in 1859 and Brisbane the capital.

Brisbane was declared a city in 1902 and is truly a scenic city. Its character is moulded by the river around which the city is built. There are seven bridges that cross the Brisbane River from the latest and longest, the Gateway, to the best known and the prettiest, the Story Bridge. This bridge was designed by Dr John Bradfield, the man who designed the Sydney Harbour Bridge, and built in the same way with the spans projecting from the north and south banks. In the early hours of the morning of 28 October 1939 the main span was joined. At night, the bridge is lit up by thousands of light bulbs which outline the structure. The lights were installed as part of the bridge's fiftieth anniversary celebrations in 1990.

The river is also a busy thoroughfare. Ferries carry passengers from bank to bank while motorised gondolas and large coal ferries go about their business. Paddle-steamers are great for seeing the river along with cruise boats that ply up and down the river day and night. Visitors can get an unrestricted view of the city while they float past the Cultural Centre, Maritime Museum, University of Queensland, Botanic Gardens and Newstead House. This low-set stately house in Newstead Park was built in 1846 and is the oldest surviving homestead in the city. Much of the administration of the growing colony of Queensland was carried out from this house. Walter Hill, the Colonial Botanist, laid the foundations for the gardens and was instrumental in introducing the jacaranda and poinciana to the city. During spring and summer the trees light up the suburbs with their covering of pale blue and red blossoms.

On the outskirts of the city's business district is Fortitude Valley— named after the ship that brought 256 immigrants to the growing settlement in 1849. They settled in the area which has now been taken over by a variety of industries, shops in an attractive mall and a Chinatown. Over the years Fortitude Valley was known as a 'red light district' and that reputation seems to have stayed with it, even though The Valley, as it is known, is now a mix of many nationalities and peoples working together.

Brisbane is an outdoor city with an average minimum temperature of 15° C and a maximum of 25° C. On weekends the city comes alive with sightseers and picnickers at the botanic gardens, at the riverside markets and one of the city's popular spots, the South Bank Park-lands. Situated on the river overlooking the city, on the site where the World Expo 88 was held, is a conglomeration of restaurants and cafés, a beach and swimming lagoon, the Butterfly and Insect House, Gondwana Rainforest Sanctuary, BBQ and picnic areas. Buskers and wandering performers parade along the esplanade and the area is vibrant and full of colour. Next to the Parklands is the Queensland Cultural Centre, one of Australia's most exciting art centres. It incorporates the Queens-land Museum, Queensland Art Gallery and the Queensland Performing Arts Complex.

Even though the skyline has changed greatly since the 1960s when the tallest building in the city was the very imposing Town Hall, at 91 metres

The skyline of Brisbane at night reflected in the Brisbane River

above street level, the compact central business district has remained mainly within the loop of the river.

Sandstone, taken from the quarry at Helidon south of Toowoomba, was used liberally in the construction of many of Brisbane's imposing buildings. The National Bank welcomes visitors with its tall Corinthian columns and pilasters of limestone with an ornate interior bathed in natural light from the leadlight dome, an extravagant example of the Victorian period. The Treasury Building, with its palazzo occupying an entire block, is considered to be the finest example of Italian Renaissance architecture in the southern hemisphere. This building was reopened in 1995 as the Treasury Casino and although the interior was completely renovated the exterior was left untouched. The latest addition to Brisbane's impressive sandstone buildings was the University of Queensland. The central core of sandstone buildings is set around a cloistered court.

The Observatory in Wickham Terrace, just north of the city centre, was built by convict labour in 1828 as a windmill. It failed dismally as a windmill and so was utilised as a convict-powered treadmill to punish prisoners and grind grain for food. When free settlers took over Brisbane the convicts were sent to one of Moreton Bay's most beautiful islands, St Helena. This hell-hole of the Pacific, existed from 1867 to 1932 and was built, and dismantled, by the residents of the prison. Day trips by launch are available to tour the ruins of this infamous prison.

Brisbane is not only a vibrant and exciting city, but it is also the heart of a dynamic and exciting tourist region. North of the city are the Glasshouse Mountains and the subtropical valleys of the Caboolture Shire along with the beaches of Bribie Island and the Sunshine Coast. Fraser Island, the largest sand island in the world, is only some two hours driving from Brisbane. To the south, between Brisbane and the Gold Coast, is Logan City, the second most populous city in the state and one of the fastest growing. The ever popular Gold Coast, with its theme parks, surfing and swimming beaches, is barely an hour away and now can be accessed by electric train to Nerang and Robina. Moreton Bay and the islands of the Bay are a stone's throw away.

The Australian Woolshed is great for that country atmosphere. There are sheep-shearing demonstrations, cows can be milked or baby lambs bottle-fed. Visit Lone Pine Sanctuary to cuddle a koala and some of Australia's unique animals and birds. The Alma Park Zoo has an abundance of native animals plus some from other parts of the world. The Brisbane Forest Park is an area of 26 500 hectares about 6 km from the city centre and consists of natural bushland with camping and picnic areas.

Brisbane is blessed with a range of restaurants offering cuisine from around the world. The Queen Street Mall features outdoor cafés and eating places in a relaxed atmosphere. Late night entertainment is provided with plenty of night clubs and bars.

The choices in accommodation range from five-star luxury hotels to more economic hotels, hostels and caravan parks. The CBD has excellent choices, many with views of the river and the city. The inner western suburbs towards the airport have a great range of hotels, motels and holiday apartments and generally offer lower rates than the city centre.

The major festival held each September in Brisbane is what used to be called the Warana Festival but is now called the Brisbane Festival. This is a major arts festival with plays, shows and exhibitions mainly centred around the Performing Arts Complex and its three superb theatres at the Queensland Cultural Centre down on the river bank.

The Springhill Festival is generally held around the middle of September and is a gathering of arts and crafts in a market-style setting.

ACCOMMODATION

CBD: Conrad International Treasury Casino, ph (07) 3306 8888; Quay West Brisbane Hotel, ph (07) 3853 6000; Sheraton Brisbane Hotel, ph (07) 3835 3535; Explorers Inn Motel, ph (07) 3211 3488; Gregory Terrace Motor Inn, ph

An aerial view of Brisbane taken from a hot-air balloon

(07) 3832 1769; Dahri Court Serviced Units, ph (07) 3832 3458; Ruth Fairfax House–QCWA Club (B&B), ph (07) 3831 8188; The Astor Apartments Holiday Units, ph (07) 3839 9022; New Brisbane City YHA Hostel, ph (07) 3236 1004

North side: Airport 85 Motel, ph (07) 3268 4966; Ascot Motel, ph (07) 3268 5266; Aspley Motor Inn, ph (07) 3263 5400; Womga Villa (B&B), ph (07) 3862 2183; Aspley Acres Caravan Park, ph (07) 3263 2668

North-west side: Clear Mountain Health Lodge Resort, ph (07) 3298 5100; Paddington B&B, ph (07) 3369 8973; Haslemere Guest House (B&B), ph (07) 3289 7190; Newmarket Gardens Caravan Park, ph (07) 3356 1458

North-east side: Northgate Airport Motel, ph (07) 3256 7222; Powerhouse Boutique Hotel, ph (07) 3862 1800; Airport International Motel, ph (07) 3268 6388; Airport Admiralty Motel, ph (07) 3268 7899

South side: Acacia Ridge Hotel/Motel, ph (07) 3275 1444; Coopers Colonial Motor Inn, ph (07) 3875 1874; Inn on the Park Motel, ph (07) 3870 9222; Lang Parade Lodge, ph (07) 3871 1780; Wesley Apartments Holiday Units, ph (07) 3368 3683; Alexandra Apartments Holiday Units, ph (07) 3393 1846; Dress Circle Mobile Village Caravan Park, ph (07) 3341 6133

South-east side: Wellington Point Hotel/Motel, ph (07) 3207 2511; Redland Bay Motor Inn, ph (07) 3206 8188; Glentrace Bed & Breakfast, ph (07) 3207 4442; Redlands Mobile Village Caravan Park, ph (07) 3822 2444

South-west side: Regatta Hotel, ph (07) 3870 7063; Centenary Motor Inn, ph (07) 3375 3077; Oxley Motor Inn, ph (07) 3375 3188; Palm Lodge Health Retreat Guesthouse, ph (07) 3297 5180; Forest Lodge Holiday Units, ph (07) 3371 6600; Oxley Pines Caravan Park, ph (07) 3375 4465

East side: McGuire's Alexandra Hills Hotel/Motel, ph (07) 3824 4444; Carindale Hotel, ph (07) 3395 0122; Lancaster Court Motel, ph (07) 3892 5700; Cornwall Crest Serviced Apartments, ph (07) 3891 2411; Georgia's Place (B&B), ph (07) 3390 2795; Greenacres Caravan Park, ph (07) 3206 4444

West side: Jindalee Hotel, ph (07) 3376 2122; Mt Ommaney Plaza Hotel, ph (07) 3279 1288; Darra Motor Inn, ph (07) 3375 5468; Casa Vivere Serviced Apartments, ph (07) 3368 3016

TOURIST INFORMATION: Ph (07) 3221 8411

FRASER ISLAND–GREAT SANDY NATIONAL PARK

First-time visitors to Fraser Island are often left fumbling for the right adjectives when asked how to describe the beauty and variety of life on this magical sand island off the Queensland coast. Here one can find an amazing range of vegetation.

MAP REFERENCE: PAGE 225 N2

LOCATION: ON FRASER ISLAND, 250 KM NORTH OF BRISBANE, 4WD ONLY

BEST TIME: ALL YEAR ROUND

MAIN ATTRACTIONS: FISHING, FRESHWATER LAKES, RAINFOREST, WILDLIFE, WORLD'S LARGEST SAND ISLAND

INFORMATION: RAINBOW BEACH, PH (07) 5486 3160; EURONG, PH (07) 4127 9128

ACCOMMODATION: SEE TOWN LISTING FOR FRASER ISLAND

BARGE SERVICES: FROM HOOK POINT TO INSKIP POINT, PH (07) 5486 3227; FROM HERVEY BAY TO WANGGOOLBA CREEK, PH (07) 5486 3227; FROM HERVEY BAY TO KINGFISHER BAY, PH (08) 4125 5511; FROM URANGAN BOAT HARBOUR TO MOON POINT, PH (07) 4125 3325

PRIVATE AIRCRAFT PERMIT: PH (07) 4123 7100

VEHICLE PERMIT: PH (07) 5486 3160, (07) 3227 8185, OR (07) 4125 7133

There are luxuriant subtropical rainforests growing out of the sand, melaleuca swamps, eucalypt forests, heathland, mangrove-lined estuaries and kilometres of magnificent deserted beaches. Add to this already impressive list the perched dune lakes—including one which is the biggest in the world—fantastic fishing, in both the surf and calm water, and over 230 species of birds, and you will have some idea why this World Heritage listed island has become one of Australia's most visited and best known national parks.

Great Sandy National Park has two sections: one is on the northern half of Fraser Island and the other is further south on the Queensland mainland at Cooloola. The two parks are both part of the Great Sandy Region, but each is administered separately.

Running 120 km from north to south, and 25 km across at its widest point, Fraser is the largest sand island in the world. Covering an area of 165 280 hectares, the island is part of the Great Sandy Region which was formed over millions of years from eroding sandstone in the Great Dividing Range. Rivers in northern New South Wales washed this sand out to sea, where it was picked up by ocean currents and transported north along the coast. The northerly dispersion of sand was, and still is, stopped by rocky outcrops such as Indian Head. The sand piled up over thousands of years, forming dunes and beaches. Seeds, carried by birds and ocean currents, germinated in the sand, providing a layer of vegetation to stabilise the dunes.

History

Aborigines from the Butchalla tribe are thought to have inhabited Fraser Island, which they called K'gari, for more than 5000 years. Since the island was extremely rich in food from the sea, lakes and forest, the number of

Lake Wabby, the deepest lake on Fraser Island

Aboriginal people on the island was relatively high. It has been estimated that nearly 2000 people were living on the island up to the 1830s. Their rapid decline began with the discovery of gold in Gympie in the late 1860s when the island became a quarantine and immigration station for ships bringing in supplies and men to the nearby goldfields. Over the next 40 years, a combination of smallpox, venereal disease, influenza, alcohol and the occasional massacre reduced the numbers of this once proud people to less than 150 individuals. The survivors of this genocide were transported to a number of mainland Aboriginal reserves, including Yarrabah near Cairns, in 1905.

Captain James Cook was the first known European to sight Fraser Island in 1770. He named Sandy Cape, Indian Head and Seventy-Five Mile Beach before continuing north. Matthew Flinders, in his ship *Norfolk*, sailed by 19 years later and returned in 1802 in another ship, the *Investigator*, to explore more of Fraser's sandy coast.

The Great Sandy Island became a household name in the fledgling colony with the rescue of Eliza Fraser. The drama began on 13 May 1836 when a ship called the *Stirling Castle* struck a coral reef off Rockhampton. The captain, James Fraser, and his pregnant wife Eliza, managed to escape in a longboat with the 16 other passengers and crew. With dwindling fresh water and virtually no food available, the longboat was beached at Fraser Island. The entire party was quickly rounded up by members of the Butchalla tribe who kept Mrs Fraser captive for nearly seven weeks. During that time Captain Fraser and a few others died while the remaining crew members managed to escape and walk south towards Moreton Bay. Once the authorities learned of Mrs Fraser's fate, an expedition was formed to rescue her. Within ten years of her lucky escape, the Great Sandy Island, as it was formerly known, was being called Fraser Island.

The logging of Fraser Island's beautiful forests began in the early 1860s and continued until all commercial cutting ceased in 1992. During the first 70 years of operations, bullock drays hauled the timber out of the forests to loading points on the coast. Giant satinay (turpentine) trees *(Syncarpia hillii)*, were one of the favourites of the loggers due to their rot-resistant qualities in salt water. Many of the largest specimens were sent to Egypt for the construction of the Suez Canal in the nineteenth century.

Today, the most impressive stands of satinay are found around Pile Valley, close to Lake McKenzie.

Fraser Island became a base for the famous Z Force commando units during World War II. Thousands of soldiers trained on the island, preparing themselves in Fraser's rainforests and mangrove-lined coast for battling the Japanese in similar conditions on the Pacific Islands. Today, a few rusted relics of the war years can be found on the west coast.

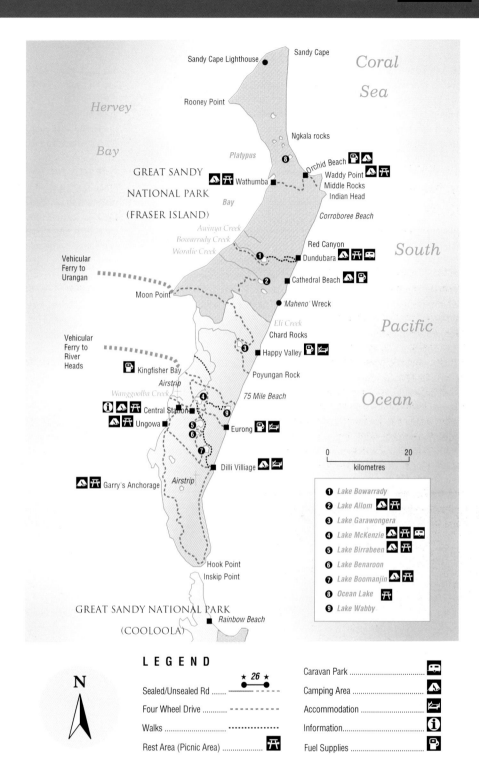

FRASER ISLAND–GREAT SANDY NATIONAL PARK

Fraser is formed from many different types of sand, including the white oceanic sands which make up most of the island's mass. Much of this sand contains concentrations of heavy minerals such as rutile, zircon and ilmenite. The beaches on the eastern side of Fraser are continually changing due to the action of waves pounding against the shore. Winds and tides form and reform sandbars, gutters and small bays along the coast. During periods of violent cyclonic weather there can be dramatic changes to the shape and slope of the eastern beaches.

The Coloured Sands

Fraser is also famous for its coloured sands which are similar to those found in the southern section of Great Sandy National Park at Cooloola on the mainland. One of the most striking examples of these coloured sands can be seen at the Cathedral on the eastern coast. Also known as the Teewah Sands, the coloured sands were formed over countless thousands of years from decaying vegetation leaching down into the sand. Shades of yellow and brown are the dominant colours, although rusty reds and orange can also be seen at certain levels. Dig down to any great depth on Fraser and you can see that the coloured sands form much of the underground mass of the island.

Perched Dune Lakes

There are more than 40 perched dune lakes on Fraser including the world's largest, the 200 hectare Lake Boomanjin. These lakes have some of the purest drinking water found anywhere in the world. Some are crystal clear with white sandy bottoms, such as Lake McKenzie, while others have a reddish brown colour which comes from humus staining from decaying vegetation such as tea-trees growing near the lake. The stain has no effect on the drinking qualities of the water.

The water is so pure in the lakes that only three species of small fish live in them. Tortoises are quite common in some of the lakes, especially Lake Bowarrady.

Apart from the dune lakes, the island has a number of freshwater streams which flow consistently throughout the year. In many respects the sand on Fraser acts like a large sponge, with rain falling on the island being held in a large underground water table. The biggest stream on the island is Eli Creek, which flows onto the eastern beach a few kilometres south of the *Maheno* wreck. At numerous other places along the beach fresh water bubbles out of the sand, providing visitors with easy access to good drinking water. None of this water has to be boiled as the sand filters out any impurities.

Great for Fishing

For more than 70 years visitors have been travelling to Fraser Island to experience its fantastic fishing. At the height of the season, between July and October, hundreds of anglers gather on the surf beaches of the island's east coast to try their luck and skills against the huge schools of tailor that migrate up the coast. Pilchards are the preferred bait for these great fighting fish, although they have been known to bite on virtually anything when in a feeding frenzy.

Other fish found on the east coast beaches include silver bream, jewfish and golden trevally. In the calm waters on the western side of the island whiting, flathead and bream can be caught throughout the year. Anglers can gather their own bait by either digging for bloodworms or pumping up yabbies from the sandflats at low tide. Nimble-fingered anglers with good eyesight can even try to catch some of the big sand worms which are common on the eastern surf beaches. The best way to do this is to place some stale fish or meat (the smellier the better) in an onion bag and drag it slowly over the sand. When the worm sticks its head up through the sand, bend down, holding a small piece of meat in your fingers, and try to grab the worm when it attaches itself to the meat. More often than not you will miss, but it is fun trying.

Another good form of bait which can be easily gathered along the surf beaches is the pipi. These little triangular shaped shellfish bury themselves a few centimetres under the sand, but can easily be found by dragging your toes along the beach. Apart from being used as bait, pipis can be cooked over an open fire and eaten from the shell or boiled and used in stews or other camp-cooked meals. Mud crabs are also present in good numbers around the mangrove-lined estuaries on the western side of the island, although you will probably need a small boat to get to the places where you can drop your crab pots.

A Mecca for 4WDs

Since there are no formed roads on Fraser, a 4WD vehicle is necessary if you want to explore the island. It is best to keep tyres deflated to around 175 kPa (25 psi), although you may have to drop them back to 140 kPa (20 psi) if you get stuck in soft sand. Due to the popularity of the island, accidents on the inland sandy tracks are becoming all too common. Never drive too fast on these tracks, particularly around blind corners. Always carry a spade in your vehicle to dig yourself out of bogs. During prolonged dry spells some of the inland tracks are difficult to negotiate due to the soft sand. Try to keep your beach driving within two hours either side of low tide. Apart from being better for your vehicle, since you will not have to drive through salt water, it is less destructive on the foredunes.

A Great Place to Go Walking

Apart from walking along Fraser's beautiful beaches, there are numerous forest hiking trails in the central and southern parts of the island.

One excellent track to start out on is the 6 km Lake Birrabeen to Central Station walk, which would take about two and a half hours one way. Birdwatchers will love this track as it meanders through a wide variety of the park's vegetation including banksia heathland, eucalypt woodland and finally rainforest around Central Station. During late winter and early spring, the heath country around the lakes becomes alive with the many varieties of colourful wildflowers.

Although rainforest covers only about 5 per cent of the island—approximately 8000 hectares—it is extremely interesting and home to a wide variety of fauna and flora.

A short walking track at Central Station (25 minutes one way) follows the crystal clear Wanggoolba Creek past towering brush box, hoop pine, white beech, ribbon wood and strangler figs. Both the piccabeen palm and

Beach fishing for tailor on Fraser Island

the shorter walking-stick palm reach up for the sunlight, entangled in an understorey of tree-ferns, vines and decaying branches. Uncommon rainforest dwellers such as the noisy pitta, emerald dove, white-headed

The Aquarium or Champagne Rock Pools forming a natural ocean swimming pool at low tide

pigeon and wompoo pigeon are sometimes sighted here. Two very conspicuous birds on this trail are the rufous fantail and the eastern yellow robin. Often these birds will fly within a few metres of walkers to 'check out the intruders' before flying back into the forest.

Don't Feed the Dingoes

Fraser is probably the best place in Australia to see wild dingoes at close quarters. While in most other parts of the country they have interbred with domestic dogs, the dingoes on Fraser are a pure strain. People who feed them or leave scraps lying around are interfering with the dingoes' ability to hunt their natural prey.

Island Access

Fraser is approximately 250 km north of Brisbane. The island can be reached by a number of methods including vehicular barges, passenger launches, aircraft or private boats.

There are four vehicular barges which service Fraser Island. On the southern end of Fraser a barge operates between Hook Point and Inskip Point near Rainbow Beach. From Hervey Bay, barges to Wanggoolba Creek and Kingfisher Bay depart from River Heads. The barge to Moon Point leaves from Urangan boat harbour. Bookings are required for the three Hervey Bay barges.

Visitors who arrive by light aircraft will land either at Toby's Gap which is managed by the Queensland National Parks and Wildlife Service (NPWS), or at Wanggoolba Creek which is managed by the Eurong Beach Resort. Landing permission and entry permits are needed for private aircraft before arrival.

A number of commercial tour operators run 4WD day trips and two to three day camping safaris to the island from Brisbane, the Sunshine Coast, Hervey Bay and Rainbow Beach. A 4WD vehicle is essential for driving on the island. If you do not have your own, they can be hired at Hervey Bay, Rainbow Beach, the Sunshine Coast and Brisbane.

People bringing a vehicle to Fraser must get a vehicle access permit and attach it to their car windscreen. The permit is valid for one month. Unregistered vehicles are not permitted on Fraser Island. Normal road rules apply for beach driving, and motorists should use their indicators to show oncoming vehicles which side they are going to pass them on.

Camping and Accommodation

The Queensland National Parks and Wildlife Service has camping grounds at Lake Boomanjin, Central Station, Lake Allom, Waddy Point, Wathumba, Lake McKenzie and Dundubara. Facilities in these places include toilets, picnic tables and showers (except for Lake Allom). Lake McKenzie and Dundubara are the only places suitable for caravans or camper trailers.

Visitors are allowed to camp at most spots along the coast unless signs indicate otherwise. Always make sure your toilet is dug to a depth of 40–60 cm and at least 50 metres away from the high-tide mark. Never bury your rubbish: take it out with you, so that Fraser remains pristine.

Visitors to the island who do not wish to camp can find motel type accommodation at Happy Valley, Eurong, and Dilli Village.

If you want to try real luxury in one of Australia's most awarded resorts for environmental awareness, you cannot go past Kingfisher Bay on the western side of the island. Visitors can go birdwatching and participate in other nature tours at the resort.

THE FRASER ISLAND TREK

We have chosen to take the barge across from Rainbow Beach, probably the most popular access point, and to leave the island from Kingfisher Bay, which puts you back on the mainland at River Heads, just south of Hervey Bay.

Rainbow Beach

Situated 187 km north of Brisbane, the small beachside resort of Rainbow Beach can be accessed via bitumen road from Gympie, via dirt roads through the Cooloola section of the Great Sandy National Park or via the coast, north along the beach from Noosa Heads. It can provide all a traveller's basic requirements.

Getting onto the Island

From the centre of Rainbow Beach head north out of town following the signs to Inskip Point. The 12 km to the ferry point start off as bitumen but then turn to dirt, which can be quite rough at times and is often dusty. The last few hundred metres may be across deep soft sand to the ferry itself—and it does not look good if you get bogged here! Lower your tyre pressures at the sign, because even if you do not bog down here you may do so as you are coming off the ferry onto the island (**GPS** 25°47'54"S, 153°03'09"E). The short trip across to the island takes only a few minutes but because of the traffic at peak holiday times you may have to wait quite some time before you get your ride.

Zero your trip meter, and once off the barge head up off the beach and take the inland road north. While this road leads all the way north to Dilli Village, a distance of around 23 km from the barge point, we would suggest you cut across to the beach, which is just a couple of hundred metres on your right, around the 7 km mark or just before the 13 km point.

Doing the Right Thing

How easy you find the beach will depend on what the tide is like. Within an hour of high tide or—if there is a storm surf pounding the shore, possibly within a couple of hours of the high tide—you will be pushed up onto the soft sand just below the frontal dunes. Here you will growl along in first or second with a real chance of getting bogged. However, if the tide is low or even half low, the beach will be anything up to a hundred metres wide, with clean hard-packed sand, and you can cruise easily along the beach at the speed limit of 80 kph.

You will need to take care where a rocky headland bars your way north. In these cases, play it safe, and take the diversion track off the beach and across the headland to the other side. As well, many small creeks and soaks flood out across the beach and these can cut shallow but steep-sided banks which can be dangerous to hit at any speed. Take care and cruise slowly—you are here to enjoy yourself anyway, so why rush?

Whatever you do, stick to the open beach or the established tracks. DO NOT drive over vegetation or make your own track over the dunes. Not only is it against the law, it really does make a mess of the environment, and as yours is one of 60 000 vehicles a year that come to this place we all must do the right thing for Fraser to stay the magic place it is.

Dilli Village to Happy Valley

Dilli Village, a little back from the beach (**GPS** 25°36'07"S, 153°05'30"E) and 23 km north of the barge landing point, has camping and accommodation units available but these must be booked before you arrive. A track leads inland from the village via a slow but scenic route which winds its way north past a number of perched freshwater lakes to Central Station and Lake McKenzie, and then back to the coast north of Eurong. It is a slower but enjoyable way north. See our Southern Lakes Drive below.

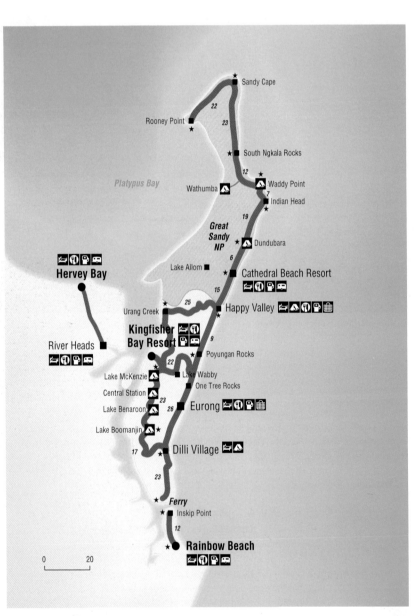

LEGEND

Road Distance in km	★ 26 ★
National Park	
Aboriginal Land	
Accommodation	
Camping Area	
Caravan Park	
Fuel Supplies	
General Store	
Meals Available	
Rest Area (Picnic Area)	
Tourist Information	

Our trek continues up the beach 10 km to the small township of Eurong. Here you will find a general store that supplies a fair range of food items, fishing gear and fuel. The hotel serves a cool beer or two and the Eurong Beach Resort has motel style accommodation and holiday flats (**GPS** 25°30'43"S, 153°07'17"E).

Eurong also gives access to Central Station (formerly a forestry station) and Lake McKenzie, 10 and 16 km away respectively in the verdant centre of the island. Both have camping facilities.

Just a few hundred metres north of the track into Eurong is the Eurong Information Centre where a DEH ranger is based. Very limited first aid facilities are located here.

One Tree Rocks, 3 km north of Eurong, can be bypassed via a track that leads up and off the beach. Once back on the beach, and just over 4 km from Eurong, there is a walking trail to Lake Wabby, the deepest lake on the island and one of the most beautiful. We highly recommend the walk. From this point it is around 3 km each way and crosses a large sandblow (which can be very hot); it is a little easier and definitely shorter to take the walking trail that leads steeply downhill from a point inland from the lake, reached via a main track, just over a kilometre north of the walking trail and about 40.5 km north of the barge landing point.

This track is also where the Southern Lakes Drive, described below, finishes on the coast and is an interesting, but slower, alternative to the drive up the coast.

Five kilometres further on are the Poyungan Rocks, which once again have a bypass around them. At low tide you can stick to the beach, but if in doubt play it safe and take the high road.

Rainbow Gorge, 2 km further along the beach, is an area of spectacular coloured sands with a walking trail that leads from the beach up to the head of the gorge.

The bypass around the Yidney Rocks (54 km north of the barge point) leads back onto the beach in front of Happy Valley, the largest settlement on the island. The Happy Valley Resort (**GPS** 25°20'17"S, 153°11'52"E) can cater for all your accommodation requirements while the nearby store can supply food and fuel.

Happy Valley is also the start of the drive, described later in this section, to the west coast of the island via Lake Garawongera, ending at Kingfisher Bay.

Happy Valley to Waddy Point

Heading north, it is just 6 km to Eli Creek, one of the delights of Fraser. Here water, crystal clear from its journey through the filtering sand, rushes out from between the dunes and floods across the beach, making the largest creek on the island and one of the major obstacles for vehicle travel along the beach. Take care!

Eli Creek is a popular spot for a picnic and the place is rarely deserted. A short boardwalk leads inland along the edge of the creek, and kids will love to float down the fast-flowing stream on a boogie board to the beach.

The rusting wreck of the *Maheno* lies on the beach 4 km north of Eli; the battered hulk is a favourite fishing spot that during the peak of the tailor season sees hundreds of fishermen crowding its seaward edge. Blown ashore during a cyclone in 1935, the wreck of the once luxury passenger liner is probably the most popular landmark on the island.

Goannas can be seen on Fraser Island

The rusting wreck of the *Maheno*, once a luxury passenger liner, lies on the beach near Eli Creek

For much of the run north from here to Indian Head imposing cliffs tower over the white sands of the beach. Called the Cathedrals, they have some of the most spectacular coloured sands on the island, ranging from pure white through reds and yellows to jet black.

Just off the beach and 6 km north from the wreck is the Cathedral Beach Resort (**GPS** 25°13'18"S, 153°15'29"E) which offers accommodation, camping and a general store with limited food supplies and fuel. Note that this is the furthest north that you can get fuel and supplies, so be prepared.

Dundubara, 6 km further north and 76 km from the barge landing spot, offers a DEH ranger and information office and a camping area.

From Dundubara it is nearly 20 km to Indian Head; the bypass track skirting this great basalt rock headland is 95 km north of the barge point. The top of the headland gives some magnificent views while the waters around here are considered to offer the best fishing on Fraser. On the northern side of the headland, where the track comes back onto the beach, there is a short protected stretch of beach popular with swimmers and picnickers.

Less than 3 km further north a soft sandy track leads off the beach again, bypassing Middle Rocks and Waddy Point. Just off the beach is a small car park with a walking trail to the Aquarium or Champagne Pools. These rock pools form a natural ocean swimming pool at low tide and they are popular with visitors, though you need to be aware of waves breaking over the rocks.

A track junction about 4 km from the beach exit spot leads right, up and over a hill, to a pleasant national park camping ground amongst coastal banksias. A DEH ranger office is located here. A little further down the hill the track meets the beach again, and beach camping along this protected north-facing beach is very popular. A small creek provides safe swimming while the protected beach offers boat fishermen a place to launch quite large boats. You are just 103 km north from the barge point.

North to Sandy Cape and Beyond

Orchid Beach, just a couple of kilometres north of Waddy Point, once housed a resort of the same name, but today expensive chalets dot the scene and supplies and fuel are no longer available.

The long run north from Waddy Point to Sandy Cape and its lighthouse is undertaken by few. The sand is softer, and the Ngkala Rocks pose a hazard at all times apart from low tide. South Ngkala Rocks are 10 km north from the entry onto the Waddy Point beach, North Ngkala is 3 km further on. Both these groups of rocks have bypass tracks around them, but even they are difficult. It is important that you plan your trip to coincide with low tide. The area inland from the beach north of Orchid Beach is closed to all vehicles.

Once past these obstacles the 21 km run north to Sandy Cape is along a wide beach. At the Cape itself a sandbar, Breaksea Spit, stretches for 30 km out to sea and the combination of tide and wind often causes a distinct change in the water condition. It can be a treacherous place for a small boat as the wrecks that abound here testify.

Turning the corner at Sandy Cape (**GPS** 24°41'56"S, 153°15'48"E), 34 km north of Waddy Point and 137 km north of the barge, the beach narrows and is steeper. Camping is allowed along here and as the beach is protected from the prevailing south-east winds it is a special spot to enjoy.

The walking track to the Sandy Cape Lighthouse is 8 km south-west of the cape itself, and it is worth the walk up the steep hill for the view along.

The beach run ends at Rooney Point (**GPS** 24°49'03"S, 153°07'02"E), 14 km further south. No vehicle access is allowed from here south, so it is a matter of backtracking.

Southern Lakes Drive

Leave the beach near Dilli Village, skirt the northern edge of the hamlet, and follow the road inland. Keep right at all the minor track junctions and right again at the major track junction 6 km from the beach.

Just over 3 km past this junction you reach Lake Boomanjin, the largest perched lake in the world. Amongst the tall trees there is a good camping ground which has toilets, cold showers and fireplaces but no other facilities. It is just a short walk down the hill to the lake shore, where a trail circumnavigates the lake.

Heading north from Lake Boomanjin, the track can be lumpy and slow going, like most of the inland tracks on Fraser. Within 11 km you pass Lake Benaroon and its camping area and then come to the shores of Lake Birrabeen. For first-time visitors to the island this place is an eye opener. Its crystal clear turquoise waters and white sands are an ideal place to stop, have lunch and a swim. Camping is not allowed.

About 3 km later you will come to a road junction where either track will take you to Central Station, another 6 km away. This was once the heart of the forestry operation on the island and looking at the magnificent trees here you can understand why loggers pioneered this island. There is an excellent camping area at Central Station with toilets, showers, fireplaces and rubbish disposal. A magnificent walk along Wanggoolba Creek is a must. A ranger is based here and limited first aid facilities can also be found.

Take the track to Eurong from Central Station, and about 1 km along the road turn left, or north, to Pile Valley, the heart of which is reached in another 2 km. You need to get out of the vehicle here to really appreciate the tall satinay trees.

Keep left at the next couple of junctions and just over 5 km from Pile Valley you will come to the car park and camping area for Lake McKenzie. The distance from the beach at Dilli Village to Lake McKenzie via the route described is around 37 km. Lake McKenzie is surely one of the most picturesque lakes on the whole island. The white sand and brilliant blue water, with a backdrop of verdant forest, make this probably the most popular lake on Fraser. Toilets, showers and fireplaces are provided in the camping ground.

Leaving Lake McKenzie can be a little confusing, so it is best to backtrack 1 km to a road junction where you will turn left, or northwards. You need to continue straight ahead at the first crossroads and then, just 2 km since turning onto this north-running road, you will come to a major crossroads where you need to turn right for the east coast.

Nearly 8 km later there is a track on your right which leads a short distance to the Lake Wabby Lookout car park and the walking trail to the lake itself. While the walk to the lake is downhill, the walk back seems to be twice as steep—though at least you are under the trees and not in the blazing sun as the walk from the beach is. Lake Wabby, the deepest on Fraser, is slowly being engulfed by a vast sandblow. The sandhill crowds steeply up to the very water's edge and it is a popular swimming spot, but be warned—many people have been injured running down the hill and diving into the water which is shallower than it looks!

From the Lake Wabby Lookout track junction the main road continues to wind through thick forest, coming to the junction with Smith Road nearly 4 km later. Turn right here and you will soon crest the hill where a car park is on your left with a lookout over the large sandblow called Stonetool. This sandblow, like many others on the island, is a mobile area of sand slowly being driven inland by the prevailing south-easterly winds.

From the lookout the track drops steeply down the hill; this was once a terror strip before a series of chained wood rails were put down to stop vehicles bogging in the soft steep sand. Less than 5 km later, and just under 20 km from Lake McKenzie, you come out on the beach, a little over 5 km north of Eurong.

West Coast via Lake Garawongera

At Happy Valley take the track inland through the settlement, and 3 km from the beach keep left at the road junction on the main road to Lake Garawongera, which is reached in another 6 km. Once again this is a pleasant spot to stop and enjoy a swim or a picnic.

Less than 3 km past the car park at the lake you will find a faint track junction on a fairly sharp bend in the main road. Turn right at this point and follow this narrow track which passes through some magnificent vine forest dominated by old tall trees. Get out of your vehicle along here to admire these forest giants. For most of the way the track skirts the southern edge of Bogimbah Creek, with the valley becoming more pronounced as you head west. This track pretty much follows the route of the 1905 tramline used to cart logs down to the barge at Urang Creek.

Note that this track is poorly maintained and overhanging branches may scratch your vehicle or logs may bar the way.

The site of the 1882 Mitchell Nursery is about 3 km along the road; kauri pine and blackbutt dominate this plantation area. The site of the Dipuying Nursery, which dates back to 1914, is just over 2 km further on, and the site of Petries Camp, dating from 1913, is just a few hundred metres on.

A track comes in on the left, 1 km further on and 6 km from the previous road junction. Now the country becomes more open and the forest a drier eucalyptus dominated one.

The country becomes more coastal scrub and swampy as you head west, and just over 6 km later you come to a T-junction (**GPS** 25°18'32"S, 155°02'43"E) where you turn left. Follow this road for another kilometre and then turn left again, following this for another 1.5 km before veering right for a short distance to the old barge point at Urang Creek. A shelter shed and numerous tracks in this area indicate it is a popular spot for campers, especially anglers, who can catch a feed and more in the nearby creek. Mangroves line the coastline and the sea is not far away.

To continue to Kingfisher Bay, backtrack to the last track junction, less than 500 metres back, and turn right, crossing Urang Creek, then Poyungan Creek, all within 4 km of the road junction. The road continues to parallel Poyungun Creek for the next few kilometres before winding its way up to the crest of Leading Hill which offers reasonable views of the surrounding area. There are a few tracks around this area, so stick to the main, obvious route and you will get to the crest of the hill, 10 km from crossing Poyungan Creek.

A track junction 3 km further on requires you to veer right and you will begin to see the occasional signpost to Kingfisher Bay from this point. Keep on the main road and keep right at the major junctions, and just over 3 km later you will be on Cornwells Road, heading almost due west to Kingfisher Bay, which you will reach in 5 km.

Kingfisher Bay (**GPS** 25°27'02"S, 152°59'25"E) is the most luxurious resort on Fraser Island, with accommodation in hotel rooms or private bungalows. There is a small shopping village where you can get basic food requirements, cool drinks, takeaways and souvenirs, and a service station where you can get fuel. The resort also has vehicle hire, runs 4WD basic courses, and offers excursions, boat hire and fishing trips for guests.

Veer right as you come down the hill into the resort, 52 km from Happy Valley, pass the service station and follow signs to the jetty and barge landing point, another kilometre away. Your travels on Fraser end here as far as this trek is concerned, but you can always head back and try a dozen other drives that are just as interesting.

AGNES WATER

491 KM NORTH OF BRISBANE
POPULATION: 120   MAP REF: PAGE 227 L10

Agnes Water is situated on 5 km of curving white sand believed to be the most northerly surfing beach in Australia. The great weather and quiet, get-away-from-it-all location make for a perfect holiday. Six kilometres north of Agnes Water is the Town of 1770, so named after Cook made his second landfall in Australia. The locals consider that reason enough to claim the town as the birthplace of Queensland.

Eurimbula National Park, covering the area where Joseph Banks collected plant specimens, is about 14 km from Agnes Water. There is a camp ground at Bustard Beach but campers must be self-sufficient. Mt Colosseum National Park is accessed some 6 km out of Miriam Vale and again the park is undeveloped so visitors must be self-sufficient.

ACCOMMODATION: Mango Tree Motel, ph (07) 4974 9132; 1770 Holiday Cabin Retreat, ph (07) 4974 9270; Hoban's Hideaway B&B, ph (07) 4974 9144; Agnes Water Caravan Park, ph (07) 4974 9193
ACTIVITIES: Boating, bushwalking, crabbing, fishing, 4WD tours, national park access
TOURIST INFORMATION: Ph (07) 4974 5100

AIRLIE BEACH

1122 KM NORTH OF BRISBANE
POPULATION: 1440   MAP REF: PAGE 226 F2

Airlie Beach is the gateway to the Whitsunday Islands. In 1987 Airlie Beach, Shute Harbour and Cannonvale were incorporated into the new town of Whitsunday. Airlie Beach in the 1960s consisted of a single shop and a small group of holiday shacks. The Seventies and Eighties saw an influx of residents with a corresponding growth in visitors. The trend has continued and the completion of Lake Proserpine, a dam on the Proserpine River, will ensure a plentiful water supply for agriculture and the growing population. The population is well catered for by restaurants and top quality holiday accommodation.

The tropical island resorts of Hayman, Hamilton, Daydream and South Molle, to name a few of the 74 islands that are just off the coast of Whitsunday and which lie inside the Great Barrier Reef, are only some of the attractions of the area. Sunshine, blue water and sandy beaches are the theme of the Whitsundays. Hire a yacht and cruise the blue water between the islands; take a seaplane out to the Great Barrier Reef for a snorkel, or try a kayak.

The calm, protected waters lend themselves to many boating events, including the Hamilton Island Race Week in August, Great Whitsunday Fun Race in September, the Grand Prix Series for 18 ft skiffs, and the Hayman Big Boat Race. Nearby Conway National Park, known for butterflies, is worth a visit.

ACCOMMODATION: Airlie Apartments, ph (07) 4946 6222; Boathaven Lodge Holiday Units, ph (07) 4946 6421; McDowalls Holiday Flats, ph (07) 4946 6176; Airlie Resort Van Park, ph (07) 4946 6727

ACTIVITIES: Charter boat tours, fishing, hiking, national park access, scenic drives, water sports
TOURIST INFORMATION: Ph (07) 4946 6673

ANAKIE

939 KM NORTH-WEST OF BRISBANE
POPULATION: 400   MAP REF: PAGE 226 E9

A house and water tower north of Anakie

Anakie is situated in probably the world's largest known sapphire deposit covering some 216 sq km. Rubies and the occasional diamond have also been found in the gemfields. The word Anakie comes from the Aboriginal word meaning 'twin peaks'.

Millaa Millaa Falls, to the south of Atherton

The gemfield became commercially productive in the 1890s, and today most of the sapphires are sent to Thailand for cutting. The world's most valuable black sapphire was discovered in Anakie in 1935. Cut as the Presidents Heads Sapphire, it is now in the Smithsonian Institute in Washington D. C.

The satellite towns of Sapphire and Rubyvale, located just north of Anakie, grew to cater for miners.

The Gemfields Reserve, an area of 9000 hectares, is set aside for fossicking. Fossicking licences are available on the fields or from the Department of Minerals & Energy at Emerald. In August Anakie holds its Gemfest Festival.

ACCOMMODATION: Gemfields Caravan Park, ph (07) 4985 4142; Bedford Gardens (holiday units), ph (07) 4985 4142
ACTIVITIES: Fossicking
TOURIST INFORMATION: Ph (07) 4935 7101

ATHERTON

1727 KM NORTH OF BRISBANE
POPULATION: 10 200   MAP REF: PAGE 229 L6

At 760 metres above sea level with an equable climate, Atherton sits on the Atherton Tableland between Cairns and Innisfail. It is the centre of a rich agricultural district of which maize is the main crop.

The town was named after John Atherton who settled in the area around 1877. The town's beginnings were as a camp for timber-getters chasing the elusive cedar trees. Later, European and Chinese

pioneers drawn to the area by the promise of gold and tin, stayed and laid the foundations of the rich agricultural industry and also established the beef and dairy herds. The Chinese built a joss house in 1900 which has been classified by the National Trust. Atherton's old post office houses a gallery, museum, visitor's centre and tearooms. US Flying Fortresses were based in the area during World War II.

There is a walking track to the top of Hallorans Hill with splendid views. North-east of the town is the Tinnaroo Falls Dam where you can swim or fish. Millaa Millaa Falls, to the south, is also attractive.

For a different experience, take a steam train ride to Herberton. Railco Steam Railways is a non-profit organisation staffed mainly by volunteers and operates the only full-sized steam locomotives in Northern Queensland.

Crystal Caves, located in Main Street, house a unique underground cave museum with fascinating giant crystal formations, fossils and fluorescent minerals from around the world.

Two major festivals are held in Atherton: the Maize Festival in September and the Tableland Folk Festival in October.

ACCOMMODATION: Hinterland Motel, ph (07) 4091 1885; Wrights Motor Inn, ph (07) 4095 4141; Atherton Woodslands Tourist Caravan Park, ph (07) 4091 1407

ACTIVITIES: Scenic tours

TOURIST INFORMATION: Ph (07) 4051 3588

AYR

1276 KM NORTH OF BRISBANE
POPULATION: 8300   MAP REF: PAGE 226 D1

Ayr is a sugar town and, due to irrigation, is now Australia's most productive sugarcane growing area. Rice growing is also a major industry in the area.

Ayr was named after the birthplace in Scotland of the Queensland premier of the early 1880s. The town was almost completely rebuilt after a disastrous cyclone in 1903. The town also suffered severe damage in the cyclone of 1959.

Home Hill, situated some 7 km to the south, is Ayr's sister town and the two towns are linked by the bridge over the Burdekin River. This is often referred to as the 'Silver Link'.

The Ayr Nature Display houses one of the major collections of butterflies, shells, rocks and native fauna in Australia.

ACCOMMODATION: Country Ayr Motel, ph (07) 4783 1700; Max Motel, ph (07) 4783 2033; Burdekin Motor Inn, ph (07) 4782 1511; Bartons Caravan Park, ph (07) 4782 1101

ACTIVITIES: Fishing, local tours, swimming

TOURIST INFORMATION: Ph (07) 4771 3061

BAMAGA

2688 KM NORTH OF BRISBANE
POPULATION: 815   MAP REF: PAGE 234 C2

Bamaga is the most northerly township in Queensland and is located 33 km south of the tip of Cape York. The area was settled by islanders from Saibai in

The tip of Cape York, 33 km north of Bamaga

the Torres Strait in 1948. It was named after one of the islanders' leaders and has an Aboriginal Council.

Jackey Jackey Airfield, located near the town and an important staging point for aircraft during World War II, is named after the Aborigine who accompanied Edmund Kennedy on the ill-fated 1848 Cape York expedition. Of the three survivors of that expedition, Jackey Jackey was the only one to reach the tip and the waiting ship. Travelling to the tip is less hazardous these days and travellers can now enjoy a remote holiday at the wilderness lodge located within walking distance of the most northerly point of Australia.

ACCOMMODATION: Seisia Seaview Lodge, ph (07) 4069 3243; Seisia Village Campground & Caravan Park, ph (07) 4069 3243

ACTIVITIES: Fishing, sightseeing, tours of the Torres Strait islands

TOURIST INFORMATION: Ph (07) 4069 3285

BARCALDINE

1066 KM NORTH-WEST OF BRISBANE
POPULATION: 1730   MAP REF: PAGE 231 N9

Known as the Garden City of the West and a major wool-growing and cattle-raising district, Barcaldine was established in 1886 as the terminus of the Rockhampton railway. Cobb & Co coaches set out from the town across the state up until 1914. In 1887 artesian water was located, giving Barcaldine a ready source of water. The town's citrus orchards attest to the quality of the bore water; however, the water made the locally brewed beer totally undrinkable!

Barcaldine is famous as the strike headquarters for the six-month shearers' strike in 1891. Over 1000 shearers camped in and around the town and their march in May 1891 was Australia's first May Day march. From this turbulent period the Australian Workers Party was created, which eventually became the Australian Labor Party. The 'Tree of Knowledge', a large gum tree at least 200 years old, is where the

striking shearers gathered for their meetings. This tree is now the focal point of a garden area which features a monument shaped as shearing blades bearing the names of the 13 men who were jailed as a result of the shearers' strike.

Mad Micks Hoppers and Huts Funny Farm in Pine Street is worth a visit. Enjoy billy tea and damper and see relics of Outback history, including a bush shearing shed, a slab-style Cobb & Co changeover station, an art gallery and a fantastic doll display.

ACCOMMODATION: Landsborough Lodge Motel, ph (07) 4651 1100; Lee Garden Motel, ph (07) 4651 1488; Barcaldine Motel, ph (07) 4651 1244; Homestead Caravan Park, ph (07) 4651 1308

ACTIVITIES: Historic interest, scenic drives

TOURIST INFORMATION: Ph (07) 4778 3555

BEAUDESERT

69 KM SOUTH OF BRISBANE
POPULATION: 4120   MAP REF: PAGE 225 M8

Beaudesert was named after a station near Mudgee in New South Wales although the name can be also traced back to Britain. Originally settled in the 1840s,

An 1875 slab-hut in Beaudesert

the district is a rich agricultural, beef and dairying producer and utilises the water of the Logan and Albert Rivers for irrigation. A prized pumpkin, the Beaudesert Blue, bears the name of the town.

Boys Town, which was established in the early 1960s and based on the American organisation that aimed to reintegrate young offenders, is located on the outskirts of the town. The Beaudesert racecourse holds a race meeting each year in support of this very worthy establishment.

Jubilee Park contains a museum with an 1875 slab hut which illustrates early building techniques.

There are many national parks in the area, including Lamington National Park.

ACCOMMODATION: Kooralbyn Resort, ph (07) 5544 6226; Kerry Court Motel, ph (07) 5541 1593; Cedar Glen Host Farm, ph (07) 5544 8170; Beaudesert Caravan Park, ph (07) 55 41 1368

ACTIVITIES: Bushwalking, national park access, scenic drives

TOURIST INFORMATION: Ph (07) 5540 5199

BILOELA

570 KM NORTH OF BRISBANE
POPULATION: 6180   MAP REF: PAGE 225 H1

Biloela comes from the Aboriginal word for 'white cockatoo', and though it is the service centre for an agricultural area producing grain and cotton, it is probably more widely known for coal from the Callide open-cut mine. The town is situated south-west of Rockhampton in the fertile Callide Valley at the junction of the Dawson and Burnett Highways.

A rural theme park called Advance Australia Fair is a living museum of the district's industries. Greycliffe, an old homestead, is open to the public as are the Callide Power Station and the cotton ginnery. The nearby Callide Dam is used by local residents for swimming and boating. Cania Gorge National Park, with its spectacular sandstone cliffs, is not far away.
ACCOMMODATION: Apollo Motel, ph (07) 4992 1122; Biloela Countryman Motel, ph (07) 4992 1488; Biloela Caravan Park, ph (07) 4992 1211; Kroombit Tourist Park Cattle Property, ph (07) 4992 2186
ACTIVITIES: Fishing, national park access, water sports
TOURIST INFORMATION: Ph (07) 4992 2405

BIRDSVILLE

1573 KM WEST OF BRISBANE
POPULATION: 100   MAP REF: PAGE 232 C4

Birdsville, of all Australian towns, most typifies the Outback: the hazards and perils of travelling in this very dry continent, and the remoteness, harshness and rugged beauty of the land. The town is on the eastern edge of the Simpson Desert in the extreme south-western corner of Queensland, 170 km from Poeppels Corner. The famous Birdsville Track starts here and runs 536 km to Marree in South Australia. The track can be travelled at most times by conventional vehicles, but should be treated with respect: it can be extremely treacherous, especially during the Wet (October to March).

Diamantina Crossing, as Birdsville was first known, was at the junction of a number of stock routes from west and central Queensland to Adelaide. There was a border customs post here which closed after Federation. In 1923 one of Birdsville's hotels became a hospital of the Australian Inland Mission and there is still a medical station in the town. The Annual Birdsville Races are held in

Big Red, a massive sand dune near Birdsville

September and the town's population explodes to between 5000 and 7000. All proceeds from the race meeting go to the Royal Flying Doctor Service and Birdsville Hospital. The only remaining hostelry, the historic 1885 Birdsville Hotel, does a roaring trade during race week.

The town's water supply is drawn from a 280-metre-deep artesian bore. The water is so hot when it reaches the surface that it is put into holding ponds to cool before being pumped around the town.

About 8 km northwards on the Bedourie road is a small stand of one of Australia's rarest trees, the waddy-wood (*Acacia peuce*). Only three stands of these trees are known in Australia. The trees are very slow growing, very prickly particularly when small, and the wood is extremely hard.
ACCOMMODATION: Birdsville Hotel, ph (07) 4656 3244; Birdsville Caravan Park, ph (07) 4656 3244
ACTIVITIES: Fishing, 4WD touring, sightseeing
TOURIST INFORMATION: Ph (07) 4746 1202

BLACKALL

959 KM NORTH-WEST OF BRISBANE
POPULATION: 2000   MAP REF: PAGE 231 N10

This district was originally explored by Thomas Mitchell in the mid-nineteenth century as he followed the Barcoo River, and Blackall is named after the second governor of Queensland, Samuel Wensley Blackall. Blackall has also established a reputation for producing some of the best sheep and cattle in Queensland. In 1885 the first artesian bore in Queensland was sunk, but the water was undrinkable.

The shearer Jacky Howe set a world record for hand-shearing in 1892 when he shore 321 sheep in under eight hours. In the same year Jacky set a machine-shearing record of 237 in eight hours at Barcaldine Station. It was not until 1950 that his record was broken by machine shearing.

The steam-driven Blackall Wool Scour, 5 km north of town, was built in 1908. It is a rare link to the past as it is the only remaining example of the 52 steam-driven wool scours that were built in Australia..

In September the Spring Time Affair is held, and this is followed in October by the annual rodeo.
ACCOMMODATION: Avington Outback Holiday Station, ph (07) 4657 5952; Blackall Motel, ph (07) 4657 4491; Blackall Coolibah Motel, ph (07) 4657 4380; Blackall Caravan Park, ph (07) 4657 4816
ACTIVITIES: Scenic tours
TOURIST INFORMATION: Ph (07) 4657 4255

BLACKWATER

823 KM NORTH-WEST OF BRISBANE
POPULATION: 8000   MAP REF: PAGE 227 F9

From the late nineteenth century to the 1960s Blackwater was a service centre for beef cattle. In 1962 a 7-metre-thick coal seam was discovered 20 km south-west of Blackwater and by the late 1960s three mining companies were operating in the area. Branch lines to Blackwater gave direct rail access to the

power station and Gladstone, and the town is now the coal capital of Queensland. Blackwater Mine, an open-cut operation south of Blackwater, produces coking coal which is exported.

The International Flag Display in the town consists of 36 flags representing the different nationalities that established Blackwater from 1965 to 1970. It is the largest flag display in the world except for the United Nations Building in New York.

Blacktown Tableland National Park, to the south, has spectacular cliffs and gorges and good bushwalks.
ACCOMMODATION: Black Diamond Motel, ph (07) 4982 5944; Bottletree Motel & Caravan Park, ph (07) 4982 5367; Capricorn Hotel Motor Inn, ph (07) 4982 5466
ACTIVITIES: Fossicking, national park access, scenic tours
TOURIST INFORMATION: Ph (07) 4982 4142

BOONAH

100 KM SOUTH-WEST OF BRISBANE
POPULATION: 6970   MAP REF: PAGE 225 M8

Boonah is the centre of an agricultural region in the Fassifern Valley that forms a part of the 'Valleys of the Scenic Rim'. Initially the area relied on dairying, pigs and timber; now its mainstay is beef cattle and cultivated crops such as potatoes and carrots. It was also the railhead for the rail line from Ipswich until the trains stopped running in 1964.

The region was first opened up by the explorer and botanist Allan Cunningham and originally named Blumbergville after the Blumberg brothers who opened the first store. The name was changed to Boonah in 1887 after an Aboriginal word 'buna'. Moogerah Dam is close by and popular with anglers and waterskiiers.
ACCOMMODATION: Boonah Motel, ph (07) 5463 1944
ACTIVITIES: Boating, fishing, waterskiing
TOURIST INFORMATION: Ph (07) 5463 0288

BOULIA

1593 KM NORTH-WEST OF BRISBANE
POPULATION: 520   MAP REF: PAGE 230 D7

Boulia is the centre of a massive shire of around 600 people with more than 5 times as many sheep and cattle. Burke and Wills passed through the area in 1860 and named the Burke River and Wills Creek. The town is on the edge of the Simpson Desert, and the Red Stump in the main street warns travellers of the dangers of travel in this desolate place.

This is the area where the eerie 'Min Min' light can be seen. The light, described as resembling a car headlight or a luminous football, seems to be especially visible around the Min Min Hotel which burnt down in the early twentieth century. None of the explanations that have been suggested has been accepted by the hundreds that have seen this light.
ACCOMMODATION: Australian Hotel/Motel, ph (07) 4746 3144; Boulia Desert Sands Motel, ph (07) 4746 3144; Boulia Caravan Park, ph (07) 4746 3359
ACTIVITIES: Fishing, 4WD touring, sightseeing
TOURIST INFORMATION: Ph (07) 4746 3386

BOWEN

1162 KM NORTH OF BRISBANE
POPULATION: 13 400   MAP REF: PAGE 226 E2

Bowen—named after George Bowen, Queensland's first governor—was the first settlement in North Queensland, founded in 1861. In 1862 the North Australian Hotel opened its doors and is the oldest licence-holder in north Queensland.

Bowen is widely known for its produce, in particular mangoes and tomatoes: the district is often referred to as the market garden of Queensland. The claim to having the best climate in Australia with an average of eight hours of sunshine daily no doubt accounts for the district's high production rate. Bowen also supports a major fishing fleet while the beef industry is also flourishing.

The high, white stacks of salt, visible from the main road on nearing the town, are the result of evaporating the water from the saltwater ponds. North of the town is Abbot Point, the most northerly coal shipping port in Australia. Here coal from the Collinsville and Newlands fields is loaded from a jetty that extends almost 3 km into the sea.

Scattered throughout the town are murals which depict Bowen's history and are becoming famous.

ACCOMMODATION: Whitsunday Sands Resort Motel, ph (07) 4786 3333; Crystal Beach Holiday Units, ph (07) 4786 2561; North Australian Hotel, ph (07) 4786 1244; Queens Beach Caravan Park, ph (07) 4785 1313

ACTIVITIES: Fishing, reef tours, water sports

TOURIST INFORMATION: Ph (07) 4786 4494

BRIBIE ISLAND

60 KM NORTH OF BRISBANE
POPULATION: 10 740   MAP REF: PAGE 225 N6

Bribie, as it is referred to by the locals, is just 51 km long and 7 km wide and joined to the mainland by a bridge that crosses Pumiceston Passage.

At the mainland end of the bridge, a monument honours the last of Bribie's Aborigines, Kalma-Kutha, who died in 1897. Less than a hundred years before her death, the island had been home to about 600 Aborigines living in substantial huts. The first European to explore Bribie was Matthew Flinders, who visited in 1799 and named Point Skirmish after an altercation with the local people.

A water paradise, Bribie offers fishing and surfing on its open beaches, and safe boating on the calm waters of Pumiceston Passage. The northern end of the island, and its beaches, are protected in Bribie Island National Park. In spring this becomes a picture of pink boronia, wattle, bottlebrush and other wildflowers.

ACCOMMODATION: Placid Waters Holiday Apartments, ph (07) 3408 2122; Bribie Island Hotel, ph (07) 3408 7477; Tanderra Lodge Holiday Units, ph (07) 3408 7888; Bribie Island Caravan Park, ph (07) 3408 1134

ACTIVITIES: Bushwalking, fishing, 4WD touring, national park access, water sports

TOURIST INFORMATION: Ph (07) 3408 9026

BUNDABERG

368 KM NORTH OF BRISBANE
POPULATION: 54 821   MAP REF: PAGE 225 L2

Bundaberg is at the centre of one of the major sugar-producing areas of Australia. The district is also renowned for its rum, timber, beef and avocados. Located some 15 km from the coast on the banks of the Burnett River, Bundaberg is a city of tree-lined streets, parks and gardens. The streets are ribbons of colour when the poincianas bloom in spring.

Bundaberg provides the southernmost access to the Great Barrier Reef and in particular to the 'two ladies of the reef', Lady Elliott and Lady Musgrave Islands. These magnificent islands are true coral cays which visitors can stay on or explore on a day cruise.

From mid-August to October whale watching is high on the agenda as the humpback whales pass close to the Bundaberg coastline. The townships of Elliott Heads, Bargara, Innes Park and Burnett Heads, all on the coast and 15 km from Bundaberg, are highly sought after as holiday destinations, and boast some of the most pristine beaches in Australia.

Just north of Bargara is the Mon Repos Environmental Park, one of the southern hemisphere's most significant turtle rookeries. Here between November and January each year loggerheads, leatherback and the rarer flatback turtles leave the ocean to nest.

Bundaberg is the birthplace of the pioneer aviator Bert Hinkler. His ambition for flying was fuelled by his studies of the ibis on the area's lagoons and in the Bundaberg Botanical Gardens. In 1928 he completed the first solo flight from England to Australia. During 1983–84, Hinkler's house was moved from England to the Hinkler House Memorial Museum in the Bundaberg Botanical Gardens.

Bundy Rum is another famous product of Bundaberg. Even the setback in the early 1930s when the distillery was completely gutted by fire has not stopped Bundy becoming the most widely known liquor in Australia. Tours of the distillery are conducted each day and are well worth a visit.

ACCOMMODATION: Alexandra Park Motor Inn, ph (07) 4152 7255; Acacia Motor Inn, ph (07) 4152 3666; Cane Village Holiday Caravan Park, ph (07) 4155 1022; Oakwood Caravan Park, ph (07) 4159 9332

ACTIVITIES: Fishing, reef tours, sightseeing, water sports, whale watching

TOURIST INFORMATION: Ph (07) 4152 2333

BURKETOWN

2093 KM NORTH-WEST OF BRISBANE
POPULATION: 210   MAP REF: PAGE 228 C7

The oldest town on the Gulf of Carpentaria, Burketown was first settled in 1861 when pastoralists opened up enormous cattle runs in the region. With wetlands to the north and drier grasslands to the south, the area continues to support a substantial beef industry. From its early days Burketown was considered wild and lawless, much like the cowboy towns of the American Wild West.

The town was originally known as Carpentaria Township but was later renamed after the explorer Robert Burke who crossed the region in 1861 during his ill-fated expedition from Melbourne to the Gulf.

Burketown hosts the world barramundi fishing championship at Easter while in May the Gregory Canoe Race is held,. Races and rodeos are in July.

ACCOMMODATION: Burketown Pub, ph (07) 4745 5104; Escott Barramundi Lodge Cattle Station, ph (07) 4748 5577; Burketown Caravan Park, ph (07) 4745 5118

ACTIVITIES: Fishing, 4WD touring

TOURIST INFORMATION: Ph (07) 4745 5101

CAIRNS

1703 KM NORTH OF BRISBANE
POPULATION: 101 000   MAP REF: PAGE 229 L5

Cairns is the perfect starting point for exploring Far North Queensland. The coastal attractions include

An aerial view of the beautiful city of Cairns

the magnificent Great Barrier Reef and, further north, the tropical beaches of the Marlin Coast. Inland you will find the rainforests and plains of the Atherton Tableland and the Gulf Savannah. To the north lie the lush Daintree National Park and the varied landscape of Cape York.

The city mixes grand colonial architecture, wonderful old pubs, high-set wooden homes of typical north Queensland style, with modern shopping malls and apartment blocks. Cairns has grown at a phenomenal rate since 1979, with new suburbs appearing as if by magic. The city is a major tourist destination for overseas travellers especially since the opening of the Cairns International Airport. It is also a popular holiday destination for Australians wanting to experience this great part of their country.

In the early days Cairns and Port Douglas were great rivals. It was not until 1924, when the railway line from Brisbane was terminated at Cairns, that Cairns became the major city in north Queensland.

There is a stunning array of things to see and do here which should satisfy even the most critical tastes. Accommodation ranges from luxury island resorts and five star hotels to rainforest retreats, family units, camping and backpacker hostels.

Explore the deserted mining ghost towns and the small isolated communities that still service the mining and pastoral industries. Take a trip out to the Great Barrier Reef for snorkelling, SCUBA diving, swimming or just admiring the myriad life forms and fascinating colours of the coral. The Kuranda Scenic Rail ride up the range west of Cairns goes through tunnels, over bridged ravines and past the Barron Gorge waterfalls arriving at the station of Kuranda, reputed to be the prettiest railway station in the country. The markets of Kuranda are famous for their variety and quality. Alternatively, there is the 7.5 km trip to Kuranda on the Skyrail, the world's longest gondola cableway, which rides above the World Heritage rainforest canopy with spectacular views of the Coral Sea beaches, canefields and the mountains.

Other activities include whitewater rafting down the Tully River, a thrilling hot-air balloon flight at sunrise, a 4WD safari through the rugged Outback country, or a Tiger Moth or helicopter sightseeing ride over spectacular waterfalls and rainforests. The Australian Woolshed puts on shearing and working sheep dog demonstrations, while Barron Gorge Power Station, an underground hydro-electric power station, is also open for tours.

The future of Cairns seems assured with the tourist industry continuing to grow, the 100 million dollar Sherga RAAF Base near Weipa currently under construction, the multi-million dollar Tully Millstream hydro-electric scheme and the possibility of the Cape York Space Station project finally becoming a reality.

Cairns' main annual festival, 'Fun in the Sun', is held in October.
ACCOMMODATION: Cairns International Hotel, ph (07) 4031 1300; Radisson Plaza Hotel, ph (07) 4031 1411; Bay Village Tropical Retreat Motel, ph (07) 4051 4622; Adobe Motel, ph (07) 4051 5511; Homestyle Bed & Breakfast, ph (07) 4058 1889; Cairns Coconut Caravan Resort, ph (07) 4054 6644;
ACTIVITIES: Bushwalking, fishing, 4WD touring, national park access, reef and scenic tours, water sports
TOURIST INFORMATION: Ph (07) 4051 3588

CAMOOWEAL

1989 KM NORTH-WEST OF BRISBANE
POPULATION: 200   MAP REF: PAGE 230 A1
It is worth noting that Camooweal is some 200 km north-west of Mount Isa but comes under the same city council. This must be one of the largest city council areas in the world, with part of the Barkly Highway as its main street. The town's only claim to fame today is that it is the last town before the Northern Territory border. However, in the old droving days it was the main dipping centre for cattle crossing the state border. The Shire Hall, built in 1922–23 and extended in 1938, is classified by the National Trust for its architecture.

The Camooweal Caves National Park has some of the biggest and least explored limestone caves in Australia. Cavers need to be experienced and well equipped and are restricted to the dry season as the caves fill with water during the wet season. During the day, the caves are home to roosting bats and owls, as well as other birds and animals escaping the heat.
ACCOMMODATION: Camooweal Roadhouse Motel, ph (07) 4748 2155; BP Camooweal Driveway Cabins, ph (07) 4748 2137
ACTIVITIES: Caving, national park access
TOURIST INFORMATION: Ph (07) 4749 1555

CARDWELL

1523 KM NORTH OF BRISBANE
POPULATION: 8850   MAP REF: PAGE 229 M7
Cardwell is sandwiched between ocean and mountains. With a rainfall that is the highest in Australia, the rich hinterland yields a great variety of produce, including beef, tea, sugarcane and bananas. One of the first northern towns to be settled, Cardwell was once the only port between Bowen and Somerset at the tip of Cape York, but the rapid growth of Townsville put an end to any further development.

Cardwell is a popular fishing and holiday town and within easy reach of its main attraction, Hinchinbrook Island. Australia's largest island national park is dominated by its rugged mountain range, which is offset by the eastern sandy beaches and the western mangrove swamps. For the very fit, the East Coast Trail is a 30 km trek considered to be among the world's greatest walking tracks.
ACCOMMODATION: Sunrise Village & Leisure Park Motel, ph (07) 4066 8550; Aquarius Motel & Holiday Units, ph (07) 4066 8755; Kookaburra Holiday Caravan Park, ph (07) 4066 8776
ACTIVITIES: Bushwalking, fishing, national park access, scenic drives, water sports
TOURIST INFORMATION: Ph (07) 4771 3061

CHARLEVILLE

744 KM WEST OF BRISBANE
POPULATION: 3400   MAP REF: PAGE 224 A5
Charleville is a well-known town of western Queensland, centre of a rich pastoral district, and in

Wills Street in the centre of Charleville

1922 it was where the first regular flight service was commenced, between Charleville and Cloncurry, by the Australian icon, QANTAS (Queensland and Northern Territory Aerial Services). Charleville also prides itself on being at the heart of the mulga country. Mulga, or to give it its Aboriginal name, 'Booga Woongaroo', is a lifesaving tree. In times of drought, when the graziers and landowners talk about being out 'cutting mulga', it means the drought is bad, all the feed is burnt and useless, and only the mulga survives to feed the sheep and cattle.

At the end of the nineteenth century Charleville was a thriving community with ten pubs and with up to 500 bullock teams passing through during the wool season. Cobb & Co moved their coach-building factory here from Bathurst, New South Wales, in 1893 and continued building 'the tall ships of Charleville', as the coaches became known, until 1920 when lack of demand forced the closure of the factory.

The Stiger Vortex guns located south of the town are an indication of the schemes devised to break the drought of 1902. These tall cones were filled with gunpowder which was fired into the air in the hope of making rain. They were not successful.

The massive rains of April 1990 almost completely devastated Charleville, but with typical country resilience, the town has slowly recovered.

Charleville contains a base for the Royal Flying Doctor Service, the Charleville School of Distance Education, and a pastoral research laboratory. In September the Booga Woongaroo Festival is held.
ACCOMMODATION: Charleville Motel, ph (07) 4654 1566; Corones Motel, ph (07) 4654 1022; Charleville Waltzing Matilda Motor Inn, ph (07) 4654 1720; Cobb & Co Caravan Park, ph (07) 4654 1053
ACTIVITIES: Fishing, sightseeing
TOURIST INFORMATION: Ph (07) 4657 4450

CHARTERS TOWERS

1367 KM NORTH OF BRISBANE
POPULATION: 9650   MAP REF: PAGE 226 B2
Back in its 'golden years', between 1872 and 1916, the locals called Charters Towers 'The World'. With its own stock exchange (which was open around the clock, seven days a week), something like 100 gold

mines, the same amount of pubs and taverns and a population around the 30 000 mark, it certainly was their world. Gold brought prosperity and many grand buildings were constructed—Charters Towers has more National Trust properties than any other place in Queensland. The classical Victorian style featured wide verandahs and cast-iron lattice work. The last mine was closed in 1926, although with modern extraction methods many of the old mine dumps are being reworked.

Charters Towers has a thriving beef industry while cotton, tobacco, citrus trees, grapes and vegetables flourish on the fertile river flats. Charters Towers is renowned for its boarding schools, which cater mainly for students from Papua New Guinea, the Torres Strait islands and northern Australia.

The old Venus gold treatment plant and stock exchange have been restored and are open for viewing. The old Civic Club, built by a group of businessmen around 1900, is a striking building that is worth a visit.

ACCOMMODATION: Cattlemans Rest Motor Inn, ph (07) 4787 3555; Country Road Motel, ph (07) 4787 2422; York Street Bed & Breakfast, ph (07) 4787 1028; Mexican Tourist Caravan Park, ph (07) 4787 1161
ACTIVITIES: Fossicking, scenic drives, sightseeing
TOURIST INFORMATION: Ph (07) 4771 3061

The township of Charters Towers

CHILDERS

311 KM NORTH OF BRISBANE
POPULATION: 1500   MAP REF: PAGE 225 L2
Childers is a sugar town as well as a National Trust town. Even though a 1902 fire destroyed much of the town, many impressive Victorian buildings remain and are listed by the National Trust. Sugarcane, the major crop, has been grown in the area since the 1870s, but now avocados and vegetables are also produced and are irrigated from the Monduran Dam.

A visit to the Pharmaceutical Museum containing the original cedar fixtures, a 1906 cash register and leather-bound prescription books is a must. At the Isis sugar mill you can see raw cane turned into familiar white sugar crystals. There is also an historic walk through the town.

ACCOMMODATION: Motel Childers, ph (07) 4126 1177; Avocado Motor Inn, ph (07) 4126 1608; Sugarbowl Caravan Park, ph (07) 4126 1521
ACTIVITIES: Scenic drives, tours
TOURIST INFORMATION: Ph (07) 4126 1994

The Donna Caves in Chillagoe–Mungana National Park

CHILLAGOE

1899 KM NORTH-WEST OF BRISBANE
POPULATION: 220   MAP REF: PAGE 229 K6
Chillagoe is situated on the Burke Development Road, 209 km south-west of Cairns, and what was once a major mining town now relies almost solely on the tourist dollar. In the early 1900s a large proportion of the lead, silver and copper mined in Queensland came from around Chillagoe. The mines also yielded gold, tin, zinc, fluorspar, wolfram and molybdenum. Mining is now confined to one quarry which crushes limestone, although a recent discovery of rare blue marble deposits may again bring Chillagoe to the attention of world markets. An excellent museum displays the old copper smelters.

The Chillagoe–Mungana Caves National Park, 8 km south of the town, is noted for its splendid limestone caves.

In May crowds pour into Chillagoe for the annual rodeo and races.

ACCOMMODATION: Chillagoe Caves Lodge Motel, ph (07) 4094 7106; Chillagoe Caravan Park and Roadhouse, ph (07) 4094 7177
ACTIVITIES: Guided tours, national park access, scenic drives
TOURIST INFORMATION: Ph (07) 4051 3588

CHINCHILLA

293 KM WEST OF BRISBANE
POPULATION: 6020   MAP REF: PAGE 225 J5
The name of this town is said to come from the Aboriginal name 'jinchilla' meaning 'cypress pine'. The district relies on grain growing, timber and grazing and is also known as the polocrosse (a hybrid of polo and lacrosse) centre of Queensland. This area contains one of the world's largest known deposits of petrified wood, reputed to be 140 to 180 million years old. You can fossick for the wood around Baking Board and Magic Stone, where you might also come across gemstones such as agate and jasper. The Folk Museum and Sawmill are interesting.

Boonarga, east of Chinchilla, has a memorial to the cactoblastis moth, the insect imported to eliminate the prickly pear plague. In 1925 over a quarter of a million hectares were inundated by prickly pear but within ten years the moth had eradicated it.

ACCOMMODATION: Chinchilla Great Western Motor Inn, ph (07) 4662 8288; Chinchilla Motel,

ph (07) 4662 7314; Little Hollow Farm, ph (07) 4662 8511; O'Shea's Chinchilla Caravan Park, ph (07) 4662 7741
ACTIVITIES: Gem and petrified wood fossicking, scenic drives
TOURIST INFORMATION: Ph (07) 4661 3122

CLERMONT

1000 KM NORTH-WEST OF BRISBANE
POPULATION: 2800   MAP REF: PAGE 226 D7
Clermont is the oldest inland settlement in northern Queensland and again it was the discovery of gold in the 1870s that started the boom. Now the region breeds cattle and sheep and produces timber, wheat, sorghum and safflower. The town has a chequered history. In 1870 and again in 1916 the Wolfgang and Sandy Creeks flooded Clermont, causing major loss of life. After these floods the town's houses, shops, school and even the two-storey hotel were hauled to their current site on higher ground.

Tours of the nearby Blair Athol coalfields, which contain the world's largest deposit of steaming coal, are available. Copperfield, a deserted copper mining town, is located 6 km south-west of Clermont; a single chimney, rusted machinery and a cemetery are the only reminders of the long-gone boom days.

The Clermont rodeo is held in September.
ACCOMMODATION: Clermont Motor Inn, ph (07) 4983 3133; Grand Hotel, ph (07) 4983 1188; Leo Hotel, ph (07) 4983 1566; Clermont Caravan Park, ph (07) 4983 1927
ACTIVITIES: Mine tours, scenic drives
TOURIST INFORMATION: Ph (07) 4983 1133

CLONCURRY

1689 KM NORTH-WEST OF BRISBANE
POPULATION: 3900   MAP REF: PAGE 230 E3
The Cloncurry Shire is mainly cattle country although mining still plays a major part in the economy, as it did during World War I when Cloncurry was Australia's biggest producer of copper. The explorer Robert Burke named the Cloncurry River after his cousin Lady Elizabeth Cloncurry, and later the town was named after the river. As late as 1974, 22 carat straw gold was discovered in the area. This type of gold, occurring near the surface, looks like lengths of wire and is very rare. The only other place it has been found is South Africa.

Cloncurry has the reputation of being very hot and this is supported by the recording in 1889 of a temperature of 124°F (51.1°C), which has never been exceeded anywhere in Australia.

Cloncurry is proud to lay claim to some of the most important firsts in the areas of aviation, health and education. The first commercial flight of the fledgling QANTAS was between Winton and Cloncurry in 1920. The Royal Flying Doctor Service's (RFDS) first base was set up in Cloncurry in 1928. This unique Australian service was the brainchild of a Presbyterian minister, John Flynn, and now spreads a mantle of safety between Derby in Western Australia, Cairns in Queensland, Broken Hill in New South

Wales and Port Augusta in South Australia. This was followed in 1960 by the first Queensland broadcast of the School of the Air using the RFDS radio network. This service is now the School of Distant Education.

There is much to see around Cloncurry. Just a few kilometres down the Landsborough Highway is McKinlay and the Walkabout Creek Hotel made famous in the film *Crocodile Dundee*. The Cloncurry/Mary Kathleen Memorial Park in McIlwraith Street includes buildings moved there from the abandoned uranium mining town of Mary Kathleen. The John Flynn Place incorporating the Fred McKay Art Gallery and RFDS Museum pays tribute to a man who saw a need and filled it despite enormous odds.

The Gidgee Inn built by the Pearson family is an example of recycling and Outback ingenuity. Rammed earth walls, corrugated iron, recycled hardwood and jarrah logs reclaimed from the old railway bridge in Cloncurry all contribute to this distinctive motel. Take a quiet walk through the Afghan Cemetery in Henry Street or the Chinese Cemetery on the Flinders Highway where the remains of some hundreds of Chinese miners are buried. There is a memorial cairn to Burke and Wills located some 43 km west of Cloncurry on the banks of the Corella River.

ACCOMMODATION: Gilbert Park Cabins & Great North West Caravan Park, ph (07) 4742 2300; Gidgee Inn Motel, ph (07) 4742 2429; Wagon Wheel Motel, ph (07) 4742 1866; Cloncurry Caravan Park Oasis, ph (07) 4742 1313
ACTIVITIES: Fishing, historic interest, scenic drives
TOURIST INFORMATION: Ph (07) 4657 4255

COOKTOWN

1930 KM NORTH OF BRISBANE
POPULATION: 1300   MAP REF: PAGE 229 L3
Cooktown was founded as a port for the Palmer River goldfields, more than a century after Captain James Cook spent 48 days on the banks of the river that bears his ship's name, *Endeavour*, repairing the vessel after it had been damaged on a coral reef off Cape Tribulation. In the mid 1870s Cooktown was Queensland's third busiest port. As the gold started to run out, tin was discovered nearby and the town

The beautiful port of Cooktown

continued to prosper as a port for the Burns Philp Company's island trade and as an access point for traders into Papua New Guinea. Nowadays Cooktown is a tourist town and the gateway to Cape York.

A visit to the Lion's Den Inn is a must. It is an old pub on the coast road from Cape Tribulation. It has heaps of character and camping is available behind the pub towards the creek. Cooktown also has many fine buildings built in the gold rush era, notably the Bank of New South Wales, an imposing building with wooden counters and the gold scales on display. The Captain Cook Historical Museum is housed in what was initially built in 1888 as a school run by Irish nuns, and displays 200 years of Cooktown's history. The Chinese Joss House is the legacy left by the thousands of Chinese who flocked to the area during the gold rush years, many of whom are buried in the Cooktown cemetery.

Lizard Island, north-east of Cooktown, was the scene of a tragedy when Mary Watson, her small son and Chinese servant were attacked by Aborigines and fled the island in an iron tank. All three died of thirst on an uninhabited island 18 km off the mainland. She is buried in the Cooktown cemetery and there is a monument to her in the town.

In June the town puts on the Cooktown Discovery Festival and re-enacts Cook's landing.
ACCOMMODATION: The Sovereign Resort Hotel, ph (07) 4069 582; Sea View Motel, ph (07) 4069 5377; Hillcrest Guest House, ph (07) 4069 5893; Cooktown Alamanda Inn, ph (07) 4069 5203; Cooktown Tropical Breeze Caravan Park, ph (07) 4069 5417
ACTIVITIES: Fishing, scenic drives, touring
TOURIST INFORMATION: Ph (07) 4051 3588

CUNNAMULLA

848 KM WEST OF BRISBANE
POPULATION: 1630   MAP REF: PAGE 233 P8
Cunnamulla is the southernmost town on the Matilda Highway which winds through western Queensland from Cunnamulla near the New South Wales border to Karumba on the Gulf of Carpentaria. Cunnamulla is the major town in the Paroo Shire, which produces cattle, sheep and wool. The Warrego River passes through the town and is famous for its Murray cod and golden perch.

Currawinya National Park, about 90 km from Cunnamulla, is one of the most remote parks in the state. Its most fascinating feature is the two lakes which even though only kilometres apart are entirely different. Lake Wyara is a salt lake while Lake Numalla is fresh water. These lakes support an incredible array of waterbirds with each lake catering for different communities of birds. The Cunnamulla–Eulo Festival of Opals, held in August/September, is a colourful event with a Sandhill Digging Championship, Dingo Derby and culminating with the World Lizard Racing Championship, held in Eulo.
ACCOMMODATION: Corella Motor Inn, ph (07) 4655 1593; Warrego Hotel, ph (07) 4655 1737; Aldville Station (guesthouse), ph (07) 4655 4814; Jack Tonkin Caravan Park, ph (07) 4655 1421
ACTIVITIES: Fishing, fossicking, national park access, scenic drives
TOURIST INFORMATION: Ph (07) 4655 1416

DAINTREE

1801 KM NORTH OF BRISBANE
POPULATION: 150   MAP REF: PAGE 229 L4
Daintree is a small village tucked away on a bend of the Daintree River. Some 11 km before the town, a ferry takes cars across the river. From there the road is sealed to Cape Tribulation, but after this it is unsealed and 4WD vehicles are recommended, especially after rain. This part of the coast is referred to as the Reef and Rainforest Coast as the lush tropical rainforest sweeps right down to the beach to meet the beautiful Great Barrier Reef.

Cruising through the Daintree National Park

Daintree was once the heart of a thriving timber industry based around the prized red cedar. Now, tourism is increasingly becoming the main industry for the town.

Take a leisurely cruise on the Daintree River and maybe catch a glimpse of that creature of the stone age—the saltwater crocodile. The bird life is extremely varied and spectacular.

The Daintree Village Timber Museum keeps alive the heady days of the timber-getters.
ACCOMMODATION: Daintree Eco Lodge, ph (07) 4098 6100; Kenadon Homestead Cabins (guesthouse), ph (07) 4098 6142; Coconut Beach Resort Motel, ph (07) 4098 0033; Red Mill House (B&B), ph (07) 4098 6169; Daintree Riverview Caravan Park, ph (07) 4098 6119
ACTIVITIES: Boating, bushwalking, fishing, national park access, river cruises
TOURIST INFORMATION: Ph (07) 4099 4588

EMERALD

896 KM NORTH-WEST OF BRISBANE
POPULATION: 13 300   MAP REF: PAGE 226 E9
Emerald is the hub of the Central Highlands and the centre for cattle, agriculture and tourism. It is also the centre for a major irrigation scheme based on water from Lake Maraboon, one of Queensland's largest water storages.

There is only one old building in Emerald, for between 1936 and 1968 four devastating fires destroyed all but the railway station. This quaint timber station was built in 1901 and is classified by the National Trust; it still services the Central Highlands area. Outside the town hall there is a 250-million-year-old fossilised tree, given to the people of

Emerald by BHP after it was found in 1979 during bridge building for the Gregory Mine.

Lake Maraboon is a magnificent recreation area with a background of mountains and parks on its shore. A visit to the Pioneer Village and Museum is a must, as it depicts the life in the highlands in the early days. The town's cotton ginnery and the Gregory Mine are also open for tours.

ACCOMMODATION: Emerald Maraboon Tavern and Motor Inn, ph (07) 4982 0777; A & A Lodge Motel, ph (07) 4982 2355; Western Gateway Motel, ph (07) 4982 3899; Freshfields Guesthouse Farm, ph (07) 4984 9656; Emerald Cabin & Caravan Village, ph (07) 4982 1300
ACTIVITIES: Fishing, fossicking, water sports
TOURIST INFORMATION: Ph (07) 4935 7101

ESK

98 KM WEST OF BRISBANE
POPULATION: 1175   MAP REF: PAGE 225 L6
Esk is the administrative centre for the shire of the same name. Its mountain setting in the upper Brisbane Valley and its broad streets lined with typical country Queensland buildings of the late nineteenth and early twentieth century make this a truly pretty town. The two-storey timber Club Hotel is a classic example with its wide verandahs and cast-iron railings on each floor. Descendants of fallow deer given to Queensland by Queen Victoria in 1873 may be seen at times in the Brisbane Valley.

Lake Wivenhoe, Somerset Dam and Atkinson Dam all have excellent facilities and provide venues for many water sports including rowing, boating, waterskiing and swimming.

The historical homesteads of Bellevue and Caboonbah are nearby and well worth a visit.
ACCOMMODATION: Glenn Rocks Motel, ph (07) 5424 1304; Wivenhoe Motel, ph (07) 5424 1677; Esk Motel, ph (07) 5424 1289; Esk Caravan Park, ph (07) 5424 1466
ACTIVITIES: Bushwalking, camping, fishing, scenic drives, water sports
TOURIST INFORMATION: Ph (07) 5424 1200

EULO

918 KM WEST OF BRISBANE
POPULATION: 90   MAP REF: PAGE 233 N8
Eulo is located some 68 km west of Cunnamulla and even though the population may be sparse the place literally hums—with bees. For years beekeepers have been coming to Eulo—some from as far away as Dubbo in New South Wales—during the winter to gather the pollen and honey from the yapunyah trees. The yapunyah honey has a taste all its own, a taste of the Outback.

The opal fields of Yowal and Duck Creek are a short distance away and there is a fossicking field set aside for visitors. The Cunnamulla–Eulo Festival of Opals, held in August/September each year, culminates on a Sunday at Eulo with the World Lizard Racing Championships. A specially constructed track is used and the day normally starts with a lizard

auction followed by a five-race program. In what must be a first, Eulo boasts a granite memorial to a racing cockroach called Destructo which was brought to an untimely end by being accidentally squashed underfoot by an excited punter.

A visit to Palm Grove, surely Australia's remotest winery, is very interesting; you can also sample their date wine and other date products.
ACCOMMODATION: Carpet Springs Tourist Retreat Guesthouse, ph (07) 4655 4064; Eulo Queen Hotel, ph (07) 4655 4867; Eulo Caravan Park, ph (07) 4655 4890
ACTIVITIES: Fishing, fossicking, sightseeing, wineries
TOURIST INFORMATION: Ph (07) 4655 1416

FRASER ISLAND

245 KM NORTH OF BRISBANE
POPULATION: 100   MAP REF: PAGE 225 N3
Measuring 120 km long by 15 km wide, Fraser Island is the largest sand island in the world. It was formed from the runoff of the northern New South Wales rivers. The grains of sand were swept north by wind and currents where they accumulated against the edge of the continental shelf and over numerous years have built up to form the sandy chain of islands dominated by Fraser. The island was named after Mrs Eliza Fraser, who spent many weeks on the island with the local Aborigines after she was shipwrecked when the *Stirling Castle* ran aground on a reef in 1836. The island is now, along with Cooloola, a part of the Great Sandy National Park and has World Heritage listing. Both sand mining and logging have been stopped on Fraser Island and the island is under the control of the Department of Environment.

The only way to see the island is with a 4WD vehicle—make sure that the tyre pressures are reduced to save chopping up the tracks. There are any number of camping spots on the island but campers need to be self-sufficient.

There is so much to see on Fraser that visitors should spend at least a fortnight. Lake Waddy,

probably Fraser's deepest lake and the home for seven out of ten of the native fish on the island, is slowly being engulfed by a massive sand blow that is moving relentlessly year by year. Probably within the next generation Lake Waddy will be swallowed up by the moving sand. The run along the ocean beach to Sandy Cape will take a full day but the visit to the lighthouse is well worth the time and effort.

Driving around the island tracks and seeing the massive satinays, strangler fig trees and dense rainforest in the centre of the island, it is hard to believe that all this growth thrives in sand. Eli Creek, the largest freshwater creek on the island, which empties some four million litres of water into the ocean each day, is wonderful for a cooling swim, but watch the crossing on the beach as it can be gouged out and dangerous at times.

Kingfisher Bay Resort on the mainland side of Fraser has been built to blend in with its surroundings and landscaped with native plants. It welcomes day visitors and is a great spot for rest and recuperation.
ACCOMMODATION: Kingfisher Bay & Village Resort, ph (07) 4120 3333; Fraser Island Retreat Serviced Apartments, ph (07) 4127 9144; Eurong Beach Resort Holiday Units, ph (07) 4127 9122; Waddy Lodge Holiday Flats, ph (07) 3862 4433; Cathedral Beach Resort & Caravan Park, ph (07) 4127 9177
ACTIVITIES: Bushwalking, fishing, 4WD touring, national park access, scenic drives, swimming
TOURIST INFORMATION: Ph (07) 4122 3444

GEORGETOWN

1955 KM NORTH-WEST OF BRISBANE
POPULATION: 340   MAP REF: PAGE 229 H7
Georgetown started life as a gold town serving the booming Etheridge Goldfields. Its population is much reduced from the 3000 of the heady days of the 1870s. The area still supports cattle-raising and mining. Positioned at a major intersection, the town is a popular stop for the beef road trains.

Fraser Island, the world's largest sand island, forms part of Great Sandy National Park

The Kidston Gold Mine was reopened in 1985 and is now one of Australia's major producers, delivering up to six tonnes of the yellow metal each year. Georgetown is a favourite with fossickers and gem collectors as Agate Creek Mineral Reserve is located south of the town and contains some of the world's best quality coloured agates.

Visit the small town of Forsayth, 40 km south of Georgetown, which is the terminus for the train from Cairns. The Cairns–Forsayth rail journey only takes 24 hours. The Tallaroo Hot Springs are worth seeing.
ACCOMMODATION: La Tara Resort Motel, ph (07) 4062 1190; Midway Caravan Park, ph (07) 4062 1219
ACTIVITIES: Fishing, gold and gem fossicking
TOURIST INFORMATION: Ph (07) 4062 1233

GIN GIN

366 KM NORTH OF BRISBANE
POPULATION: 1200 MAP REF: PAGE 225 L2
Gin Gin is a pretty town, situated on the Bruce Highway, at the turn-off to Bundaberg. Some of the earliest settlements of the Burnett Valley were around Gin Gin. Gregory Blaxland, one of the team that crossed the Blue Mountains—the mountain barrier to the east of Sydney—settled in Gin Gin around 1842. Another resident was the infamous James McPherson, Queensland's only bushranger, known as the 'Wild Scotsman', who held up the Royal Mail on several occasions. The Wild Scotsman Bushranger Festival is held each March.

Attractions in town include the Historical Museum, the Currajong Gardens and the Moonara Craft Spinning Inn. East of Gin Gin on the Bundaberg road are the Mystery Craters. These strange sandstone formations were probably made by meteors. Nearby is Haig Dam for the boating and fishing enthusiast.
ACCOMMODATION: Wild Scotsman Motor Inn, ph (07) 4157 2522; Gin Gin Village Motor Inn, ph (07) 4157 2599; Gin Gin Motel, ph (07) 4157 2260
ACTIVITIES: Boating, fishing, scenic drives
TOURIST INFORMATION: Ph (07) 4152 2333

GLADSTONE

545 KM NORTH OF BRISBANE
POPULATION: 37 500 MAP REF: PAGE 227 K9
The key to Gladstone's industrial growth is its excellent harbour, supported by the natural resources needed by industry—land, water, transport, coal, limestone and electricity. Twenty-five years ago Gladstone was a small community of some 6000 people with a meatworks and some port trade. Today, it is an area of giants, with the world's largest alumina plant, the state's largest power station and the state's busiest port, handling more tonnage than even Sydney, and soon to have Australia's largest aluminium smelter. This industrial growth has not been at the expense of quality of life.

Gladstone's growth from the time the Port Curtis pastoral district was proclaimed in 1854 to the 1960s was fairly slow although it expanded rapidly after World War II when the port became a bulk handling facility for coal from the vast Callide and Blackwater fields and for grain from inland Queensland. The building of the alumina plant in the 1960s and 1970s signalled an unprecedented growth rate.

Gladstone is the departure point for the southern section of the Great Barrier Reef. Charter boats cater for all, mainly servicing Heron Island (the most southerly resort island on the reef), and the uninhabited Masthead Island and North-West Islands where permit campers are welcome.

The Gladstone Tondoon Botanic Garden is one of Australia's totally native botanic gardens specialising in plants of the Port Curtis and Far North Queensland regions. The gardens extend over 55 hectares and are located some 8 km from the city.

Lake Awoonga has had its capacity increased over the years to service the power station and aluminium smelter. In so doing it has also provided a superb setting for the Lake Awoonga Recreation Park which provides water-based recreations, magnificent scenery, family picnic areas and a tree-top restaurant.

A walk from the Auckland Park Waterfall, which is floodlit at night, up the 111 steps to Victoria Park gives panoramic views of the harbour and the islands.

The major festival for the town is the Harbour Festival held over Easter for ten days and timed to coincide with the finish of the Brisbane to Gladstone Yacht Race.
ACCOMMODATION: Country Plaza International Motel, ph (07) 4972 4499; Country Club Motor Inn, ph (07) 4972 4322; Rusty Anchor Motor Inn, ph (07) 4972 2099; Queens Hotel, ph (07) 4972 6615; Kin Kora Village Caravan Park, ph (07) 4978 5461; Barney Beach Caravan Park, ph (07) 4972 1366
ACTIVITIES: Fishing, reef tours, water sports
TOURIST INFORMATION: Ph (07) 4972 9922

GOLD COAST

66 KM SOUTH OF BRISBANE
POPULATION: 334 000 MAP REF: PAGE 225 N8
It was only in 1996 that the Gold Coast and Albert Shires were amalgamated to form the second largest council in Queensland—the Gold Coast City Council. The Gold Coast stretches from Beenleigh in the north, taking in South Stradbroke Island, right down to the Queensland/New South Wales border and the towns of Coolangatta and Tweed Heads. The Gold Coast region has one of the highest growth rates in Australia, something like four times the national average, and lays claim to being the tourist capital of Australia, with a million overseas and several million Australian visitors a year. With a climate providing more than 300 days of sunshine per year, some of the best surfing and swimming beaches in Australia patrolled by the largest body of lifesavers in the country, many exciting theme parks, and a lush hinterland of national parks, mountain hideaways and spectacular views, it is no wonder the area draws visitors like a magnet.

The building boom from the 1960s to the 1980s saw Surfers Paradise, in particular, go from a relatively small holiday community to a bustling, glittering strip of high-rise buildings. At the same time developers have turned vast areas of the Gold Coast into a maze of canals and expensive residential subdivisions.

Probably the greatest attraction, particularly for families, is the theme parks. You can visit Movie World for insights into movie-making, stunts and pyrotechnics; Sea World for sea lion and shark shows; Dreamworld for action rides and white tigers on Tiger Island; Wet 'n' Wild for spectacular water rides and twisters; and Cable Ski World for waterskiing, bungee jumping and go-cart racing. Parks and sanctuaries where visitors can 'talk to the animals' include Fleay's Wildlife Park, Currumbin Bird Sanctuary, Royal Pines, Pioneer Plantation, Paradise Country, Aussie Country Down Under and Tropical Fruit World.

For the golf enthusiast the Gold Coast is paradise, with a choice of about 60 courses, some designed by international golfing greats.

For a complete change of pace spend a few days exploring the hinterland, which offers spectacular views, bushwalking, camping and even abseiling. Lamington National Park is Australia's largest reserve of subtropical rainforest with some 160 km of walking tracks. Near O'Reilly's Rainforest Guesthouse is Australia's first treetop walkway where visitors can stroll into the forest canopy some 16 metres above the

The skyline of Surfers Paradise on the Gold Coast

ground. Springbrook and Tamborine National Parks offer spectacular scenery, waterfalls, rockpools and a huge array of flora and fauna. The hinterland is dotted with guesthouses, restaurants, craft galleries and farm-type resorts offering a whole new dimension to a Gold Coast holiday.

For the shopper the Coast has some of the biggest shopping centres in the southern hemisphere offering goods ranging from resort wear and accessories to artworks and antiques.

ACCOMMODATION: *Ashmore:* Royal Pines Resort, ph (07) 5597 1111; Ashmore Palms Holiday Units, ph (07) 5539 3222

Biggera Waters: Runaway Cove Serviced Apartments, ph (07) 5529 1000; Pelican Cove Holiday Units, ph (07) 5537 7001; Treasure Island Caravan Village, ph (07) 5537 1649

Bilinga Beach: Oceanside Resort Holiday Units, ph (07) 5534 7000; Coolangatta YHA Hostel, ph (07) 5536 7644

Broadbeach: Conrad Jupiters Hotel, ph (07) 5592 1133; Golden Rainbow Motel, ph (07) 5570 3400; Talisman Holiday Units, ph (07) 5592 0100; Barbados Holiday Apartments, ph (07) 5570 1166;

Burleigh Heads: Fifth Avenue Motel, ph (07) 5535 3588; Burleigh Surf Holiday Units, ph (07) 5535 8866; Gemini Court Holiday Units, ph (07) 5576 0300; Burleigh Beach Caravan Park, ph (07) 5581 7755

Carrara: River Gardens Caravan Park, ph (07) 5594 4211

Coolangatta: Greenmount Beach Resort Hotel, ph (07) 5536 1222; Beachcomber International Resort Hotel, ph (07) 5574 2800; Aries Apartments, ph (07) 5536 2711; Eden Tower Holiday Units, ph (07) 5536 8213

Coomera: Coomera Motor Inn, ph (07) 5573 2311; Dreamtime Caravan Park, ph (07) 5573 1665

Currumbin: The Hill Apartments, ph (07) 5598 1233; The Rocks Resort, ph (07) 5534 4466; Little Cove Holiday Units, ph (07) 5534 4922

Kirra: At the Beach Motel & Holiday Units, ph (07) 5536 3599; Kirra Beach Hotel, ph (07) 5536 3311; Kirra Vista Holiday Units, ph (07) 5536 7375; Kirra Caravan Park, ph (07) 5581 7744

Labrador: Limassol Motel, ph (07) 5591 6766; Champelli Palms Apartments, ph (07) 5591 8155; Golden Shores Holiday Units, ph (07) 5574 2800; Pine Ridge Caravan Village, ph (07) 5591 1488

Main Beach: Sheraton Mirage Hotel, ph (07) 5591 1488; Sea World Nara Resort Hotel, ph (07) 5591 0000; Carrington Court Holiday Units, ph (07) 55 32 8822; Sunbird Plaza Holiday Units, ph (07) 5532 9888

Mermaid Beach: Camden Colonial Motor Inn, ph (07) 5575 1066; Heron Motel, ph (07) 5572 6655; Montana Palms Holiday Units, ph (07) 5572 6833

Miami: Kristine Court Motel, ph (07) 5572 7171; Miami Shore Motel & Apartments, ph (07) 5572 4333; Mariner Shores Club Holiday Units, ph (07) 5535 2177; Miami Caravan Park, ph (07) 5572 7533

Nobby Beach: Magic Mountain Quest Resort Holiday Units, ph (07) 5572 8088; Sandrift Apartments, ph (07) 5575 3677

Ormeau: Ormeau Motel & Cabin Park, ph (07) 5546 6285

Oxenford: Garden Vale Caravan Park, ph (07) 5573 1185

Palm Beach: Tropic Sands on the Beach Motel, ph (07) 5535 1044; Surf N Sand Motel, ph (07) 5576 3804; Palm Winds Holiday Units, ph (07) 5576 5833

Southport: Earls Court Motor Inn, ph (07) 5591 4144; Park Regis Hotel, ph (07) 5532 7922; Palmerston Tower Holiday Units, ph (07) 5532 0566; Marine Parade Holiday Units, ph (07) 5591 6666; Southport Tourist Caravan Park, ph (07) 5531 2281

Surfers Paradise: ANA Hotel Gold Coast, ph (07) 5579 1000; Marriot Surfers Paradise Resort Hotel, ph (07) 5592 9800; Ramada Hotel, ph (07) 5579 3499; Cavill Inn Motel, ph (07) 5531 5559; Paradise Inn Motel, ph (07) 5592 0585; International Beach Resort Hotel, ph (07) 5530 0099; Budds Beach Apartments, ph (07) 5592 2779; Narrowneck Court Holiday Units, ph (07) 5592 2455; Coolamon Apartments, ph (07) 5538 9600; Ashleigh Lodge Holiday Units, ph (07) 5539 8541

Tallebudgera: Tallebudgera Creek Beach Tourist Park, ph (07) 5581 7700

Tugan: Surfside Motel, ph (07) 5534 2461; Crystal Beach Apartments, ph (07) 5534 6560

ACTIVITIES: Bushwalking, fishing, golf, national park access, scenic tours and drives, theme parks, water sports

TOURIST INFORMATION: Ph (07) 5538 4419

GOONDIWINDI

360 KM WEST OF BRISBANE
POPULATION: 5000   MAP REF: PAGE 225 H9

The same river red gums still line the banks of the Macintyre River as when Allan Cunningham came through this area in 1827. When Queensland became a separate colony in 1854 a customs house was built on the ferry crossing because the river forms the border between New South Wales and Queensland. This building still stands today and houses a fascinating collection of memorabilia put together by the Historical Society. The name Goondiwindi (pronounced Gundawindy), is said to come from the Aboriginal word 'goonawinna' which officially means 'resting place of the birds'.

Goondiwindi is a modern, prosperous town, the commercial, service and recreation centre for a vast area producing some of Australia's best wool, wheat, beef cattle and cotton. In a good season, the Waggamba Shire is rated with the best of Australia's primary producing regions.

The town's hero is Gunsynd, 'The Goondiwindi Grey', a racehorse owned by a local syndicate; it went on to win 29 races and became one of the best loved racehorses in racing history. A statue of it now stands in Apex Park near the Border Bridge.

Goondiwindi Botanic Gardens set on 25 hectares of land is being developed to house those inland plants that cannot survive in coastal climates. This is a wonderful community project offering family recreation with sweeping lawns, BBQ areas and a 5 hectare lake encircling a bird-nesting island. Boobera Lagoon, a permanent deep-water lagoon on the river, is a wildlife sanctuary and a great waterskiing venue.

Goondiwindi's annual spring festival takes place in October.

ACCOMMODATION: Town House Motor Inn, ph (07) 4671 1855; Border Motel, ph (07) 4671 1688;

Bales of cotton grown in Goondiwindi

Gunsynd Motor Inn, ph (07) 4671 1555; Railway Hotel, ph (07) 4671 1035; Goondiwindi Mobile Village, ph (07) 46712566

ACTIVITIES: Fishing, sightseeing, touring, waterskiing
TOURIST INFORMATION: Ph (07) 4671 2653

GYMPIE

161 KM NORTH OF BRISBANE
POPULATION: 11 825   MAP REF: PAGE 225 M4

Gympie is the town reputed to have saved the young colony of Queensland from bankruptcy back in the 1860s. Drought had devastated the colony's farms, but then James Nash discovered gold in 1867 and the rush was on. The town's name comes from 'gimpi gimpi'—the Aboriginal name for a stinging nettle bush that covered the banks of the Mary River.

When the gold ran out around 1925 dairy farming, fruit and vegetable production, and Forestry Department plantations took over and continue to be the region's chief industries.

Mary Street, the main street, meanders through the town, mainly because the road follows the old bullock route. Even though rebuilding has eliminated the greatest kinks, it still has a case of the 'wanders'.

Gympie is the main entrance into the delights of Cooloola Beach, Great Sandy National Park and the glories of Fraser Island. At the Deep Creek Gold Fossicking Park you can explore an old goldmining site and pick, shovel or pan for gold.

On the northern side of town is a timber museum which has timber exhibits and displays early timber cutting techniques and a fully working steam-driven sawmill. On the Brisbane Road adjacent to Lake Alford is a goldmining museum, the main attraction being a simple four room timber cottage that was once the home of the first Labor prime minister of Australia, Andrew Fisher. Another interesting building is the original retort house of the Scottish Gympie Gold Mining Company where gold was extracted from quartz.

The Gympie Country Music Muster, held in August, is a must for all country music fans, and the Goldrush Festival takes place in October.

ACCOMMODATION: Fox Glenn Motor Inn, ph (07) 5482 3199; Hilltop Motel, ph (07) 5482 3577; Northumberland Hotel, ph (07) 5482 2477; Gympie Caravan Park, ph (07) 5483 6800; Silver Fern Caravan

Gympie's town park

Park, ph (07) 5483 5171; Bingara Rainforest Camp
(tent sites), ph (07) 5486 7296
ACTIVITIES: Fishing, fossicking, national park access,
scenic drives
TOURIST INFORMATION: Ph (07) 5482 5444

HERVEY BAY

291 KM NORTH OF BRISBANE
POPULATION: 42 300   MAP REF: PAGE 225 M3
Hervey Bay is a large expanse of water protected by
the bulk of Fraser Island and was named by James
Cook in 1770 after Captain Hervey, who became the
Earl of Bristol. It is also the collective name given to
the seaside resorts that dot the southern shore of the
bay, which include Gatakers Bay, Urangan, Toogoom
and Torquay, and the inland town of Howard.

Hervey Bay is an aquatic paradise and caters for
all sports and pastimes. Boating and fishing
enthusiasts have a choice of jetty, reef, beach and
estuary and may even indulge in some game fishing.
Because the bay is protected, it has little or no surf
and provides safe swimming. Hervey Bay is an ideal
spot for diving, featuring coral and artificial reefs
teeming with marine life. Neptune's Reefworld at
Urangan with its coral reefs and fish life exhibits will
appeal to non-divers as much as to divers. There is a
ferry to Fraser Island from Urangan.

Over recent years, the region has become famous
as the playground of the gentle giants of the sea, the
humpback whales. From August to October families
of these majestic creatures stop in the bay to rest and
play. They are on their return journey to the Antarctic
after calving in the northern waters. An industry of
whale-watching has grown up to cater for the
thousands of visitors who come to catch a glimpse of
the beautiful and playful humpbacks.

To celebrate the return of the whales, Hervey Bay
stages a Whale Festival for two weeks each August.
The Blessing of the Fleet, an illuminated procession of
floats, is the highlight of this exciting fortnight.

To experience the early settlement of Hervey Bay
and Fraser Island, visit the Hervey Bay Historical
Museum at Pialba, or Woody Island National Park
with its ruined lighthouse, graves and buildings.

Brooklyn House in Howard is a gracious
Queensland-style timber home which was built in
1870 predominantly of cedar and beech and has since
been lovingly restored to its former glory. The house
is still a family home and offers guided tours and
Devonshire teas.
ACCOMMODATION: Hervey Bay Resort Motel, ph
(07) 4128 1555; Kondari Resort Hotel, ph (07) 4128 9702;
Beachside Motor Inn, ph (07) 4124 1999; The Bay Bed &
Breakfast, ph (07) 4125 6919; Biarra Holiday Units,
ph (07) 4125 1315; Australiana Village Caravan Park,
ph (07) 4128 2762; Shelly Beach Caravan Park, ph
07) 4125 1105
ACTIVITIES: Coral viewing, fishing, national park
access, scenic drives, water sports, whale watching
TOURIST INFORMATION: Ph (07) 4125 2333

HUGHENDEN

1610 KM NORTH-WEST OF BRISBANE
POPULATION: 1900   MAP REF: PAGE 231 L3
Hughenden lies 250 km east of Charters Towers, at
the junction of the Townsville–Mount Isa railway line.
The centre of local government for the massive
Flinders Shire, the town is located on the banks of the
Flinders River and is surrounded by cattle and sheep
country. When Ernest Henry drove his cattle into the
Jardine Valley in 1863 he named his station
Hughenden, after his grandfather's English manor.

In recent years, Hughenden has become famous
for the almost complete dinosaur skeleton fossil that
was unearthed at Roseberry Downs.

The Porcupine Gorge National Park, located some
60 km north of the town, resembles a small-scale
Grand Canyon. Forty kilometres north of Porcupine
Gorge are the Cheviot Hills where high quality
peridot gemstones may be found. Brazil is the only
other place on earth where this unique and rare
stone has been discovered.
ACCOMMODATION: Hughenden Rest Easi Motel, ph
(07) 4741 1633; Royal Hotel, ph (07) 4741 1183; Wrights
Motel & Rest, ph (07) 4741 1677; Allan Terry Caravan
Park, ph (07) 4741 1190
ACTIVITIES: Fossicking, national park access, scenic
drives
TOURIST INFORMATION: Ph (07) 4741 1288

INGHAM

1471 KM NORTH OF BRISBANE
POPULATION: 5700   MAP REF: PAGE 229 M8
The climate and soil were perfectly suited to the
introduction of sugarcane back in the early 1870s
and Ingham continues to prosper from its sugar
production. The region produces some three million
tonnes of sugarcane a year.

The region has a strong Italian and Spanish
Basque background, illustrated by the ornate family
mausoleums in the Ingham cemetery.

The ballad, *Pub with No Beer*, is said to have its
origins at Lee's pub in Ingham. From all accounts, in
1942, after the Battle of the Coral Sea, the Americans
drank the pub dry in celebration of the victory.

The Wallaman Falls National Park with its
300 metre falls, bushwalks, spectacular rainforest and
swimming and picnic spots is well worth a visit.
Jourama Falls National Park, south of Ingham, has an
attractive picnic and camping ground beside
Waterview Creek and its waterfalls.

The Maraka Festival, which takes place each
October, highlights the town's sugar industry. The
Italian Festival, held in May, is a major event
celebrating the town's heritage.
ACCOMMODATION: Herbert Valley Motel, ph
(07) 4776 1777; Ingham Motel, ph (07) 4776 2355; Lees
Hotel, ph (07) 4776 1577; Como Estate Homestay B&B,
ph (07) 4777 2165; Palm Tree Caravan Park, ph
(07) 4776 2403
ACTIVITIES: Bushwalking, fishing, national park
access, scenic drives, sugar mill tours, swimming
TOURIST INFORMATION: Ph (07) 4776 5211

HERVEY BAY

N

Hervey   Bay

0   250   500
metres

To Point
Vernon
Jetty
Sailing
Club
To Point
Vernon
ESPLANADE
Rd
ESPLANADE
Freshwater
Freshwater St
Gossner St
Frank St
Freshwater
Freshwater St
Rd
Torquay
St
East
St
Rd
Queens
Tingira
St
Boongala Tce
John
BOAT
Winbirra
Parkway Dr
Camp
Holiday Pde
Gordon
St
To
Maryborough Hillcrest
Wuruma St
Turrum
Moonbi
Wonga
St
Kululu
Melong St
Koloi
Kuruman St
Minguin St
Ave
St
Denman
Barry St
St
Mabel
Ct
King
Henry
Ct
Dartmouth
Tavistock
West
St
Exeter
Pineapple
Ave
Bideford
HARBOUR
Urangan
Dr
Jacaranda
Snow
St
Cochrane
Barnstaple St
Patridge
Torquay
Tce
Torquay St
Fraser St
Totness
Campbell St
Truro
St
Cypress
St
Ocean
St
Macks Rd
Robert
St
Eric
St
Keys
St
Truro
St
Ann St
Ahembo
Dr
DRIVE
Ann St
Mylne Ct
Toohey
Southerden St
Honiton
St
Garden
St
Robert
St
Howard
St
To Bingham
Glenray
St
Bruce St
Dayman
St
To Bingham
Shelly
Beach
To Bingham
Witt St
St
Ave
ESPLANADE
Sailing
Club
Surf Life
Saving Club

INJUNE

570 KM NORTH-WEST OF BRISBANE
POPULATION: 395   MAP REF: PAGE 224 E4

Injune, a small cattle and timber town, is located approximately 90 km north of Roma and is the southern entrance to Carnarvon Gorge. The Gorge, which brings many visitors through the area, plays a large part in the economy of the town.

The Carnarvon National Park encompasses 251 000 hectares of the Consuelo Tableland, a plateau of the Great Dividing Range. The gorge itself is over 30 km long and follows the twisting course of the creek, with walls rising vertically 200 metres. Over 50 Aboriginal sites have been identified, and most are decorated with engravings and paintings. Stencils are predominant and the areas known as the Cathedral Cave and Art Gallery are the most impressive.

An Aboriginal dance festival held in Injune

Lonesome National Park, a small park north-east of Injune, has spectacular views from the plateau of the Dawson and Arcadia river valleys.
ACCOMMODATION: Grace's Hotel, ph (07) 4626 1205; Injune Motel, ph (07) 4626 1328; Injune Caravan Park, ph (07) 4626 1222
ACTIVITIES: Bushwalking, national park access, scenic drives
TOURIST INFORMATION: Ph (07) 4622 1266

INNISFAIL

1614 KM NORTH OF BRISBANE
POPULATION: 8150   MAP REF: PAGE 229 M6

Innisfail's economy is primarily based on sugar although tea, fishing, timber and dairying also play a big role. Like Ingham, the character of the district was established with the influx of migrants, mainly Italian, after World War I. The town and the area have retained that very cosmopolitan mix ever since. Many Chinese settled in the area and erected the Joss House that still stands in Ernest Street.

Fishing is a very important industry and prawn trawlers, line fishing boats and mackerel boats can be seen anchored in the Johnstone River.

In the 1950s, Dr Alan Maruff started growing tea commercially at Nerada, west of Innisfail, and over the years the production of tea from the Nerada Plantation has continued to rise. Tours of the plantation are conducted regularly.

At Mena Creek south of Innisfail are the ruins of Paronella Park, a Spanish-style castle built by a migrant named Jose Paronella. There are also walks through rainforest and stands of bamboo and kauri pine to Mena Creek and Teresa Falls.

Mt Bartle Frere, north of the town, is the highest mountain in Queensland and a hiking track leads to magnificent views at the top.
ACCOMMODATION: Barrier Reef Motel, ph (07) 4061 4988; Black Marlin Motel, ph (07) 4061 2533; The Robert Johnstone Motel, ph (07) 4061 2444; Flying Fish Point Caravan Park, ph (07) 4061 3131; River Drive Van Park, ph (07) 4061 2515
ACTIVITIES: Boating, bushwalking, fishing, scenic drives
TOURIST INFORMATION: Ph (07) 4061 6448

IPSWICH

40 KM WEST OF BRISBANE
POPULATION: 131 514   MAP REF: PAGE 225 M7

Ipswich is Queensland's oldest provincial city. In 1827 it was called Limestone Hills because of the limestone that was mined by the convicts, but its name was later changed by Governor Brisbane. Ipswich has large deposits of coal and has become a major industrial centre with the state's most diversified manufacturing base outside of Brisbane. It was an important river port for produce until the railway arrived in 1876.

Ipswich has many examples of the classical timber Queensland home and also fine, nineteenth century buildings, among them the Civic Group consisting of the Town Hall, Post Office and Bank of Australasia.

The Amberley Air Force Base, south of the city, is the largest RAAF base in Australia and the home of the F111 fighter bomber. Rosewood, a small village south of Amberley, has a charming church built in the early 1900s that is said to be the largest wooden church in the South Pacific.
ACCOMMODATION: Ipswich Flag Inn Motel, ph (07) 3281 2633; Homestead International Motel, ph (07) 3202 4622; Villiers Bed & Breakfast, ph (07) 3281 7364; Amberley Caravan Park, ph (07) 5464 3388
ACTIVITIES: Fishing, historic interest, water sports
TOURIST INFORMATION: Ph (07) 3281 0555

The Technical College building in Ipswich

JULIA CREEK

1686 KM NORTH-WEST OF BRISBANE
POPULATION: 602   MAP REF: PAGE 230 G3

Even though Julia Creek is the administrative centre for the McKinley Shire, a shire of 41 000 sq km, it is fairly isolated, being 550 km from Townsville and 250 km from Mount Isa on the Flinders Highway. The district has massive shale oil deposits containing the rare element vanadium, used in the production of high quality steel. If an economical way to extract the vanadium can be devised, Julia Creek may one day become a booming mining town.

There are four bores all within 2 km of the town but their water is hot and most houses have installed special systems to cool it.

The Julia Creek Dirt & Dust Triathlon weekend held generally around May is a part of the Saucony Adventure Series when the town plays host to upwards of 500 triathletes from around the world.
ACCOMMODATION: Julia Creek Motel, ph (07) 4746 7305; Gannons Motel, ph (07) 4746 7103; Julia Creek Caravan Park, ph (07) 4746 7108
ACTIVITIES: Fossicking, scenic drives
TOURIST INFORMATION: Ph (07) 4657 4255

KARUMBA

2125 KM NORTH-WEST OF BRISBANE
POPULATION: 620   MAP REF: PAGE 228 E6

Karumba, situated at the northern end of the Matilda Highway, was named after a local Aboriginal tribe. Eight kilometres from the town is Karumba Point which is the only stretch of beach in the Central Savannah that can be accessed by road. The sunsets from this beach are exceptionally beautiful. Karumba is considered by many to be extremely friendly, casual and laid-back, perhaps a bit rough around the edges but a great town to visit and stay awhile.

The only Queensland port in the Gulf of Carpentaria, Karumba is a major stop for the prawn trawlers operating in the Gulf and the Arafura Sea and is one of Australia's largest prawn processing centres. The Empire Flying Boats used Karumba for repairs and refuelling on their way to Britain from Australia. It was also a base for the flying-boat Catalinas during World War II and the old slipway is still used today as a boat ramp.

Anglers know of Karumba because of the barramundi in its wetlands, which extend for some 30 km towards Normanton. In 1992 a group of anglers formed the Gulf Barramundi Restocking Association. They spawn their own fingerlings to replenish the barramundi stocks in the Gulf rivers. The Barraball is held at the end of the year and people come from all over to celebrate the end of another barramundi fishing season.
ACCOMMODATION: Karumba Lodge Hotel, ph (07) 4745 9121; Ash's Holiday Units, ph (07) 4745 9132; Gee Dee's Family Cabins, ph (07) 4745 9433; Gulf Country Caravan Park, ph (07) 4745 9148; Karumba Point Caravan Park, ph (07) 4745 9306
ACTIVITIES: Fishing
TOURIST INFORMATION: Ph (07) 4051 3588

KINGAROY

209 KM NORTH-WEST OF BRISBANE
POPULATION: 11 590   MAP REF: PAGE 225 L5
Dominated by enormous peanut silos and the home of
Queensland's former premier Joh Bjelke-Petersen,
the town of Kingaroy is the peanut capital of
Australia. The town services the productive South
Burnett district and has also earned a name as the
nation's baked bean capital, with 75 per cent of
Australia's navy bean crop grown in the region.

The Aboriginal word for red ant, 'kinkerroy', gave
the town its name. Kingaroy had a slow start until the
railway opened in 1904, followed, in 1924, by the first
major plantings of peanuts.

The Peanut Heritage Museum located in the
town's old powerhouse is the only peanut museum in
Australia and well worth a visit. The Peanut Van in
Kingaroy Street has been operating for 25 years and
there are 12 flavours of peanut to choose from.

The Peanut Festival is held in early March and the
Taabinga Music Festival in October.
ACCOMMODATION: Burke & Wills Motor Inn,
ph (07) 4162 2933; Holliday Motel, ph (07) 4162 1822;
Taabinga Host Farm, ph (07) 4164 5543; Kingaroy
Caravan Park, ph (07) 4162 1808
ACTIVITIES: Bushwalking, scenic drives
TOURIST INFORMATION: Ph (07) 4162 3199

KYNUNA

1509 KM NORTH-WEST OF BRISBANE
POPULATION: 85   MAP REF: PAGE 230 G5
Kynuna is a small, remote town almost midway
between Winton and Cloncurry and located on the old
Diamantina stock route. The Blue Heeler Hotel is well
known in the district and the flashing tongue of the
blue heeler dog in the pub's neon sign is a very
welcome sight after a hot day.

Twelve kilometres south of the town is the Combo
Waterhole reputed to be the billabong that A. B.
'Banjo' Paterson featured in *Waltzing Matilda*.

Just up the road towards Cloncurry is the small
town of McKinlay with another popular watering hole:
the Walkabout Creek Hotel, made famous in
Crocodile Dundee.
ACCOMMODATION: Blue Heeler Hotel & Van Park,
ph (07) 4746 8650; Never Never Caravan Park,
ph (07) 4746 8683
ACTIVITIES: Scenic drives
TOURIST INFORMATION: Ph (07) 5465 3241

LONGREACH

1173 KM NORTH-WEST OF BRISBANE
POPULATION: 4452   MAP REF: PAGE 231 L8
Longreach is the centre of a pastoral industry, a
major tourist attraction in its own right, and a
commercial and administrative base for the region. It
has been said that Longreach has had a greater
influence on Australian life than any other town or
city, certainly far beyond what one would expect of a

town of its location and size. Although the region is
semi-arid, the country is excellent for grazing
because it is at the centre of Mitchell grass country—
the only natural grasslands in Australia.

The town was named after a nine-kilometre-long
reach of the Thomson River. The rapid expansion of
Longreach in the early twentieth century was due to
the wool industry, but this was followed in the 1920s
by a boost of a different nature—flying. The establishment of QANTAS (Queensland and Northern
Territory Aerial Services), and the building of the first
hangar in Longreach, were the beginning. Between
1926 and 1927, seven DH 50 bi-plane aircraft were
built in this hangar. Not only is QANTAS the second
longest-serving airline in the world it is the only
airline to build its own aircraft. This historic hangar
now houses a fascinating display.

The railway station at Longreach

The Australian Stockman's Hall of Fame and
Outback Heritage Centre were officially opened by
the Queen in 1988. It pays tribute to the early
pioneers, the stockmen, the women, the ringers, the
Aborigines and all the other people who pioneered
and worked in Outback Australia. The Outback
Muster and Drovers' Reunion is the most important
annual occasion at the Hall of Fame. Bush poetry,
yarn telling, music, novelty events and book launches
all form a part of this festival.

Also in Longreach are the Longreach School of
Distance Education, with students spread over an
area twice the size of Victoria, and Pamela's Dolls
and Crafts with over 1500 dolls and a fascinating
collection of Outback memorabilia.
ACCOMMODATION: Albert Park Motel, ph
(07) 4658 2411; Longreach Motor Inn, ph (07) 4658 2322;
Hallview Lodge B&B, ph (07) 4658 3777; Aussie Betta
Cabins, ph (07) 4658 3811; Gunnadoo Caravan Park,
ph (07) 4658 1781
ACTIVITIES: Fishing, historic interest, swimming
TOURIST INFORMATION: Ph (07) 4778 3555

MACKAY

975 KM NORTH OF BRISBANE
POPULATION: 58 641   MAP REF: PAGE 226 G4
Mackay started life as a port for the export of wool
and tallow from the hinterland's sheep and cattle.
Around 1865 the first sugarcane was planted and by
the mid-1880s there were 30 sugar mills processing
the cane. Mackay became the leading sugar district in
Australia—a position it still holds as the producer of
one-third of Australia's sugar harvest. Between 1863
and 1906 the bulk of the labour in the canefields was

provided by South Sea islanders who worked as
indentured labourers. When the government later
prohibited non-European immigration, hundreds of
Italians, Greeks, Maltese, Spanish and Scandinavians
flocked to North Queensland, and the sugar industry
in particular. These many nationalities are reflected
in the population of modern Mackay.

Just to the north of Mackay is one of the best
artificial harbours on the east coast which boasts the
world's largest sugar terminal.

South of Mackay is Hay Point, one of the biggest
coal loading complexes in the world with an annual
capacity of 50 million tonnes.

During the crushing season (July to November)
Farleigh Mill, a working sugar mill, and Polstone
Sugar Cane Farm offer tours.

Mackay's heritage walk takes in the Police
Station, the Court House and Commonwealth Bank,
buildings that are all over 100 years old and listed
with the National Trust. Greenmount Homestead,
18 km west of Mackay, houses possessions of the Cook
family, original settlers in the region.

West of the town is Eungella National Park, one of
Queensland's most spectacular parks, with cloud-
shrouded peaks, deep gorges and lush rainforest.
Cape Hillsborough National Park to the north is
noted for its rainforest that runs down to the beach
and rocky headlands.

Regular cruises take visitors out to Brampton,
Lindeman and Hamilton Islands and beyond to the
Great Barrier Reef and Whitsunday Islands.
ACCOMMODATION: Ocean International Hotel, ph
(07) 4957 2044; Alara Motor Inn, ph (07) 4951 2699;
White Lace Motor Inn, ph (07) 4951 4466; Dolphin
Heads Resort Motel, ph (07) 4954 9666; Illawong Lakes
Resort Holiday Units, ph (07) 4957 8427; Eagle Nest
Farm B&B, ph (07) 4959 0552; Pacific Palms Holiday
Units, ph (07) 4954 6277; Andergrove Caravan Park,
ph (07) 4942 4922
ACTIVITIES: Bushwalking, fishing, island cruises,
national park access, scenic drives, water sports
TOURIST INFORMATION: Ph (07) 4952 2677

MAGNETIC ISLAND

1379 KM NORTH OF BRISBANE
POPULATION: 2013   MAP REF: PAGE 229 N9
Magnetic Island is situated just 8 km and 20 minutes
by fast ferry from Townsville. Over 2000 people live on
this beautiful island, which has more than half of its
5184 hectares protected as national park. Captain
Cook named the island in June 1770 when his
'compass would not travis well when near it'.

There is a host of activities to satisfy most visitors,
including water sports such as snorkelling, SCUBA
diving, waterskiing and swimming and, of course,
fishing. There are 23 bays and beaches all around the
island, and buses run regularly between the towns.
Bicycles, mopeds or mini-mokes may be hired.

Wildlife abounds on Magnetic Island, particularly
koalas which are numerous and roam freely. For the
birdwatchers there are some 160 species to record.

There are over 20 km of walking tracks, and tours
of animal reserves and trips to the Great Barrier
Reef. Accommodation caters for all budgets while the
shopping facilities and eating houses are excellent.

One of Magnetic Island's many attractive beaches

ACCOMMODATION: Arcadia Hotel Resort, ph (07) 4778 5177; Magnetic Island Tropical Resort Motel, ph (07) 4778 5955; Magnetic International Resort Motel, ph (07) 4778 5200; Marshall's Bed & Breakfast, ph (07) 4778 5112; Tropical Palms Inn Serviced Apartments, ph (07) 4778 5076; Dunoon Resort Holiday Units, ph (07) 4778 5161
ACTIVITIES: Bushwalking, fishing, horse riding, national park access, water sports
TOURIST INFORMATION: Ph (07) 4721 3660

MAREEBA

1759 KM NORTH OF BRISBANE
POPULATION: 17 310   MAP REF: PAGE 229 L5
Mareeba is situated where the Barron River and Granite Creek meet—the name is derived from an

The Rodeo Festival in Mareeba

Aboriginal word that means 'meeting of the waters' or 'place to meet'. The first thing visitors notice on entering Mareeba is its massive concrete water tower. The town is the hub of Australia's main tobacco growing region but also grows cash crops such as pineapples and mangoes.

All around the district are signposts marking the camp sites where American and Australian service-men were based during World War II. It was from the airfield, south of Mareeba, that Allied aircraft flew many missions in the Battle of the Coral Sea.

A walk through Granite Gorge, to the south of Mareeba, allows you to experience the mass of grey granite boulders which were produced by volcanic action many centuries ago.

In July the town hosts the Rodeo Festival.
ACCOMMODATION: Jackaroo Motel, ph (07) 4092 2677; Mareeba Motel Golden Leaf, ph (07) 4092 2266; Arriga Park Host Farm, ph (07) 4092 2114; Riverside Caravan Park, ph (07) 4092 2309
ACTIVITIES: Bushwalking, fishing, golf, water sports
TOURIST INFORMATION: Ph (07) 4091 4222

MARYBOROUGH

250 KM NORTH OF BRISBANE
POPULATION: 25 527   MAP REF: PAGE 225 M3
Maryborough is one of Queensland's oldest cities and was first settled in 1843. The town developed as a port to service the influx of free settlers. When steam-driven machinery was introduced, timber such as kauri was harvested from the extensive forests and the region provided most of Queensland with timber. Around 1860 sugarcane was first planted and this industry is still one of the region's major activities.

Many European immigrants arrived in the town during the second half of the nineteenth century. The splendid old houses, mostly built of local timber and reflecting the classic timber 'Queenslander' design, have given Maryborough its reputation as one of the most beautiful historic towns in Queensland. This can best be appreciated by following the Heritage Walk which takes in 28 historic buildings in the central business district. There is a Driving Tour, which covers nearly 80 buildings and historic sites.

Each Thursday is Heritage Market Day high-lighted by the firing of the 'Time Cannon' at 1 pm and attended by the Town Crier. The Maryborough Heritage City Festival is held in early September with the Maryborough Masters Games in late September.
ACCOMMODATION: McNevin's Parkway Motel, ph (07) 4122 2888; Blue Shades Motor Inn, ph (07) 4122 2777; Royal Centre Point Hotel, ph (07) 4121 2241; Country Stopover Caravan Park, ph (07) 4121 2764; Kell's Colonial Caravan Park, ph (07) 4121 4681
ACTIVITIES: Fishing, golf, historic interest, water sports
TOURIST INFORMATION: Ph (07) 4121 4111

MILLMERRAN

208 KM SOUTH-WEST OF BRISBANE
POPULATION: 3127   MAP REF: PAGE 225 K8
The local Aborigines once used this place as a lookout, and the Aboriginal words for 'eye' ('meel') and 'to look out' ('merran') gave the town its name. The region has a history of producing excellent wool, but the future may bring new industries as extensive coal deposits were discovered just outside of Millmerran in the 1970s.

The oldest building in the shire, All Saints Chapel which dates back to 1877, is in the nearby township of Yandilla. Originally erected as a private chapel, it has been an Anglican church since the early 1900s.
ACCOMMODATION: Millmerran Motel, ph (07) 4695 1155; Dandarriga Homestead Host Farm, ph (07) 4695 7125; Stonehenge Homestead Host Farm, ph (07) 4695 7183; Millmerran Caravan Park, ph (07) 4695 1572
ACTIVITIES: Scenic drives
TOURIST INFORMATION: Ph (07) 4661 3122

MISSION BEACH

1608 KM NORTH OF BRISBANE
POPULATION: 3525   MAP REF: PAGE 229 M7
Fourteen kilometres of coastline and wide, white sandy beaches met by rainforest make up the Mission Beach area. It includes the settlements of Bingal Bay, Garners Beach, Narragon Beach, Clump Point and Wongaling Beach.

The Cutten brothers established a farming industry here in the 1880s by growing pineapples, tea and coffee. Now, sugarcane and bananas dominate the region's agriculture. In 1912 an Aboriginal mission was established on what is now South Mission Beach, hence the name. Tourism is a growth industry in North Queensland and Mission Beach attracts more than its fair share of the visitors.

The pier at Bedarra Island, off Mission Beach

From Clump Point you can take a day trip to Dunk Island, just 4 km away. Dunk Island is the access point, by water taxi, to Bedarra Island which is famous for its exclusive resorts.

ACCOMMODATION: Castaways Beach Resort Motel, ph (07) 4068 7444; Mission Beach Resort Hotel, ph (07) 4068 8288; Watersedge Beachside Holiday Apartments, ph (07) 4068 8479; Eco Village Mission Beach (cottages), ph (07) 4068 7534; Mission Beach Hideaway Caravan Village, ph (07) 4068 7104; Tropical Hibiscus Caravan Park, ph (07) 4068 8138

ACTIVITIES: Bushwalking, fishing, water sports

TOURIST INFORMATION: Ph (07) 4068 7099

MITCHELL

567 KM WEST OF BRISBANE
POPULATION: 1300   MAP REF: PAGE 224 D5

Mitchell is situated on the Warrego Highway on the banks of the Maranoa River between Roma and Charleville. The town is named for the explorer Thomas Mitchell who passed through the area in 1845. Mitchell is also the birthplace of Australia's shortest serving prime minister, Francis Forde, who led the nation for just 6 days in 1945.

A monument near Arrest Creek records the arrest of the 'last of the bushrangers', Patrick and James Kenniff, who murdered two men at Lethbridge Pocket in 1902.

Mitchell is the southern gateway to the Mt Moffat section of the Carnarvon National Park. The park has no facilities so visitors must be self-sufficient.

ACCOMMODATION: Berkeley Lodge Motor Inn, ph (07) 4623 1666; Mitchell Motel, ph (07) 4623 1355

ACTIVITIES: Historic interest, national park access

TOURIST INFORMATION: Ph (07) 4622 1266

MOUNT ISA

1804 KM NORTH-WEST OF BRISBANE
POPULATION: 24 100   MAP REF: PAGE 230 C3

There are some interesting statistics attributed to Mount Isa, not the least being that it is the site of Australia's largest underground mine. The city administers an area the size of Switzerland—about 50 000 sq km. Were it not for the towns of Mount Isa and Cloncurry, though, this vast area would be almost unpopulated. A remarkable statistic from 1973 is that there were more than 2.5 vehicles per resident.

The enormous mine at Mount Isa is the basis of Queensland's mining industry with an annual output of 11 million tonnes of ore. This is one of the few areas in the world where the four minerals—copper, lead, silver and zinc—are found in close proximity.

In a hot and isolated region, the people of Mount Isa, consisting of more than 50 nationalities, have made their city into a modern inland oasis which contrasts sharply with the surrounding Outback. Lake Moondarra, an artificial lake 20 km north of the town, and Lake Julius, a further 80 km away, are great spots to cool off from the heat. Lake Julius is noted for its fishing and water sports.

The area around Mount Isa is a fossicker's dream, with occasional finds of the prized Maltese crosses.

The railway depot at Mount Isa

The Riversleigh Fossils Interpretive Centre and the Royal Flying Doctor Service base are both worth a visit. The city features the Gregory River Canoe Race in May and the Rodeo and Mardi Gras in August.

ACCOMMODATION: Mercure Hotel Verona, ph (07) 4743 3024; Mount Isa Outback Motor Inn, ph (07) 4743 2311; Burke & Wills Isa Motel, ph (07) 4743 8000; Riverside Tourist Caravan Park, ph (07) 4743 3904; Lake Julius (cabins and caravan sites), ph (07) 4742 5998

ACTIVITIES: Gem fossicking, mine tours, scenic drives, water sports

TOURIST INFORMATION: Ph (07) 4743 7966

MOUNT MORGAN

671 KM NORTH OF BRISBANE
POPULATION: 3164   MAP REF: PAGE 227 J9

Driving into Mount Morgan is like going back in time. This former gold and copper mining town, a 30-minute drive south-west of Rockhampton, is now quiet and peaceful after 100 years of mining. The result of all this mining is the awe-inspiring 300-metre-deep crater. The town has so much history and so many fine buildings that the National Trust of Queensland and the Australian Heritage Commission have listed the town as an historic site.

The Coronation Light in Anzac Park was built in 1902 to celebrate the coronation of King Edward VII. The Mafeking Bell—cast at the Mount Morgan mine from English pennies donated by children to celebrate the relief of Mafeking, South Africa, during the Boer War—is outside the Scout Hut in Dee Street. Rides are offered behind one of the fully restored Hunslett locomotives that were purchased in 1904 and used at the mine until 1947.

Not far from town is Big Dam, where the local residents go for picnics, water sports and fishing.

ACCOMMODATION: Silver Wattle Caravan Park, ph (07) 4938 1550

ACTIVITIES: Bushwalking, fishing, historic interest, water sports

TOURIST INFORMATION: Ph (07) 4927 2055

MUNDUBBERA

363 KM NORTH-WEST OF BRISBANE
POPULATION: 2299   MAP REF: PAGE 225 K3

Mundubbera is the citrus centre of Queensland, noted for its mandarins. Among its many citrus orchards is the Gold Mile Orchard, the largest in the southern hemisphere. Beef cattle, grain, peanuts, dairying and timber also feature highly in the economy. The town is located east of Maryborough, near the point where the Boyne, Auburn and Burnett Rivers meet.

There are two claims for the origin of the name, one proposing it came from the Aboriginal words for 'foot' and 'step', after the footholds cut into the area's tall trees, while the other cites the Aboriginal word meaning 'meeting of the waters'.

The Big Mandarin acts as the town's information centre and as a window for the citrus industry.

ACCOMMODATION: Billabong Motor Inn, ph (07) 4165 4533; Mundubbera Motel, ph (07) 4165 4131; Host Farm Albaradoran, ph (07) 4165 6188; Citrus Country Caravan Park, ph (07) 4165 4549

ACTIVITIES: Horse riding, scenic drives, water sports

TOURIST INFORMATION: Ph (07) 4165 4549

MUTTABURRA

1217 KM NORTH-WEST OF BRISBANE
POPULATION: 200   MAP REF: PAGE 231 M7

Muttaburra is a small town famous among palaeontologists for *Muttaburrasaurus*, the dinosaur fossil discovered in the area. The town is situated

119 km north of Longreach and 152 km north of Barcaldine and is in sheep and cattle country.

Lake Dunn, or as the residents call it, 'The Lake', is a very remarkable inland waterway 3 km long and 1.6 km wide. It is home to more than 80 species of birds. It is also perfect for water sports and is a great spot for a picnic. Lake Galilee, a saltwater lake some 40 km long and a wildlife sanctuary, is worth visiting if it has water, so check with Tourist Information first.

Aramac, 95 km south, is worth a visit, even if it is just to see the statue of the white bull, a replica of a bull in the herd stolen and driven to South Australia by Harry Redford.

ACCOMMODATION: Exchange Hotel, ph (07) 4658 7125
ACTIVITIES: Fishing, fossils, water sports
TOURIST INFORMATION: Ph (07) 4658 7147

NAMBOUR

98 KM NORTH OF BRISBANE
POPULATION: 22 746   MAP REF: PAGE 225 M5

Nambour, from the Aboriginal word meaning 'red-flowering tea-tree', is the administrative centre for the Maroochy Shire. It is primarily a sugar town, but also has industries based on dairying, timber, bananas, pineapples and citrus fruits.

The shire is one of the fastest growing in the state and the population is expected to exceed 100 000 by the year 2001. With more than a quarter of the population over 50, the Sunshine Coast University of the Third Age has more than 1200 students.

The Sunshine Plantation, just south of Nambour, has an enormous fibreglass pineapple as its emblem, one of the local landmarks, and on its 12 hectares produces some 60 varieties of tropical fruits, nuts and spices. The plantation is open to visitors, with a train ride around the property being the highlight.

ACCOMMODATION: Nambour Motor Inn, ph (07) 5441 5500; Centrepoint Motel, ph (07) 5441 4811;

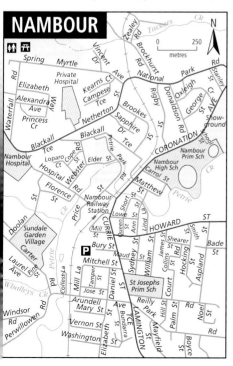

Commercial Hotel, ph (07) 5441 1144; Nambour Rainforest Holiday Cabin Village, ph (07) 5442 1153
ACTIVITIES: Golf, scenic drives, swimming
TOURIST INFORMATION: Ph (07) 5443 6400

NANANGO

185 KM NORTH-WEST OF BRISBANE
POPULATION: 8321   MAP REF: PAGE 225 L5

Nanango initially developed around a single general store, but boomed when gold was discovered in the 1860s, at what came to be called Seven Mile Diggings. The town's name comes from the area's first sheep run, which was established in 1842. Nowadays beef cattle have replaced sheep, and beans and grain are grown. The Boondooma Dam is a recreational area with camping sites and picnic facilities and is stocked with perch and bass. Nearby is the National Trust listed Boondooma Homestead, an old stone house constructed during the mid-nineteenth century.

The Nanango Astronomical Observatory is well worth a visit as it runs on solar power, a world first.
ACCOMMODATION: Copper Country Motor Inn, ph (07) 4163 1011; Antler Motel, ph (07) 4163 1444; Nanango Star Motel, ph (07) 4163 1666; Twin Gums Caravan Park, ph (07) 4163 1376; Tarong Village Caravan Park, ph (07) 4163 1376
ACTIVITIES: Bushwalking, fishing, fossicking
TOURIST INFORMATION: Ph (07) 4163 1374

NOOSA HEADS

144 KM NORTH OF BRISBANE
POPULATION: 11 690   MAP REF: PAGE 225 N5

Noosa Heads, located at the most northerly point of the Sunshine Coast, is one of Australia's most enticing resort destinations. The sophisticated cafés, boutiques, hotels and restaurants have given the area a cosmopolitan air, and a strict building law has ensured that no building is higher than the trees. The northerly aspect of the ocean beach with its excellent waves makes it popular with surfers. The name Noosa is said to derive from the Aboriginal term for 'shade' or 'shadow'.

Noosa Heads is the southern entry point to the Cooloola Section of the Great Sandy National Park, Cooloola Beach and onto Rainbow Beach from where the barge leaves for Fraser Island. The southern section of Cooloola–Great Sandy National Park is dominated by a complex system of rivers and streams that forms what is referred to as the Noosa 'lakes district'. The extensive waterways provide a superb venue for boating, sailing, canoeing and windsurfing.

Many anglers consider the section of the river known as the Narrows to be the best fishing spot on the east coast, particularly for the elusive bass. The Everglades, not far from Lake Cootharaba, is also popular, particularly with nature lovers.

In the nineteenth century loggers cut timber such as kauri, hoop pine, and cypress from upriver forests and floated it down to the mills at Tewantin. The ruins of their camps can still be seen along the river.

The Festival of Waters is held around the end of August to early September.

Oyster Rocks in Noosa National Park

ACCOMMODATION: Sheraton Noosa Resort Hotel, ph (07) 5449 4888; Caribbean Noosa Motel, ph (07) 5447 2247; Noosa Village Motel, ph (07) 5447 5800; The French Quarter Serviced Apartments, ph (07) 5430 7100; Noosa Valley Bed & Breakfast, ph (07) 5471 0058; Bali Hai Apartments, ph (07) 5447 2381; Noosa Quays Holiday Units, ph (07) 5449 2699; Uncles Lodges Holiday Units, ph (07) 5447 4490; Munna Point Caravan Park, ph (07) 5449 7050; Noosa Bougainvillia Caravan Park, ph (07) 5447 1712
ACTIVITIES: National park access, scenic drives, water sports
TOURIST INFORMATION: Ph (07) 5447 5506

NORMANTON

2053 KM NORTH OF BRISBANE
POPULATION: 1150   MAP REF: PAGE 228 E7

Normanton is situated on the Norman River, 80 km upstream, and is the administrative centre for the Carpentaria Shire. The explorer Ludwig Leichhardt and the Burke and Wills expedition passed through this area in 1844 and 1861 respectively.

Normanton started life as a cattle port but later boomed during the goldmining at Croydon and the copper and silver mining at Cloncurry. It was around that time, between 1888 and 1891, that the quaint and unusual railway line was constructed between Normanton and Croydon. The famous railmotor known as the Gulflander leaves a grand old station at Normanton each Wednesday on its leisurely trip to Croydon 152 km away. The trip takes over four hours, overnights in Croydon and then makes its unhurried way back to Normanton. The sleepers are of a hollow steel construction that can be filled with mud, sand, or whatever, making ballast unnecessary on the track. Amazingly, 95 per cent of the track is original and in surprisingly good condition.

In the Carpentaria Shire Council Park is a replica of 'Krys, the Savannah King', the largest recorded saltwater crocodile taken in Australia. It measured 8.6 metres and was shot in the Norman River in 1958 by Krystina Pawloski.

The National Hotel, or Purple Pub as it is better known, was built in the early 1900s and has survived floods (boats were hitched to the verandah in 1974) and fire to become a major attraction.

Camp 119, the last camp of Burke and Wills before they reached the Gulf of Carpentaria, is on the road to Burketown on the banks of the Little Bynoe River.

Normanton from the air

The Normanton Barra Classic fishing competition is held on the weekend before Easter and is followed by the World Barramundi Championship at nearby Burketown on the Easter weekend.

ACCOMMODATION: Albion Motel, ph (07) 4745 1218; Normanton Caravan Park, ph (07) 4745 1121; Shady Lagoons Campsites, ph (07) 4745 1160

ACTIVITIES: Fishing, riding the Gulflander, scenic drives

TOURIST INFORMATION: Ph (07) 4745 1268

PORT DOUGLAS

1759 KM NORTH OF BRISBANE
POPULATION: 2100   MAP REF: PAGE 229 L5

Port Douglas, once a fishing village, is now one of the leading tourist towns of Far North Queensland due mainly to its proximity to the wonders of the reef and the rainforest (it is the closest Australian town to the Great Barrier Reef), and its superb year-round climate. All the natural beauty is supported by numerous restaurants, delightful shops, luxury hotels and resorts and historic Queenslander buildings.

Back in the gold rush days of the Hodgkinson River during the 1880s, Port Douglas boomed and became a major shipping port for sugar. Its decline, and losing battle with Cairns as the major northern port, started in 1885 when the decision was made to build a railway line from the inland mining regions to Cairns. The cyclone of 1911 which destroyed most of the town's buildings compounded the population

slide. The decline was complete when the railway line from Brisbane terminated at Cairns in 1924. By the early 1980s, however, Port Douglas's population started to increase, due to tourism.

Port Douglas is a great base for exploring the region. You can take day tours to the reef, join a 4WD safari, ride the Bally Hooley sugar train, and travel along the coast to the Daintree and Cape Tribulation rainforests. The Low Isles, part of the reef, lie just offshore Port Douglas.

The region is also a well-known fishing ground for the mighty black marlin, although anglers who prefer smaller challenges such as coral trout, red emperor or the tenacious barrumundi, should try Dickson Inlet. What should not be missed is a visit to the award-winning Rainforest Habitat which gives a taste of life within the rainforest environment.

Port Douglas's Reef and Rainforest Festival is held each May.

ACCOMMODATION: Sheraton Mirage Resort Hotel, ph (07) 4099 5888; Lazy Lizard Motor Inn, ph (07) 4099 5900; Port Douglas Motel, ph (07) 4099 5248; Ocean View Lodge B&B, ph (07) 4098 5407; Marae Bed & Breakfast, ph (07) 4098 4900; Beaches Holiday Units, ph (07) 4099 4150; The White House Holiday Units, ph (07) 4099 5600; Glengarry Caravan Park, ph (07) 4098 5922

ACTIVITIES: Big-game fishing, bushwalking, scenic drives, tours of reef and rainforest, water sports

TOURIST INFORMATION: Ph (07) 4099 4588

PROSERPINE

1097 KM NORTH OF BRISBANE
POPULATION: 3100   MAP REF: PAGE 226 F2

Proserpine is located 30 km from Whitsunday and is the departure point for Airlie Beach, Shute Harbour and the Whitsunday Islands. This productive valley was named after Proserpina, the Roman goddess of fertility, and supports a prosperous sugar industry.

A visit to the folk museum which displays the clothing and furniture of the early pioneers is a must. Also worth a stop is the wildlife sanctuary which features a reptile house and a walk-through aviary. At the nearby aquarium you can watch colourful tropical fish being fed. There is a pleasant hike to Cedar Creek in the rainforest-clad hills behind the town.

ACCOMMODATION: Proserpine Motor Lodge, ph (07) 4945 1788; Whitsunday Palms Motel, ph (07) 4945 1288; Pine Caravan Park, ph (07) 4945 1540

ACTIVITIES: Bushwalking, sightseeing, swimming

TOURIST INFORMATION: Ph (07) 4946 6673

QUILPIE

953 KM WEST OF BRISBANE
POPULATION: 734   MAP REF: PAGE 233 L5

This part of western Queensland is the land of colour—opal colour. Quilpie is in the middle of opal country although it is also the centre for the area's beef and sheep properties.

The late Des Burton, a Quilpie chemist, is credited with having the boulder opal recognised on world markets. A visit to the town's Catholic church is a must, for the altar, lectern and font are covered with brilliant opal slabs made and donated by Des Burton.

Duck Creek and Sheep Station Creek are the places to visit for opal fossicking. There are 800 hectares in which to fossick but permits are required for both fossicking and camping. These are best obtained from the Courthouse in Cunnamulla. Visitors travelling from the south who arrive at Cunnamulla should take the 'opal byway' to Charleville, detour west to Eulo, take a short detour to Yowal and then go on to Toompine and Quilpie.

ACCOMMODATION: Imperial Hotel, ph (07) 4656 1300; Quilpie Motor Inn, ph (07) 4656 1277; L. R. McManus Caravan Park, ph (07) 4656 2160

ACTIVITIES: Opal fossicking, scenic tours

TOURIST INFORMATION: Ph (07) 4656 1133

ROCKHAMPTON

633 KM NORTH OF BRISBANE
POPULATION: 65 000   MAP REF: PAGE 227 J8

Driving into Rockhampton from the south, visitors cross the Tropic of Capricorn which is marked by a huge metal sundial known as the 'The Capricorn Spire'. This is the heartland of Australia's premium beef cattle region, and recent estimates have calculated that the Fitzroy Basin beef herds number more than 2.5 million.

In 1855 Colin Archer sailed up the Fitzroy River as far as he could, bringing supplies to his property Gracemere. The spot where the cargo was unloaded is the site of present-day Rockhampton.

A stroll around the Quay Street Historical Precinct will show you a number of outstanding buildings, including the city's second customs house, the former offices of the Mount Morgan Gold Mining Company, the Criterion Hotel, the former Queensland National Bank building and the former Union Bank of Australia building.

There is plenty to do and see on the Capricorn Coast. A short distance away on the coast is Yeppoon, the stepping-off place for visits to Great Keppel Island. Byfield State Forest just north of Yeppoon is a pleasant, secluded spot in a rainforest environment; at Cooberrie Park Flora and Fauna Centre visitors can cuddle a koala or feed a kangaroo; and Koorana Crocodile Farm offers something different.

Emu Park, down the coast from Yeppoon, has a 12-metre-high structure of pipes in the shape of a large sail which commemorates James Cook's voyage in the *Endeavour*.

North of Rockhampton are the Cammoo Caves and the Capricorn Taverns. Both cave systems are

Port Douglas's large marina, from where boats can be chartered to go to the Great Barrier Reef

ROCKHAMPTON

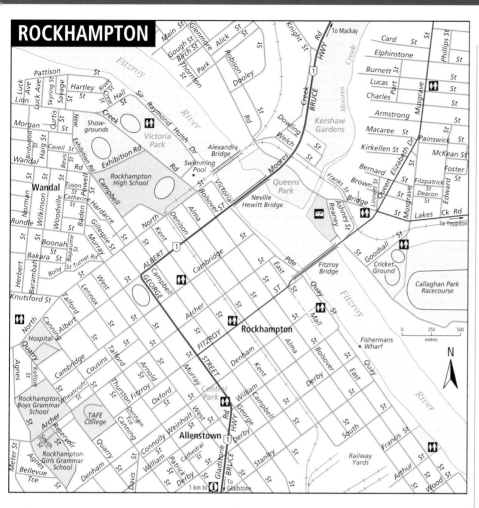

worth exploring, in particular the Cathedral cave in the Capricorn Taverns.

There are any number of festivals, rural shows and carnivals happening around Rockhampton. Central Queensland University's Multicultural Fair, held in August, and Rockhampton's Family Festival, in September, are just two of them.

ACCOMMODATION: Cattle City Motor Inn, ph (07) 4927 7811; Country Comfort Inn Motel, ph (07) 4927 9933; Archer Park Motel, ph (07) 4927 9266; Mamelon Bed & Breakfast, ph (07) 4928 8484; Big 4 Tropical Wanderer Caravan Village, ph (07) 4926 3822; Southside Caravan Village, ph (07) 4927 3013

ACTIVITIES: Boat cruises, bushwalking, fishing, scenic drives, waterskiing

TOURIST INFORMATION: Ph (07) 4927 2055

ROMA

480 KM WEST OF BRISBANE
POPULATION: 6775   MAP REF: PAGE 224 E5

Roma is the 'Gateway to the Outback' and the commercial centre of the Maranoa District which produces wool, wheat, citrus fruit, timber and beef. The town is named after Lady Diamantina Roma Bowen who was the wife of the first governor of Queensland, George Bowen. Back in 1859, when Queensland separated from New South Wales and became a colony in its own right, Roma was the first settlement to be gazetted.

In 1863 a Mr S. Bassett planted a vineyard at Roma which is still operating as 'Romavilla', the oldest and one of the largest vineyards in the state.

Memorial Avenue, with its 93 bottle trees, each one dedicated to a man lost in World War I, extends from the railway station to the cenotaph.

The Big Rig, one of the best preserved oil drilling rigs of its era, is on display near Roma's Information Centre east of the town and will form the centrepiece of the proposed National Oil and Gas Museum.

ACCOMMODATION: Overlander Homestead Motel, ph (07) 4622 3555; Bryants Motel, ph (07) 4622 3777; Mandalay Motel, ph (07) 4622 2711; Richmond Down Bed & Breakfast, ph (07) 4622 2731; Villa Tourist Caravan Park, ph (07) 4622 1309; Roma Big Rig Van Park, ph (07) 4622 2538

ACTIVITIES: Fishing, historic interest, scenic drives

TOURIST INFORMATION: Ph (07) 4622 3399

ST GEORGE

569 KM SOUTH-WEST OF BRISBANE
POPULATION: 2500   MAP REF: PAGE 224 E8

Three major highways lead to the town of St George. Sitting on banks of the Balonne River, it is known as the 'inland fishing capital'. The site received its name on St George's Day, 23 April 1846, when the explorer Thomas Mitchell crossed the Balonne.

The heavily irrigated district produces much of Queensland's cotton crop. Other crops include grain, sunflowers and grapes and, of course, sheep and

cattle are raised. The water comes from the E. J. Beardmore Dam, not from the annual rainfall which is less than 500 mm. This dam not only supplies the water for the crops and stock but also provides some excellent fishing for the yellowbelly.

Birdwatchers will delight in the diverse bird life among the white gums along its banks. Rosehill Aviaries, 64 km west of St George, houses the most comprehensive collection of Australian parrots in the world. Over 60 species are housed in some 80 aviaries, totalling more than 600 birds.

ACCOMMODATION: Merino Motor Inn, ph (07) 4625 3333; Motel Balonne, ph (07) 4625 5155; Kamarooka Caravan Park, ph (07) 4625 3120; St George Tourist Caravan Park, ph (07) 4625 5778

ACTIVITIES: Fishing, scenic drives, water sports

TOURIST INFORMATION: Ph (07) 4625 3222

STANTHORPE

219 KM SOUTH-WEST OF BRISBANE
POPULATION: 10 601   MAP REF: PAGE 225 L9

Stanthorpe, at 811 metres above sea level, is one of the highest towns in Queensland and consistently records the state's lowest temperature. The mild summers grant the region a virtual monopoly on the growing of stone fruit. Grapes and wine are also produced, and wineries are now Stanthorpe's leading tourist attraction. All offer tastings and sales.

Stanthorpe had a late start and it was not until the discovery of tin that a hastily planned township developed at the Quart Pot crossing, which had merely been the site of an inn catering for passing traffic. Tin also gave the settlement its name: 'stannum' is the Latin word for 'tin'.

Within a short distance of Stanthorpe are several national parks, notably Girraween and Sundown.

The Granite Belt Spring Wine Festival in October sees the town booked out as visitors come from all over to join in the festivities.

ACCOMMODATION: Apple & Grape Motel, ph (07) 4681 1288; Happy Valley Vineyard Retreat, ph (07) 4681 3250; Stannum Lodge Motor Inn, ph (07) 4681 2000; Country Club Hotel, ph (07) 4681 1033; Das Helwig Haus Guesthouse, ph (07) 4683 4227; Rowanbrae Bed & Breakfast, ph (07) 4681 2101; Callemondah Host Farm, ph (07) 4685 6162; Blue Topaz Caravan Park, ph (07) 4683 5279

ACTIVITIES: Bushwalking, fishing, gem fossicking, golf, horse riding, national park access, wineries

TOURIST INFORMATION: Ph (07) 4681 2057

SUNSHINE COAST

85 KM NORTH OF BRISBANE
POPULATION: 166 000   MAP REF: PAGE 225 N5

The Sunshine Coast is the name given to the coastal region stretching from Bribie Island and Caloundra in the south, to Noosa Heads and beyond in the north, and all this just an hour's drive north of Brisbane. It is one of the fastest growing regions in Queensland, if not in Australia. The Sunshine Coast has 150 km of perfect surf beaches, tropical fruit plantations and larger-than-life tourist attractions.

The Glass House Mountains, named by James Cook in 1770 because they appeared to be inside a glasshouse, are weirdly beautiful and are the first landmark visitors see when travelling up from Brisbane. Inland is Nambour, one of the prettiest sugar towns in south-east Queensland. Buderim, located on a plateau between the Blackall Range and the coast, is noted for its beautiful homes and gardens. Australia's only ginger factory, and the world's largest, is at Yandina, 9 km north of Nambour. Eumundi's brewery can be toured and the Saturday market at Eumundi is one of the best on the coast.

The Blackall Range and the popular villages of Monteville, Flaxton and Mapleton are all craft and art orientated and are well worth visiting any day of the week. The Mapleton and Kondilla National Parks with their dramatic waterfalls and walking tracks are a pleasant alternative to the coastal regions.

The Sunshine Coast has much to offer the surfer looking for the perfect waves, from Moffat Beach at Caloundra, to Alexandra Headland at Maroochydore, to Coolum and Peregian Beaches and the near perfect conditions of Laguna Bay at Noosa.

The Sunshine Coast is experiencing growth both in its tourism industry and in its population. The region takes a low-key approach to its expansion, avoiding the proliferation of high-rise buildings that distinguish the Gold Coast, south of Brisbane.

ACCOMMODATION: *Alexandra Headland:* Club Boolarong Holiday Units, ph (07) 5444 3099; Mandolin Holiday Units, ph (07) 5443 5011; Sorrento Holiday Units, ph (07) 5444 4099

Boreen Point: Apollonian Hotel, ph (07) 5485 3100; Everglades Caravan Park, ph (07) 5485 3213

Buderim: Buderim Sunshine Motel, ph (07) 5445 1102; Buderim Pines Motel, ph (07) 5445 1119

Caloundra: Norm Provan's Oasis Resort, ph (07) 5491 0333; Caloundra Safari Motel, ph (07) 5491 3301; Dolphins Motel, ph (07) 5491 2511; Belvedere Apartments, ph (07) 5492 3963; Burgess Holiday Units, ph (07) 5491 4594; Norfolks on Moffat Beach Holiday Units, ph (07) 5492 6666; Caloundra Holiday Resort, ph (07) 5491 3342; Hibiscus & Tripcony Holiday Park, ph (07) 5491 1564; Alexandra Caravan Park, ph (07) 5491 3428

Coolum Beach: Stewarts Coolum Beach Hotel/Motel, ph (07) 5446 1899; Hyatt Regency Resort Hotel Coolum, ph (07) 5446 1234; Coolum Sands Holiday Units, ph (07) 5446 4523; Coolum Beach Motel Lodges, ph (07) 5446 1155; Coolum Gardens Caravan Park, ph (07) 5446 1177

Kawana Waters: Kawana International Motor Inn, ph (07) 5444 6900; Sun Surf Motel, ph (07) 5493 3377; Beachside Resort Holiday Units, ph (07) 5478 4000

Maroochydore: Coachman's Court Motor Inn, ph (07) 5443 4099; Avenue Motor Inn, ph (07) 5443 3600; Blue Waters Motel, ph (07) 5443 6700; Chateau Royale Beach Resort, ph (07) 5443 0300; Banyandah Towers Holiday Units, ph (07) 5443 6911; Beach Houses Holiday Units, ph (07) 5443 3049; Majorca Isle Holiday Units, ph (07) 5443 9437; Alexandra Gardens Tourist Park, ph (07) 5443 2356; Maroochy River Cabin Village & Carapark, ph (07) 5443 3033

Mooloolaba: Headland Motel, ph (07) 5444 1600; Mooloolaba Motel, ph (07) 5444 2988; Sandcastles on the Beach Serviced Apartments, ph (07) 5478 0666; Sailport Apartments, ph (07) 5444 1844; Dockside Holiday Units, ph (07) 5478 2044; Alexandra on the Pacific Holiday Units, ph (07) 5443 4262; Maroochy Beach Caravan Park, ph (07) 5478 3000

ACTIVITIES: Bushwalking, fishing, scenic tours, sightseeing, water sports

TOURIST INFORMATION: Ph (07) 5443 6400

TAMBO

861 KM NORTH-WEST OF BRISBANE
POPULATION: 592   MAP REF: PAGE 224 A2

Tambo, on the banks of the Barcoo River, has perhaps the best grazing land in western Queensland. It also has some of the oldest buildings in that part of Queensland and some of the most unusual. McLeod's House, once a part of the Live and Let Live Hotel, has unusual foundations—a bed of logs laid on the ground, instead of stumps. Another building of note is the Old Post Office Museum which is where the Tambo Teddies are manufactured. This cottage industry has grown so much that in 1996 the 10 000th Tambo Teddy was made. All Tambo Teddies are individuals and each has a name.

Take note of the bottle trees in the town, in particular the huge one in Edward Street that stands on the site of the first Catholic church in town.

The Salvator Rosa Section of Carnarvon National Park, located 120 km east of Tambo, is a part of the history of the area and also has some wonderful natural attractions. A 4WD vehicle is necessary to visit this park.

ACCOMMODATION: Tambo Mill Motel, ph (07) 4654 6466; Club Motel, ph (07) 4654 6109; Yandarlo Host Farm, ph (07) 4654 9319; Tambo Caravan Park, ph (07) 4654 6463

ACTIVITIES: Fishing, 4WD touring, national park access, scenic drives

TOURIST INFORMATION: Ph (07) 4654 6133

TAROOM

464 KM NORTH-WEST OF BRISBANE
POPULATION: 2981   MAP REF: PAGE 224 G3

Taroom, on the Dawson River, like so many other towns, was first settled by sheep farmers but the sheep have been replaced by beef, wheat and sorghum. The name of the town comes from an Aboriginal word 'taroom'—'wild lime tree'—which the Aborigines used for perfume and as a food. The town boasts a coolibah tree on which the explorer Ludwig Leichhardt carved his initials, during his expedition to Darwin in 1844. The tree now stands on the main street of Taroom.

In 1857 eleven Europeans were killed by Aborigines at Hornet Bank Homestead and in the aftermath the local Jiman tribe was decimated, with 300 Aborigines indiscriminately killed.

The Isla Gorge National Park is 50 km north of Taroom; at the 14 km mark, look for the rare *Livistona* palms which are visible from the highway.

ACCOMMODATION: Cattle Camp Motel, ph (07) 4627 3412; Leichhardt Motel, ph (07) 4627 3137; Taroom Caravan Park, ph (07) 4627 3218

ACTIVITIES: Historic interest, national park access

TOURIST INFORMATION: Ph (07) 4627 3211

TEXAS

312 KM SOUTH-WEST OF BRISBANE
POPULATION: 900   MAP REF: PAGE 225 J10

Texas is a small town on the Dumaresq River where it forms the border with New South Wales. Tobacco crops once surrounded the town but these have given way to other products like lucerne, wool, cattle and timber. The McDougall brothers established a station in the area in about 1840. They later had a bitter dispute with a claim-jumper that they likened to a US border war, and so named their property 'Texas'. The town developed in the mid-1880s.

A feed-lot, south of Texas, and established some years ago, has grown to be the biggest in the southern hemisphere. This has provided much needed employment for the town as well as a ready market for many of the grain and lucerne crops. Tours of the feed-lot can be arranged.

ACCOMMODATION: Texas Motel, ph (07) 4653 1300; Yellow Rose B&B, ph (07) 4653 1592; Texas 3 Rivers Caravan Park, ph (07) 4653 1194

ACTIVITIES: Fishing, scenic drives, swimming

TOURIST INFORMATION: Ph (07) 4653 1277

THURSDAY ISLAND

2738 KM NORTH-WEST OF BRISBANE
POPULATION: 4000   MAP REF: PAGE 234 C2

Thursday Island, off the tip of Cape York Peninsula, is Australia's most northerly settlement and the centre for the 14 inhabited islands of the Torres Strait. Ferry and plane services operate from Bamaga on the mainland. Thursday Island has a fine natural harbour in Port Kennedy, and visitors will notice the profusion of small aluminium boats, known as 'tinnies'. Fishing is the favourite pastime of the islanders.

Thursday Island was a major base for the pearling fleets in the early days and many Japanese pearl fishermen are buried in the local cemetery.

Indulge in a conducted tour of the island and visit Green Hill Fort built in 1892 during the Russian invasion scare, and Quetta Rock, the site of the sinking of the SS *Quetta* in February 1890. 'The Coming of the Light' Festival is held each year in July.

Thursday Island, looking south across to Prince of Wales Island

ACCOMMODATION: Jardine Hotel, ph (07) 4069 1555
ACTIVITIES: Fishing, sightseeing
TOURIST INFORMATION: Ph (07) 4069 2277

TOOWOOMBA

125 KM WEST OF BRISBANE
POPULATION: 90 563   MAP REF: PAGE 225 L7

Toowoomba is Queensland's largest inland city and
marks the start of the Darling Downs. Perched on the
edge of the Great Dividing Range at an elevation of
800 metres and with over 1000 hectares of parks and
gardens, Toowoomba has deservedly earned the title
of the Garden City of Queensland.

The prosperity of Toowoomba is based to a large
extent on the fertile soil of the Darling Downs. Allan
Cunningham first sighted the Downs in 1827 and he
was soon followed by squatters; by the 1900s intensive
agriculture had taken over. The Downs is a prolific
producer of all types of grain crops and in good
seasons two crops may be harvested. In recent years,
cotton has been more extensively grown.

The first settlement started at Drayton around a
store, pub and blacksmith's shop. Lack of water
prompted many of the town's residents to move to
'The Swamp', as Toowoomba was first called. There
are any number of theories as to where the name
originated although it is known that Thomas Alford,
one of the early settlers in the region, named his
house 'Toowoomba', and by the 1860s this had become
the name of the town.

When the railway arrived in 1867, the position of
Toowoomba as the commercial and service centre for
the Downs was assured. Over the same period many
of the city's finest buildings were constructed. The city
has many reminders of its colourful past including the
magnificently restored City Hall, the impressive
Empire Theatre, and the Royal Bulls Head Inn at
Drayton, now a museum operated by the National
Trust. The Cobb & Co Museum houses Australia's
largest collection of horse-drawn carriages and is the
national centre for the research and conservation of
Australia's horse-drawn vehicles.

The University of Southern Queensland is based
in Toowoomba, and some of its schools date back to
the nineteenth century.

Heritage walks and tourist drives are laid out
around the city and outskirts and provide an insight
into the history and beauty of this very country, inland
city. Toowoomba celebrates the coming of spring with
the Carnival of Flowers held in the last full week of
September. A major attraction of this festival is the
number of private residences that open their gardens
to the public. The owners work for months to prepare
for this home garden competition.

ACCOMMODATION: Grammar View Motor Inn, ph
(07) 4638 3366; Applegum Inn Motel, ph (07) 4632 2088;
Toowoomba Motel, ph (07) 4639 3993; Wilsonton
Hotel, ph (07) 4634 2033; Bellhaven Homestay Bed &
Breakfast, ph (07) 4635 3402; Mrs Bee's Bed &
Breakfast, ph (07) 4639 1659; Clewleys Country Haven
(cottages), ph (07) 4638 3466; Toowoomba Motor
Village Caravan Park, ph (07) 4635 8186; Garden City
Caravan Park, ph (07) 4635 1747
ACTIVITIES: Fishing, scenic tours, sightseeing
TOURIST INFORMATION: Ph (07) 4639 3797

Townsville, Australia's largest tropical city

TOWNSVILLE

1363 KM NORTH OF BRISBANE
POPULATION: 124 925   MAP REF: PAGE 229 N9

Townsville is a thriving international port and
Australia's largest tropical city. It lays claim to having
320 days of sunshine a year and to receive three-
quarters of its annual rainfall in the wet season
between October and March. Cyclones also feature
in the city's tropical climate.

The small settlement on Cleveland Bay at the
mouth of Ross Creek had a slow start and it was not
until John Melton Black persuaded Robert Towns,
from Sydney, to invest in a boiling-down works for
the cattle industry that there was some growth.
Thousands of labourers from the South Pacific
worked the sugar and cotton fields and the coffee
plantations. Copper was found at Einasleigh in 1866,

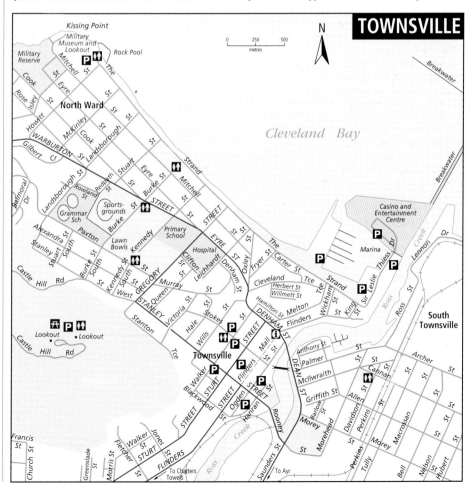

and the discovery of gold at Cape River, Ravenswood and Charters Towers soon followed, establishing Townsville as a regional centre. Other factors in the city's growth were the railway from the west, which terminated at Townsville, and the region's first meat freezing works, established in 1892 at Ross River.

During World War II, Townsville was a major staging base for American and Australian troops due mainly to its strategic position near the South Pacific region. In 1942, the town was bombed three times by Japanese aircraft but no damage was done.

There are many historic buildings in Townsville particularly around the waterfront park area. The typical Queenslander, high-set on stilts, of timber construction and with verandahs, is very common.

Townsville is also the northern centre for higher education. One of the new public buildings in the town is the James Cook University, formerly the University College of Townsville, which specialises in marine biology. The Great Barrier Reef Marine Park Authority and the Australian Institute of Marine Science are both based in the city.

In 1986 the city of Thuringowa was officially declared; it shares a common boundary with Townsville, and the two are promoted as twin cities. Thuringowa is the fastest growing city in Queensland and currently has a population of 40 000 living in an area of 1872 sq km. With a growth rate exceeding 6 per cent per annum this city is attracting many businesses to meet the demand. The city is also home to the North Queensland Cowboys rugby league team.

The beautiful Magnetic Island is only 20 minutes away by 'fast cat' from Townsville and it offers secluded beaches, 24 km of walking tracks, a range of accommodation and great restaurants.

The Townsville Town Common Environmental Park is a refuge for brolgas, jabirus and other wetland birds during the wet season. They move out when the swamps dry up and crack. The Great Barrier Reef Wonderland is well worth a visit with its walk-through underwater tunnel, giving a great all-round view of the coral and the fish.

ACCOMMODATION: Centra Townsville Hotel, ph (07) 4772 2477; Sheraton Breakwater Hotel, ph (07) 4722 2333; Beach House Motel, ph (07) 4721 1333; South Bank Motor Inn, ph (07) 4721 1474; Castle Lodge Motel, ph (07) 4721 2290; The Rocks Historic Guesthouse, ph (07) 4771 5700; Civic Guesthouse & Backpacker Inn, ph (07) 4771 5381; Coonambelah Caravan Park, ph (07) 4774 5205; The Lakes Caravan Park, ph (07) 4725 1577
ACTIVITIES: Fishing, historic interest, water sports
TOURIST INFORMATION: Ph (07) 4721 3660

TULLY

1565 KM NORTH OF BRISBANE
POPULATION: 3100   MAP REF: PAGE 229 M7
Tully lies south of Innisfail in one of Australia's highest rainfall areas. It supports a thriving sugar-cane, tea and banana growing area. Tully was originally a pastoral area known as Banyan. When the township was surveyed it was named Tully after a member of Dalrymple's 1864 expedition.

The Tully Sugar Mill was constructed in 1925, the last of the sugar mills built in Queensland. The mill

has an assigned area of 24 000 hectares from which an annual crop of some two million tonnes is harvested between June and November each year. Twenty-nine harvesters are employed and the cane travels over 200 km of light gauge rail to the mill for crushing. This results in 230 000 tonnes of sugar which is exported through the bulk sugar terminal at Mourilyan Harbour. The mill is open for tours during the crushing season, June to December.

The Kareeya Power Station is on the wild Tully River and is open to the public. The Tully River is famous for whitewater rafting.
ACCOMMODATION: Tully Motel, ph (07) 4068 2233; Googarra Beach Caravan Park, ph (07) 4066 9325; Tully Heads Van Park, ph (07) 4066 9260
ACTIVITIES: Bushwalking, fishing, whitewater rafting
TOURIST INFORMATION: Ph (07) 4061 6448

WARWICK

164 KM SOUTH-WEST OF BRISBANE
POPULATION: 11 300   MAP REF: PAGE 225 L8
Warwick is the second largest city on the Darling Downs, situated in the southern region, on the banks of the Condamine River. Patrick Leslie set up a sheep station on the Condamine River back in 1847. The local sandstone is an excellent building material as can be seen in St Mary's Church and the Town Hall.

The red rose is Warwick's floral emblem and the Australian Rough Riders Association is based in the town which has become known as the Rose and Rodeo City. The Rose and Rodeo Festival is held in late October and since 1929, only war and severe drought have stopped the annual rodeo.

The area around Warwick is popular among fossickers with gold, silver, agate, shell fossils and petrified wood being some of the treasures found in the region. People come from around the world for the annual Rock Swap Festival held over Easter.
ACCOMMODATION: McNevin's Gunyah Motel, ph (07) 4661 5588; Country Rose Motel, ph (07) 4661 7700; Alexander Motel, ph (07) 4661 3888; Cherrabah Homestead Resort, ph (07) 4667 9177; Kahlers Oasis Caravan Park, ph (07) 4661 1473; Rose City Caravan Park, ph (07) 4661 1662
ACTIVITIES: Fishing, gem fossicking, scenic drives, water sports
TOURIST INFORMATION: Ph (07) 4661 3122

St Mary's Church in Warwick, built from local sandstone

WEIPA

2507 KM NORTH-WEST OF BRISBANE
POPULATION: 2359   MAP REF: PAGE 234 B6
Weipa is an isolated town on the eastern coastline of the Gulf of Carpentaria.

It is the site of the world's largest and richest bauxite deposit. Bauxite is the raw material for aluminium and is extracted by the open-cut method. The bulk of the output, after washing and grading, is shipped to the smelter in Gladstone. Kaolin, a fine white clay used in paper manufacturing, is also mined in the area.

The township of Weipa North accommodates many hundreds of miners. It was built in the 1960s by the Queensland Government and the mining company Comalco. Napranum, formerly known as Weipa South, is where most of the area's large Aboriginal community is based.

Weipa is a major supply point for visitors to Cape York and it has some fine fishing spots north of the town. Sherga, a major strategic air base, has been under construction for some years and is located south of the town.
ACCOMMODATION: Paxhaven Camping Ground, ph (07) 4069 9159; Weipa Riverview Cabins, ph (07) 4069 7871
ACTIVITIES: Fishing, mine tour, scenic drives
TOURIST INFORMATION: Ph (07) 4051 3588

WINTON

1345 KM NORTH-WEST OF BRISBANE
POPULATION: 1667   MAP REF: PAGE 231 J6
Pelican Waterhole, as Winton was first known, was, apparently, too long and cumbersome to hand-frank onto stamps so the postmaster called the town Winton after his birthplace in Bournemouth, England.

The first board meeting of QANTAS was held in the Winton Club in 1920 and the first registered office of the company was opened in the town in the same year. A. B. 'Banjo' Paterson wrote the words to Australia's unofficial national anthem, *Waltzing Matilda*, when he visited Dagworth Station near Winton in 1895, and gave the first reading at Winton's North Gregory Hotel.

Winton, located as it is on two major highways and being the terminus for the railways from Townsville and Rockhampton, is the major road and rail centre for western Queensland. It is here that the massive road trains from the Gulf country bring cattle which are then loaded onto the trains.

The Waltzing Matilda Centre was opened in early 1998 and commemorates the song and Australian bush poets. The Bronze Swagman Award is an annual presentation recognising bush verse.
ACCOMMODATION: Matilda Motel, ph (07) 4657 1433; Winton Outback Motel, ph (07) 4657 1422; Banjo's Overnight Family Cabins, ph (07) 4657 1213; Matilda Country Caravan Park, ph (07) 4657 1607; Pelican Fuel Stop Caravan Park, ph (07) 4657 1478
ACTIVITIES: Gem fossicking, historic interest, scenic drives
TOURIST INFORMATION: Ph (07) 4657 1188

A knob-tailed gecko, Simpson Desert National Park

BLACKDOWN TABLELAND NATIONAL PARK

Blackdown Tableland rises like a green island from flat plains about 185 km west of Rockhampton. It is moist, cool and heavily forested, while the land below is hot, dry and largely cleared. The plateau is dissected by deep gorges where ferns and mosses thrive; waterfalls cascade over sheer sandstone cliffs. The last town on the eastern side is Dingo, 12 km before the turn-off to the national park. There are a number of walking tracks and scenic lookouts in the park, as well as abundant bird life and Aboriginal art.

BUNYA MOUNTAINS NATIONAL PARK

Set amidst cool mountain forests, and only four hours west of Brisbane, this park is the ideal place to escape from the city's humid summers. It has the largest stand of bunya pines in the world. Aborigines from the Waka Waka tribe used to collect the tasty nuts which grew at the top of the trees. But axemen in search of valuable timber entered the area in the mid-1870s and soon most of the trees had gone. The park has beautiful waterfalls and abundant wildlife.

CANIA GORGE NATIONAL PARK

Cania Gorge National Park, about 500 km north of Brisbane, is sometimes described as a smaller Carnarvon Gorge. Like Carnarvon, it has spectacular sandstone cliffs, caves and rock formations, plus a dammed lake for water sports. Cania Gorge National Park is mostly thick bush, with some pockets of rainforest, and cut by creeks. The park is 26 km from Monto. A sealed road follows Three Moon Creek into the main gorge, and several of the most popular walks begin from a picnic area on the creek bank. About 12 km further on the road ends at Cania Dam, where a wall has been built between cliffs to block the creek and provide, along with irrigation water for the district, waterskiing, sailing, canoeing, swimming and fishing. Other activities include bushwalking, rock climbing, gold panning in the creeks, and fossicking for semi-precious stones in the gorge area. Camping is not allowed in the park.

CARNARVON NATIONAL PARK

The rugged, isolated Consuelo Tableland in central Queensland guards one of Australia's most spectacular natural gems: Carnarvon Gorge. The original visitors to this scenic wonderland, the Aborigines, have long since vanished but their unique artistry remains. Cathedral Cave, one of the largest Aboriginal rock art sites so far discovered, is 10 km from the camping ground. Another is 500 metres off the main track at the 'Art Gallery', dated at over 4000 years old. Carnarvon Gorge occupies only a fraction of the park, but it is by far the most scenic and easily accessible section. A diversity of plant life can be found in the park and wildlife is abundant, including platypus in Carnarvon Creek. The park is 720 km north-west of Brisbane.

CHILLAGOE–MUNGANA CAVES NATIONAL PARK

The Chillagoe–Mungana Caves National Park is reached via Mareeba and Dimbulah. It is 210 km from Cairns. The limestone seen around Chillagoe is part of a belt deposited as reef when this area was a shallow sea 400 million years ago. It has weathered into 'towers' up to 70 metres high and large caves. Tours are available most days of the year. A tour of the large Royal Arch Cave takes over an hour and you can explore a labyrinth of tunnels and lofty caverns with the aid of hand-held lamps. There are also galleries of Aboriginal rock paintings. The area was once important for its copper and lead mining and you can fossick for minerals and inspect the ruins of the old smelters.

CONWAY NATIONAL PARK

Another of northern Queensland's coastal national parks in a beautiful location, part of this park's attraction is that it is in the heart of the Whitsunday region. Within sight of lookouts in Conway National Park are resort islands like Daydream, Hamilton, Hayman, Lindeman and South Molle, and the park's camping ground is just a few kilometres from Shute Harbour and Airlie Beach. Access to Conway National Park is from the Bruce Highway, 1 km north of Proserpine. One popular walking track climbs to a lookout on Mount Rooper with a spectacular view over the Whitsunday islands. Swimming is popular but marine stingers might be present in summer.

CURRAWINYA NATIONAL PARK

One of Queensland's largest national parks, Currawinya, in semi-arid mulga country, ironically provides inland eastern Australia's most extensive waterbird habitat. The park is well and truly in the Outback: south-west of Cunnamulla and north of Hungerford on the New South Wales border. However, the Paroo, the major river in the region, borders or flows through most of the eastern section of the park. It has long deep waterholes never known to dry up. Other creeks, lakes and lagoons also seasonally carry large quantities of water. Access to the park is via Cunnamulla and Eulo, Thargomindah or Bourke. All tracks in the park are unsealed and 4WD vehicles are recommended. Lake Numalla is a large freshwater lake covering more than 2200 hectares. However, after rain, hundreds of small lakes, swamps and claypans form a mosaic through the dunes. The largest lake, Wyara, is salt but still attracts large numbers of waterbirds. Apart from the striking beauty and contrast of the countryside itself, wildlife is one of the attractions at Currawinya, especially the great variety of bird life.

D'AGUILAR RANGE NATIONAL PARK

The D'Aguilar Range overlooks Brisbane from the north-west and its ridges provide views over the city and out across Moreton Bay. Just 30 minutes drive from the centre of Brisbane, it has the closest rainforest to the city and offers a quiet and cool escape from the hustle and bustle. One of the easiest areas for walking and camping is between Bellbird Grove and Camp Mountain in the south-eastern corner of the park. Rangers recommend late August and September as a good period to walk and camp in the park, particularly for the wildflowers. Wildlife is a major attraction in the park. Wrens, finches, flycatchers and other small colourful birds flit through the undergrowth all day, and parrots feed in taller trees morning and afternoon. After dark, possums can be spotted by torch in the trees.

DAINTREE NATIONAL PARK

The Daintree National Park stretches along the coast from the Daintree River in the south to the Bloomfield River in the north. It is divided into two parts: the Mossman Gorge section and the smaller Cape Tribulation section, both north of Cairns. This spectacular wilderness of rugged mountains, fast-flowing streams and towering rainforest is an important component in the Wet Tropics World Heritage Area. It has some of Australia's rarest mammals, the most interesting being the Bennett's tree-kangaroo. Bird life is varied and prolific and the large flightless cassowary is occasionally sighted by bushwalkers. Most of the Mossman Gorge section of the park is virtually inaccessible, and hikers should be experienced bushwalkers. At Oliver Creek, near Noah Beach, the very interesting Maffdja Boardwalk winds its way for 800 metres through mangroves and rainforest. There are crocodiles in the Daintree and Bloomfields Rivers, so never swim there!

EUNGELLA NATIONAL PARK

This park in the mountain ranges north-west of Mackay protects a mix of tropical and subtropical rainforest. Much of it is rugged and inaccessible but the southern section, adjacent to the access road, is popular with campers and day visitors. The park can provide a special treat for visitors lucky enough to see one of the resident platypus in the creek by the camping area. Eungella National Park is adjacent to the township of the same name, 80 km west of Mackay. The most popular activity in the park is bushwalking. The northern section is for experienced, well-prepared walkers only; the southern section around Broken River has a number of walking tracks. Back on the other side of Eungella township, a road turns off north to Finch Hatton Gorge, which is worth seeing. More walking tracks start here.

GEMFIELDS RESERVE

This reserve in western central Queensland, famous for sapphires, has produced world class gems, some found by fossickers. The gateway to the Gemfields is the township of Anakie, on the Capricorn Highway 42 km west of Emerald. Other townships on the fields are Sapphire and Rubyvale, respectively 10 and 18 km directly north of Anakie, and The Willows, about 37 km to the south-west. To escape the heat and wet, the best time to visit is March to October.

GIRRAWEEN NATIONAL PARK

Girraween National Park is about 260 km by road from Brisbane, about 26 km south of Stanthorpe. It is dominated by granite domes, tors and boulders. Bald Rock Creek is one of the park's best features, with rocky rapids and deep waterholes, one near the main picnic ground and another delightful rock pool further down the creek. These are great places to explore. Walking is the main activity in the park. Trails varying in length from 600 metres to 7.5 km lead to The Pyramid, Castle Rock, Sphinx and Turtle Rocks, and Mt Norman. This region can be very hot during the day in summer, while winter temperatures can plunge to –8°C. Bushwalkers prefer the cooler weather of autumn and spring. Spring has a marvellous wildflower display: thick flowering heath and a wide variety of flowering shrubs, such as wattles, pea-flowers, mint bushes, daisies and rock roses.

GREAT SANDY NATIONAL PARK
Cooloola Section

This section of Great Sandy National Park, beginning just north of Noosa, protects the largest tract of natural land along the southern Queensland coast. The landscape is based on sand and one of the many special features of Cooloola is its rainforests

which grow in sand. The best ways to see the park are by 4WD along the beach north from Noosa or by canoeing on the Noosa River. Several walking trails cut through Cooloola National Park. More or less parallel with the river, but separated by forest, heath and high dunes, is the open Cooloola Beach, also called Teewah Beach and Forty Mile Beach.

HINCHINBROOK ISLAND NATIONAL PARK

This is Australia's largest island national park, rugged and richly vegetated, about halfway between Townsville and Cairns. The island cannot be reached by vehicle and its tracks are wide enough only for walkers. The backbone of the island is a chain of rugged granite peaks in the south, giving way to lesser peaks in the north-west. The highest point is Mt Bowen, 1142 metres; its spectacular north face drops in cliffs and rocky forested slopes almost to sea level. Bushwalking and camping are popular on the island and there are a number of tracks. A boardwalk along one of Missionary Bay's southern creeks provides a path through dense mangroves. Then a track leads through a sandy area and over dunes to the open eastern beach at Ramsay Bay. From here, a 32 km track (Thorsborne Trail) runs down the eastern side of the island, sometimes paralleling the beach, sometimes winding inland.

LAMINGTON NATIONAL PARK

Dominant on the skyline behind the Gold Coast beaches are the green peaks and plateaus of the border ranges. Here Lamington National Park protects magnificent subtropical rainforest rising to more than 1100 metres. The two main starting points for exploring Lamington National Park are Binna Burra and Green Mountains (also known as O'Reilly's because of the well-known guesthouse), each about an hour-and-a-half's drive from Brisbane and an hour from the Gold Coast. Binna Burra is well known for its long-established lodge with pleasant accommodation. For a visit to Lamington National Park, three items are essential: a raincoat, insect repellent and a bird identification book. This splendid rainforest retreat is overrun with birds. The repellent is for the abundant leeches. Of course the raincoat is needed for the rain that gives rainforest its name. At both Binna Burra

and Green Mountains, pademelons graze the lawns early and late in the day, and spotlighting in the forest at night will reveal possums, bandicoots, frogs and geckoes.

LAWN HILL NATIONAL PARK

This spectacular oasis in arid far north-western Queensland boasts a beautiful creek lined by lush tropical vegetation winding through a gorge of multi-coloured sandstone. This park has been progressively enlarged, making it one of Queensland's largest. A notable inclusion in 1992 was the Riversleigh Section, protecting internationally significant fossil deposits. The large Lawn Hill Creek, fed by numerous springs, flows through fissures in the Constance Range, with walls of red, orange and grey sandstone falling 60 metres to the pools and waterholes. Rainforest vegetation in this oasis includes cabbage palms, figs and the prominent dark green, broad-leaved Leichhardt trees. Among the large numbers of birds and other animals are wallaroos, the rare rock ringtail possum and fairy martins. The creek is home to crocodiles but they are the harmless freshwater variety. The upper and middle sections of the gorge offer swimming and boating.

LUMHOLTZ NATIONAL PARK

Lumholtz is one of a number of national parks and forestry reserves in the Ingham–Cardwell–Tully region, between Townsville and Cairns, where ranges rise sharply from a narrow coastal plain, and rock, water and rainforests tumble down the hillsides. This large park protects part of the Wet Tropics World Heritage Area; its best known feature is Wallaman Falls, the largest permanent 'clear drop' waterfall in Australia. There is a camping area, on the gorge top above Wallaman Falls. From the camping area a short track leads to a swimming hole in the rocky creek. A road leads 2 km to a lookout over the falls and then there is a very steep 2 km walking track to the base of the falls. Other parts of the park can be reached by fit walkers, and some by 4WD.

MAIN RANGE NATIONAL PARK

This park, south-west of Brisbane, takes in the peaks and ramparts of the Great Dividing Range stretching approximately 55 km north and south of Cunninghams Gap. Roads and walking tracks cut through rainforest and eucalypts to lookouts with

spectacular views. The park includes historic Spicers Gap, which took drays laden with Darling Downs produce to the port of Brisbane. You can still follow the pioneers' route through Spicers Gap (part by 4WD, part only on foot) and search out historic relics along the way. The major feature of the park is the Governor's Chair, a rocky bluff providing views south to the border ranges and north towards Brisbane, with Moogerah Dam and surrounding hills far below. The southern end of the park also has some delightful features, including Queen Mary Falls, near the small town of Killarney, 34 km from Warwick.

SUNDOWN NATIONAL PARK

Sundown National Park, 250 km south-west of Brisbane, was created in the late 1970s from parts of three large sheep stations which, over time, had become uneconomic to run. Copper, tin and arsenic were once mined in the Red Rock area in the north of Sundown, but very little wealth was gained from the low-grade ore. Sundown's most striking feature is the Severn River. At most times of the year it is a series of large rocky waterholes in its upper reaches but after prolonged heavy rain it becomes a raging torrent. It is enjoyable walking along the banks of the river or up one of the many narrow gorges. Sundown's rugged terrain of steep gullies, eroded ridge tops, gorges and creek flats makes the park a mecca for wilderness seekers. The park has a wide range of vegetation including eucalypts, white box and cypress. Kangaroos and wallabies are commonly seen in the park.

WHITSUNDAY ISLANDS NATIONAL PARK

Azure blue seas, white sandy beaches, forest-covered slopes, abundant wildlife and isolated camping spots are just some of the more inviting aspects of a trip to the Whitsunday Islands National Park. The islands lie off the Queensland coast between Bowen and Mackay. One of the main attractions of the park is swimming among the colourful fish and coral in the Great Barrier Reef Marine Park. The variety is staggering and it is easy for divers and snorkellers to become spellbound when they enter this amazing world. But currents are strong so make sure you do not drift too far, and don't swim alone.

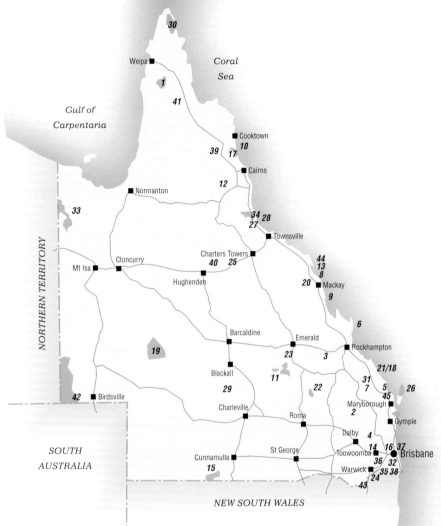

Popular Parks	Camping	Caravans	Wheel Chairs	4WD Access	Picnic Area	Toilets	Walking Trks	Kiosk	Information
1 Archer Bend NP				●					
2 Auburn River NP	●				●	●	●		
3 Blackdown Tableland NP	●				●	●	●		
4 Bunya Mountains NP	●		●		●	●	●	●	●
5 Burrum Coast NP	●			●			●		
6 Byfield SF & NP	●			●					
7 Cania Gorge NP	●	●			●	●	●	●	●
8 Cape Hillsborough NP	●				●	●	●		
9 Cape Palmerston NP	●			●					
10 Cape Tribulation NP	●				●	●	●		●
11 Carnarvon NP									
– Carnarvon Gorge	●				●	●	●		●
– Mount Moffatt	●				●				
– Salvator Rosa	●				●				
12 Chillagoe-Mungana Caves NP	●				●	●	●		●
13 Conway NP	●	●			●	●	●		●
14 Crows Nest Falls NP	●				●	●	●		
15 Currawinya NP	●			●					
16 D'Aguilar Range NP	●		●		●	●	●		●
17 Daintree NP					●	●	●		
18 Deepwater NP	●	●			●	●	●		
19 Diamantina Gate NP									
20 Eungella NP	●				●	●	●	●	●
21 Eurimbula NP	●			●					
22 Expedition NP	●				●	●	●	●	

Popular Parks	Camping	Caravans	Wheel Chairs	4WD Access	Picnic Area	Toilets	Walking Trks	Kiosk	Information
23 Gemfields Reserve	●	●		●					
24 Girraween NP	●	●			●	●	●		●
25 Great Basalt Wall NP	●			●					
26 Great Sandy NP									
– Cooloola	●	●			●	●	●		●
– Fraser Island North	●			●	●	●	●		●
27 Herbert River Falls NP	●								
28 Hinchinbrook Island NP	●						●		
29 Idalia NP	●								●
30 Jardine River NP	●			●					
31 Kroombit Tops SF	●			●					
32 Lamington NP	●		●		●	●	●	●	●
33 Lawn Hill NP	●				●	●	●		●
34 Lumholtz NP	●				●		●		
35 Main Range NP	●						●		
36 Moogerah Peaks NP	●						●		
37 Moreton Island NP	●			●					●
38 Mount Barney NP							●		
39 Palmer Goldfields Reserve	●			●					
40 Porcupine Gorge NP	●			●			●		
41 Rokeby NP	●			●					
42 Simpson Desert NP				●					
43 Sundown NP	●			●	●	●	●		●
44 Whitsunday Islands NP	●			●	●	●	●		
45 Woodgate NP	●			●	●	●	●		●

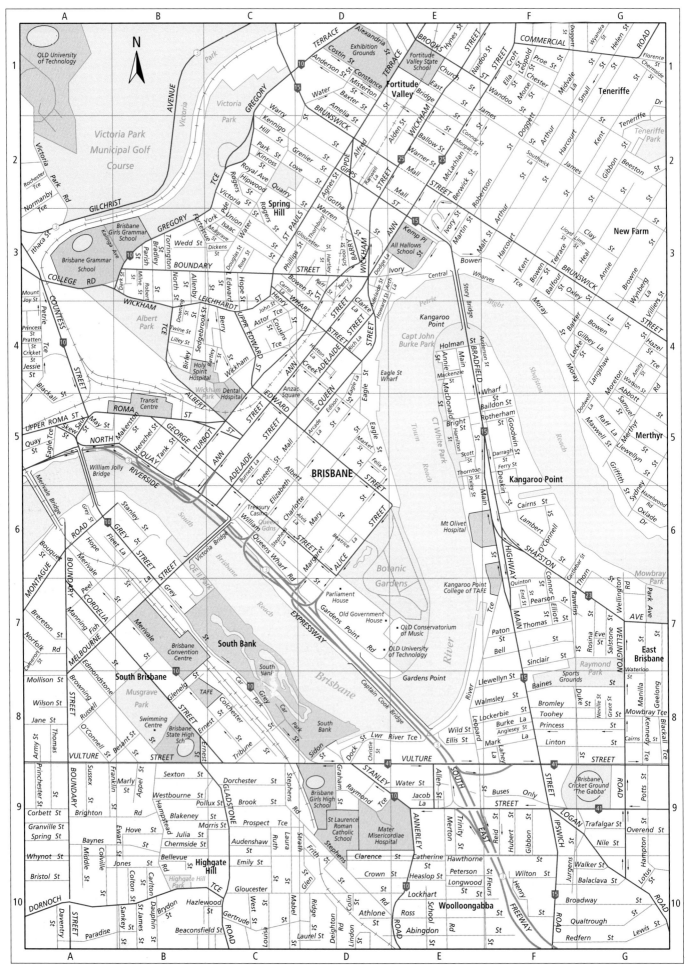

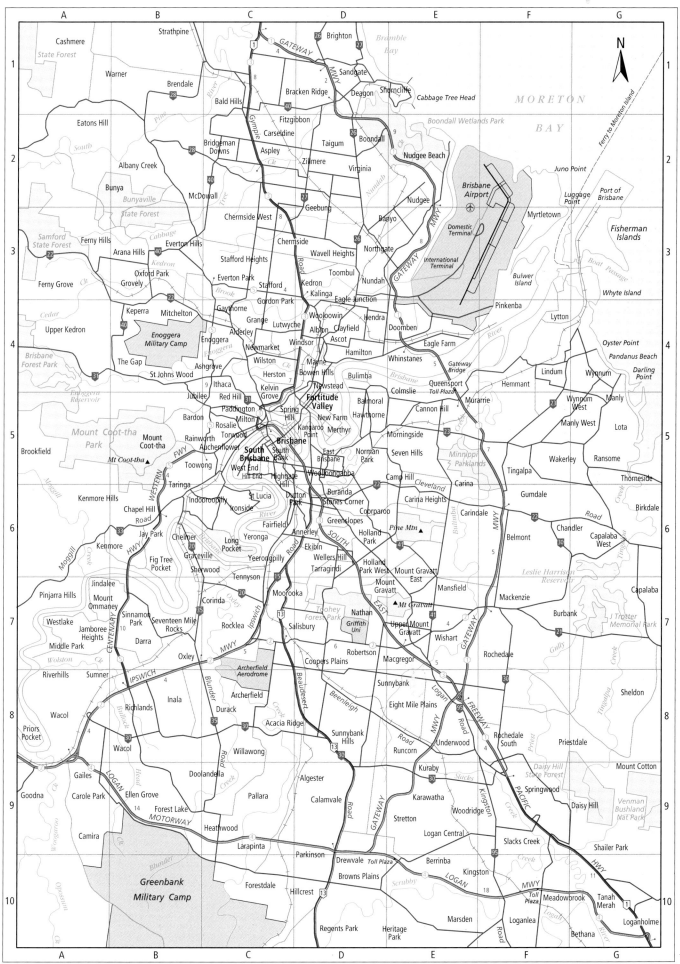

kilometres
0 10 20 30 40 50

225

N

Column A
▲ Mt Barbara
Windera
Lake Boondooma
Proston
Cloyna
Mondure
Hivesville
Goode R
Wondai
Tingoora
Dangore Mtn ▲
Memerambi
Kingaroy
Ironpot
Kumbia
173
Bunya Mtns Nat Park
Bell
Kaimkillenbun
Quinalow
Peranga
Kulpi
Bowenville
Acland
Jondaryan
84
Oakey
Mount Tyson
Springside
Cambooya
Yarranlea
Pittsworth
Brookstead
Greenmount
Tummaville
Felton East
Clifton
Ryeford
Leyburn
Pratten
Thane
Karara
Lake Leslie
108
▲ Mt Burrabaranga
▲ Tank Mtn
Dalveen
Wylie Creek
The Summit
Stanthorpe
Pikedale
Glen Aplin
Ballandean
Glenlyon
Sundown Nat Park
Mingoola
Tarban
Mole River
Riverton

Column B
152
Woologa
Tansey
Kilkivan **76**
Murgon
Goomeri
Glastonbury
Widgee Mtn ▲
Amamoor
Kandanga
Manumbar
Elgin Vale
Mt Gibbarnee ▲
Nanango
Yarraman
D'AGUILAR
Linville
Moore
Blackbutt
140
Cooyar
Wutul
Toogoolawah
Haden
Crows Nest
Goombungee
Murphys Creek
Meringandan
Toowoomba
Helidon
Grantham
Gatton
Fordsdale
Mulgowie
Mt Cooper ▲
Mt Lowe
Townson
Mt Mistake Nat Park
Spring Creek
Allora
Goomburra
Maryvale
Mt Huntley ▲
Rockbrae
Warwick
Allan
Killarney
Legume
Dalveen
Rivertree Peak
Liston
Tooloom
Amosfield
Girraween Nat Pk
Boonoo Boonoo NP
Wallangarra
Bryans Gap
Leechs Gully
Tenterfield
Sandy Flat

Column C
Glenwood
Gunalda
Mt Coora ▲
Barambah Ck
Lake Borumba
Jimna
Conondale
Yednia
Lake Somerset
Kilcoy
Somerset Dam
Esk
Lake Wivenhoe
125
Coominya
Fernvale
Hatton Vale
Laidley
Marburg
Rosewood
Rosevale
164
Warrill View
Mt Castle ▲
Tarome
Kalbar
Coulson
Boonah
Maroon
Main Range Nat Park
Lake Moogerah
Mt Barney ▲
Dalman
Woodenbong
Urbenville
Old Bonalbo
Paddys Flat
Bonalbo
Mummulgum
Tabulam
128
Alice
Camira Creek

Column D
Tin Can Bay
35
48
Goomboorian
Wolvi
Gympie
14
Kin Kin
Cooran
Pomona
Tewantin
Imbil
Brooloo
Yandina
Kenilworth
Mapleton
Montville
Palmwoods
Maleny
Landsborough
Beerwah
Woodford
Beerburrum
Wamuran
Mount Mee
Caboolture
Dayboro
Strathpine
Samford
Mount Nebo
Browns Plains
Park Ridge
Ipswich
Purga
Mt Elliott
Harrisville
Milbong
Laravale
Rathdowney
Numinbah Valley
Bald Mtn ▲
Border Ranges NP
Wiangaree
Eden Creek
Ettrick
Leeville
Mallanganee
Coombell
Wyan
Rappville
Baryulgil
Whiporie

Column E
Rainbow Beach
Double Island Point
30
Great Sandy National Park
Lake Cootharaba
Boreen
Noosa Heads
Noosa Nat Park
Lake Weyba
Eumundi
Coolum Beach
Nambour
Maroochydore
Mooloolaba
Buderim
Caloundra
Bribie Island
Bribie Island Nat Park
Bongaree
Beachmere
Deception Bay
Redcliffe
Sandgate
Petrie
Mud Is
Moreton
BRISBANE
Capalaba
Cleveland
Victoria Point
Loganholme
Beenleigh
Wolffdene
Pimpama
Tamborine
Oxenford
Nerang
Mudgeeraba
Numinbah
Tumbulgum
Murwillumbah
Uki
Blue Knob
Nimbin
89
Kyogle
Dunoon
Cedar Point
Fairy Hill
Goolmangar
Casino
Alstonville
Yorklea
Ellangowan
Coraki
Woodburn

Column F
154
SOUTH
PACIFIC
Sunshine Coast
OCEAN
Cape Moreton
Moreton Island
Moreton Island National Park
Bay
Amity Point
Point Lookout
North Stradbroke Island
Woongoolba
Eden Island
Jacobs Well
South Stradbroke Island
Paradise Point
Southport
140
Surfers Paradise
Burleigh Heads
Coolangatta
Tweed Heads
Banora Point
Kingscliff
Burringbar
Wooyung
79
Brunswick Heads
Mullumbimby
Byron Bay
Bangalow
Suffolk Park
Lismore
Ballina
Empire Vale
Wardell
Dungarubba
Broadwater NP
Evans Head
Snapper Point
Bundjalung National Park

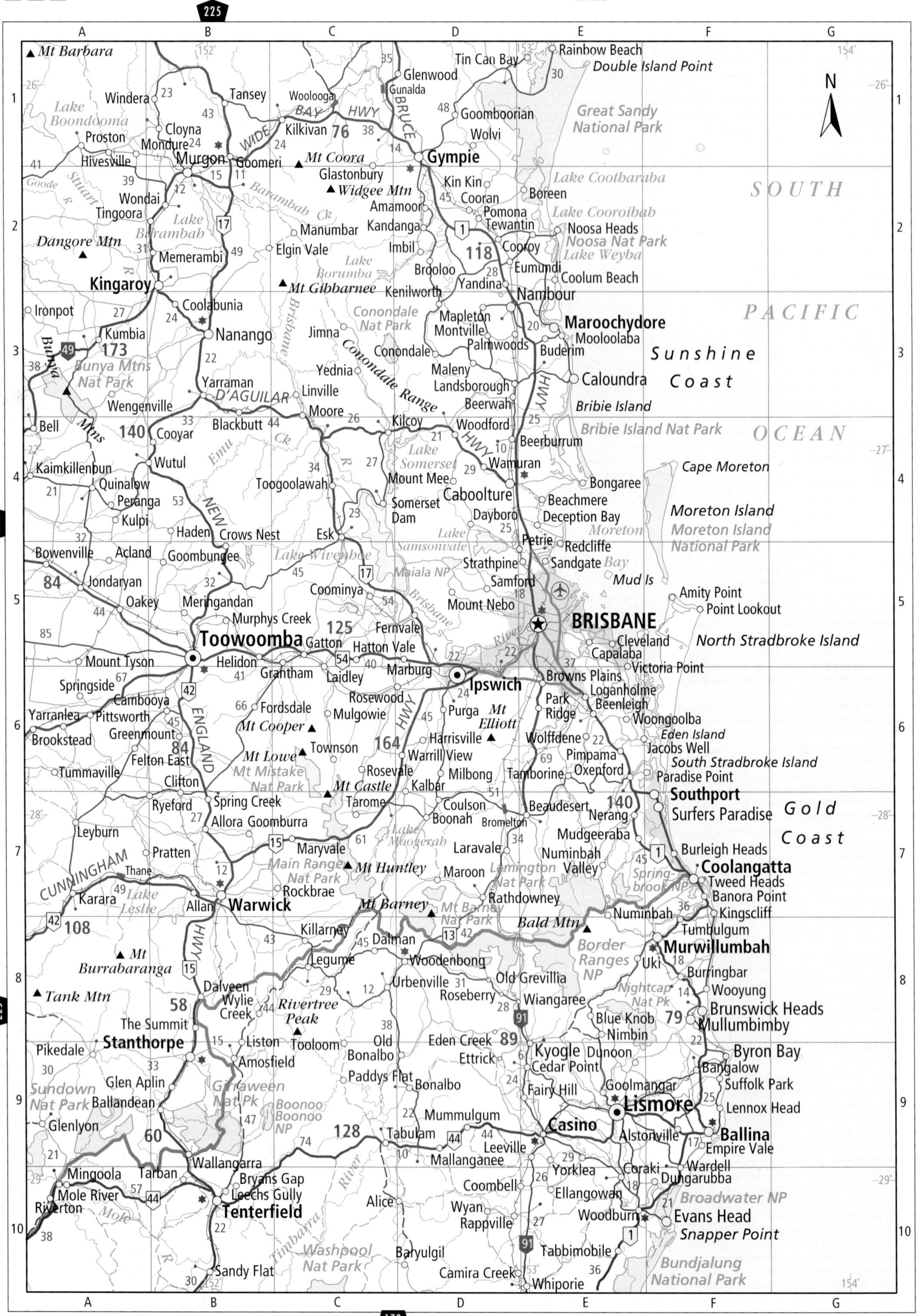

© Random House Australia Pty Ltd

179

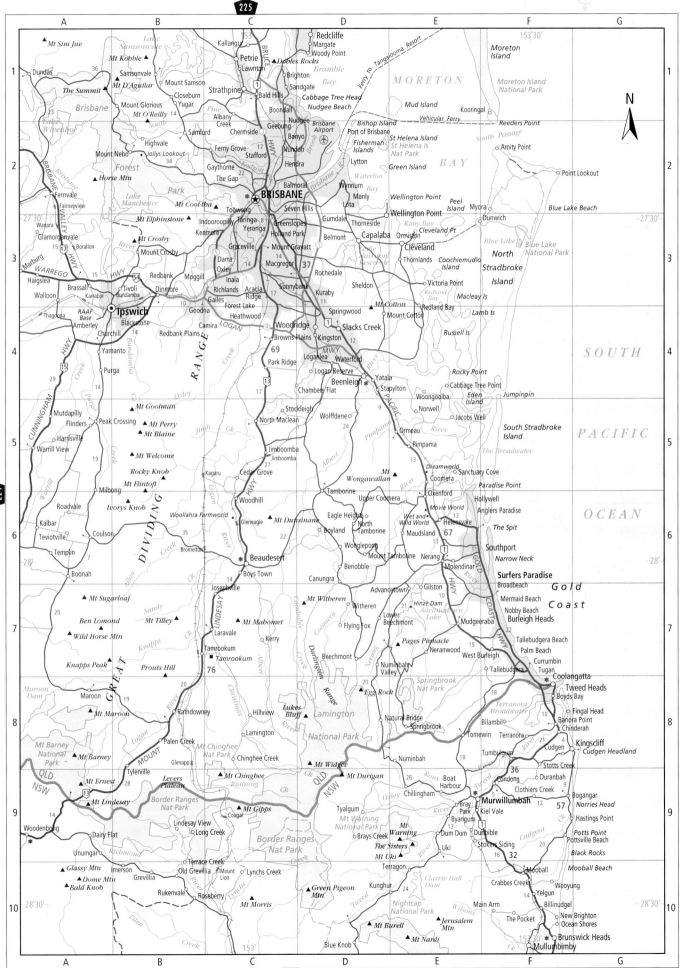

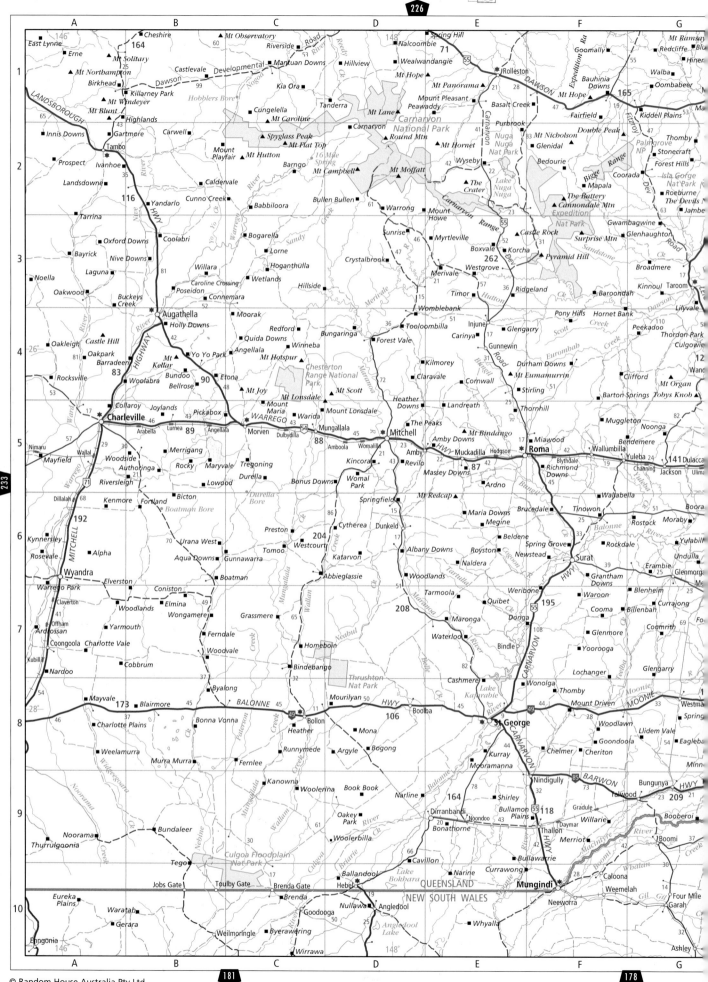

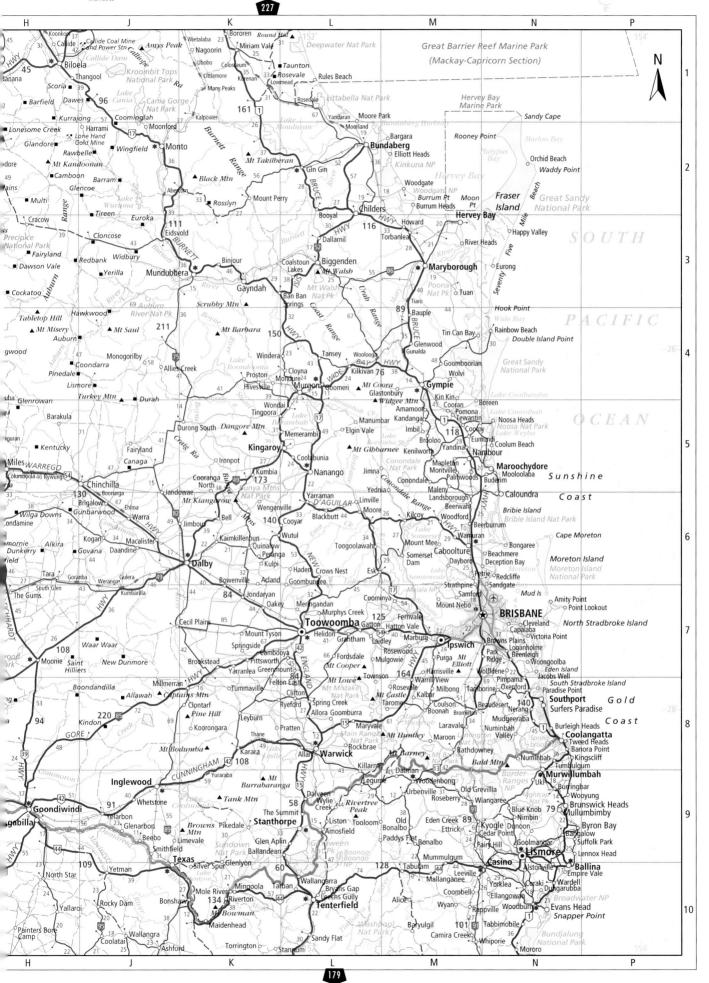

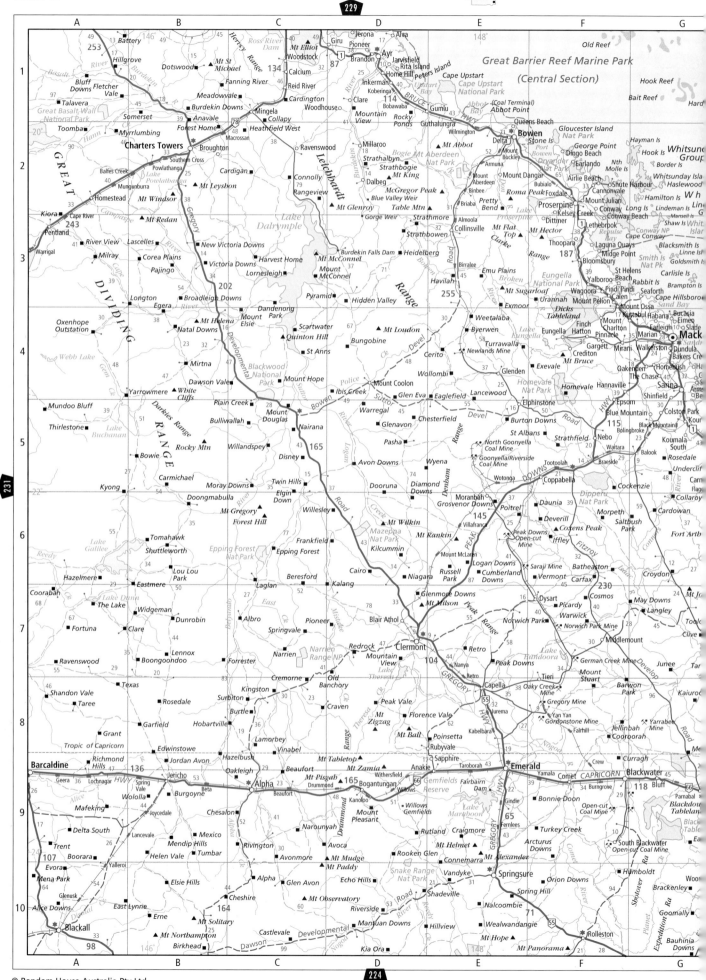

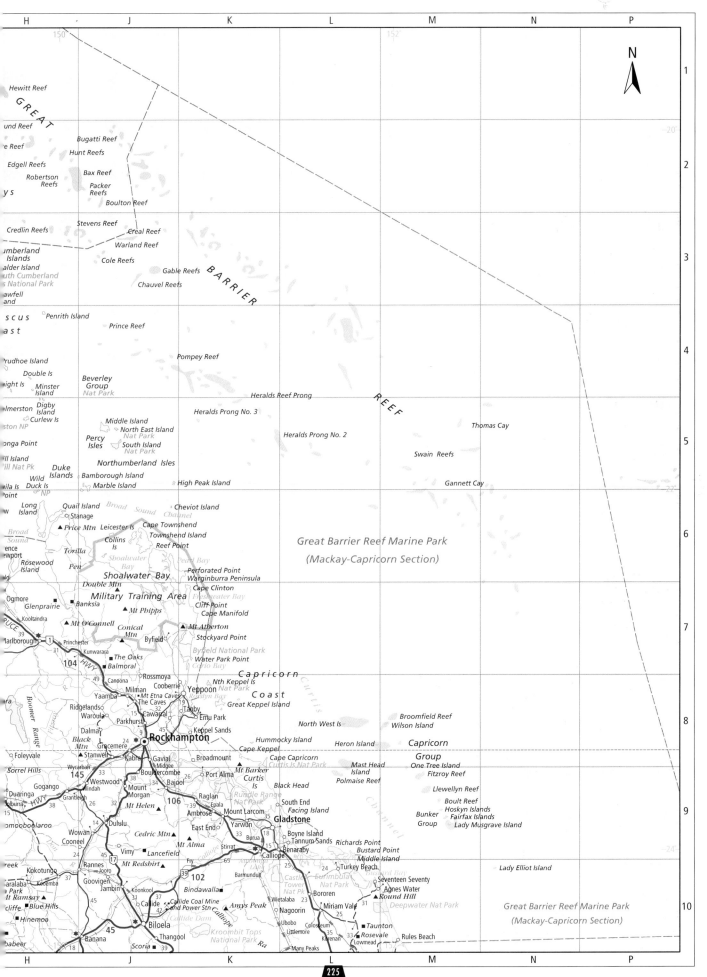

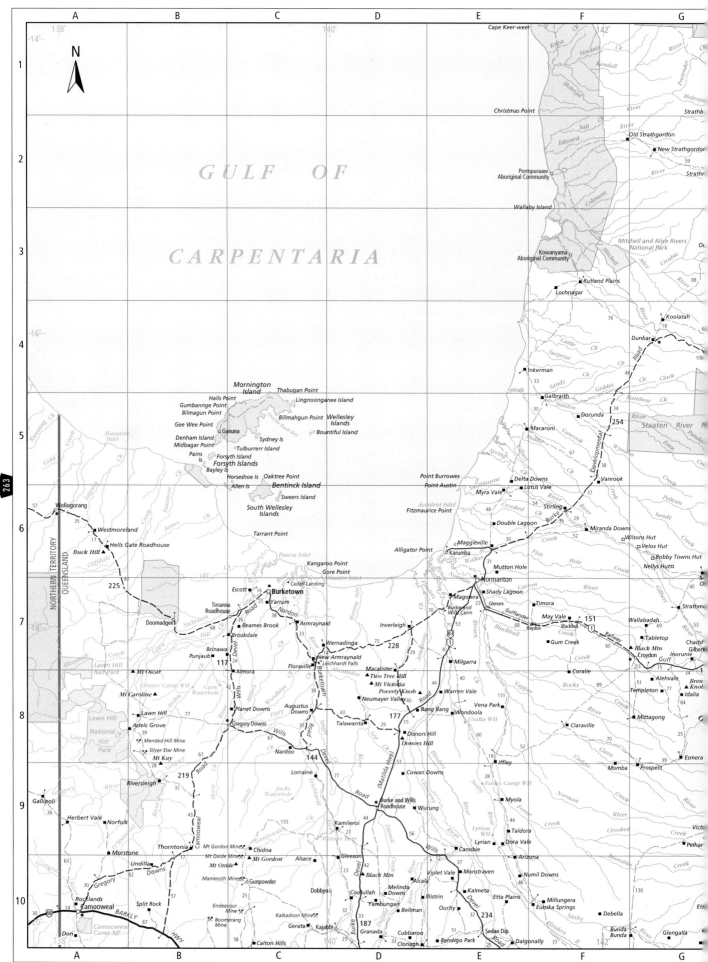

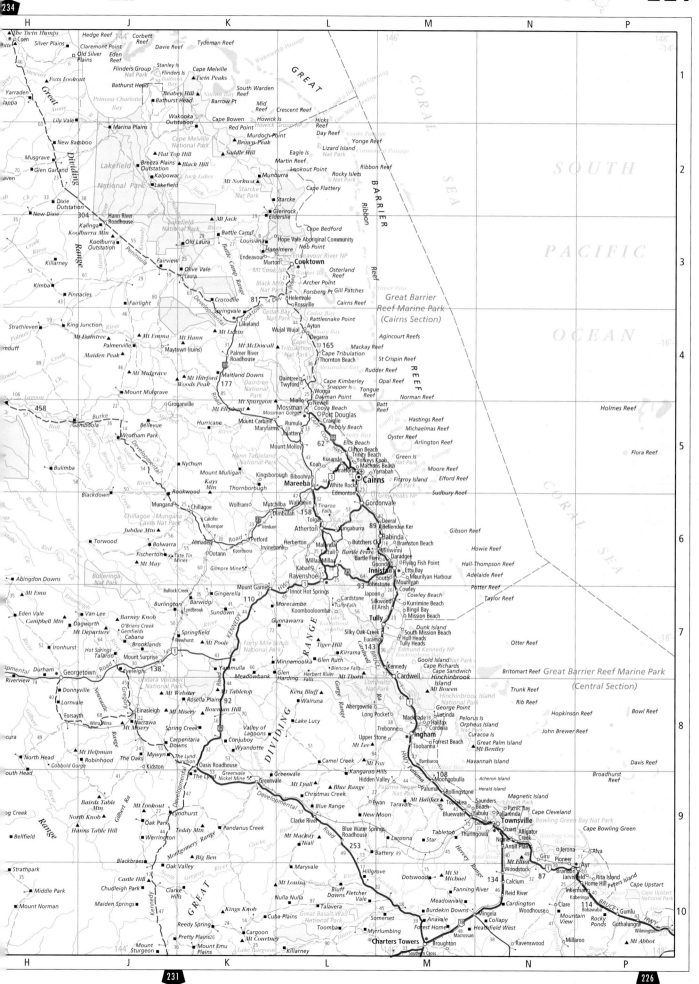

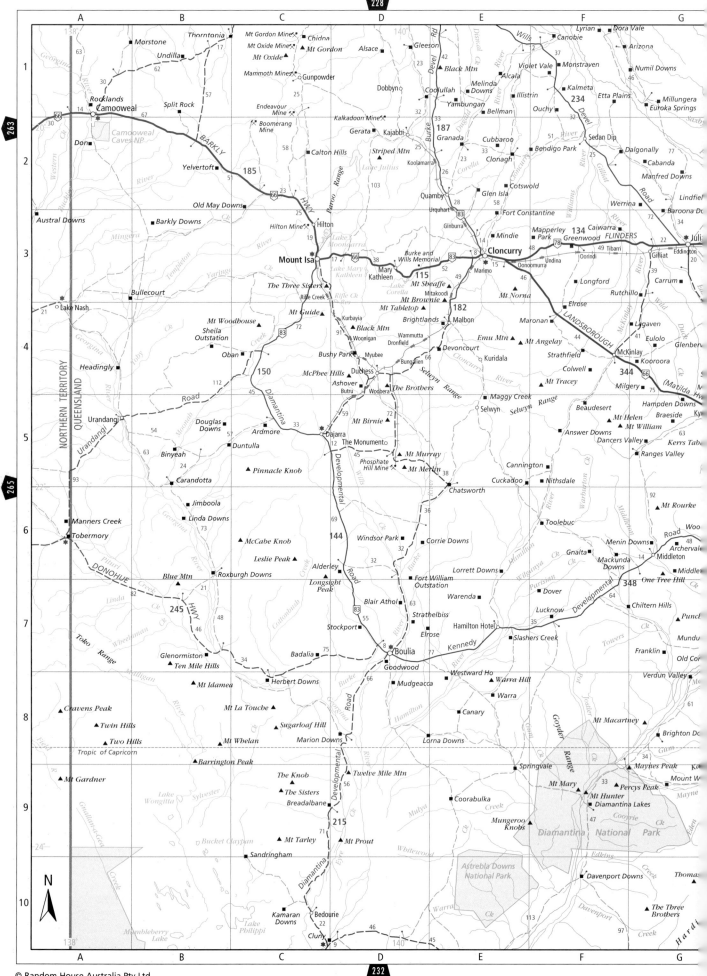

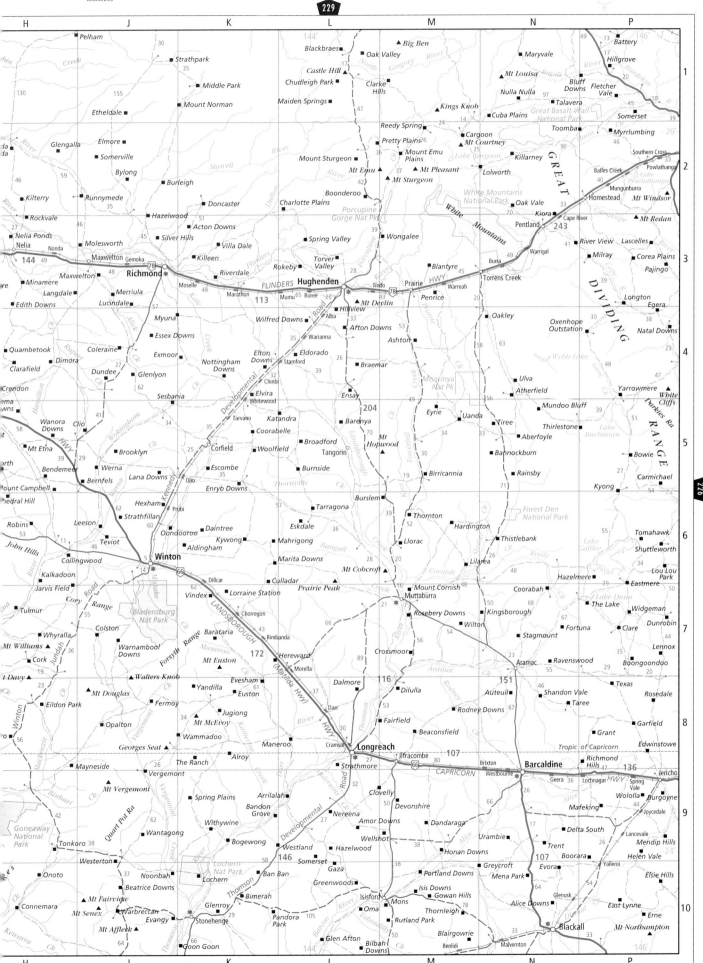

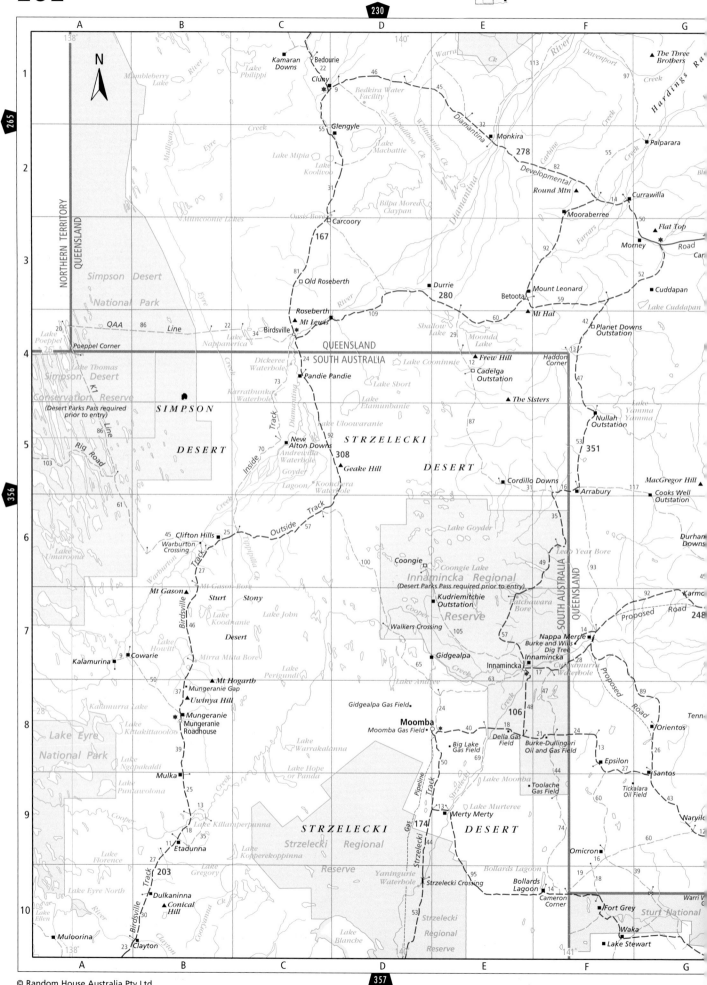

© Random House Australia Pty Ltd

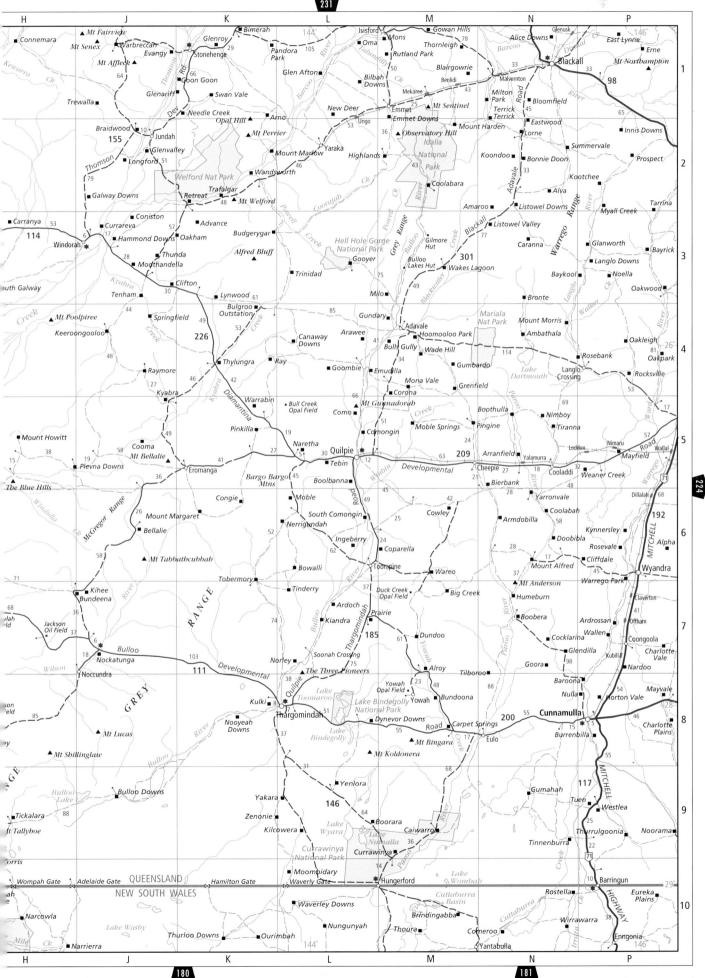

kilometres
0   20   40   60   80

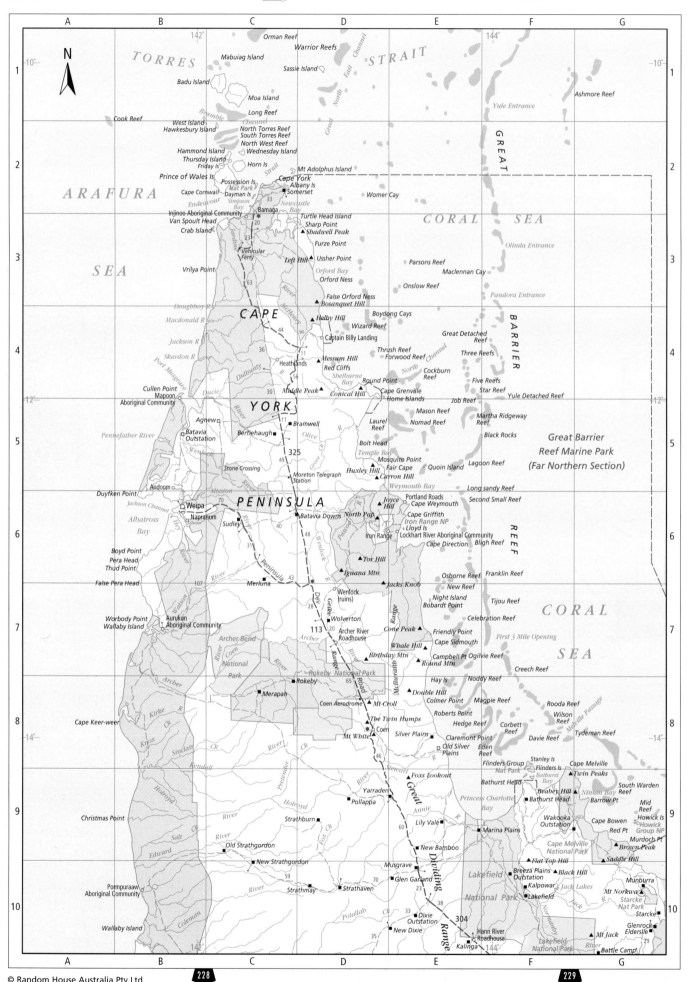

kilometres

0 10 20 30 40 50

229

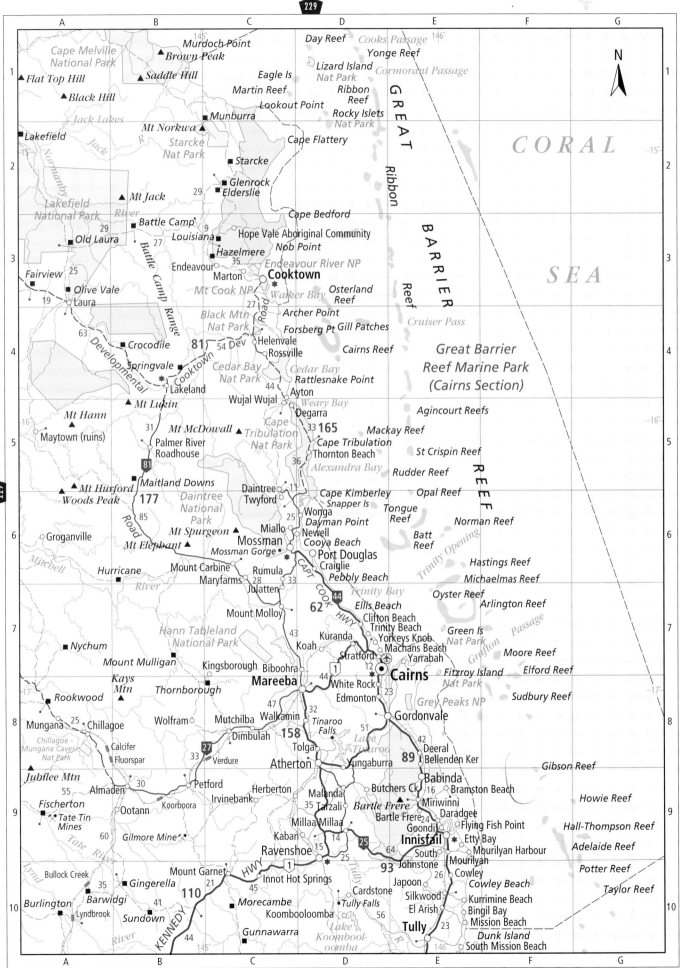

Cape Melville National Park
Flat Top Hill
Murdoch Point
Brown Peak
Saddle Hill
Black Hill
Day Reef
Cooks Passage
Yonge Reef
Lizard Island Nat Park
Cormorant Passage
Eagle Is
Martin Reef
Lookout Point
Ribbon Reef
Rocky Islets Nat Park
Lakefield
Jack Lakes
Mt Norkwa
Munburra
Cape Flattery

GREAT

CORAL

Starcke Nat Park
Starcke
Glenrock
Elderslie
Cape Bedford
Mt Jack
Lakefield National Park
Battle Camp
Louisiana
Hazelmere
Hope Vale Aboriginal Community
Nob Point
SEA
29
9
Old Laura
27
Endeavour
Marton
Cooktown
Endeavour River NP
BARRIER

Fairview
25
Olive Vale
19 Laura
63
Crocodile
81 54 Dev
Mt Cook NP
Walker Bay
Osterland Reef
Archer Point
Forsberg Pt Gill Patches
Cairns Reef
Cruiser Pass

Springvale
Lakeland
Black Mtn Nat Park
Helenvale
Rossville
Cedar Bay Nat Park
Rattlesnake Point
Ayton
Weary Bay
Great Barrier Reef Marine Park (Cairns Section)

Mt Lukin
Mt Hann
Maytown (ruins)
Wujal Wujal
Degarra
33 165
Mackay Reef
Agincourt Reefs

31 Mt McDowall
Palmer River Roadhouse
Cape Tribulation Nat Park
Cape Tribulation
Thornton Beach
St Crispin Reef

81
36
Rudder Reef
Alexandra Bay

Mt Hurford
Woods Peak
177
Maitland Downs
85
Daintree National Park
Daintree
Twyford
Cape Kimberley
Snapper Is
Opal Reef

REEF
Groganville
Mt Spurgeon
Mt Elephant
Miallo
Newell
Wonga
Dayman Point
Cooya Beach
Tongue Reef
Norman Reef
Batt Reef

Mitchell
Hurricane
Mossman
Mossman Gorge
Port Douglas
Craiglie
Hastings Reef

Mount Carbine
Maryfarms
28 33
Rumula
Julatten
Pebbly Beach
Trinity Bay
Michaelmas Reef

Nychum
Hann Tableland National Park
Mount Molloy
62
44
Ellis Beach
Clifton Beach
Trinity Beach
Oyster Reef
Arlington Reef

Mount Mulligan
43
Kuranda
Koah
Yorkeys Knob
Machans Beach
Green Is Nat Park
Moore Reef
Passage

Kingsborough
Biboohra
Stratford
12
Cairns
Yarrabah
Fitzroy Island Nat Park
Elford Reef

Rookwood
Kays Mtn
Thornborough
Mareeba
44
White Rock
Edmonton
23
Grey Peaks NP
Sudbury Reef

Mungana
25 Chillagoe
Wolfram
Mutchilba
Walkamin
47
32
Tinaroo Falls
51
Gordonvale
42
Gibson Reef

Chillagoe-Mungana Caves Nat Park
Calcifer
Fluorspar
Dimbulah
158
Tolga
Lake Tinaroo
Deeral
89 Bellenden Ker

Jubilee Mtn
55 Almaden
30
Petford
Koorboora
Irvinebank
Herberton
Verdure
33
Atherton
Yungaburra
Babinda
Butchers Ck 16
Bramston Beach

Fischerton
Ootann
Malanda
35 Tarzali
Bartle Frere
Miriwinni
Daradgee
Howie Reef

Tate Tin Mines
60
Gilmore Mine
Kaban
14
Bartle Frere
24
Goondi
Flying Fish Point
Hall-Thompson Reef

Millaa Millaa
25
Innisfail
Etty Bay
Adelaide Reef

Bullock Creek
Mount Garnet
Ravenshoe
15
25
64
South Johnstone
Mourilyan
Mourilyan Harbour
Potter Reef

Burlington
Barwidgi
Gingerella
41
110
21
45
Innot Hot Springs
93
Japoon
26
Cowley
Cowley Beach
Taylor Reef

Lyndbrook
Sundown
Morecambe
Koombooloomba
Tully Falls
Cardstone
Silkwood
El Arish
Kurrimine Beach
Bingil Bay

Tate River
Lynd River
44
145
Gunnawarra
Lake Koombool-oomba
56
Tully
23
Dunk Island
Mission Beach
South Mission Beach
146

229

© Random House Australia Pty Ltd

THE NORTHERN TERRITORY

The Northern Territory—the Outback—Australia's last frontier—even the official name, 'Northern Territory', has a wild romantic ring about it, that sets the scene and provides the allure for modern-day travellers. For a hundred years the Territory has attracted adventurers, incurable romantics and pioneers whether they are tough cattlemen, rough-around-the-edges crocodile shooters, aspiring gold hunters, or hardened business men wanting and willing to take a gamble on the trucking game, running a store, or throwing in their hand to look for diamonds, oil, or gas.

For many the reality is not all that far from the truth. While you will not find buffalo or crocodile shooters any more travelling the Territory, you will still find tall, whippet-like young men and women riding a horse, cracking a whip and wheeling cattle through the dust, and older, more weather-beaten souls behind the wheel of a three-dog (trailers) semi, or sitting in the cab—an air-conditioned cab—of a grader or dump truck in a mine somewhere. It is in their spare time that they will sit down in an air-conditioned house to play a computer game, watch a video, and drink a beer that is more than just 'Kimberley cool'.

You no longer have to be 'tough' to live in the Territory, and while today's Territorian has almost certainly just come up from down south, they have more than likely cruised up the Stuart Highway or come in along Highway 1—both fully bituminised these days—in their Holden Commodore or Ford Falcon. Still, the image is of tough men, and tougher women, in a wild, harsh land and there is certainly no dispute about that!

It is a big land. The Territory takes up about one-sixth of Australia, covering over 1.4 million sq km, and in that huge expanse there are less than 180 000 people. Half of those live in the Darwin metro region and a big percentage of the rest live in Alice Springs, Katherine, Tennant Creek, Nhulunbuy and Yulara. A sprinkling of other towns and Aboriginal communities leaves the greater part of the state to very few people. Around 23 per cent of the population is Aboriginal, with over 50 per cent of the Territory classed as Aboriginal land, whether that be reserve, community land, pastoral land or freehold.

The distances between habitations are great. Even on the Stuart, where a big percentage of the towns are located, you will still travel over 200 km between them. Head off on the lesser, but even so bituminised roads, and you may well travel twice that distance between dwellings. Once onto the dirt, 400 km between points of civilisation is not uncommon.

But for all that the road network is pretty good. The great ribbon of the Stuart Highway cuts right through the heart of the state, stretching from the Northern Territory/South Australia border all the way north to Darwin.

The moon setting over the eastern bluff of Mt Connor

Do not expect dual lanes, but it is a good road. The Barkly Highway comes in from Queensland, across the billiard table flatness of the golden grassed Barkly Tablelands, meeting the Stuart at Three Ways, while the Victoria Highway heads west from Katherine, as part of Highway 1 into Western Australia. Add the Kakadu Highway, the Roper, Tablelands, and the Lasseter Highway out to Uluru (Ayers Rock), and these are the main bituminised roads. Of course there is more blacktop, mainly out to tourist attractions such as the road into Litchfield National Park, the road skirting the southern edge of the West MacDonnell Ranges and the road out to Kings Canyon. The Territory prides itself in the fact that 90 per cent of the major tourist attractions are reached by blacktop and are therefore accessible by the traveller in their normal car.

However, even on these highways, at times, the blacktop is just one lane wide and you will need to drop a set of wheels into the dirt when passing another vehicle. A word of warning may be opportune here: if a road train is approaching, do not expect them to shift off the bitumen. With 50 tonnes on the back and up to three dogs, they are king of the road.

Much of the road network and the blacktop owes its existence to the planned expansion of the beef road network of the 1970s which saw a general upgrading of roads to service the pastoral industry. Before then most of the roads, even the highways, were dirt, with only the Stuart between Alice and Darwin being blacktop, a hangover from World War II.

The Stuart Highway owes its existence to the man from whom it takes its name: John McDouall Stuart, who in the early 1860s led a number of expeditions north from South Australia and finally crossed the continent in 1862. The Overland Telegraph Line followed his route and a track sprang up beside this ribbon of wire, that was dotted with the signs of civilisation in the form of repeater stations, such as Alice Springs, Tennant Creek, Elliott, Katherine and others.

Until 1911 the Territory was deemed to be part of South Australia and then the Federal Government took over for a while. Between 1926 and 1931 the Territory was divided in two, with Northern Australia being looked after by Darwin, and Central Australia being administered from Alice. In 1931 the Federal Government took control again and it was not until 1978 that the Territory was finally granted self-government, although not full statehood. Many decisions, much to most Territorians' grief, are still made in far-away Canberra.

The thorny devil, an unmistakable lizard

The last section of the Stuart Highway was bituminised in the late 1980s, while the round Australia high-way was completed about the same time. For the most part that means Highway 1, but observant road atlas users will see that Highway 1 heads east from near Daly Waters on the Stuart to Borroloola, where it turns to dirt and heads across the Gulf into Queensland. And, while that is a great trip for adventurous four-wheelers, most travellers prefer the bitumen of the Barkly Highway further south.

Being such a large area and stretching from the arid interior north into the tropics, the Territory has extremes in not only climate but vegetation.

To the south and north of Alice Springs, the country is dry, with sand-ridges and sandplains, cut here and there with low rocky ranges covered in vegetation that is at home in this arid landscape. The weather varies from hot, dry summers, with the occasional storm, to drier, cooler winters. In summer, temperatures of 45°C are not uncommon, while in winter, at night, temperatures as low as –7°C have been recorded. However, for the most part winter day temperatures are a mild 15 to 23°C. Rainfall varies, with September being the driest month in Alice with an average of 10 mm, while the wettest month is February with an average of just 50 mm of rain.

In the Top End the climate is tropical with two main seasons, the Dry from May to November, and the Wet. Most of Darwin's 1500 mm of rain falls during the Wet, especially in the first three months of the year, with virtually none in June, July and August. The temperature range is pretty static with maximums in the low thirties nearly all the time, and minimums in the mid twenties, except for the three driest months already mentioned, when the minimum temperatures are around 20°C. We should mention humidity, which some people find is very high and unbearable in the Wet, and especially in the month before the Wet begins.

It is no wonder the Dry is the most popular time to visit the Centre and the Top End, but what you will see is a drier, more tame country than you would see in summer. With a good road network and air-conditioned cars and motels, it may pay to see the Territory when most of the other travellers are back down south. Certainly you will find a different, more verdant countryside that is more subject to the vagaries of the weather, and with that, you will capture a wilder side of the Territory—one that is closer to its reputation. Wouldn't that be one of the best reasons for travelling then?

Yulara, seen from the air, with Uluru (Ayers Rock) rising up in the background

DARWIN-BRISBANE
Via Cunningham Hwy 15, & Warrego Hwy 54
Landsborough Hwy 71 & 61, Barkly Hwy 66
& Stuart Hwy 87, 3484 Kilometres

DARWIN	36	*Jabiru*
112		
Adelaide River	148 / 3328	
114		
Pine Creek		*Jabiru*
113		
Port Hedland / Perth	**Katherine**	375 / 3109
106		
Mataranka		
75		
	Larrimah	556 / 2928
84		
Daly Waters	44	*Borroloola*
Dunmarra		
101		
785 / 2699	Elliott	
67		
	Renner Springs	
169		
Tenant Creek / Alice Springs / Adelaide	Three Ways Roadhouse	1021 / 2463
188		
Barkly Homestead		*Borroloola*
NORTHERN TERRITORY	272	
1481 / 2003 Camooweal	STATE BORDER	
188	**QUEENSLAND**	
Boulia	**Mt Isa**	1669 / 1815
117		
Cloncurry		*Normanton / Hughenden*
105	McKinlay	
1891 / 1593		
78		
Kynuna		
165		
Boulia	Winton	*Hughenden*
174		
2308 / 1176 **Longreach**		
107		
Barcaldine		*Emerald*
107		
	Blackall	
97		
2619 / 865	Tambo	
116		
Charleville	Augathella	
92		
Charleville	Morven	2827 / 657
89		
	Mitchell	
88		
St George	**Roma**	3004 / 480
58		
Yuleba		
81		
Goondiwindi	Miles	Banana
45		
3143 / 296	Chinchilla	
81		
St George		*Kingaroy*
	Dalby	
83		
Warwick	**Toowoomba**	*Goomeri*
89		
Ipswich		*Esk*
Warwick	43	
	BRISBANE	

DARWIN

POPULATION: 100 000

MAP REFERENCE: PAGE 259 C2

The most cosmopolitan of Australian cities, Darwin is Australia's only tropical capital and is the closest Australian city to the equator. It is also closer to much of Asia than it is to much of southern Australia, with Jakarta in Indonesia being closer than Brisbane, and Singapore closer than Hobart.

This sprawling capital sits on the eastern shore of Port Darwin, which is a convoluted inlet on the Beagle Gulf, itself a large inlet of the Timor Sea. While the centre of the city and the port are located on a wide isthmus of land between Frances Bay and Fannie Bay, most of the suburbs are either directly to the north, or spread along the string of the Stuart Highway. For most travellers heading up the long haul of 'the Track', as the highway is more often called, the city's outskirts seem to start an awfully long way out. This is accentuated by the satellite city of Palmerston, 25 km south of the heart of Darwin, that heralds the beginning of the metropolitan area.

All told, there are just under 100 000 people in this greater metro area, making it the smallest capital city in Australia, but what it lacks in population, it makes up for in variety. There are more than 50 ethnic groups represented in the city, with a large number of these having been here almost from the very first days of the settlement. As is to be expected, Darwin is also home to a vibrant Aboriginal culture, with Aboriginal language, art and craft, dance and music being an everyday affair.

Aboriginal people have been living along the northern coastline of Australia for 40 000 years or more, while Macassan *bêche-de-mer* fishermen from the islands of modern-day Indonesia were probably sailing this coast for at least the last few hundred years. In the 1500s Dutch navigators first discovered the Great South Land, and in 1644 Abel Tasman sailed and mapped much of the north-west coast and the Gulf of Carpentaria.

Port Darwin was named and mapped by John Stokes and John Wickham on the *Beagle* in 1839. Charles Darwin and his ship were yet to become famous, as it was to be another 20 years before he wrote *The Origin of the Species*, and while Charles Darwin was not on board when the ship came into this mangrove-lined inlet, Stokes named it after his longtime friend.

Already Britain had tried to establish a base in northern Australia, but each and every one had failed, the most spectacular being the settlement

The Darwin Crocodile Farm

at Port Essington on the Cobourg Peninsula which lasted just over 10 years from 1838. In 1863 Escape Cliff, near the mouth of the Adelaide River, was established and abandoned four years later. Just a couple of years on, in 1869, Port Darwin, officially called Palmerston but the name never really caught on, was established.

Darwin's Parliament House at night

A year later the construction of the Overland Telegraph Line between Darwin and Adelaide began and this was the real start of the city. With the discovery of gold at Pine Creek 200 km south of Darwin, over 7000 Chinese and a handful of Europeans streamed through the port on their way to the diggings. A railway line south to the fields brought more workers from India and Malaya, while the port also attracted pearlers with

their crews of Japanese and islanders. By the early 1900s the port was more Asian than European.

In World War II Darwin became Australia's front line, suffering greatly from the Japanese bombing raids, as well as becoming the headquarters for the Allied effort to the north.

During the late 1940s to the early 1960s the city was more a frontier town with crocodile shooters, buffalo shooters, pioneer cattlemen and other 'wild west' characters calling it home. In 1974 Cyclone Tracy devastated the town, killing 64 people and injuring thousands. It was the rebirth of the city, with a huge redevelopment occurring soon afterwards. With the regeneration, much of the old character was lost, traffic lights appeared and the city took on its modern appearance.

For travellers and visitors there is a host of things to do in and around the city. For those who enjoy looking into the past and admiring fine old architecture, there are the old Town Hall and Government House (1883), old Court House and Police Station (1884) and Hotel Darwin, originally called the Palmerston (1883). As well, a wander around the Fannie Bay Gaol, a registered heritage site and in use from 1883 until 1979, gives visitors an insight into the penal system and the conditions endured by its prisoners.

There are also many reminders of World War II, such as the Oil Storage Tunnels (some open to the public), the anti-submarine boom net tower and the East Point gun emplacements, to name just a few.

The Museum and Art Gallery of the Northern Territory is a must for any visitor, with displays covering just about every aspect of the Territory, its history and art. The Australian Aviation Centre has an impressive display of Territory aviation history and is dominated by a US Air Force B52 bomber. The Australian Pearling Exhibition and the Indo-Pacific Marine facility can both be found down at the Wharf Precinct, while Lyons Cottage, built in 1925 to house workers from the Australian Telegraph Company, has a marvellous collection of old photographs.

For those who love to wander around local markets there is quite a few to choose from in Darwin. A stroll around the Mindil Beach Sunset Market, with its local and regional handicrafts and food stalls is popular, as is the Parap Market. Darwin's oldest market is the Rapid Creek Markets, held every Sunday morning, and food lovers will be overwhelmed by the choices from the many Asian and Australian food stalls.

The rich cultural heritage of Darwin means that there are a wide variety of restaurants to enjoy in the city including Asian, Chinese, Mongolian, Greek, Latin American and original Australian with buffalo, camel, barra, mud crabs and more on the menu.

The city also makes a fine base from which to experience many of the delights of the Top End, most of which are within an easy hour or two's drive. There are the Darwin Crocodile Farm and the Territory Wildlife Park, and the delightful Windows on the Wetlands, on the Arnhem Highway, 60 km south-east of Darwin. A little further along the highway are the jumping crocodiles of the Adelaide River. Now if you want to see a croc up close, this is the spot!

Of course there is more, including the Marrakai and Fogg Dam Conservation Reserves with their waterbirds, and the Wildman and Shady Camp Reserves which are well-known fishing spots. Offshore and reached by boat or aircraft are the Tiwi Aboriginal islands of Bathurst and Melville. There is a great cultural experience to be had on the islands and tours are regularly run from Darwin. The fishing, as is to be expected, is brilliant. There are plenty of places to throw a line in and you can be lucky enough to catch barra almost everywhere. Close to the port there are a number of wrecks that act as artificial reefs and around the area you will find barra, cod and black jewfish, as well as tuna, queenfish and Spanish mackerel.

Special annual events include the Corroboree Park Challenge fishing competition in April, the Top End Country Music Festival in May, the Top End Camp Draft and Rodeo in May/June, the Royal Darwin Show in July, the Saltwater Festival and Darwin Cup Carnival in July, the famous Darwin Beer Can Regatta and the Festival of Darwin in August. The Darwin Symphony Orchestra also performs on numerous occasions throughout the year with special evening concerts.

ACCOMMODATION

CBD: The Beaufort Darwin, ph (08) 8980 0800; All Seasons Frontier Darwin, ph (08) 8981 5333; Poinciana Inn Motel, ph (08) 8981 8111; Metro Inn Darwin, ph (08) 8981 1544; Tiwi Lodge Motel, ph (08) 8981 6471; City Gardens Holiday Units, ph (08) 8941 2888; Palms Caravan Park, Darwin, ph (08) 8932 1202

North: Coconut Grove Holiday Apartments, ph (08) 8985 0500; Darwin Phoenix Motel, Nightcliff, ph (08) 8985 4144; Coolibah Holiday Units, Nightcliff, ph (08) 8985 4166; Comfort Inn Paravista, Parap, ph (08) 8981 9200; Stuart Park Holiday Apartments, ph (08) 8981 6408

North-west: Seabreeze Motel, Fannie Bay, ph (08) 8981 8433; MGM Grand Darwin, The Gardens, ph (08) 8943 8888; Botanic Gardens Apartments, The Gardens, ph (08) 8946 0300

South-east: Darwin Boomerang Motel & Caravan Park, Virginia, ph (08) 8983 1202; La Escondida Homestead B&B, McMinns Lagoon, ph (08) 8988 1598; Howard Springs Caravan Park, Howard Springs, ph (08) 8983 1169; Overlander Caravan Park, Berrimah, ph (08) 8984 3025

East: Leprechaun Motel & Caravan Park, Winnellie, ph (08) 8984 3400

West: Banyan View Lodge, Larrakeyah, ph (08) 8981 8644; Coolalinga Caravan Tourist Resort, Winnellie, ph (08) 8983 1026; Shady Glen Caravan Park, Winnellie, ph (08) 8984 3330

TOURIST INFORMATION: Ph (08) 8981 4300

A corroboree on a beach in Darwin

KAKADU NATIONAL PARK

Kakadu National Park is not only Australia's biggest national park measuring almost 20 000 sq km, but is unquestionably one of the country's national treasures.

MAP REFERENCE: PAGE 260 F4

LOCATION: 147 KM SOUTH-EAST OF DARWIN

BEST TIME: APRIL TO OCTOBER

MAIN ATTRACTIONS: WORLD HERITAGE LISTED, SCENIC GORGES, WATERFALLS, WETLANDS, BUSHWALKING, FISHING, PHOTOGRAPHY, BIRDWATCHING, ABORIGINAL ROCK ART, CAMPING

RANGER HEADQUARTERS: BOWALI VISITOR CENTRE, PHONE (08) 8938 1100

ACCOMMODATION: SEE TOWN LISTING FOR JABIRU

Towering over the park's wetlands is the huge 500 km long Arnhem Land escarpment which was created about 2 billion years ago. This ancient landscape will leave you with a feeling of majesty and awe. Its natural geological features, including rock formations, powerful waterways, towering cliffs, spectacular waterfalls and quiet, peaceful streams and lagoons, as well as its diverse wildlife, and unique plant life, together with some of the country's best Aboriginal art galleries, add up to a truly magnificent area.

The value of Kakadu's treasures is also reflected in the park's World Heritage listing, awarded for both cultural and natural significance.

Access

From Darwin go south along the Stuart Highway for 40 km, then turn east onto the Arnhem Highway for a further 107 km to the western park boundary. Soon after entering the park the road leads to the park entrance station manned by rangers. An entry fee applies and your permit is valid for 14 days (or multiple entries to the park within the 14 day period).

When coming from the south, turn off the Stuart Highway 90 km north of Katherine at Pine Creek. It is then 59 km to the park boundary; 6 km into the park you reach the southern entrance station where you can obtain your 14 day permit, maps and information notes on the park.

History

A large portion of this magnificent park in the Top End of the Northern Territory is owned by Aboriginal people (the Gagudju Association) who have maintained strong personal and spiritual links with these traditional lands for at least 60 000 years.

Kakadu's Aboriginal rock art sites are of world significance, and Ubirr Rock has been added in its own right to the World Heritage listing for its cultural, anthropological and archaeological value. Ubirr Rock, together with the other significant art sites in the park at Nourlangie, Nanguluwur and Anbangbang, give the whole area an historical aura unmatched anywhere else in the country. The many art galleries found in the park on cliffs, rock faces and in large natural rock shelters, record Aboriginal history, culture and beliefs. They also record the visits of Macassans who came from the north to fish, gather trepangs and search for pearls. Visits by the Dutch, and later the British, shown with their ships, axes and firearms, all feature in Kakadu's ochre art galleries.

The East Alligator, South Alligator and West Alligator Rivers were named in 1818 by surveyor Phillip Parker King, who mistook the many crocodiles he saw on the river banks for alligators. Ludwig Leichhardt, leader of the first land-based expedition to the area, was the first

The rugged, ancient landscape of Kakadu

European to stand on the Arnhem Land escarpment. This happened during his 15 month trek from Moreton Bay in Queensland in 1845.

The first stage of Kakadu National Park was proclaimed in 1979, and in 1981 it was World Heritage listed. The park was subsequently extended in various stages and now occupies 19 799 sq km. The park is managed by a specially selected board on which the traditional owners sit.

Within the park boundaries special title exclusions apply to the Ranger, Jabiluka and Koongarra mineral leases.

Today Kakadu draws visitors from around Australia and, indeed, all around the world, at a rate of well over 200 000 people every year. Most come in the dry season, from April to October, when the climate is almost perfect for exploring. For those few who come during the Wet and are prepared to put up with the heat and humidity, some of the rewards on offer are even more spectacular—the waterfalls flow strongly, the billabongs are full, the area is lush and green. In contrast, by late in the dry season, much of the bushland is tinder dry and grass fires, lit in the park as part of its management control system, have blackened much of the bushland area. Roads to some of the more remote attractions may, however, be flooded and impassable during the Wet.

MAIN ATTRACTIONS

Kakadu has some splendid bushwalks leading off from car parks (as well as other cross-country treks) usually incorporating one of the park's many attractions, such as art sites, waterfalls and billabongs. Some tracks are accessible only by 4WD.

Fishing, birdwatching, photography, exploring and swimming are only some of the activities at Kakadu. To see and enjoy the park properly, allow at least 4 or 5 days. Take insect repellent, a hat and good comfortable walking gear.

The following are some of the park's most interesting areas.

Bowali Visitor Centre and Park Headquarters
Located on the edge of Jabiru on the Kakadu Highway, this provides everything you need to know about the park. In addition, local souvenirs, Aboriginal art, as well as displays on the park, all make this an ideal starting off place for your Kakadu visit. Guided walks around most of the park's main art sites, some led by experienced Aboriginal guides, are held daily.

Jabiru
This centre is Kakadu's residential hub. The town, originally built for workers from the Ranger Uranium Mine, also houses many of the park employees. Fuel, supplies, a post office, supermarket, a wide range of services and accommodation (including the famous Gagudju Crocodile Hotel) are all available here. The airport is 6 km east of town, on the way to the mine. From here you can take scenic flights over Kakadu and the Arnhem Land escarpment. The Ranger Uranium Mine is 4 km further on.

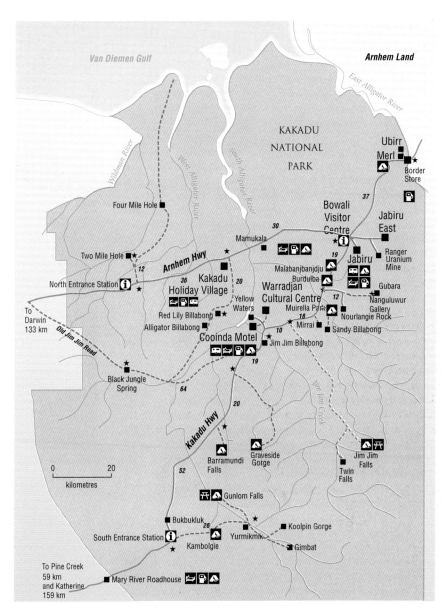

Royalties from the mine have been used by the Gagudju Association to fund the building of the Crocodile Hotel and other ventures within the park. Tours of the mine are conducted regularly.

Art Sites
UBIRR: 3 km north of the Border Store (which has fuel and supplies) is Ubirr. It is some 40 km from Jabiru and is where the main road crosses the East Alligator River into Arnhem Land (which is accessible only with a permit). Ubirr, reached by sealed road on this side of the river, is one of the main accessible art sites in the park, including by wheelchair. A 1 km, easy walking circuit trail leads from the car park.

There are various art styles here, including the stick-like Mimi figures, some estimated to be up to 20 000 years old, but the more recent, dramatic, X-ray style is the most striking.

Whilst at Ubirr, climb to the top of the rocky escarpment for splendid views out over the Kakadu countryside. You will also get a panoramic vista over the nearby billabongs of the Arnhem wetlands and the huge Arnhem Land escarpment which lies across the East Alligator River.

BARDEDJILIDJI: The upstream picnic area near the Border Store is where the boat ramps are located. Here you will also find the start of the highly recommended Bardedjilidji Sandstone Walk, which covers 2.5 km. An easy walk, the trail wanders through tall, tropical grasses, amongst oddly shaped sandstone outcrops. You will also encounter tall termite mounds, pandanus, fig and native peach trees, and pass under rocky overhangs where you will see more good examples of Aboriginal art.

NOURLANGIE ROCK: 19 km south of the visitor centre are the Nourlangie Rock and Anbangbang rock shelter, art sites of great significance to the traditional owners. Nourlangie is the anglicised version of the Aboriginal word Nawurlandja. The main circuit trail of 1.5 km is a relatively easy stroll of about one hour—most of it is accessible by wheelchair. The main galleries here include some excellent artwork with signboards explaining the figures and the stories behind them.

The paintings along the rock face of Anbangbang were painted by Nayombolmi, also known as Barramundi Charlie, in 1964. Other paintings in this area date back to much earlier times. The paintings are of Namonjok, a dangerous spirit, and Namarrgon, the Lightning Man. On the other side of the Anbangbang billabong and also part of Nawurlandja are the famous Blue paintings. These paintings, which date from the early 1960s, are unusual in their innovative use of Reckitt's laundry blue.

Much repainting has taken place both here and at Ubirr, with some of the much older, faded works seen underneath the more recent art. Repainting at Aboriginal sites was a traditional practice.

To the north of Nourlangie Rock is the Koongarra Saddle, from where there is a pleasant 3 km walk to the crystal clear Dubara pools.

There is an excellent extended bushwalk linking Nourlangie and Nanguluwur art sites. This involves some fairly strenuous climbing, so you need to be quite fit. You should allow between 6 and 8 hours for the return walk. It is important that you sign in with the rangers, and sign out again on your return. The rangers can provide a trail map.

NANGULUWUR GALLERY WALK: This easy, 3.4 km return walk—allow 1½–2 hours—through flat, open woodlands is on the western side of Nourlangie Rock and leads to one of the most interesting galleries in Kakadu. Its walls are like pages in a history book illustrating aspects of the lives of Aboriginal people from ancient to modern times. In these protected rock shelters evidence of meals of fish, mussels, turtles and wallabies has been found. This was their living room and dining room area.

Jim Jim Falls and Twin Falls

These falls are spectacular in the wet season when water thunders over the top of the Arnhem escarpment and plummets 200 metres to the creek below. The pool at the bottom is cold, but ideal to cool off in or to enjoy an invigorating swim. The falls are usually reduced to not much more than a trickle as the dry season progresses. Camping is allowed at Jim Jim where toilets, BBQs and tables are provided. Access to this area is suitable for 4WD vehicles only.

For a great day trip only (no camping), a visit to the nearby Twin Falls is thoroughly recommended. The mostly sandy 10 km track from Jim Jim is slow and winding and will take about an hour in a 4WD vehicle. On reaching the end of the trail at one of the creek's white sandy beaches, it's

Aboriginal cave drawing depicting the arrival of Europeans

then into the water—take an inflatable mattress for a great paddle (about 1 km) towards the falls. Look up at the rock faces as you make your way upstream. There are a few rocks to cross over before you reach a lovely sandy beach and the huge, clear, natural splash pool at the foot of the falls.

Yellow Waters

Located virtually in the centre of the park, Yellow Waters is a magnificent billabong on the South Alligator River. A boardwalk extending several hundred metres along the edge of this picturesque waterway is a must for birdwatchers. Boat cruises on this beautiful stretch of water are popular, and you can also watch for crocodiles and fish for barramundi.

Camping is not allowed here, but just 1 km away is the Cooinda Motel which has motel, caravan and camping facilities, as well as food, general supplies and fuel.

Also located here is the Warradjan Aboriginal Cultural Centre. This excellent centre gives a good insight into local Aboriginal culture with artefacts and locally produced works of art available for sale.

Barramundi Falls and Maguk

Further south in the park, the Barramundi Falls are the next place to stop. The 4WD track leads 12 km to a small waterfall which tumbles down through the sandstone escarpment into a large, clear pool at the bottom. There are some lovely swimming spots with sandy beaches along the trail to the falls. Camping is allowed here at Maguk but there are no facilities.

Gunlom Falls

The Gunlom Falls are in the southern section of the park, 37 km off the main Kakadu Highway. The conventional vehicle access road leads to a pretty grassed picnic area with the falls and its large, sandy bottomed, plunge pool only around 100 metres away. The walk trail to the falls is suitable for wheelchair access. This is a particularly appealing picnic and swimming spot (great also for children) with several different walk trails. When the Waterfall Creek is in flood, the 70-metres-high Gunlom Falls are indeed a splendid sight.

Fully recommended for those of reasonable fitness is a walk and climb trail to the top of the falls. Allow ½ hour to reach the top. Here there are several small, appealing rockpools in which to cool off. You can take in the sweeping view from the escarpment, out over the Kakadu countryside, and more immediately, down to the large pandanus-lined splash pool at the foot of the falls. Ludwig Leichhardt is reputed to have stood at this very spot during his epic overland journey in 1845.

The camping facilities are good here.

Wildlife

Wallabies, euros, wild black pigs, and even the occasional wild Timor pony are found in the park, as are crocodiles.

Many varieties of large waterbirds, including egrets and jabirus, brolgas, as well as many grass and bushland species of birds, can be seen in Kakadu. A total of over 300 species of birds has been recorded.

Camping

Kakadu offers some superb camping experiences —often near waterfalls, billabongs, or with rocky escarpment outlooks. They range from caravan parks (including those at Jabiru and Cooinda), to several formal camping areas also quite suitable for caravans at Merl (near Ubirr), Muirella Park (between Jabiru and Yellow Waters), Mardugal (near Yellow Waters) and at Gunlom Falls. These areas are all equipped with showers, flushing toilets and water, and have facilities for the disabled. A camping fee is charged at these spots. A free camping area with pit toilets only, and quite suitable for caravans, is Malabanjbanjdju (13 km south of Jabiru).

Throughout the park there are a number of other, less developed, tent camping areas, most with toilets, BBQs, but not showers. There are some in more remote locations with no facilities at all. Your park permit allows you to camp in these less developed areas at no extra charge.

In addition to camp sites there are day picnic areas located near many of the main attractions throughout the park, most with BBQs and tables.

WARNING

Dangerous estuarine (saltwater or 'salty') crocodiles inhabit a number of the Kakadu waterways. Do not go into, and be very careful near, the water in these areas—look out for the crocodile warning signs. Many of the popular swimming holes are safe, but if in doubt, check with the local rangers.

THE KAKADU TREK

This trek guides you round the major features of Kakadu National Park which are dealt with in greater detail above.

Two Mile Hole, Four Mile Hole and West Alligator Head

Almost 18 km from the park entrance, take a signposted track to the left. This track winds for 12 km through eucalypt forest with occasional sand-ridges to Two Mile Hole. There is a shady camp site beside the waterhole, but no facilities; water from the billabong should be boiled before use. Two Mile Hole offers boat access and good fishing, particularly for barramundi.

It is a further 26 km to Four Mile Hole (**GPS** 12°33'53"S, 132°14'26"E), first through forest, then open plain. When you pass a large swamp, watch out for the jacana bird, with a red crest and very long legs and toes, which

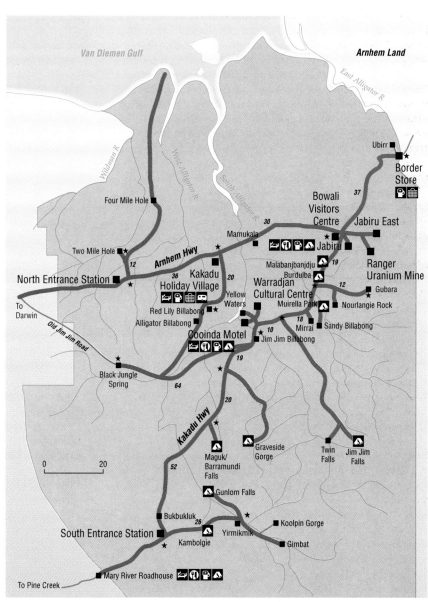

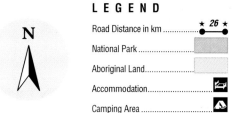

cannot only walk on the water but even builds its nest on a platform of floating leaves. Four Mile Hole is very scenic and a popular fishing spot, but again the camping area has no facilities and there is not much shade. Saltwater crocodiles are prevalent in these waterholes, so do not swim.

You are now in 4WD country. The track continues across plains and mangrove swamps for 43 km, to the head of the West Alligator River (**GPS** 12°10'21"S, 132°13'55"E). This is the only track in the park that goes to the sea; there are no facilities but you can beach camp. Watch for sandflies.

Red Lily Billabong and Alligator Billabong

Return to the Arnhem Highway, turn left and travel 36 km. Turn right here and follow the 4WD track south for 20 km, then take a turn-off on the left to Red Lily Billabong (**GPS** 12°49'55"S, 132°28'38"E), a pleasant spot with lots of bird life and crocodiles. Do not camp close to the water's edge! There is boating and fishing for barramundi—definitely no swimming. A few fireplaces are provided, but otherwise it is bush camping with mosquitoes!

Backtrack the short distance to where you turned left, and turn left again towards Alligator Billabong with two very interesting water crossings on the way. There are good camping sites, a boat ramp and plenty of firewood at Alligator Billabong, but also very large crocodiles.

Continuing south-west, the track winds across open plains and through remnant rainforest pockets to its junction with the Old Jim Jim Road (also called the Old Darwin Road) (**GPS** 13°08'13"S, 132°16'00"E). You may see wild Timor ponies and any number of black feral pigs.

At the Old Jim Jim Road, turn right and drive 24 km to Black Jungle Spring (**GPS** 13°02'00"S, 132°07'19"E). This spring, the headwaters of a tributary of the South Alligator, is a pleasant camp site, but has no facilities.

Return eastwards to the low level South Alligator River crossing, just east of where you first met the Old Jim Jim Road. From here it is about 40 km on to Cooinda Motel and Yellow Waters. Alternatively, you can return along the Red Lily Billabong track to the Arnhem Highway and Kakadu Village, which has all the amenities of a small resort. Tours can be arranged from here, or it can be used as a base to explore the area.

Just 2 km east of Kakadu Village, the Arnhem Highway crosses the mighty South Alligator River. This river, whose headwaters are high up in the Arnhem Land escarpment, is tidal for 120 km, well upstream of the road bridge, and the outgoing tide flows at 10 knots. The South Alligator is popular for barramundi fishing, but crocodiles pose a threat for the unwary. Cruise vessels once plied the river, but continuously shifting sandbanks made it hazardous and finally unworkable. Near the road bridge there are picnic tables, toilets and a boat ramp.

Merl, Ubirr, the Border Store and Cahills Crossing

From the South Alligator bridge, continue east along the Arnhem Highway. About 7 km on, near a car park, is the short but informative Mamukala Nature Walk. About 30 km further on, a turn-off on the left heads north-west to the Ubirr art site. This sealed road takes you past the Magela Swamp (home to thousands of waterbirds but closed to the public), Jabiluka Billabong and Mineral Lease (also closed), and rocky outliers which form the western edge of the Arnhem Land escarpment, to the road crossing of the East Alligator River and the border of the Arnhem Land Aboriginal Reserve (which you need a permit to enter).

After 39 km you come to the Merl caravan and camping area; close by is the Border Store which sells basic foods, soft drinks, souvenirs, diesel and unleaded petrol. At nearby Cahills Crossing of the East Alligator River picnic tables and two boat ramps are provided, and three bushwalking tracks start from here. Once again, observe the crocodile warnings.

From the Border Store, a sealed road takes you 3 km north to Ubirr rock art site, one of the main accessible art sites within the park.

Backtrack to the Arnhem Highway and turn left (east) towards Jabiru, which is just a few kilometres further on.

Aboriginal art gallery in Kakadu

Jabiru and Bowali Visitor Centre

The town of Jabiru was built to accommodate workers at the nearby Ranger Uranium Mine; initially it was to be a closed mining town, but tourism has brought a shopping centre, post office, service station and caravan park, and the Crocodile Hotel, built to the form of a stylistic crocodile. Legend has it that Ginga the giant crocodile, totem to the Gagudju people, who came from the sea at the beginning of the Dreamtime, was responsible for creating all the rocky outcrops. One day, however, when Ginga was in the shape of a man, he caught fire and had to rush towards the river to cool off. When he reached the water he turned into a crocodile. At night when the lights come on, the eyes of the Crocodile Hotel light up.

From Jabiru head back west along the Arnhem Highway, then turn left (south) onto the Kakadu Highway; just 2 km on is the park headquarters and the Bowali Visitor Centre, which gives an insight into both natural and cultural aspects of Kakadu National Park.

The Malabanjbanjdju camping area, 13 km south from the visitor centre along the Kakadu Highway, has facilities for caravans and campers as well as fireplaces and toilets; but no drinking water or swimming. A few kilometres further on is the Burdulba camping area, for tent camping only. It has fireplaces and toilets, but there is no tap water and no swimming.

Between Malabanjbanjdju and Burdulba camping areas is the Iligadjarr Walk; this 3.8 km walking trail across a grassy floodplain and wooded areas offers an opportunity to view waterbirds—you may even see a crocodile.

Continue south-west along the Kakadu Highway 19 km from the visitor centre to a road junction on the left, leading to Nourlangie Rock, one of the park's most important art galleries.

Muirella Park and Sandy Billabong

Returning to the Kakadu Highway, turn left and drive 7 km to the Muirella Park turn-off; 6 km along this sealed road is Muirella Park, with sites for caravans with and without generators. This pleasant camping area has toilets, showers, facilities for the disabled and tap water. There is also a boat ramp. It offers good opportunities for fishing or relaxing. A nature walk along a guided track begins and ends at the park.

A further 6 km along a 4WD track from Muirella Park is Sandy Billabong (**GPS** 12°54'00"S, 132°46'17"E), with a variety of bird life and aquatic plants. Fireplaces have been provided for bush camping, but there are no other facilities.

Back on the Kakadu Highway, head south-west a short distance to Mirrai Lookout. A walk of about 1½ hours return takes you to the top of the hill for a magnificent view of the central part of Kakadu.

Jim Jim Falls and Twin Falls

About 13 km south from Mirrai, the road to the Arnhem Land escarpment turns off. This track was intended to give 2WD access, but when reopened after the Wet it quickly deteriorates into corrugations and long stretches of thick bulldust and can be hazardous even in a 4WD. It is 60 km to Jim Jim Falls (**GPS** 13°16'35"S, 132°49'04"E) and a further 10 km to Twin Falls. The 60 km journey should take around 2 hours.

During the wet season Jim Jim Falls (no one knows where the name originated) thunders over the top of the escarpment, but with a relatively small catchment area, by July it is merely a trickle. It is however a pleasant walk to the pool at the bottom of the falls, which probably has the coldest water in the Northern Territory.

To get to Twin Falls (for day visits only) you have to cross Jim Jim Creek: take care when crossing as it can be over a metre deep. The next 10 km along a sandy track wind to the foot of the escarpment. It is a short walk from the car park to the creek. From the creek's white sandy beaches the only access to the falls is by water. Take an inflatable mattress and paddle to the falls.

Cooinda Motel, Yellow Waters and Jim Jim Billabong

Cooinda Motel is located 4 km off the Kakadu Highway and 6 km from the Jim Jim Falls turn-off. Just a short walk away is the famous Yellow Waters Billabong on the South Alligator River which has boat cruises to view the wildlife that inhabits these waters.

Back on the Kakadu Highway, a track opposite the turn-off to Cooinda leads 6 km to Jim Jim Billabong; there is bush camping, with toilets provided. The fishing is good, but there is no swimming.

Mardugal and Graveside Gorge

Close to Cooinda, with its sealed access road 2 km south of the Cooinda turn-off, is the Mardugal camping area. It caters for caravans and tents; it has showers, toilets, tap water and facilities for the disabled, but again there is no swimming.

Continuing south-west along Kakadu Highway, the road soon becomes unsealed and just over 8 km from the Cooinda turn-off the Old Jim Jim Road veers off to the right. Veer left here, and 26 km from the Cooinda turn-off a rough 4WD track on the left heads for Graveside Gorge, 44 km away. This gorge represents the beginning of the southern part of Kakadu National Park, the traditional land of the Jawoyn people. The camping area is close to the gorge, which winds quite a long way up into the escarpment. Despite its name, Graveside Gorge (**GPS** 13°15'06"S, 132°34'22"E) is a nice quiet place to relax.

Maguk and Barramundi Falls

Backtrack to the Kakadu Highway and turn left. The next track off to the left (4WD only), 46 km south of the Cooinda turn-off, leads to Maguk camping area (no facilities) and Barramundi Falls. This small waterfall tumbles through a series of weathered sandstone formations, then drops down into a large clear pool. It is possible to swim to the falls and climb up and along the weathered rocks. Be careful, though, as a rather large resident freshwater crocodile lives in this pool; freshwater crocodiles are generally harmless and shy, but if you corner one inadvertently it may bite.

Continue along the Kakadu Highway for another 32 km south of the Barramundi Falls track. On the left is the lofty Bukbukluk Lookout. Picnic tables are provided but no camping is allowed.

Gunlom Falls and Gimbat

Now it is 8 km to the Gunlom Falls Road, again on the left. Along this road, you pass Kambolgie camping area, a bush camping site beside a creek but there are no facilities.

From the Yirmikmik car park a number of walks can be taken: a 2 km return walk to Small Gorge (Plumtree Falls), 5 km return to Yirmikmik Lookout, 8 km return to Motor Car Falls, 11 km return to Kurrundie Falls. Camping permits are required if you wish to camp.

Continue along this road to a Y-junction. Left takes you 11 km to Gunlom Falls, where you can camp: there are hot showers and toilets. Right takes you 12 km into Gimbat day use picnic area.

The Gimbat picnic area is set along the upper reaches of the South Alligator River, a short way from the Old Gimbat Station Homestead.

This is the end of the track to the east in Kakadu. Right at this point is the controversial Coronation Hill. The mining giant BHP wanted to mine gold and platinum here. But the traditional owners of the land, the Jawoyn people, believe that this is Sickness country guarded by the spirit Bula. If the earth is disturbed a great sickness will overcome all who have entered this area. After an investigation, the Federal Government placed a 50-year ban on mining in the area. Other considerations were that cyanide residue from mining operations could leak into the South Alligator River floodplain and destroy the delicately balanced ecosystems.

Return to the Y-junction, turn right, and 6 km on, after crossing the shallow waters of the South Alligator River, a track heads off to the left. The next 8 km to Koolpin Gorge will take an hour to drive as the track is not maintained. The camping area is located away from the creek and to collect water you have to walk a short distance. Koolpin Gorge (**GPS** 13°20'22"S, 132°34'48"E) is a pretty spot and worth exploring. Permits, available from the ranger station, are required to camp in this area.

Backtrack to the main road and turn left onto the Kakadu Highway and go south to exit the park at the Mary River. From Gimbat it is 43 km to the park's southern entrance and ranger station, and a further 6 km to the Mary River and the park boundary. Beyond the park boundary lies the Mary River Roadhouse, and 59 km on you come to Pine Creek and the Stuart Highway. Turn right for Darwin (230 km), or left for Katherine (90 km). This is the end of the Kakadu Trek, and from here the remainder of the Northern Territory and its 4WD tracks are waiting for you.

Ubirr, one of the main accessible art sites in Kakadu National Park

ADELAIDE RIVER

119 KM SOUTH OF DARWIN
POPULATION: 370 MAP REF: PAGE 260 D5

Just over an hour's drive south of Darwin, the
township of Adelaide River, on a stream of the same
name, is a popular stopover for travellers. There is a
lot to see and do, with several museums such as the
Motor Cycle Haven and the Adelaide River Railway
Station, as well as a number of World War II sites,
including the War Cemetery and the large
ammunition depot at Snake Gully.

The township played an important role during
World War II: after the bombing raid on Darwin in
February 1942, Adelaide River became the centre of
military activity as the Australian and American
headquarters were relocated there, along with
camps, hospitals, airfields and army supply depots.

Back in the early 1880s the town site became an
overnight stop for the miners heading to the Pine
Creek goldfields, and so it continued when the rail
arrived later that same decade.

Today the town offers easy access to the delights
of Litchfield National Park and the Daly River and
there is good fishing in the nearby streams and rivers.

Annual events include the Adelaide River Show,
rodeo, campdraft and gymkhana which are held in
June, along with the Country Race Meeting and
Country Music Festival.

Railway Station Museum in Adelaide River

ACCOMMODATION: Adelaide River Inn,
ph (08) 8976 7037; Mt Bundy Station, ph (08) 8976 7009;
Adelaide River Show Society Caravan Park,
ph (08) 8976 7032; Shady River Caravan Park,
ph (08) 8976 7047
ACTIVITIES: Fishing, national park access, scenic
drives, swimming
TOURIST INFORMATION: Ph (08) 8981 4300

ALICE SPRINGS

1513 KM SOUTH OF DARWIN
POPULATION: 27 520 MAP REF: PAGE 265 H6

Located almost in the centre of the continent, Alice
Springs is to many the epitome of the 'Red Centre',
gaining international fame as one of the places to
visit in Australia.

Alice Springs is located at the very foot of the
rugged MacDonnell Ranges, near Heavitree Gap,
where the Todd River has cut its way through this

The Alice Springs Rodeo

rocky barrier and gives access through the range. It
began life as a repeater station on the Overland
Telegraph Line in 1871. The station takes its name
from the spring, or waterhole, in the bed of the Todd
River, close to the original telegraph station, which
was named after Alice, the wife of the Superintendent
of Telegraphs, Charles Todd. These stations, the first
European buildings in Central Australia, are now an
excellent museum, and are located just a short
distance north of the town centre.

Initially the town was called Stuart, after the great
explorer who blazed a way north across the continent
in 1860–61, and while his route passed through
another gap in the range a little to the west, it is on
the whole his route that the telegraph line and the
original railway line followed.

Cattle stations were taken up in this region in the
1870s and a police station was soon located here. In
1887 gold was found at Arltunga, 130 km east of the
telegraph station. At its height, this small outpost
supported over 400 people, making it the biggest
enclave of Europeans in the Centre, and most of those
followed the telegraph line to Alice before pushing
into the more remote, harsh country further east.

Between 1926 and 1931 the separate territory of
Central Australia was formed, and its administrative
centre was Alice. In 1929 the railway finally arrived
from the south and soon after the name of the town
was officially changed to Alice Springs. As a railhead,
a position it still enjoys today, the town grew as a
major supply centre, not only to the outlying cattle
stations but also to the rest of the Territory. During
World War II the Stuart Highway north to Darwin was
bituminised as part of the war effort to supply the
thousands of troops in the Top End.

In the 1950s a novel by Neville Shute, *A Town Like
Alice*, along with the subsequent film and TV show,
brought wide acclaim to this remote town, and really
started the tourist industry on which much of the
town now bases its economy.

The town and the surrounds have much to offer. In
the centre of Alice Springs are the historic buildings
of the old town gaol (1909), Adelaide House (1926)
designed by the Reverend John Flynn (founder of the

Royal Flying Doctor Service, which was established
here in 1939 and still operates from near here), and
the old Hartley Street School (1930), the first school
in the region.

Within a few kilometres from the centre of town
are the buildings and pleasant surrounds of the old
Telegraph Station, the Strehlow Research Centre
with its great Aboriginal cultural display, the
stunning displays of the Alice Springs Desert Park,
the Transport Heritage Centre and the Central
Australian Museum, to name just a few.

The area is also well endowed with natural
attractions, with the West MacDonnell National Park,
incorporating such well-known attractions as
Standley Chasm, Simpson's Gap, Ormiston Gorge and
Pound and Redbank Gorge. In the eastern
MacDonnells there are the less visited Trephina
Gorge, N'Dhala Gorge, the well established Ross
River homestead, and the well preserved historic site
of the Arltunga goldfields.

Further afield are such international attractions
as Rainbow Valley, Uluru (Ayers Rock), Kings Canyon
and the Simpson Desert.

You can enjoy camel rides, horse rides, balloon
trips and 4WD excursions in and around the local
area, as well as Aboriginal cultural tours that take in
traditional foods, art or Dreaming trails.

When it comes to food, the Alice has a good range
of restaurants to enjoy. You can share your dinner
with a camel, take a balloon ride to breakfast, or
enjoy the friendship of a bush gourmet BBQ. The
Overlander Steakhouse, like a number of eating
places in town, has buffalo, kangaroo, emu, crocodile,
camel, barramundi and more traditional fare on
the menu. There is also a good range of international
cuisine available in the Alice.

There is a host of annual events including
Heritage Week in April; the Central Australian
Country Music Festival in April/May; the Bangtail
Muster, which incorporates a parade of floats down
the Todd Mall in May; the Finke Desert Race,
Australia's fastest desert race for motorcycles and
vehicles, in June; the Alice Springs Show and the
famous Lions Camel Cup in July; the Central

ALICE SPRINGS

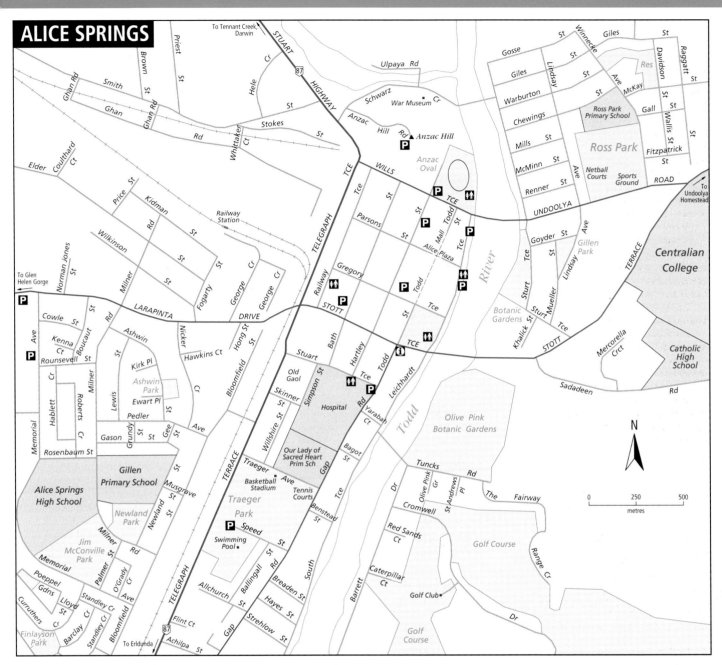

Australian Aboriginal Art and Craft Exhibition in July/August; the Alice Springs Rodeo also in August, while the Henley-On-Todd, the world-famous waterless regatta where 'boats' are run down the sandy bed of the Todd, occurs in September. In October there is the International Cultural Festival, and the Corkwood Festival in November.

ACCOMMODATION: All Seasons Frontier Oasis Motel, ph (08) 8952 1444; Lasseters Hotel Casino, ph (08) 8950 7777; Desert Rose Inn Motel, ph (08) 8952 1411; Heavitree Gap Outback Resort Motel and Caravan Park, ph (08) 8952 4866; MacDonnell Range Caravan Park, ph (08) 8952 6111; Ross River Homestead, ph (08) 8956 9711; Ooraminna Bush Camp & Cattle Station, ph (08) 8953 0170

ACTIVITIES: Ballooning, bowls, bushwalking, camel riding, 4WD touring, golf, horse riding, national park access, scenic drives, swimming

TOURIST INFORMATION: Ph (08) 8952 5800 or 1800 621 336

BARKLY HOMESTEAD

1158 KM SOUTH-EAST OF DARWIN
POPULATION: 10   MAP REF: PAGE 263 L8

Barkly Homestead, 210 km east of Tennant Creek, is located on the Barkly Highway close to the junction with the north–south Tablelands Highway which leads to Cape Crawford and Borroloola on the Gulf.

This small roadhouse, the only sign of habitation on the flat grassy plains of the Barkly Tableland, is the only supply point between Three Ways on the Stuart Highway and Camooweal in Queensland, a distance of 450 km. The roadhouse will meet most of a traveller's requirements, and even has a five hole golf course!

ACCOMMODATION: Barkly Roadhouse Motel and Caravan Park, ph (08) 8964 4549

ACTIVITIES: Birdwatching, golf

TOURIST INFORMATION: Ph (08) 8962 3388

BATCHELOR

106 KM SOUTH OF DARWIN
POPULATION: 650   MAP REF: PAGE 260 D5

Batchelor is a small township 14 km off the Stuart Highway and was once the main town for Rum Jungle, Australia's first uranium mine and one of the largest economic influences on the Top End's development at that time. Uranium was discovered in the area in 1949, and in 1952 the township of Batchelor was established to service the nearby mine site. Today, apart from a couple of jungle-clad and deep man-made lakes, little remains of this mining venture.

The area had been first settled in the late 1800s and up until the 1940s had seen a steady and varying stream of tin miners, Chinese market gardeners and copper prospectors. During World War II the town was an important base and was bombed by the Japanese.

Termite mounds outside Batchelor

Since the closing of the mine in 1963 and the cessation of ore processing in 1971, the town has been a lot quieter, and today is the site of a TAFE college specialising in Aboriginal tourism, as well as an export abattoir.

The big attraction of Batchelor these days is its proximity to Litchfield National Park: it is just 25 minutes driving time to Florence Falls, one of the highlights of this park. The town also offers the closest accommodation to the park.

ACCOMMODATION: Rum Jungle Motor Inn, ph (08) 8976 0123; Batchelor Caravillage, ph (08) 8976 0166; Banyan Tree Caravan Park, ph (08) 8976 0330

ACTIVITIES: Birdwatching, bowls, bushwalking, canoeing, gliding, national park access, scenic drives, sky diving, swimming

TOURIST INFORMATION: Ph (08) 8981 4300

BORROLOOLA

976 KM SOUTH-EAST OF DARWIN
POPULATION: 1450   MAP REF: PAGE 263 M1

Set on the banks of the McArthur River, 80 km inland from the muddy waters of the Gulf of Carpentaria, Borroloola has a rich historical past. Today it serves the fishing and mining industries, along with its traditional role as a service centre for the surrounding pastoral properties.

The town was established as a port in 1885 for the mining camps inland and the pastoral properties on the Barkly Tablelands to the south. It was a wild town with sly-grog shops, and horse and cattle stealing commonplace, inhabited by, as one government official described the locals, 'the scum of the earth'.

The Heritage Walk winds its way through the old town past grave sites, old buildings, and along the McArthur River, and is a good way to explore the town. The old Police Station, now an excellent museum, was constructed in 1886, and is the oldest surviving example of an outpost police station in the Northern Territory.

Cape Crawford, 116 km south-west of Borroloola, is little more than the Heartbreak Hotel/Motel at the junction of the Carpentaria and Tablelands Highways. The small settlement acts as the gateway to the Gulf country and as a base for seeing the amazing Lost City rock formations, which are only accessible via helicopter.

The fishing is the prime attraction of this region, with the river and the Sir Edward Pellew Group of islands just offshore being the main drawcards. The town also acts as a stepping-off point for those 4WD tourers heading across the Gulf Track to Queensland.

The premium social event is the Heartbreak Bushball which takes place in October, while the Borroloola Fishing Classic is held in April and attracts fishing people from all over the Territory and north Queensland. The Borroloola Rodeo, which includes bush races and campdrafting, attracts the crowds in August.

A dry riverbed near Borroloola

ACCOMMODATION: Borroloola Holiday Village, ph (08) 8975 8742; Borroloola Inn, ph (08) 8975 8766; McArthur River Caravan Park, ph (08) 8975 8734; Heartbreak Hotel, ph (08) 8975 9928

ACTIVITIES: Boating, bushwalking, fishing, 4WD touring,

TOURIST INFORMATION: Ph (08) 8972 2650

DALY RIVER

232 KM SOUTH OF DARWIN
POPULATION: 150   MAP REF: PAGE 260 C6

South-west of Adelaide River is the small riverside community of Daly River, which for tourists is to all intents the end of the road, as to the west is the Daly River/Port Keats Aboriginal Land Trust.

A Jesuit mission opened here in 1885 and for a time copper was mined nearby, while a government-

Crossing the Daly River

run smelter operated in the area in the early 1900s.

There is great fishing in the Daly River for barramundi, threadfin salmon, catfish and sooty grunter. For the travelling angler there are a number of fishing lodges, and boats are available for hire.

Aboriginal arts and crafts are available at the Aboriginal art centre, and the area is richly endowed with native flora and fauna. Other attractions include the old Jesuit mission and old mine sites.

Annual events include the Northern Territory Barra Nationals in April, and the Northern Territory Barramundi Classic in May.

ACCOMMODATION: Daly River Pub, ph (08) 8978 2418; Woolianna Tourist Park, ph (08) 8978 2478; Daly River Mango Farm, ph (08) 8978 2464; Perrys on the Daly, ph (08) 8978 2452

ACTIVITIES: Boating, bushwalking, fishing

TOURIST INFORMATION: Ph (08) 8972 2650

DALY WATERS

595 KM SOUTH OF DARWIN
POPULATION: 25   MAP REF: PAGE 262 G2

Located just off the main Stuart Highway, the small hamlet of Daly Waters has been, almost right from the time of first settlement, nothing more than a pub, although after being named by John McDouall Stuart in 1862, it became, in 1871, the site of a repeater station for the Overland Telegraph Line.

Llicensed in 1893, the Daly Waters pub has the distinction of being the oldest hotel in the Territory and was originally a watering hole for the stockmen on the long cattle drive across the Territory from Queensland to the Kimberley in Western Australia.

In 1926 it was a refuelling point for the London to Sydney Air Race, and in the 1930s was an important stopover for QANTAS, while the passengers were given a meal at the pub. During World War II, the airstrip was a refuelling point for the bombers flying north, and today the old aerodrome hangar has been restored by the National Trust and is a museum.

Just to the south of the old town, on the main highway, is the turn-off to Borroloola, and located at the junction of these two highways is the Hi-Way Inn.

The Daly Waters Rodeo, Campdraft and Gymkhana is held every September.

ACCOMMODATION: Daly Waters Hotel & Caravan Park, ph (08) 8975 9927; Hi-Way Inn Motel & Caravan Park, ph (08) 8975 9925
ACTIVITIES: Tennis
TOURIST INFORMATION: Ph (08) 8972 2650

ELLIOTT

740 KM SOUTH OF DARWIN
POPULATION: 430   MAP REF: PAGE 263 H4
Situated approximately halfway between Alice Springs and Darwin on the Stuart Highway is the small township of Elliott. Like many towns and hamlets on this route north, the town started out as a repeater station on the Overland Telegraph Line. During World War II it became a major stopping point and an interim camp for the large numbers of troops and supplies heading north, at which time the road was upgraded from a two-wheel track to a bitumen road. The town is named after a Captain Elliott who was the officer in charge of the camp.

Heading north it is 100 km to the roadhouse at Dunmarra and another 45 km to the Hi-Way Inn at Daly Waters. South, on the long run to Tennant Creek, the only signs of habitation are Renner Springs (92 km south) and Three Ways (226 km south), the latter just 24 km north of Tennant Creek.
ACCOMMODATION: Elliott Hotel, ph (08) 8969 2069; Halfway Caravan Park, ph (08) 8969 2025
ACTIVITIES: Golf
TOURIST INFORMATION: Ph (08) 8972 2650

GEMTREE

1513 KM SOUTH OF DARWIN
POPULATION: 10   MAP REF: PAGE 265 H4
Located 140 km north-east of Alice Springs on the Plenty Highway, Gemtree, as its name suggests, was established purely to look after the growing number of people who come to this part of the Harts Range to look for gemstones. These are some of the richest gem fields in Australia and contain beryl, garnets, iolite and zircons. The caravan park in Gemtree runs regular tours of the fields and fossicking equipment can be hired here, as well as any stones cut and polished. Basic supplies and fuel are also available.

The Plenty Highway, which continues east towards Queensland, becomes a dirt road a short distance beyond Gemtree.
ACCOMMODATION: Gemtree Caravan Park, ph (08) 8956 9855
ACTIVITIES: 4WD touring, gem fossicking
TOURIST INFORMATION: Ph (08) 8952 5800

JABIRU

254 KM EAST OF DARWIN
POPULATION: 1735   MAP REF: PAGE 260 G4
Surrounded by the World Heritage and internationally acclaimed Kakadu National Park, and the subject of a fair amount of controversy, Jabiru is a mining town which was established in 1981 to house

the workers for the uranium mines of Ranger, Jabiluka and Koongarra.

It makes a fine base from which to explore the surrounding park while other resorts, with camping grounds, are located at Cooinda to the south, or on the banks of the South Alligator River to the west.

The town is a modern, sparkling clean mining community that has all the services a traveller requires. The surrounding national park offers some of the finest Aboriginal art sites imaginable, fantastic barra fishing, as well as spectacular scenery and incredible bird life.

Annual events include the Kakadu Barra Bash in March, the Oenpelli Open Day in August, and the Jabiru Wind Festival in August/September.

The wetlands at Jabiru

ACCOMMODATION: Gagudju Crocodile Hotel, ph (08) 8979 2800; All Seasons Frontier Lodge & Caravan Park, ph (08) 8979 2422; Cooinda Motel & Caravan Park, ph (08) 8979 0145; All Seasons Frontier Kakadu Village & Caravan Park, ph (08) 8979 0166
ACTIVITIES: Boating, bowls, fishing, golf, national park access, scenic drives, tennis
TOURIST INFORMATION: Ph (08) 8981 4300

JERVOIS HOMESTEAD

1715 KM SOUTH-EAST OF DARWIN
POPULATION: 15   MAP REF: PAGE 265 L5
Jervois Station, 356 km east of Alice Springs, is one of the newest properties in Central Australia and was originally purchased by the Broad family in the early 1960s. The homestead is situated on the Plenty Highway, and although there is bitumen from Alice Springs east to Gemtree, from there on to the Queensland border the road is graded and unsealed, and a 4WD is recommended.

The homestead store carries limited supplies for travellers. It also has fuel, as well as shower and toilet facilities. It is open during daylight hours, seven days a week.

A unique feature worthy of an inspection is the huge rocket-proof shelter which was built at the homestead during the 1960s. This was to serve as protection from any wayward Blue Streak rockets which were being launched from Woomera in South Australia during that period.
ACCOMMODATION: Camping only, away from the homestead
ACTIVITIES: 4 WD touring, fuel supply, stopover
TOURIST INFORMATION: Ph (08) 8956 6307

KALKARINDJI

779 KM SOUTH-WEST OF DARWIN
POPULATION: 150   MAP REF: PAGE 262 D4
Located on the banks of the Victoria River, 170 km south-west of Top Springs on the Buchanan Highway, this small township was once known as Wave Hill, an outpost of law and order since its early days. It still has a police station, along with a caravan park and service station that dispenses limited supplies, fuel and takeaway food. It is also the spot where the bitumen runs out, and from this point west the road is all dirt.

While travellers use this route through Kalkarindji as they head west to the West Australian border, the other major road junction just east of town is the Lajamanu Road which leads south to the Tanami Road and Rabbit Flat.
ACCOMMODATION: Caravan Park, ph (08) 8975 0788
ACTIVITIES: Fuel, overnight stop
TOURIST INFORMATION: Ph (08) 8972 2650

KATHERINE

321KM SOUTH-EAST OF DARWIN
POPULATION: 11 200   MAP REF: PAGE 260 F8
Katherine is a bustling community on the southern bank of the Katherine River and astride the Stuart Highway, at its junction with the Victoria Highway, the main route to the west. This major Top End town services an area the size of the state of Victoria, and has a multicultural mix which enhances its 'Outback' image. In recent years the town has become a major military centre, with the RAAF Base Tindal, and army units and training areas close by.

The river was named by John McDouall Stuart in 1862 and nine years later the Overland Telegraph Line crossed this major permanent stream at Knotts Crossing, where a store was soon established, selling grog by the gallon! In 1876 Springvale became the first lease to be taken up in the Northern Territory and the homestead, 100 metres from the river, was built three years later. It was the focal point for much of the activity—business and social—in the area for the next few years. The homestead and surrounds, a short distance to the west of the town, are now an idyllic camping ground and resort, with the homestead housing a fine display of memorabilia.

A post office was established in 1883 and that same year the gold rush to Halls Creek in Western Australia saw many hopefuls pass through the town.

In 1902 Mrs Aeneas Gunn arrived in Katherine staying at the Sportsman's Arms Hotel on her way to Elsey Station, 60 km to the south. Her book, *We of the Never Never*, has become a classic.

The railway from Darwin arrived on the north side of the Katherine River, at what became known as Emungalan, in 1917, but it was another six years before the bridge across the river was completed. This ensured the town's growing importance as a railhead for the expanding Vestey's cattle empire that, amongst others, were shipping thousands of head of cattle to the recently established Vestey's Freezing Works in Darwin.

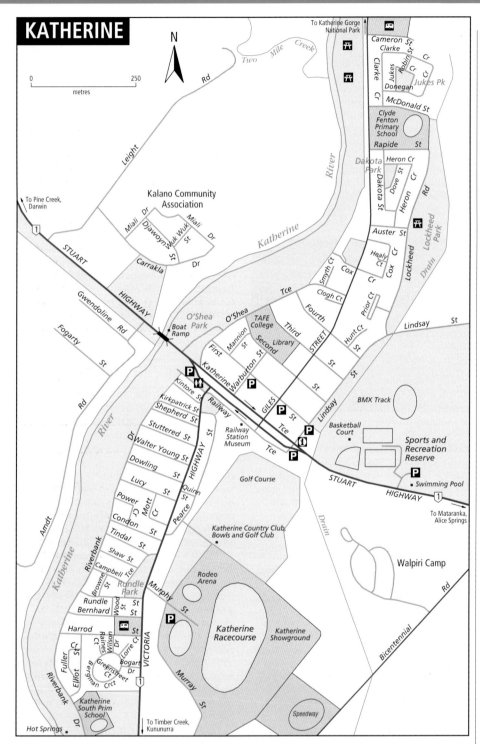

KATHERINE

N

0 _____ 250
metres

To Katherine Gorge
National Park

Two Mile Creek

Cameron
Clarke
Clarke Cr
Robin St
Jukes St
Jukes Pk
Donegan Cr
McDonald St

Clyde
Fenton
Primary
School

Rapide St

Dakota
Park
Heron Cr
Dove St
Heron Cr
Dakota St
Lockheed
Drain Park

Auster St

Healy Ct
Cox Cr
Cox Cr
Smrth Ct
Clogh Ct

Lockheed Rd

Leight Dr

Rd

River

Katherine

Kalano Community
Association

Djawoyn Wuk Wuk St
Miali Dr
Miali Dr

Carrakla Dr

To Pine Creek,
Darwin

STUART

HIGHWAY

Gwendoline Rd

Fogarty St

O'Shea
Park
O'Shea
Boat
Ramp

Mannion St
First St
Second St
Third St
Library
Fourth STREET
St
St
Lindsay St
St

TAFE
College

Tce

Lindsay St

BMX Track

Basketball
Court

Sports and
Recreation
Reserve

Rd

River

Kintore St
Kirkpatrick St
Shepherd St
Stuttered St
Walter Young St
Dowling St
Lucy St
Power St
Condon St
Tindal St
Shaw St
Campbell Tce
Browne St
Rundle
Park
Rundle St
Bernhard St
Harrod St

Katherine St
Warburton St
GILES St

Railway

Railway
Station
Museum

HIGHWAY

Quinn St
Mott Cr
Pearce St

Murphy St

Golf Course

Katherine Country Club,
Bowls and Golf Club

STUART
HIGHWAY

Swimming Pool

To Mataranka,
Alice Springs

Walpiri Camp

Drain

Arndt Rd

Katherine River

Riverbank

Fuller Ct
Elliot Ct
Raines Ct
Wilson Dr
Bergman Ct
Greenstreet Dr
Bogart Ct
Lorre Ct

VICTORIA

Rodeo
Arena

Katherine
Racecourse

Katherine
Showground

Murray St

Bicentennial Rd

Katherine
South Prim
School

Riverbank Dr

Hot Springs

To Timber Creek,
Kununurra

Speedway

Katherine Gorge in Nitmiluk National Park

In World War II the town came under army control, as most of the civilians had been evacuated south, a process that was hurried along when the Japanese bombed the Katherine airfield in March 1942. This caused the road, really a track, south to Alice Springs to be upgraded and bituminised.

After the war a meatworks was established in town and Katherine became a centre for the rapidly expanding roadtrain network. In 1963 the Katherine Gorge National Park was proclaimed setting the town on course to becoming a major tourist centre.

Today Katherine can offer travellers all they require. The town itself has many places of interest, including the historic Springvale Homestead, the Katherine School of the Air, the Katherine Railway Museum and Gallery and the Katherine Museum. The Katherine Hot Springs, and the Katherine Low Level (a small park along the river), are pleasant spots to swim and have a picnic, just on the edge of town.

The major attraction of the town and the area is Katherine Gorge, which lies within the Nitmiluk National Park, 30 km east of town. You can camp out in the park, go on a cruise (which should not be missed), go canoeing, swimming or bushwalking. It really is a spectacular place and there are a number of gorges separated by rock bars and rapids.

A boat ramp is located close to the camping ground (10 hp motors are the maximum allowed), and

there is some excellent fishing in the waters below the gorge and in the first gorge itself.

For walkers there are a number of trails that meander across the rocky tops of the escarpment to the edge of the gorge. For longer, overnight jaunts you need to register with the ranger.

Accessed north of Katherine, but still within the park, is Edith Falls, another very pleasant swimming and walking area.

Further north of town, and west of the small settlement of Pine Creek, is the Umbrawarra Gorge Nature Park, while a little further on is the Tjuwaliyn (Douglas Hot Springs) Nature Park, one of the real delights of the region.

South of the town is the Cutta Cutta Caves Nature Park with its weirdly shaped rock formations and underground caves. Guided tours of the caves are conducted every day and a short walking trail takes people through a typical tropical woodland.

About 120 km north-west of Katherine is the recently proclaimed Flora River National Park which has some spectacular stretches of river backed up behind tall, natural limestone barriers called turfa dams. The river is spring fed and there is good fishing, excellent canoeing, boating and walking along this delightful rainforest-shrouded waterway.

Annual events include the Red Cross Canoe Marathon and horseracing in June; the Katherine Show and the Katherine Campdraft & Rodeo in July; and in the same month the Australian Red Cross Triathlon: swim, cycle, run in the beautiful Nitmiluk National Park.

ACCOMMODATION: All Seasons Frontier Motel & Caravan Park, ph (08) 8972 1744; Knotts Crossing Resort & Caravan Park, ph (08) 8972 2511; Katherine Hotel/Motel, ph (08) 8972 1622; Palm Court Backpackers, ph (08) 8972 2722; Springvale Homestead Tourist Park, ph (08) 8972 1355; Katherine Gorge Caravan Park, ph (08) 8972 1253

ACTIVITIES: Bowls, bushwalking, canoeing, fishing, 4WD touring, golf, horse riding, national park access, water sports

TOURIST INFORMATION: Ph (08) 8972 2650

KULGERA

1762 KM SOUTH OF DARWIN
POPULATION: 25   MAP REF: PAGE 264 G9

A small settlement on the Stuart Highway, just 20 km north of the Northern Territory/South Australia border, Kulgera is little more than a wayside stop for

A museum in an old homestead at Kulgera

travellers. It is 278 km south of Alice Springs and 156 km north of Marla in South Australia.

The town is surrounded by stark rocky outcrops, some as high as 600 metres, but there is little else to attract the traveller.

A dirt road heads east from the blacktop at Kulgera to the small settlement of Finke, where adventurous travellers can either head north to Alice Springs along the Old Ghan Line or south-east into the Simpson Desert.

To the south, just before the border, another sandy track heads west to Mulga Park homestead and then north to Curtin Springs on the main road to Uluru.
ACCOMMODATION: Kulgera Roadhouse Hotel/Motel, ph (08) 8956 0973; Kulgera Caravan Park, ph (08) 8956 0973
ACTIVITIES: 4WD touring
TOURIST INFORMATION: Ph (08) 8956 0973

MATARANKA

427 KM SOUTH OF DARWIN
POPULATION: 245   MAP REF: PAGE 260 G8
Situated 110 km south of Katherine, Mataranka is known as the capital of the Never Never Country, as it was near here, at Elsey Station, that Mrs Aeneas 'Jeannie' Gunn lived, and later wrote her acclaimed book, *We of the Never Never*.

The town of Mataranka, located on the main north–south highway, boasts a small number of shops and stores and the Never Never Museum, which houses a good display of the area's early history.

Just a couple of kilometres south of the township is the turn-off to Mataranka Homestead, which was established in 1916 as an experimental station for sheep and horses. The homestead is the centre of activities for the surrounding Elsey National Park and offers accommodation and camping. Near the homestead is a replica of the original hand-hewn timber Elsey homestead. The original Elsey homestead can be visited, along with the graves of

many of the characters in the book, about 22 km south of the present-day township.

The thermal pool, which has been the main attraction here for generations, is close to the main Mataranka homestead, but included in the park. The fabulous pool is a constant 34°C and flows at something like 30 million litres a day.

The Roper River, which has its source not far from the homestead, picks up the water from the thermal pool and flows through the park. A good road skirts the southern edge of the river, giving access to pleasant picnic grounds and a small camping ground. A walking trail leads from here about 3 km to Mataranka Falls.

Annual events to look out for include the Australia Day Cricket Match in January, the Back to the Never Never Festival in May, and the Mataranka Bushman's Festival including a campdraft, night rodeo, and gymkhana in August.
ACCOMMODATION: Old Elsey Roadside Inn, ph (08) 8975 4512; Mataranka Homestead Tourist Resort, ph (08) 8975 4544; Territory Manor, ph (08) 8975 4516
ACTIVITIES: Bushwalking, canoeing, horse riding, national park access, swimming
TOURIST INFORMATION: Ph (08) 8972 2650

NHULUNBUY

1042 KM EAST OF DARWIN
POPULATION: 3500   MAP REF: PAGE 261 M4
There are only two ways to reach the modern mining town of Nhulunbuy, located on the Gove Peninsula in north-eastern Arnhem Land, and that is either to fly, or take a long 4WD trip via Katherine and then the Mainoru Road north-east to Nhulunbuy.

You require a permit to drive this route which can be obtained from the Northern Land Council in Darwin, Katherine or Nhulunbuy.

Access is only possible via this route from late April to November—in the Wet, rains close the roads.

There are designated camping areas along the way and the total distance from Katherine is 700 km, the last fuel being at Bulman. No other supplies are available, so be prepared.

Nhulunbuy was established as a service centre for the very large bauxite mine nearby, owned and operated by mining giant, Nabalco.

The adventurous traveller who gets to Nhulunbuy will find an almost tourist-free area, undiscovered by the masses. If you are into fishing or diving, then the surrounding coast and islands provide a host of attractions. Boats can be hired for fishing and you will catch barra, mangrove jack, Spanish mackerel, queenfish and a lot more.

As the town is surrounded by Aboriginal land there are a number of art and craft galleries and museums, including Yirrkala Arts and Crafts and Nambara Arts and Crafts. Tours are available to outlying Aboriginal communities, and Aboriginal guides will take you on food gathering trips. Tours of the mine and the alumina plant are also available.
ACCOMMODATION: Gove Peninsula Motel, ph (08) 8987 0700; Walkabout Arnhem Land Resort, ph (08) 8987 1777; Hideaway Safari Lodge, ph (08) 8987 3933
ACTIVITIES: Bowls, fishing, golf, scenic drives, water sports
TOURIST INFORMATION: Ph (08) 8981 4300

PINE CREEK

230 KM SOUTH OF DARWIN
POPULATION: 610   MAP REF: PAGE 260 E6
The area around Pine Creek was the scene of extensive mining in the 1870s and 1880s and the region is rich with historic sites, such as Grove Hill and Mt Wells. One of the largest open-cut gold mines in the Territory was in operation here until 1995.

The railway station was built in 1888 and is now an historical display of the North Australia Railway, while nearby is an 1877 steam engine with carriages which were used on the railway from 1880 to 1943. The museum is housed in the original mining warden's house and has a display on the Overland Telegraph Line and the mining years. The Miners Park houses machinery used on the old mines.

The Northern Goldfields Loop, a marked, well-maintained dirt road, starts outside Pine Creek and leads north to just beyond Hayes Creek. This is an alternative route to Darwin.

North-west of the town, and reached by a good dirt road, is delightful Tjuwaliyn (Douglas Hot Springs). You can camp here, or the nearby Douglas Daly Park offers good camping and accommodation.

A little further on, past Tjuwaliyn, on a route which is now really a 4WD track, is Butterfly Gorge. You need to be a little active to take the walk through the riverine forest to the pool at the mouth of the gorge, but it is well worth the effort.

To the west of Pine Creek is the less visited but peaceful and picturesque Umbrawarra Gorge Nature Park, while closer to town is the Copperfield Recreation Reserve, which is a pleasant spot for a swim, picnic or even to camp for a while. The town is also a good jumping-off point to Kakadu National Park via the Kakadu Highway.

Annual events include the Pioneer Goldrush Weekend and Horse Races in May.

ACCOMMODATION: Pine Creek Hotel/Motel, ph (08) 8976 1288; Diggers Rest Motel, ph (08) 8976 1442; Bonrook Lodge Guest House, ph (08) 8976 1232; Pine Creek Caravan Park, ph (08) 8976 1217; Douglas Daly Park, ph (08) 8978 2479

ACTIVITIES: Boating, fishing, 4WD touring, gold prospecting, national park access, swimming

TOURIST INFORMATION: Ph (08) 8976 1391

RABBIT FLAT ROADHOUSE

1161 KM SOUTH-WEST OF DARWIN
POPULATION: 2   MAP REF: PAGE 262 B9

The very isolated Rabbit Flat Roadhouse is located on the Tanami Road in the Tanami Desert. Travellers use this road for access between Halls Creek in Western Australia and Alice Springs in the Northern Territory, and for the most part the road is pretty reasonable, although it really is 4WD country. Travellers should be well prepared for crossing this harsh region.

The Rabbit Flat Roadhouse is a little oasis in the surrounding desert with limited trading days, being only opened between 7 am and 10 pm, four days a week: closed Tuesday, Wednesday and Thursday. The roadhouse dispenses fuel (diesel, petrol), beer, soft drinks, takeaway foods and payment is cash only.

ACCOMMODATION: Camp site, ph (08) 8956 8744

ACTIVITIES: 4WD touring, fuel, roadside stop

TOURIST INFORMATION: Ph (08) 8952 5800

ROSS RIVER

1592 KM SOUTH OF DARWIN
POPULATION: 20   MAP REF: PAGE 265 J6

The Ross River Homestead is 88 km east of Alice Springs. An historic homestead, it is a tourist destination that offers travellers a chance to experience the East MacDonnell Ranges. There is plenty to do, including bushwalking, while those with a 4WD can enjoy N'Dhala Gorge to the south, Trephina Gorge to the north, or Ruby Gap Nature Park and the Arltunga Historical Reserve to the east.

Gold was discovered at Arltunga in 1887, as were garnets, the latter being reported as rubies, which started a rush into the area. The best place to stop if you want to fossick is the Arltunga Hotel.

ACCOMMODATION: Ross River Homestead and Camping Ground, ph (08) 8956 9711; Arltunga Hotel, ph (08) 8956 9797

ACTIVITIES: Bushwalking, 4WD touring, gold and gem fossicking, horse riding, swimming

TOURIST INFORMATION: Ph (08) 8952 5800

TENNANT CREEK

994 KM SOUTH OF DARWIN
POPULATION: 3500   MAP REF: PAGE 263 H8

Tennant Creek, situated on the Stuart Highway, is the main regional centre for the Barkly Tablelands, and is just over 500 km from Alice Springs. It is also 25 km

south of the road junction and roadhouse known as Three Ways, from where you can continue north to Darwin or turn east to Queensland and Mount Isa.

The creek itself was discovered and named in 1860 by John McDouall Stuart on his trek across the continent, and in 1872 it became the site for a repeater station on the Overland Telegraph Line. The town sprang up a few kilometres to the south of the station. Gold was discovered in the area in 1930 and Australia's last great gold rush began. It turned out to be the third richest goldfield in Australia, and while mining is still carried out, the boom years have gone.

Today, Tennant Creek is a vigorous, friendly community with modern amenities. Its strategic position on the Stuart Highway and a variety of attractions make it a popular stop for travellers.

Much of the town's history can be seen at Battery Hill, home of the Tennant Creek gold stamping battery and mining museum. The different mines can be toured, including the Burnt Shirt Mine, the Golden Forty, or Noble's Nob Open Cut Mine, once the richest goldmine in Australia. There is also an historic walk to some of the notable relics of those golden days.

Other buildings of interest include the Overland Telegraph Station, and the old Australian Inland Mission built in 1932. Tuxworth Fulwood House was constructed as an army hospital in 1942, and today houses photographs and displays of early mining life, machinery and equipment.

The Aboriginal culture is very strong in Tennant Creek and you can view a number of murals here, watch art and craft being made, purchase items at the local art and craft centre or go on a bush tucker tour.

Just north of Tennant Creek is the Attack Creek Historical Reserve. The creek received its name following an incident between explorer John McDouall Stuart and local Waramunga Aborigines. Stuart was forced to retreat to South Australia, before finally crossing the continent in 1862.

Mary Ann Dam, 5 km north of town, is a man-made lake suitable for small boats and canoes, an ideal spot for a swim and a picnic.

The Pebbles, located 17 km to the north, is an extensive area of granite boulders that are miniatures of the Devils Marbles.

Just to the north of the small outpost and hotel of Wauchope 115 km to the south, are the Devils Marbles, A stopover in Wauchope is worthwhile.

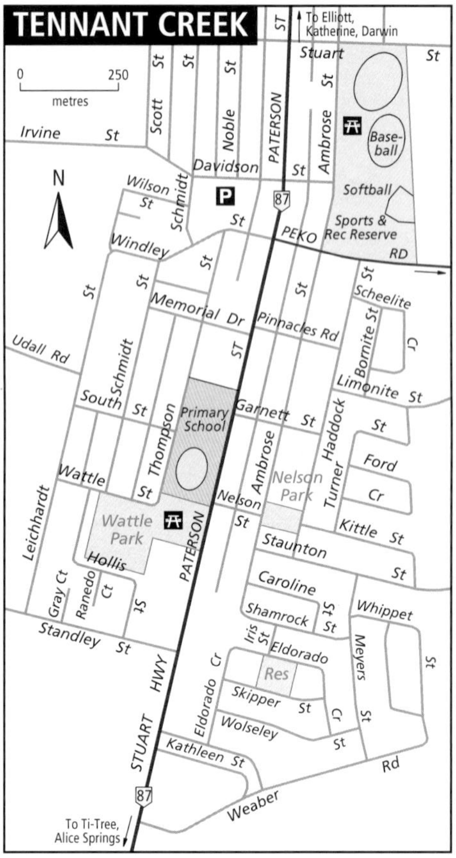

TENNANT CREEK

[Map of Tennant Creek showing streets including Stuart St, Scott St, Noble St, Davidson St, Ambrose St, Paterson, Irvine St, Wilson St, Schmidt St, Windley St, Peko Rd, Memorial Dr, Pinnacles Rd, Scheelite Cr, Bornite St, Limonite St, Udall Rd, South St, Schmidt St, Garnett St, Haddock St, Ford Cr, Wattle St, Nelson, Ambrose, Turner St, Kittle St, Leichhardt St, Wattle Park, Hollis, Staunton St, Caroline St, Whippet St, Gray Ct, Ranedo Ct, Shamrock St, Eldorado Cr, Meyers St, Standley St, Iris St, Res, Skipper St, Wolseley St, Eldorado Cr, Kathleen St, Weaber Rd, Stuart Hwy. Landmarks: Base-ball, Softball, Sports & Rec Reserve, Primary School, Nelson Park. "To Elliott, Katherine, Darwin" at top; "To Ti-Tree, Alice Springs" at bottom. Scale 0–250 metres.]

The Northern Territory Street Circuit Go-Kart Grand Prix is held in April; the Tennant Creek Art Award and Tennant Creek Cup in May; the Tennant Creek District Show in July; and the Spring Flower Show and Goldrush Folk Festival in August.

ACCOMMODATION: Bluestone Motor Inn, ph (08) 8962 2617; Goldfields Hotel/Motel, ph (08) 8962 2030; Desert Sands Serviced Apartments, ph (08) 8962 1346; Outback Caravan Park, ph (08) 8962 2459; Three Ways: Three Ways Roadhouse Caravan Park, ph (08) 8962 2744; Wauchope: Wauchope Well Hotel, ph (08) 8964 1963; Wauchope Well Camping Ground, ph (08) 8964 1963

ACTIVITIES: Bowls, canoeing, gold prospecting, golf, horse riding, swimming, yachting

TOURIST INFORMATION: Ph (08) 8962 3388

The Devils Marbles, granite boulders south of Tennant Creek

TILMOUTH WELL

1667 KM SOUTH OF DARWIN
POPULATION: 8   MAP REF: PAGE 264 F4

Along the formed, unsealed road known as the Tanami Road, Tilmouth Well is situated 195 km north-west of Alice Springs on Napperby Station. While one of the larger working cattle stations in Central Australia, Tilmouth Well, surrounded by green lawns, has been set up with a restaurant and bar, swimming pool, BBQ, golf course and clay shooting range. There are also bushwalking trips and a bore run.

The roadhouse also supplies travellers with limited grocery supplies, hardware, car accessories, take-away food, ice and alcohol, as well as fuel. Basic mechanical repairs, tyres and tyre repairs are also available, and major credit cards are accepted.

Four-wheel drives are recommended for travelling the Tanami Road, while caravans and conventional trailers are not.

ACCOMMODATION: Air-conditioned cabins and camping, ph (08) 8956 8777
ACTIVITIES: Bushwalking, clay shooting, 4WD touring, golf, horse riding, station activities, swimming (pool)
TOURIST INFORMATION: Ph (08) 8952 5800

TIMBER CREEK

602 KM SOUTH OF DARWIN
POPULATION: 150   MAP REF: PAGE 260 C10

Located less than 100 km west of the Victoria River Roadhouse, on the Victoria Highway and alongside the mighty Victoria River, is the town of Timber Creek.

Established as a police post in the late 1800s, the town now services the surrounding region and cattle properties, as well as catering for passing travellers. It is also a good base from which to explore the spectacular nearby Gregory National Park, while anglers will find it hard to drag themselves away from the great fishing on offer in the river. For something a little more tranquil, you can put your own boat in the river and cruise this wide waterway, or join a river cruise past rugged gorges and dramatic landscapes.

The town has various services available, along with a general store that can supply most needs.

If you are passing through in September, join in the day's fun and activities of the Timber Creek Races with campdraft events, races, gymkhana and ball.

ACCOMMODATION: Timber Creek Wayside Inn Hotel/Motel, ph (08) 8975 0732; Timber Creek Wayside Inn Caravan Park, ph (08) 8975 0732.
ACTIVITIES: Fishing, heritage walk, national park access, river cruises, scenic drives
TOURIST INFORMATION: Ph (08) 8972 2650

VICTORIA RIVER CROSSING

522 KM SOUTH-WEST OF DARWIN
POPULATION: 10   MAP REF: PAGE 260 D9

The Victoria Highway, as it heads west from Katherine, is one of the most scenic in the Territory, passing through a variety of country, none more spectacular than the rugged escarpment country around the Victoria River Crossing.

The Victoria River, thought by the first European explorers to lead to an inland sea, makes a modest start south-west of Kalkarindji and wanders north to the sea through the Victoria River District. The river was named and navigated by Captain Wickham in the *Beagle* in 1839, and it was to be another 17 years before Augustus Gregory landed at the mouth of this river for his explorations inland.

Victoria River Crossing is little more than a roadhouse, motel and caravan park, located on the western edge of the Victoria River.

The eastern and smaller section of the Gregory National Park surrounds this small hamlet, and includes a number of attractions such as Joe's Creek Walk, which takes visitors up to the face of the escarpment, while the Escarpment Lookout gives good views from the top of the Stokes Range, east up to the entrance of the Victoria Gorge. A little further downstream from the Crossing is the original crossing point, while further west is Kuwang Lookout.

There is some good fishing in the river and a lot of crocodiles! West of the Crossing a road south to the famous Victoria River Downs station leads through the spectacular Jasper Gorge.

ACCOMMODATION: Victoria River Roadhouse Hotel/Motel, ph (08) 8975 0744; Victoria River Roadhouse Caravan Park, ph (08) 8975 0755
ACTIVITIES: Bushwalking, fishing, 4WD touring, national park access
TOURIST INFORMATION: Ph (08) 8972 2650

YULARA

1925 KM SOUTH OF DARWIN
POPULATION: 2350   MAP REF: PAGE 264 D9

Kata Tjuta National Park is some 450 km south-west of Alice Springs and within its boundaries is the most recognised Australian landmark, Ayers Rock, or as it is now known, from the local Aboriginal language, Uluru. For the more technical minded it is the world's second largest monolith, but for most Australians it is the epitome of Central Australia and the closest this continent comes to a pilgrimage site.

It is, as well, an important Aboriginal sacred site, being sacred to a number of Aboriginal groups in the surrounding area.

Yulara is located just outside the park and is the village that services the huge number of travellers who come from far and wide to view this great rock. Most will try and make the tough 1.6 km ascent to the top; it is best to do it in the cool of early morning. Better to take a walking tour around Uluru with an Aboriginal guide, learning about its fascinating stories, and its importance in Dreamtime legend for the people. At sunset do not miss out on going to Sunset Strip, a low sandridge, which, if the weather is right, gives an unforgettable view of Uluru as it changes colour in the fading light.

The Mulgara Gallery has working resident artists and houses an impressive collection of prestigious Australian arts, crafts and gifts, while the Maruku Arts & Crafts is an Aboriginal owned outdoor gallery selling the works of more than 800 artists and crafts people of the region. The Sails in the Desert Hotel Garden is an award-winning native garden and can be inspected on a free one-hour tour.

Also in this park are the Olgas, or to give them their Aboriginal name, Kata Tjuta. They are a dramatic series of 36 dome-like rock formations which stand up to 546 metres high and cover an area of 35 sq km. Like Uluru, they produce an incredible light show at sunset, and to walk amongst them is a memorable experience.

You can also take a camel to dinner, enjoy a scenic flight around the Rock or just marvel at the stars. You'll never forget the experience!

ACCOMMODATION: Sails in the Desert Hotel; Desert Gardens Hotel, Outback Pioneer Hotel, Emu Walk Serviced Apartments, Spinifex Lodge, ph (02) 9360 9099; Ayers Rock Campground, ph (08) 8956 2055
ACTIVITIES: Aboriginal sites, camel rides, national park access, nature walks, scenic drives and flights
TOURIST INFORMATION: Ph (08) 8956 2240 or 1800 089 622

An aerial view of Uluru (Ayers Rock)

Glen Helen Gorge in West Macdonnell National Park

ALICE SPRINGS TELEGRAPH STATION

This telegraph station is the reason for the existence of the town of Alice Springs. The station was completed in 1872 near the spring which Charles Todd, builder of the Overland Telegraph Line, named after his wife, Alice. The location was also near a regularly used ceremonial ground of the Arrernte Aboriginal clan. Today the station is a popular picnic spot and historical museum.

ARLTUNGA HISTORICAL RESERVE

In 1887 gold was discovered near Arltunga and central Australia's first gold rush was on. Many of the fortune seekers were already in the area as they had rushed up to the 'ruby' fields at Ruby Gap (the rubies turned out to be semi-precious garnets). Some miners pushed their barrows 600 km from the Oodnadatta railhead in South Australia to reach the Arltunga field. Later a government battery was established at Arltunga and the town was larger than the outpost of Alice Springs. Today there is a visitor centre with a small museum and slide shows and a working two-stamp battery. Adjacent to the historical reserve there is a fossicking reserve and with the right permits you may try your luck at fossicking for an elusive nugget, and you can also explore some of the old mines

in the area. Arltunga lies 110 km east of Alice Springs along the Ross Highway.

CHAMBERS PILLAR HISTORICAL RESERVE

This reserve lies 163 km south of Alice Springs along the Old South Road; en route you pass the Ewaninga rock carvings. The road is sandy and corrugated in places, with river and dune crossings, and the drive takes you through some picturesque country along the fringe of the Simpson Desert. John McDouall Stuart in 1860 was the first European to sight this solitary sandstone pillar which stands high above the dune landscape, and he named it after James Chambers, one of his expedition sponsors. Until the advent of the railway line, subsequent explorers and overlanders all used Chambers Pillar as a landmark on their journeys through the centre, and carved their names in the soft sandstone rock face.

CUTTA CUTTA CAVES NATURE PARK

These ancient limestone caves, up to 15 metres deep, are managed as a commercial venture and are open to the public seven days a week. Recently the Tindal Cave was added to the complex. The caves are home to orange horseshoe bats and brown tree snakes. Picnic tables and toilets are provided. May to October is the

best time to visit. The park is 30 km south of Katherine, just off the Stuart Highway.

DAVENPORT RANGE NATIONAL PARK

This is one of the newest parks in the Northern Territory and development of the area has yet to commence. The access track heads east off the Stuart Highway 27 km north of the Wauchope Roadhouse. At present there is only one camping area open, at Old Police Station Waterhole, and this is accessible only by 4WD. It is envisaged that the park will eventually have access for conventional vehicles and that three other 4WD tracks will be opened. The Davenport Range is a biological interzone of flora and fauna between the tropical north and the arid centre of the Northern Territory. It has a rich Aboriginal history and a notable recent history in mining and pastoralism. The park is bordered by four cattle stations and until proper fencing can be erected the park will maintain its fair share of wild cattle and feral donkeys. Dingoes live throughout the park and so do feral cats which are a threat to all the small animal inhabitants. Moves are afoot to control the unwanted animals and introduced plants within the park. Swimming in the Old Police Station Waterhole is a favourite pastime, as is canoeing.

DEVILS MARBLES CONSERVATION RESERVE

This pile of huge rounded granite boulders is an awesome sight next to the Stuart Highway 90 km south of Tennant Creek. The boulders are the result of exposure and weathering over millions of years. Visitors may wander through the boulders for a chance at that quintessential photograph. This is an Aboriginal sacred site and visitors are asked to respect the cultural heritage of the area. Picnic tables, toilets, camping facilities and unpowered caravan sites are provided.

ELSEY NATIONAL PARK

The headwaters of the Roper River near the township of Mataranka on the Stuart Highway provide tranquil spots for canoeing, swimming and fishing. There are a few good walks through the monsoon forests along the Roper, especially one to Elsey Falls. Camping and caravan facilities are provided. The Mataranka thermal pool on the Waterhouse

River is the other popular feature of this park. Situated near Mataranka Homestead, a commercial venture within the park where a replica of the old Elsey Homestead (of *We of the Never Never* fame) has been built, the warm waters attract many visitors during winter.

EWANINGA CONSERVATION RESERVE

A small reserve protects the low hills of Ewaninga which are covered in petroglyphs. So ancient are these rock carvings that their meanings are not known by the traditional owners of the land. The reserve is open to the public and lies 25 km south of Alice Springs along the Old South Road. A walking track from the car park with interpretive signs has been provided so that visitors may get an insight into the way people lived in this area so long ago. This reserve is for day use only.

FINKE GORGE NATIONAL PARK

This park was established to protect the incredible gorges which the Finke River and its tributary the Palm River have carved through the ancient mountains of central Australia. In these gorges the red rock walls have eroded to incredible shapes. The spectacular Palm Valley is home to 2000 red cabbage palms, unique in the world, and remnants of an era when this region was part of the wet tropics. Palm Valley is 138 km west of Alice Springs along Larapinta Drive; past the Hermannsburg Community, you turn left (south), and the last 16 km along the bed of the Finke River is for 4WD vehicles only. It is an easy drive, however, and very picturesque, culminating at the Palm Valley car park. Two pleasant walks take the adventurer through the valley. There are other walks along the way as well as picnic areas. There is a camping area, 4 km back from the car park.

GREGORY NATIONAL PARK

This park, 160 km south-west of Katherine on the Victoria Highway, was named after the explorer A. C. Gregory who trekked through this country in 1855. It features magnificent gorges, important Aboriginal cultural and art sites, and protects the plant and animal communities of this fragile area that is part tropical, part semi-arid. The park has an interesting diversity of flora with heathlands, spinifex, melaleuca

forests, nutwood, turpentine and giant boab trees in abundance; flowering eucalypts dominate other sections of the park. Feral donkeys, wild pigs, brumbies and stray cattle compete with the native animals, and both saltwater and freshwater crocodiles inhabit the creeks and billabongs. The area is very rich in bird life. Camping areas are located at Limestone Gorge and near the Bullita Homestead.

GURIG NATIONAL PARK & COBOURG MARINE PARK

The remote Gurig National Park lies 570 km east and north of Darwin. Permits are required to enter the park, and only 15 vehicles at any one time are allowed in the park. Bookings are essential. The road is sealed up to the East Alligator River crossing and from there it deteriorates. The last 70 km into Black Point on Cobourg Peninsula is sandy and corrugated. This national park is the traditional home of four clans of Aboriginal people who today live within the boundaries of the park. The camping area is at Smith Point, only about 100 metres from a sandy white beach. Here you can swim (but keep an eye out for crocodiles), walk along the beach, and watch turtles lay their eggs at night. Fishing for certain species of fish is permitted within the Cobourg Marine Park, and you can also join a tour by boat to explore the ruins of the Victoria Settlement at Port Essington, abandoned in 1848.

KEEP RIVER NATIONAL PARK

This park, 48 km east of Kununurra, is not far from the Northern Territory/Western Australia border and a short distance from the Victoria Highway. It offers red sandstone cliffs, sweeping views and giant boab trees along the banks of the Keep River. In the Wet, the river is a raging torrent, but during the Dry you can walk along its bed to view the wealth of Aboriginal rock art in caves and rock shelters and on the walls of the gorge. Some of the rock formations resemble the Bungle Bungles in Western Australia. Camping and picnic facilities and walking tracks are available. Visitors are asked not to venture into several sacred sites in the park, which are fenced off and signposted.

LITCHFIELD NATIONAL PARK

This park, with its magnetic termite mounds, its rainforest pockets and magnificent waterfalls splashing down from the plateau into crystal-clear pools, is only two hours drive from Darwin via the town of Batchelor. On the perimeter of the park are a motel and caravan parks; bush camping and unpowered caravan sites are provided in the park. Walking tracks lead to several lookouts with spectacular views. Highlights of the park are the Florence, Tolmer, Wangi and Sandy Creek falls; an area of spectacular eroded sandstone formations called the Lost City. Blyth Homestead, a magnetic termite plain and the Reynolds River.

N'DHALA GORGE NATURE PARK

Just 8 km from Ross River Homestead and 88 km from Alice Springs, N'Dhala Gorge is of great cultural significance to the Eastern Arrernte Aboriginal clan. Around 6000 petroglyphs (rock carvings) have been recorded in the gorge and one can only wonder at the unknown history of these magnificent yet mysterious works of art. The track from Ross River Homestead, for 4WD vehicles only, winds along the picturesque river bed and through a valley where great forces of nature have twisted the rock ledges under incredible pressure. Picnic tables, a bush toilet and limited camping facilities are provided.

NITMILUK (KATHERINE GORGE) NATIONAL PARK

Over millions of years the Katherine River has cut through the sandstone plateau to form a series of 13 gorges, though most visitors see only the lower two. Nitmiluk is part of the traditional land of the Jawoyn people; they have now been granted title to the park, which is leased to the Northern Territory Conservation Commission, and managed jointly by the Jawoyn and the commission. Katherine Gorge is one of the great natural wonders of the north. Abundant bird and fish life, as well as crocodiles, inhabit this area. The gorge is 32 km from Katherine town along a sealed road. Tour boat cruises operate on the Katherine River and canoes can be hired. The park has more than 100 km of walking tracks; scenic flights, swimming and photography also attract visitors. The Edith Falls section of the park is 45 km north from Katherine along the Stuart Highway and 20 km in along a sealed road. This small waterfall tumbles over a series of ridges and through a number of pools to a large pool fringed by monsoon forest. The pool is safe for swimming, and there are pleasant walks along the river bank. There are camping grounds near Katherine Gorge and at Edith Falls, plus several bush camping areas along walking trails.

TJUWALIYN (DOUGLAS HOT SPRINGS) NATURE PARK

Camping and caravanning are the order of the day at these hot springs. The artesian waters bubble up from the depths of the earth and some say that they have therapeutic powers. In certain areas the water is too hot to enter, but in others you can spend a relaxing time in the heated water. Be careful not to have an alcohol intake whilst in the springs as both cause dehydration. The springs are located 180 km from Darwin along the Oolloo Road off the Old Stuart Highway; only 8 km of this road is unsealed.

TREPHINA GORGE NATURE PARK

This park is noted for its massive quartzite cliffs and its sandy creeks lined with river red gums. Access is possible by conventional vehicle, but to get to John Hayes Rockhole a high clearance 4WD vehicle is required. Like many other gorges in the Eastern MacDonnell Ranges, Trephina offers excellent bushwalking tracks and a chance to view the surrounding ranges and some of the more elusive rock wallabies that inhabit this area. On the drive into the gorge, turn off at the signpost to admire the biggest ghost gum in central Australia. The park is 85 km east of Alice Springs along the Ross Highway.

ULURU–KATA TJUTA NATIONAL PARK

This park, whose main attractions are Uluru (Ayers Rock) and Kata Tjuta (Mt Olga), is probably the best known, most visited and most photographed place in the Northern Territory. It is a World Heritage Area, managed jointly by the Aboriginal traditional owners and the Australian Nature Conservation Agency. There is a great deal to enjoy in the park including photography, magnificent views, sunsets and the changing colours of Uluru, especially at sunrise and sunset or during a storm. Uluru can also be climbed although visitors are asked to respect the traditional owners' sacred areas. There are interesting walks around the base of Uluru, and walks through the Valley of the Winds at Kata Tjuta. Vantage points have been constructed throughout the park with interpretive signs. At Yulara Tourist Village, 20 km from Uluru, hotel and motel accommodation is available as well as caravan and camping sites. Camping is not allowed in the park itself. Scenic flights of the area can be arranged at Yulara.

WATARRKA (KINGS CANYON) NATIONAL PARK

The magnificent Kings Canyon, with sheer sandstone cliffs to 270 metres high, is found in this park. Set in the western end of the George Gill Range, north of Yulara and 302 km south-west of Alice Springs, the canyon with its permanent waterholes and lush vegetation of cycads, palms, ferns and desert oaks is in sharp contrast with the spinifex and stunted bushes of the surrounding arid hills. A range of fauna shares this oasis including rock wallabies and euros in the gorges, parrots, honeyeaters, native pigeons and birds of prey, and giant perenties (goannas) and other lizards and snakes. There are a number of walks, including two constructed walking tracks in the canyon area: one along the creek and one around the rim of the canyon. All camping and accommodation is provided by commercial operators in the park.

WEST MACDONNELL NATIONAL PARK

West of Alice Springs, the parallel ridges of the MacDonnell Ranges contain an amazing array of canyons, cliffs and ridges, ancient hills and valleys, permanent waterholes and sandy creek beds. The West MacDonnell National Park incorporates a number of smaller parks and reserves. Some of the places worth visiting are: Ellery Creek Big Hole, a large permanent waterhole just 90 km west of Alice Springs along Namatjira Drive; the Ochre Pits, where for thousands of years the local Arrernte people collected ochre for ceremonial purposes; Ormiston Gorge, which offers perhaps the most striking scenery and brilliant colours in the West MacDonnells; Redbank Gorge; Serpentine Chalet, a small bush camping area; Serpentine Gorge; Simpsons Gap; Glen Helen Gorge and Standley Chasm.

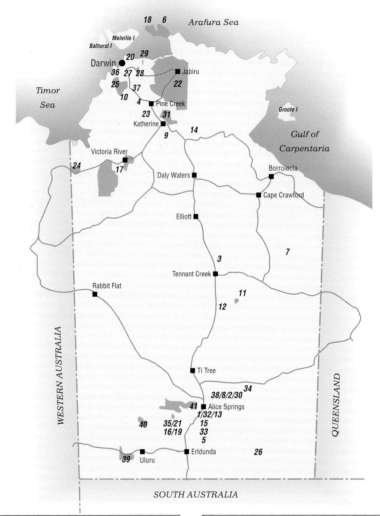

Popular Parks

#	Park	Camping	Caravans	Wheel Chairs	4WD Access	Picnic Area	Toilets	Walking Trks	Kiosk	Information
1	Alice Springs TS			●		●	●	●		●
2	Arltunga HR			●		●	●	●		●
3	Attack Creek HR					●				
4	Butterfly Gorge Nature P				●	●		●		
5	Chambers Pillar HR	●			●	●	●	●		
6	Cobourg Marine Park									
7	Connells Lagoon CR				●					
8	Corroboree Rock CR					●	●	●		
9	Cutta Cutta Caves Nature P	●				●	●			●
10	Daly River Nature P	●	●			●	●			
11	Davenport Range NP	●			●	●				
12	Devils Marbles CR	●	●			●	●	●		
13	Emily & Jessie Gaps Nature P				●	●	●	●		
14	Elsey NP	●	●			●	●	●		●
15	Ewaninga CR					●		●		
16	Finke Gorge NP	●			●	●	●	●		
17	Gregory NP	●			●	●	●	●		●
18	Gurig NP	●				●	●	●		●
19	Henbury Meteorite Craters CR					●	●	●		
20	Howard Springs Nature P					●	●	●		
21	Illamurta Springs CR				●	●		●		
22	Kakadu NP	●	●		●	●	●	●	●	●
23	Katherine Low Level Nature P				●	●	●			
24	Keep River NP	●				●	●	●		
25	Litchfield NP	●	●		●	●	●	●		●
26	Mac Clark CR				●					

#	Park	Camping	Caravans	Wheel Chairs	4WD Access	Picnic Area	Toilets	Walking Trks	Kiosk	Information
27	Manton Dam CR					●	●	●		
28	Marrakai CR				●					
29	Mary River Wetlands CR	●				●	●	●		●
30	N'Dhala Gorge Nature P	●				●	●	●		
31	Nitmiluk NP									
	– Edith Falls									
	– Katherine Gorge	●	●	●		●	●	●	●	●
32	Olive Pink Nature P					●	●	●		●
33	Rainbow Valley CR	●			●	●		●		
34	Ruby Gap Nature P	●			●			●		
35	Ryans Well HR									
36	Territory Wildlife Park				●	●	●	●		●
37	Tjuwaliyn (Douglas Hot Springs) Nature P	●	●			●	●	●		
38	Trephina Gorge Nature P	●			●	●	●	●		
39	Uluru-Kata Tjuta NP					●	●	●	●	●
40	Watarrka (Kings Canyon) NP	●	●			●	●	●		●
41	West MacDonnell NP									
	– Ellery Creek Big Hole	●						●		
	– Glen Helen							●		
	– Ochre Pits				●			●		
	– Ormiston Gorge							●		
	– Redbank Gorge	●				●	●	●		
	– Serpentine Gorge					●	●	●		
	– Simpsons Gap				●	●	●	●		●
	– Standley Chasm					●	●		●	

Scale:
0 — 250 — 500
metres

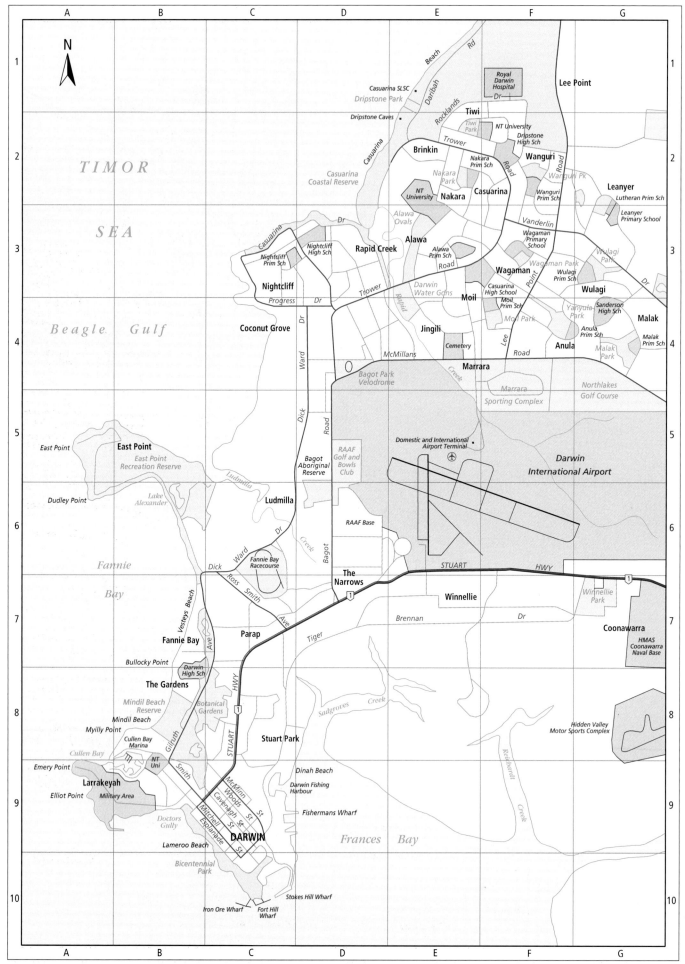

kilometres
0 10 20 30 40 50

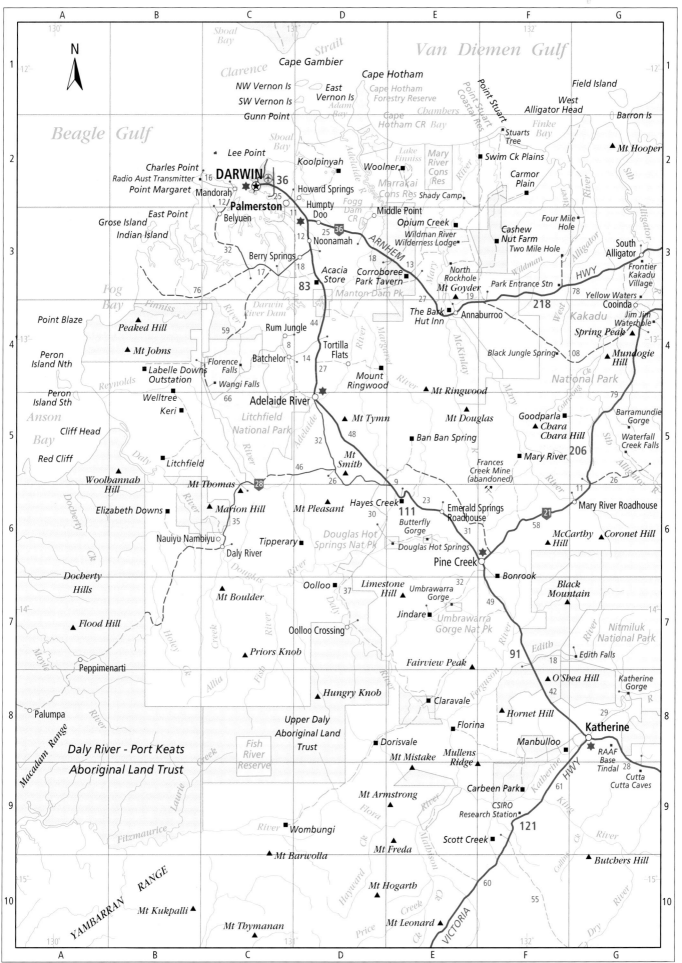

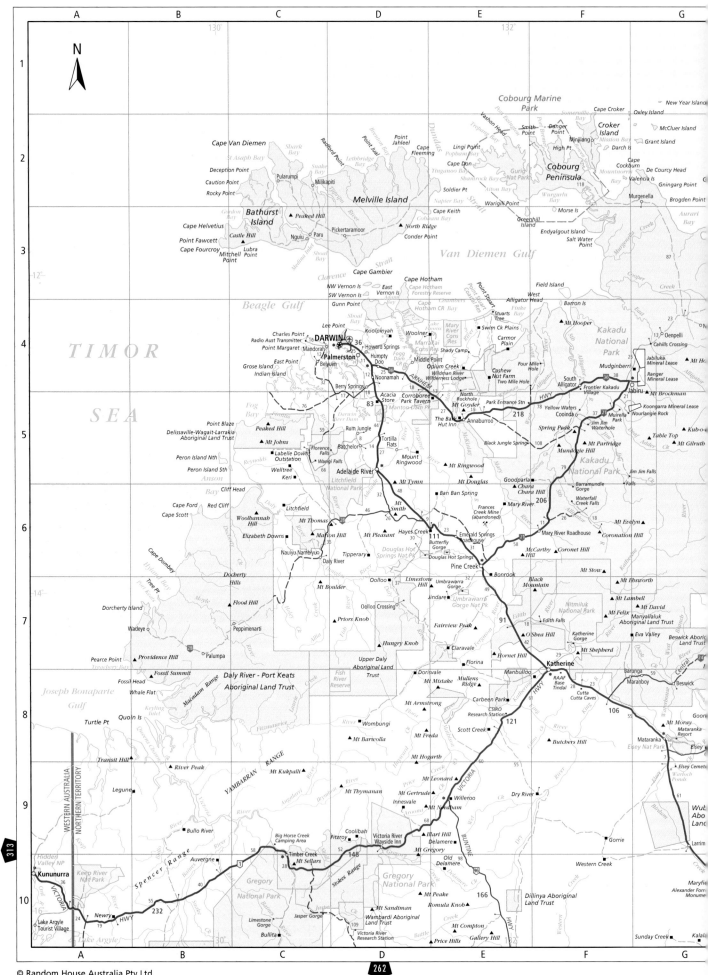

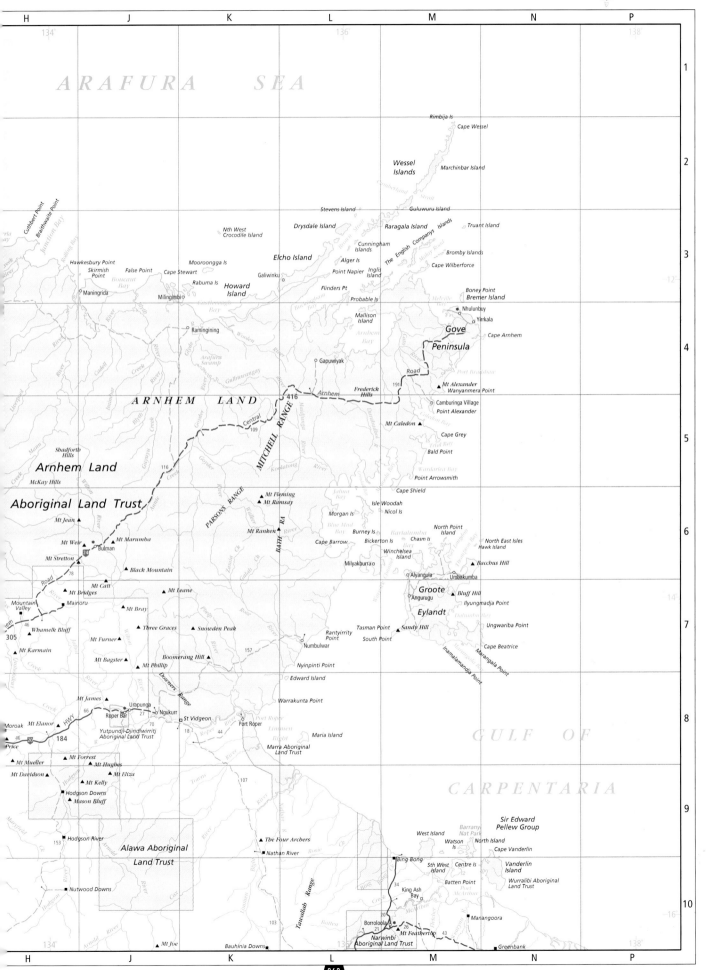

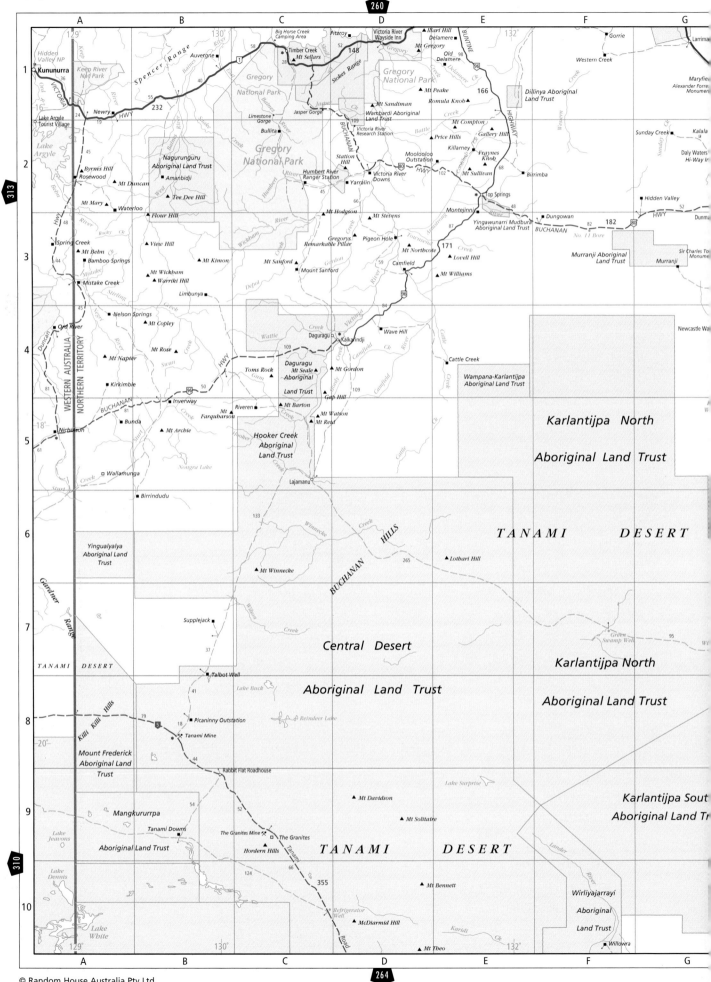

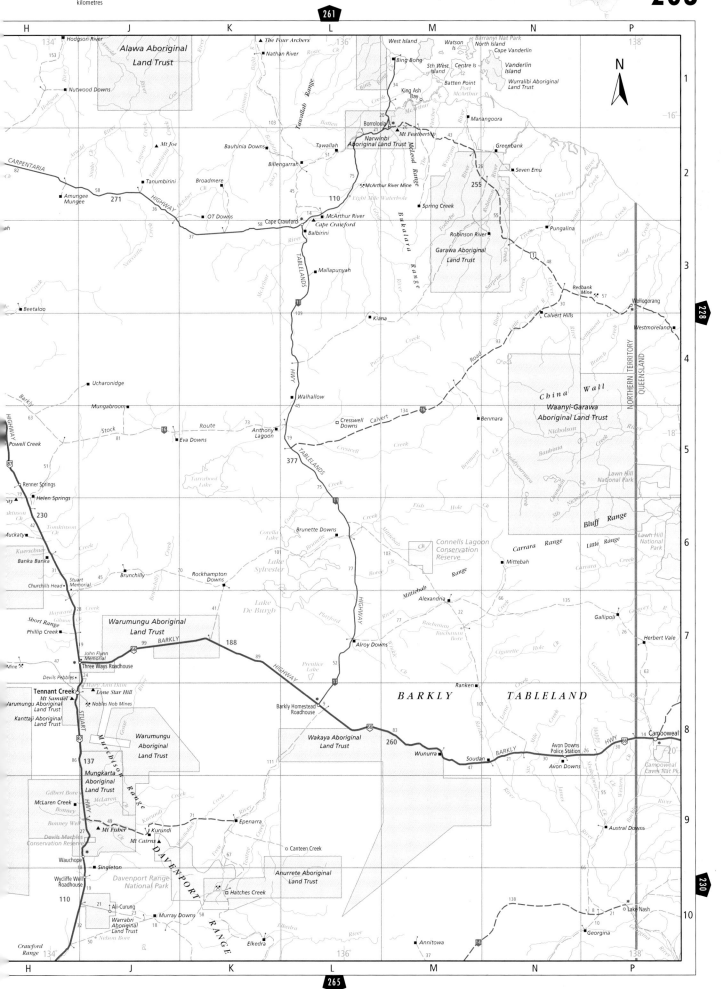

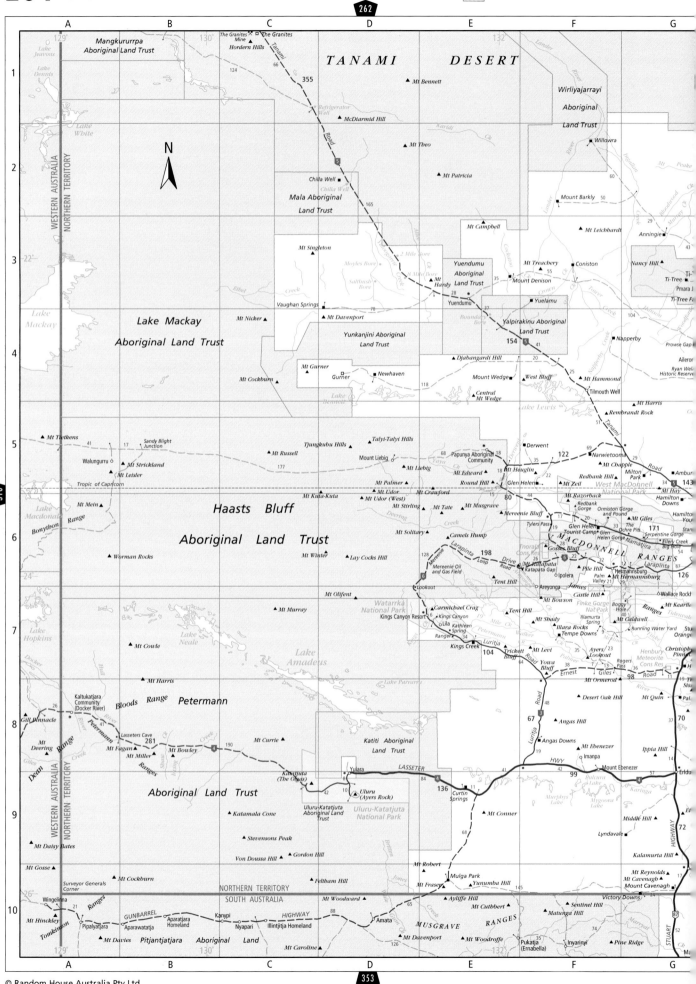

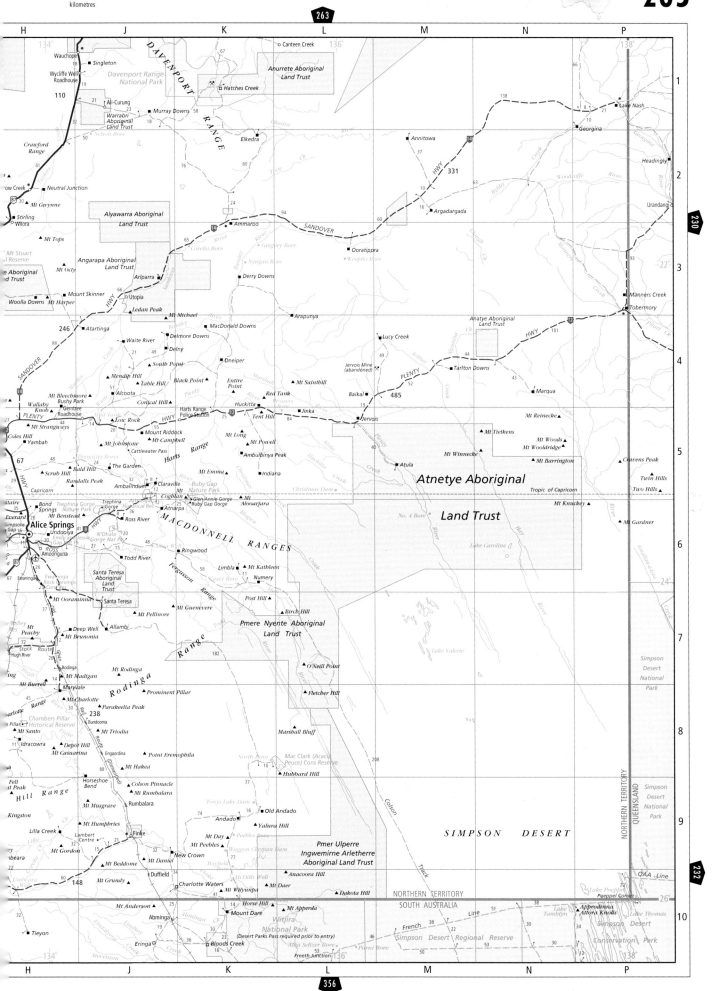

WESTERN AUSTRALIA

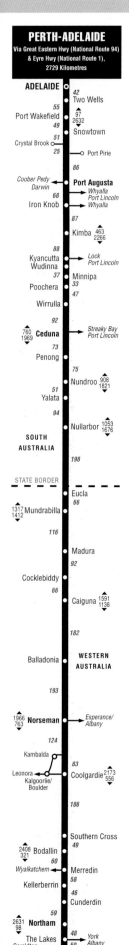

For most visitors driving across the Nullarbor the first impression is daunting, not the least being that it is over 1400 km from the border outpost of Eucla to the state capital. If that is not enough, the thought that 1400 km will only get you from Perth to Onslow on the mid-north coast, and that there is still another 1800 km to go before you reach the northernmost settlements of the state at Kununurra or Wyndham, is mind blowing, and, for most, a little terrifying. To a West Australian travelling anywhere means travelling long distances; many locals will think nothing of journeying over a thousand kilometres for a few days' fishing.

Taking up over 2.5 million sq km, Western Australia is by far the largest state in Australia, occupying more than a third of our island continent. But being big is not everything, and in this state there are enough attractions and delights to keep the most jaded traveller happy and contented. Not only that, the state has a sense of newness—almost rawness—about it, a vitality that transcends its boom-and-bust mineral-based economy, and an open, friendly, independent, outdoor-based lifestyle that makes it feel different from the rest of Australia.

With a population of 1.8 million, and over 1.2 million of those in Perth, the state is very sparsely populated. Over 90 per cent of the population lives in the more temperate southwest, so once you head inland, there are only a handful of towns that have more than a thousand people, and all those towns owe their livelihood and prosperity to mining.

In the south-west of the state, the Mediterranean climate and higher rainfall have resulted in rich farming land, forests of tall trees, and delightful rivers and streams, creating a lushness and verdancy found nowhere else in Western Australia. The area is, in the main, rolling hills and plains, but two mountain ranges—the Stirling and the Porongurup—have created a unique habitat, complete with their own flora, and to a lesser degree, fauna. The Darling Ranges behind Perth are little more than a line of hills bordering what was once in a more natural state a swampy sandplain.

Vast areas of the state are uninhabited, with much of it being classed as semi-desert or desert country. The deserts of the Great Victoria, Gibson, Little Sandy and the Great Sandy stretch from near the southern coast all the way to the northwest coast north of Port Hedland and to the southern edges of the Kimberley, making up two-thirds of the state.

But it would be quite wrong to write this desert country off as uninteresting and always the same. Here, in this vastness, subtle changes continually occur and nothing is the same for long. Stretches of spinifex country give way to mallee and mulga, changing again to desert oak dotted plains, or low, red-raw rocky ranges marked by the occasional vivid ghost gum.

Amongst this desert and semi-desert country are the two other mountainous regions of Western Australia. Not that the mountains reach great heights: the tallest in the state is Mt Meharry in the Pilbara region, reaching just 1245 metres. In

One of Western Australia's small desert settlements

The beautiful, still waters of the Denmark River, crossed by a bridge at Denmark

the far north of the state is the rugged Kimberley, where the highest peak lies within the Durack Ranges at 983 metres.

If there is variety in these desert lands, then the coast offers a real kaleidoscope of habitats, experiences and images. The coastline stretches for over 15 000 km, from Eucla across the western half of the cliff-lined Great Australian Bight, to Esperance and onwards, past hundreds of rocky headlands interspersed with bays of glistening white beaches and turquoise blue water, to Cape Leeuwin. Here the cool waters of the Southern Ocean meets with the warmer waters of the Indian Ocean, and it is this ocean that laps the shores of Western Australia all the way north to its meeting with the Timor Sea and the Northern Territory border. Long stretches of sand intermingle with lines of cliffs, small bays, islands and reefs, including the Ningaloo Reef, the second longest fringing coral reef in Australia, and one more readily accessible than Queensland's Great Barrier Reef. North of Broome, along the Kimberley coast, the sea and ocean mix in a virtual battle-ground where roaring tides and raging currents have carved great rents into the coast, leaving the coastline littered with dozens of islands and reefs. Needless to say, it is one of the most dangerous coasts in the world—and one of the most spectacular.

The climate is as varied as the land. In the south, the Mediterranean climate brings hot, dry summers and mild, wet winters. Perth has the mildest climate of any Australian capital with average summer maximums of about 30°C, while winter minimums are around 8°C.

The desert country has very hot, dry summers with temperatures often in the high 40s, with mild, dry winters and temperatures in the mid 20s. Marble Bar, in the north-west of the state, is recognised as the hottest place in Australia.

The tropics have hot, muggy and wet summers, called the Wet, where the temperature is often 30°C or more with high humidity. Occasionally there are tropical cyclones along the coast and when these go inland they become low depressions bringing heavy rain to a large area of the state. For travellers, the Wet can bring road closures and dirt roads can stay closed for weeks. The Dry, or winter, is mild and sunny and is the time when people head north to escape the chill of the south.

The road network through the south-west of the state is well maintained and in the main bitumen capped. Once away from settled areas bitumen is reserved for the major highways and for around town.

Only two highways make the border in a bitumen state: these are the Eyre Highway in the south across the Nullarbor, and the Victoria Highway in the north, east of Kununurra. The others are dirt, and in some cases very rough dirt.

Once north of Geraldton on the coast, or Meekatharra inland, the only roads that are blacktop are the main North West Coastal Highway, the Great Northern Highway, plus a couple of major roads to Tom Price and Exmouth. You will have to get used to travelling on gravel roads if you want to experience the delights of the Pilbara, the Gascoyne or the Kimberley. Once away from the major mining towns, the roads and tracks are really the home of the 4WD.

Many of the state's wildlife species have evolved slightly differently from those in the east. Some of its species, including the state emblem, the numbat, are found only in this state.

Western Australia offers the visitor vast expanse and tranquillity with a diverse range of landscape, flora and fauna. The hugeness and the very seasonal differences that the state endures means a number of visits—perhaps at varying times of the year—are really the best way to experience some of the delights of this state.

Banksias growing in Drovers Cave National Park

PERTH - DARWIN
Via Stuart, Victoria, Great Northern,
North West Coastal & Brand Hwys
(National Route 1), 4156 Kilometres

PERTH	56		Northam/ Adelaide
Newman Port Headland	115		
Badgingarra			Cervantes
	184		
Mingenew			Dongara
Mt. Magnet	63		**Geraldton** 418 / 3738
Northhampton	52		
	228		
Overlander Roadhouse			Denham
	201		
		899 / 3257	Carnarvon
Minilya Roadhouse	136		Exmouth 220
	228		
Tom Price Newman			Nanutarra Roadhouse 1263 / 2853
	45		Onslow
Fortescue River Roadhouse	120		
	137		Roebourne 1560 / 2596
Newman	84		Whim Creek
Perth	80		Port Hedland
	291		
Sandfire Roadhouse			2015 / 2141
	285		
	2300 / 1856	Roebuck Roadhouse	Broome
	145		Derby
	214		2659 / 1497
Fitzroy Crossing			
	288		**WESTERN AUSTRALIA**
2947 / 1209 Halls Creek			
	163		
Turkey Creek			
	151		Wyndham
Kununurra	88		
STATE BORDER			3349 / 807
NORTHERN TERRITORY	185		
			Timber Creek
3623 / 533	89		Victoria River
Top Springs	68		
	125		
Adelaide			**Katherine** 3816 / 340
Jabiru	113		Pine Creek
	114		Adelaide River
	113		**DARWIN**

PERTH

POPULATION: 1.2 MILLION

MAP REFERENCE: PAGE 305 B5

Perth, on the northern banks of the Swan River, 18 km inland from its port of Fremantle, is arguably Australia's most modern city, with the mining boom of the 1970s and 1980s transforming Perth's skyline, and everything below it.

The city and its greater metro area sprawls over more than 5700 sq km of undulating sandplain, from Rockingham on the south coast, north for 55 km to the northern coastal suburbs of Burns Beach and Mindarie. Inland the metro area stretches to the rolling hills of the Darling Ranges and the city of Armadale, and along the Swan River north and east, beyond Midland to Upper Swan and Brigadoon.

Vast areas within this region have been kept as open land, while much of the Swan River frontage is open to the public. The beaches, stretching from the south to the north and beyond, are considered by the locals to be the best of any Australian capital, while the surf is in a similar category. The southern beaches in the lee of Garden Island are somewhat protected and offer calmer waters, while the Swan River has many delightful bays and areas to swim in. Further offshore there are a number of islands, including Rottnest Island.

With a population of over 1.2 million, Perth is the fourth biggest city in Australia, but because of the gold rushes of the 1890s and the more modern mineral boom of the late twentieth century, the city has been rebuilt a couple of times since it was founded in 1829.

Britain's fear of a French or Dutch colony being established on this far west coast of Australia led in 1826 the push for a colony in Western Australia. In that year Albany was established, and the following year Captain James Stirling arrived to explore the Swan River. Britain agreed to support another colony, but only in a minimal way, so Australia's first free settlers, devoid of convict labour, arrived with Captain Fremantle on 2 May 1829. Stirling, the colony's first Lieutenant-Governor, arrived in June and headed inland to find a site for the settlement. It was not until 12 August that the foundation of Perth was declared.

For the first few decades growth was slow, and there was a huge shortage of labour. Convicts arrived in 1850 to bolster the workforce, but even after another 20 years, by which time the transportation of convicts to Australia had ceased, the population of the city was still less than 5000.

In the 1870s the Overland Telegraph Line between Adelaide and Perth was completed, and the following decade a number of railways around the city and further afield helped the settlement to grow.

That slow growth was, in hindsight, a blessing, for it allowed the city to be laid out to plan. The surveyor, John Septimus Roe, laid out his main boulevard, St George Terrace, along the flat land parallel to the river, while Hay and Murray Streets, which were to be his retail sector of the city, were on hillier ground, but also parallel to the main boulevard. Other streets ran at right angles to these forming what was, and still is,

the heart of the city. Today, many of those streets are one-way thoroughfares to cope with the ever increasing vehicle traffic, while the retail area of Hay and Murray Streets are pedestrian shopping malls.

The Government Legislative Council of Western Australia was formed in 1832 and the old legislative building erected four years later. That same year, Perth's oldest surviving building, the Courthouse, was built. Other buildings pre-dating the gold rushes of the 1890s, include the Old Perth Boys' School (1854), Bishop's House (1859), Wesley Uniting Church (1870), and the former Government Printers Office (1879).

Mt Eliza, which blocked the city's expansion to the west, is today Kings Park, one of the jewels in Perth's crown. Looking over the city, the 400 hectares of park and bushland provide many fine panoramas of the city and the river, while being a showcase for much of Western Australia's floral wealth and its colourful bird life. While a couple of roads wind through the park, a number of walking and bike paths, picnic areas and playgrounds are also available.

Moonrise over the modern skyline of Perth

Perth's, and Western Australia's, fortunes changed when gold was discovered. First it was far away in the Kimberley and Pilbara, but as more and more prospectors went looking for the golden metal the finds got closer and richer, until almost unbelievable discoveries occurred at Coolgardie and Kalgoorlie in the 1890s. The population of the state rocketed and by the turn of the century the city had over 29 000 people and a burgeoning public works program. Many of Perth's finer old buildings date from this boom period, including the refurbished commercial buildings along King Street, the Central Government Building (1874-1902), His Majesty's Theatre (1904) and the Perth Mint (1898), where even today, each and every day, you can see pure gold bars being poured.

Perth's fortune waned during the 1920s and 1930s and did not really revive until after World War II when, with increased immigration and growing mineral exploration and development, the city began to prosper. The mineral boom began in the 1960s and 1970s with iron ore, oil and natural gas. Perth grew with the development of the state's resources into the city of today—modern, cosmopolitan, egalitarian and friendly.

Northbridge, just on the northern side of the city, with its migrant heritage, comes to life at night with one of the highest concentrations of restaurants to be found anywhere in Australia. Riverside restaurants can be found in South Perth, Crawley and Nedlands, as well as down at Fremantle. Fraser's Restaurant and the Kings Park Tea Rooms are favourites because of their outstanding views of the city. And, if you want to partake in food and a little flutter, there is always the Burswood Casino.

Fremantle is very much part of the Perth experience. Perth's port had become a city in its own right by 1929, and had survived the building demolitions of the 1890s and the 1960s to emerge in 1987, when it was the host city for the America's Cup challenge, as a city rich with heritage and soul.

'Freo', as nearly everyone calls the port, is home to a 500-strong fishing fleet, a vast number of yachts and pleasure craft that on most summer weekends see the waterways busy, and the island of Rottnest surrounded by the white hulls of fishing boats, dive boats, and cruising yachts.

Over 150 buildings are classified by the National Trust in the port, such as The Round House (built in 1831 and Western Australia's oldest public building), the Esplanade Hotel (1890s) and the Fremantle Prison, (built by convict labour and used from 1855 to 1991). The National Trust Fremantle Markets, established in 1897, are still open every weekend with just about everything on offer from bric-a-brac and fashions to fresh produce.

Another spot to visit is the Fremantle Arts Centre and History Museum housed in a magnificent building, constructed by convicts in the 1860s to serve as the colony's first lunatic asylum. The WA Maritime Museum, down near the harbour, contains a first-class international exhibit of the early Dutch wrecks that litter the West Australian coast.

If you enjoy fine food, alfresco cafés or a quirky beer such as 'Redback', or 'Dogbolter', then Freo is the place for you. South Terrace is known as the cappuccino strip, while the E Shed Markets down on Victoria Quay have an international food court and restaurants with some great seafood.

As you would expect, there are plenty of good fishing opportunities in and around Perth and Fremantle, with estuary fishing in the Swan and Canning Rivers, throughout the port area and off the beaches, where you can get tailor, whiting, garfish, flathead, mulloway and tommy ruff.

The Perth Royal Show is held during September/October, while the Kings Park Wildflower Festival is on around the same time. In late October, Perth hosts the Australian round of the FIA World Rally Championships, while the Highland Games are held at Armadale in November/December. Then there's the Australia Day Celebration in January and down in Fremantle, the Sardine Festival, also in January, while in November there is the Fremantle Festival.

The Swan River, flowing through Perth to Freemantle

ACCOMMODATION

CBD: Airways City Hotel, ph (08) 9323 7799; Bailey's Parkside Hotel/Motel, ph (08) 9325 3788; Burswood Resort Hotel, ph (08) 9362 7777; Brownelea Holiday Apartment, ph (08) 9328 4840; CWA House Residential (B&B), ph (08) 9321 6081; Briannia International YHA, ph (08) 9328 6121

Fremantle: Esplanade Hotel, ph (08) 9432 4000; Fremantle Hotel, ph (08) 9430 4300; Danum House B&B, ph (08) 9336 3735; Fremantle Village Caravan Park and Chalet Centre, ph (08) 9430 4866

North side: Bayswater Motel/Hotel, ph (08) 9271 7111; Joondalup Resort Hotel, ph (08) 9400 8888; Mindarie Marina Hotel, ph (08) 9305 1057; Burns Beach Caravan Park, ph (08) 9305 5000

North-east: Ballajura Inn Homes B&B, ph (08) 9249 1230; Guildford Rose & Crown Hotel, ph (08) 9279 8444; Maylands Motel, ph (08) 9370 5505; Swan Valley Tourist Village Caravan Park, Guildford, ph (08) 9274 2828

North-west: Nookenburra Hotel, Innaloo, ph (08) 9445 3111; Ocean View Motel, North Beach, ph (08) 9246 4699; Scarborough Starhaven Caravan Park, ph (08) 9341 1770

South: Swanview Motel, Como, ph (08) 9367 5755; Airport Chalet Centre, Jandakot, ph (08) 9414 1040; Metro Inn Perth, ph (08) 9367 6122

South-east: Bentley Motor Inn, ph (08) 9451 6344; Heritage View (B&B), Bedfordale, ph (08) 9497 1635; Pioneer Motel/Hotel, Armadale, ph (08) 9399 5122; Carlisle Motel/Hotel, ph (08) 9361 1544; Kelmscott Caravan Park, ph (08) 9390 6137

South-west: Raffles Riverfront Hotel, Canning Bridge, ph (08) 9364 7400; Applecross Bed & Breakfast, ph (08) 9364 7742; Captain Stirling Hotel, Nedlands, ph (08) 9386 2200; Coogee Beach Caravan Resort, ph (08) 9418 1810

East: Ascot Inn, ph (08) 9277 8999; Bel Eyre Motel, Belmont, ph (08) 9277 2733; Southglen Llamas Cottages, Glen Forrest, ph (08) 9298 8617; Springvale Park Homes & Caravan Park, High Wycombe, ph (08) 9454 6829

West: Kings Park Motel, Subiaco, ph (08) 9381 0000; Swanbourne Hotel, ph (08) 9384 2733; Murray Lodge Motel, West Perth, ph (08) 9321 7441

TOURIST INFORMATION: Ph (08) 9483 1111

THE SOUTH-WEST

The south-west corner has some of the most picturesque country in the state. Margaret River is an easy three hour drive from Perth and is situated between the 'Two Capes', Cape Naturaliste in the north and the state's most south-westerly point, Cape Leeuwin, near Augusta, to the south.

MAP REFERENCE: PAGE 306 A8

LOCATION: 261 KM SOUTH OF PERTH TO CAPE NATURALISTE, 324 KM SOUTH OF PERTH TO CAPE LEEUWIN

BEST TIME: OCTOBER TO MAY

MAIN ATTRACTIONS: COASTAL AND FOREST SCENERY, FISHING, SWIMMING, LIMESTONE CAVES, BUSHWALKING, DIVING, 4WD TOURING, WINERIES

INFORMATION: DEPARTMENT OF CONSERVATION AND LAND MANAGEMENT, AT BUSSELTON, (08) 9752 1677; MARGARET RIVER, (08) 9757 2322; NANNUP, (08) 9756 1101; PEMBERTON, (08) 9776 1107

ACCOMMODATION: SEE TOWN LISTINGS FOR AUGUSTA, MARGARET RIVER, PEMBERTON AND YALLINGUP

NOTE: CARRY DRINKING WATER AND A PORTABLE STOVE

The economic backbone of this region has been the dairy, beef and timber industries since the area was first settled in the early 1920s as part of the Group Settlement Scheme. But over the past 20 years tourism has become one of the district's more important industries, receiving national and world-wide recognition for things as diverse as its premium wines, an international surfing competition and the annual black-tie outdoor concert at the Leeuwin Estate winery.

This area is host to a rough, extremely dramatic coastline and to some of the smallest, most delicate formations to be found underground anywhere. The Leeuwin–Naturaliste Ridge, a 600-million-year-old geological formation of granite, is capped by limestone and sand dunes. It is around 40 km from the ridge to the sea.

Aboriginal occupation of the area has been dated to around 40 000 years ago with bones, implements and other evidence found at sites, including caves, throughout the region.

The earliest recorded European account of the area is a mention in 1622 of 'Leeuwin's Land' in the log of the Dutch East India Company ship *Leeuwin*. A second reference was made by J. P. Poereboom, who, in 1685, anchored in what is thought to be Flinders Bay. Many explorers followed, including Matthew Flinders, who named Cape Leeuwin in 1801, and Nicholas Baudin from whom Hamelin Bay, Cape Naturaliste and Geographe Bay got their names.

South of Pemberton is Point D'Entrecasteaux, named in honour of Bruni D'Entrecasteaux, who led a French scientific expedition along the coast of Western Australia in 1792. One hundred and thirty kilometres of this coastline, between Augusta and Walpole, are now protected in D'Entrecasteaux National Park.

Access
The region is easily accessible on major roads south of Perth.

LEEUWIN–NATURALISTE NATIONAL PARK
Covering an area of 19 700 hectares of the Limestone Coast, this long, thin park is a popular holiday destination for West Australians. They are attracted by the sheltered bays and beaches, good fishing, dramatic wind-swept coastal scenery, limestone caves, jarrah and karri forests, excellent surfing and the local wineries.

The coastal strip is a bushwalker's delight with many short, easy trails, as well as other, more demanding treks. Roads lead to the main scenic

Ellen Brook, near the estuary of the Margaret River in Leeuwin–Naturaliste National Park

attractions and from many of the car parks, walk trails head off along clifftops and beaches, through heathland and rocky outcrops.

On the Coast
CAPE NATURALISTE
Sealed roads lead to the lighthouse built in 1903 (an excellent vantage point to look out over the cape and Geographe Bay), and to Sugarloaf Rock (a rough exposed section of coastline featuring a tall, pyramid-shaped rock). Watch out for dangerous waves when walking around the rocky shoreline. A 4WD track leads from near the lighthouse to the coast, good for surfing and fishing. A 3 km walking trail connects the lighthouse with Bunker Bay, a picturesque spot. Toilets and tables are available.

YALLINGUP
This popular holiday destination is a real favourite for surfers keen to tackle the huge rolling swells. A caravan park and wide range of other accommodation are available here.

SMITHS BEACH
A popular surfing spot on this extensive stretch of clean, sandy beach, this is also good for swimming. Fishing here is a favourite sport. There is a caravan park and other accommodation 200 metres from the beach.

CANAL ROCKS
A series of rocks extend into the ocean from the headland, making a natural canal. This is a good fishing spot, but dangerous for swimming.

A walkway and bridge lead out into the rocks to view the canal and see the power of the ocean as it surges through the passageways. There is a protected boat ramp here.

COWARAMUP BAY GRACETOWN

A lovely scenic bay, this has a good lookout on the right before reaching the town. Fishing is popular here and when the swells are right, some excellent waves for surfing come in across the bay. There are picnic facilities, toilets and a caravan park in the town opposite the bay.

PREVELLY PARK

Located at the mouth of the Margaret River, just outside the park, this area is famous for its magnificent surfing. The annual Margaret River Classic attracts top surfers from all around the world. There are headlands and vantage points from which to watch the surfers. Canoeing here is a popular pastime. The Margaret River is a lovely pristine waterway with plenty of bird life.

HAMELIN BAY

Set in a protected bay behind Hamelin Island and the surrounding reef, this pretty bay is very popular with families and anglers. The swimming is good and there are some excellent SCUBA diving and snorkelling areas. A boat ramp is available for launching small craft. The long beach is ideal for walking, while a climb to the headland gives nice views. There is a caravan park right beside the beach.

Last century, Hamelin Bay was used for exporting karri timber. In its heyday, the port had a jetty and heavy moorings for ships in the bay. The rotting stumps of the jetty can still be seen in the water, and where the old timber yard once stood is now the camping area.

CAPE LEEUWIN

This is the point where the Indian and the Southern Oceans meet, with the impressive Leeuwin Lighthouse right on the cape. In 1895, during the building of the lighthouse (opened in 1896), a spring was tapped to provide fresh water for the workers. The spring water was carried along a narrow wooden channel to the wooden water wheel. This rudimentary system was used until 1928. Since then, salt

LEGEND

Sealed/Unsealed Rd	★ 26 ★
Four Wheel Drive	- - - - -
Walks	··········
Rest Area (Picnic Area)	⊞

Caravan Park	🚐
Camping Area	⛺
Accommodation	🛏
Information	ℹ
Fuel Supplies	⛽

deposits have steadily encrusted the wheel, virtually encasing it in stone.

WHALE WATCHING

The annual whale migration to and from Antarctica can be seen close up along the Leeuwin–Naturaliste coastline. Both humpback and southern right whales swim past these shores in July on their way to northern breeding grounds and southwards between October and November. The southern right whales are often seen lazing about in some of the shallow bays along the coast. Part of this behaviour is to enable adult females to give birth, then nurture their young in the shallows away from the danger of predators, particularly sharks, in the deeper waters. The best vantage points to see the humpback whales are Cape Leeuwin, Cape Naturaliste, Gracetown Lookout at Cowaramup Bay, and around Sugarloaf Rock. It is estimated that 3000 to 4000 humpbacks make their way along this coast each year.

WATER SPORTS

With the warm Leeuwin Current running off-shore from this coastline, the fishing from the beach, off rocks and over reefs in small boats is excellent all year. Good catches of skippy, dhufish, snapper, whiting, school and gummy sharks and flathead are regularly made. During late summer and early autumn the Australian salmon make their migratory run up the coast to around Perth and then back again. Abalone and cray fishing are popular in a number of bays, but licences are needed.

The coastline offers many great SCUBA diving spots in protected bays around the islands and reefs. Fourteen ships are known to have sunk during storms and after hitting reefs around Hamelin Bay. A dive trail has been set up which takes in four of these ships.

Sailing and windsurfing are also popular summertime attractions along the coastline.

Inland

BORANUP FOREST

Boranup Forest is the largest known karri forest growing in limestone sands, and covers 3200 hectares. It is around 100 km from Western Australia's other main forest areas where the trees are usually found growing in red clay loams. Boranup was mostly clear-felled between 1882 and 1913. The karri forest has since regenerated with most trees (some up to 60 metres high) now less than a hundred years old.

There is a pleasant, tall timber drive through the forest, and the Boranup camping area, set in the bush, is quite basic with BBQs, tables and toilet facilities, but no water. Some of the most spectacular multi-headed grass-trees you will ever see grow here. Some of these old giants are over 5 metres high, with more than 15 heads! It is also a great place to enjoy the forest and birds, and at night you should look out for possums.

CAVES

Beneath the sweeping landscape of the park lies an intriguing underground world containing stalagmites and stalactites. Over the years, fossils of long-extinct marsupial lions, Tasmanian tigers, a shark, koalas, and even the remains of a gigantic wombat-like creature the size of a horse (dated around 37 000 years ago) have been found here. The cave systems are among the oldest and most valuable archaeological sites in Australia.

The extent of this underground limestone system is extraordinary with over 360 caves having been discovered in the park. They range from narrow tunnels to enormous caverns measuring over 14 km long.

Four of the most spectacular of the caves are open to the public with regular guided tours. These are Yallingup Cave, to the north of the park, Mammoth and Lake Caves in Boranup Forest, and Jewel Cave in the south near Augusta. In addition there are two adventure caves in Boranup Forest: self-guided experiences where no lights are provided. Take a torch and wear strong footwear and old protective clothing—the caves are a lot of fun, but care must be taken.

Other Attractions

Whilst travelling between various sections of the park, you will encounter other notable features: wineries, cheese factories, craft shops, galleries and studios making anything from gumnut ornaments to jewellery, pottery and furniture. In recent years this area has developed a name for its cottage industries.

A visit to the old Ellensbrook Homestead, situated near the mouth of the Margaret River, is also popular. Ellensbrook was built in 1857 by Alfred Bussell for himself and his young wife, Ellen. The building has now been restored by the National Trust and is open to the public.

Animals found here include western grey kangaroos, brush-tail possums, honey possums and fat-tail dunnarts. There is a wide range of seabirds, as well as wedge-tailed eagles, kites and the red-tailed tropic bird. In all, around 200 species of birds have been recorded.

The wildflowers are particularly colourful around headlands and in low heath areas in spring and early summer. Acacias, tiny orchids, coastal daisy bush, cocky's tongue, banksias and one-sided bottlebrush are all found in the park.

Access

Roads to all the main areas in the park are either sealed or good gravel.

D'ENTRECASTEAUX NATIONAL PARK

D'Entrecasteaux National Park covers some 115 000 hectares of diverse, mainly untouched country. It has huge sand dunes, limestone cliffs and long, white, sandy beaches. Inland there

are lakes, wetlands, the Shannon, Donnelly and Warren Rivers, areas of heathland and tracts of tall karri and jarrah forest.

Several conventional access trails lead off the Vasse Highway, Windy Harbour Road and South-Western Highway to the park's main features. There are also rough, narrow and sandy 4WD tracks going to various sections of the park and to the coast, mostly to great fishing spots.

No supplies are available in the park—bring all your requirements, including water. The nearest fuel and supplies are at Pemberton, Northcliffe and Walpole.

Wildlife here includes a small number of quokkas, chuditch, ringtail, brush-tail and pygmy possums, wallabies and bandicoots, while southern right whales migrate along the coast.

In 1990 archaeological studies were carried out in Lake Jasper in the park's northern sector. Divers found Aboriginal artefacts, trees and grass-tree stumps deep underwater, and ancient camp sites dating from 40 000 years ago when the Aboriginal Minang people lived in the region.

THE SOUTH WEST TREK
Margaret River to Augusta

From Margaret River you can take any of the roads west of the town (the Wallcliffe–Prevelly road just north of town is a good one) to get onto Caves Road, which is a sealed road running parallel to the main Bussell Highway between Yallingup and Augusta. Turn left onto Caves Road and you will pass through mostly open farmland for about 10 km until you hit the forest areas around Mammoth and Lake Caves.

Just past Lake Cave, turn right onto Conto Road and a limestone track will take you over peppermint woodland and coastal heath down to the spectacular scenery around Cape Freycinet. There are two designated camp sites in this area, the well-established and popular one at Conto's Field and a smaller one a little further on, just off Point Road. Toilets, BBQs, firewood and basic facilities are provided for a small fee, but there is neither water nor a rubbish bin at these sites.

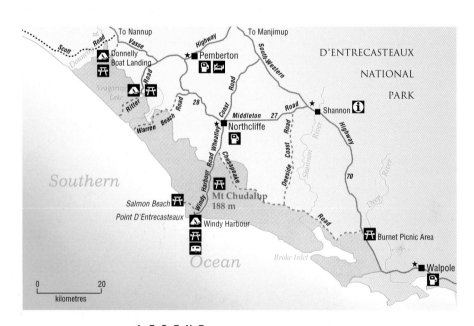

LEGEND

★ 26 ★	
Sealed/Unsealed Rd .... ●━━● - - -	Caravan Park .... 🚐
Four Wheel Drive .... - - - - - -	Camping Area .... 🏕
Walks .... ••••••	Accommodation .... 🛏
Rest Area (Picnic Area) .... 🏕	Information........................ ℹ
	Fuel Supplies .... ⛽

A limestone cave, one of the many in the south-west of Western Australia

The Cape Freycinet area has some great fishing spots, particularly for herring, trevally or whiting. But please use extreme caution when fishing the rock platforms along this whole south coastal region. Many lives have been lost to the big Southern Ocean swells.

From Cape Freycinet you can exit via Point Road, then bear right onto Love Spring Road which runs into Boranup Drive and eventually, after about 18 km, back onto Caves Road. Just before you reach Caves Road on Boranup Drive is the Boranup Forest camping area.

At the Boranup Drive–Caves Road junction, turn right onto Caves Road and head south for about 8 km until you reach the delightful caravan park at Hamelin Bay.

Backtracking 2 km on the Hamelin road brings you to the junction with Caves Road. Turn right here and you can access the good SCUBA diving and fishing areas at Cosy Corner or the Jewel Caves a little further on, before Caves Road terminates 14 km later at the Bussell Highway. Turn right and it is only 3 km to Augusta, which is the second major town in this area and your last chance to stock up before the 4WD section and the next supply point of Pemberton, about 170 km to the east.

Situated at the southern tip of the Leeuwin–Naturaliste National Park, Augusta is ideally placed for a wealth of aquatic activities. There is plenty of varied fishing on the ocean beaches and rocks and in the Blackwood estuary, as well as good surfing, diving and windsurfing. The town has excellent services for a small community offering banks, medical facilities and a good range of shops.

Augusta to Black Point

From Augusta backtrack 14 km to Karridale on the Bussell Highway. Alternatively, if you are coming from Hamelin Bay, bear left onto Caves Road (heading north) for about 5 km until you hit the Bushby Road junction; turn right here and in a couple of kilometres you will be at the Karridale town site. Karridale has a small store with fuel available. From Karridale head east on the Brockman Highway towards Nannup through dairy farms and the scattered remnants of forest. In about 9 km the road passes over the Alexandra Bridge on the magnificent Blackwood River which is navigable up to about this point. About 300 metres after crossing the bridge you will notice a road on the left; this short road runs down to the 'old' Alexandra Bridge and a great camping and picnic area on the Blackwood. It is a good spot for a brew or to wet a line for black bream.

From Alexandra Bridge continue east on the Brockman Road for about another 7.5 km until you meet Scott River Highway coming in from the

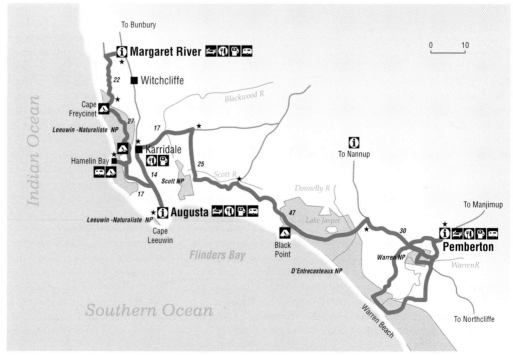

right. Turn right here and follow the formed gravel road south through farming properties for 14 km, crossing the Scott River at Brennan Bridge.

About 2.5 km past the bridge, Scott River Road takes a right turn to the west. However we turn *left* here onto the Milyeannup Coast Road and the start of the offroad section of this trip.

Lower tyre pressures to around 10–15 psi (70–105 kPa) and engage the front hubs if necessary. Make sure everything is secured, with nothing protruding from the vehicle before heading off through the coastal scrub and heathland. This section of the track is fairly sandy with a few soft patches but if you keep the momentum up it shouldn't pose any problems.

In around 12.5 km you will come across a track off to the right; it is not signposted, but this is Roberts Road (**GPS** 34°17'55"S, 115°23'03"E), the only all-weather access track to Black Point from the west. If you miss this turn-off you will end up at a small bridge over the Scott River—you have gone too far! Retrace your steps about 1.5 km south of the bridge and look for the track, now on your left. There is a CALM sign giving Black Point information about 200 metres in on the left.

Once you turn onto Roberts Road you are in 4WD country, so select the gear that suits your vehicle and the track conditions. You may have to experiment, but for many vehicles low-range third will keep you moving at a comfortable pace with enough power to prevent you from stalling.

Roberts Road runs through a mixture of coastal heathland, acacia and wattle scrub with some low-lying areas in between. The track is mainly black sand and can vary greatly in its standard. Stay with the main track which runs around the vegetated coastal dunes, bordering private property on the right; it can be a bit soft and rough in this area depending on how much traffic it has seen, but it should not cause any problems.

About 20 km on, Roberts Road links up with Black Point Road coming in on the left; proceed straight ahead. (*Note:* If you were to turn left here onto Black Point Road the track joins up with a major gravel road after about 13 km. This goes off to a mine site and eventually out onto the Vasse Highway. However, this 13 km section is closed to all traffic from May to January because of the large bogholes which are impassable.)

Continue for another 2.5 km until you reach the junction with Wapet Track; turn right here and it is just a short 1.5 km run to Black Point (**GPS** 34°25'17"S, 115°32'24"E). You are now in the D'Entrecasteaux National Park. There are two areas of sheltered undefined camp sites with pit toilets tucked away in the peppermint gums before you come over the last rise and down to the beach. These are the only designated camping areas, and they are much more sheltered than the wind-blown day use area down near the beach which has a toilet, BBQ tables and a BBQ ring provided.

The beach area and the 'stepping-stones' on the north-west side of Cape Beaufort (Black Point) are the best places for a swim or snorkel, and there are several good breaks around the point with excellent waves if you are into surfing. A rough vehicle track south of the beach car park runs out over capstone and heathland, skirting around Bolghinup Lake and on to the southern part of the point to several fishing spots with spectacular scenery along the dark basalt cliffs, their curiously carved vertical columns etched out by the Southern Ocean. But please take care here—the big seas come out of nowhere on this very exposed section of coast.

Black Point to Pemberton

Backtracking 1.5 km out from the camp sites brings you to the junction with the Wapet Track. Turn right here and follow the winding track across the coastal scrub and heathland for about 7.5 km, until you come to a right turn which will take you another 1 km down to Jasper Beach. There are a couple of badly rutted sandhills in this section that may require a bit of a run-up to get over, but if you stay in the right gear and keep the power on they should be no trouble. The coastal scrub is very close in places, so watch the paintwork and do not speed over these narrow one-lane tracks. It is a good idea to sound your horn when approaching blind corners.

Lefroy Brook near Pemberton

It is possible to drive down onto Jasper Beach, as a lot of surf fishermen do, but just be aware that you have to be able to get yourself back up again! Beach conditions can vary greatly and there is no shelter down there to make a comfortable camp. If you do decide to camp here to fish, swim or just to beachcomb this magnificent stretch of beach, a much more sheltered proposition is the small nook carved into the peppermints just back over the first dunes that you passed on the way in.

Turning right again out of Jasper Beach, the track begins to slowly wind its way inland. There are one or two small crests here that can be fairly soft in summer, but they should not present too many problems if you get a bit of a run-up.

Coming off the coastal heathland, the track turns back into the forest and some overgrown sections of vine thickets and big timber. There are quite a few blind corners and right turns in this section, so put your lights on and be aware of oncoming traffic, keeping in mind areas to back-up into for passing if need be. About 5.7 km from the Jasper Beach turn-off you will come to the junction with Scott Road; turn left here and continue for approximately another 4.7 km until you meet Lake Jasper Road coming in from the left. Turn left again here and it is only 5.4 km on the loose sandy track to the camp sites at Lake Jasper (**GPS** 34°25'36"S, 115°41'20"E).

The camping area has a boat ramp, toilets, BBQs and tables and a nice little white sandy beach all set amongst the shady peppermint trees, making it an ideal spot for the family to relax. A short 1 km track leads around the edge of the camping area and across a paperbark swamp to an expanse of beautiful white beach on the south-eastern corner of the lake. This is an ideal place for a picnic and a swim and is very popular with the locals over the summer months for waterskiing. There are several other tracks leading away from the camp ground that make interesting walks.

From the Jasper camp site it is about 14 km out to the Vasse Highway. Head back out the way you came in on Lake Jasper Road until it links up with Scott Road, then turn left and follow Scott Road out to the small bridge over the Donnelly River. The bridge marks the end of this 4WD section and the track gradually improves as it winds through the karri forest and out to the main road.

Once you reach the bitumen, turn right onto the highway and it is a very pleasant 25 km into Pemberton through some of the most scenic country in the south-west.

Pemberton has a lot to offer the off-road traveller, even if you are not into general tourist activities. Being centrally situated in the main karri belt and one of the oldest timber towns in the south-west, there is plenty of history around with interesting places to visit just a short distance from town. You can make a base at the caravan park down on the banks of the Lefroy Brook (within walking distance of town), or bush camp on the coast or at one of the other previously mentioned areas away from Pemberton.

The Pemberton–Warren Beach–Yeagarup Circuit

The last 4WD section of this trek is a circuit route from Pemberton and may be done as a run-on from the previous section or at your leisure at a later time. It is basically a summer only track (November to April) as it involves crossing the mouth of the Warren River which can only be done when the water levels are low, and even then only after a thorough inspection of the crossing. For this reason it is essential that you get up-to-date information on track conditions, tides and the state of the river crossing from the CALM office in Pemberton before you go. It is recommended that you do this circuit in the company of another vehicle if possible, and make sure you have your recovery gear on board.

If it is not possible to get across the mouth of the Warren you can still get beach access from the Yeagarup Dunes side and complete half of the circuit, which is almost equally interesting. To complete the whole 90 km circuit should take you around four to five hours without major stops, but it is really easy to lose several days camping, fishing or just taking in the surroundings in this beautiful area that combines the ocean with the forest.

Zero your trip meter at the Pemberton post office and head out of town on the Pemberton–Northcliffe road. Go past the Vasse Highway coming in on the right just out of town and continue for 10 km before turning right into Callcup Road. There are forestry tracks crossing your route everywhere in this region so follow these kilometre notes to get you through to Warren Beach.

Veer left at the Y-junction about 0.4 km from the main road turn-off, and continue straight ahead over the crossroads for 1.5 km. Bear left at the Y-junction 0.8 km further on, then in another 0.7 km turn right at the T-junction onto Allis Road. Continue straight ahead onto the Malimup Track for about 5 km, where you cross the bridge over the Dombakup River. Keep going straight ahead through the next track junction onto Richardson Road and over the 3 tonne bridge.

About 2.5 km from the Dombakup River you will come to the junction with Lewis Road. Turn right onto Lewis Road and continue straight ahead into the D'Entrecasteaux National Park. In about 5.5 km Lewis Road runs onto Callcup Road; continue straight ahead for about 0.5 km, then veer left onto Warren Beach Road.

About 5.3 km from here, you need to bear right at the Y-junction and continue straight ahead for just over 1 km until you reach the top of Callcup Hill (**GPS** 34°37'34"S, 115°52'42"E).

This is the start of the 4WD section and a good place to take in the impressive views of Warren Beach and the Southern Ocean while you let your tyres down to 10 psi (70 kPa) before descending the hill.

Take a good look at the condition of the track down Warren Hill; if you think that to get back up again may be beyond you or your vehicle's capabilities, *do not descend it!* Once you do you are committed, so it may be better to opt for the Yeagarup Dunes alternative.

The descent down Warren Hill to the beach is about 2.5 km; turn right at the bottom and it is around 5 km to the river mouth. There are some good fishing gutters and holes along this whole expanse of beach where you can usually pick up a feed of herring, whiting and tarwhine or even bigger species like salmon and mulloway in season. It is possible to drive south along the beach for about 8 km, crossing the Meerup River and on to another exit point at the Summertime Track, but again it is dependent on seasonal conditions.

After carefully selecting a safe place to cross the Warren River and having a look around the estuary, do the crossing, then follow the track north for about 0.5 km, turning right back into the dunes. There are a couple of rough camp sites in this area if you wish to stay on the beach.

Follow the track for another 1.8 km where you go up over a steep dune, turning left at the top, then straight ahead for the 4 km run up the sandhill. This hill is a long steep climb, so make sure you are in the right gear to keep the power on, and reduce tyre pressures further to around 8 psi (55 kPa) if you are having problems. But keep your speed down.

Bear left at the Y-junction and continue for about 1 km, where you veer right around a steep dune on the left. You are now entering the Yeagarup Dunes area, a large expanse of sandhills that are slowly moving inland. Follow the marker posts across the dunes for about 4.5 km until you come down to the Yeagarup Lake picnic site and the end of the 4WD section.

Heathland is part of the diverse landscape of the D'Entrecasteaux National Park

Back now on the formed gravel of Ritter Road, follow it inland and back into the forest for just over 11 km until you hit the crossroad with the Old Vasse Road. Turn right here and continue into the big timber of the Warren National Park for a further 3.8 km before turning right onto the scenic drive and the Heartbreak Trail.

After about 1.7 km, bear left and you are onto the Maiden Bush fishing trail. Along this 5 km trail which follows the Warren River there are several good picnic and camping sites. These provide basic facilities such as toilets, BBQs and picnic tables. All the sites are secluded, tucked away under the dense canopy of the karri forest, making great places to hole-up for a few days to fish for the wily trout and big redfin perch for which the area is renowned.

Do not forget that you need a freshwater fishing licence to fish inland waters in Western Australia. These licences are obtainable through any post office).

Canoeing is also a popular activity on the Warren River, although it can be frustrating in times of low water due to the many log-jams that have to be portaged.

After your stay in the karri forest, follow the one-way Maiden Bush Trail out to the junction with the Old Vasse Road, stopping along the way to take in the views of the river valley from the Warren River Lookout. Turn right at the T-junction and follow the Old Vasse Road for 2 km until it hits the Pemberton–Northcliffe road. A left turn here will take you 8 km back into Pemberton and the end of this trek.

ALBANY

417 KM SOUTH-EAST OF PERTH
POPULATION: 16 400   MAP REF: PAGE 306 F10

Albany is one of Western Australia's top tourist destinations and it is easy to understand why. Known for its many local natural attractions, its rich heritage and its unique arts and crafts, as well as cultural activity, there is something for everyone here.

It is the state's most historically significant town and its oldest settlement, having been founded in 1826, but many of the names that dot the coast, including King George Sound, Princess Royal Harbour and Point Possession, recall the first European visitor, Captain Vancouver, who claimed the area in 1791 for Britain. Other visitors included the French explorer Bruni d'Entrecasteaux who arrived in the same year, and Matthew Flinders who arrived 10 years later. Britain took formal possession, sending the ship, *Amity*, with troops and convicts, to form a colony. Originally called Frederickstown, in 1832 the first governor of the new Swan River Colony, Governor Stirling, changed its name to Albany.

The town's perfect natural harbour helped make it a major port, and from the 1850s steamers from England and naval ships operating in the Indian

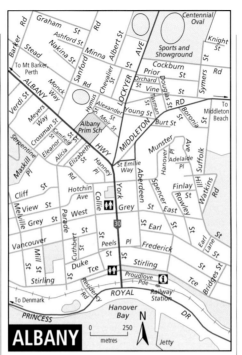

The town lost a lot of its importance as Fremantle developed in the early part of this century. However, it has evolved into an important business centre and

The beautiful coastline of Albany

Ocean began using Albany as a coaling station. This continued until the turn of the century when Fremantle was established.

Since the early 1800s seals and whales had been hunted and in the 1840s a land-based whaling station was established at Albany. Initially hunting southern right whales, in later years the station hunted sperm whales. It was the last whaling station in Australian waters, closing its slipway finally in 1978. Today, the rich marine life along the coast is a major tourist attraction, with the southern right whales arriving in the waters off Albany between July and October. An added attraction is that seals can often be seen along the coast and also off nearby islands.

supply centre for the fishing fleet and processing operation that are based there, in particular the meat processing plant and the sawmilling interests in and around the town. It also services the many farms in the local region. The town has now become a popular tourist destination.

In the town itself there are over 50 historic buildings, many of which have been developed as museums, display galleries or restaurants. Patrick Taylor's Cottage, built just one year after the town was officially surveyed in 1832, is now a museum. The Old Gaol, built in 1851, is also a museum. The whaling museum, named Whaleworld, details the whales and the whaling operation that once flourished here.

The Old Farm, on Strawberry Hill, was the first farm in the region and its two-storey brick building, one of the oldest in the state, was erected in the 1830s. The National Trust eventually took it over in 1963 and it is now furnished in various styles, representing the different eras it has experienced.

There are a number of national parks and reserves in the area, with Torndirrup National Park just out of town. The spectacular coastline is worth at least a daytrip to view the Gap, Natural Bridge, the Blowholes and Jimmy Newhills Harbour.

A little further to the east is Two Peoples Bay Nature Reserve, an important bird and animal habitat, while 70 km inland is the outstanding botanical environment of the Stirling Ranges National Park. Over a thousand species of plants exist here, and while there is always something in flower, the best time to visit is between August and November. There are magnificent wildflower displays all around Albany during this time and they really should not be missed.

The whole coast is captivating and the fishing from beach or boat can be excellent, especially for salmon, tarwhine, tommy ruff, shark, groper, queen snapper and whiting. The protected waters of Oyster Harbour are good for garfish, flounder and whiting.

Surfing and diving are also popular activities in the area and a wreck has been sunk in the Sound as an artificial reef, making it a popular dive site.

A variety of cultural, social and sporting events takes place in Albany throughout the year. The Festival of Albany is held in April, the Wildflowers Festivals in September and October, and the Summer Street Fair in November.

ACCOMMODATION: Royal Gorge Hotel/Motel, ph (08) 9841 1013; Dog Rock Motel, ph (08) 9441 4422; Brackenhurst B&B, ph (08) 9842 3158; Channel Resort, ph (08) 9844 8100; Emu Beach Caravan Park, ph (08) 9844 1147

ACTIVITIES: Bushwalking, bowls, fishing, golf, historical walks, horse riding, national park access, scenic drives, water sports, whale watching, wineries

TOURIST INFORMATION: Ph (08) 9841 1088

AUGUSTA

325 KM SOUTH OF PERTH
POPULATION: 465   MAP REF: PAGE 306 B8

Augusta is a small town located on the more protected eastern side of the promontory of land that ends at Cape Leeuwin, the far south-western tip of the state, where the waters of the Indian Ocean and the Southern Ocean clash. The Blackwood and Scott Rivers form Hardy Inlet, and much of the town stretches along its shores and those of Flinders Bay.

The first settlers arrived here in 1830, making it the state's third oldest settlement. A monument to the *Emily Taylor*, the ship that brought the first Europeans here, stands on the shores of the bay.

About a kilometre further south, near Barrack Point, is a whaling memorial and a whale rescue information shelter. It was here that in 1986 the world's most successful whale-saving operation was carried out when over 100 false killer whales were returned to the sea. The Augusta Historical Museum is located in the heart of town and has historical information on the town's early days, and details on the Leeuwin Lighthouse and the many shipwrecks that dot the coast.

The area's history is closely aligned with the timber industry, the cutting of jarrah, marri and karri, and the museum has an excellent display on the period during the 1880s that brought the town to prominence.

The area is richly endowed with natural attractions, including the Leeuwin-Naturaliste National Park where you can bushwalk, picnic and camp. Hamelin Bay, 17 km north of the town and on the west coast within the park, is a magnificent spot popular with campers, divers, surfers and anglers.

A disused water-wheel in Augusta

There are more than 300 caves in the area with Jewel Cave being a popular place to visit. Further north, towards the small hamlet of Margaret River, there are other well-known caves to visit, including Lake and Mammoth Caves, while the more adventurous can explore the Moondyne Cave system.

The Spring Flower Show is held every September/ October.
ACCOMMODATION: Augusta Sheoak Chalets, ph (08) 9758 1958; Baywatch Manor Resort (backpackers), ph (08) 9758 1290; Georgiana Molloy Motel, ph (08) 9758 1255; Doonbanks Chalets & Caravan Park, ph (08) 9758 1517
ACTIVITIES: Bushwalking, fishing, golf, historical walks, national park access, water sports, wineries
TOURIST INFORMATION: Ph (08) 9758 1695

BALLADONIA

939 KM EAST OF PERTH
POPULATION: 20   MAP REF: PAGE 311 A8
The tiny township of Balladonia is located 193 km east of Norseman, and 182 km west of Cocklebiddy on the Eyre Highway. Between the tiny settlement of Caiguna in the west and Balladonia is one of the longest straight stretches of bitumen in the world, 145 km in length.

Once the site of a telegraph station, today Balladonia consists of only a hotel/motel and a service station. The site of the nearby Balladonia Station Homestead was chosen back in 1879 by the

Ponton brothers and John Sharp for their sheep station, while rock from the surrounding granite outcrops was used to build the original homestead in 1880, as well as the fences.

There is a gallery of oil paintings at the homestead which will be of interest to visitors as the paintings depict Balladonia's history.
ACCOMMODATION: Balladonia Hotel/Motel, ph (08) 9039 3453; Balladonia Caravan Facility, ph (08) 9039 3453
ACTIVITIES: Fuel and rest stop
TOURIST INFORMATION: Ph (08) 9039 3453

BEVERLEY

127 KM EAST OF PERTH
POPULATION: 760   MAP REF: PAGE 306 D5
This small town in the Avon River valley was once one of the major towns in the area. Settled in the 1830s, it wasn't until the Great Southern Railway passed through that the town took on any real importance or substance. When the last passenger train made its call in 1975, the town went back to being a quiet village servicing the local mixed farms in the valley.

There are many fine old historic buildings such as the old police station, court house and railway station, and the town has a very good Aeronautical Museum that traces the development of aviation in the state.

Less than 50 km south of the town are the Yenyening Lakes which are popular for sailing, waterskiing and swimming. For walkers the nearby County Peak makes for a pleasant interlude.

Join in the family fun at the annual Beverley Duck Races held each September on the Avon River, while an Arts and Gallery Purchase Exhibition is held around the Easter period.
ACCOMMODATION: Beverley Hotel, ph (08) 9646 1190; Rosedale Holiday Farm, ph (08) 9648 1031; Beverley Caravan Park, ph (08) 9646 120
ACTIVITIES: Bushwalking, golf, historical walks, horse riding, water sports
TOURIST INFORMATION: Ph (08) 9646 1555

BREMER BAY

594 KM SOUTH-EAST OF PERTH
POPULATION: 190   MAP REF: PAGE 306 H9
This small holiday resort is situated at the mouth of the Bremer River, on the horseshoe-shaped bay of the same name. It is one of the best fishing spots on the south coast and good catches of salmon, whiting, tommy ruff, trevally and queen snapper are common from around the bay, while you can add groper to the list when fishing from the rocks. There are also good diving and surfing along the local coast.

Matthew Flinders had first sailed this coast in 1802 and sealers and whalers no doubt sheltered in the protected waters of the bay. Edward John Eyre passed through here on his epic crossing of the Bight in 1841 and the area was slowly opened up by pioneer pastoralists. Gold and other minerals were found in the surrounding area, but nothing ever really boomed, leaving the area for today's nature lover.

The town is one of two places, the other being Hopetoun, that gives conventional vehicles access into the Fitzgerald River National Park, with its spectacular scenery and magnificent floral display in late winter through to spring. Over 1800 plant species, with 80 or so endemic, are found in this park, which was declared a World Biosphere Reserve in 1978 because of its virgin bush and verdant variety.

Within the park, on the banks of the Gairdner River is the 1858 cottage of Quaalup Homestead, established by an early settler. It contains a good display of memorabilia and is furnished in the style of the day. There is a self-contained guest house and a camping ground located at this spot. Wellstead Homestead, west of the town, was established around the same time and is still owned by members of the same family.
ACCOMMODATION: Adventurers B&B, ph (08) 9837 4067; Bremer Bay Hotel, ph (08) 9837 4133; Bremer Bay Caravan Park, ph (08) 9837 4018
ACTIVITIES: Bushwalking, fishing, golf, national park access, water sports
TOURIST INFORMATION: Ph (08) 9837 4093

BRIDGETOWN

274 KM SOUTH OF PERTH
POPULATION: 1520   MAP REF: PAGE 306 C8
Situated in scenic surroundings on the Blackwood River, Bridgetown is the commercial centre for the region, which produces apples and stone fruits. It is also an important timber region with jarrah forests and pine plantations.

Some tin mining is carried out around the district, but first and foremost the area is known for its natural beauty of rolling hills, and with its rivers, forests and magnificent displays of wildflowers, is considered by many to be one of the prettiest parts of Western Australia.

The region was first settled in the 1850s and there are a number of places to visit that date from those early days. The home of the first settler, John Blechynden, is located on the banks of the Blackwood River, while to the north-east, just out of Boyup Brook, is a tree blazed by the 1840 explorer, A. C. Gregory.

There are galleries and museums to stroll through and those people interested in craft markets and the like should visit the River Markets held every second Sunday at the Blackwood River Park.

Scenic drives in and around the area include the Geegeelup Heritage Trail, a 52 km loop taking in the historic towns of Bridgetown and Greenbushes. You can also take a walk or a picnic through the Bridgetown Jarrah Park, which is located 20 km from the town.

Annual events include the Greenbushes Dry Land Regatta held in March, the Blues Festival in November, and the local show in late November.
ACCOMMODATION: Bridgetown Motel, ph (08) 9761 1641; Campbells B&B, ph (08) 9761 2710; Country Cottages, ph (08) 9761 1370; Bridgetown Caravan Park, ph (08) 9761 1053
ACTIVITIES: Bushwalking, canoeing, fishing, horse riding, swimming
TOURIST INFORMATION: Ph (08) 9761 1740

BROOME

2356 KM NORTH OF PERTH
POPULATION: 11 151   MAP REF: PAGE 315 N1

This subtropical town has a fascinating, colourful history and a unique, cosmopolitan feel about it which originates from its early pearling days when over 400 luggers plied the coast as part of its pearling fleet. Although pearling still plays an important role in Broome's economy and development, the town of Broome today is one of Western Australia's most popular tourist destinations, with the fabulous and beautiful Cable Beach one of its major drawcards.

While Aboriginal people lived along this coast for thousands of years, the Malays and Macassareses sailed the coastline well before the coming of Europeans, the first being William Dampier who journeyed along the coastline in 1688. It wasn't until 1821 that the British sent Phillip Parker King to survey the coast; he named Roebuck Bay.

By the 1870s pearling was a major activity along the Kimberley coast, with about 80 boats working from Cossack, near Roebourne, and by 1880 a settlement had grown up near the mouth of Dampier Creek. In 1883 the township of Broome was officially proclaimed by Sir Frederick Napier Broome, the then governor of Western Australia, and pastoralists soon followed the pearling industry, opening up the inland.

In 1889 Broome became connected to the Overland Telegraph Line from the south. As well, a submarine telegraph cable was laid between Broome and Banjawangie in Indonesia. Between 1900 and 1914 Broome was at its height, but World War I saw trade in pearl shell suspended and the town never again rose to its pre-war heights, even though pearling began again in earnest once the war finished.

Divers paid a high price for removing the pearl shells from the sea, with hundreds of divers over the heady days of the pearling industry losing their lives, most to the dreaded 'bends'.

With the demise of markets for mother-of-pearl shell after World War II, the cultured pearl industry was born and still thrives today.

Broome's rich heritage and culture provide plenty of things to see and do. A visit to the Japanese and

The Court House in Broome

Pioneer Cemeteries gives a good insight into the harsh life these people endured and the Historical Society Museum is well worth a visit.

A telephone booth reflecting Broome's Asian connections

Chinatown, once a mix of pearl sheds, Japanese boarding houses, saloons and hotels, is today a hive of business, centred on the commercial pearling industries, with many fine old buildings and structures still standing. After admiring the exquisite, lustrous pearls in the many pearl emporiums, you can take a drive out to the Willie Creek Pearl Farm and observe pearl farming at close quarters and learn how cultured pearls are grown.

Also found in Chinatown, and a must for any visitor, is the Sun Pictures movie house, believed to be the world's oldest open-air picture garden.

Broome is renowned for its fabulous Cable Beach, its name taken from the cable which linked Broome with what is present-day Indonesia. With its miles upon miles of clean white sand and turquoise blue sea offering safe swimming, it is a gem along this coastline. Vehicles are even permitted to drive along the beach north from the boat ramp at Cable Beach, which is also a nude bathing area!

Not far from Cable Beach is the Malcolm Douglas Crocodile Park where visitors get the chance to see mature crocodiles and many other reptiles at close hand in their natural habitats.

Anglers will find plenty of places to drop a line close by to Broome, such as Crab Creek, Barred Creek, Willie Creek, Fisherman's Bend and Prices Point. Gamefishing is also becoming a major attraction in Broome, with the Sailfish Fly Rod Challenge being held in June, and the Broome Gamefish Tournament competition in July—both 'tag and release' events.

Just out of Broome is the Broome Bird Observatory, a research base for Birds Australia and recognised as one of the top five wader bird viewing locations in the world. Various guided tours and ornithological courses are run during the year and there is a variety of interesting walks and excursions along the beach, mangroves, plains and bushlands. Accommodation and caravan/camping facilities are also available at the Observatory.

The Dampier Peninsula, north of Broome, features miles of great coastline, secluded bays, spectacular red pindan cliffs (especially in the evening light), blue waters and some great fishing, as well as a good variety of bird and animal life. Access is pretty good, but it is definitely 4WD country.

A number of Aboriginal communities have opened their doors to travellers, as have one or two cattle stations, making the Peninsula a great destination during your stay in Broome.

Several special events are held in Broome, with the O-Bon Festival in August and the Shinju Matsuri (Festival of the Pearl) held in August/September a must for any visitor. Accommodation is always short at this time of year, so it pays to book ahead.
ACCOMMODATION: Cable Beach Club, ph (08) 9192 0400; Harmony Broome B&B, ph (08) 9193 7439; Roebuck Bay Hotel/Motel, ph (08) 9192 1221; Broome Caravan Park, ph (08) 9192 1776
ACTIVITIES: Beach driving, birdwatching, camel riding, fishing, 4WD touring, horse riding, swimming
TOURIST INFORMATION: Ph (08) 9192 2222

BUNBURY

184 KM SOUTH OF PERTH
POPULATION: 21 750   MAP REF: PAGE 306 B7

This city on the south-west coast of Western Australia is the region's major port, centred on its deep water harbour and its bulk storage and handling facilities. Those extensive facilities testify to the fact that inland lies some of Western Australia's richest agricultural land, while the whole area is also rich in minerals. Ilmenite, rutile and zircon were discovered in the sands along the coast and have been heavily exploited since the 1950s, while bauxite, used in the production of alumina, has also been found nearby. The timber industry has always been important to Bunbury, with two-thirds of the state's hardwood forests found in the region, while woodchip, a contentious export, is also serviced by the port.

The first European sighting was that of French explorer Captain de Freycinet, on the *Geographe* in 1803. In 1829, the then governor in charge of the new Swan River Colony sent a detachment south to look for good land. They explored the estuary and the two rivers, the Collie and the Preston, that now carry their names. However, it wasn't until a Lieutenant Bunbury arrived in 1836 that real development took place. The early settlers traded with the sealers and whalers who anchored in the bay until the government placed a handling charge on them. They moved and Bunbury nearly died, staying subdued until the railway arrived in 1891.

Now it is the major city in the south-west, acting as the region's administration and business centre. In recent years, the area around the port has seen a lot of improvement, and Bunbury combines city and country in a pleasant blend, making it a popular place

to live and visit, and an ideal base for touring the beautiful south-west.

Around the town there are a number of art and craft galleries with a fine range of local craft, including some delightful woodcraft made from local West Australian timbers.

King Cottage Museum, built in the 1880s, is a five-room cottage that houses a good display of colonial artefacts, while St Mark's Anglican Church is the second oldest in the state.

Wild dolphins visit the beach along Koombana Bay on a regular basis and have become a major attraction in their own right, prompting the building of the Dolphin Discovery Centre nearby. The beaches, bays and inlets close to town offer a range of safe

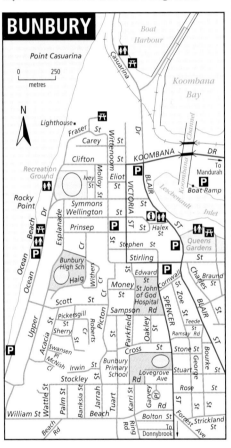

swimming and surfing beaches, ideal for boat cruising, yachting, fishing and crabbing.

The surrounding forests have a number of pleasant scenic drives and you can drive and walk through the Tuart Forest, one of the finest stands of tuart in the state, and unique to the south-west.

The *Leschenault Lady* is a vintage steam train that once hauled logs from the forests, and now takes people on a pleasant day trip through those same forests to towns dotted along the coast and inland.

Just to the north of Bunbury on the long arm of the Leschenault Estuary is the pleasant hamlet of Australind. A scenic drive along the inlet can be quite delightful and the town has a number of historic buildings, and a fine gemstone collection housed in Henton Cottage, built in 1883.

Annual events include the Agricultural Show in March, the Art Extraordinaire in August and the Bunbury Festival in November.

ACCOMMODATION: Clifton Beach Motel, ph (08) 9721 4300; Fawlty Towers Lodge, ph (08) 9721 2427; Ecotel Wellington Mill Cottages, ph (08) 9728 3043; Bunbury Inlet B&B, ph (08) 9721 4140; Bunbury Village Caravan Park, ph (08) 9795 7100

ACTIVITIES: Bushwalking, fishing, horse riding, water sports, yachting

TOURIST INFORMATION: Ph (08) 9721 7922

BUSSELTON

236 KM SOUTH OF PERTH
POPULATION: 18 000   MAP REF: PAGE 306 B7

This seaside town sits on the shores of Geographe Bay, a bay of calm waters, long beaches and sheltered coves, which is ideal for water-based activities.

While the primary industries of dairy and beef cattle, sheep, fruit and vegetable markets, and forestry have well supported the region, the relatively new venture of winemaking is making headway.

In 1801 a French sailor named Vasse drowned in what is today known as Geographe Bay. A small river bears his name. The first pioneers in the region were the Bussell brothers in 1832, and a town soon developed around the timber and dairying industries and the shipping of products from the bay.

The Busselton Jetty, all 2 km of it, is the longest wooden jetty in the southern hemisphere. Today it is a major landmark, and daily train rides are conducted along its length. To see marine life up close, visit the Oceanarium, or if you are into diving, this is one of the best dives around. The amount of marine life in, on, and around the pylons has to be seen to be believed!

For those who enjoy browsing through local markets, the Vasse and the Railway Markets are held regularly. There are also plenty of art and craft galleries and many old buildings, such as the Old Butter Factory, Court House and Newton House.

Special events include the Busselton Antique Fair and Collectors' Exhibition in January, the Old Machinery Rally in March, the Wildflower and Craft Exhibition in September, and the Agricultural Show in November.

ACCOMMODATION: Busselton Backpackers Hostel, ph (08) 9754 2763; Geographe Guest House B&B, ph (08) 9752 1451; Motel Busselton, ph (08) 9752 1908; Acacia Caravan Park, ph (08) 9755 4034; Kookaburra Caravan Park, ph (08) 9752 1516

ACTIVITIES: Abseiling, bushwalking, cycling, fishing, horse riding, parasailing, water sports

TOURIST INFORMATION: Ph (08) 9752 1288

CARNARVON

905 KM NORTH OF PERTH
POPULATION: 8500   MAP REF: PAGE 308 B2

The tropical gateway to the north, Carnarvon is located on the southern side of the mouth of the Gascoyne River. Most of its port facilities are located on Babbage Island, which is just offshore and connected to the mainland by a causeway, or at South Carnarvon near Mangrove Point.

The Dutch explorer Dirk Hartog sailed along this coast in 1616, landing on an island that now bears his name, just a short distance south in Shark Bay. William Dampier followed and left unimpressed.

It was not until the explorer George Grey visited Shark Bay that any land exploration was carried out. His 1839 expedition resulted in a number of names being bestowed around this region, including the Gascoyne River, which he discovered and named after a friend.

The town was gazetted in 1883, seven years after the first settlers drove sheep north from York to take up land in the district. It became an important port as the vast pastoral holdings produced large quantities of wool. The One-Mile Jetty juts out from Babbage Island nearly 1.5 km and was built in 1904 to service the growing trade with the town and the hinterland. Nearby is the Lighthouse Keeper's Cottage, which was built around the same time and is now a museum.

The wide streets of Carnarvon too, are a result of these early years, when a camel train was required to be able to turn in the main street.

In 1950 a whaling station was based here, which eventually closed down in 1962, and today this building is the prawning factory where tours are conducted during the winter months. The town has also seen some high-tech establishments, including the satellite tracking station used by OTC, the former overseas arm of Telstra, Radio Australia and a NASA tracking station. All of these have closed, while the prominent dish of the station is used as a pedestal for a fine viewing platform.

The town is an important agricultural centre, with bananas and exotic fruits available from a number of

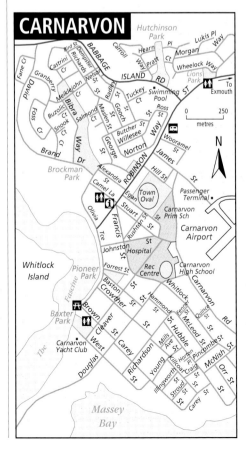

plantations. A rich prawn and scallop fishery is also based in Carnarvon, and 65 km north is the Lake Macleod Salt Mine.

Carnarvon is a fine base from which to explore the surrounding area and the coast is well known for its many attractions and great fishing. Offshore there are the long thin islands of Bernier and Dorre, while further south are the bays, inlets, rugged bluffs and headlands of Shark Bay and its encompassing marine park. If you are into surfing, 3-Mile Beach is considered by many to have the best left-hand break in the world.

Inland are the Rocky Pools on the Gascoyne River, while further afield are a number of semi-desert parks and reserves.

The major celebration of the year is the Carnarvon Festival, held in July. Other festivities include the Mirari Festival in May and the Carnar-Fin Fishing Competition run in June.

ACCOMMODATION: Hospitality Inn Carnarvon, ph (08) 9941 1600; Port Hotel, ph (08) 9941 1704; Carnarvon Beach Holiday Resort, ph (08) 9941 2226; The Outcamp B&B, ph (08) 9941 2421; Carnarvon Tourist Centre Caravan Park, ph (08) 9941 1438; Wintersun Caravan Park, ph (08) 9941 8150
ACTIVITIES: Fishing, golf, scenic drives, water sports
TOURIST INFORMATION: Ph (08) 9941 1146

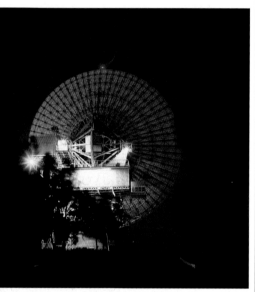

The OTC Satellite dish at Carnarvon

CARNEGIE HOMESTEAD

1296 KM NORTH-EAST OF PERTH
POPULATION: 10   MAP REF: PAGE 309 N4
Located on the western end of the famous Gunbarrel Highway, Carnegie Homestead offers an important re-fuelling point for travellers who venture along these lonely dirt roads. Located nearly 350 km east of the nearest town, Wiluna, Carnegie is first and foremost a sheep station covering a vast area of this semi-desert scrub country.

Although inhospitable country, this area saw a flurry of explorers in the late nineteenth century. John Forrest passed through in 1874, while Ernest Giles journeyed to the north in 1876. David Carnegie,

Dried mudflats by the Gunbarrel Highway near Carnegie

and another expedition led by Lawrence Wells, both heading for Halls Creek, passed through this region in late 1896/early 1897.

For those travelling east this is the last homestead and the final spot for fuel before Warburton Aboriginal Community, nearly 500 km away. To the east of Carnegie is Mungali Claypan Nature Reserve and a little further on, the Gibson Desert Nature Reserve, centred around a lonely track junction called Everard Junction.
ACCOMMODATION: Cabin accommodation and camping is available at the homestead, ph (08) 9981 2991
ACTIVITIES: A long scenic drive!
TOURIST INFORMATION: Ph (08) 9981 2991

CERVANTES

243 KM NORTH OF PERTH
POPULATION: 650   MAP REF: PAGE 306 B2
A two-masted American whaling ship gave its name to a small island when it was wrecked there in the early 1800s, and that, in turn, gave its name to the small fishing village that sprang up on the nearby coast. Today this small fishing town is popular with beach lovers and fishermen, many of whom make the trip north from Perth for the weekend.

The town's beaches are ideal for swimming, boating and especially windsurfing. So good and predictable are the winds that a round of the World Cup Slalom Sailboarding Championships is held in Cervantes each year in December.

Nambung National Park almost surrounds the town, and its major draw, the Pinnacles, are 29 km to the south. Here thousands of limestone pillars, standing up to 4 metres tall, dot the barren landscape. A one-way loop drive takes visitors, in normal cars, through the heart of this unique region.

To the north is Jurien Bay, another enjoyable fishing village, while inland are a number of other, not so well known, but interesting, national parks.
ACCOMMODATION: Cervantes Pinnacles Motel, ph (08) 9652 7145; Cervantes Holiday Homes, ph (08) 9652 7115; Cervantes Beachfront Units, ph (08) 9652 7194; Cervantes Pinnacles Caravan Park, ph (08) 9652 7060
ACTIVITIES: Bowls, fishing, golf, national park access, scenic drives, water sports
TOURIST INFORMATION: Ph (08) 9652 7041

COCKLEBIDDY

1164 KM EAST OF PERTH
POPULATION: 25   MAP REF: PAGE 311 D8
Hardly worth a mention, apart from the fact that on most people's run across the Nullarbor, between the towns of Ceduna in South Australia and Norseman in Western Australia, this is one of the few places for fuel, refreshments and accommodation. We have always found Cocklebiddy to be one of the dearest places, if not the dearest place, for fuel on the Nullarbor. Mind you, there are no bargains on the Nullarbor crossing at any of the places!

Just to the north-west of this small hamlet are the Cocklebiddy Caves, one of a number of sub-terranean caverns that are under the surface of the Nullarbor. A number of cave diving records have been set in this area, but a major rainstorm caused a large cave-in a few years ago, trapping a caving team for a few days, and it is still considered too unsafe to explore.

To the south, close to the coast, is the Eyre Bird Observatory, one of four major bird study bases around Australia. This complex is reached via a track that turns off the main highway 17 km east of the motel complex at Cocklebiddy. Accommodation and nature-based courses are run from the Observatory, but space is limited, so ring beforehand.
ACCOMMODATION: Wedgetail Inn Motel/Hotel, ph (08) 9039 3462; Cocklebiddy Caravan Park, ph (08) 9039 3462; Eyre Bird Observatory, ph (08) 9039 3450
ACTIVITIES: Birdwatching, caving, fishing, scenic drives
TOURIST INFORMATION: Ph (08) 9039 3462

COLLIE

206 KM SOUTH OF PERTH
POPULATION: 9500   MAP REF: PAGE 306 C7
This coalmining town is centred on the state's only coalfield. It is picturesque with its parks and gardens and is surrounded by heavily timbered jarrah forests and the Collie River Valley in the Darling Range.

The town was established in 1883, when a shepherd discovered coal here, nearly 60 years after the river had been named by a visiting naval surgeon, Dr Alexander Collie.

Places of interest include the Historical and Mining Museum, the Muja Power Station (which has tours), and a drive along the scenic Collie River. A couple of nearby dams, Wellington and Harris, offer some very pleasant picnic areas, while Honeymoon Pool is a delightful camping and picnic spot.

Special events include the Country and Western Roundup in March, Griffin Festival in May and the Collie Show in November.
ACCOMMODATION: Collie Forest Motor Lodge, ph (08) 9734 3388; Club Motel/Hotel, ph (08) 9734 1722; Victoria Hotel, ph (08) 9734 1138; Mr Marron Holiday Village (Caravan Park), ph (08) 9734 5088
ACTIVITIES: Bushwalking, canoeing, fishing, horse riding, scenic drives, swimming
TOURIST INFORMATION: Ph (08) 9734 2051

COOLGARDIE

554 KM EAST OF PERTH
POPULATION: 1400   MAP REF: PAGE 307 L3

Located at the junction of the Great Eastern Highway, the Coolgardie–Esperance Highway and the main road to Kalgoorlie and the goldfield towns further north, Coolgardie is today more a service town for the passing traffic than anything else.

Once it was the boom town on the newly discovered goldfields: during the 1890s it had a population of over 15 000 thirsty miners, 20 plus hotels to slake their thirst, three breweries to keep the pubs supplied and six banks to process the thousands of ounces of gold that were found.

The architecture of the main street, part of the Great Eastern Highway, is reminiscent of those early days and there are a number of old buildings gracing the roadway. The wide streets are lined with a variety of styles from corrugated iron and wood homes to large grand stone buildings. The Marble Bar Hotel is one of the 20 or so pubs still standing and dates back to the turn of the century. The Wardens Court Building, erected in 1898 using local stone and one of the largest buildings on the main thoroughfare, houses the Mining Registrar's Office, the Tourist Bureau, and the Goldfields Exhibition, an excellent display of photos, life-size models and old memorabilia from the goldrush days.

The Railway Station Museum, built in 1896, also has a fine display relating to transport, while the Ben Prior's Open Air Museum features machinery and mining equipment from the early days.

The main annual event is the Coolgardie Day Celebrations, held in September.

ACCOMMODATION: Coolgardie Motel, ph (08) 9026 6080; Coolgardie Caravan Park, ph (08) 9026 6009; The Haven Caravan Park, ph (08) 9026 6123
ACTIVITIES: Bowls, bushwalking, gem fossicking, golf, horse riding, rock climbing, scenic drives
TOURIST INFORMATION: Ph (08) 9026 6090

CORAL BAY

1145 KM NORTH OF PERTH
POPULATION: 300   MAP REF: PAGE 314 B9

This small village, situated on the 'Coral Coast' south of Exmouth and the Cape Range National Park, is located on the edge of the Ningaloo Marine Park. The park protects the reef of the same name, the longest coral reef in Western Australia, and the second longest in Australia after Queensland's Great Barrier Reef. However, the Ningaloo reef is much closer to shore and more readily accessible, so it is a place to be enjoyed by all the family. Whether you are into fishing from shore or boat, diving, swimming or just relaxing, this place has it all.

Coral Bay is the southern gateway to the park and a wide range of accommodation and facilities are located here, all within an easy walk from the beach.

Children and adults can swim amongst a mass of tropical fish just metres from the shore at Coral Bay, while the more adventurous can head off on a snorkel or SCUBA dive with the local dive operator. If you are in the area at the right time of the year you might even get the chance to snorkel with the giant but harmless whale sharks.

The sailing and boating are fantastic, and the well-equipped angler and diver have the whole coast to explore. However, a number of sanctuaries have been established along the coast and for the most part these exclude any fishing. It pays to check with the local tourist outlet or the Fisheries Department for bag limits and for areas where you can fish and dive.
ACCOMMODATION: Ningaloo Reef Resort Hotel/Motel, ph (08) 9942 5934; Coral Bay Lodge, ph (08) 9385 7411; Bayview Coral Bay Backpackers, ph (08) 9942 5932; Bayview Holiday Village Caravan Park, ph (08) 9942 5932
ACTIVITIES: Fishing, water sports, whale watching
TOURIST INFORMATION: Ph (08) 9942 5988

COSSACK

1587 KM NORTH OF PERTH
POPULATION: 115   MAP REF: PAGE 314 F5

Located at the mouth of the Harding River, Cossack has had a chequered past since it was founded in 1863 and called Tien Tien, after the boat that landed the first settlers there. It soon became the major port for the area and was the base for a large pearling fleet that operated from the port. It was re-named Cossack in 1873, after the warship of the same name which brought the governor of the day to the port for a visit.

During the late 1880s the port was busy as gold prospectors bustled through to the new, rich finds of the Pilbara. Many of the town's fine buildings date from this time, but in the following decade the town went into decline as the port silted up and the growing demand for port facilities saw nearby Port Sampson take over as the major town in the region. By the 1930s less than a dozen buildings remained in Cossack and 20 years later the town was abandoned. In 1979 restoration work was begun and in the early 1990s the Heritage Council of Western Australia took over control of the town, continuing with extensive restoration work to the present day.

Apart from the faithfully restored buildings in the town there is a museum with a wonderful display of early Cossack memorabilia, an art gallery, home to the annual art awards, and tearooms located in the old Customs House, while a large stone warehouse now has on display a selection of Aboriginal art and local products.

A wide safe beach will win over the children while there is good fishing from the wharf, along the beaches or amongst the mangroves in the river. You can expect to catch barra, mangrove jack, bream, threadfin salmon and mackerel. Mud crabs and blue swimmer crabs can also be found along the shoreline.

The annual Cossack Fair, in June, attracts a lot of visitors, while the Cossack Art Ball and Art Award is held in July.
ACCOMMODATION: Cossack Historic Town Lodge, ph (08) 9182 1190
ACTIVITIES: Boating, fishing, historic walk, swimming
TOURIST INFORMATION: Ph (08) 9182 1190

CRANBROOK

328 KM SOUTH-EAST OF PERTH
POPULATION: 320   MAP REF: PAGE 306 E8

A picturesque town situated just off the Albany Highway amongst rolling hills, Cranbrook is a wheat and sheep farming centre. For most travellers it is also the gateway to the nearby Stirling Ranges.

The town was declared in 1899 and was initially a watering point on the Great Southern Railway. Early on it was an important centre for the extraction of sandalwood which was exported to China for use in temples, but today the area is better known for its

The beautiful beach at Coral Bay

vineyards, wool production and wildflowers. From Sukey Hill Lookout, 5 km from town, you get a fine view of the surrounding area, including salt lakes, undulating farmland and the Stirling Ranges.

The annual event of the year is the Wildflower Show in late September/early October.

ACCOMMODATION: Cranbrook Hotel, ph (08) 9826 1002; Karinya B&B, ph (08) 9826 1199; Cranbrook Caravan Park, ph (08) 9826 1068

ACTIVITIES: Bushwalking, national park access, scenic drives, wineries

TOURIST INFORMATION: Ph (08) 9826 1018

CUE

646 KM NORTH-EAST OF PERTH
POPULATION: 600   MAP REF: PAGE 308 G6

The glory days of Cue, 'Queen of the Murchison', once the site of the richest goldfields in Western Australia, are long gone. Today all that remains are the fine buildings that were built in the 1890s. The main street is classified by the National Trust, as are a number of other buildings, including the primary school, the Masonic Lodge and the old jail.

Extensive mining was carried out at the turn of the century, including the Big Bell and Day Dawn mines nearby. Today's activity depends on the current price of gold, but still there are many prospectors willing to try their luck in and around these old mine sites. Mind you, you do require a Miners Right, and need to check areas for mining leases before prospecting for any gold.

Walga Rock, 50 km south of Cue, is a large monolith that deserves a visit. During spring the wildflowers are worth the trip alone.

ACCOMMODATION: Murchison Club Motel/Hotel, ph (08) 9963 1020; Dorsett Guest House, ph (08) 9963 1286; Nallan Station, ph (08) 9963 1054; Cue Caravan Park, ph (08) 9963 1107

ACTIVITIES: Fossicking, historic walk

TOURIST INFORMATION: Ph (08) 9963 1216

DAMPIER

1573 KM NORTH OF PERTH
POPULATION: 2500   MAP REF: PAGE 314 F5

The port of Dampier is the focus of much of the activity in the north-west, including the massive North-West Shelf Project, situated on the nearby Burrup Peninsula. The port really got its start when Hamersley Iron P/L built the ore-loading facility in 1966. Today it is the biggest tonnage port in Australia with over 1500 ships loading more than sixty million tonnes of iron ore from mines as far away as Tom Price, Paraburdoo, Brockman, and the new mine at Marandoo. As well, large quantities of salt, gas and condensate pass through the port.

The town takes its name from the nearby Dampier Archipelago, a group of 42 islands that were first visited and named by William Dampier in 1688. Its major attractions and recreational activities centre around these islands which have a fascinating history of shipwrecks, whaling, pearling and farming. Today they are mainly reserves.

The jetty at Dampier built for loading iron ore

The diving around the coast is good, and the fishing fantastic. You can expect to catch a good range of fish from big tuna, coral trout, red emperor, giant trevally, cobia and more.

On the Burrup Peninsula can be found one of the best collections of Aboriginal rock engravings—there could hardly be a more spectacular setting for this ancient art.

The annual Dampier Classic and Game Fishing Classic are held the first weekend in August.

ACCOMMODATION: Mercure Inn Hotel Dampier, ph (08) 9183 1222; Peninsula Palms Motel, ph (08) 9183 1888; Dampier Transit Caravan Park, ph (08) 9183 1109

ACTIVITIES: Fishing, mine tours, scenic drives, water sports

TOURIST INFORMATION: Ph (08) 9183 1440

DENHAM

830 KM NORTH OF PERTH
POPULATION: 1130   MAP REF: PAGE 308 B4

The World Heritage listed Shark Bay, a huge gulf on the Indian Ocean coast of Western Australia, is cut neatly into two by the long finger of the Peron Peninsula. On the peninsula's western shore is Denham, a small seaside town, the most westerly town in Australia, which was once, last century, the centre of the pearling industry.

Dirk Hartog Island, directly opposite, was the site of the first European landfall in Australia in 1616, while the first pioneers arrived in the area in the 1860s bringing their sheep to the freshwater soaks along the coast. They were followed by the pearlers and sandalwood harvesters. In 1898 the town was gazetted and named after Captain Henry Denham who had charted the bay 30 years earlier. On his trip he blazed a rock at Eagle Bluff, a section of which collapsed into the sea, and has now been recovered and relocated at the Pioneer Park, a couple of hundred metres back from the jetty.

A salt mine across the water at Useless Loop, the dolphins at Monkey Mia and the World Heritage listing of Shark Bay make up more recent history. The François Peron National Park was proclaimed in 1990 and takes up much of the peninsula, north of the town. The original Peron Homestead can be reached by normal car while trips further north to Cape Peron require a 4WD.

The Department of Conservation and Land Management (CALM) have instigated Project Eden which plans to eradicate all the feral cats and foxes from the peninsula, north from the narrow isthmus, which is about 25 km south of Denham, and make the park and intervening area into a haven for rare native animals. So far the plan is working and a number of animals that have been extinct on the mainland for over 100 years have been released.

The town has safe swimming beaches and is an excellent spot to dangle a line: anglers can expect to catch salmon, whiting and flathead from the beach or jetty. Outside the protection of the bay and from the cliffs of Steep Point, the most westerly point on the mainland, you can have some real action with cobia, tuna, Spanish mackerel and more.

The major event of the year takes place in the first week of August when the Shark Bay Fishing Fiesta, a fishing competition, gets under way.

The coastline near Denham

ACCOMMODATION: Heritage Resort Shark Bay, ph (08) 9948 1133; Shark Bay Hotel/Motel, ph (08) 9948 1203; Shark Bay Holiday Cottages, ph (08) 9948 1206; Monkey Mia Dolphin Resort Caravan Park, ph (08) 9948 1320; Denham Seaside Caravan Park, ph (08) 9948 1242

ACTIVITIES: Fishing, national park access, scenic drives, water sports

TOURIST INFORMATION: Ph (08) 9948 1253

DENMARK

470 KM SOUTH-EAST OF PERTH
POPULATION: 990   MAP REF: PAGE 306 E10

The township of Denmark nestles along the idyllic banks of the Denmark River and is surrounded by picturesque hinterlands and forests.

There are a number of scenic drives from Denmark, such as the Scotsdale and Mount Shadforth Scenic Drives, which give superb panoramic vistas of both the nearby ocean and encircling landscape.

During the wildflower season, the scene becomes a kaleidoscope of beautiful colours.

For history buffs there is the Historical Museum, while art and craft enthusiasts will find plenty of galleries to wander around.

There are wineries too numerous to mention open for cellar tastings and wine sales, and for something a little different, Bartholomew's Meadery produces mead, a fortified drink made from honey. Bridgart's Farm for seasonal produce, Mount Romance Emu Farm, and Pentland Alpaca Stud and Tourist Farm are all worth a visit.

Denmark also makes a great base from which to explore the nearby coastal scenery and the William Bay National Park with its spectacularly beautiful, yet rugged coastline. There are plenty of fabulous beaches to visit, with one of the most popular spots on the coast being Peaceful Bay. The more tranquil waters around Wilson Inlet are alive with bird life and there is a variety of boat cruises available on the Inlet.

The Art and Craft Markets, held in December, January and Easter are a great occurrence, as is the Denmark Country Farm in March.

ACCOMMODATION: Denmark Motel & Hillside Cottages, ph (08) 9848 1147; Denmark Unit Hotel/Motel, ph (08) 9848 2206; Misty Valley Farmstay, ph (08) 9840 9239; The Peppermints B&B, ph (08) 9840 9305; Ocean Beach Caravan Park, ph (08) 9848 1105

ACTIVITIES: Bushwalking, fishing, horse riding, national park access, prawning, water sports

TOURIST INFORMATION: Ph (08) 9848 2055

DERBY

2509 KM NORTH OF PERTH
POPULATION: 2300   MAP REF: PAGE 312 E7

Derby is located on King Sound, near the mouth of the Fitzroy River, just 220 km north of Broome, with Wyndham some 914 km away via Highway 1, and by the Gibb River Road just over 690 km.

While Aborigines inhabited this area well before the coming of the white man, it was Alexander Forrest who blazed his way through this region in 1879 and started a land rush that quickly saw Europeans take up land along the Fitzroy River in huge pastoral properties. Derby was proclaimed officially in 1883. With the discovery of gold at far away Halls Creek in 1885, Derby became established as a major port.

While the cattle industry still plays a major role in Derby's economy, mineral wealth, tourism and a number of defence establishments are today changing the face of the town. It has also become the gateway to the magnificent gorge country of the central Kimberley, as well as the maze of islands that dot the Kimberley's rugged coastline.

There are a number of historic attractions to interest the visitor, such as the Pigeon Heritage Trail, the Boab Prison Tree (a giant, hollowed out boab tree with a girth of 14 metres), and the Old Derby Gaol and Police Yard built in the 1880s.

Anglers will not be able to resist casting a line from the jetty, and there is a boat ramp that gives access to the sea. While the fishing is good, even spectacular, the tides and currents must be watched.

Derby, in fact, has the second highest tidal range in the world at 11 metres.

There are quite a few special events and festivals during the year, such as the Boab Festival in July, the Kimberley Music and Art Fair and Craft Festival in September, and the fun and frivolity of the cockroach racing, seed spitting, stubby sipping and frog racing events held at the Spinifex Hotel on Boxing Day.

Derby's jetty at sunset

ACCOMMODATION: King Sound Resort Hotel, ph (08) 9193 1044; Derby Boab Inn, ph (08) 9191 1044; Spinifex Hotel, ph (08) 9191 1233; West Kimberley Lodge, ph (08) 9191 1031; Kimberley Entrance Caravan Park, ph (08) 9193 1055

ACTIVITIES: Boating, fishing, heritage drive, scenic drives

TOURIST INFORMATION: Ph (08) 9182 1190

DONGARA

357 KM NORTH OF PERTH
POPULATION: 2500   MAP REF: PAGE 308 C9

While the township of Dongara is located on the Brand Highway on the banks of the Irwin River, its port is located 3 km away at Port Denison. These twin towns act as the centre for the Irwin Shire, a mixed farming district which has gained even more prominence through the discovery of oil and natural gas in the 1960s and which have been piped to Perth since 1970. The fishing boat harbour at Port Denison, one of the largest in the state, acts as a base for the crayfishing fleet, which during the lobster season—December to June—is busy bringing the catches back to the local processing factory.

The area was first explored by George Grey in 1839, and in 1846 Augustus Gregory discovered a coal seam. Settlement followed Gregory's report of good land, coal and other minerals and the district was soon a rich wheat producer, with a flour mill operating by 1859.

Russ Cottage, built during the 1870s and home to the Dent family, has been restored in its original

manner, while the old police station houses the Dongara–Denison tourist centre and also an historic display.

The nearby coast is popular with anglers, divers and windsurfers, while the town makes an ideal base from which to explore the surrounding countryside. Ellendale Pool, a pleasant swimming and picnic area, the beautiful Coalseam Conservation Park with its wildflowers, the Burma Road and the Yardanogo Nature Reserves are some of the attractions. The tourist centre can give up-to-date information on the best wildflower displays as well as the enjoyable 1.6 km walk along the Dongara Heritage Trail.

Annual events and activities include the Batavia Coast Craft Market Day held in April, the Lions Rodeo the same month, and the Blessing of the Fleet in November.

ACCOMMODATION: Dongara Motor Hotel, ph (08) 9927 1023; Seaspray Villas, ph (08) 9927 1165; Obawara B&B, ph (08) 9927 1043; Dongara/Denison Tourist Park, ph (08) 9927 1210; Dongara Denison Beach Caravan Park, ph (08) 9927 1131

ACTIVITIES: Bowls, fishing, golf, historic walks, water sports, wildflowers

TOURIST INFORMATION: Ph (08) 9927 1404

DONNYBROOK

219 KM SOUTH OF PERTH
POPULATION: 2300   MAP REF: PAGE 306 C7

First settled in 1842 by a group of Irishmen, Donnybrook today is notable for its quality fruit and vegetables, while sheep, dairy cattle and timber also play an important part in the region's economy. Back in the 1880s, however, Donnybrook was a goldmining centre, albeit short lived.

Well worth a visit is the historic Anchor and Hope Inn, built in 1862 as a coaching inn, and now restored to its original glory. Of interest also is the old Goldfields Orchard and Cider Factory, where you can have a go at gold panning and fishing.

For canoeists, there is a canoe course, Trigwell Place, on the Preston River, where there are also BBQ and picnic facilities.

If you are in the area at Easter, join in the activities of the Apple Festival.

ACCOMMODATION: Donnybrook Motel Motorlodge, ph (08) 9731 1499; Rosedeane Tourist Farm (B&B), ph (08) 9732 1332; Donnybrook Caravan Park, ph (08) 9731 1263

ACTIVITIES: Canoeing, fishing, scenic drives, swimming, waterskiing

TOURIST INFORMATION: Ph (08) 9731 1720

DWELLINGUP

119 KM SOUTH OF PERTH
POPULATION: 455   MAP REF: PAGE 306 C6

This town was ravaged by fire in 1951, and again 10 years later, the last time leaving only the hotel, a few houses and outbuildings standing.

Situated in the heart of the forest country, Dwellingup has always been a forestry town since its founding at the turn of the century. In 1918 it became a base for the management of and research into the local jarrah forests. The many roads through the forest give people a chance to view these magnificent trees up close, some of which are over 40 metres in height. To learn more about the timber and associated industries, the Forest Heritage Centre in town details the resources and the conservation that have gone into the surrounding forests.

The Dwellingup History and Visitor Centre is a good place to start your touring. From here you can head out to several pleasant picnic and walking spots, including Scarp Pool, Nanga Mill and Pool, Island Pool, Marrinup Falls, and Oakley Dam and Falls.

The Lane Pool Reserve, located south of the town, is a 50 000 hectare reserve, situated along the Murray River where trout, marron and freshwater cobbler can be caught. The Bibbulmun long distance walking trail passes through this reserve and bushwalkers can join it from here for a day or longer.

For a more unusual outing, the Hotham Valley Tourist Railway runs on the original 1910 line between Dwellingup and Pinjarra through farmland and jarrah forest, making a pleasant trip for steam buffs.

The special event for the year is the Dwellingup Long Chop, held every February.

ACCOMMODATION: Dwellingup Hotel, ph (08) 9538 1056; Berryvale Lodge B&B, ph (08) 9538 1239; Dwellingup Chalets and Caravan Park, ph (08) 9538 1157; Baden Powell Camping Facility, ph (08) 9538 1001
ACTIVITIES: Boating, bushwalking, canoeing, fishing
TOURIST INFORMATION: Ph (08) 9538 1108

ESPERANCE

743 KM SOUTH-EAST OF PERTH
POPULATION: 8500   MAP REF: PAGE 307 M8

Esperance is delightfully situated on a coast that has near-perfect white sandy beaches, azure water, and rocky headlands, all sheltered by the islands of the Recherche Archipelago, which stretch across the bay and along the coast. Long considered a summer holiday town by the people of the inland goldfields, Esperance has much to attract and delight the visitor.

This coast was first sighted by Dutch mariners in 1627 and then by George Vancouver in 1791. A year later the French arrived, giving their names to many of the islands and headlands along the coast.

In 1841 Edward John Eyre passed through, and it was at tranquil Rossiter Bay, east of present-day Esperance, that Eyre met Captain Rossiter of the French whaling ship, *Mississippi,* and secured badly needed supplies. However, it was to be another 20 plus years before pioneer settlers made their way to this coast. In the 1890s the town became an important port for the goldfields, but its importance waned when the Perth to Kalgoorlie railway line was opened in 1896. The area remained poor farming land until, in the 1950s, it was discovered that the soil was missing trace elements, and since then the surrounding area has been transformed into a valuable farming region.

The town has a rich heritage and the Museum Village and the Esperance Municipal Museum help preserve that, while the Old Cannery Arts and Crafts Centre houses workshops, exhibitions and the Society of Artists, with locally made products for sale.

The town is centrally situated to a number of excellent parks and reserves, the best known being those along the coast to the east, consisting of Cape Le Grand National Park, and further afield, Cape Arid National Park. Magnificent white sandy beaches, delightful bays and islands and bulky granite outcrops, many of them rolling in a graceful arc into the blue waters of the Southern Ocean, make this an outstanding coastal area. Offshore the sea is dotted with dozens of islands and the fishing, diving, surfing and windsurfing can be superb.

Further east again is the long strip of protected land along the cliff-lined coast, the Nuytsland Nature Reserve, encompassing the historic Israelite Bay Telegraph Station. Built in 1877, the station was an essential link in the communication network that once stretched across this coast, and linked Perth to the rest of the country.

To the west of Esperance is the smaller Stokes National Park, while inland there is the small Peak Charles National Park and the much bigger Dundas Nature Reserve. The wildflowers are a great attraction during spring in all these parks,

The clear waters at West Beach, Esperance

particularly at Cape Le Grand, with over 200 species being recorded. The Wildflower Society conducts guided walks from September to November from the Helms Arboretum.

In recent years, from July to November, there have been regular sightings of southern right whales along the coast, as they rest in the sheltered bays to calve. They have become another drawcard to the town and the area.

Annual events and festivities include the Agricultural Show in October and the Sailboard Classic in late December/early January.

ACCOMMODATION: Bay of Isles Motel, ph (08) 9071 3999; Esperance Motor Hotel/Motel, ph (08) 9071 1555; Esperance All Seasons Holiday Units, ph (08) 9071 2257; Pink Lake Lodge, ph (08) 9071 2075; Croker's Park Holiday Resort, ph (08) 9071 4100
ACTIVITIES: Bowls, fishing, 4WD touring, golf, horse riding, scenic drives, water sports, wineries
TOURIST INFORMATION: Ph (08) (08) 9071 2330

EUCLA

1438 KM EAST OF PERTH
POPULATION: 45   MAP REF: PAGE 311 G7

Now better known as a truck stop for the passing parade of motorists making the run across the Nullarbor from Perth to the eastern states, or vice versa, Eucla sits 11 km on the West Australian side of the border, close to a great escarpment that overlooks the flat coastal plain and the band of mobile white dunes along the coast itself. It is a popular spot to stop and refuel or even stay overnight.

Close to the beach and 4 km away are the notable relics of the old Overland Telegraph Line repeater station, connecting Western Australia to the rest of Australia. This station was once the busiest on the whole line as the base was staffed with both West and South Australians, since two morse code systems were used. In 1929 the station was abandoned and the

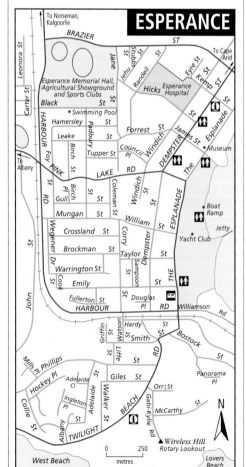

Map of Esperance showing streets including Brazier St, Jane St, Randell St, Eyre St, Kemp St, Leonora St, Carter St, Black St, Hamersley St, Leake St, Padbury St, Birch St, Tupper St, Forrest St, Council St, Windich St, Dempster St, James St, Harbour Rd, Foy, Pink Rd, Lake Rd, The Esplanade, Coleman St, Mungan St, William St, Crossland St, Corry St, Taylor St, Wegener Dr, Brockman St, Sampson St, Warrington St, Cook St, Emily St, Fullerton St, Douglas Pl, Harbour Rd, Williamson Rd, John St, Griffin St, Watson St, Hardy St, Smith St, Bostock St, Liffe St, Mills Pl, Phillips St, Giles St, Panorama Pl, Hockey Pl, Adelaide Cl, Ingleton St, Walker St, Orr St, McCarthy St, Gabi-Kylie Rd, Collie St, Albany St, Twilight Beach Rd, West Beach, Wireless Hill Rotary Lookout, Lovers Beach. Markers include Esperance Memorial Hall, Agricultural Showground and Sports Clubs, Swimming Pool, Esperance Hospital, Museum, Boat Ramp, Jetty, Yacht Club. To Norseman, Kalgoorlie; To Cape Arid; To Albany. Scale 0–250 metres. N compass.

shifting sands now cover and uncover its remains.

A town was proclaimed here in 1885 but it never eventuated, while in the early 1890s hopeful prospectors tramped the long distances across the Nullarbor Plain on their way to find their fortunes in the West Australian goldfields.

The Bunda Cliffs and a couple of lookouts near the present-day hamlet of Eucla give good views of these 90-metre tall cliffs plunging into the sea.

The Eucla National Park takes in a sea of mallee, heathland and scrub, inland from the cliffs of the Great Australian Bight.

ACCOMMODATION: Eucla Motor Hotel, ph (08) 9039 3468; Eucla Caravan Park, ph (08) 9039 3468

ACTIVITIES: Caving, fishing, golf, national park access, tennis

TOURIST INFORMATION: Ph (08) 9039 4368

Shifting sand dunes in Eucla National Park

EXMOUTH

1272 KM NORTH OF PERTH
POPULATION: 2600   MAP REF: PAGE 314 C7

Exmouth, near the top end of North West Cape, really came into being in 1967 when a support town was required for the US–Australian Naval Communication Base which was established nearby. It was not the first time that the strategic position of the Cape had been used: during World War II, Exmouth Gulf, lying within the protection of the Cape, had been a re-supply base for submarines operating in the Indian Ocean.

Dutch navigators first visited this western coast in the early 1600s, but it was left to Phillip Parker King in 1818 to survey the gulf and give it a name. Whalers and pearlers plied this coast and pioneer pastoralists took up land throughout the region during the 1880s. In 1912 the Vlaming Head Lighthouse was erected at the northern tip of the Cape and still overlooks the reefs and sea.

In the 1950s the Cape Range was subjected to the search for oil and a number of roads and tracks within the Cape Range National Park date from those days and give access into the heart of the park, which lies just to the south-west of the town. Both the Charles Knife and the Shothole Canyon Roads are

Yardie Creek in Cape Range National Park south-west of Exmouth

worthwhile scenic drives, giving good views of the surrounding range country, as well as access to a number of walking trails within the park. Further afield, still within the park, and reached via a good dirt road that skirts along the western side of the Cape, is Yardie Creek, with its boat tours, walking trails and unique wildlife. There are pleasant camping areas near the creek.

Exmouth itself acts as a fine base for fishing and diving enthusiasts and there are a number of boat ramps close by, giving access to the waters of the Indian Ocean, or the calmer waters of Exmouth Gulf. In the Gulf you can throw a line in for whiting and bream, while offshore you can expect to catch queenfish, marlin tuna, and sailfish, and along the reefs snapper, cobia, cod, wahoo, mackerel, barracuda, spangled emperor and giant trevally. In the mangrove creeks along the shoreline of the Cape you are likely to strike tarwhine and mangrove jack. Fishing is permitted in the waters of the Ningaloo Reef Marine Park, however there are special bag limits and regulations that apply.

In more recent years the town and the nearby coral reefs of the Ningaloo Marine Park have become a world-wide mecca for divers wanting to swim with giant whale sharks. This is the only place in the world where it can be virtually guaranteed that a trip out for the day will result in a swim with these gentle plankton-eating giants. The peak time for the whale sharks is from March to June, while the humpback whales begin to appear in the winter months, as do the huge schools of manta rays.

The turtle nesting season, when hundreds of green, loggerhead and hawksbill turtles come up onto the beaches at night, runs from November to January.

Annual major fishing competitions are the Billfish Bonanza in April and the Ultralight Tackle Gamefishing Competition in August, while other festivities include the Arts and Crafts Show in July and the Festival of Trees in November.

ACCOMMODATION: Potshot Hotel Resort, ph (08) 9949 1200; Exmouth Cape Tourist Village, ph (08) 9949 1101; Lighthouse Caravan Park, ph (08) 9949 1478; Exmouth Accommodation & Caravan Park, ph (08) 9949 1389; Exmouth Caravan Park, ph (08) 9949 1331

ACTIVITIES: Boating, bushwalking, diving, fishing, national park access, scenic drives, snorkelling, whale shark watching

TOURIST INFORMATION: Ph (08) 9949 1176

FITZROY CROSSING

2696 KM NORTH OF PERTH
POPULATION: 430   MAP REF: PAGE 313 H9

Fitzroy Crossing is a small settlement on Highway 1, some 255 km east of Derby and 290 km west of Halls Creek. Once a sleepy little hamlet on the banks of the mighty Fitzroy River, it began life as a watering hole for travellers stranded by floods at the crossing of the river. With the construction of a bridge across the Fitzroy in 1974, a new town grew up to the south.

This is cattle country and the town services the outlying stations, and has all the important facilities (fuel, stores and repairs) for travellers.

There are a number of things to see and do in and around the town. The Crossing Inn, built by Joseph Blythe in the 1890s as a shanty inn and trading store, is located near the old townsite and ford crossing, and today still offers travellers a cold beer. Also at the old townsite you can still see reminders of a past era such as the former post office and police station.

A visit to the nearby Geikie Gorge National Park, where the Fitzroy River flows through a striking slash in the range, is not to be missed. There are a number of walking trails, as well as boat tours operated by CALM which take visitors for a cruise up the best section of the gorge.

The freshwater fishing in the Fitzroy River can be rewarding, with catches of barramundi and sooty grunter available.

Annual events to enjoy when in the area include the Fitzroy Valley Rodeo held in June and the Beer Can Regatta in September.

ACCOMMODATION: Fitzroy River Lodge, Safari Tents and Caravan Park, ph (08) 9191 5141; Crossing Motor Inn, ph (08) 9191 5080; Darlngunaya Backpackers, ph (08) 9191 5140; Crossing Inn Caravan Park, ph (08) 9191 5208; Tarunda Caravan Park, ph (08) 9191 5176

ACTIVITIES: Fishing, gorges, historic drives, national park access, walking trails

TOURIST INFORMATION: Ph (08) 9191 5355

GASCOYNE JUNCTION

1065 KM NORTH OF PERTH
POPULATION: 35   MAP REF: PAGE 308 D3

If you are heading to the Burringurrah (Mt Augustus) National Park, then it is more than likely that you will drive through Gascoyne Junction, and while there might not be much to keep you in this tiny township, it is the last icy cold beer this side of Meekatharra.

The Junction, located on the southern side of the Gascoyne River, is the centre of the desert Merino fine wool industry, and its small and only pub comes straight out of olden droving days. It also doubles as a general store for the tiny town and passing travellers.

The Kennedy Ranges National Park is reached by a reasonable dirt road from Gascoyne Junction and this large park of rugged breakaway and gorge country has a number of walking trails and basic camping sites. Winter and spring are the best times to visit when wildflowers can be profuse. Gemstone and mineral specimen prospectors can collect petrified wood, opalite, chalcedony and many other different kinds of semi-precious stones in a number of areas around the town.

Rocky Pool, 54 km from town on the main road to Carnarvon and located on the Gascoyne River, is a popular spot for swimming, fishing and camping.

The Junction Race meet is held at Gascoyne Junction in the middle of July and is a great occasion if you are in the area.

ACCOMMODATION: Junction Hotel, ph (08) 9943 0504; Erong Springs Station (170 km south of Mt Augustus), ph (08) 9981 2910

ACTIVITIES: Birdwatching, fossicking, 4WD touring, national park access, gem collecting, swimming

TOURIST INFORMATION: Ph (08) 9981 2910

GERALDTON

423 KM NORTH OF PERTH
POPULATION: 21 300   MAP REF: PAGE 308 C8

A year-round holiday climate, and a location just five hours' drive north of Perth, make Geraldton one of the most popular places in the state, especially in winter. Good beaches, offshore islands and reefs, an inland ablaze with wildflowers in spring, and an interesting history that dates back to the first European contact with Australia, 350 years ago, along with good facilities in and around the town, and you have the finest makings of a great holiday destination.

The islands of the Abrolhos, which lie 100 km offshore, were the scene in 1629 of one of the greatest shipwrecks and mutinies in Australian history. Here the Dutch ship *Batavia* was wrecked, and in the ensuing months the drama of mutiny, murder, survival and rescue were played out on the islands and nearby mainland.

George Grey, on his walk back to Perth after being wrecked at the mouth of the Murchison River in 1839, was the first to bring back good reports of the area. The first British ship anchored here in 1841, naming it Champion Bay after the ship, but this was changed to Geraldton when the town was surveyed 10 years later.

Minerals and pioneer pastoralists opened up this region and today the area is rich farming land, with

St Francis Xavier Cathedral, Geraldton

market gardens along the river being fed from this all-year underground stream, while the port acts as a major base for the crayfishing fleet which operates from Geraldton.

There are plenty of fishing opportunities in and around Geraldton. The harbour is home to tommy ruff and garfish, while further offshore the reefs produce pink snapper, baldchin tuskfish, Westralian jewfish, sweetlip and mackerel, while off the beaches you can catch tailor, mulloway and whiting.

Diving and surfing are popular, and fishing and diving trips to the Abrolhos Islands can be organised.

Annual events and festivities include the Geraldton Classic Windsurfing in January, Batavia Coast Fishing Classic in April, Batavia Seafood Festival in June and the Festival of Geraldton in October.

ACCOMMODATION: African Reef Resort Hotel, ph (08) 9964 5566; Geraldton Motor Inn, ph (08) 9964 4777; Ocean Centre Hotel, ph (08) 9921 7777; Grantown Guest House, ph (08) 9921 3275; Sun City Tourist Park, ph (08) 9938 1655; Separation Point Caravan Park, ph (08) 9921 2763

ACTIVITIES: Bowls, fishing, golf, horse riding, water sports

TOURIST INFORMATION: Ph (08) 9921 3999

HALLS CREEK

2989 KM NORTH OF PERTH
POPULATION: 1200   MAP REF: PAGE 313 L9

China Wall, an eroded 'wall' of quartz at Halls Creek

Halls Creek, in the East Kimberley, was the site of Western Australia's first gold rush in 1886. Today, the town is headquarters for the vast Halls Creek Shire, as well as a major service centre for the surrounding pastoral area, while tourism and mining are becoming increasingly important.

The town is also close to the junction of the Tanami Road to Alice Springs, as well as being at the junction of the Duncan Highway which leads east to Katherine, via Wave Hill.

Of interest are places such as Old Halls Creek, the site of the original township, and old gold mines of the Ruby Queen Mine and Bradley Mines. Other attractions include the China Wall, Palm Springs and Sawpit Gorge.

The Halls Creek Agricultural Show is held in July, while the horseracing and rodeo runs in August.

ACCOMMODATION: Kimberley Hotel/Motel, ph (08) 9168 6101; Halls Creek Motel, ph (08) 9168 6001; Shell Roadhouse Halls Creek Backpackers, ph (08) 9168 6060; Halls Creek Caravan Park, ph (08) 9168 6169; Old Halls Creek Lodge and Caravan Park, ph (08) 9168 8999

ACTIVITIES: 4WD touring, exploring old mining sites, gold fossicking, swimming

TOURIST INFORMATION: Ph (08) 9168 6262

HOPETOUN

605 KM SOUTH-EAST OF PERTH
POPULATION: NOMINAL   MAP REF: PAGE 307 J8

This tiny town on the southern coast of Western Australia flourished as a port for the inland gold-fields earlier this century, while previously it had served early settlers and sealing and whaling ships when it was known as Mary Anne Harbour. The town was declared in 1901 and its name was changed to Hopetoun. Today it features a substantial jetty and breakwaters on a lovely bay.

This delightful spot offers a wide range of fishing opportunities within close proximity to the town, whether you like to fish from the beach, off the jetty, rocks, offshore, or in the land-locked Culham Inlet and nearby rivers.

To the west and easily accessible from Hopetoun is the large Fitzgerald River National Park, where nearly 1800 species of plants flourish along a wild untamed coastline. A number of walking trails in the park, at East Mount Barrens and No Tree Hill, are excellent ways to experience this reserve.

Dunn's Swamp, 5 km north of the town, is a peaceful spot, ideal for bushwalks and birdwatching.

The main festivities occur during the Summer Festival when a host of activities take place, including concerts, fishing competitions and exhibitions.

ACCOMMODATION: Hopetoun Motel & Chalet Village, ph (08) 9838 3219; CWA Hopetoun Cottage, ph (08) 9838 3128; Hopetoun Caravan Park, ph (08) 9838 3096

ACTIVITIES: Bushwalking, fishing, golf, national park access, scenic drives, water sports

TOURIST INFORMATION: Ph (08) 9838 1277

HYDEN

346 KM SOUTH-EAST OF PERTH
POPULATION: 190   MAP REF: PAGE 306 G5

This small town is in the heart of the wheat belt and is best known for the rock formation called Wave Rock. Located about 4 km from town, this granite rock has the appearance of a breaking wave, with the over-hang more than 15 metres high. A low retaining wall above the lip of the wave is a man-made scar, built in the 1950s to channel water into Hyden's reservoir.

European pioneers first came to this semi-arid area in search of sandalwood, while settlement only occurred in the 1920s.

The town and the surrounding area have a number of other attractions including Mulka's Cave, the Gnamma Holes, the collection of the region's memorabilia at the Pioneer Town, a wildlife park (adjacent to the caravan park), and a seasonal display of native orchids, the best in the state and some extremely rare, that burst from the ground between June and August.

ACCOMMODATION: Hyden Wave Rock Hotel, ph (08) 9880 5052; Omeo Farm Cottage, ph (08) 9866 8023; Wave Rock Caravan Park, ph (08) 9880 5022
ACTIVITIES: Bushwalking, golf
TOURIST INFORMATION: Ph (08) 9880 5182

JURIEN

240 KM NORTH OF PERTH
POPULATION: 1100   MAP REF: PAGE 306 A1

The crayfishing fleet which operates out of this large protected bay is the main employer in the town, together with tourism. The tourism centres around the coast, the offshore reefs, and the great fishing and diving that can be enjoyed here.

The old jetties are available for the public to fish and swim from and there is equally good fishing and swimming off the beaches. Boat fishermen, who are well serviced with boat ramps, can expect to catch jewfish, baldchin, mackerel and snapper. The area is also popular with divers and windsurfers.

Only a few kilometres inland is the Drovers Cave National Park and a little further on is the larger Lesueur National Park. The former park has a range of limestone caves while the latter is one of the finest wildflower areas in Western Australia.

ACCOMMODATION: Jurien Bay Hotel/Motel, ph (08) 9652 1022; Jurien Bay Holiday Flats, ph (08) 9652 1172; Jurien Bay Caravan Park, ph (08) 9652 1595
ACTIVITIES: Bowls, fishing, golf, national park access, water sports
TOURIST INFORMATION: Ph (08) 9652 1444

The protected waters of Jurien Bay

KALBARRI

590 KM NORTH OF PERTH
POPULATION: 830   MAP REF: PAGE 308 C7

Located at the mouth of the Murchison River, Kalbarri has grown from virtually nothing in 1950 to a pleasant seaside town, offering all amenities.

The rocky wild coast north and south of the town has claimed many ships, dating back to the very first Europeans to venture this way. In 1629, two suspected mutineers were marooned on this coast near Wittecarra Gully, just to the south of the town, making them the first Europeans to settle on the continent.

The Murchison River cutting through Kalbarri National Park

In 1712 the *Zuytdorp* was wrecked along the cliffs that now bear that ship's name, while George Grey's ship was wrecked at the mouth of the river he named the Murchison, when he was exploring the coast in 1839. His forced march south along the coast to Perth resulted in much of the region being opened up to pioneer pastoralists.

Kalbarri National Park is right on the doorstep of the town and covers 186 000 sq km, through the heart of which flows the Murchison River with some 85 km of gorges, several of which are accessible to tourists. A number of unsealed roads give good access to the gorge country along the river at such places as the Loop, Nature's Window and the Z Bend, while the two lookouts, Hawks Head and Ross Graham, give fine views of the river. The spring wildflower display in the park is magnificent with over 500 species on show, while the park also contains over 170 species of birds and a number of mammals.

Travel companies based in Kalbarri can arrange canoeing, rock climbing, abseiling, camel trekking, and more, through the park and along the coast.

The surrounding coast provides fabulous fishing and while the boat fishing is excellent, fishing from the rocks, beach or in the river is more rewarding. Coral trout, mulloway, snapper, tailor, Spanish mackerel and more are all on the menu at such places as Chinaman's Rock, Red Bluff, Rainbow Valley and Pot Alley Gorge.

There is also good surfing, windsurfing and diving in the local area, and whale watching is becoming more common as the whales return to the region. There is a beautiful bird park, known as Rainbow Jungle, just south of town, while the Kalbarri Wildflower Centre is close to town and situated on 16 hectares of undisturbed bushland.

The annual Blessing of the Fleet is held each November.

ACCOMMODATION: Kalbarri Resort, ph (08) 9937 2333; Kalbarri Hotel/Motel, ph (08) 9937 1000; Kalbarri Beach Resort, ph (08) 9937 1061; Sun River Chalets, ph (08) 9937 1119; Kalbarri Tudor Caravan Park, ph (08) 9937 1077; Red Bluff Caravan Park, ph (08) 9937 1080
ACTIVITIES: Abseiling, bowls, bushwalking, fishing, golf, national park access, rock climbing, water sports, whale watching, wildflower viewing
TOURIST INFORMATION: Ph (08) 9937 1104

KALGOORLIE

593 KM EAST OF PERTH
POPULATION: 26 100   MAP REF: PAGE 307 L2

When Paddy Hannan struck gold here in 1893 he found the last great goldfield in Australia—and the largest. It changed the history of Western Australia. Within a month of his discovery hundreds of miners were on the field, and two years later the town, originally known as Hannans, had 6000 people with over another 1000 in nearby Boulder. By 1902, after the swelling population of the goldfields had ensured Western Australia stayed within the newly founded Commonwealth, the number reached over 30 000.

Since then the fortunes of this historic town have ridden the roller-coaster ride of fluctuating gold prices. The 'Golden Mile', one of the richest ore bodies on earth, yielded most of the early great mines. It has more recently been turned into a gigantic open cut, the Superpit, in the never-ending quest for the elusive metal.

In the 1970s a nickel boom brought added prosperity and action to the town and a nickel smelter was built. While nickel and gold remain the mainstay of the local economy, the twin towns of Kalgoorlie and Boulder are important service centres for the outlying pastoral properties and a growing tourist trade.

In the early days a lack of water was a huge problem on the field and this was solved by the construction of the Mundaring–Kalgoorlie Pipeline, a technical feat that many said could not be done.

There are also a large number of buildings dating from the turn of the century still to be seen in 'Kal', as the locals call the town—these include those along Hannan Street in Kalgoorlie and Burt Street in Boulder, the towns' main streets. The town halls in both Kal and Boulder are especially good.

There are a number of museums, including the School of Mines Museum, the Museum of the Goldfields, the Goldfields War Museum and the Historical Society Display. The last of these, a fine photographic collection of the area, is housed in the Boulder Railway Station.

Hannans North is one of the original mines and tours underground and around the above-ground

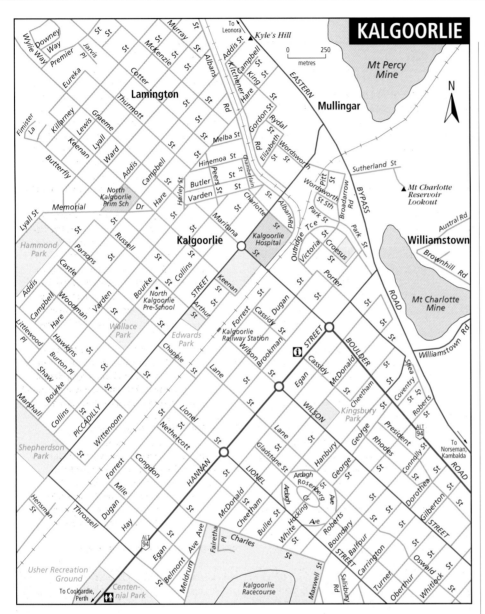

KALGOORLIE

KALGOORLIE map labels: To Leonora, Kyle's Hill, Mt Percy Mine, 0 250 metres, N, Downey Way, Wylie Way, Premier St, Jarvis St, Murray St, McKenzie St, Addis Rd, Campbell St, King St, Hare St, Kitchener, EASTERN, Mullingar, Mt Charlotte Reservoir Lookout, Eureka St, Cotter St, Thurmott St, Lamington, Albans St, Rydal St, Gordon St, Sutherland St, Williamstown, Fimister La, Killarney, Lewis, Graeme St, Melba St, Elizabeth St, Wordsworth St, Chamberlain St, Brownhill Rd, Keenan, Lyall, Ward, Addis, Hinemoa St, Butler St, Peers St, Pitt St, Wordsworth, St Sth, Broadarrow Py, BYPASS, Mt Charlotte Mine, Austral Rd, Butterfly, Campbell, Harley St, Varden St, Charlotte St, Albans Rd, Park St, Victoria St, Croesus St, North Kalgoorlie Prim Sch, Memorial Dr, Hare, Mariana St, Outridge Tce, ROAD, Williamstown Rd, Lyall St, Hammond Park, Russell St, Kalgoorlie, Kalgoorlie Hospital, Porter St, Parsons, Collins St, Keenan St, Dugan St, Castle St, Bourke St, STREET, Arthur, Forrest St, Cassidy St, Addis, Campbell, Woodman, Varden, North Kalgoorlie Pre-School, Kalgoorlie Railway Station, Wilson, Brookman, STREET, BOULDER, Littlewood Pl, Hare, Hawkins, Wallace Park, Edwards Park, Chapple, Lane, Cassidy, McDonald, Shea St, Coventry St, Shaw St, Burton Pl, Bourke, Egan, Cheetham St, Roberts St, Marshall, Collins, PICCADILLY, Wittenoom, Lionel, Nethercott, WILSON, Lane, Kingsbury Park, George St, President, Rhodes St, Connolly St, To Norseman, Kambalda, ALT 94, Shepherdson Park, Forrest, Congdon, HANNAN, LIONEL, Gladstone St, Hanbury, George St, Dorothea St, Gilberton St, Hensman St, Mile, Ardagh, Rosenberg, Hacking Ave, Roberts St, Dugan, Throssell, Hay, Egan, Belmont Ave Ave, Meldrum, Fairetha Pl, McDonald, Cheetham, Buller St, White St, Ave, Boundary St, Balfour St, Carrington St, Turner St, Oberthur St, Whitlock St, ALT 94, Usher Recreation Ground, To Coolgardie, Perth, Centennial Park, Charles St, Maxwell St, Salisbury Rd, Kalgoorlie Racecourse, STREET, Oswald St

workings are held each day. The Golden Mile Superpit Lookout offers expansive views of this vast working and is open each day, blasting permitting.

There is much more to see and do around the town, including trying your luck at the Boorara Fossicking Area, 18 km from town. You can take an enjoyable day trip along the 22-km-long Kanowna Heritage trail or alternatively, board an old steam-powered rattler for an hour-long run on the Loopline Railway.

In March you can try your hand at the Western Australia Gold Panning Championships, or enjoy the Kalgoorlie–Boulder Community Fair which is also held in March. There is the Great Gold Festival in July and the Spring Festival in September. This latter event includs the world two-up championships.
ACCOMMODATION: Albion Shamrock Motor Lodge, ph (08) 9093 1399; Cornwall Hotel, ph (08) 9093 2510; Old Australia Guesthouse, ph (08) 90211320; Kalgoorlie Village Caravan Park, ph (08) 9093 2780
ACTIVITIES: Bowls, fossicking, golf, heritage drives and walks, mine tours, swimming
TOURIST INFORMATION: Ph (08) 9021 1966

The Exchange Hotel in Kalgoorlie

KALUMBURU

3170 KM NORTH OF PERTH
POPULATION: 600   MAP REF: PAGE 313 K2
Kalumburu is an Aboriginal community in the far north of Western Australia. The community was established in 1932 when a mission was entrenched here by Benedictine monks who had previously started a mission at nearby Pago 24 years earlier.

The township was bombed by the Japanese during World War II and the place near-abandoned until after the war, when both the missionaries and the Aboriginal people returned.

Today the community runs their own affairs, while the mission maintains a school and church area. The town can provide basic requirements, while the mission supplies limited fuel.

You require a permit to stay on the Aboriginal community lands and this can be arranged from the community office. Camping and fishing are allowed at a wide variety of places along the coast north of the township, and the fishing is nothing short of fantastic. Visits to the nearby Drysdale River National Park can be arranged from here but you must be self-sufficient to visit this remote park.
ACCOMMODATION: Camping permits, ph (08) 9161 4300; McGowan Island Fishing Camp, ph (08) 9161 4300
ACTIVITIES: Camping, fishing, national park access
TOURIST INFORMATION: Ph (08) 9161 4300

KAMBALDA

635 KM EAST OF PERTH
POPULATION: 4510   MAP REF: PAGE 307 L3
Kambalda is a town reborn. First settled when gold was discovered in 1897, the town, then called Red Hill, was abandoned and forgotten when the gold ran out 10 years later. In the mid-1960s, though, vast deposits of nickel were found and by 1967 a treatment plant and modern town was in operation at this site.

On Lake Lefroy, a vast flat salt pan of over 500 sq km, just to the south-east of the town, land yachts can be seen racing nearly every Sunday. The Red Hill Lookout, John Hill Viewpoint and Defiance Open Cut Lookout all give different views of the vast mining operation carried out in Kambalda.

In June there is the annual Sky Diving Gathering.
ACCOMMODATION: Kambalda Hotel/Motel, ph (08) 9027 1333; Kambalda Caravan Park, ph (08) 9027 1582
ACTIVITIES: Bowls, bushwalking, golf, land yachting, skydiving
TOURIST INFORMATION: Ph (08) 9027 1446

KARRATHA

1553 KM NORTH OF PERTH
POPULATION: 8350   MAP REF: PAGE 314 F5
The Pilbara's largest and best serviced town, Karratha is located a short distance off the North West Coastal Highway and has a large selection of facilities,

accommodation levels and things to see and to do, while only 20 km away is the major port of Dampier and its massive ore-loading facilities.

The name Karratha derives from an Aboriginal word meaning 'good country' and was the name of the first station property in the area taken up in the 1860s. The present-day town was established by Hamersley Iron, when Dampier outgrew its available land, and with continual development in the area, the town is sure to grow even bigger.

While Karratha is mainly used by visitors as a base for exploring the surrounding area, coast and islands, there are also many inland delights such as the Millstream–Chichester National Park and the gorges around Wittenoom.

The Karratha Festival is held on the second weekend in June.

ACCOMMODATION: Karratha International Hotel, ph (08) 9185 3111; Mercure Inn, ph (08) 9185 1155; Rosemary Road Caravan Park, ph (08) 9185 1855; Balmoral Caravan Park, ph (08) 9185 3628; Karratha Caravan Park, ph (08) 9185 1012

ACTIVITIES: Fishing, golf, industry tours, national park access, scenic drives, water sports

TOURIST INFORMATION: Ph (08) 9144 4600

KATANNING

287 KM SOUTH-EAST OF PERTH
POPULATION: 5100   MAP REF: PAGE 306 E7

Located in the heart of one of the most prosperous agricultural regions in the state, Katanning is well known for its annual stud Merino sales, as well as being a major producer of cereal grains.

Before the coming of Europeans, the natural springs in the area were a meeting place for the local Aborigines, and the name of the town supposedly comes from the term meaning 'a place to meet'.

The first Europeans arrived in 1835 and within five years much of the land was taken up by sheep properties. The first flour mill, started in 1891, still stands and was also the site of the first electric power plant in Western Australia, which not only supplied the mill but also the street lighting. The local tourist office is located at the Old Mill which has been restored to its original condition.

The town has a couple of other old buildings including the Anglican church, built last century, and the King George Hostel, built in the early 1900s to house men working at the Old Mill.

Lake Dumbleyung, north of the town and famous as the site for Donald Campbell's successful world record attempt in his boat *Bluebird* in 1964, is a popular spot for water activities as well as a sanctuary for bird life.

In the early 1970s a strong Muslim community settled here and each July sees the Islamic Celebrations, while in October there is the annual Art Prize and the Agricultural Show. The Great Southern Cycling Classic is run in October.

ACCOMMODATION: Federal Hotel, ph (08) 9821 1010; Katanning Motel, ph (08) 9821 1657; Katanning Caravan Park, ph (08) 9821 1066; Sunbeam Caravan Park, ph (08) 9821 2165

ACTIVITIES: Bowls, scenic drives, swimming

TOURIST INFORMATION: Ph (08) 9821 2634

KUNUNURRA

3345 KM NORTH-EAST OF PERTH
POPULATION: 4950   MAP REF: PAGE 313 N5

The 'green' capital of the north, Kununurra owes its existence and its verdant looks to the great man-made lakes that lie close by.

Established when the Ord River Scheme was first built in 1961, the town slumbered on for many years as a number of different ideas were tried to make the hugely expensive irrigation scheme work.

Finally, more than 30 years after it was finished, the scheme looks like fulfilling most of its early promises with a large variety of crops, especially sugar, now being grown over the flat, fertile plains of the lower Ord River.

This area was first explored by Alexander Forrest during his 1875 expedition which opened up the Kimberley for pastoral development. The famous Durack family established their cattle empire over much of the land that was to be resumed and flooded when the Ord River dam was built in the 1960s.

In recent years diamond finds south of the town, and oil and gas discoveries in the Timor Sea, have seen the town take on a new vitality. It is well serviced with all that a traveller requires in this vast region, far from a major capital city.

Just on the east side of town is the Mirima National Park which has as its heart the Hidden Valley. The rock formations here are spectacular and a number of walking trails lead through the park which give a visitor a tantalising glimpse of the natural wonder of the area.

On the other side of town is Lake Kununurra, the smaller of the two dams on the Ord and used as a regulating dam for the irrigation areas nearby. The waters of the dam are a popular swimming, boating

and waterskiing area, while the backwater, locally known as the 'Everglades', is a birdwatcher's delight. It's also a top spot to enjoy a little canoeing.

The main dam on the Ord is some 70 km away and holds back the waters of Lake Argyle, which is the largest man-made lake in Australia. There are boating, fishing and swimming activities to enjoy on the lake and a small camping and accommodation resort looks after visitors. The river, from below the dam wall to Lake Kununurra, is a popular stretch of water with both small boat owners and canoeists.

The irrigation area is also worth a lookover, while more natural delights can be found at Valentine's Rock Pool, Black Rock Falls or Middle Springs. Point Spring Nature Reserve is a small area of rainforest about 50 km north of the town that is an idyllic picnic spot and home for many different bird species.

There is a good choice of fish and fishing spots in and around Kununurra, with catches of black bream, sooty grunter, catfish, and of course barra, to excite and entice. Popular fishing spots include Ivanhoe Crossing, Bullocks Crossing, Fords Beach and Valentine's Creek.

There are also a number of festivals and events held throughout the year for visitors to participate in and enjoy, such as the Dam to Dam Dinghy Race in late March/early April, Ord Tiki Day and Agricultural Show in July, and rodeos, race meetings and art exhibitions in August.

ACCOMMODATION: Hotel Kununurra, ph (08) 91681 344; Country Club Hotel, ph (08) 9168 1024; Kimberley Court, ph (08) 9168 1411; Kona Lakeside Tourist Park, ph (08) 9168 1031; Hidden Valley Caravan Park, ph (08) 9168 1790; Ivanhoe Village Caravan Park, ph (08) 9169 1995

ACTIVITIES: Birdwatching, bowls, bushwalking, canoeing, fishing, golf, national park access, water sports

TOURIST INFORMATION: Ph (08) 9168 1177

The dam wall on Lake Argyle, Kununurra, which is the largest man-made lake in Australia

LAKE KING

465 KM SOUTH-EAST OF PERTH
POPULATION: 150   MAP REF: PAGE 307 H6

This small community, located on the edge of the wheat belt, acts as a service centre for the surrounding farmers. Located 130 km south of Wave Rock, and 70 km north of Ravensthorpe, the town's major claim to fame is the profusion of wildflowers that erupt each spring.

The first white explorer through this area was J. S. Roe in 1848, but it was not until settlement of the area, in the late 1920s, that the town of Lake King was finally established.

The town acts as an access point for the sandy track west through the Frank Hann and Peak Charles National Parks, meeting with the main Norseman–Esperance road, 155 km north of the coastal town.

ACCOMMODATION: Lake King Caravan Park, ph (08) 9874 4060
ACTIVITIES: Bushwalking, national park access, scenic drives, wildflowers
TOURIST INFORMATION: Ph (08) 9874 4060

LANCELIN

127 KM NORTH OF PERTH
POPULATION: 400   MAP REF: PAGE 306 B3

This is the sailboard mecca of Western Australia. Its long stretches of white sandy beach are ideal for swimming, while the reefs and breaks offshore make this *the* place to practice sailboarding. A couple of close inshore islands make for a well-protected anchorage, as well as adding to the area's attractions for divers and fishermen. The town is also a major commercial rock lobster centre, while amateur anglers will find plenty of spots to cast a line. Off the beach you can catch tailor, mulloway and shark, and offshore are silver trevally, mulloway, samson fish, Westralian jewfish and snapper.

The extensive bare dunes just out of town are the perfect location for the offroad enthusiast, while a run north along a sandy 4WD track, just behind the first line of dunes, takes you to some excellent swimming, fishing and diving spots.

Special events include the Ocean Classic Windsurfing competition in January, sand dune buggy racing at Easter and the Leisure Expo in April.

ACCOMMODATION: Lancelin Inn, ph (08) 9655 1005; Lancelin Family Villas, ph (08) 9655 1100; Lancelin Caravan Park, ph (08) 9655 1056
ACTIVITIES: Fishing, 4WD touring, water sports
TOURIST INFORMATION: Ph (08) 9655 1100

LAVERTON

935 KM NORTH-EAST OF PERTH
POPULATION: 880   MAP REF: PAGE 309 N8

Laverton is situated 361 km north of Kalgoorlie, on the road to Warburton, and services the mining and grazing industries surrounding it.

Sandalwooders were early visitors to the area to gather this valuable timber, but it was not until the discovery of gold in 1896 that the town became established, with the field being one of the richest in Western Australia. The town was originally named British Flag after the first mineral lease; by 1901 there were a number of large mines in the area and a population of about 3500. After time, however, the gold pickings became lean and the town declined, to revive once again with the discovery of nickel at nearby Windarra in 1969.

That led to the infamous Poseidon share rise and fall where some investors won millions, while others lost everything. The mining site is silent today and its old buildings now house a visitors' centre, while a heritage trail takes walkers around the mine and old processing site.

The town itself sees an increasing number of tourists stop to use its services and prepare for the trip across the Great Victoria Desert to Uluru (Ayers Rock) and onto Alice Springs. Two permits are required to travel this road. Applications should be made to the Aboriginal Affairs Planning Authority in Perth, ph (08) 9483 1333 and the Central Land Council in Alice Springs, ph (08) 8952 3800.

To get a good view of Laverton and its surrounds, take the short climb up Billy Goat Hill. Those who love to explore around old mining fields and towns will find several in the Laverton district including Burtville, Gladiator, Heffernans and Just in Time. The Mines Department has a large scale map available for travellers to help get the most out of their explorations.

ACCOMMODATION: Desert Inn, ph (08) 9031 1188; Laverton Motel, ph (08) 9031 1130; Laverton Downs Station, ph (08) 9037 5998; Desert Pea Caravan Park, ph (08) 9031 1072
ACTIVITIES: Explore old ghost mining towns and fields
TOURIST INFORMATION: Ph (08) 9031 1202

LEONORA

830 KM NORTH-EAST OF PERTH
POPULATION: 530   MAP REF: PAGE 309 L8

The once flourishing goldmining town of Leonora is found 237 km north of Kalgoorlie, and the town still leaves a unique impression on visitors with many vestiges of a past era.

The explorer John Forrest first wandered through this area in 1869 with a party searching for the lost Leichhardt Expedition. He named Mt Leonora in honour of the wife of the then Western Australian governor. He was not, however, too impressed with the countryside. In 1896 the first gold claims were pegged at Leonora, and at its twin town Gwalia (the Gaelic name for Wales), and in those busy, hard-working times it was the largest centre in the north-eastern goldfields.

Today it still maintains that role and is the railhead for copper from the northern copper mines and nickel from Leinster. Gold continues to play an exciting and important part in Leonora's future, while the surrounding pastoral industry produces a substantial wool clip during good years. While once you could have journeyed around town in the state's

An open-cut mine at Leonora

first electric trams, today you will have to walk along the Gwalia Heritage Trail to experience at first-hand the town's history. There are plenty of buildings dating back to the 1890s to admire. For those who love to delve and learn more about the town's past, visits to both the Gwalia Historical Museum and Historical Gallery are a must.

ACCOMMODATION: Whitehouse Hotel, ph (08) 9037 6030; Leonora Motel, ph (08) 9037 6181; Central Hotel, ph (08) 9037 6042; Leonora Caravan Park, ph (08) 9037 6568; Mine Site Village, ph (08) 9037 6200
ACTIVITIES: Gold fossicking, heritage walking trail
TOURIST INFORMATION: Ph (08) 9037 6044

MANDURAH

83 KM SOUTH OF PERTH
POPULATION: 42 000   MAP REF: PAGE 306 B5

A popular year-round holiday resort, about an hour's drive from Perth, the township is set on a maze of waterways on the expansive Harvey Estuary and Peel Inlet.

The area was settled in the 1830s by Thomas Peel, who took up a vast spread of land in the immediate area. However, his enterprise failed and he died penniless 35 years later. The town and surrounding area today have a large number of accommodation houses, places to eat and a good range of entertainment, so there is always something to do.

There are also plenty of fishing opportunities, with one of the easiest spots, especially for children, being the old road bridge in the heart of town, where you stand a good chance of catching tailor, mulloway, whiting, garfish and tarwhine. Other spots to try are the jetties, beaches, estuary and inlet, while offshore the fishing is good for Westralian jewfish, snapper and King George whiting. Crabbing is also a popular pastime.

There are a number of events and festivities that occur throughout the year, including the Mandurah Festival in January, Art and Craft Festival

in March, Blessing the Fleet in October, a fishing competition in November and the Mandurah Community Fair in December.

ACCOMMODATION: All Seasons Atrium Resort Hotel, ph (08) 9535 6633; Blue Bay Motel, ph (08) 9535 2743; Mandurah Holiday Village, ph (08) 9535 4963; Albatross House, ph (08) 9581 5597; Peninsula Caravan Park, ph (08) 9535 2792; Belvedere Caravan Park, ph (08) 9535 1213

ACTIVITIES: Bowls, crabbing, fishing, golf, water sports

TOURIST INFORMATION: Ph (08) 9535 1155

MANJIMUP

310 KM SOUTH OF PERTH
POPULATION: 5000   MAP REF: PAGE 306 C8

The imposing timber arches which you drive under as you enter the township at its northern and southern

Imposing jarrah trees at Manjimup

entrances are indicative of what this area is well known for—its impressive surrounding tall timber. As such, many of the tourist attractions are timber related, and a visit to the Manjimup Regional Timber Park is a must. Here visitors can take a close look at the state's only timber museum, along with Bunnings's Age of Steam Museum, Historical Hamlet and a display of vintage machinery. For a first-hand look at the timber industry, the Forest Industries Federation runs guided tours into the forest.

For a closer, awe-inspiring look at the giants of the forest, take a drive out to the Four Aces and see the four massive towering karri trees, each believed to be hundreds of years old.

There are also a number of wineries in the area open for cellar tasting and wine sales, or you can enjoy a picnic or BBQ in the orchard at Fontanini's Nut Farm, and when in season, pick your own chestnuts, walnuts and fruit.

The region around Manjimup also abounds with many delightful and varied walking trails through

these magnificent karri forests, or you could cool off at Fontys Pool and enjoy a picnic in its delightful gardens. Another enjoyment for visitors is the colourful, dazzling display of flowers in the region during the wildflower season in spring.

The Agricultural Show is held in March, while the Chestnut Festival happens in April.

ACCOMMODATION: Kingsley Motel, ph (08) 9771 1177; Greenfields Farm Stay, ph (08) 9772 1364; Nyamup Holiday Village, ph (08) 9773 1273; Manjimup Caravan Park, ph (08) 9771 2093

ACTIVITIES: Bushwalking, scenic drives, waterskiing, wineries

TOURIST INFORMATION: Ph (08) 9771 1831

MARBLE BAR

1980 KM NORTH OF PERTH
POPULATION: 360   MAP REF: PAGE 315 J6

Marble Bar is famous as the hottest locality in Australia and in the 1920s recorded 160 days in a row over the old 100°F, or 38°C.

The town is just over 200 km from Port Hedland, the last 58 km of which are unsealed, but the road is still pretty good, most of the time.

Gold was discovered in the region in the 1890s, but by the early 1900s the gold had petered out and the miners had left. In 1936 there was a major find which was worked until 1955.

Marble Bar shares with the goldfields town of Nullagine the distinction of being on 'Mad Man's Track', a frontier track which lured prospectors eager to find their fortune, and thousands headed this way during the boom days. Today, a few hundred people make a living from tin and manganese, and from the occasional tourists who come to this historic, remote settlement.

Worth seeing is the 'marble bar', really a band of jasper, across the Coongan River, about 5 km from town; Chinaman's Pool, a popular swimming spot;

Jasper Rocks, originally thought to be marble, near Marble Bar

and Coppins Gap a little further out and another good swimming spot; while in town there are a number of old stone buildings dating from the 1880s. The Ironclad Hotel, named after the ironclad battleships of the American Civil War, is worthy of some time as well.

The Marble Bar Cup and Ball is usually held in June or July.

ACCOMMODATION: Iron Clad Hotel, ph (08) 9176 1066; Marble Bar Travellers' Stop Roadhouse, ph (08) 9176 1166; Caravan Park, ph (08) 9176 1067

ACTIVITIES: Gold prospecting, horseracing, scenic drives, swimming

TOURIST INFORMATION: Ph (08) 9176 1166

MARGARET RIVER

282 KM SOUTH OF PERTH
POPULATION: 800   MAP REF: PAGE 306 B8

Originally founded on dairy, cattle and timber, the region has become more recently renowned as an

Vineyards are abundant throughout Margaret River

excellent wine-producing area and holiday spot.

While the wineries are drawcards, swimming and fishing are favourite pastimes. This is also cave country, and Mammoth and Lake Caves, found near Margaret River, are open for guided tours daily.

The town boasts many fine old buildings, such as Ellensbrook Homestead built in 1851 and the Old Settlement Craft Village, both well worth a visit.

Events not to be missed are the Margaret River Wine and Food Festival held in February, the Show, and Surf Classic in November.

ACCOMMODATION: Blue Gum Farm Stay (B&B), ph (08) 9757 6338; Margaret River Hotel, ph (08) 9757 2655; Wallcliffe Lodge, ph (08) 9757 2699; Margaret River Caravan Park, ph (08) 9757 2180

ACTIVITIES: Abseiling, bushwalking, caving, climbing, fishing, scenic drives, water sports, wineries

TOURIST INFORMATION: Ph (08) 9757 2911

MEEKATHARRA

763 KM NORTH OF PERTH
POPULATION: 1000   MAP REF: PAGE 309 H5

The township of Meekatharra is found on the Great Northern Highway, 196 km north of Mt Magnet, and is part of Western Australia's Outback Mid West region.

Mt Augustus near Meekatharra

It is an area that is transformed during the wildflower season from July to September, with the countryside becoming a mass of beautiful colour from plants such as everlasting daisies.

The town has had a new lease of life in the last 15 or so years as more and more mines have opened up. The town is once again a major service centre for the outlying mines and vast pastoral holdings. Many old buildings still exist, including the Old Courthouse (1912) which is classified by the National Trust. Throughout the local area there are also many old ghost towns to explore and fossick around.

Meekatharra is also the closest town to Mt Augustus, the world's largest monolith, over two times bigger than Uluru (Ayers Rock). The rock is protected in the surrounding Burringurrah National Park, which is home to a number of rare plants.

The special event of the year is the horseracing in October.

ACCOMMODATION: Auski Inland Motel, ph (08) 9981 1433; Commercial Hotel, ph (08) 9981 1020; Royal Mail Hotel, ph (08) 9981 1148; Meekatharra Caravan Park, ph (08) 9981 1253
ACTIVITIES: Bushwalking, fossicking, gold prospecting, national park access
TOURIST INFORMATION: Ph (08) 9981 1002

MENZIES

687 KM EAST OF PERTH
POPULATION: 235   MAP REF: PAGE 309 L9

Located 132 km north of Kalgoorlie on the road to Leonora, the birth of the town began with the discovery of gold in 1894 and the opening of the nearby Lady Shenton Mine. At its peak in 1905, this once-bustling town had a population of over 10 000, and included 13 hotels and three breweries. Visitors today will find it a lot quieter, with the only reminders of its past history visible in the many historical buildings, made from local stone.

Buildings of note include the Town Hall and Shire Offices built in 1896, and the Railway Station, now renovated. The cemetery is also a place to wander round and try to envisage what hardships and isolation those early miners had to endure.

Nearby attractions include the Coongarrie National Park, and the ghost towns of Kookynie and Niagara.

ACCOMMODATION: Menzies Railway Hotel, ph (08) 9024 2043; Menzies Caravan Park, ph (08) 9024 2041
ACTIVITIES: Exploring old goldmining town, fossicking, national park access
TOURIST INFORMATION: Ph (08) 9024 2041

MERREDIN

258 KM EAST OF PERTH
POPULATION: 3520   MAP REF: PAGE 306 F4

The largest centre in the eastern wheat belt, Merredin is situated on the Great Eastern Highway beside the Perth–Kalgoorlie railway line. Once an important stop for those en route to the goldfields, today Merredin has all the services and facilities for travellers and the surrounding pastoral properties which mainly produce wheat, wool and pigs.

Its early history began when the goldfields were discovered in Coolgardie in 1892, which led to the construction of a railway link which reached Merredin a year later. The railway played an important part in the town's history and much of that heritage is displayed in the Railway Museum in the station which was built in 1893. A walk around the Merredin Park Heritage Trail is a great way to learn more about the town. Another interesting building is the Cummins Theatre (1928), built from pressed brick.

Special events and festivals held during the year include the Vintage Fair and Country Music Festival in September/October and the Central Wheat Belt Games in October.

ACCOMMODATION: Potts Motor Inn, ph (08) 9041 1755; Merredin Oasis Hotel, ph (08) 9041 1133; Merredin Motel, ph (08) 9041 1886; Commercial Hotel, ph (08) 9041 1052; Merredin Caravan Park, ph (08) 9041 1535
ACTIVITIES: Bushwalking, historic walks
TOURIST INFORMATION: Ph (08) 9041 1666

MONKEY MIA

855 KM NORTH OF PERTH
POPULATION: 135   MAP REF: PAGE 308 B4

The dolphins of Monkey Mia have become world famous, resulting in this small hamlet on the east coast of the Peron Peninsula, 25 km from the township of Denham, taking on a more prosperous look.

The dolphins have been visiting the beach since the 1960s and today the feeding times are controlled in such a way as to allow human contact while ensuring that these beautiful wild animals do not become dependent on humans for food. There are no regular feeding times, but rangers will randomly allow visitors to feed the dolphins with fresh fish.

Shark Bay, which surrounds the peninsula on which Monkey Mia is located, is a World Heritage area, acclaimed for its dugong population, visiting whales, and the ancient life forms of stromatolites located at the southern extremity of the bay in Hamelin Pool. The offshore islands have provided sanctuary for a number of animals that have become extinct on the mainland.

A pearl farm, 5 km to the north of the town, is worth a visit. As is to be expected, the surrounding waters offer excellent fishing, sailing and boating.

ACCOMMODATION: Monkey Mia Dolphin Resort, ph (08) 9948 1320; Nanga Bay Resort, ph (08) 9948 3992
ACTIVITIES: Dolphin feeding, fishing, water sports
TOURIST INFORMATION: Ph (08) 9948 1445

MORAWA

395 KM NORTH OF PERTH
POPULATION: 1200   MAP REF: PAGE 308 E9

Situated 179 km from Geraldton, in the state's mid-west, many tourists flock to this area during the wildflower season. That is usually from July to October, when the countryside is covered with colourful blooms, with plants such as everlasting and wreath flowers, wild pomegranates and orchids forming a veritable multicoloured carpet.

The primary agriculture of the region, however, is cereal farming. Sheep, pig and cattle raising, together with newer markets for emu, ostrich and marron, are also of importance.

History buffs will enjoy a wander through the police station and gaol, and a walk along the Hawes Heritage Trail.

Nearby scenic spots include Koolanooka Springs and Bilya Rock.

The major annual event is the Morawa Music and Art Spectacular in October.

ACCOMMODATION: Morawa Motel/Hotel, ph (08) 9971 1060; Bellaranga Farmstay (B&B), ph (08) 9971 6038; Morawa Caravan Park, ph (08) 9971 1380
ACTIVITIES: Bushwalking, scenic drives, gliding, historic walks
TOURIST INFORMATION: Ph (08) 9971 1421

MOUNT BARKER

367 KM SOUTH-EAST OF PERTH
POPULATION: 1520   MAP REF: PAGE 306 E9

One of Western Australia's earliest settlements, Mount Barker is situated along the Albany Highway within a region of diverse ecological features and natural attractions. It is also a rich agricultural area, and while sheep and cattle still play a significant role, the newer enterprises of viticulture and wildflowers are finding a market.

Some of the original buildings are well preserved, such as the St Werburgh's Chapel (1872), the Grain Mill (1842) and the Old Police Station, built by convicts in 1868, and now a museum.

The old police station at Mount Barker

There are also a number of art and craft galleries, while outdoor enthusiasts will enjoy the nearby Stirling Range and Porongurup National Parks, both of which are famous for their resplendent array of wildflowers during spring.

Special events include the Machinery Field Day in March and the Great Southern Wine Festival in October.

ACCOMMODATION: Valley Views Motel, ph (08) 9851 1899; Plantagenet Hotel, ph (08) 9851 1008; Mt Barker Hotel, ph (08) 9851 1477; Hayrocks (B&B), ph (08) 9851 2196; Mt Barker Caravan Park, ph (08) 9851 1691
ACTIVITIES: National park access, scenic drives, wineries
TOURIST INFORMATION: Ph (08) 9851 1163

MOUNT BARNETT

2809 KM NORTH OF PERTH
POPULATION: 250 MAP REF: PAGE 313 J6

Originally Mount Barnett was the name given to the surrounding cattle station, but it now refers more to the roadhouse situated on the Gibb River Road. The station and roadhouse are owned by the Kupungarri Aboriginal community, which has a large housing estate on the opposite side of the main road, a little to the south of the roadhouse.

Situated over 300 km north-east of Derby and 400 km south-west of Kununurra, Mount Barnett has been a spot for many years where travellers have stopped, refuelled and refreshed as they travel along the Gibb River Road.

The camping area down on the Barnett River, just below the Lower Manning Gorge, is pleasant, while the swimming hole is delightful. There is a good day walk to the Upper Manning Gorge and a number of Aboriginal art sites close by. The camping ground makes a good base from which to explore the other gorges, found through the ranges, to the south.

ACCOMMODATION: Mount Barnett Camping Ground, ph (08) 9191 7007
ACTIVITIES: Aboriginal art sites, bushwalking, canoeing, swimming
TOURIST INFORMATION: Ph (08) 9191 1426

MOUNT MAGNET

566 KM NORTH OF PERTH
POPULATION: 620 MAP REF: PAGE 308 G7

Situated on the Great Northern Highway, 247 km east of Geraldton, this is the region's oldest surviving gold settlement of the Murchison field. While pastoralists ventured into the area with their sheep in the late 1870s, the rush for gold began in 1891 when the first rich diggings were discovered, and the township of Mount Magnet was proclaimed soon after.

The town is still the service centre for the surrounding goldmining operations and pastoral properties, and tourists will find plenty to see in an overnight stop.

There are both heritage walks and drives which will take you past notable relics of the gold-rush era, as well as historic buildings and sites, such as the

Post Office and Shire Building (1898) and the Old School House (1896), while the Historical Society Museum has a remarkable collection of memorabilia.

The nearby scenic spectacle of the Granites is a great place to explore, and wildflowers are prolific from August to September.

Annual events include the race meetings in February and May and the gymkhana in October.

ACCOMMODATION: Grand Hotel, ph (08) 9963 4110; Commercial Hotel, ph (08) 9963 4021; Goldview Lodgings, ph (08) 9963 4495; Wogarno Homestead, ph (08) 9963 5846; Murrum Station, ph (08) 9963 5843
ACTIVITIES: Bushwalking, gold and gem fossicking, historic walk, scenic drives
TOURIST INFORMATION: Ph (08) 9963 4172

MULLEWA

521 KM NORTH OF PERTH
POPULATION: 1400 MAP REF: PAGE 308 D8

Situated 99 km east of Geraldton, in the Northern Midlands, Mullewa is in the midst of wildflower country and surrounded by sheep and wheat country.

Wreath flowers growing in the sand at Mullewa

Of interest to visitors would be an outing with the family to the Jack Murray Wildlife Sanctuary, and a visit to the small but delightful church of Our Lady of Mount Carmel. Architecturally a mixture of Byzantine, Romanesque, Greek Orthodox and Spanish styles, the priesthouse, now a museum, gives visitors an insight into the life of Monsignor John Hawes, an extraordinary architect, stonemason and carpenter. This church was the culmination of his achievements.

Nearby is the stone-pitched Tenindewa Pioneer Well, as well as a natural glacier bed, which is also a great place for wildflowers.

Major annual events are the Wildflower Show held in August/September and the Agricultural Show also in September.

ACCOMMODATION: Railway Hotel/Motel, ph (08) 9961 1050; Club Hotel, ph (08) 9961 1131; Pindar Pub, ph (08) 9962 3024; Tallering Station, ph (08) 9962 3045; Mullewa Caravan Park, ph (08) 9961 1007
ACTIVITIES: Bushwalking, historic walk, scenic drives
TOURIST INFORMATION: Ph (08) 9961 1505

MUNDARING

34 KM EAST OF PERTH
POPULATION: PART OF PERTH
MAP REF: PAGE 306 C4

Nestled in the Darling Range, Mundaring was the name of a vineyard owned by the Jacob family, originally established by the Gugeri family in 1882. The vineyards, however, were not to be the town's claim to fame, and in 1898 to 1902 the Mundaring Weir and Number 1 pumping station were designed and built to supply water to the goldfields in Kalgoorlie, 550 km away. The water pipeline first reached Kalgoorlie in 1903, and the weir continues to supply this water under the Great Southern Towns and Goldfields Water Supply Scheme.

A pleasant picnic area is established at the weir, and of interest is a visit to the C. Y. O'Connor Historical Museum (named after Charles O'Connor who designed the weir). There is another museum nearby in the Old Mahogany Inn, built in 1837.

Other attractions include the Mundaring Arts Centre, the hillside garden of the Lavender Path and its tearooms, and the Community Sculpture Park with a display of interactive sculptures, amphitheatre and walking trail.

For those who enjoy the outdoors, then a drive to the Hills Forest, with its walking trails through ancient jarrah forests and nature-based activity centre, is a must, as is a trip to the nearby John Forrest National Park.

ACCOMMODATION: Mahogany Inn, ph (08) 9295 1118; Mundaring Weir Hotel, ph (08) 9295 1106; Travellers Rest Motel, ph (08) 9295 2950; Faversham Cottages and Gardens (B&B), ph (08) 9295 1312; Mundaring Caravan Park, ph (08) 9295 1125
ACTIVITIES: Bushwalking, national park access, scenic drives
TOURIST INFORMATION: Ph (08) 9483 1111

MUNDRABILLA

1377 KM EAST OF PERTH
POPULATION: 15 MAP REF: PAGE 311 E7

The first Europeans to settle in this remote and desolate area were Thomas and William Kennedy, who established Mundrabilla Homestead in the early 1870s. The motel and service station complex, situated 66 km west of Eucla on the Eyre Highway, was named after that original homestead.

Although considered just a stopover point for travellers crossing the Nullarbor, the surrounding region is a known meteorite site, where the shattered fragments of a huge meteor that plummeted to earth during the Ice Age are strewn over a 60 km area, making it one of the largest meteor sites in the world.

Also of interest is a bird and animal sanctuary which has been established at the rear of the Mundrabilla motel.

ACCOMMODATION: Mundrabilla Motel/Hotel, ph (08) 9039 3465; Mundrabilla Caravan Facility, ph (08) 9039 3465
ACTIVITIES: Meteor site, stopover
TOURIST INFORMATION: Ph (08) 9039 3465

NANNUP

294 KM SOUTH OF PERTH
POPULATION: 550   MAP REF: PAGE 306 C8

Graziers were the first European settlers into the region in the mid-1850s and today this historic town is still a farming district, with dairy farming and fruit-growing, along with timber, playing important roles.

The town itself has charm and character, with many original buildings still in use. You can walk along the Nannup Heritage Trail, or take a variety of scenic drives in the picturesque surrounding countryside. You can also sample some of the local wines produced at Oldfields Donnelly River Wines.

The Blackwood River is pleasant canoeing, while birdwatchers will delight in the Blackwood Billabong Bird Hide.

Special events include the Daffodil Display in August, and Wildflower Display and Discovery Week in September.

ACCOMMODATION: Nannup Tiger Cottages, ph (08) 9756 1188; Nannup Bush Cabins, ph (08) 9756 1170; Nannup Caravan Park, ph (08) 9756 1211

ACTIVITIES: Bushwalking, canoeing, fishing, historic walk, scenic drives, swimming

TOURIST INFORMATION: Ph (08) 9756 1211

NARROGIN

196 KM SOUTH-EAST OF PERTH
POPULATION: 4970   MAP REF: PAGE 306 E6

Situated within the heart of the state's richest farming land, Narrogin is a major railway junction and the largest service centre in the region, meeting the needs of the surrounding agricultural industries of sheep and pig raising and cereal growing.

Although the first settlers moved into the area in the 1860s, development was slow until the Great Southern Railway reached Narrogin in the 1880s. With the building of the Hordern Hotel beside the railway line, the settlement grew and the town site was declared in 1897.

Those interested in the town's heritage and history will enjoy the Heritage Trails, of both the township and district, while the old Court House Museum (1893) has displays of Narrogin's pioneer days. If you have read the book *A Fortunate Life* by Albert Facey, then a visit to his house is a must.

Bird and nature lovers will delight in a trip to the nearby Dryandra State Forest where there is an abundance of fauna and flora and some great bushwalks, with a profusion of wildflowers in spring.

Annual festivals and events include the Arts Festival in March, the Agricultural Show and Spring Festival in October.

ACCOMMODATION: Narrogin Motel, ph (08) 9881 1660; Wagon Way Motel, ph (08) 9881 1899; Chuckem Cottages, ph (08) 9885 9050; Stoke Farm Guest House, ph (08) 9885 9018; Town of Narrogin Caravan Park, ph (08) 9881 1260

ACTIVITIES: Birdwatching, bowls, bushwalking, croquet, golf, historic trails, horseracing

TOURIST INFORMATION: Ph (08) 9881 2064

NEW NORCIA

129 KM NORTH-EAST OF PERTH
POPULATION: 140   MAP REF: PAGE 306 C3

The Benedictine abbey at New Norcia

Founded by the Benedictine monk, Dom Rosendo Salvado, in March 1846, this small, historic township is situated on the Victoria Plains, along the Great Northern Highway.

A small self-sufficient village was built by the monks around their church, and New Norcia today, with its extraordinary buildings and olive trees, has a definite Spanish feel about it. While the monks continue with their ecclesiastic work, visitors will find much to interest them in this unique settlement.

The self-guided walk along the New Norcia Heritage Trail takes you past many of the town's landmarks, such as the still operating flour mill built in 1879 and the ornate structure of the St Gertrude's College, built in the early 1900s. Also well worth a visit is the Museum and Art Gallery, where you can also purchase a wide range of local goods from the shop, many produced by the monks themselves, including their famous bread and olive oil.

If you are in the region in July, you can participate in the Newdale Horse Trials and Country Fair.

ACCOMMODATION: New Norcia Hotel, ph (08) 9654 8034; Napier Downs Farm Cottages, ph (08) 9655 9015; Monastery Guesthouse, ph (08) 9654 8002

ACTIVITIES: Historic walk, scenic walks and drives

TOURIST INFORMATION: Ph (08) 9654 8056

NEWMAN

1180 KM NORTH OF PERTH
POPULATION: 4500   MAP REF: PAGE 315 J9

Located in the heart of the Pilbara, Newman is a modern mining town built to service the workers and their families who live close to Mt Whaleback, the largest single open-cut iron ore mine in the world. It is the administrative centre of the East Pilbara Shire—the largest shire in Australia, and the only shire to completely split the state, with an area bigger than the State of Victoria, or the country of Italy. Being such an important centre it has a large range of facilities and everything a traveller would require.

The town takes its name from nearby Mt Newman, which was named in 1896 after the local explorer, Aubrey Newman. In 1957 a massive iron ore deposit was discovered at Mt Whaleback.

Things to see in town include the BHP Iron Ore Silver Jubilee Museum Gallery with its magnificent leadlight window depicting the Pilbara landscape, and the Mining and Pastoral Museum, while a tour of the local mining operation is sure to impress by its sheer size and the massive equipment being used.

Ophthalmia Dam, 15 km north of town, supplies the town with water, and has a pleasant picnic area on its banks, while Radio Hill Lookout takes in expansive views of the area and the townsite.

The Newman Waterhole Circuit is a very pleasant 4WD day trip that takes in a number of waterholes and Aboriginal art sites in the region. You will be surprised at the diversity of bird life and plants on this trip, as well as the sheer grandeur of the gorges and waterholes. Maps are available from the local tourist centre.

Karijini National Park to the north-west of the town takes in a large area of rugged range and gorge country that is well worth exploring.

Newman is also a jumping-off point for the remote Karlamilyi (Rudall River) National Park and the Canning Stock Route, both areas being the domain of the well set-up and experienced four wheel driver.

The mining of iron ore at Newman

ACCOMMODATION: All Seasons Newman Hotel, ph (08) 9177 8666; Mercure Inn, ph (08) 9175 1101; Dearlove's Caravan Park, ph (08) 9175 2802; Newman Caravan Park, ph (08) 9175 1428

ACTIVITIES: 4WD touring, mine tours, national park access, sailing, scenic drives, swimming,

TOURIST INFORMATION: Ph (08) 9175 2888

NORSEMAN

724 KM EAST OF PERTH
POPULATION: 1900   MAP REF: PAGE 307 L5

Known as 'The Golden Gate to the Western State', the goldmining town of Norseman is located at the junction of the Eyre and Eastern Highways, 207 km south of Coolgardie.

A horse is said to have made the first discovery, stumbling over a large gold nugget in the 1890s. Today Norseman's quartz reef is the richest in Australia. Those interested in mining and those early gold rush days will enjoy a visit to the Historical and Geological Collection exhibited in the School of Mines.

Gem fossickers can scratch around on the gemstone leases north and east of town, while gold seekers and those interested in old mining sites should take a drive on the Dundas Coach Road Heritage Trail.

There are also a number of interesting geological sites such as the Salt Lakes, Dundas Rocks and Mt Jimberlana, while a pleasant picnic and swimming spot can be found at Bromus Dam.

Norseman is also an important quarantine checkpoint for travellers from the eastern states.

Annual events include the CWA Art and Craft Expo in August/September and the Gala Day in December.

ACCOMMODATION: Norseman Eyre Motel, ph (08) 9039 1130; Great Western Motel, ph (08) 9039 1633; Railway Motel ph (08) 9039 1115; Gateway Caravan Park, ph (08) 9039 1500
ACTIVITIES: Gem fossicking, gold prospecting, scenic drives
TOURIST INFORMATION: Ph (08) 9039 1071

NORTHAM

95 KM EAST OF PERTH
POPULATION: 7500   MAP REF: PAGE 306 D4
Set astride the Avon River in the heart of the valley of the same name, Northam is the largest town in the region. First settled in 1836, the area did not develop until 1886 when Northam was linked to Perth by rail, and this important part of the town's heritage is displayed in the old Railway Station Museum.

There are also a number of unique attractions in the town including the Austwide Sheepskin Products, the largest sheepskin tannery in Australia, and the pedestrian suspension bridge, which offers visitors a good chance to glimpse the large colony of regal white swans as they gracefully glide up and down the Avon River.

There are several art and craft outlets to browse through, or for something a little more exhilarating there is hot-air ballooning which will give a bird's-eye view of the area.

Festivals and events include the Avon Descent White Water Classic and River Festival in August, Agricultural Show in September and the Avon Valley Country Music Festival in November.

ACCOMMODATION: Shamrock Hotel, ph (08) 9622 1092; Northam Motel, ph (08) 9622 1755; Brackson House B&B, ph (08) 9622 5262; Northam Guest House, ph (08) 9622 2301; Mortlock Caravan Park, ph (08) 9622 1620
ACTIVITIES: Camel riding, canoeing, golf, hot-air ballooning, whitewater rafting
TOURIST INFORMATION: Ph (08) 9622 2100

ONSLOW

1404 KM NORTH OF PERTH
POPULATION: 650   MAP REF: 314 D7
The original town site was established in 1885, at the former mouth of the Ashburton River, as a port for the surrounding sheep stations and a centre to supply goods and services to the pearling and mining industries. A deeper port with better facilities was needed, however, and most of the buildings, along with the residents, were moved during 1925 to the new town site along the coast at Beadon Bay. The vestiges of the old town site still remain as a stark reminder of yesteryear.

Although small and isolated, set in a harsh climate, it is a green town, with plenty of shady trees. Mining and pastoral properties of sheep and cattle are the town's lifeblood, yet tourism is also beginning to play an important role.

Onslow has had its share of historic events and misfortunes. Cyclones have devastated the town on numerous occasions, forcing the closure of the port in 1963, and during World War II its airfield was bombed by the Japanese. For a look back into the town's history visit the Shell Museum and the Onslow Goods Shed Museum.

There are also excellent fishing opportunities both along the coast and offshore, with the most popular spots being Beadon Creek and Four Mile Creek where you can fish for mangrove jack, bream and estuary cod.

ACCOMMODATION: Onslow Sun Chalets, ph (08) 9184 6058; Mackerel Islands, ph (08) 9388 2020; Ocean View Caravan Park, ph (08) 9184 6053; Onslow Beadon Bay Village, ph (08) 9184 6042
ACTIVITIES: Boating, fishing, swimming
TOURIST INFORMATION: Ph (08) 9184 6113

PEMBERTON

344 KM SOUTH OF PERTH
POPULATION: 870   MAP REF: PAGE 306 C9
Pemberton has a splendid, picture-postcard setting, surrounded by lofty forests of karri, jarrah and marri.

Tall karri trees, typical of the area around Pemberton

The Karri Visitor Centre should not be missed, and there is a unique ride through the timber on the 1907 replica Pemberton Tramway.

To get a bird's-eye view of the forest, you can climb 60 metres up the trunk of the Gloucester Tree, to the highest fire lookout in a tree in the world.

Trout fishermen will find plenty of waterways and dams to cast a line in, while wine lovers are well catered for with a number of wineries in the area. For craft enthusiasts there are a number of excellent woodcraft galleries on hand.

The Pemberton Forest Festival is held in October.

ACCOMMODATION: Karri Forest Motel, ph (08) 9776 1019; Pemberton Hotel, ph (08) 9776 1017; Pemberton Lavender & Berry Farm Cottages, ph (08) 9776 1661; Pemberton Caravan Park, ph (08) 9776 1300
ACTIVITIES: Bushwalking, canoeing, fishing, horse riding, scenic drives, wineries
TOURIST INFORMATION: Ph (08) 9776 1133

PINJARRA

96 KM SOUTH OF PERTH
POPULATION: 1340   MAP REF: PAGE 306 C5
Straddling the South Western Highway, alongside the Murray River, Pinjarra is one of the oldest towns in the state, with the first Europeans arriving in the early 1830s. It did not take long for these early farmers to begin producing bountiful harvests in this fertile landscape, calling the region Pinjarrup, the Aboriginal name meaning 'place of swamps'.

The surrounding Murray District is not only rich in agriculture and history, but has a wide range of landscapes, from a maze of waterways to undulating grazing pastures and verdant jarrah forests. There are plenty of attractions both in and around Pinjarra for the visitor.

The many fine old and restored buildings in town, reminders of a past era, can be admired by taking the Pinjarra Heritage Trail, past buildings such as the Edenvale residence, St John's Church (1861), Original School House (1862), Post Office (1880s) and the Old Blythewood Homestead.

Somewhat unusual is Cooper's Mill, built in 1843 to grind wheat and corn, which can only be reached by boat and is one of only two wind-driven mills still standing in Western Australia today.

For flower lovers, a stroll around the Heritage Rose Garden which features 364 old-fashioned roses, is a must, while the surrounding area is a patchwork of colourful wildflowers during the season.

The nearby Alcoa Refinery also conducts tours of the mine site and refinery.

Special events not to miss, if you are in the area, are the Old Blythewood Music Evening in February, Rotary Art Exhibition and Sale in June, Alcoa Fairbridge International Horse Trial in September and the Lions Rodeo in November.

ACCOMMODATION: Pinjarra Motel, ph (08) 9531 1811; Bonny Farm B&B, ph (08) 9530 3203; Pinjarra Caravan Park, ph (08) 9531 1374; Pinjarra Park Country Camping, ph (08) 9531 1604
ACTIVITIES: Birdwatching, bushwalking, heritage walks
TOURIST INFORMATION: Ph (08) 9531 1438

PORT HEDLAND

1779 KM NORTH OF PERTH
POPULATION: 15 000   MAP REF: PAGE 315 H5

Port Hedland was originally a quiet country town with the first settlers taking land up for cattle grazing in 1863. Times have certainly changed and the Port Hedland of today is a busy administrative centre and port, servicing not only the mining community but the surrounding cattle stations.

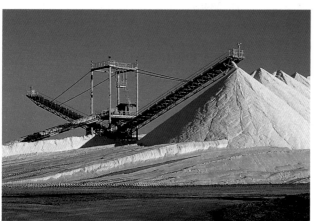

Salt stacks at the docks of Port Hedland

Originally named Mangrove Harbour in 1863, the port became a busy base and thoroughfare for pearling luggers in the 1870s, and then the gold prospectors when colour was found at Marble Bar. The town site was not officially gazetted until 1896, with its first jetty built a few years later. A second jetty was completed in 1911, while a rail link between Port Hedland and Marble Bar was built to help with the movement of people and goods.

While the extraction of tin, copper, gold and manganese over the years brought prosperity to the region, it was the discovery of the astounding rich body of iron ore in the 1960s in the hinterland that saw the huge development of Port Hedland and its surrounds take place. The accompanying explosion in population required the building of a new satellite city in South Hedland, while a deep-water port was also needed to cater for the world's biggest ore carriers that constantly call into the port. Much of what relates to mining here is on a massive scale: the machinery is huge, and the BHP Iron Ore Railroad carries the world's longest, regularly scheduled trains, bringing the ore from outlying mining sites into the port. No visit to Port Hedland would be complete without a tour of the BHP iron ore facilities at Nelson Point.

Another important mineral extracted from the land is salt, and the large expanses of white conical towers stand starkly against the landscape, waiting for shipment overseas.

Port Hedland has four Heritage Trails which take visitors past many of the historical landmarks giving an insight into the town's early days. Other notable relics are the Pioneers and Pearlers Cemetery, the Don Rhodes Mining Museum, Police Station and Jail (1903), Court House (1900), Olde St Matthews Church Art Gallery and Exhibition Centre, Pretty Pool and the Redbank Bridge Lookout.

Day outings from Port Hedland, for those with a 4WD vehicle, can lead to such attractions as the Ord Ranges, Poonthune Pool and Whim Creek, which is the site of one of the oldest pubs in the Pilbara.

Extended forays to consider are trips out to Marble Bar and Nullagine; the Newman Waterhole Circuit; Karijini National Park; Millstream–Chichester National Park and Eighty Mile Beach.

Again, four-wheel drivers can also get to some well-known but isolated fishing and camping spots such as Twelve Mile Creek, Tichilla, Pardoo Station and Cape Keraudren. Closer to Port Hedland the harbour is an excellent fishing area with chances of landing black jewfish and Spanish mackerel, while Spoil Bank, a sand spit just west of the jetty, is the spot for threadfin salmon. Those with a boat will find endless places to fish, not only offshore, but along the mangrove-lined coast where you can catch queenfish and barramundi, while the mangrove crabs are plentiful, and reputed to be the biggest in Australia. If you find yourself in the region some time between September to April, you may see flatback turtles nesting at the town beaches, while humpback whales pass through between June and October.

This busy community runs quite a few events during the year, such as the Beerfest and Heritage Week in April, a game fishing tournament in July, the Music Festival in September and the Arts Foundation Art Show in November.

ACCOMMODATION: Hospitality Inn Port Hedland, ph (08) 9173 1044; South Hedland Motel, ph (08) 9172 2222; Pier Hotel, ph (08) 9173 1488; Cooke Point Ocean Beach Caravan Park, ph (08) 9173 1271

ACTIVITIES: Boating, fishing, 4WD touring, heritage walks, turtle and whale watching

TOURIST INFORMATION: Ph (08) 9173 1711

ROCKINGHAM

47 KM SOUTH OF PERTH
POPULATION: 50 000   MAP REF: PAGE 306 B5

This once peaceful seafront village on Cockburn Sound was one of Western Australia's earliest settlements and by the turn of the century the port was one of the busiest in the state, loading timber from Jarrahdale for shipping to England. Times got quieter when the port of Fremantle took its place, and the town again took on a sleepy facade. Its delightful settings and surrounds, though, were slowly being discovered by travellers and it soon became a popular tourist destination, the sheltered waters of Cockburn Sound and Mangles Bay ideal for water sports.

While the beaches are popular, away from the water nature lovers and birdwatchers will enjoy the Karnup Nature Reserve, or the Lake Richmond–Anne Mueller Environmental Walk. For history buffs there are the Rockingham Museum and the Granary, and a walk along the Old Rockingham Heritage Trail leads past notable landmarks pertaining to the early settlement in East Rockingham.

There are also wineries to visit, and art and craft outlets to browse through, and market devotees will not want to miss the Sunday markets.

Anglers can expect catches of tommy ruff, tailor, snapper, mulloway and trevally.

Annual events include the Navy Open Day in October/November, Baldivis Fair and the Spring Festival in November.

ACCOMMODATION: Leisure Inn, ph (08) 9527 7777; Rockingham Motel/Hotel, ph (08) 9592 1828; The Anchorage (B&B), ph (08) 9527 4214; Palm Beach Caravan & Camping Holiday Village, ph (08) 9527 1515

ACTIVITIES: Bushwalking, fishing, heritage walks, scenic drives, water sports, wineries

TOURIST INFORMATION: Ph (08) 9592 3464

ROEBOURNE

1577 KM NORTH OF PERTH
POPULATION: 1695   MAP REF: PAGE 314 F6

Located on the North West Coastal Highway at the junction of the road to Wickham, Cossack and Point Samson, Roebourne can boast of being the oldest

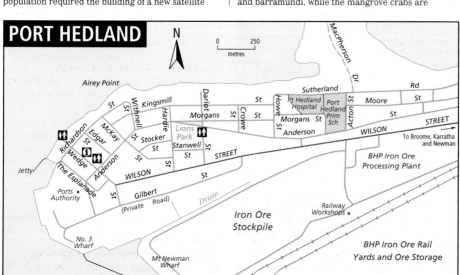

PORT HEDLAND

N

0   250
metres

Airey Point

Kingsmill St

Withnell St

Richardson St

McKay St

Edgar St

Wedge St

The Esplanade

Anderson St

Jetty

Ports Authority

Gilbert St
(Private) Road

WILSON ST

Hardie St

Darlot St

Morgans St

Stocker St

Stanwell St

Lions Park

Crowe St

Howe St

St

STREET

Sutherland St

Pt Hedland Hospital

Morgans St

Anderson St

Port Hedland Prim Sch

Moore St

Acton St

WILSON

Rd

St

Macpherson Dr

STREET

To Broome, Karratha and Newman

BHP Iron Ore Processing Plant

Drain

Iron Ore Stockpile

Railway Workshops

BHP Iron Ore Rail Yards and Ore Storage

No. 3 Wharf

Mt Newman Wharf

town on the north-west coast. Named after the state's first surveyor general, John Roe, the town was settled in 1866, the area having been explored just five years earlier. Many pioneers took up pastoral leases in the area and the town became the administrative centre for the region until the railway line was built between Marble Bar and Port Hedland. With the building of the railway, the town declined, until the 1960s when the iron ore boom ensured its future.

A walk or drive around the town reveals many old buildings dating from the 1880s, with the old gaol now the town's tourist bureau and museum.

The 52 km long Emma Withnell Heritage Trail commences in the heart of Roebourne and takes travellers out to historic Cossack, on to Wickham—built during the 1970s for the ever-expanding workforce of the iron ore industry—and ending at Point Samson, the old port for the area and a tranquil seaside town with excellent beaches and good fishing.

The annual events include the Roebourne Royal Show in June, and the Roebourne Cup and Ball which takes place in July.

ACCOMMODATION: Mt Welcome Motel, ph (08) 9182 1282; Wickham Lodge, ph (08) 9187 1439; Point Sampson Lodge, ph (08) 9187 1052; Harding River Caravan Park, ph (08) 9182 1063
ACTIVITIES: Fishing, gem fossicking, gold prospecting, historic walks, scenic drives
TOURIST INFORMATION: Ph (08) 9182 1060

SANDFIRE

2070 KM NORTH OF PERTH
POPULATION: 20 MAP REF: PAGE 315 L4
A small oasis on the long run north from Port Hedland to Broome and the Kimberley, Sandfire originated in the 1970s when a fuel truck broke down here and suddenly found itself dispensing petrol to passing motorists. It was a lonely and hard life for much of the time but this small haven is still an important one for travellers. It can provide the basic requirements of travellers as well as a cold drink, meals and accommodation.

Access to the long Eighty Mile Beach is possible near here, while a small caravan and camping park is located a little further south at Nallal Downs homestead. The beach is a good fishing spot and a well-known locality for shells which are washed up on the beach in incredible numbers.

Further north, and about 160 km south of Broome, is Port Smith with its camping and caravan park.
ACCOMMODATION: Sandfire Roadhouse Hotel and Caravan Park, ph (08) 9176 5944; Eighty Mile Beach Caravan Park, ph (08) 9176 5941
ACTIVITIES: Fishing, 4WD touring, swimming
TOURIST INFORMATION: Ph (08) 9176 5944

SOUTHERN CROSS

366 KM EAST OF PERTH
POPULATION: 800 MAP REF: 307 H3
Gold was discovered here in 1888 by two prospectors who, at the time, were more interested in finding water. The town received its name from the fact that

they used the stars of the Southern Cross to find their way. A number of mines were developed in the area; however, the finds were to be overshadowed by the gold discovered further east a few years later.

While some mining is still carried on, the town is now well known as the centre for a rich agricultural area, with a profusion of wildflowers in spring. Frog Rock, 34 km south of Southern Cross, is a popular place for flowers and a good picnic spot as well.

Reminders of the days of gold are preserved in the Old Court House (1892) that is now the local museum, at the old cemetery, and the Mining Registrar's office. Wimmera Hill, on the highway just west of the town, was the site of the first major gold discovery in Western Australia and gives good views over the town and surrounding farmland.

Koolyanobbing, 50 km north from Southern Cross, is a 'modern' ghost town having closed down in 1983 after less than 30 years in existence. Hope's Hill, just 6 km from town, is the now desolate site of what was a booming gold town of the 1890s, while Mount Palmer, another rich gold town of that era, is nothing more than a pleasant picnic area.

The annual 'King of the Cross' motocross championship draws competitors from far and wide.
ACCOMMODATION: Southern Cross Motel, ph (08) 9049 1144; Palace Hotel, ph (08) 9049 1555; Elouera Holiday Farm Guest House, ph (08) 9047 5010; Southern Cross Caravan Park, ph (08) 9049 1212
ACTIVITIES: Bowls, motocross, scenic drives, wildflowers
TOURIST INFORMATION: Ph (08) 9049 1001

TOM PRICE

1632 KM NORTH OF PERTH
POPULATION: 3560 MAP REF: PAGE 314 G8
The town of Tom Price was built at the base of Mt Nameless, after the discovery of the huge iron deposit at nearby Mt Tom Price in the 1960s. This discovery of probably the largest iron ore body ever found was the trigger for the establishment of Hamersley Iron P/L,

Open-cut mining in operation at Tom Price

the construction of the mine, the port of Dampier and the railway between the two towns.

The town also acts as the administrative centre for the surrounding Ashburton Shire, and takes its name from a minerals expert and surveyor for the US-based Kaiser Steel Corporation who was an enthusiastic supporter of the development of the iron ore potential of the Pilbara.

The town is close to the gorges and rugged ranges of Karijini National Park, and because of the natural attractions of the area and the vast mine workings it is a popular stopover for visitors travelling through the Pilbara.

Annual events include the Tom Price Nameless Festival in August and the State Go-kart Championships in October.
ACCOMMODATION: Tom Price Mercure Inn, ph (08) 9189 1101; Hillview Lodge Motel, ph (08) 9189 1110; Tom Price Caravan Park, ph (08) 9189 1515
ACTIVITIES: Bowls, bushwalking, national park access, scenic drives, swimming
TOURIST INFORMATION: Ph (08) 9188 1112

TOODYAY

98 KM NORTH-EAST OF PERTH
POPULATION: 550 MAP REF: PAGE 306 D4
The small pleasant town of Toodyay, on the banks of the Avon River, was one of the first inland towns in the state, and has many fine old buildings dating from the 1860s when the town was moved from its original flood-prone position to its present site. Because of the wealth of old buildings, the whole town has been classified as historic by the National Trust. Places of interest include Connors Mill (1870), the third steam-powered flour mill to grace the town and now the tourist centre. The old gaol houses a museum.

Toodyay offers plenty of other attractions including Coorinja Winery, the pleasant picnic areas of Reservoir Lookout and Drummond's Park, and Duidgee Park on the banks of the Avon.

The Avon Valley National Park nearby is a wealth of wildflowers in spring.

The Moondyne Colonial & Convict Festival is held in May, the Avon Descent passes through in August, the Highland Games and Festival of the Celts are in September, and the Toodyay Festival and Agricultural Show in October.
ACCOMMODATION: Victoria Hotel/Motel, ph (08) 9574 2206; Freemasons Hotel, ph (08) 9574 2201; Ipswich View Homestead, (B&B), ph (08) 9574 4038; Toodyay Caravan Park, ph (08) 9574 2612
ACTIVITIES: Bowls, bushwalking, canoeing, fishing, national park access, scenic drives, swimming, wineries
TOURIST INFORMATION: Ph (08) 9574 2435

WALPOLE

431 KM SOUTH-EAST OF PERTH
POPULATION: 290 MAP REF: PAGE 306 D10
Nestled around Walpole Inlet and surrounded by extraordinary red tingle and karri forests, Walpole is

Karri forests surround the town of Walpole

both a picturesque and quiet town, making it a great holiday destination.

Truly unrivalled is the Tree Top Walk in the Valley of the Giants. Here a 420-metre-long walkway has been erected in the tingle forest canopy, at times 40 metres above the ground, and this breathtaking experience, accessible for children, wheelchairs and the elderly, should not be missed.

On the water, the Walpole and Nornalup Inlets can be explored by houseboat or ferry, while a pleasant outing can be had visiting the Thurlby Herbal Farm. Nature lovers will find the wildflowers in springtime, especially in the surrounding Walpole–Nornalup National Park, a delight.

Annual events include the Easter Sunday Market Day and the Orchid Show in October.
ACCOMMODATION: Bow River Cottages, ph (08) 9840 1192; Inlet View (B&B); ph (08) 9840 1226; Coalmine Beach Caravan Park, ph (08) 9840 1026
ACTIVITIES: Bushwalking, canoeing, fishing, national park access, scenic drives, wildflowers
TOURIST INFORMATION: Ph (08) 9840 1111

WARBURTON

1536 KM NORTH-EAST OF PERTH
POPULATION: 910   MAP REF: PAGE 310 D10
Located on what most people know as the Gunbarrel Highway, Warburton is an important Aboriginal community, nearly 700 km north-east of Leonora and 560 km west of Uluru (Ayers Rock).

The road is dirt for all its length and can be rough, so the roadhouse with its fuel and supplies is a popular and necessary stop for those heading

through from Western Australia to Uluru or Alice Springs. However, it should be noted that the roadhouse is not open 24 hours a day. The main route is from the south from Laverton while a rougher 4WD route follows the original Gunbarrel to Carnegie Homestead and Wiluna.

Two permits are required to travel these roads. You should apply to the Aboriginal Affairs Planning Authority in Perth, ph (08) 9483 1333 and the Central Land Council in Alice, ph (08) 8952 3800. The Aboriginal community itself is out of bounds for travellers, but artefacts can sometimes be bought from the store.
ACCOMMODATION: Warburton Roadhouse Caravan Park, ph (08) 8956 7656
ACTIVITIES: Overnight stop
TOURIST INFORMATION: Ph (08) 8956 7656

WILUNA

946 KM NORTH-EAST OF PERTH
POPULATION: 230   MAP REF: PAGE 309 K5
Located at the junction of the 4WD Gunbarrel Highway to the east, the long and arduous 4WD route of the Canning Stock Route to the north, and the main dirt road west to Meekatharra or south to Leonora, Wiluna is a service town for the surrounding and even more remote sheep and cattle properties, the mining camps and the Aboriginal communities.

Gold was discovered here in 1896 and the mine became the largest in Australia. However, when the

A fuel drop on the Canning Stock Route near Wiluna

mine closed in 1947 the town declined. Today mining activities are still carried on close to the town, but the current population is far short of the 10 000 that once lived here.

The town has two fuel outlets, but they are sometimes out of one or more fuels, so it pays to check in advance.
ACCOMMODATION: Club Hotel/Motel, ph (08) 9981 7012; Wiluna Caravan Park, ph (08) 9981 7021
ACTIVITIES: 4WD touring
TOURIST INFORMATION: Ph (08) 9981 7010

WITTENOOM

1660 KM NORTH OF PERTH
POPULATION: 10   MAP REF: PAGE 315 H8
The town of Wittenoom has refused to die completely, even though it has been officially abandoned and

declared inhabitable. This is due to the mining of blue asbestos which continued from the 1930s through to 1966, when the mines closed because of economic reasons. The health hazards of this mineral were fairly well known, caused by the asbestos fibres which readily float through the air once disturbed.

However, the town is located close to some magnificent gorges, which are readily accessible to normal vehicles, while a 4WD will give access to

Town Pool in Wittenoom Gorge near Wittenoom

others. Many of the gorges have magnificent waterfalls when the rivers flow after heavy rain. Fortescue Falls are especially noteworthy.

The attractions include the original town site and the natural pool—called Town Pool—in Wittenoom Gorge, the old asbestos mine in Vampire Gorge, as well as the vast Karijini National Park. A road from the old town leads south into the park and another gorge, Hancock Gorge. The Fortescue River, reached by a good dirt road north of the town, is also very pleasant with many fine waterholes and patches of palm and paperbark forests.
ACCOMMODATION: Fortescue Hotel, ph (08) 9189 7055; Wittenoom Holiday Homes, ph (08) 9189 7096; Gorges Caravan Park, ph (08) 9189 7075
ACTIVITIES: 4WD touring, national park access, scenic drives, swimming
TOURIST INFORMATION: Ph (08) 9189 7075

WYNDHAM

3355 KM NORTH OF PERTH
POPULATION: 1550   MAP REF: PAGE 313 M4
The northernmost town in Western Australia, Wyndham sits beside the muddy grey waters of the Cambridge Gulf. It is the administrative centre for the East Kimberley Shire but has lost much of its importance to the 'new' town of Kununurra, 100 km to the south-east.

Phillip Parker King surveyed this coast in 1818, naming the great gulf that the town is located on, while the port came into existence when gold was discovered at Halls Creek in 1886. The town remained an important outlet for the beef industry which grew

up in the Kimberley, and a large jetty was built here in the 1890s to handle the ever increasing cargo, while a meatworks, which was started in 1919, closed down in 1985.

During World War II the town was bombed by the Japanese and today there are two main parts to the town. The 'Old Port' is located close to the old meatworks and is the site of the original town, while the newer part of town is 5 km away on slightly higher ground.

One of the best views possible, and a fine panorama of the gulf and the five rivers that flow into it, is from the top of the Bastion at Five Rivers Lookout. Just south of town is the Parry Lagoons Nature Reserve, which is one of the finest bird habitats and birdwatching areas in the state.

Other attractions include Moochalabra Dam and the nearby Aboriginal art sites, the pioneer cemeteries, both close to town, the Prison Tree and the Grotto. The local museum and tourist information centre is located down at the Old Port.

Annual events include the Top of the West Festival in July/August and the Bastion Billy Cart Race in August.

ACCOMMODATION: Wyndham Community Club Hotel, ph (08) 9161 1130; Wyndham Town Hotel, ph (08) 9161 1003; Three Mile Caravan Park, ph (08) 9161 1064
ACTIVITIES: Bowls, fishing, 4WD touring
TOURIST INFORMATION: Ph (08) 9161 1054

YALLINGUP

266 KM SOUTH OF PERTH
POPULATION: 50   MAP REF: PAGE 306 A7

Situated as it is along a spectacular coast and surrounded by the Leeuwin–Naturaliste National Park, Yallingup makes a great place to explore Cape Naturaliste, including its extraordinary cave systems.

Drinkers can savour the local wines, or watch ales being brewed at the Bootleg Winery or Abbey Vale Vineyard. Local flower farms specialise in fresh and dried flowers, and there is a range of galleries.

Surfers can revel in the excellent waves along Yallingup beach, and the area is a magnet for anglers and divers. The Malibu Surfing Competition is held in December.

ACCOMMODATION: Caves House Hotel, ph (08) 9755 2131; Canal Rocks Beach Resort, ph (08) 9755 2116; Crayfish Lodge Guest House, ph (08) 9755 2028; Yallingup Farm Cottages, ph (08) 9755 2261; Yallingup Beach Caravan Park, ph (08) 9755 2164
ACTIVITIES: Bushwalking, fishing, horse riding, national park access, scenic drives, water sports
TOURIST INFORMATION: Ph (08) 9755 6311

YANCHEP

57 KM NORTH OF PERTH
POPULATION: 490   MAP REF: PAGE 306 B4

Originally called Two Rocks, the more modern and catchy 'Yanchep Sun City' gained wider acclaim as the base for one of the America's Cup's yachting

challenges. Today Yanchep is one of Perth's most popular tourist destinations and recreational areas, catering for those who love to go boating, fishing, diving, surfing and windsurfing. Lagoon Beach is one such spot, while if you want to get away from the beach scene you can experience some pleasant walking in the nearby Yanchep National Park. This small park is home to a number of native mammals including western grey kangaroos and bandicoots, and a host of waterbirds. There are a number of caves in the area and also in the park, as well as several lakes. Rowboats can be hired so you can enjoy the waters of the verdant-rimmed Lake McNess.

The Yaberoo Budjara Heritage Trail is a walking trail that extends for 28 km north of Joondalup along the chain of coastal lakes that makes this part of Western Australia so picturesque.

ACCOMMODATION: Club Capricorn Motel and Chalets, ph (08) 9561 1106; Yanchep Holiday Village, ph (08) 9561 2244; Yanchep Lagoon Lodge, ph (08) 9561 1033
ACTIVITIES: Boating, bushwalking, fishing, golf, horse riding, national park access
TOURIST INFORMATION: Ph (08) 9561 2244

YORK

94 KM EAST OF PERTH
POPULATION: 1140   MAP REF: PAGE 306 D4

York, in the Avon Valley, is Western Australia's most historic town as well as being its first inland town.

Settled in 1830, the town was proclaimed the following year, with wool being the main produce. The

town was a convict depot in the 1850s, and when gold was discovered at nearby Yilgarn in 1889, York got another boost to its posterity.

The town is a very popular weekend trip for Perth people and has much to offer.

Balladong Farm, established in 1831, is the oldest farm in the state and is now a working museum, and here the children can feed the farm animals. The Residency, where the resident magistrate was based, dates back to 1843 and is now a museum.

The York Motor Museum houses one of the finest collections of vintage cars, motorcycles and horsedrawn-vehicles in Australia and is well worth a visit. The old two-storey railway station, built in 1886 and one of the few remaining two-storey station buildings in Australia, houses an historic railway collection. The Sandalwood Press is Western Australia's only working printing museum.

The picturesque Avon Park, alongside the Avon River, is a pleasant picnic area, while the Mt Brown Lookout, just east of town, offers a 360 degree panorama of the surrounding countryside.

Events include the EarthCare Festival in March, the Antique Collectors Fair and Heritage Week in April, the Veteran Car Rally in August, the York Arts and Crafts Award and the York Jazz Festival in October, and the York Rose Festival in November.

ACCOMMODATION: Avon Motel, ph (08) 9641 2066; Castle Hotel, ph (08) 9641 1007; King's Head Cottage, ph (08) 9641 1817; Out of Town Inn (B&B), ph (08) 9641 2214; Mt Bakewell Caravan Park, ph (08) 9641 1421
ACTIVITIES: Archery, canoeing, scenic drives, swimming
TOURIST INFORMATION: Ph (08) 9641 1301

Settlers' houses, built around 1835, in York

The Fitzroy River running through Geikie Gorge National Park

BURRINGURRAH (MOUNT AUGUSTUS) NATIONAL PARK

Mt Augustus is the biggest rock in the world, almost twice the size of Uluru. To the Wadjeri tribe, the Aboriginal people who inhabited this region, Mt Augustus was known as Burringurrah. They left behind many rock engravings, and a large number of stone tools have also been discovered. Water draining from the rock and then seeping underground supports stands of white-barked river gums while mulga, myall, gidgi and other wattles are scattered across the plains. A circuit drive of 49 km provides access to all the points of interest.

CAPE ARID NATIONAL PARK

This park, 80 km north-east of Perth, is famous for its magnificent beaches and headlands. In the northern section is Mt Ragged, the highest peak of the Russell Range at 594 metres. The granite hills and pools of permanent water provide habitats for rare plants and animals and around Mt Ragged a variety of ferns and orchids grow. The bird life is prolific, the rare Cape Barren goose is a regular visitor and flocks of the endangered ground parrots are surviving here. During winter southern right whales can be spotted close inshore and seals on the beaches. Bushwalking is popular, and coastal fishing is good all year.

CAPE LE GRAND NATIONAL PARK

Cape Le Grand National Park, about 40 km east of Esperance, is known for its sandy beaches, beautiful bays and rocky headlands. The most spectacular feature is a chain of massive outcrops of granite and gneiss in the south-west corner: Mt Le Grand (352 metres), Frenchman Peak (262 metres) and Mississippi Hill (180 metres). Heathland, banksia and paperbarks, as well as several species of mallee grow in the park. Mammals and birds abound. Fishing and boating are popular activities.

CAPE RANGE NATIONAL PARK

Winter is the best time to visit Cape Range National Park, which is on North West Cape about 1250 km north of Perth, since summer temperatures can reach 40°C and cyclones are not uncommon. Cape Range itself is a rough, stony, limestone ridge, only 311 metres above sea level at its highest point, eroded into caves and gullies and intersected by deep gorges and chasms. The national park extends west to the Indian Ocean, protecting the sandy beaches and shifting dunes of the Coral Coast. With the superb Ningaloo Reef, it is now incorporated as the Ningaloo Marine Park. The main attractions of Cape Range National Park are the unspoilt beaches, and good fishing, diving and swimming in the Ningaloo Marine Park. Numerous mammals and bird species live in the park.

DRYSDALE RIVER NATIONAL PARK

This is Western Australia's most northerly park, in the north of the Kimberley. It is a wilderness park which provides great opportunities for walking and nature observation as there are no facilities and no authorised vehicle tracks. The rivers and creeks contain many steep-sided gorges, cliffs and magnificent waterfalls, the largest being Morgan Falls and Solea Falls. Remnant pockets of rainforest are found along the 48 km of the Carson Escarpment and in some gorges such as Worriga Gorge. The bird and animal life is diverse: short-eared rock wallabies, sugar gliders, purple-crowned fairy wrens, Gouldian finches and grey and peregrine falcons. Not to be forgotten are the many species of reptiles, frogs, and freshwater fish. This park is best visited in the Dry season (May–October) as most rivers of the Kimberley are in flood during the Wet. A 4WD vehicle is essential as the only way into the park is via station tracks. Visitors must obtain prior permission from the stations.

FITZGERALD RIVER NATIONAL PARK

This large park, on the south coast between the towns of Bremer Bay and Hopetoun, is important botanically as a world biosphere reserve. Access is restricted to either end of the park in an effort to control the spread of dieback disease. From the east, the scenic Hamersley Drive gives access to Four Mile, Barrens, Mylies and West beaches. Many of the tracks are 4WD only. The landscape varies from protected beaches, sea cliffs, steep ranges and extensive plains to river systems emptying into the ocean via broad estuaries. There is an abundance of flora and fauna. The extensive coastline offers whale watching from August to November, excellent bushwalking, and good fishing (fishing regulations apply).

FRANCOIS PERON NATIONAL PARK

Located 835 km north of Perth on a peninsula in Shark Bay, both park and peninsula are named for the French explorer and naturalist Francois Péron. It was established as a sheep station in the 1880s and purchased by the state government in 1990, and the homestead now gives visitors a taste of life in the 1880s. Most of the Shark Bay area was given World Heritage listing in 1991. This park protects rare wildlife while offering the visitor a wilderness experience, impressive coastal scenery, boating, fishing and swimming. The road in to the homestead can be used by cars but a high-clearance 4WD is needed for travel further in the park. There is a wide variety of land and sea birds and the region also boasts euros, other small marsupials and lizards. From the cliffs at Cape Peron it is possible to see dugong, dolphins, turtles and even large manta rays.

KALBARRI NATIONAL PARK

Kalbarri National Park, on the west coast north of Geraldton, is a paradise for walkers, with magnificent scenery both along the coast and in the river gorges. These spectacular red and white banded gorges, created by the Murchison River as it meanders to the sea, stretch for over 80 km. The wettest months are June and July, and after that the wildflowers, for which the area is famous, begin to bloom. These cooler months are the best time for exploring the park. Along the coastline are some dramatic rock formations, and the views from the cliffs are stunning. There is excellent fishing along the rock platforms and beaches or in the estuary. The nearby town of Kalbarri, which is 150 km north of Geraldton, is a fishing port and a good base for visitors.

KARIJINI (HAMERSLEY RANGE) NATIONAL PARK

Karijini is part of the Hamersley Range in the Pilbara region, 310 km from Roebourne and 285 km from Port Hedland. The best time to visit is May–October; the Wet is a time of thunderstorms, cyclones, and temperatures over 40°C. The mountains and escarpments have been eroded to form a series of magnificent gorges and deep, narrow chasms. This is rugged and ancient land, the spectacular banded-iron formation of the gorge dates back more than 2500 million years. Wildflowers vary with the season and rainfall; in the cooler months you may see yellow flowering sennas and acacias, and purple mulla-mullas. The area is also rich in bird life and fauna.

LESUEUR NATIONAL PARK

Lesueur National Park, an important area for flora conservation in southern Western Australia, was gazetted in 1992 after a proposal to mine coal and construct a power station in the area was defeated. The variety of landforms has produced an enormous diversity of flora. Mammals include bats, echidnas,

dunnarts, honey possums and kanga-roos. Bird life is prolific, and Lesueur is thought to be the only place where four species of fairy wren occur together. The salt lakes are also important refuges for several resident and migratory wading birds. Walking is the best way to explore the park but you must carry your own water as there are no facilities or designated camping areas. A good tick repellent is also strongly recom-mended. Access to the park is by 4WD only.

MILLSTREAM–CHICHESTER NATIONAL PARK

Millstream is an oasis of green in this park of the central Pilbara. In the north is the Chichester Range with its rocky peaks, gorges and hidden rock pools, sloping gradually down to the plains of the Fortescue River; then the land rises again to the bulk of the Hamersley Range. The Millstream oasis on the Fortescue River is a series of deep spring-fed pools surounded by plam trees and eucalypts. Most plants here flower after the winter rains, so the best wildflower display is June to August. The Millstream palm is unique to this area, and the date palms were planted last century by Afghan camel drivers. A variety of birds and mammals can be seen. Activities at Millstream include swimming in waterholes at Deep Reach and Crossing Pool, and some boating (however, no power boats are allowed).

PURNULULU (BUNGLE BUNGLE) NATIONAL PARK

Located in the far northern Kimberley region, Purnululu National Park was declared in 1987 to protect the spectacular Bungle Bungle Range. The best time to visit is May to September; the park is closed from 1 January to 31 March each year. This park is definitely 4WD only and good ground clear-ance is vital as Spring Creek Track, the only access into the park, has jagged rocks, bulldust, soaks and creeks which are often impassable until well into the Dry. The Bungle Bungle Range is around 360 million years old; it has been home to the Aboriginal people for at least 20 000 years and contains many sacred sites and galleries of rock art. The beehive domes with their striped orange and black bands are remnants of an ancient sandstone plateau. Wind and water have carved

deep gorges and sheer-sided chasms, and in some sections the strange towers stand alone. Walking is the main activity as any exploration into the Bungle Bungles must be on foot. The park is 109 km north of Halls Creek or 250 km south of Jununurra.

STIRLING RANGE NATIONAL PARK

Bluff Knoll, the highest peak in the Stirling Range, rises 1073 metres above sea level and is typical of the rugged peaks of this area with their sheer cliffs and breathtaking views. The climate is variable: in winter (June–August) it is cold and wet, and higher in the ranges even spring weather is unpredictable. Sudden cold changes can bring rain or hail, even snow. The best time to visit is late spring and early summer as the days are warming up and the wild-flowers are in bloom. Birds include western rosellas, red-capped parrots, splendid wrens and golden whistlers, while wedge-tailed eagles can be sighted riding the thermals. Common but seldom seen are western grey kangaroos, black-glove wallabies, emus, quokkas and honey and pygmy possums. The park is 330 km south-east of Perth, north of Albany.

STOKES NATIONAL PARK

Located west of Esperance, this park protects Stokes Inlet and the sur-rounding lakes, also beautiful beaches, rugged headlands, sand dunes and low hills. Vegetation ranges from heaths, yate, swamp yate and paperbarks which have formed a low, dense forest which is home to numerous species of water-birds. Stokes Inlet is popular for boating and canoeing but take care as there are extensive shallow areas and rock outcrops. Fishing in the inlet and along the beaches can be rewarding for Australian salmon, black bream, mullet and King George whiting. A 'heritage trail' bushwalk is an easy 45 minute trip giving excellent views of the inlet and surrounding area.

WALPOLE–NORNALUP NATIONAL PARK

Surrounding the Walpole and Nornalup inlets on the south coast, this park contains forests of gigantic karri and the unique tingle trees. The Frankland River and the Deep River flow through it and empty into sheltered inlets. The park also offers 40 km of magnificent coastline from

Irwin Inlet in the east to Mandalay Beach in the west. The rugged Nuyts Wilderness has been isolated so visitors can enjoy the wild pristine environment. No vehicles, pets or fires are allowed here, and access is via a small footbridge across Deep River near Tinglewood Lodge. An absolute must-see is the Valley of the Giants, where a 400 metre walking track traverses the forest of giant karri and red tingle trees. Scenic drives display the grandeur of the park, its waterfalls, mountains, forests, rivers and wild ocean beaches. Canoeing is popular on the rivers, there are several boat launch-ing facilities, and fishing is always good in the inlets, the rivers or from the beach. The park is 430 km south of Perth and 121 km west of Albany.

WILLIAM BAY NATIONAL PARK

William Bay National Park, off the South Coast Highway about 14 km west of Denmark, includes 10 km of coastline, sandy beaches, low head-lands and sand dunes, plus heath-land. Seepages and permanent streams in the heathland support scattered groves of peppermint trees and on the sheltered side of Tower Hill is a spectacular stand of giant karri trees. Along the coast between Greens Pool and Madfish Bay a series of granite boulders and rock shelves extend about 100 metres out to sea, dramatically reducing the heavy seas of the Southern Ocean and forming protected pools and channels for swimming. A viewing platform overlooking Greens Pool is designed for easy access by the disabled. The beaches and headlands of the park offer good fishing, swimming and interesting walking. No camping is allowed in the park.

WINDJANA GORGE, TUNNEL CREEK & GEIKIE GORGE NATIONAL PARKS

These three parks in the Kimberley are also known as the Devonian Reef National Parks as the geology of this region provides an idea of life 350 million years ago, before the existence of reptiles or mammals. Much of the area was then covered by sea and in the warm shallow water was an immense coral reef. At Windjana Gorge, Tunnel Creek and Geikie Gorge, flood waters over mil-lennia have deeply eroded the ranges and exposed layers of fossils and a cross-section of the limestone strata of the ancient reef. The best time to visit the area is May–

September, the Dry season, when the days are clear and hot and the nights are cool.

Windjana Gorge:
The Lennard River has cut through the limestone range to form this gorge. It is flooded during the Wet, but in the Dry the river forms large pools with tall Leichhardt trees, native figs and paperbarks along the banks. The area is home to many species of birds, and freshwater crocodiles are often seen basking on the banks. Windjana is 145 km from Derby and 150 km from Fitzroy Crossing.

Tunnel Creek:
This park preserves a cavern or tunnel 750 metres long, carved out of the limestone by water seeping through over thousands of years. The tunnel varies between 3 metres and 12 metres high and it is about 15 metres wide. In one section the roof has fallen in, leaving an opening to the top of the range. Tunnel Creek is 180 km from Derby and 115 km from Fitzroy Crossing.

Geikie Gorge:
Situated where the Oscar and Geikie ranges meet, this gorge was formed by the mighty Fitzroy River carving a canyon 30 metres deep through the limestone. The Aboriginal people from this region operate a boat tour of Geikie Gorge providing visitors with a unique perspective of the park, its plants and animals. The river banks are a wildlife sanctuary and, apart from a permitted area along the west bank, no one is allowed within 200 metres of either bank. The park is 16 km from Fitzroy Crossing, around 280 km from Derby.

YANCHEP NATIONAL PARK

Established in 1905, Yanchep is one of Western Australia's oldest parks and one of the most popular for day trips from Perth. Located 51 km north of the city, it has a picturesque setting around Loch McNess with plenty of grassy, shaded areas, ideal for picnics. There are a number of easy walking trails, providing oppor-tunities for birdwatching and photo-graphy of wildlife, World War II bunkers and scenic lake and bushland subjects. There is a koala sanctuary near one of the main car parks where visitors can see the animals at close range. Rowing boats and paddle-boats are available for hire, but camping is not allowed.

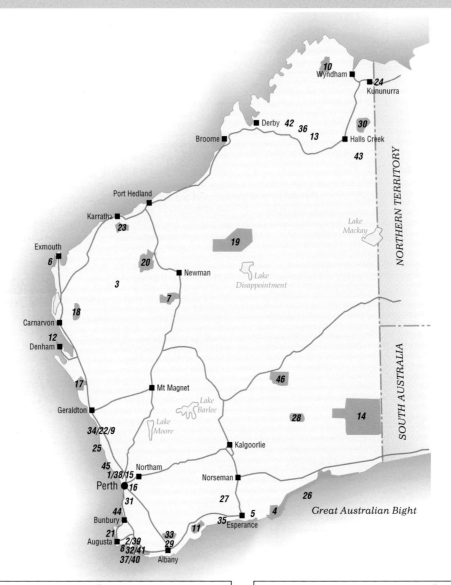

Popular Parks

		Camping	Caravans	Wheel Chairs	4WD Access	Picnic Area	Toilets	Walking Trks	Kiosk	Information
1	Avon Valley NP	■				■	■	■		
2	Beedelup NP					■		■		
3	Burringurrah (Mt Augustus) NP					■		■		
4	Cape Arid NP	■	■		■	■	■	■		
5	Cape Le Grand NP	■	■	■		■	■	■		■
6	Cape Range NP	■	■			■	■			■
7	Collier Range NP					■		■		
8	D'Entrecasteaux NP	■			■	■		■		
9	Drovers Cave NP				■	■		■		
10	Drysdale River NP	■				■				
11	Fitzgerald River NP	■				■	■	■		
12	Francois Peron NP	■			■	■	■			
13	Geikie Gorge NP				■	■		■		
14	Great Victoria Desert NR									
15	John Forrest NP					■	■	■		■
16	Kalamunda NP									
17	Kalbarri NP					■	■	■		■
18	Karijini (Hamersley Ra) NP	■				■	■	■		
19	Karlamilyi (Rudall River) NP	■			■					
20	Kennedy Range NP	■						■		
21	Leeuwin-Naturaliste NP	■	■			■		■		■
22	Lesueur NP					■		■		
23	Millstream-Chichester NP	■	■		■	■	■	■		■

		Camping	Caravans	Wheel Chairs	4WD Access	Picnic Area	Toilets	Walking Trks	Kiosk	Information
24	Mirima (Hidden Valley) NP				■	■	■	■		
25	Nambung NP			■	■	■	■	■		■
26	Nuytsland NR				■					
27	Peak Charles NP	■						■		
28	Plumbridge Lakes NR									
29	Porongurup NP			■		■	■	■		
30	Purnululu NP	■			■	■		■		■
31	Serpentine NP	■				■	■	■		
32	Shannon NP	■	■	■		■	■	■		
33	Stirling Range NP	■	■			■	■	■		■
34	Stockyard Gully NP							■		
35	Stokes NP	■	■			■	■	■		
36	Tunnel Creek NP							■		
37	Walpole-Nornalup NP	■				■	■	■		
38	Walyunga NP					■	■	■		
39	Warren (Pemberton) NP	■				■		■		
40	West Cape Howe NP	■						■		
41	William Bay NP					■		■		
42	Windjana Gorge NP	■	■			■	■			■
43	Wolfe Creek Crater NP							■		
44	Yalgorup NP	■				■		■		
45	Yanchep NP			■		■	■	■	■	■
46	Yeo Lake NR									

0   250   500
metres

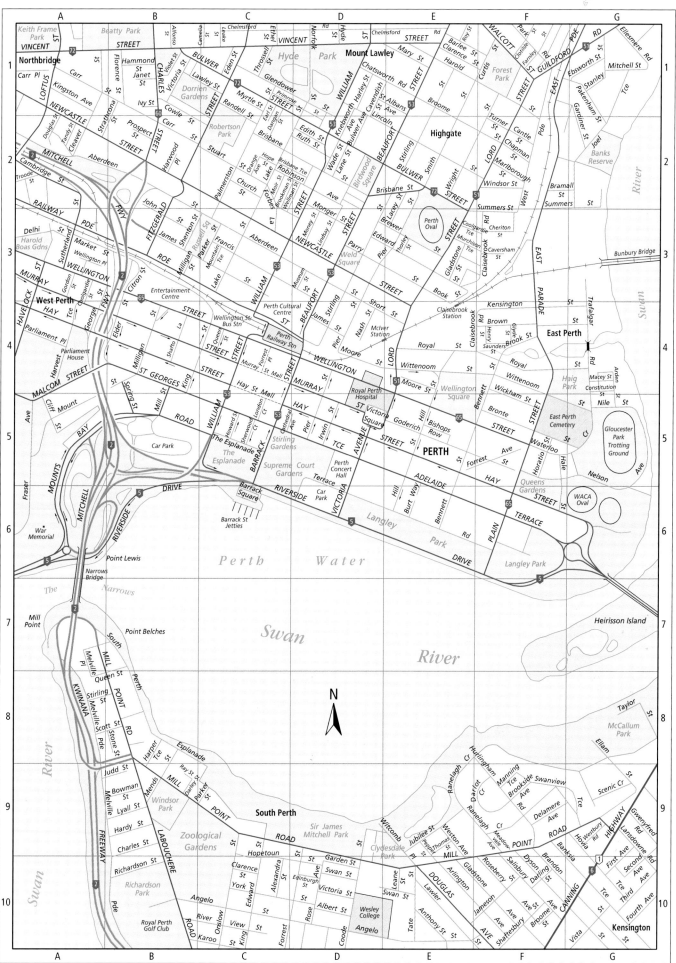

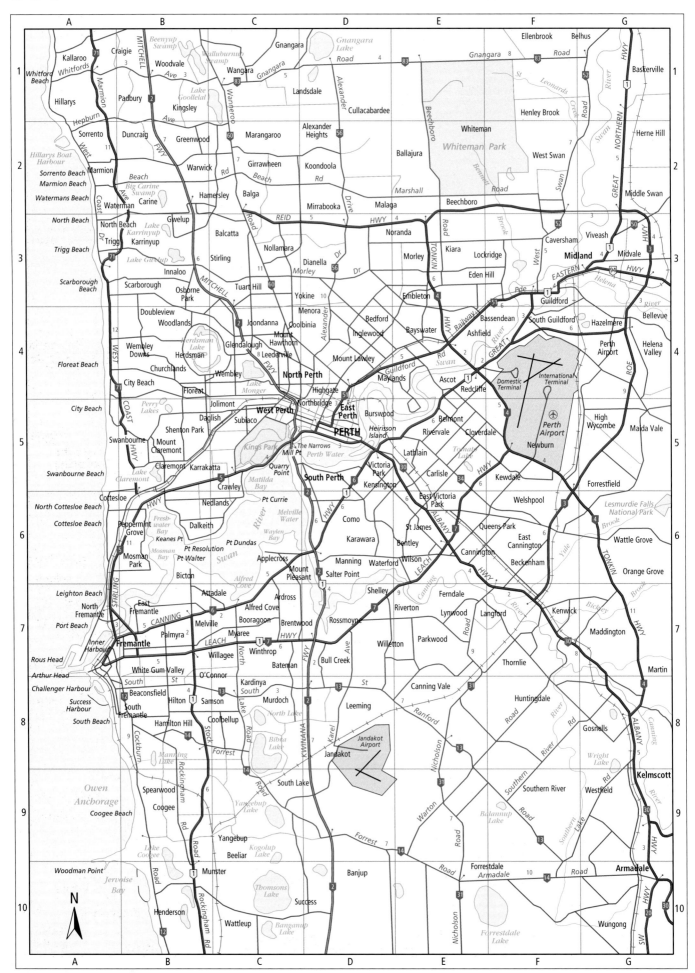

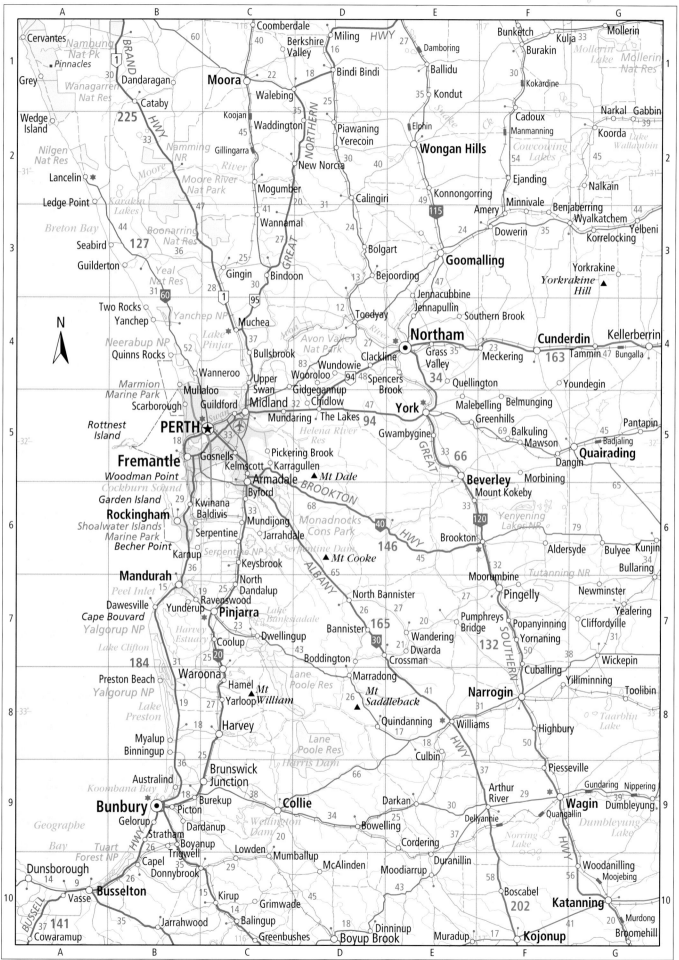

kilometres
0 10 20 30 40 50

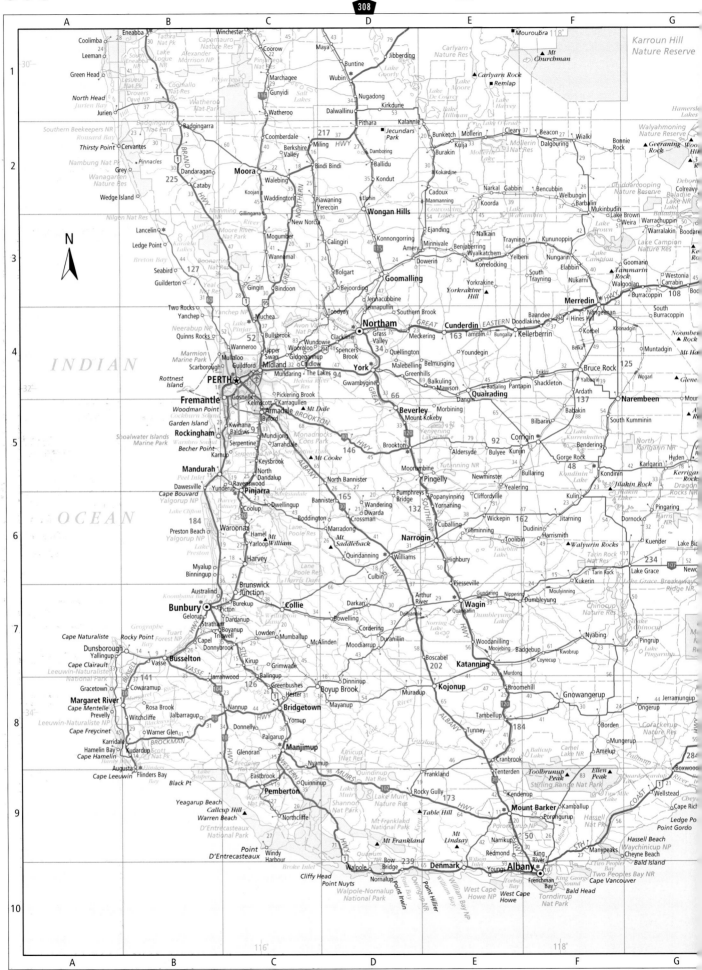

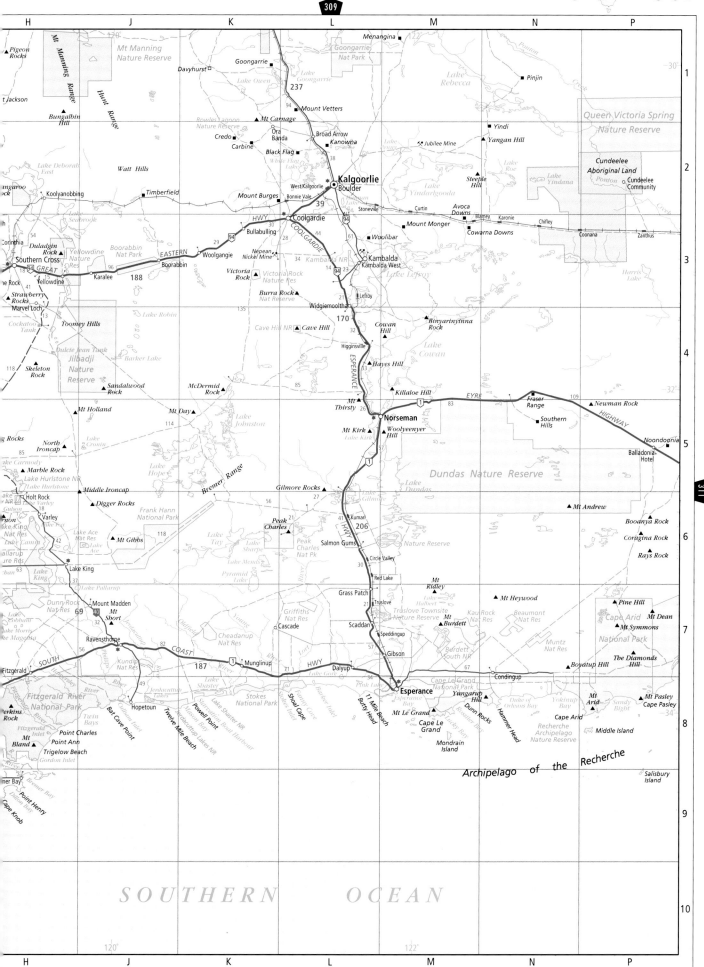

0 20 40 60 80 100
kilometres

H   J   K   L   M   N   P

Pigeon Rocks
Mt Manning Nature Reserve
Mt Jackson
Bungalbin Hill
Davyhurst
Goongarrie
Menangina
Goongarrie Nat Park
Lake Rebecca
Pinjin
Queen Victoria Spring Nature Reserve

Lake Owen
Lake Goongarrie
237
Watt Hills
Mount Vetters
94
Mt Carnage
Rowles Lagoon Nature Reserve
Credo
Ora Banda
Broad Arrow
Kanowna
Jubilee Mine
Yindi
Yangan Hill
Cundeelee Aboriginal Land
Ponton
Cundeelee Community

Koolyanobbing
Timberfield
Carbine
Black Flag
38
Lake Carey
Steeple Hill
Lake Yindarlgooda
Lake Yindana

Lake Deborah East
West Kalgoorlie
Kalgoorlie
Boulder
Mount Burges
Bonnie Vale
Stoneville
Curtin
Avoca Downs
Blamey
Karonie
Chifley
Coonana
Zanthus

Koolyanobbing
39
Coolgardie
Mount Monger
Woolibar
Cowarna Downs

54
Corinthia
Duladgin Rock
Yellowdine Nature Res
29
Bullabulling
Boorabbin Nat Park
Woolgangie
Nepean Nickel Mine
28
Kambalda NR
Woolibar
Kambalda
Kambalda West

Southern Cross
94
Karalee
96
Boorabbin
188
Victoria Rock
34
14
23
Lake Lefroy

Yellowdine
Strawberry Rocks
Marvel Loch
13
Cockatoo Tank
Toomey Hills
Dulcie Jean Tank
Barker Lake
Burra Rock Nat Reserve
Widgiemooltha
170
Lefroy
Harris Lake

118
Jilbadji Nature Reserve
Lake Robin
135
Cave Hill NR
Cave Hill
32
Cowan Hill
Binyarinytnna Rock
Lake Cowan

Skeleton Rock
Sandalwood Rock
McDermid Rock
85
Higginsville
Hayes Hill

Mt Holland
Mt Day
114
Lake Johnston
Killaloe Hill
EYRE
83
Fraser Range
Newman Rock
109
HIGHWAY

Rocks
North Ironcap
Lake Cronin
Mt Thirsty
26
Norseman
Southern Hills
Noondoonia

Lake Carmody
Marble Rock
Lake Hurlstone NR
Middle Ironcap
Digger Rocks
Frank Hann National Park
Mt Kirk
Lake Kirk
57
Woolyeenyer Hill
Balladonia Hotel

Lake Hope
Bremer Range
Gilmore Rocks
27
Lake Gilmore
Lake Dundas
Dundas Nature Reserve
Mt Andrew

NR
Holt Rock
Lake Varley
Varley
56
Peak Charles
21
Kumari
HWY
206
Nature Reserve
Booanya Rock
Coragina Rock

Gibson
42
Mt Gibbs
Lake Tay
Lake Sharpe
Peak Charles Nat Pk
Salmon Gums
Rays Rock

Lake King Nat Res
Lake Ace Nat Res
118
Lake Ace
Lake Magenta
Pyramid Lake
Lake Monjil
Circle Valley
30
Red Lake
Mt Ridley

allarup re Res
63
Lake King
Lake King
37
Lake Pallarup
Grass Patch
Truslove
Mt Heywood
Pine Hill
Mt Dean

Dunn Rock Nat Res
Mount Madden
69
Mt Short
32
Griffiths Nat Res
Cascade
Young River
Scaddan
Truslove Townsite Nature Reserve
Mt Burdett
Kau Rock Nat Res
Beaumont Nat Res
Cape Arid
Mt Symmons
National Park
The Diamonds Hill

Ravensthorpe
82
COAST
Cheadanup Nat Res
Speddingup
Burdett South NR
Muntz Nat Res

Fitzgerald
SOUTH
56
187
Munglinup
71
HWY
Dalyup
Gibson
57
67
Condingup
Boyatup Hill

Fitzgerald River National Park
49
Hopetoun
Jerdacuttup Lakes
Lake Shaster NR
Stokes National Park
Shoal Cape
Dalyup
34
Esperance
Cape Le Grand National Park
Yungarup Hill
Mt Arid
Mt Pasley
Cape Pasley

Perkins Rock
Bat Cave Point
Powell Point
Twelve Mile Beach
11 Mile Beach
Barry Head
Esperance Bay
Mt Le Grand
Cape Le Grand
Dunn Rocks
Hammer Head
Duke of Orleans Bay
Yoktaup Bay
Cape Arid
Recherche Archipelago Nature Reserve
Middle Island
Sandy Bight

Mt Bland
Point Charles
Point Ann
Trigelow Beach
Gordon Inlet
Mondrain Island

Bremer Bay
Point Henry
Cape Knob
Archipelago of the Recherche
Salisbury Island

SOUTHERN   OCEAN

120°   122°

H   J   K   L   M   N   P

311

1
2
3
4
5
6
7
8
9
10

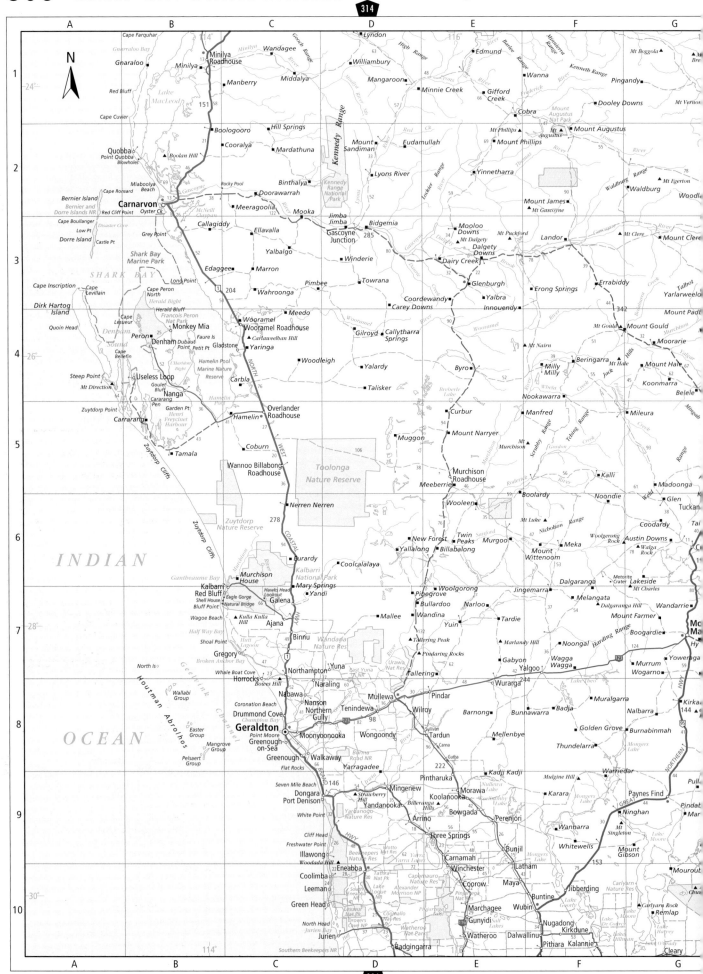

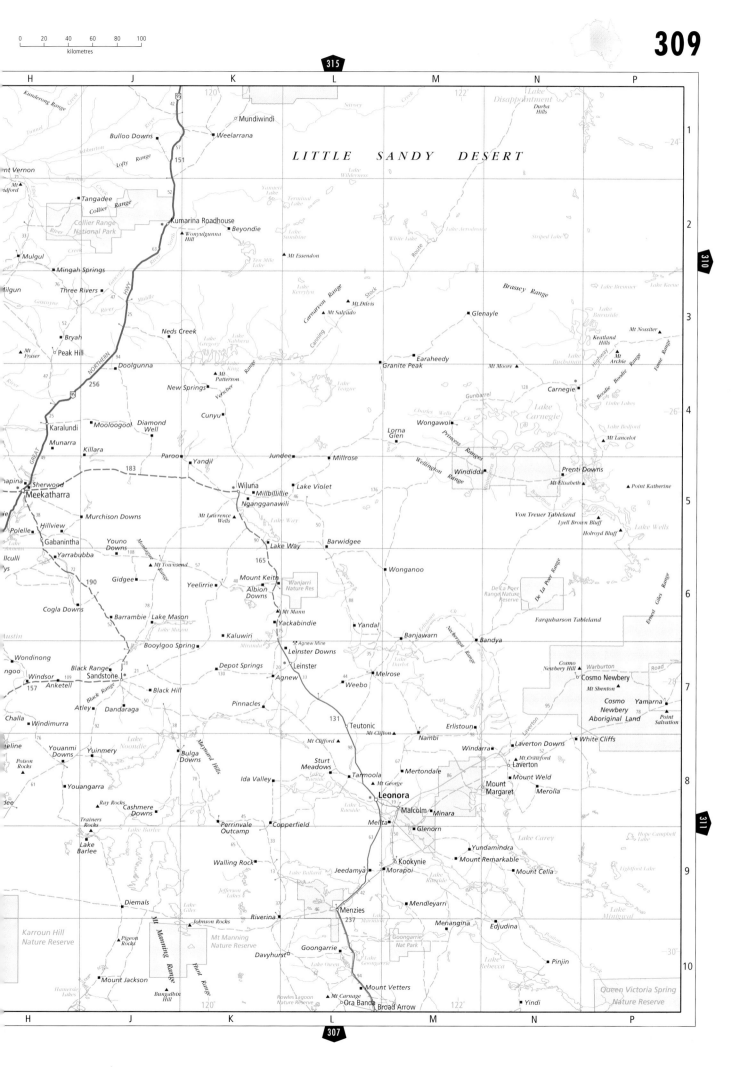

0 20 40 60 80 100
kilometres

LITTLE   SANDY   DESERT

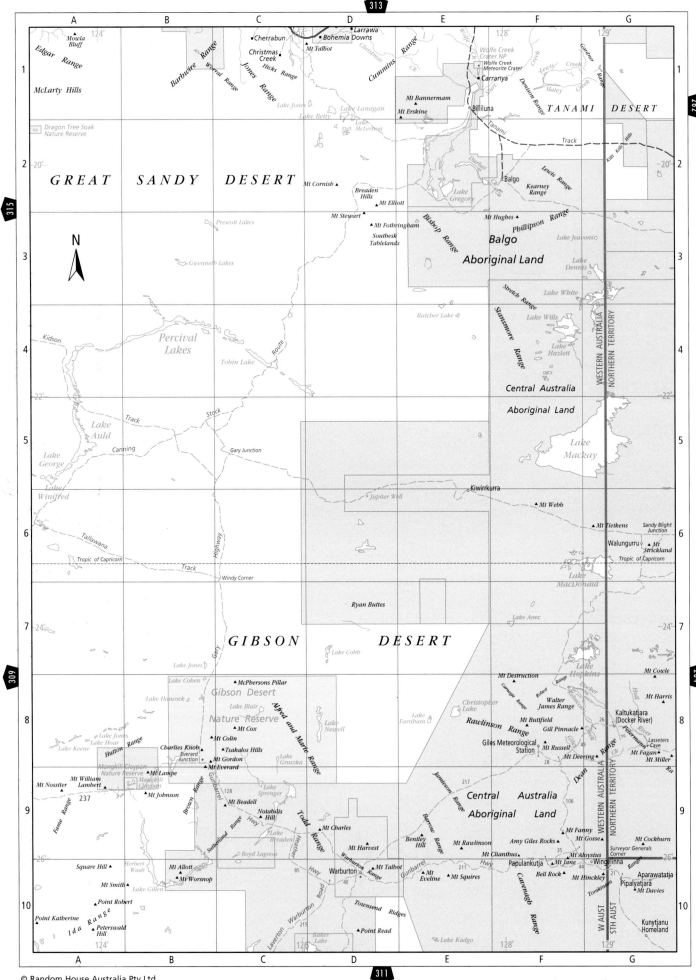

kilometres

0 25 50 75 100

kilometres

0 25 50 75 100

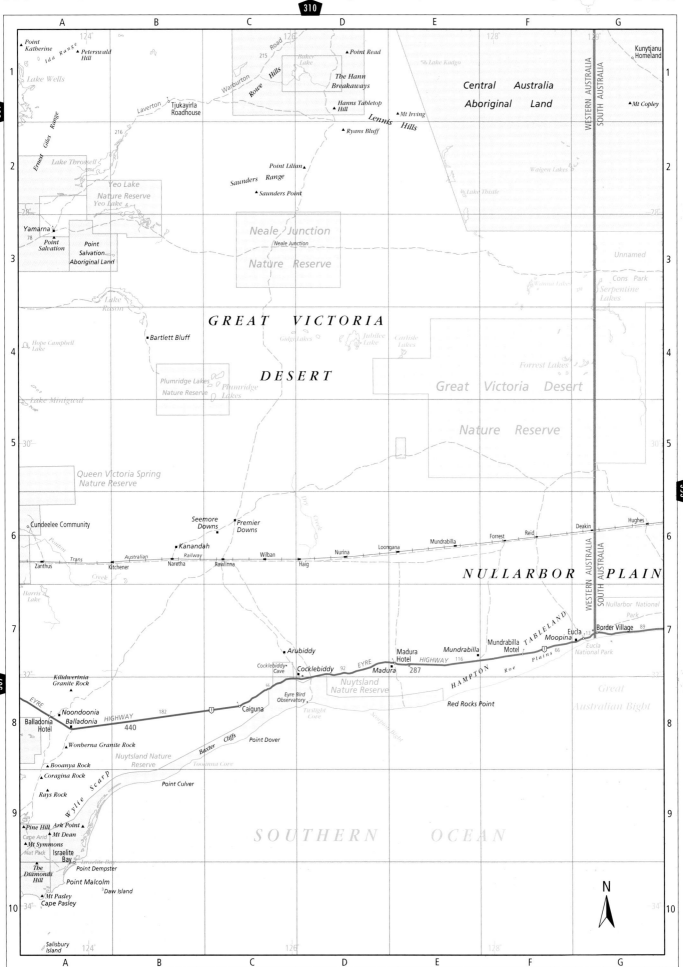

310

307

353

307

A B C D E F G

▪ Point Katherine

Ida Range

124°

▪ Peterswald Hill

126°

▪ Point Read

215

Rowe Hills

Baker Lake

The Hann Breakaways

Lake Kaigo

128°

Central Australia Aboriginal Land

WESTERN AUSTRALIA
SOUTH AUSTRALIA

129°

Kunytjanu Homeland

Lake Wells

1

Warburton Road

Laverton

Tjukayirla Roadhouse

Hanns Tabletop Hill

Lennis Hills

▪ Mt Irving

▪ Mt Copley

Ernest Giles Range

216

▪ Ryans Bluff

2

Lake Throssell

Point Lilian Range

Saunders

Walgen Lakes

Yeo Lake Nature Reserve
Yeo Lake

▪ Saunders Point

Lake Thistle

28°

Yamarna ▪
78
Point Salvation ▪

Point Salvation Aboriginal Land

Neale Junction

Neale Junction

Unnamed

3

Lake Raeside

Nature Reserve

Wanna Lakes

Serpentine Lakes

Cons Park

Hope Campbell Lake

▪ Bartlett Bluff

GREAT VICTORIA

Gidgi Lakes

Jubilee Lake

Carlisle Lakes

4

Lake Minigwal

DESERT

Plumridge Lakes Nature Reserve

Plumridge Lakes

Forrest Lakes

Great Victoria Desert

5

30°

Queen Victoria Spring Nature Reserve

Nature Reserve

30°

Cundeelee Community

Seemore Downs

Premier Downs

Dry Creek

Deakin

Hughes

6

Panton

Trans

Australian

Railway

Kanandah

Wilban

Nurina

Loongana

Mundrabilla

Forrest

Reid

WESTERN AUSTRALIA
SOUTH AUSTRALIA

Zanthus

Kitchener

Naretha

Rawlinna

Haig

NULLARBOR PLAIN

Harris Lake

Nullarbor National Park

7

Border Village
89

Eucla 113

Eucla National Park

Moopina

Mundrabilla Motel

TABLELAND

Madura Hotel

Mundrabilla

Arubiddy

HIGHWAY 116

66 Plains

Roe

Kilidwerinia Granite Rock

Cocklebiddy Cave

Cocklebiddy 92

EYRE

Madura 287

HAMPTON

32°

Great Australian Bight

32°

EYRE

Noondoonia

66

Nuytsland Nature Reserve

Eyre Bird Observatory

Red Rocks Point

8

Balladonia Hotel

Balladonia

HIGHWAY 182

440

Caiguna

Twilight Cove

Spragots Bight

▪ Wonberna Granite Rock

Baxter Cliffs

Point Dover

Toolinna Cove

▪ Booanya Rock

Nuytsland Nature Reserve

Point Culver

Wylie Scarp

▪ Coragina Rock

▪ Rays Rock

9

Pine Hill ▪ Ark Point ▪
Cape Arid ▪ Mt Dean
Mt Symmons ▪
Nat Pack
Israelite Bay

SOUTHERN OCEAN

The Diamonds Hill

Point Dempster

Point Malcolm

Daw Island

▪ Mt Pasley
Cape Pasley

N

10

Salisbury Island

124°

126°

128°

34°

A B C D E F G

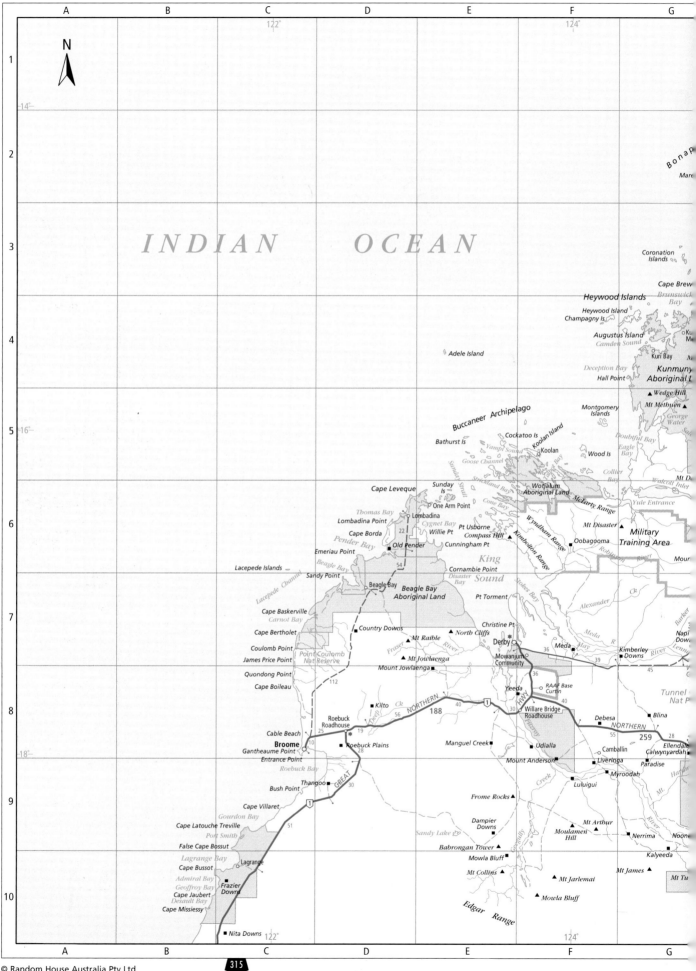

INDIAN OCEAN

Bonap

Mare

Coronation
Islands

Cape Brew

Heywood Islands   *Brunswick Bay*
                  Heywood Island
                  Champagny Is

                  Augustus Island   Ku
                  Camden Sound   Me

                  Kuri Bay

                  Deception Bay   Kunmuny
                  Hall Point   Aboriginal L

                              ▲Wedge Hill
                              ▲Mt Methuen
        Montgomery   *George
        Islands   Water*

Buccaneer Archipelago

                    Cockatoo Is Koolan Island   *Doubtful Bay*
        Bathurst Is *Yampi Sound* ○Koolan   *Eagle
                    Goose Channel   Wood Is   Bay*   Mt D

                                              Collier   Watcott Inlet
                                              Bay*

Cape Leveque   Sunday   *McLarty Range*   *Yule Entrance*
                  Is   Wotjalum
            ○One Arm Point   Aboriginal Land
  Thomas Bay   *Cone Bay*
Lombadina Point   ●Lombadina   *Wyndham Range* ▲Mt Disaster   Military
            Cygnet Bay   Training Area
Cape Borda   22 Pt Usborne Compass Hill ▲   Oobagooma
  Pender Bay   Willie Pt   *Kimbolton Range*
Emeriau Point   ○Old Pender   Cunningham Pt   *Robin*   Mour
        Beagle Bay 54   King
  Sandy Point   Cornambie Point   Sound   *Alexander*   Ck
Lacepede Islands   *Disaster   *Stokes Bay*
                    ●Beagle Bay   Bay*   *Meda*   Napi
        Lacepede Channel Beagle Bay   Pt Torment   *R*   Dow
Cape Baskerville   Aboriginal Land
  Carnot Bay   Christine Pt
Cape Bertholet   ■Country Downs   ▲Mt Raible ●North Cliffs   Derby ○   36 ○Meda   Kimberley
Coulomb Point   *Fraser*   Mowanjum   39   Downs
James Price Point   Point Coulomb ▲Mt Jowlaenga   Community   36   45
                    Nat Reserve Mount Jowlaenga■   Tunnel
Quondong Point   112   Yeeda ○   ○RAAF Base   Nat P
Cape Boileau   HWY Curtin 40
                          Ck ●Kilto   Willare Bridge
        ■Roebuck   *Thangoo* 56 NORTHERN 40 30 Roadhouse   Debesa   ●Blina
        Roadhouse   188   1   55 NORTHERN 28
  Cable Beach* 25   19   *Fitzroy* Udialla   259 ○Ellendal
  Broome   10   ●Roebuck Plains Manguel Creek■   Camballin ○Calwynyardah
Gantheaume Point   28   ○Liveringa Paradise
Entrance Point   Mount Anderson●   ○Myroodah
  Roebuck Bay   Luluigui●   *Mt*
  Bush Point ●Thangoo 30   Frome Rocks*
Cape Villaret   1   ▲Mt Arthur ■Nerrima Noon
  Gourdon Bay   Dampier   Moulamen
Cape Latouche Treville   51   *Sandy Lake* Downs   Hill   *River*
  Port Smith   Babrongan Tower●   ○Kalyeeda
False Cape Bossut   Mowla Bluff●
  Lagrange Bay   Mt Collins▲   ▲Mt Jarlemai   Mt James▲ Mt Tu
Cape Bussot   Lagrange
  Admiral Bay   Mowla Bluff▲
  Geoffroy Bay Frazier
Cape Jaubert Downs   *Edgar Range*
  Desault Bay
Cape Missiessy

        ●Nita Downs

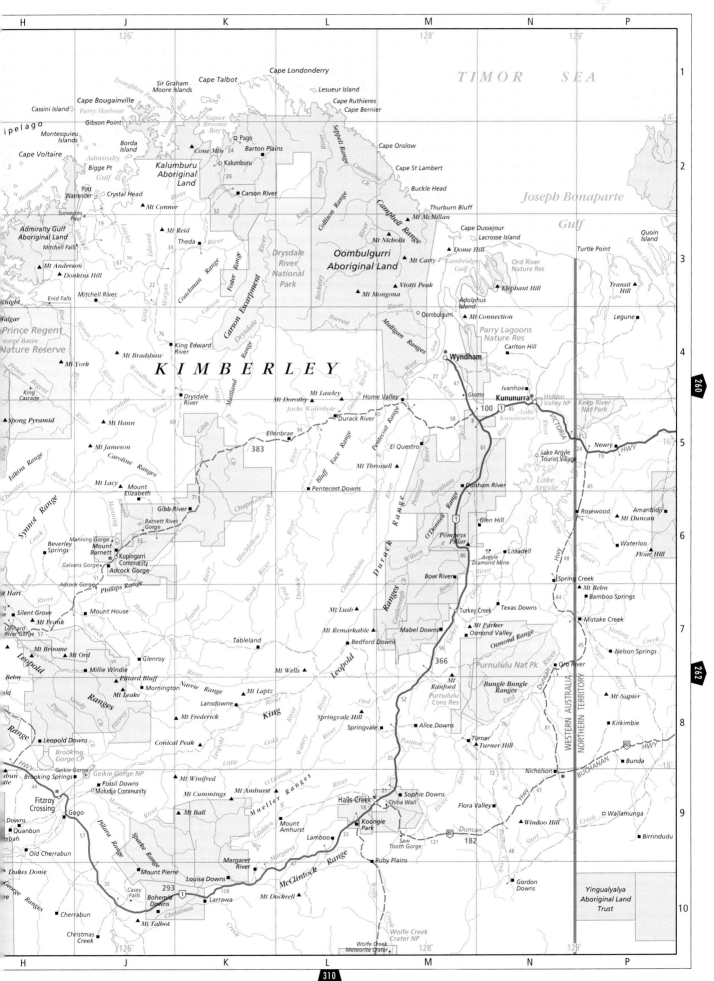

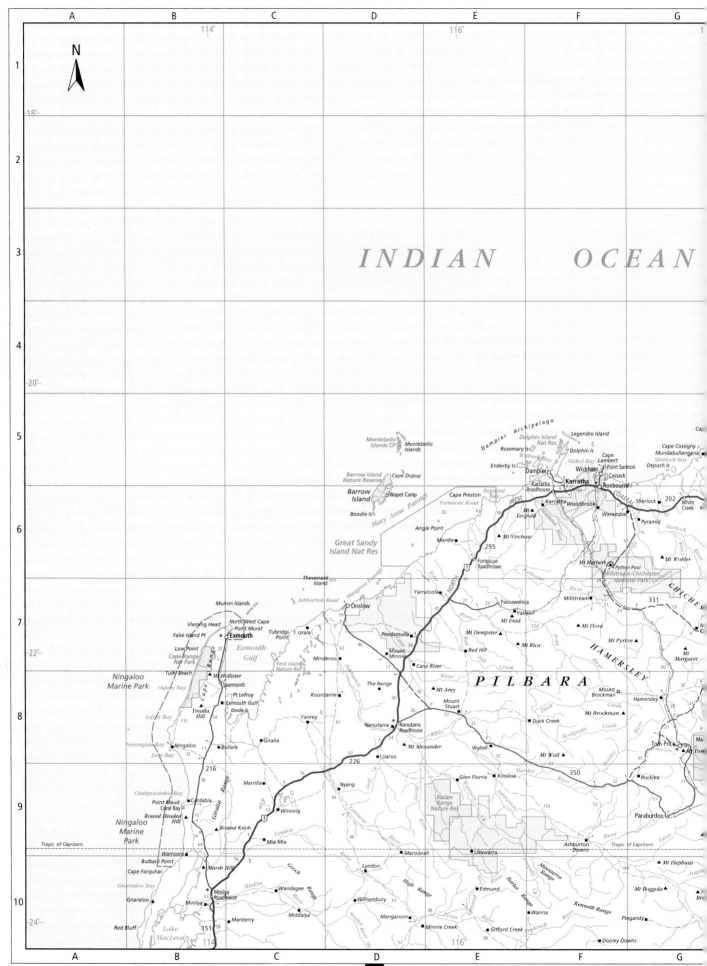

0 20 40 60 80 100
kilometres

H J K L M N P

120° 122°

Rowley Shoals
Marine Park

Point Coulomb
Nat Reserve
James Price Point
Quondong Point
Cape Boileau

▲ Mt Jowlaenga
Mount Jowlaenga

Mowanjum
Community
■ Yeeda
Willare Bridge
Roadhouse

NORTHERN HWY

Kilto ■ Ck
Roebuck
Roadhouse
19
Cable Beach 25
Broome
Gantheaume Point
Entrance Point 10
Roebuck Plains
28

188 40 30 36
-18

Manguel Creek Udialla

GREAT

Roebuck Bay
Thangoo 30
Bush Point
Cape Villaret 51

▲ Frome Rocks

Dampier
Downs
Babrongan Tower ▲
Mowla Bluff

Sandy Lake

Gourdon Bay
Cape Latouche Treville
Port Smith
False Cape Bossut
Lagrange Bay
Cape Bussot ■ Lagrange
Admiral Bay
Geoffroy Bay
Cape Jaubert
Desault Bay
Cape Missiessy

■ Frazier
Downs

Mt Collins ▲

Edgar Range

Beach
HWY
142
Nita Downs
251
Anna Plains ■

McLarty Hills

Shovel Lake

Mile

Eighty Mile Beach ■
Mandora
45
Sandfire
Roadhouse

Dragon Tree Soak
Nature Reserve

-20°

Poissonnier Point
Breaker Inlet
Cape Keraudren
Eighty
44 49
NORTHERN
Kidson
Track

Spit Point
Pardoo ■ 50
Pardoo
Roadhouse 291

Port Hedland
De Grey
GREAT
53
Goldsworthy
Strelley 45
Carlindi
Wallareenya
Shay Gap
De Grey
River
Warralong
Coongan
Muccan
Yarrie
Callawa
Oakover River

Isabella Range
Gregory Range

Lake
Waukarlycarly

Kidon

Track

Indee
Tabba Tabba
Lalla Rookh
124
55
Eginbah
16
Bamboo Creek
Warrawagine
Nullagine River
Yilgalong
Creek

Private
Road
Paterson Range
Throssell Range
Telfer Mine

261
95
Abydos
Pilga
Woodstock
Hillside
Marble Bar
Comet Mine
9
26
Mount Edgar
Corunna
Downs 103
Carawine
Gorge
Woodie Woodie

Coolbro

▲ Mt Isdell

Lake
Dora

Eva Broadhurst Lake

Nullagine
40
Bamboo
Springs

Nullagine

RANGE
Wittenoom
42
Yampire
Gorge
Forrescue
Falls 31
Auski Roadhouse
68
Marillana
78
Roy Hill
38

NORTHERN

Bonney
Downs
52
Noreena Downs

Davis

Mt Divide ▲
Mt Hodgson ▲

Broadhurst Range

Rudall

Rudall River
National Park

Mt Connaughton ▲

Lake
Blanche

Lake
George

Lake
Winifred

Juna Downs
Mt Mcharry
212 131
Opthalmia
Range
Mt Newman ▲
Newman
10
Capricorn
Roadhouse
42
95

Yandicoogina
Ethel Creek
Jigalong
Billinnooka
Walgun
Jigalong
Robertson
Range
Robertson Range
Garranulla Creek
Kalgan
Jimblebar
Balfour
Downs
Tallawana

Track

Harbutt Range
McKay Range

Tropic of Capricorn

Turee
Creek
Prairie
Downs
Kunderong Range
Sylvania
Mundiwindi

Jigalong
Aboriginal
Land

Savory

Lake
Disappointment
Durba
Hills

Runton Range

Emu Lake

Bulloo Downs
Weelarrana
Lofty Range
Tunnel
151
120° 122°

LITTLE SANDY DESERT

-24°

H J K L M N P
1 2 3 4 5 6 7 8 9 10

SOUTH AUSTRALIA

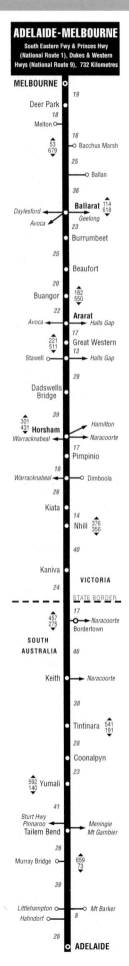

Most people, when they think of South Australia picture Adelaide, its fine elegant capital, or the wine-growing regions of the Barossa Valley or the Coonawarra, or perhaps the spine of mountains that is the Flinders Ranges, the great expanse of shifting sand of the Simpson Desert or the flatness that is the Nullarbor Plain.

All these are, most definitely, images of South Australia, but the state has much more to offer a traveller than just a few isolated images and experiences stretched across a large slice of Australia.

Most of the population of just over one million people live in Adelaide, while the remainder of the 1.4 million that call the state home live in and around the coast. Even so, some of the larger provincial cities, including the industrial trio of Port Pirie, Port Augusta and Whyalla, are situated in the semi-arid country in the heart of the state at the top end of Spencer Gulf. Less than one per cent of the population lives north of Port Augusta, which is just 315 km from Adelaide. Getting away from it all has, therefore, never been a problem for the residents of South Australia.

South Australia, hemmed in by the Great Southern Ocean to the south, has land borders with every other state, a unique occurrence in this country. Taking up 984 000 sq km, the state occupies about one-eighth of the total land mass of Australia with over 80 per cent of it receiving less than 250 mm of rain a year. That makes South Australia the driest state in the driest continent on earth—anywhere away from the more luxuriant south-east of the state the country ranges from semi-arid to desert. This gives the impression that the state has little to offer the traveller; it has, however, many hidden jewels.

The imposing Straun House in Narracoorte

Much of the state is also flat with over 80 per cent less than 250 metres in height. Only the Mt Lofty Ranges and their more spectacular continuation, the Flinders Ranges, can really boast mountains of any sort. With the highest peak, St Mary Peak, in the heart of the Flinders topping out at just 1170 metres, you would be hard-pressed to call it tall. Even so, the Flinders are

The view over the Spencer Gulf from Hancocks Lookout at the top of Horrocks Pass

rugged, imposing and very impressive. They cut right into the heart of the state, beginning their trail north in the more well-watered, manicured part of the state around Gladstone and ending up surrounded by stark desert country at Mt Hopeless, just south of the Strzelecki Track.

The Murray River, or at least the lower section of it, is the only major river in South Australia. It enters from the east, where it has formed the boundary between New South Wales and Victoria, winds its way west to the foothills of the eastern edge of the Mt Lofty Ranges and then turns south. It follows a slow, tortuous path through Lake Alexandrina and Lake Albert, forming the long arm of the Coorong in the process. The river eventually makes it to the ocean after negotiating the man-made barrage that pro-tects this part of the river from the incursion of saltwater from the sea.

Other rivers in the state are short, small or ephemeral. The only contradiction to that is in the far north of the state where the streams of inland Australia flow towards Lake Eyre. Rarely do these streams, their waters feeding down from Queensland, reach the lake, whose catchment area covers 25 per cent of the Australian continent, the greater portion of which lies within South Australia. These rivers offer long coolibah-shrouded waterholes. In many parts of the north-east these are the only source of surface water for hundreds of kilometres.

The long, indented coastline of the state is very spectacular, offering a diversity of landscapes from sweeping beaches devoid of human footprints and pounded by marching lines of tall ocean swells, to sheer, rugged cliffs plunging into a boiling sea, to small, protected bays fringed by reef and rocks. There are also many offshore islands, the biggest being Kangaroo Island (the third biggest island off the Australian mainland after Tasmania and Melville). Apart from all its sea-related activities, Kangaroo Island offers pleasant touring. The fishing around the whole state is excellent, the surfing second to none, and the diving superb.

Deciding on where to go in South Australia will depend on the time of year. Adelaide's Mediterranean climate means that in mid-summer its average maximum temperature is around 29°C, while mid-winter's maximum is around 15°C. The south of the state is cooler all year round and late spring, summer and early autumn are the best times to visit. Summer is delightful along the coast, but if you are like many who want to see the ever-growing population of whales that are now visiting the coast, then winter is the time. Winter is also, by far, the best season during which to visit the far north of the state, when the crossing of the Simpson Desert, one of the great 4WD destinations, is a crowded thoroughfare! For those who want to experience the delights of the Flinders Ranges, one of the great attractions of South Australia, the best time to visit is late winter and early spring, when the wildflowers bloom.

For travellers the road network also varies depending on which area of the state you are in. Major highways cut through the state from east to west, converging on Adelaide from Broken Hill in New South Wales, from Mildura and Ouyen in northern Victoria and from Horsham and Portland in central and southern Victoria. The latter is a part of the round Australia Highway 1, while the highway from Horsham is the main road link to Melbourne. From the west and the north come the two great highways that lead, respectively, from Perth and Darwin and converge at Port Augusta, before heading south to Adelaide. These routes, the Eyre Highway to

the west and the Stuart Highway to the north, are the only bituminised routes through these vast areas. The Eyre Highway cuts across the flat, treeless Nullarbor Plain close to the spectacular coastline of the Great Australian Bight, while the Stuart Highway runs through the heart of the state, past the opal mining centre of Coober Pedy to the Northern Territory border south of Alice Springs. Both these routes are, to those used to travelling the more crowded east coast, daunting, as they are devoid of habitation for hundreds of kilometres. It pays to stop at each and every lonely and remote roadhouse to revive and survive.

The rest of the road network, in the far south, through the Murraylands, around Adelaide and throughout Yorke Peninsula and Eyre Peninsula is, for the most part, extensive, with much of it bituminised. The dirt roads are, in the main, very good and maintained to a high standard. However, for those not used to travelling on such surfaces the smoothness can be seductive and quite high speeds can be reached and maintained. But take care—a slight dusting of dirt on an otherwise hard clay or limestone bed can sometimes mean it is easy to lose control.

In the Flinders Ranges the bitumen only goes as far north as Wilpena, while the road along the western flank of the range is bitumen to Lyndhurst. North of here the well-known

The Blue Lake, in an extinct volcano near Mount Gambier

outback routes of the Strzelecki, Birdsville and Oodnadatta Tracks are dirt. These long dusty dirt tracks, while not as bad as their once fearsome reputation, can be a little daunting in the normal family car. It comes as no surprise that these routes are the home of the 4WD. Elsewhere in the far north and north-west of the state the routes are rough, sandy and not the place to be in a normal car.

From desert landscapes to beautiful coastlines, opal mining town to festival city, world-class wineries to fabulous national parks—South Australia has something that will appeal to each and every visitor.

ADELAIDE-PERTH
Via Great Eastern Hwy (National Route 94)
& Eyre Hwy (National Route 1),
2729 Kilometres

ADELAIDE
42 Two Wells
55
Port Wakefield 97 / 2632
49 Snowtown
Crystal Brook 51
25 Port Pirie
86
Coober Pedy / Darwin Port Augusta
68 Whyalla / Port Lincoln
Iron Knob Whyalla
87
Kimba 463 / 2266
88
Kyancutta / Wudinna Lock / Port Lincoln
37 Minnipa
Poochera 33
47
Wirrulla
92
760 / 1969 Ceduna Streaky Bay / Port Lincoln
73
Penong
75 Nundroo 908 / 1821
51
Yalata
94
Nullarbor 1053 / 1676
SOUTH AUSTRALIA
198
STATE BORDER
Eucla
1317 / 1412 Mundrabilla 66
116
Madura
92
Cocklebiddy
66 Caiguna 1591 / 1138
182
Balladonia WESTERN AUSTRALIA
193
1966 / 763 Norseman Esperance / Albany
124
Kambalda
83
Leonora / Kalgoorlie / Boulder Coolgardie 2173 / 556
186
Southern Cross
2408 / 321 Bodallin 49
60
Wyalkatchem Merredin
Kellerberrin 58
46 Cunderdin
59
2631 / 98 Northam
The Lakes 48 York / Albany
Geraldton / Darwin 50
PERTH

ADELAIDE

POPULATION: 1.1 MILLION

MAP REFERENCE: PAGE 351 D6

Australia's fifth largest city after Perth, Adelaide is an orderly, dignified city that owes much of its charm and delight to the man who first designed its layout—Colonel William Light.

He surveyed the city in 1837 and his plan was simple: a rectangular grid pattern centred around five squares—the largest and central one being Victoria Square—and bordered by the River Torrens to the north. North of the Torrens he planned North Adelaide, equally well laid out but around a single square called Wellington Square. His thoroughfares were wide and tree lined, with the widest and grandest (King William Street) running north–south, linking North Adelaide and Adelaide itself. Around the new city's perimeter he planned a vast area of parklands, nearly a thousand hectares in all, while along North Terrace, just to the south of the Torrens, he placed Government House. To the founding forefathers' credit, the plan is essentially intact: Adelaide has a charm and character all its own.

The Adelaide Arts Centre at dusk

Located about halfway along the eastern shores of the Gulf St Vincent, Adelaide and its metropolitan area stretch for about 80 km from the beachside suburb of Aldinga north-east to the delightful township of Gawler. For nearly the whole length of this sprawling metro region, the Mt Lofty Ranges form a backdrop of low hills and deep valleys. The suburbs of the ever-enlarging city have crowded up to the ranges and even climbed their flanks in some places. However, for the most part the scene is a natural green one protected by a string of parks and reserves.

The city was founded as the colony of South Australia and was proclaimed in 1836, down near the shores of Glenelg, still Adelaide's premier seaside suburb. Named after Queen Adelaide, the city's location was chosen by Light, who laid out the city 10 km from its port at Port Adelaide. His vision for his city was not without opposition and he came under increasing attack from the first governor, Governor Hindmarsh, and he was to die a broken man a few years later. 'Light's Vision', a bronze figure of Light overlooking the city he planned, stands on Montefiore Hill in a park separating the heart of Adelaide from North Adelaide.

During the 1840s the city, riding on the back of rich discoveries of copper at Kapunda and Burra, began to take shape: temporary mud and timber buildings gave way to more substantial ones. The first churches, the Holy Trinity Anglican Church and Christ Church, were built around that time; Government House and the Adelaide Gaol were both begun in 1840, while Old Parliament House, now beautifully restored as a museum to the state's political history, was built in the 1850s. The Supreme Court was built in 1868, while the suburban railway to Glenelg was opened in 1873. A year earlier the Overland Telegraph Line was completed between Adelaide and Darwin and the city became the first in the country to be connected to London via the telegraph.

It was during those early years that other villages sprung up along the routes that led to the city. Unley, Prospect, Hindmarsh and a dozen others came into existence as wayside stops and watering points; these were later to become suburbs of the expanding city of Adelaide. Now, stretching over the flat plains and bordered by the ranges to the east and the Gulf to the west, the city covers nearly 2000 sq km.

Today, driving along King William Street from the north and down the hill towards the Torrens, the design and charm of this city is immediately evident. Past the Adelaide Oval, considered by many to be one of the finest looking, traditional cricket grounds in the world and surrounded by lawns and gardens, you cross the Torrens River with its lawns, decorative rotunda, and the magnificent Festival Centre, to arrive at North Terrace.

This tree-lined boulevard to the east presents an impressive scene with many fine buildings dotting its length. Government House, the State Library, the South Australian Museum, the Art Gallery of South Australia and the Adelaide University are all found here. A little further along the terrace, just past the Royal Adelaide Hospital, the next series of buildings past the university, is the Botanical Gardens and the State Herbarium, begun in 1855. These gardens feature the oldest glasshouse in an Australian botanical garden, and the only Museum of Economic Botany, while the Conservatory contains a magnificent tropical rainforest.

To the west of King William Street are the imposing marble columns of Parliament House, completed in 1939, while a little further along, in what once was the Adelaide Railway Station, is the Adelaide Casino. This imposing building was built in the 1920s.

Continuing along King William you come to Rundle and Hindley Streets, the former the shopping heart of Adelaide, while the latter is the night spot centre with discos, hotels, nightclubs and restaurants. Further along the main thoroughfare is the town hall, housing the oldest municipal council body in Australia, and testimony to the fact that South Australia was never a convict colony, but grew from the endeavours of free settlers.

Just a short distance further south along King William is the centre of the city—Victoria Square, with its lawns, impressive fountain and the terminus for the Glenelg tram. Surrounded by many state government buildings, the square is dominated by the clock tower of the GPO.

King William Street continues past shop fronts to South Terrace, the southern boundary of the city proper, where a number of gardens and parks make up the southern perimeter. These include the rose garden and conservatory, the Himeji Gardens (a traditional Japanese garden), along with other areas that are not so formally laid out.

For visitors to this elegant city there is plenty to do and see. Apart from the surrounding parks and the state art gallery and museum in North Terrace—the latter having the largest collection of Aboriginal artefacts in the world—there are a host of other places to see and experience. For the history buff there is the Mortlock Library of historical material, the Migration and Settlement Museum and the South Australian Police Museum, and, befitting a city with the premium arts festival in the country, is the SA Theatre Museum, a magnificent complex of halls and theatres.

For those who want to experience the culinary delights of fine food, and wine, there could hardly be a better place. Being so close to the hills, the Barossa Valley, and the wineries of the Vales to the south, it is no wonder that Adelaide boasts more restaurants per capita than any other city in Australia. Hindley and Rundle Streets in the heart of the city, Gouger Street close to Victoria Square, and O'Connell and Melbourne Streets in North Adelaide would have to be the diner's choice of places to go.

For those with children, a trip on *Popeye*, a small launch that plies the river from the banks of the Torrens near the Festival Centre to the Adelaide Zoo, makes for a great outing.

Then, of course, there are the suburbs.

Glenelg, on the coast just 10 km from the city centre, and a city in its own right, is the summer playground for its residents and visitors. Along the foreshore and the wide sandy beach is the largest amusement park in the state, with Magic Mountain, games and rides. There are many restaurants, while a wander along the Glenelg Jetty is enjoyable to all.

Port Adelaide, an easy 25 minutes' drive west of the city, had its heyday during the late 1880s, which probably accounts for the area's historic buildings, ships' chandlers, warehouses and old pubs. There are the South Australian Maritime Museum, the Historic Military Vehicles Museum, and the South Australian Historical Aviation Museum among others. Around

One of the many beautiful parks to be found in Adelaide

the Port you can also join a cruise on an old sailing ketch, or take a steam train ride along the old Semaphore Railway.

The beaches south of Port Adelaide and including Glenelg are wide, white, clean and sandy. They make ideal places to enjoy a safe swim and many have a jetty where you will often see kids and adults dangling a line for garfish or tommy ruff. Further south the beaches are even better and surfers will love the breaks in and around Christies Beach, Moana and Seaford. Divers can enjoy the reefs and marine sanctuaries, the first in Australia, at Port Noarlunga or at Aldinga, while at Aldinga the beach is so wide and firm you can drive your car on it.

The nearby Mt Lofty Ranges offer another natural experience to enjoy, from seeing native animals close-up at Cleland Wildlife Park, to picnics and day bushwalks at Belair National Park, to rock climbing at Morialta Falls Conservation Park.

No mention of Adelaide can be complete without reference to its major international festival, The Adelaide Festival of Arts, when artists come from all around the world to dance, sing and entertain. There is a host of other festivals and events, including the Italian Carnevale in February, the Comedy Festival and the Dragonboat Championships in March, the Adelaide Cup race meet in May, and the Royal Adelaide Show in late August/early September. Nearby in the Adelaide Hills, the Barossa Valley or down along the Fleurieu Peninsula there is a plethora of other festivals to keep the state and the people, locals and visitors alike, hopping.

ACCOMMODATION

CBD: Hilton International Adelaide, ph (08) 8217 2000; Hindley Parkroyal, ph (08) 8231 5552; Country Comfort Inn, ph (08) 8223 4355; Grosvenor Hotel, ph (08) 8407 8888; Adelaide City Parklands Motel, ph (08) 8223 1444; Apartments on the Park, ph (08) 8232 0555; The Old Terrace Cottages, ph (08) 8364 5437

North: Sombrero Motel, Blair Athol, ph (08) 8269 3655; Prasads Gawler Motel, ph (08) 8522 5900; Adelaide Beachfront Tourist Park, Semaphore Park, ph (08) 8449 7726; Hillier Park Caravan Park, Gawler, ph (08) 8522 2511

North-east: Highlander Hotel/Motel, Gilles Plains, ph (08) 8261 5288; Clovercrest Hotel/Motel, Modbury, ph (08) 8264 5266; Paradise Hotel, ph (08) 8337 5055; Levi Park Caravan Park, Walkerville, ph (08) 8344 2209

North-west: Largs Pier Hotel/Motel, Largs Bay, ph (08) 8449 5666; Hendon Hotel, Royal Park, ph (08) 8445 6161; Lakes Resort, West Lakes, ph (08) 8356 4444

South: Uniting Church Accommodation, Belair, ph (08) 8212 4066; Christies Beach Hotel/Motel, ph (08) 8382 1166; The Old Clarendon Winery, ph (08) 8383 6166; McLaren Vale Motel, ph (08) 8323 8265; St Francis Winery Resort, Reynella, ph (08) 8322 2246; McLaren Vale Lakeside Caravan Park, ph (08) 8323 9255

South-east: Runnymede Lodge Private Hotel, Aldgate, ph (08) 8370 9968; Eagle on the Hill Hotel/Motel, ph (08) 8339 2211; Princes Highway Motel, Frewville, ph (08) 8379 9253; Warrawong Sanctuary Tent Cabins, Mylor, ph (08) 8370 9422

South-west: Esplanade Hotel, Brighton, ph (08) 8296 7177; Capri Lodge Holiday Units, Everard Park, ph (08) 8297 1168; Patawalonga Motor Inn, Glenelg, ph (08) 8294 2122; Brighton Caravan Park & Holiday Village, ph (08) 8377 0833

East: Bishops of Basket Range Cottages, ph (08) 8390 3469; Petts Wood Lodge Holiday Units, Burnside, ph (08) 8331 9924; Kensington Apartments, ph (08) 8364 6030; Adelaide Caravan Park, Hackney, ph (08) 8363 1566

West: Adelaide International Airport Motel, Brooklyn Park, ph (08) 8234 4000; Lockleys Hotel, Fulham, ph (08) 8356 4822; Marineland Holiday Village Villas, West Beach, ph (08) 8353 2655

TOURIST INFORMATION: Ph (08) 8303 2033

THE FLINDERS RANGES

MAP REFERENCE: PAGE 355 J3

LOCATION: 446 KM NORTH OF ADELAIDE

BEST TIME: APRIL TO OCTOBER, PARTICULARLY EARLY SPRING

MAIN ATTRACTIONS: MAGNIFICENT MOUNTAIN SCENERY, WILDFLOWERS, CAMPING

INFORMATION: WILPENA, PHONE (08) 8648 0048; ORAPARINNA, PHONE (08) 8648 0047

ACCOMMODATION: SEE TOWN LISTINGS FOR HAWKER, QUORN, WILPENA

NOTE: CARRY WATER AT ALL TIMES

For many people this spectacular region of semi-arid mountain country is their first experience of the Australian Outback.

At sunrise the changing light colours the mountains with varying hues of blue, then pink, gold and yellow, before they take on their daytime appearance of raw-coloured rock and dull green of the native scrub. At sunset the ranges are etched in darkening blues as the sky above changes from cobalt blue to rich golds and reds, then finally to purple just as the light fades. Often kangaroos—mainly stockily built euros in this part of the range, but sometimes tall, powerful red kangaroos—grace the landscape.

From the great Australian artist Sir Hans Heysen who 'discovered' these ranges in the 1930s to the latest artists, who with both brush and camera have tried to capture the changing moods and magic of these mountains, the Flinders have enchanted all who see them.

No other comparable area of Australia has had so many glossy coffee-table books produced on it as these ranges that stretch 300 km from near Gladstone in the relatively well-watered parts of the state, north to the low hill of Mt Hopeless on the edge of the Strzelecki Desert.

The Flinders were, long before the coming of the white man, an important area for the Aboriginal nomads of Australia. The relatively well-watered ranges with their more permanent waterholes, rich vegetation and bountiful game were in stark contrast to the surrounding arid plains. The Adnyamathanha people, or 'Hill People' as they are called today, have left a rich heritage behind in the art sites that dot the region.

While Matthew Flinders was the first European to see the ranges on his circumnavigation of Australia in 1802, and after whom the great sweep of mountains is named, it was Edward John Eyre in 1839 and 1840 who opened the area up for settlement. Then came the pioneer pastoralists searching for rich grazing and farming land.

Access

You can travel from Adelaide to the motel at the entrance to Wilpena Pound on the bitumen via Wilmington and Quorn (456 km); the slightly shorter way (370 km) through Orroroo and Jamestown has a 50 km section of good dirt road south of Hawker. The latter route also misses out on some of the delightful range country between Melrose and Quorn.

Elsewhere, good dirt roads suitable for the family car lead through the park to all the points of interest. Only after occasional severe rains or floods are any of the roads closed, and then generally only for a short time.

FLINDERS RANGES NATIONAL PARK

The Flinders Ranges National Park has, to its south, the great battlements of the northeastern wall of Wilpena Pound and the highest point in South Australia, St Mary Peak, while to the west, the peaks of the ABC Range are

Good dirt roads make driving in the Flinders Ranges easy

lower and smoother than the craggy tops of the Heysen Range above them. But it is the central Flinders, around the unique geological structure of Wilpena Pound, that the ranges take on their grandest and most distinctive character.

In 1970 the government bought Oraparinna Station and a national park was founded to the northeast of Wilpena Pound. In fact, since the early 1950s, the Pound has had a tourist motel located at the Wilpena Creek entrance, and the Pound itself had been declared a reserve. In 1972 the new national park was amalgamated with the Pound and four years later the park was enlarged. In 1988 Wilpena Station, which took in much of the eastern flank of the Wilpena Pound Range, was included in the park which now covers 92 746 hectares.

Wilpena Pound

Wilpena Pound is still the major attraction and the centrepiece of the Flinders Ranges National Park, attracting most of the visitors and the acclaim.

Taking its name from the early settlers' name for a stock enclosure, the name Wilpena is said to mean in the local Aboriginal dialect, 'a cupped hand', which is a magnificent description of this huge natural amphitheatre. Nearly 5 km wide and 11 km long, the rolling pine-clad grassland inside the Pound sweeps up on its edges to the lofty craggy peaks of the all-encircling Wilpena Pound Range, that on the very outside plummet to the surrounding plains.

There are only two exits from the Pound. One, in the north, through Edeowie Gorge is narrow and rock and cliff strewn, while the other follows the gum-lined Wilpena Creek through a steep-sided valley on the eastern side of the Pound.

Few people would come to this area and not take at least a short stroll through the gap carved by Wilpena Creek. Ancient, giant red gums tower over the track and crowd the rocky, often reed-shrouded creek bed, making the walk a shady delight, especially welcome after a long walk across rocky ridges or sun-scorched open plains.

The shorter walks take you into the old homestead and then up the ridge on a short but steep climb to Wangara Lookout. The return walk of 2 to 3 km will take between 1 to 2 hours, depending on your fitness and how long you stop to admire the view over the Pound and surrounding countryside.

From the entrance into the Pound there is also an hour long walk along a nature trail and a more strenuous walk of about 2 hours to the lookout on top of Mt Ohlssen Bagge.

Longer walks of a day or more can take you south to Bridle Gap or north to Edeowie Gorge, while a circuit route via the heart of the Pound and Cooinda Camp can take you north to Tanderra Saddle and the top of St Mary Peak. From there it is south along the battlements of the range back to the starting point at Wilpena Creek.

Part of the long-distance Heysen Walking Trail cuts through the park entering at the southern end of the Pound via Bridle Gap and heads north from Wilpena Creek along the ABC Range to the Aroona Valley and out of the park to Parachilna Gorge and beyond. You can enjoy this trail for a day —or longer, but you must be experienced for any extended walk.

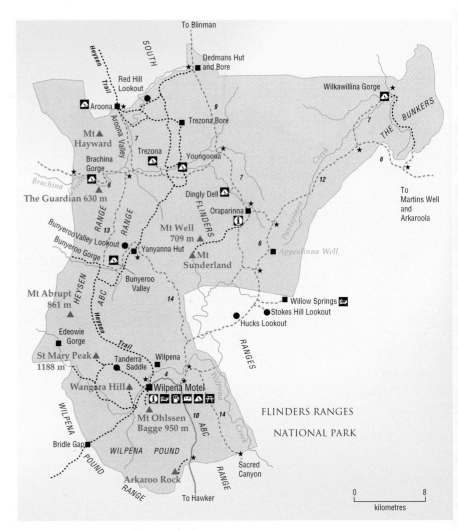

LEGEND

Sealed/Unsealed Rd	★ 26 ★
Four Wheel Drive	- - - - - - -
Walks	· · · · · · ·
Rest Area (Picnic Area)	⊼

Caravan Park	🚐
Camping Area	⛺
Accommodation	🛏
Information	ℹ
Fuel Supplies	⛽

Sacred Canyon

One of the best Aboriginal art sites in the Flinders Ranges is Sacred Canyon. This small chasm is accessible via a 14 km, good dirt road that heads off the main Blinman road just north of the Wilpena Pound Motel turn-off. A brief walk from the car park along a tree-lined creek brings you to the short narrow canyon. There are rock engravings, or petroglyphs, which can be seen on the sheer rock faces on both sides of the canyon. This ancient form of Aboriginal art includes animal tracks, circles and other symbols.

Aroona Valley

The picturesque Aroona Valley tucks in beside the northern peaks of the ABC Range, but it is the Heysen Range immediately to the west that dominates the scene. The ruins of the Aroona homestead are perfectly situated to make the most of the view.

The Heysen Walking Trail passes by the ruins and you can enjoy a short or long stroll along that or along the nearby creek. Another walking trail leads out to Red Hill Lookout, a 7 km, 1½–2 hours, return trip, while the walk east leads to Trezona Bore at the headwaters of Brachina Creek. Instead of returning the same way (a 14 km round trip), you can head south along the creek to the main road near the camping area of Trezona. From there you can complete the circuit back to Aroona by following the road and Brachina Creek west to the track that leads to the Aroona camp site and ruins. All up, this is a 25 km walk and takes over a day. But with a car shuffle you could make it a long day walk of about 16 km.

Brachina Gorge

Where the Brachina Creek cuts its meandering course through the Heysen Range it forms one of the most delightful features in the area. Gums line the creek which often has a slow trickle of water running along it. In places, quite large pools, protected by a rugged bluff or group of shady trees, provide a permanent water source for the corellas and brightly coloured parrots. In the evening small roos and wallabies come for a drink.

While there are no designated walks as such, a stroll along the creek is a must and for those who feel energetic a climb of one of the nearby peaks will give a grand view of the gorge and the surrounding mountains.

A Top Scenic Drive

One of the best drives in the place is to take the Yanyanna Hut–Bunyeroo Valley road in the early morning. It is especially colourful after rain when the wildflowers bloom. Once you are off the main Blinman road red kangaroos are very common and as you get closer to the main range and the hills begin to crowd in, euros and western grey kangaroos will be seen.

The views are fantastic, with the pine-clad hills rolling away to the sheer bluffs of the Heysen Range. If you want to make a day of it, head up to the Prairie Hotel in Parachilna for lunch and then in the evening head back taking the Moralana Scenic Drive to Wilpena. This 36 km drive gives great views of the western walls of Wilpena and in the dying light of day they are just fabulous.

Wilkawillina Gorge

Located in the very northeast of the park is Wilkawillina Gorge where the Mt Billy Creek has cut its way through the Bunker Range. There is a camping ground located close to the vehicle track end and a walk of about a kilometre will take you into the gorge proper.

This part of the Flinders is much drier than the Wilpena side but water can often be found in the heart of the gorge. As well, there are fewer travellers in this region and you may have the place to yourself.

Camping

At Wilpena Pound there is a well-established caravan park with all facilities and a motel complete with general store, fuel outlet, ranger base and information centre. This place does get crowded at holiday times so it is best to book well in advance.

There is some very pleasant camping in the Aroona Valley. The main camp area to the east of the Aroona homestead ruins has toilets and water.

Further east along the headwaters of Brachina Creek at Slippery Dip, Trezona and Youngoona, bush camping areas have been established and

An old pioneer's cottage close to Quorn

while all have toilets, you will need to take your own water. Camping areas are also located at Dingly Dell on the Blinman road 30 km north of Wilpena Pound; along the main road through Bunyeroo Gorge, just north of the Pound proper but 27 km by road from the motel; and at Wilkawillina Gorge in the far northeast of the park.

An excellent area for camping is along Brachina Gorge where a good dirt road leads from the Aroona Valley through the Heysen Range to exit the park. Here the western ramparts of the rugged range country meet with the flat plains of the desert country surrounding the great salt lake of Lake Torrens. There are no facilities, so you need to be prepared.

The magnificently colourful Flinders Ranges

FLINDERS RANGES TREK

This trek starts in Quorn, 34 km east of Port Augusta via the scenic Pichi Richi Pass, or 33 km north of Wilmington via the edge of the range and the starkly beautiful Willochra Plain. No matter which way you come from Adelaide you are about 350 km north of the capital on good bitumen roads. Close to the centre of town is the railway station, which recaptures its bygone glory when, on school holidays or long weekends, the locomotives are rolled out, and people can take a short trip on the Pichi Richi Railway.

Quorn nestles beside the main bulk of the Flinders Ranges. Established as a farming community, by the 1930s Quorn had become the centre of the

Yourambulla Peak gives fine views of the Flinders Ranges

Australian Outback rail system. The Ghan set off from here for its run north to Alice Springs, and trains from the east and west would also pass through. With the re-routing of the train system to Port Augusta, Quorn became a backwater in the 1950s, only to find salvation in recent years in the tourist industry. Today it is a thriving little town, full of character and charm and all the facilities a traveller requires.

Quorn to Hawker

From the railway station take the road heading west towards Port Augusta, but instead of following the main road once you have crossed the railway line, continue straight ahead, keeping the mountains on your left.

Rolling hills and farmland stretch away on your right, while in contrast, almost beside you on the other side, the ranges rear up towards their lofty ragged battlements. The Dutchmans Stern is the most obvious peak and within 7 km from town you will come to the turn-off to the conservation park that incorporates this peak.

The small park encompasses some of the most rugged country in the Flinders, and from the main ridge spectacular views of the ranges to the east and Spencer Gulf to the west can be admired. Walking trails give access from the parking area.

Continuing along the main dirt road, a track junction 21 km from Quorn marks the turn-off to Warrens Gorge. A short drive down this side track takes you into a small, sheer-sided, red gum shaded gorge (**GPS** 32°11'26"S, 138°02'31"E) that has water trickling through it in all but the driest years. As you exit on the far side you enter an area of rolling hills dotted with native pine, while a creek trickles beside the rocky spine of the range. This popular area makes a good camp or lunch spot.

Another 8 km further on along the main dirt road from Quorn, yet another junction is reached. The road we need to take continues straight ahead, but first a small detour to the left is worthwhile.

This track, within 1 km of the junction, passes through Buckaringa Gorge; the red rock wall on the right as you enter the small gorge is a popular rock climbing venue, and there are a few camp sites located at

each end of the gorge. Once through the gorge, the track continues less than 2 km to a car park on the right which is a reasonable camp site and a stepping-off spot for Middle Gorge, just a short walk away. If you follow the creek down to the southern extremity of this gorge you will come to a viewing platform which overlooks a rocky bluff—the home for a small group of the rare yellow-footed rock wallaby. You need to be quiet here, of course, and if you want to see these beautiful creatures the hotter part of the day should be avoided.

Back at the main road junction before you turned into Buckaringa, the dirt road skirts the eastern side of the range and 6 km later comes to Proby's grave. Hugh Proby drowned in Willochra Creek while mustering sheep one stormy night in 1852. He had established Kanyaka Station, which we pass a little later on this trek.

You cross the wadi-like Willochra Creek just past Proby's grave and then come to another junction, 6 km from the grave site, where you need to turn right. The few scattered ruins of Simmonston are on your left, as you head south for another 6 km before turning left again, with the last 9 km over dirt road to the main Quorn–Hawker road, which is bitumen. By the route you have followed you are 56 km from Quorn, but by the blacktop Quorn is just 34 km south.

When you reach the bitumen and the Quorn–Hawker road junction, turn left. You are now travelling across the heart of the Willochra Plain and the ruins of Gordon lie around this road junction. Gordon, like many small hamlets that were established in the late 1800s in this area on the promise of good seasons and a rich bounty of wheat, is today nothing but scattered mounds of building rubble.

The ruins of Kanyaka homestead (**GPS** 32°04'23"S, 138°18'13"E) and its outbuildings lie just off the road, 7 km further on along the main road to Hawker. Proby, whose grave you passed just a few kilometres back, founded this 100 000 hectare station; at its height in the early 1870s over 70 families lived here, working the 40 000 sheep that made Kanyaka one of the richest properties in the area.

The bearded dragon, often seen in the Flinders Ranges

The turn-off to Yourambulla Peak, with its fine views and Aboriginal cave art, is just 16 km north, past the ruins of another farming dream, called Wilson.

The small township of Hawker comes up on your right, 9 km north of Yourambulla and 88 km since leaving Quorn, although you are just 66 km from Quorn via the bitumen. You need to swing off the main road, into the centre of Hawker, at the signposted junction, marked Wilpena Pound.

Founded in 1880 during the farming land boom times, Hawker became the centre for the many small wheat farms that once dotted the surrounding plain. When the normal dry seasons returned and the farms turned to ruins, Hawker survived as a railway town. Today it caters for the ever increasing number of travellers heading for the central Flinders Ranges. There are a number of food stores, general stores and fuel outlets in the town, plus a range of accommodation.

Hawker to Wilpena Pound and Parachilna

The road from Hawker to Wilpena Pound strikes northeast across gently undulating country, with the ranges becoming more prominent. On your left is the striking ridge of the Elder Range, to your right the Lower, Druid and then Chace Ranges, while almost directly ahead are the southern ramparts of Wilpena Pound. Although the road maintains its good bitumen status, take your time and enjoy the views.

The Arkaba Station Woolshed, 19 km north of Hawker, sits on a low rise with a panoramic view of the nearby Elder Range. This historic woolshed is open most days and can supply the traveller with coffee, tea and scones, as well as souvenirs and local art. The station also runs guided tag-along tours on their property, which is one of the most spectacular in the region, and there is a delightful cabin to rent if you feel like staying for longer.

The Moralana Scenic Drive leaves the main road (**GPS** 31°43'04"S, 138°31'52"E) 5 km further on past Arkaba, and this dirt road skirts the southern rim of Wilpena Pound before exiting on the main Hawker–Leigh Creek road. This road crosses Arkaba Station and although it is a private road, the owners allow people to use it.

Rawnsley Park Station, with its camping ground and accommodation, sits under Wilpena Pound's main bluff, Rawnsley Bluff; you can get basic supplies here as well as fuel.

Heading north, the ranges crowd in from the west and dense stands of native pines push right up to the edge of the road. Just before entering the Flinders Ranges National Park, 44 km from Hawker, you pass the turn-off to Arkaroo Rock which contains a small collection of Aboriginal rock art. The site is reached via a short walk from the car park through open forest.

The turn-off to Wilpena Pound is 8 km further on, 52 km from Hawker. Turning left at the junction will take you 4 km to the Wilpena Pound Motel, with camping ground, motel, store and ranger's office. The camping ground offers all facilities for vanners and campers; set amongst big river red gums, it is a very pleasant spot to spend a few days. The motel can also organise flights over the Pound and further afield.

Whatever you do, do not miss this spectacular geological formation. Make the effort at least to walk into the Pound and up to the closest viewing point, Wangara Lookout.

Back on the main road heading north, the bitumen very quickly expires just north of the motel turn-off, and within 1 km a track on the right leads to Sacred Canyon (**GPS** 31°36'00"S, 138°43'02"E). The Aboriginal art site contains some of the best rock engravings in the whole of the Flinders—well worth the 14 km drive.

At a major road junction 5 km north of the motel turn-off, you need to turn left towards Yanyanna Hut and Bunyeroo Valley. This dirt road initially winds across low hills and through valleys of red gums. It then climbs through native pine, finally cresting a ridge after 14 km; from here there are expansive views down the Bunyeroo Valley and across the rounded domes of the ABC Range to the main ramparts of the Heysen Range. Named after the great Australian landscape painter, the ranges around here inspired many of his finest works.

From the Bunyeroo Valley Lookout (**GPS** 31°33'42"S, 138°38'56"E), the road follows the ridgeline for a short distance before winding its way carefully down to Bunyeroo Creek. The next couple of kilometres are through a rocky gorge, the track in the creek bed itself, and while this is generally no problem to a 4WD, the rocks and boulders can be a hassle to a low-slung car. Generally the creek has at least a trickle of water in it and there are some very pleasant small camp sites tucked in along the edge.

Once the road leaves the creek it swings north, travelling between the ABC and Heysen Ranges. At a T-junction (**GPS** 31°29'17"S, 138°38'51"E) 10 km north of the creek and 28 km from the Wilpena Motel turn-off, you need to turn left towards Brachina Gorge.

Almost straight away you are going along Brachina Creek and within a couple of kilometres you enter the gorge proper. Once again there is normally water through this gorge, but the track is generally easy for a 4WD. There are also a number of camp sites here and these are some of the best places to camp in the whole of the Flinders.

The road crosses the creek for the last time 7 km from the T-junction and climbs a low hill where, from a car park, you can get a good view back across the creek and down the Heysen Range to the northern walls of Wilpena Pound. From this point the road heads due west for 12 km until it strikes the main Hawker–Leigh Creek road. Turn left here for the drive back down the blacktop to Hawker, or turn right for Parachilna, Marree and the Outback beyond! At this point you are just 43 km from Hawker, 109 km from Quorn via the main road and 418 km from Adelaide, via Orroroo.

LEGEND

Road Distance in km	★ 26 ★
National Park	
Aboriginal Land	
Accommodation	
Camping Area	
Caravan Park	
Fuel Supplies	
General Store	
Meals Available	
Rest Area (Picnic Area)	
Tourist Information	

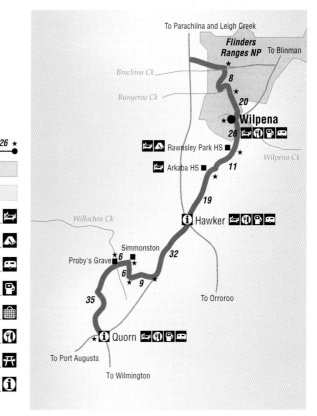

AMERICAN RIVER

140 KM SOUTH-WEST OF ADELAIDE, ON KANGAROO ISLAND
POPULATION: 260   MAP REF: PAGE 352 B4

A pleasant base from which to explore Kangaroo Island, American River received its name when an American ship sailed into the wide river mouth in 1803 and stayed while some of its crew built a small schooner, the *Independence*, from local timber.

Today it is a quiet beachside resort, the tranquil waters of the river and Eastern Cove adding to the serenity. The river flows into Pelican Lagoon and its conservation park. With five small islands, the park is an aquatic reserve where fish breed and is also an important waterbird refuge, particularly for pelicans. They make instant friends with the anglers who fish from the wharf or the waters of Eastern Cove.

On an evening walk around the town you often see wallabies, possums and other nocturnal animals, while during the day the foreshore is excellent for birdwatching. There is also good canoeing and boating in the protected waterways. A major feature of the town is the colourful carpet of small freesias that bloom around the end of August.
ACCOMMODATION: Wanderers Rest, ph (08) 8559 7201; The Fig Tree B&B, ph (08) 8553 1229; Linnetts Island Caravan Park and Holiday Flats, ph (08) 8483 3053
ACTIVITIES: Birdwatching, bushwalking, fishing, horse riding, water sports
TOURIST INFORMATION: Ph (08) 8553 1185

ANGASTON

77 KM NORTH-EAST OF ADELAIDE
POPULATION: 2000   MAP REF: PAGE 355 K9

Situated in the east of the famous and largest wine-growing area in Australia, the Barossa Valley, Angaston can be reached via Gawler and Nuriootpa, or via a pleasant run through the Eden Valley passing through Birdwood and Hahndorf.

Just south of the town is Yalumba Wines, the oldest family-owned winery in the country. The Henschke Estate, established in 1847 just a couple of

Collingrove Homestead (1853), south of Angaston

years before the Yalumba winery, has an exceptional reputation for fine wines and is located a few kilometres east, while the Saltram Wine Estate, with its heritage going back to 1859, is a couple of kilometres north. All offer wine-tasting and sales.

The town, a rich blend of English and German cultures, contains many fine public buildings, numerous art and craft shops, galleries and tearooms. The Lutheran church was built in the 1850s of pink marble, while the town hall was constructed from local white marble, which is still cut from a nearby quarry. The Angas Park Fruit Co. provides visitors with a sample of some of the other fare that this region produces: dried fruit, nuts, chocolate, and honey. The Angaston Blacksmith Shop has been restored and is open to the public.

Just to the south of the town is Collingrove Homestead. Built for John Angas in 1853, it is now owned by the National Trust. Nearby is the racehorse stud of Lindsay Park, built in 1848 by George Fife Angas, who was responsible for taking up much of the area.

About 10 km south-west of the town is the Kaiser Stuhl Conservation Park which protects a rugged area of natural bushland and is ideal for day walks.

Annual events include the show in February and the Yalumba Christmas Carols which take place at Yalumba Wines in December.
ACCOMMODATION: Vineyards Motel, ph (08) 8564 2404; Hillview Guesthouse, ph (08) 8564 2761; Collingrove Homestead, ph (08) 8564 2061
ACTIVITIES: Bushwalking, cycling, scenic drives, wineries
TOURIST INFORMATION: Ph (08) 8563 0600

ARDROSSAN

144 KM NORTH-WEST OF ADELAIDE
POPULATION: 980   MAP REF: PAGE 355 H9

Named after the town in Ayrshire, Scotland, Ardrossan is one of the largest ports on the Yorke Peninsula and the third largest grain handling outlet in the state. The area is dominated by the wheat silos down near the wharf. It also handles the shipping of dolomite which is mined nearby for BHP.

Situated on the north-east coast of the Peninsula, the area boasts great fishing and crabbing. The long jetty at Ardrossan is ideal for garfish, tommy ruff, and whiting. Blue crabs can be caught in the shallows at low tide or from the jetty. Diving in this area is centred on the wreck of the *Zanoni*, 10 nautical miles off the coast and acknowledged as one of the most interesting wrecks in South Australian waters.

On the clifftop near the town is a monument to the stump-jump plough which was developed here. This invention allowed the cultivation of fields previously deemed useless because of the many mallee roots buried in the ground. The Smith Plough Museum has a series of exhibits, while the National Trust Museum is nearby.
ACCOMMODATION: Ardrossan Hotel/Motel, ph (08) 8837 3468; Ardrossan Caravan Park, ph (08) 8837 3262; Highview Holiday Village, ph (08) 8837 3399
ACTIVITIES: Bowls, fishing, golf, water sports
TOURIST INFORMATION: Ph (08) 8837 3048

Sillers Lookout, at the end of Arkaroola Ridge

ARKAROOLA

702 KM NORTH OF ADELAIDE
POPULATION: 45   MAP REF: PAGE 357 L10

This wildlife sanctuary-cum-resort in the very north of the Flinders Ranges was once a run-down sheep station, and is reached via good dirt roads from either Copley (the closest bitumen) or via Yunta. Today, Arkaroola is one of the best Outback resorts in South Australia, offering visitors a rich experience of natural attractions in a rugged, wild, inland setting.

Located on the edge of the Gammon Ranges National Park and close to a number of historic sites such as the Bolla Bollana smelter ruins, as well as the geological wonders of the Paralana Hot Springs and Mt Painter, the resort is an ideal base from which to explore the surrounding area. There are a number of pleasant 4WD routes and a host of walking tracks.

One of the best ways to experience this place is on the Ridgetop Tour, a 4WD trip, which ends at the spectacular Sillers Lookout. Another unique attraction is the large astronomical telescope located on a peak close to the heart of the resort.
ACCOMMODATION: Arkaroola Resort (motel and camping), ph (08) 8648 4848
ACTIVITIES: Bushwalking, 4WD touring, national park access, scenic drives
TOURIST INFORMATION: Ph 1800 676 042

BARMERA

215 KM EAST OF ADELAIDE
POPULATION: 4470   MAP REF: PAGE 355 N8

This pretty little town, located in the heart of the Murray Riverland, on the shores of Lake Bonney, is known today as the capital of the South Australian country music scene. Each June long weekend, the town hosts the state's Country Music Awards. Rocky's Country Music Hall of Fame is always worth a visit.

Being in the centre of the Riverland and the irrigation area, the town and surrounds produce a vast quantity of fruit, particularly grapes. The Bonneyview Winery, established in 1967, is located just west of town along the Sturt Highway.

Lake Bonney itself has many sandy beaches and is popular for swimming and waterskiing. In 1964 the flat water of the lake was the site of Donald Campbell's attempt at the world water-speed record.

Europeans first came across the lake in the 1830s and by 1850 Nappers Old Accommodation House was

in operation. Its ruins, at the mouth of Chambers Creek, are now classified by the National Trust, while the Cobdogla Irrigation and Steam Museum houses the only working Humphrey Pump in the world. This National Trust museum has many other interesting displays and photographs.

Other annual events in Barmera include the Easter Sailing Regatta and the Riverland Autumn Floral Spectacular in April and the National Sheepdog Trials in September.

Lake Bonney at sunset, at Barmera

ACCOMMODATION: Lake Resort Motel, ph (08) 8588 2555; Barmera Hotel/Motel, ph (08) 8588 2111; Lake Bonney Holiday Park, ph (08) 8588 2234; Pelican Point Nudist Resort Caravan Park, ph (08) 8588 7366
ACTIVITIES: Bowls, fishing, golf, water sports, wineries
TOURIST INFORMATION: Ph (08) 8588 2289

BERRI

230 KM EAST OF ADELAIDE
POPULATION: 7100 MAP REF: PAGE 355 N8
Fruit, fruit juice and wine are what make the town of Berri tick. Located on a bend on the Murray River, from where it gains its name—'berri berri' is Aboriginal for 'big bend'—the surrounding area is a mosaic of different fruit orchards and vineyards.

Berrivale Orchards is one of the largest manufacturers of fruit and juice in Australia. Berri Estates, founded in 1922 and located 13 km west of the town, is one of the largest wineries in Australia.

Set on the cliffs overlooking the Murray is the old Reiners homestead, now part of the Wilabalangaloo Reserve. It has a fine collection of riverboat photos and a outdoor display including a small paddleboat. There are numerous walking tracks in this reserve.

Crossing the Murray River at Berri

Just a few kilometres south of town is the Katarapko section of the Murray River National Park, while upstream is the park's Lyrup Flats section. These areas of bushland protect the riverflats bordering the river and offer excellent camping, canoeing and fishing. The most common fish caught are yellowbelly, redfin and the occasional Murray cod.

Annual events include the Berri Easter Festival and the Berri/Loxton Bowling Carnival in September.
ACCOMMODATION: Riverbush Holiday Cottages, ph (08) 8582 3455; Berri Resort Hotel, ph (08) 8582 1411; Big River Motor Inn, ph (08) 8582 2688; Berri Riverside Caravan Park, ph (08) 8582 3723
ACTIVITIES: Bowls, fishing, golf, national park access, wineries, water sports
TOURIST INFORMATION: Ph (08) 8584 7919

BIRDWOOD

42 KM EAST OF ADELAIDE
POPULATION: 500 MAP REF: PAGE 355 K10
Located in the picturesque Adelaide Hills, Birdwood is home to the National Motor Museum, Australia's largest, and most important, collection of motor vehicles. It rates as one of the world's finest collection of vintage, veteran and classic cars and motorcycles dating back from the present day to 1899. The museum is also the focus of the annual Bay to Birdwood Run by vintage vehicles.

This small town also hosts the annual Rock & Roll Rendezvous and the very different Medieval Festival.

Back 6 km along the main road to Adelaide is the small town of Gumeracha with its Toy Factory, while at Cudlee Creek, another 7 km west, the Gorge Wildlife Park has one of the largest, private, native animal collections in Australia.
ACCOMMODATION: Birdwood Country Retreat B&B, ph (08) 8568 5321; Birdwood Cabins, ph (08) 8568 5436
ACTIVITIES: Horse riding, scenic drives, wineries
TOURIST INFORMATION: Ph (08) 8389 6996

BLINMAN

525 KM NORTH OF ADELAIDE
POPULATION: 55 MAP REF: PAGE 355 J2
Located in the heart of the Flinders Ranges, the last 32 km, or 55 km, of road, depending if you come from

Parachilna or from Wilpena, is reasonable dirt, passable to a normal car. The drive from Parachilna is exceptional as it winds its way through Parachilna Gorge, while the southern route from Wilpena passes what is known as 'The Great Wall of China'.

Other natural attractions include Glass Gorge and the secluded, spring-fed Blinman Pools, most easily accessible by following Blinman Creek up from the Angorichina Tourist Village. Further afield is Chambers Gorge with rugged country, ancient Aboriginal stone engravings and wildflowers.

This small town was once a booming copper mining town, the remains of which are well signposted. The self-guided walk is excellent.

In October, there is fun and excitement at the annual Blinman Picnic Race Meeting and Gymkhana.
ACCOMMODATION: Blinman Hotel/Motel, ph (08) 8648 4867; The Captains Cottage, ph (08) 8648 4894; Gum Creek Station, ph (08) 8648 4883; Angorichina Tourist Village and Caravan Park, ph (08) 8648 4842
ACTIVITIES: Historic walks, scenic drives
TOURIST INFORMATION: Ph 1800 633 060

BORDERTOWN

281 KM SOUTH-EAST OF ADELAIDE
POPULATION: 2200 MAP REF: PAGE 352 C10
Situated on the Dukes Highway just west of the South Australia/Victoria border, this town acts as a major service centre for those travelling between Adelaide and Melbourne, as well as for the rich cereal growing and sheep grazing areas that surround it.

Located in the Tatiara (Aboriginal for 'the good country') district, Bordertown came into prominence during the gold rush days of the 1850s when gold was taken by horseback from the Victorian diggings to Adelaide. Robert 'Bob' Hawke, Prime Minister of Australia during the 1980s, was born here in 1929 and Hawke House, his childhood home, can be toured.

South of the town is the rich wine-growing area of the Coonawarra, while to the north is the mallee scrubland of the Ngarkat Group of Conservation Parks, attractive for remote touring and camping.

A 40 km historic drive starts near the Bordertown Civic Centre and takes you to 11 heritage sites. Just

Old farm equipment at Clayton Farm, Bordertown

10 km from town is the historic township of Mundulla, with its National Trust hotel and museum. The bird life at the nearby Moot-Yang-Gunya Swamp and at the Poocher Swamp closer to Bordertown is varied.

Those interested in old machinery will not want to miss the Clayton Farm Vintage Field Day held in April. Other festivities include the Concert Band and Fiesta in September.

ACCOMMODATION: Dukes Motor Inn, ph (08) 8752 1177; Woolshed Inn Hotel/Motel, ph (08) 8752 1144; Bordertown Hotel, ph (08) 8752 1016; Bordertown Caravan Park, ph (08) 8752 1752
ACTIVITIES: Birdwatching, bowls, golf, historic drive
TOURIST INFORMATION: Ph (08) 8752 1044

BURRA

176 KM NORTH OF ADELAIDE
POPULATION: 1200   MAP REF: PAGE 355 K7
This historic town once had a population of over 5000 when Adelaide had just 18 000! Its importance in the 1850s was due to the discovery of copper—'The Monster Mine' became the richest mine of its time in Australia. The Burra Burra, as the area was first called, had several distinct villages, Redruth (Cornish), Aberdeen (Scottish), Llywchwr (Welsh), Hampton (English), and the mining company town of Kooringa. The villages eventually became Burra.

The mine was abandoned in 1877 but was reworked during the 1980s. Today, however, the town relies more on tourism and servicing its surrounding rich Merino sheep country than anything else.

Restored mine buildings at Burra

Burra was declared a State Heritage Town in 1994. There is a self-guided walk or drive leading past 43 heritage sites. The Unicorn Brewery Cellars give an indication of how hard men used to work and drink in that period, while the 'Dugouts' in the Burra Creek are mute testimony to the life many of these workers lived away from the danger of the mines. The Paxton Square Cottages, built around 1850 to provide the mineworkers with decent housing, are now refurbished and open for visitors to stay in.

Annual events include the South Australian Stud Merino Field Days in March and the Antique Fair and Cultural Weekend in May.

ACCOMMODATION: Burra Motor Inn, ph (08) 8892 2777; Burra Hotel, ph (08) 8892 2389;

Paxton Square Cottages, ph (08) 8892 2622; Burra Caravan Park, ph (08) 8892 2442
ACTIVITIES: Bowls, golf, historic walks and drives, horse riding
TOURIST INFORMATION: Ph (08) 8892 2154

CEDUNA

795 KM WEST OF ADELAIDE
POPULATION: 4050   MAP REF: PAGE 354 A4
The largest town in the far west of the state, Ceduna, with nearby Thevenard—a deep-sea port just 4 km away,—services a vast hinterland of cereal land and a fishing fleet that chases fish, abalone and crayfish. Grain, salt and gypsum are stored for export in the huge silos and stockpiles that dominate the skyline of Thevenard when seen from across the bay at Ceduna.

For many travellers Ceduna is the last town of any note before reaching the Nullarbor, or the first of any size after driving from Western Australia. The town's name is supposed to come from the Aboriginal word 'chedoona' which means 'a resting place', an apt name for a place at one end of the Nullarbor.

Matthew Flinders came this way in 1802 naming the larger, outer bay, Denial Bay, while the French explorer, Nicholas Baudin, named the smaller bay, on which Ceduna is located, Murat Bay.

The original township was established in the 1840s at Denial Bay, 13 km to the west of present-day Ceduna and on the western side of the bay. The original McKenzie Landing at the bay and the McKenzie Ruins located on the road to Davenport Creek are heritage listed. The present-day jetty at Denial Bay is only a third of its former length and is excellent for fishing and crabbing. The surrounding waters are also gaining acclaim as a top oyster-growing area. Ceduna was proclaimed in 1901 and soon grew into the major port it is today.

Apart from the swimming, fishing, diving, surfing, or boating that this area offers, there are other attractions: the Old Schoolhouse National Trust Museum in Ceduna has a wide range of pioneer artefacts on display as well as items from the Maralinga atomic bomb test sites.

On the October long weekend, Ceduna holds Oysterfest with beach sport events, the opening of the sailing season, a Red Faces competition, and a variety of other entertainment. Watching whales from the cliffs as they come to these waters to calve is a fascinating experience.

ACCOMMODATION: East West Motel, ph (08) 8625 2101; Ceduna Foreshore Hotel/Motel, ph (08) 8625 2008; Ceduna Foreshore Caravan Park, ph (08) 8625 2290
ACTIVITIES: Caving, fishing, water sports, whale watching
TOURIST INFORMATION: Ph (08) 8625 2780

CLARE

132 KM NORTH OF ADELAIDE
POPULATION: 3000   MAP REF: PAGE 355 J8
Just one and a half hour's drive north from Adelaide is the charming Clare Valley. Vineyards and gum

trees colour the scene and in the space of a few kilometres you will pass through the small villages of Auburn, Watervale and Sevenhill and will finally arrive in delightful Clare.

Home to over 28 wineries, the valley is arguably the finest riesling producing area in Australia, but others would say its shiraz isn't bad. The Riesling Trail—a walking, bike or horse-riding path from Watervale to Sevenhill—emphasises the importance of riesling in the valley.

In 1851 the Jesuit Fathers set up a church and school at Sevenhills, and planted a vineyard. The Sevenhill Cellars, the oldest and one of the most famous wineries in the area, is still operated by the Jesuit Society. St Aloysius Church, with its crypt, is well worth a look. Other wineries in the area include Taylors Wine, Tim Knappstein, Pikes, Leasingham and Jim Barry Wines.

The region has a rich European heritage, with Edward John Eyre passing through this way in 1839—his reports soon had pastoralists taking up land. The Hawker brothers set up Bungaree Station, today one of the most respected Merino studs in Australia, while nearby John Hope established Wolta Wolta, another famous stud and historic homestead.

C. J. Dennis, poet, famous for his 'Sentimental Bloke' was born in nearby Auburn in 1876 and is commemorated in an annual festival in the village.

Clare has a large number of heritage-listed buildings, including the former courthouse and police station which are now the National Trust Museum and Hill River Station with its coach-house and stables.

In mid-May there is the Clare Valley Gourmet Weekend, while the Anzac weekend has a Spanish Festival. Easter sees big racing meets and there is the Summer Festival in early December.

ACCOMMODATION: Clare Country Club Motel, ph (08) 8842 1060; Bungaree Station, ph (08) 8842 2677; The Palms B&B, ph (08) 8842 3911; Clare Caravan Park, ph (08) 8842 2724
ACTIVITIES: Bowls, bushwalking, cycling, horse riding, wineries
TOURIST INFORMATION: Ph (08) 8842 2131

CLEVE

541 KM NORTH-WEST OF ADELAIDE
POPULATION: 820   MAP REF: PAGE 354 F7
This small town on Eyre Peninsula lies 25 km inland from Arno Bay and services the surrounding rich cereal and grazing land. It is an easy 20 minute drive to the coast. The Cowell Hills give great views of the surrounding plain and Spencer Gulf, while the Carappee Hill Conservation Park offers flora and fauna as well as camping and bushwalking.

The town has an agricultural and folk museum which is opened on request.

The Eyre Peninsula Field Days, held in August every two years (1998, 2000, etc.), are huge, attracting exhibits from all over Australia. The Cleve Show, held in October, is one of the biggest on the peninsula.

ACCOMMODATION: Cleve Hotel/Motel, ph (08) 8628 2011
ACTIVITIES: Bowls, bushwalking, golf, horse riding, scenic drives, swimming (pool), tennis
TOURIST INFORMATION: Ph (08) 8628 2004

COFFIN BAY

700 KM WEST OF ADELAIDE
POPULATION: 350   MAP REF: PAGE 354 D9
The small resident population of this idyllic holiday resort is often outnumbered by its many visitors. The town is located on the protected waters of Coffin Bay, and nearly surrounded by the national park of the same name. Reached by a bitumen road off the Flinders Highway, 35 km north-west of Port Lincoln, Coffin Bay is known as a top spot to fish for whiting, sail or boat on the protected waters, or just go swimming. The oysters from this bay are considered among the best in Australia. A graded walking track—the Oyster Walk—winds for 2.5 km around the foreshore of the bay.

Just a short drive away through the national park, along a graded dirt road, is a wild untamed coast, vastly different from Coffin Bay. The national park offers a good choice of bush camping sites and some great fishing from rock or beach.

Yachties will not want to miss the 'Queen of the Gulf' Yacht Race held in March.
ACCOMMODATION: Coffin Bay Motel, ph (08) 8685 4111; Alpine Cottage, ph (08) 8685 4068; Siesta Lodge Holiday Units, ph (08) 8685 4001; Coffin Bay Caravan & Camping Park, ph (08) 8685 4170
ACTIVITIES: Bushwalking, fishing, national park access, water sports
TOURIST INFORMATION: Ph (08) 8685 4057

Sand dunes in Coffin Bay National Park

COOBER PEDY

857 KM NORTH OF ADELAIDE
POPULATION: 3500   MAP REF: PAGE 356 C7
The famed opal mining town of Coober Pedy lies on the Stuart Highway near the centre of the state, on the main route to the Northern Territory.

It is not a pretty place, the harsh climate where summer temperatures are often in the high 40°Cs makes many of the locals live underground. Some shops and motels are buried in the earth to escape the heat. Added to that are the white mounds of clay, littering the red-brown landscape, testimony to how

Underground living in Coober Pedy

many holes have been dug in search of the elusive opal. While you don't need a permit to 'noodle' for opal, only selected areas are open to noodlers.

The oldest and biggest opal mining town in South Australia, Coober Pedy acts as the centre for over 70 different small opal fields scattered around the town. Founded in 1915, the town was only proclaimed in 1969. Over 45 nationalities live in the town; however, it is the Greek population that are the most obvious, and each July they hold their Greek Glendi carnival.

There are three underground churches which should not be missed. The Umoona Mine Museum features the Aboriginal heritage of the area, and there are also underground mine tours.

The Breakaways Reserve, located 32 km north along the Stuart Highway, protects an area of stark sandstone mesas and buttes.
ACCOMMODATION: Desert Cave Motel, ph (08) 8672 5688; The Underground Motel, ph (08) 8672 5324; Desert View Apartments, ph (08) 8672 3330; Stuart Range Caravan Park, ph (08) 8672 5179
ACTIVITIES: Fossicking, mine tours
TOURIST INFORMATION: Ph 1800 637 076

COPLEY

573 KM NORTH OF ADELAIDE
POPULATION: 95   MAP REF: PAGE 355 J1
There is still a little confusion surrounding the naming of Copley which dates back to when it was just a railway siding, then known as Leigh Creek. When the town of Copley was proclaimed in 1891 the siding was absorbed into the new town but the locals retained the name of Leigh Creek for the pub, the railway station and the post office. While today the much larger township of Leigh Creek is just down the road, the Leigh Creek Hotel remains in Copley!

The small town, with its population of hardy souls, lies at the junction of the main bitumen road north to Marree and the dirt road east to Arkaroola and the Gammon Ranges. It makes a good base from which to explore the surrounding area.
ACCOMMODATION: Leigh Creek Hotel, ph (08) 8675 2281; Agnews Spread, ph (08) 8675 2635; Copley Roadhouse & Caravan Park, ph (08) 8675 2288
ACTIVITIES: Exploring the region
TOURIST INFORMATION: Ph 1800 633 060

COWELL

498 KM WEST OF ADELAIDE
POPULATION: 710   MAP REF: PAGE 354 F7
Located on the protected waters of Franklin Harbour on the east coast of Eyre Peninsula, Cowell is a major port servicing the inland grazing and cereal growing area. As well, fishing is an important industry while jade, mined in the nearby Minbrie Ranges, has put Cowell on the world gem market. The nephrite jade, from one of the biggest deposits in the world, has a variety of colour and patterns not found elsewhere, and the jade boulders, sometimes weighing tonnes, are brought into the town-based factory for cutting prior to export or further processing. It is Australia's only commercial jade mining operation.

The first pioneers arrived in the area in the 1850s, although the bay had been seen, and described as a lagoon, by Matthew Flinders 50 years earlier. The local museum, once the post office, was built in 1885.

The real attraction for the visitor is the large bay and its great fishing for whiting, snapper, garfish and snook. Crabbing at night is fun and Entrance Island has small, lovely beaches. South of the town the shallow waters of the bay are a birdwatcher's delight.

The Cowell Show is held in September.
ACCOMMODATION: Cowell Jade Motel, ph (08) 8629 2002; Cowell Commercial Hotel, ph (08) 8629 2181; Elbow Hill Inn B&B, ph (08) 8628 5012; Cowell Foreshore Caravan Park, ph (08) 8629 2307
ACTIVITIES: Birdwatching, bushwalking, crabbing, fishing, gem fossicking, scenic drives, water sports
TOURIST INFORMATION: Ph (08) 8629 2019

CRYSTAL BROOK

198 KM NORTH OF ADELAIDE
POPULATION: 2100   MAP REF: PAGE 355 J7
The 'Gateway to the Flinders Ranges', Crystal Brook lies just off the main highway north, amongst the gentle folds of hills where the Mt Lofty Ranges begin to give way to the more rugged slopes of the Flinders.

Edward Eyre was the first European into this rich farming area in 1840 and named the creek Crystal Brook. The land was soon taken up by graziers, while the town came into existence in the 1870s. The town now services the surrounding farming community.

The local museum in the old bakehouse is worth a visit, while the two hotels in the town date back to the 1870s. The Bowman Fauna Park, located 5 km east of town, includes the ruins of the original Bowman homestead which was the heart of one of South Australia's largest sheep stations. Today, it offers backpacker-type accommodation and restricted camping, and a chance to experience quiet bushland.

An agricultural show is held in August, while in October there is an antiques and collectables fair.
ACCOMMODATION: Crystal Brook Hotel, ph (08) 8636 2023; Royal Hotel, ph (08) 8636 2018; Crystal Brook Caravan Park, ph (08) 8636 2640
ACTIVITIES: Bowls, bushwalking, croquet, horse riding, rock climbing
TOURIST INFORMATION: Ph (08) 8636 2150

EDITHBURGH

226 KM WEST OF ADELAIDE
POPULATION: 450   MAP REF: PAGE 355 H10
Situated on the 'heel' of Yorke Peninsula, Edithburgh is a quiet seaside town and is an easy three hours' drive from Adelaide.

The large jetty is a reminder of the days when the port was used to ship large quantities of salt, which was mined on the numerous saltlakes nearby. Surveyed in 1869, the town retains much of its old-style charm, including the local hotel built in 1872. Today recollections of the old days are relived when the tall ships, *One and All* and *Falie*, visit the port as they cruise the waters of Gulf St Vincent.

For divers the nearby coast boasts a number of shipwrecks, the best known being the *Clan Ranald* off Troubridge Point. So many ships were lost that the Troubridge Light was built on an island lying just offshore Edithburgh in 1856. Today the island with its light is included in a conservation park and is home to penguins and crested terns. A pleasant scenic drive takes you out to Troubridge Point and Troubridge Hill, with its modern light.

For the angler the surrounding waters offer excellent fishing for whiting, snapper, tommy ruff and snook, while the jetty is probably the best fishing jetty in the region.

During October in Edithburgh sees the annual Gala Day.
ACCOMMODATION: Edithburgh Seaside Hotel/Motel, ph (08) 8852 6172; Anchorage Edithburgh Motel, ph (08) 8852 6262; Clan Ranald Holiday Units, ph (08) 8852 6172; Edithburgh Caravan Park, ph (08) 8852 6056
ACTIVITIES: Fishing, scenic drives, water sports
TOURIST INFORMATION: Ph (08) 8852 6109

ELLISTON

664 KM WEST OF ADELAIDE
POPULATION: 250   MAP REF: PAGE 354 C7
This tiny hamlet is located on the shores of the cliff-lined Waterloo Bay, which is further protected by a near continuous reef across its mouth. This is one of the larger towns on the Eyre Peninsula coast. It is an important service town for the surrounding farms and also serves as a port for the fishing, crayfish and abalone industries.

The nearby coastline is spectacular, with a number of sheltered bays and offshore islands to attract anglers and divers. The surfing too is great, with the famous 'Blackfellows' waves running to the

Elliston's Agricultural Hall decorated with murals

north in Anxious Bay. Locks Well and Sheringa Beach are both superb surf fishing areas.

Walkers Rocks, 11 km to the north, is a popular wild beach, while the Talia Caves region further north is an area of natural beauty with caves, white sand dunes and a beautiful beach. Lake Newland Conservation Park is excellent for bird life.
ACCOMMODATION: Elliston Motel, ph (08) 8687 9028; Elliston Hotel/Motel, ph (08) 8687 9009; Elliston Holiday Units, ph (08) 8687 9028; Elliston Waterloo Bay Caravan Park, ph (08) 8687 9076
ACTIVITIES: Birdwatching, fishing, scenic drives, water sports
TOURIST INFORMATION: Ph (08) 8687 9177

GAWLER

41 KM NORTH OF ADELAIDE
POPULATION: 11 500   MAP REF: PAGE 355 K9
Just 35 minutes north of Adelaide, Gawler is a pleasant rural town nestling between the two arms of the Para River and backed by the rolling hills of the Mt Lofty Ranges. Ordered streets and three town

Grass-trees, a common sight near Gawler

squares are due to Colonel William Light, the foresighted planner of Adelaide. Fine Victorian architecture complements a town that British poet laureate, Sir John Betjeman, said, 'was one of the most delightful towns [he] had seen anywhere'.

One of the first major settlements north of Adelaide, the town, begun in 1839, was a wayside stop for the miners and load carriers heading for the Burra mine or the copper mines on Yorke Peninsula. The railway arrived in 1857, and the present station, built in 1879, is also a telecommunications museum .

Acting as the western gateway to the Barossa Valley, the town is also the centre of a rich agricultural district that favours fat lambs, wool, wheat, poultry and dairy products. The Roseworthy Agricultural College is the oldest agricultural college in Australia and one of the most prestigious.

The regular Gawler races are an important social event, while the annual Gawler Three Day Horse Show, held in June, is a major event.
ACCOMMODATION: Prasads Gawler Motel, ph (08) 8522 5900; Eagle Foundry B&B, ph (08) 8522 3808; Gawler Cottages, ph (08) 8522 2727; Gawler Caravan Park, ph (08) 8522 3805

ACTIVITIES: Bowls, bushwalking, golf, horse riding, horseracing, swimming
TOURIST BUREAU: Ph (08) 8522 6814

GLADSTONE

210 KM NORTH OF ADELAIDE
POPULATION: 790   MAP REF: PAGE 355 J6
Located on the banks of the Rocky River, Gladstone was once two separate towns: the government town of Booyoolie, and the private town of Gladstone, separated by the railway tracks. While the two towns amalgamated some time ago, it was not until 1940 that the town became officially known as Gladstone.

The town became a major railway junction with all three gauges used in Australia—broad, narrow and standard—running side by side. Today the town is of less importance as far as the railway is concerned but it still acts as a major service centre for the surrounding grazing region.

The local gaol, built in 1879, was finally closed in 1975 and opened to the public a few years later. It is the town's most famous landmark.
ACCOMMODATION: Gladstone Hotel, ph (08) 8662 2015; Commercial Hotel, ph (08) 8662 2148; Gladstone Caravan Park, ph (08) 8662 2036
ACTIVITIES: Bowls, golf, swimming (pool)
TOURIST INFORMATION: Ph (08) 8662 2018

GOOLWA

82 KM SOUTH OF ADELAIDE
POPULATION: 3000   MAP REF: PAGE 352 A6
Goolwa is located close to the mouth of the Murray River where a barrage across the Goolwa Channel is part of a series of man-made barriers to stop saltwater from entering the great freshwater expanse of Lake Alexandrina and the river itself.

Once an important inland port that linked the Murray River trade with the ocean port of Port Elliot, the town is now more a tourism and holiday centre. The paddle-steamers tied up to the wharf are a vivid reminder of days gone by and offer an excellent way to see the river, while the *Captain Sturt* is the only Mississippi paddleboat on display in Australia.

A free car ferry operates across to Hindmarsh Island, a tranquil holiday retreat and dairy farming community. Captain Charles Sturt landed here on his epic trip down and back up the Murray in 1829–30. At the southern end of the island are the sand-filled channels which lead to the Murray Mouth and the open ocean. These have always proved to be a barrier to the sea.

The Coorong, one of Australia's great waterbird habitats, lies on the eastern side of the mouth and is now protected in the long sweep of the Coorong National Park. Cruises from Goolwa take in the river mouth and the delights of the Coorong.

The town's railway station is a base for a number of steam trains operating between Goolwa and nearby Port Elliot, as well as Mount Barker, further inland.

The Armfield Slip still features the building of wooden boats and from here a wooden boat festival is held each year. Other annual events include the

Paddle-steamers moored at Goolwa wharf

Goolwa to Milang Sailing Classic in February, and the 'Markets on the Wharf', held on a weekend each month between December and March.
ACCOMMODATION: Goolwa Central Motel, ph (08) 8555 1155; Birks Harbour B&B, ph (08) 8555 5393; Riverbank Lodge Cottage, ph (08) 8555 2002; Goolwa Caravan Park, ph (08) 8555 2737
ACTIVITIES: Bowls, fishing, golf, national park access, water sports
TOURIST INFORMATION: Ph (08) 8555 3488

HAHNDORF

25 KM SOUTH-EAST OF ADELAIDE
POPULATION: 1750   MAP REF: PAGE 355 K10
Claimed to be South Australia's most popular tourist attraction, Hahndorf is an historic German village situated in the delightful Adelaide Hills, just off the South Eastern Freeway. It is the oldest German village still surviving in Australia and was originally settled by 52 German migrants in 1839. More than 10 buildings are listed on the National Estate, including the Hahndorf Old Mill, now a motel and restaurant.

Hans Heysen, the brilliant painter who celebrated much of the grandeur of the Flinders Ranges in his paintings, lived here until his death in 1968. The Cedars, his home, has been preserved, as has his studio, as he left it. The Hahndorf Academy originally opened as a school in 1857, but is now an art gallery specialising in Heysen's work and that of local artists.

In January the famous Schutzenfest German Festival takes place; in March the town holds the

German Arms Hotel, Hahndorf, built in 1839

Hahndorf Founders Celebration, while in December is the 'St Nicholas Comes to Hahndorf' weekend.
ACCOMMODATION: Hahndorf Old Mill Motel, ph (08) 8388 7888; The Stables Restaurant & Inn, ph (08) 8388 7988; Storison Cottages, ph (08) 8388 7247; Hochstens Hahndorf Caravan Park, ph (08) 8388 7361
ACTIVITIES: Bowls, golf, horse riding, scenic drives
TOURIST INFORMATION: Ph (08) 8388 1185

HAWKER

409 KM NORTH OF ADELAIDE
POPULATION: 350   MAP REF: PAGE 355 J3
Promoted as 'The Hub of the Flinders', Hawker sits in a broad valley of the central Flinders Ranges. Reached by bitumen via Wilmington and Quorn, the shortest route to Adelaide is via Oororoo, but that still has around 100 km of dirt—good dirt—road.

This small town relies nearly completely on tourism since the railway left in 1970. Founded in the 1880s on the promise of wheat, the area was just a little too far north to ensure consistent, good rainfall, but the town took on a more important role, and a lot more substance, when the Great Northern Railway passed through in the same decade.

For most travellers it is the last major town before heading further north to the Flinders' major attraction, Wilpena Pound, or onwards to the Gammon Ranges and Arkaroola.

The town makes a good base from which to explore the surrounding area: just south of the town is Yourambulla Peak with its caves, where there are a number of Aboriginal paintings.

A walking trail and scenic lookout have been established on Jarvis Hill, while to the north is the magnificent Arkaba homestead with its cottage and camping facilities. The Moralana Scenic Drive runs from Parachilna to Wilpena and provides wonderful views of the western wall of Wilpena Pound.
ACCOMMODATION: Outback Chapmanton Motor Inn, ph (08) 8648 4100; Hawker Hotel/Motel, ph (08) 8648 4102; Arkaba Homestead (cottage and camping), ph (08) 8648 4195; Flinders Ranges Caravan Park, ph (08) 8648 4266
ACTIVITIES: Bowls, bushwalking, golf, national park access, scenic drives, swimming
TOURIST INFORMATION: Ph (08) 8648 4014

INNAMINCKA

1081 KM NORTH OF ADELAIDE
POPULATION: 105   MAP REF: PAGE 357 N4
In the far north-east of South Australia, surrounded by deserts in all directions, is an oasis fed by the slow moving waters of Cooper Creek.

Located on the southern bank of the Cooper, not far from the Queensland border, is a motley collection of buildings known as Innamincka. The pub and the general store are the heart of the township, while the national park headquarters, with its fine photographic display, is housed in the recently refurbished Australian Inland Mission (AIM) Nursing Home.

You can't get to Innamincka without travelling a long way on dirt roads, the closest bitumen being to the east, in Queensland, 160 km away. South is the infamous Strzelecki Track, now tamed because of the Moomba gas fields. While you could take a normal car to the Cooper, via the Strzelecki, it really is the home of the 4WD, so in anything less, take care!

Charles Sturt came this way in 1844 and the Burke and Wills tragedy was played out along the Cooper 16 years later. A number of monuments are located near the AIM home as well as by the stream.

Before Federation in 1901, the town was an important stopping point for the drovers taking cattle down the Strzelecki Track. A pub was soon followed by a customs office, police station and the AIM home.

By the 1950s, however, the town was deserted and it was not until gas was found around Moomba that a new pub was built at Innamincka in the early 1970s. The town is now the biggest it has ever been!

While the Cooper is the major attraction, the town also acts as a stepping-off point for the magical Coongie Lakes, 112 km to the north-west.

If you are in the area in August, the picnic race meeting is not to be missed.
ACCOMMODATION: Innamincka Hotel, ph 08) 8675 9901; Innamincka Cabins, ph (08) 8675 9900
ACTIVITIES: Birdwatching, canoeing, fishing, 4WD touring, swimming
TOURIST INFORMATION: Ph (08) 8675 9900

Cooper Creek in Innamincka Regional Reserve

IRON KNOB

385 KM NORTH-WEST OF ADELAIDE
POPULATION: 325   MAP REF: PAGE 354 G5
Just off the Eyre Highway, 70 km west of Port
Augusta, is Iron Knob. The small town has little to
offer except to those interested in mining history.

It was here that iron ore was first discovered in
Australia in the 1870s, making it the birthplace of the
Australian steel industry. BHP first started mining the
iron ore deposit in 1897. Ore is still supplied to the
BHP steelworks in Whyalla from these mines and
others in the area. Tours of the Iron Knob mine are
available, and the tourist centre is a mining museum.

To the north are the remote Gawler Ranges,
known for their wildflower displays in spring.
ACCOMMODATION: Iron Knob Motel, ph (08) 8646 2058;
Iron Knob Hotel, ph (08) 8646 2013; Pandurra Station,
ph (08) 8643 8941; Mt Ive Station (accommodation and
camping), ph (08) 8648 1817
ACTIVITIES: Scenic drive, mine visits
TOURIST INFORMATION: Ph (08) 8646 2129

JAMESTOWN

206 KM NORTH OF ADELAIDE
POPULATION: 1360   MAP REF: PAGE 355 J6
A pleasant rural township in the southern Flinders
Ranges, Jamestown derives most of its income from
the surrounding wheat and sheep farms. Founded in
1871, it was the arrival of the railway soon afterwards
that lent permanence to the town.

South of the town is the Bundaleer Forest, which
was the first government forest reserve in Australia.
Tasmanian blue gums and pines were first planted in
1876 and today the forest produces more than 6000
tonnes of timber annually. There is a pleasant scenic
drive in the forest as well as a number of walks.

The National Trust Museum, located in the old
railway station, has displays of regional interest.

The Jamestown Show, held every October Labour
Day weekend, is one of the biggest shows in the mid-
north of South Australia.
ACCOMMODATION: Railway Hotel/Motel, ph
(08) 8664 1035; Commercial Hotel/Motel,
ph (08) 8664 1013; Jamestown Country Retreat Holiday
Units and Caravan Park, ph (08) 8664 0077
ACTIVITIES: Bowls, horseracing, horse riding,
swimming
TOURIST INFORMATION: Ph 1800 633 060

KADINA

144 KM NORTH-WEST OF ADELAIDE
POPULATION: 3600   MAP REF: PAGE 355 H8
One of the three towns of the 'Copper Triangle', the
other two being Wallaroo and Moonta, Kadina is the
biggest town on the Yorke Peninsula and the service
centre for the rich surrounding agricultural district.

The town was founded after the discovery of
copper and the opening of the Wallaroo Mine, a large
mine, with workings down to 800 metres or so. The

mine is located just south of town and the remains of
the pumping station and the tall square Cornish-built
chimney dominate the old mine site.

The town has many reminders of its past and a
number of historic buildings listed by the National
Trust. Kadina has two museums, one of which
includes a former mine manager's residence.

In celebration of the area's Cornish, Welsh and
Scottish heritage, 'Kernewek Lowender' is held every
two years in May with highland games, caber tossing,
haggis-eating competitions and more. The events
take place around the three towns of the Triangle.
ACCOMMODATION: Kadina Gateway Motor Inn,
ph (08) 8821 2777; Kadina Hotel, ph (08) 8821 1008;
Miners Rest Cottage, ph (08) 8821 3422; Kadina
Caravan Park, ph (08) 8821 2259
ACTIVITIES: Bowls, golf, mining history
TOURIST INFORMATION: Ph (08) 8821 2093

KAPUNDA

81 KM NORTH-EAST OF ADELAIDE
POPULATION: 1625   MAP REF: PAGE 355 K9
The rich heritage of Kapunda is easily visible in its
fine old buildings, museums and churches, over 50 of
which are listed by the National Trust. Of interest are
the fine examples of patterned iron work, 'Kapunda
Lace', that graces many of the buildings and fences.

The site of Australia's first significant copper
mine, the town was established in the 1840s. For
the next 30 years the town was one of the biggest
in the state, but when the copper finally ran out,
the town was nearly deserted. Today it services the
surrounding grazing and farming lands.

The Kapunda Copper Mine Walking Trail
meanders through the old mine workings, and past
one of the earliest miners' cottages in the state.

The Kapunda Celtic Festival is held in March,
while the Country Music Festival is in August.
ACCOMMODATION: Sir John Franklin Hotel,
ph (08) 8566 3233; Ford House, ph (08) 8566 2280;
Blue Gum Retreat Cottage, ph (08) 8563 4020; Dutton
Park Caravan Park, ph (08) 8566 2094
ACTIVITIES: Bowls, bushwalking, golf, mining history,
trotting
TOURIST INFORMATION: Ph (08) 8566 2288

KEITH

236 KM SOUTH-EAST OF ADELAIDE
POPULATION: 1180   MAP REF: PAGE 352 C9
Located in the centre of a rich farming area, Keith
is found on the Dukes Highway in the region that
was once called 'The 90-Mile Desert'. Originally
settled in the 1840s, it was not until after World War II
that it was discovered that the 'desert' was short of
trace elements in the soil. With the addition of those
minerals the land was soon intensely cultivated.

To the north of the town is a series of parks
and reserves, the largest of which is the Ngarkat
Conservation Park, a sea of rolling dunes covered
with mallee and desert oaks.

The main street, called Heritage Street, has a
fine collection of historic buildings.

Hereford cattle grazing near Keith

Annual events include the Country Music Festival
in March and Horse Trials in April.
ACCOMMODATION: Keith Hotel/Motel,
ph (08) 8755 1122; Keith Motor Inn, ph (08) 8755 1500;
Keith Caravan Park, ph (08) 8755 1630
ACTIVITIES: Bowls, golf, national park access,
swimming
TOURIST INFORMATION: Ph (08) 8755 1061

KIMBA

484 KM NORTH-WEST OF ADELAIDE
POPULATION: 680   MAP REF: PAGE 354 E6
Located in the central north of Eyre Peninsula, Kimba
is one of the largest towns in the region, being the
service centre for one of South Australia's major
wheat growing areas. To the north are the granite
domes of the Gawler Ranges, while to the north-east
is the Lake Gilles Conservation Park, to the north-
west the Pinkawillinie Conservation Park and to the
south-west the Hambridge Conservation Park and
Carappee Hill Conservation Park.

The region was settled in the 1870s but it was not
until 1915 that the town was proclaimed. An excellent
local museum opposite the wheat silos traces the
development of the area.

The annual show is held in September, while the
rodeo takes place in October.
ACCOMMODATION: Kimba Community Hotel/Motel,
ph (08) 8627 2007; Kimba Motel and Caravan Park,
ph (08) 8627 2040
ACTIVITIES: Bowls, bushwalking, gem fossicking, golf,
horse riding, swimming (pool)
TOURIST INFORMATION: Ph (08) 8627 2112

KINGSCOTE

**120 KM SOUTH-WEST OF ADELAIDE, ON
KANGAROO ISLAND**
POPULATION: 1450   MAP REF: PAGE 352 B3
The 'capital' of Kangaroo Island, Kingscote is the
largest town on this delightful island. It is the island's
trade centre and is serviced by a regular air service
from Adelaide as well as the daily *SuperFlyte* fast
passenger ferry from the Adelaide suburb of Glenelg.

Established in 1836 as the first 'official' settlement in the then new colony of South Australia, Kingscote is situated on Nepean Bay, with the sweep of cliffs leading south to the mouth of Cygnet River where the surrounding swampland is home to a multitude of bird life. To the north the cliffs descend to Reeves Point, the most famous heritage site in South Australia, where the first settlement was located, while out in Nepean Bay are the Beatrice Island and Busby Islet Conservation Parks.

Kangaroo Island is the third largest island off the Australian mainland, being smaller only than Tasmania and Melville Island in the Northern Territory. Intensive farming on the island only became possible after the discovery that the soil lacked trace minerals. The island is a popular tourist destination, with fine beaches and great fishing, diving and surfing. Much of the island is protected in national parks and these are another delightful attraction.

The Hope Cottage Folk Museum, operated by the National Trust, is housed in one of the island's most historic homes. The surrounding grounds have a number of buildings, including the reconstructed light from Cape Willoughby Lighthouse. There is a eucalyptus oil distilling plant and yacca gum is also produced, both relics from earlier times.

In the cliffs in the front of the town little penguins nest, and guided tours are run by the National Parks and Wildlife Service. Nearby, on the northern side of the wharf area, pelicans are fed daily.

ACCOMMODATION: Wisteria Lodge Motel, ph (08) 8553 2707; The Island Resort Motel, ph (08) 8553 2100; Queenscliffe Family Hotel, ph (08) 8553 2254; Kingscote Nepean Bay Tourist Park, ph (08) 8553 2394

ACTIVITIES: Bushwalking, fishing, golf, horse riding, national park access, water sports

TOURIST INFORMATION: Ph (08) 8553 1185

KINGSTON S.E.

305 KM SOUTH-EAST OF ADELAIDE
POPULATION: 1430   MAP REF: PAGE 352 D8

Kingston S.E. is located on the shores of Lacepede Bay just to the south of the Coorong National Park. The S.E., for south-east, is to avoid confusion with Kingston-on-Murray, another town in South Australia.

As you approach this fishing and tourist destination you will either come past the very large lobster known as 'Larry' on the Princes Highway, or via the old Cape Jaffa Lighthouse, erected on the foreshore. The town is an important fishing port, especially for crayfish—or lobster. Snapper, shark, salmon, whiting and garfish are also caught regularly.

Lacepede Bay is considered by the locals to be the safest area of water in the state and is ideal for swimming, windsurfing and sailing.

The area was first settled in the 1850s, but not before a group of survivors from the ship, *Maria*, were massacred by Aborigines in 1840. The town was proclaimed in 1866, the same year the post office and police station were built. The famous lighthouse was built on Margaret Brock Reef, just off Cape Jaffa, a few kilometres south of Kingston, in 1870. Cape Jaffa today is a small holiday and fishing community, ideal for those who want to get away from it all.

'Larry', the giant lobster, just outside Kingston S. E.

In January there is the annual Lions Surf Fishing Competition, while the annual show is in October.

ACCOMMODATION: Beehive Motor Inn, ph (08) 8767 2444; Kingston Lobster Motel, ph (08) 8767 2322; Kingston Caravan Park, ph (08) 8767 2050; Cape Jaffa Caravan Park, ph (08) 8768 5056

ACTIVITIES: Bowls, fishing, golf, horse riding, national park access, water sports

TOURIST INFORMATION: Ph (08) 8767 2555

LEIGH CREEK

569 KM NORTH OF ADELAIDE
POPULATION: 1950   MAP REF: PAGE 355 J1

Located on the edge of the Flinders Ranges, this is the state's source of coal which is shipped south to the power stations at Port Augusta.

The town was moved to its present location in 1981 when the original site proved to be in the way of the mining operation. Coal was originally discovered here in 1888, but it was not until the 1940s that it was mined in earnest and now the fields produce over two million tonnes annually. The area was first settled in 1841 and the town was named after Harry Leigh, the head stockman on the surrounding sheep station.

Today the town houses the miners and their families and offers passing travellers a pleasant spot to stop and refresh, although accommodation is very limited. The nearby Aroona Dam is a pleasant spot to visit, while tours of the coalfields can be arranged.

ACCOMMODATION: Leigh Creek Motel, ph (08) 8675 2406; Leigh Creek Caravan Park, ph (08) 8675 2476

ACTIVITIES: Bushwalking, mine tours, scenic drives

TOURIST INFORMATION: Ph 1800 633 060

LOXTON

243 KM EAST OF ADELAIDE
POPULATION: 3380   MAP REF: PAGE 355 N9

Situated on a sweep of the Murray River, Loxton is a pleasant town with a number of parks and gardens. Established in the 1850s, the town was proclaimed in 1907, taking its name from a boundary rider who lived in a log hut near the site of the township. After World War II the town became the centre of a large soldier settlement scheme based around the newly declared irrigation area and with that, the town boomed. Today the area is rich with vineyards and orchards. A number of co-ops were formed in the 1950s, including a winery and distillery which, combined, crush more than 20 000 tonnes of grapes a year.

Much of the early history of the region is re-created in the Loxton Historical Village with more than 30 fully furnished buildings.

The Katarapko Island section of the Murray River National Park encompasses a vast area of river flats across the river from the town nearly all the way to the township of Berri. There is good fishing and excellent walking and canoeing in this region of the

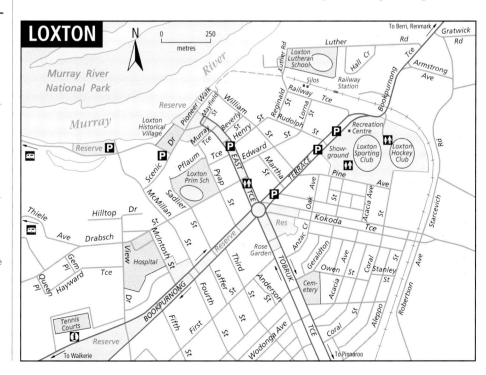

Marks on a tree in Loxton, showing the dates and heights of the Murray River in flood

park and it is easily accessible, with many fine camping spots dotted along the river. The river also provides an excellent spot for water sports.

The Pyap Reserve, also known as the Daisy Bates Reserve, commemorates the life of a remarkable woman who spent much of her life working with and for Aboriginal people.

Annual events include the Apex Fisherama in January and the Show Day in October.

ACCOMMODATION: Loxton Hotel/Motel, ph (08) 8584 7266; Erehwon Estate Vineyard Retreat, ph (08) 8584 7240; Loxton B&B, ph (08) 8584 5350; Loxton Riverfront Caravan Park, ph (08) 8584 7862

ACTIVITIES: Bowls, bushwalking, fishing, golf, national park access, water sports

TOURIST INFORMATION: Ph (08) 8584 7919

LYNDOCH

56 KM NORTH-EAST OF ADELAIDE
POPULATION: 950   MAP REF: PAGE 355 K9

Situated in the south of the Barossa Valley, the town is the first one you enter in this famous wine-growing area when you come from Adelaide via Gawler. One of the most famous wineries in the valley is located close by. Chateau Yaldara is not only a fine winery but also has an outstanding collection of artwork, antiques and European porcelain.

Given the name of Lyndoch by Colonel Light in 1837, it was once known as Hoffnungsthal, the 'Valley of Hope'. A flood in 1854 forced the mainly Lutheran people to move their settlement to higher ground.

The South Australian Museum of Mechanical Music, with a fine collection of music boxes, player organs and other instruments run by clockwork can be found in town. Nearby is Lyndoch Lavender Farm.

A short distance west of the town is the Sandy Creek Conservation Park, a birdwatcher's delight with over 100 species of birds found in an area of native bush dominated by native pine and pink gum.

ACCOMMODATION: Chateau Yaldara Estate Motel, ph (08) 8524 4268; Woodlands Vineyard Homestead, ph (08) 8524 4511; Barossa Country Cottages, ph (08) 8524 4426; Barossa Caravan Park, ph (08) 8524 4262

ACTIVITIES: Birdwatching, bushwalking, horse riding, swimming, wineries

TOURIST INFORMATION: Ph (08) 8524 4110

McLAREN VALE

38 KM SOUTH OF ADELAIDE
POPULATION: 1200   MAP REF: PAGE 355 J10

Home to the famous Hardy and Seaview wineries, McLaren Vale is located in the heart of the Fleurieu Peninsula's 'wine coast' in the rolling plains at the foot of the Mt Lofty Ranges. Dotted amongst the vineyards are orchards of olives, almonds, avocados, stone fruits and berries, all of which grow well in this temperate region.

While the Almond Train in the main street sells the largest range of almond products in Australia, it is the area's 50 plus wineries for which the district is most famous. Wines have been made here since the region was first settled in the 1850s, but the industry took off with Thomas Hardy's arrival in 1873.

The nearby beaches and reefs offer excellent swimming, diving and surfing.

Throughout October visitors can participate in the annual Wine Bushing Festival.

ACCOMMODATION: Wirilda Creek Winery, ph (08) 8323 9260; Aunt Amanda's Cottage, ph (08) 8383 7122; McLaren Vale Lakeside Caravan Park, ph (08) 8323 9255

ACTIVITIES: Bushwalking, horse riding, swimming, wineries

TOURIST INFORMATION: Ph (08) 8323 9455

MANNUM

78 KM EAST OF ADELAIDE
POPULATION: 2030   MAP REF: PAGE 355 L10

Founded in 1852, Mannum became a major port when paddleboats plied the Murray River from its mouth upstream as far as Albury in New South Wales. The town is still an important river town servicing the surrounding community and an interesting place.

A number of vessels are based at Mannum, including the paddle-steamers, PS *Marion*, *Proud Mary*, and *Murray Princess*, the latter being the largest paddleboat in the southern hemisphere. The National Trust museum, housed in an old paddle-steamer, pays homage to the river trade and Charles Sturt, the first European explorer to come this way.

There is good fishing along the river, while the Cowirra Historic Reserve north-east of the township is important to the Aborigines who once lived here.

In July there is the annual River Festival.

ACCOMMODATION: Mannum Motel, ph (08) 8569 1808; Cygnet Houseboat, ph (08) 8569 2018; Mannum Caravan Park, ph (08) 8569 1402; Mannum Holiday Village, ph (08) 8569 1179

ACTIVITIES: Bushwalking, fishing, horse riding, water sports

TOURIST INFORMATION: Ph (08) 8569 1303

MARLA

1092 KM NORTH-WEST OF ADELAIDE
POPULATION: 100   MAP REF: PAGE 356 A4

Proclaimed in 1981, the modern township of Marla acts as the government administration centre in northern South Australia. Situated at the junction of the bituminised Stuart Highway and the all-gravel Oodnadatta Track, Marla is located at the site of a reliable water supply, the Marla Bore, an important consideration in this semi-desert country.

Just 35 km to the west are the Mintabie opal fields which have, in recent years, outstripped Coober Pedy as the largest supplier of opals. The Dalhousie Mound Springs in the Witjira National Park are 350 km to the north-east, a virtual stone's throw in this vast desert country, but you will need a 4WD to get there.

The Marla Race Meeting is held annually in April.

ACCOMMODATION: Marla Travellers Rest Hotel/Motel and Caravan Park, ph (08) 8670 7001

ACTIVITIES: 4WD touring, gem fossicking

TOURIST INFORMATION: Ph 1800 633 060

MARREE

689 KM NORTH OF ADELAIDE
POPULATION: 385   MAP REF: PAGE 357 H8

Located at the junction of the Birdsville Track, the Oodnadatta Track and the main road south to Port Augusta, Marree has always been an important service town for this outback area of South Australia.

Located close to Hergott Springs, a natural spring discovered by John McDouall Stuart in 1860, and by which name the town was first known, the area was put on the map by the construction of the Overland Telegraph Line in 1871. By the time the railway line arrived in 1882, the town had become an important staging post for the camel trains carrying supplies further north. Only when the railway was shifted west in the 1970s did Marree lose its strategic importance. Today it continues to service the travellers passing through and the surrounding cattle and sheep stations. A few decaying reminders of the glory days stand close to the old railway siding.

The town is bustling in June when the Picnic Race Meeting and Gymkhana are held.

ACCOMMODATION: Marree Hotel, ph (08) 8675 8344; Marree Caravan & Campers Park, ph (08) 8675 8371

ACTIVITIES: 4WD touring

TOURIST INFORMATION: Ph 1800 633 060

MELROSE

271 KM NORTH OF ADELAIDE
POPULATION: 210   MAP REF: PAGE 355 J5

A delightful town in the Flinders Ranges, Melrose nestles at the foot of Mt Remarkable, one of the

highest peaks in the range. Melrose was established in 1853 and is one of the oldest towns, with the North Star Hotel being licensed one year later, in 1854.

The town is an excellent base from which to explore the surrounding area and the nearby Mt Remarkable National Park. A walking trail from just outside town leads to the top of the mount, giving splendid views of the countryside, including the Willochra Plain. Another walking trail goes past the old copper mines to Bald Hill Lookout. A heritage walk in the town is also of interest to history buffs.

The Melrose Show held in October of each year is one of the largest in the region.

ACCOMMODATION: Melrose Hotel/Motel, ph (08) 8666 2119; North Star Hotel, ph (08) 8666 2110; Melrose Holiday Units, ph (08) 8666 4201; Melrose Caravan Park, ph (08) 8666 2060
ACTIVITIES: Bushwalking, golf, horse riding, national park access, scenic drives
TOURIST INFORMATION: Ph (08) 8666 2060

MILLICENT

411 KM SOUTH-EAST OF ADELAIDE
POPULATION: 5120   MAP REF: PAGE 352 F9
Located astride the Princes Highway, north-west of Mount Gambier, Millicent is an important township servicing the rich surrounding farming land. It also acts as a gateway to Canunda National Park which stretches along the rugged windswept coast.

A busy commercial centre, Millicent also has many pleasant parks and gardens, including the Memorial Garden with its quaint rotunda.

The area was first settled in 1851 and the surrounding swamps were drained in a huge scheme that started in 1863 and continued into the 1900s. Nearly 1500 km of drains were built, along with 500 bridges. In the very early 1900s pine plantations were established and two paper mills were later constructed south of the town.

The Millicent National Trust Museum is recognised as one of the best regional museums in South Australia and has many award-winning displays, including a fully equipped blacksmith's shop and a shipwreck room containing artefacts from

The Shell Gardens of Millicent

wrecks along the nearby coast. Also worth a visit are the Millicent Shell Gardens and the local art gallery.

The nearby Canunda National Park offers camping and excellent 4WD touring along the beach, although some experience is necessary. Fishing and surfing are also popular pastimes.

The Tantanoola Caves Conservation Park is located just a short drive south of Millicent and guided tours are available of these unique limestone caves. A number of lakes, including the Lake McIntyre Reserve, are well-known bird habitats.

ACCOMMODATION: Diplomat Motel, ph (08) 8733 2211; Somerset Hotel/Motel, ph (08) 8733 2888; Millicent Motel, ph (08) 8733 2655; Millicent Lakeside Caravan Park, ph (08) 8733 3947
ACTIVITIES: Bushwalking, fishing, golf, horse riding, national park access, scenic drives, water sports
TOURIST INFORMATION: Ph (08) 8733 3205

MINTARO

122 KM NORTH OF ADELAIDE
POPULATION: 90   MAP REF: PAGE 355 K8
This small town, located 15 km south-east of Clare, is a declared heritage site, the first complete town in South Australia to be so recognised. Many of the old cottages and buildings date from when the town was first settled in 1849. The magnificent Martindale Hall, just 2 km south of the centre of town, is a fine example of an old-style Georgian mansion. Many cottages offer self-contained accommodation and the town makes a good base from which to explore the Clare Valley and the many local wineries.

The town is also known for its enormous slate deposit which has been worked for over 150 years. It has not only been used a great deal in local construction, but also in fine buildings overseas and in billiard tables around the world.

The annual Paddy's Market and Street Fair is held in March.

ACCOMMODATION: Martindale Hall B&B, ph (08) 8843 9088; Olde Devonshire House, ph (08) 8843 9058; Mintaro Mews, ph (08) 8843 9001; Oldfields Cottages, ph (08) 8843 9038
ACTIVITIES: Historic town walk, wineries
TOURIST INFORMATION: Ph (08) 8842 2131

MOONTA

161 KM NORTH-WEST OF ADELAIDE
POPULATION: 2750   MAP REF: PAGE 355 H8
Located just a short distance inland from Moonta Bay and the shores of Yorke Peninsula, Moonta is rich in heritage and fine old buildings. It owes its existence to the discovery of copper in 1861 and the establishment of the Moonta Mining Co.

Most of the mining was undertaken by Cornish miners and by 1875 the population had reached 12 000. Many of the buildings associated with this era are still standing. The Moonta Mines State Heritage Area, which covers most of the old Moonta Mines lease area, includes Cornish cottages, the local church, a couple of shafts and ore processing plants. The Moonta Mines School is a very good museum.

Nearby Moonta Bay is a popular holiday centre with good beaches for water sports and fishing.

In May the 'Kernewek Lowender Festival' celebrates the Cornish heritage of the Copper Triangle towns of Moonta, Kadina and Wallaroo. The annual Moonta Show takes place in October.

ACCOMMODATION: Patio Motel, ph (08) 8825 2473; Royal Hotel, ph (08) 8825 2108; Baroona Cottages B&B, ph (08) 8825 3430; Moonta Bay Caravan Park, ph (08) 8825 2406
ACTIVITIES: Fishing, golf, heritage walks, mining history, water sports
TOURIST INFORMATION: Ph (08) 8825 2622

MORGAN

166 KM EAST OF ADELAIDE
POPULATION: 445   MAP REF: PAGE 355 L8
Located on the great bend of the Murray River where the river turns south towards the sea, Morgan is a quiet, pleasant town that relies mainly on tourism and servicing the local farm country for its existence.

This has not always been the case, as Morgan was once one of the most important ports in the state servicing the paddle-steamers along the Murray. When the railway arrived from Adelaide it was one of only a couple of towns connected to the coast by rail. The area around the port and the railway siding is still preserved, as is a section of the long high wharf.

There is an excellent heritage walk around the wharf and nearby town area, while a museum is located down at the railway siding. The PS *Mayflower* still plies the river and, being built in 1844, is the oldest operating paddle-steamer in South Australia.

There are a number of art and craft places in the town, while trail rides can be arranged through the nearby bushland on carts, horses or camels.

ACCOMMODATION: Colonial Motel, ph (08) 8540 2277; Commercial Hotel, ph (08) 8540 2107; Morgan Riverside Caravan Park, ph (08) 8540 2207; Kanyaka Houseboats, ph (08) 8540 4014
ACTIVITIES: Bushwalking, fishing, heritage walk, horse riding, swimming
TOURIST INFORMATION: Ph (08) 8540 2354

MOUNT GAMBIER

462 KM SOUTH-EAST OF ADELAIDE
POPULATION: 21 160   MAP REF: PAGE 352 F10
Mount Gambier is the South East's unofficial capital and is a well-known tourist focal point, as well as an industry and business centre. Set in pleasant rolling landscape, the area produces fat lambs, fine cheeses, dairy products, as well as wool and wheat.

Apart from the surrounding rich farmland, the region is also home to the largest softwood timber milling industry in Australia. There are many plantation forests of radiata pine and the occasional large timber mill. The district is also famous for its Mount Gambier limestone which is used as a building material all over southern Australia.

The town is located at the base of Mt Gambier which is the highest point of an extinct volcanic crater that has, as its heart, a number of lakes, including

Mount Gambier's town hall

Valley Lake and Browne Lake. Here you will find a very pleasant picnic area and a steep walk to Centenary Tower on top of the peak with views of the surrounding countryside. There are walking trails and boardwalks around the lake shore and the bird life will enchant everyone. Nearby is Blue Lake, set in another extinct volcano, and the deepest of the lakes near the city. It turns a deep cobalt blue in November before changing back to grey in late summer.

Mt Gambier was the first part of South Australia to be named in 1800 by Lieutenant James Grant, sailing by in the *Lady Nelson*, but it was not until 1839 that settlement took place. That was a couple of years before the explorer Thomas Mitchell arrived, who was surprised to find George Henty already working the area. The town was surveyed in 1861 and the railway arrived in 1879. The poet, Adam Lindsay Gordon, served here with the mounted police in the 1850s and obtained lasting fame, not only for his poetry but by jumping a horse over a wooden fence onto a ledge on the very lip of the Blue Lake crater.

Much of the surrounding area is limestone: the Cave Gardens in the centre of the city are a very pleasant attraction. Umpherstone Cave has been planted with terraced gardens and is floodlit at night, while Engelbrecht Cave is open to the public, as well as to divers.

Piccaninnie Ponds and Ewen Ponds, both closer to the coast, have crystal clear water bubbling up from deep underground, and are excellent for snorkelling or diving.

Mt Schank further south is another extinct volcano that was again named as the *Lady Nelson* sailed the coast. A walking trail climbs this peak, and continues into the crater itself.

The city is a well-known sporting location and regularly hosts a number of national and state events, including shooting and tennis. Annual events include the Country Music Festival in February, Blue Lake Festival in March, Field Days in April and the Eisteddfod in August.

ACCOMMODATION: Presidential Motel, ph (08) 8724 9966; Blue Lake Motel, ph (08) 8725 5211; Garden Cottage, ph (08) 8726 8052; Blue Lake City Caravan Park, ph (08) 8725 9856

ACTIVITIES: Bowls, bushwalking, cave diving, fishing, golf, horseracing, scenic drives, tennis, trotting, water sports, wineries

TOURIST INFORMATION: Ph (08) 8724 9750 or 1800 087 187

MURRAY BRIDGE

80 KM EAST OF ADELAIDE
POPULATION: 12 750   MAP REF: PAGE 355 L10

Murray Bridge is an important rural riverside town as well as being a popular tourist retreat. It is sited on the Princes Highway and connected to Adelaide via the South East Freeway,

Charles Sturt first passed this way in 1829–30, but it was another 25 years before settlement took place. In the 1860s cattle on the overland route from the eastern states swam the Murray at this point, then known as Edward's Crossing and later as Mobilong. The first bridge was built in 1879 and in 1886 the railway passed through. In 1906 the swamps were drained and the land irrigated, allowing for farming of pigs, dairy cattle, fruit and vegetables. The new bridge, just to the south of town, was built in 1979.

The area is well endowed with water sports activities with everything from swimming and fishing to cruising in a houseboat. Another favourite attraction is the Butterfly House which is a tropical greenhouse filled with hundreds of Australian butterflies. Just south of the town is the pioneer village of Old Tailem Town.

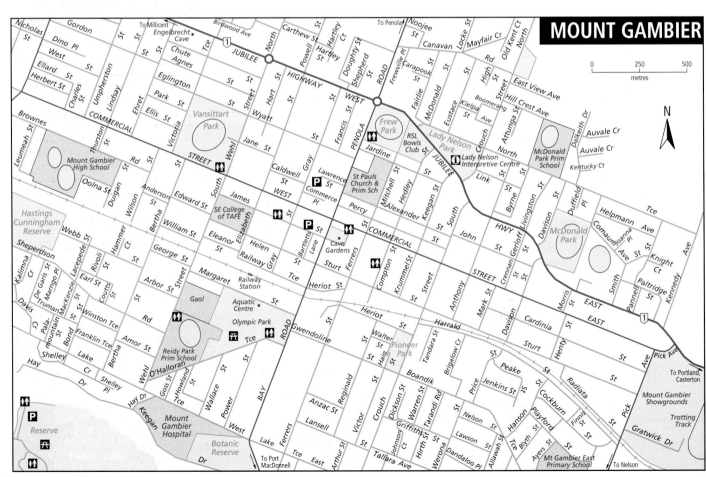

An old bridge at Murray Bridge

West of Murray Bridge is the Monarto Zoological Park featuring Asian and African animals. Here you will also find some pleasant walking trails.
ACCOMMODATION: Murray Bridge Motor Inn, ph (08) 8532 1144; Murray Bridge Hotel, ph (08) 8532 2024; Flipper IV Houseboat, ph (08) 8532 2230; Long Island Caravan Park, ph (08) 8532 6900
ACTIVITIES: Bowls, bushwalking, fishing, horseracing, water sports
TOURIST INFORMATION: Ph (08) 8532 2900

NARACOORTE

346 KM SOUTH-EAST OF ADELAIDE
POPULATION: 4720   MAP REF: PAGE 352 E9
Located in the south-east of the state, Naracoorte owes its fame mostly to the caves that are nearby. The largest and most significant of the 60 plus caves along the Cave Range is the Victoria Fossil Cave. First discovered in 1894, it won worldwide acclaim when in 1969 an amazing diversity of fossils was found. In all, over 93 species of animal fossils have been found, including many that are extinct, such as a marsupial lion, a large echidna, a giant tree-browsing kangaroo and a hippo-size wombat. A modern interpretive centre recaptures the prehistoric landscape. A number of caves contained within the Naracoorte Caves Conservation Park are also open to the public.

The area was first settled in the 1840s when it was known as Mosquito Plain. The railway arrived in 1876 and several buildings from this era still grace the town. Today the town is a major service centre for the rich agricultural area that surrounds it and produces fat lambs, wool and cattle.

Bool Lagoon, 17 km south of the town, is a vast wetland that is alive with birds. Over 155 species, including brolgas, Cape Barren geese and numerous species of ducks and waders, use this reserve. There are boardwalks and hides for watching the birds.

Calendar events include the Swap Meet and Three Day Equestrian Event in May and the Underground Music Festival in October.

ACCOMMODATION: William MacIntosh Motor Lodge, ph (08) 8762 1644; Naracoorte Hotel/Motel, ph (08) 8762 2400; The Shepherds Cave Apartment, ph (08) 8762 0246; Naracoorte Caravan park, ph (08) 8762 2128
ACTIVITIES: Bowls, bushwalking, golf, horse riding, scenic drives, swimming, wineries
TOURIST INFORMATION: Ph (08) 8762 1518

NULLARBOR

1097 KM WEST OF ADELAIDE
POPULATION: 15   MAP REF: PAGE 353 C9
Nothing more than a roadhouse, motel and caravan park on the edge of the main highway, Nullarbor is 300 km west of Ceduna on the edge of the vast, treeless Nullarbor Plain. For most it is nothing more than an overnight stay, or an even shorter refuel stop, but in winter a major event takes place,

This tiny outpost of civilisation is the closest habitation to the Head of the Bight where southern right whales come to give birth and to mate. From the cliffs you get a great view of the animals frolicking in the waters. You will need a permit to travel across the Yalata Aboriginal land and these are available from the motel. This section of coast is one of the premier whale viewing areas in the world.

North of the roadhouse is the Murrawijinie Cave, just one of several large caves found on the Nullarbor but this one is approved for the public to visit.
ACCOMMODATION: Nullarbor Hotel/Motel & Caravan Park, ph (08) 8625 6271
ACTIVITIES: Caving, whale watching
TOURIST INFORMATION: Ph (08) 8625 2780

NURIOOTPA

72 KM NORTH-EAST OF ADELAIDE
POPULATION: 3350   MAP REF: PAGE 355 K9
The largest town in the Barossa Valley this delightful place is excellent as a base to experience the many

wineries in the immediate area. Nuriootpa is the commercial centre of the valley and home to some of Australia's largest wineries. On the edge of town is Penfolds, who for over 150 years have been producing wines, while a few kilometres to the west is the Seppelt's winery and to the north Wolf Blass. Smaller, lesser known wineries dot the intervening areas. All have wine-tasting and cellar door sales.

Europeans first arrived here in the 1840s and William Coulthard built an inn. A town soon sprang up around this watering hole and while the original building has long gone a hotel is still on the site. Coulthard's House, an impressive bluestone building, is now the National Trust Museum.

In May of each year there is a hot-air balloon regatta, while the Barossa in Bloom weekend is held every September.
ACCOMMODATION: Vine Inn Hotel/Motel, ph (08) 8562 2133; Kaesler Cottages B&B, ph (08) 8562 2711; Seppeltsfield Holiday Log Cabins, ph (08) 8562 8240; Barossa Valley Tourist Park, ph (08) 8562 1404
ACTIVITIES: Bowls, bushwalking, gem fossicking, swimming, wineries
TOURIST INFORMATION: Ph (08) 8562 2627

OODNADATTA

1093 KM NORTH OF ADELAIDE
POPULATION: 235   MAP REF: PAGE 356 D4
A small historic backwater in the desert region of South Australia's far north, Oodnadatta owes its existence to the trains that once ran through here.

John McDouall Stuart blazed a route through here on his crossing of the continent in 1861. The Overland Telegraph Line arrived in 1870. A few years later a town was laid out and from 1891 to 1929 Oodnadatta was the railhead servicing the outposts further north. Tough Afghan camel drivers took their strings of camels loaded with supplies far and wide through the desert country and when the train line was finally pushed further north to Alice Springs it received the name The Ghan. The old Ghan operated through Oodnadatta until 1980, and while the new train line is much further west, it still carries the name of these pioneer camel men.

A small section of track and the old railway station, now a museum, are reminders of those heady days of steam, and hustle and bustle.

The famous, or infamous, Oodnadatta Track links the town with Marree, 410 km to the south, and Marla 220 km to the west. To the north, over rough sandy

The Pink Roadhouse in Oodnadatta

tracks, is the Witjira National Park, while 200 km to the south-west is the mining town of Coober Pedy.

Probably the most famous establishment in town is the Pink Roadhouse, run by Adam and Lynnie Plate and home to the famous Oodna-burger.

In May Oodnadatta holds its Picnic Race Meeting.

ACCOMMODATION: Transcontinental Hotel, ph (08) 8670 7804; Pink Roadhouse Caravan Park, ph (08) 8670 7822

ACTIVITIES: 4WD touring, national park access

TOURIST INFORMATION: Ph (08) 8670 7822

PINNAROO

244 KM EAST OF ADELAIDE
POPULATION: 650   MAP REF: PAGE 355 N10

Pinnaroo is a small town in far eastern South Australia, situated on the Ouyen Highway almost on the South Australia–Victoria border. The township gains its living from the wheat, barley and oat farms that surround it. Established in the 1860s, it was not until the railway arrived in 1906 that the town took on any real importance.

Pinnaroo's main street

Part of the mallee lands that once dominated the whole region, Pinnaroo is close to a number of large parks that preserve vast tracks of mallee scrub and heath-covered plains. The Scorpion Springs, Mt Shaugh, Mt Rescue and Ngarkat—the largest of the four parks—Conservation Parks all lie to the south and are easily reached on a good dirt road from Pinnaroo. However, a 4WD vehicle would be best to take advantage of this wilderness. To the north-west is the Karte Conservation Park with a number of good walking trails that allow you to experience the park at your leisure.

The town has a big aviary and a large collection of grain varieties. The local museum specialises in farm machinery.

ACCOMMODATION: Pinnaroo Motel, ph (08) 8577 8261; Alcheringa Homestead B&B, ph (08) 8576 6171; Pepper Tree Cottage, ph (08) 8577 8121; Pinnaroo Caravan Park, ph (08) 8577 8224

ACTIVITIES: Bowls, bushwalking, golf, swimming, tennis

TOURIST INFORMATION: Ph (08) 8577 8002

PENOLA

397 KM SOUTH-EAST OF ADELAIDE
POPULATION: 1150   MAP REF: PAGE 352 E10

Penola lays claim to being the gateway to the famous wine-growing area of the Coonawarra, probably Australia's premium red wine growing region. Wynns Coonawarra Estate winery, the Padthaway winery, Haselgrove, and more than a dozen others have wine-tasting, cellar door sales and tours, so it is easy to enjoy the results of this great grape-growing region.

The town itself is historic, being on the crossroads of traffic travelling between Adelaide and Melbourne, including the carts and drays that headed further south in earlier days. It was the first town in the South East, established in 1850, six years after the first settlers arrived. There is a good collection of heritage buildings including John Riddoch's magnificent 1880s mansion, and Yallum Park, said by some to be Australia's best preserved Victorian house. The first vines in the area were planted on this property. The former post office which was built in 1865 houses the National Trust Museum.

Mary MacKillop, the nun who founded the Sisters of St Joseph and started a small school for poor children in Penola, is commemorated by a sign-posted, wide-ranging tourist drive and by a display housed in the school house she had built in 1867.

The town is also famous for a number of poets and writers who found inspiration here, amongst them Adam Lindsay Gordon and Will Ogilvie.

A short distance out of town on the road to Robe is the Penola Conservation Park, while the Greenrise Recreation Ground close to town is a peaceful venue for boating, fishing or a picnic.

In April is the Penola Founders Day, in June the annual festival and in October the Penola Show.

ACCOMMODATION: Coonawarra Motor Lodge, ph (08) 8737 2364; Prince of Wales Hotel/Motel, ph (08) 8737 2402; Cobb & Co Cottages, ph (08) 8737 2526; Penola Caravan Park, ph (08) 8737 2381

ACTIVITIES: Bowls, golf, swimming, wineries

TOURIST INFORMATION: Ph (08) 8737 2855

PETERBOROUGH

248 KM NORTH OF ADELAIDE
POPULATION: 2140   MAP REF: PAGE 355 K6

The town of Peterborough was, and still is, a railway town. A year after it was founded in 1880, the railway arrived from Adelaide, and seven years later the line from Broken Hill to Port Pirie passed through. A short time later the railway to Port Augusta arrived and Peterborough became one of the few places in the world where three railway gauges—broad, standard and narrow—met. Now most of the lines have been standardised but the local, active Steamtown Railway Preservation Society still uses some of the narrow gauge lines in the town and around the area to run steam train excursions.

The town services the surrounding wheat and sheep properties while the only state gold battery is located here. This battery has been crushing ore for 100 years and has yielded more than 400 kg of gold.

The town has many old buildings and a number of museums, mainly centred around the railway and the importance it played for Peterborough and Australia. Being located on the eastern edge of the Flinders Ranges the town acts as a gateway to this area.

A night rodeo is held every February.

ACCOMMODATION: Peterborough Motor Inn, ph (08) 8651 2078; Peterborough Hotel/Motel, ph (08) 8651 2006; Peterborough Caravan Park, ph (08) 8651 2545

ACTIVITIES: Bowls, golf, horse riding, steam train rides, swimming

TOURIST INFORMATION: Ph (08) 8651 2708

PORT AUGUSTA

318 KM NORTH OF ADELAIDE
POPULATION: 14 600   MAP REF: PAGE 355 H5

Situated at the head of Spencer Gulf, Port Augusta is one of South Australia's major towns and is known as 'The Crossroads of the North'. It acts for many travellers as a gateway to Outback South Australia, to Central Australia and the Northern Territory, and to Eyre Peninsula and places further west. It is also a major rail terminal and is literally the powerhouse of the state, with the state's major electricity generating stations located just south of the town on the shores of Spencer Gulf.

Matthew Flinders on the *Investigator* was the first European to see this semi-desert country. In 1839 Edward John Eyre pushed north along the coastal plain and followed the western edge of the Flinders Ranges north on his failed quest to find a way inland.

The town was founded in 1854 as a major port for the pastoral lands and mining endeavours taking place further north at that time. In the 1870s it became an important base for the construction of the Overland Telegraph Line, linking Adelaide and the rest of Australia with Darwin and the world. In 1878 it also became the major railway town for the Ghan line heading to Alice Springs, and then in 1917 it was joined to Perth via the Transcontinental Line. In 1944 the Morgan-Whyalla pipeline was completed, assuring Port Augusta of a steady supply of good water, while 10 years later the first of the state's major power stations was opened. The ships stopped calling at the port in 1973, but by then the large Australian National Railways workshops were located here.

The town is also the operational base for the Royal Flying Doctor Service and the School of the Air. Tours of both bases can be arranged.

Located on the shores of Spencer Gulf, the fishing is an attraction, with the mighty 'reds', big snapper, being the fish to chase. Of course, other fish are around, including whiting, mullet and flathead.

The Arid Lands Botanical Garden is a large area dedicated to Australia's unique arid land plants, while the Wadlata Outback Centre is an award-winning display that will take you from the present day back 15 million years. There are a number of historic buildings in the town, including the Institute of Mechanics building built in 1875. A heritage walk gives a good insight into the history and importance of this town in opening up the Outback of Australia. The town also has several other museums including the Homestead Park

Pioneer Museum which includes a fully furnished 130-year-old homestead as well as hundreds of other historic items and displays.

Being close to the Flinders Ranges, the town acts as a good base from which to explore the immediate area, through Pitchi Richi Pass to Quorn, or south-east via Horrocks Pass to Wilmington and Melrose, or south to Mt Remarkable National Park inland from historic Port Germein.

The Australia Day Breakfast and Swimming Carnival is held in January, the Apex Summer Festival and Surf Boat Carnival in March, the Blues & Country Music Festival in April, the Racing Carnival in June, Golf Week and the Camel Cup in August and the BMX Carnival in October.

ACCOMMODATION: Augusta Westside Motel, ph (08) 8642 2488; Flinders Hotel/Motel, ph (08) 8642 2544; Port Augusta East Motel, ph (08) 8642 2555; Port Augusta Holiday Park, ph (08) 8642 2974

ACTIVITIES: Bowls, bushwalking, fishing, golf, horse riding, national park access, scenic drives, tennis, water sports

TOURIST INFORMATION: Ph (08) 8641 0793

PORT BROUGHTON

285 KM NORTH OF ADELAIDE
POPULATION: 680   MAP REF: PAGE 355 H7

Located on a very well protected arm of Mundoora Bay, Port Broughton, with its safe family beach, has become a very popular seaside holiday resort. The town has a protected anchorage where the fishing fleet, renowned for its catches of prawns, is moored.

The town was named and established in 1871 after the surrounding area had been divided into wheat farms and a port was needed from which to ship the grain . The first jetty was completed in 1874 and today's long T-shaped jetty makes a good fishing platform for young and old. The town's local museum is housed in the old council chambers.

Just to the north of the town is the small village of Fisherman's Bay while to the south are the copper towns of Moonta, Kadina and Wallaroo.

ACCOMMODATION: Sunnyside Hotel/Motel, ph (08) 8635 2100; Port Broughton Hotel, ph (08) 8635 2004; Port Broughton Caravan Park, ph (08) 8635 2188; Broughton Bayside Caravan Park, ph (08) 8635 2140

ACTIVITIES: Boating, bowls, fishing, golf, swimming

TOURIST INFORMATION: Ph (08) 8635 2107

PORT LINCOLN

653 KM WEST OF ADELAIDE
POPULATION: 11 350   MAP REF: PAGE 354 D9

Port Lincoln, one of the largest towns on the Eyre Peninsula, as well as one of the busiest ports, is situated on Boston Bay, which has over three times the expanse of Sydney Harbour.

The bay was named by Matthew Flinders in 1802 and was used by whalers and sealers before a permanent settlement was established. In 1839 it was mooted to be the site for the capital of the new

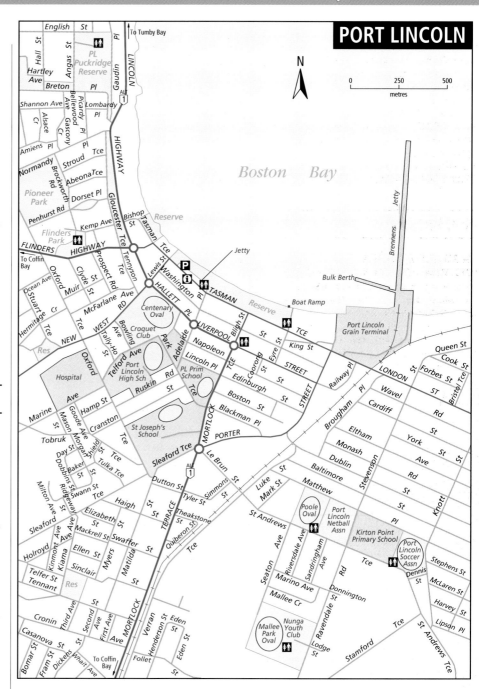

PORT LINCOLN

colony of South Australia, but Colonel William Light was concerned about the lack of fresh water and chose the site of Adelaide instead.

The Lincoln Hotel, built in 1840, still stands on the waterfront. The first jetty was built in 1875 to handle the ever increasing load of wheat and wool being shipped from the port. As the 1900s progressed a web of railway lines brought even more primary products to the harbour and in 1980 Port Lincoln became the second port in Australia to handle bulk grain export.

A cannery was opened in the 1950s, mainly processing tuna, and today the calm waters around Boston Island are dotted with the circular enclosures of great fish traps that house and fatten the tuna. The harbour is also a base for the cray fishing and abalone industries, both of which abound in these waters.

For travellers the city makes a fine base from which to explore the surrounding area and to take in the many delights the region has to offer. The town

itself has a number of attractions including the Mill Cottage Museum operated by the National Trust, the Settler's Cottage Museum, and the nearby Rose-Wal Memorial Shell Museum. The Apex Wheelhouse commemorates the commercial fishing industry while the Alex Stenross Maritime Museum features an extensive collection of sailing ship memorabilia.

A number of local art galleries include the Constantia Designer Craftsmen who have been internationally recognised for their fine work, while the Mayne Gallery and the Arteyrea Gallery display a wide selection of local arts and crafts.

Just out of town is the fully restored Mikkira Station, the oldest sheep station on the Peninsula. The station has picnic and camping areas but visits must be booked in advance.

To the south is a magnificent coastline of white sandy beaches and rugged headlands, much of it protected in the Lincoln National Park, and this park offers excellent bush camping, fishing, diving and surfing. To the west of the town and readily accessible are the town and waters of Coffin Bay.

Whaler's Way is a privately owned scenic drive to the south of the town that takes in some of the most spectacular coastal scenery in Australia. You have to pay to obtain the key to open the gates to the drive. The key, and details on camping on Whaler's Way, are obtainable from the tourist offices in the city.

Offshore there is a host of islands to attract the traveller, including Boston Island and the Spilsby Island group to the north. Dangerous Reef, one of the best known great white shark locations in the world, is offshore and charter boats and cruises include this area on their tours. The reef is also home to one of the largest sea lion colonies in Australia and an underwater viewing platform allows visitors to see these magnificent animals in their own environment.

With such a protected waterway and a host of islands it is no wonder that Port Lincoln is a great yachting destination; there are a number of charter boats for hire from here. The fishing is not only varied but excellent. Offshore there are shark, whiting, snapper and kingfish, while from the jetty and beach there are tommy ruff, whiting and garfish.

There are a number of walking trails in the nearby national park and in the town the Parnkalla Walking Trail winds around the delightful harbour.

Annual events include the Adelaide to Port Lincoln Yacht Race in January, as well as the Tunarama Festival at the end of that month.

ACCOMMODATION: First Landing Motel, ph (08) 8682 2344; Blue Seas Motel, ph (08) 8682 3022; Port Lincoln Hotel, ph (08) 8682 1277; Harbourview Apartments, ph (08) 8682 4251; Kirton Point Caravan Park, ph (08) 8682 2537
ACTIVITIES: Bowls, bushwalking, fishing, golf, horse riding, national park access, scenic drives, water sports
TOURIST INFORMATION: Ph (08) 8683 3544

PORT MacDONNELL

490 KM SOUTH-EAST OF ADELAIDE
POPULATION: 680   MAP REF: PAGE 352 G9
The most southerly port in South Australia, much has changed since this was the second busiest port in the state, loading wool and wheat for Melbourne and Adelaide. Today, it is a quiet seaside port but still with the biggest cray fishing fleet in the state. Reminders of the old days are the historic 1862 customs house, the 1882 lighthouse and local courthouse. The Maritime Museum gives a good indication of how dangerous this coast once was to the sailing ships that transported the goods which made the port busy.

The cottage of poet Adam Lindsay Gordon is located in the nearby Dingley Dell Conservation Park, while the Piccaninnie Ponds and Ewen Ponds Conservation Parks are a short distance away along the coast. To the north is Mt Schank with its walking trails, while to the east, just across the border in Victoria, is Lower Glenelg National Park and the tranquil waters of the Glenelg River.

It is the coast around Port MacDonnell that is the main attraction for visitors, and surfers and anglers will love its wild, windswept nature.

Summer activities include the Bayside Festival held in January.
ACCOMMODATION: Seaview Motel & Holiday Units, ph (08) 8738 2243; Port MacDonnell Harbour View Caravan Park, ph (08) 8738 2085
ACTIVITIES: Bowls, bushwalking, fishing, golf, horse riding, national park access, water sports
TOURIST INFORMATION: Ph (08) 8738 2207

PORT PIRIE

228 KM NORTH OF ADELAIDE
POPULATION: 15 120 MAP REF: PAGE 355 H6
Port Pirie, located just off Highway One, on the eastern side of Spencer Gulf and just a short distance from the ragged bluffs of the southern Flinders

Ruins of a homestead in Mt Remarkable National Park, near Port Pirie

Ranges, is one of South Australia's major cities and ports. It is also the site of the world's largest lead-smelting and refining plant, as well as a site for a huge bulk silo complex which is used for the storing of grain before export.

The town got its start in 1845, when local pastoralists requested a ship be sent to transport sheep and the schooner, *John Pirie*, navigated the mangrove-lined creek that was soon to see a jetty and harbour established. The town was surveyed in 1871 and in 1877 the railway line to Broken Hill was opened, bringing with it the ore that was to see the town grow into the state's first provincial city.

At one stage three railway gauges converged at Port Pirie and ran down the main street, but while these have been standardised, the town remains an important railway town which services the Indian–Pacific and Ghan railways.

A number of historic buildings exist within the town, including the railway station, Sampson's Cottage which dates from the 1890s, and the majestic mansion of Carn Brae, built in 1901.

Being close to the Flinders Ranges, the town is a good base from which to explore the area around the Mt Remarkable National Park, or the Telowie Gorge Conservation Park and Nelshaby Reserve. All three of these parks have a number of walking trails, the most spectacular being the one into Alligator Gorge which is in the national park and accessible from the small township of Wilmington. The walking trail in the Nelshaby Reserve has wheelchair access.

Just up the coast is the small hamlet of Port Germein, once an important wheat shipping port but now nothing more than a beachside holiday destination with a long wooden jetty, ideal for fishing.

There is good crabbing along this coastline, while the fishing from the jetty or shore is good for whiting, salmon and garfish. Offshore there is snapper.

A number of festivals and events are held each year. The Easter Speedway and Motocross in March/April; the Blessing of the Fleet in late August/early September; the Country Music Festival and a round of the National Offroad Championships in October. The Athletic and Cycling Carnival is a big event in November.

ACCOMMODATION: John Pirie Motor Inn, ph (08) 8632 4200; Flinders Ranges Motor Inn, ph (08) 8632 3555; Sampson's Cottages, ph (08) 8632 2272; Port Pirie Caravan Park, ph (08) 8632 4275
ACTIVITIES: Bowls, bushwalking, crabbing, fishing, golf, horse riding, national park access, scenic drives, water sports
TOURIST INFORMATION: Ph (08) 8633 0439

PORT VICTORIA

181 KM WEST OF ADELAIDE
POPULATION: 315   MAP REF: PAGE 354 G9
This tranquil, seaside town nestles on the eastern coastline of Spencer Gulf, on Yorke Peninsula, and overlooks a protected bay sheltered by the bulk of Wardang Island, a few kilometres offshore. A busy commercial port for grain in the early 1900s, it is known as 'the last of the windjammer ports'. It was from here that the final, great grain race to Great Britain began in June 1939. History buffs can learn more about the area's past by visiting the Maritime Museum, while divers can explore a number of wrecks around Wardang Island which are part of the Maritime Heritage Underwater Trail.

The area abounds with water-based activities and anglers are likely to get catches of snapper, flathead, snook and whiting.
ACCOMMODATION: Ventnor Hotel, ph (08) 8853 7036; Guides SA Accommodation, ph (08) 8853 7285; Gulf View Holiday Units, ph (08) 8853 7302; Gulfhaven Caravan Park, ph (08) 8834 2012
ACTIVITIES: Bushwalking, fishing, golf, water sports
TOURIST INFORMATION: Ph (08) 8834 2098

The harbour at Port Victoria

PORT WAKEFIELD

93 KM NORTH-WEST OF ADELAIDE
POPULATION: 515   MAP REF: PAGE 355 J8

This historic township, at the northern end of Gulf St Vincent, is at the crossroads of the main route to Yorke Peninsula or the road further north to Port Augusta, so its main thoroughfare is cluttered with fuel outlets and roadhouses.

Port Wakefield was the first government town north of Adelaide and traces its beginnings back to 1838 when it was known as Port Henry; it was established to ship copper ore from Burra. The link between Burra and Port Wakefield was of such importance that a horse-drawn tramway was constructed between the two towns and used until the coming of the railway in 1857. Later the port was used to export wheat and wool from the surrounding districts.

Today, the town is tranquil, with many of its original buildings still standing and well preserved, and a walk around town and along the jetty is most interesting. The jetty is also irresistible to anglers and the surrounding shallow waters and mangrove habitats make for excellent fishing, with catches of whiting, snapper, mullet and Australian salmon.

ACCOMMODATION: Port Wakefield Motel, ph (08) 8867 1271; Port Wakefield Caravan Park, ph (08) 8867 1151
ACTIVITIES: Boating, bowls, croquet, fishing
TOURIST INFORMATION: Ph (08) 8867 1008

QUORN

344 KM NORTH OF ADELAIDE
POPULATION: 1390   MAP REF: PAGE 355 H4

Nestled in the south-central Flinders Ranges, Quorn, proclaimed in 1878, was founded on farming. It became an important railway centre when the Great Northern Railway pushed north from Port Augusta to Quorn in 1879, eventually to reach Alice Springs some 50 years later. With the closure of the railway in 1956, the town struggled to survive, but today tourism has put vitality back into this wonderful little country town with its unique character.

A ride on the historic narrow gauge Pichi Richi Railway, one of the oldest intact railway systems in

The Pichi Richi Railway near Quorn

the world, should not be missed while nature lovers will enjoy a tour into the nearby spectacular Dutchmans Stern Conservation Park.

A stroll around the town will take you past many fine old buildings and there are also numerous art and craft galleries.

The Quorn Show and a country music event under the stars are held in September.

ACCOMMODATION: The Mill Motel, ph (08) 8648 6016; Transcontinental Hotel, ph (08) 8648 6076; Tulloch House B&B, ph (08) 8648 6477; Quorn Caravan Park, ph (08) 8648 6206
ACTIVITIES: Bushwalking, horse riding, national park access, scenic drives
TOURIST INFORMATION: Ph (08) 8648 6419

RENMARK

251 KM EAST OF ADELAIDE
POPULATION: 4260   MAP REF: PAGE 355 N8

Renmark, initially named Bookmark, is located on the Sturt Highway, alongside the Murray River and around 145 km west of Mildura and 256 km from Adelaide. It is the oldest and largest town in the Riverland and is the centre for South Australia's largest irrigation scheme along the Murray River, covering an area of nearly 7000 hectares. In fact, it was here that two Canadian brothers, George and William Chaffey, established Australia's first irrigation settlement. Their original home in the district, Olivewood Historical Homestead, is open to the public and gives a fine introduction to the region and the development of the scheme.

The lifegiving flow of water allows the growing of grapes, citrus, stone fruit, vegetables and flowers, while wheat and wool are produced from the region as well. Like many towns along the river Renmark's

businesses were built with a strong sense of community involvement. Australia's first co-operative winery was opened here in 1916, six years after the first winery and distillery in the Riverland.

Renmark's rich history is portrayed to visitors in many forms, from its magnificent and well preserved old buildings and monuments, to the romantic age of paddle-steamers. These haven't quite disappeared from the river, with the PS *Industry* now a floating museum. The *Murray Princess*, the largest stern paddle-steamer in the southern hemisphere, plies the waterways taking passengers on cruises. For others, a houseboat is an idyllic way to cruise up and down the Murray and there are many to choose from which are based in Renmark.

Other water sports including swimming, sailing and waterskiing are popular activities along the river. Fishing for golden perch and Murray cod is also on the agenda and it is a great way to spend time.

Visitors will find plenty to keep them occupied in and around Renmark. One of Australia's largest reptile parks is located here with more than 450 reptiles, birds, and animals, while Ruston's Rose Garden is the largest in the southern hemisphere.

Across the river from town is Paringa, which has excellent picnic and recreational facilities centred around the river and water activities.

There are many conservation and games parks surrounding Renmark. Just to the north of the city is the Bulyong section of the Murray River National Park, with its natural flood plains, and the Ral Ral Creek canoe trail. In fact, canoeing is a pleasant way to enjoy much of the river and you can hire a canoe at a number of places in town.

A short distance south of the town is the Lyrup Flats section of the same national park with its pleasant camping and walking trails. Birdwatchers will find plenty of bird life to keep them occupied along the river and amongst its wetlands and

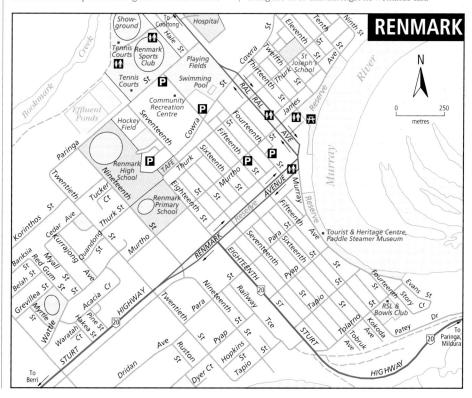

An unusual fountain in Renmark

tributaries. When the Calperum Wetlands have water, they become one of the major centres for breeding waterbirds in southern Australia.

Orange Week, the local festival, is held in August/September of each year.

ACCOMMODATION: Citrus Valley Motel, ph (08) 8586 6717; Willows and Waterbirds Cottage, ph (08) 8586 6566; En-V-Us Houseboat, ph (08) 8586 4623; Renmark Riverfront Caravan Park, ph (08) 8586 6315

ACTIVITIES: Bowling, bushwalking, golf, national park access, water sports, wineries

TOURIST INFORMATION: Ph (08) 8586 6704

ROBE

350 KM SOUTH-EAST OF ADELAIDE
POPULATION: 730   MAP REF: PAGE 352 E8
Settled along the shores of Guichen Bay and just 130 km north of Mount Gambier, Robe is a charming seaside village with the character of yesteryear.

While Aborigines were the earliest known inhabitants, pioneer settlers followed in the footsteps of the early explorers and by 1846 Robe had become South Australia's third most important port, exporting wool and horses. From the mid-1800s it saw a rabble of gold seekers pass through on their way to the Victorian goldfields, including 16 500 Chinese. The port is somewhat quieter today, with professional crayfish and shark fishing fleets operating out of the sheltered anchorage.

Robe has many fine old buildings including such impressive examples as the Customs House, Robe House and the Caledonian Inn.

Water-based activities, especially fishing, are popular pastimes. Dropping a line at the breakwater or jetty could hook you garfish, mullet and trevally, while the bay yields delicious King George whiting.

The nearby Little Dip Conservation Park protects a rugged, windswept, imposing limestone coastline and sand dune range just south of Robe. A drive through the park along its 4WD tracks takes you through wind-swept dunal areas and along treacherous beaches offering a driving challenge. Behind the dunes are a number of lakes, and with

such a varied range of habitats and vegetation, it is no wonder that this area is home to a wide variety of flora and fauna, with bird life being especially prolific.

ACCOMMODATION: Melaleuca Motel, ph (08) 8768 2599; Criterion Cottage, ph (08) 8768 2137; Grey Masks B&B, ph (08) 8768 2203; Robe Long Beach Caravan Park, ph (08) 8768 2237

ACTIVITIES: Fishing, 4WD touring, national park access, water sports

TOURIST INFORMATION: Ph (08) 8768 2465

ROXBY DOWNS

570 KM NORTH-WEST OF ADELAIDE
POPULATION: 3030   MAP REF: PAGE 354 F1
This modern mining town is reached by bitumen road on the way to Andamooka and is 85 km from Pimba, off the Stuart Highway. It can also be accessed via the Oodnadatta Track, which is to the north.

The community was established in 1987 to service the employees and their families of the Olympic Dam mining operations. With the availability of water, thanks to the Great Artesian Basin, the town is developing into a verdant, treed oasis in an otherwise parched landscape.

Surface tours of the mine site, 15 km north of the town, give you an idea how copper, uranium oxide, gold and silver are extracted and refined.

ACCOMMODATION: Roxby Downs Motor Inn, ph (08) 8671 0311; Roxby Downs Caravan Park, ph (08) 8671 1000

ACTIVITIES: Bowling, golf, mine tours, swimming (pool), squash, tennis

TOURIST INFORMATION: Ph (08) 8671 0788

STRATHALBYN

61 KM SOUTH-EAST OF ADELAIDE
POPULATION: 2630   MAP REF: PAGE 355 K10
Established beside the peaceful Angas River on the Fleurieu Peninsula in 1839 by Scottish immigrants, Strathalbyn is one of the most attractive towns in South Australia.

Copper was one of its first enterprises and was mined and smelted in and around the district from 1848 to 1914. Other operations included flour milling, brewing, a foundry and a gasworks. Today, however, its primary industries revolve around the production of butter, cheese and cereal crops.

Some of the area's earliest history is depicted within the Anthony's Hill Historic Reserve, where a small sandstone rock shelter was used as an art gallery by the Aborigines to paint unusual human figures in red ochre on the walls and ceiling.

Strathalbyn has been declared a heritage town, with over 30 vintage heritage-listed buildings. There is even a roving, resident town crier. There are also plenty of delicious dining concerns, and handicraft enthusiasts will find a wide range of antique, craft and gift shops to browse through.

A pleasant day can be spent visiting the nearby wine-growing districts of Langhorne Creek, or take a drive to Milang and see the largest freshwater lake in Australia, Lake Alexandrina.

For nature lovers, a worthwhile trip is a visit to the Cox Scrub Conservation Park and Kuipto Forest, west of the town. Here you can enjoy a drive or go for a walk through the natural bushland.

Annual events include the Collectors Hobbies and Antiques Fair in August and the Rotary Duck Race in November.

ACCOMMODATION: Victoria on the Park Hotel/ Motel, ph (08) 8530 2202; Watervilla House B&B, ph (08) 8536 4099; The Railway Cottages, ph 015 601692; Strathalbyn Caravan Park, ph (08) 8536 3681

ACTIVITIES: Bowls, bushwalking, golf, historic walks, scenic drives, wineries

TOURIST INFORMATION: Ph (08) 8536 3212

STREAKY BAY

722 KM WEST OF ADELAIDE
POPULATION: 960   MAP REF: PAGE 354 B5
The coastal township of Streaky Bay is located in the southern corner of the bay of the same name, on the Flinders Highway and 112 km south of Ceduna.

Matthew Flinders sailed into the bay in 1802, naming it after the streaks of colour in the water created by the seaweed. The town itself was not proclaimed until 1865 and its early history can be gleaned by a visit to the National Trust Museum.

The harvesting of wheat played an important role in Streaky Bay's early development, and continues today, along with the production of barley, wool and fat lambs. Fishing has also been a major part of the town's economy, along with tourism, and granite mining, the latest commercial venture.

The spectacularly beautiful coastline around Streaky Bay is dotted with bays and coves, many protected from the relentless motion of the Southern Ocean, and the fishing is excellent. You can also fish close to town where you stand a chance of catching snook, snapper, garfish, squid and tommy ruff.

Of special interest and well worth the drive are a couple of unique attractions within 60 km of Streaky Bay. At Point Labat you can observe the only sea lion colony on the Australian mainland, while the impressive rocky outcrops of pink granite boulders known as 'Murphy's Haystacks', 1500-million-year-old granite iselbergs, are a phenomenal sight.

Regular events and shows include the Agricultural Show in September, the Snapper Contest in November/December and Camel Cup Races in November.

The jetty at Streaky Bay

ACCOMMODATION: Streaky Bay Community
Hotel/Motel, ph (08) 8626 1008; Headland House
B&B, ph (08) 8626 1315; Koolangatta Cottage,
ph (08) 8626 1174; Streaky Bay Foreshore Tourist
Park, ph (08) 8626 1666
ACTIVITIES: Bowls, fishing, golf, scenic drives, water
sports
TOURIST INFORMATION: Ph (08) 8626 1126

SWAN REACH

138 KM NORTH-EAST OF ADELAIDE
POPULATION: 240   MAP REF: PAGE 355 L9
Delightful Swan Reach has long been a popular
holiday destination, as the holiday shacks that line
the river front attest. Located 26 km south of
Blanchetown on the Sturt Highway, the small
township, settled by Europeans during the late 1830s,
is perched high on the clifftop on the eastern bank of
the Murray River. Spectacular cliff faces tower above
the waterline while a line of vivid green, hugging the
cliff base along the water's edge, provides a delightful
setting for the houseboats that pull up along here.
The vehicle ferry that crosses the river here provides
the only access from one side of the river to the other.

Well known for its excellent water sports, there
are launching facilities on the river and anglers can
pursue golden perch and cod, but are more likely to
catch carp. The surrounding area teems with bird life,
while the flora and fauna are well safeguarded within
the Swan Reach and Ridley Conservation Parks.
ACCOMMODATION: Swan Reach Hotel, ph
(08) 8570 2003; Punyelroo Caravan Park,
ph (08) 8570 2021
ACTIVITIES: Fishing, river cruising, water sports
TOURIST INFORMATION: Ph (08) 8586 6704

TAILEM BEND

106 KM EAST OF ADELAIDE
POPULATION: 1600   MAP REF: PAGE 352 A7
Located near the junction of the Duke, Ouyen and
Princes Highways, 26 km south of Murray Bridge,
Tailem Bend is close to the last great bend of the
Murray River. Proclaimed in 1887, the town is laid
out atop the lofty east bank of the river and is a
major road and railway junction, with railway
workshops and marshalling yards. It also provides
many necessary services for the surrounding mixed
farming communities.

The town's interesting colonial history has been
re-created in the pioneer village at Old Tailem Town
a few kilometres north, where you can saunter
around the many exhibits and buildings that have
captured the atmosphere of bygone days.

A ferry operates from Tailem Bend, taking
vehicles across the river to disembark at Jervois.
From there it is just an 11 km drive to Wellington at
the junction of the river and Lake Alexandrina.
ACCOMMODATION: River Bend Motel, ph
(08) 8572 3633; Rivers Edge Caravan Park,
ph (08) 8572 3307
ACTIVITIES: Bowls, fishing, golf, water sports
TOURIST INFORMATION: Ph (08) 8572 3537

TANUNDA

91 KM NORTH-EAST OF ADELAIDE
POPULATION: 3100   MAP REF: PAGE 355 K9
The settlement of Tanunda was established along the
banks of the North Para River in 1843, and was
originally called Langmeil, later renamed Tanunda.

A focal point in Barossa Central, Tanunda is
surrounded by wineries. The area was first settled by
German Lutherans who established farms and
villages in the valley, while English settlers took up
the surrounding grazing land. Although well known
for its vineyards, the region around Tanunda also
produces wool and wheat.

One of the oldest towns in the Barossa, the first
vines were planted by Samuel Hoffman in the mid-
1800s and the town was basically a German enclave,
with all the stores, school and church German. The
Tabor Lutheran Church was built in 1849, and is one
of four in the town today, its towering spire seeming
to overlook the town like a guardian angel.

To sample the rich heritage and culture of this
delightful town, a stroll around the streets is a must.
A feeling of wandering round a German village is
probably most noticeable whilst in the vicinity of the
old market square, Goat Square—which is classified
by the National Trust—as the square is surrounded by
century-old cottages. The historical museum is
housed in the old Post Office, built in 1866.

To discover all that Tanunda and its surrounds has
to offer, visit the Barossa Wine and Visitor Centre in
Murray Street. Apart from information on the many
attractions and services available, the wine centre
will teach you about the art of making good wine and
the history of this wine-growing region. There are
wine-tasting tours of the many vineyards in the area,
such as Langmeil Winery which is set amongst the old
Tanunda Langmeil settlement..

Other attractions of special interest include the
Keg Factory, makers of traditional handcrafted pot
kegs, and Norm's Collies Performing Sheep Dogs, a
working team of sheep dogs.

There is a hectic calendar of events for the
Barossa region and of special interest in Tanunda are
the Jazz and German Night in February, and the
Melodienacht in May.
ACCOMMODATION: Barossa Weintal Hotel,
ph (08) 8563 2303; Barossa Motor Lodge, ph
(08) 8563 2988; Paranook B&B, ph (08) 8563 0208;
Tanunda Caravan Park, ph (08) 8563 2784
ACTIVITIES: Bowls, golf, swimming, wineries
TOURIST INFORMATION: Ph (08) 8563 0600

TEROWIE

239 KM NORTH OF ADELAIDE
POPULATION: 230   MAP REF: PAGE 355 K6
The small settlement of Terowie is passed on the
Barrier Highway, 63 km north of Burra, in the rural
area of the mid-north.

Its life began in the 1800s as an important railway
town, and it was not long before the outlying stations
to the north-east became reliant on it for supplies.
With the re-direction of the railway line in the 1980s,
the town's significance and its economy diminished.
However, Terowie has been declared an historic
township and a walk along the main street is like
stepping back in time. The verandah shop fronts have
retained their original character and architecture,
while the small museum, hardware store and
blacksmith shop exhibit artefacts from a bygone era.
Other attractions include the Terowie Antique Linen
and Lace and Collectables.
ACCOMMODATION: Terowie Hotel, ph (08) 8659 1012;
Terowie Roadhouse & Motel, ph (08) 8659 1082
ACTIVITIES: Historic town walk
TOURIST INFORMATION: Ph (08) 8894 2100

TUMBY BAY

608 KM WEST OF ADELAIDE
POPULATION: 1150   MAP REF: PAGE 354 E9
The small scenic coastal town of Tumby Bay lies on
the western shore of Spencer Gulf on Eyre Peninsula,
49 km north of Port Lincoln. The blue water of its
sheltered bay and white sandy beaches are
backdropped by a grassy foreshore, lined with
majestic Norfolk Island pines.

Named by Matthew Flinders in 1802, the town was
settled in the 1840s. It became an important port for
vessels visiting the communities which farmed sheep
and grew wheat on the offshore islands of the Sir
Joseph Banks Group. Two jetties were built in the
1870s for the handling of supplies and produce.

Fishing is a favourite activity in and around the
bay and there is good fishing around the jetties.
ACCOMMODATION: Tumby Bay Hotel,
ph (08) 8688 2005; Tumby Bay Motel, ph (08) 8688 2311;
Tumby Bay Caravan Park, ph (08) 8688 2208
ACTIVITIES: Bowls, fishing, scenic drives, water
sports
TOURIST INFORMATION: Ph (08) 8688 2584

VICTOR HARBOR

81 KM SOUTH OF ADELAIDE
POPULATION: 5950   MAP REF: PAGE 352 B5
Situated along the wide, sandy shore of Encounter
Bay, this picturesque and often breathtakingly
beautiful part of South Australia has long been a very
popular holiday destination.

Named after HMS *Victor* by its commander in
1837, Victor Harbor's beginnings in the early 1830s
were a somewhat gruesome affair, with hardy
pioneers harvesting whales and seals from the
surrounding waters. By 1837 a whaling station had
been established on Granite Island, which lies just
offshore, to process the catches. The island is now
connected to the mainland by a causeway.

The first permanent settlers did not arrive until
1839 and Victor Harbor became an important trading
port, initially because of the whaling station, and later
as a shipping port for the wool and primary industries
developing along the Murray River. By World War I
the port had lost its importance; today, it is a popular
holiday and retirement town.

The town boasts a number of historic homes and
buildings including the railway station, St Augustine's

A tram ride is a popular way of going from Victor Harbor to Granite Island

The Cockle Train, a superbly restored steam train, runs between Victor and Goolwa, recalling the days when steam was king and Victor and Goolwa were a part of the rich Murray River trade.

Nature lovers will enjoy the wildlife of the nearby Urimbirra Wildlife Park or the native plants and trees in the Nangawooka Flora Park. Further afield a number of other parks, including the Newland Head Conservation Park, offer a wider, natural experience.

Victor Harbor is one of the state's most popular fishing destinations, and keen anglers can cast a line from the jetties, rocks, around the bay, or in the nearby streams, all with more than a good chance of catching salmon and mulloway, while garfish, whiting, and Australian salmon are common around the bay.

The town attracts artists and photographers. Their works are exhibited at the Rotary Art Show held in January. Other annual events are the Apex Easter Craft Fair and the start of the whale season in June—when the coast is crammed with people watching the whales. The Folk Festival is in October.

Church (1869), the Warringa Guesthouse built early this century, and the 1890s mansion, Adare.

Most visitors to Victor cross the causeway to Granite Island. For those not up to the walk, you can take a ride on the famous horse-drawn trams. Alternatively, a chairlift goes to the high point in the centre of the island for a bird's-eye view of the surrounding bay, other islands and the nearby mainland. The Penguin Interpretive Centre, on Granite Island, is worth a visit. There are fairy penguin walks.

ACCOMMODATION: Hotel Victor Harbor, ph (08) 8552 1288; City Motor Inn, ph (08) 8552 2455; Whalers Inn Resort, ph (08) 8552 4400; Victor Harbor Council Caravan Park, ph (08) 8552 1111
ACTIVITIES: Bowls, bushwalking, fishing, golf, scenic drives, water sports
TOURIST INFORMATION: Ph (08) 8552 5738

WAIKERIE

170 KM NORTH-EAST OF ADELAIDE
POPULATION: 1750   MAP REF: PAGE 355 M8

The biggest citrus-growing centre in Australia, Waikerie is the largest town in the Riverland.

Founded as a communal settlement in 1894, created to relieve unemployment in Adelaide at the time, the new settlers set to with their government-supplied tools and began carving out an oasis in the dry mallee scrub. With irrigation the area boomed and today the town is home to one of the largest citrus-packing sheds in the southern hemisphere, as well as the popular 'Crusta' fruit juice company.

It is considered by many who know to be one of the best gliding areas in Australia, and each year sees many making the pilgrimage to this pleasant riverside town to take to the clear blue skies.

A large riverside park caters for many sporting activities and from the nearby Rotary clifftop lookout there is a fine view of the surrounding area and some of Waikerie's one million or so orange trees.

On the main highway is The Orange Tree where you can buy a wide selection of local produce and where you'll find the Heritage Room which depicts life as it was during the early years of this settlement.

Like most of the riverside towns there is a great selection of bird life along the river and in the nearby lagoons and backwaters, and, of course, fishing.

The Waikerie International Food Fair takes place in March.
ACCOMMODATION: Kirriemuir Motel, ph (08) 8541 2488; Waikerie Hotel/Motel, ph (08) 8541 2999; Jo's B&B, ph (08) 8541 3491; Green & Gold Houseboats, ph (08) 8541 2001; Waikerie District Council Caravan Park, ph (08) 8541 2651
ACTIVITIES: Bowls, fishing, gliding, golf, horse riding, scenic drives, water sports
TOURIST INFORMATION: Ph (08) 8541 2332

WALLAROO

153 KM NORTH-WEST OF ADELAIDE
POPULATION: 2470   MAP REF: PAGE 355 H8

The third town of the Copper Triangle—the other two being Kadina and Moonta—Wallaroo is now one of the major ports in the state, exporting barley and wheat while shipping in phosphate rock.

Surveyed in 1860, the town was established a year later when rich discoveries of copper were found at Kadina and Moonta. The first jetty was constructed that year to ship the ore from the Wallaroo Mine, located near Kadina. A smelter was built and that led to the port becoming one of the busiest in the state.

The town is a pleasant reminder of those past days with many of the buildings listed by the National

VICTOR HARBOR

Map of Victor Harbor showing streets including Greenhill Road, Richardson Rd, Folkstone Tce, Galpin Ave, Tudor Ave, Oxford Ave, Harvey Ave, James Tce, Seaview Ave, Hillview St, Cornhill St, Canterbury Rd, Keithalan Ave, Thorne St, Crozier Rd, Holder Rd, Edbell Rd, Adey Rd, Baudin Rd, Swain St, River Rd, Almond Ave, Kullaroo Rd, Leeworthy Oval, Lindsay St, Park Rd, Sturt St, Kingsford St, Hinkler St, Burke St, George St, Main Rd, Newland St, Esplanade, Inman St, Bay Rd, Kent Harbor Dr, Malin Ave, Norfolk, Warland Rd, Nurton Ave, Pine Ave, Marlborough Ave, Fernbank Rd, Dorset Ave, Renown St, Hay St, Connell St, Wheaton Ct, Brand Ave, Grantley St, Breckan Ave, Cornhill Rd, Seymour St, Carlisle Rd, O'Leary St, William St, Lawson St, Hill Ct, Hill St, Graham St, Forrest St, Churchill Rd, Acraman St, Torrens Lane, Coral St, Stuart St, Railway Tce, Albert St, Wills St, Victoria St, King St, Island St, Memorial Dr, Soldiers, Riverview Rd, High St, Broadway Ave, Bridge, Ocean St, McKinlay St, Flinders St, Eyre Tce, Hindmarsh Rd, Reserve Tce, Pearson Dr, Anderson Gr, Wattle Dr, Cherington Rd, Bluffview Rd, Honeyman Gr, Adare Ave, Laxton St, Dinan Rd, Wattle, Ives Gr, The Parkway, Sowden Ave, Gum Ave, Day Rd, Heath St. Labelled: To Hindmarsh Valley, To Port Elliot & Goolwa, 'Cockle Train', Victor Harbor to Goolwa, Reserve, Henderson Rd, Dene Ave, Ozone St, To Yankalilla, Victor Harbor Holiday Park, Victor Harbor Council Caravan Park, To Waitpinga, Trotting Track, Kent Reserve, Kent View Tce, Railway Station, Warland Reserve, Pedestrian and Horse-drawn Tram Causeway, Granite Island. Scale 0–250 metres. North arrow.

Trust. The 'Big Stack' of the smelter still stands as testimony to the craftsmanship of the Welsh builders who built it, while many others owe their heritage to Cornish immigrants who made up the bulk of the early population. The whitewashed limestone buildings of the Heritage and Nautical Museum, dating back to 1865 and once the post office, now house a fine display of the region's early history.

While the offshore fishing is good, for those without a boat the grain jetty provides a perfect platform from which to fish for snapper, yellowtail kingfish, mulloway, snook, garfish, and others.

Two low-lying islands just offshore Wallaroo, the Bird Islands, are protected in a conservation park as a breeding area for a good variety of seabirds.

The major annual festivity that takes place in Wallaroo and surrounding areas is the Kernewek Lowender, an 11 day event celebrating the Cornish history of the Copper Triangle.
ACCOMMODATION: Sonbern Lodge Motel, ph (08) 8823 2291; Anglers Inn Hotel/Motel, ph (08) 8823 2545; Alicias Cottage, ph (08) 8823 2682; Office Beach Holiday Cabins & Caravan Park, ph (08) 8823 2722
ACTIVITIES: Bowls, fishing, golf, historic walks, horse riding, water sports
TOURIST INFORMATION: Ph (08) 8823 2023

WHYALLA

391 KM NORTH-WEST OF ADELAIDE
POPULATION: 25 260   MAP REF: PAGE 354 G6
Located nearly 80 km south of Port Augusta on the Lincoln Highway, in the north of the Spencer Gulf and on the east side of Eyre Peninsula, Whyalla is the largest provincial town in South Australia. It owes its existence to the nearby great iron ore deposits of Iron Knob, Iron Monarch and Iron Baron, with Iron Knob being the first iron ore deposit to be exploited in Australia at the end of the nineteenth century.

Whyalla, called Hummock Hill when Flinders first sailed the Gulf in 1802, became a port for the ore when a tramway was built from the mine. In 1941 the town got a blast furnace and soon became a shipbuilding town and in 1965 received a big shot in the arm when BHP opened a steelworks there. The shipyard has closed and the steel mill running down, but the town is still an industrial giant with oil and gas production and a shipping terminal nearby at Port Bonython, while tourism and aquaculture are playing a more important part in recent times.

The town has a number of attractions including the Maritime Museum, home of the biggest land-locked ship in Australia, the former warship *Whyalla*; the largest model railway in Australia; the Whyalla Wildlife and Reptile Sanctuary with its large collection of native reptiles, birds and animals; and the Ada Ryan Gardens, one of the first parks established in the city and still one of the most popular. The National Trust museum is housed in the Mount Laura Homestead, a former sheep station, and consists of a number of buildings relocated and refurbished here as well as displays of stationary engines and many old photographs. For something different you can always try the Steelworks Tour, the only one of its kind in Australia.

There are other attractions further afield including the historic Point Lowly Lighthouse, Port Bonython and a scenic coastal drive along the Gulf.

The Tanderra Craft Village, located next to the Tourist Centre has a variety of craft markets and speciality shops, a pottery workshop and gallery.

Whyalla is considered to be the best fishing spot for snapper in Australia, with the Australian Amateur Snapper Fishing Championship held in January. While the fishing is great offshore for salmon and yellowtail kingfish, closer in there are whiting, snook and garfish; along the foreshore you might just catch blue swimmer crabs.

Whyalla is very active when it comes to festivals and events, with some of the major highlights being the Sportsfishing Convention held in March or April, the local show in August and Proclamation Day Concert in December, while harness racing is a favourite spectacle throughout the year.
ACCOMMODATION: Alexandra Motor Inn, ph (08) 8645 9488; Sundowner Hotel/Motel, ph (08) 8645 7688; Derhams Heritage Cottage B&B, ph (08) 8645 5444; Red Gum Cottage, ph 0419 213853; West Whyalla Foreshore Caravan Park, ph (08) 8645 7474
ACTIVITIES: Bowls, fishing, golf, horseracing, water sports
TOURIST INFORMATION: Ph (08) 8645 7900

WILMINGTON

295 KM NORTH OF ADELAIDE
POPULATION: 250   MAP REF: PAGE 355 H5
Located 23 km north of Melrose and 51 km west of Orroroo in the mid-north of the state, Wilmington lies tucked in beside the Flinders Ranges with the vast flat Willochra Plain stretching away to the east and north.

Formerly known as Beautiful Valley, the name was changed when the town was officially founded in 1876. The town, located near Horrocks Pass, with its access to the coast and Port Augusta, became an important service centre for the surrounding farms. The railway arrived in 1915. Today the town still services the surrounding district and the tourists who travel through here experiencing the Flinders.

Located at the northern end of Mt Remarkable National Park, Wilmington gives easy access to

Alligator Gorge, probably the most spectacular gorge in the Flinders and certainly the most accessible. Walking trails start from near the gorge car park.

In town there is a small museum and a number of historic buildings. Further afield there are the Spring Creek Copper Mine ruins, which are worth a look, and the historic settlements of Hammond and Bruce. Hancock's Lookout, accessed from the road through Horrocks Pass, gives spectacular views of Spencer Gulf and Port Augusta.

The major events for the town are the show in September and the Night Rodeo in January.
ACCOMMODATION: Wilmington Hotel, ph (08) 8667 5154; My-Ora Cottage, ph (08) 8641 0552; Beautiful Valley Caravan Park, ph (08) 8667 5197; Nobes Tourist Park, ph (08) 8667 5002
ACTIVITIES: Bowls, golf, bushwalking, national park access, scenic drives
TOURIST INFORMATION: Ph 1800 633 060

WILPENA

456 KM NORTH OF ADELAIDE
POPULATION: NOMINAL   MAP REF: PAGE 355 J3
Arguably South Australia's most famous tourist attraction, Wilpena Pound is located within the confines of the Flinders Ranges National Park. At the only access to the pound is the small hamlet of Wilpena, little more than a caravan park, motel complex and the national park headquarters. It is a delightful place. Recently upgraded, the motel and camping area have lost none of their charm.

You can enjoy a host of walks and some of the best scenic drives in the state while based at Wilpena. For the more active there are some long, hard walks in and around the pound, or further through the ranges along the Heysen Trail. Rock climbers can test their mettle on the walls of the pound near Arkaroo Rock.

If you live in South Australia, make a trip to Wilpena; if you are passing through, stop for a day or two.
ACCOMMODATION: Wilpena Motel, ph (08) 8648 0004; Arkaba Station Cottage, ph (08) 8648 4195; Rawnsley Park Holiday Units & Tourist Park, ph (08) 8648 0030; Wilpena Camping & Caravan Park, ph (08) 8648 0004
ACTIVITIES: Bushwalking, national park access, scenic drives, scenic flights
TOURIST INFORMATION: Ph (08) 8648 0004

The stunning ramparts of Wilpena Pound

Camels resting near Coongie Lakes, Innamincka Regional Reserve

BOOL LAGOON GAME RESERVE

Consisting of a series of shallow lakes, Bool Lagoon is the largest waterbird breeding wetland in south-eastern Australia. A high natural embankment traps the water, forming the swamp, and the lagoon is also used as a way of controlling floods along Mosquito Creek. Large concentrations of brolgas can be seen around the lagoon, while the dense tea-tree stands around the main lagoon are an important rookery for up to 10 000 ibis. The reserve is 370 km south-east of Adelaide, and is easily accessible from Naracoorte.

COFFIN BAY NATIONAL PARK

The Coffin Bay Peninsula is a large wilderness area, almost surrounded by water, reaching out into the Great Australian Bight. Rich in flora, the peninsula is covered in dense coastal heathland and mallee. The park also has a good variety of birds, and the beaches are breeding grounds for many seabirds. Western grey kangaroos are easily seen. The area is popular with bushwalkers, divers, campers and birdwatchers; and it also has excellent fishing. A 4WD is needed to get around the majority of the park. The park is 720 km west of Adelaide and 50 km west of Port Lincoln.

COORONG NATIONAL PARK

This beautiful part of South Australia protects ancient shifting dune formations, tranquil waterways and marshlands, with the pounding surf of the Southern Ocean crashing against 60 km of coastline from the Murray River mouth south. Having reached the end of its journey, the Murray River seldom gains access to the sea and its sluggish and silted waters fan out into Lake Alexandrina and Lake Albert and down into the shallow Coorong, creating perfect wetland environments and breeding grounds for bird life. Activities to enjoy are beach-combing, fishing, photography, birdwatching, bushwalking, canoeing and boating. The park is 210 km south-east of Adelaide.

DUTCHMANS STERN CONSERVATION PARK

Dutchmans Stern Conservation Park, 7 km north of Quorn, is renowned not only for its dramatic scenery, but also for its bird life and orchids. The car park and picnic area is 3 km from the main road and from this point access to the park is on foot, or by joining one of the 4WD tour operators who are allowed to run trips into the area. To appreciate the wild grandeur of this park you need to venture into its interior. The view from the top of the range over the flat plains to the distant gulf and back towards the bluffs and escarpments is astonishing, especially in the soft evening light. The rare Quorn wattle is found in this park, and the animal life is varied, with euros and the occasional yellow-footed rock wallaby.

FLINDERS CHASE NATIONAL PARK

This park occupies the entire western end of Kangaroo Island. The area is a major sanctuary for a wide variety of native animals, there being no dingoes or introduced predators on the island. The scenery here is striking and spectacular. High rocky cliffs drop into a wild and rugged ocean. The constant battering of the Southern Ocean's swell and nature's elements have carved into the limestone and ironstone formations creating the most sensational geological configurations, such as those at Remarkable Rocks. Here groups of graphic orange coloured granite boulders seem to balance precariously on a smooth granite dome. The park is also rich in flora and in spring the heathland flowers are a riot of colour, competing with native orchids and other flowering shrubs. At Rocky River camping area the wildlife is very much 'at hand', with wallabies, emus and koalas easily seen. Scenic spots not to be missed are the Admirals Arch, a natural arch below the Cape du Couedic lighthouse, Weirs Cove, where supplies were loaded for the lighthouse, and Cape Borda and its historic lighthouse settlement. The park is 210 km south-west of Adelaide and 100 km west of Kingscote on Kangaroo Island.

GAMMON RANGES NATIONAL PARK

This wild and formidable country forms the far north-east of the Flinders Ranges. The park takes in not only the rough and craggy heart of the ranges, but also a section of the surrounding plain leading to the salt expanse of Lake Frome. Geologically the ranges consist mainly of heavily dissected granites and allied rocks, and after millions of years of battling nature's elements are now worn down to awesome chasms, gorges, sheer bluffs and overhangs, with creeks that sometimes plunge downwards as waterfalls. The magnificent Sturt's desert pea and the delicate Sturt's desert rose are found here. Animal life is plentiful, if a little elusive, and includes euros, red kangaroos and the rare yellow-footed rock wallaby. Birdwatching is especially rewarding around the park's water points. The view from Grindells Hut, overlooking the Illinawortinna Pound and the Gammons, is breathtaking. The park is 750 km north of Adelaide and 110 km east of Leigh Creek.

INNAMINCKA REGIONAL RESERVE

This reserve covers a unique and historic part of Australia, with a contrasting but impressive landscape of sand dunes, claypans and gibber desert and the oasis of the mighty Cooper Creek. The reserve is rich in flora and fauna and one of the most significant habitats in the reserve is the Coongie Lakes system, in the north-west. This large wetland area, made up of a myriad lakes, is an important retreat for birds. Unfortunately visitors are only allowed access to Coongie Lake itself, which is the southernmost lake of the system. Cooper Creek and its waterholes are well stocked with fish, and there is a good chance of catching a feed of yellowbelly.

INNES NATIONAL PARK

The first glimpse of the coast as you head towards the tip of Yorke Peninsula, once seen, is never forgotten. The striking coastline with its rocky cliffs and extrusive headlands is broken up by beautiful sandy beaches and secluded coves, with a number of offshore islands in a shimmering sea. The park was originally established to protect the rare western whipbird and its habitat of dense heath and mallee scrub, which is the most prevalent flora. Gravel roads circle the park, leading to idyllic sheltered bays and scenic lookouts; the area is a favourite destination for nature lovers, birdwatchers, campers, anglers, divers and surfers. Pondalowie is a popular camping spot. The park is 300 km west of Adelaide.

LAKE EYRE NATIONAL PARK

Lake Eyre National Park protects a major part of the heat-hazed, shimmering salt flats of Lake Eyre, the largest salt lake in Australia. This park encircles all of Lake Eyre North and the adjoining Tirari Desert. A drier, more inhospitable landscape you could hardly imagine. Lake Eyre is both a dry salt lake and a playa lake (one that occasionally floods), and is split in two, with the north and south lakes joined by the 13 km long Goyder Channel. When the great rivers of the channel country far to the north flood, they set course for Lake Eyre, and occasionally the life-giving waters arrive at the lower reaches of Lake Eyre and may even span out to fill both lakes, creating an inland sea nearly one-sixth the size of Australia. This then was the inland sea that Charles Sturt and his party set out to discover back in 1844—a sea of salt. At times of flooding, the lakes' waters, fresh for a short time, teem with fish from the rivers, and the lake is a utopia for a variety of waterbirds, such as pelicans, gulls and ducks. The park is 720 km from Adelaide.

LINCOLN NATIONAL PARK

The park is situated on the Eyre Peninsula, 13 km south of Port Lincoln. It is the wild coastline and the fishing and diving that attract most people to this park. A rough walking trail leads down the cliffs on the western side of Wanna Cove giving access to a short section of rocks that in calm weather is a good spot to cast a line for sweep, salmon and groper. There are also some popular surf fishing spots. There are many pleasant walks in the park, along the beach or the clifftops.

LITTLE DIP CONSERVATION PARK

This park is part of a group of parks which stretches from the South Australian/Victorian border north towards Kingston, and includes the Canunda National Park. The parks preserve a coastal wilderness of complex dune systems and low trees further inland. The region also encompasses numerous inland fresh and saltwater lagoons and lakes which provide a sanctuary for large numbers of waders and waterbirds. Vehicle access tracks are limited; however there are designated tracks that follow the coastline and meander through the sand dunes and these are definitely 4WD only. Fishing enthusiasts will find plenty of places for some good beach fishing, but swimming is not recommended as all the beaches along this coastline are dangerous, with strong tides, rips and undertows. While the wildlife is not abundant, occasionally you will see a seal resting on the beach. The bird life is prolific and there have been 200 species of birds recorded, with many migratory waders. It is 410 km from Adelaide.

MOUNT REMARKABLE NATIONAL PARK

Mount Remarkable National Park, in the southern Flinders Ranges, is divided into two sections: the Alligator Gorge section in the west and the Mount Remarkable section in the east. A circle of ridges, which encompass a basin of valleys and creeks, form the Alligator Gorge section of the park. The gorge and the creek it feeds are the main attractions of the park. With a varied habitat and a reasonably reliable rainfall for this part of the state, the park is rich in wildflowers and birds and is home to many animals, including euros and yellow-footed rock wallabies. From Melrose, in the eastern section of the park, a

number of walking trails take people to the top of Mt Remarkable. Alligator Creek, in the west, has cut a deep path through the red quartzite along the creek bed, creating a number of impressive cliff-lined gorges. The park is 270 km north of Adelaide and 50 km north of Port Pirie.

MURRAY RIVER NATIONAL PARK

This park, about 240 km east of Adelaide, is made up of three distinct sections of floodplain spread along the Murray River from above Renmark to just north of Loxton. The Katarapko section covers river flats and is the largest, while the Bulyong Island and Lyrup Flats sections are smaller. Fishing, cruising on a houseboat, canoeing, camping and bird-watching are all popular pastimes in the park.

NARACOORTE CAVES CONSERVATION PARK

This small park, 370 km south-east of Adelaide, is on the World Heritage List because of the discovery of rich fossil beds in Victoria Cave. First found in 1969, this bed of fossils continues to arouse interest as the remains of marsupials and other animals, some of which are extinct, are unearthed. Provision has been made for visitors to view the dig. Within the park a number of other caves are open to tourists. Between November and February thousands of common bentwing bats inhabit the caves, which are ideal for breeding and raising young. They leave the caves at dusk to search for food, making a spectacular sight.

NGARKAT GROUP OF CONSERVATION PARKS

The park takes in the Ngarkat, Scorpion Springs, Mount Rescue and Mount Shaugh Conservation Parks and is considered a significant wilderness area, linking with Victoria's Big Desert region. Its landscape of disordered, undulating sandhills is covered in a mantle of mallee eucalypts, while heath blankets the plains between the dunes. In a few places where surface soaks provide water, larger trees take advantage of the moisture. The wildflowers in spring attract not only birds and bees, but also apiarists. The parks are also home to some unusual animals such as the ningau, silky mouse and pygmy mouse, along with the more common echidnas and western grey kangaroos. This region

can get extremely hot during the summer months. The park is 300 km south-east of Adelaide.

NULLARBOR NATIONAL PARK

The Nullarbor Plain, on first appearance, looks a desolate and featureless countryside of saltbush and bluebush with the occasional patch of mallee scrub, with little to offer the visitor in the way of scenic attractions or interest. The natural wonders of the park are hidden. The area has an underground labyrinth of cave systems and caverns formed by water dissolving and eroding through the limestone layers. In places, where the surface has collapsed to form sinkholes, these caverns are exposed and provide shelter for birds and mammals. The other outstanding feature of the park is the dramatic coastline of the Great Australian Bight. Here the plains end suddenly in confrontation with the great Southern Ocean. The spectacle is that of precipitous towering cliffs, with the indigo of the ocean contrasting with the mottled brown and greens of the rocky plain high above. The coastal waters at the head of the Great Australian Bight are frequented by southern right whales in winter and spring. The park is 330 km west of Ceduna.

PICCANINNIE PONDS CONSERVATION PARK

This small reserve is on a section of coast in the far south-east of South Australia, about 430 km south-east of Adelaide, just over the border from Victoria. Behind the beach a large reed swamp is surrounded by a dense band of tea-tree and sedge. At the heart of the swamp lies the jewel—Piccaninnie Ponds. It is one of the world's most famous cave dives, the crystal-clear water being a huge attraction. The Chasm, with its white walls and curtains of algae, is superb, while The Cathedral at the far end is a large cavern accessible to scuba divers. The best time to visit the area is in spring and summer.

SEAL BAY CONSERVATION PARK

Seal Bay, on Kangaroo Island, 190 km south of Adelaide, must be one of the best places in the world to see sea lions and fur seals at close quarters. The wide white beach of Seal Bay plays host to dozens of these animals which are surprisingly tolerant of humans. Often, if you are lucky, a young seal will approach you as you sit on the beach—a great experience!

Access to other beaches and bays along the coast from Seal Bay is totally prohibited, and no swimming, boating or fishing are allowed in the adjoining aquatic reserve. Camping is not allowed.

SIMPSON DESERT REGIONAL RESERVE

Abutting the eastern boundary of the Witjira National Park, the Simpson Desert Regional Reserve is joined by the Conservation Park and in Queensland the Simpson Desert National Park, creating a forbidding yet extraordinarily beautiful wilderness area of Australia. Endless sand dunes of varying earthy red colours crest in enormous waves and run unimpaired the full length of the park from south-east to north-west. The landscape is scattered with dry playa lakes and claypans. Hardy plants such as spinifex and sandhill cane grass cover the sandy slopes and valleys, along with good growths of acacia. In more sheltered areas shrubs such as wattles, grevilleas and emu bush endure. On the rare occasions when it rains, the Simpson's salt lakes fill with water, the clay flats become wet and boggy and a major hazard to cross by vehicle, and the desert blooms. Though you may not see them, the desert is home to a large number of animals such as the hopping mouse, dunnart and rabbit-eared bandicoot. The area also supports an abundant and varied bird life, even more so after rain when wildflowers and rabbits are abundant. The park is located 1200 km from Adelaide.

WITJIRA NATIONAL PARK

The Witjira National Park, forming the western edge of the Simpson Desert, protects a vast desert landscape of sand, stony tablelands, gibber plains, mound springs and transitory river systems that include the Finke River floodplains. The jewel in the crown of this park is Dalhousie Springs, the most active artesian spring in Australia. The mounds and springs are an important habitat for invertebrates, fish and birds. The animal life is not easy to see, most being nocturnal. The Dalhousie ruins lie some 9 km south of Dalhousie Springs and are located near another spring complex that is dominated by date palms. Travel within the park is definitely by 4WD only. The Witjira National Park is 120 km north of Oodnadatta and 1200 km from Adelaide.

SOUTH AUSTRALIA PARKS & RESERVES

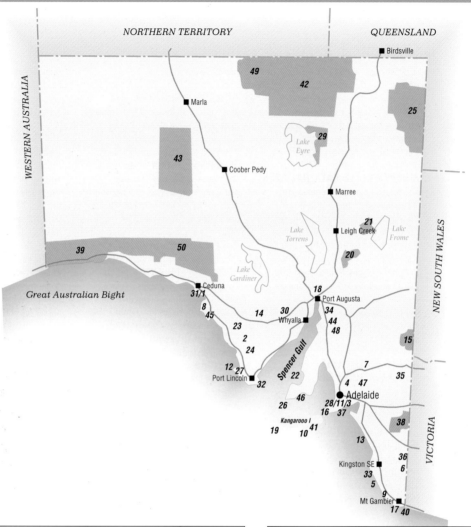

Popular Parks	Camping	Caravans	Wheel Chairs	4WD Access	Picnic Area	Toilets	Walking Trks	Kiosk	Information
1 Acraman Creek CP	■			■	■		■		
2 Bascombe Well CP	■			■	■				
3 Belair NP	■	■			■	■	■	■	■
4 Black Hill NP					■	■	■		■
5 Beachport CP	■			■		■			
6 Bool Lagoon Game Reserve	■	■			■	■	■		■
7 Brookfield CP				■		■	■		
8 Calpatana Waterhole CP	■			■	■				
9 Canunda NP	■			■	■	■	■		
10 Cape Gantheaume CP	■			■	■	■			
11 Cleland NP			■		■	■	■	■	■
12 Coffin Bay NP	■			■	■	■	■		■
13 Coorong NP	■			■	■	■	■		
14 Corobinnie Hill CP	■			■	■				
15 Danggali CP	■			■			■		
16 Deep Creek CP	■	■		■	■	■	■		■
17 Dingley Dell					■	■			
18 Dutchmans Stern CP							■		
19 Flinders Chase NP	■			■	■	■	■	■	■
20 Flinders Ranges NP	■	■		■	■	■	■	■	■
21 Gammon Ranges NP	■			■		■	■		
22 Goose Island CP	■			■					
23 Hambidge CP	■			■	■				
24 Hincks CP	■			■	■				
25 Innamincka RR	■	■		■	■	■	■	■	■

Popular Parks	Camping	Caravans	Wheel Chairs	4WD Access	Picnic Area	Toilets	Walking Trks	Kiosk	Information
26 Innes NP	■	■		■	■	■	■	■	■
27 Kellidie Bay CP	■			■	■		■		
28 Kyeema CP	■				■	■	■		
29 Lake Eyre NP	■			■					
30 Lake Giles CP	■			■					
31 Laura Bay	■	■		■			■		
32 Lincoln NP	■			■	■	■	■		
33 Little Dip CP	■			■		■			
34 Mt Remarkable NP	■				■	■	■		■
35 Murray River NP	■			■		■			
36 Naracoorte Cave CP	■	■			■	■	■	■	■
37 Newland Head CP	■		■		■	■	■		
38 Ngarkat Group of CP	■			■		■	■		
39 Nullarbor NP & RR	■	■		■					
40 Piccaninnie Ponds CP	■					■	■		
41 Seal Bay CP	■					■	■		■
42 Simpson Desert NP/CP/RR	■			■			■		
43 Tallaringa CP	■			■					
44 Telowie Gorge CP	■						■		
45 Venus Bay CP	■					■			
46 Warrenben CP	■			■			■		
47 Warrens Gorge Reserve	■			■	■	■			
48 Wirrabara Forest Reserve	■			■	■	■	■		
49 Witjira NP	■			■					■
50 Yumbarra CP/Pureba CP & Yellabinna RR	■			■			■		

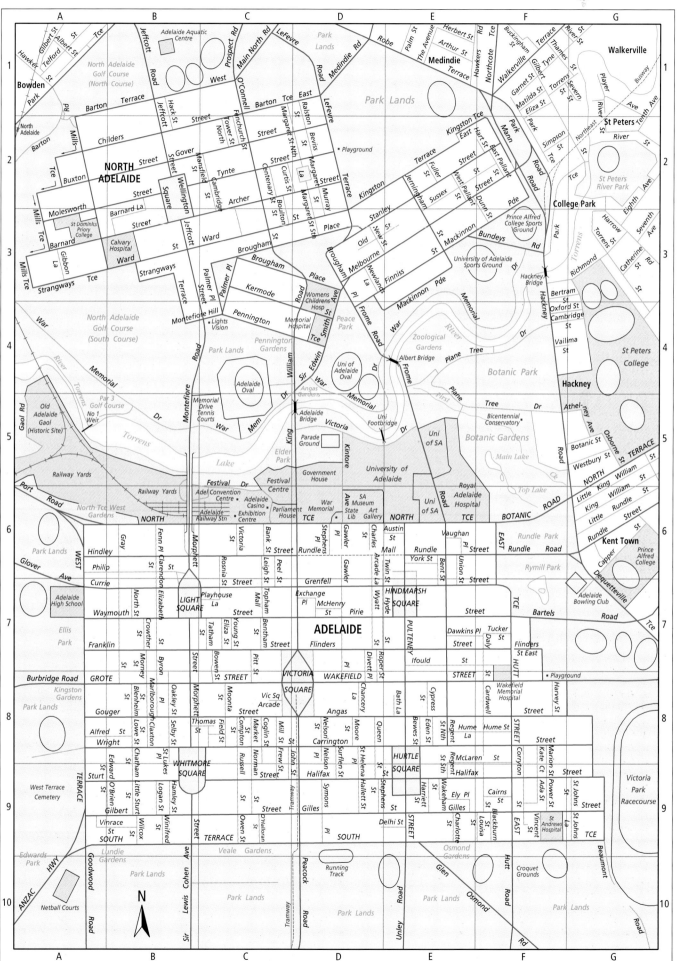

Adelaide City Centre map

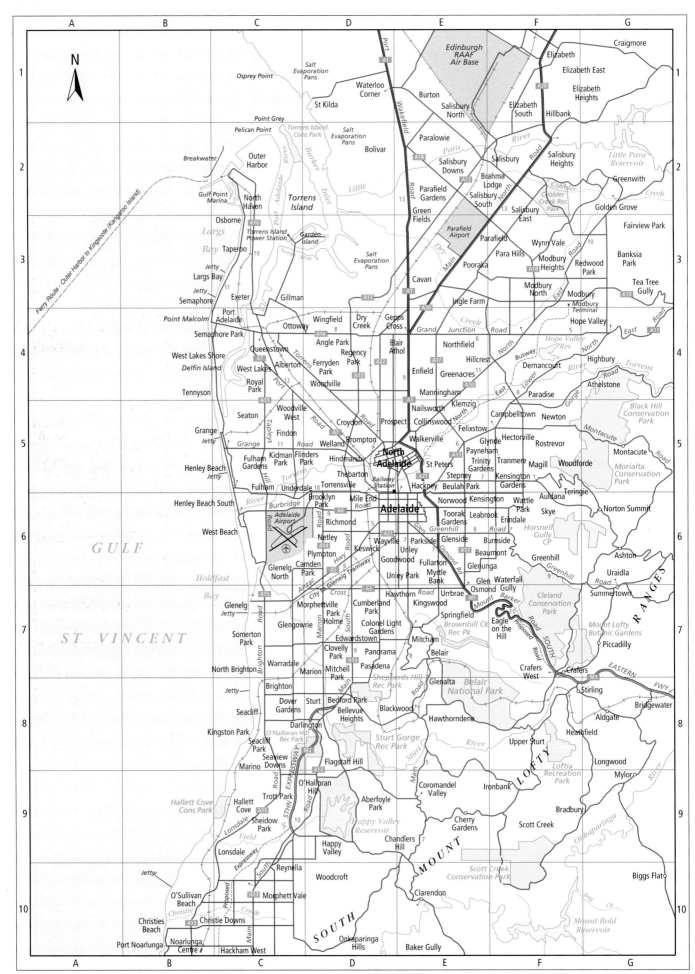

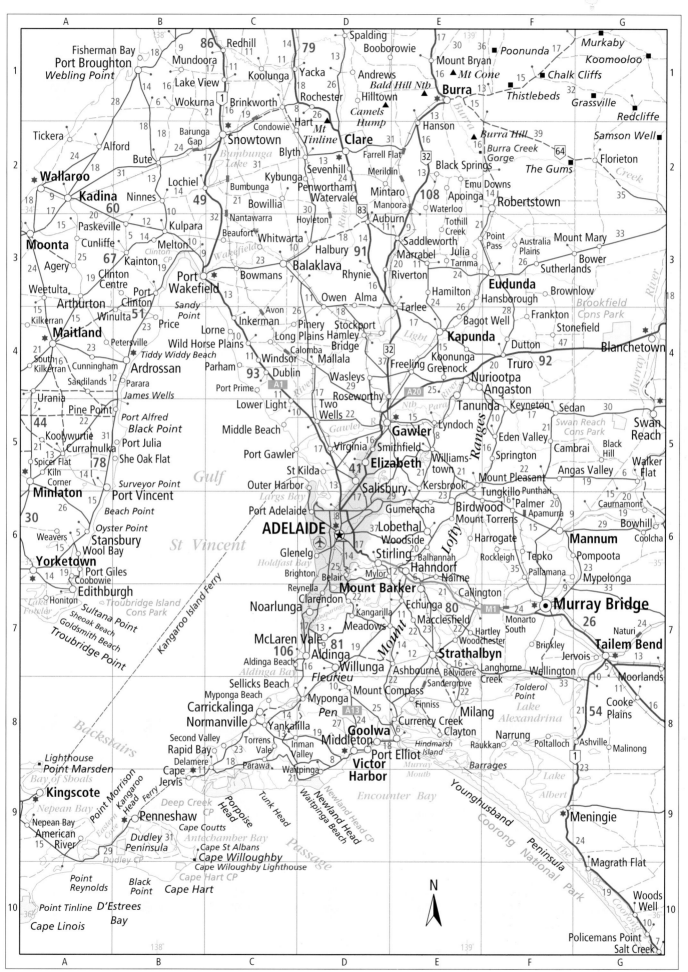

kilometres

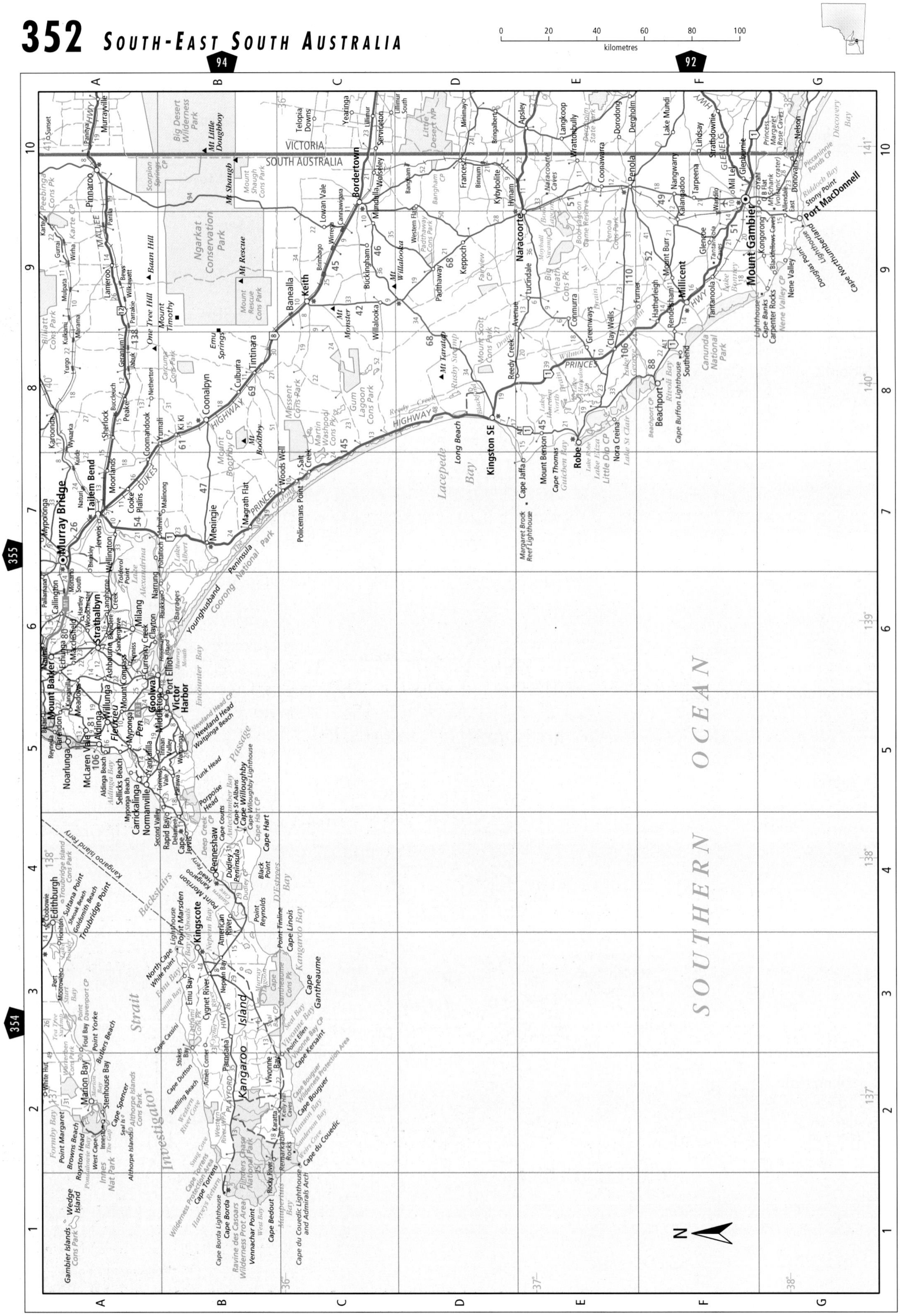

kilometres

VICTORIA
SOUTH AUSTRALIA

SOUTHERN OCEAN

Investigator Strait

Kangaroo Island

Big Desert Wilderness Park
Ngarkat Conservation Park

Murray Bridge
Tailem Bend
Bordertown
Keith
Naracoorte
Penola
Mount Gambier
Port MacDonnell
Millicent
Kingston SE
Robe
Goolwa
Victor Harbor
Mount Barker
McLaren Vale
Kingscote
Edithburgh
Marion Bay

Encounter Bay
Lacepede Bay
Backstairs Passage
Spencer

Coorong National Park
Canunda National Park

© Random House Australia Pty Ltd

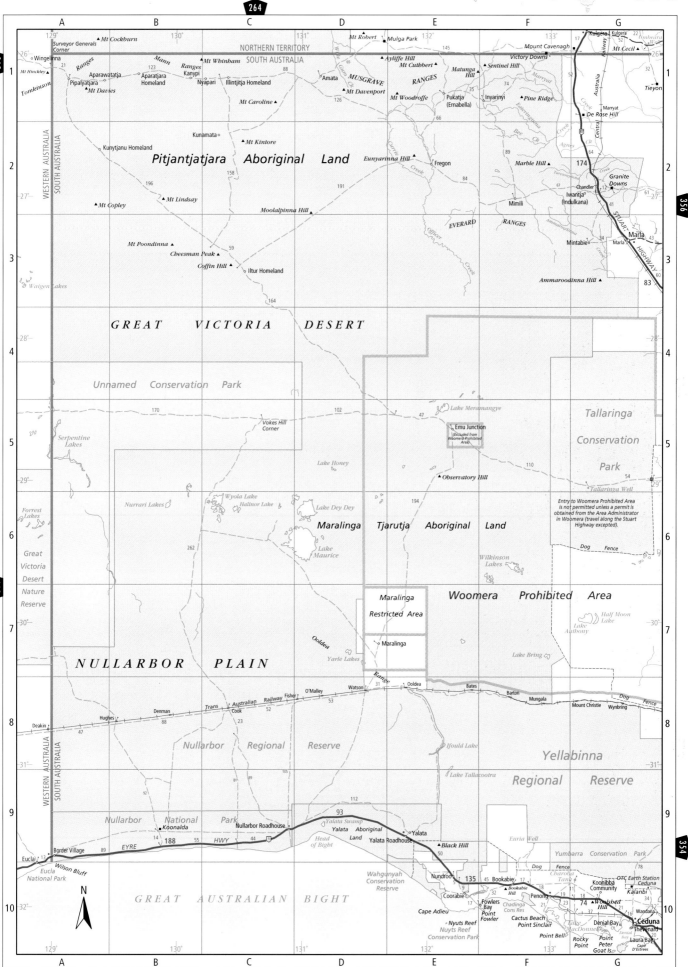

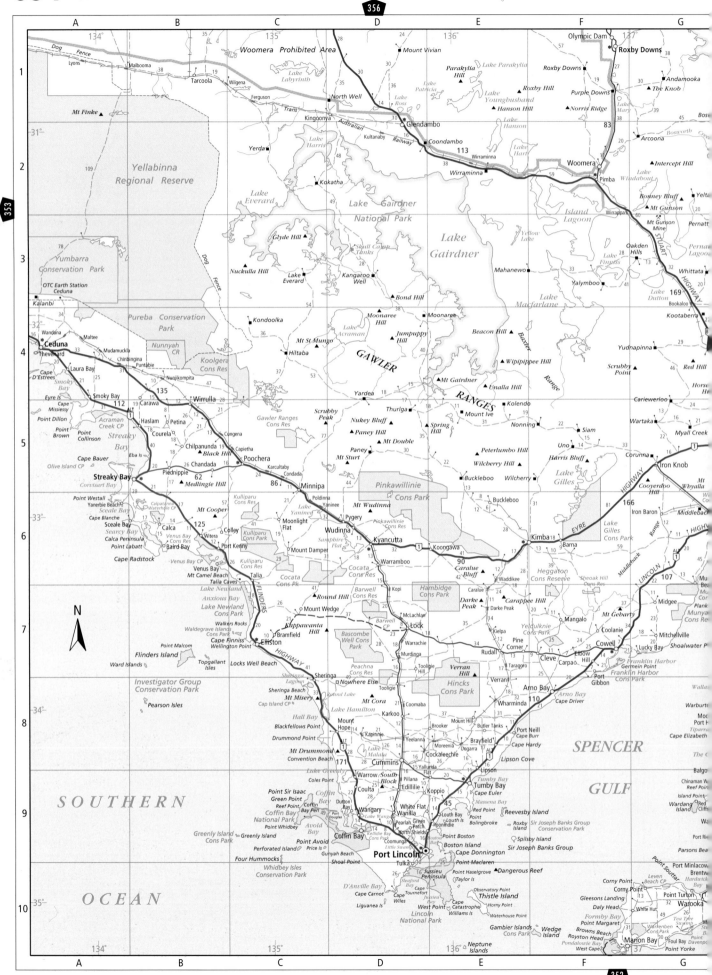

kilometres
0 20 40 60 80

H J K L M N P

Major places and labels:

Leigh Creek, Copley, Mount Serle, Mt McKinlay Gorge, Italowie Gorge, Balcanoona, Wertaloona, Nepabunna, Angepena, Maynards Well, North Moolooloo, Beltana Mine, Beltana Roadhouse, Beltana, Nuccaleena Mine (ruin), Moolooloo

NORTH FLINDERS RANGES, Nantawarrina Aboriginal Land, Warraweena, Nantawarrina, Teatree Outstation, Mulga View, Chambers Gorge, Mt Chambers

Lake Frome, Lake Frome Regional Reserve, Lake Elder, Green Lake, Lake Matjanapa, Pine Dam, Quinyambie, Sanpah, Joulnie, Avenel

Lake Torrens, Lake Torrens National Park, Ediacara Cons Reserve, Nilpena, Parachilna, Parachilna Gorge, Motpena, Commodore, Angorichina Village, Glass Gorge, Blinman, Brachina Gorge, Mt Emily, Artimore, Wirrealpa, Frome Downs, Lake Namba, Lake Kuturu, Lake Karpi, Lake Moko, Lake Tarkarooloo, McDougalls Well, Mount Woowoolahra, Kantappa

Aroona, Wilkawillina Gorge, Oraparinna, Mt Caernarvon, Appealinna Station, Martins Well, Erudina Woolshed, Erudina, St Marys Peak, Edeowie, Bunyeroo Gorge, Edeowie Gorge, Stokes Hill Lookout, Upalinna, Wilpena, Wilpena Pound, Rawnsley Bluff, Rawnsley Park, Sacred Canyon, Mernmerna, Cotabena, Wilangee, Mt Ellie, Mulyungarie, Yarramba, Mooleulooloo

Wallerberdina, Lake Torrens, Mt Neville, Mt Josephine, Arkaba, Warcowie, Mt Plantagenet, Willippa, Curnamona, Strathearn, Nancatee Hill, Kalkaroo, Killawarra, Glenorchy, Kalabity, Wiperaminga Hill, Boolcoomata, Silverton, Broken Hill

Hawker, SOUTH FLINDERS RANGES, Warrakimbo, Yadlamalka, Middle Gorge, Buckaringa Gorge, Wilkatana, Wilson, Kanyaka, Holowilena South, Yednalue, Cradock, Gordon, Mt Victor, Mount Victor, Koonamore, Plumbago, Bimbowrie, Bulloo Creek, Cockburn, Burta, Netley

Depot Creek, Warren Gorge, Willochra, Belton, Witchitie, Spotswood Hill, Melton, Waukaringa, Florina, Outalpa, Weekeroo, Olary, Waiwera, Eringa, Mingary, Pine Creek, Corella, Ballara, Mutooroo

Quorn, Bruce, Mt Brown, Carrieton, Oladdie Plain, Minburra Plain, Johnburgh, Minburra, Moockra, Hammond, Eurelia, Meadow Downs, Chinamans Hat, One Tree Hill, McCoys Well, Paratoo, Yunta, Mannahill, Wadnaminga, Devonborough Downs

Port Augusta, Stirling North, Woolshed Flat, Horrocks Pass, Wilmington, Willowie, Morchard, Orroroo, Black Rock, Dawson, Mergenia, Paratoo, Panaramitee, Tiverton, Benda, Oulnina Park, Netley Gap, Diorah Downs, Kimberley, South Ita

Melrose, Booleroo Centre, Pekina, Yatina, Murray Town, Tarcowie, Oodla Wirra, Nackara, Manunda, Oak Park, Lilydale, Sturt Vale, Oakbank, Quondong Vale, Oakvale, Loch Lilly, Nanya

Port Germein, Wirrabara, Mannanarie, Appila, Yongala, Belalie North, Terowie, Franklyn, Pine Creek, Loch Winnoch, Faraway Hill, Morgan Vale, Ennisvale

Port Pirie, Napperby, Nelshaby, Laura, Caltowie, Jamestown, Whyte-Yarcowie, Mallett, Ketchowla, Collinsville, Bendigo, Braemar, Pine Valley, Danggali Conservation Park, Loch Lilly

Gladstone, Belalie East, Georgetown, Washpool, Hallett, Mt Bryan, Hog Back, Caroona, Glenora, Murkaby, Woolgangi, Fords Lagoon, Lords Well, Canopus, Hyperna, Belmore

Crystal Brook, Huddleston, Campbell Hill, The Bluff, Hallett Hill, Mt Scrub, Koomooloo, Old Koomooloo, Canegrass, Parcoola

Merriton, Redhill, Narridy, Spalding, Booborowie, Andrews, Bald Hill Nth, Mount Bryan, Chalk Cliffs, Koomooloo, Chowilla Regional Reserve, Lake Victoria

Mundoora, Koolunga, Yacka, Hilltown, Burra, Thistlebeds, Grassville, Redcliffe, Balah, Bunyung

Wokurna, Brinkworth, Rochester, Hanson, Camels Hump, Burra Hill, Samson Well, Florieton, Lake Victoria

Snowtown, Blyth, Clare, Condowie, Mt Tinline, Burra Creek Gorge, The Gums, Chowilla Game Reserve, Nelwood, Border Cliffs, Cal Lal, Rufus River

Bute, Lochiel, Kybunga, Sevenhill, Merildin, Black Springs, Emu Downs, Pooginook Cons Park, Calperum, Cooltong, Chowilla, Lindsay Point

Kadina, Ninnes, Bumbunga, Penwortham, Watervale, Waterloo, Apoinga, Robertstown, Morgan, Cadell, Renmark, Paringa

Kulpara, Nantawarra, Bowillia, Hoyleton, Auburn, Mintaro, Manoora, Tothill, Mount Mary, Qualco, Ramco, Barmera, Berri, Lyrup

Paskeville, Cunliffe, Melton, Kainton, Whitwarta, Halbury, Marrabel, Saddleworth, Julia, Tarnma, Sutherlands, Murbko, Waikerie, Kingston-on-Murray, Moorook, Yinkanie, Winki, Glossop

Port Wakefield, Bowmans, Balaklava, Rhynie, Riverton, Hamilton, Springton, Brownlow, Blanchetown, Notts Well, Maggea, Wunkar, Loxton, Gerard, Taldra

Inkerman, Lorne, Avon, Owen, Alma, Tarlee, Hansborough, Frankton, STURT HIGHWAY, Maggea, Cobera, Taplan, Paruna, Meribah

Price, Sandy Point, Long Plains, Hamley Bridge, Stockport, Wasleys, Kapunda, Dutton, Eudunda, Stonefield, Sedan, Swan Reach, Bakara, Mantung, Mercunda, Galga, Wanbi, Alawoona

Wild Horse Plains, Pinery, Windsor, Mallala, Freeling, Greenock, Koonunga, Nuriootpa, Angaston, Truro, Keyneton, Swan Reach, Cambrai, Nildottie, Walker Flat, Copeville, Mindarie, Peebinga, Billiatt Conservation Park

Two Wells, Roseworthy, Lower Light, Lyndoch, Tanunda, Eden Valley, Angas Valley, Purnong, Sandalwood, Wynarka, Karte CP

Middle Beach, Gawler, Smithfield, Williamstown, Mount Pleasant, Springton, Black Hill, Halidon, Bowhill, Borrika, Peebinga Cons Pk

Port Gawler, Virginia, Elizabeth, Salisbury, Kersbrook, Birdwood, Palmer, Apamurra, Caurnamont, Purnong, Coolcha, Perponda, Murray-Sunset National Park

Adelaide, Port Adelaide, Glenelg, Brighton, Stirling, Lobethal, Woodside, Hahndorf, Mount Torrens, Tungkillo, Punthari, Kalyan, Wanbi, Pinnaroo, Murrayville

Noarlunga, Mylor, Balhannah, Nairne, Kanmantoo, Callington, Tepko, Pompoota, Mypolonga, Mannum, Bowhill, Karoonda, Kulde, Marama, Wirha

Mount Barker, Echunga, Macclesfield, Monarto South, Murray Bridge, Tailem Bend, Jervois, Kulkami, Wynarka, Yurgo, Mulpata, Cowangie

McLaren Vale, Aldinga, Strathalbyn, Kanmantoo, Hartley, Wellington, Sunset, Pinnaroo

Port Vincent, Stansbury, Wool Bay, Oyster Point, Edithburgh, Coobowie, Troubridge Island Cons Park, Kangaroo Island Ferry

St Vincent Gulf, Spencer Gulf, Gulf St Vincent

SOUTH AUSTRALIA / NEW SOUTH WALES border, Dog Fence, SOUTH AUSTRALIA / VICTORIA, Murray River, Barrier Highway, North Road

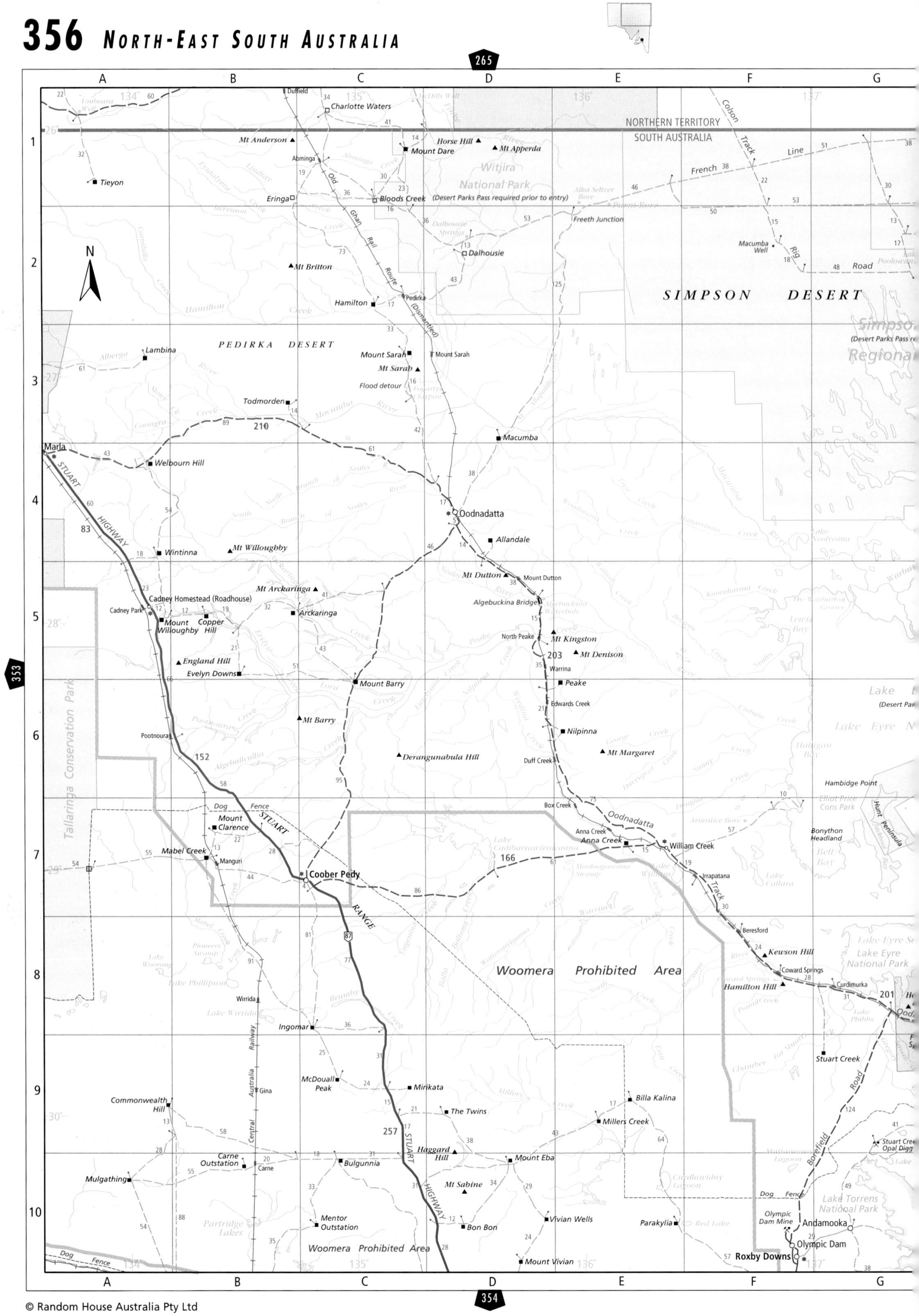

265
NORTHERN TERRITORY
SOUTH AUSTRALIA
Charlotte Waters
Mt Anderson
Horse Hill
Mt Apperda
Mount Dare
Witjira National Park
(Desert Parks Pass required prior to entry)
Tieyon
Eringa
Bloods Creek
Colson Track
French Line
Freeth Junction
Dalhousie
Macumba Well
Rig Road
Mt Britton
Hamilton
Pedirka
SIMPSON DESERT
PEDIRKA DESERT
Lambina
Mount Sarah
Mt Sarah
Flood detour
Todmorden
Macumba
Marla
Welbourn Hill
Oodnadatta
STUART HIGHWAY
Wintinna
Mt Willoughby
Allandale
Mt Dutton
Mount Dutton
Algebuckina Bridge
Mt Arckaringa
Cadney Homestead (Roadhouse)
Cadney Park
Mount Willoughby
Copper Hill
Arckaringa
North Peake
Mt Kingston
Mt Denison
England Hill
Evelyn Downs
Warrina
Mount Barry
Peake
Edwards Creek
Mt Barry
Nilpinna
Pootnoura
Mt Margaret
Derangunabula Hill
Duff Creek
Tallaringa Conservation Park
Hambidge Point
Box Creek
Oodnadatta Track
Mount Clarence
Dog Fence
Anna Creek
William Creek
Mabel Creek
Manguri
Coober Pedy
Irrapatana
Beresford
Woomera Prohibited Area
Keewson Hill
Coward Springs
Hamilton Hill
Curdimurka
Lake Eyre National Park
Wirrida
Ingomar
Stuart Creek
McDouall Peak
Mirikata
Gina
Commonwealth Hill
The Twins
Billa Kalina
Millers Creek
Central Australia Railway
Carne Outstation
Carne
Bulgunnia
Haggard Hill
Mount Eba
Mulgathing
Mt Sabine
Borefield Road
Mentor Outstation
Bon Bon
Vivian Wells
Parakylia
Olympic Dam Mine
Andamooka
Olympic Dam
Roxby Downs
Mount Vivian
Lake Torrens National Park
Stuart Creek Opal Diggings
354
353

© Random House Australia Pty Ltd

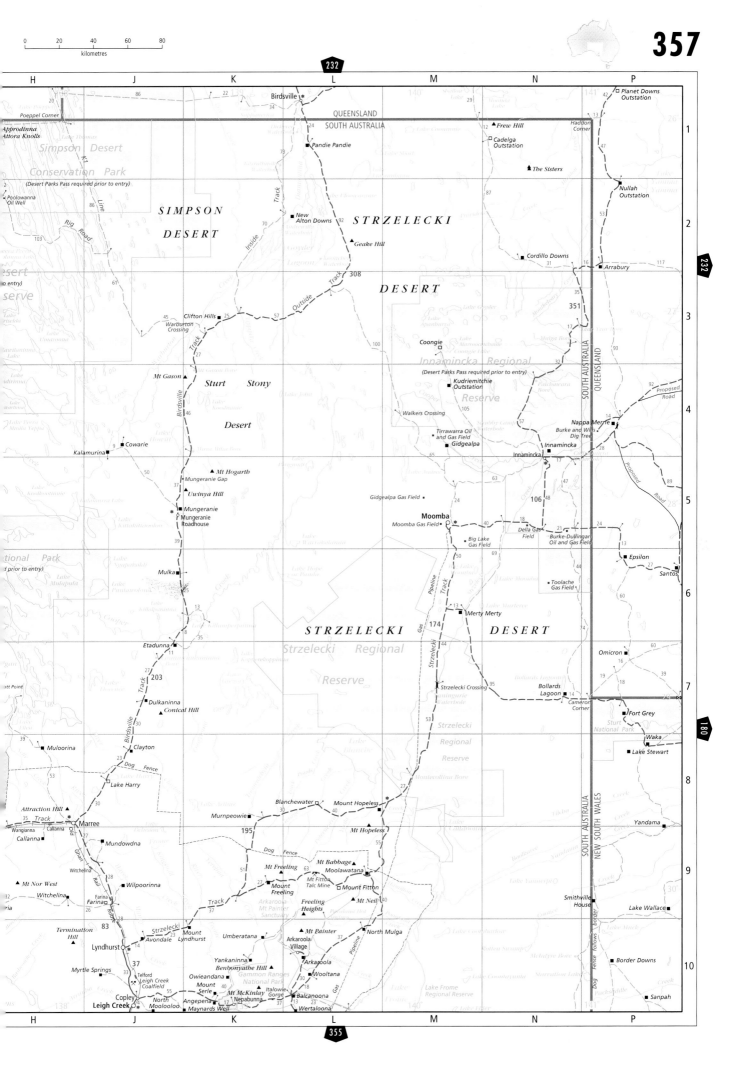

TASMANIA

HOBART-GEORGETOWN
Via Midland Highway (National Route 1),
East Tamar Highway,
272 Kilometres

GEORGETOWN

16

Exeter ◄

24

→ *Underwood*

7   Launceston
47   *Exeter* ← *Scottsdale*
225
5
Westbury/
Deloraine
(national route 1)

13

Perth

14

Cressy ◄

43

→ *St Marys*

11

133   Campell Town
139
12

3   ○ Ross

14

2   ○ Tunbridge

22

186
86
○ Oatlands

29

Bothwell ◄
215
57
8
Kempton

27

250
22
Bridgewater

1
New Norfolk ←

21

HOBART

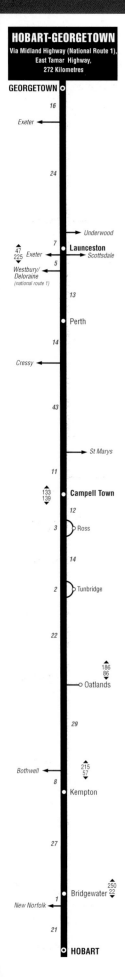

Tasmania may be small in size, but it is one of the most diverse and interesting states of Australia. Separated from the mainland by the Bass Strait, it was once the forgotten state, but nowadays the historical and wilderness delights of this magnificent island bring visitors flocking to its shores. While many come by air for their visit, the ferry which transports both vehicle and passenger is becoming a more popular way of exploring Tasmania. With a good highway system and a multitude of reasonably priced hotels or bed and breakfast establishments to be found, motoring really is the best way to experience this small island.

Tasmania covers an area of 68 331 sq km, making it roughly the same size as Scotland. The shallow channel known as the Bass Strait can be extremely treacherous, and while it is seen by some sailors as a challenge, many vessels have met their end on its rough waters. It does, however, play host to the famous Sydney to Hobart Yacht Race held each year between Christmas and New Year.

A diverse state, each region across the island offers quite different natural landscapes and features. The northern part of Tasmania consists of gentle farmlands and rolling pastures in between large outcrops such as the Great Western Tiers. This huge range extends across the centre of Tasmania separating the rugged wilderness of the Cradle Mountain–Lake St Clair National Park from the agricultural region and Launceston to the north.

The Tamar Valley, the state's premier winegrowing region, is near Launceston. Along the north and east coast are magnificent beaches, some stretching for many kilometres; there are quaint fishing villages with excellent surfing to the north-west. The east is also rich in agricultural lands, while the west coast of Tasmania features wild rivers which cut through an area of rugged beauty that is rich in mineral wealth and important for the large forestry industry.

The south of the state houses the magnificent Huon and Derwent Valleys and is home to Tasmania's capital city, Hobart. There are also many other towns, such as Richmond, which feature magnificent historic buildings. The Tasman Peninsula in the far south-east is home to Australia's most notorious convict settlement, Port Arthur, while Bruny Island is a popular holiday destination, especially in summer.

The climate in Tasmania is mild throughout the year and ideal for a motoring holiday. Spring and autumn offer mild to warm days with magnificent blooms and the golden hues of autumn leaves, but the nights can become very chilly and rainfall is possible. Summer sees long warm to hot days, whereas the nights are pleasant and never uncomfortable. During winter much of the mountainous country is coated in crisp white snow, ideal for skiing. Down from the mountain tops the climate will be chilly and nights cold, perfect for relaxing around a log fire. The west coast of Tasmania boasts 360 days of rain each year so pack a raincoat if you are heading in that direction and during winter check with tourist authorities on road conditions for the higher peaks.

It is the historic interest and charm of the Holiday Isle that bring flocks of visitors from the mainland and overseas.

Steep bluffs in the Walls of Jerusalem National Park

The island was first sighted by Europeans in 1624. The Dutch navigator Abel Tasman arrived off the west coast of this mountainous body of land and named it Van Diemen's Land after the Dutch Governor of Jakarta. It was many years later, in 1777, that Captain James Cook anchored off Bruny Island in the south-east of Tasmania and a further 27 years before the settlement of Hobart was established by Colonel David Collins.

The white settlement of Tasmania brought with it the near extinction of the local Aborigines. During the 1800s authorities took it upon themselves to rid the state of the Aboriginal people and the last remaining Aborigines were sent to Flinders Island. When Truganini died in Hobart in 1876, it was thought that she was the last of the Tasmanian Aborigines. However, there are Aborigines in mainland Australia that are descendants of the Tasmanian tribes.

Tasmania's early beginnings were as a convict penal colony and many men and women were shipped from the 'Mother Country' to serve their sentences in harsh and often barbaric conditions in the penal settlements. Remnants of these penal settlements can be found all over Tasmania, the most notable being Port Arthur, on the Tasman Peninsula in the far south-east of the state. The Port Arthur penal settlement was set up in 1830 and over the 57 years of its operation it is estimated

Wooden huts on Lake Pedder in Southwest National Park

that 12 500 convicts passed through its gates. The settlement is extensive with many of the buildings restored, giving an insight into the conditions endured by the prisoners. These include solitary confinement cells where frequently prisoners went insane. Tours, including the eerie night tours, are recommended when visiting what is considered Australia's most significant penal settlement.

Sarah Island on the wild west coast is another notable site, where the most hardened prisoners were kept in conditions not unlike Port Arthur and endured harsh treatment.

Convicts continued to be shipped to Tasmania until 1852 and during this time they were used as free labour to construct buildings, roads and bridges, many of which are still standing. Many of the old colonial buildings are utilised as bed and breakfast (B&B) establishments. There are literally hundreds of these scattered throughout Tasmania.

Mineral wealth has led to the establishment and growth of many towns, particularly on the west coast where you will find the mining towns of Zeehan and Queenstown. Originally gold was mined in the hills around Queenstown, but after most of the gold had been extracted, copper was mined, a process that caused considerable damage to the surrounding countryside and is still evident today. Silver, lead and tin have all been mined at Zeehan, with tin mining continuing today.

With turbulent rivers gorging through the rugged mountain ranges, hydro-electricity is the best source of power for Tasmania. The island produces more energy than is needed to power the whole state. You will find plenty of these power stations on a journey through Tasmania, many of which are open to the public for inspection.

Much of the landscape was forested when Europeans first arrived and the rich timbers of Tasmania were used for buildings both here and on the mainland. Today there are still paper mills to be found in Tasmania, including the Australian Newsprint Mill in Boyer which produces more than 250 000 tonnes of paper annually, the Australian Paper Mill in Burnie and the Tasmanian Pulp and Forest Holdings in Triabunna which produces woodchip, mostly for export to Japan.

Much of the island World Heritage listed or national park land. The raging rivers, rainforests, scenic coastal reserves and the crisp mountain air give Tasmania the title of Wilderness Capital of Australia. Some areas are so rugged it is likely that they have never been explored by Europeans.

A journey into the parks will reveal stunning lakes such as St Clair or Dove Lakes, towering sheer precipices such as those found in the Ben Lomond National Park, the limestone caves found near Mole Creek, or the vivid coloured rocks of the Freycinet National Park. The most popular, however, is the Franklin–Gordon Rivers region which was steeped in controversy during the 1980s when it was proposed the Franklin River be dammed. The plans for the dam were abolished and today the wild waters form part of the World Heritage Listing and are a major drawcard for visitors to Tasmania.

There are many outdoor activities on offer in Tasmania, including bushwalking. Numerous books have been written on the large number of walks available through the Tasmanian wilderness. There is everything ranging from easy strolls in gentle, rolling countryside or along coastal heathlands, to more rigorous and lengthy treks through inhospitable remote areas of the national parks.

Horse riders will enjoy trekking along the beaches or across mountain ranges, while there are also opportunities for rock climbing, downhill and cross-country skiing, canoeing, whitewater rafting, abseiling or hang gliding. Trails and roads provide a base for mountain biking while tourists can experience the wild rivers in a jet boat ride or the rugged mountain terrain in a 4WD vehicle. You will even find camel riding on the agenda if that is what you desire. Marine reserves which protect the marine environment also provide for excellent diving and snorkelling.

Tasmania has much to offer the gourmet, with excellent wines in the Tamar Valley including Piper's Brook Vineyard—which produces excellent chardonnay, pinot noir and riesling—or the nearby vineyards of Heemskerk, Dalmere or Dairymple. Dairy produce is superb and you will find a large selection of cheeses and creams, including rich and creamy camembert and brie.

Seafood is abundant and there is always a great selection of fresh fish and delicacies such as prawns and crayfish on the menu of most restaurants throughout Tasmania.

Being small, most of the attractions in Tasmania are only a short drive away. It is a great destination for all ages, with plenty of family fun, natural thrills and action for the outdoor enthusiast, historical interest and impressive scenery that rivals that of most countries.

Tasmania really is an isle of contrasts, with rugged mountain ranges, magnificent scenery, sandy beaches, historic towns and fine food and wine—no wonder it is called the Holiday Isle.

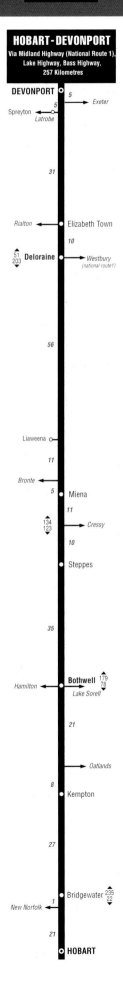

HOBART-DEVONPORT
Via Midland Highway (National Route 1),
Lake Highway, Bass Highway,
257 Kilometres

DEVONPORT
5
Spreyton ← 5 → Exeter
Latrobe
31
Rialton ← ● Elizabeth Town
10
51 / 203 Deloraine ● → Westbury (national route 1)
56
Liaweena ○
11
Bronte ←
5 ● Miena
11
134 / 123 → Cressy
10
● Steppes
35
Hamilton ← ● Bothwell 179 / 78
Lake Sorell
21
→ Oatlands
8
● Kempton
27
Bridgewater 235 / 22
New Norfolk ← 1
21
● HOBART

HOBART

POPULATION: 128 603
MAP REFERENCE: PAGE 386 C5

Nestled on the Derwent River on the south-east coast of Tasmania is the state's capital, Hobart, the smallest capital city in Australia, but one of the oldest, second only to Sydney.

Occupying both banks of the Derwent River this picturesque city offers a lifestyle not found in other Australian capitals. With impressive views of Mt Wellington, the general atmosphere is one of relaxation which is why it is so popular with mainland Australians. Dining is exquisite, with seafood a speciality along with other choice produce from the state, including delicious dairy products, fresh vegetables and fruits, and fine wines.

The region was founded by Colonel David Collins in 1804 and a township was soon established and named after Robert Hobart, Earl of Buckinghamshire and Secretary for the Colonies. Van Diemen's Land, as Tasmania was first known, was not a separate state until 1825 when it was declared independent of New South Wales and the bustling town of Hobart named as its capital.

The township lies around its busy docks and it is here you can watch the local catch coming in from the fishing trawlers, and the large icebreaker ships being loaded before heading south on their dangerous journey to the freezing climate of Antarctica. Constitution Dock is a popular marina, especially around New Year's Eve when the yachts arrive from the annual Sydney to Hobart Race, which is held every year leaving Sydney Harbour on Boxing Day. This race, Australia's premier yacht race, has been navigating the dangerous waters of Bass Strait since 1949 and is regarded as one of the toughest races in the world.

The docks area and city centre features many delightful cafés and restaurants along with boutique stores. Shoppers will be satisfied by Hobart's shopping precinct at Elizabeth Street Mall as well as by the large array of retail stores which can be found along Collins, Murray, Liverpool and Argyle Streets. So you do not lose track of time while working out the credit cards, a large clock in the Cat and Fiddler Arcade chimes nursery rhymes on the hour.

A walk through the town will reveal that Hobart has resisted pressure to modernise—the rustic charm of the old buildings adds to this city's delight. Tasmania's Parliament House was built by convicts in the late 1830s and originally set up as a customs house, now fully restored. The Penitentiary, Chapel and Criminal Courts, a National Trust Property and one of Tasmania's oldest convict buildings sits on Brisbane Street and a tour of this site will reveal eerie underground tunnels which once led to execution yards.

Historic homes can be found throughout the state and in Hobart there are fine examples of the Colonial, Georgian and Victorian period, many of which are owned by the National Trust.

Cape Barren geese, found in the north of Tasmania

Wrest Point Casino on Sandy Bay with the Yacht Club in the foreground

Runnymede House, a colonial building, was built by a lawyer, Robert Picton, in 1840 and is situated in New Town to the north, while Theatre Royal in Campbell Street is Australia's oldest theatre. Originally opened in 1837, it still boasts a full program of theatre and music under an extensively decorated dome ceiling.

A heritage walk is the best way to appreciate the history of Hobart and tours depart the Wrest Point Casino at 2 pm every Saturday afternoon.

Hobart has many attractions for visitors including the Anglesea Barracks and Museum on Davey Street. This military museum is set in the oldest military barracks in Australia and is, in fact, still occupied by the Australian Army. Apart from memorabilia dating back to convict days you can view some of the tombstones that were situated at the original burial ground of Hobart Town.

Hobart has a rich convict past and the Cascade Female Factory Site is an illustration of where women were sent for rehabilitation. The first inmates of this prison arrived in 1828 and the complex continued to operate until 1877, during which time many of the women got quite out of hand. It is said that corruption and crime were rife throughout the prison, with frequent riots by the prisoners. Most of the site on Degraves Street was demolished but what was left standing has been restored.

The Tasmanian Transport Museum at Glenorchy in Hobart is a must for tram and train buffs. It boasts a wide collection of steam trains, rail cars, trams and trolley buses. There is even a railway station and signal box on site. For a train ride to remember, the Hobart-based Classic Rail Tours Tasmania has restored two 1939 rail carriages which are available for tours and charter bookings. The cars run from the museum in Glenorchy to the historical town of Ross every third Sunday during the warmer months.

Sandy Bay is a suburb only 2.5 km south of Hobart and it is home to Australia's first casino. The Wrest Point Casino opened in 1973 and Australians used to flock to the holiday isle to legally play blackjack, roulette and keno. Some of the excitement has gone since casinos have been built in other states throughout Australia, but the centre is still popular and features many fine restaurants and a large convention centre.

Sandy Bay is also home to the John Elliot Classics Museum, which, situated in the University of Tasmania, contains artefacts from Ancient Mesopotamia, Egypt, Greece and Rome. Those who appreciate art may also like to visit the nearby Masterpiece Fine Art and Antique Gallery in Sandy Bay. Australian paintings from the Impressionist, Colonial and Modern periods feature in this gallery along with many Aboriginal paintings and antique furniture.

North of the town you will find Plasminco Metals–EZ, a zinc mining plant, on the shores of the Derwent River, where tours are conducted Monday to Friday. Suitable clothing is required. Further north, Risdon Cove Historical Site is where the first European settlement was formed in Tasmania during 1803. You will find a visitors' centre, monument, theatre and housing displays on the site.

If you fancy heading outdoors, nearby Mt Wellington is excellent for a full or half day's adventure. Being so close to town, the mountain offers superb views of both Hobart and the Derwent River. There are many walking trails: one of the most popular is the 3 km walk from the Springs which treks to the Pinnacle and halfway up the mountain passes the Organ Pipes. Brake Out Cycling Tours conduct a half-day tour of Mt Wellington that begins up on the mountain so it is easy, downhill all the way, 21 km in total. If less energy expenditure is required, sit in the side car of a Harley Davidson and experience the mountain in a totally different way. Harley Tours of Tassie also offer other tours of the area.

For the food and wine lover, gourmet tours of the state and details of the wineries can be arranged through the Tasmanian Wine Centre in Collins Street. Wine-tastings are also held here by arrangement while the Trout Fishing Guides of Tasmania offer tours and advice on fishing Tasmania's inland waters for this sought-after delicacy.

The Royal Harbour Regatta is held each February and sailors and onlookers see in the New Year with a celebration on the docks at Hobart. The Hobart Film Festival is held in September while the Royal Hobart Show is on in October.

Tasmania is renowned world-wide for its quality beers, and Cascade Brewery on Cascade Road in South Hobart opens the brewery, museum and gardens to the public on weekdays. The brewery is the oldest in Australia and was founded by Peter Degraves in 1824 and today still uses traditional methods to manufacture the beer.

Even more popular than beer is chocolate and in Claremont, south of Hobart, the Cadbury Chocolate Factory, Australia's largest confectionery factory, opens the doors of its manufacturing plant for tours. The huge factory covers an area of nearly 15 hectares and the tour shows the manu-facturing process along with offering samples for those with a sweet tooth. Tours operate most days except public holidays and late December to January when the factory shuts down. It is essential to book for this tour.

Near the Cadbury Factory is the Alpenrail, a piece of Switzerland in Tasmania. An indoor village and model railway display places you in the Alps of Switzerland and you listen to Swiss music while gazing upon rivers, lakes and the magnificent scenery that can only be found in Switzerland. Alpenrail is on Abbotsfield Road.

Ten kilometres south of Hobart at Taroona you will find the Tudor Court Model Village, another intricate village model. This magnificent project was undertaken by John Palotta who was unfortunately crippled by polio.

ACCOMMODATION

CBD: Hotel Grand Chancellor, ph (03) 6235 4535; Country Comfort Hadleys Hotel, ph (03) 6223 4355; Hobart Mid City Motor Inn, ph (03) 6234 6333; Domain View Apartments, ph (03) 6234 1181; Transit Centre Backpackers, ph (03) 6231 2400

North side: Hobart Tower Hotel, ph (03) 6228 0166; Wendover Hotel, ph (03) 6278 2066; Roseneath (B&B), ph (03) 6243 6530

South side: Wrest Point Hotel Casino (hotel/motel), ph (03) 6225 0112; Lenna of Hobart (hotel), ph (03) 6232 3900; Blue Hills, ph (03) 6223 1777

West side: Motel Mayfair, ph (03) 6231 1188; Crows Nest (B&B), ph (03) 6234 9853; Valley Lodge Motel, ph (03) 6228 0125

East side: Lindisfarne Motor Inn, ph (03) 6243 8666; Silwood Park (HU), ph (03) 6244 4278; Sun Valley Motor Inn, ph (03) 6244 3855

TOURIST INFORMATION: Ph (03) 6230 8233

THE WEST COAST

The west coast, in particular Queenstown, Strahan and, to a lesser extent, Zeehan, are on the itinerary of almost every visitor to Tasmania.

MAP REFERENCE: PAGE 388 D2
LOCATION: 258 KM WEST OF HOBART
BEST TIME: LATE SPRING AND SUMMER
MAIN ATTRACTIONS: BEAUTIFUL RIVERS, MAGNIFICENT SCENERY, RAFTING, WALKS, WILD COAST BEACHES, 4WD
INFORMATION: QUEENSTOWN, PH (03) 6471 2511; STRAHAN, PH (03) 6471 7140
ACCOMMODATION: SEE TOWN LISTINGS FOR QUEENSTOWN, STRAHAN, ZEEHAN

Their famous attractions, such as the Queenstown mine and the Gordon River Cruise, are definitely worth following up.

There are still a number of areas the driver can find solitude in some beautifully wild country, although there is very little of this central west coast that has not been worked over by humans. For peace you either go further north to the Arthur and Pieman River areas or south into the World Heritage Wilderness Area and the Southwest National Park. The latter can only be done on foot, by the very fit; and the Pieman has only one track in, to Corinna, then a wonderful river cruise is the only route of exploration. From Hobart follow Highway 1 north for 20 km, then take the Lyell Highway (A10) along the south bank of the Derwent, crossing the river at New Norfolk, 53 km from Hobart. You travel through pretty, hop-growing country along the Derwent Valley.

The Lyell Highway parallels the Derwent River for the next 65 km, with numerous dams and power stations of the Hydro Electricity Commission, to Tarraleah. From here you pass some of the many lakes of the trout fishing regions of the central plateau. Then you travel on to Derwent Bridge near the source of the Derwent River.

Beyond Derwent Bridge you enter spectacular wilderness areas, with the Lyell Highway forming the border between the Franklin–Gordon Wild Rivers National Park and Cradle Mountain–Lake St Clair National Park. Following, more or less, the route taken by the early explorers and prospectors, it is one of the most scenic drives in the state as it skirts mountains, lakes and river gorges with alpine peaks dominating the horizon. Along the way are a number of signposted places of interest: lookouts, short walks and the start of numerous long and strenuous treks.

Winding through open eucalypt forest and button-grass plains, the road ascends the King William Saddle, the main divide between the Derwent River system and the Franklin–Gordon system to the west. A lookout here offers extensive views across the King William Range.

A word of caution: this road across the high country can be subject to snow or ice at any time of year, so it should be treated with caution. You would be very fortunate to strike really good weather, as it rains more often than not in this western region of Tasmania.

The vegetation changes to verdant rainforest as the road winds around Mt Arrowsmith and the Surprise Valley Lookout over a glacial valley, before dropping down to the Franklin River, a mere stream here with a pleasant picnic area. A few more kilometres brings you to a car park for Donaghys Hill Wilderness Lookout on the left.

FRANKLIN–GORDON WILD RIVERS NATIONAL PARK

One of the greatest wilderness adventure trips in Australia is to float down the often tranquil, sometimes rapid-churned Franklin River to its junction with the reflective wide waters of the mighty Gordon River in south-west

Tasmania. Born out of the greatest environmental battle fought in this country, the Franklin–Gordon Wild Rivers National Park now protects the Franklin River and much of the lower reaches of the Gordon River.

While for many the rivers are a remote, challenging experience, for others who are not so fit or adventurous, there are 'softer' adventures that one can enjoy and gain an experience of this great natural expanse of forested mountains, gnarled peaks and tumultuous rivers. Here you can touch a tree that has lived for over 2000 years, marvel at the thought that this area has been inhabited for over 20 000 years or thrill to the sound of rapids that are known to rafters around the world as 'Thunder Rush' or the 'Churn'.

History

Carved and shaped by glaciers, the great valleys of the Gordon and Franklin Rivers have played host to one of the oldest records of human habitation in Australia. Between 13 000 and 20 000 years ago Kutikina

Cruising on the Franklin River in south-west Tasmania

Cave, on the edge of the Franklin River not far upstream from its confluence with the Gordon, was continually occupied by Ice Age people. As weather patterns changed and the ice retreated, dense temperate rainforest re-invaded the valleys and the evidence of human activity decreased—the people probably moved closer to the coast. The large numbers of shell middens dotted along the beaches and cliffs testify to their occupation there 6000 years ago.

European exploration began with the voyage of Abel Tasman in 1642 but it was not for another 160 years, when the first English settlement began on what was Van Diemen's Land, that real exploration began. In 1815 Macquarie Harbour was discovered along with the source of the fabled Huon pine.

By 1821 one of the most notorious penal colonies in history had been established on Sarah Island at the head of Macquarie Harbour. This was set up to harvest the rich bounty of timber from the banks of the surrounding rivers. Working in atrocious conditions, the convicts not only harvested the Huon pine but also built a number of ships and smaller craft.

By the time the prison closed in 1834, other tough individuals were using the rivers to bring down the wealth in logs. In 1842 Governor Franklin journeyed from Hobart to the west coast via Lake St Clair. He passed Frenchmans Cap and crossed the Franklin, which was named after him, just above a major tributary of that river now called the Jane, named in honour of his wife and companion.

For the next 100 years only weatherbeaten loggers plied the region searching for the rich Huon which was floated down the Franklin and Gordon Rivers to be milled at small towns that had sprung up on the wild and wet west coast.

It was not until the 1950s that the Franklin River was first canoed over its entire length, and in that same decade a young emigrant, Olegas Truchanas, paddled a canoe from Lake Pedder to Strahan via the Gordon

The vegetation on the hills of Queenstown slowly regenerating after years of copper smelting in the area

River. In the late 1960s the dam that was to flood the pristine natural surrounds of Lake Pedder was begun on the upper reaches of the Gordon. The fight to prevent this was a fight that the fledgling conservation movement lost, but when the Tasmanian Hydro-Electric Commission released plans to flood the lower Gordon and the Franklin Rivers, the battle lines were drawn and the conservation movement was determined that this time it would win.

It was during this time that world focus was directed onto these two great rivers and the first commercial rafting trips began down the Franklin, while pleasure cruises took in the lower, tannin-stained waters of the picturesque Gordon River.

In 1981 the threat of a dam on these rivers was finally defeated in the High Court and soon after the Wild Rivers National Park was formed, amalgamating some smaller, older parks and joining two bigger parks, the Southwest National Park and Cradle Mountain–Lake St Clair National Park into one continuous band of green which is now a declared World Heritage Area.

Access

There is very limited vehicle access to the Franklin and Gordon areas: in fact, there is only one vehicle track which takes you anywhere near the river and it is accessible only by 4WD. This is the Mt McCall Track, constructed by the hydro-electric commission in the days when it was thought the dam was going to be built. It gives access to the Franklin River just below the Great Ravine. There has been an ongoing fight about this track but it remains open—though you will more than likely have difficulty getting a key for the gate from the Queenstown office of the Parks and Wildlife Service.

The track takes you through some pretty spectacular country and ends, 22 km later, near Mt McCall above the Franklin River. It is well above the river, and it is a fit person who can walk down beside the ruins of the steep railway to the river and back and not feel completely exhausted!

Some of the commercial rafting operators start or finish sections of their rafting trip here. Driving time for this track is approximately one hour each way.

The Last Wild River

The Franklin River is the largest river in Tasmania to run free for its entire length from its source in the Cheyne Range, just to the west of Lake St Clair, to its meeting with the Gordon River 45 km from the sea at Macquarie Harbour.

For most, a rafting trip on the Franklin begins on one of the Franklin's tributaries, the Collingwood on the Lyell Highway. It is only a short run to join the Franklin. The Franklin begins its great arc around the sheer gigantic bluff of Frenchmans Cap, but unless you leave the river for a hard day's hike you will never see it, for the peak remains hidden behind high walls of rock and veils of green vegetation.

The Irenabyss is one of the delightful glens to be found on the upper Franklin and here, beside the slowly eddying current, a small camp site is located which is a good stepping-off point for the climb to the top of Frenchmans Cap. As the giant rock buttresses of Frenchmans Cap disap-

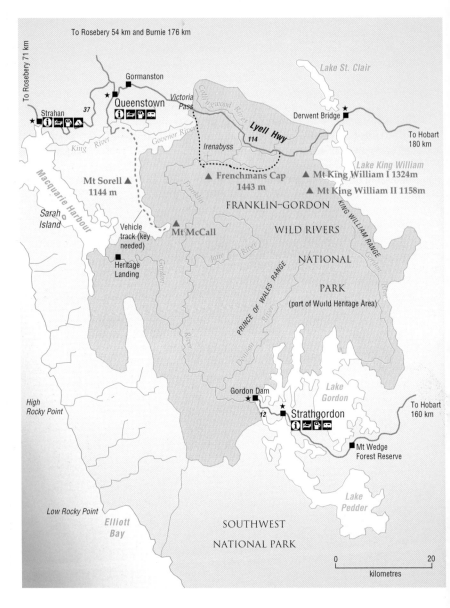

pear from view, the river enters a series of gorges separated by rapids of varying intensity. Inception Reach, Serenity Sound and Transcendence Reach are cut by rapids that carry such descriptive names as the Churn, Coruscades, Thunder Rush and the Cauldron, the latter depositing you in Deliverance Reach, the last great stretch of placid water in the Great Ravine. You breathe a little easier once you get here!

From here the river passes through a number of lesser but still spectacular gorges as well as delightful peaceful reaches and over a number of rapids, some quite long while others are just a single drop of white water.

Below Big Fall the river slows and spreads out, waiting to join the Gordon, and you need to put a bit of paddling in. It depends on which

LEGEND

Sealed/Unsealed Rd	★ 26 ★
Four Wheel Drive	----------
Walks	············
Rest Area (Picnic Area)	🏕

Caravan Park	🚐
Camping Area	⛺
Accommodation	🛏
Information	ℹ
Fuel Supplies	⛽

operator and what sort of craft picks you up, on how much paddling you have to do downstream. No matter what, you will be glad to see the pick-up boat, or floatplane or chopper.

The Tranquil Gordon

The Gordon is regarded by many as the monarch of all rivers. Rising in the King William Range south of the Lyell Highway, it too was a wild river until the great dams were built, forming those fabulous stretches of trout-filled water now known as Lake Gordon and Lake Pedder. Below here the river flows through ever narrowing gorges until it passes through the Gordon Splits. Further on, just below its junction with the Franklin, the river divides and runs around Butler Island, turns north and then west to Heritage Landing and finally to the sea at the eastern end of Macquarie Harbour.

Today, because of water released at unexpected times from the dams, the river is out of bounds. It is too dangerous to raft or paddle, apart from the placid stretches of the lower Gordon which are accessible by boat from Strahan on the northwestern shores of Macquarie Harbour.

That does not mean to say the Gordon River has lost any of its beauty—far from it. The lower reaches are magnificent, known for their fantastic reflections that, like the very best mirror, refract the images of the dense forests crowding the pristine river bank.

By Walking

A number of walks leave the Lyell Highway, including some short ones and others that are really only suitable for the well-equipped, experienced bushwalker.

The Donaghys Hill Wilderness Walk is a short, easy walk of 2 km return that gives great views of the Franklin River and Frenchmans Cap. Far below, hidden amid the rainforest, is the Collingwood River and, beyond, the peaks of Cradle Mountain–Lake St Clair National Park. To the south, trackless wilderness and a deep gorge of the Upper Franklin River. You should allow about 40 minutes return.

You can reach the Irenabyss on the Franklin River by leaving the Lyell Highway at Victoria Pass and heading south. This is a much tougher walk and once you have crossed the Franklin you can take the well-worn track to the top of Frenchmans Cap. It is a three day return walk of about 54 km and it is difficult.

By Raft

For more people wanting to experience the Franklin, a rafting trip is the best way; the most exciting and the most rewarding.

You can do it yourself but it takes experience, planning and the right equipment—the Franklin trip is not a trip to be undertaken lightly. It would be much better to join one of the commercial operators—such as Peregrine Adventures—who run a variety of trips down the river in summer.

By Boat

There are any number of cruise boats operating daily out of Strahan, taking sightseers to the lower reaches of the Gordon. Powered craft are only allowed up the river as far as Horseshoe Bend. Near here, at Heritage Landing, a loop walkway of about ten minutes through the rainforest has been constructed to allow you to experience this ancient forest. A large Huon pine, some 2000 years old, is the highlight here.

West Coast Yacht Charters also operate trips out of Strahan on a classic yacht that takes you up the Gordon, generally further than any of the other boat companies.

Contact the Tourist Visitor Information Centre in Strahan, at the wharf, for a detailed list of the choices you have.

By Plane and Helicopter

A number of companies with float planes, such as Wilderness Air, operate out of Strahan taking tourists over the great rivers and around the high peaks. The standard flight takes you up the Gordon as far as a small landing where you can walk to the Sir John Falls—this is much further upstream than most of the boats are allowed to go. It is also a great way to see this region.

Camping

There are a few bush camps suitable for bushwalkers scattered through the area. The bridge over the Collingwood is one, Irenabyss Camp on the Franklin is another, along with Warners Landing on the Gordon. Otherwise you pitch a tent where you find room in amongst the dense forest or on a flattish slope on the edge of a cliff!

The township of Strahan has all facilities and is a really delightful place to spend a few days. It was named after Major Sir George Strahan, governor of tasmania from 1881 to 1886.

Rafting is the most exciting way to experience the Franklin River

THE WILD WEST COAST TREK

The road from Hobart to Derwent Bridge as described at the beginning would make a good three day trip when added to this trek. The trek starts at Victoria Pass, the top of the range, where the road leaves the World Heritage Area. Look for the Nelson Falls car park on your left, 4 km further on, by the Nelson River Bridge. There is a short but very pretty boardwalk, among giant tree-ferns, through the rainforest to a beautiful 35 metre waterfall with interpretive boards en route to explain these ancient forests.

Now the highway drops down to 53 sq km Lake Burbury, feeding the King River Power Station, below Mt Jukes. A steep, winding descent through the Linda Valley leads to Queenstown, 256 km from Hobart and all bitumen to this point.

The approach to Queenstown is impressive; starkly barren hills of orange, purple and grey tower above this mining town on the Queen River. The Mt Lyell Copper Mine dominates the town, but it was gold and silver that attracted the earliest prospectors in the 1870s. The Mt Lyell Mining Company was formed in 1891, by Bowes Kelly; it was originally based at nearby Penghana until it was wiped out by bushfires; the town was then moved to Queenstown.

The barren landscape is the result of decades of timber felling for the smelters, plus the sulphur fumes they produced destroying any regrowth. Erosion from the extremely high rainfall (annual average 2500 mm) totally denuded the hills of soil, creating an ecological disaster which became a tourist attraction. Now greenery is gradually creeping back up the mountainsides as regeneration programs begin to be effective. (Not all tourism operators are happy about this!)

Surface tours of Mt Lyell Mine are a must, as is the Galley Museum, located in a lovely old two-storey building in the centre of town and featuring photographs, memorabilia and household items of early west coast life.

Opposite the museum is the most interesting Miners Siding Park, with a large bronze/Huon pine sculpture of a miner's family, plus an old ABT railway engine. Here, too, are eleven wonderful bronze relief sculptures, by artist Stephen Walker, showing the history of Queenstown mining.

The ABT Railway to Macquarie Harbour was Queenstown's only link with the world until the Lyell Highway was built in 1932. The 3 ft 6 in gauge line followed the Queen and King Rivers to the river port of Teepookana and, later, to near Regatta Point on Macquarie Harbour. It was such a steep route it required a 'rack' or cog rail. After 63 years, and a million miles, the railway closed in 1963, but you can still drive part of this route along the King River out of Strahan.

A rival railway, the North Lyell, took a longer and much easier route, via Gormanstown and Crotty, to Pillinger in the Kelly Basin much further south in Macquarie Harbour. You can also drive part of this by following the Queen River south from Queenstown on the Mt Jukes Road for a scenic mountain drive through Lynchtown, around Mt Jukes, Lake Burbury and the old mining town of Crotty.

After 37 km, turn right through a tunnel of greenery (look for a small sign) onto the Kelly Basin Track, which is actually the old North Lyell railway track. You can drive a further 5 km to the Bird River Bridge—now decrepit and rotted—where there is a car park (**GPS** 42°18'45"S, 145°36'56"E). From here (for the really energetic) a three hour walking trail, through magnificent rainforest of sassafras, myrtle and King Billy pine, alongside the Bird River, leads to Kelly Basin and the overgrown ghost town of Pillinger.

There are numerous 4WD tracks in this area south of Queenstown; however they are being progressively closed to public access, so you must check with the National Parks and Wildlife Service in Queenstown first. NPWS fees and regulations apply to the Mt Jukes/Kelly Basin tracks.

Queenstown has all the facilities of a large regional town, with numerous motels, hotels and caravan parks.

Queenstown to Zeehan

From Queenstown, take the Zeehan–Murchison Highway (A10) past the large mining operation at Renison Bell and the upper reaches of Lake Pieman, 58 km to Rosebery, which has limited accommodation and a caravan park.

Continue north for 18 km to Tullah, on Lake Rosebery, then turn left, after 3 km, onto the Reece Dam Road (C249). This lonely road meanders 55 km across open forest country (much of it scarred by old bushfires), heathlands and across numerous rivers feeding into Lake Pieman, of which you will see little until you reach Reece Dam, which holds back the mighty Pieman River. There is a good picnic area here.

Just a few kilometres downstream (but 170 km by road!) is the picturesque little fishing hamlet of Corinna, on the north bank, from whence runs the excellent Pieman River Cruise downstream to Pieman Heads; unfortunately, though, it is inaccessible from Reece Dam.

About 5 km past Reece Dam a track wanders some 20 km out to Pieman Heads (the south bank of the Pieman) and Hardwicke Bay. It is well used by anglers with shacks at Pieman Heads.

Continue 14 km along route C249, then turn right to Granville Harbour, 9 km on, for your first glimpse of the wild west coast, lashed by surf which has travelled 20 000 km from South America.

(It is theoretically possible to travel some 40 km south along the coast from Pieman Heads, through Granville Harbour to Trial Harbour on a strictly 4WD track.)

Granville Harbour (**GPS** 41°48'21"S, 145°01'53"E) is a small holiday/fishing hamlet on a pretty little bay. There are no commercial facilities at all here, in fact nothing along this route between Rosebery and Zeehan, a total of 114 km.

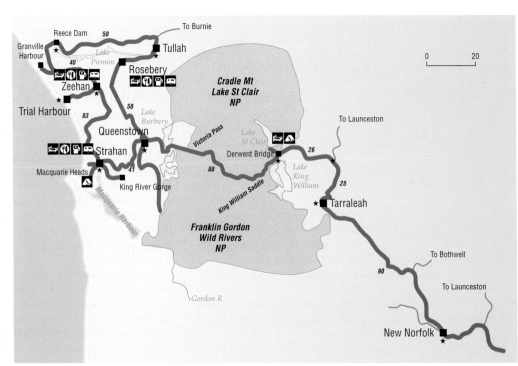

LEGEND

Road Distance in km	★ 26 ★
National Park	
Aboriginal Land	
Accommodation	
Camping Area	
Caravan Park	
Fuel Supplies	
General Store	
Meals Available	
Rest Area (Picnic Area)	
Tourist Information	

Unless you can get accurate information on the 4WD track to Trial Harbour, return to C249 and on to Zeehan, a further 26 km. This route crosses high buttongrass plains dominated by the bulk of Mt Heemskirk, an isolated but easy run.

A century ago Zeehan was a booming silver mining town with a population of 10 000, plus 26 pubs and the largest theatre in Australia—the Gaiety—which attracted such famous artists as Dame Nellie Melba and the great Caruso. Abel Tasman's flagship was the *Zeehan*, and he gave nearby Mt Zeehan its name. Around the 1950s the ore ran out and today Zeehan is pretty much a backwater, although some splendid buildings still line the main street including the Grand Hotel and the Gaiety Theatre. Zeehan has a motel, a hotel and a caravan park.

The big attraction in Zeehan is the West Coast Pioneers' Memorial Museum, a huge complex spread through several buildings. Outdoor lots are filled with old mining machinery, steam trains and other memorabilia to fascinate those with mechanical interests. Inside are old photographs and documents, Aboriginal artefacts, historic west coast memorabilia and a very large collection of minerals.

From Zeehan a very rough track (C248) runs west for 20 km to Trial Harbour (**GPS** 41°55'46"S, 145°10'25"E), another collection of fishing shacks around a rocky little harbour. Abalone and crayfish are plentiful here.

The drive itself is most attractive; surrounded by rugged hills of granite and lush greenery but few trees; you could well believe that you were on the west coast of Ireland.

Zeehan to Strahan

Return to Zeehan and back onto bitumen again for a picturesque run south, on B27, for 83 km to Strahan. This fairly new road follows an old railway line, including an old railway bridge over the Henty River, and offers glimpses of the vast 24 km long, 30 metre high Henty Dunes bordering the Southern Ocean.

One of the world's largest harbours, Macquarie Harbour is the only port on Tasmania's west coast and has had a colourful past, from the convict era through timber, mining and fishing industries to today's tourist throngs. Strahan, at the northern end of the harbour, is the only town, while the Gordon River, flowing in at the southern end, is the main reason for the tourist boom. Originating 193 km inland in Lake Richmond, the Gordon River is navigable for 41 km upriver from the harbour.

Named after Governor Macquarie, the harbour is Australia's second largest—after Port Phillip Bay—and was discovered in 1815 by Captain James Kelly who explored much of the Tasmanian coast in a small boat.

During the convict era Sarah Island, at the southern end of the harbour, was chosen for a penal settlement because of its isolation and also because of the availability of supplies of coal and the much-prized Huon pine. The brutal cruelty of the convict regime can be partly relived by a visit to Sarah Island. Only a few ruins remain, but interpretive boards contain old photo-graphs and drawings showing how Sarah Island was until it was disbanded in 1833 in favour of Port Arthur. The main industries in which the convicts were employed were shipbuilding and timber felling. Up to 370 second-offender convicts were kept here at a time, in ghastly conditions; some escaped to become bushrangers and even cannibals!

Although today the island is forested with trees, it was very barren back then. So much so that a huge palisade was built around the perimeter, as much to keep the bitter winds out as to keep the convicts in. Of the original 30-plus buildings only 13 remain and these are just ruins; the penitentiary on a headland is the most impressive.

Free settlers, known as 'piners', continued the arduous work of logging, floating the timber downriver to the harbour, enduring conditions little better than those of the convicts.

With the inland mining boom, the town of Strahan (and Pillinger, to the south, now deserted) became vitally important for supplying the mining towns. It was the world-wide publicity, and ensuing conservation battles over the proposed damming of the Gordon River, that started the area's tourism boom which continues unabated.

Strahan is a pretty little town with an old pub, a motel and a wealth of B&B accommodation, including some delightful restored period cottages around the waterfront.

Once steam ships from Strahan plied the sea routes to Hobart and Melbourne. Now, morning and afternoon, the wharf area seethes with tourists, buses, cruise boats, float planes and fishing boats.

A Gordon River cruise is a must. Sleek, fast cruise boats speed across the vast expanse of Lake Macquarie to Hells Gates, the entrance to the harbour, and south past Sarah Island into the Gordon River. The rainforest is reflected on the mirrorlike surface of this tannin-stained river as you glide upstream to Heritage Landing, where a boardwalk meanders through the forest past Huon pines more than 2000 years old.

Apart from the famed Huon pine, the rainforest consists of blackwood, myrtle, sassafras, beech and celery-top pine forming a dense canopy above giant tree-ferns, moss-coated laurels and leatherwoods.

Huon pine, so valued for shipbuilding because of its long-lasting qualities, was named after a Frenchman in Bruni d'Entrecasteaux's exploration party. This temperate rainforest, now confined to the west coast of Tasmania, once covered much of Australia, New Zealand and Chile.

In the Gordon River there are cod, rainbow and brown trout, eels, platypus and yabbies. From the deck of the cruise boat you will enjoy the ever-changing vista as you round each bend.

Another tourist option is to cruise one way and take a seaplane flight returning over the World Heritage Wilderness. Strahan Wharf Centre, an award-winning information and interpretive centre handles cruises, 4WD tour and wilderness flight bookings.

South of Strahan

Having done the tourist bit, drive west from Strahan for 6 km to the Ocean Beach which stretches northwards for over 30 km, offering magnificent scenery, surfing and fishing, plus giant muttonbird rookeries. The high sandy cliffs are a popular place to watch the sun set.

Then retrace your tracks for 4 km, turn right and travel for 12 km to Macquarie Heads (**GPS** 42°13'16"S, 145°13'39"E). It is a teeth-jarring track, but leads to a marvellous camping area (WCs only) among the dunes and banksias situated between ocean and harbour. With views across Hells Gates and the all-important lighthouse to Cape Sorell, this area is very popular with the fishing fraternity and a great place for an overnight stop.

Swan Basin, 6 km from Strahan on the Macquarie Heads track, is a very pleasant little harbour, dotted with yachts and home to many waterbirds.

From Strahan drive south around the harbour, through Regatta Point and around Letts Bay. You will see the old railway station and the remains of the old port which served the aforementioned ABT Railway, whose course you can follow along the north bank of the King River. It is an easy, if extremely muddy track, carved through rocks at some points, alongside the heavily polluted and silted-up King River on whose sand banks ghostly dead trees look like a desert scene amid the enclosing rainforest.

Mining effluent made the Queen River the world's most polluted—a problem which will take generations to repair—and, as it flows into the King River, the latter cannot be far behind. It is an eerie, ugly–beautiful drive which once went much further but now ends, after about 5 km, at the big iron Teepookana Bridge (**GPS** 42°11'23"S, 145°25'19"E), which is rotting and has been closed to traffic.

Backtrack to Strahan and take the Lyell Highway (B24) once more to Queenstown; this is a breathtaking, 37 km cliffside rollercoaster ride which has scared the wits out of more than a few visitors! And then it is back on the Lyell Highway for the 256 km run to Hobart, equally scenic on the return journey.

The wharf at Bicheno

BICHENO

187 KM NORTH-EAST OF HOBART
POPULATION: 705   MAP REF: PAGE 391 P9

One of Tasmania's most popular holiday resorts, Bicheno offers visitors pristine white beaches, sailing on sparkling ocean waters, and the bustling atmosphere of a seaside town.

An important port and fishing area, the safe waters of the Maclean Bay were first used in the early 1800s by European sealers and whalers as a harbour. Today Bicheno is a favourite with anglers who fish off the rocks, in the surf or go deep-sea fishing. Two lookouts offer magnificent views of the harbour via walking tracks. Whaler's Lookout in particular allows visitors to take in much of the coastline.

The passageway (the Gulch) between nearby Governor's Island and the township of Bicheno on the mainland is generally a mass of colour with sailboats and fishing vessels which use this waterway as a safe refuge. Diving is also popular here while a glass-bottom boat is a dry alternative for those interested in marine life. Underwater life can also be viewed at the Bicheno Sea Centre.

Further north, on the edge of town, is Diamond Island, joined to the mainland by the Penguin Sandbar which is accessible at low tide. The fairy penguins that live here can be viewed at night.

Nearby is the Douglas–Apsley National Park, which is home to a large dry sclerophyll forest. Over half Tasmania's eucalypt species can be found here, including rare species.

ACCOMMODATION: Beachfront Family Resort (motel units), ph (03) 6375 1111; Silver Sands Resort (motel units), ph (03) 6375 1266; Greenlawn Cottage, ph (03) 6375 1114; Bicheno Cabins and Tourist Park, ph (03) 6375 1117; Bicheno Caravan Park, ph (03) 6375 1280
ACTIVITIES: Fishing, golf, horse riding, national park access. tennis, walking, water sports
TOURIST INFORMATION: Ph (03) 6375 1333

BOAT HARBOUR

355 KM NORTH-WEST OF HOBART
POPULATION: 390   MAP REF: PAGE 390 D4

A popular beach resort on the north coast of the state, Boat Harbour has protected beaches and crystal clear waters which lead out into the Bass Strait. These waters are perfect for fishing, swimming, waterskiing and diving. At low tide rock pools provide an insight into the local marine life.

Further west along the coast is the Rocky Cape National Park, Tasmania's smallest national park. It has good walking trails, picnic areas and a large number of Aboriginal sites. The small township of Sisters Beach offers magnificent views of the coastline and boasts accommodation in delightful cottages.

ACCOMMODATION: Boat Harbour Beach Resort, ph (03) 6445 1107; Country Garden Cottages (farmland property), ph (03) 6445 1233; Boat Harbour Beach Seaside Garden (cottage), ph (03) 6445 1111
ACTIVITIES: Fishing, national park access, water sports
TOURIST INFORMATION: Ph (03) 6336 3122

BOTHWELL

77 KM NORTH-WEST OF HOBART
POPULATION: 400   MAP REF: PAGE 389 J2

Set around the magnificent Queens Park, this historic town is built along the banks of the Clyde River and boasts more than 18 National Trust buildings. Amongst those is a building which was opened in 1837 and became Tasmania's first public library.

Other interesting buildings include the Castle Hotel—which has held its licence since 1829—and Wentworth House—which was built in 1833 for Major D'Arcy Wentworth. Visitors, attracted by the history of the area often stay in one of the many historic hotels. Bothwell Grange, a heritage building circa 1836, puts on 'Murder Mystery Weekends'.

ACCOMMODATION: Bothwell Grange (heritage B&B), ph (03) 6259 5556; Mrs Woods Farmhouse (farming property), ph (03) 6259 5612; Bothwell Camping Ground, ph (03) 6286 3202
ACTIVITIES: Fishing, golf, hang gliding, historic interest, swimming
TOURIST INFORMATION: Ph (03) 6336 3122

BRIDPORT

289 KM NORTH-EAST OF HOBART
POPULATION: 1165   MAP REF: PAGE 391 L4

Bridport lies at the mouth of the Forester River which opens up into Anderson Bay on Tasmania's northern coast. Once a haunt of those wishing to escape the law, it is now an excellent destination for those escaping city life. Lush green forests extend to white sandy beaches which are safe for swimming.

Early settlers include Janet and Andrew Anderson, the first landowners, and after whom the picturesque bay is named. Bowood, a nearby homestead built in 1839, includes the remains of a schoolhouse, a cemetery and wildlife park. At certain times of the year, the impressive gardens around the homestead are open for public viewing.

The Foreshore Walking Trail extends from the Old Pier Beach in the north of the town along the shoreline, continuing past Goftons Beach and the mouth of the Great Forester River to the bridge. Another walking track which can be linked to the Foreshore Trail begins near the golf course and heads north to Adams Beach.

There are also tours to the Double Sandy Point Coastal Reserve, or to the sand dunes of Waterhouse.

The nearby region is a renowned grape-growing area and wineries such as Pipers Brook give tastings and have cellar door sales.

A seaside market is held in town on the first and third Sundays of each month. The Bridport triathlon is an event staged every January while the Art Exhibition is held in early November.

ACCOMMODATION: Platypus Park Farm Chalets, ph (03) 6356 1873; Bridport Motor Inn, ph (03) 6356 1238; Bridport Indra Holiday Units, ph (03) 6356 1196
ACTIVITIES: Fishing, golf, horse riding, tennis, walking, water sports, wineries
TOURIST INFORMATION: Ph (03) 6336 3122

BRUNY ISLAND

33 KM SOUTH OF HOBART
POPULATION: 520   MAP REF: PAGE 389 K8

Situated just off the coast of southern Tasmania is Bruny Island. Joined by a slender stretch of sand shoreline, known as the Neck, are North and South Bruny, two distinctly different areas. The north comprises mainly cleared pastoral land with only a scattering of light brush land areas. The south, however, is quite different: it is a rugged, mountainous region which is heavily timbered.

Many explorers navigated their way around this small tract of land including Tobias Furneaux, James Cook who came ashore in 1777, William Bligh and Matthew Flinders. The Bligh Museum in Adventure

The Neck which joins North and South Bruny

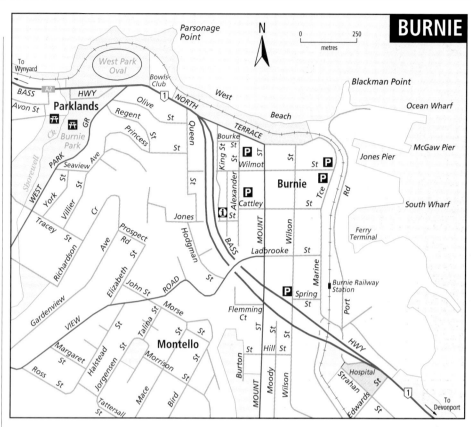

Bay has excellent displays highlighting the travels of these explorers and the whalers who used Bruny as a base from which to hunt.

Bruny also has important significance for the Aborigines as the birthplace of Truganini. She was the daughter of an island chief and the last of the full-blooded Tasmanian Aborigines. She died in 1876.

A car and passenger ferry operates from Kettering to North Bruny. The island, although only 55 km in length, has much to offer the visitor and while many people come on a day trip from Hobart, the island is best appreciated over two or three days. The island's main town is Alonnah.

South Bruny National Park is Tasmania's newest national park. It has wild and rugged scenery and spectacular views. Some areas of the park are inaccessible, whereas others can be reached by walking or following 4WD tracks.

The Barnes Bay Regatta is held in early March, while there is a rodeo over the Easter weekend.

ACCOMMODATION: Belmont Bruny Island Hotel, ph (03) 6244 7155; Barnes Bay Villas, ph (03) 6206 6287; Whalers Inn Holiday Village, ph (03) 6293 1271
ACTIVITIES: Fishing, 4WD touring, national park access, walking, water sports
TOURIST INFORMATION: Ph (03) 6267 4494

BURNIE

328 KM NORTH-WEST OF HOBART
POPULATION: 20 505   MAP REF: PAGE 390 E5

Burnie, on the northern coast, is the fourth largest city in Tasmania. It was named after William Burnie, a director of the Van Diemen's Land Company. The original town was established on Emu Bay where the port is today. It remained a fairly peaceful town until tin was discovered in the hills during the 1870s. It was then that the town began to grow. First a tramway was built, to move tin from Mt Bischoff to the port. Then, in 1900, the Emu Bay Railway was extended to service the mining towns of Zeehan and Rosebery. Today the large deep-water port handles a major portion of the produce exported from Tasmania.

In 1938 Associated Pulp and Paper Mills opened a factory in South Burnie and now it is Australia's largest fine-paper manufacturer. The mill can be toured, as can the Lactos Cheese Company, while tastings are available at the Cheese Tasting Centre on Old Surrey Road.

The Burnie Regional Art Gallery at the Civic Centre displays Australian contemporary artwork. Burnie Inn, the oldest building in town, has been relocated to Burnie Park. The Pioneer Village contains replicas of stores such as a blacksmith shop, general store and boot shop from the early 1900s.

Outside of Burnie lies the Emu Valley Rhododendron Garden, a 12 hectare property which contains thousands of rhododendrons. Annsleigh Gardens and Tea Rooms is another delightful garden.

The Burnie Athletics Carnival, including the Burnie Gift, is run on New Year's Day. The Burnie Festival comes alive in September and the Burnie Agricultural Show, the Orchid Show and Rhododendron Show are all held during October.

ACCOMMODATION: Voyager Motor Inn, ph (03) 6431 4866; Glen Osborne House (B&B), ph (03) 6431 9866; West Beach Villas, ph (03) 6431 5708

The Pioneer Museum in Burnie

ACTIVITIES: Fishing, golf, nature walks, tennis, water sports
TOURIST INFORMATION: Ph (03) 6434 6111

CAMPBELL TOWN

130 KM NORTH OF HOBART
POPULATION: 820   MAP REF: PAGE 391 L9

The centre of the fine wool industry, historic Campbell Town is situated on the Midland Highway between Hobart and Launceston. Today the area is a major primary producer, renowned for its wool, beef cattle and timber.

There was much bushranger activity in the early 1800s with raids from the infamous Matthew Brady and an unfortunate bushranger, John Quigley, who, in his attempt to hold up a coach on its way to the races, was shot in the leg and captured. The town was established as one of the five garrisons built along the main route between Hobart and Launceston.

Today the town is far more sedate and offers buildings of historic interest including the Campbell Town Inn and the Catholic church, which is the oldest such building in Australia.

The Red Bridge, which takes the main street over the Elizabeth River in the middle of town, was built by convicts in the 1830s.

Campbell Town markets are held on the fourth Sunday of each month while the Agricultural Show is on the first Tuesday and Wednesday in June.

ACCOMMODATION: Powells Hotel/Motel, ph (03) 6381 1161; Foxhunters Return (B&B), ph (03) 6381 1602; The Grange (B&B), ph (03) 6381 1686
ACTIVITIES: Golf, historic interest, swimming, tennis
TOURIST INFORMATION: Ph (03) 6381 1283

The village of Coles Bay

COLES BAY

203 KM NORTH-EAST OF HOBART
POPULATION: 120 MAP REF: PAGE 391 P10
The tiny township of Coles Bay on the east coast of
Tasmania is nestled beside the world-famous
Freycinet National Park where spectacular red
granite boulders plunge deep into the ocean. As the
closest town to this park, Coles Bay is the last stop for
supplies before venturing into the park.

The park itself has long been recognised and was
proclaimed in 1916 as a flora and fauna reserve. Now
it covers 11 000 hectares and boasts a variety of
vegetation including wattles, oyster bay pines, grass-
trees and banksias with the predominant feature
being its coastal heathlands. The three peaks of the
Hazards dominate the skyline from all directions.
Bushwalking is the main activity here as the road only
ventures about 6 km into the park, and there are a
number of excellent walks to choose from.

Secluded swimming areas can be found on the
east coast of the park such as Wineglass Bay with
spectacular sandy beaches. A sea cruise or fishing
charter is available from Coles Bay.
ACCOMMODATION Freycinet Lodge (motel), ph
(03) 6257 0101; Freycinet Holiday Homes,
ph (03) 6257 0218; Pine Lodge (cabins), ph
(03) 6257 0113
ACTIVITIES: Bushwalking, cruises, fishing, golf,
national park access, rock climbing, scenic flights,
tennis, water sports
TOURIST INFORMATION: Ph (03) 6257 0107

CYGNET

58 KM SOUTH OF HOBART
POPULATION: 925 MAP REF: PAGE 389 J6
The centre of a large fruit-growing region, Cygnet
sits on the banks of Port Cygnet, where the Huon
River flows out into the D'Entrecasteaux Channel.
Agriculture has always been the mainstay of this
town and convicts, who were housed for a short
period in probation settlements, were used to clear
the surrounding land.

Unlike much of Tasmania where buildings are
traditionally built from stone, Cygnet's buildings were
mainly constructed using the timbers that were
cleared from the land. This tradition continues today:
the wood-turner at the Deepings, on the way to

Nicholls Rivulet south-east of town, manufactures
bowls and ornaments from the magnificent
Tasmanian timbers.

Nearby, the Talune Wildlife Park and Koala
Gardens has local native wildlife, including the
infamous Tasmanian devil.

There are two wineries in the region, Panorama
Winery and the Hartzview Vineyard, both of which
offer tastings and cellar door sales.

The Huon Folk Festival is held in late January or
early February.
ACCOMMODATION: Howard Cygnet Central Hotel,
ph (03) 6295 1244; Cygnet Hotel, ph (03) 6295 1267;
Leumeah Lodge (B&B), ph (03) 6295 1839
ACTIVITIES: Fishing (trout), golf, nature park, tennis,
water sports, wineries
TOURIST INFORMATION: Ph (03) 6297 1836

DELORAINE

231 KM NORTH-WEST OF HOBART
POPULATION: 2100 MAP REF: PAGE 391 H7
Sitting at the base of the towering Cluan and Great
Western Tiers, the district of Deloraine boasts fertile
soils and a temperate climate, making it rich in
dairying, lamb, cattle, and vegetable farming.

Established in 1840, the township has historical
classification. Many impressive buildings have been
restored and are open to the public. The Bowerbank
Mill Gallery was built in 1853 and has a selection of
paintings, crafts and handmade furniture using
Tasmanian wood.

Deloraine is surrounded by beautiful scenery—
Liffey Falls to the south are spectacular. Popular with

artists, Deloraine's proximity to the Lakes area and
Mt St Clair means bushwalkers use it as a base.

Showground markets are held on the first
Saturday of each month while the Deloraine
Agricultural Show takes place in November and the
Grand National Steeple Chase on Easter Monday.
ACCOMMODATION: Mountain View Country
Inn Motel, ph (03) 6362 2633; Arcoona (B&B),
ph (03) 6363 3443; Boney's Inn (B&B), ph (03) 6362 2974
ACTIVITIES: Fishing, golf, historic interest,
horseracing, horse riding, swimming, tennis
TOURIST INFORMATION: Ph (03) 6362 2046

DEVONPORT

280 KM NORTH-WEST OF HOBART
POPULATION: 25 400 MAP REF: PAGE 390 G5
For many Australians Devonport is the first town they
visit in Tasmania as it has been the port for ferry
crossings from Melbourne since 1959. Today the *Spirit
of Tasmania* departs from Melbourne three times a
week. The port in this town also handles the export of
much of the fresh produce from the surrounding
agricultural areas.

Because many visitors land in Devonport, it is the
perfect starting point for a self-drive Tasmanian
holiday. Visitors use the town as a base to see the
northern part of the island. Popular features such as
Cradle Mountain, Boat Harbour, Stanley, Burnie,
Launceston and Deloraine can all be undertaken as
day trips, either in your own vehicle, or on a tour.

International cruise ships visit this port during the
year and each summer Devonport comes alive with
yachts heading south from Victoria across the

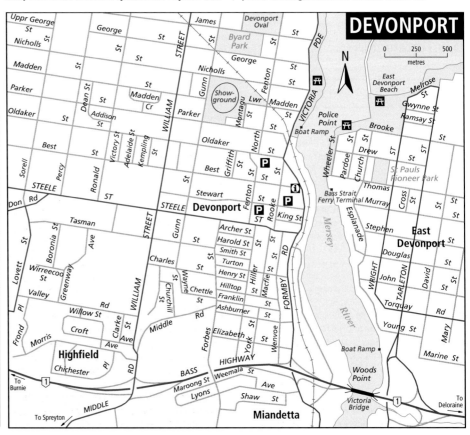

Don River Railway Museum in Devonport

treacherous Bass Strait. Perched alongside the Mersey River is the Maritime Museum, with its library and research centre which contains hundreds of detailed models of sailboats, steamboats and ferries.

Devonport puts on regular exhibitions of local artwork at the Gallery and Art Centre. Exhibits of earlier inhabitants can be found at Tiagarra, a Tasmanian Aboriginal Cultural Museum where Aboriginal crafts, artefacts and rock engravings, many of which are thousands of years old, are on show. The carvings were discovered at Mersey Bluff in 1929 and the site has since been protected with the museum established in 1972. The bluff offers commanding views of the Mersey and Don Rivers, which flank the town, as well as of the majestic coastline.

Also popular with visitors is the Don River Railway: the train takes passengers on scenic rides from Don, on the western side of Devonport. During weekdays the train is drawn by a diesel engine, while on the weekends passengers step back in time as the carriages are hauled by a steam engine.

The Melbourne–Devonport Yacht Race is held in late December as is the Cycling and Athletics Carnival. The Devonport Cup takes place in early January and the Food and Wine Fun Fiesta in late February. The Devonport Agricultural Show is held in November.

ACCOMMODATION: Gateway Inn Hotel, ph (03) 6424 4922; Birchmore of Devonport, (B&B), ph (03) 6423 1336; Mersey Bluff Lodge (units), ph (03) 6424 5289

ACTIVITIES: Bass Strait ferry access, golf, steam train rides, swimming, tennis

TOURIST INFORMATION: Ph (03) 6424 8176 For information on the *Spirit of Tasmania* ph 1800 636 110, visit their web site on www.tt-line.com.au or e-mail reservations@tt-line.com.au

DOVER

87 KM SOUTH OF HOBART
POPULATION: 570   MAP REF: PAGE 389 H8
Originally a convict station, today Dover is a popular fishing town, its sheltered harbour facing the D'Entrecasteaux Channel and the west side of Bruny Island. The Huon pine was once heavily processed and exported from Dover, but since this magnificent timber has become scarce, fishing and fruit growing are now the major sources of income. Tourism is also

a growth industry and there are charming cottages which offer bed and breakfast.

Dover is an excellent base for exploring the nearby Hartz Mountains National Park, which is part of the World Heritage Area and offers spectacular scenery with a number of walking trails through rainforests, rugged ranges, mountain lakes and alpine heathlands. There is a short walk to Waratah Lookout where you can view the grandeur of Mt Wellington and take in the beauty of the Huon Valley.

ACCOMMODATION: Annes Old Rectory (B&B), ph (03) 6298 1222; Dover Hotel, ph (03) 6298 1210; 3 Island Holiday Apartments, ph (03) 6298 1396

ACTIVITIES: Fishing, golf, national park access, scenic river cruises, water sports

TOURIST INFORMATION: Ph (03) 6336 3122

DUNALLEY

61 KM EAST OF HOBART
POPULATION: 310   MAP REF: PAGE 389 M5
The small township of Dunalley stands on the narrow isthmus which connects the Forestier Peninsula to mainland Tasmania and it was the site of the first European landing in December 1642. The Tasman Memorial 2 km north-east of the town bears testament to the landing by Dutch sailors from the ships *Heemskirk* and *Zeehan* under the command of Abel Tasman more than 350 years ago.

Tasman named the island Van Diemen's Land after Anthony Van Diemen, who was then the governor-in-chief of the Dutch East India Company. This name was only changed to Tasmania in 1855.

The Dennison Bridge connects the peninsula to the mainland and occasionally vehicles wanting to use the bridge will have to wait for boats to pass under the swing-style bridge.

Dunalley has small cafés and local arts and crafts which are sold in small shops and galleries.

There are guided tours of bushland around Dunalley which take in large tracts of grasslands and native bush, ideal for bushwalking. The local lagoons and coastal areas are also of interest to the visitor.

ACCOMMODATION: Potters Croft (B&B), ph (03) 6235 5469; Fullham Cottages, ph (03) 6253 5247

ACTIVITIES: Bushwalking, fishing, golf, surfing

TOURIST INFORMATION: Ph (03) 6336 3122

EVANDALE

182 KM NORTH OF HOBART
POPULATION: 775   MAP REF: PAGE 391 K7
Classified as an historic town, Evandale boasts some of the country's best preserved colonial buildings. Although the town is set in some of Tasmania's most picturesque countryside—Ben Lomond National Park is just to the north-west—it is the lover of history who heads to Evandale to view the town's many original and now restored buildings. Of particular interest is Clarendon, a grand Georgian mansion which lies on the South Esk River, 8 km from town at Nile. Originally built in 1836, it has been restored by the National Trust. Formal gardens and parkland surround the three-storey mansion.

There are also art galleries and antique shops, and in nearby Breadalbane is a traditional glassblower who uses the sand mined from the Savage River on Tasmania's west coast to produce some of the world's finest glassware.

Evandale can also claim some significant former residents: John Batman, the founder of Melbourne, lived in the Evandale region for 15 years.

Evandale hosts the World Pennyfarthing Championships each year in February. Here riders from all around the world gather to exhibit their prowess on this incredible cycle.

Other events include the Sunday markets, The Village Fair (held in February), and the Agricultural Show which takes place in mid-March.

ACCOMMODATION: Harland Rise (B&B), ph (03) 6391 8283; Strathmore (B&B), ph (03) 6398 6213; Greg and Jills Place (holiday units), ph (03) 6391 8248

ACTIVITIES: Fishing, historic interest, national park access, swimming

TOURIST INFORMATION: Ph (03) 6391 8128

FLINDERS ISLAND

198 KM NORTH OF HOBART
POPULATION: 1130   MAP REF: 391 J2
Measuring 60 km in length and 20 km wide, Flinders is the largest of the Furneaux Group of islands off the north-east coast of Tasmania. First visited by Tobias Furneaux in 1773, this island was later named after the explorer Matthew Flinders.

In the early days, sealers established a base on the island. Today fishing is the main industry and visitors flock to this isolated island to enjoy its water sports: diving around the many shipwrecks which dot the coastline is very popular. Walking is also a favourite activity and Mt Strzelecki in the Strzelecki National Park rises 756 metres above sea level, attracting rock climbers.

In the early 1800s as the Aboriginal population decreased at an alarming rate on mainland Tasmania, Aborigines were relocated onto the island. Today, near the township of Emita, lies the Wybalenna Historic Site. Here and at the Emita Museum visitors can appreciate the cultural richness of the island's previous inhabitants including the Aborigines, sealers, sailors and fishermen.

The island supports much wildlife including Cape Barren geese and muttonbirds which fly thousands of kilometres each year, then return to the same burrow.

The wreck of the *Farsund* off Flinders Island

Other interests for visitors include fossicking for Killecranke diamonds (really white topaz).

ACCOMMODATION: Flinders Island Lodge, Lady Barron, ph (03) 6359 3521; Flinders Island Interstate Hotel, Whitemark, ph (03) 6359 2114; Boat Harbour Beach House, ph (03) 6359 6510

ACTIVITIES: Bowls, bushwalking, fishing, gem fossicking, golf, horse riding, national park access, rock climbing, scenic drives, tennis, water sports

TOURIST INFORMATION: Ph (03) 6359 2217

FRANKLIN

62 KM SOUTH-WEST OF HOBART
POPULATION: 465   MAP REF: PAGE 389 J6

Not to be confused with the well-known Franklin River of Tasmania, this small timber milling and orchard town is one of the oldest to be found along the Huon River in the state's south-west. Only a short drive from Hobart, Franklin was named after Governor Sir John Franklin who, with his wife Lady Jane Franklin, lived on the banks of the Huon. The settlement expanded rapidly near their home.

There are a number of historic buildings in the town including three churches which were constructed in the mid-1800s.

Although the main industry has always been timber milling, there is a museum in the town which highlights the orchard industry of the region.

ACCOMMODATION: Franklin Lodge (B&B), ph (03) 6265 3506; Homestead Cottage Accommodation (B&B), ph (03) 6266 3686

ACTIVITIES: Historic interest, scenic walks

TOURIST INFORMATION: Ph (03) 6336 3122

GEEVESTON

65 KM SOUTH OF HOBART
POPULATION: 830   MAP REF: PAGE 389 H6

The timber town of Geeveston was first settled in 1842 by William Geeves who came to the richly treed region and began clearing timber, a process that has lasted more than 150 years.

There are many walking trails, some of which, such as the walks off Arve Road, feature labelled trees for easy identification. Further west along the Arve Road is the Tahune Reserve where there is a natural stand of the rare Huon pine.

The Forest and Heritage Centre allows you to smell and feel the magnificent local timber. There are also photographs and displays of wooden artefacts handcrafted by the local wood-turners.

Geeveston is the perfect starting point for a journey to the Hartz Mountains National Park, a rugged mountain range which is popular with walkers and day trippers in milder months and cross-country skiers in the winter season.

ACCOMMODATION: Eringa (B&B), ph (03) 6297 1561

ACTIVITIES: Bushwalking, fishing, golf, national park access, tennis

TOURIST INFORMATION: Ph (03) 6297 1836

GEORGE TOWN

254 KM NORTH OF HOBART
POPULATION: 5030   MAP REF: PAGE 391 J5

George Town, situated near the mouth of the Tamar River, was first settled in 1811 and was one of the first major towns in the north of Tasmania. It was not, however, until the 1950s that the town grew rapidly when the Comalco Mining Company set up a smelter at the nearby port of Bell Bay.

George Town has many historic homes which can be viewed by taking the George Town Discovery Trail, a four-part self-guided tour which includes one of the finest Georgian mansions in Tasmania: the Grove.

The Discovery Trail also stops by the Paterson Monument which marks the location on the banks of the Tamar River where Lieutenant-Colonel Paterson proclaimed the north of Tasmania in 1804 and named the town in honour of King George III.

There is a ferry service from George Town across the river to Beauty Point. Other cruises are available on the river and out to sea, visiting local bird and seal colonies. The SS *Furneaux Explorer* cruises around the Furneaux Group of islands.

There is a fairy penguin colony at Low Head which can be viewed every evening. During the day Low

Head, which is only 5 minutes north of George Town, offers magnificent beaches for swimming and surfing.

Outside town there are orchards selling delicious local produce such as apples. This is also home to the popular Pipers Brook regional wineries including Delamere, Pipers Brook and Rochcombe, which offer wine tastings and cellar-door sales.

During March the Bass Strait Challenge, Australia's oldest yacht race, heads across the Strait from Queenscliff in Victoria to its finish at George Town. Other events in the town include the Tamar Valley Folk Festival which is held in January and an arts and craft market which is held on the second Saturday of each month.

ACCOMMODATION: The Pier Motel, ph (03) 6382 1300; Grays The George Town Hotel, ph (03) 6382 2655; Central Court Apartments, ph (03) 6382 2215

ACTIVITIES: Golf, historic interest, water sports, wineries

TOURIST INFORMATION: Ph (03) 6382 1700

Apple picking in the Huon Valley near Huonville

HUONVILLE

42 KM SOUTH-WEST OF HOBART
POPULATION: 1525   MAP REF: PAGE 389 J6

The French admiral, Bruni D'Entrecasteaux, who explored much of the region south of Hobart in the early 1790s was the first European to sight the Huon River. He named it after Captain Huon de Kermedec, his second-in-command. The small township of Huonville sits beside the fast flowing Huon River, on which jet boat rides have become extremely popular. With the coming of settlers, the Huon Valley developed into an excellent fruit-growing district.

The fresh produce is easily obtained from laden roadside stalls, while just outside town is the Huon Apple and Heritage Museum. This commemorates the early orchard industry with exhibits of restored machinery. There are also the many locally grown varieties of apple on hand for sampling.

To the north of the town in Ranelagh is the Tasmanian Antique Motor Museum which has more than 40 beautifully restored vehicles on display.

On the Denison River at nearby Judbury is the Snowy Range Trout Fishery. Its ponds are stocked

The Arve River near Geeveston

with Tasmanian rainbow trout weighing up to 4 kg. Atlantic salmon are available too.

Sunday markets are held down by the river bank while the Festival on the Bank is held in April.

ACCOMMODATION: Grand Hotel, ph (03) 6264 1004; Crabtree House (guesthouse), ph (03) 6266 4227; Barnes Camp Site, ph (03) 6266 0279

ACTIVITIES: Fishing, golf, horse riding, jet boat rides, tennis, water sports

TOURIST INFORMATION: Ph (03) 6297 1836

KETTERING

33 KM SOUTH OF HOBART
POPULATION: 295   MAP REF: PAGE 389 K6

Kettering is the gateway to Bruny Island, being the car and passenger ferry terminal. North of Kettering is Oyster Cove, home of a thriving berry industry, while the larger fruit-growing district of Cygnet is only a short drive to the south-west.

On the outskirts of Kettering is the Herons Rise Vineyard which produces a range of wines including pinot noir, Rhine riesling and Müller Thurgau. Wine tastings and cellar door sales are available by appointment, while accommodation is also offered on this scenic property.

Only 8 km north of town on the Channel Highway is the delightful township of Snug. It is here you will find Mother's Favourites, Tasmania's finest bakery for pies and quiches. To the south-west of Snug are Snug Falls, accessible via a walking track.

ACCOMMODATION: Oyster Cove Inn (motel), ph (03) 6267 7446; Herons Rise Vineyard (guesthouse), ph (03) 6267 4339

ACTIVITIES: Boating, sailing, walking, wineries

TOURIST INFORMATION: Ph (03) 6267 44947

KINGSTON

13 KM SOUTH OF HOBART
POPULATION: 12 910   MAP REF: PAGE 389 K5

The largest town south of Hobart and known as the gateway to southern Tasmania, Kingston could almost be described as a southern suburb of Hobart. Both the town site and river were named Browns River after the botanist Robert Brown who explored this region in 1804. The town's name was later changed to Kingston after Lieutenant Philip Gidley King, the officer in charge of the first settlement in Tasmania. Browns River flows through the Kingston Beach Golf Course, considered one of the finest in Tasmania, before reaching the sea at Kingston Beach, which is a magnificent safe swimming area.

Kingston is also the home of Australia's Antarctic Division Research Facility which provides the necessary back-up to the research stations in Antarctica—a section of the facility is open to the public on weekdays.

The region around Kingston is perfect for scenic drives. The road south of the town follows the coastline for much of the way to Cygnet, taking in towns such as Snug, Woodbridge and Middleton. Along the way there are many vantage points to view Bruny Island. Continuing north along the Channel

Highway to Huonville you can pick up the Huon Highway and make the round trip back to Kingston.

The Kingborough Festival is held in March, and the Dutch Oliebollen Festival during October.

ACCOMMODATION: Welcome Inn Hotel, ph (03) 6229 4800; Tranquilla (B&B), ph (03) 6229 6282

ACTIVITIES: Antarctic Division Headquarters, golf, scenic drives, tennis, water sports

TOURIST INFORMATION: Ph (03) 6230 8233

LATROBE

273 KM NORTH-WEST OF HOBART
POPULATION: 2550   MAP REF: PAGE 390 G5

Latrobe was once a bustling port and major commercial centre during the 1800s, but today visitors come to the quiet town to sample the fine restaurants and view the historic buildings.

There are many things to do in the town, including picnicking in the delightful Bells Parade Park on the banks of the Mersey River. Sherwood Hall, the 1848 home of Thomas and Dolly Johnson, early pioneers of the region, is in the park, as are a reconstructed wharf and sculptures, reminders of Latrobe's earlier years as a busy port and regional centre. The Court House Museum is also worth a visit.

Numerous walking tracks offer excellent views of the town, one of which, the Teddy Shean Walk, heads off from the car park on Gilbert Street.

Each Christmas the township comes alive as it hosts the Latrobe Wheel Race. Established in 1890, this is one of Australia's biggest cycling carnivals where cyclists and sprinters compete for the Latrobe Wheel and the Latrobe Gift. The famous Tasmanian Axemen are also in action here.

A market is held in Latrobe each Sunday while the Latrobe Summer Festival takes place each year around Australia Day.

ACCOMMODATION: Lucas Hotel, ph (03) 6426 1101; Old Latrobe Motel, ph (03) 6426 2030; Erica Cottage (guesthouse), ph (03) 6426 2717

ACTIVITIES: Fishing, tennis, water sports

TOURIST INFORMATION: Ph (03) 6426 2693

LAUNCESTON

201 KM NORTH OF HOBART
POPULATION: 68 779   MAP REF: PAGE 391 K6

Tasmania's second biggest city, Launceston is an important northern regional centre for the surrounding agricultural industry. Situated on the edge of the magnificent Tamar Valley, it is the ideal base for visitors.

Launceston is a city of parks and gardens; a major attraction is City Park which was established in the 1820s. This sanctuary features manicured lawns, colourful flowerbeds and towering English deciduous trees such as oaks and elms. Punchbowl Reserve is

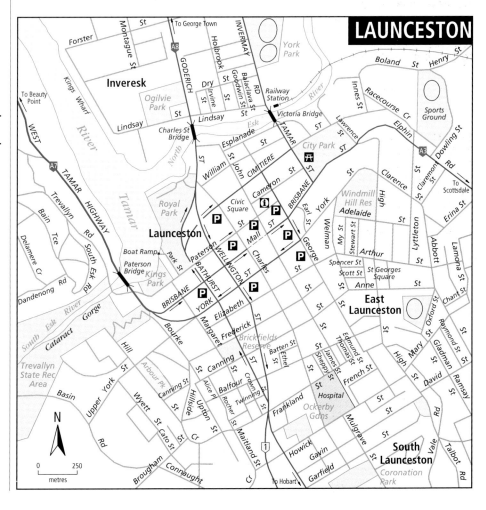

Penny Royal World in Launceston

5 km south of the town. This is a 24 hectare reserve with extensive lawns, huge multi-coloured rhododendrons and native trees, while nestled on the edge of the South Esk River only 2 km from the town are Trevallyn Dam and the State Recreation Reserve. The dam is the storage area for the Trevallyn power station and is open for inspection. The reserve is ideal for horse riding, swimming and bushwalking.

Settled in 1804, Launceston is rich in history. It has a number of museums including the Community History Museum which is situated in an historic warehouse, built in 1842. The Queen Victoria Museum and Art Gallery exhibits fine pieces of colonial artwork alongside contemporary Australian artwork.

The National Trust of Tasmania has restored many fine historic properties throughout Tasmania; an excellent example is Franklin House, 8 km south of Launceston. Built in 1838, this Georgian home has been fully restored and decorated with furniture from the 1800s. Another fine building is Macquarie House at Civic Square, a colonial warehouse which was built in 1830 and now houses displays relating to Tasmania's convict past.

Other fascinating attractions of Launceston include the National Automotive Museum of Tasmania, opposite City Park, which contains over 40 classic vintage cars. There is also a large collection of motorcycles that date back as far as 1914.

Penny Royal World, an impressive tourist attraction, sits in an old quarry in the centre of town. Features include a nineteenth-century gunpowder mill, lakes, windmill, waterfalls and a traditional confectionery factory, while an underground museum shows how the gunpowder was manufactured. Penny Royal World is adjacent to Cataract Gorge and Paterson Bridge from where the *Lady Stelfox* paddle-steamer offers daily cruises of the picturesque gorge.

The Launceston Planetarium is one of only four such displays in Australia where visitors can view the night-time skies of the southern hemisphere. A solar telescope also allows safe viewing of the sun.

The sheep and wool industry has been a mainstay for Tasmanians and the Waverley Woollen Mills, established in 1874 and the oldest in Australia, can be toured. The milling process—from fleece to the finished product—is demonstrated to visitors. The Tasmanian Woollie Crafts illustrate the sheepskin

process where the hides are tanned. The Tamar Knitting Mill, Tasmania's largest, also offers tours of its working mill.

Festivale, featuring food, wine, arts and entertainment, takes place in February as does the Country Club Casino Skyrace. Three Peaks Race is held at Easter, followed by the Launceston Show in September, and the Royal Launceston Show takes place in October.

ACCOMMODATION: Country Club Casino Hotel, ph (03) 6355 5777; Colonial Motor Inn, ph (03) 6331 6588; Tamar River Villas, ph (03) 6327 1022; Able Tasman Airport Motor Inn, ph (03) 6344 5244

ACTIVITIES: Golf, greyhound racing, historic sites, horseracing, tennis, water sports

TOURIST INFORMATION: Ph (03) 6336 3122

LILYDALE

230 KM NORTH OF HOBART
POPULATION: 335   MAP REF: PAGE 391 K5

In the 1800s the small township of Lilydale was renowned for its wine production, but surrounded as it was by forest it was the logging industry that became the major source of income. Today this pretty town is popular with artists and there are many arts and craft shops which feature paintings, wood-turning, drawings, sculptures and leather work.

To the south-east of the town stands Mt Arthur, which is popular with bushwalkers using Lilydale as their base. Tracks which once serviced the nearby Lisle goldfields allow walkers and climbers to gain excellent views from its peak.

Lilydale Falls is 3 km north of the town in a popular picnic reserve with an easy walking track to the falls. The notable W. A. G. Walker Rhododendron Reserve in nearby Lalla has plants that are 60 years old and tower more than 6 metres tall.

The Bridestowe Estate Lavender Farm at Nabowla north of Lilydale is the largest oil-producing lavender farm in the southern hemisphere. Open only during January, it is a delight when plants are in full bloom.

ACCOMMODATION: Plovers Ridge Country Retreat (B&B), ph (03) 6395 1102; Falls Farm (B&B), ph (03) 6395 1598; Callamoor Host Farm (holiday units), ph (03) 6395 4125

ACTIVITIES: Sightseeing, swimming, walking

TOURIST INFORMATION: Ph (03) 6336 3122

LONGFORD

189 KM NORTH OF HOBART
POPULATION: 2605   MAP REF: PAGE 391 K7

Longford is an historic village situated where the South Esk and Macquarie Rivers meet and is noted for its rich agricultural land which supports the local beef and dairy industry. Longford's origins were influenced by the early British settlers who first moved here from Norfolk Island in 1813. Stately homes and rural properties are scattered around the rolling countryside.

Two notable properties worth visiting are Brickendon and Woolmers Estate. Brickendon is one of Tasmania's oldest rural properties, established

in 1824 by William Archer, and now farmed by Archer's descendants. Located 5 km out of Longford, Woolmers Estate offers cottage accommodation and guided house tours.

In the town centre there are antique shops, art and craft stores and The Ye Olde Dolls House Shop and Museum which specialises in dolls and miniatures. Christ Church, built in 1839, features the graves of many of the early pioneers of this region.

Twelve kilometres north of town is the Longford Wildlife Park, the first to import deer into Tasmania (in 1834) and these splendid creatures roam in this pleasant park.

The Blessing of the Harvest takes place in March while the Longford Show is held during October, and the Longford Village Green Garden Fair in November.

ACCOMMODATION: The Racecourse Inn Hotel, ph (03) 6391 12352; Brickendon Historic Cottages, ph (03) 6391 1251; Kingsley House Olde World Accommodation (holiday units), ph (03) 6391 2318

ACTIVITIES: Fishing, golf, historic interest

TOURIST INFORMATION: Ph (03) 6391 1181

MOLE CREEK

256 KM NORTH-WEST OF HOBART
POPULATION: 250   MAP REF: PAGE 390 G7

This is the apiarists' centre of Tasmania and the honey produced at Mole Creek is considered 'liquid gold'—the finest in Australia. It is the leatherwood forests of the west coast of Tasmania that are responsible for the honey's distinctive flavour. The Stephens Honey Factory offers tastings and sales.

Mole Creek is the perfect starting point for a journey through the Great Western Tiers. To the south-west is Mole Creek Karst National Park with over 200 caves including Scotts, Baldock and Marakoopa Caves. The latter is a glow-worm cave with a magnificent fern-glade walk near by. King Solomon Cave, further north on the edge of the Emu Plains, has stalactites which hang from the cave top glittering in the light. The nearby Trowunna Wildlife Park allows visitors to see Tasmanian animals in their native settings.

ACCOMMODATION: Mole Creek Hotel, ph (03) 6363 1102; Mole Creek Guest House, ph (03) 6363 1399; Rosewick Cottage, ph (03) 6363 1354

ACTIVITIES: Bushwalking, caves, national park access, nature study

TOURIST INFORMATION: Ph (03) 6363 1399

NEW NORFOLK

39 KM NORTH-WEST OF HOBART
POPULATION: 5820   MAP REF: PAGE 389 J4

Located on the banks of the Derwent River, not far from Hobart, New Norfolk is a major town, offering visitors history, good restaurants and museums.

The town took its name from the settlers who arrived here from Norfolk Island after the penal colony was abandoned in 1808. These country men built a superb colonial village (registered in its entirety with the National Trust) which is best appreciated through a town walk. Of particular

The beautiful Derwent River near New Norfolk

interest are the Old Colony Inn with its art and craft shop and magnificent gardens, and the Bush Inn, built in 1816 and overlooking the Derwent River.

During the mid-1800s hops were introduced to the region. Bushy Park produced the first commercial hops in the district and was once the largest hop farm in the southern hemisphere. Each March Bushy Park hosts the Derwent Valley Hop Festival.

For thrillseekers there are jet boat rides over the rapids of the Derwent River. Train enthusiasts will enjoy the Derwent Valley Railway which offers steam train rides through the valley. Tulips make a colourful display when in bloom from the first week in October.

Nearby Plenty is home to the Salmon Ponds where the first brown and rainbow trout were bred in captivity in Australia in 1864.

ACCOMMODATION: Bush Inn Hotel, ph (03) 6261 2256; Glen Derwent (B&B), ph (03) 6261 3244; New Norfolk Caravan Park, ph (03) 6261 1268

ACTIVITIES: Fishing, golf, historic interest, hop farming, jet boat rides, tennis, water sports

TOURIST INFORMATION: Ph (03) 6261 2777

OATLANDS

85 KM NORTH OF HOBART
POPULATION: 525   MAP REF: PAGE 389 K2

Before the delightful township of Oatlands was established this area was home in 1827 to a military garrison, one of four which controlled the state from the south to the north. It was to be five more years before the township was surveyed on the shores of Lake Dulverston and the community of sandstone buildings erected: High Street has 87 colonial sandstone buildings. It is claimed that Oatlands has the best collection of pre-1837 houses in Australia, including the Carrington Mill (extensively renovated by the National Trust in the 1980s), the courthouse, gaoler's residence and three magnificent churches.

Among the more interesting shops is the Scottish, Irish and Welsh Shop which stocks over 500 different tartans on display. The Craft Bear, housed in an

historic building circa 1845, has a large range of teddy bears, biscuits and chocolates, while Wood and Wife has a wide choice of collectables and antiques.

To the north-west of Oatlands are Lakes Sorell and Crescent, which sit at the base of Mt Franklin, and the Lake Sorell Wildlife Sanctuary. There are many activities involving the lakeland area including a walking track which runs through Lake Dulverton Aquatic Reserve, a scenic golf course built on the shores of Lake Dulverton and trout fishing in the lake.

In February there is a rodeo held in Oatlands.

ACCOMMODATION: Oatlands Lodge (B&B), ph (03) 6254 1444; Currajong Cottages, ph (03) 6252 2150; Oatlands YHA, ph (03) 6254 1320

ACTIVITIES: Golf, historic interest, swimming, tennis, walking

TOURIST INFORMATION: Ph (03) 6254 1212

ORFORD

79 KM NORTH-EAST OF HOBART
POPULATION: 505   MAP REF: PAGE 389 M3

Orford is a popular holiday resort and fishing village on the east coast of Tasmania where the Prosser River opens out into the Prosser Bay. As a seaside resort Orford's activities include fishing and swimming off sandy beaches such as the popular Shelly Beach or Raspins Beach.

Maria Island, which lies off the coast, was named after Anthony Van Diemen's wife, and a penal settlement was established there in 1825. There have since been many different ventures on the island, but it is now a national park and wildlife sanctuary. There are still many convict buildings to investigate on the island. Much of the western side of the island is perfect for swimming, snorkelling and diving while the island has a variety of wildlife including wallabies, Cape Barren geese and emus.

Access to the island is via ferry and charter boats operate in the bay and are available for fishing or for cruises. There are also scenic flights over Maria Island leaving from Triabunna.

The Wielangta Road Forest Drive, south of Orford, is a great alternative route down to the Tasman Peninsula. The road passes through the Sandspit Forest Reserve with walks which highlight the trees and plants through information boards. Another walk goes through the old Wielangta saw-milling town, most of which is now ruined.

ACCOMMODATION: The Eastcoaster Hotel, ph (03) 6257 1172; Blue Waters Motel, ph (03) 6257 1102; Riverside Villas, ph 1800 817 533

ACTIVITIES: Charter boat cruises, fishing, golf, horse riding, national park access, tennis, water sports

TOURIST INFORMATION: Ph (03) 6257 1372

PENGUIN

309 KM NORTH-WEST OF HOBART
POPULATION: 2880   MAP REF: PAGE 390 F5

Nestled between Bass Strait and the mountain ranges of northern Tasmania, this town offers magnificent parklands and a beautiful bay lined with pristine sandy beaches. Penguin's beginnings were as a timber town, when it supplied timber from the lush hinterland to both Australia and New Zealand. This seaside resort is famous for the fairy penguins which inhabit the eastern edge of the Penguin Beach. Hiscutt Park has the town's Bicentennial Project, a large windmill which was built by the Dutch community of Penguin.

Main Road travels along the water's edge and is the perfect location for a walk or picnic. For shoppers, the Old School Markets are held in King Edward Street off Main Road every second Sunday and are full of arts and crafts from the region.

The journey between Penguin and Ulverstone provides excellent views of the coastline. The Three Sisters Seabird Sanctuary, on offshore islands which offer refuge to thousands of seabirds, is worth a visit.

To the south lies Mt Montgomery which has many walking tracks, while a day drive could be taken down to the caving district south of Gunns Plains.

ACCOMMODATION: Neptune Grand Hotel, ph (03) 6437 2406; Beachfront Lodge Hotel, ph (03) 6435 4134; Penguin Caravan Park, ph (03) 6437 2785

ACTIVITIES: Fairy penguin viewing, fishing, golf, horse riding, scenic drives, swimming, tennis

TOURIST INFORMATION: Ph (03) 6437 1421

PERTH

182 KM NORTH OF HOBART
POPULATION: 1575   MAP REF: PAGE 391 K7

The quaint township of Perth was established in 1821 by Governor Lachlan Macquarie when travelling through the South Esk River region towards Hobart. A ferry service was established on the river for transport before the road was built to Launceston. The bridge across the South Esk River, which replaced the ferry, has had an unfortunate history: the first bridge built in 1836 was destroyed by floods in 1929. The structure was replaced within two years, but was once again washed away in floods 50 years later. Fortunately the current bridge has remained intact since 1971.

Many buildings from last century remain, including the Uniting Church, Old Post Office, Jolly Farmer, Leather Bottell and the Old Crown Inn. The Tasmanian Honey Company, producer of fine Tasmanian honey, is open to the public.
ACCOMMODATION: Flinty Creek (B&B), ph (03) 6398 2704; Old Perth Jail (B&B), ph (03) 6398 2100; Queens Head Inn (hotel/motel), ph (03) 6398 2218
ACTIVITIES: Fishing, 4WD touring, swimming
TOURIST INFORMATION: Ph (03) 6230 8233

POATINA

203 KM NORTH OF HOBART
POPULATION: 120   MAP REF: PAGE 391 J8
Located on the edge of the Great Western Tiers, the small township of Poatina was built in the 1950s to house workers for the hydro-electric power station 5 km south-west of town. In 1977 the Great Lake Power Development Scheme was completed, with water diverted north towards Poatina inaugurating Tasmania's first underground power station. Tours are available of the power station. South-west of the historic towns of Longford and Perth, Poatina is perfect for a day drive and a chance to view part of this state's power system.
ACCOMMODATION: Poatina Chalet Motel, ph (03) 6397 8290
ACTIVITIES: Golf, power station tours
TOURIST INFORMATION: Ph (03) 6336 3122

PONTVILLE

31 KM NORTH OF HOBART
POPULATION: 1125   MAP REF: PAGE 389 K4
This mid-nineteenth century garrison town was built near a quarry which supplied most of the freestone used in Tasmania last century. The town is classified as an historic town and has many interesting buildings from the 1800s, including St Matthew's Catholic Church and St Mark's Church of England. The Barracks, formerly the local store, and the Sheiling, built in 1825, are both restored as accommodation houses. There is also an historic bridge, built by convicts, which spans the Jordan River.
Less than 20 km north is the Chauncy Vale Wildlife Sanctuary while south of the town is the Bonorong Park Wildlife Centre near Brighton.
ACCOMMODATION: The Sheiling (B&B), ph (03) 6268 1951; The Barracks (units), ph (03) 6268 1665
ACTIVITIES: Historic interest, wildlife parks
TOURIST INFORMATION: Ph (03) 6336 3122

PORT ARTHUR

102 KM SOUTH-EAST OF HOBART
POPULATION OF TASMAN PENINSULA: 1595
MAP REF: PAGE 389 M6
A visit to the historic state of Tasmania is not complete without a tour of the Port Arthur Penal Settlement. In 1830 Lieutenant-Governor Arthur chose this site to incarcerate the worst of Tasmania's

The Penitentiary at Port Arthur

convicts as there was only one route for escape on land. This made the job of confining the prisoners easier. Tales of man-eating sharks in the waters surrounding the settlement deterred escape by sea.
The penal settlement operated until 1877. An estimated 12 500 convicts served time here. There are still more than 30 buildings which can be inspected including the church, penitentiary, the commandant's residence and the model prison, where prisoners were put into solitary confinement. The Isle of the Dead near Point Puer is where nearly 2000 convicts and residents are buried.
The township of Port Arthur boasted a sawmill operation, shipbuilding yards, coalmining and brick manufacturing industries. The Bush Mill Steam Railway gives an insight into the area's timber industry. This railway, based on the narrow gauge system, takes passengers on a breathtaking 4 km journey around the hillside.
Stewarts Bay State Reserve to the north of the town has a walking track which leads from the penitentiary and follows the foreshore around Lakes Bay before joining back up with a track leading into the Reserve and down to Garden Point.
The Tasmanian Devil Park to the north of the town is a wildlife rescue centre. There are up to 25 species of injured and orphaned animals on display at any time, including Tasmanian devils, quolls, owls, eagles and kangaroos.
Further north again is Eaglehawk Neck, the small tract of land that connects the Tasman Peninsula with the mainland. Here was installed the notorious Dog Line, which was yet another means of preventing the prisoners from escaping from the prison. This area's natural attractions, preserved in state reserves, include the Tessellated Pavement, Tasman Blowhole, Tasman Arch and Devils Kitchen.
The township of Port Arthur holds a regatta, triathlon and woodchopping festival on Boxing Day.
ACCOMMODATION: Port Arthur Motor Inn, ph (03) 6250 2101; Port Arthur Villas, ph (03) 6250 2239; Port Arthur Holiday World, ph (03) 6250 2262
ACTIVITIES: Boat cruises, golf, historic interest, scenic flights, swimming, walking
TOURIST INFORMATION: Ph (03) 6250 2363

PORT SORELL

293 KM NORTH-WEST OF HOBART
POPULATION: 1495   MAP REF: PAGE 391 H5
This popular seaside resort is nestled amongst the surrounding hills making the protected waters of the Port Sorell estuary particularly good for water sports. Freers Beach is a favourite with swimmers.
The town, once known as Burgess, was established in the early 1800s, and was a base for sealers, whalers and fishermen.
To the east of Port Sorell across the bay is the Asbestos Range National Park with its sandy beaches and a wide variety of walks. Because of its proximity to Devonport this park is popular with day trippers and campers, who use the marked walking trails to explore the heathlands and open plains of the park.
ACCOMMODATION: Shearwater Country Club Hotel, ph (03) 6428 6205; Tudor Cabins, ph (03) 6428 6390; Arklow House (B&B), ph (03) 6428 6424
ACTIVITIES: Fishing, golf, nature walks, national park access, tennis, water sports
TOURIST INFORMATION: Ph (03) 6426 2693

QUEENSTOWN

262 KM NORTH-WEST OF HOBART
POPULATION: 3370   MAP REF: PAGE 390 D10
Cresting the mountain range and heading into Queenstown, it is evident from the bare surrounding hills that this town's history evolved around mining. Gold was discovered in 1881 and the Mt Lyell Gold Mining Company formed to extract the precious metal. Mining of gold was completed in 1891 but then the copper, which had been discarded as rubbish, was mined and this continues today. The mining process has stripped the vegetation and left scarred hillsides.
The remains of the West Lyell Open Cut Mine, once Australia's largest mine, and the Mt Lyell Mine can both be toured. The CMT Underground tour takes in the working areas of the copper mine, 6 km down

the main shaft and 340 metres below sea level. This is only the second working mine in the world to allow visitors access to the underground face.

Beyond the hills of Queenstown lie Tasmania's magnificent rainforests. 4WD tours are available which offer spectacular views of the west coast as well as an opportunity to walk some of the Kelly Basin Track, formerly part of the North Lyell Railway Line. Queenstown provides access to both the Franklin–Gordon Wild Rivers and the Cradle Mountain–Lake St Clair National Parks. Whitewater rafting trips on the Franklin River are also on offer. A scenic drive to the King River Power Development south of Queenstown travels through forest with Huon pine, King Billy pine and celery-top pine trees.
ACCOMMODATION: Westcoaster Motor Inn, ph (03) 6471 1033; Queenstown Motor Lodge, ph (03) 6471 1866; Queenstown Cabin and Tourist Park, ph (03) 6471 1332
ACTIVITIES: Fishing, golf, mining tours, national park access, swimming, tennis, whitewater rafting
TOURIST INFORMATION: Ph (03) 6471 2388

RICHMOND

28 KM NORTH-EAST OF HOBART
POPULATION: 755   MAP REF: PAGE 389 K4
Only 20 minutes' drive from Hobart, the small town of Richmond is one of the finest examples of a Georgian village in Australia, some buildings dating back to the 1820s. The Richmond Gaol, which is the oldest and best preserved colonial gaol in Australia, was built between 1825 and 1840. Australia's oldest complete freestone bridge crosses the Coal River in Richmond. Built by convicts between 1823 and 1825, it gave access from Hobart to the east coast and Tasman Peninsula. Other structures of interest in the town include the post office building (1828) and Prospect House mansion.

The Peppercorn Gallery, an 1850s convict-built cottage, features local art work. The Old Hobart Town Historical Model Village depicts Hobart as it was in the 1920s in a scale model. Always fun for both children and adults is the Richmond Maze. With toys dating back to 1900, the Richmond Toy Museum contains many reminders of the past. There are Matchbox and Hornby toys, teddy bears and dolls.

The Richmond Village Fair is held in October while a harvest festival is staged during May.

Richmond Bridge crossing the Coal River

ACCOMMODATION: Richmond Arms Hotel, ph (03) 6260 2109; The Leys (B&B), ph (03) 6260 4378; Richmond Barracks (B&B), ph (03) 6260 2453
ACTIVITIES: Golf, historic interest
TOURIST INFORMATION: Ph (03) 6260 2127

ROSEBERY

308 KM NORTH-WEST OF HOBART
POPULATION: 1640   MAP REF: PAGE 390 D8
The mining town of Rosebery is situated on the mineral-rich west coast of Tasmania where gold was first discovered in 1893. Only one year later, lead, zinc and copper were also found; however, by 1912, the mines had ceased to operate.

Only 2 km from Rosebery is the magnificent Montezuma Falls, one of the highest in Tasmania, with a drop of 104 metres.

Lake Pieman and the Pieman River lie on the edge of town and legend has it that the river took its name from the criminal Alexander 'Pieman' Pearce who was jailed for selling food unfit for humans. He escaped and is alleged to have eaten his fellow escapees in the process.

Rosebery's sporting carnival is held in mid-December.
ACCOMMODATION: Plandome Hotel, ph (03) 6473 1351; Milners Cottage, ph (03) 6473 1796; Rosebery Caravan Park, ph (03) 6473 1336
ACTIVITIES: Fishing, golf, mine tour, swimming, tennis, walking trails
TOURIST INFORMATION: Ph (03) 6471 6225

ROSS

119 KM NORTH OF HOBART
POPULATION: 285   MAP REF: PAGE 391 L9
The small township of Ross was named by Governor Lachlan Macquarie in 1821 after a town in Scotland, but the town had already been established some ten years earlier as a military outpost.

While there are a number of historic buildings, the town's most splendid feature is the bridge across the Macquarie River. This intricately designed bridge was built by convicts, the job being completed in 1836. It is one of the oldest such bridges in Australia.

Ross was the site of one of only two female convict settlements in Tasmania and the 'Female Factory' has been partially restored by the Department of National Parks and Wildlife. The station was opened in 1847 and housed female convicts and their babies until the transportation of convicts to Tasmania ceased in 1853.

This region of midland Tasmania is famous for producing fine Merino wool; Ross is home to the Tasmanian Wool Centre which features wool garments, arts and crafts along with a retail store. There are other fine examples of the local crafts in the Ross Nursery, Crafts and Antiques Store, and the Village Toymaker.
ACCOMMODATION: The Elms Inn Hotel, ph (03) 6381 5246; Man O'Ross Hotel, ph (03) 6381 5240; Colonial Cottages of Ross, ph (03) 6381 5354
ACTIVITIES: Historic interest
TOURIST INFORMATION: Ph (03) 6381 5466

ST HELENS

267 KM NORTH-EAST OF HOBART
POPULATION: 1145   MAP REF: PAGE 391 P6
Protected by Georges Bay, St Helens is the easternmost town in Tasmania and popular with holiday-makers. The beaches offer safe swimming and other water sports, such as sailing and water-skiing. A cycling and walking track follows this magnificent foreshore from the bridge at St Helens.

Fishing is one of the main industries and there are three fish processing plants in town. Many fishing charter boats operate out of St Helens.

With many reserves and parks, the area is ideal for walking and St Helens Point State Recreation Area is a great place to start, with coastal views, impressive sand dunes and camp sites. Other walks in the area can be found at Humbug Point Reserve, Bay of Fires Coastal Reserve and Goblin Forest Walk.

Only 20 minutes north-west of town is Pyengana, a small village which has an early history of tin mining. From here you can access the St Columba Falls, which drop 100 metres to South George River.

On the St Columba Falls Road is Healeys Pyengana Cheese Factory where traditional, old-style cheddar cheese is produced.

The Game Fishing Championship is held over a long weekend in March while the Surf Angling Champion is determined in late April. A huge jazz festival takes place over the June long weekend.
ACCOMMODATION: Anchor Wheel Motel, ph (03) 6376 1358; Bayside Inn (hotel/motel), ph (03) 6376 1466; Cockle Grove Beachfront (apartments), ph (03) 6376 3036
ACTIVITIES: Fishing, golf, rowing, tennis, walking, water sports
TOURIST INFORMATION: Ph (03) 6376 1329

ST MARYS

232 KM NORTH-EAST OF HOBART
POPULATION: 630   MAP REF: PAGE 391 N7
St Marys is situated on the headwaters of the South Esk River, surrounded by spectacular mountain peaks and is only ten minutes' drive from the east coast. The small township once supported a local dairy industry, but most of the farms have since gone and the main industries are now cattle, coalmining and timber.

St Patricks Head State Reserve is 7 km east of town. From the top of St Patricks Head, which takes about an hour to climb, there are spectacular views. To the north a trek along the Grey Mare Trail leads to a picnic area and small waterfall, while Elephant Pass south of the town also offers splendid coastal views. The drive from Bicheno through St Marys to the seaside town of St Helens gives excellent views.

Fingal, 20 km west on the Esk Highway, was originally a goldmining town, but now supports farming and a coalmining industry. The Tasmanian Hotel, built in 1860, was constructed of stone removed from the local prison barracks.
ACCOMMODATION: St Marys Hotel, ph (03) 6372 2181
ACTIVITIES: Fishing, golf, scenic lookouts, tennis
TOURIST INFORMATION: Ph (03) 6372 2529

SCAMANDER

247 KM NORTH-EAST OF HOBART
POPULATION: 410   MAP REF: PAGE 391 P6
Situated at the mouth of the Scamander River, Scamander's small resident population rises to nearer 1000 during the peak holiday season when holiday-makers head to this east coast resort for sun, water sports and its magnificent sandy beaches.

Fishing is a popular recreation, both in the river and out at sea, with bream the main catch in this seaside estuary. Steels Beach and Wrinklers Beach, either side of the river mouth, offer safe swimming in the protected waters. Beaumaris, which is 5 km to the north, has beaches, and lagoon areas for water sports.

Scamander Forest Reserve is perfect for a picnic, fishing for trout or bushwalking. At Trout Creek Reserve, only ten minutes from Scamander, anglers will find a platform built for trout and bream fishing.
ACCOMMODATION: Scamander Beach Resort, ph (03) 6372 5255; Surfside Motel, ph (03) 6372 5177; Blue Seas Motel, ph (03) 6372 5211
ACTIVITIES: Fishing, walking, water sports
TOURIST INFORMATION: Ph (03) 6376 1329

SCOTTSDALE

267 KM NORTH-EAST OF HOBART
POPULATION: 2020   MAP REF: PAGE 391 L5
Situated in the regional heart of the north-east of Tasmania, Scottsdale is the centre of a rich agriculture, dairy and forest industry. The tall pine trees that cover the local hillsides are milled at Tonganah, 7 km south-east of town. Potatoes are harvested here mainly for the frozen-food company Birdseye.

The area was first viewed by Europeans in 1855 when the government surveyor, James Scott, came across this fertile land. It took less than 10 years for the first sawmill to begin production of the local timber, but over 40 years for the railway to stretch from Launceston, 65 km to the south.

The visitor information centre is in the old Lyric Theatre, which closed in 1972. On show here are old photographs and artefacts from the town's past. A bike museum is housed at the historic Beulah B&B.

Sliding Range Lookout on the highway west of town offers superb views of the countryside while North-East Park on the Tasman Highway to the east is a pleasant picnic location with interesting walking trails. Cuckoo Falls and the Tonganah hop fields are located just outside of the town, and the Bridestowe Lavender Farm to the west is delightful, especially in January when the lavender is in full bloom.

The Derby Tin Mine Centre, an authentically reconstructed mining town, also has a tin mine museum with displays, old photographs and artefacts.

Scottsdale Markets are held each Saturday and the Scottsdale Show is in early November.
ACCOMMODATION: Beulah of Scottsdale (B&B), ph (03) 6352 3723; Anabels of Scottsdale Motel, ph (03) 6352 3277; Lords Hotel, ph (03) 6352 2319
ACTIVITIES: Historic interest, sightseeing, swimming (pool), tennis, walks
TOURIST INFORMATION: Ph (03) 6352 3095

SHEFFIELD

269 KM NORTH-WEST OF HOBART
POPULATION: 995   MAP REF: PAGE 390 G6
Sheffield is near the beautiful Lake Barrington on the edge of the Great Western Tiers. The town boasts a most unusual outdoor art gallery, with more than 30 historic murals painted on walls and shop fronts. The project began in 1986 to help boost tourism and Sheffield is now known as the 'Town of Murals'.

In the main street you will find art and craft stores, a blacksmith gallery, pottery, the Kentish School Community Museum as well as the Diversity Theatre which screens films about the town's murals.

During December and January, and for the first weekend each month, the Redwater Creek Steam Railway Society offers steam train rides.

A short drive from Sheffield is the Mount Roland Emu Ranch, which is open to the public. Mount Roland is also home to the Paradise Park Deer Farm—you can tour the farm, or fish for trout here.

Markets are held every third Saturday in March, June, September and December, while the Model Railways and Collectables Show is held on Australia Day. Daffodil Week is in full bloom in mid-September and the Triple Top Running Race is held in October.
ACCOMMODATION: Sheffield Country Motor Inn, ph (03) 6491 1800; Badgers Host Farm (apartments), ph (03) 6491 1816; Silver Ridge Retreat (holiday units), ph (03) 6491 1727
ACTIVITIES: Golf, historic interest, tennis, walks
TOURIST INFORMATION: Ph (03) 6491 1036

SMITHTON

415 KM NORTH-WEST OF HOBART
POPULATION: 3495   MAP REF: PAGE 390 C3
Smithton sits at the mouth of the Duck River in the far north-west of Tasmania. Not far from Stanley and the Arthur Pieman Protected Areas, it is the administrative centre of this northern region of Tasmania. Forestry and farming provide the basis of employment in the region and Gunn's Timber Mill, the largest mill of its type in the southern hemisphere, is open for tours. There is also a strong fishing industry and dolomite is now being mined in the area.

The mouth of the Duck River is popular for boating and fishing. Much of the area, however, is reclaimed swampland and fossilised bones, including those of a giant wombat and kangaroo, were found by locals in the swamps. These bones are now on display at the Hobart and Launceston museums.

The Smithton–Circular Head Heritage Centre features local history of the area, including the history of the Aborigines who lived in the region.

One of the more exciting ways to experience this region's remote wilderness is on a 4-wheeler quad bike; these are specifically designed to tackle the beaches and rugged timbered terrain.

To the west is the small town of Marrawah on the coast which offers excellent surfing, while the surrounding west coast region forms part of the Arthur Pieman Protected Area, a popular area with bushwalkers and campers.

A food festival is held during February every even-numbered year and is run in conjunction with the Tasmanian circumnavigational yacht race. Tasmania Day Regatta, held in November, is another popular event .
ACCOMMODATION: Bridge Hotel Motel, ph (03) 6452 1389; Tall Timbers (motel), ph (03) 6452 2755; Macvillas (holiday units), ph (03) 6452 1278
ACTIVITIES: Golf, fishing, scenic walks, water sports
TOURIST INFORMATION: Ph (03) 6452 1265

SORELL

27 KM NORTH-EAST OF HOBART
POPULATION: 3200   MAP REF: PAGE 389 L4
Not to be mistaken for Port Sorell, the town of Sorell is connected to Midway Point by a large causeway which took eight years to build. This route is a major link between Hobart and Port Arthur and shortens the distance to the Tasman Peninsula.

In the early days this town was an important supplier of grain, but now sheep farming is the main industry through the region.

Bushranger Matthew Brady came upon the small settlement of Sorell not long after it had been established and captured the guards of the garrison, along with most of the locals. The audacious act, however, was short lived, and Brady was caught some two years later and, in 1826, hanged for his crimes.

The town has many historical attractions, including the Blue Bell Inn, which was built in 1863, and two churches, St George's and Scots Church.

A short drive from Sorell is the Orani Vineyard, which offers wine tastings and cellar sales.

A food festival is held in Sorell in November.
ACCOMMODATION: Sorell Barracks Motel, ph (03) 6265 1236; Blue Bell Inn (B&B), ph (03) 6265 2804; Flimby (B&B), ph (03) 6265 1632
ACTIVITIES: Historic interest, wineries
TOURIST INFORMATION: Ph (03) 6265 2201

Scots Church in Sorell

STANLEY

408 KM NORTH-WEST OF HOBART
POPULATION: 580   MAP REF: PAGE 390 C3

An historic town and fishing port in the far north-west of the state, Stanley has a most prominent feature: Circular Head. This was named by Bass and Flinders who sailed this region in 1798. This landmass forms the Nut State Reserve and 'the Nut', as it is commonly known, is a giant 152-metre-high mound of lava which has set hard, with sheer cliffs on three sides that drop into the water. A chairlift operates from behind the Nut Shop Tea Rooms or there is a walking track to the top. From here there are spectacular views across Bass Strait and the township of Stanley.

Originally a port for sailors and whalers who fished the rough seas of the Bass Strait, today Stanley is the base for many cray and shark fishermen. The waterfront features quaint, old, bluestone buildings including the old grain store and the customs bond store. Other historic buildings in town include Lyons Cottage which was once the home of the former Australian Prime Minister Joseph Lyons.

The Circular Head Spring Flower Festival offers a colourful display of local blooms in early October, while the port comes alive on Melbourne Cup Weekend in November, when the Melbourne to Stanley Yacht Race takes place.

ACCOMMODATION: Stanley Village (motel), ph (03) 6458 1404; Stanley Guest House (B&B), ph (03) 6458 1488; Captains Cottage (holiday units), ph (03) 6458 1109
ACTIVITIES: Fishing, golf, historic interest, tennis, water sports
TOURIST INFORMATION: Ph (03) 6452 1265

STRAHAN

302 KM WEST OF HOBART
POPULATION: 600   MAP REF: PAGE 390 C10

The quaint town of Strahan sits beside the protected waters of Macquarie Harbour in the south-west. From here visitors can experience some of the best natural wilderness in Tasmania. Surrounded by lush forests, this was once home to a booming timber industry along with mining and fishing. These declined, and then, during the 1980s, came the controversy over the proposed damming of the Franklin River.

Macquarie Harbour is a magnificent bay and best appreciated from the air. Apart from the seaplane flights, the region is accessible only to walkers or rafters. Within the harbour lies Sarah Island, an old convict settlement whose history makes Port Arthur seem like a resort. Established in 1822, it was known for the harsh treatment inflicted on prisoners and the appalling conditions in which they lived. The island is accessible by boat only but tours are available.

Most visitors take the opportunity to cruise the still waters of the Gordon River into the remote wilderness of the Franklin–Gordon Wild Rivers National Park, passing through lush verdant forests and magnificent Huon pines. This region is part of the Tasmanian Wilderness World Heritage Area with rainforests that are thousands of years old.

The wharf at Strahan

Tours by 4WD take in Ocean Beach, Tasmania's longest, along with the Henty sand dunes which are close to Strahan. Horse rides through the heavily timbered forests or along the sandy beaches at sunset are also a great way to explore the region.

In town you can wander along the wharf, investigate the local arts and craft stores, gaze at the gem and mineral display or just enjoy the fine dining at the many restaurants.

The Strahan–Lyell Picnic Day is held on Australia Day and the Tin Miner's Marathon is in February.
ACCOMMODATION: Franklin Manor (historical B&B), ph (03) 6471 7311; Strachan Village Cottages, ph (03) 6471 7191; Strachan Motor Inn, ph (03) 6471 7160
ACTIVITIES: Fishing, 4WD tours, golf, historic tours, horse riding, national park access, river cruises, scenic flights, water sports
TOURIST INFORMATION: Ph (03) 6471 7488

SWANSEA

137 KM NORTH-EAST OF HOBART
POPULATION: 550   MAP REF: PAGE 389 N1

Swansea lies on the brilliant blue waters of the Great Oyster Bay and is a popular fishing destination and seaside resort. The views from the town are spectacular, with the famous Freycinet National Park on the other side of the bay. Anglers fish in the bay or head out to the Tasman Sea to cast their lines.

The town was first settled in 1821 and six years later a military garrison was established on Waterloo Point. Now this point features a park and picnic area which leads down to the Schouten House Beach on the southern edge of the point.

Whalers set up a base in Swansea but it is the bark factory, established in 1885, for which Swansea is renowned. The Swansea Bark Mill and East Coast Museum on the Tasman Highway is the only restored black wattle bark mill in Australia. (The bark from the black wattle was used for tanning leather.)

There is an historic walk which takes in the council chambers, Swan Inn, Morris General Store and the Community Centre, said to house Australia's last remaining full-sized billiard table.

Mayfield and Boltons Beach Coastal Reserves to the south are easily accessible from the highway while other seaside attractions include the Rocky Hills Convict Station and the unusual, convict-built stone bridge at Spiky Beach.

Two vineyards, Craigie Knowe and Spring Vale, feature in the area. The cellar at Spring Vale was originally a stable built by convicts, and the stone walls and pine rafters are still intact.

The Swansea Show is held in September and the Craft Fair in December.
ACCOMMODATION: Meredith House (B&B), ph (03) 6257 8119; Piermont Resort (holiday units), ph (03) 6257 8131; Swansea Ocean Villas (holiday units), ph (03) 6257 8656
ACTIVITIES: Fishing, golf, tennis, water sports, wineries
TOURIST INFORMATION: Ph (03) 6257 8677

TRIABUNNA

88 KM NORTH-EAST OF HOBART
POPULATION: 925   MAP REF: PAGE 389 M3

Triabunna's early claim to fame was as a whaling station which kept it alive during its early years as a garrison town. Today the small township boasts a large woodchip mill; the paper produced from the woodchip is mainly exported to Japan. Fishing is also a big industry in this seaside town.

The grand old buildings in the town can be appreciated on an historic walk which takes in the police watch house and the magistrates office, both built in the 1840s, as well as the Girraween Gardens and Tearooms. These gardens are a magnificent sight in spring and summer when they are in full bloom.

Maria Island to the south was in the early 1800s a penal settlement, but today it is a national park. A ferry goes from the Eastcoaster Resort, just south of Triabunna, to Darlington on Maria Island. You can visit the ruins of the settlement, and also go bushwalking, swimming and fishing.

An important attraction is the Spring Bay Crayfish Derby. Held on 4 January, it is a gourmet's delight.

ACCOMMODATION: Tandara Motor Inn, ph
(03) 6257 3333; Triabunna YHA, ph (03) 6257 3439;
Triabunna Caravan Park, ph (03) 6257 3375
ACTIVITIES: Fishing, horse riding, national park
access, tennis, water sports
TOURIST INFORMATION: Ph: (03) 6230 8233

ULVERSTONE

300 KM NORTH-WEST OF HOBART
POPULATION: 9925   MAP REF: PAGE 390 F5

The seaside resorts of Ulverstone and nearby Turners
Beach are a little over an hour's drive from
Devonport. Ulverstone is at the mouth of the Leven
River. With excellent beaches and spectacular parks
lining the river and foreshore, this town is ideal for
water sports, fishing, or just relaxing in the sun.

As with much of Tasmania, the timber industry
was the first to thrive in Ulverstone when paling
splitters worked the region's forests for timber to
build houses in Tasmania and the mainland. It was
here that Australia's first axe man competition was
held in the 1870s.

In the town there are antique stores with a large
selection of fine furniture and heirlooms. The Local
History Museum features artefacts and photographs
which will help preserve the history of the region.

Between Ulverstone and Devonport is Turners
Beach with 2 km of pristine sandy beaches which
attract beach lovers and anglers.

The Twilight Rodeo is the highlight in February
and the Agricultural Show in October.
ACCOMMODATION: The Lighthouse Hotel, ph
(03) 6425 1197; Boscobel of Ulverstone (B&B), ph
(03) 6425 1727; Ocean View (B&B), ph (03) 6425 5401
ACTIVITIES: Fishing, golf, tennis, walking, water
sports
TOURIST INFORMATION: Ph (03) 6425 2839

WESTBURY

216 KM NORTH-WEST OF HOBART
POPULATION: 1295   MAP REF: PAGE 391 J7

Originally a farming village established in 1828,
Westbury is an historic town with Georgian and
Victorian homes, brilliant green pastures and hedges.

There are many historic buildings including the
White House, a National Trust property situated on
the village green. Built in the 1840s, it has been
completely restored and furnished with eighteenth-
century oak. Culzean is another historic home which
was built in 1841 and is surrounded by a magnificent
English-style garden.

Mazes often go hand in hand with historic colonial
towns and Westbury's young maze, which was planted
only in 1984, is sure to provide plenty of family fun.

Gem collectors will delight in the Westbury
Minerals and Gemstones store which features more
than 30 000 specimens of minerals and gemstones.
Visitors can also purchase Tasmanian stones either
polished or roughly cut.

The St Patrick's Day Festival is great fun, while
over Easter and during November Pearn's Steam
World activates its extensive exhibit of steam engines.

The Westbury Markets are held at St Andrew's
Church on the third Saturday of each month.
ACCOMMODATION: The Regiments Retreat (B&B), ph
(03) 6393 2025; Westbury Hotel, ph (03) 6393 1151; Old
Bakehouse Westbury (holiday units), ph (03) 6393 1140
ACTIVITIES: Historic interest, steam engines,
swimming, tennis, walking
TOURIST INFORMATION: Ph (03) 6393 1140

WYNYARD

345 KM NORTH-WEST OF HOBART
POPULATION: 4680   MAP REF: PAGE 390 E4

Not far from Burnie, on the state's north coast, is
Wynyard, nestled between the Inglis River and the
Table Cape. This is a rich agricultural area with forest
reserves, rhododendron gardens and colourful crops
of poppies or tulips. Wynyard is an excellent base for
a visit to King Island. Once on the island you can
sample the beef and cheeses for which it is famous.

To Wynard's west is Rocky Cape National Park
and its magnificent Sisters Beach. You can choose
between leisurely 15 minute strolls or more energetic
walks on the park's well-signposted tracks. One of the
smallest parks in Tasmania, Rocky Cape features
coastal heathlands, beaches and Aboriginal sites.

One of Wynyard's biggest events is the annual
Tulip Festival, held in early October. The festival is
very much a community event and, apart from the
magnificent tulip displays, there are sailing races,
music, fireworks and a running event along with the
crowning of the Festival Queen. A must during this
festival time is a visit to the Van Diemen's Quality
Bulb Farm where rows of brightly coloured tulips,
irises and daffodils cover more than 3 hectares.

The Wynyard Agricultural Show takes place in
March.
ACCOMMODATION: Alexandria (B&B), ph
(03) 6442 4411; Wynyard Motor Inn, ph (03) 6442 2351;
Leisure Ville Caravan Park, ph (03) 6442 2291
ACTIVITIES: Fishing, golf, horse riding, national park
access, scenic flights, tennis, water sports
TOURIST INFORMATION: Ph (03) 6442 4143

Henty Sand Dunes, south of Zeehan

ZEEHAN

295 KM NORTH-WEST OF HOBART
POPULATION: 1135   MAP REF: PAGE 390 C9

Zeehan, in the state's west, is rich in both history and
minerals, and the discovery of silver and lead in 1882
saw it become the third largest settlement in the
early 1900s. In this peak period there were 26 hotels
in town, but after the boom in around 1914, most of
the residents left and there are now only two hotels.
Today Zeehan is a tourist town although the opening
of the Renison Bell tin mine outside of town has
boosted the town's economy.

Many historic buildings line the main street of
Zeehan including the Gaiety Theatre, post office,
Grand Hotel, the local bank and St Lukes Church.
Much of the history of the region and one of the best
mining displays can be found at the West Coast
Pioneers Memorial Museum.

Spray Tunnel Road leads to an old mine site. Also
worth a visit are the pioneers' cemetery, and Zeehan
smelters, built in 1898.

Granville Harbour, to the north, was originally
opened up as a soldier settlement at the end of World
War I. It is an excellent spot for fishing. Today it has
few permanent residents but many holiday shacks
line the coast from Granville to Trial Harbour.

From Zeehan you can visit the Henty Sand Dunes
to the south which are ideal for 4WD, or follow the old
railway line, now a road from Zeehan to Strahan.

Cruises leave from the old goldmining town of
Corinna to the north and take in the spectacular
wilderness of the Pieman River State Forest. The
Reece Dam and Lake Pieman are also in the region.

In February each year Zeehan plays host to the
Tin Miners' Marathon.
ACCOMMODATION: Heemskirk Motor Hotel (B&B),
ph (03) 6471 6107; Hotel Cecil, ph (03) 6471 6372;
Treasure Island West Coast Caravan Park, ph
(03) 6471 6633
ACTIVITIES: Fishing, 4WD touring, golf, historic
interest, mining tours, tennis
TOURIST INFORMATION: Ph (03) 6471 6225

Native flora in the Cradle Mountain–Lake St Clair National Park

BEN LOMOND NATIONAL PARK

Ben Lomond National Park is a 1300 metre high plateau, just 60 km from Launceston, and the massive bulk of Ben Lomond Plateau can be seen from all points of the compass. In winter this park becomes the state's major ski resort offering all levels of cross-country and downhill skiing. In spring, when the snow melts, Ben Lomond becomes a popular spot for day visitors. While lacking the dramatic wilderness scenery of Tasmania's west and south, the park is a pleasant, unspoilt spot for walkers. The plateau also attracts rock climbers. The road up to Ben Lomond is not for the faint-hearted: the final ascent is steep, winding and narrow. The section known as Jacobs Ladder has six hairpin bends, vertical drops and no safety barriers, and it is often closed in winter. A shuttle bus operates from the snowline or you can get a bus from Launceston.

CRADLE MOUNTAIN–LAKE ST CLAIR NATIONAL PARK

This park is part of the Tasmanian Wilderness World Heritage Area. It lies in the central west of the state, its landscape contrasting craggy mountain pinnacles, deep forested valleys with gorges and waterfalls, and alpine moorlands. The wildlife most commonly seen in the park are Bennett's wallabies, rufus wallabies and potoroos. Bird life consists of parrots, birds of prey, and numerous smaller bush birds. Vehicle access is only possible to Cradle Valley in the north of the park, and Lake St Clair in the south. Lake St Clair is the deepest lake in Australia. It is ideal for canoeing and windsurfing, and swimming is popular in the warmer months. Fishing for trout in the lakes and rivers is allowed in season, provided you have a licence. The park is a bushwalker's paradise. Cradle Valley, 95 km south of Devonport, is the northernmost point of entry into the World Heritage Area.

DOUGLAS–APSLEY NATIONAL PARK

Tasmania's newest national park is situated on the east coast and covers a range of landforms and habitats which preserves an area rich in fauna and flora, especially rare eucalypts. Its scenic splendour is made up of river gorges, waterfalls, deep pools and rainforest patches, while the hillsides are covered in dry sclerophyll forest. There is a variety of walks throughout the park. The park is approximately 150 km south-east of Launceston.

FREYCINET NATIONAL PARK

Jutting from the sea along the east coast, remarkable red granite cliffs plunge straight down into the ocean's depths on both sides of the peninsula, broken only where stark white beaches, such as Wineglass Bay, soften the otherwise rugged coastline. A variety of vegetation, including grass trees, banksia, wattles, oyster bay pine and bull oak, also add to the park's scenic attractions, and around Wineglass Bay the shoreline is quickly swallowed up by the marshy heathlands that abut it. Vehicle access to the park extends for only 6 km; after that, the way to explore this park is on foot, and it is well worth the effort. While bushwalking is the main recreational activity, there is some excellent offshore fishing around the peninsula and water sports such as swimming, sailing, canoeing, waterskiing and skindiving are popular. The park is 200 km north of Hobart.

HARTZ MOUNTAINS NATIONAL PARK

The wild and rugged primeval landscape of this park is made up of alpine heathlands, snow gum woodlands, glacially carved mountain lakes and rugged dolerite ranges which run north–south between the catchments of the Arve and Picton Rivers. In winter the highlands are popular with cross-country skiers, while the bright red blooms of the Tasmanian waratah, along with other wildflowers, soften the landscape in spring and summer, and intrepid bushwalkers venture into what can still be an exposed, cold and windswept region. The park is 85 km south-west of Hobart.

MARIA ISLAND NATIONAL PARK

This tranquil and beautiful island, just 15 km off Tasmania's east coast, boasts magnificent coastal scenery and a mountain range high enough to support a rainforest habitat. There are walking tracks which vary from half an hour to several days, taking in the wilder southern areas. Near Darlington lie the Painted Cliffs. The Fossil Cliffs, full of millions of fossilised shellfish, are found to the east of Darlington. Wildlife is abundant and includes large numbers of tame Bennett's wallabies. The numerous birds include the introduced Cape Barren goose and the endangered forty-spotted pardalote. Seals and whales are frequent visitors and some of the waters have been declared a marine reserve. Orford is 77 km from Hobart.

MOLE CREEK KARST NATIONAL PARK

Two of Tasmania's finest cave systems, Marakoopa and King Solomons, are now combined into one national park, together with over 200 caves and sinkholes. King Solomons Caves are small, dry caves with a profusion of light-reflecting calcite crystals that glisten like diamonds. They have some interesting formations such as 'The Temple' and the vast 'Bridal Chamber'. A path leads to the larger Marakoopa Caves which have two underground streams and stretch for 6 km. Marakoopa is the only cave system in Tasmania that is open to the public with glow-worm colonies. Nearby are shelter huts with log fires which are welcome in winter. The park is 85 km west of Launceston.

MOUNT FIELD NATIONAL PARK

In the last ice age, glacial movements shaped the landforms of the plateau and the myriad lakes and tarns of this, Tasmania's oldest national park. The striking landscape of the park is bountiful in flora, from rainforest to towering forests of swamp gum, stringybarks and conifers, while gnarled snow gums and alpine moorlands are found on the high country. The bird and animal life, too, is abundant. Lady Barron, Horseshoe and Russell falls are major attractions. Bushwalking is popular. For winter sport enthusiasts, the high country has been a favourite for over 70 years, although the snowfall in the area is unreliable. Trout fishing in Lakes Webster and Dobson is also popular. The park is 75 km west from Hobart.

MOUNT WILLIAM NATIONAL PARK

This park is situated on the northeastern tip of Tasmania with a diverse landscape of sweeping sandy beaches, dunes, coastal heathlands and granite rock pools along the coast, while the inland slopes feature dry sclerophyll forest. The area as a whole provides refuge for a variety of mammals, and there is also a thriving and varied bird population.

Mt William itself is 216 metres high, and the short walk to the top is well worth the effort. Recreations are swimming, surfing, diving, fishing and boating, and horse riding is permitted on special horse trails. The park is 160 km east of Launceston.

PIEMAN RIVER STATE RESERVE

In the south of the Arthur–Pieman Protected Area, 206 km south-west of Devonport, lies the serene beauty of the Pieman River, along which an 800 metre wide reserve protects the cool-temperate rainforest growing along the river's banks. Ferns and shrubs grow under the protective canopy of towering beech forests, with lichens and mosses coating trunks of trees, rocks and fallen logs. Stands of Huon pine can also be found, along with the rare and elegant Cunningham tree-fern. As there is no vehicle access within the reserve, you have to get out on the river to fully discover its charm. Visitors can explore the river by canoe, or join one of the wilderness cruises. Other activities to be enjoyed include swimming, fishing, boating and bushwalking.

PORT ARTHUR HISTORIC SITE

This historic site is on the beautiful Tasman Peninsula in the south-east of the island. Started as a timber station in 1828, it was a penal settlement from 1830 to 1877. A bushfire ravaged the settlement in 1897, and a second has swept through the area since, but many of the buildings have survived, although badly damaged, as poignant reminders of the harsh conditions the convicts endured. Visitors can wander through the area with its lush green lawns, surveying the Penitentiary, Church, Model Prison, Hospital and the Guard House, and marvel at these incredible structures, their heritage and their surrounds. From the man-made formations of Port Arthur, nearby, around Eaglehawk Neck, are the natural attractions of the Tasman Arch, the Devils Kitchen, the Blowhole and the Tessellated Pavement. The Port Arthur Historic Site is 102 km south-east of Hobart.

ROCKY CAPE NATIONAL PARK

Tasmania's smallest national park contains rocky, north coast headlands, small, sheltered beaches, hills covered in heath and woodlands, plus some of the state's richest Aboriginal sites. Vehicular access is limited to Sisters Beach in the east

and Rocky Cape Road in the west. Beautiful Sisters Beach is wide, clean and shaded by she-oaks. At the western end of Sisters Beach signs lead to cave shelters—Wet Cave and Lee Archer Cave—with interpretive signs detailing some of the history of the Aborigines who lived here up to 10 000 years ago. At the western end of the park the Rocky Cape lighthouse towers above orange-coated rocks, and sea caves dot the cliffs. The Rocky Cape National Park is about 90 km west of Devonport via the Bass Highway.

SEAL ROCKS STATE RESERVE, KING ISLAND

King Island's most famous natural features are its storm-lashed cliffs which claimed over 70 ships last century. Few places are wilder and more forbidding than Seal Rocks in the south-west, where giant cliffs overlook jagged, rocky outcrops, once home to a great many seals. Although almost wiped out early last century, the number of seals has increased, but you will see more muttonbirds and penguins here than seals. The adventurous visitor can explore caves in these steep and dangerous cliffs. On the nearby cliff top is the Petrified Forest, a lunar-like landscape of 30 million year old fossilised tree stumps and branches. Now fenced off for protection, there is a walkway and a windblown lookout. Seal Rocks is about 32 km south of Currie via South Road.

SOUTH BRUNY NATIONAL PARK

This is Tasmania's newest national park. Encompassing the south coast of Bruny Island, it stretches from Partridge Island and Labillardiere Peninsula across Cape Bruny, Cloudy Bay and Tasman Head, then up the east coast to Adventure Bay. The convict-built Cape Bruny Lighthouse is Australia's oldest manned lighthouse. It offers breathtaking views of Lighthouse Bay, rugged West Cloudy Head and across to East Cloudy Head, Tasman Head and the Friars Rocks. Cloudy Bay, a popular surfing spot, can become wild in winter. There is excellent fishing in most areas with swimming at Great Taylor and Adventure Bays, a range of other bushwalks and 4WD tracks. Ferries run frequently from Kettering. Adventure Bay is the 'holiday resort' of Bruny. It has a long sweep of white sands lapped by clear waters, and is safe for swimming and boating.

SOUTHWEST NATIONAL PARK

The largest park in Tasmania, the area encompasses the Frankland and Arthur ranges to the west and south coasts, forming the remote southern portion of the World Heritage Area. The only way to see much of this breathtakingly beautiful part of Tasmania is to walk. In the northern end of the park the Gordon River and Scotts Peak roads wind through forest, scrub and moorland giving access to the north-western and south-eastern shores of Lake Pedder. Here it is possible to launch a boat and enjoy the trout fishing. It is also possible by vehicle to reach Cockle Creek, south of Dover, in the eastern portion of the park. Here the activity of the whaling, coal mining and logging days in the region have long passed, and nature once again reigns. The park is located 160 km west of Hobart.

STRZELECKI NATIONAL PARK

Strzelecki National Park on the south-western tip of Flinders Island is made up of extremely rugged country with towering granite peaks rising almost sheer from the sea. The highest peak, Mt Strzelecki, is only 756 metres but the range dominates the south of the island behind a narrow coastal band. A rough 4WD track runs along the south coast to Big River. Along this narrow coastal plain are pretty little coves, tannin-stained rivers and salmon-coloured rocks. Bennett's wallabies, wombats, pademelons, echidnas and brush-tail possums are very common throughout the island and care should be taken on all roads. Some 150 bird species have been recorded. In the park's west is the stunningly beautiful Trousers Point, with headlands of jumbled granite boulders encrusted with orange lichen. There is just one, steep, walking track to the peaks offering sweeping views from the summit of Mt Strzelecki. Flinders Island is an hour's flight from Melbourne.

TESSELLATED PAVEMENT STATE RESERVE

This reserve, together with Tasman Arch State Reserve, are possibly the most visited state reserves in Tasmania, being at the entrance to the Tasman Peninsula and Port Arthur. The Tessellated Pavement is at Pirates Bay, one of the best fishing and surfing spots in the area. A five minute walk from the car park leads to intriguing geological features at

the water's edge which have an appearance remarkably like paving stones. At low tide a beach walk to Clydes Island reveals fascinating sea life in many rockpools. The Tasman Arch Reserve includes the spectacular Blowhole and the Devils Kitchen, a crevice in which the sea boils and churns. These reserves are 70 km from Hobart on the Arthur Highway.

THE NUT STATE RESERVE

The Nut is a giant, 152 metre high, lump of solidified lava looming above the historic town of Stanley. This windy plateau, believed to be millions of years old, and the town are connected to the mainland by a 7 km isthmus and are thus almost surrounded by water. Sheer on three sides, the Nut offers spectacular views up and down the north coast, inland across Stanley and out over Bass Strait. Large muttonbird colonies inhabit this reserve and a short nature walk circumnavigates the summit. A walking track to the top starts opposite the post office, or you can take the chairlift. Stanley is 130 km west of Devonport via the Bass Highway.

WALLS OF JERUSALEM NATIONAL PARK

A subalpine wilderness, this national park is a stunningly beautiful, but very fragile place. It is 110 km west of Launceston, wedged between Cradle Mountain National Park and the windswept Central Plateau and is part of the World Heritage Area. This park is strictly for the very fit. Bushwalking, plus some rock climbing and cross-country skiing are the activities here; there is no vehicular access. From the car park at Fish River Road a rough walking track heads off into the park. From here, also, a strenuous three hour walk entails a steep climb to Trappers Hut and on to Solomons Jewels, a chain of little lakes.

WATERHOUSE PROTECTED AREA

This lovely area is found in the far north-east, protecting an area east of Bridport, along Anderson Bay north, and across to Ringarooma Bay. Pristine rockpools and sand dunes, along with tranquil beaches, make it an ideal spot for recreational activities such as swimming, fishing, bushwalking and horse riding. The Waterhouse Road, easy 4WD, gives access to the protected area. Driving on the beaches is not permitted. The area is 85 km from Launceston.

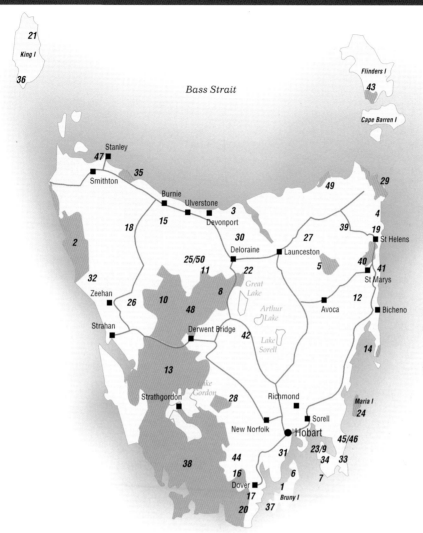

King I — 21, 36

Flinders I — 43

Cape Barren I

Bass Strait

Stanley — 47, 35
Smithton
Burnie, Ulverstone — 15
Devonport — 3
18, 2
49, 29, 4
39, 19 — St Helens
30 — Deloraine
27 — Launceston
25/50, 11, 22
Great Lake
8
40, 41 — St Marys
32 — Zeehan
26, 10, 48
Arthur Lake
5
Avoca — 12
Bicheno
Strahan
Derwent Bridge — 42
Lake Sorell
14
13
Strathgordon
Lake Gordon
28
Richmond — Maria I — 24
New Norfolk
Sorell
Hobart
44, 16 — Dover
38
31, 23/9, 45/46, 34, 33
6, 7
17, 1 — Bruny I
20, 37

Popular Parks

	Camping	Caravans	Wheel Chairs	4WD Access	Picnic Area	Toilets	Walking Trks	Kiosk	Information
1 Adventure Bay CR					■	■	■		
2 Arthur Pieman Protected Area	■	■	■	■	■	■			■
3 Asbestos Range NP	■	■			■	■	■		■
4 Bay of Fires CR	■	■			■	■			
5 Ben Lomond NP					■	■	■	■	■
6 Bruny Island Neck Game Res	■				■	■			
7 Cape Raoul SR							■		
8 Central Plateau CA	■	■			■	■	■	■	■
9 Coal Mines Historic Site	■	■			■	■	■		
10 Cradle Mountain-Lake St Clair	■	■	■		■	■	■	■	■
11 Devils Gullet SR							■		
12 Douglas-Apsley NP	■				■	■	■		■
13 Franklin-Gordon Wild Rivers NP	■		■		■	■	■		■
14 Freycinet NP	■	■			■	■	■		■
15 Gunns Plains Cave SR					■	■			
16 Hartz Mountains NP					■	■	■		
17 Hastings Caves SR				■	■	■	■	■	■
18 Hellyer Gorge SR					■	■			
19 Humbug Point SRA	■				■	■	■		
20 Ida Bay SR							■	■	
21 Lavinia NR	■								
22 Liffey Falls SR	■				■	■	■		
23 Lime Bay NR	■	■			■	■	■		
24 Maria Island NP	■	■		■	■	■	■		■
25 Mole Creek Karst NP					■	■	■		■

Popular Parks

	Camping	Caravans	Wheel Chairs	4WD Access	Picnic Area	Toilets	Walking Trks	Kiosk	Information
26 Montezuma Falls				■			■		
27 Mt Barrow SR					■	■	■		
28 Mt Field NP	■	■	■		■	■	■	■	■
29 Mt William NP	■	■			■	■	■		■
30 Notley Gorge SR					■	■	■		
31 Peggs Beach CR	■	■			■	■	■		
32 Pieman River SR	■				■	■	■		
33 Point Puer–Crescent Bay SR							■		
34 Port Arthur Historic Site	■	■	■		■	■	■	■	■
35 Rocky Cape NP					■	■	■		■
36 Seal Rock SR							■		
37 South Bruny NP	■	■		■	■	■	■		■
38 Southwest NP	■	■			■	■	■		■
39 St Columba Falls SR							■		
40 St Marys Pass SR							■		
41 St Patricks Head SR							■		
42 Steepes SR							■		
43 Strzelecki NP	■	■			■	■	■		
44 Tahune Forest Reserve	■				■	■	■		
45 Tasman Arch SR					■	■	■		
46 Tessellated Pavement SR							■		
47 The Nut SR					■	■	■	■	■
48 Walls of Jerusalem NP	■						■		
49 Waterhouse Protected Area	■	■			■	■	■		■
50 Wellington Park					■	■	■	■	

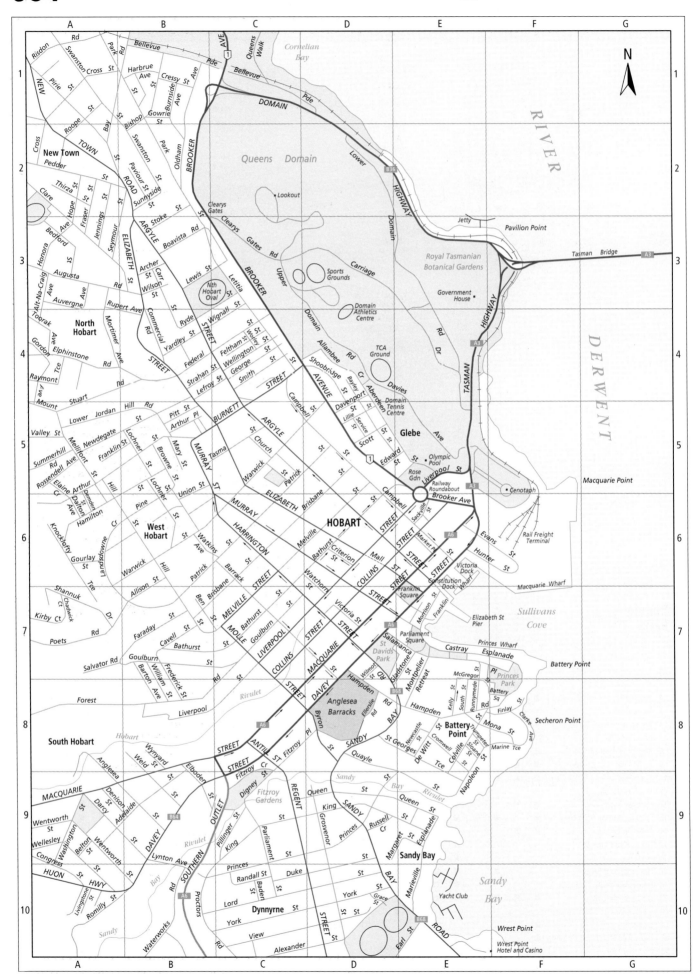

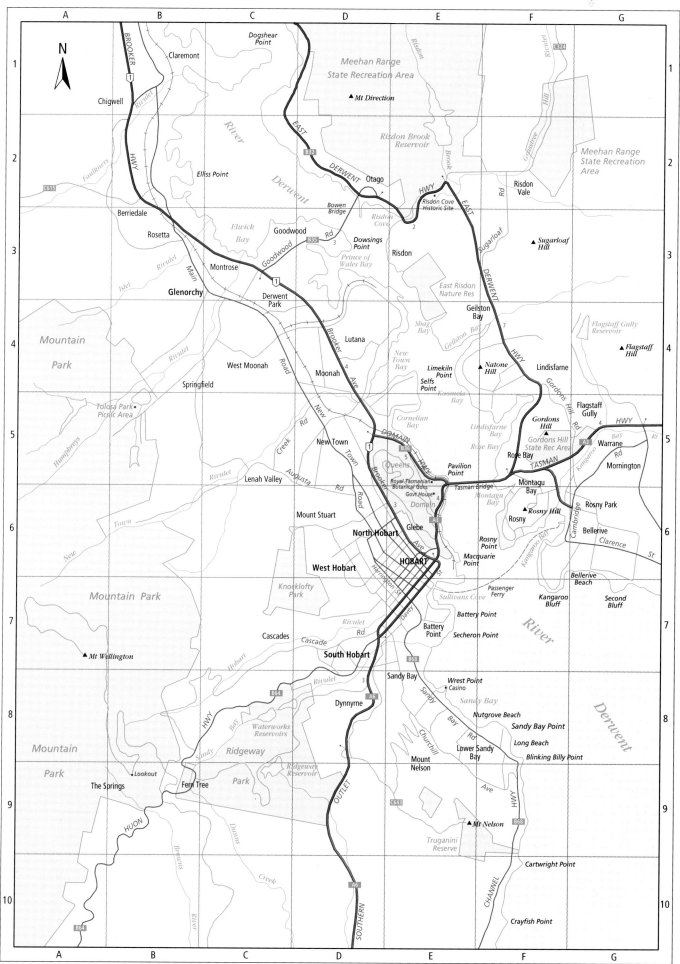

kilometres

0   1   2

N

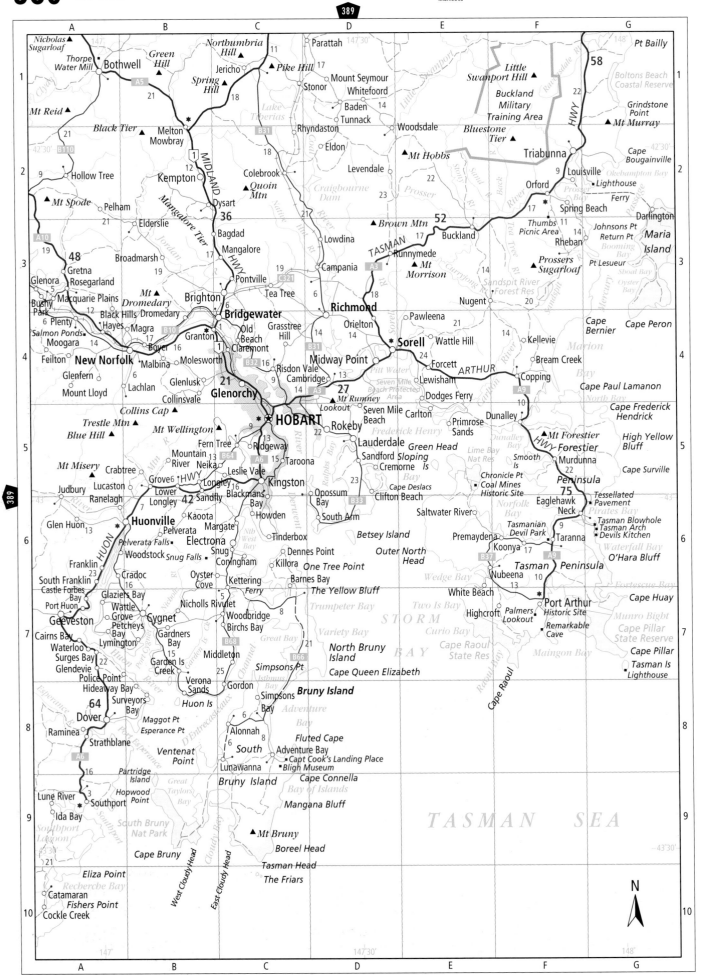

kilometres
0   5   10   15   20

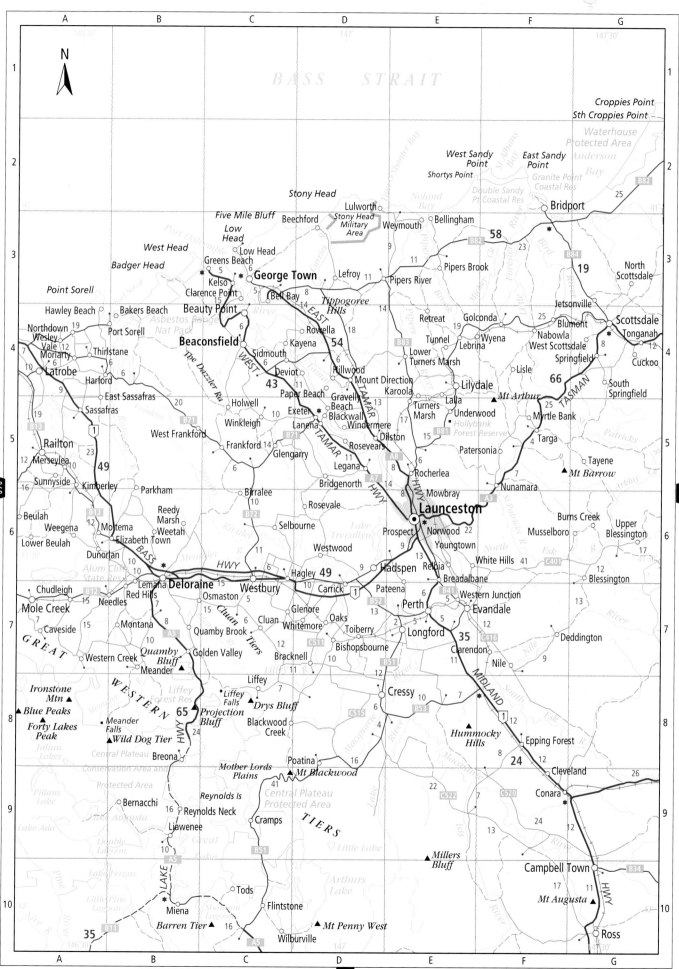

BASS STRAIT

Croppies Point
Sth Croppies Point

Waterhouse
Protected Area
Anderson
Bay

West Sandy
Point
East Sandy
Point
Shortys Point
Granite Point
Coastal Res

Double Sandy
Pt Coastal Res

Bridport

Stony Head

Lulworth
Stony Head
Military
Area
Weymouth
Bellingham

B82 58 23

B84 19

North
Scottsdale

Five Mile Bluff
Beechford

Low
Head

West Head
Low Head
Greens Beach
Kelso
Clarence Point
Bell Bay
George Town
Lefroy
Pipers River
Pipers Brook

Retreat
Golconda
Jetsonville

Badger Head

Beauty Point

EAST

Tippogoree
Hills

Scottsdale
Tonganah

Point Sorell

Hawley Beach
Bakers Beach
Port Sorell
Asbestos Range
Nat Park

Beaconsfield
Sidmouth
Deviot

Rowella
Kayena

54

Tunnel
Wyena
Lebrina

Lower
Turners Marsh

Blumont
Nabowla
West Scottsdale
Springfield
South
Springfield

Cuckoo

Lisle

66

Northdown
Wesley
Vale
Moriarty

Thirlstane

43

Hillwood
Mount Direction
Paper Beach

Lilydale

Mt Arthur

Latrobe
Harford

Holwell

Gravelly
Beach
Blackwall
Lanena

Karoola

Lalla
Underwood

Myrtle Bank

East Sassafras

Winkleigh

Exeter
Windermere

Turners
Marsh

Hollybank
Forest Reserve

Targa

Sassafras

West Frankford

Frankford

Glengarry

Dilston
Rosevears

Patersonia

Tayene

Railton

Merseylea
Sunnyside

Kimberley
Parkham

Birralee

Bridgenorth

Legana

Rocherlea

Mt Barrow

Nunamara

49

Beulah
Weegena
Moltema
Weetah
Reedy
Marsh

Rosevale

Mowbray

Burns Creek

Upper
Blessington

Lower Beulah
Elizabeth Town

Selbourne

Launceston

Musselboro

Dunorlan

Westwood

Prospect
Norwood
Youngtown

White Hills

Blessington

Chudleigh
Red Hills
Needles

Lemana
Deloraine
Osmaston

BASS HWY

Westbury
Hagley
49
Carrick

Hadspen
Relbia
Breadalbane

Western Junction

Mole Creek
Montana

Caveside

GREAT

Quamby Brook

Cluan
Whitemore

Glenore
Oaks
Toiberry
Pateena

Perth

Evandale

Deddington

Western Creek

Quamby
Bluff
Golden Valley
Meander

Bracknell

Bishopsbourne

Longford

35

Clarendon
Nile

Ironstone
Mtn

Liffey
Forest Res

Liffey
Liffey
Falls

Drys Bluff

Cressy

Blue Peaks

Projection
Bluff

Blackwood
Creek

Hummocky
Hills

Epping Forest

Forty Lakes
Peak

Meander
Falls

Wild Dog Tier

65

WESTERN

HWY

Breona

Mother Lords
Plains

Poatina

Mt Blackwood

24

Cleveland

Conara

Bernacchi

Reynolds Is

Reynolds Neck

Cramps

Central Plateau
Protected Area

TIERS

Millers
Bluff

Campbell Town

Liawenee

Tods

Miena

Flintstone

Mt Penny West

Mt Augusta

Ross

35

Barren Tier

Wilburville

MIDLAND HWY

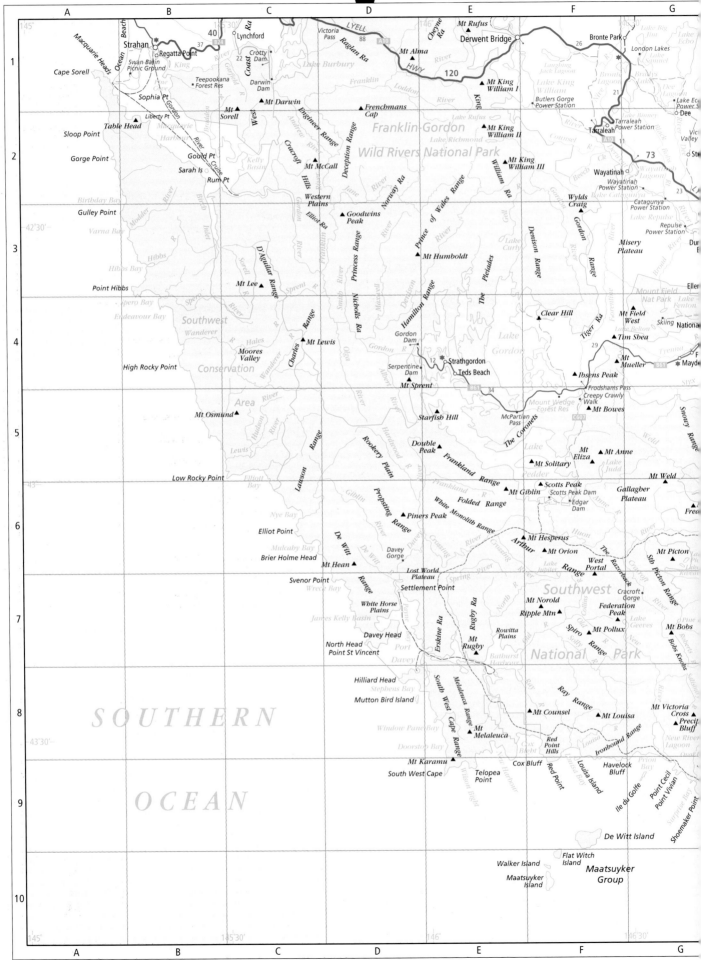

391

kilometres

0   10   20   30

TASMAN SEA

N

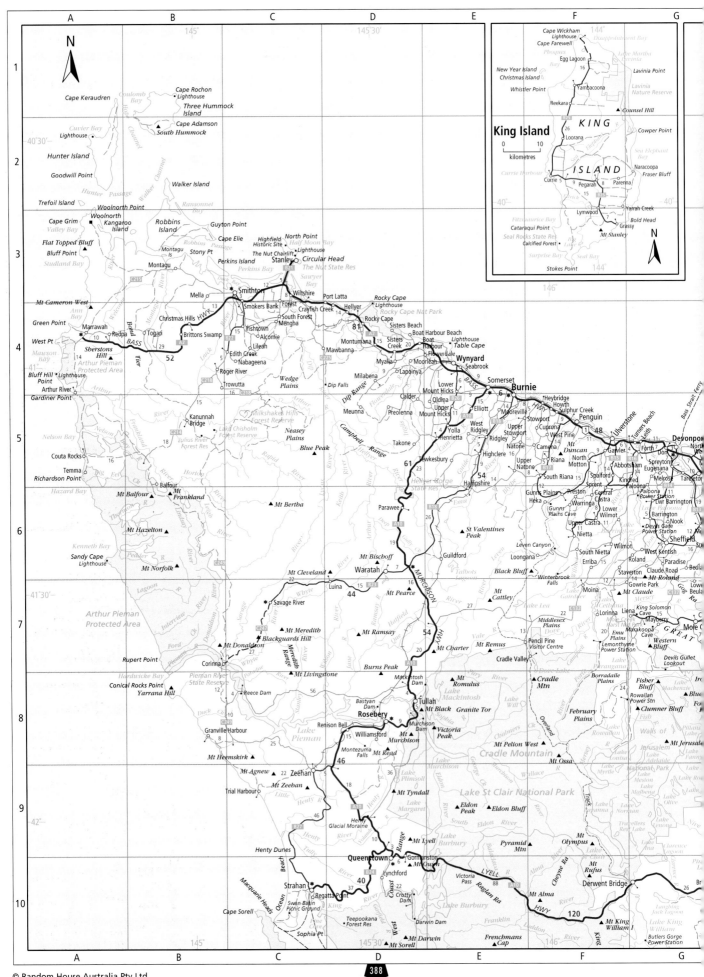

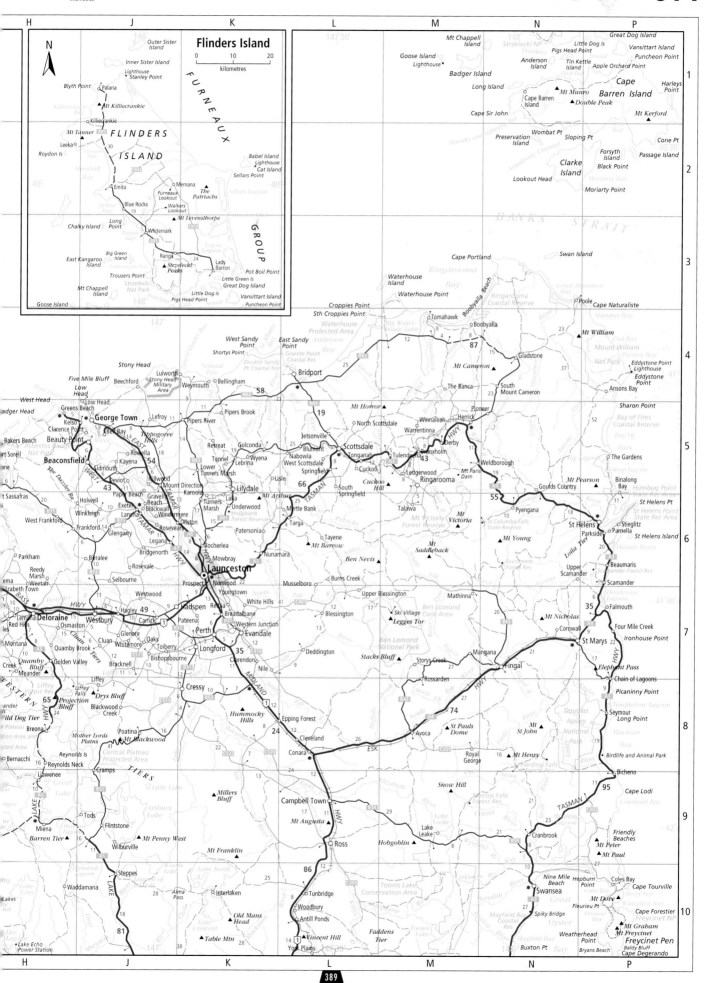

Flinders Island

0 10 20
kilometres

FURNEAUX

FLINDERS ISLAND

GROUP

INDEX

Abbreviations used in the index

CA	Conservation Area		RP	Recreation Park
CP	Conservation Park		RR	Regional Reserve
CR	Conservation Reserve		SF	State Forest
FP	Forest Park		SP	State Park
FR	Forest Reserve		SR	State Reserve
GR	Game Reserve		SRA	State Recreation Area
NP	National Park		WP	Wildlife Park
NR	Nature Reserve		WPA	Wilderness Protection Area
PA	Protected Area			

Numbers in bold indicate an entry in text.

The Pinnacles in Nambung National Park, Western Australia